RETHINKING THE COLOR LINE

RETHINKING THE COLOR LINE
Readings in Race and Ethnicity

Third Edition

Charles A. Gallagher
Georgia State University

Boston   Burr Ridge, IL   Dubuque, IA   Madison, WI   New York   San Francisco   St. Louis
Bangkok   Bogotá   Caracas   Kuala Lumpur   Lisbon   London   Madrid   Mexico City
Milan   Montreal   New Delhi   Santiago   Seoul   Singapore   Sydney   Taipei   Toronto

Higher Education

RETHINKING THE COLOR LINE

Published by McGraw-Hill, a business unit of The McGraw-Hill Companies, Inc., 1221 Avenue of the Americas, New York, NY, 10020. Copyright © 2007 by The McGraw-Hill Companies, Inc. All rights reserved. No part of this publication may be reproduced or distributed in any form or by any means, or stored in a database or retrieval system, without the prior written consent of The McGraw-Hill Companies, Inc., including, but not limited to, in any network or other electronic storage or transmission, or broadcast for distance learning.

Some ancillaries, including electronic and print components, may not be available to customers outside the United States.

This book is printed on acid-free paper.

1 2 3 4 5 6 7 8 9 0 AGM/AGM 0 9 8 7 6

ISBN-13: 978-0-07-313574-8
ISBN-10: 0-07-313574-7

Publisher: *Phil Butcher*
Sponsoring Editor: *Sherith Pankratz*
Development Editor and Permissions Coordinator: *Robin Reed, Carlisle Communications*
Marketing Manager: *Dan Loch*
Media Producer: *Nancy Garcia*
Project Manager: *Roger Geissler*
Designer: *Srdj Savanovic*
Production Supervisor: *Rich DeVitto*
Compositor: *International Typesetting & Composition*
Printer: *Quebecor World—Martinsburg*

Library of Congress Cataloging-in-Publication Data

Rethinking the color line : readings in race and ethnicity / [edited by] Charles A.
  Gallagher.—3rd ed.
    p. cm.
  Includes bibliographical references.
  ISBN 0-07-313574-7 (softcover)
  1. United States—Race relations. 2. United States—Ethnic relations. 3.
  Minorities—Civil rights—United States. I. Gallagher, Charles A. (Charles Andrew), 1962–
E184.AIR4485 2006
305.800973—dc22   2006042046

www.mhhe.com

Contents

Preface

When it comes to race and ethnic relations in the United States, we are two nations. The nation we imagine ourselves to be as depicted in the media, and the communities in which we live. Reflect for a moment about how race is depicted in popular culture. Turn on the television and you enter a fantasyland where whites, blacks, Latinos, and Asians gather together to shop, eat, work, and interact in spaces where race is meaningless. Typical is an advertisement for Checker's fast food. With a hip-hop jingle playing in the background, young adults pack into a car to get a snack at the drive-thru window. What is now totally unremarkable is that the group in the car is composed of a racially integrated group of actors; the new formula to sell products to youth markets is interracial, interethnic chic. In Hollywood's version of U.S. race relations, your best friends are always from a different race. It is almost a requirement to have a multiracial cast of characters selling Gap, Old Navy, or Pepsi products. In this racial nirvana, handsome, middle class men of varying races relax in upper middle class living rooms, back slapping and bonding over football, Coor's Beer, and Domino's Pizza. Car commercials, advertisements for antacids, snack foods, soda, and fast food restaurants routinely show an America that is integrated, assimilated, beautiful, and colorblind. In this carefully manufactured racial utopia, television commercials depict actors of different races interacting in race-neutral environments like Chili's or Applebee's. America's racial "presentation of self" in the media is overwhelmingly depicted as an environment that is integrated, multiracial and for the most part colorblind. The media, particularly in advertisements, presents America as a kind of United Nations reunion party where everyone has equal social standing, equal opportunity and everyone is middle class.

These representations of a colorblind America seriously misrepresent the extent to which race continues to shape the life chances of racial minorities in the United States. Take for example racial diversity in corporate America. Significant movement into the upper ranks of top management would indicate that racial barriers have fallen. Yes, progress into the executive ranks has been minuscule. The Glass Ceiling Report produced by the U.S. Department of Labor found that "97% of the senior managers of Fortune 1000 industrial and Fortune 500 are white; 95 to 97% are male." (racial minorities make up about 30% of the U.S. population.) All things being equal, we should expect to see about 30% of the top jobs going to racial minorities. What we see however is that only 3%, not 30% of senior managers at Fortune 1000 and Fortune 500 companies are racial minorities. What does this figure say about the notion that we are now a colorblind nation?

The United States Senate provides a rather good test of the fit between how groups are presented on television dramas like CSI or in the movie theatre multiplex and the clout racial minorities have achieved politically. Since there are 100 members in the U.S. Senate, then there should be 30 Senators who are members of racial minorities. When we look at the membership of the 109th Congress we find only **five** racial minorities in the U.S. Senate, which means that 95 senators are white. Since whites constitute about 70% of the U.S. population, proportional representation suggests whites should hold 70 Senate seats, not 95. How do we explain this discrepancy? There are currently no American Indians in the U.S. Senate. Women too are underrepresented in the Senate. Although women comprise about 52% of the adult population (which means we should see 52 women in the Senate) there are only 14 female U.S. Senators.

We are two nations in yet another way. Reflect for a moment on these rather schizophrenic events in American social and cultural life: a black Texan is tied to the back of a pick-up truck and dragged to his death by racist whites while white rapper Eminem wins three Grammy awards; challenges to University of Michigan's affirmative action program move up to the Supreme Court, creating a national dialogue on the extent to which the racial "playing field" is level. After 9/11 tougher immigration laws are called for by politicians, while U.S. farmers and agra-business discuss institution of a new *bracero* farm labor program that would ease restrictions on seasonal immigrant farm workers. Oprah Winfrey has a net worth of over one billion dollars while almost a quarter of the total black population live below the poverty line. Racial profiling brings about a new term, DWB (driving while black) while Colin Powell, Denzel Washington, and Tiger Woods are consistently voted among America's most celebrated and respected people. White suburban teenagers continue to be the largest consumers of rap and hip-hop, yet racially motivated hate crimes continue to happen on campuses throughout the country. Latinos are now larger than the black population, yet each group is significantly underrepresented in Congress and in corporate America. The readings in *Rethinking the Color Line* will allow you to examine the contradictions of race and ethnicity and prepare us

to live in an increasingly racially and ethnically diverse society.

Although the media has seized on a U.S. Census Bureau figure that predicts that by the year 2060 whites will be outnumbered by Asians, blacks, Hispanics, and American Indians, this rather simplistic demographic forecast misses the conflicts, contradictions, and cultural convergences that currently define race and ethnic relations in the United States. *Rethinking the Color Line* is designed to help make sense of how race and ethnicity influence aspects of social life in ways that are often made invisible by culture, politics, and economics. This theoretically informed, empirically grounded reader uses a social constructionist perspective to frame and define the concept of race and ethnicity in the United States. The selections should stimulate conversation in the classroom and allow students to think through solutions to what often seem to be intractable problems. As a pedagogical strategy, this text raises a number of questions in the part introductions that guide students through the readings by providing an overview of how each reading is conceptually linked to the others. Each chapter starts with "Questions to Consider," which ask students to focus their attention on specific themes, issues, or questions raised in the reading. It was important to me that my students be exposed to the classic paradigms in the study of race and ethnic relations in the United States. However, just as important was my desire that students be exposed to and explore new theories and paradigms that were challenging, supplanting, and redefining the classic race and ethnicity "canon," which itself changes over time. The biologically-based, pseudo-scientific assumptions that defined and guided race and ethnicity scholarship for much of this century have been debunked, discredited, and discarded. What has emerged in the last 30 years are competing narratives of what race and ethnic identity mean and the social pressures that shape those meanings. Post-colonial, post-modern, post-ethnic, class-based, or primordialist perspectives each claim to elucidate how race and ethnicity in the last 30 years are competing narratives of what race and ethnic identity mean and how the meaning of race and ethnicity has been and continues to be thoroughly rethought.

The readings in the first part of this text provide students with the theoretical framework and analytical tools they will use throughout the book. Students come to understand what is meant by race and ethnicity as a social construction. The news, situation comedies, MTV, the racial topography of neighborhoods—each become subjects for sociological scrutiny. *Rethinking the Color Line* allows students to learn how race and ethnicity influence life in ways that many students routinely take for granted. It has been my experience that a majority of students who read these articles internalize a version of the "sociological imagination" that forever changes how they understand race and ethnic relations. Raising consciousness about how each of us influence and in turn are influenced by race and ethnic relations is an explicit goal of this book.

Over the last decade I have had the luxury of testing a large and varied number of readings on hundreds of students in dozens of race and ethnic relations classes at large public universities as well as small, elite liberal arts colleges. The readings in this book represent the final outcome of classroom "hits" or "misses." I have used classroom experiences, the results of examinations, and how easily students were able to integrate the readings into research papers to gauge (1) the extent to which the reading contributed to students' understanding of a particular theory or concept, (2) if the reading was intellectually engaging,

and (3) if it lent itself to active learning in the classroom. If a reading could pass these hurdles in at least three of my classes, then it made it into this book. Teaching at both public universities and private colleges also provided me with the opportunity to observe how students from different regions, class backgrounds, and racial and ethnic identities reacted to the assigned readings. The articles speak to, challenge, and find common ground among students from racially, ethnically, culturally, and economically diverse backgrounds. *Rethinking the Color Line* is a response to my students' calls for a book that was user-friendly but did not sacrifice intellectual or theoretical rigor.

This book has been designed to be relevant for students on an individual level while also helping them understand that race and ethnic relations are embedded in the institutions that structure their lives. The readings require students to constantly negotiate the tensions between individual agency and the often-determining constraints of social structure. The common thread that links these readings is the ongoing debate about the relationship between agency and structure. It is this conceptual framework that will allow students to think about race and ethnicity in fluid rather than static terms.

Changes to the Third Edition

Race and ethnic relations are never static. The fourteen new readings in the third edition reflect this fact. An insightful article by David R. Williams and Chiquita Collins explore the extent to which access to health care varies by race, a finding that is quite literally about life and death. Thomas Shapiro's research examines the wealth gap between whites and blacks, demonstrating how invisible transfers of family money throughout the life course creates opportunities along racial lines. Jennifer Lee and Frank Bean ask us to rethink how we classify racial categories as a sizable part of the U.S. population has come to define themselves as "multiracial." What does this term "multiracial" mean and what are the implications for future generations and contemporary racial politics? Law professors Lani Guinier and Gerald Torres challenge the widespread belief that we are a colorblind nation. Colorblindness is a laudable goal but as these authors point out, the United States is generations away from becoming a nation where color does not significantly shape life chances. Susan M. Akram and Kevin R. Johnson argue that since 9/11 Arab-Americans have become the unfortunate targets of stereotyping, racial profiling, and discrimination. They argue that the terrorist attacks on the United States have had the effect of "racializing" this group, that is, Arab-American racial identity has been redefined through politics. Shannon Zenk and her colleagues demonstrate that residential segregation results in communities that lack important amenities—in this case, full service supermarkets. What are the implications when individuals do not have access to fresh fruit, vegetables, and dairy products and perhaps more importantly, why does this happen and how does race figure into the answer? Devah Pager's study exposes the extent to which the interplay between race and having a criminal record shapes in the hiring preferences of employers. Amy Braverman points outs that it is not just the color of one's skin that is used to discriminate job applicants but how "non-white" your name sounds to employers. Xiaolan Bao, William Kandel, and Emilio A. Parrado help us understand how immigrants from Asian and South and Central America are radically transforming urban and rural America. Expanding on past

readings concerning the media, Roger Klein and Stacy Naccarato update how bias creeps into news coverage of racial minorities. In similar fashion Debra Merskin deconstructs why stereotypes of American Indians persist in the media and the sociological meaning of American Indian sports mascots. New to the Race and Romance section is Randall Kennedy's article on how perceptions of interracial romance have changed in the media but not necessarily among the American public.

Instructor's Resource CD

My colleague Kristin Wilson has designed an instructor's manual (appearing on the IRCD) to accompany the third edition. The manual is designed to provide instructors with relevant questions, theoretical overviews, discussion points, multiple choice questions, and essay questions about each reading.

Rethinking the Color Line Supersite

A Web site has been designed and updated to accompany the third edition. The Web site contains flashcard exercises, Web and U.S. Census links, practice test questions, and other material which focus on race and ethnic relations in the United States. Visit the site at *www.mhhe.com/gallagher3e.*

Appendix

New to the third edition is an appendix meant to capture almost every quality of life measure (income, education, health . . .) by race and ethnicity. The appendix is linked to the text in the Seeing the Big Picture questions, appearing at the end of most readings.

The appendix was designed for faculty and students to have a ready comparative reference of racial and ethnic social statistics relevant for classroom discussions and research assignments.

Acknowledgements

The selections in this reader and the questions that frame each chapter reflect thousands of conversations I've had with friends and family about race in America. I have benefited greatly from the research and insights of Richard Alba, Robert Adelman, Eli Anderson, Maggie Anderson, Amy Ansell, Alexis Bender, Kathy Blee, Eduardo Bonilla-Silva, Dave Brunsma, Erica Chito Childs, Rodney Coates, Francesca Coin, Heather Dalmage, Nancy Ditomaso, Woody Doane, Mitch Duneier, Jennifer Eichstedt, Abby Ferber, Joe Feagin, Tyrone Foreman, Doug Hartmann, Elizabeth Higginbotham, Charlie Jaret, Kathleen Odell Korgan, Karyn Lacy, Amanda Lewis, Melinda Mills, Bob Moore, Pamela Perry, Jennifer Pierce, Dave Roediger, Mary Romero, Tom Shapiro, Steve Steinberg, Hernan Vera, Winddance Twine, Sarah Willie, Frank Whittington, Howie Winant, Caroline Woods, George Yancey and Al Young Jr.

My thanks go to the following reviewers who provided suggestions about the form and content of the second edition reader: Karyn McKinney, Pennsylvania State University at Altoona; Emily Ignacio, Loyola University; Gregory DeFreitas, Hofstra University; Harriett Romo, University of Texas at San Antonio; Jennifer Lerner, Northern Virginia Community College; Leonda Keniston, Virginia Commonwealth University; Shelly Brown, University of North Carolina at Greensboro; Linda Rodriguez, University at Albany; and Garvey Lundy, University of Pennsylvania.

Many thanks to my colleague Kristin Wilson who once again took up the very difficult task of preparing the Instructor's Guide and supersite information.

Lastly, I thank the McGraw-Hill production team: Project Manager, Roger Geissler, Production Supervisor, Rich DeVitto, Designer, Srdj Savanovic, and Media Producer, Nancy Garcia.

I welcome any comments, suggestions, or criticism concerning this reader. Please feel free to contact me about which readings work, which do not, or readings I might include in future editions. Please send any comments directly to me. I look forward to your feedback.

Charles A. Gallagher
Department of Sociology
Georgia State University
University Plaza
Atlanta, GA 30303-3083
E-mail: cgallagher@gsu.edu

About the Contributors

Susan Akram (Reading 18) is an associate professor at the Boston University School of Law. She is the founding director of the Immigration Project at the public interest law firm of Public Counsel in Los Angeles, and of the Political Asylum/Immigration Representation Project in Boston and the interim director of the Joint Voluntary Agency for resettlement of Iraqi refugees in refugee camps in Saudi Arabia after the Gulf War. She has authored articles on U.S. immigration law and policy, refugee law and policy, and human rights and the Middle East. She is currently a Fulbright Senior Scholar at Al-Quds University.

Daniel R. Amundson (Reading 37) is research director of the Center for Media and Public Affairs. He is co-author (with S. Robert Lichter) of *Solid Waste Management: Comparing Expert Opinion, Media Coverage, and Public Opinion* (1992).

Elijah Anderson (Reading 22) is the Charles and William L. Day Professor of the Social Sciences, professor of sociology, and director of the Philadelphia Ethnography Project at the University of Pennsylvania. An expert on the sociology of black America, he is the author of *A Place on the Corner: A Study of Black Streetcorner Men* (1978), numerous articles on the black experience, and the forthcoming *The Code of the Streets*. For his ethnographic study *Streetwise: Race, Class, and Change in an Urban Community* (1990), he was honored with the Robert E. Park Award of the American Sociological Association. Anderson is also associate editor of *Qualitative Sociology* and a member of the board of

directors of the American Academy of Political and Social Science.

Frank D. Bean (Reading 12) is a professor of sociology at the University of California, Irvine, and the co-director of the Center for Research on Immigration, Population and Public Policy. He is former director of the Center for U.S./Mexico Border and Migration Research at the University of Texas, Austin. His current research examines four areas: the intersection of race/ethnicity in the United States, immigration and U.S. welfare patterns, migration within and from Mexico, and the effects of immigration on labor markets. He is the author of *America's Newcomers and the Dynamics of Diversity* (2003).

Rebecca M. Blank (Reading 6) is dean of the Gerald R. Ford School of Public Policy, Henry Carter Adams Collegiate Professor of Public Policy, and professor of economics at the University of Michigan. Prior to going to Michigan, she served as a member of the President's Council of Economic Advisers from 1997–1999. Blank's research has focused on the interaction between the macro-economy, government antipoverty programs, and the behavior and well-being of low-income families. She is the author of *It Takes a Nation: A New Agenda for Fighting Poverty* (1997), *Finding Jobs: Work and Welfare Reform* (2000), and *The New World of Welfare* (2001).

Herbert Blumer (Reading 16) spent most of his professional career at the University of Chicago and the University of California, Berkeley. Blumer established symbolic interactionism as a major sociological perspective in American sociology.

Eduardo Bonilla-Silva (Reading 5) is an associate professor of sociology at Texas A&M University. He is best known for his 1997 piece in the *American Sociological Review* entitled "Rethinking Racism: Toward a Structural Interpretation." He is also the author of three books: *White Supremacy and Racism in the Post–Civil Rights Era* (2001), *Racism Without Racists: Color Blind Racism and the Persistence of Racial Inequality in the USA* (2003), and *Whiteout: The Continuing Significance of Racism* (with Ashley Doane, 2003). He is currently working on a project examining the idea that race relations in the United States are becoming Latin America–like, and a book-length manuscript entitled *Anything but Racism: How Social Scientists Limit the Significance of Racism.*

Robert D. Bullard (Reading 23) is Ware Professor of Sociology and director of the Environmental Justice Resource Center at Clark Atlanta University. He is the author of numerous articles, monographs, and scholarly papers that address environmental justice and public participation concerns. His book, *Dumping in Dixie: Race, Class and Environmental Quality* (1990, 1994, 2000), has become a standard text in the environmental justice field. His most recent books are *People of Color Environmental Groups Directory 2000* (2000) and *Sprawl City: Race, Politics, and Planning in Atlanta* (2000).

David Cole (Reading 26) was named one of the forty-five outstanding lawyers under the age of forty-five by *The American Lawyer*. He is a professor at Georgetown University Law Center, an attorney with the Center for Constitutional Rights, the chief litigator for *Karen Finley v. National Endowment for the Arts*, and a regular contributor to NPR's *All Things Considered, The Nation,* and op-ed pages in major newspapers nationwide. He is the author of *No Equal Justice* (1999).

Chiquita A. Collins (Reading 7) is an assistant professor in the department of sociology and research associate with the Population Research Center at the University of Texas at Austin. She also has a joint appointment with the Center for African and African American Studies, and adjunct appointments with the Center for Health Promotion and Disease Prevention in Underserved Populations in the school of nursing, and the Institute of Gerontology. Before joining the faculty at the University of Texas, she was a Fellow of the Robert Wood Johnson Foundation Scholars in Health Policy Research Program (1999–2001) at the University of California (Berkeley and San Francisco). Her publications have appeared in the *Annals of the New York Academy of Sciences, Annual Review of Sociology, Public Health Reports*, and *Sociological Forum.*

Hector Cordero-Guzman (Reading 9) is an urban poverty fellow in the Department of Sociology at the University of Chicago and a researcher at the Center for Puerto Rican Studies.

Heather M. Dalmage (Reading 45) is an associate professor of sociology at the School of Policy Studies at Roosevelt University, Chicago. She is the author of *Tripping on the Color Line: Black–White Multiracial Families in a Racially Divided World* (2000) and a national expert on interracial relationships. She is editor of *The Multiracial Movement: The Politics of Color* (2003).

Angela Y. Davis (Reading 27) is professor of history of consciousness at the University of California, Santa Cruz. During the last twenty-five years, she has lectured in all fifty states, as well as in Africa, Europe, the Caribbean, and the former Soviet Union. Her articles and essays have appeared in numerous journals and anthologies, and she is the author of five books, including *Angela Davis: An Autobiography; Women, Race & Class;* and the recently published *Blues Legacies and Black Feminism: Gertrude "Ma" Rainey, Bessie Smith, and Billie Holiday. The Angela Y. Davis Reader,* a collection of Davis's writings that spans nearly three decades, was published in 1998.

Catherine Ellis (Reading 32) is a visiting scholar at Radcliffe's Murray Center for the Study of Lives and is examining racial attitudes and memories of segregation among older whites and African Americans.

Yen Le Espiritu (Reading 11) teaches race and ethnic relations and Asian American studies in the ethnic studies department at the University of California, San Diego. She is the author of *Asian American Women and Men: Labor, Laws, and Love* (1997); *Filipino American Lives* (1995); and *Asian American Panethnicity: Bridging Institutions and Identities* (1992). She is also review editor of the *Journal of Asian-American Studies.*

Clairece Booher Feagin (Reading 4) is the author of *What Will School Be Like?* (1991) and co-author of *Stories for Parents* (1990) and *Discrimination American Style: Institutional Racism and Sexism* (1978).

Joe R. Feagin (Readings 4 and 20) is a professor of sociology at the University of Florida. He does research mainly on gender and racial discrimination. He has completed a major research project on the discrimination faced by successful black Americans, a major portion of which was published in 1994 as *Living with Racism: The Black Middle Class Experience.* He has also published a

book, *White Racism: The Basics* (1995), with co-author and professor Hernan Vera and has served as scholar-in-residence at the U.S. Commission on Civil Rights. Feagin was nominated for a Pulitzer Prize for *Ghetto Revolts* (1973).

Charles Gallagher (Readings 13 and 48) is an assistant professor of sociology at Georgia State University. He has written extensively about race and ethnic relations in the United States. He has written on the changing nature of racial categories, specifically the ways in which whiteness can expand; the social functions of color-blind political narrative and the accounts individuals give for their misrepresentations of racial group size. He has been honored with four teaching awards, most recently the Michael Harrington Distinguished Teaching Award (2002) from the National Forum on Poverty and Inequality. He is currently finishing his manuscript based on interviews with whites from around the country.

Herbert J. Gans (Reading 15) is the Robert Lynd Professor of Sociology at Columbia University. He received his Ph.D. from the University of Pennsylvania. He has worked as a research planner for public and private agencies, and prior to coming to Columbia taught at the University of Pennsylvania, MIT, and Teachers College of Columbia University. He is the author of nine books and over 160 articles. His first book was *The Urban Villagers* (1962). Recent works include *War Against the Poor* (1995) *Making Sense of America* (1999), and *Democracy and the News* (2003).

Lani Guinier (Reading 14) is the Bennett Boskey professor of law at Harvard University. She was nominated by President Clinton to be the first black woman to head the civil rights division of the Department of

Justice. She has authored ninety-seven publications, many examining the intersection of race, gender, and the law.

Marvin Harris (Reading 1) spent a portion of his life teaching in the anthropology department at Columbia University, where he served as department chair. He has published sixteen books, including *Cannibals and Kings; Culture, People, and Nature;* and *Our Kind.*

Sut Jhally (Reading 36) is author of *The Codes of Advertising: Social Communication in Advertising* and *Enlightened Racism* and co-editor of *Cultural Politics in Contemporary America* and the forthcoming *The Fantasy Factory.* He is founder and executive director of The Media Education Foundation. He is the producer of videotapes *Dreamworlds, Pack of Lies, The Killing Screens, The Date Rape Backlash, Slim Hopes, Tough Guise, Killing Us Softly III, Off the Straight and Narrow,* and *Advertising and the End of the World.*

Kevin R. Johnson (Reading 18) is associate dean for academic affairs and Mabie-Apallas Public Interest Professor of Law and Chicana/o Studies at the University of California at Davis. He has published extensively on immigration law and policy, racial identity, and civil rights in national and international journals. His book *How Did You Get to Be Mexican? A White/Brown Man's Search for Identity* (1999) was nominated for the 2000 Robert F. Kennedy Book Award. He also has published *Race, Civil Rights, and American Law. A Multiracial Approach and Mixed Race America and the Law: A Reader.* A regular participant in national and international conferences, Johnson has also held leadership positions in the Association of American Law Schools. He has been honored for his service by the Minority Groups Section of the Association of American Law Schools with the Clyde Ferguson Award in 2004 and previously by the UC Davis campus. In 2003, he was elected to the American Law Institute.

William Kandel (Reading 34) is a sociologist with the Economic Research Service of the U.S. Department of Agriculture, where he conducts research on the geographic dispersion of immigrants and minorities in rural areas and the role of industrial restructuring in demographic change. He obtained his doctorate in sociology from the University of Chicago, where his dissertation research examined impacts of temporary U.S. migration on Mexican children's educational attainment. He also held a postdoctoral fellowship in international demography and income inequality at the Population Research Institute at the Pennsylvania State University.

Randall L. Kennedy (Reading 44) is a professor of law at Harvard Law School. His areas of research and interest include the intersection of racial conflict and legal institutions in American life. He is author of *Interracial Intimacies: Sex, Marriage, Identity and Adoption* (2003) and *Race, Crime, and the Law* (1997).

Roger D. Klein (Reading 35) is an associate professor of psychology in education at the University of Pittsburgh.

Jonathan Kozol (Reading 24) taught in public schools for several years and is the award-winning author of many books, including *Death at an Early Age, Illiterate America, Free Schools,* and *Rachel and Her Children.*

Richard E. Lapchick (Reading 39) is the DeVos Eminent Scholar Chair and director of the Business Sports Management graduate program in the College of Business Administration at the University of Central Florida. He founded both Northeastern University's Center for the Study of Sport in Society as well as the National Consortium for Academics and Sport and is now director emeritus of the center and director of the consortium. He is the son of Joe Lapchick, the former coach of the New York Knicks, who pioneered integrating the NBA. Among many honors, he was inducted into the Sports Hall of Fame of the Commonwealth Nations in the humanitarian category along with Nelson Mandela and Arthur Ashe. He has published eleven books and is a columnist for the *Sport Business Journal* and the *Sporting News*.

Jennifer Lee (Reading 12) is an associate professor in the department of sociology at the University of California, Irvine, and received her B.A. and Ph.D. degrees from Columbia University. She is author of *Civility in the City: Blacks, Jews, and Koreans in Urban America* (2002) and co-editor of *Asian American Youth: Culture, Identity, and Ethnicity* (with Min Zhou), (2004). In 2003, she received the Robert E. Park Best Scholarly Article Award from the American Sociological Association's Community and Urban Sociology Section and honorable mention for the Thomas and Znaniecki Distinguished Book Award from the International Migration Section. In 2003, she was a Fellow at the Center for Advanced Study in the Behavioral Sciences at Stanford, California.

Justin Lewis (Reading 36) is professor of communication and deputy head of the School of Journalism, Media and Cultural Studies at Cardiff University. He has written many books and articles on media, politics and culture, and is currently series editor for the list in *Media and Culture* for Peter Lang Publishers.

S. Robert Lichter (Reading 37) is the founder of the Center for Media and Public Affairs, a nonpartisan, nonprofit research and educational organization that conducts scientific studies of news and entertainment media. He is the co-author (with Daniel Amundson) of *Solid Waste Management: Comparing Expert Opinion, Media Coverage, and Public Opinion* (1992).

George Lipsitz (Reading 19) researches racialization in U.S. society, including the racialization of space, urban culture, collective memory, and movements for social change. He is the author of *American Studies in a Moment of Danger* (2001), *The Possessive Investment in Whiteness: How White People Profit from Identity Politics* (1998), *Dangerous Crossroads: Postmodernism, Politics, and the Poetics of Place* (1994), *Rainbow at Midnight: Labor and Culture in the 1940s* (1991), *Time Passages: Collective Memory and American Pop Culture* (1990), *A Life in the Struggle: Ivory Perry and the Culture of Opposition* (1988, 1995).

Douglas S. Massey (Reading 21) is chair and professor of sociology at the University of Pennsylvania. His book *American Apartheid* (co-authored with Nancy A. Denton) won the 1995 Distinguished Scholarly Publication Award from the American Sociological Association.

Debra Merskin (Reading 38) is an associate professor at the University of Oregon and was the recipient of the School of Journalism's Marshall Award for Innovative Teaching in 1997. Her research interests focus on the representation of women and minorities in media, historical studies, and the social influences of the media. Her research appears in several journals, including *Journalism & Mass Communication Quarterly, American Behavioral Science, Sex Roles, Journal* *of Communication Inquiry, Feminist Media Studies*, and the *Howard Journal of Communication*. She has written chapters for several books including *Dressing in Feathers: The Construction of the Indian in American Popular Culture; Growing Up Girls: Popular Culture and the Construction of Identity; Sexual Rhetoric; The Girl Wide Web;* and *Bring 'Em on: Media and Politics in the Iraq War*.

Robert K. Merton (Reading 17) is an adjunct professor at Rockefeller University, a resident scholar at the Russell Sage Foundation, and a professor emeritus at Columbia University. He is an eminent sociological theorist and a well-known defender of sociology as a genuine science. His publications include *On the Shoulders of Giants: A Shandean Postscript* (1965) and *The Sociology of Science: Theoretical and Empirical Investigations* (1973).

Stacy Naccarato (Reading 35) has an M.Ed. from the University of Pittsburgh.

Katherine S. Newman (Reading 32) is Malcolm Wiener Professor of Urban Studies, dean of Social Science at the Radcliffe Institute for Advanced Study, and chair of joint doctoral programs in sociology, government, and social policy. She is the author of several books on middle-class economic insecurity, including *Falling From Grace* (1988) and *Declining Fortunes* (1993). Her 1999 book, *No Shame in My Game: The Working Poor in the Inner City*, won both the Sidney Hillman Book Prize and the Robert F. Kennedy Book Award.

Michael Omi (Reading 3) is a professor in the Department of Ethnic Studies at the University of California, Berkeley, and the co-author of *Racial Formation in the United States from the 1960s to the 1980s* (1986). He has also written about racial theory and politics, right-wing political movements, Asian Americans and race relations, and race and popular culture. In 1990, he was the recipient of Berkeley's Distinguished Teaching Award.

Devah Pager (Reading 29) is an assistant professor of sociology and faculty associate of the Office of Population Research at Princeton University. Her research focuses on institutions affecting racial stratification, including education, labor markets, and the criminal justice system. Pager's current research has involved a series of field experiments studying discrimination against minorities and ex-offenders in the low-wage labor market. As a separate line of work, Pager recently spent a year in Paris on a Fulbright grant studying changes in crime policy and its relationship to patterns of immigration and ethnic tension in contemporary France.

Emilio A Parrado (Reading 34) is an assistant professor of sociology at Duke University. He writes: "Broadly, my research entails the study of the interaction between social change and population processes with particular emphasis on Latin America. Most of my work falls into three categories: 1) marriage, employment, and fertility behavior, 2) international migration, and 3) the Latino population of the United States." He is "currently conducting a study of migration from Paraguay and Peru to Argentina that investigates the role of gender, family strategies, and macro-economic crises in affecting migration decisions."

Jeffrey Reiman (Reading 28) is the William Fraser McDowell Professor of Philosophy at American University in Washington D.C. He is the author of *In Defense of Political Philosophy* (1972), *The Rich Get Richer and the Poor Get Prison: Ideology, Class, and Criminal Justice* (1979), *Justice and Modern Moral Philosophy*

(1990), *Critical Moral Liberalism: Theory and Practice* (1997), *The Death Penalty: For and Against* (with Louis P. Pojman, 1998), *Abortion and the Ways We Value Human Life* (1999), and more than 50 articles in philosophy and criminal justice journals and anthologies.

Clara E. Rodriguez (Reading 9) is a professor in the Division of Social Sciences at Fordham University. Her major areas of research and interest include race and ethnicity, Latino studies, media, labor markets, and migration.

Maria Root (Reading 47) is a clinical psychologist and president-elect of the Washington State Psychological Association. She is the leading published authority in the nation on the developmental and social issues raised by the "biracial baby boom." She has researched and published extensively on the topic of identity development and related topics such as minority mental health, gender, and trauma. Root has edited and authored six books. She has two award-winning books, *Racially Mixed People in America* (1992) and *The Multiracial Experience: Racial Borders As the New Frontier* (1996). Her last book is *Love's Revolution: Racial Intermarriage* (2001).

Thomas M. Shapiro (Reading 8) is a professor of sociology and anthropology at Northeastern University. Shapiro and Melvin L. Oliver have been awarded the C. Wright Mills Award and the American Sociological Association's Distinguished Scholarly Publication Award for *Black Wealth/White Wealth*. Shapiro's books include *Population Control Politics: Women, Sterilization, and Reproductive Choice* and *Great Divides: Readings in Social Inequality in the United States.*

Stephen Steinberg (Reading 40) is the assistant chair of day studies and a sociologist in the Urban Studies Department at Queens College. His most recent book, *Turning Back: The Retreat from Racial Justice in American Thought and Policy* (1995), was awarded the Oliver Cromwell Cox Award for Distinguished Anti-Racist Scholarship by the Race and Ethnicity Section of the American Sociological Association. His previous works include *The Ethnic Myth, The Academic Melting Pot* and *The Tenacity of Prejudice.*

Michael W. Suleiman (Reading 42) is University Distinguished Professor in the Department of Political Science at Kansas State University. He has written and co-edited numerous works in the field of Arab American studies, including *U.S. Policy on Palestine from Wilson to Clinton* and *Arab Americans: Continuity and Change.*

Gerald Torres (Reading 14) is the H.O. Head Centennial Professor of Real Property Law at the University of Texas. He was previously professor of law and associate dean at the University of Minnesota Law School and also served in the U.S. Department of Justice, first as deputy assistant attorney general for Environment and Natural Resources and then as counsel to Attorney General Janet Reno. His publications include *Environmental Justice: The Legal Meaning of a Social Movement* (1996), *Understanding Environmental Racism* (1992), and *Critical Race Theory: The Decline of the Universalist Ideal and the Hope of Plural Justice* (1991).

Roger Waldinger (Reading 31) is a professor of race/ethnic/minority relations, urban sociology, and migration and immigration at the University of California, Los Angeles. He is the author of *Still the Promised City? New Immigrants and African-Americans in Post-Industrial New York* (1996) and *Ethnic Los Angeles,* co-edited with Medhi Bozorgmehr (1996).

Mary C. Waters (Reading 43) is a professor of sociology at Harvard University. She is the author of *Ethnic Options: Choosing Identities in America* and the co-author of *From Many Strands: Ethnic and Racial Groups in Contemporary America.* She has consulted with the Census Bureau on issues of measurement of race and ethnicity, and was a member of the National Academy of Science's Study Panel on the Demographic and Economic Consequences of Immigration to the United States. She has been a Guggenheim Fellow and a visiting scholar at the Russell Sage Foundation, and is a member of the International Committee of the Social Science Research Council.

David E. Wilkins (Reading 10) is an associate professor of American Indian studies, political science, and law. He has authored several books and a number of articles dealing with the political/legal relationship between indigenous nations and the United States and state governments. His most recent book is *American Indian Politics and the American Political System* (2002).

David R. Williams (Reading 7) is the Harold W. Cruse Collegiate Professor of Sociology at the University of Michigan. His major areas of research and interest include medical sociology, social psychology, race and SES differences in health, racism and health, and religion and mental health.

Howard Winant (Reading 3) is a professor of sociology at the University of California, Santa Barbara. He is the author of numerous books and articles, including *Racial Formation in the United States from the 1960s to the 1990s* (1994) (with Michael Omi), *Racial Conditions: Politics, Theory, Comparisons* (1994), and *Stalemate: Political Economic Origins of Supply-Side Policy* (1988). Winant states: "My abiding interests are in the sociology of race, particularly in the dynamics of racial politics and the theoretical logic of race. I have conducted research and taught in Brazil and Mexico. My current research focuses on the global dynamics of race at the end of the twentieth century."

Frank H. Wu (Reading 46) is the first Asian American to serve as a law professor at Howard University Law School. He has written for a range of publications, including the *Washington Post, L.A. Times, Chicago Tribune,* and *The Nation,* and writes a regular column for *Asian Week.* Wu participated in a major debate against Dinesh D'Souza on affirmative action that was televised by C-Span and was the host of the syndicated talk show *Asian America* on PBS. His most recent book is *Yellow: Race in America Beyond Black and White* (2002).

Shannon N. Zenk (Reading 25) is a post-doctorate research associate at the Institute for Health Research and Policy at the University of Illinois Chicago.

Min Zhou (Reading 41) is professor of sociology and chair of the Asian American Studies Interdepartmental Degree Program at the University of California, Los Angeles. Her main areas of research are immigration and immigrant adaptation, ethnic and racial studies, Asian Americans, entrepreneurship and ethnic economies, and the community and urban sociology. She is the author of *Chinatown: The Socioeconomic Potential of an Urban Enclave* (1992), co-author of *Growing Up American: How Vietnamese Children Adapt to Life in the United States* (1997), and co-editor of *Contemporary Asian American: A Multidisciplinary Reader* (2000).

Howard Zinn (Reading 2), professor, activist, and author, has dedicated his life to the notion that the knowledge of history is important to people's everyday lives and can be a powerful force for social change. Zinn is a champion of the idea that historical change occurs more through mass movements of ordinary people than through the wisdom and insight of so-called Great Men. His best-known book, *A People's History of the United States,* was one of the first major looks at American history from such a perspective.

Rethinking the Color Line: Understanding How Boundaries Shift

The sociological promise implicit in the title, *Rethinking the Color Line,* is that we will explore the contemporary meaning of race and ethnicity and examine how social, political, economic, and cultural forces shape those meanings. This may seem like a straightforward task. It is not. Race and ethnicity are slippery concepts because they are always in a state of flux. Imagine for a moment the shape of the United States as analogous to a definition of race or ethnicity. It may appear that an outline or sketch of the U.S. border, like a definition of race or ethnicity, can be neatly described or mapped out. That is, just as we can imagine the borders of the United States, we can, with reasonable certainty, identify someone as black, white, Asian, or American Indian. We place people in these racial categories because we have been trained to focus on a combination of traits like skin color, hair texture, and eye shape. After we have placed individuals in racial categories, we typically use cultural markers, such as their ethnic background or ancestry, to further sort them. For instance, if a white person walks into a room, we *see* that individual's race. What happens when he or she starts talking and we pick up on an Irish brogue or a New York City accent or a southern dialect? What happens when the brown woman in front of us in the supermarket talks to the cashier and we recognize her accent as Jamaican or English? We tend to sort first by color and then by cultural background.

Since the founding of the United States more than two hundred years ago, the lines that have defined the nation's borders have been redrawn dozens of times. Just as there was no United States of America prior to 1776, the idea of race as it is currently understood did not exist until the Europeans colonized the Americas, Africa, and parts of Asia. The mental map of the United States we conjure up today is only about forty years old. The map was last redrawn in 1959 when Hawaii was admitted into the Union as the fiftieth state. Previously, the map had been redrawn after the Louisiana Purchase of 1803 and again after the Missouri Compromise of 1820, as well as after the admittance of every new state to the Union. And we will have to redraw our mental map yet again if the Commonwealth of Puerto Rico votes to enter the Union as the fifty-first state.

The problem with definitions of race and ethnicity, as with the shape of the United States, is that the borders or contours that give form and meaning to these concepts change over time. A person defined as white in the year 2007 might have been defined as black or Irish or Italian at various times in American history. For example, around the turn of the century, Irish and Italian immigrants were *not* viewed as white when they first arrived in the United States. At that time, members of those groups did not easily fit into the existing racial hierarchy; they were in a racial limbo—not white, not black, not Asian. Their ethnic background—that is, the language, culture, and religious beliefs that distinguished these Irish and Italian immigrants from the dominant group—was used in various ways to define them as a racial group. Within a generation or two, these so-called Irish and Italian

1

racial groups assimilated and were absorbed into the category we now know as white. The journey from being considered not white or racially ambiguous to white was rather swift. It may seem odd, and may even shock our racial sensibilities, to think of Supreme Court Justice Antonin Scalia's or Senator Ted Kennedy's parents or grandparents as possibly being defined as nonwhite Italians or nonwhite Irish at different times in American history. But is a nonwhite Italian or nonwhite Irish any less curious an idea than a black-Irish American or an Asian-Italian American? If one's ethnic identity is subsumed or taken over by a racial identity, the question we need to ask as sociologists is why?

Just as the shape of the United States has changed over time, so have the definitions of race and ethnicity. Do you think your view of race and ethnicity is different from that of your parents or grandparents? How you understand race and ethnicity reflects a definition specific to this moment in time, one that, in all likelihood, will look quite different in three or four decades. *Rethinking the Color Line* will provide you with a theoretical framework for understanding how and why definitions of race and ethnicity change over time, what sociological forces bring about these changes, and what these categories might look like in the next century.

What these examples suggest, and what many of the readings in *Rethinking the Color Line* consciously explore, is how race and ethnicity are socially constructed. When we say that something is socially constructed, we mean that the characteristics deemed relevant to that definition are based on societal and cultural values. Race and ethnicity are social constructions because we derive their meanings by focusing on arbitrary characteristics that a given society deems important. Race and ethnicity are social products based on cultural values, not scientific facts.

Think for a moment about gravity. If you push this book off your desk, do you expect it to fall to the ground? Obviously, you do. If you lived in Brazil or South Africa or Puerto Rico, would you expect the same thing to happen to your book? Of course you would because you know that gravity is a universal constant. However, someone defined as black in the United States could be defined as white in Brazil, Trigueno (intermediate) in Puerto Rico, and "coloured" in South Africa. Gravity is the same everywhere, but racial classifications vary across place and time because definitions of race and ethnicity are based on the physical traits a society chooses to value or devalue. Because each society's values are based on a different set of historical experiences, cultural circumstances, and political definitions, ideas about race and ethnicity can vary quite a bit, not only between countries but within them as well. For example, historically, it was not uncommon for someone to have been socially and legally defined as black in the southern part of the United States but to "pass" for white after migrating north. The beliefs and definitions that undergird the idea of race are very unstable and, as we will see in the readings, quite susceptible to political manipulation.

Racial and ethnic identity is culturally meaningful only because we define and understand it in that way. In other words, race exists because we say race exists. And because the characteristics that make up the idea of race and ethnicity reflect a social process, it is possible to imagine these concepts in a different way. Instead of looking at skin color, facial features, or hair texture as a way to sort individuals, we could create a racial category based on the size of people's feet. People with shoe sizes between 4 and 7 would be labeled the Petite Race, those with sizes 8–11 would be designated the Bigger Race, and the 12–15 shoe size crowd would be categorized as the

Monster Foot Race. Those with feet smaller or larger than the existing categories would be the "Other" Race. Likewise, we could use eye color, height, glove size, or nose length to create racial categories. Because the physical markers we use to define race are arbitrary and have no basis in genetics, biology, anthropology, or sociology, using shoe size as the criterion to fashion a new definition of race would be just as valid as the system currently in place. Similarly, we could redefine ethnicity by changing the focus from language, culture, religion, or nationality as a method of sorting people and instead create categories of people based on the amount of meat they eat or the way they style their hair.

What complicates our ability to accurately and easily map these definitions of race and ethnicity is that the definitions are constantly changing. Are the thirty million Latinos in the United States an ethnic group because they are defined by the U.S. Census Bureau as such, or are Latinos a racial group? If the current census categories of white, black, Asian, and American Indian do not adequately reflect what Latinos experience or how Latinos are viewed by non-Latinos, should a "brown category be added to the census? Would a newly created "brown" category link Puerto Ricans in New York City with Cuban Americans in Miami and Mexican Americans in San Diego? Why or why not? How should we define the race of a child whose father was Mexican-African American and whose mother was Japanese-Irish American? What is this child's ethnicity?

For that matter, how and in what ways are race and ethnicity related?

In 1903, sociologist W. E. B. Du Bois wrote that "the problem of the twentieth century is the problem of the color-line." It appears that a key problem of the twenty-first century, while different in degree and context from the one Du Bois chronicled, will still be the color line. A topic or issue may not initially seem to be linked to race or ethnicity, but on closer sociological scrutiny, patterns often emerge that make it clear that race and ethnicity matter quite a bit. How do you see race and ethnicity being connected to who gets a good education or adequate health care, who is likely to be poor, where toxic waste sites are built, who gets hired or promoted, or which racial or ethnic groups are more likely to have members sentenced to death and executed? Race and ethnicity are intertwined in every aspect of our lives.

Rethinking the Color Line will provide you with the tools necessary to navigate the complicated and often contradictory meaning of race and ethnicity in the United States. The readings will take you on a sociological journey and explore how you, your classmates, your family, and your friends fit into the racial and ethnic mosaic of the United States. If you focus carefully on the readings, the "Questions to Consider" chapter introductions, and the "Seeing the Big Picture" discussion at the end of most chapters, your perspective on race and ethnic relations in the United States will be changed forever.

PART I
Sorting by Color:
Why We Attach Meaning to Race

How would you answer these questions? Who taught you how to "be" black or American Indian or white or Asian? Did you learn to "do" your race by watching sitcoms on television or by watching your peers in the schoolyard? Was it your parents or an older sibling or cousin who taught you how to act both your age and your race? In what social situations do you think about your racial identity? Is it only when you interact with an individual from a different racial background? Do you think about your race, about other racial groups, or about race relations when you watch football games or MTV or the nightly news? Do you think about your race while you are in your neighborhood or only when you drive through an area with a different racial population? Were you ever in a social setting in which you were the only person of your color? How did that make you feel?

How did you learn to "be" Korean or Jamaican or German? In what situations do you think about your ancestry? Is it during the holidays or when you spend time with your family? Or has your family been in the United States for so many generations that the family tree linking you to the homeland is unimportant, nonexistent, or untraceable? Does that mean you have a racial identity but not an ethnic identity? Or does "American" best mirror your social identity?

The readings in Part I answer these questions by exposing you to the social theories used to define and understand the dynamics of race and ethnicity. The first five readings in "Race and Ethnicity: Sociohistoric Constructions" examine how the natural variation in human skin color has been used as a way to sort people into groups, create a racial hierarchy, and justify exploitation based on skin color. Marvin Harris explains why gradations of color, from black to white, are "beautiful" sociocultural responses to the environment. Howard Zinn charts the evolution of the idea of race in early U.S. history and how the idea of racial categories were synonymous with who would be free and who would be enslaved. Michael Omi and Howard Winant explain the emergence of racial categories as a "sociohistoric" process they call racial formation; that is, the way we define ourselves racially reflects a political and social process that was hundreds of years in the making. Joe Feagin and Clairece Booher Feagin provide an overview of the theories central to ethnic and racial studies, theories that will reemerge throughout the book. Eduardo Bonilla-Silva suggests that race, like class or gender, takes on a "life of its own" creating hierarchical social relations that are exploitive and coercive. As you will see throughout the text, many of the articles in this reader draw on one or more of these theories to explain a particular aspect of racial inequality and race and ethnic relations.

The next three readings in "Contemporary Socioeconomic Trends" draw on theories outlined in the first section while emphasizing socioeconomic disparities between racial and ethnic groups. Rebecca Blank provides descriptive statistics of the social and economic well-being of non-Hispanic whites, non-Hispanic blacks, Hispanics, Asian and

Pacific Islanders, and American Indians and Alaska natives. Very real differences exist between groups in terms of income, rates of poverty and incarceration, access to computers, and health status. How might you explain these between group differences in quality of life markers? David Williams and Chiquita Collins present a rather disturbing overview of racial disparities in health. Not only are racial minorities worse off compared to whites on almost every health measure but it is likely that this gap will continue to grow as the United States limits access to public health care for the poor. Using national data on wealth, Thomas Shapiro examines the racial dynamics of how transformative assets, the financial assistance one gets from families, shape life chances.

In "Race as Chameleon: How the Idea of Race Changes over Time and Place" Clara Rodriguez and Hector Cordero-Guzman explain how the social and political organization of slavery in Puerto Rico differed from that in the United States, resulting in an understanding and definition of race that may seem peculiar to those of us accustomed to the white-versus-black view of race relations so dominant in the United States. Although the specific historical circumstances of Asians and American Indians are quite different, Yen Le Espiritu and David Wilkins demonstrate how, why, and in what situations racial and ethnic identities are used to organize politically. Throughout this book I will be arguing that the idea of race is not static. Jennifer Lee and Frank D. Bean suggest that we are yet again at a crossroads in the construction of how we think about racial categories with the growing number of individuals who define themselves "multiracial." As these readings demonstrate, the creation of racial categories is as much a historical process as it is a political one.

In the next section, "Colorblind America: Fact, Fantasy, or Our Future," the three readings focus on how different social conditions can exacerbate racial and ethnic relations and what might be done at both the macro and micro levels to ameliorate racial inequality. Charles A. Gallagher notes that current trends in popular culture have blurred the color line by linking the consumption of products across racial groups to racial harmony. Gallagher asks, if groups from various races now share and consume the same products (hip-hop, McDonald's, reality TV), has racial equality been achieved? Lani Guinier and Gerald Torres make the case that descriptions of America as a colorblind nation are quite premature while Herbert Gans argues that a "beige-ing" of America is taking place that will incorporate some parts of the Latino and Asian populations but not blacks. The color line will shift, Gans argues, but not necessarily in a way that is inclusive. Each of these readings points to the various social, economic, and cultural barriers to racial equality and the rather lofty goal of becoming a truly colorblind nation.

RACE AND ETHNICITY: SOCIOHISTORIC CONSTRUCTIONS AND . . .

1

HOW OUR SKINS GOT THEIR COLOR

Marvin Harris

QUESTIONS TO CONSIDER

Cultural anthropologist Marvin Harris links the variations in skin color one can observe in traveling around the world to the human body's ability to adapt physically to changes in exposure to solar radiation. How do you explain his assertion that "white was beautiful because white was healthy" and "black was beautiful because black was healthy"?

Most human beings are neither very fair nor very dark, but brown. The extremely fair skin of northern Europeans and their descendants, and the very black skins of central Africans and their descendants, are probably special adaptations. Brown-skinned ancestors may have been shared by modern-day blacks and whites as recently as 10,000 years ago. Human skin owes its color to the presence of particles known as melanin. The primary function of melanin is to protect the upper levels of the skin from being damaged by the sun's ultraviolet rays. This radiation poses a critical problem for our kind because we lack the dense coat of hair that acts as a sunscreen for most mammals. . . . Hairlessness exposes us to two kinds of radiation hazards: ordinary sunburn, with its blisters, rashes, and risk of infection; and skin cancers, including malignant melanoma, one of the deadliest diseases known. Melanin is the body's first line of defense against these afflictions. The more melanin particles, the darker the skin, and the lower the risk of sunburn and all forms of skin cancer. This explains why the highest rates for skin cancer are found in sun-drenched lands such as Australia, where light-skinned people of European descent spend a good part of their lives outdoors wearing scanty attire. Very dark-skinned people such as heavily pigmented Africans of Zaire seldom get skin cancer, but when they do, they get it on depigmented parts of their bodies—palms and lips.

Marvin Harris, "How Our Skins Got Their Color" from *Our Kind: Who We Are, Where We Came from and Where We Are Going*, pp. 112–114. Copyright © 1989 by Marvin Harris. Reprinted by permission of HarperCollins Publishers, Inc.

If exposure to solar radiation had nothing but harmful effects, natural selection would have favored inky black as the color for all human populations. But the sun's rays do not present an unmitigated threat. As it falls on the skin, sunshine converts a fatty substance in the epidermis into vitamin D. The blood carries vitamin D from the skin to the intestines (technically making it a hormone rather than a vitamin), where it plays a vital role in the absorption of calcium. In turn, calcium is vital for strong bones. Without it, people fall victim to the crippling diseases rickets and osteomalacia. In women, calcium deficiencies can result in a deformed birth canal, which makes childbirth lethal for both mother and fetus.

Vitamin D can be obtained from a few foods, primarily the oils and livers of marine fish. But inland populations must rely on the sun's rays and their own skins for the supply of this crucial substance. The particular color of a human population's skin, therefore, represents in large degree a trade-off between the hazards of too much versus too little solar radiation: acute sunburn and skin cancer on the one hand, and rickets and osteomalacia on the other. It is this trade-off that largely accounts for the preponderance of brown people in the world and for the general tendency for skin color to be darkest among equatorial populations and lightest among populations dwelling at higher latitudes.

At middle latitudes, the skin follows a strategy of changing colors with the seasons. Around the Mediterranean basin, for example, exposure to the summer sun brings high risk of cancer but low risk for rickets; the body produces more melanin and people grow darker (i.e., they get suntans). Winter reduces the risk of sunburn and cancer; the body produces less melanin, and the tan wears off.

The correlation between skin color and latitude is not perfect because other factors—such as the availability of foods containing vitamin D and calcium, regional cloud cover during the winter, amount of clothing worn, and cultural preferences—may work for or against the predicted relationship. Arctic-dwelling Eskimo, for example, are not as light-skinned as expected, but their habitat and economy afford them a diet that is exceptionally rich in both vitamin D and calcium.

Northern Europeans, obliged to wear heavy garments for protection against the long, cold, cloudy winters, were always at risk for rickets and osteomalacia from too little vitamin D and calcium. This risk increased sometime after 6000 B.C., when pioneer cattle herders who did not exploit marine resources began to appear in northern Europe. The risk would have been especially great for the brown-skinned Mediterranean peoples who migrated northward along with the crops and farm animals. Samples of Caucasian skin (infant penile foreskin obtained at the time of circumcision) exposed to sunlight on cloudless days in Boston (42°N) from November through February produced no vitamin D. In Edmonton (52°N) this period extended from October to March. But further south (34°N) sunlight was effective in producing vitamin D in the middle of the winter. Almost all of Europe lies north of 42°N. Fair-skinned, non-tanning individuals who could utilize the weakest and briefest doses of sunlight to synthesize vitamin D were strongly favored by natural selection. During the frigid winters, only a small circle of a child's face could be left to peek out at the sun through the heavy clothing, thereby favoring the survival of individuals with translucent patches of pink on their cheeks characteristic of many northern Europeans. (People who could get calcium by drinking cow's milk would also be favored by natural selection.)

If light-skinned individuals on the average had only 2 percent more children survive per generation, the changeover in their skin color could have begun 5,000 years ago and reached present levels well before the beginning of the Christian era. But natural selection need not have acted alone. Cultural selection may also have played a role. It seems likely that whenever people consciously or unconsciously had to decide which infants to nourish and which to neglect, the advantage would go to those with lighter skin, experience having shown that such individuals tended to grow up to be taller, stronger, and healthier than their darker siblings. White was beautiful because white was healthy.

To account for the evolution of black skin in equatorial latitudes, one has merely to reverse the combined effects of natural and cultural selection. With the sun directly overhead most of the year, and clothing a hindrance to work and survival, vitamin D was never in short supply (and calcium was easily obtained from vegetables). Rickets and osteomalacia were rare. Skin cancer was the main problem, and what nature started, culture amplified. Darker infants were favored by parents because experience showed that they grew up to be freer of disfiguring and lethal malignancies. Black was beautiful because black was healthy.

2

DRAWING THE COLOR LINE

Howard Zinn

QUESTIONS TO CONSIDER

In this article Howard Zinn chronicles the beginning of slavery in North America. How did law, custom, and culture reconcile the emergence of chattel slavery with Christian precepts, which reject the idea that one human could own or forcibly control another human being? What arguments were used to justify slavery? List which groups profited from the slave trade.

A black American writer, J. Saunders Redding, describes the arrival of a ship in North America in the year 1619:

Sails furled, flag drooping at her rounded stern, she rode the tide in from the sea. She was a strange ship, indeed, by all accounts, a frightening ship, a ship of mystery. Whether she was trader, privateer, or man-of-war no one knows. Through her bulwarks black-mouthed cannon yawned. The flag she flew was Dutch; her crew a motley. Her port of call, an English settlement, Jamestown, in the colony of Virginia. She came, she traded, and shortly afterwards was gone. Probably no ship in modern history has carried a more portentous freight. Her cargo? Twenty slaves.

From *A People's History of the United States,* pp. 23–38, by Howard Zinn. Copyright © 1980 by Howard Zinn. Reprinted by permission of HarperCollins Publishers, Inc.

There is not a country in world history in which racism has been more important, for so long a time, as the United States. And the problem of "the color line," as W. E. B. Du Bois put it, is still with us. So it is more than a purely historical question to ask: How does it start?—and an even more urgent question: How might it end? Or, to put it differently: Is it possible for whites and blacks to live together without hatred?

If history can help answer these questions, then the beginnings of slavery in North America—a continent where we can trace the coming of the first whites and the first blacks—might supply at least a few clues.

Some historians think those first blacks in Virginia were considered as servants, like the white indentured servants brought from Europe. But the strong probability is that, even if they were listed as "servants" (a more familiar category to the English), they were viewed as being different from white servants, were treated differently, and in fact were slaves. In any case, slavery developed quickly into a regular institution, into the normal labor relation of blacks to whites in the New World. With it developed that special racial feeling—whether hatred, or contempt, or pity, or patronization—that accompanied the inferior position of blacks in America for the next 350 years—that combination of inferior status and derogatory thought we call racism.

Everything in the experience of the first white settlers acted as a pressure for the enslavement of blacks.

The Virginians of 1619 were desperate for labor, to grow enough food to stay alive. Among them were survivors from the winter of 1609–1610, the "starving time," when, crazed for want of food, they roamed the woods for nuts and berries, dug up graves to eat the corpses, and died in batches until five hundred colonists were reduced to sixty.

In the *Journals* of the House of Burgesses of Virginia is a document of 1619 which tells of the first twelve years of the Jamestown colony. The first settlement had a hundred persons, who had one small ladle of barley per meal. When more people arrived, there was even less food. Many of the people lived in cavelike holes dug into the ground, and in the winter of 1609–1610, they were

> . . . driven thru insufferable hunger to eat those things which nature most abhorred, the flesh and excrements of man as well of our own nation as of an Indian, digged by some out of his grave after he had lain buried three days and wholly devoured him; others, envying the better state of body of any whom hunger has not yet so much wasted as their own, lay wait and threatened to kill and eat them; one among them slew his wife as she slept in his bosom, cut her in pieces, salted her and fed upon her till he had clean devoured all parts saving her head. . . .

A petition by thirty colonists to the House of Burgesses, complaining against the twelve-year governorship of Sir Thomas Smith, said:

> In those 12 years of Sir Thomas Smith, his government, we aver that the colony for the most part remained in great want and misery under most severe and cruel laws. . . . The allowance in those times for a man was only eight ounces of meale and half a pint of peas for a day . . . mouldy, rotten, full of cobwebs and maggots, loathsome to man and not fit for beasts, which forced many to flee for relief to the savage enemy, who being taken again were put to sundry deaths as by hanging, shooting and breaking upon the wheel . . . of whom one for stealing two or three pints of oatmeal had a bodkin thrust through his tongue and was tied with a chain to a tree until he starved. . . .

The Virginians needed labor, to grow corn for subsistence, to grow tobacco for export. They had just figured out how to grow tobacco, and in 1617 they sent off the first cargo to England. Finding that, like all pleasurable drugs tainted with moral disapproval, it brought a high price, the planters, despite their high religious talk, were not going to ask questions about something so profitable.

They couldn't force Indians to work for them, as Columbus had done. They were outnumbered, and while, with superior fire-arms, they could massacre Indians, they would face massacre in return. They could not capture them and keep them enslaved; the Indians were tough, resourceful, defiant, and at home in these woods, as the transplanted Englishmen were not.

White servants had not yet been brought over in sufficient quantity. Besides, they did not come out of slavery, and did not have to do more than contract their labor for a few years to get their passage and a start in the New World. As for the free white settlers, many of them were skilled craftsmen, or even men of leisure back in England, who were so little inclined to work the land that John Smith, in those early years, had to declare a kind of martial law, organize them into work gangs, and force them into the fields for survival.

There may have been a kind of frustrated rage at their own ineptitude, at the Indian superiority at taking care of themselves, that made the Virginians especially ready to become the masters of slaves. Edmund Morgan imagines their mood as he writes in his book *American Slavery, American Freedom:*

If you were a colonist, you knew that your technology was superior to the Indians'. You knew that you were civilized, and they were savages. . . . But your superior technology had proved insufficient to extract anything. The Indians, keeping to them-selves, laughed at your superior methods and lived from the land more abundantly and with less labor than you did. . . . And when your own people started deserting in order to live with them, it was too much. . . . So you killed the Indians, tortured them, burned their villages, burned their

cornfields. It proved your superiority, in spite of your failures. And you gave similar treatment to any of your own people who succumbed to their savage ways of life. But you still did not grow much corn. . . .

Black slaves were the answer. And it was natural to consider imported blacks as slaves, even if the institution of slavery would not be regularized and legalized for several decades. Because, by 1619, a million blacks had already been brought from Africa to South America and the Caribbean, to the Portuguese and Spanish colonies, to work as slaves. Fifty years before Columbus, the Portuguese took ten African blacks to Lisbon—this was the start of a regular trade in slaves. African blacks had been stamped as slave labor for a hundred years. So it would have been strange if those twenty blacks, forcibly transported to Jamestown, and sold as objects to settlers anxious for a steadfast source of labor, were considered as anything but slaves.

Their helplessness made enslavement easier. The Indians were on their own land. The whites were in their own European cul-ture. The blacks had been torn from their land and culture, forced into a situation where the heritage of language, dress, custom, family relations, was bit by bit obliterated except for the remnants that blacks could hold on to by sheer, extraordinary persistence.

Was their culture inferior—and so subject to easy destruction? Inferior in military capa-bility, yes—vulnerable to whites with guns and ships. But in no other way—except that cultures that are different are often taken as inferior, especially when such a judgment is practical and profitable. Even militarily, while the Westerners could secure forts on the Afri-can coast, they were unable to subdue the inte-rior and had to come to terms with its chiefs.

The African civilization was as advanced in its own way as that of Europe. In certain ways, it was more admirable; but it also included cruelties, hierarchical privilege, and the readiness to sacrifice human lives for religion or profit. It was a civilization of 100 million people, using iron implements and skilled in farming. It had large urban centers and remarkable achievements in weaving, ceramics, sculpture.

European travelers in the sixteenth century were impressed with the African kingdoms of Timbuktu and Mali, already stable and organized at a time when European states were just beginning to develop into the modern nation. In 1563, Ramusio, secretary to the rulers in Venice, wrote to the Italian merchants: "Let them go and do business with the King of Timbuktu and Mali and there is no doubt that they will be well-received there with their ships and their goods and treated well, and granted the favours that they ask. . . ."

A Dutch report, around 1602, on the West African kingdom of Benin, said: "The Towne seemeth to be very great, when you enter it. You go into a great broad street, not paved, which seemeth to be seven or eight times broader than the Warmoes Street in Amsterdam. . . . The Houses in this Towne stand in good order, one close and even with the other, as the Houses in Holland stand."

The inhabitants of the Guinea Coast were described by one traveler around 1680 as "very civil and good-natured people, easy to be dealt with, condescending to what Europeans require of them in a civil way, and very ready to return double the presents we make them."

Africa had a kind of feudalism, like Europe based on agriculture, and with hierarchies of lords and vassals. But African feudalism did not come, as did Europe's, out of the slave societies of Greece and Rome, which had destroyed ancient tribal life. In Africa, tribal life was still powerful, and some of its better features—a communal spirit, more kindness in law and punishment—still existed. And because the lords did not have

the weapons that European lords had, they could not command obedience as easily.

In his book *The African Slave Trade,* Basil Davidson contrasts law in the Congo in the early sixteenth century with law in Portugal and England. In those European countries, where the idea of private property was becoming powerful, theft was punished brutally. In England, even as late as 1740, a child could be hanged for stealing a rag of cotton. But in the Congo, communal life persisted, the idea of private property was a strange one, and thefts were punished with fines or various degrees of servitude. A Congolese leader, told of the Portuguese legal codes, asked a Portuguese once, teasingly: "What is the penalty in Portugal for anyone who puts his feet on the ground?"

Slavery existed in the African states, and it was sometimes used by Europeans to justify their own slave trade. But, as Davidson points out, the "slaves" of Africa were more like the serfs of Europe—in other words, like most of the population of Europe. It was a harsh servitude, but they had rights which slaves brought to America did not have, and they were "altogether different from the human cattle of the slave ships and the American plantations." In the Ashanti Kingdom of West Africa, one observer noted that "a slave might marry; own property; himself own a slave; swear an oath; be a competent witness and ultimately become heir to his master. . . . An Ashanti slave, nine cases out of ten, possibly became an adopted member of the family, and in time his descendants so merged and intermarried with the owner's kinsmen that only a few would know their origin."

One slave trader, John Newton (who later became an antislavery leader), wrote about the people of what is now Sierra Leone:

> The state of slavery, among these wild barbarous people, as we esteem them, is much milder than in our colonies. For as,

on the one hand, they have no land in high cultivation, like our West India plantations, and therefore no call for that excessive, unintermitted labour, which exhausts our slaves: so, on the other hand, no man is permitted to draw blood even from a slave.

African slavery is hardly to be praised. But it was far different from plantation or mining slavery in the Americas, which was lifelong, morally crippling, destructive of family ties, without hope of any future. African slavery lacked two elements that made American slavery the most cruel form of slavery in history: the frenzy for limitless profit that comes from capitalistic agriculture; the reduction of the slave to less than human status by the use of racial hatred, with that relentless clarity based on color, where white was master, black was slave.

In fact, it was because they came from a settled culture, of tribal customs and family ties, of communal life and traditional ritual, that African blacks found themselves especially helpless when removed from this. They were captured in the interior (frequently by blacks caught up in the slave trade themselves), sold on the coast, then shoved into pens with blacks of other tribes, often speaking different languages.

The conditions of capture and sale were crushing affirmations to the black African of his helplessness in the face of superior force. The marches to the coast, sometimes for 1,000 miles, with people shackled around the neck, under whip and gun, were death marches, in which two of every five blacks died. On the coast, they were kept in cages until they were picked and sold. One John Barbot, at the end of the seventeenth century, described these cages on the Gold Coast:

As the slaves come down to Fida from the inland country, they are put into a booth or prison . . . near the beach, and when the Europeans are to receive them, they are brought out onto a large plain, where the

ship's surgeons examine every part of everyone of them, to the smallest member, men and women being stark naked. . . . Such as are allowed good and sound are set on one side . . . marked on the breast with a red-hot iron, imprinting the mark of the French, English, or Dutch companies. . . . The branded slaves after this are returned to their former booths where they await shipment, sometimes 10–15 days. . . .

Then they were packed aboard the slave ships, in spaces not much bigger than coffins, chained together in the dark, wet slime of the ship's bottom, choking in the stench of their own excrement. Documents of the time describe the conditions:

The height, sometimes, between decks, was only eighteen inches; so that the unfortunate human beings could not turn around, or even on their sides, the elevation being less than the breadth of their shoulders; and here they are usually chained to the decks by the neck and legs. In such a place the sense of misery and suffocation is so great, that the Negroes . . . are driven to frenzy.

On one occasion, hearing a great noise from belowdecks where the blacks were chained together, the sailors opened the hatches and found the slaves in different stages of suffocation, many dead, some having killed others in desperate attempts to breathe. Slaves often jumped overboard to drown rather than continue their suffering. To one observer a slave-deck was "so covered with blood and mucus that it resembled a slaughter house."

Under these conditions, perhaps one of every three blacks transported overseas died, but the huge profits (often double the investment on one trip) made it worthwhile for the slave trader, and so the blacks were packed into the holds like fish.

First the Dutch, then the English, dominated the slave trade. (By 1795 Liverpool had more than a hundred ships carrying slaves and accounted for half of all the European slave trade.) Some Americans in New England entered the business, and in 1637 the first American slave ship, the *Desire,* sailed from Marblehead. Its holds were partitioned into racks, 2 feet by 6 feet, with leg irons and bars.

By 1800, 10 to 15 million blacks had been transported as slaves to the Americas, representing perhaps one-third of those originally seized in Africa. It is roughly estimated that Africa lost 50 million human beings to death and slavery in those centuries we call the beginnings of modern Western civilization, at the hands of slave traders and plantation owners in Western Europe and America, the countries deemed the most advanced in the world.

In the year 1610, a Catholic priest in the Americas named Father Sandoval wrote back to a church functionary in Europe to ask if the capture, transport, and enslavement of African blacks was legal by church doctrine. A letter dated March 12, 1610, from Brother Luis Brandaon to Father Sandoval gives the answer:

> Your Reverence writes me that you would like to know whether the Negroes who are sent to your parts have been legally captured. To this I reply that I think your Reverence should have no scruples on this point, because this is a matter which has been questioned by the Board of Conscience in Lisbon, and all its members are learned and conscientious men. Nor did the bishops who were in Sao Thome, Cape Verde, and here in Loando—all learned and virtuous men—find fault with it. We have been here ourselves for forty years and there have been among us very learned Fathers . . . never did they consider the trade as illicit. Therefore we and the Fathers of Brazil buy these slaves for our service without any scruple. . . .

With all of this—the desperation of the Jamestown settlers for labor, the impossibility of using Indians and the difficulty of using whites, the availability of blacks offered in greater and greater numbers by profit-seeking dealers in human flesh, and with such blacks possible to control because they had just gone through an ordeal which if it did not kill them must have left them in a state of psychic and physical helplessness—is it any wonder that such blacks were ripe for enslavement?

And under these conditions, even if some blacks might have been considered servants, would blacks be treated the same as white servants?

The evidence, from the court records of colonial Virginia, shows that in 1630 a white man named Hugh Davis was ordered "to be soundly whipt . . . for abusing himself . . . by defiling his body in lying with a Negro." Ten years later, six servants and "a negro of Mr. Reynolds" started to run away. While the whites received lighter sentences, "Emanuel the Negro to receive thirty stripes and to be burnt in the cheek with the letter R, and to work in shackle one year or more as his master shall see cause."

Although slavery was not yet regularized or legalized in those first years, the lists of servants show blacks listed separately. A law passed in 1639 decreed that "all persons except Negroes" were to get arms and ammunition— probably to fight off Indians. When in 1640 three servants tried to run away, the two whites were punished with a lengthening of their service. But, as the court put it, "the third being a negro named John Punch shall serve his master or his assigns for the time of his natural life." Also in 1640, we have the case of a Negro woman servant who begot a child by Robert Sweat, a white man. The court ruled "that the said negro woman shall be whipt at the whipping post and the said Sweat shall tomorrow in the forenoon do public penance for his offense at James citychurch. . . ."

This unequal treatment, this developing combination of contempt and oppression, feeling and action, which we call "racism"— was this the result of a "natural" antipathy of white against black? The question is important, not just as a matter of historical accuracy, but because any emphasis on "natural" racism lightens the responsibility of the social system. If racism can't be shown to be natural, then it is the result of certain conditions, and we are impelled to eliminate those conditions.

We have no way of testing the behavior of whites and blacks toward one another under favorable conditions—with no history of subordination, no money incentive for exploitation and enslavement, no desperation for survival requiring forced labor. All the conditions for black and white in seventeenth-century America were the opposite of that, all powerfully directed toward antagonism and mistreatment. Under such conditions even the slightest display of humanity between the races might be considered evidence of a basic human drive toward community.

Sometimes it is noted that, even before 1600, when the slave trade had just begun, before Africans were stamped by it—literally and symbolically the color black was distasteful. In England, before 1600, it meant, according to the *Oxford English Dictionary*: "Deeply stained with dirt; soiled, dirty, foul. Having dark or deadly purposes, malignant; pertaining to or involving death, deadly; baneful, disastrous, sinister. Foul, iniquitous, atrocious, horribly wicked. Indicating disgrace, censure, liability to punishment, etc." And Elizabethan poetry often used the color white in connection with beauty.

It may be that, in the absence of any other overriding factor, darkness and blackness, associated with night and unknown, would take on those meanings. But the presence of another human being is a powerful fact, and the conditions of that presence are crucial in determining whether an initial prejudice,

against a mere color, divorced from humankind, is turned into brutality and hatred.

In spite of such preconceptions about blackness, in spite of special subordination of blacks in the Americas in the seventeenth century, there is evidence that where whites and blacks found themselves with common problems, common work, common enemy in their master, they behaved toward one another as equals. As one scholar of slavery, Kenneth Stampp, has put it, Negro and white servants of the seventeenth century were "remarkably unconcerned about the visible physical differences."

Black and white worked together, fraternized together. The very fact that laws had to be passed after a while to forbid such relations indicates the strength of that tendency. In 1661 a law was passed in Virginia that "in case any English servant shall run away in company of any Negroes" he would have to give special service for extra years to the master of the runaway Negro. In 1691, Virginia provided for the banishment of any "white man or woman being free who shall intermarry with a negro, mulatoo, or Indian man or woman bond or free."

There is an enormous difference between a feeling of racial strangeness, perhaps fear, and the mass enslavement of millions of black people that took place in the Americas. The transition from one to the other cannot be explained easily by "natural" tendencies. It is not hard to understand as the outcome of historical conditions.

Slavery grew as the plantation system grew. The reason is easily traceable to something other than natural racial repugnance: the number of arriving whites, whether free or indentured servants (under four to seven years contract), was not enough to meet the need of the plantations. By 1700, in Virginia, there were 6,000 slaves, one-twelfth of the population. By 1763, there were 170,000 slaves, about half the population.

Blacks were easier to enslave than whites or Indians. But they were still not easy to enslave. From the beginning, the imported black men and women resisted their enslavement. Ultimately their resistance was controlled, and slavery was established for 3 million blacks in the South. Still, under the most difficult conditions, under pain of mutilation and death, throughout their two hundred years of enslavement in North America, these Afro-Americans continued to rebel. Only occasionally was there an organized insurrection. More often they showed their refusal to submit by running away. Even more often, they engaged in sabotage, slowdowns, and subtle forms of resistance which asserted, if only to themselves and their brothers and sisters, their dignity as human beings.

The refusal began in Africa. One slave trader reported that Negroes were "so wilful and loth to leave their own country, that they have often leap'd out of the canoes, boat and ship into the sea, and kept under water till they were drowned."

When the very first black slaves were brought into Hispaniola in 1503, the Spanish governor of Hispaniola complained to the Spanish court that fugitive Negro slaves were teaching disobedience to the Indians. In the 1520s and 1530s, there were slave revolts in Hispaniola, Puerto Rico, Santa Marta, and what is now Panama. Shortly after those rebellions, the Spanish established a special police for chasing fugitive slaves.

A Virginia statute of 1669 referred to "the obstinacy of many of them," and in 1680 the Assembly took note of slave meetings "under the pretense of feasts and brawls" which they considered of "dangerous consequence." In 1687, in the colony's Northern Neck, a plot was discovered in which slaves planned to kill all the whites in the area and escape during a mass funeral.

Gerald Mullin, who studied slave resistance in eighteenth-century Virginia in his work *Flight and Rebellion,* reports:

> The available sources on slavery in 18th-century Virginia—plantation and county records, the newspaper advertisements for runaways—describe rebellious slaves and few others. The slaves described were lazy and thieving; they feigned illnesses, destroyed crops, stores, tools, and sometimes attacked or killed overseers. They operated blackmarkets in stolen goods. Runaways were defined as various types, they were truants (who usually returned voluntarily), "outlaws" . . . and slaves who were actually fugitives: men who visited relatives, went to town to pass as free, or tried to escape slavery completely, either by boarding ships and leaving the colony, or banding together in cooperative efforts to establish villages or hide-outs in the frontier. The commitment of another type of rebellious slave was total; these men became killers, arsonists, and insurrectionists.

Slaves recently from Africa, still holding on to the heritage of their communal society, would run away in groups and try to establish villages of runaways out in the wilderness, on the frontier. Slaves born in America, on the other hand, were more likely to run off alone, and, with the skills they had learned on the plantation, try to pass as free men.

In the colonial papers of England, a 1729 report from the lieutenant governor of Virginia to the British Board of Trade tells how "a number of Negroes, about fifteen . . . formed a design to withdraw from their Master and to fix themselves in the fastnesses of the neighboring Mountains. They had found means to get into their possession some Arms and Ammunition, and they took along with them some Provisions, their Cloths, bedding and working Tools. . . . Tho' this attempt has happily been defeated, it ought nevertheless to awaken us into some effectual measures. . . ."

Slavery was immensely profitable to some masters. James Madison told a British visitor shortly after the American Revolution that he could make $257 on every Negro in a year, and spend only $12 or $13 on his keep. Another viewpoint was of slaveowner Landon Carter, writing about fifty years earlier, complaining that his slaves so neglected their work and were so uncooperative ("either cannot or will not work") that he began to wonder if keeping them was worthwhile.

Some historians have painted a picture—based on the infrequency of organized rebellions and the ability of the South to maintain slavery for two hundred years—of a slave population made submissive by their condition; with their African heritage destroyed, they were, as Stanley Elkins said, made into "Sambos," "a society of helpless dependents." Or as another historian, Ulrich Phillips, said, "by racial quality submissive." But looking at the totality of slave behavior, at the resistance of everyday life, from quiet noncooperation in work to running away, the picture becomes different.

In 1710, warning the Virginia Assembly, Governor Alexander Spotswood said:

> . . . freedom wears a cap which can without a tongue, call together all those who long to shake off the fetters of slavery and as such an Insurrection would surely be attended with most dreadful consequences so I think we cannot be too early in providing against it, both by putting our selves in a better posture of defence and by making a law to prevent the consultations of those Negroes.

Indeed, considering the harshness of punishment for running away, that so many blacks did run away must be a sign of a powerful rebelliousness. All through the 1700s, the Virginia slave code read:

> Whereas many times slaves run away and lie hid and lurking in swamps, woods, and other obscure places, killing hogs, and commiting

other injuries to the inhabitants . . . if the slave does not immediately return, anyone whatsoever may kill or destroy such slaves by such ways and means as he . . . shall think fit . . . . If the slave is apprehended . . . it shall . . . be lawful for the county court, to order such punishment for the said slave, either by dismembering, or in any other way . . . as they in their discretion shall think fit, for the reclaiming any such incorrigible slave, and terrifying others from the like practices. . . .

Mullin found newspaper advertisements between 1736 and 1801 for 1,138 men runaways, and 141 women. One consistent reason for running away was to find members of one's family—showing that despite the attempts of the slave system to destroy family ties by not allowing marriages and by separating families, slaves would face death and mutilation to get together.

In Maryland, where slaves were about one-third of the population in 1750, slavery had been written into law since the 1660s, and statutes for controlling rebellious slaves were passed. There were cases where slave women killed their masters, sometimes by poisoning them, sometimes by burning tobacco houses and homes. Punishments ranged from whipping and branding to execution, but the trouble continued. In 1742, seven slaves were put to death for murdering their master.

Fear of slave revolt seems to have been a permanent fact of plantation life. William Byrd, a wealthy Virginia slaveowner, wrote in 1736:

> We have already at least 10,000 men of these descendants of Ham, fit to bear arms, and these numbers increase every day, as well by birth as by importation. And in case there should arise a man of desperate fortune, he might with more advantage than Cataline kindle a servile war . . . and tinge our rivers wide as they are with blood.

It was an intricate and powerful system of control that the slaveowners developed to maintain their labor supply and their way of life, a system both subtle and crude, involving every device that social orders employ for keeping power and wealth where it is. As Kenneth Stampp puts it:

> A wise master did not take seriously the belief that Negroes were natural-born slaves. He knew better. He knew that Negroes freshly imported from Africa had to be broken into bondage; that each succeeding generation had to be carefully trained. This was no easy task, for the bondsman rarely submitted willingly. Moreover, he rarely submitted completely. In most cases there was no end to the need for control—at least not until old age reduced the slave to a condition of helplessness.

The system was psychological and physical at the same time. The slaves were taught discipline, were impressed again and again with the idea of their own inferiority to "know their place," to see blackness as a sign of subordination, to be awed by the power of the master, to merge their interest with the master's, destroying their own individual needs. To accomplish this there was the discipline of hard labor, the breakup of the slave family, the lulling effects of religion (which sometimes led to "great mischief," as one slaveholder reported), the creation of disunity among slaves by separating them into field slaves and more privileged house slaves, and finally the power of law and the immediate power of the overseer to invoke whipping, burning, mutilation, and death. Dismemberment was provided for in the Virginia Code of 1705. Maryland passed a law in 1723 providing for cutting off the ears of blacks who struck whites, and that for certain serious crimes, slaves should be hanged and the body quartered and exposed.

Still, rebellions took place—not many, but enough to create constant fear among white planters. The first large-scale revolt in the North American colonies took place in New York in 1712. In New York, slaves were 10 percent of the population, the highest proportion in the northern states, where economic conditions usually did not require large numbers of field slaves. About twenty-five blacks and two Indians set fire to a building, then killed nine whites who came on the scene. They were captured by soldiers, put on trial, and twenty-one were executed. The governor's report to England said: "Some were burnt, others were hanged, one broke on the wheel, and one hung alive in chains in the town. . . ." One had been burned over a slow fire for eight to ten hours—all this to serve notice to other slaves.

A letter to London from South Carolina in 1720 reports:

> I am now to acquaint you that very lately we have had a very wicked and barbarous plot of the designe of the negroes rising with a designe to destroy all the white people in the country and then to take Charles Town in full body but it pleased God it was discovered and many of them taken prisoners and some burnt and some hang'd and some banish'd.

Around this time there were a number of fires in Boston and New Haven, suspected to be the work of Negro slaves. As a result, one Negro was executed in Boston, and the Boston Council ruled that any slaves who on their own gathered in groups of two or more were to be punished by whipping.

At Stono, South Carolina, in 1739, about twenty slaves rebelled, killed two warehouse guards, stole guns and gunpowder, and headed south, killing people in their way, and burning buildings. They were joined by others, until there were perhaps eighty slaves in all and, according to one account of the time, "they called out Liberty, marched on with Colours displayed, and two Drums beating." The militia found and attacked them. In the ensuing battle perhaps fifty slaves and twenty-five whites were killed before the uprising was crushed.

Herbert Aptheker, who did detailed research on slave resistance in North America for his book *American Negro Slave Revolts,* found about 250 instances where a minimum of ten slaves joined in a revolt or conspiracy.

From time to time, whites were involved in the slave resistance. As early as 1663, indentured white servants and black slaves in Gloucester County, Virginia, formed a conspiracy to rebel and gain their freedom. The plot was betrayed, and ended with executions. Mullin reports that the newspaper notices of runaways in Virginia often warned "ill-disposed" whites about harboring fugitives. Sometimes slaves and free men ran off together, or cooperated in crimes together. Sometimes, black male slaves ran off and joined white women. From time to time, white ship captains and watermen dealt with runaways, perhaps making the slave a part of the crew.

In New York in 1741, there were ten thousand whites in the city and two thousand black slaves. It had been a hard winter and the poor—slave and free—had suffered greatly. When mysterious fires broke out, blacks and whites were accused of conspiring together. Mass hysteria developed against the accused. After a trial full of lurid accusations by informers, and forced confessions, two white men and two white women were executed, eighteen slaves were hanged, and thirteen slaves were burned alive.

Only one fear was greater than the fear of black rebellion in the new American colonies. That was the fear that discontented whites would join black slaves to overthrow the existing order. In the early years of slavery, especially, before racism as a way of thinking was firmly ingrained, while white indentured servants were often treated as badly as black slaves, there was a possibility of cooperation. As Edmund Morgan sees it:

There are hints that the two despised groups initially saw each other as sharing the same predicament. It was common, for example, for servants and slaves to run away together, steal hogs together, get drunk together. It was not uncommon for them to make love together. In Bacon's Rebellion, one of the last groups to surrender was a mixed band of eighty negroes and twenty English servants.

As Morgan says, masters, "initially at least, perceived slaves in much the same way they had always perceived servants . . . shiftless, irresponsible, unfaithful, ungrateful, dishonest. . . ." And "if freemen with disappointed hopes should make common cause with slaves of desperate hope, the results might be worse than anything Bacon had done."

And so, measures were taken. About the same time that slave codes, involving discipline and punishment, were passed by the Virginia Assembly,

Virginia's ruling class, having proclaimed that all white men were superior to black, went on to offer their social (but white) inferiors a number of benefits previously denied them. In 1705 a law was passed requiring masters to provide white servants whose indenture time was up with ten bushels of corn, thirty shillings, and a gun, while women servants were to get 15 bushels of corn and forty shillings. Also, the newly freed servants were to get 50 acres of land.

Morgan concludes: "Once the small planter felt less exploited by taxation and began to prosper a little, he became less turbulent, less dangerous, more respectable. He could begin to see his big neighbor not as an extortionist but as a powerful protector of their common interests."

We see now a complex web of historical threads to ensnare blacks for slavery in America: the desperation of starving settlers, the special helplessness of the displaced

African, the powerful incentive of profit for slave trader and planter, the temptation of superior status for poor whites, the elaborate controls against escape and rebellion, the legal and social punishment of black and white collaboration.

The point is that the elements of this web are historical, not "natural." This does not mean that they are easily disentangled, dismantled. It means only that there is a possibility for something else, under historical conditions not yet realized. And one of these conditions would be the elimination of that class exploitation which has made poor whites desperate for small gifts of status, and has prevented that unity of black and white necessary for joint rebellion and reconstruction.

Around 1700, the Virginia House of Burgesses declared:

> The Christian Servants in this country for the most part consists of the Worser Sort of the people of Europe. And since . . . such numbers of Irish and other Nations have been brought in of which a great many have been soldiers in the late warrs that according to our present Circumstances we can hardly governe them and if they were fitted with Armes and had the Opertunity of meeting together by Musters we have just reason to fears they may rise upon us.

It was a kind of class consciousness, a class fear. There were things happening in early Virginia, and in the other colonies, to warrant it.

REFERENCES

Aptheker, Herbert, ed. 1974. *A Documentary History of the Negro People in the United States.* Secaucus, NJ: Citadel.

Boskin, Joseph. 1966. *Into Slavery: Radical Decisions in the Virginia Colony.* Philadelphia: Lippincott.

Catterall, Helen. 1937. *Judicial Cases Concerning American Slavery and the Negro.* 5 vols. Washington, DC: Negro University Press.

Davidson, Basil. 1961. *The African Slave Trade.* Boston: Little, Brown.

Donnan, Elizabeth, ed. 1965. *Documents Illustrative of the History of the Slave Trade to America.* 4 vols. New York: Octagon.

Elkins, Stanley. 1976. *Slavery: A Problem in American Institutional and Intellectual Life.* Chicago: University of Chicago Press.

Federal Writers Project. 1969. *The Negro in Virginia.* New York: Arno.

Franklin, John Hope. 1974. *From Slavery to Freedom: A History of American Negroes.* New York: Knopf.

Jordan, Winthrop. 1968. *White over Black: American Attitudes toward the Negro, 1550–1812.* Chapel Hill: University of North Carolina Press.

Morgan, Edmund S. 1975. *American Slavery, American Freedom: The Ordeal of Colonial Virginia.* New York: Norton.

Mullin, Gerald. 1974. *Flight and Rebellion: Slave Resistance in Eighteenth-Century Virginia.* New York: Oxford University Press.

Mullin, Michael, ed. 1975. *American Negro Slavery: A Documentary History.* New York: Harper & Row.

Phillips, Ulrich B. 1966. *American Negro Slavery: A Survey of the Supply, Employment and Control of Negro Labor as Determined by the Plantation Regime.* Baton Rouge: Louisiana State University Press.

Redding, J. Saunders. 1973. *They Came in Chains.* Philadelphia: Lippincott.

Stampp, Kenneth M. 1956. *The Peculiar Institution.* New York: Knopf.

Tannenbaum, Frank. 1963. *Slave and Citizen: The Negro in the Americas.* New York: Random House.

3
———————

RACIAL FORMATIONS

Michael Omi • *Howard Winant*

QUESTIONS TO CONSIDER

If race is not "real" in a scientific sense, why can I look around the classroom or campus and see that someone is black or Asian or white? What is the difference between something being "real" (like the book in front of you) and something being a "social construction" (like race or gender)? Use Omi and Winant's theory of racial formation to explain how and why we "see" race as we do.

In 1982–83, Susie Guillory Phipps unsuccessfully sued the Louisiana Bureau of Vital Records to change her racial classification from black to white. The descendant of an eighteenth-century white planter and a black slave, Phipps was designated "black" in her birth certificate in accordance with a 1970 state law which declared anyone with at least one-thirty-second "Negro blood" to be black. The legal battle raised intriguing questions about the concept of race, its meaning in contemporary society, and its use (and abuse) in public policy. Assistant Attorney General Ron Davis defended the law by pointing out that some type of racial classification was necessary to comply with federal record-keeping requirements and to facilitate programs for the prevention of genetic diseases. Phipps's attorney, Brian Begue, argued that the assignment of racial categories on birth certificates was unconstitutional and that the one-thirty-second designation was inaccurate. He called

on a retired Tulane University professor who cited research indicating that most whites have one-twentieth "Negro" ancestry. In the end, Phipps lost. The court upheld a state law which quantified racial identity, and in so doing affirmed the legality of assigning individuals to specific racial groupings.[1]

The Phipps case illustrates the continuing dilemma of defining race and establishing its meaning in institutional life. Today, to assert that variations in human physiognomy are racially based is to enter a constant and intense debate. *Scientific* interpretations of race have not been alone in sparking heated controversy; *religious* perspectives have done so as well.[2] Most centrally, of course, race has been a matter of *political* contention. This has been particularly true in the United States, where the concept of race has varied enormously over time without ever leaving the center stage of US history.

What Is Race?

Race consciousness, and its articulation in theories of race, is largely a modern phenomenon. When European explorers in the

From *Racial Formation in the United States*, Second Edition, Michael Omi and Howard Winant, eds. Copyright © 1994 by Routledge, Inc. Reproduced by permission of Routledge, Inc., part of the Taylor & Francis Group.

New World "discovered" people who looked different than themselves, these "natives" challenged then existing conceptions of the origins of the human species, and raised disturbing questions as to whether *all* could be considered in the same "family of man."[3] Religious debates flared over the attempt to reconcile the Bible with the existence of "racially distinct" people. Arguments took place over creation itself, as theories of polygenesis questioned whether God had made only one species of humanity ("monogenesis"). Europeans wondered if the natives of the New World were indeed human beings with redeemable souls. At stake were not only the prospects for conversion, but the types of treatment to be accorded them. The expropriation of property, the denial of political rights, the introduction of slavery and other forms of coercive labor, as well as outright extermination, all presupposed a worldview which distinguished Europeans—children of God, human beings, etc.—from "others." Such a worldview was needed to explain why some should be "free" and others enslaved, why some had rights to land and property while others did not. Race, and the interpretation of racial differences, was a central factor in that worldview.

In the colonial epoch science was no less a field of controversy than religion in attempts to comprehend the concept of race and its meaning. Spurred on by the classificatory scheme of living organisms devised by Linnaeus in *Systema Naturae*, many scholars in the eighteenth and nineteenth centuries dedicated themselves to the identification and ranking of variations in humankind. Race was thought of as a *biological* concept, yet its precise definition was the subject of debates which, as we have noted, continue to rage today. Despite efforts ranging from Dr. Samuel Morton's studies of cranial capacity[4] to contemporary attempts to base racial classification on

shared gene pools,[5] the concept of race has defied biological definition. . . .

Attempts to discern the *scientific meaning* of race continue to the present day. Although most physical anthropologists and biologists have abandoned the quest for a scientific basis to determine racial categories, controversies have recently flared in the area of genetics and educational psychology. For instance, an essay by Arthur Jensen argued that hereditary factors shape intelligence not only revived the "nature or nurture" controversy, but raised highly volatile questions about racial equality itself.[6] Clearly the attempt to establish a *biological* basis of race has not been swept into the dustbin of history, but is being resurrected in various scientific arenas. All such attempts seek to remove the concept of race from fundamental social, political, or economic determination. They suggest instead that the truth of race lies in the terrain of innate characteristics, of which skin color and other physical attributes provide only the most obvious, and in some respects most superficial, indicators.

Race as a Social Concept

The social sciences have come to reject biologistic notions of race in favor of an approach which regards race as a *social* concept. Beginning in the eighteenth century, this trend has been slow and uneven, but its direction clear. In the nineteenth century Max Weber discounted biological explanations for racial conflict and instead highlighted the social and political factors which engendered such conflict.[7] The work of pioneering cultural anthropologist Franz Boas was crucial in refuting the scientific racism of the early twentieth century by rejecting the connection between race and culture, and the assumption of a continuum of "higher" and "lower" cultural groups. Within the contemporary social science literature, race is assumed to be a variable which is shaped by broader societal forces.

Race is indeed a pre-eminently *socio-historical* concept. Racial categories and the meaning of race are given concrete expression by the specific social relations and historical context in which they are embedded. Racial meanings have varied tremendously over time and between different societies.

In the United States, the black/white color line has historically been rigidly defined and enforced. White is seen as a "pure" category. Any racial intermixture makes one "nonwhite." In the movie *Raintree County*, Elizabeth Taylor describes the worst of fates to befall whites as "havin' a little Negra blood in ya'—just one little teeny drop and a person's all Negra."[8] This thinking flows from what Marvin Harris has characterized as the principle of *hypo-descent:*

> By what ingenious computation is the genetic tracery of a million years of evolution unraveled and each man [sic] assigned his proper social box? In the United States, the mechanism employed is the rule of hypo-descent. This descent rule requires Americans to believe that anyone who is known to have had a Negro ancestor is a Negro. We admit nothing in between. . . . "Hypo-descent" means affiliation with the subordinate rather than the superordinate group in order to avoid the ambiguity of intermediate identity. . . . The rule of hypo-descent is, therefore, an invention, which we in the United States have made in order to keep biological facts from intruding into our collective racist fantasies.[9]

The Susie Guillory Phipps case merely represents the contemporary expression of this racial logic.

By contrast, a striking feature of race relations in the lowland areas of Latin America since the abolition of slavery has been the relative absence of sharply defined racial groupings. No such rigid descent rule characterizes racial identity in many Latin American societies. Brazil, for example, has historically had less rigid conceptions of race, and thus a variety of "intermediate" racial categories exist. Indeed, as Harris notes, "One of the most striking consequences of the Brazilian system of racial identification is that parents and children and even brothers and sisters are frequently accepted as representatives of quite opposite racial types."[10] Such a possibility is incomprehensible within the logic of racial categories in the US.

To suggest another example: the notion of "passing" takes on new meaning if we compare various American cultures' means of assigning racial identity. In the United States, individuals who are actually "black" by the logic of hypo-descent have attempted to skirt the discriminatory barriers imposed by law and custom by attempting to "pass" for white.[11] Ironically, these same individuals would not be able to pass for "black" in many Latin American societies.

Consideration of the term "black" illustrates the diversity of racial meanings which can be found among different societies and historically within a given society. In contemporary British politics the term "black" is used to refer to all nonwhites. Interestingly this designation has not arisen through the racist discourse of groups such as the National Front. Rather, in political and cultural movements, Asian as well as Afro-Caribbean youth are adopting the term as an expression of self-identity.[12] The wide-ranging meanings of "black" illustrate the manner in which racial categories are shaped politically.[13]

The meaning of race is defined and contested throughout society, in both collective action and personal practice. In the process, racial categories themselves are formed, transformed, destroyed and reformed. We use the term *racial formation* to refer to the process by which social, economic and political forces determine the content and importance of racial categories, and by which they are in turn shaped by racial meanings. Crucial to this formulation is the treatment of race as a *central axis* of social relations which cannot be subsumed under or reduced to some broader category or conception.

Racial Ideology and Racial Identity

The seemingly obvious, "natural" and "common sense" qualities which the existing racial order exhibits themselves testify to the effectiveness of the racial formation process in constructing racial meanings and racial identities.

One of the first things we notice about people when we meet them (along with their sex) is their race. We utilize race to provide clues abut *who* a person is. This fact is made painfully obvious when we encounter someone whom we cannot conveniently racially categorize—someone who is, for example, racially "mixed" or of an ethnic/racial group with which we are not familiar. Such an encounter becomes a source of discomfort and momentarily a crisis of racial meaning. Without a racial identity, one is in danger of having no identity.

Our compass for navigating race relations depends on preconceived notions of what each specific racial group looks like. Comments such as, "Funny, you don't look black," betray an underlying image of what black should be. We also become disoriented when people do not act "black," "Latino," or indeed "white." The content of such stereotypes reveals a series of unsubstantiated beliefs about who these groups are and what "they" are like.[14]

In US society, then, a kind of "racial etiquette" exists, a set of interpretative codes and racial meanings which operate in the interactions of daily life. Rules shaped by our perception of race in a comprehensively racial society determine the "presentation of self,"[15] distinctions of status, and appropriate modes of conduct. "Etiquette" is not mere universal adherence to the dominant group's rules, but a more dynamic combination of these rules with the values and beliefs of subordinated groupings. This racial "subjection" is quintessentially ideological. Everybody learns some combination, some version, of the rules of racial classification, and of their own racial identity, often without obvious teaching or conscious inculcation. Race becomes "common sense"—a way of comprehending, explaining and acting in the world.

Racial beliefs operate as an "amateur biology," a way of explaining the variations in "human nature."[16] Differences in skin color and other obvious physical characteristics supposedly provide visible clues to differences lurking underneath. Temperament, sexuality, intelligence, athletic ability, aesthetic preferences and so on are presumed to be fixed and discernible from the palpable mark of race. Such diverse questions as our confidence and trust in others (for example, clerks or salespeople, media figures, neighbors), our sexual preferences and romantic images, our tastes in music, films, dance, or sports, and our very ways of talking, walking, eating and dreaming are ineluctably shaped by notions of race. Skin color "differences" are thought to explain perceived differences in intellectual, physical and artistic temperaments, and to justify distinct treatment of racially identified individuals and groups.

The continuing persistence of racial ideology suggests that these racial myths and stereotypes cannot be exposed as such in the popular imagination. They are, we think, too essential, too integral, to the maintenance of the US social order. Of course, particular meanings, stereotypes and myths can change, but the presence of a *system* of racial meanings and stereotypes, of racial ideology, seems to be a permanent feature of US culture.

Film and television, for example, have been notorious in disseminating images of racial minorities which establish for audiences what people from these groups look like, how they behave, and "who they are."[17] The power of the media lies not only in their ability to reflect the dominant racial ideology, but in their capacity to shape that ideology in the first place. D.W. Griffith's epic *Birth of a Nation*, a sympathetic treatment of the rise of the Ku Klux Klan during Reconstruction, helped to generate, consolidate and "nationalize" images of blacks which had been more disparate (more regionally specific, for example) prior to the film's appearance.[18] In US television, the necessity to define characters in the briefest and most condensed manner has led to the perpetuation of racial caricatures, as racial stereotypes serve as shorthand for scriptwriters, directors and actors, in commercials, etc. Television's tendency to address the "lowest common denominator" in order to render programs "familiar" to an enormous and diverse audience leads it regularly to assign and reassign racial characteristics to particular groups, both minority and majority.

These and innumerable other examples show that we tend to view race as something fixed and immutable—something rooted in "nature." Thus we mask the historical construction of racial categories, the shifting meaning of race, and the crucial role of politics and ideology in shaping race relations. Races do not emerge full-blown. They are the results of diverse historical practices and are continually subject to challenge over their definition and meaning.

Racialization: The Historical Development of Race

In the United States, the racial category of "black" evolved with the consolidation of racial slavery. By the end of the seventeenth century, Africans whose specific identity was Ibo, Yoruba, Fulani, etc., were rendered "black" by an ideology of exploitation based on racial logic—the establishment and maintenance of a "color line." This of course did not occur overnight. A period of indentured servitude which was not rooted in racial logic preceded the consolidation of racial slavery. With slavery, however, a racially based understanding of society was set in motion which resulted in the shaping of a specific *racial* identity not only for the slaves but for the European settlers as well. Winthrop Jordan has observed: "From the initially common term *Christian*, at mid-century there was a marked shift toward the terms *English* and *free*. After about 1680, taking the colonies as a whole, a new term of self-identification appeared—*white*."[19]

We employ the term *racialization* to signify the extension of racial meaning to a previously racially unclassified relationship, social practice or group. Racialization is an ideological process, an historically specific one. Racial ideology is constructed from pre-existing conceptual (or, if one prefers, "discursive") elements and emerges from the struggles of competing political projects and ideas seeking to articulate similar elements differently. An account of racialization processes that avoids the pitfalls of US ethnic history[20] remains to be written.

Particularly during the nineteenth century, the category of "white" was subject to challenges brought about by the influx of diverse groups who were not of the same Anglo-Saxon stock as the founding immigrants. In the nineteenth century, political and ideological struggles emerged over the classification of Southern Europeans, the Irish and Jews, among other "nonwhite" categories.[21] Nativism was only effectively curbed by the institutionalization of a racial order that drew the color line *around,* rather than *within,* Europe.

By stopping short of racializing immigrants from Europe after the Civil War, and by subsequently allowing their assimilation, the American racial order was reconsolidated in the wake of the tremendous challenge placed before it by the abolition of racial slavery.[22] With the end of Reconstruction in 1877, an effective program for limiting the emergent class struggles of the later nineteenth century was forged: the definition of the working class *in racial terms*—as "white." This was not accomplished by any legislative decree or capitalist maneuvering to divide the working class, but rather by white workers themselves. Many of them were recent immigrants, who organized on racial lines as much as on traditionally defined class lines.[23] The Irish on the West Coast, for example, engaged in vicious anti-Chinese race-baiting and committed many pogrom-type assaults on Chinese in the course of consolidating the trade union movement in California.

Thus the very political organization of the working class was in important ways a racial project. The legacy of racial conflicts and arrangements shaped the definition of interests and in turn led to the consolidation of institutional patterns (e.g., segregated unions, dual labor markets, exclusionary legislation) which perpetuated the color line *within* the working class. Selig Perlman, whose study of the development of the labor movement is fairly sympathetic to this process, notes that:

> The political issue after 1877 was racial, not financial, and the weapon was not merely the ballot, but also "direct action"—violence. The anti-Chinese agitation in California, culminating as it did in the Exclusion Law passed by Congress in 1882, was doubtless the most important single factor in the history of American labor, for without it the entire country might have been overrun by Mongolian [sic] labor and *the labor movement might have become a conflict of races instead of one of classes.*[24]

More recent economic transformations in the US have also altered interpretations of racial identities and meanings. The automation of southern agriculture and the augmented labor demand of the postwar boom transformed blacks from a largely rural, impoverished labor force to a largely urban, working-class group by 1970.[25] When boom became bust and liberal welfare statism moved rightwards, the majority of blacks came to be seen, increasingly, as part of the "underclass," as state "dependents." Thus the particularly deleterious effects on blacks of global and national economic shifts (generally rising unemployment rates, changes in the employment structure away from reliance on labor intensive work, etc.) were explained once again in the late 1970s and 1980s (as they had been in the 1940s and mid-1960s) as the result of defective black cultural norms, of familial disorganization, etc.[26] In this way new racial attributions, new racial myths, are affixed to "blacks."[27] Similar changes in racial identity are presently affecting Asians and Latinos, as such economic forces as increasing Third World impoverishment and indebtedness fuel immigration and high interest rates, Japanese competition spurs resentments, and US jobs seem to fly away to Korea and Singapore.[28] . . .

Once we understand that race overflows the boundaries of skin color, superexploitation, social stratification, discrimination and prejudice, cultural domination and cultural resistance, state policy (or of any other particular social relationship we list), once we recognize the racial dimension present to some degree in *every* identity, institution and social practice in the United States—once we have done this, it becomes possible to speak of *racial formation.* This recognition is hard-won; there is a continuous temptation to think of race as an *essence,* as something fixed, concrete and objective, as (for example) one of the categories just enumerated. And there is also an opposite temptation: to see it as a mere illusion, which an ideal social order would eliminate.

In our view it is crucial to break with these habits of thought. The effort must be made to understand race as *an unstable and "decentered" complex of social meanings constantly being transformed by political struggle.*

NOTES

1. *San Francisco Chronicle,* 14 September 1982, 19 May 1983. Ironically, the 1970 Louisiana law was enacted to supersede an old Jim Crow statute which relied on the idea of "common report" in determining an infant's race. Following Phipps's unsuccessful attempt to change her classification and have the law declared unconstitutional, a legislative effort arose which culminated in the repeal of the law. See *San Francisco Chronicle,* 23 June 1983.

2. The Mormon church, for example, has been heavily criticized for its doctrine of black inferiority.

3. Thomas F. Gossett notes:

   Race theory . . . had up until fairly modern times no firm hold on European thought. On the other hand, race theory and race prejudice were by no means unknown at the time when the English colonists came to North America. Undoubtedly, the age of exploration led many to speculate on race differences at a period when neither Europeans nor Englishmen were prepared to make allowances for vast cultural diversities. Even though race theories had not then secured wide acceptance or even sophisticated formulation, the first contacts of the Spanish with the Indians in the Americas can now be recognized as the beginning of a struggle between conceptions of the nature of primitive peoples which has not yet been wholly settled. (Thomas F. Gossett, *Race: The History of an Idea in America* [New York: Schocken Books, 1965], p. 16.)

   Winthrop Jordan provides a detailed account of early European colonialists' attitudes about color and race in *White over Black: American Attitudes Toward the Negro, 1550–1812* (New York: Norton, 1977 [1968]), pp. 3–43.

4. Pro-slavery physician Samuel George Morton (1799–1851) compiled a collection of 800 crania from all parts of the world which formed the sample for his studies of race. Assuming that the larger the size of the cranium translated into greater intelligence, Morton established a relationship between race and skull capacity. Gossett reports that:

   In 1849, one of his studies included the following results: The English skulls in his collection proved to be the largest, with an average cranial capacity of 96 cubic inches. The Americans and Germans were rather poor seconds, both with cranial capacities of 90 cubic inches. At the bottom of the list were the Negroes with 83 cubic inches, the Chinese with 82, and the Indians with 79. (Ibid., p. 74.)

   On Morton's methods, see Stephen J. Gould, "The Finagle Factor," *Human Nature* (July 1978).

5. Definitions of race founded upon a common pool of genes have not held up when confronted by scientific research which suggests that the differences *within* a given human population are greater than those between populations. See L.L. Cavalli-Sforza, "The Genetics of Human Populations," *Scientific American,* September 1974, pp. 81–89.

6. Arthur Jensen, "How Much Can We Boost IQ and Scholastic Achievement?" *Harvard Educational Review* 39 (1969):1–123.

7. Ernst Moritz Manasse, "Max Weber on Race," *Social Research* 14 (1947):191–221.

8. Quoted in Edward D. C. Campbell, Jr., *The Celluloid South: Hollywood and the Southern Myth* (Knoxville: University of Tennessee Press, 1981), pp. 168–70.

9. Marvin Harris, *Patterns of Race in the Americas* (New York: Norton, 1964), p. 56.

10. Ibid., p. 57.

11. After James Meredith had been admitted as the first black student at the University of Mississippi, Harry S. Murphy announced that he, and not Meredith, was the first black student to attend "Ole Miss." Murphy described himself as black but was able to pass for white and spent nine months at the institution without attracting any notice (ibid., p. 56).

12. A. Sivanandan, "From Resistance to Rebellion: Asian and Afro-Caribbean Struggles in Britain," *Race and Class* 23(2–3) (Autumn–Winter 1981).

13. Consider the contradictions in racial status which abound in the country with the most rigidly defined racial categories—South Africa. There a race classification agency is employed to adjudicate claims for upgrading of official racial identity. This is particularly necessary for the "coloured" category. The apartheid system considers Chinese as "Asians" while the Japanese are accorded the status of "honorary whites." This logic nearly detaches race from any grounding in skin color and other physical attributes and nakedly exposes race as a juridical category subject to economic, social and political influences. (We are indebted to Steve Talbot for clarification of some of these points.)

14. Gordon W. Allport, *The Nature of Prejudice* (Garden City, NY: Doubleday, 1958), pp. 184–200.

15. We wish to use this phrase loosely, without committing ourselves to a particular position on such social psychological approaches as symbolic interactionism, which are outside the scope of this study. An interesting study on this subject is S.M. Lyman and W.A. Douglass, "Ethnicity: Strategies of Individual and Collective Impression Management," *Social Research* 40(2) (1973).

16. Michael Billig, "Patterns of Racism: Interviews with National Front Members," *Race and Class* 20(2) (Autumn 1978):161–79.

17. "Miss San Antonio USA Lisa Fernandez and other Hispanics auditioning for a role in a television soap-opera did not fit the Hollywood image of real Mexicans and had to darken their faces before filming." Model Aurora Garza said that their faces were bronzed with powder because they looked too white. "'I'm a real Mexican [Garza said] and very dark anyway. I'm even darker right now because I have a tan. But they kept wanting me to make my face darker and darker'" (*San Francisco Chronicle,* 21 September 1984). A similar dilemma faces Asian American actors who feel that Asian character lead roles inevitably go to white actors who make themselves up to be Asian. Scores of Charlie Chan films, for example, have been made with white leads (the last one was the 1981 *Charlie Chan and the Curse of the Dragon Queen*). Roland Winters, who played in six Chan features, was asked by playwright Frank Chin to explain the logic of casting a white man in the role of Charlie Chan: "'The only thing I can think of is, if you want to cast a homosexual in a show, and get a homosexual, it'll be awful. It won't be funny . . . and may be there's something there . . .'" (Frank Chin, "Confessions of the Chinatown Cowboy," *Bulletin of Concerned Asian Scholars* 4(3) (Fall 1972)).

18. Melanie Martindale-Sikes, "Nationalizing 'Nigger' Imagery Through 'Birth of a Nation'," paper prepared for the 73rd Annual Meeting of the American Sociological Association, 4–8 September 1978, San Francisco.

19. Jordan, *White over Black,* p. 95; emphasis added.

20. Historical focus has been placed either on particular racially defined groups or on immigration and the "incorporation" of ethnic groups. In the former case the characteristic ethnicity theory pitfalls and apologetics such as functionalism and cultural pluralism may be avoided, but only by sacrificing much of the focus on race. In the latter case, race is considered a manifestation of ethnicity.

21. The degree of antipathy for these groups should not be minimized. A northern commentator observed in the 1850s: "An Irish Catholic seldom attempts to rise to a higher condition than that in which he is placed, while the Negro often makes the attempt with success." Quoted in Gossett, op. cit., p. 288.

22. This analysis, as will perhaps be obvious, is essentially DuBoisian. Its main source will be found in the monumental (and still largely unappreciated) *Black Reconstruction in the United States, 1860–1880* (New York: Atheneum, 1977 [1935]).

23. Alexander Saxton argues that:
    North Americans of European background have experienced three great

racial confrontations: with the Indian, with the African, and with the Oriental. Central to each transaction has been a totally one-sided preponderance of power, exerted for the exploitation of nonwhites by the dominant white society. In each case (but especially in the two that began with systems of enforced labor), white workingmen have played a crucial, yet ambivalent, role. They have been both exploited and exploiters. On the one hand, thrown into competition with nonwhites as enslaved or "cheap" labor they suffered economically; on the other hand, being white, they benefited by that very exploitation which was compelling the nonwhites to work for low wages or for nothing. Ideologically they were drawn in opposite directions. *Racial identification cut at right angles to class consciousness.* (Alexander Saxton, *The Indispensable Enemy: Labor and the Anti-Chinese Movement in California* [Berkeley and Los Angeles: University of California Press, 1971], p. 1; emphasis added.)

24. Selig Perlman, *The History of Trade Unionism in the United States* (New York: Augustus Kelley, 1950), p. 52; emphasis added.

25. Whether southern blacks were "peasants" or rural workers is unimportant in this context. Some time during the 1960s blacks attained a higher degree of urbanization than whites. Before World War II most blacks had been rural dwellers and nearly 80 percent lived in the South.

26. See George Gilder, *Wealth and Poverty* (New York: Basic Books, 1981); Charles Murray, *Losing Ground* (New York: Basic Books, 1984).

27. A brilliant study of the racialization process in Britain, focused on the rise of "mugging" as a popular fear in the 1970s, is Stuart Hall et al., *Policing the Crisis* (London: Macmillan, 1978).

28. The case of Vincent Chin, a Chinese American man beaten to death in 1982 by a laid-off Detroit auto worker and his stepson who mistook him for Japanese and blamed him for the loss of their jobs, has been widely publicized in Asian American communities. On immigration conflicts and pressures, see Michael Omi, "New Wave Dread: Immigration and Intra-Third World Conflict," *Socialist Review* 60 (November–December 1981).

4

THEORETICAL PERSPECTIVES IN RACE AND ETHNIC RELATIONS

Joe R. Feagin • *Clairece Booher Feagin*

QUESTIONS TO CONSIDER

Which theories outlined by Feagin and Feagin do you believe best explain contemporary race relations in the United States? Do you need to pull together theories in this reading to explain the experiences of different racial and ethnic groups in the United States? Can one theory explain or fully capture the dynamics of race and ethnic relations in the United States? Why or why not?

Assimilation and Other
Order Perspectives

In the United States much social theorizing has emphasized assimilation, the more or less orderly adaptation of a migrating group to the ways and institutions of an established group. Hirschman has noted that "the assimilation perspective, broadly defined, continues to be the primary theoretical framework for sociological research on racial and ethnic inequality." The reason for this dominance, he suggests, is the "lack of convincing alternatives."[1] The English word *assimilate* comes from the Latin *assimulare,* "to make similar."

Robert E. Park

Robert E. Park, a major sociological theorist, argued that European out-migration was a major catalyst for societal reorganization around the globe. In his view intergroup contacts regularly go through stages of a *race relations cycle.* Fundamental social forces such as out-migration lead to recurring cycles in intergroup history: "The race relations cycle which takes the form, to state it abstractly, of *contacts, competition, accommodation* and eventual *assimilation,* is apparently progressive and irreversible."[2] In the contact stage migration and exploration bring people together, which in turn leads to economic competition and thus to new social organization. Competition and conflict flow from the contacts between host peoples and the migrating groups. Accommodation, an unstable condition in the race relations cycle, often takes place rapidly. It involves a forced

From *Racial and Ethnic Relations*, Sixth Edition, by Joe R. Feagin and Clairece Booher Feagin. Copyright © 1999 Pearson Education. Reprinted by permission of Pearson Education, Inc., Upper Saddle River, NJ.

adjustment by a migrating group to a new social situation. . . . Nonetheless, Park and most scholars working in this tradition have argued that there is a long-term trend toward assimilation of racial and ethnic minorities in modern societies. "Assimilation is a process of interpenetration and fusion in which persons and groups acquire the memories, sentiments, and attitudes of other persons or groups, and, by sharing their experience and history, are incorporated with them in a common cultural life."[3] Even racially subordinate groups are expected to assimilate.[4]

Stages of Assimilation:
Milton Gordon

Since Park's pioneering analysis in the 1920s, many U.S. theorists of racial and ethnic relations and numerous textbook writers have adopted an assimilationist perspective, although most have departed from Park's framework in a number of important ways. Milton Gordon, author of the influential *Assimilation in American Life,* distinguishes a variety of initial encounters between race and ethnic groups and an array of possible assimilation outcomes. While Gordon presents three competing images of assimilation—the melting pot, cultural pluralism, and Anglo-conformity—he focuses on Anglo-conformity as the descriptive reality. That is, immigrant groups in the United States, in Gordon's view, have typically tended to give up much of their heritage for the dominant, preexisting Anglo-Saxon core culture and society. The touchstone of adjustment is viewed thus: "If there is anything in American life which can be described as an overall American culture which serves as a reference point for immigrants and their children, it can best be described, it seems to us, as the middle-class cultural patterns of, largely, white Protestant, Anglo-Saxon origins, leaving aside for the moment the question of minor reciprocal influences on this culture exercised by the cultures of later entry into the United States."[5]

Gordon notes that Anglo-conformity has been substantially achieved for most immigrant groups in the United States, especially in regard to cultural assimilation. Most groups following the English have adapted to the Anglo core culture. Gordon distinguishes seven dimensions of adaptation:

1. *cultural assimilation:* change of cultural patterns to those of the core society;
2. *structural assimilation:* penetration of cliques and associations of the core society at the primary-group level;
3. *marital assimilation:* significant intermarriage;
4. *identification assimilation:* development of a sense of identity linked to the core society;
5. *attitude-receptional assimilation:* absence of prejudice and stereotyping;
6. *behavior-receptional assimilation:* absence of intentional discrimination;
7. *civic assimilation:* absence of value and power conflict.[6]

Whereas Park believed structural assimilation, including primary-group ties such as intergroup friendships, flowed from cultural assimilation, Gordon stresses that these are separate stages of assimilation and may take place at different rates.

Gordon conceptualizes structural assimilation as relating to primary-group cliques and relations. Significantly, he does not highlight as a separate type of structural assimilation the movement of a new immigrant group into the *secondary groups* of the host society—that is, into the employing organizations, such as corporations or public bureaucracies, and the critical educational and political institutions.

The omission of secondary-structural assimilation is a major flaw in Gordon's theory. Looking at U.S. history, one would conclude that assimilating into the core society's secondary groups does *not necessarily* mean entering the dominant group's friendship cliques. In addition, the dimension Gordon calls *civic assimilation* is confusing since he includes in it "values," which are really part of cultural assimilation, and "power," which is a central aspect of structural assimilation at the secondary-group level.

Gordon's assimilation theory has influenced a generation of researchers. . . . In a recent examination of Gordon's seven dimensions of assimilation, J. Allen Williams and Suzanne Ortega drew on interviews with a midwestern sample to substantiate that cultural assimilation was not necessarily the first type of assimilation to occur. For example, the Mexican Americans in the sample were found to be less culturally assimilated than African Americans, yet were more assimilated structurally. Those of Swiss and Swedish backgrounds ranked about the same on the study's measure of cultural assimilation, but the Swedish Americans were less assimilated structurally. Williams and Ortega conclude that assimilation varies considerably from one group to another and that Gordon's seven types can be grouped into three more general categories of structural, cultural, and receptional assimilation.[7]

In a later book, *Human Nature, Class, and Ethnicity* (1978), Gordon has recognized that his assimilation theory neglects power issues and proposed bringing these into his model, but so far he has provided only a brief and inadequate analysis. Gordon mentions in passing the different resources available to competing racial groups and refers briefly to black-white conflict, but gives little attention to the impact of economic power, inequalities in material resources, or capitalistic economic history on U.S. racial and ethnic relations.[8]

Focused on the millions of white European immigrants and their adjustments, Gordon's model emphasizes *generational* changes within immigrant groups over time. Substantial acculturation to the Anglo-Protestant core culture has often been completed by the second or third generation for many European immigrant groups. The partially acculturated first generation formed protective communities and associations, but the children of those immigrants were considerably more exposed to Anglo-conformity pressures in the mass media and in schools.[9] Gordon also suggests that substantial assimilation along certain other dimensions, such as the civic, behavior-receptional, and attitude-receptional ones, has occurred for numerous European groups. Most white groups have also made considerable progress toward equality at the secondary-structural levels of employment and politics, although the dimensions of this assimilation are neither named nor discussed in any detail by Gordon.

For many white groups, particularly non-Protestant ones, structural assimilation at the primary-group level is underway, yet far from complete. Gordon suggests that substantially complete cultural assimilation (for example, adoption of the English language) along with structural (primary-group) pluralism form a characteristic pattern of adaptation for many white ethnic groups. Even these relatively acculturated groups tend to limit their informal friendships and marriage ties either to their immediate ethnic groups or to *similar* groups that are part of their general religious community. Following Will Herberg, who argued that there are three great community "melting pots" in the United States—Jews, Protestants, and Catholics—Gordon suggests that primary-group ties beyond one's own group are often developed with one's broad socioreligious community, whether that be Protestant, Catholic, or Jewish.[10]

In his influential books and articles Gordon recognizes that structural assimilation has been retarded by racial prejudice and discrimination, but he seems to suggest that non-European Americans, including African Americans, will eventually be absorbed into the core culture and society. He gives the most attention to the gradual assimilation of middle-class non-Europeans. In regard to blacks he argues, optimistically, that the United States has "moved decisively down the road toward implementing the implications of the American credo of [equality and justice] for race relations"—as in employment and housing. This perceived tremendous progress for black Americans has created a policy dilemma for the government: should it adopt a traditional political liberalism that ignores race, or a "corporate liberalism" that recognizes group rights along racial lines? Gordon includes under corporate liberalism government programs of affirmative action, which he rejects.[11] . . .

Some assimilation-oriented analysts such as Gordon and Alba have argued that the once prominent ethnic identities, especially of European American groups, are fading over time. Alba suggests that there is still an ethnic identity of consequence for non-Latino whites, but declares that "a new ethnic group is forming—one based on a vague *ancestry* from anywhere on the European continent."[12] In other words, such distinct ethnic identities as English American and Irish American are gradually becoming only a vague identification as "European American," although Alba emphasizes this as a trend, not a fact. Interestingly, research on intermarriages between members of different white ethnic groups has revealed that large proportions of the children of such marriages see themselves as having multiple ethnic identities, while others choose one of their heritages, or simply "American," as their ethnic identity.[13]

Ethnogenesis and Ethnic Pluralism

Some theorists working in the assimilation tradition reject the argument that most European American groups have become substantially assimilated to a generic Anglo-Protestant or Euro-American identity and way of life. A few have explored models of adjustment that depart from Anglo-conformity in the direction of ethnic or cultural pluralism. Most analysts of pluralism accept some Anglo-conformity as inevitable, if not desirable. In *Beyond the Melting Pot*, Glazer and Moynihan agree that the original customs and home-country ways of European immigrants were mostly lost by the third generation. But this did not mean the decline of ethnicity. The European immigrant groups usually remained distinct in terms of name, identity, and, for the most part, primary-group ties.[14]

Andrew Greeley has developed the interesting concept of *ethnogenesis* and applied it to white immigrant groups, those set off by nationality and religion. Greeley is critical of the traditional assimilation perspective because it assumes "that the strain toward homogenization in a modern industrial society is so great as to be virtually irresistible."[15] Traditionally, the direction of this assimilation in the United States is assumed to be toward the Anglo-Protestant core culture. But from the ethnogenesis perspective, adaptation has meant more than this one-way conformity. The traditional assimilation model does not explain the persistence of ethnicity in the United States— the emphasis among immigrants on ethnicity as a way of becoming American and, in recent decades, the self-conscious attempts to create ethnic identity and manipulate ethnic symbols.[16]

. . . Greeley suggests that in many cases host and immigrant groups had a somewhat similar *cultural* inheritance. For example, some later European immigrant groups had a cultural background initially similar to that of earlier English settlers. As a result of interaction in schools and the influence of the media over several generations the number of cultural traits common to the host and immigrant groups often grew. Yet late in the adaptive process certain aspects of the heritage of the home country remained very important to the character of the immigrant-ethnic group. From this perspective, ethnic groups share traits with the host group *and* retain major nationality characteristics as well. A modern ethnic group is one part home-country heritage and one part common culture, mixed together in a distinctive way because of a unique history of development within the North American crucible.[17]

A number of research studies have documented the persistence of distinctive white ethnic groups such as Italian Americans and Jewish Americans in U.S. cities, not just in New York and Chicago but in San Francisco, New Orleans, and Tucson as well. Yancey and his associates have suggested that ethnicity is an "emergent phenomenon"—that its importance varies in cities and that its character and strength depend on the specific historical conditions in which it emerges and grows.[18]

Some Problems with Assimilation Theories

Most assimilation theorists take as their examples of ethnic adaptation white European groups migrating more or less voluntarily to the United States. But what of the adaptation and assimilation of non-European groups beyond the stage of initial contact? Some analysts of assimilation include non-white groups in their theories, despite the problems that arise from such an inclusion. Some analysts have argued that assimilation, cultural and structural, is the necessary, if long-term, answer to the racial problem in the United States. . . .

More optimistic analysts have emphasized progressive inclusion, which will eventually provide black Americans and other minority groups with full citizenship, in fact as well as principle. For that reason, they expect ethnic and racial conflict to disappear as various groups become fully assimilated into the core culture and society. Nathan Glazer, Milton Gordon, and Talcott Parsons have stressed the egalitarianism of U.S. institutions and what they view as the progressive emancipation of non-European groups. Gordon and others have underscored the gradual assimilation of middle-class black Americans over the last several decades. Full membership for black Americans seems inevitable, notes Parsons, for "the only tolerable solution to the enormous [racial] tensions lies in constituting a single societal community with full membership for all."[19] The importance of racial, as well as ethnic, stratification is expected to decline as powerful, universalistic societal forces wipe out the vestiges of earlier ethnocentric value systems. White immigrants have desired substantial assimilation, and most have been absorbed. The same is expected to happen eventually for non-European groups.

Assimilation theories have been criticized as having an "establishment" bias, as not distinguishing carefully enough between what *has* happened to a given group and what the establishment at some point felt *should have* happened. For example, a number of Asian American scholars and leaders have reacted vigorously to the application of the concept of assimilation to Asian Americans, arguing that the very concept originated in a period (1870–1925) of intense attacks by white Americans on Asian Americans. The term was thus tainted from the beginning by its association with the dominant European American group's ideology that the only "good groups" were those that assimilated (or could assimilate) in Anglo-conformity fashion.

Unlike Park, who paid substantial attention to the historical and world-economy context of migration, many of today's assimilation theorists do not analyze sufficiently the historical background and development of a particular racial or ethnic group within a national or world context. In addition, assimilation analysts such as Gordon tend to neglect the power imbalance and inequality in racial and ethnic relations, which are seen most clearly in the cases of non-European Americans. As Geschwender has noted, "they seem to have forgotten that exploitation is the driving force that gives meaning to the study of racial and ethnic relations."[20]

Biosocial Perspectives

Some U.S. theorists, including assimilationists, now accent a biosocial perspective on racial and ethnic relations. The idea of race and ethnicity being deeply rooted in the biological makeup of human beings is an old European and American notion that has received renewed attention from a few social scientists and biologists in the United States since the 1970s. In *Human Nature, Class, and Ethnicity*, for example, Gordon suggests that ethnic ties are rooted in the "biological organism of man." Ethnicity is a fundamental part of the physiological as well as the psychological self. Ethnicity "cannot be shed by social mobility, as for instance social class background can, since society insists on its inalienable ascription from cradle to grave." What Gordon seems to have in mind is not the old racist notion of the unchanging biological character and separateness of racial groups, but rather the rootedness of inter-group relation, including racial and ethnic relations, in the everyday realities of kinship and other socially constructed group boundaries. Gordon goes further, however, emphasizing that human beings tend to be "selfish, narcissistic and perpetually poised on the edge of aggression." And it is these selfish tendencies that lie behind racial and ethnic tensions.[21] Gordon is here adopting a Hobbesian (dog-eat-dog) view of human nature. . . .

Although decidedly different from the earlier biological theories, the modern biosocial analysis remains problematical. The exact linkages between the deep genetic underpinnings of human nature and concrete racial or ethnic behavior are not spelled out beyond some vague analysis of kin selection and selfish behavior. . . .

Another difficulty with the biosocial approach is that in the everyday world, racial and ethnic relations are *immediately social* rather than biological. As Edna Bonacich has pointed out, many racial and ethnic groups have mixed biological ancestry. Jewish Americans, for example, have a very mixed ancestry: as a group, they share no distinct biological characteristics. Biologically diverse Italian immigrants from different regions of Italy gained a sense of being Italian American (even Italian) in the United States. The bonds holding Jewish Americans together and Italian Americans together were not genetically based or biologically primordial, but rather the result of real *historical* experiences as these groups settled into the United States. Moreover, if ethnicity is primordial in a biological sense, it should always be a prominent force in human affairs. Sometimes ethnicity leads to recurring conflict, as in the case of Jews and Gentiles in the United States; in other cases, as with Scottish and English Americans, it quietly disappears in the assimilation process. Sentiments based on common

ancestry are important, but they are activated primarily in the concrete experiences and histories of specific migrating and host groups.[22]

Emphasizing Migration: Competition Theory

. . . The *human ecology* tradition in sociological thought draws on the ideas of Park and other ecologists and emphasizes the "struggle of human groups for survival" within their physical environments. This tradition, which highlights demographic trends such as the migration of groups and population concentration in cities, has been adopted by competition analysts researching racial and ethnic groups.[23]

Competition theorists such as Susan Olzak and Joane Nagel view ethnicity as a social phenomenon distinguished by boundaries of language, skin color, and culture. They consider the tradition of human ecology valuable because it emphasizes the stability of ethnic population boundaries over time, as well as the impact of shifts in these boundaries resulting from migration; ethnic group membership often coincides with the creation of a distinctive group niche in the labor force. Competition occurs when two or more ethnic groups attempt to secure the same resources, such as jobs or housing. Competition theorists have accented the ways in which ethnic group competition and the accompanying ethnic solidarity lead to collective action, mobilization, and protest.[24]

According to competition theorists, collective action is fostered by immigration across borders and by the expansion of once-segregated minorities into the same labor and housing markets to which other ethnic groups have access. A central argument of these theorists is that collective attacks on a subordinate ethnic group—immigrant and black workers, for instance—increase at the local city level when the group moves up and out of segregated jobs and challenges other groups and not, as one might expect, in cities where ethnic groups are locked into residential segregation and poverty. . . .

Competition theorists explicitly contrast their analyses with the power-conflict views we will discuss in the next section, perspectives that emphasize the role of capitalism, economic subordination, and institutionalized discrimination. Competition theorists write about urban ethnic worlds as though institutionalized racism and capitalism-generated exploitation of workers are not major forces in recurring ethnic and racial competition in cities. As we have seen, they emphasize migration and population concentration, as well as other demographic factors. . . .

Power-Conflict Theories

The last few decades have witnessed the development of power-conflict frameworks explaining U.S. racial and ethnic relations, perspectives that place much greater emphasis on economic stratification and power issues than one finds in assimilation and competition theories. Within this broad category of power-conflict theories are a number of subcategories, including the internal colonialism viewpoint, and a variety of class-based and neo-Marxist theories. . . .

Internal Colonialism

Analysts of internal colonialism prefer to see the racial stratification and the class stratification of U.S. capitalism as *separate but related* systems of oppression. Neither should be reduced in social science theories to the other. An emphasis on power and resource inequalities, particularly white-minority inequalities, is at the heart of the internal colonialism model.

The framework of internal colonialism is built in part upon the work of analysts of *external colonialism*—the worldwide imperialism of certain capitalist nations, including the United States and European nations.[25] For example, Balandier has noted that capitalist expansion has affected non-European peoples since the fifteenth century: "Until very recently the greater part of the world population, not belonging to the white race (if we exclude China and Japan), knew only a status of dependency on one or another of the European colonial powers."[26] External colonialism involves the running of a country's economy and politics by an outside colonial power. Many colonies eventually became independent of their colonizers, such as Britain or France, but continued to have their economies directed by the capitalists and corporations of the colonial powers. This system of continuing dependency has been called *neocolonialism*. Neocolonialism is common today where there are few white settlers in the colonized country. Colonies experiencing a large in-migration of white settlers often show a different pattern. In such cases external colonialism becomes *internal colonialism* when the control and exploitation of non-European groups in the colonized country passes from whites in the home country to white immigrant groups within the newly independent country.[27]

Non-European groups entering later, such as African slaves and Mexican farm workers in the United States, can also be viewed in terms of internal colonialism. Internal colonialism here emerged out of classical European colonialism and imperialism and took on a life of its own. The origin and initial stabilization of internal colonialism in North America predate the Revolutionary War. The systematic subordination of non-Europeans began with "genocidal attempts by colonizing settlers to uproot native populations and force them into other regions."[28] Native Americans were killed or driven off desirable lands. Slaves from Africa were a cheap source of labor for capital accumulation before and after the Revolution. Later, Asians and Pacific peoples were imported as contract workers or annexed in an expansionist period of U.S. development. Robert Blauner, a colonialism theorist, notes that agriculture in the South depended on black labor; in the Southwest, Mexican agricultural development was forcibly taken over by European settlers, and later agricultural development was based substantially on cheap Mexican labor coming into what was once northern Mexico.[29]

In exploiting the labor of non European peoples, who were made slaves or were paid low wages, white agricultural and industrial capitalists reaped enormous profits. From the internal colonialism perspective, contemporary racial and ethnic inequality is grounded in the economic *interests* of whites in low-wage labor—the underpinning of capitalistic economic exploitation. Non-European groups were subordinated to European American desires for *labor* and *land*. Internal colonialism theorists have recognized the central role of *government* support of the exploitation of minorities. The colonial and U.S. governments played an important role in legitimating slavery in the sixteenth through the nineteenth centuries and in providing the government soldiers who subordinated Native Americans across the nation and Mexicans in the Southwest.

Most internal colonialism theorists are not concerned primarily with white immigrant groups, many of which entered the United States after non-European groups were subordinated. Instead, they wish to analyze the establishment of racial stratification and the control processes that maintain persisting white dominance and ideological racism. Stokely Carmichael and Charles Hamilton, who in their writings in the 1960s were among the first to use the term *internal colonialism*, accented institutional racism—

discrimination by the white community against blacks as a group.[30] From this perspective African Americans are still a "colony" in the United States in regard to education, economics, and politics. . . .

A Neo-Marxist Emphasis on Class

Analysts of racial and ethnic relations have combined an internal colonialism perspective with an emphasis on class stratification that draws on the Marxist research pioneered by [black sociologists W. E. B.] Du Bois and [Oliver] Cox. Mario Barrera, for example, has suggested that the heart of current internal colonialism is an interactive structure of class *and* race stratification that divides our society. Class, in the economic-exploitation sense of that term, needs to be central to a colonialism perspective. Basic to the U.S. system of internal colonialism are four classes that have developed in U.S. capitalism:

1. *capitalists:* that small group of people who control capital investments and the means of production and who buy the labor of many others;

2. *managers:* that modest-sized group of people who work as administrators for the capitalists and have been granted control over the work of others;

3. *petit bourgeoisie:* that small group of merchants who control their own businesses and do most of their work themselves, buying little labor power from others;

4. *working class:* that huge group of blue-collar and white-collar workers who sell their labor to employers in return for wages and salaries.

The dominant class in the U.S. political-economic system is the capitalist class, which in the workplace subordinates working

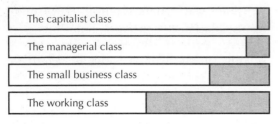

FIGURE 1   The Class and Race Structure of Internal Colonialism. *Note:* Shaded area represents nonwhite segment.

people, both nonwhite and white, to its profit and investment needs. And it is the capitalists who decide whether and where to create jobs. They are responsible for the flight of capital and jobs from many central cities to the suburbs and overseas.

Barrera argues that each of these classes contains important segments that are set off in terms of race and ethnicity. Figure 1 suggests how this works. Each of the major classes is crosscut by a line of racial segmentation that separates those suffering institutionalized discrimination, such as black Americans and Mexican Americans, from those who do not. Take the example of the working class. Although black, Latino, and other minority workers share a similar *class* position with white workers, in that they are struggling against capitalist employers for better wages and working conditions, they are *also* in a subordinate position because of structural discrimination along racial lines within that working class. Barrera notes that the dimensions of this discrimination often include lower wages for many minority workers, as well as their concentration in lower-status occupations. Many Americans suffer from both class exploitation (as wage workers) and racial exploitation (as workers of color).

Ideology and Oppositional Culture

Internal colonialism theorists have studied the role of cultural stereotyping and ideology

in limiting the opportunities of subordinate groups of color. A racist ideology dominates an internal colonialist society, intellectually dehumanizing the colonized. Stereotyping and prejudice, seen in many traditional assimilation theories as more or less temporary problems, are viewed by colonialism analysts as a way of rationalizing exploitation over a very long period, if not permanently. Discrimination is a question not of individual bigots but rather of a system of racial exploitation rationalized by prejudice.[31]

In his book on the English colonization of Ireland, Michael Hechter has developed a theory of internal colonialism that emphasizes how the subordinate group utilizes its own culture to *resist* subordination. Hechter argues that in a system of internal colonialism, cultural as well as racial markers are used to set off subordinate groups such as African Americans in the United States and the Irish in the United Kingdom. Resistance to the dominant group by the subordinate group often takes the form of cultural solidarity in opposition to the dominant culture. This solidarity can become the basis for protest movements by the subordinated group.[32]

Beginning in the 1960s, a number of power-conflict scholars and activists have further developed this idea of *oppositional culture* as a basis for understanding the resistance of non-European groups to the Euro-American core culture. Bonnie Mitchell and Joe Feagin have built on the idea of oppositional culture suggested in the work of Hechter and Blauner.[33] They note that in the centuries of contact before the creation of the United States, Mexico, and Canada, North America was populated by a diverse mixture of European, African, and Native American cultures. The U.S. nation created in the late 1700s encompassed African enslavement and the genocide of Native Americans. Faced with oppression, these and other victims of internal colonialism have long drawn on their own cultural resources, as well as their distinctive knowledge of Euro-American culture and society, to resist oppression in every way possible.

The cultures of those oppressed by European Americans have not only provided a source of individual, family, and community resistance to racial oppression and colonialism but have also infused, albeit often in unheralded ways, some significant elements into the evolving cultural mix that constitutes the core culture of the United States. The oppositional cultures of colonized groups such as African Americans, Latino Americans, and Native Americans have helped preserve several key elements of U.S. society, including its tradition of civil rights and social justice. Another key element, ironically enough given the usual white image of minority families, is the value of extended kinship relations. The tendency toward extended kin networks is both culturally encouraged and economically beneficial for oppressed minority groups. For example, research on black and Latino communities has found extensive kinship networks to be the basis of social and economic support in difficult times. Native American groups have also been known for their communalism and extended family networks.[34]

. . . This reality contrasts with the exaggerated stereotypes of endemic family pathology in these groups. Internal colonialism theories accent both the oppression of minority Americans and the oppositional cultures that enable minority groups not only to survive but also to resist oppression, passively and actively.

Criticism of Internal Colonialism Theories

. . . Joan Moore has criticized the term *neocolonialism*. As we have noted, a neocolonial situation is one in which a Third World country (for example, an African country) has separated itself politically from a European colonial power but continues to be dependent on that country. The former colony needs "foreign experts." It has a class of indigenous leaders who help the former colonial power exploit the local population. It has a distinct territorial boundary. Moore suggests that this neocolonialism model does not apply very well to subordinate nonwhite groups in the United States, in that these groups are not generally confined to a specific bounded territory, nor do they contain the exploitative intermediary elite of Third World neocolonialism. This space-centered critique has been repeated by Omi and Winant, who argue that the social and spatial intermixing of white and nonwhite groups in the United States casts serious doubt on the internal colonialism argument about territorially bounded colonization.[35]

However, most internal colonialism researchers have recognized the differences between internal colonial and neocolonial oppression. These theorists note that the situations of minority groups in the United States are different from those of, for instance, Africans in a newly independent nation still dependent on a European country. In response to Moore's critique, internal colonialism analysts might argue that there are many aspects of colonialism evident in U.S. racial and ethnic relations; they might emphasize that non-European groups in the United States (1) are usually residentially segregated, (2) are typically "super-exploited" in employment and deficient in other material conditions when compared with white immigrants, (3) are culturally stigmatized, and (4) have had some of their leaders co-opted by whites. While these conditions in the United States are not defined as precisely as they are in the case of Third World neocolonialism, they are similar enough to allow the use of the idea of colonialism to assess racial and ethnic relations in the United States.

The Split Labor Market View: Another Class-Based Theory

Colonialism analysts such as Blauner are sometimes unclear about whether all classes of whites benefit from the colonization of nonwhites, or just the dominant class of capitalist employers. A power-conflict perspective that helps in assessing this question is the *split labor market* view, which treats class in the sense of position in the "means of production." This viewpoint has been defended by Edna Bonacich. She argues that in U.S. society the majority-group (white) workers do not share the interests of the dominant political and economic class, the capitalists. Yet both the dominant employer class and the white part of the working class discriminate against the nonwhite part of the working class.[36]

. . . Bonacich emphasizes that discrimination against minority workers by ordinary white workers seeking to protect their own privileges, however limited these may be, is important. Capitalists bring in nonwhite laborers to decrease labor costs, but white workers resist because they fear job displacement or lower wages. For example, over the last century white workers' unions have restricted the access of black workers to many job ladders, thus splitting the labor market and reducing black incomes. . . . White workers gain and lose from this structural racism. They gain in the short run, because there is less competition for privileged job categories from the nonwhites they have excluded. But they lose in the long run because employers can use this cordoned-off sector of nonwhites to undercut them.[37]

"Middleman" Minorities and Ethnic Enclaves

Drawing on insights of earlier scholars, Bonacich has explored the in-between position, in terms of power and resources, that

certain racial and ethnic groups have occupied in stratified societies. These groups find their economic niche serving elites and workers as small-business people positioned between producers and consumers. Some ethnic and racial groups become small-scale traders and merchants doing jobs that dominant groups are not eager to do. For example, many first-generation Jewish and Japanese Americans, excluded from mainstream employment by white Protestants, became small-scale merchants, tailors, restaurant operators, or gardeners. These groups have held "a distinctive class position that is of special use to the ruling class." They "act as a go-between to this society's more subordinate groups."[38]

Bonacich and Modell have found that Japanese Americans fit the middleman minority model. Before World War II Japanese Americans resided in highly organized communities. Their local economies were based on self-employment, including gardening and truck farming, and on other nonindustrial family businesses. The group solidarity of the first generation of Japanese Americans helped them establish successful small businesses. However, they faced hostility from the surrounding society, and in fact were driven into the businesses they developed because they were denied other employment opportunities. By the second generation there was some breakdown in the middleman position of Japanese Americans, for many of that generation moved into professional occupations outside the niche economy.[39]

Some middleman minorities, such as Jewish and Korean American merchants in central cities, have become targets of hostility from less well off groups, such as poor African Americans. In addition, strong ethnic bonds can make the middleman group an effective competitor, and even Anglo-Protestant capitalists may become hostile toward an immigrant middleman minority that competes too effectively. Thus Jewish

Americans have been viewed negatively by better-off Anglo-Protestant merchants, who have the power to discriminate against them, as well as by poor black renters and customers with whom Jews deal as middle-man landlords and merchants. . . .

A somewhat similar perspective, *enclave theory*, examines secondary-structural incorporation into the economy, especially the ways in which certain non-European immigrant groups have created social and economic enclaves in cities. Both the middleman and the enclave perspectives give more emphasis to economic inequality and discrimination than assimilation perspectives, and they stress the incorporation of certain groups, such as Asians and Cubans, into the United States through the means of small businesses and specialized ethnic economies. The major differences between the two viewpoints seem to stem from the examples emphasized. Groups accented by enclave theorists, such as Cuban Americans, have created ethnic enclaves that are more than merchant or trading economies—they often include manufacturing enterprises, for example. In addition, ethnic enclaves usually compete with established Anglo-Protestant business elites. In contrast, the middleman minorities and those described as enclave minorities develop trading economies and are likely to fill an economic niche that *complements* that of established white elites. However, the aforementioned research of Bonacich on Jewish Americans suggests that there is little difference between the real-world experiences of those described as middleman minorities. . . .

Women and Gendered Racism: New Perspectives

Most theories of racial and ethnic relations have neglected gender stratification, the hierarchy in which men as a group dominate women as a group in terms of power and resources. In recent years a number of scholars have researched the situations of women within racial and ethnic groups in the United States. Their analyses assess the ways in which male supremacy, or a patriarchal system, interacts with and operates within a system of racial and ethnic stratification. Discussing racial and ethnic cultures around the globe, Adrienne Rich has defined a *patriarchal system* as "a familial-social, ideological, political system in which men—by force, direct pressure, or through ritual, tradition, law and language, customs, etiquette, education, and the division of labor—determine what part women shall or shall not play, and in which the female is everywhere subsumed under the male."[40]

Asking whether racism or patriarchy has been the primary source of oppression, social psychologist Philomena Essed examined black women in the United States and the Netherlands.[41] She found racism and sexism interacting regularly. The oppression of black women can be seen as *gendered racism*. For example, under slavery African American women were exploited not only for labor but also as sex objects for white men. And after slavery they were excluded from most job categories available to white men and white women; major employment changes came only with the civil rights movement of the 1960s. Today racism has many gendered forms. In the U.S. mass media the white female is the standard for female beauty. Minority women are often stereotyped as matriarchs in female-headed families and are found disproportionately in lower-status "female jobs," such as typists. Some women of color are closely bound in their social relations with those who oppress them in such areas as domestic employment ("maids") and other low-paid service work.[42]

In her book *Black Feminist Thought* Patricia Hill Collins argues that a black feminist theoretical framework can help highlight and analyze the negative stereotypes of black women in white society—the stereotypes of the docile mammy, the domineering matriarch, the promiscuous whore, and the irresponsible welfare mother. These severely negative images persist among many whites because they undergird white discrimination against black women in the United States.[43]

Scholars assessing the situations of other women of color, including Native American, Asian, and Latino women, have similarly emphasized the cumulative and interactive character of racial and gender oppression and the necessity of liberating these women from white stereotypes and discrimination. For example, Denise Segura has examined labor-force data on Mexican American women and developed the concept of "triple oppression," the mutually reinforcing and interactive set of race, class, and gender forces whose cumulative effects "place women of color in a subordinate social and economic position relative to men of color and the majority white population."[44]

Class, the State, and Racial Formation

Looking at the important role of governments in creating racial and ethnic designations and institutionalizing discrimination, Michael Omi and Howard Winant have developed a theory of *racial formation*. Racial tensions and oppression, in their view, cannot be explained solely in terms of class or nationalism. Racial and ethnic relations are substantially defined by the actions of governments, ranging from the passing of legislation, such as restrictive immigration laws, to the imprisonment of groups defined as a threat (for example, Japanese Americans in World War II). Although the internal colonialism viewpoint gives some emphasis to the state's role in the exploitation of non-white

minorities, it has not developed this argument sufficiently.

Omi and Winant note that the U.S. government has shaped the politics of race: the U.S. Constitution and a lengthy series of laws openly defined racial groups and interracial relationships (for example, slavery) in racist terms. The U.S. Constitution counted each African American slave as three-fifths of a person, and the Naturalization Law of 1790 explicitly declared that only *white* immigrants could qualify for naturalization. Many non-Europeans, including Africans and Asians, were prevented from becoming citizens. Japanese and other Asian immigrants, for example, were until the 1950s banned by law from becoming citizens. In 1854 the California Supreme Court ruled that Chinese immigrants should be classified as "Indians"(!), therefore denying them the political rights available to white Americans.[45]

For centuries, the U.S. government officially favored northern European immigrant groups over non-European and southern European groups such as Italians. For example, the Immigration Act of 1924 was used to exclude Asian immigrants and most immigrants from southern and eastern Europe, whom political leaders in Congress saw as racially inferior and as a threat to their control of the society. North European Americans working through the government thereby shaped the subsequent racial and ethnic mix that is the United States.

Another idea accented by Omi and Winant is that of *social rearticulation*, the recurring historical process of rupturing and reconstructing the understandings of race in this country. The social protest movements of various racial and ethnic groups periodically challenge the governments' definition of racial realities, as well as individual definitions of those realities. The 1960s civil rights movement, for instance, rearticulated traditional cultural and political ideas about race in the United States, and in the process changed the U.S. government and broadened the involvement of minority Americans in the politics of that government. New social movements regularly emerge, sometimes bringing new identities and political norms.[46]

Resistance to the Dominant Group

Recent research has highlighted the many ways in which powerless groups fight back against the powerful. One power-conflict theorist who has made an important contribution to our understanding of how the oppressed react to oppression is James Scott. Influenced by the work of scholars such as John Gaventa on the many "faces of power" Scott has shown that at the heart of much interaction between the powerless and the powerful is intentional deception.[47] For example, the African American slaves were not free to speak their minds to their white masters, but they did create a crucial discourse among themselves that was critical of their white oppressors. Scott cites a proverb of African slaves on the Caribbean island of Jamaica: "Play fool, to catch wise." Looking closely at the lives of slaves and the poor everywhere, Scott has developed the idea of a backstage discourse by the oppressed that includes views that cannot be discussed in public for fear of retaliation. In addition to secret ideological resistance on the part of slaves and other poor people, a variety of other resistance tactics are used, including foot-dragging, pilfering, dissimulation, and flight. Scott cites Afro-Christianity as an example of how African American slaves resisted the "ideological hegemony" (attempts to brainwash) of white slavemasters. In public religious services African American slaves controlled their gestures and facial expressions and pretended to accept Christian preaching about meekness and obedience. Backstage, where no whites were present,

Afro-Christianity emphasized "themes of deliverance and redemption, Moses and the Promised Land, the Egyptian captivity, and emancipation."[48] For slaves the Promised Land meant the North and freedom, and the afterlife was often viewed as a place where the slaves' enemies would be severely punished.

Historian Sterling Stuckey has noted that slave spirituals, although obviously affected by Christianity, "take on an altogether new coloration when one looks at slave religion on the plantations where most slaves were found and where African religion, contrary to the accepted scholarly wisdom, was practiced." The religion of African Americans mixed African and European elements from the beginning. Yet at its core the expressive, often protest-inclined African values prevailed over the European values.[49] Stuckey has shown that African culture and religion were major sources of the slaves' inclination to rebellion. The work of Scott and Stuckey can be linked to the analyses of Hechter and Mitchell and Feagin that we cited previously, for they too have accented the role of an oppositional culture in providing the foundation of resistance to racial oppression.

We can conclude this discussion of the most important critical power-conflict theories by underscoring certain recurring themes:

1. a central concern for racial and ethnic inequalities in economic position, power, and resources;
2. an emphasis on the links of racial inequalities to the economic institutions of capitalism and to the subordination of women under patriarchal systems;
3. an emphasis on the role of the government in legalizing exploitation and segregation and in defining racial and ethnic relations;
4. an emphasis on resistance to domination and oppression by those oppressed.

NOTES

1. Charles Hirschman, "America's Melting Pot Reconsidered," *Annual Review of Sociology* 9 (1983): 397–423.

2. Robert E. Park, *Race and Culture* (Glencoe, IL: Free Press, 1950), p. 150 (italics added).

3. Robert E. Park and Ernest W. Burgess, *Introduction to the Science of Society* (Chicago: University of Chicago Press, 1924), p. 735.

4. Janice R. Hullum, "Robert E. Park's Theory of Race Relations" (M.A. thesis, University of Texas, 1973), pp. 81–88; Park and Burgess, *Introduction to the Science of Society,* p. 760.

5. Milton M. Gordon, *Assimilation in American Life* (New York: Oxford University Press, 1964), pp. 72–73.

6. Ibid., p. 71.

7. Silvia Pedraza, *Political and Economic Migrants in America: Cubans and Mexicans* (Austin: University of Texas Press, 1985), pp. 5–7; Richard Alba, *Ethnic Identity: The Transformation of White America* (New Haven, CT: Yale University Press, 1990), p. 311; J. Allen Williams and Suzanne T. Ortega, "Dimensions of Assimilation," *Social Science Quarterly* 71 (1990):697–709.

8. Milton M. Gordon, *Human Nature, Class, and Ethnicity* (New York: Oxford University Press, 1978), pp. 67–89.

9. Gordon, *Assimilation in American Life,* pp. 78–108.

10. See Will Herberg, *Protestant–Catholic–Jew,* rev. ed. (Garden City, NY: Doubleday, Anchor Books, 1960).

11. Milton M. Gordon, "Models of Pluralism: The New American Dilemma," *Annals of the American Academy of Political and Social Science* 454 (1981):178–88.

12. Alba, *Ethnic Identity,* p. 3.

13. Stanley Lieberson and Mary Waters, "Ethnic Mixtures in the United States," *Sociology and Social Research* 70 (1985):43–53: Cookie White Stephan and Walter Stephan, "After Intermarriage," *Journal of Marriage and the Family* 51 (May 1989):507–19.

14. Nathan Glazer and Daniel P. Moynihan, *Beyond the Melting Pot* (Cambridge, MA: M.I.T. Press and Harvard University Press, 1963).

15. Andrew M. Greeley, *Ethnicity in the United States* (New York: Wiley, 1974), p. 293.

16. Ibid., pp. 295–301.

17. Ibid., p. 309.

18. William L. Yancey, D. P. Ericksen, and R. N. Juliani, "Emergent Ethnicity: A Review and Reformulation," *American Sociological Review* 41 (June 1976):391–93. See also Greeley, *Ethnicity in the United States,* pp. 290–317.

19. Talcott Parsons, "Full Citizenship for the Negro American? A Sociological Problem," in *The Negro American,* edited by Talcott Parsons and Kenneth B. Clark (Boston: Houghton Mifflin, 1965–66), p. 740.

20. James Geschwender, *Racial Stratification in America* (Dubuque, IA: Brown, 1978), p. 58.

21. Gordon, *Human Nature, Class, and Ethnicity,* pp. 73–78. See also Clifford Geertz, "The Integrative Revolution," in *Old Societies and New States,* edited by Clifford Geertz (New York: Free Press, 1963), p. 109.

22. Edna Bonacich, "Class Approaches to Ethnicity and Race," *Insurgent Sociologist* 10 (Fall 1980):11.

23. Frederik Barth, "Introduction," in *Ethnic Groups and Boundaries: The Social Organization of Culture Difference* (Oslo: Universitets Forlaget, 1969), pp. 10–17.

24. Susan Olzak, "A Competition Model of Collective Action in American Cities," in *Competitive Ethnic Relations,* edited by Susan Olzak and Joane Nagel (Orlando, FL: Academic Press, 1986), pp. 17–46.

25. Ronald Bailey and Guillermo Flores, "Internal Colonialism and Racial Minorities in the U.S.: An Overview," in *Structures of Dependency,* edited by Frank Bonilla and Robert Girling (Stanford, CA: privately published by a Stanford faculty–student seminar, 1973), pp. 151–53.

26. G. Balandier, "The Colonial Situation: A Theoretical Approach," in *Social Change,* ed. Immanuel Wallerstein (New York: Wiley, 1966), p. 35.

27. Pablo Gonzalez-Cassanova, "Internal Colonialism and National Development," in *Latin American Radicalism,* edited by Irving L. Horowitz et al. (New York: Random House, 1969), p. 130; Bailey and Flores, "Internal Colonialism," p. 156.

28. Bailey and Flores, "Internal Colonialism," p. 156.

29. Blauner, *Racial Oppression in America,* p. 55. Our analysis of internal colonialism draws

throughout on Blauner's provocative discussion.

30. Stokely Carmichael and Charles Hamilton, *Black Power* (New York: Random House, Vintage Books, 1967), pp. 2–7.

31. Guillermo B. Flores, "Race and Culture in the Internal Colony: Keeping the Chicano in His Place," in *Structures of Dependency,* edited by Bonilla and Girling, p. 192.

32. Michael Hechter, *Internal Colonialism* (Berkeley: University of California Press, 1975), pp. 9–12; Michael Hechter, "Group Formation and the Cultural Division of Labor," *American Journal of Sociology* 84 (1978): 293–318; Michael Hechter, Debra Friedman, and Malka Applebaum, "A Theory of Ethnic Collective Action," *International Migration Review* 16 (1982).412–34. See also Geschwender, *Racial Stratification in America,* p. 87.

33. Joe Feagin and Bonnie Mitchell, "America's Non-European Cultures: The Myth of the Melting Pot," in *The Inclusive University: Multicultural Perspectives in Higher Education,* edited by Benjamin Bowser, Gale Auletta, and Terry Jones (forthcoming).

34. Carol B. Stack, "Sex Roles and Survival Strategies in an Urban Black Community," in *Women, Culture and Society,* edited by Michelle Zimbalist Rosaldo and Louise Lamphere (Stanford, CA: Stanford University Press, 1974), p. 128; Ronald Angel and Marta Tienda, "Determinants of Extended Household Structure: Cultural Pattern or Economic Need?" *American Journal of Sociology* 87 (1981–82):1360–83.

35. Joan W. Moore, "American Minorities and 'New Nation' Perspectives," *Pacific Sociological Review* 19 (October 1976):448–55; Michael Omi and Howard Winant, *Racial Formation in the United States* (New York: Routledge & Kegan Paul, 1986), pp. 47–49.

36. Bonacich, "Class Approaches to Ethnicity and Race," p. 14.

37. Barrera, *Race and Class in the Southwest,* pp. 201–203; Bonacich, "Class Approaches to Ethnicity and Race," p. 14.

38. Bonacich, "Class Approaches to Ethnicity and Race," pp. 14–15.

39. Edna Bonacich and John Modell, *The Economic Basis of Ethnic Solidarity* (Berkeley: University of California Press, 1980), pp. 1–37. For a critique, see Eugene Wong, "Asian American Middleman Minority Theory: The Framework of an American Myth," *Journal of Ethnic Studies* 13 (Spring 1985): 51–87.

40. Quoted in Michael Albert et al., *Liberating Theory* (Boston: South End Press, 1986), p. 35.

41. Philomena Essed, *Understanding Everyday Racism* (Newbury Park, CA: Sage, 1991), pp. 30–32.

42. Ibid., p. 32.

43. Patricia Hill Collins, *Black Feminist Thought: Knowledge, Consciousness, and the Politics of Empowerment* (Boston: Unwin Hyman, 1990), pp. 40–48.

44. Denise A. Segura, "Chicanas and Triple Oppression in the Labor Force," in *Chicana Voices: Intersections of Class, Race and Gender,* edited by Teresa Cordova et al. (Austin, TX: Center for Mexican American Studies, 1986), p. 48.

45. Omi and Winant, *Racial Formation in the United States,* pp. 75–76.

46. Howard Winant, "Racial Formation Theory and Contemporary U.S. Politics," in *Exploitation and Exclusion,* edited by Abebe Zegeye, Leonard Harris, and Julia Maxted (London: Hans Zell, 1991), pp. 130–40.

47. James C. Scott, *Domination and the Arts of Resistance* (New Haven, CT: Yale University Press, 1990); John Gaventa, *Power and Powerlessness* (Urbana: University of Illinois Press, 1980).

48. Scott, *Domination and the Arts of Resistance,* p. 116.

49. Sterling Stuckey, *Slave Culture* (New York: Oxford University Press, 1987), pp. 27, 42–46.

5

RACIALIZED SOCIAL SYSTEM APPROACH TO RACISM

Eduardo Bonilla-Silva

QUESTIONS TO CONSIDER

Eduardo Bonilla-Silva argues that "after a society becomes racialized, racialization develops a life of its own." What does this mean? How does society become "racialized" and how is it possible that the idea of race can develop a "life" of its own? How, according to the author, is the United States characterized by racialized social systems?

In order to capture the society-wide, organized, and institutional character of racism I build my alternative theory around the notion of *racialized social systems.*[1] This term refers to societies in which economic, political, social, and ideological levels are partially structured by the placement of actors in racial categories or races. Races typically are identified by their phenotype, but (as we see later) the selection of some human traits to designate a racial group is always socially rather than biologically based.

These systems are structured partially by race because modern social systems incorporate two or more forms of hierarchical patterns. Although processes of racialization are always embedded in other forms of hierarchy, they acquire autonomy and have independent social effects. This implies that the phenomenon that has been conceived as a

free-floating ideology in fact has its own structural foundation.

In all racialized social systems the placement of actors in racial categories involves some form of hierarchy[2] that produces definite social relations among the races. The race placed in the superior position tends to receive greater economic remuneration and access to better occupations and prospects in the labor market, occupies a primary position in the political system, is granted higher social estimation (e.g., is viewed as "smarter" or "better looking"), often has the license to draw physical (segregation) as well as social (racial etiquette) boundaries between itself and other races, and receives what W.E.B. Du Bois called a "psychological wage."[3] The totality of these racialized social relations and practices constitutes the racial structure of a society.

Although all racialized social systems are hierarchical, the particular character of the hierarchy, and, thus, of the racial structure, is variable. For example, the domination of blacks in the United States was achieved through dictatorial means during slavery, but in the post–civil rights period this domination has been *hegemonic,* that is in the Gramscian sense of the term, achieved through consent rather than coercion.[4] Similarly, the form of securing domination and white privilege is variable too. For instance, the racial practices and mechanisms that kept blacks subordinated changed from overt and eminently racist in the Jim Crow era to covert and indirectly racist in the contemporary period. The unchanging element of these systems is racial inequality—that the subordinated races' life chances are significantly lower than those of the dominant race. This is the feature that ultimately distinguishes this form of hierarchical social organization. Generally, the higher the level of racial inequality, the more racialized the social system, and vice versa.

Because the races receive different social rewards at all levels, they develop different interests, which can be detected in their struggles to either transform or maintain a particular racial order. These interests are collective rather than individual, are based on relations among races rather than on particular group needs, and are practical; that is, they are related to concrete struggles. Although one race's general interest may ultimately lie in the complete elimination of a society's racial structure, its array of alternatives may not include that possibility. For instance, the historical struggle against chattel slavery led not to the development of race-free societies but to the establishment of social systems with a different kind of racialization. Race-free societies were not among the available alternatives because the nonslave populations had the capacity to preserve some type of racial privilege. The historical "exceptions" occurred in racialized societies in which the nonslaves' power was almost completely superseded by that of the slave population.[5]

A simple criticism of the argument I have advanced so far is that it ignores the internal divisions of the races along class and gender lines. Such criticism, however, does not deal squarely with the issue at hand. The fact that not all members of the dominant race receive the same level of rewards and (conversely) that not all members of the subordinate race or races are at the bottom of the social order does not negate the fact that races, as social groups, are in either a superordinate or a subordinate position in a social system. Historically the racialization of social systems did not imply the exclusion of other forms of oppression. In fact, racialization occurred in social formations also structured by class and gender. Hence, in these societies, the racialization of subjects is fragmented along class and gender lines. The important question— Which interests move actors to struggle?—is historically contingent and cannot be ascertained a priori.[6] Depending on the character of racialization in a social order, class interests may take precedence over racial interests as in contemporary Brazil, Cuba, and Puerto Rico. In other situations, racial interests may take precedence over class interests as in the case of blacks throughout most of U.S. history.

In general, the systemic salience of class in relation to race increases when the economic, political, and social inequality among the races decreases substantially. Yet this broad argument generates at least one warning: The narrowing of within-class differences among racial actors usually causes *more* rather than *less* racial conflict, at least in the short run, as the competition for resources increases.[7] More significantly, even when class-based conflict becomes more salient in a social order, this cannot be interpreted as prima facie evidence that race has subsided as a social factor. For instance, because of the way in which Latin American racial formations rearticulated race and racial discourse in the nineteenth-century–post-emancipation era,[8] these societies silenced from above the political space for public racial contestation. Yet more than 100 years after these societies developed the myth of racial democracy, they have more rather than less racial inequality than countries such as the United States.[9]

Because racial actors are also classed and gendered (that is, they belong to class and gender groups), analysts must control for class and gender to ascertain the material advantages enjoyed by a dominant race. In a racialized society such as the United States, the independent effects of race are assessed by analysts who (1) compare data between whites and nonwhites in the *same* class and gender positions, (2) evaluate the proportion as well as the general character of the races' participation in some domain of life, and (3) examine racial data at all levels— social, political, economic, and ideological— to ascertain the general position of racial groups in a social system.

The first of these procedures has become standard practice in sociology. No serious sociologist would present racial statistics without controlling for gender and class (or at least the class of persons' socioeconomic status). By doing this, analysts assume they can measure the unadulterated effects of "discrimination" manifested in unexplained "residuals." Despite its usefulness, however, this technique provides only a partial account of the "race effect" because (1) a significant amount of racial data cannot be retrieved through surveys and (2) the technique of "controlling for" a variable neglects the obvious—why a group is over- or underrepresented in certain categories of the control variables in the first place.[10] Moreover, these analysts presume that it is possible to analyze the amount of discrimination in one domain (e.g., income, occupational status) "without analyzing the extent to which discrimination also affects the factors they hold constant."[11] Hence to evaluate "race effects" in any domain, an-

alysts must attempt to make sense of their findings in relation to a race's standing in other domains.

But what is the nature of races or, more properly, of racialized social groups? Omi and Winant state that races are the outcome of the racialization process, which they define as "the extension of racial meaning to a previously racially unclassified relationship, social practice, or group."[12] Historically the classification of a people in racial terms has been a highly political act associated with practices such as conquest and colonization, enslavement, peonage, indentured servitude, and, more recently, colonial and neocolonial labor immigration. Categories such as "Indians" and "Negroes" were invented in the sixteenth and seventeenth centuries to justify the conquest and exploitation of various peoples.[13] The invention of such categories entails a dialectical process of construction; that is, the creation of the category "Other" involves the creation of a category "Same." If "Indians" are depicted as "savages," Europeans are characterized as "civilized"; if "blacks" are defined as natural candidates for slavery, "whites" are defined as free subjects.[14] Yet although the racialization of peoples was socially invented and did not override previous forms of social distinction based on class or gender, it did not lead to imaginary relations but generated new forms of human association with definite status differences. After the process of attaching meaning to a "people" is instituted, race becomes a real category of group association and identity.[15]

Because racial classifications partially organize and limit actors' life chances, racial practices of opposition emerge. Regardless of the form of racial interaction (overt, covert, or inert), races can be recognized in the realm of racial relations and positions. Viewed in this light, races are the effect of racial practices of opposition ("we" versus "them") at the economic, political, social, and ideological levels.[16]

Races, as most social scientists acknowledge, are not biologically but socially determined categories of identity and group association. In this regard, they are analogous to class and gender.[17] Actors in racial positions do not occupy those positions because they are of X or Y race, but because X or Y has been socially defined as a race. Actors' phenotypic (i.e., biologically inherited) characteristics, such as skin tone and hair color and texture, are usually, although not always, used to denote racial distinctions.[18] For example, Jews in many European nations and the Irish in England have been treated as racial groups.[19] Also, Indians in the United States have been viewed as one race despite the tremendous phenotypic and cultural variation among nations. Because races are socially constructed, both the meaning and the position assigned to races in the racial structure are always contested. Who is to be black or white or Indian reflects and affects the social, political, ideological, and economic struggles among the races. The global effects of these struggles can change the meaning of the racial categories as well as the position of a racialized group in a social formation.

This latter point is illustrated clearly by the historical struggles of several "white ethnic" groups in the United States in their efforts to become accepted as legitimate whites or "Americans."[20] Neither light-skinned nor, for that matter, dark-skinned immigrants necessarily came to this country as members of X or Y race. Light-skinned Europeans, after brief periods of "not-yet white," became "white" but did not lose their "ethnic character.[21] Their struggle for inclusion had specific implications: racial inclusion as members of the white community allowed Americanization and class mobility. On the other hand, among dark-skinned immigrants from Africa, Latin America, and the

Caribbean, the struggle was to avoid classification as "black." These immigrants challenged the reclassification of their identity for a single reason: In the United States "black" signified a subordinate status in society. Hence many of these groups struggled to keep their own ethnic or cultural identity, as denoted in expressions such as "I am not black; I am Jamaican," or "I am not black; I am Senegalese."[22] Yet eventually many of these groups resolved this contradictory situation by accepting the duality of their situation: In the United States, they were classified socially as black yet they retained and nourished their own cultural or ethnic heritage—a heritage deeply influenced by African traditions.

Although the content of racial categories changes over time through manifold processes and struggles, race is not a secondary category of group association. The meaning of black and white, the "racial formation," changes within the larger racial structure. This does not mean that the racial structure is immutable and completely independent of the action of racialized actors. It means only that the social relations among the races become institutionalized (form a structure as well as a culture) and affect social life whether or not individual members of the races want it to. In Frederick Barth's words, "Ethnic identity implies a series of constraints on the kinds of roles an individual is allowed to play [and] is similar to sex and rank, in that it constrains the incumbent in all his activities."[23] For instance, free blacks during the slavery period struggled to change the meaning of "blackness," specifically to dissociate it from slavery. Yet they could not escape the larger racial structure that restricted their life chances and their freedom.[24]

The placement of a group of people in a racial category stemmed initially[25] from the interests of powerful actors in the social system (e.g., the capitalist class, the planter class, and colonizers). After racial categories were employed to organize social relations in societies, however, race became an independent element of the operation of the social system.

What are the dynamics of racial issues in racialized systems? Most important, after a social formation is racialized, its "normal" dynamics always include a racial component. Societal struggles based on class or gender contain a racial component because both of these social categories are also racialized; that is, both class and gender are constructed along racial lines. In 1922, for example, white South African workers in the middle of a strike inspired by the Russian revolution rallied under the slogan "Workers of the world unite for a white South Africa." One of the state's "concessions" to this "class" struggle was the passage of the Apprenticeship Act of 1922, "which prevented Black workers acquiring apprenticeships."[26] In another example, the struggle of women in the United States to attain their civil and human rights has always been plagued by deep racial tensions.[27]

Nonetheless, some of the strife that exists in a racialized social formation has a distinct racial character; I call such strife *racial contestation*—the struggle of racial groups for systemic changes regarding their position at one or more levels. Such a struggle may be social (Who can be here? Who belongs here?), political (Who can vote? How much power should they have? Should they be citizens?), economic (Who should work, and what should they do? They are taking our jobs!), or ideological (Black is beautiful!).

Although much of this contestation is expressed at the individual level and is disjointed, sometimes it becomes collective and general and can effect meaningful systemic changes in a society's racial organization. The form of contestation may be relatively passive and subtle (e.g., in situations of fundamental overt racial domination such as slavery and apartheid) or more active and overt (e.g., in

quasi-democratic situations such as the contemporary United States). As a rule, however, fundamental changes in racialized social systems are accompanied by struggles that reach the point of overt protest.[28] This does not mean that a violent racially based revolution is the only way of accomplishing effective changes in the relative position of racial groups. It is simply an extension of the argument that social systems and their supporters must be "shaken" if fundamental transformations are to take place.[29] On this structural foundation rests the phenomenon labeled racism by social scientists.

I reserve the term *racial ideology* for the segment of the ideological structure of a social system that crystallizes racial notions and stereotypes. Racial ideology provides the rationalization for social, political, and economic interactions among the races. Depending on the particular character of a racialized social system and on the struggles of the subordinated races, racial ideology may be developed highly (as in apartheid) or loosely (as in slavery) and its content expressed in overt or covert terms.

Although racial ideology originates in race relations, it acquires relative autonomy in the social system and performs practical functions.[30] In Paul Gilroy's words, racial ideology "mediates the world of agents and the structures which are created by their social praxis."[31] Racism crystallizes the changing "dogma" on which actors in the social system operate and becomes "common sense"; it provides the rules for perceiving and dealing with the Other in a racialized society. In the United States, for instance, because racial notions about what blacks and whites are or ought to be pervade their encounters, whites still have difficulty in dealing with black bankers, lawyers, professors, and doctors.[32] Thus, although racist ideology is ultimately false, it fulfills a practical role in racialized societies.

At this point it is possible to sketch the framework of the racialized social system. First, racialized social systems are societies that allocate differential economic, political, social, and even psychological rewards to groups along racial lines, lines that are socially constructed. After a society becomes racialized, a set of social relations and practices based on racial distinctions develops at all societal levels. I designate the aggregate of those relations and practices as the racial structure of a society. Second, races historically are constituted according to the process of racialization; they become the effect of relations of opposition among racialized groups at all levels of a social formation. Third, on the basis of this structure, a racial ideology develops. This ideology is not simply a "superstructural" phenomenon (a mere reflection of the racialized system) but becomes the organizational map that guides actions of racial actors in society. It becomes as real as the racial relations it organizes. Fourth, most struggles in a racialized social system contain a racial component, but sometimes they acquire or exhibit a distinct racial character. Racial contestation is the logical outcome of a society with a racial hierarchy. A social formation that includes some form of racial contestation. Finally, the process of racial contestation reveals the different objective interests of the races in a racialized social system.

Conclusion

My central argument in this chapter is that the commonsense understanding of racism, which is not much different than the definition developed by mainstream social scientists or even by many critical analysts, does not provide an adequate theoretical foundation for understanding racial phenomena. With notable exceptions,[33] analysts in academia are still entangled in ungrounded ideological interpretations of racism. Lacking a structural view, they tend to reduce racial phenomena to a derivation of the class structure (as Marxist interpreters do) or the result of an irrational ideology (as mainstream social scientists do).

In the racialized social system framework, I suggest, as do Omi and Winant, that racism should be studied from the viewpoint of racialization. I contend that after a society becomes racialized, racialization develops a life of its own.[34] Although racism interacts with class and gender structurations in society, it becomes an organizing principle of social relations in itself. Race, as most analysts suggest, is a social construct, but that construct, like class and gender, has independent effects in social life. After racial stratification is established, race becomes an independent criterion for vertical hierarchy in society. Therefore different races experience positions of subordination and superordination in society and develop different interests. This framework has the following advantages over traditional views of racism:

Racial phenomena are regarded as the "normal" outcome of the racial structure of a society. Thus we can account for all racial manifestations. Instead of explaining racial phenomena as deriving from other structures or from racism (conceived of as a free-floating ideology), we can trace cultural, political, economic, social, and even psychological racial phenomena to the racial organization of that society.

The changing nature of what analysts label "racism" is explained as the normal outcome of racial contestation in a racialized social system. In this framework, changes in racism are explained rather than described. Changes are due to specific struggles at different levels among the races, resulting from differences in interests. Such changes may transform the nature of racialization and the global character of racial relations in the system (the racial structure). Therefore, change is viewed as a normal component of the racialized system.

The racialized social system framework allows analysts to explain overt as well as covert racial behavior. The covert or overt nature of racial contacts depends on how the process of racialization is manifested; this in turns depends on how race originally was articulated in a social formation and on the process of racial contestation. This point implies that rather than conceiving of racism as a universal and uniformly orchestrated phenomenon, analysts should study "historically-specific racisms."[35] This insight is not new: Robert Park, Oliver Cox, Pierre van den Bergue, and Marvin Harris described varieties of "situations of race relations" with distinct forms of racial interaction.

Racially motivated behavior, whether or not the actors are conscious of it, is regarded as "rational"—that is, based on the given race's individual interests.[36] This framework accounts for Archie Bunker–type racial behavior as well as for more "sophisticated" varieties of racial conduct. Racial phenomena are viewed as systemic; therefore all actors in the system participate in racial affairs. Some members of the dominant racial group tend to exhibit less virulence toward members of the subordinated races because they have greater control over the form and outcome of their racial interactions. When they cannot control that interaction—as in the case of revolts or blacks moving into "their" neighborhood—they behave much like other members of the dominant race.

The reproduction of racial phenomena in contemporary societies is explained in this framework not by reference to a long-distant past but in relation to its contemporary structure. Because racism is viewed as systemic (possessing a racial structure) and as organized around the races' different interests, racial aspects of social

systems today are viewed as fundamentally related to hierarchical relations among the races in those systems. Elimination of the racialized character of a social system entails the end of racialization, and hence of races altogether. This argument clashes with social scientists' most popular policy prescription for "curing" racism, namely education. This "solution" is the logical outcome of defining racism as a belief. Most analysts regard racism as a matter of individuals subscribing to an irrational view, thus the cure is educating them to realize that racism is wrong. Education is also the choice pill prescribed by Marxists for healing workers from racism. The alternative theory offered here implies that because the phenomenon has structural consequences for the races, the only way to cure society of racism is by eliminating its systemic roots. Whether this can be accomplished democratically or only through revolutionary means is an open question, and one that depends on the particular racial structure of the society in question.

A racialization framework accounts for the ways in which racial and ethnic stereotypes emerge, are transformed, and disappear. Racial stereotypes are crystallized at the ideological level of a social system. These images ultimately indicate—although in distorted ways—and justify the stereotyped group's position in a society. Stereotypes may originate out of (1) material realities or conditions endured by the group, (2) genuine ignorance about the group, or (3) rigid, distorted views on the group's physical, cultural, or moral nature. Once they emerge, however, stereotypes must relate—although not necessarily fit perfectly—to the group's true social position in the racialized system if they are to perform their ideological function. Stereotypes that do not tend to reflect a group's situation do not work and are bound to disappear. For example, notions of the Irish as stupid or of Jews as athletically talented have all but vanished since the 1940s, as the Irish moved up the educational ladder and Jews gained access to multiple routes of social mobility. Generally, then, stereotypes are reproduced because they reflect a group's distinct position and status in society. As a corollary, racial or ethnic notions about a group disappear only when the group's status mirrors that of the dominant racial or ethnic group in the society.

The framework of the racialized social system is not a universal theory explaining racial phenomena in societies. It is intended to trigger a serious discussion of how race shapes social systems. Moreover, the important question of how race interacts and intersects with class and gender has not yet been addressed satisfactorily. Provisionally I maintain that a nonfunctionalist reading of the concept of social system may give us clues for comprehending societies *structured in dominance*, to use Stuart Hall's term. If societies are viewed as systems that articulate different structures (organizing principles on which sets of social relations are systematically patterned), it is possible to claim that race—as well as gender—has both individual and combined (interactive) effects in society.

To test the usefulness of the racialized social system framework as a theoretical basis for research, we must perform comparative work on racialization in various societies. One of the main objectives of this comparative work should be to determine the specific mechanisms, practices, and social relations that produce and reproduce racial inequality at all levels—that is, uncover the society's racial structure. Unlike analysts who believe that "racism" has withered away, I argue that the persistent inequality experienced by blacks and other racial minorities in the United States today is due to the *continued* albeit *changed* existence of a racial structure. In contrast to race relations in the Jim Crow period, however, racial practices that reproduce racial inequality in contemporary America are (1) increasingly covert, (2) embedded in normal operations of institutions, (3) void of direct racial terminology, and (4) invisible to most whites.

NOTES

1. All racialized social systems operate along white supremacist lines. See Mills, *Blackness Visible* (Ithaca, NY: Cornell University Press, 1998).
2. I make a distinction between race and ethnicity. Ethnicity has a primarily sociocultural foundation, and ethnic groups have exhibited tremendous malleability in terms of who belongs. In contrast, racial ascriptions (initially) are imposed externally to justify the collective exploitation of a people and are maintained to preserve status differences. The distinction I make was part of a debate that appeared recently in the *American Sociological Review*. For specialists interested in this matter, see Bonilla-Silva, "The Essential Social Fact of Race," *American Sociological Review* 64, no. 6 (1999): 899–906.
3. Herbert Blumer was one of the first analysts to make this argument about systemic rewards received by the races ascribed the primary position in a racial order. See Herbert Blumer, "Reflections on Theory of Race Relations," pp. 3–21 in *Race Relations in World Perspective*, edited by A. W. Lind (Honolulu, HI: University of Hawaii Press, 1955). Du Bois's argument about the psychological wages of whiteness has been used recently by Manning Marable, *How Capitalism Underdeveloped Black America*; and by David Roediger, *The Wages of Whiteness*.
4. This point has been made by Omi and Winant, *Racial Formation in the United States*; Winant, *Racial Conditions*.
5. I am referring to cases such as Haiti. Nonetheless, recent research has suggested that even in such places, the abolition of slavery did not end the racialized character of the social formation. See Michel-Rolph Troillot, *Haiti, State Agency Nation: Origins and Legacy of Duvalierism* (New York: Monthly Review Press, 1990).
6. For a similar argument, see Floya Anthias and Nira Yuval-Davis, *Racialized Boundaries: Race,*

Nation, Gender, Colour, and the Anti-Racist Struggle (London, England: Tavistock, 1992).

7. For an early statement on this matter, see Hubert M. Blalock, Jr., *Toward a Theory of Minority-Majority Group Relations* (New York: John Wiley and Sons, 1967). For a more recent statement, see Susan Olzack, *The Dynamics of Ethnic Competition and Conflict* (Stanford, CA: Stanford University Press, 1992).

8. Nineteenth century nation-building processes throughout Latin America included the myth of racial democracy and color- or race-blindness. This facilitated the struggles for independence and the maintenance of white supremacy in societies wherein white elites were demographically insignificant. For discussions pertinent to this argument see the excellent collection edited by Michael Hanchard, *Racial Politics in Contemporary Brazil* (Durham and London: Duke University Press, 1999).

9. See my "The Essential Social Fact of Race," *American Sociological Review* 64, no. 6 (December 1999): 899–906.

10. On this point, see Warren Whatley and Gavin Wright, *Race, Human Capital, and Labor Markets in American History*, Working Paper #7 (Ann Arbor, MI: Center for Afroamerican and Africa Studies, University of Michigan, 1994). For an incisive discussion, see Samuel L. Meyers, Jr., "Measuring and Detecting Discrimination in the Post–Civil Rights Era," pp. 172–197 in *Race and Ethnicity in Research Methods*, edited by John H. Stanfield II and Rutledge M. Dennis (London: Sage Publications, 1993).

11. Michael Reich, "The Economics of Racism," in *Racial Conflict, Discrimination, and Power: Historical and Contemporary Studies*, edited by William Barclay, Krishma Kumar, and Ruth P. Simms (New York: AMS Press, 1976), p. 224.

12. Omi and Winant, *Racial Formation in the United States*, 64.

13. On the invention of the white race, see Theodore W. Allen *The Invention of the White Race*, Vol. I (London: Verso, 1994). On the invention of the "Indian" race, see Robert E. Berkhoffer, *The White Man's Indian* (New York: Vintage, 1978). On the invention of the black and white races, see Winthrop Jordan, *White over Black.*

14. A classic book on the ideological binary construction of the races in the United States is Thomas Gossett, *Race: The History of an Idea in America* (Dallas, TX: Southern Methodist University Press, 1963). For an analysis of an earlier period in the Americas, see Tzevetan Todorov, *The Conquest of America: The Question of the Other* (New York: Harper Colophon, 1984).

15. On this matter, I stated in my recent debate in the pages of the *American Sociological Review* with Mara Loveman that "'race,' like 'class' or 'gender,' is *always contingent* but is also *socially real.* Race operates 'as a shuttle between socially constructed meanings and practices, between subjective and lived, material reality' (Hanchard 1994:4)." (901). Michael G. Hanchard, *Orpheus and Power* (Princeton, NJ: Princeton University Press, 1994).

16. This last point is an extension of Poulantza's view on class. Races—as classes—are not an "empirical thing"; they denote racialized social relations or racial practices at all levels. Poulantzas, *Political Power and Social Classes* (London: Verso, 1982), p. 67.

17. For a full discussion, see my "The Essential Social Fact of Race." For a similar argument, see Teresa Amott and Julie Matthaei, *Race, Gender, and Work: A Multicultural Economic History of Women in the United States* (Boston, MA: South End Press, 1996).

18. Frederick Barth, "Introduction," pp. 9–38 in *Ethnic Groups and Boundaries: The Social Organization of Culture Difference*, edited by F. Barth (Bergen, Norway: Universitetsforlaget, 1969).

19. For the case of the Jews, see Miles, *Racism After "Race Relations"* (London: Routledge, 1993). For the case of the Irish, see Allen, *The Invention of the White Race.*

20. For a recent excellent discussion on ethnicity with many examples from the United States, see Stephen Cornell and Douglas Hartmann, *Ethnicity and Race: Making Identities in a Changing World* (London: Pine Forge Press, 1998).

21. Roediger, *The Wages of Whiteness*. See also Noel Ignatiev, *How the Irish Became White* (New York: Routledge, 1995).

22. For identity issues among Caribbean immigrants, see the excellent edited collection by Constance R. Sutton and E. M. Chaney, *Caribbean Life in New York City: Sociocultural Dimensions* (New York: Center for Migration Studies of New York, 1987).

23. Barth, "Introduction," 17.

24. A few notable discussions on this matter are Ira Berlin, *Slaves Without Masters: The Free Negro in Antebellum South* (New York: Pantheon, 1975); John Hope Franklin, *From Slavery to Freedom: A History of the Negro Americans* (New York: Alfred Knopf, 1974); August Meir and Elliot Rudwick, *From Plantation to Ghetto* (New York: Hill and Wang, 1970).

25. The motivation for racializing human relations may have originated in the interests of powerful actors, but after social systems are racialized, all members of the dominant race participate in defending and reproducing the racial structure. This is the crucial reason why Marxist analysts (e.g., Cox, Reich) have not succeeded in successfully analyzing racism. They have not been able to accept the fact that after the phenomenon originated with the expansion of European capitalism into the New World, it acquired a life of its own. The subjects who were racialized as belonging to the superior race, whether or not they were members of the dominant class, became zealous defenders of the racial order. For an interesting Marxist-inspired treatment, see Bush, *We Are Not What We Seem.*

26. Hillel Ticktin, *The Politics of Race: Discrimination in South Africa* (London: Pluto, 1991), p. 26.

27. The classic book on this is Paula Giddings, *When and Where I Enter: The Impact of Black Women on Race and Sex in America* (New York: Bantam, 1984). See also Nancy Caraway, *Segregated Sisterhood: Racism and the Politics of American Feminism* (Knoxville, TN: University of Tennessee Press, 1991).

28. This argument is not new. Analysts of the racial history of the United States have always pointed out that most of the significant historical changes in this country's race relations were accompanied by some degree of overt violence. See Harold Cruse, *Rebellion or Revolution* (New York: William Morrow, 1968); Franklin, *From Slavery to Freedom;* and James W. Button, *Blacks and Social Change: Impact of the Civil Rights Movement in Southern Communities* (Princeton, NJ: Princeton University Press, 1989).

29. This point is important in literature on revolutions and democracy. On the role of violence in the establishment of bourgeois democracies, see Barrington Moore, Jr., *Social Origins of Dictatorship and Democracy* (Boston, MA: Beacon Press, 1966). On the pivotal role of violence in social movements, see Frances Fox Piven and Richard A. Cloward, *Poor People's Movements: Why They Succeed, How They Fail* (New York: Vintage, 1979).

30. The notion of relative autonomy comes from the work of Poulantzas (*Power and Social Classes*) and implies that the ideological and political levels in a society are partially autonomous in relation to the economic level; that is, they are not merely expressions of the economic level.

31. Paul Gilroy, *"There Ain't No Black in the Union Jack": The Cultural Politics of Race and Nation* (Chicago, IL: University of Chicago Press, 1991), p. 17.

32. See Ellis Cose, *The Rage of a Privileged Class: Why Are Black Middle Class Angry? Why Should America Care?* (New York: HarperCollins, 1993); Lawrence Otis-Graham, *Member of the Club: Reflections on Life in a Racially Polarized World* (New York: HarperCollins, 1995).

33. In addition to the work by Joe R. Feagin and Hernán Vera already cited, see Lawrence Bobo, J. Kluegel, and R. Smith, "Laissez Faire Racism: The Crystallization of a Kinder, Gentler, Antiblack Ideology," and, particularly, Mary R. Jackman, *Velvet Glove: Paternalism and Conflict in Gender, Class and Race Relations* (Berkeley, CA: University of California Press, 1994).

34. Curiously, historian Eugene Genovese made a similar argument in his book *Red and Black.* Although he still regarded racism as an ideology, he stated that once it "arises it alters profoundly the material reality and in fact becomes a partially autonomous feature of that reality." *Red and Black: Marxian Explorations in Southern and Afroamerican History* (New York: Pantheon, 1971), p. 340.

35. Hall, "Race Articulation and Societies Structured in Dominance," in *Sociological Theories: Race and Colonialism,* edited by UNESCO (Paris: UNESCO, 1980), p. 336.

36. Actions by the Ku Klux Klan have an unmistakably racial tone, but many other actions (choosing to live in a suburban neighborhood, sending one's children to a private school, and opposing government intervention in hiring policies) also have racial undertones.

. . . CONTEMPORY SOCIOECONOMIC TRENDS

6

AN OVERVIEW OF TRENDS IN SOCIAL AND ECONOMIC WELL-BEING, BY RACE

Rebecca M. Blank

QUESTIONS TO CONSIDER

In this reading, Rebecca Blank discusses seven indicators of "well-being" for various racial and ethnic groups in the United States. As you read this chapter take note of which racial groups appear to be socially disadvantaged relative to one another. How do you explain group level disparities in these quality of life indicators? Do you agree with the three explanations she provides at the end of this chapter as to why these quality of life disparities exist?

Introduction

In general, there are many signs of improvement across all racial and ethnic groups in a wide variety of measures of measures of well-being, such as educational achievement, health status, and housing quality. In some cases, disparities between different racial groups have narrowed, as all groups have experienced improvements. But in too many cases, overall improvement in well-being among all groups has brought about no lessening of racial or ethnic disparities. In a few key mea-

Rebecca M. Blank, "An Overview of Trends in Social and Economic Well-Being, by Race" from *America Becoming: Racial Trends and Their Consequences*, Vol. 1, National Academies Press, 2001, pp. 21–39. Reprinted with permission from *America Becoming*.

sures, disparities have actually widened. The primary conclusion of this paper is that race and ethnicity continue to be salient predictors of well-being in American society. To understand what is happening in America today and what will be happening in America tomorrow, one must understand the role of race.

Indicators of Well-Being

This chapter discusses trends in seven areas:

1. population/demographic change,
2. education,
3. labor markets,
4. economic status,
5. health status,
6. crime and criminal justice, and
7. housing and neighborhoods.

Wherever possible, trends over time are presented for key variables, focusing on five major population groups: non-Hispanic Whites, non-Hispanic Blacks, Hispanics, Asian and Pacific Islanders, and American Indians and Alaska Natives. These data are taken almost entirely from U.S. government sources. In many cases, however, data for all groups are not available, or not available for the entire time period. Data available for as many groups as possible are presented in the 14 figures. The term "minority" is used to refer to a group that composes a minority of the total population. Although these five groups are currently minorities in the population, current trends project they will, together, constitute more than half the U.S. population by 2050.

This brief introduction does not attempt to provide anything like a comprehensive discussion of the available data. Provided here is an overview of some of the more interesting trends, particularly focusing on issues that introduce key topics that will be addressed in this book. One particular limitation of these data is that they present averages across very large aggregate categories of racial and ethnic classification. This hides much of the rather important information about subgroups. For instance, although data for Dominican and Cuban Americans might show very different trends, they are both combined within the Hispanic category. Similarly, Japanese and Laotian Americans are grouped together in the Asian and Pacific Islander category; Italian and Norwegian Americans are grouped together as non-Hispanic Whites.

An Increasingly Diverse Population

The U.S. population is becoming increasingly diverse. Hispanics, non-Hispanic Blacks, Asian and Pacific Islanders, and American Indians and Alaska Natives currently constitute 27 percent of the population. By 2005, Hispanics will be the largest of these groups in the United States, surpassing non-Hispanic Blacks. These changes will present this nation with a variety of social and economic opportunities and challenges.

Recent high levels of immigration are also increasing diversity within these groups. At present, 38 percent of Hispanics are foreign-born; 61 percent of Asian and Pacific Islanders are foreign-born. This raises questions of assimilation and generational change. Will the second generation among these groups show a narrowing of the disparities that distinguish their foreign-born parents from the U.S.-born population?

Where people live and who they live next to is important in determining how individuals experience racial and ethnic diversity. The population in the West is the most diverse, with more than one-third of the population composed of racial and ethnic minorities. The West is also the region where a higher percentage of Hispanics, Asian and Pacific Islanders, and American Indians and Alaska Natives reside. The South is the second most diverse region and has the largest percentage of non-Hispanic Blacks. The Midwest is the region with the least population diversity; 85 percent of its population is non-Hispanic Whites.

The household structure of these different groups varies greatly. Household structure, based on data for 1970 and 1996, correlates with a variety of other variables, particularly variables relating to economic well-being. More adults in a family means more potential earnings as well as more available adults to care for children. Single-parent households are among the poorest groups in the country. Individuals who live alone are also often more economically vulnerable than are persons who live with other family members.

All groups show significant increases in the number of people living alone or in single-parent families between 1970 and 1996, but the percentage living in single-parent families is much larger among Blacks, Hispanics, and American Indians and Alaska Natives. In fact, the biggest recent percentage of all families are in single-father families, rather than single-mother families, although single-father families continue to be a small percentage of all families. The reasons for these trends—and why some groups have much larger percentages of single-parent families in particular—are much debated.

Household structure is closely related to age distribution as well. Minority populations have a significantly larger percentage of children under the age of 17 than do non-Hispanic Whites, whereas Whites have a much larger percentage of elderly persons. The result is that the school-aged population—persons aged 5 to 17—is more racially and ethnically diverse than the population as a whole, so that today's schools reflect tomorrow's more diverse adult

population—and also mirror some of the conflicts and the benefits that accompany growing diversity.

Educational Attainment

In a society growing increasingly complex, educational skills are key to future life opportunities. Disparities in education are fundamental because they can determine lifetime earning opportunities and influence an individual's ability to participate in civic activities as well.

The labor market of the twenty-first century will rely increasingly on computers; thus, obtaining computer skills is fundamental. Figure 1 shows how children's access to computers has changed over time, both in their schools and in their homes. Clearly, more and more children have access to computers, particularly in their schools; but there

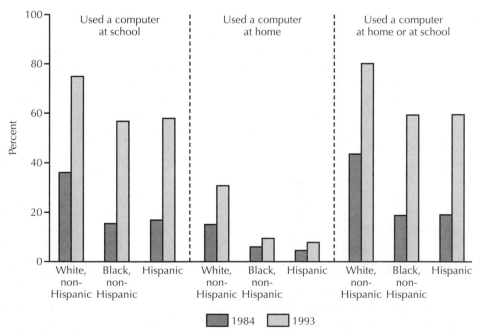

FIGURE 1   Computer Use by Children in First Through Sixth Grades. *Source:* Council of Economic Advisers (1998).

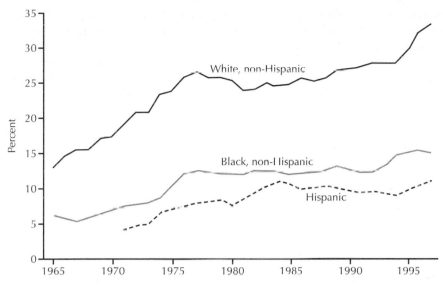

FIGURE 2   Persons Aged 25 to 29 with a Four-Year College Degree or Higher. Prior to 1971, data for Whites include Hispanic Whites, and data for Blacks include Hispanic Blacks. Data for non-Hispanic Blacks and Hispanics are three-year centered averages. Prior to 1991, data are for persons having completed four or more years of college. *Source:* Council of Economic Advisers (1998).

is an ongoing gap in computer use between White children versus Black and Hispanic children. Between 1984 and 1993, the years for which these data are available, this gap increased for computer use at home, leaving children in minority groups further behind.

Other more conventional measures of achievement in elementary and secondary schooling have generally shown narrowing gaps across racial groups. Mathematics proficiency scores, as measured among children of different ages by the National Assessment of Educational Progress, have shown ongoing gains, particularly by Black children. High school completion continues to inch up among both Whites and Blacks, with substantially greater progress among Blacks; so that the White-Black high school dropout rates are slowly converging over time. Among Hispanics, high school completion has been stagnant at approximately 60 percent since the early 1980s. Hence, the gap

between Hispanics and other groups in terms of educational achievement is widening.

Figure 2 shows trends in attainment of college degrees, through 1997, among Whites, Blacks, and Hispanics. Economic returns to a college education have increased dramatically in recent years, and college degrees continue to be an important credential for entry into many white-collar jobs. Although college completion has increased steeply among Whites, it has increased only modestly among Blacks, leading to a widening gap since the early 1990s. Among Hispanics, college completion rates are not much higher now than they were in the mid-1980s.

The more stagnant educational trends among Hispanics reflect, in part, the growing immigrant percentage of that population. Immigrants are less likely to hold high school or college degrees. U.S.-born Hispanics are making progress in increasing both their high school and college completion levels, but this progress is being diluted by the growing pool of less-educated immigrants. This re-emphasizes the question of how second-generation Hispanic children will fare. If they follow the trends of other U.S.-born populations, Hispanic educational attainment will start to increase over time.

Labor-Market Involvement

Involvement in the labor force means integration with the mainstream U.S. economy. Earnings are the primary source of income for most persons. Although job-holding may create some stress, it also produces economic rewards. Access to jobs is key for economic progress.

Figure 3 plots the labor-force participation rates from the 1950s to 1997 for Whites, Blacks, and Hispanics, by gender. The chart shows rapidly increasing convergence in labor-force participation rates, as men's rates have slowly decreased while women's rates have increased steadily. White women, who used to be much less likely to work than Black

women, are now just as likely to be in the labor force. In fact, both White women's and Black women's labor-force participation rates are rapidly converging with those of Black men, who have experienced steady decreases in work involvement.

Hispanic women also have shown increases in labor-force participation, but remain much less likely to work than other women. A major question for the Hispanic population is whether adult women will show rapid increases in labor-force participation, to the level of women from other groups. Such changes in women's labor-market involvement not only mean changes in the economic base of families—and probably in the economic security and decision-making power of husbands versus wives—but may also mean substantial changes in family functioning and in child-rearing practices.

Along with labor-force participation, unemployment is another measure of access (or lack of access) to jobs. After two decades of higher unemployment rates, unemployment in the late 1990s was at 25-to-30-year lows

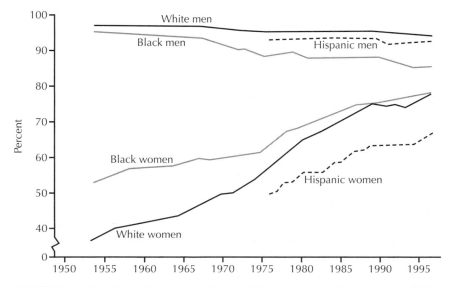

FIGURE 3   Labor Force Participation Rates of Persons Aged 25 to 54. Prior to 1972, data for Blacks include all non-Whites. *Source:* Council of Economic Advisers (1998).

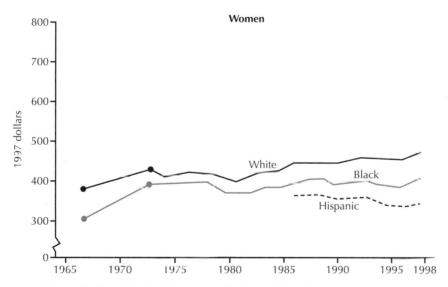

FIGURE 4 Median Weekly Earnings of Male and Female Full-Time Workers. Straight line between dots indicates data are not available for intervening years. Prior to 1979, data for Blacks include all non-Whites. Data for 1998 are from the first two quarters. *Source:* Council of Economic Advisers (1998).

among all groups. The differentials between groups, however, remained quite large. For instance, unemployment rates among Blacks have consistently been at least twice as high as those of Whites.

The labor-market issue that has received the most attention in recent years is wage opportunities. Figure 4 plots median weekly earnings among male and female full-time workers from 1965 through the first two

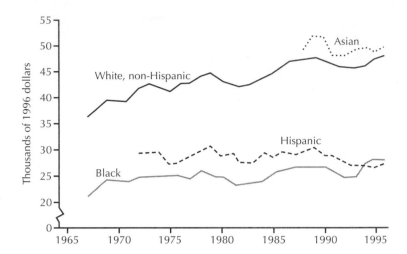

FIGURE 5 Median Family Income. Prior to 1972, data for Whites include Hispanic Whites. *Source:* Council of Economic Advisers (1998).

quarters of 1998. Among all groups, men's wages decreased steadily from 1980 until 1995, when there was evidence of an upturn. The pay gap between White and Black men changed little, however, with no sign of relative progress in wages for Black men. Hispanic men have actually seen decreases in both absolute and relative wages, compared with White and Black men. Again, this pattern is at least partially the result of the growing percentage of less-educated immigrants in the Hispanic population.

In contrast, women have not experienced wage decreases. In fact, White women's wages have grown slowly since the 1980s, so that they now earn more than both Hispanic and Black men. Black women's wages have been largely stagnant, although they show a recent upturn; and Hispanic women's wages have decreased slightly. Thus, the wage gap between White women and both Black and Hispanic women has increased.

Economic Status

Continued and even growing gaps in earnings imply that the economic situation is not improving for minority populations relative to the White population. Other measures of family economic well-being reinforce this conclusion. Figure 5 shows median family income for Asian and Pacific Islanders, non-Hispanics Whites, Hispanics, and Blacks through 1996. Family income is probably the most widely used measure of overall economic well-being. Among non-Hispanic Whites, family income has been rising steadily. Essentially, the growth in female labor-force participation and increases in White women's wages have resulted in more family income, even though men's earnings have deteriorated somewhat. Asian families earn even more than Whites. Black family income has been relatively stagnant since the 1970s, although there were signs of increase after 1993. Hispanic family income decreased in the 1990s.

This means that income differentials have widened between Whites and Asian and Pacific Islanders on the upper end of the income brackets and Blacks and Hispanics on the lower end. American Indians and Alaska Natives, for whom we only have data from the 1990 Census, show lower income than Blacks in that year.

These median family income numbers hide very different experiences at different

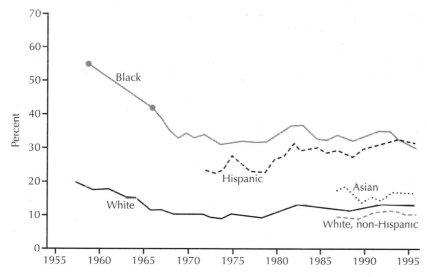

FIGURE 6   Poverty Rates for Individuals. Straight line between dots indicates data not available for intervening years. *Source:* Council of Economic Advisers (1998).

points in the income distribution. Households headed by less skilled workers—particularly those headed by single parents—have generally experienced income decreases over the past several decades. Households headed by a person with a college degree have generally experienced income increases.

One might be particularly concerned with the number of families at very low income levels. Figure 6 shows poverty rates among individuals by racial group, indicating the percentage of the population in each group living in families with incomes below the official U.S. poverty line, which was less than $8,000 per year in the late 1990s. In general, poverty rates have been relatively flat since the early 1970s. About 10 percent of the White population has been poor over this period. Asian and Pacific Islanders show a slightly higher poverty rate, underscoring the diversity within the Asian and Pacific Islander populations—they have both higher median incomes than Whites as well as higher poverty rates, reflecting the fact that at least some Asian groups are experiencing economic difficulties.

Black poverty has also been relatively constant, but at nearly 30 percent—three times the White poverty rate. Hispanic poverty rates are now higher than Black poverty rates. Poverty rates among subgroups, such as children or the elderly, show similar differentials between racial and ethnic groups.

Health Status

Economic well-being is often closely linked to other aspects of well-being, such as health status. Interestingly, health differences do not necessarily show the same patterns as economic differences. Infant-mortality rates provide a primary indicator of both health status and access to health care in a population. Figure 7 plots infant-mortality rates by race from the early 1980s through 1995. Infant mortality has been steadily decreasing among all groups, indicating major health improvements within all populations. The disparities between groups, however, have remained largely constant. Black infant-mortality rates

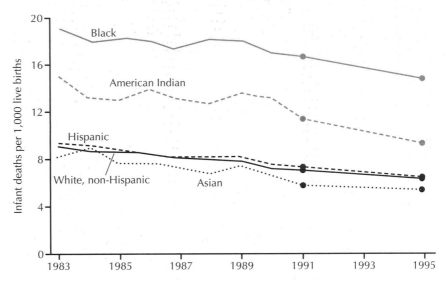

FIGURE 7   Infant Mortality Rates. Straight line between dots indicates data not available for intervening years. *Source:* Council of Economic Advisers (1998).

are about two-and-a-half times White rates. American Indian and Alaska Native rates have fallen a bit faster than other groups, but remain well above White rates.

Figure 7 also shows a pattern visible in much health data—namely, although Hispanics show substantial educational and economic differentials, they show far fewer health differentials. Hispanic infant-mortality rates are almost identical to White and Asian and Pacific Islander infant mortality rates.

Clearly, smoking is a health issue that emerges in adolescence. Smoking is correlated with a shorter life expectancy and greater health risks. In general, smoking rates have fallen for both young women and men over the past 30 years; and this is one of the few indicators where Blacks and Hispanics do better than Whites. Black smoking rates have fallen faster than White rates, so that young Blacks, who used to be more likely to smoke than Whites, are now less likely to smoke.

In contrast, Figure 8 shows death rates among 15- to 34-year-olds in the mid-1990s. There are very large differences in death rates

by cause among different racial groups. American Indians and Alaska Natives are far more likely to die as a result of unintentional injuries—typically automobile accidents—and suicide. Blacks are far more likely to die as a result of homicide and HIV infection. These differences emphasize that living conditions and health-risk factors are quite different among different populations.

Crime and Criminal Justice

There is no single aggregate measure of the likelihood of being a victim of crime. Figure 9 plots homicide rates, which constitute a small percentage of all crimes but are among the best measured crime statistics (few homicides go unnoticed or unreported). Figure 9 shows that Blacks are far more likely to be homicide victims than is any other group. The homicide victimization rate of Blacks is more than twice that of Hispanics and six times that of non-Hispanic Whites and Asian and Pacific Islanders. American Indian and Alaska Native homicide rates are about twice those of Whites

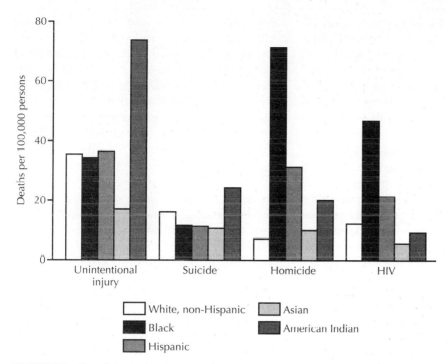

FIGURE 8 Death Rates by Cause, for Persons Aged 15 to 34, 1996 to 1995. Data for 1994 and 1995 are averaged to provide more reliable estimates. HIV data for American Indians are for 1993–1995. *Source:* Council of Economic Advisers (1998).

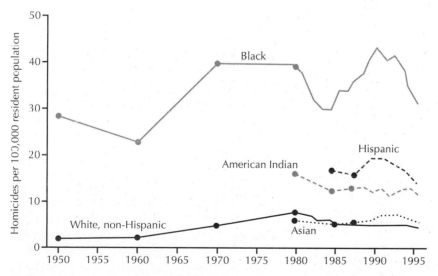

FIGURE 9 Victims of Homicide. Straight line between dots indicates data not available for intervening years. Data include deaths from "legal intervention" (use of police force). Prior to 1985, data for Whites include Hispanic Whites. Prior to 1970, data include nonresidents. *Source:* Council of Economic Advisers (1998).

and Asian and Pacific Islanders, and slightly below those of Hispanics. Although public discussion often focuses on the higher likelihood that Blacks will be arrested for crimes, there is little discussion of the fact that Blacks are also much more likely to be victims. There are large disparities by race in both the likelihood of being a victim of a crime, as well as in the likelihood of being arrested and incarcerated by the criminal justice system. Although other crime statistics, such as property crimes, show smaller racial disparities, they also show higher victimization among minority groups.

Data on experience within the criminal justice system are largely tabulated only for Whites and Blacks, and hence provide less comprehensive measures across racial groups. Blacks are far more likely to be arrested and incarcerated than are Whites. Some of these differences reflect differences in the crimes for which Blacks are disproportionately arrested, and some may reflect discriminatory behavior on the part of the police and other persons within the criminal justice system. In 1995, more than 9 percent of the Black population was under correctional supervision, either on probation or parole, or in jail or prison, compared to 2 percent of the White population. Among young Black men 20 to 29 years old, more than 25 percent are under correctional supervision. Because arrests and prison stays often fracture families and reduce future labor-market opportunities, these high rates of involvement with the criminal justice system are correlated with the reduced economic opportunities of Black families.

Housing and Neighborhoods

Where people live, and the housing they live in, is correlated with their health and economic status. Increasing concern among social scientists about "neighborhood effects"—the influence of peers and of neighborhood characteristics on individual health and behavior—has raised interest in housing and neighborhood issues. Figure 10 shows the percentage of populations living in housing units with physical problems, such as substandard plumbing or heating as well as electrical and other serious upkeep problems. All groups for which we have data, from the mid-1970s to the mid-1990s, show substantial improvement in housing quality; but, as in other areas, large disparities remain across groups. Non-Hispanic Blacks, Hispanics, and American Indians and Alaska Natives are far more likely to live in substandard housing than are Whites or Asian and Pacific Islanders. Other measures of housing adequacy, such as crowding, show similar trends, with overall improvement among all groups, but continuing large disparities between groups.

Information about neighborhoods raises again the question of where people live and who they live next to. The diversity of a person's neighborhood can affect his or her overall sense of national diversity and knowledge of members of other races or ethnicities.

Whites are by far the most segregated population, even more than their larger population percentage would justify. The average White person lives in a neighborhood that is more than 80 percent White. Blacks are the next most segregated, living in neighborhoods that are, on average, about 60 percent Black and 30 percent White.

Hispanics live in neighborhoods that have close to equal amounts (about 40 percent each) of Whites and Hispanics. Asian and Pacific Islanders live in the most diverse neighborhoods, composed of a mix of Whites, Blacks, Hispanics, and other Asian and Pacific Islanders. This suggests that these two population groups are experiencing and living in

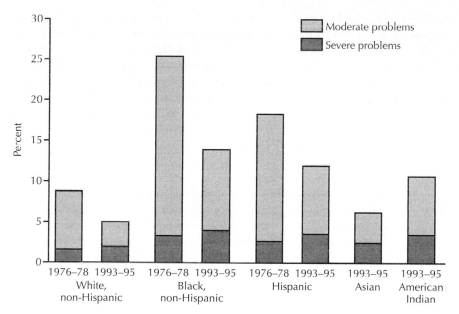

FIGURE 10 Housing Units with Physical Problems. Data for 1976 and 1978, or 1993 and 1995, are averaged to provide more reliable estimates. Data for Asians exclude Hispanic Asians, and data for American Indians exclude Hispanic American Indians. *Source:* Council of Economic Advisers (1998)

the midst of diversity in this country to a much greater degree than Whites or Blacks.

What Do These Disparities Mean?

This very quick and quite limited review of some of the key indicators of economic and social well-being underscores the ongoing importance of disparities by race and by Hispanic origin in U.S. society. Of course, there are multiple reasons behind these disparities. Many of the other chapters in this book summarize what the research literature indicates about the causes and effects of racial disparities in key areas of society. Three overarching conclusions, based on the data, are presented here.

First, race and Hispanic origin continue to be defining characteristics for many

Americans. They are correlated with educational and economic opportunities, with health status, and with where people live and who they live next to. The magnitude of these differences, especially for Blacks and Hispanics, is extremely significant on average, suggesting that these disparities are widely experienced. Relative to the White and Asian populations, the Black population on average has only two-fifths as many college graduates, three-fourths as much earnings, and only slightly more than one-half as much income. The Hispanic population fares even worse. Although we do not have as much comparable information for American Indians and Alaska Natives, their data tend to be closer to those of Blacks and Hispanics than to those of Whites. Whatever their causes, these are substantial differentials; they shape our life opportunities and they shape our opinions about behavior toward each other. To repeat the point I started with at the beginning of this chapter, race continues to be a salient predictor of well-being in America.

Second, the growing presence of Hispanic and Asian and Pacific Islander populations is fundamentally changing the face of America. The displacement of Blacks as the largest minority group in the population in the early 2000s may cause some political and social tension. High numbers of immigrants within the Hispanic and Asian and Pacific Islander groups make questions of assimilation and second-generation progress particularly important in the years ahead. If second-generation Hispanic women behave more like other U.S.-born women, there will be many more Hispanic families with wives in the labor market two decades from now. If second-generation Hispanics acquire education at the rate of other U.S.-born populations, the education levels within the Hispanic community will rise substantially.

Third, Whites may be less aware of the changes and the challenges of growing population diversity than any other group. In part, there is often a "blindness" among the majority to the situation of other groups, because their own situation is typically taken as the norm. This "blindness" is reinforced by locational patterns and neighborhood choice. Whites are much more likely to live in the Midwest than other groups, the least diverse part of the nation; and they tend to live in the most segregated neighborhoods in the other regions. In contrast, Asian and Pacific Islanders—who do as well as Whites on many measures of well-being—live in much more diverse neighborhoods and are almost surely more aware of issues relating to diversity and difference, even when these issues do not translate into personal economic differentials. In short, the growing population of Hispanics and Asian and Pacific Islanders, as well as many Blacks, may be better prepared to address the challenges, and to take the advantage of the benefits, of an increasingly diverse population than are Whites.

REFERENCE

Council of Economic Advisers. 1998. *Changing America: Indicators of Social and Economic Well-Being by Race and Hispanic Origin.* Washington, D.C.: U.S. Government Printing Office.

SEEING THE BIG PICTURE

Think for a moment about three important indicators of "living the good life" (for example, good health, high income, and a college degree). Now look up those indicators in the Appendix and determine whether those indicators vary by race and ethnicity. How do you explain group-level differences in these quality of life indicators?

7
_____

THE COLOR OF HEALTH IN THE UNITED STATES

David R. Williams • *Chiquita Collins*

QUESTIONS TO CONSIDER

We tend to think about health in individual terms: a parent's battle with cancer, a brother struggling with diabetes, or a sister coping with acute asthma. But upon closer inspection, what appears to be an individual malady or a family tragedy is linked to racial inequality. Medical researchers found that the odds of babies dying in Central Harlem before their first birthday was one in fifty while just one zip code away in the Upper East Side the death odds were only one in six hundred. Put another way, babies are twelve times more likely to die before they reach their first birthday in Central Harlem than are babies on the Upper East Side of New York City. In this reading Williams and Collins explain how race, poverty, and health outcomes are linked. How likely is it, given increased levels of socioeconomic inequality and health care cuts by both federal and state governments, that the United States can follow the policy recommendations suggested by the authors?

• • •

The United States is relatively unusual among industrialized countries in that it reports the health status of its population based on race.[1] Most other countries focus on social class differences. For most of this century, the contrast between whites and nonwhites (a category that consisted almost exclusively of blacks) was the basis of differentiation. Since the late 1970s there has been a growing emphasis on collecting more data on the racial and ethnic minority populations that constitute an increasing proportion of the American population. Recent reviews reveal that race and ethnicity remain potent predictors of variations in health status.[2-5]

The most recent report card on the health of the U.S. population presents infant and adult mortality rates by race.[6] Infant mortality rates are reported for major subgroups of the Asian and Pacific Islander American (APIA) and the Hispanic population, but subgroup differences were not available for adult mortality. The infant mortality rate for blacks is twice that of whites, and American Indians also have elevated infant mortality rates compared to the white population. The APIA population and its four major subgroups have rates that are lower than those of whites, while the rate for Hispanics is equivalent to that of whites. However, variation occurs within the Hispanic category: Puerto Ricans have higher infant mortality rates than do the other Hispanic groups and the white population. The report also revealed that the age-adjusted death rate for the entire black population is dramatically higher than that of whites, but all of the other racial/ethnic populations have death rates lower than the white population, with the APIA population having the lowest death rates.

These overall data mask important patterns of variation for subgroups of these populations and for specific health conditions, a point readily evident in recent overviews of the health of the Hispanic population.[7,8] While Latinos have lower death rates for the two leading causes of death (heart disease and cancer) than do non-Hispanics, they also have higher mortality rates than do non-Hispanic whites for tuberculosis, septicemia, chronic liver disease and cirrhosis, diabetes, and homicide. Death rates of Hispanics also exceed those of whites in the fifteen to forty-four age group.[9] Moreover, Hispanics have elevated rates of infectious diseases such as measles, rubella, tetanus, tuberculosis, syphilis, and AIDS. The prevalence of obesity and glucose intolerance are also particularly high, especially among Mexican Americans. Similar to the findings for infant mortality, adult mortality rates for Puerto Ricans are higher than the rates of other Hispanic groups. However, even among Puerto Ricans, the mortality rate is lower than for white non-Hispanics and considerably lower than for African Americans.

Specific subgroups of the APIA population have elevated rates of morbidity and mortality across a number of health indicators. The Native Hawaiian population has the highest cancer rates of any APIA population in the United States[10] and the highest death rates due to heart disease of any racial

group in the United States.[11] Rates of stomach cancer are high among Japanese Americans, and Chinese Americans have an incidence of liver cancer that is four times higher than that of the white population.[10] Very high rates of obesity are evident for Native Hawaiians and Samoans, and these populations, along with Asian Indians, Japanese Americans, and Korean Americans, have prevalence rates of diabetes that are more similar to those of the black population than those of the white population.[12] Death rates for Native Americans are high for the under-forty-five age group, and suicide rates for American Indian youth are two to four times higher than those of any other racial group.[9] Native American youth also have higher levels of alcohol and other drug use than does any other racial group.[13]

Worsening Health Status

As part of the increasing income inequality in the United States, the gains in economic status of blacks relative to that of whites have stagnated in recent years.[14] Moreover, on several economic indicators there has been an absolute decline in the economic status of African Americans. For example, unlike the pattern for white families, the pattern for low-income black and Hispanic families shows an absolute decline in family income since 1973, and weekly wage and salary income declined for all black and Hispanic males below the 90th percentile of income between 1979 and 1987. Similarly, the percentage of black children living in poverty increased from 41 percent to 44 percent between 1979 and 1988.[15] Similar to the findings noted earlier for [socioeconomic status] SES, this decline in black economic well-being and increase in black-white inequality is associated with worsening black health across a number of health status indicators.

The gap in life expectancy between blacks and whites widened between 1980 and 1991 from 6.9 years to 8.3 years for males and from 5.6 years to 5.8 years for females.[16] Moreover, for every year between 1985 and 1989, the life expectancy for both African American men and women declined from the 1984 level, although an upturn has been reported in the most recent data.[6] A slower rate of decline among blacks than whites for heart disease is the chief contributor to the widening racial gap in life expectancy, while HIV infection, homicide, diabetes, and pneumonia are major causes of decreasing life expectancy for blacks.[17]

The age-adjusted death ratios for blacks and whites were greater in 1991 than in 1980, and the annual number of excess deaths for the African American population, compared to the white population, increased from 60,000 in 1980 to 66,000 in 1991.[16] During this period, the overall age-adjusted death rate decreased more rapidly for white males and females than for their black counterparts. Under the age of seventy, three causes of death—cardiovascular disease, cancer, and problems resulting in infant mortality—account for 50 percent of the excess deaths for black males and 63 percent of the excess deaths for black females. Homicide accounts for 19 percent of the excess deaths for black males and 6 percent for black females. An analysis of death rates between 1900 and the present reveals that black-white health inequality among men is currently at an all-time high for this century.[18] In some depressed urban environments there has been no improvement in the health status of the black population over time. For example, Freeman[19] shows that in contrast to a steady decline in national mortality rates for both blacks and whites between 1960 and 1980, there was no change in mortality for African Americans in Harlem over this twenty-year period. However, the potential contribution

of selection processes via migration to this pattern was not assessed.

The gap in infant mortality rates for white and black babies widened for each sex between 1980 and 1991.[16] Rates of both pre-term delivery[20] and low birth-weight[16] have remained stable for white women but have been increasing among African Americans. A widening differential between African Americans and whites is also evident for rates of sexually transmitted diseases.[21] Between 1986 and 1989, cases of gonorrhea and syphilis decreased by 50 percent and 11 percent, respectively, for whites. In contrast, gonorrhea declined by only 13 percent for blacks while syphilis increased by 100 percent. The increase in syphilis is thought to be associated with increases in the use of crack cocaine and related increases in prostitution.

Major Historical Events

This recent evidence of deterioration in the health of the African American population emphasizes the importance of considering the larger historical context in understanding the health status of population groups. Mullings has suggested that the civil rights movement, for example, has had important positive effects on black health.[22] By reducing occupational and educational segregation, it improved the SES position of at least a segment of the black population and also influenced public policy to make health care accessible to larger numbers of people. Consistent with this hypothesis, one study found that between 1968 and 1978, blacks experienced a larger decline in mortality rates (both on a percentage and absolute basis) than whites.[23]

More recently, the presidential campaign of Jesse Jackson may have had a positive short-term impact on the health of the African American population. Using four-wave data from the National Study of Black Americans that span the period 1979–80 to 1992, Jackson et al. found that during the third wave of data collection (1988), the reported levels of physical and mental well-being were at their highest.[24] In addition, the proportions of respondents reporting that they had experienced racial discrimination and that they perceived whites as wanting to keep blacks down were at their lowest levels. Contemporaneously, Jesse Jackson, a black male, was making the most successful run for the presidency of the United States that had ever been made by an African American in the history of the United States. These researchers suggest that this political event may have had spillover effects for black adults' perceptions of America's racial climate and their health status.

The massive internal migration of blacks in the United States earlier this century has been an important influence on the African American population. Although the initial economic and longer-term political gains linked to migration may have had positive health consequences, the black migration may have also had profound adverse effects on health.[25] First, the black migration disproportionately distributed the African American population to urban residential areas where living conditions are hostile to life and health. Unlike the white urban poor who are dispersed throughout the city, with many residing in relatively safe and comfortable neighborhoods, the black poor are concentrated in depressed central-city neighborhoods[26] where the stress of poor urban environments can lead to illness.[27,28] A recent study in Harlem, one of the poorest areas of New York City, documented that black males between the ages of twenty-five and forty-four in Harlem are six times more likely to die than are their white counterparts in the United States.[29] Moreover, the life expectancy of blacks in Harlem is

lower than that of persons in Bangladesh, one of the poorest countries in the world.

Wilson suggests that the concentration of black poverty in the inner city is due to the out-migration of middle-class blacks to other areas.[26] In contrast, Massey and Gross found that three complementary mechanisms were responsible:[30] the wholesale abandonment of black and racially mixed areas by middle-class whites, the selective migration of poor people into black neighborhoods, and the net movement into poverty of blacks living in segregated areas. Living conditions in inner-city areas are also deteriorating over time. The economic status of central-city African Americans has declined relative to other urban blacks. In 1940, central-city blacks earned 10 percent more than did other black urban dwellers, but by 1980 they were receiving 10 percent less.[14] There is also growing concern about the health consequences of stress in residential environments, such as the high level of community violence in many depressed urban environments.[31]

The internal migration of the African American population also affected health by changing health behaviors in ways that lead to high risks of disease and death. With the great migration and urbanization of black Americans came a dramatic rise in their use of alcohol and tobacco, and a reversal in the racial distribution of alcohol and tobacco use.[32] During the first half of the twentieth century, the prevalence of cigarette smoking and alcohol abuse was higher for whites than for blacks. The great migration shifted a considerable portion of the black population from the relatively "dry" rural South, where social life revolved around churches and family associations, to the "wet" areas of the urban North, where taverns and associated alcohol use were an integral part of social life.[33] Moreover, by producing feelings of alienation, powerlessness, and helplessness, life in urban settings created the need for individuals to mask these feelings or obtain temporary relief from them by consuming tobacco and alcohol. African Americans have been special targets of the advertising of both the tobacco and the alcohol industries,[34,35] targeting that dates back to the 1950s.[36]

A recent provocative theory designed to account for the high rates of hypertension among African Americans also gives a central role to historical factors.[37] According to the "slavery hypothesis," the historic conditions of slavery, especially those linked to capture in Africa and the transatlantic slave voyage, resulted in the preferential survival of those Africans who had a genetic propensity to conserve sodium and water. Contemporary African Americans have inherited this trait, which is responsible for the elevated rates of high blood pressure. Despite its deceptive simplicity and intuitive appeal, like earlier biological explanations, this hypothesis locates racial disparities in health inside the individual and pays scant attention to current living conditions. Serious questions have been raised regarding the plausibility of a historic genetic "bottleneck" being a key determinant of current genetic characteristics,[38] and about the validity of the historic data that have been invoked to support this theory.[39] Moreover, there is abundant evidence that the current social circumstances of African Americans play a major role in accounting for their elevated rates of high blood pressure.[40]

Race and SES

Socioeconomic differences between racial groups are largely responsible for the observed patterns of racial disparities in health status. Race is strongly correlated with SES and is sometimes used as an indicator of SES. For example, while 11 percent of the white population is poor, poverty rates for the African American and Hispanic population are 33 percent and 29 percent, respectively. Not surprisingly, differentials in health status associated with race are smaller than those associated with SES. For example, in 1986, persons with an annual household income of $10,000 or less were 4.6 times more likely to be in poor health than those with income over $35,000, while blacks were 1.9 times more likely to be in poor health than whites.[1] Thus, race differentials were less than half of the SES differentials.

Researchers frequently find that adjusting racial disparities in health for SES substantially reduces these differences. In some cases the race disparity disappears altogether when adjusted for SES.[41,42] Two recent studies provide striking evidence of the contribution of SES to observed racial differences in violence and illegal drug use. Greenberg and Schneider[43] showed that rates of violent deaths in New Jersey were associated not with race per se, but with residence in urban areas with a high concentration of undesirable environmental characteristics such as waste incinerators, landfills, and deserted factories. Violent deaths from homicide, poisoning/drug use, falls, fires, and suicide in these marginal areas were ten times higher for males and six times higher for females than for their counterparts in the rest of New Jersey. Moreover, deaths in these marginal areas were high for whites and Hispanics as well as blacks, females as well as males, and middle-aged and elderly populations as well as youthful populations. Lillie-Blanton et al.[44] also found that a twofold higher prevalence of crack cocaine use for blacks and Hispanics compared to whites was reduced to nonsignificance when adjusted for census indicators of social environmental risk factors. Thus, failure to adjust racial differences for SES can reinforce racial prejudices and perpetuate racist stereotypes, diverting both public opinion and research dollars from

TABLE 1   Median Net Worth in 1991 by Monthly Household Income Quintiles for Whites, Blacks, and Hispanics

Household Income	White	Black	Hispanic
All	$44,408	$4,604	$5,345
Lowest quintile	$10,257	$1	$645
Second quintile	$25,602	$3,299	$3,182
Third quintile	$33,503	$7,987	$7,150
Fourth quintile	$52,767	$20,547	$19,413
Highest quintile	$129,394	$54,449	$67,435

Source: Eller, T. J. (1994). *Household wealth and asset ownership, 1991* (U.S. Bureau of the Census, Current Population Reports, P70–34). Washington DC: U.S. Government Printing Office.

the underlying social factors that are responsible for the pattern of risk distribution.

More frequently, it is found that adjustment for SES substantially reduces but does not eliminate racial disparities in health.[18, 45, 46] That is, within each level of SES, blacks generally have worse health status than whites. One recent study found higher infant mortality rates among college-educated black women than among their similarly situated white peers.[47] Moreover, some studies find that the black-white mortality ratio actually increases with rising SES. This is clearly the case for infant mortality, where the black-white gap is narrowest among women who have not completed high school, and highest among women with a college education.[48]

Kessler and Neighbors emphasize the importance of systematically testing for interactions between race and socioeconomic status.[49] They reanalyzed data from eight epidemiologic surveys and demonstrated that although controlling for SES reduced to nonsignificance the association between race and psychological distress, low-SES blacks had higher rates of distress than did low-SES whites. However, the findings have not been uniform. Analyses of data from the large ECA study found that low-SES white males had higher rates of psychiatric disorders than did their black peers.[50] Among women,

low-SES black females had higher levels of substance abuse disorders than did their white peers. These findings suggest the importance of distinguishing distress from disorder, as well as the need to understand the interactions among race, gender, and class.

One reason for the persistence of racial differences despite adjustment for SES is that the commonly used SES indicators do not fully capture the economic status difference between households of different races. For example, racial differences in wealth are much larger than those for income. There are large racial differences in the inheritance of wealth and intergenerational transfers of wealth. Table 1 shows that while white households have a median net worth of $44,408, the net worth was $4,604 for black households and $5,345 for Hispanic households.[51] Compared to white households, black households had a significantly greater percentage of their net worth in durable goods such as housing and motor vehicles, and a significantly lower percentage of their net worth in financial assets. Moreover, at every income level, the net worth of black and Hispanic households is dramatically less than that of white households. Thus, in studies of racial comparisons, measures of assets are necessary for the identification of the economic status of the household.

TABLE 2   Median Earnings in 1990 by Education (Years of School Completed) for White, Black, and Hispanic, Male and Female Full-Time Workers

Education Level	Males		
	White	*Black*	*Hispanic*
8 years or less	16,906	16,961	13,913
9–11 years	21,048	16,778	17,868
12 years	26,526	20,271	20,932
Some college	31,336	25,863	26,380
College degree	28,263	30,532	33,074
Graduate	47,787	36,851	42,315
Education Level	Females		
	White	*Black*	*Hispanic*
8 years or less	11,826	11,364	11,231
9–11 years	14,010	13,643	12,586
12 years	17,552	16,531	16,298
Some college	21,547	19,922	20,881
College degree	26,822	26,881	22,555
Graduate	31,991	31,119	30,133

Source: U.S. Bureau of the Census. (1991). *Money income of households, families, and persons in the United States* (Current Population Reports, P-60, No. 174). Washington, DC: U.S. Government Printing Office.

In some cases where blacks are more exposed to particular risk factors, these risk factors appear to have weaker effects for the black population. In a national study in which black children constituted 75 percent of those in the category of lowest long-term income, persistent poverty was unrelated to either stunting or wasting for blacks, unlike the strong pattern evident for non-Hispanic whites and Hispanics.[52] Similarly, although black infants have twice the low birthweight risk of whites, low birthweight is more strongly linked to infant mortality in the neonatal period for blacks than for whites.[53]

Racism

Another reason for the failure of SES indicators to completely account for racial differences in health is the failure of most studies to consider the effects of racism on health. A growing body of theoretical and empirical work suggest that racism is a central determinant of health status of oppressed racial and ethnic populations.[18,48,54,55,56] Racism is viewed as incorporating ideologies of superiority, negative attitudes and beliefs toward racial and ethnic outgroups, and differential treatment of members of those groups by both individuals and societal institutions. Racism can affect health in at least three ways.[18,54]

First, it can transform social status so that SES indicators are not equivalent across race. There are large differences related to race in the quality of elementary and high school education, so that blacks bring fewer basic skills to the labor market than whites do.[57] In addition, as Table 2 indicates, whites receive higher income returns from education than blacks and Hispanics.[58]

These racial differences are larger among males than among females, and the black-white income gap for males does not become narrower with increasing years of education. In addition, although Hispanic males do better than their black peers at the higher levels of education, the same is not true for Hispanic females. These data indicate that simply equalizing levels of education would still leave a large racial gap in earned income.

Dressler also indicates that the pattern of income production varies for black and white households.[59] Black households are more likely than white ones to rely on several wage earners to contribute to total household income. Middle-class blacks are also more likely than their white peers to be recent and tenuous in that class status.[60] College-educated blacks, for example, are almost four times more likely than their white peers to experience unemployment.[61] Researchers have also emphasized that the purchasing power of a given level of income varies by race,[55,62] with blacks paying higher prices than whites for a broad range of goods and services in society, including food and housing. African Americans also have higher rates of unemployment and underemployment than do whites. Moreover, employed blacks are more likely than their white peers to be exposed to occupational hazards and carcinogens, even after adjusting for job experience and education.[63]

Second, racism can restrict access to the quantity and quality of health-related desirable services such as public education, health care, housing, and recreational facilities. Recent studies have found a positive association between residential segregation and mortality rates for both adults[64] and infants.[65,66] The relationship between segregation and infant mortality exists for blacks but not for whites. A recent review of racial differences in medical care found that even after adjusting for severity of illness, SES, and/or insurance status, blacks were less likely to receive a wide range of medical services than were whites.[67]

Third, the experience of racial discrimination and other forms of racism may induce psychological distress than may adversely affect physical and mental health status as well as the likelihood of engaging in violence and addiction. Recent reviews reveal that a small but growing body of evidence indicates that the experience of racial discrimination is adversely related to a broad range of health outcomes.[48,54] In addition, the internalization of racist ideology is also adversely associated with morbidity.[54]

In color-conscious American society, skin color may be an important determinant of the degree of exposure to racial discrimination, access to valued resources, and the intensity of the effort necessary to obtain those resources.[59] Dressler[59] has employed darker skin color as an objective indicator of low social status within the black population and found that status inconsistency based on the relation of skin color to lifestyle (ownership of material goods and engaging in status-enhancing behaviors) is associated with elevated rates of hypertension. Independent of education level, persons with darker skin color and higher lifestyle had the highest levels of blood pressure. Klag et al. also found an interaction between skin color and SES in a sample of blacks.[68] Darker skin color was associated with elevated rates of hypertension for low- but not high-SES blacks. Consistent with the notion that darker-skinned African Americans may experience higher levels of discrimination, analyses of data from the National Study of Black Americans found that skin color was a stronger predictor of occupational status and income of blacks than was parental SES.[69]

• • •

Racial and socioeconomic inequality in health is arguably the single most important public health issue in the United States. The evidence reviewed indicates that SES inequalities in health are widening, and the health status of at least some racial groups has worsened over time. The ranking of the United States relative to other industrialized countries in terms of health has been declining over time, while America continues to spend more on medical care per capita than any other country in the world. The evidence reviewed suggests that a serious and sustained investment in reducing societal inequalities can enhance the quantity and quality of life of all Americans and create the necessary liberty for the pursuit of health and happiness.

NOTES

1. Navarro, V. (1990). Race or class versus race and class: Mortality differentials in the United States. *Lancet, 336,* 1238–1240.

2. Braithwaite, R. L., & Taylor, S. E. (1992). *Health issues in the black community.* San Francisco: Jossey-Bass.

3. Furino, A. (Ed.). (1992). *Health policy and the Hispanic.* Boulder, CO: Westview Press.

4. Livingston, I. L. (1994). *Handbook of black American health: The mosaic of conditions, issues, policies, and prospects.* Westport, CT: Greenwood Press.

5. Zane, N. W. S., Takeuchi, D. T., & Young, K. N. S., (Eds.). (1994). *Confronting critical health issues of Asian and Pacific Islander Americans.* Thousand Oaks, CA: Sage.

6. National Center for Health Statistics. (1994). *Health, United States, 1993.* Hyattsville, MD: U.S. Department of Health and Human Services.

7. Sorlie, P. D., Backlund, E., Johnson, N. J., & Rogot, E. (1993). Mortality by Hispanic status in the United States. *JAMA, 270,* 2464–2468.

8. Vega, W. A., & Amaro, H. (1994). Latino outlook: Good health, uncertain prognosis. *Annu Rev Public Health, 15,* 39–67.

9. Fingerhut, L. A., & Makuc, D. M. (1992). Mortality among minority populations in the United States. *Am J Public Health, 82,* 1168–1170.

10. Lin-Fu, J. S. (1993). Asian and Pacific Islander Americans: An overview of demographic characteristics and health care issues. *Asian Am Pacific Islander J Health, 1,* 20–36.

11. Chen, M. S. (1993). A 1993 status report on the health status of Asian American and Pacific Islanders: Comparisons with *Healthy People 2000* objectives. *Asian Am Pacific Islander J Health, 1,* 37–55.

12. Crews, D. E. (1994). Obesity and diabetes. In N.W.S. Zane, D. T. Takeuchi, & K.N.J. Young (Eds.), *Confronting critical health issues of Asian and Pacific Islander Americans* (pp. 174–208). Thousand Oaks, CA: Sage.

13. Smith, E. M. (1993). Race or racism? Addiction in the United States. *Ann Epidemiol, 3,* 165–170.

14. Smith, J. P., & Welch, F. R. (1989). Black economic progress after Myrdal. *J Econ Lit, 27,* 519–564.

15. Hernandez, D. J. (1993). *America's children: Resources from family, government and the economy.* New York: Russell Sage Foundation.

16. National Center for Health Statistics. (1994). *Excess deaths and other mortality measures for the black population: 1979–81 and 1991.* Hyattsville, MD: U.S. Public Health Service.

17. Kochanek, K. D., Maurer, J. D., & Rosenberg, H. M. (1994). Why did black life expectancy decline from 1984 through 1989 in the United States? *Am J Public Health, 84,* 938–944.

18. Cooper, R. S. (1993). Health and the social status of blacks in the United States. *Ann Epidemiol, 3,* 137–144.

19. Freeman, H. P. (1993). Poverty, race, racism, and survival. *Ann Epidemiol, 3,* 145–149.

20. Rowley, D. L., Hogue, C.J.R., Blackmore, A. C., Ferre, C. D., Hatfield-Timajchy, K., et al. (1993). Preterm delivery among African-American women: A research strategy. *Am J Prev Med, 9*(Suppl.), 1–6.

21. Castro, K. G. (1993). Distribution of acquired immunodeficiency syndrome and other sexually transmitted diseases in racial and ethnic populations, United States: Influences of life-style and socioeconomic status. *Ann Epidemiol, 3,* 181–184.

22. Mullings, L. (1989). Inequality and African-American health status: Policies and prospects. In W. A. VanHorne & T. V. Tonnesen (Eds.), *Twentieth century dilemmas—Twenty-first century prognoses* (pp. 154–182). Madison: University of Wisconsin, Institute on Race and Ethnicity.

23. Cooper, R. S., Steinhauer, M., Schatzkin, A., & Miller, W. (1981). Improved mortality among U.S. blacks, 1968–78: The role of antiracist struggle. *Int J Health Serv, 11,* 511–522.

24. Jackson, J. S., Brown, T. N., Williams, D. R., Torres, M., Sellers, S. L., & Brown, K. (1995). Perceptions and experiences of racism and the physical and mental health status of African Americans: A thirteen year national panel study. *Ethn Dis, 5*(1).

25. Williams, D. R. (1995). Poverty, racism and migration: The health of the African American population. In S. Pedraza & R. G. Rumbaut (Eds.), *Immigration, race, and ethnicity in America. Historical and contemporary perspectives.* Belmont, CA: Wadsworth.

26. Wilson, W. J. (1987). *The truly disadvantaged.* Chicago: University of Chicago Press.

27. Haan, M., Kaplan, G., & Camacho, T. (1987). Poverty and health: Prospective evidence from the Alameda County Study. *Am J Epidemiol, 15,* 989–998.

28. Harburg, E., Erfurt, J., Chape, C., Havenstein, L., Scholl, W., & Schork, M. A. (1973). Sociological stressor areas and black-white blood pressure: Detroit. *J Chronic Dis, 26,* 595–611.

29. McCord, C., & Freeman, H. P. (1990). Excess mortality in Harlem. *N Engl J Med, 322,* 173–177.

30. Massey, D. S., & Gross, A. B. (1993). *Black migration, segregation, and the spatial concentration of poverty.* Irving B. Harris Graduate School of Public Policy Studies Working Paper, Ser. 93-3, University of Chicago.

31. Gabarino, J., Dubrow, N., Kostelney, K., & Pardo, C. (1992). *Children in danger: Coping with the consequences of community violence.* San Francisco: Jossey-Bass.

32. Williams, D. R. (1991). Social structure and the health behavior of blacks. In K. W. Schaie, J. S. House, & D. Blazer (Eds.), *Aging, health behaviors and health outcomes* (pp. 59–64). Hillsdale, NJ: Erlbaum.

33. Herd, D. (1985). Migration, cultural transformation and the rise of black liver cirrhosis mortality. *Br J Addict, 80,* 397–410.

34. Davis, R. M. (1987). Current trends in cigarette advertising and marketing. *N Engl J Med, 316,* 725–732.

35. Singer, M. (1986). Toward a political economy of alcoholism. *Soc Sci Med, 23,* 113–130.

36. Levin, M. (1988). The tobacco industry's strange bedfellows. *Bus Soc Rev, 65,* 11–17.

37. Wilson, T. W., & Grim, C. E. (1991). Biohistory of slavery and blood pressure differences in blacks today. *Hypertension, 17*(Suppl. I), 122–128.

38. Jackson, F.L.C. (1991). An evolutionary perspective on salt, hypertension, and human genetic variability. *Hypertension, 17*(1, Suppl. 1), 129–132.

39. Curtin, P. D. (1992). The slavery hypothesis for hypertension among African Americans: The historical evidence. *Am J Public Health, 82,* 1681–1686.

40. Williams, D. R. (1992). Black-white differences in blood pressure: The role of social factors. *Ethn Dis, 2,* 126–141.

41. Baquet, C. R., Horm, J. W., Gibbs, T., & Greenwald, P. (1991). Socioeconomic factors and cancer incidence among blacks and whites. *J Natl Cancer Inst, 83,* 551–557.

42. Rogers, R. G. (1992). Living and dying in the U.S.A.: Sociodemographic determinants of death among blacks and whites. *Demography, 29,* 287–303.

43. Greenberg, M., & Schneider, D. (1994). Violence in American cities: Young black males is the answer, but what was the question? *Soc Sci Med, 39,* 179–187.

44. Lillie-Blanton, M., Anthony, J. C., & Schuster, C. R. (1993). Probing the meaning of racial or ethnic group comparisons in crack cocaine smoking. *JAMA, 269,* 993–997.

45. Krieger, N., & Fee, E. (1994). Social class: The missing link in U.S. health data. *J Health Serv, 24,* 25–44.

46. Otten, M. C., Teutsch, S. M., Williamson, D. F., & Marks, J. S. (1990). The effect of known risk factors on the excess mortality of black adults in the United States. *JAMA, 263,* 845–850.

47. Schoendorf, K. C., Hogue, C.J.R., Kleinman, J. C., & Rowley, D. (1992). Mortality among infants of black as compared with white college-educated parents. *N Engl J Med, 326,* 1522–1526.

48. Krieger, N., Rowley, D. L., Herman, A. A., Avery, B., & Phillips, M. T. (1993). Racism, sexism, and social class: Implications for studies of health, disease, and well-being. *Am J Prev Med, 9*(Suppl.), 82–122.

49. Kessler, R. C., & Neighbors, H. W. (1986). A new perspective on the relationships among race, social class, and psychological distress. *J Health Soc Behav, 27,* 107–115.

50. Williams, D. R., Takeuchi, D., & Adair, R. (1992). Socioeconomic status and psychiatric disorder among blacks and whites. *Soc Forces, 71,* 179–194.

51. Eller, T. J. (1994). *Household wealth and asset ownership, 1991* (U.S. Bureau of the Census, Current Population Reports, P70–34). Washington, DC: U.S. Government Printing Office.

52. Miller, J. E., & Korenman, S. (1994). Poverty and children's nutritional status in the United States. *Am J Epidemiol, 140,* 233–243.

53. Hogue, C.J.R., Buehler, J. W., Strauss, L. T., & Smith, J. C. (1987). Overview of the National Infant Mortality Surveillance (NIMS) project: Design, methods, results. *Pub Health Rep, 102,* 126–138.

54. Williams, D. R., Lavizzo-Mourey, R., & Warren, R. C. (1994). The concept of race and health status in America. *Pub Health Rep, 109,* 26–41.

55. King, G., & Williams, D. R. (1995). Race and health: A multi-dimensional approach to African American health. In S. Levine, D. C. Walsh, B. C. Amick, & A. R. Tarlov (Eds.), *Society and health: Foundation for a nation.* New York: Oxford University Press.

56. Williams, D. R. (Ed.). (1995). Special issue on racism and health. *Ethn Dis, 5.*

57. Maxwell, N. L. (1994). The effect on black-white wage differences in the quantity and quality of education. *Indust Labor Relations Rev, 47,* 249–264.

58. U.S. Bureau of the Census. (1991). *Money income of households, families, and persons in the United States* (Current Population Reports, Ser. P-60, No. 174). Washington, DC: U.S. Government Printing Office.

59. Dressler, W. W. (1993). Health in the African American community: Accounting for health inequalities. *Med Anthropol Q, 7,* 325–345.

60. Collins, S. M. (1983). The making of the black middle class. *Soc Problems, 10,* 369–382.

61. Wilhelm, S. M. (1987). Economic demise of blacks in America: A prelude to genocide? *J Black Studies, 17,* 201–254.

62. Cooper, R. (1984). A note on the biological concept of race and its application in epidemiologic research. *Am Heart J, 108,* 715–723.

63. Robinson, J. (1984). Racial inequality and the probability of occupation-related injury or illness. *Milbank Q, 62,* 567–590.

64. Polednak, A. P. (1993). Poverty, residential segregation, and black/white mortality rates in urban areas. *J Health Care Poor Underserved, 4,* 363–373.

65. LaVeist, T. A. (1989). Linking residential segregation and infant mortality in U.S. cities. *Social Soc Res, 73,* 90–94.

66. Polednak, A. P. (1991). Black-white differences in infant mortality in 38 standard metropolitan statistical areas. *Am J Public Health, 81,* 1480–1482.

67. Council on Ethical and Judicial Affairs, American Medical Association. (1990). Black-white disparities in health care. *JAMA, 263,* 2344–2346.

68. Klag, M. H., Whelton, P. K., Coresh, J., Grim, C. E., & Kuller, L. H. (1991). The Association of skin color with blood pressure in U.S. blacks with low socioeconomic status. *JAMA, 265,* 599–602.

69. Keith, V. M., & Herring, C. (1991). Skin tone and stratification in the black community. *Am J Sociol, 97,* 760–778.

SEEING THE BIG PICTURE

Look at Section III in the Appendix on race and health. What trends do you observe? Why do certain diseases affect one group more than others? Are you able to discern the role of race and class in these health disparities?

8

TRANSFORMATIVE ASSETS, THE RACIAL WEALTH GAP AND THE AMERICAN DREAM

Thomas M. Shapiro

QUESTIONS TO CONSIDER

There is a saying that the color of America is green (money!). But using income as a way to measure the relative success of racial groups does not, according to Professor Tom Shapiro, paint an accurate portrait of social inequality or who is likely to achieve the American Dream. What are "transformative assets," who is likely to have them, and how are these intergenerational perks a form of unearned privilege? Are these intergenerational transfers of wealth throughout the life course "fair"? Are they racist? Do these transfers of wealth undermine the deeply held belief that individuals should pull themselves up by their OWN bootstraps?

Race and Wealth

Racial inequality remains a festering public and private issue in American society. After dismantling the most oppressive racist policies and practices of its past, many have come to believe that the United States has moved beyond race and that our most pressing racial concerns should center now on race-neutrality and color blindness. Proclaiming the successes of the civil rights agenda and the dawning of a postracial age in America, books by Shelby Steele, Abigail and Stephan Thernstrom, and others influenced not only the academic debates but elite, media, and popular opinion as well.[1] Indeed, a review of the record shows impressive gains since the mid-1960s, most particularly in the areas

of law, education, jobs, and earnings. During the 2004 Presidential election, for instance, and into the second term of the Bush Administration, politicians and the media treat racial inequality as a non-issue, or as if it no longer existed. Even though progress is real, this new political sensibility about racial progress and equality incorporates illusions that mask an enduring and robust racial hierarchy and continue to hinder efforts to achieve our ideals of democracy and justice.

In fact, we can consider seriously the declining economic significance of race because the measures we have traditionally used to gauge racial inequality focus almost exclusively on salaries and jobs. The black-white earning gap narrowed considerably throughout the 1960s and 1970s. The earnings gap has remained relatively stable since then, with inequality rising again in the 1980s and closing once more during tight labor markets in the 1990s. The average black family earned

The Racial Wealth Gap, by Thomas Shapiro. Reprinted by permission of the National Urban League.

55 cents for every [9] dollar earned by the average white family in 1989; by 2000, it reached an all-time high of 64 cents on the dollar. For black men working full-time, the gains are more impressive, as their wages reached 67 percent of those of fully employed white men, up from 62 percent in 1980 and only 50 percent in 1960. How much the racial wage gap has closed, why it has closed, and what it means are the subjects of academic and political debate. One study, for example, argues that the racial wage gap is really 23 percent higher than the official figures because incarceration rates hide low wages and joblessness among blacks. In any case, it takes more African American family members to work to earn the same money as white families. For example, middle-income black families worked the equivalent of 12 more weeks than white families to earn the same family income in 2000.[2]

The tremendous growth of the black middle class often is cited as the triumphant sign of progress toward racial equality. The raw numbers appear to justify celebration: In 1960, a little more than three-quarters of a million black men and women worked in middle class occupations. By 1980, the number increased to nearly three and a half million and nearly seven million African Americans worked in middle class jobs in 1995. This impressive growth in achieving middle class status, however, does not tell the whole story, as one can point out that stagnating economic conditions and blacks' lower middle class occupational profile have stalled the march into the great American middle class since the mid-1970s.

The case I want to make is that the real story of the meaning of race in modern America, however, must include a serious consideration of how one generation passes advantage and disadvantage to the next— how individuals' starting points are determined. While ending the old ways of outright exclusion and violence, our nation continues to reproduce racial inequality, racial hierarchy, and social injustice that is very real and formidable for those who experience [it]. This contribution will explore the bedrock of racial inequality in modern America.

The racial wealth gap—which has more to do with race than with merit or accomplishments—translates into different worlds, opportunities, and rewards for black and white families. My argument is grounded in three big ideas. First, I argue that family inheritance and continuing discrimination in really vital areas like home-ownership are reversing gains earned in schools and on the job and making racial inequality worse. In addition to money passed at death, family inheritance includes paying for college education, substantial down payment assistance in buying a first home, and other continuing parental financial assistance. Consequently, it is virtually impossible for people of color to earn their way to equal wealth through wages. No matter how much blacks earn, they cannot pass their occupational status along to their children; they cannot outearn the wealth gap. Many believe that African Americans do not do as well as whites, other minorities, or immigrants because they spend too much money rather than save and invest in the future of their families. They are unable to defer gratification, do not sacrifice for the future, and consume excessively. The facts speak otherwise. Second, these inheritances amount to transformative assets. This involves the capacity of unearned, inherited wealth to lift a family economically and socially beyond where their own achievements, jobs, and earnings would place them. Since the vast majority of African Americans were first excluded and later precluded from the kind of occupations, investments, and government policies and programs that lead to wealth generation, transformative assets typically apply to whites from financial advantaged families and not blacks. These head-start assets set up different starting lines, establish different rules for success, fix different rewards for accomplishments, and ultimately perpetuate racial inequality. Third, the way families use head-start assets to transform their own lives—within current structures that reward them for doing so—has racial and class consequences for the homes they buy, the communities they live in, and the quality of schools their children attend. The same set of processes typically advantages whites while disadvantaging African Americans.

These big ideas help us understand one of the most important issues facing America as we start the twenty-first century. African American were frozen out of the mainstream of American life over the first half of the last century, but since 1954 the civil rights movement has won many battles against racial injustice, and America has reached a broad national consensus in favor of a more tolerant, more inclusive society. Yet we live with a great paradox: Why is racial inequality increasing in this new era?

The Racial Wealth Gap

The typical black household makes 59 cents earned by the typical white household. This income comparison is the most widely used indicator of current racial and ethnic material inequality.[3] However, changing the lens of analysis to wealth dramatically shifts the perspective. For example, the 1999 net worth (all assets minus all liabilities) of typical white families is $81,000 compared to $8,000 for black families. This baseline racial wealth gap, then, shows the black families possess only 10 cents for every dollar of wealth held by white families. The

socioeconomic yardstick is no longer how to get from 59 cents on the dollar to parity but how to think about going from 10 cents on the dollar to a figure approaching parity. In dollars, the baseline racial wealth gap is robust: The typical white family's wealth is almost $74,000 more than the typical black family's. Even though both white and black families increased their net worth between 1988 and 1999, the black-white gap actually grew by $16,000 (in 1999 dollars). During this period, typical white and black families improved financially but inequality grew. The figures for net financial assets (excluding home equity and vehicles) do not paint a better picture. Later we will examine the impact of the recession and jobless recovery that started in the late 1990s.

The classic argument is that racial inequality in significant areas like family wealth represents huge disparities in education, jobs, and income. Once these disparities are alleviated, our traditional understanding and theory lead to an expectation that racial inequality will be diminished to a great extent.[4] Confounding this traditional understanding, and demonstrating the need for new thinking about civil rights in the twenty-first century, examining middle class families demonstrates that even black and white families with equal accomplishments are separated by a dramatic wealth gap. Defining middle class by income, we see a reduction in the baseline racial wealth gap to $44,500 for whites and $17,000 for blacks. Clearly, income is important to wealth accumulation. At the same time, however, middle class black families with similar incomes to white own only 26 cents of wealth for every dollar owned by whites. Defining middle class by occupation changes the ratio to 22 cents on the dollar. And, using a college education as a hallmark of middle class status moves the wealth ratio to 27 cents on the dollar. One need to be asking how it is that blacks with equal accomplishments in income, jobs, and degrees possess only about a quarter of the wealth of their white counterparts.

The black middle class that emerged between the mid-1960s and early 1980s is a success story written in the accomplishments of education, occupation, and earnings. An asset perspective, however, shows that the white middle class stands for the most part on the two legs of good earning and substantial financial assets while the black middle class stands for the most part on the earning leg alone. Middle class status is thus more precarious for blacks than it is for whites; blacks are more susceptible to falling from middle-class grace, less capable of cushioning hard times, and less able to retool careers or change directions. And, of course, they are far less able to pass along their hard-earned successes to their children.

We can examine the relationship between family wealth and what we think predicts wealth, such as education, income, age, marital status, family size, region, and job. To make our findings more graphic, we can estimate the cost of being African American, that is, the wealth difference between typical white and black families with equal accomplishments on all the factors that we think lead to wealth accumulation. The cost of being black amounts to $136,174. This is a measure of the accumulative disadvantage of being African-American. Flipping the perspective, the accumulative advantage or the legacy of whiteness for the typical white family also is $136,174.[5]

Is the Racial Wealth Gap Narrowing or Growing?

Among the crucial issues facing families today is how the recent recession and jobless recovery has affected family economic security. My recent research argues that a widen-ing wealth gap between minorities and whites is reversing gains earned in schools and on jobs and making inequality worse. A 2004 report from the Pew Hispanic Center provides new data on family wealth and offers a sobering assessment of the precarious and fragile status of middle-class families, including whites, but most particularly Hispanics and African-Americans.[6]

In the years prior to the 2001 recession, white, Hispanic, and African-American families were generating wealth through savings, investment, and homeownership. More families were acquiring assets and family portfolios were growing. In this context of wealth accumulation, however, the wealth gap between minority and white families was widening. The recession and recovery brought wealth growth to an abrupt halt for millions of American families. During the recession and jobless recovery, Hispanic and African-American families lost over one-quarter of their wealth while the wealth of white families grew slowly. In 2002, a typical Hispanic family owned 11 cents of wealth for every dollar owned by a typical white family, and African American families owned only 7 cents.

Net wealth losses illustrate how Hispanic and African-American families, and low-to-middle income families in general, have shouldered the burden of tightening economic times in the Bush administration. And the wealth data show that the current combination of recession and recovery has tightened the financial vice on millions of American families. Over one in four Hispanic and African-American families are asset-poor, having no liquid financial assets, compared to 6 percent of whites. Families with small or moderate amounts of wealth drew down their meager stockpile of savings to use as private safety nets. In addition to making tough choices like giving up health insurance or spacing out medical appointments and refilling prescriptions, this is the real story of how families are adapting to the recession, jobless recovery, stagnating wages, outsourcing, and dwindling federal commitment to important safety nets like unemployment benefits and the minimum wage, which are not keeping pace with inflation.

For example, interest-earning assets like savings bonds, IRA and Keogh accounts, 401(k) and thrift accounts, stocks and mutual funds, and business capital declined precipitously in Hispanic families with assets. In African-American families, stock and mutual fund investments plummeted by nearly two-thirds. Surely, this reflects investment losses, but it also represents families tapping accounts to cover insecurities about employment and losses of job-related income. These families are adapting by eating the acorns they were storing for their future economic mobility and security. These setbacks will not be made up easily or in a short time span.

While the income, educational achievement, and job gaps among Hispanics, African-Americans and whites remain steady or show some slight narrowing, the wealth gap increases. I made this argument in my recent book, *The Hidden Cost of Being African American.* The report and current data from the Pew Hispanic Center further corroborate how a growing wealth gap reverses gains in schools, on jobs, and in paychecks. An added compounding change is that the financial portfolios of Hispanics and African-Americans have been shrinking in the current economy.

More than any other economic attribute, wealth represents the sedimentation of historical inequalities in the American experience, in a sense the accumulation of advantagesand disadvantages for different racial, class, and ethnic groups. In this way, it allows us a window to explore how our past influences realities today.

This is not simply a story about counting money, because families think about us ing wealth first as a private safety net, and then as a vehicle to launch mobility into middle-class status, homeownership, business development, or a more secure retirement. The recent recession and recovery—along with public policies—are a real step backward for the self-reliance and independence of Hispanics, African-Americans, and other low-to-middle income families. They are a double blow against equality and family well-being in America. Missing from the current national political scene is a serious conversation about the economic status of America's families and the role of government in enabling families to build a wealth pillar for their mobility, stability, and well-being. Finally, family wealth is not a story about counting dollars to determine who has played the game best. Far more importantly, family wealth is crucial to opportunities and success in a way that allows families to launch their own social mobility in a self-reliant and independent manner. Closing the racial wealth gap needs to be at the forefront of the civil rights agenda moving into the twenty-first century.

NOTES

1. Most particularly and influential, Steele's book *The Content of Our Character: A New Vision of Race in Race,* published in 1990; and Thernstrom's 1997 book, *America in Black and White: One Nation, Indivisible.*

2. Mary Patillo-McCoy's book, *Black Picket Fences,* traces the development of the black middle class.

3. Data from this section, as well as a fuller discussion of the details, can be found in *The Hidden Cost of Being African American.*

4. William Julius Wilson makes this case, especially for jobs, in his 1987 book *The Truly Disadvantaged.* Christopher Jencks and Meredith Phillips present the black-white education gap argument in *The Black-White Test Score Gap,* 1998.

5. The full multiple regression results can be found in *The Hidden Cost of Being African American.*

6. *The Wealth of Hispanic Households: 1996 to 2002.* Kochhar, Rakesh. The Pew Hispanic Center. October, 2004.

SEEING THE BIG PICTURE

Section VI in the Appendix lists households making over $250,000 and those in poverty, which the government defines as $19,484 for a family of four (2004). Using these two income categories as your reference point, explain how race is linked to transformative assets and upward mobility.

RACE AS CHAMELEON: HOW THE IDEA OF RACE CHANGES OVER TIME AND PLACE

9

PLACING RACE IN CONTEXT

Clara E. Rodriguez • Hector Cordero-Guzman

QUESTIONS TO CONSIDER

How and in what specific ways have definitions of race and ethnicity changed over time and place? How is it possible to be defined as belonging to one race in one country and to a different race in another country? What insight into this question do Rodriguez and Cordero-Guzman provide in their description of how and why the definition of race is different in the United States and Puerto Rico? If there is a "social context" to race, as Rodriguez and Cordero-Guzman suggest, what are the sociological factors that make that "context" vary from country to country?

Clara Rodriguez and Hector Cordero-Guzman, "Placing Race in Context" from *Ethnic and Racial Studies,* 1992, Vol. 14, 4, October, pp. 523–529, 539–541. Copyright © 1992. Reprinted with permission of Routledge, Inc., part of the Taylor & Francis Group. Journal's Web site: http://www.tandf.co.uk/journals.

Introduction

By the 1960s a consensus had been reached that race as a biological concept was useless (Alland 1971; Harris 1968; Mead et al. 1968; Montagu 1964). There was only one human race and it had infinite variation and some population clusters. Yet, race, as people experience it, is a cultural construct (Sanjek 1990). Thus, how "races" or racial paradigms are determined also varies from culture to culture, as does the meaning of the term "race."

For example, in the United States of America race is conceived as being biologically or genetically based. The White race was defined by the absence of any non-White blood, and the Black race was defined by the presence of any Black blood. This cultural conception of race differed from that which evolved in Latin America. In Latin America, race may have had blood lines as a referent, but there were also other dimensions brought into "racial classification": for example, class, physical type, and ethnic background. Thus, in the US and in Latin America, two different cultural definitions of "race" arose, each of which took different referents. Each system of racial classification was seen, by those who utilized it, to be the only correct way of viewing individuals.

The fact that popular definitions of "race" vary from culture to culture suggests the importance of historical events, developments or context in determining "race." That there are different systems of racial classification in different countries (and sometimes within countries) is quite counter to the usual perception that most White Americans hold of race in the United States. This is because of the particular way in which race is popularly viewed in the US where race is seen to be genetically based and therefore unchanging. In the words of American sociologists, it is an ascribed characteristic.

An example of how race changes from context to context is the description of the man who, in travelling from Puerto Rico to Mexico to the United States, changes his race from "White to Mulatto to Black" (Mintz 1971). Then there is the case of the Japanese who were accorded the status of honorary Whites in South Africa because of the changing business context. Again, there is the example of the Jews in Europe, who were classified by the Germans as a race apart from other Europeans, despite the fact that they were a group with highly varied phenotypes and quite diverse genetic strains. In nineteenth-century US and in the early twentieth-century immigration laws, race was used to describe not only Blacks and Whites, but also Slavs, Italians, Anglo-Saxons, etc. A basic white-non-white dichotomous categorization was present, but many European groups were also viewed as sub-races, different from Anglo-Saxon stock.

Given the significance of context in determining popular conceptions of race, it is also important to understand what happens to the conceptions of race and racial self-identity of individuals when they move from a country with one racial paradigm to a country with another. Are dual racial paradigms maintained? Do individuals adhere to their own perceptions of race? What determines whether they adopt or maintain their own perceptions of race? Are responses to questions of racial identity altered depending on how respondents interpret the question and its context?

These issues are brought into sharp relief when studying Puerto Ricans, a group with a history of contact with the US but with a different racial paradigm. In this article we study the way in which Puerto Ricans, who have been exposed to both cultures, identify themselves racially, how they are identified by interviewers and how they think that they would be viewed by North

Americans. This research sheds light on these two racial paradigms—that of the US and Puerto Rico— and what happens when they come into contact with each other.

Race in Historical Perspective

Although both the United States and Latin America relied on the importation of African slaves to meet labour needs, the conception and incorporation of peoples of African-descent as a "race" took different directions in the two areas (Denton and Massey 1989; Pitt-Rivers 1975; Wagley 1965). Of special interest is the case of the Spanish Caribbean and, in particular, Puerto Rico. In Puerto Rico race came to be seen as a continuum of categories, with different gradations and shades of colour as the norm. In the US race was conceived as a dichotomous concept in which individuals were envisaged, and legally defined, as being either White or Black. Although both areas had instituted slavery and both had clear demarcations between free whites and slaves, the category "White" included more people in Puerto Rico than it would have done in the United States. In addition, there was a variety of race categories in Puerto Rico and many were fluid.[1]

The population of Puerto Rico is mostly descended from the original Taino Indian settlers, white Spanish colonizers, black slaves brought from Africa, and countless other immigrants. The variety of phenotypes in Puerto Rico, then, is mostly the result of a relatively unexamined history of racial mixing and diverse migratory flows. A number of works have touched on the issue of racial mixing in the island, but there is no real consensus on its extent. Puerto Rican and American researchers at different times have discussed or found Puerto Rico to be everything from a mulatto country to a

predominantly white country with small subgroups of blacks and mulattos. Compare, for example, the accounts of Seda Bonilla (1961) with those of Gordon (1949), Mills, Senior and Goldsen (1950), and Senior (1965).

The historical formation of race relations in Puerto Rico was accompanied by the development of a distinct nomenclature to describe the different groups. This nomenclature and the racial discourse in Puerto Rico reflected the fact that race was seen to be multidimensional. This was quite distinct from the conception of race that developed in the United States, where new "racial" categories and terms were not developed. On some occasions the US census did separately count mulattos and other mixtures of European and African peoples, but this practice fluctuated and by 1930 the census used only the "Negro" category to describe those with any trait of African descent (Martin et al. 1990). Thus, the offspring of Native American Indians, Asians or Europeans who intermarried with Blacks would simply be counted as Negro.

The 1896 decision of the US Supreme Court in the *Plessy v Ferguson* case legitimated the more dichotomous black/white view of "race." In this case, the petitioner averred that since he was ". . . seven eighths Caucasian and one eighth African blood; and that the mixture of colored blood was not discernible in him . . . ," he was entitled to the rights and privileges of citizens of the white race. The Supreme Court, however, decided against the plaintiff, thus further legitimating the genetic or blood quantum definition of race and sanctioning Jim Crow legislation (Blaustein and Zangrando 1968). The "separate but equal" doctrine elaborated in *Plessy v Ferguson* regulated the level of contact between White and Black Americans and went so far as to define as "Black" any individual who had even a small fraction of "Black" ancestry (Chang 1985, p. 52).

In Puerto Rico and in other parts of Latin America, race was based more on phenotypic and socio-economic definitions of the person rather than on genotypic definitions. Thus, in the US race is generally seen as a fact of biology, while in many parts of Latin America—particularly in the Spanish Caribbean—a more socio-economic conception of race has been the norm. This more socio-economic conception of race has emphasized dimensions that are freely varying, such as physical appearance (as opposed to genetic make-up), social class, and cultural modes of behaviour. For example, Sanjek (1971, p. 1128) notes that in Brazil classification is affected by contextual variables, that is, by situational and sociological variables that would include

> economic class, the dress, personality, education, and relation of the referent to the speaker; the presence of other actors and their relations to the speaker and referent; and contexts of speech, such as gossip, insult, joking, showing affection, maintenance of equality or of differential social status, or pointing out the referent in a group.

This perspective of race is opposed to the US conception, which relies mainly on genetic inheritance. In the United States race is an ascribed characteristic that does not change after birth, or from country to country. It is more dependent on a person's supposed genetic make-up and physical appearance than on socio-economic characteristics. The US conception of race with its emphasis on genetic or biological inheritance privileges a static conception of race. One is and always will be the race into which one was born, one is one's blood. This conception also disallows or ignores more contextual definitions.

In many Latin American countries, race is not a meta-concept based on biological categories, but rather a classification dependent on time and context. According to this more

fluid view of race, the determination and relative salience of race categories depend not on their "inherent" nature as physical characteristics but on the historical development of the contexts in which these categories are valued. Within this framework, the points of social reference in which a given individual operates are important determinants of racial identity.

A number of arguments seek to account for the different racial conceptions that evolved in the United States and in Puerto Rico. For example, Denton and Massey (1989) cite three elements of the Spanish colonial system that contributed to a greater blending of the peoples in the Spanish Caribbean. First, they argue that the Spanish history of contact with northern African populations made them more tolerant of different colour groups than were northeastern Europeans. Hence, groups of Mediterranean origin, in contrast to northeastern Europeans, tend to see darker people as white. Second, they maintain that the Spanish conceived of slaves and Indians as being subjects or vassals of the crown and as having certain rights. This differed from the North American conception of slaves as being property. (That is not to say, however, that the Spanish treatment of slaves was necessarily more benevolent, merely that it was sanctioned and conceived of differently.) The third factor that Denton and Massey (1989) discuss is the Spanish Catholic Church. They argue that the Church had a central role in the conquest and promoted the conversion, baptism, and attendance of slaves at integrated religious services. Thus, the role of the Church was analogous to that of the Spanish legal code. It promoted ". . . a positive cultural attitude towards persons of color in theory" but failed "to implement the idea in practice."

The history of a country's economic development has also been seen as an important determinant of race relations and racial conceptions. Duany (1985), for example, has argued that Puerto Rico's economy was less dependent on slaves than was that of other countries in the Caribbean. Thus, there was less commitment to slavery as an institution and there were fewer slaves in Puerto Rico, both absolutely and proportionately. This, together with substantial immigration into the island of Europeans and former slaves in the nineteenth century, made for a conception of race that was rather fluid as opposed to strictly dichotomous. Lastly, the greater migration of European women and families to North America as compared with Latin America—where men predominated and European women were scarce—may also have influenced the relations between races and the consequent conceptions of race that evolved.

The differences between these two conceptions of race have been accentuated and made more apparent with the increasing number of Latinos in the United States. In this article, we explore responses by Puerto Ricans to questions about racial identity. We contend that these responses reflect a conception of race that is different from that generally found in the classical social science literature and from that conventionally held in the US. We also argue that racial identity is contextually influenced, determined and defined.

Race and the United States Census

In the 1980 decennial census results the Puerto Rican conception of race appears to have been manifested. In response to the race item, which asked respondents to identify themselves as White, Black, or Other, 48 percent of Puerto Ricans living in New York City replied that they were "Other" and wrote in a Spanish descriptor. Another 4 percent

replied that they were "Other" but did not write in any additional comment, 44 percent said they were "White," and 3.9 percent said they were "Black." This unique distribution of responses to the race item ran parallel with the national level where a full 40 percent of all Hispanics (or 7.5 million) replied that they were "Other."

On the national level, where over 60 percent of the nation's Hispanics are of Mexican origin and Puerto Ricans constitute about 12 percent, there were similar results. The distribution of Latinos on the race item is particularly surprising in the light of the fact that in no state, including Hawaii, did more than 2 percent of the general population indicate that they were of "other race" (Rodriguez 1991). See also Denton and Massey (1989) for a detailed discussion of racial identity among Mexican-Americans and Telles and Murguia (1990) for an interesting discussion of the effects of phenotype on the incomes of Mexicans in the United States.

It has been well documented (Denton and Massey 1989; Martin et al. 1990; Tienda and Ortiz 1986) that the Hispanic responses to the race item differed considerably from those of the general population. It is less clear why this is so. One interpretation stresses that the format of the race question may have led to misinterpretation. The question did not include the word race, but rather asked, "Is this person . . . ?" and provided tick-off categories. Included as possible answers were various Asian groups. This may have induced some Latino respondents to respond culturally, namely, to say that they were "Other" and write in "Mexican," "Dominican," etc. (Tienda and Ortiz 1986). In addition, the fact that the race question preceded the Hispanic identifier may have caused a cultural response to the race item. However, Martin et al. (1990) altered the sequence of the race and Hispanic identifier items and found that this affected the responses only of those Hispanics born in the US; it did not affect the tendency of foreign-born Hispanics to report that they were "Other."

Other research also suggests that there are contextual factors that affect the way in which Latinos respond to questions about race. A Content Reinterview Study by census personnel found that of those who reported that they were "Other" in the census, only 10 percent were similarly classified in the reinterviewing (McKenney, Fernandez and Masamura 1985). Martin et al. (1990) conclude: "[I]t appears that many Hispanic people will report themselves as 'Other race' on a self-administered questionnaire, but will be classified as 'White' by enumerators." Chevan (1990) reports on a Current Population Survey in March 1980 in which Hispanics identified themselves overwhelmingly as "White." Thus, in the presence of an interviewer who presented them with four non-Hispanic choices, 97 percent of Hispanics identified themselves as "White," while "one month later in filling out the Census form in the privacy of their home, almost 40 percent of Hispanics chose 'Other' and were prompted to write in the meaning of 'Other' on the form." Of those who specified a meaning 90 percent wrote in a Hispanic identifier (Chevan 1990, p. 8). . . .

Our results also provide insight into the racial responses by Hispanics reported in the 1980 Census. The findings indicate that, regardless of how the "race" question was asked, many Puerto Ricans chose *not* to use the conventional racial categories of White and Black. The "Other" response did not represent a misunderstanding. Nor did it represent self-classification as a racially intermediate person in all cases. These results suggest a more complex reality than that which assumes that this "Other" response simply represented a misunderstanding of

the question, or that it represented a homogeneous middle category of mestizos or mulattos.

The findings indicate that we cannot automatically assume that because Puerto Ricans choose to identify as "Other" they are placing themselves in a racially intermediate situation. For some Puerto Ricans a cultural response also carries a racial implication, that is, they see race and culture as being fused. They emphasize the greater validity of ethnic or cultural identity. Culture is race, regardless of the physical types within the culture.

Others see their culture as representing a "mixed" people. Still others view these concepts as independent, and a cultural response does not imply a racial designation for them. In this latter case, a respondent may identify as "Other-Puerto Rican" because he or she is not culturally or politically like White Americans or Black Americans, regardless of his or her particular race. In essence, the United States of America may choose to divide its culture into White and Black races, but a Puerto Rican will not (Rodriguez et al. 1991).

The findings suggest that race can be viewed in more than one way. For many of our respondents, race was something more than phenotype and genotype and was influenced by contextual factors such as class, education, language, and birthplace. These findings challenge the hegemonic and more static biological view of race prevalent in the US and its data-collection agencies. They challenge the arrogance behind the biological view of race implying, as it does, that there is no other view of race. These findings also raise questions about the extent to which culture, class and race are inextricably tied together even within a classification system that purports to be "biologically" anchored. Thus, "race" in the US may also, in practice, be more of a social construction than is generally admitted.

Acknowledgments

Dr. Clara Rodriguez would like to acknowledge the financial assistance of the Rockefeller Foundation and the Inter-University Program for Latino Research/Social Science Research Council.

NOTES

1. Clearly, the fact that there are different conceptions of race in Puerto Rico and in the US is not meant to imply that there is no racism in Puerto Rico.

REFERENCES

Alland, Alexander. 1971. *Human Diversity*. New York: Columbia University Press.

Blaustein, Albert P., and Robert L. Zangrando. 1968. *Civil Rights and the American Negro: A Documentary History*. New York: Washington Square Press.

Chang, Harry. 1985. "Toward a Marxist Theory of Racism: Two Essays by Harry Chang." *Review of Radical Political Economics*, 17(3):34–45.

Chevan, Albert. 1990. "Hispanic Racial Identity: Beyond Social Class." Paper presented at the American Sociological Association meetings, Washington, DC, 14 August 1990.

Denton, Nancy, and Douglas S. Massey. 1989. "Racial Identity Among Caribbean Hispanics: The Effect of Double Minority Status on Residential Segregation." *American Sociological Review* 54:790–808.

Duany, Jorge. 1985. "Ethnicity in the Spanish Caribbean: Notes on the Consolidation of Creole Identity in Cuba and Puerto Rico, 1762–1868." *Ethnic Groups* 6:99–123.

Gordon, Maxine W. 1949. "Race Patterns and Prejudice in Puerto Rico," *American Sociological Review* 14:294–301.

Harris, Marvin. 1968. *Patterns of Race in the Americas*. New York: Walker.

Martin, Elizabeth, Theresa J. Demaio, and Pamela C. Campanelli. 1990. "Context Effects for Census Measures of Race and Hispanic Origin." *Public Opinion Quarterly* 54(4):551–66.

Mckenney, Nampeo R., Edward W. Fernandez, and Wilfred T. Masamura. 1985. "The Quality of the Race and Hispanic Origin Information Reported in the 1980 Census," *Proceedings of the Survey Research Methods Section* (American Statistical Association), pp. 46–50.

Mead, Margaret, Theodosius Dobzhansky, Ethel Tobach, and Robert Light, eds. 1968. *Science and the Concept of Race*. New York: Columbia University Press.

Mills, C. Wright, Clarence Senior, and Rose Goldsen. 1950. *The Puerto Rican Journey: New York's Newest Migrants*. New York: Harper & Row.

Mintz, Sidney W. 1971. "Groups, Group Boundaries and the Perception of Race." *Comparative Studies in Society and History* 13(4):437–50.

Montagu, Ashley, ed. 1964. *The Concept of Race*. New York: Free Press

Pitt-Rivers, Julian. 1975. "Race, Color and Class in Central America and the Andes." In *Majority and Minority*, edited by Norman Yetman and C. Hoy Steele. Boston: Allyn & Bacon.

Rodriguez, Clara E. 1974. "Puerto Ricans: Between Black and White." *New York Affairs* I(4):92–101.

———. 1991. *Puerto Ricans: Born in the USA*. Boulder, CO: Westview Press.

Rodriguez, Clara E., Aida Castro, Oscar Garcia, and Analisa Torres. 1991. "Latino Racial Identity: In the Eye of the Beholder?" *Latino Studies Journal* 2(3):33–48.

Sanjek, Roger. 1971. "Brazilian Racial Terms: Some Aspects of Meaning and Learning." *American Anthropology* 73(5):1126–43.

———. 1990. "Conceptualizing Caribbean Asians: Race, Acculturation, Creolization." Asian/American Center Working Papers, Queens College/City University of New York.

Seda Bonilla, E. 1961. "Social Structure and Race Relation." *Social Forces* 40:141–48.

Senior, Clarence. 1965. *Strangers, Then Neighbors: From Pilgrims to Puerto Ricans*. Chicago: Quadrangle.

Telles, Edward, and Edward Murguia. 1990. "Phenotypic Discrimination and Income Differences Among Mexican Americans." *Social Science Quarterly* 71(4):682–96.

Tienda, Marta, and Vilma Ortiz. 1986. " 'Hispanicity' and the 1980 Census." *Social Science Quarterly* 67:3–20.

Wagley, Charles. 1965. "On the Concept of Social Race in the Americas." In *Contemporary Cultures and Societies of Latin America: A Reader in the Social Anthropology of Middle and South America and the Caribbean*, edited by Dwight B. Heath and Richard N. Adams. New York: Random House.

10

A TOUR OF INDIAN PEOPLES
AND INDIAN LANDS

David E. Wilkins

QUESTIONS TO CONSIDER

Why has it been so difficult to find a political and cultural definition of who is an American Indian, what constitutes a tribe, and what criteria need to be met to claim tribal membership? How are race, culture, identity, and politics linked in David Wilkins's discussion of American Indians?

One of the greatest obstacles faced by the Indian today in his desire for self-determination . . . is the American public's ignorance of the historical relationship of the United States with Indian tribes and the lack of general awareness of the status of the American Indian in our society today.

American Indian Policy Review
Commission, 1977[1]

This chapter provides descriptions, definitions, and analysis of the most important concepts necessary for a solid foundation for the study of Indian politics. I will attempt to clarify how indigenous peoples, variously grouped, are defined, and discuss why such definitions are necessary. I will then analyze how the term Indian is defined and discuss what constitutes a reservation or Indian Country. Finally, I will conclude the chapter with a description of the basic demographic

facts and socioeconomic data that applies throughout Indian lands.

What Is an Indian Tribe?

American Indians, tribal nations, Indian tribes, indigenous nations, Fourth World Peoples, Native American Peoples, Aboriginal Peoples First Nations, and Native peoples—these are just a sample of current terms that are used to refer to indigenous peoples in the continental United States in a collective sense. Alaska Natives, including Aleuts, Inuit, and Indians, and Native Hawaiians are the indigenous people of those respective territories. While I will provide some descriptive details about Alaska Natives, I will have less to say about Native Hawaiians because their legal status is unique among aboriginal peoples of the United States.[2]

This was brought to light in the Supreme Court's 2000 ruling in *Rice v. Cayetano.*[3] In that case, the Court struck down restrictions that had allowed only persons with Native Hawaiian blood to vote for the trustees of the Office of Hawaiian Affairs, a state agency created to better the lives of Hawaii's aboriginal people. While *Cayetano* did not specifically address the political relationship of the Native Hawaiians to the federal government, it called into question the status of the more than 150 federal statutes that recognize that Hawaii's native peoples do, in fact, have a unique legal status.

The departments of the Interior and Justice issued a preliminary report of August 23, 2000, that recommended that Congress "enact further legislation to clarify Native Hawaiians' political status and to create a framework for recognizing a government-to-government relationship with a representative Native Hawaiian governing body."[4] If Congress acts to create such a framework, and a bill was introduced on July 20, 2000 (S. 2898), by Senator Daniel K. Akaka (D-HI), then Hawaii's Natives would have a political relationship with the federal government similar to that of federally recognized tribes. The sovereignty movement in Hawaii is very complex, however, and some segments of the population desire more than mere federal recognition of their status because of their nation's preexisting sovereign status.[5]

Indigenous communities expect to be referred to by their own names—Navajo or Diné, Ojibwe or Anishinabe, Sioux or Lakota, Suquamish, or Tohono O'odham—since they constitute separate political, legal, and cultural entities. In fact, before Europeans arrived in the Americas, it is highly doubtful whether any tribes held a "conception of that racial character which today we categorize as 'Indian.' People recognized their neighbors as co-owners of the lands given to them by the Great Spirit and saw themselves sharing a basic status within creation as a life form."[6] However, when discussing Indian people generically, *American Indian tribes* and *Native Americans* remain the most widely used terms despite the inherent problems with both. For instance, America's indige-

nous people are not *from* India, and the term *Native American* was "used during the nativist (anti-immigration, anti-foreign) movement (1860s–1925) and the anti-black, anti-Catholic, and anti-Jewish Ku Klux Klan resurgence during the early 1900s."[7]

There is no universally agreed upon definition of what constitutes an Indian tribe, in part because each tribal community defines itself differently and because the U.S. government in its relations with tribes has operated from conflicting sets of cultural and political premises across time. Although no universal definition exists, many statutes give definitions for purposes of particular laws, federal agencies like the Bureau of Indian Affairs generate their own definitions, numerous courts have crafted definitions, and the term *tribe* is found—though not defined—in the Constitution's commerce clause.

For example, the Indian Self-Determination Act of 1975 (as amended) defines an Indian tribe as "any Indian tribe, band, nation, or other organized group or community . . . which is recognized as eligible for the special programs and services provided by the United States to Indians because of their status as Indians." By contrast, the Supreme Court in *Montoya v. United States* (1901) even more ambiguously said that "by a 'tribe' we understand a body of Indians of the same or a similar race united in a community under one leadership or government, and inhabiting a particular though sometimes ill-defined territory."[8]

Broadly, the term *tribe* can be defined from two perspectives—*ethnological* and *political-legal.*[9] From an ethnological perspective, a tribe may be defined as a group of indigenous people connected by biology or blood; kinship, cultural, and spiritual values; language; political authority; and a territorial land base. But for our purposes, it is the political-legal definition (since there is no single definitive legal definition) of tribe, especially by the federal government, which is crucial since whether or not a tribal group is *recognized* as a tribe by the federal government has important political, cultural, and economic consequences, as we shall see shortly.

Federally Recognized Tribal and Alaska Native Entities

The extension of federal recognition by the United States to a tribal nation is the formal diplomatic acknowledgment by the federal government of a tribe's legal status as a sovereign. This is comparable to when the United States extended "recognition" to the former republics of the Soviet Union after that state's political disintegration. It is the beginning point of a government-to-government relationship between an indigenous people and the U.S. government.[10] The reality is that an American Indian tribe is not a legally recognized entity in the eyes of the federal government unless some explicit action by an arm of the government (i.e., congressional statute, administrative ruling by the BIA, presidential executive order, or a judicial opinion) decides that it exists in a formal manner.

Federal recognition has historically had two distinctive meanings. Before the 1870s, "recognize" or "recognition" was used in the cognitive sense. In other words, federal officials simply acknowledged that a tribe existed, usually by negotiating treaties with them or enacting specific laws to fulfill specific treaty pledges.[11] During the 1870s, however, "recognition," or more accurately, "acknowledgment," began to be used in a formal jurisdictional sense. It is this later usage that the federal government most often employs to describe its relationship to tribes. In short, federal acknowledgment is a formal act that establishes a political relationship between a tribe and the United States. It affirms a tribe's sovereign status.

Simultaneously, it outlines the federal government's responsibilities to the tribe.

More specifically, federal acknowledgment means that a tribe is not only entitled to the immunities and privileges available to other tribes, but is also subject to the same federal powers, limitations, and other obligations of recognized tribes. What this means, particularly the "limitations" term, is that "acknowledgment shall subject the Indian tribe to the same authority of Congress and the United States to which other federally acknowledged tribes are subjected."[12] In other words, tribes are informed that they are now subject to federal plenary power and may, ironically, benefit from the virtually unlimited and still largely unreviewable authority of the federal government. For example, recognized tribes have exemptions from most state tax laws, enjoy sovereign immunity, and are not subject to the same constitutional constraints as are the federal and state governments.

Until 1978, federal recognition or acknowledgment was usually bestowed by congressional act or presidential action. But in 1978 the BIA, the Department of the Interior agency primarily responsible for carrying out the federal government's treaty and trust obligations to tribal nations, published regulations which contained specific criteria that unacknowledged or nonrecognized tribal groups had to meet in order to be formally recognized by the United States. The set of guidelines was based mainly on confirmation by individuals and groups outside the petitioning tribe that members of the group were Indians. The mandatory criteria were the following: the identification of the petitioners "from historical times until the present on a substantially continuous basis, as 'American Indian' or 'Aboriginal'" by the federal government, state or local governments, scholars, or other Indian tribes; the habitation of the tribe on land identified as

Indian; a functioning government that had authority over its members; a constitution; a roll of members based on criteria acceptable to the secretary of the interior; not being a terminated tribe, and members not belonging to other tribes.[13]

These criteria largely were designed to fit the "aboriginal" or "mythic" image of the western and already recognized tribes. They were problematic for many eastern tribes who sought recognition, since they paid little heed to the massive historical, cultural, economic, and legal barriers those tribes had to endure merely to survive as tribes into the late twentieth century, lacking any semblance of federal support or protection.

Since the late 1970s there has been tension between those who support BIA or administrative recognition versus those who believe that only the Congress has authority to recognize tribes. The debate over administrative versus legislative recognition rages on, with some advocates from each camp asserting their exclusive right to extend or withhold recognition. This raises an important question: Is there a qualitative difference between the two types of recognition? There are two important differences. First, tribes that opt for administrative variety must meet the formalized set of criteria mentioned earlier. Tribes that pursue congressional recognition, provided they can muster enough proof that they are a legitimate group composed of people of Indian ancestry, have only to make a compelling case to the congressional representative(s) of the state they reside in. The congressional sponsor(s) then make(s) the case for the tribe via legislation.

The second major difference involves the administrative law component known as "subordinate delegation." The major grant of authority the Congress has delegated to the secretary of the interior is located in title 25—*Indians*—of the *U.S. Code*. Section 1 states that the head of Indian affairs, formerly the com-missioner of Indian Affairs, today the assistant secretary of Indian Affairs, is "appointed by the President, by and with the advice and consent of the Senate."[14] In section 2, the head is authorized to "have the management of all Indian affairs and of all matters arising out of Indian relations."[15] As William Quinn states, this law "would arguably not authorize the Secretary or Commissioner to establish a perpetual government-to-government relationship via federal acknowledgment with an Indian group not already under the Department's aegis."[16] Nevertheless, Quinn asserts that the secretary of the interior, with the U.S. Supreme Court's approval, has historically exercised the authority to "recognize" tribes "when a vacuum of responsibility existed over decades, resulting in a gradual and unchallenged accretion of this authority."[17]

The problem, however, is not that the secretary is usurping unused congressional authority; instead, it is the manner and degree to which secretarial discretion and interpretation of federal laws have been discharged by BIA officials. As Felix Cohen said more than forty years ago, "Indians for some decades have had neither armies nor lawyers to oppose increasingly broad interpretations of the power of the Commissioner of Indian Affairs, and so little by little 'the management of all Indian affairs' has come to be read as 'the management of all the affairs of Indians.'"[18] This statement has relevance today, notwithstanding the federal government's policy of Indian self-determination and the more recent policy of tribal self-governance.

The Congress's track record is problematic as well. Generally speaking, however, tribes with explicit congressional acknowledgment have found their status less subject to the whims of BIA officials, though even that is no guarantee of smooth affairs, because BIA oversees and administers most of the government's political relationship with tribes.

A prime example involves the Pascua Yaqui tribe of southern Arizona. The Yaqui were legislatively recognized in 1978. However, in the late 1980s, when they solicited the approval of the BIA on some changes in their constitution, they were informed by bureau officials that they were limited in what governmental powers they could exercise because they were not a "historic tribe," but were instead merely a "created adult Indian community":

> A historic tribe has existed since time immemorial. Its powers derive from its unextinguished, inherent sovereignty. Such a tribe has the full range of governmental powers except where it has been removed by Federal law in favor of either the United States or the state in which the tribe is located. By contrast, a community of adult Indians is composed simply of Indian people who reside together on trust land. A community of adult Indians may have a certain status which entitles it to certain privileges and immunities. . . . However, that status is derived as a necessary scheme to benefit Indians, not from some historical inherent sovereignty.[19]

The bureau's attempt to create two categories of recognized tribes, a novel and disturbing approach to determining tribal identity, was halted by Congress, which declared that no department or agency of the government could develop regulations that negated or diminished the privileges and immunities of any federally recognized tribes.[20] The Congress has, moreover, in recent years tried to reassert its constitutional authority in the field by introducing legislation that would transfer administrative and congressional consideration of applications for federal recognition to an independent commission.[21]

Congress's actions, along with the increasing politicization of the administrative recognition process because of Indian gaming operations and state concerns, compelled Kevin Gover, the assistant secretary of Indian Affairs (head of the BIA), in May 2000 to testify before Congress that his agency was no longer able to do the job of recognizing tribes. Gover admitted that he had been unable to streamline the recognition process, which in some cases had taken years to resolve, but he placed larger blame on the fact that Indian gaming revenues had enabled some groups to wage protracted legal battles that often involved nonrecognized tribes, non-Indian citizens and towns, and recognized tribes.[22]

As of 2001, the Department of the Interior officially recognizes 561 indigenous entities—332 are Indian nations, tribes, bands, organized communities, or Pueblos in the lower forty-eight states; 229 are Alaska Native villages or corporations—on a list annually prepared by the BIA (see appendix A for a list of recognized native entities). These constitute the indigenous people eligible for special programs and services provided by the United States to indigenous communities because of their status as Indians or Alaska Natives.

The situation of Alaska Native villages and corporations is complicated not only by distinctive ethnological differences but also by their unique political and legal status. Although Alaska Natives are eligible to receive services from the BIA, their political sovereignty as self-governing bodies has been questioned and at times constrained by the federal government. A recent Supreme Court case, *Alaska v. Native Village of Venetie Tribal Government* (1998),[23] cast some doubts on the sovereign status of Alaskan villages. *Venetie* dealt with the jurisdictional status of Alaska Native villages and whether or not lands owned in fee simple by these communities—a type of ownership defined by the Alaska Native Claims Settlement Act of 1971—constituted "Indian Country."

In a major victory for Alaskan state authorities and a blow to the sovereignty of the village of Venetie, an Athabaskan community of some 350 people, Justice Clarence Thomas for a unanimous court held that Venetie's 1.8 million acres of fee-simple lands did not qualify as "Indian Country" because they had not been set aside by the federal government for tribal use and were not "under federal supervision." Thus, the tribal government lacked the inherent authority to impose a 5 percent business tax on a contractor building a state-funded school in the village. In denying Venetie, and by extension every other Alaskan village, the power to tax, this ruling called into question what the actual political status of these villages was.

In addition, the indigenous people of Hawaii, who prefer to be called Hawaiians, Hawaiian Natives, or Native Hawaiians, although they are treated as Native Americans for some legal purposes, are not on the Department of the Interior's list of federally recognized tribal entities and have a unique status under federal law.[24]

But there are other indigenous people in the United States who are *not federally recognized*, who had their recognized status *terminated* by the federal government, or who have *state recognition* only. I will discuss these three categories briefly.

Nonrecognized or Unacknowledged Groups

These are groups exhibiting a tremendous degree of racial, ethnic, and cultural diversity. In some cases, they are descendants of tribes who never fought the United States, had no resources desired by the federal government, or lived in geographic isolation and were simply ignored, and hence may never have participated in a treaty or benefited from the trust relationship which forms the basis of most contemporary recognized tribes' status. Despite these circumstances, some of these groups retain their aboriginal language, hold some lands in common, and in some cases have retained some degree of traditional structures of governance. These groups feel entitled to recognition status and have petitioned the United States to be so recognized.[25]

In other cases, groups have questionable genealogical connections to legitimate historical tribes but, for varying reasons, have chosen to self-identify as particular tribes and desire to be recognized by the federal government.[26] As of 2000, the BIA had received a total of 237 letters of intent and petitions for federal recognition. The acknowledgment process, established in 1978 and administered by the Branch of Acknowledgment and Research (BAR) in the BIA, proved to be an extremely slow, expensive, and politicized process that required excessive historical documentation and was greatly influenced by already recognized tribes who were reluctant to let other groups, regardless of their historical legitimacy, gain politically recognized status.[27] Because of these and other problems, the bureau surrendered its power to administratively recognize tribal groups in the fall of 2000. Between 1978 and 2000, the BIA officially recognized only fifteen tribes (e.g., Grand Traverse Band of Ottawa & Chippewa and Jamestown S'Klallam) and denied the petitions of fifteen groups (e.g., Lower Muscogee Creek Tribe east of Mississippi, Kaweah Indian Nation, Southeastern Cherokee Confederacy).[28]

Terminated Tribes

From 1953 to the mid-1960s, the federal government's Indian policy was called "termination" because the United States wanted to sever the trust relationship and end federal benefits and support services to as many tribes, bands, and California rancherias as was feasible in an effort to expedite Indian assimilation and to lift discriminatory practices and policies that negatively affected indigenous peoples.[29] This policy was exemplified by House Concurrent Resolution No. 108, passed in 1953. This measure declared that,

> Whereas it is the policy of Congress, as rapidly as possible, to make the Indians within the territorial limits of the United States subject to the same laws and entitled to the same privileges and responsibilities as are applicable to other citizens of the United States, to end their status as wards of the United States, and to grant them all the rights and prerogatives pertaining to American citizenship; and Whereas the Indians within the territorial limits of the United States should assume their full responsibilities as American citizens: Now, therefore, be it resolved . . . that it is declared to be the sense of Congress that, at the earliest possible time, all of the Indian tribes and the individual members thereof located within the States of California, Florida, New York . . . should be freed from Federal supervision and control and from all disabilities and limitations specially applicable to Indians.[30]

Over one hundred tribes, bands, and California rancherias—totaling a little more than eleven thousand Indians—were "terminated" and lost their status as "recognized" and sovereign Indian communities. Termination thus subjected the tribes and their members to state law, their trust assets were usually individualized and either sold or held by the banks, and they were no longer eligible for the other benefits and exemptions recognized tribes enjoy.

The terminated tribes, other tribes faced with termination, and Indian and non-Indian interest groups began to lobby Congress to end this disastrous policy, because of the economic and political hardships it was causing. By the mid-1960s, the policy was stifled. Gradually, terminated tribes began

to push for "restoration" of their recognized status. The first tribe terminated, the Menominee of Wisconsin (terminated in 1954), was also the first tribe to be legislatively "restored," in 1973.

Although discredited as policy by the mid-1960s, and rejected by presidents Nixon and Reagan in their Indian policy statements, termination was not officially rejected by Congress until 1988 in a largely symbolic gesture that declared that "the Congress hereby repudiates and rejects HCR 108 of the 83rd Congress and any policy of unilateral termination of federal relations with any Indian nation."[31]

State-Recognized Tribes

Some Indian tribes have been recognized by their host states since the colonial era (e.g., Pamunkey Tribe of Virginia), although others have been recognized by state decrees (governor's action or state statute) in contemporary times. There are currently over fifty state-recognized tribes in Alabama, Connecticut, Georgia, Louisiana, Massachusetts, Michigan, Montana, New Jersey, North Carolina, New York, Oklahoma, Virginia, Washington, and West Virginia. See Table 1 for a list of these tribes. Depending on the policy established by the individual state, state recognition may or may not depend on prior federal recognition. Importantly, state recognition is not a prerequisite for federal recognition, although a long-standing relationship with a state is one factor in the federal recognition criteria that the BIA weighs in its determination of whether a group has historical longevity in a particular place.

For example, the Lumbee Tribe of North Carolina was legislatively recognized by the state in 1953.[32] Confident, the Lumbee leadership two years later asked Representative Frank Carlyle (D-NC) to introduce a bill before Congress that would extend federal

TABLE 1   State Recognized Tribes

Alabama
Echota Cherokee
Northeast Alabama Cherokee
MaChis Lower Creek
Southeast Alabama Cherokee
Star Muscogee Creek
Mowa Band of Choctaw

Georgia
Georgia Eastern Cherokee
Cherokee of Georgia
Lower Muskogee Creek
Tama Tribal Town

New Jersey
Nanticoke Lenni-Lanape
Powhatan Renape
Ramapough Mountain

Michigan
Burt Lake Band of Ottawa & Chippewa Indians
Gun Lake Band of Grand River Ottawa Indians
Grand River Band of Ottawa Indians
Swan Creek Black River Confederated Tribes

North Carolina
Coharie Intra-Tribal Council
Haliwa Saponi Tribe
Lumbee
Meherrin Tribe
Person County Indians
Waccamaw-Siouan Tribe

Virginia
Chickahominy Indian Tribe
Eastern Chickahominy Indian Tribe
Mattaponi Indian Tribe
Monacan Indian Tribe

Nansemond Indian Tribe
Pamunkey Indian Tribe
United Rappahannock Tribe
Upper Mattaponi Indian Tribe

West Virginia
Appalachian American Indians of West Virginia

Connecticut
Golden Hill Paugussett
Paucatuck Eastern Pequot
Schagticoke

Louisiana
Choctaw-Apache of Ebarb
Caddo Tribe
Clifton Choctaw
Four Winds Cherokee
United Houma Nation

New York
Shinnecock
Poospatuk

Montana
Little Shell Tribe of Chippewa

Oklahoma
Delaware Tribe of East Oklahoma
Loyal Shawnee Tribe
Yuchi Tribe

Washington
Chinook Indian Tribe
Duwamish Tribe
Kikiallus Indian Nation
Marietta Band of Nooksack Indians
Steilacoom Indian Tribe
Snohomish Tribe of Indians

Source: http://www.thespike.com/tablest.htm

recognition to the Lumbee. On June 7, 1956, the Congress passed an act which provided a measure of recognition to the Lumbee Nation,[33] without giving them the full range of benefits and services other federally recognized tribes received because federal policy at the time was focused on terminating the unique trust relationship between tribes and the United States. To date, the Lumbee Tribe is still not considered a federally recognized tribe by the BIA or the Indian Health Service, though they qualify for and receive other federal services as a recognized tribe.[34]

Who Is an American Indian?

Having established the complexity of determining what an Indian tribe is from a legal-political perspective, we now turn to a brief but necessary examination of the equally if not more cumbersome question of "Who is an Indian?" This is important, as McClain and Stewart note, because "the question of who is an Indian is central to any discussion of American Indian politics."[35] The political relationship that exists between tribes and the federal government, bloated with issues of disparate power, cultural biases, and race and ethnicity, makes this so. Of course, like the concept of "Indian tribe," before Columbus arrived in 1492 there were no peoples in the Americas known as "Indians" or "Native Americans." Each indigenous community had its own name relating to the character of its people and the lands they inhabited.

With the political status of Indian nations defined, the question of deciding just "who is an Indian" would not appear to be a difficult one to answer. The decision rests with the tribal nations who retain, as one of their inherent sovereign powers, the power to decide who belongs in their nation. Unless this right has been expressly ceded in a treaty, it remains probably the most essential component of self-government. If tribes were to lose the right to decide who their citizens/members were, then it would logically follow that any government could dictate or influence what the tribe's membership should entail.

Since the identification of individuals as Indians depends upon or coincides with their association in a unique body politic and distinctive cultural and linguistic systems, historically, at least, "allegiance rather than ancestry per se [was] the deciding factor" in determining who was an Indian.[36] In other words, historically, to be considered an Indian one had to meet certain basic tribally defined criteria, including the social, cultural, linguistic, territorial, sociopsychological, and ceremonial. These criteria, of course, varied from tribal nation to tribal nation. However, as the federal government's power waxed by the late nineteenth century, with the corresponding waning of tribal power, indigenous cultural-social-territorial–based definitions of tribal identity were sometimes

ignored and replaced by purely legal and frequently race-based definitions often arbitrarily articulated in congressional laws, administrative regulations, or court cases.

Congress, in particular, began to employ and still uses ethnological data, including varying fractions of blood quantum. In fact, blood quantum remains one of the most important criteria used by the federal government and tribal governments to determine Indian status, despite the fact that its continued use "poses enormous conceptual and practical problems" since blood is not the carrier of genetic material and cultural traits as was thought in the nineteenth century.[37]

When blood quantum was first used in the Indian context in the early part of the twentieth century as a mechanism to reduce federal expenditures for Indian education, it "was meant to measure the amount of Indian blood possessed by an individual. Because racial blood types could not be observed directly, Indian blood quantum was inferred from the racial backgrounds of parents. If both parents were reputed to have 'unadulterated' Indian blood, then the blood quantum of their children was fixed at 100 percent. For children of racially mixed parents, their Indian blood quantum might be some fractional amount such as ¾, ½, or ⅛."[38]

The federal government's principal function in formulating definitions of "Indian," since like the concept "tribe" there is no single constitutional or universally accepted definition, is to "establish a test whereby it may be determined whether a given individual is to be excluded from the scope of legislation dealing with Indians."[39] The most widely accepted "legal" definition of "Indian" is from Felix Cohen, who wrote in 1943 that:

> The term "Indian" may be used in an ethnological or in a legal sense. Ethnologically, the Indian race may be distinguished from the Caucasian, Negro, Mongolian, and other races. If a person is three-fourths

Caucasian and one-fourth Indian, it is absurd, from the ethnological standpoint, to assign him to the Indian race. Yet legally such a person may be an Indian. From a legal standpoint, then, the biological question of race is generally pertinent, but not conclusive. Legal status depends not only upon biological, but also upon social factors, such as the relation of the individual concerned to a white or Indian community. . . . Recognizing the possible diversity of definitions of "Indianhood," we may nevertheless find some practical value in a definition of "Indian" as a person meeting two qualifications: (a) That some of his ancestors lived in America before its discovery by the white race, and (b) That the individual is considered an "Indian" by the community in which he lives.[40]

Because of the Constitution's silence on the issue of who is an Indian, Congress, the BIA, and the federal courts have had great latitude in developing specific meanings for specific situations which only sometimes reflect the definitions of particular tribes. But because of the plenary power doctrine and the trust doctrine, these federal actors, but especially the Congress, have vested themselves with the right to define "who an Indian is" for purposes relating to legislation and have sometimes established base rolls which actually identify who a tribe's members are. This was done in the case of the so-called Five Civilized Tribes of present-day Oklahoma. Congress, in 1893, enacted a law that all but secured to the federal government the right to determine membership of these tribes.[41]

Over thirty "legal" definitions have been promulgated by various agencies, departments, and congressional committees and subcommittees that explain who is and is not an Indian eligible for federal services.[42] These definitions can be grouped into six categories. First, and most common, are those definitions that require a specific blood quantum, with one-fourth being the most widely accepted

fraction. Second, there is a set of definitions clustered under the requirement that the individual be a member of a federally recognized indigenous community.

A third category includes definitions that mandate residence "on or near" a federal Indian reservation. A fourth class includes definitions grouped under descendancy. These entail definitions that extend eligibility not only to tribal members but also to their descendants up to a specified degree. For example, the definition of Indian found in a 1998 bill, Indian Trust-Estate Planning and Land Title Management Improvement Act, declares that "the term 'Indian' means any individual who is a member, or a descendant of a member, of a North American tribe, band, pueblo, or other organized group of natives who are indigenous to the continental U.S., or who otherwise has a special relationship with the U.S. through a treaty, agreement, or other form of recognition." The bill's sponsors described an "Alaska Native" as "an individual who is an Alaskan Indian, Eskimo, Aleut, or any combination thereof, who are indigenous to Alaska."

Under the fifth grouping are several definitions that rely on self-identification. The U.S. Census Bureau, for example, allows individuals to simply declare that they are Indian. Finally, the sixth class is a miscellaneous category that includes definitions which do not easily fit in the other categories.[43]

Defining "Indian" and "tribe" are not simple tasks in part because of the political and economic resources involved and because of the number and power of the respective actors: tribal governments, individual Indians, Congress, the president, the Department of the Interior, the BIA, federal courts and, increasingly, state governments and the various agencies and individuals who constitute those sovereigns. But who does the defining and how these emotionally laden terms are defined are crucial in expanding our understanding of the politics of individual tribes, intertribal relations, and intergovernmental relations.

For example, in terms of identity, high outmarriage rates, steadily decreasing federal dollars, and an intensified tribal-state relationship have prompted questions about "whether the rules defining Indianness and tribal membership should be relaxed or tightened—that is, made more inclusionary or more exclusionary."[44] For instance, some tribes are eliminating blood quantum and adopting descent criteria, while others are pursuing an "ethnic purification strategy" by adopting a stricter set of blood quantum rules concerning tribal enrollment. These decisions impact tribes and their political relationship with the federal government.

While tribes retain the right to establish their own membership criteria, the BIA in August 2000 published proposed regulations on the documentation requirements and standards necessary for Indians to receive a "certificate of degree of Indian blood" (CDIB), which is the federal government's way of determining whether individuals possess sufficient Indian blood to be eligible for certain federal programs and services provided exclusively to American Indians or Alaska Natives.[45]

But a number of Indian leaders, like W. Ron Allen, chairman of the Jamestown S'Klallam Tribe of Washington, charged that the federal government should not be in the business of determining who is Indian. The proposed regulations, he argued, by requiring applicants to show a relationship to an enrolled member of a federally recognized tribe, would potentially exclude members of descendants of terminated tribes, state-recognized tribes, and nonrecognized tribes.

Since the BIA's standard blood quantum is one-fourth, and with the high rates of out-marriage, Russell Thornton, an anthropologist, suggests that sometime in this century the proportion of the Indian population with less than one-fourth blood quantum will rise to 60 percent. If this trend is correct, from the federal government's standpoint "decreasing blood quanta of the total Native American population may be perceived as meaning that the numbers of Native Americans to whom it is obligated have declined."[46] This will not mean the extinction of Indian tribes, but it will mean a new form of federal termination of Indians who are eligible for federal aid and services.

Questions around whether a tribe is federally recognized, state-recognized, nonrecognized, or terminated have direct bearing on the internal and external political dynamics of tribes, and directly affect intergovernmental relations, since only recognized tribes may engage in gaming operations that are not directly subject to state law, may exercise criminal jurisdiction over their members and a measure of civil jurisdiction over nonmembers, and are exempt from a variety of state and federal taxes.

What Are Indian Lands?

The first and most obvious difference between Indian peoples and all other groups in the United States is that Indians were here before anyone else. All the land in the continental United States, Alaska, and Hawaii was inhabited and revered by the over six hundred distinctive indigenous peoples who dwelt here. Gradually, however, from 1492 forward, various foreign nations—Russia, Holland, Spain, Great Britain, France, Sweden, and later the United States—competed for an economic foothold in North America. For the three most dominant European states, France, Spain, and Great Britain (and later the United States, as Britain's successor), this usually included efforts to secure title to indigenous lands through formal treaties, which were sometimes coercive and occasionally fraudulent, while some were fairly negotiated.[47]

When the United States declared independence in 1776, it wisely opted to continue the policy of negotiating treaties with tribes, which it continued to do until 1871, when Congress unilaterally declared that "hereafter no Indian nation or tribe within the territory of the United States shall be acknowledged or recognized as an independent nation, tribe, or power with whom the United States may contract by treaty."[48] However, this stance proved unworkable and within a short period the United States was again negotiating *agreements* with tribal nations that were often referred to and accorded the legal status of treaties. The negotiation of agreements continued until 1912.

Many of these documents were primarily viewed as land cession arrangements by the federal government, in which the United States purchased varying amounts of tribal lands in exchange for monies, goods, and services. In addition, tribes "reserved" their remaining lands, or agreed to relocate to new lands, which were usually designated as reservations. These reserved lands were to be held "in trust" by the United States on behalf of the tribe(s), who were deemed the beneficiaries. As the tribes' "trustee," the federal government theoretically exercised the responsibility to assist the tribes in the protection of their lands, resources, and cultural heritage and pledged that it would hold itself to the highest standards of good faith and honesty in all its dealings with the tribes.

For example, article 1 of a treaty the Kickapoo signed on October 24, 1832, contained a cession of land:

> The Kickapoo tribe of Indians, in consideration of the stipulations hereinafter made, do hereby cede to the United States, the lands assigned to them by the treaty of Edwardsville, and concluded at St. Louis ...

and all other claims to lands within the State of Missouri.[49]

The second article, however, described the lands the tribe had secured for their land cessions:

> The United States will provide for the Kickapoo tribe, a country to reside in, southwest of the Missouri river, as their permanent place of residence as long as they remain a tribe ... [and] it is hereby agreed that the country within the following boundaries shall be assigned, conveyed, and forever secured ... to the said Kickapoo tribe.[50]

In this case the Kickapoo agreed to relocate to a little over 700,000 acres of new lands in Kansas that were to serve as their permanent "reservation."

In short, a reservation is an area of land—whether aboriginal or new—that has been reserved for an Indian tribe, band, village, or nation. Generally, the United States holds, in trust for the tribe, legal title to the reserved territory. The tribe in these instances holds a beneficial title to the lands, or, in other words, an exclusive right of occupancy. Of course, reservations were not all created by treaty. Congress established a number of reservations by statute.

The president, through the use of executive order power, established many other reservations. For instance, the state of Arizona has twenty-one reservations—twenty of which were created by presidents. The core foundation of the Navajo Reservation (the largest in the country), was treaty-established in 1868, though the many additions to it were mostly by executive orders. In 1919, Congress forbade the president from establishing any more reservations via executive order. Finally, the secretary of the interior is empowered under the 1934 Indian Reorganization Act to establish, expand, or restore reservations.

As of 1998, there were 314 reservations and other restricted and trust lands in the

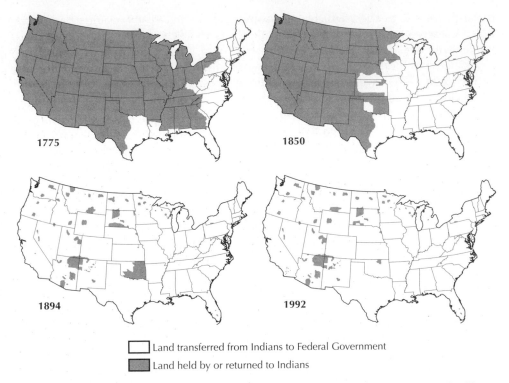

1775

1850

1894

1992

☐ Land transferred from Indians to Federal Government

■ Land held by or returned to Indians

MAP 1 American Indian Land Losses. *Source: Encyclopedia of North American Indians,* edited by Frederick E. Hoxie. Copyright © 1996 by Houghton Mifflin Company. All rights reserved.

United States. These reserved lands are located in thirty-one states, mostly in the West. There are also twelve state-established reservations in Connecticut, Massachusetts, Michigan, New York, New Jersey, South Carolina, Georgia, and Virginia. Despite the large number of federally recognized Alaska Native groups, there is only one reservation, the Annette Island Indian Reserve.[51]

At present, the indigenous land base in the United States, including Alaska, is approximately 100 million acres—fifty-six million in the continental United States, forty-four million in Alaska. This represents approximately 4 percent of all lands in the United States. Map 1 graphically shows the rapid and enormous loss of aboriginal territory to the United States from the birth of the American republic to the present day.

The roughly one hundred million acres constitutes territory over which tribal governments and Alaska Native villages and corporations exercise varying amounts of governmental jurisdiction, and where state laws are generally inapplicable, with exceptions.

In 1999, 1,397,931 Indians were identified in a BIA report out of the total U.S. Indian population in 2000 of 2,475,956 (individuals self-identifying as single race American Indian or Alaska Native).

What Is Indian Country?

For an indigenous government to be able to exercise criminal or civil jurisdiction over their territory, their own members, and, in some limited cases, non-Indians, the land in question must be designated as *Indian Country*. In the colonial era, Indian Country encompassed all the lands beyond the frontier lands "populated by tribes and bands of Indians who rejected contact with 'civilized' populations."[52] Today, however, the concept "has been elevated by federal law above other ideas because it transcends mere geographical limitations and represents that sphere of influence in which Indian traditions and federal laws passed specifically to deal with the political relationship of the United States to American Indians have primacy."[53]

Indian Country: Beyond the Reservation

Broadly, the term "Indian Country" means land within which Indian laws and customs and federal laws relating to Indians are generally applicable. But it is also defined as all the land under the supervision and protection of the federal government that has been set aside primarily for the use of Indians. Federal law defines it, first, as all land within the boundaries of an Indian reservation, whether owned by Indians or non-Indians. Second, it includes all "dependent Indian communities" in the United States. These are lands—pueblos of New Mexico, Oklahoma Indian tribal lands, and California rancherias—previously recognized by European nations and now by the successor government, the United States, as belonging to the tribes or as set aside by the federal government for use and benefit of the Indians.

Pueblo lands, because they were previously recognized as belonging to the pueblos under Spanish, Mexican, and later U.S. law, are not, strictly speaking, reservations, but are considered Indian lands and are held in trust by the federal government because

they are held in communal ownership with fee-simple title residing in each pueblo. Some Pueblo Indian lands are held in equitable ownership by various pueblos, with the United States holding legal title. These lands include reservations created by congressional statute and executive order reservations established by the president.

Oklahoma's numerous Indian tribes also have a distinctive history, though their lands also constitute Indian Country. It is important to note that the tribes in the eastern part of the state, what was called "Indian Territory," home of the Five Civilized Tribes, have a somewhat different history from tribes in the western part of the state, or what was called "Oklahoma Territory," home of the Cheyenne, Arapaho, Kiowa, Comanche, etc. Although the BIA and the Bureau of the Census have asserted that there are no Indian reservations in Oklahoma, except for the Osage, John Moore argues that the reservation status of Oklahoma tribes persists, notwithstanding allotment and other policies designed to terminate Indian communal land holdings.[54]

Some California tribes, because of heavy Spanish influence dating from 1769, live on rancherias, a Spanish term meaning "small reservation" and originally applied to Indians who had not been settled in Christian mission communities. The history of death and dispossession visited upon California's indigenous population may well be the worst of any aboriginal peoples in the United States. From a population of well over 300,000 at the time of contact, California Indians experienced a staggering rate of decline from diseases, outright genocide, and displacement.[55] That they have retained any lands at all is a remarkable testimony to their fortitude.

Finally, the Indian Country designation includes all individual Indian allotments (I will discuss the allotment policy shortly) that are still held in trust or restricted status by the federal government—whether inside or outside an Indian reservation.[56]

For political and legal purposes, the designation of Indian Country is crucial because the reach of a tribal nation's jurisdiction is generally restricted to lands so designated. And it is Indian Country where most jurisdictional disputes arise between tribes and their members, tribes and non-Indians, and tribes and the local, county, state, or federal governments.

For example, this was the central question in the recent U.S. Supreme Court case involving indigenous people, *Alaska v. Native Village of Venetie Tribal Government* (1998). In this case, the court had to decide whether the village of Venetie constituted Indian Country. If so, then the tribal government had the right to impose a tax on a construction company; if not, then it lacked such taxing power. In a harmful ruling for Alaska Native sovereignty, the Supreme Court held that the village's fee-simple lands did not constitute Indian Country, thus depriving Alaska villages and corporations of the power to exercise a number of governmental powers that tribal nations in the lower forty-eight states exercise routinely. The Supreme Court, however, need not have relied so exclusively on the question of whether or not Venetia constituted "Indian Country" since the statutes articulating this concept clearly did not encompass Alaska at the time they were enacted.

Demography and Indian Country

According to a report, *Changing America,* prepared by the Council of Economic Advisers for President Clinton's Race Initiative in 1998, the population of the United States is increasingly diverse. In recent years the four major racial/ethnic minority groups—Latinos, Asian Americans, African Americans, and

American Indians—have each grown faster than the population as a whole. Whereas in 1970 the combination of these four groups represented only 16 percent of the entire population, by 1998 this had increased to 27 percent.[57] The Bureau of the Census, the report noted, projects that by 2050, these groups will account for "almost half of the U.S. Population." Early data from the 2000 U.S. census, which shows a total population of 281,421,906, indicate the continuing transformation of race and ethnicity in America. While the categories of white (211,460,626), Hispanic or Latino (35,305,818), black or African American (34,658,190), American Indian or Alaska Native (2,475,956), Asian (10,242,998), and Native Hawaiian or other Pacific Islander (398,835) were familiar, for the first time in history individuals could choose self-identify as having more than one race. Some 6,826,228 people, 2.4 percent of the total population, claimed affiliation with two or more races.[58]

While this projected growth has potentially staggering political and economic implications, the fact is that the total indigenous population, despite the large number of indigenous nations—561 and counting—is comparatively quite small (see figures 1–5). In 2000, there were a reported 2,475,956 self-identified Indians and Alaska Natives, a 26 percent increase since 1990. This is a drastic decline from pre-European figures of over seven million, but it is far more than the nadir of perhaps only 250,000 around 1900.[59] The 2000 figure represents only 0.9 percent of the total U.S. population of 281,421,906.

Although the overall population of self-identified American Indians and Alaska Natives is still quite small, because of the new category allowing individuals to identify as belonging to more than one race (sixty-three racial options were possible), the 2000 census data are not directly comparable with data from the 1990 census or previous

FIGURE 1 American Indian Population, 1890–1990 (thousands). *Source:* Larry Hajime Shinagawa and Michael Jang, *Atlas of American Diversity* (Walnut Creek, Calif.: AltaMira, 1998), 107–8. *Notes:* 1900, partially estimated: 1930 Eskimo and Aleut populations are based on 1939 counts.

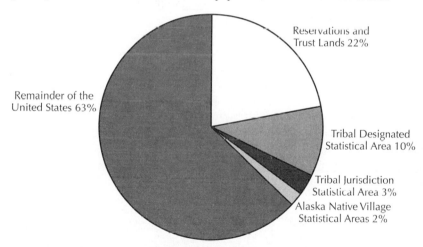

FIGURE 2 American Indian Population by Type of Area, 1990 (percent).
Source: Larry Hajime Shinagawa and Michael Jang, *Atlas of American Diversity* (Walnut Creek, Calif.: AltaMira, 1998), 107–8.

censuses. Thus, while approximately 2.5 million individuals identified themselves as American Indian and Alaska Native alone, an additional 1.6 million people reported themselves as being indigenous and belonging to "at least one other race." Within this group, the most common combinations were "American Indian and Alaska Native *and* White" (66 percent of the population reported this); "American Indian and Alaska Native *and* Black or African American" (11 percent of the population); and "American Indian and

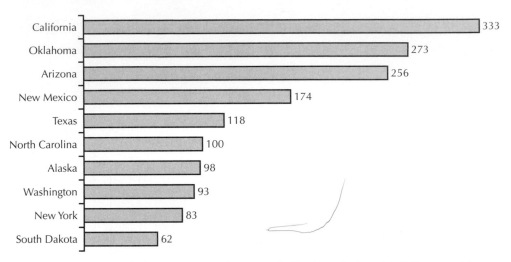

FIGURE 3   States with the Ten Largest American Indian Populations, 2000 (thousands). *Source:* www.census.gov/clo/www/redistricting.html

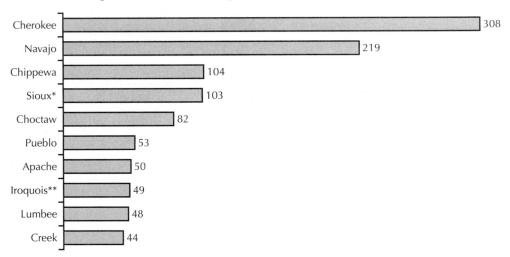

FIGURE 4   Ten Largest American Indian Tribes, 1990 (thousands). *Source:* Larry Hajime Shinagawa and Michael Jang, *Atlas of American Diversity* (Walnut Creek, Calif.: AltaMira, 1998), 107–8. *Any entry with the spelling "Siouan" was miscoded to Sioux in North Carolina. **Reporting and/or processing problems have affected the data for this tribe.

Alaska Native *and* White *and* Black or African American" (7 percent). In sum, approximately 4.1 million people reported themselves as being American Indian and Alaska Native "alone or in combination with one or more other races."[60] The wide diversity within this population will be discussed in greater detail in forthcoming Census reports not yet available.

Suffice it to say, the amount of racial mixing acknowledged in the American Indian context is extreme when compared to that of other racial/ethnic groups. As Russell Thorton, a Cherokee anthropologist,

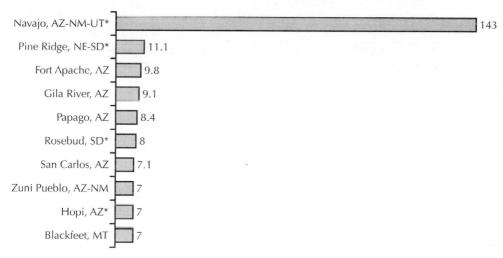

FIGURE 5 Reservations with the Largest Numbers of American Indians, 1990 (thousands).
Source: Larry Hajime Shinagawa and Michael Jang, *Atlas of American Diversity* (Walnut Creek, Calif.:
AltaMira, 1998), 107–8. *Includes trust lands

noted in his analysis of the 2000 census data, American Indians have a racial mixture of 37 percent, which "far exceeds percentages for other groups." Thornton noted that only about 5 percent of African Americans reported mixed ancestry.[61]

In Alaska, there is only one small reservation, Annette Island Reserve, though for census purposes lands are designated as "Alaska Native Village Statistical areas" that are inhabited and recognized as indigenous areas. Approximately 47,244 Alaska Natives live on these lands. In sum, more than 60 percent, over one million, of all Indian people do not live on Indian reservations.[62] A majority of indigenous peoples, in fact some 56.2 percent, live in metropolitan or suburban areas. And roughly half of all urban Indians can be found in as few as sixteen cities, largely as a result of the 1950s and 1960s termination, relocation, and educational programs of the federal government.

In the early days of relocation, the BIA generally helped send Indians to Chicago, Los Angeles, Denver, or Salt Lake City. By 1990, Indians had migrated to a number of other metropolitan areas. Cities with the largest Indian populations in 1990 were Tulsa, Oklahoma (48,348); Oklahoma City, Oklahoma (46,111); Los Angeles-Long Beach, California (43,689); Phoenix, Arizona (38,309); and Seattle-Tacoma, Washington (32,980).[63] The vast majority of Indians still live in the western half of the United States.

The states with the ten largest indigenous populations are shown in figure 4. The District of Columbia had the fewest Indians, 1,466.

There is also great variation in the population of individual tribes (see figure 5). The largest tribe is the Cherokee Nation of Oklahoma, with 369,035 members. The smallest tribes have fewer than one hundred members. The indigenous population is also a young population, with more than 35 percent younger than age seventeen. In fact, the median age for reservation Indians is more than ten years younger than that of the general U.S. population. The Indian population, like that of the Jews and the Japanese Americans in Hawaii, is also one that experiences an extremely high level of intergroup marriage (marriage between persons of different races). Although intergroup marriage couples accounted for only 4 percent of all married couples in the United States in 1990, American Indians had a 53 percent intergroup marriage rate. Potentially, this figure could have severe cultural and political implications for indigenous nations.[64]

As Snipp mused:

> The extraordinarily high level of racial intermarriage for American Indians provides a good reason to expect that growing numbers of American Indians and their descendants will choose non-Indians for spouses and to a greater or lesser degree become absorbed into the dominant culture. Some of these Indians will abandon their cultural heritage altogether, while others may make only minor accommodations as a result of having a non-Indian spouse. This raises a question that is extremely controversial within many quarters of the American Indian community: Are American Indians assimilating so quickly through racial intermarriage that they will eventually, in the not to distant future, marry themselves out of existence?[65]

Predicting the future is an impossible task and I will not hazard a guess as to whether this intermarriage rate will continue. Suffice it to say, this is viewed as a serious predicament by some tribes and raises some important questions. For instance, will Indians, like many intermarried Jews, be able to show a propensity for combining extensive intermarriage with a surge in ethnic and religious pride? For while the rate of Jewish intermarriage is higher today than at any other point, American Jewish culture and community life appear to be flourishing, including a resurgent interest in Yiddish.[66]

Other questions confront tribes as well. Will they continue to use blood quantum as their primary definitional criteria? Will the federal government claim that its legal and

moral obligations to Indians dissipate if a tribal nation's blood quantum falls below a certain percentage? Will tribes be able to exercise jurisdiction over a multiracial citizenry? These are questions some tribes are beginning to address as we begin the new millennium.

Conclusion

The power to define—what is a tribe, who is an Indian, what constitutes Indian Country, which group gets recognized—along with the power to decide whether or not to act in a colonial capacity in relation to indigenous nations are important means by which the federal government has gained and retains a dominant position vis-à-vis tribal groups. While on one hand supporting the right of indigenous polities to exercise self-determination, the United States on the other still insists that it has the power and the right to trump important tribal governmental decisions regarding identity and has shown throughout its history that it will so act if it deems it necessary to further its own economic, political, and cultural interests.

The demographic data presented glaringly show that diversity and uncertainty are hallmarks of Indian Country, with more than half the indigenous population living off reservations and Indians outmarrying at increasing rates. What the impact of such movement and marriage rates will be on tribal national identity, federal Indian policy, and the government-to-government relationship is, however, impossible to predict.

NOTES

1. U.S. Congress, *American Indian Policy Review Commission: Final Report,* vol. 1 (Washington, D.C.: Government Printing Office, 1977), 3.

2. See, e.g., Haunani-Kay Trask, *From a Native Daughter: Colonialism and Sovereignty in Hawai'i* (Monroe, Maine: Common Courage,

1993) and Roger MacPherson Furrer, ed., *He Alo á He Alo (Face to Face): Hawaiian Voices on Sovereignty* (Honolulu, Hawaii: American Friends Service Committee-Hawai'i, 1993).

3. 3528 U.S. 495 (2000).

4. Http://www.doi.gov/nativehawaiians/.

5. See, S. James Anaya, "The Native Hawaiian People and International Human Rights Law: Toward a Remedy for Past and Continuing Wrongs," *Georgia Law Review* 28 (1994), 309–64.

6. Vine Deloria Jr. "The American Indian Image in North America," *Encyclopedia of Indians of the Americas,* vol. 1 (St. Clair Shores, Mich.: Scholarly Press, 1974), 43.

7. Paula D. McClain and Joseph Stewart Jr., *"Can We All Get Along?" Racial and Ethnic Minorities in American Politics* (Boulder, Colo.: Westview, 1998), 6, citing John Higham, *Strangers in the Land: Patterns of American Nativism, 1860–1925* (Westport, Conn.: Greenwood, 1963).

8. 180 U.S. 261 (1901).

9. Felix S. Cohen, *Handbook of Federal Indian Law,* reprint ed. (Albuquerque: University of New Mexico Press, 1972), 268.

10. Jack Utter, *American Indians: Answers to Today's Questions* (Lake Ann, Mich.: National Woodlands, 1993), 1972), 30–31.

11. William Quinn Jr., "Federal Acnowledgment of American Indian Tribes? The Historical Development of a Legal Concept," *American Journal of Legal History* 34 (October 1990): 331–63.

12. 56 *Federal Register* 47, 325 (1991).

13. 25 Code of Federal Regulations 83.7 (a)–(g) (1991).

14. 25 *U.S.C.* chapter 1, section 1, 961.

15. 25 *U.S.C.* chapter 1, 962.

16. William W. Quinn Jr., "Federal Acknowledgment of American Indian Tribes: Authority, Judicial Interposition, and 25 C.F.R. Sec. 83," *American Indian Law Review* 17 (fall 1992): 48.

17. Quinn, "Federal Acknowledgment of American Indian Tribes," 52.

18. Felix Cohen, "The Erosion of Indian Rights, 1950–1953: A Case Study in Bureaucracy," *Yale Law Journal* 62 (February 1953): 352.

19. Letter from Carol A. Bacon, acting director of the Office of Tribal Services, Bureau of Indian Affairs, 3 December 1991. The author has copy of the letter.

20. 108 Stat., 709.

21. See U.S. Congress, House, "A Bill to Provide for Administrative Procedures to Extend Federal Recognition to Certain Indian Groups, and for Other Purposes," 105th Cong., 2d sess., 1998, H. Rept. 1154. As of this writing—May 1999—none of these bills has become law.

22. Ellen Barry, "Agency Willing to Relinquish Power to Recognize Tribes," *Boston Globe,* 26 May 2000, B1.

23. 118 U.S. 948 (1998).

24. See, e.g., Trask, *From a Native Daughter,* and Anaya, "The Native Hawaiian People," 309.

25. Allogan Slagle, "Unfinished Justice: Completing the Restoration and Acknowledgment of California Indian Tribes," *American Indian Journal* 13, no. 4 (fall 1989): 325–45.

26. William W. Quinn Jr., "The Southeast Syndrome: Notes on Indian Descendant Recruitment Organizations and Their Perceptions of Native American Culture," *American Indian Quarterly* 14, no. 2 (spring 1990): 147–54.

27. Jackie J. Kim, "The Indian Federal Recognition Procedures Act of 1995: A Congressional Solution to an Administrative Morass," *The Administrative Law Journal of the American University* 9, no. 3 (Fall 1995): 899–932.

28. See http://www.doi.gov/bia/bar/indexq.htm for statistical details of the acknowledgment project's efforts.

29. Donald Fixico, *Termination and Relocation: Federal Indian Policy, 1945–1960* (Albuquerque, N. Mex.: University of New Mexico Press, 1986).

30. 67 Stat., B132.

31. 110 Stat., 130.

32. N.C. Public Laws, 1953, chapter 874, p. 747.

33. 70 Stat., 254.

34. David E. Wilkins, "Breaking into the Intergovernmental Matrix: The Lumbee Tribe's Efforts to Secure Federal Acknowledgment," *Publius: The Journal of Federalism* 23 (Fall 1993): 123–42.

35. McClain and Stewart, "Can We All Get Along?" 6.

36. Bart Vogel, "Who Is an Indian in Federal Indian Law?" in *Studies in American Indian Law,* ed. Ralph Johnson (Pullman, Wash.: Washington State University, 1970), 53.

37. C. Matthew Snipp, *American Indians: The First of This Land* (New York: Russell Sage Foundation, 1989), 34.

38. Snipp, *First of This Land,* 33.

39. Cohen, *Handbook,* 2.

40. Snipp, *First of This Land,* 33.

41. 29 Stat., 321.

42. Abdul G. Kahn, *Report on the Indian Definition Study* (Washington, D.C.: Department of Education, 1980).

43. Kahn, *Indian Definition Study,* 56.

44. Joane Nagel, *American Indian Ethnic Renewal: Red Power and the Resurgence of Identity and Culture* (New York: Oxford University Press, 1996), 243.

45. Brian Stackes, "Planned Bureau of Indian Affairs Regulations Stir Concerns Among Tribal Leaders," *Indian Country Today,* 18 August 2000, 1.

46. Russell Thornton, "Tribal Membership Requirements and the Demography of 'Old' and 'New' Native Americans," in *Changing Numbers, Changing Needs: American Indian Demogrphy and Public Health,* ed. Gary D. Sandefur, Ronald R. Rindfuss, and Barney Cohen (Washington, D.C.: National Academy Press, 1996), 110–11.

47. See, e.g., Francis Paul Prucha, *American Indian Treaties: The History of a Political Anomaly* (Berkeley, Calif.: University of California Press, 1994) and Robert A. Williams Jr. *Linking Arms Together: American Indian Treaty Visions of Law and Peace, 1600–1800* (New York: Oxford University Press, 1997).

48. 16 Stat., 566.

49. 7 Stat., 391.

50. 7 Stat., 391.

51. Cesare Marino, "Reservations," in *Native America in the Twentieth Century: An Encyclopedia,* ed. Mary B. Davis (New York: Garland Publishing, Inc., 1996), 544–56.

52. Vine Deloria Jr. and Clifford M. Lytle, *American Indians, American Justice* (Austin: University of Texas Press, 1983), 58.

53. Deloria and Lytle, *American Indians,* 58.

54. John H. Moore, "The Enduring Reservations of Oklahoma," in *State & Reservation: New Perspectives on Federal Indian Policy,* ed. George Pierre Castile and Robert L. Bee (Tucson: University of Arizona Press, 1992), 92–109.

55. See, Robert F. Heizer, *The Destruction of California Indians* (Lincoln: University of Nebraska Press, 1993) for a first rate account of what these nations experienced from 1847 to 1865.

56. Title 18, *U.S. Code,* section 1151.

57. Council of Economic Advisers, *Changing America: Indicators of Social and Economic Well-Being by Race and Hispanic Origin* (Washington, D.C.: Government Printing Office, 1998), 4.

58. www.census.gov/prod/2001 pubs.

59. Russell Thornton, *American Indian Holocaust and Survival: A Population History Since 1492* (Norman: University of Oklahoma Press, 1987).

60. www.census.gov/prod/2001 pubs.

61. Russell Thornton, "What the Census Doesn't Count," *New York Times,* 23 March 2001, A21.

62. C. Matthew Snipp, "The Size and Distribution of the American Indian Population: Fertility, Mortality, Migration, and Residence," in *Changing Numbers, Changing Needs: American Indian Demography and Public Health,* ed. Gary D. Sandefur, Ronald R. Rindfuss, and Barney Cohen (Washington, D.C.: National Academy Press, 1996), 42–43.

63. Snipp, "The Size and Distribution," 39.

64. Snipp, *The First of This Land,* 171.

65. Snipp, *The First of This Land,* 165.

66. Lawrence H. Fuchs, *The American Kaleidoscope* (Hanover, N.H.: Wesleyan University Press, 1990), 329.

SEEING THE BIG PICTURE

Map 1 in this reading shows land held by Indians in 1750 and 1992. Glance at the quality of life indicators in the Appendix. Do you believe the socioeconomic standing and the loss of Indian lands are connected? How?

11

ASIAN AMERICAN PANETHNICITY: BRIDGING INSTITUTIONS AND IDENTITIES

Yen Le Espiritu

QUESTIONS TO CONSIDER

Korean, Chinese, Japanese, and Philippine Americans share very different cultural histories. Each group has their own language, culture, religious beliefs, and immigration experiences, yet they get "lumped" under the category Asian. What political function does panethnic identity serve, according to Yen Le Espiritu, for these diverse ethnic groups?

Goals, Definitions, and Scope

Pan-Asian American ethnicity is the development of bridging organizations and solidarities among several ethnic and immigrant groups of Asian ancestry. Although subject to the same general prejudice and similar discriminatory laws, Asians in the United States have rarely conceived of themselves as a single people and many still do not. "Asiatic," "Oriental," and "Mongolian" were merely convenient labels used by outsiders to refer to all Asians. The development of panethnicity among Asian Americans has a short history. While examples of white oppression of Asian Americans stretch back over a century, a meaningful pan-Asian movement was not constructed until the late 1960s (Daniels 1988, p. 113). This [reading] tells the story of this construction—of the resultant unity and division, and corresponding benefits

and costs. The emphasis here is on the *political* nature of panethnicity, that is, on the distribution and exercise of, and the struggle for, power and resources inside and outside the community. Panethnicity is political not only because it serves as a basis for interest group mobilization but also because it is linked with the expansion of the role of the polity (Enloe 1980, p. 5).

Panethnicity has not been well studied. Moreover, the few existing works on panethnicity have dealt primarily with Native American and Latino American panethnicities (Cornell 1988; Nagel 1982; Padilla 1985). Except for several essays from the proponents of the 1960s Asian American movement (Uyematsu 1971; P. Wong 1972), the process of pan-Asianization has not been well documented. While social scientists have devoted substantial attention to individual Asian groups (Bonacich and Modell 1980; Kim 1981; Montero 1979), few have focused on Asian Americans as a collectivity. Yet a host of pan-Asian organizations testify to the salience of pan-Asian consciousness, as do the numerous cooperative efforts by Asian American groups and organizations on behalf of both subgroup and pan-Asian interests.

There are two dimensions of groupness: the conceptual and the organizational. The conceptual refers to individual behavior and attitude—the ways group members view themselves; the organizational refers to political structures—the ways groups are organized as collective actors. The boundaries of these two dimensions usually but do not necessarily coincide (Cornell 1988, p. 72). Some key indicators of pan-Asian consciousness include self-identification, pan-Asian residential, friendship, and marriage patterns, and membership in pan-Asian organizations. Given the multiple levels of Asian American ethnicity, a study of individual ethnicity can also document "ethnic switching"—the relabeling of individuals' ethnic affiliation to meet situational needs. That is, a person is a Japanese American or an Asian American depending on the ethnic identities available to him or her in a particular situation. Sometimes the individual has a choice, and sometimes not (see Nagel 1986, pp. 95–96). While recognizing the importance of the conceptual dimension of panethnicity, this work is primarily a study of the organizational dimension: the institutionalization of Asian American consciousness, and not the state of panethnic consciousness itself. Thus, most of the evidence is drawn from the level of formal organizations. The research methods are basically those of the historically grounded community study, combining organization archives, public records, interviews with the leaders of organizations, participant observation, and library research.

Naturally, the rank and file's level of Asian American consciousness influences its institutionalization. On the other hand, grassroots consciousness does not necessarily precede the process of organizational consolidation. As this study documents, panethnic organizations need not merely reflect existing panethnic consciousness but can also generate and augment it. In building themselves, pan-Asian organizations also build pan-Asian consciousness. Thus, the organizational level is intrinsically worthy of examination because it tells us about the directions of the populations supposedly represented.

Moreover, pan-Asian institutions cannot survive without support; their very existence presupposes some amount of consensus. One research strategy would be to quantify this consensus. Another would be to identify the individuals who may have vested interests in promoting pan-Asian ethnicity, and in so doing name the dominant groups and sectors in the pan-Asian coalitions. The research question then becomes not who identifies with pan-Asian ethnicity, but who benefits the most from it—and at whose expense? Such an approach allows us to look beyond numbers to the power struggles and the resultant intergroup conflicts and competition.

The influx of the post-1965 Asian immigrants and refugees—who are distinct in ethnic and class composition from the more "established" Asian Americans—has exacerbated intergroup conflicts. The determination of what and whose interests will be defended often factionalizes the pan-Asian collectivity, as newcomers and old-timers pursue their separate goals (Lopez and Espiritu 1990, p. 206). On the other hand, the pan-Asian concept is now so well institutionalized that new Asian immigrants and refugees often encounter extensive pressure to consider themselves Asian Americans, regardless of whether or not they see themselves in such terms. For example, Southeast Asian refugees have had to adopt the Asian American designation because this category resonates in the larger society (Hein 1989; Skinner and Hendricks 1979). Accordingly, this study examines the benefits as well as the limitations of pan-Asian coalitions.

Scholars and laypersons alike have argued that Asian Americans are not a panethnic group because they do not share a common culture (Ignacio 1976; Trottier 1981). While Native Americans can trace their common descent to their unique relationship to the land, and Latino Americans to their common language, Asian Americans have no readily identifiable symbols of ethnicity. This view involves the implicit assumption that ethnic boundaries are unproblematic. However, as Frederick Barth (1969) suggested, when ethnic boundaries are strong and persistent, cultural solidarity will result. But ethnic groups that are merging need not exhibit such solidarity. Discussing the ongoing efforts to build an Asian American culture, John Liu (1988 pp. 123 24) stated, "The admonition that we can no longer assume that Asian Americans share a common identity and culture is not a setback in our efforts, but rather a reminder that the goals we set for ourselves need to be constantly struggled for."

The construction of pan-Asian ethnicity involves the creation of a common Asian American heritage out of diverse histories. Part of the heritage being created hinges on what Asian Americans share: a history of exploitation, oppression, and discrimination. However, individuals' being treated alike does not automatically produce new groups. "Only when people become aware of being treated alike on the basis of some arbitrary criterion do they begin to establish identity on that basis" (Shibutani and Kwan 1965, p. 210). For Asian Americans, this "arbitrary criterion" is their socially defined racial distinctiveness, or their imposed identity as "Asians." As such, an important task for pan-Asian leaders is to define racist activities against one Asian American subgroup as hostilities against all Asian Americans. In her call for pan-Asian organization, Amy Uyematsu (1971, pp. 10–11) referred to the internment of Japanese Americans as a "racist treatment of '*yellows*,'" and the mistreatment of Chinese immigrants in 1885 as mistreatment of *Asians* in America (emphasis mine).

More recently, Asian American leaders characterized the 1982 fatal beating of Chinese American Vincent Chin as a racial attack against all Asian Americans (Zia 1984). Thus, following Barth (1969), the task at hand is to document the process of culture building and its function in the construction and maintenance of panethnic boundaries—not to define and inventory cultural symbols. . . .

Social and Demographic Changes: Setting the Context

Although Asians in the United States have long been engaged in political action, their efforts never drew public attention until the 1960s (Chan 1991, p. 171). Prompted by broader political struggles and internal demographic changes, college students of Asian ancestry spearheaded the Asian American movement. Critical to its development was the mobilization of American blacks. Besides offering tactical lessons, the civil rights and the Black Power movements had a profound impact on the consciousness of Asian Americans, sensitizing them to racial issues (Uyematsu 1971). The anticolonial nationalist movements in Asia also stirred racial and cultural pride and provided a context for the emergence of the Yellow Power movement (P. Wong 1972). Influenced by these broader political struggles, Americans of Asian ancestry united to denounce racist institutional structures, demand new or unattended rights, and assert their cultural and racial distinctiveness. Normal urban issues such as housing, education, and social welfare began to take on ethnic coloration.

While important, these broader societal developments alone do not explain why the Asian American movement became panethnic. To understand this development, we first need to understand the underlying social and demographic factors that allowed pan-Asianism to take root in the 1960s but not earlier. Before World War II, pan-Asian unity was not feasible because the predominantly foreign-born Asian population did not share a common language. During the postwar years, increasing intergroup communication and contact facilitated the emergence of a pan-Asian consciousness. The breakdown of economic and residential barriers during the postwar period provided the first opportunity for an unprecedented number of Asian Americans to come into intimate, sustained contact with the larger society—and with one another.

From an Immigrant to a Native Population

Before 1940, the Asian population in the United States was primarily an immigrant population. Immigrant Asians faced practical barriers to pan-Asian unity. Foremost was their lack of a common language. Old national rivalries were another obstacle, as many early Asian immigrants carried the political memories and outlook of their homelands. For example, Japan's occupation of Korea resulted in pervasive anti-Japanese sentiments among Koreans in the United States. According to Brett Melendy (1977, p. 155), "Fear and hatred of the Japanese appeared to be the only unifying force among the various Korean groups through the years." Moreover, these historical enmities and linguistic and cultural differences reinforced one another as divisive agents.

During the postwar period, due to immigration restrictions and the growing dominance of the second and third generations, American-born Asians outnumbered immigrants. The demographic changes of the 1940s were pronounced. During this decade, nearly twenty thousand Chinese American babies were born. For the first time, the largest five-year cohort of Chinese Americans was

under five years of age (Kitano and Daniels 1988, p. 37). By 1960, approximately two-thirds of the Asian population in California had been born in the United States (Ong 1989, pp. 5–8). As the Asian population became a native-born community, linguistic and cultural differences began to blur. Although they had attended Asian-language schools, most American-born Asians possessed only a limited knowledge of their ethnic language (Chan 1991, p. 115). By 1960, with English as the common language, persons from different Asian backgrounds were able to communicate with one another (Ling 1984, p. 73), and in so doing create a common identity associated with the United States.

Moreover, unlike their immigrant parents, native-born and American-educated Asians could muster only scant loyalties to old world ties. Historical antagonisms between their mother countries thus receded in importance (P. Wong 1972, p. 34). For example, growing up in America, second-generation Koreans "had difficulty feeling the painful loss of the homeland and understanding the indignity of Japanese domination" (Takaki 1989, p. 292). Thus, while the older generation of Koreans hated all Japanese, "their children were much less hostile or had no concern at all" (Melendy 1977, p. 156). As a native-born Japanese American community advocate explained, "By 1968, we had a second generation. We could speak English; so there was no language problem. And we had little feelings of historical animosity" (Kokubun interview).

As national differences receded in subjective importance, generational differences widened. For the most part, American-born Asians considered themselves to have more in common with other American-born Asians than they did with foreign-born compatriots. According to a third-generation Japanese American who is married to a Chinese American, "As far as our experiences in America, I have more things in common than differences with a Chinese American. Being born and raised here gives us something in common. We have more in common with each other than with a Japanese from Japan, or a Chinese from China" (Ichioka interview). Much to their parents' dismay, young Asian Americans began to choose their friends and spouses from other Asian groups. Eui-Young Yu (1983, p. 47) related that second- and third-generation Koreans "identify and intermingle as much with other Asian minorities as with fellow Koreans, especially with the Japanese and Chinese." Similarly, Stephen Fugita and David O'Brien (1991, p. 146) reported that the Sansei (third-generation) were much more likely than the Nisei (second-generation) to see themselves as Asian Americans. This muting of cultural and historical divisions distressed their parents, who, more often than not, had supported these divisions for most of their lives. As a young Chinese American asserted:

> My parents mean well and I try to respect them, but they do not understand what it's all about. We have buried the old hatreds between Chinese and Japanese, and my friends and I must go beyond our parents' "hang-ups." My mother is upset because I'm engaged to a Japanese girl but she knows she can do nothing about it. (Cited in Weiss 1974, p. 235)

The Watershed of World War II

Before World War II, Asian immigrant communities were quite distinct entities, isolated from one another and from the larger society. Because of language difficulties, prejudice, and lack of business opportunities elsewhere, there was little chance for Asians in the United States to live outside their ethnic enclaves (Yuan 1966, p. 331). Shut out of the mainstream of American society, the various immigrant groups struggled separately in their respective Chinatowns, Little Tokyos, or

Manilatowns. Stanford Lyman (1970, pp. 57–63) reported that the early Chinese and Japanese communities in the western states had little to do with one another—either socially or politically. Although statistical data do not exist, ethnographic accounts confirm the ethnic homogeneity of each early Asian immigrant community. For example, according to a study of New York's Chinatown in the 1890s, "The entire triangular space bounded by Mott, Pell, and Doyers Streets and Chatham Square is given to the exclusive occupancy of these Orientals" (cited in Yuan 1966, p. 323). Within these enclaves, diversity among Asian nationalities was more salient than commonality.

Economic and residential barriers began to crumble after World War II. The war against Nazism called attention to racism at home and discredited the notions of white superiority. The fifteen years after the war was a period of largely positive change as civil rights statutes outlawed racial discrimination in employment as well as housing (Daniels 1988, ch. 7). Popular attitudes were also changing. Polls taken during World War II showed a distinct hostility toward Japan: 74 percent of the respondents favored either killing off all Japanese, destroying Japan as a political entity, or supervising it. On the West Coast, 97 percent of the people polled approved of the relocation of Japanese Americans. In contrast, by 1949, 64 percent of those polled were either friendly or neutral toward Japan (Feraru 1950).

During the postwar years, Asian American residential patterns changed significantly. Because of the lack of statistical data, a longitudinal study of the changing residential patterns of Asian Americans cannot be made. However, descriptive accounts of Asian American communities indicate that these enclaves declined in the postwar years. Edwin Hoyt (1974, p. 94) reported that in the 1940s, second-generation Chinese Americans moved

TABLE 1   Mean Segregation Indices for Chinese and Japanese Americans in 822 U.S. Suburbs, 1960, 1970, and 1980

Ethnic Groups	1960	1970	1980	Change, 1960–80
Chinese–White	38.83	31.45	28.22	−10.61
Chinese–Black	54.02	50.42	49.43	−4.59
Japanese–White	34.00	22.16	26.77	−7.23
Japanese–Black	48.62	48.46	45.97	−2.65
Chinese–Japanese	39.11	27.70	24.97	−14.14

Source: Lam (1986: tables 1, 2, and 3).

out of the Chinatowns. Although they still came back to shop or to see friends, they lived elsewhere. In 1940, Rose Hum Lee found twenty-eight cities with an area called Chinatown in the United States. By 1955, Peter Sih found only sixteen (Sung 1967, pp. 143–44). New York's Chinatown exemplifies the declining significance of Asian ethnic enclaves. In 1940, 50 percent of the Chinese in New York City lived in its Chinatown; by 1960, less than one-third lived there (Yuan 1966, p. 331). Similarly, many returning Japanese Americans abandoned their prewar settlement in old central cities and joined the migration to suburbia (Daniels 1988, p. 294). In the early 1970s, Little Tokyo in Los Angeles remained a bustling Japanese American center, "but at night the shop owners [went] home to the houses in the suburbs" (Hoyt 1974, p. 84).

Although single-ethnic communities were still the norm, residential segregation between Asian nationalities declined in the postwar years. Formerly homogeneous, the ethnic enclaves started to house other Asian groups—as well as non-Asian groups. In 1957, driving past 7th and H streets in Washington, D.C., Betty Lee Sung (1967, pp. 142–43) reported, "I passed the length of Chinatown before I suddenly realized that the place was almost deserted. The faces that I did see on the street were not Chinese but Filipinos." In 1970, due to the influx of Japanese and Filipinos, there was a proposal to rename Oakland Chinatown "Asiantown"

(Sano 1970). Multigroup urban centers also emerged. Paul Wong (1972, p. 34) reported that since the early 1960s, Asian Americans of diverse national origins have moved into the suburbs outside the major Asian communities such as Berkeley or San Mateo, California. Although a small proportion of the local population, these Asian Americans tended to congregate in pockets; consequently, in some residential blocks a majority of the residents were Asian Americans.

Moreover, recent research on suburban segregation indicates that the level of segregation between certain Asian American groups is often less than that between them and non-Asians. Using Standard Metropolitan Statistical Area (SMSA) data for 1960, 1970, and 1980, Frankie Lam (1986) computed indices of dissimilarity (ID) among Chinese, Japanese, black, and white Americans in 822 suburbs. As indicated in Table 1, from 1960 to 1980 the level of segregation between Chinese and Japanese Americans was much less than that between these two groups and blacks and, in one case, less than that between these groups and whites. But the actual level of segregation is only one issue. The decline of segregation over time is another. From 1960 to 1980, Chinese segregation from the Japanese shows a more pronounced decline (−14.14) than that of Chinese or Japanese from whites (−10.61 and −7.23 respectively) and from blacks (−4.59 and −2.65 respectively). Though not comprehensive, these studies together suggest that Asian residential seg regation declined in the postwar years.

As various Asian groups in the United States interacted, they became aware of common problems and goals that transcended parochial interests and historical antagonisms. One recurrent problem was employment discrimination. According to a 1965 report published by the California Fair Employment Practices Commission, for every $51 earned by a white male Californian, Japanese males earned $43 and Chinese males $38—even though Chinese and Japanese American men had become slightly better educated than the white majority (Daniels 1988, p. 315). Moreover, although the postwar period marked the first time that well-trained Chinese and Japanese Americans could find suitable employment with relative ease, they continued to be passed over for promotion to administrative and supervisory positions (Kitano and Daniels 1988, p. 47). Asians in the United States began to see themselves as a group that shared important common experiences: exploitation, oppression, and discrimination (Uyematsu 1971).

Because inter-Asian contact and communication were greatest on college campuses, pan-Asianism was strongest there (P. Wong 1972, pp. 33–34). Exposure to one another and to the mainstream society led some young Asian Americans to feel that they were fundamentally different from whites. Disillusioned with the white society and alienated from their traditional communities, many Asian American student activists turned to the alternative strategy of pan-Asian unification (Weiss 1974, pp. 69–70).

The Construction of Pan-Asian Ethnicity

Although broader social struggles and internal demographic changes provided the impetus

for the Asian American movement, it was the group's politics—confrontational and explicitly pan-Asian—that shaped the movement's content. Influenced by the internal colonial model, which stresses the commonalities among "colonized groups," college students of Asian ancestry declared solidarity with fellow Asian Americans— and with other Third World minorities (Blauner 1972, ch. 2). Rejecting the label "Oriental," they proclaimed themselves "Asian American." Through pan-Asian organizations, publications, and Asian American studies programs, Asian American activists built pan-Asian solidarity by point ing out their common fate in American society. The pan-Asian concept enabled diverse Asian American groups to understand their "unequal circumstances and histories as being related" (Lowe 1991, p. 30).

From "Yellow" to "Asian American"

Following the example of the Black Power movement, Asian American activists spearheaded their own Yellow Power movement to seek "freedom from racial oppression through the power of a consolidated yellow people" (Uyematsu 1971, p. 12). In the summer of 1968, more than one hundred students of diverse Asian backgrounds attended an "Are You Yellow?" conference at UCLA to discuss issues of Yellow Power, identity, and the war in Vietnam. In 1970, a new pan-Asian organization in northern California called itself the "Yellow Seed" because "Yellow [is] the common bond between Asian-Americans and Seed symboliz[es] growth as an individual and as an alliance" (Masada 1970). This "yellow" reference was dropped when Filipino Americans rejected the term, claiming that they were brown, not yellow (Ignacio 1976, p. 84; Rabaya 1971, p. 110). At the first Asian American national conference in 1972, Filipino Americans "made it clear to the conferees that we were 'Brown Asians'" by forming a Brown Asian Caucus (Ignacio 1976, pp. 139–41). It is important to note, however, that Filipino American activists did not reject the term "yellow" because they objected to the pan-Asian framework. Quite the contrary, they rejected it because it allegedly excluded them from that grouping (Rabaya 1971, p. 110).

Other community organizers used the term "Oriental" to define their organizations and service centers. In Southern California, the Council of Oriental Organizations (COO) became the political base for the diverse Asian American communities. In 1968, COO lobbied for federal funding to establish the Oriental Service Center in Los Angeles County, serving Chinese, Japanese, Filipinos, and Koreans. But Asian American activists also rejected *Oriental* because the term conjures up images of "the sexy Susie Wong, the wily Charlie Chan, and the evil Fu Manchu" (Weiss 1974, p. 234). It is also a term that smacks of European colonialism and imperialism: *Oriental* means "East"; Asia is "east" only in relationship to Europe, which was taken as the point of reference (Browne 1985). To define their own image and to claim an *American* identity, college students of Asian ancestry coined the term *Asian American* to "stand for all of us Americans of Asian descent" (Ichioka interview). While *Oriental* suggests passivity and acquiescence, *Asian Americans* connotes political activism because an Asian American "gives a damn about his life, his work, his beliefs, and is willing to do almost anything to help Orientals become Asian Americans" (cited in Weiss 1974, p. 234).

The account above suggests that the creation of a new name is a significant symbolic move in constructing an ethnic identity. In their attempt to forge a pan-Asian identity, Asian American activists first had to coin a composite term that would unify and encompass the constituent groups. Filipino Americans' rejection of the term "yellow" and the activists' objection to the cliché-ridden *Oriental* forced the group to change its name to Asian American. . . . It is noteworthy that while *Yellow, Oriental,* and *Asian American* connote different ideologies, all three terms signify panethnicity. . . .

Conclusion

The development of a pan-Asian consciousness and constituency reflected broader societal developments and demographic changes, as well as the group's political agenda. By the late 1960s, pan-Asianism was possible because of the more amicable relationships among the Asian countries, the declining residential segregation among diverse Asian groups in America, and the large number of native-born, American-educated political actors. Disillusioned with the larger society and estranged from their traditional communities, third- and fourth-generation Asian Americans turned to the alternative strategy of pan-Asian unification. Through pan-Asian organizations, media, and Asian American Studies programs, these political activists assumed the role of "cultural entrepreneurs" consciously creating a community of culture out of diverse Asian peoples. This process of pan-Asian consolidation did not proceed smoothly nor did it encompass all Asian Americans. Ethnic chauvinism, competition for scarce resources, and class cleavages continued to divide the subgroups. However, once established, the pan-Asian structure not only reinforced the cohesiveness of already existing networks but also expanded these networks. Although first conceived by young Asian American activists, the pan-Asian concept was subsequently institutionalized by professionals and community groups, as well as government agencies. The confrontational politics of the activists eventually gave way to the conventional and electoral politics of the politicians, lobbyists, and professionals, as Asian Americans continued to rely on the pan-Asian framework to enlarge their political capacities.

REFERENCES

Barth, Frederick. 1969. *Ethnic Groups and Boundaries.* Boston: Little, Brown.

Blauner, Robert. 1972. *Racial Oppression in America.* New York: Harper & Row.

Bonacich, Edna, and John Modell. 1980. *The Economic Basis of Ethnic Solidarity: A Study of Japanese Americans.* Berkeley: University of California Press.

Browne, Blain T. 1985. "A Common Thread: American Images of the Chinese and Japanese, 1930–1960." Ph.D. dissertation, University of Oklahoma.

Chan, Sucheng. 1991. *Asian Americans: An Interpretive History.* Boston: Twayne.

Cornell, Stephen. 1988. *The Return of the Native: Native American Political Resurgence.* New York: Oxford University Press.

Daniels, Roger. 1988. *Asian America: Chinese and Japanese in the United States Since 1850.* Seattle: University of Washington Press.

Enloe, Cynthia H. 1980. *Police, Military, and Ethnicity: Foundations of State Power.* New Brunswick, NJ: Transaction Books.

Feraru, Arthur N. 1950. "Public Opinion Polls on Japan." *Far Eastern Survey* 19(10):101–103.

Fugita, Stephen S., and David J. O'Brien. 1991. *Japanese American Ethnicity: The Persistence of Community.* Seattle: University of Washington Press.

Hein, Jeremy. 1989. "States and Political Migrants: The Incorporation of Indochinese Refugees in France and the United States." Ph.D. dissertation, Northwestern University.

Hoyt, Edwin P. 1974. *Asians in the West.* New York: Thomas Nelson.

Ignacio, Lemuel F. 1976. *Asian Americans and Pacific Islanders (Is There Such an Ethnic Group?)* San Jose, CA: Filipino Development Associates.

Kim, Illsoo. 1981. *New Urban Immigrants: The Korean Community in New York.* Princeton, NJ: Princeton University Press.

Kitano, Harry H. L., and Roger Daniels. 1988. *Asian Americans: Emerging Minorities.* Englewood Cliffs, NJ: Prentice-Hall.

Lam, Frankie. 1986. "Suburban Residential Segregation of Chinese and Japanese Americans, 1960, 1970, and 1980." *Sociology and Social Research* 70(4):263–65

Ling, Susie Hsiuhan. 1984. "The Mountain Movers: Asian American Women's Movement in Los Angeles." *Amerasia Journal* 15(1):51–67.

Liu, John. 1988. "The Relationship of Migration Research to Asian American Studies: Unity and Diversity Within the Curriculum." Pp. 117–25 in *Reflections on Shattered Windows,* edited by Gary Okihiro, Shirley Hune, Arthur Hansen, and John Liu. Pullman: Washington State University Press.

Lopez, David, and Yen Espiritu. 1990. "Panethnicity in the United States: A Theoretical Framework." *Ethnic and Racial Studies* 13(2): 198–224.

Lowe, Lisa. 1991. "Heterogeneity, Hybridity, Multiplicity: Marking Asian American Differences." *Diaspora* 1:24–44.

Lyman, Stanford M. 1970. *The Asian in the West.* Reno and Las Vegas: Desert Research Institute, University of Nevada.

Masada, Saburo. 1970. "Stockton's Yellow Seed." *Pacific Citizen,* 9 October.

Melendy, H. Brett. 1977. *Asians in America: Filipinos, Koreans, and East Indians.* Boston: Twayne.

Montero, Darrell. 1979. *Vietnamese Americans: Patterns of Resettlement and Socioeconomic Adaptations in the United States.* Boulder, CO: Westview Press.

Nagel, Joane. 1982. "The Political Mobilization of Native Americans." *Social Science Journal* 19: 37–45.

———. 1986. "The Political Construction of Ethnicity." Pp. 93–112 in *Competitive Ethnic Relations,* edited by Susan Olzal and Joane Nagel. San Diego: Academic Press.

Ong, Paul. 1989. "California's Asian Population: Past Trends and Projections for the Year 2000." Los Angeles: Graduate School of Architecture and Urban Planning.

Padilla, Felix M. 1985. *Latino Ethnic Consciousness: The Case of Mexican Americans and Puerto Ricans in Chicago.* Notre Dame, IN: Notre Dame University Press.

Rabaya, Violet. 1971. "I Am Curious (Yellow?)." Pp. 110–11 in *Roots: An Asian American Reader,* edited by Amy Tachiki, Eddie Wong, and Franklin Odo. Los Angeles: UCLA Asian American Studies Center.

Sano, Roy. 1970. "Asiantown in Oakland." *Pacific Citizen,* 4 August.

Shibutani, Tamotsu, and Kian M. Kwan. 1965. *Ethnic Stratification.* New York: Macmillan.

Skinner, Kenneth, and Glen Hendricks. 1979. "The Shaping of Self-Identity Among Indochinese Refugees." *Journal of Ethnic Studies* 7:25–41.

Sung, Betty Lee. 1967. *Mountain of Gold: The Story of the Chinese in America.* New York: Macmillan.

Takaki, Ronald. 1989. *Strangers from a Different Shore: A History of Asian Americans.* Boston: Little, Brown.

Trottier, Richard. 1981. "Charters of Panethnic Identity: Indigenous American Indians and Immigrant Asian Americans." Pp. 271–305 in *Ethnic Change,* edited by Charles F. Keyes. Seattle: University of Washington Press.

Uyematsu, Amy. 1971. "The Emergence of Yellow Power in America." Pp. 9–13 in *Roots: An Asian American Reader,* edited by Amy Tachiki, Eddie Wong, and Franklin Odo. Los Angeles: UCLA Asian American Studies Center.

Weiss, Melford S. 1974. *Valley City: A Chinese Community in America.* Cambridge, MA: Schenkman.

Wong, Paul. 1972. "The Emergence of the Asian American Movement." *Bridge* 2(1):33–39.

Yu, Eui-Young. 1983. "Korean Communities in America: Past, Present, and Future." *Amerasia Journal* 10(2):23–51.

Yuan, D. Y. 1966. "Chinatown and Beyond: The Chinese Population in Metropolitan New York." *Phylon* 23(4):321–32.

Zia, Helen. 1984. "The Real Violence." *Bridge* 9(2):18–23.

SEEING THE BIG PICTURE

Look at Asians relative to other groups in Section VI (Income, Wealth, and Poverty) and sections VII (Employment) and VIII (Occupations) in the Appendix. Might panethnic identity formation as a political strategy explain the relative success of Asians? How?

12

BEYOND BLACK AND WHITE: REMAKING RACE IN AMERICA

Jennifer Lee • Frank D. Bean

QUESTIONS TO CONSIDER

*Much has been made of recent U.S. Census reports that Latinos are now the largest racial minority in the United States. Equally important but not as widely addressed in the media has been the relative explosion of individuals who self-identify as "multiracial." Tiger Woods (Cablinasian: **Caucasian-Black-Indian Asian**), Vin Diesel (white Italian-American and African*

American) and Halle Berry (white mother and African American father) each have made a point to publicly celebrate and affirm their hybrid ethnic and racial identities. What do Lee and Bean say these trends mean for the future of the color line as the children of mixed race unions age out and have their own children? Will racial categories as we know them blur into one another or are we likely to see new categories emerge that serve to maintain racial hierarchy and inequality?

S tarting with the 2000 census, Americans could officially label themselves and their children as members of more than one race. Nearly 7 million Americans, 2.4 percent of the nation's population, were recorded as being multiracial. This option and these numbers signal a profound loosening of the rigid racial and ethnic boundaries that have so long divided the country. The immigration patterns behind these changes also point to potentially important realignments in America's color lines.

How might a black father and a white mother fill out official government documents, like U. S. Census forms, requiring them to designate the race of their child? Before 2000, such an intermarried couple had no alternative but to list their child as either black or white. Similarly, a child born to a white father and an Asian mother had to be listed as either Asian or white, but not Asian and white. Not any more. Americans can now officially identify themselves and their children as black and white, or white and Asian. Indeed, respondents can now choose a combination of up to six different categories of races, including "Other." The 2000 Census reported one in every forty Americans was registered as belonging to two or more racial groups. Many sociologists think this ratio could soar to one in five Americans by the year 2050.

Why does this checking of additional boxes matter? For one thing, how people report themselves racially provides information needed to implement and enforce important legislation, such as the Voting Rights Act. The Department of Justice uses the statistics to identify places where substantial minority populations exist and may be subject to disenfranchisement. For another, the counts document social and economic disparities among racial groups in America. Countries like France that do not collect data on race cannot verify the existence and effects of racial discrimination even when other evidence suggests such discrimination is a major problem. These data also signal the official recognition and hence the influence of groups that define themselves on the basis of common national origin, skin color or ancestry. Americans of Pacific Islander origin, for example, recently asked to be separately classified. On the other hand, critics worry that official data on race perpetuate rather than eliminate racial identities and divisions. A ballot initiative being circulated in California, for example, would largely ban the state's collection of racial information.

But the new opportunity to mark more than one race is also important because it indicates that people can now officially recognize the mixing of racial backgrounds in American society. If the United States was once thought of as a black-and-white society, this is certainly no longer so. Continued immigration from Latin America and Asia, the rise in intermarriage over the past 30 years, and the formal recognition of the multiracial population are moving America far beyond black and white. Yet while America's increasing diversity implies that racial divisions may be weakening, it does not mean that race has become irrelevant. Instead, new kinds of color lines may be emerging. For now, however, the rearrangement seems to leave African Americans facing a new black-nonblack, instead of the old black-white, racial divide.

Why There Are More Multiracial Americans

The growth of the multiracial population is a result both of increasing intermarriage between whites and nonwhites and of peoples' increasing willingness to report their multiracial backgrounds. The number of racial intermarriages in the United States grew from 150,000 in 1960 to 1.6 million in 1990—a tenfold increase over three decades. It is still the exception rather than the rule for whites and blacks in this country, however. Just 6 percent of whites and 10 percent of blacks marry someone of a different race. By contrast, more than one-quarter of all native-born Asians and Latinos marry someone of a different race. (For this discussion, we will speak of Latinos as if they were a "race," although government forms count Hispanic background separately, so that people who say they are Latino can report themselves as belonging to any racial group, such as white, black, or Asian.) Even more striking is that two of every five young Latinos and two of every three young Asians born in the United States marry someone of a different race, and the majority marry whites. Asians and Latinos—many of whom are either immigrants or the children of immigrants—are three times as likely to marry whites as blocks are to marry whites.

Coinciding with the rise in intermarriage has been the growth of a new immigrant stream from Latin America and Asia. Today, immigrants and their children total more than 60 million people, approximately 22 percent of the U.S. population. The increase in immigration from non-European countries over the past 35 years has converted the United States from a largely white and black society into one that is comprised of numerous racial and ethnic groups. This, plus increasing intermarriage, and the increasing willingness of Americans to call themselves multiracial has changed the way race is measured in America.

Constructing Race

Social scientists generally agree that race is not a biological category, but a social and cultural construction, meaning that racial distinctions have not existed since time immemorial, are not rooted in biology and are not fixed. Rather, they have changed and been reinterpreted throughout our nation's history. For instance, when the Irish, Italians, and Jews first arrived in the United States in the 19th century, Anglo Americans considered them racially distinct and inferior. They were not considered white. However, they successfully achieved "whiteness" by deliberately and forcefully distinguishing themselves from African Americans. Today, few would contest the claim that the Irish, Italians and Jews are white.

Race and racial boundaries have changed for other groups as well. For example, Asian ethnic groups like the Chinese in Mississippi have changed their racial status from almost black to almost white. Sociologist James Loewen details how the Chinese there achieved near-white status by becoming as economically successful as whites, copying their cultural and social practices, and distancing themselves from African Americans and Chinese Mississippians who married African Americans.

As historian Gary Gerstle explains, whiteness as a category "has survived by stretching its boundaries to include Americans—the Irish, eastern and southern Europeans—who had been deemed nonwhite. Contemporary evidence suggests that the boundaries are again being stretched as Latinos and Asians pursue whiteness much as the Irish, Italians, and Poles did before them." Given the change in racial boundaries over time, it is likely that the boundaries may continue to stretch to include newer groups. For instance, some sociologists argue that Asians are the next in line to become white. Whether or not they do, we should understand that race is a cultural product that has changed over time, rather than a fixed, primordial category rooted in biology.

The Origin of "Mark One or More Races"

Since its inception in 1790, the decennial U.S. Census has determined taxation, the numbers of representatives from each state, and the boundaries of Congressional districts. And it has always counted the U.S. population by race. The way that race is measured and even the racial categories themselves, however, have changed considerably. For example, in 1850, the Census added the category "mulatto," and in 1890, it added the categories "quadroon" and "octoroon" in an effort to more precisely measure the representation of black mixtures in the population. ("Mulatto" refers to people of mixed black and white "blood," "quadroon" to people with one-fourth black blood, and "octoroon" to those with one-eighth black blood.) However, "quadroon" and "octoroon" were promptly removed in 1900 because they caused countless statistical inaccuracies. The Census Board determined that the "mulatto" category provided clearer data on the U.S. population with mixed blood, but eventually dropped this category in 1930. By that time, the law of the country, with the census following suit, had adopted the "one-drop rule" of hypodescent (by which all persons with any trace of black ancestry were labeled racially black) as an appropriate criterion by which to attempt to measure race. Importantly, census enumerators classified the people they interviewed by race.

In the 1960s, racial categories came under scrutiny once again, and the Civil Rights Movement prompted one of the most significant changes in the political context and purpose of racial categorization. The argument spread that Americans should be able to mark their own race to identify themselves and their children rather than leaving this to enumerators. Some politicians and experts asserted that the racial categories should more accurately reflect America's diversity and lobbied for new categories, distinguishing among categories of whites, and substituting the term "ethnic" in place of "race." Changes in the 1970 Census reflected some of these currents, with self-identification replacing enumerator identification in order to satisfy public sentiments. By the mid-1970s, groups wanting to be recognized as racial minorities organized advisory committees to seek official statistical representation so that they could participate in federal programs designed to assist racial "minorities." These advisory committees lobbied for the adoption of five racial categories—white, black, Asian, Native American, and other—by the Census and all federal agencies. In 1980, the Census categories changed yet again, this time including the category of Hispanic origin separately from race, and modifying one of the racial categories to Asian-Pacific Islander.

During the early 1990s, new advocacy groups arose with a different agenda. These groups criticized the government standards for not accurately reflecting the diversity in the country brought about by increases in immigration and interracial marriage. In particular, advocates from groups such as the Association for Multi-Ethnic Americans (AMEA) and Project RACE (Reclassify All Children Equally) lobbied the Census Bureau to adopt a "multiracial" category. Advocates argued that it was an affront to force them or their children into a single racial category. Furthermore, they argued that forced mono-racial identification was inaccurate because it denies the existence of interracial marriages, and is ultimately discriminatory. A year later in 1994, the Office of Management and Budget (OMB), which managed this issue, acknowledged that the racial categories were of decreasing value and considered an alternate strategy: allowing respondents to identify with as many races as they wished. While the spokespeople for the multiracial movement were not entirely satisfied with this option, they conceded that it was an improvement over forced mono-racial identification.

Not everyone favored adding a multi-racial category or allowing Americans to mark more than one race. Civil rights groups—and in particular, black civil rights groups such as the NAACP—strongly objected. They feared that those who would otherwise be counted as black or Hispanic would now choose to identify as multiracial, and, depending on how such persons were counted, diminish their official counts. This, in turn, could undermine enforcement of the Voting Rights Act and potentially reduce the size and effectiveness of government programs aimed at helping minorities.

On October 30, 1997 the Census Bureau announced its final decision that all persons would have the option to identify with two or more races, starting with the 2000 Census and extending to all federal data systems by the year 2003. The racial options on the 2000 Census included "White," "Black," "Asian," "Native Hawaiian or Other Pacific Islander,"

"American Indian and Alaska Native," and "Other." While "Latino" or "Hispanic" was not a racial category on the 2000 Census, OMB mandated two distinct questions: one on race and a second asking whether a person is "Spanish/Hispanic/Latino." Because those who classify themselves as "Spanish/Hispanic/ Latino" can be of any race, the Census asks both questions in order to identify the Latino population in the United States.

The Census Bureau's decision to allow Americans to "mark one or more races" is a landmark change in the way the U.S. government collects data on race. Perhaps even more importantly, it gives official status and recognition to individuals who see themselves or their children as having mixed racial heritage—an acknowledgement that speaks volumes about how far the country has come since the days when the "one-drop rule" enjoyed legal legitimacy. Moreover, such changes may mean that old racial divides are beginning to fade. Multiracial reporting, however, has not been equally distributed across all racial and ethnic groups. Rather, those who choose to mark two or more races are distinctive.

Who Are the Multiracials?

Interracial marriage was illegal in 16 states as recently as 1967, but today, about 13 percent of American marriages involve persons of different races. If we go back even further to 1880, the rates of intermarriage among Asians and Latinos in this country were close to zero, but now, more than a quarter of all native-born Asians and Latinos marry someone of a different racial background, mostly whites. As we noted, in 2000, 6.8 million people, or 2.4 percent of the population, were reported as multiracial. While these figures may not appear large, a recent National Academy of Science study estimated that the multiracial population could rise to 21 percent by the

TABLE 1   Multiracial Identification by Race: People Recorded as One Race Who Are Also Recorded as One or More Other Races

	Racial Identification (millions)	Multiracial Identification (millions)	Percent Multiracial
White	216.5	5.1	2.3%
Black	36.2	1.5	4.2
Asian	11.7	1.4	12.4
Other	18.4	3.0	16.4
American Indian and Alaska Native	3.9	1.4	36.4
Native Hawaiian or other Pacific Islander	0.7	0.3	44.8

Source: U.S. Census 2000

year 2050 because of rising intermarriage, when as many as 35 percent of Asians and 45 percent of Hispanics could claim a multiracial background. Of the multiracial population in 2000, 93 percent reported two races, 6 percent reported three races, and 1 percent reported four or more races.

As Table 1 illustrates, the groups with high percentages of multiracial persons include "Native Hawaiian or Other Pacific Islander," "American Indian and Alaska Native," "Other," and "Asian." The categories with the lowest proportion of persons who claim a multiracial background are "White" and "Black."

The proportion of blacks who identify as multiracial is quite small, accounting for just 4.2 percent of the total black population. These figures stand in sharp contrast to those among American Indian/Alaska Natives and Native Hawaiian or other Pacific Islanders who have the highest percentage of multiracials as a proportion of their populations at 36.4 and 44.8 percent, respectively. The particular combinations are of interest. Among those identified as black, Asian, or Latino, 2 percent, 7 percent, and 5 percent, respectively, also claim a White identity. Among Asians, the Asian-white multiracial combination is about three and a half times more likely to occur, and among Latinos, the Latino-white combination is more than two and a half times

more likely to occur, as the black-white combination occurs among blacks. Why this is so is particularly perplexing when we consider that the Census Bureau has estimated that at least three-quarters of black Americans have some white ancestry and thus could claim a multiracial identity on this basis alone.

The tendency of black Americans not to report multiracial identifications undoubtedly owes in part to the legacy of slavery, lasting discrimination, and both the legal and de facto invocation of the "one-drop rule." For no other racial or ethnic group in the United States does the one-drop rule limit identity choices and options. Recent sociological studies find that about 50 percent of American Indian-white and Asian-white intermarried couples report a white racial identity for their children. In a study of multiracial Hispanic students, we found that 44 percent chose a Hispanic identity. Without the imposition of the "one-drop rule" that historically imposed a black racial identity on multiracial black Americans, multiracial Asians, Latinos, and American Indians appear to have much more leeway to choose among different racial options.

In addition, because a significant proportion of Latinos and Asians in the United States are either immigrants or the children of immigrants, their understanding of race, racial boundaries, and the black-white color divide is shaped by a different set of circumstances than those of African Americans. Most importantly, Latinos' and Asians' experiences are not rooted in the same legacy of slavery with its systematic and persistent patterns of legal and institutional discrimination and inequality through which the tenacious black-white divide was formed and cemented. For these reasons, racial and ethnic boundaries appear more fluid for the newest immigrants than for native-born blacks, providing multiracial Asians and Latinos more racial options than their black counterparts.

Remaking Race and Redrawing the Color Line

What do current trends and patterns in immigration, intermarriage, and multiracial identification tell us about the remaking of race in America? It appears that increases in intermarriage and the growth of the multiracial population reflect a blending of races and the shifting of color lines. Because interracial marriage and multiracial identification indicate a reduction in social distance and racial prejudice, these phenomena provide evidence of loosening racial boundaries. At first glance, these patterns offer an optimistic portrait of the weakening of color lines. For instance, interracial marriage was illegal in 16 states as recently as 1967, but today, about 13 percent of American marriages involve persons of different races. If we go back even further to 1880, the rates of intermarriage among Asians and Latinos in this country were close to zero, but now, more than a quarter of all native-born Asians and Latinos marry someone of a different racial background, mostly whites.

Yet, upon closer examination, we find that patterns of intermarriage and multiracial identification are not similar across all groups. Not only are Latinos and Asians more likely to intermarry than blacks, they are also more likely to report a multiracial identification. These different rates suggest that while racial boundaries may be fading, they are not disappearing at the same pace for all groups.

What is crucial here is how we interpret the intermarriage and multiracial identification rates for Latinos and Asians. If we consider Latinos and Asians as discriminated-against racial minorities, closer to blacks than whites in their social disadvantages, then their high levels of multiracial identification suggest that racial border lines might be fading for all nonwhite groups. Latinos and Asians look more, however, like immigrant groups whose disadvantages derive from their not having had time to join the economic mainstream, but who soon will. Their high levels of intermarriage and multiracial reporting therefore signal an experience and trajectory different from that of blacks. Their situations do not necessarily indicate that similar assimilation can be expected among blacks.

Based on the patterns of intermarriage and multiracial identification noted above, the color line appears less rigid for Latinos and Asians than blacks. Asians and Latinos have high rates of intermarriage and multiracial reporting because they were not and are not treated as blacks have been. While the color line may also be shifting for blacks, this shift is occurring more slowly, leaving Asians and Latinos socially nearer to whites. Much of America's racial history has revolved around who was white and who was not; the next phase may revolve instead around who is black and who is not.

The emergence of a black-nonblack divide in a context where diversity is increasing and other racial and ethnic boundaries are diminishing represents a good news-bad news outcome for America. That a white-nonwhite color line does not seem to be enduring is the good news. But that newer nonwhite immigrant groups appear to be jumping ahead of African Americans in a hierarchy still divided by race is the bad news. Based on immigration, intermarriage, and multiracial identification, it appears that Latinos and Asians are closer to whites than to blacks, and consequently may be participants in a new color line that continues to disadvantage blacks.

As a final matter, one might ask: What does all of this imply for the future of measuring race in the census? Critics of racial labels argue that if racial and ethnic boundaries are loosening, we should abandon the use of racial categories in the census altogether and learn to get along without them in our policy making. They argue that if racial labels could be eliminated, racial discrimination itself would be eradicated. However, in the United States today, because the practice of discrimination based on physical characteristics such as skin color continues to persist, at least for African Americans, eradicating racial labels would simply put us in a position where we know less about the disadvantages experienced by blacks and can do less about it.

REFERENCES

Bean, Frank D., and Gillian Stevens. *America's Newcomers and the Dynamics of Diversity.* New York: Russell Sage Foundation, 2003. This book explores the significance of immigration for America, including its implications for loosening racial and ethnic boundaries.

Davis, F. James. *Who is Black? One Nation's Definition.* University Park, PA: Pennsylvania State University Press, 1991. Davis details the history of the "one-drop rule" in the United States.

Gerstle, Gary. "Liberty, Coercion, and the Making of Americans." In *The Handbook of Inter-national Migration,* edited by Charles Hirschman, Philip Kasinitz, and Josh DeWind. New York: Russell Sage Foundation, 1991. A history of racial categories and how they have changed.

Loewen, James. *The Mississippi Chinese: Between Black and White.* Cambridge, MA: Harvard University Press, 1971. Loewen shows how Chinese immigrants changed their racial classification from almost black to almost white.

Nobles, Melissa. *Shades of Citizenship: Race and the Census in Modern Politics.* Stanford, CA: Stanford University Press, 2000. A history or racial categories in the Census in the United States.

Perlmann, Joel, and Mary C. Waters, eds. *The New Race Question: How the Census Counts Multiracial Individuals.* New York: Russell Sage Foundation, 2002. This anthology examines the history of racial enumeration, the likely effects of the Census change in the race question, and possible policy implications for the future.

Qian, Zhenchao. "Breaking the Racial Barriers: Variations in Interracial Marriage Between 1980 and 1990." *Demography* 34, 2 (1997), 263–276. This study illustrates the growing trends in interracial marriage.

Waters, Mary C. "Multiple Ethnicities and Identity in the United States." In *We Are a People: Narrative and Multiplicity in Constructing Identity,* edited by Paul Spikard and W. Jeffrey Burroughs. Philadelphia: Temple University Press, 2000. Water examines the different ways interracial couples identify their children.

SEEING THE BIG PICTURE

Section X in the Appendix lists the percentage of Americans who identify with more than one race. How might you interpret the fact that Latino and American Indians are more likely than whites or blacks to claim more than one race?

COLORBLIND AMERICA:
FACT, FANTASY, OR OUR FUTURE?

13

COLOR BLIND PRIVILEGE: THE SOCIAL AND POLITICAL FUNCTIONS OF ERASING THE COLOR LINE IN POST-RACE AMERICA

Charles A. Gallagher

QUESTIONS TO CONSIDER

The dominant view in the United States is that we are now a colorblind nation. Rap and hip-hop are thoroughly mainstream commodities available for sale in every mall across the country. Celebrities, CEOs, high-level politicians, and opinion makers are drawn from every racial and ethnic group. Race, the mainstream media would have us believe, no longer matters. Charles A. Gallagher argues that the story of color-blindness promoted in the mass media disguises a more troubling reality: continued racial inequality. How does presenting the United States as a colorblind nation serve various political, ideological, and social functions?

Introduction

An adolescent white male at a bar mitzvah wears a FUBU[1] shirt while his white friend preens his tightly set, perfectly braided corn rows. A black model dressed in yachting attire peddles a New England yuppie boating look in Nautica advertisements. It is quite

Charles A. Gallagher, "Color Blind Privilege: The Social and Political Functions of Erasing the Color Line in Post-Race America" from the *RGC Journal Special Edition on Privilege*, Abby L. Ferber and Dena R. Samuels, co-editors, Vol. 10, No. 4, 2003.

unremarkable to observe whites, Asians, or African Americans with dyed purple, blond, or red hair. White, black, and Asian students decorate their bodies with tattoos of Chinese characters and symbols. In cities and suburbs, young adults across the color line wear hip-hop clothing and listen to white rapper Eminem and black rapper Jay-Z. A north Georgia branch of the NAACP installs a white biology professor as its president. The music of Jimi Hendrix is used to sell Apple Computers. Du-Rag kits, complete with bandana headscarf and elastic headband, are on sale for $2.95 at hip-hop clothing stores and family-centered theme parks like Six Flags. Salsa has replaced ketchup as the best-selling condiment in the United States. Companies as diverse as Polo, McDonald's, Tommy Hilfiger, Walt Disney World, Master Card, Skechers sneakers, IBM, Giorgio Armani, and Neosporin antibiotic ointment have each crafted advertisements that show a balanced, multiracial cast of characters interacting and consuming their products in a post-race, color-blind world.[2]

Americans are constantly bombarded by depictions of race relations in the media which suggest that discriminatory racial barriers have been dismantled. Social and cultural indicators suggest that America is on the verge, or has already become, a truly color-blind nation. National polling data indicate that a majority of whites now believe discrimination against racial minorities no longer exists. A majority of whites believe that blacks have as good a chance as whites in procuring housing and employment or achieving middle-class status while a 1995 survey of white adults found that a majority of whites (58%) believed that African Americans were better off finding jobs than whites.[3] Much of white America now sees a level playing field, while a majority of black Americans see a field which is still quite uneven. Best-selling books like The *End of Racism*[4] and *Color-Blind: Seeing Beyond Race in a Race-Obsessed World* suggest the United States is not very far from making color blindness a social and political reality.[5] The color-blind or race neutral perspective holds that in an environment where institutional racism and discrimination have been replaced by equal opportunity, one's qualifications, not one's color or ethnicity, should be the mechanism by which upward mobility is achieved. Whites and blacks differ significantly, however, on their support for affirmative action, the perceived fairness of the criminal justice system, the ability to

acquire the "American Dream," and the extent to which whites have benefited from past discrimination.[6]

This article examines the social and political functions color blindness serves for whites in the United States. Drawing on information compiled from interviews and focus groups with whites around the country, I argue that color blindness maintains white privilege by negating racial inequality. Embracing a post-race, color-blind perspective provides whites with a degree of psychological comfort by allowing them to imagine that being white or black or brown has no bearing on an individual's or a group's relative place in the socioeconomic hierarchy. My research included interviews with seventeen focus groups and thirty individual whites around the country. While my sample is not representative of the total white population, I used personal contacts and snowball sampling to purposively locate respondents raised in urban, suburban, and rural environments. Twelve of the seventeen focus groups were conducted in a university setting, one in a liberal arts college in the Rocky Mountains and the other at a large urban university in the Northeast. Respondents in these focus groups were selected randomly from the student population. The occupational range for my individual interviews was quite eclectic and included a butcher, construction worker, hair stylist, partner in a prestigious corporate law firm, executive secretary, high school principal, bank president from a small town, retail workers, country lawyer, and custodial workers. Twelve of the thirty individual interviews were with respondents who were raised in rural and/or agrarian settings. The remaining respondents lived in suburbs of large cities or in urban areas.

What linked this rather disparate group of white individuals together was their belief that race-based privilege had ended. As a majority of my respondents saw it, color blindness was now the norm in the United

States. The illusion of racial equality implicit in the myth of color blindness was, for many whites, a form of comfort. This aspect of pleasure took the form of political empowerment ("what about whites' rights") and moral gratification from being liberated from "oppressor" charges ("we are not responsible for the past"). The rosy picture that color blindness presumes about race relations and the satisfying sense that one is part of a period in American history that is morally superior to the racist days of the past is, quite simply, a less stressful and more pleasurable social place for whites to inhabit.

The Norm of Color Blindness

The perception among a majority of white Americans that the socioeconomic playing field is now level, along with whites' belief that they have purged themselves of overt racist attitudes and behaviors, has made color blindness the dominant lens through which whites understand contemporary race relations. Color blindness allows whites to believe that segregation and discrimination are no longer an issue because it is now illegal for individuals to be denied access to housing, public accommodations, or jobs because of their race. Indeed, lawsuits alleging institutional racism against companies like Texaco, Denny's, Coca Cola, and Cracker Barrel validate what many whites know at a visceral level is true; firms which deviate from the color-blind norms embedded in classic liberalism will be punished. As a political ideology, the commodification and mass marketing of products that signify color but are intended for consumption across the color line further legitimate color blindness. Almost every household in the United States has a television that, according to the U.S. Census, is on for seven hours every day.[7] Individuals from any racial background can wear hip-hop clothing, listen to rap music (both purchased at Wal-Mart) and root for their favorite, majority black, professional sports team. Within the context of racial symbols that are bought and sold in the market, color blindness means that one's race has no bearing on who can purchase an SUV, live in an exclusive neighborhood, attend private schools, or own a Rolex.

The passive interaction whites have with people of color through the media creates the impression that little, if any, socioeconomic difference exists between the races. Research has found that whites who are exposed to images of upper-middle class African Americans, like the Huxtable family in *The Cosby Show*, believe that blacks have the same socioeconomic opportunities as whites.[8] Highly visible and successful racial minorities like Secretary of State Colin Powell and National Security Advisor Condoleezza Rice are further proof to white America that the nation's efforts to enforce and promote racial equality have been accomplished. Reflecting on the extent to which discrimination is an obstacle to socioeconomic advancement and the perception of seeing African Americans in leadership roles, Tom explained:

> If you look at some prominent black people in society today, and I don't really see [racial discrimination], I don't understand how they can keep bringing this problem onto themselves. If they did what society would want them to, I don't see that society is making problems for them. I don't see it.

The achievement ideology implicit in the color-blind perspective is also given legitimacy and stripped of any racist implications by black neoconservatives like antiaffirmative action advocate Ward Connerly, Shelby Steele, and Clarence Thomas, and Asian American Secretary of Labor Elaine Chou.[9] Each espouses a color-blind, raceneutral doctrine that treats race-based government programs as a violation of the sacrosanct belief that American society only recognizes the rights of individuals. These individuals also serve as an important public example that in a post-race, color-blind society climbing the occupational ladder is now a matter of individual choice.

The new color-blind ideology does not, however, ignore race; it acknowledges race while ignoring racial hierarchy by taking racially coded styles and products and reducing these symbols to commodities or experiences which whites and racial minorities can purchase and share. It is through such acts of shared consumption that race becomes nothing more than an innocuous cultural signifier. Large corporations have made American culture more homogenous through the ubiquity of fast food, television, and shopping malls but this trend has also created the illusion that we are all the same through consumption. Most adults eat at national fast-food chains like McDonald's, shop at mall anchor stores like Sears and J. C. Penney's, and watch major league sports, situation comedies, or television dramas. Defining race only as cultural symbols that are for sale allows whites to experience and view race as nothing more than a benign cultural marker that has been stripped of all forms of institutional, discriminatory or coercive power. The post-race, color-blind perspective allows whites to imagine that depictions of racial minorities working in high status jobs and consuming the same products, or at least appearing in commercials for products whites desire or consume, is the same as living in a society where color is no longer used to allocate resources or shape group outcomes. By constructing a picture of society where racial harmony is the norm, the color-blind perspective functions to make white privilege invisible while removing from public discussion the need to maintain any social programs that are race-based.

How then is color blindness linked to privilege? Starting with the deeply held belief that America is now a meritocracy, whites are able to imagine that the socioeconomic success they enjoy relative to racial minorities is a function of individual hard work, determination, thrift, and investments in education. The color-blind perspective removes from personal thought and public discussion any taint or suggestion of white supremacy or white guilt while legitimating the existing social, political, and economic arrangements that whites are privileged to receive. This perspective insinuates that class and culture, and not institutional racism, are responsible for social inequality. Color blindness allows whites to define themselves as politically progressive and racially tolerant as they proclaim their adherence to a belief system that does not see or judge individuals by the "color of their skin." This perspective ignores, as Ruth Frankenberg puts it, how whiteness is a "location of structural advantage societies structured in racial dominance."[10] Frankenberg uses the term "color and power evasiveness" rather than color blindness to convey how the ability to ignore race by members of the dominant group reflects a position of power and privilege. Color blindness hides white privilege behind a mask of assumed meritocracy while rendering invisible the institutional arrangements that perpetuate racial inequality. The veneer of equality implied in color blindness allows whites to present their place in the racialized social structure as one that was earned.

Given the pervasiveness of color blindness, it was not surprising that respondents in this study believed that using race to promote group interests was a form of racism.

Joe, a student in his early twenties from a working class background, was quite adamant that the opportunity structure in the

United States did not favor one racial group over another.

> I mean, I think that the black person of our age has as much opportunity as me, maybe he didn't have the same guidance and that might hurt him. But I mean, he's got the same opportunities that I do to go to school, maybe even more, to get more money. I can't get any aid. . . . I think that blacks have the same opportunities as whites nowadays and I think it's old hat.

Not only does Joe believe that young blacks and whites have similar educational experiences and opportunity but it is his contention that blacks are more likely or able to receive money for higher education. The idea that race matters in any way, according to Joe, is anachronistic; it is "old hat" in a color-blind society to blame one's shortcomings on something as irrelevant as race.

Believing and acting as if America is now color blind allows whites to imagine a society where institutional racism no longer exists and racial barriers to upward mobility have been removed. The use of group identity to challenge the existing racial order by making demands for the amelioration of racial inequities is viewed as racist because such claims violate the belief that we are a nation that recognizes the rights of individuals, not rights demanded by groups. Sam, an upper-middle-class respondent in his twenties, draws on a pre- and post–civil rights framework to explain racial opportunity among his peers:

> I guess I can understand my parents' generation. My parents are older, my dad is almost sixty and my mother is in her mid-fifties, ok? But the kids I'm going to school with, the minorities I'm going to school with, I don't think they should use racism as an excuse for not getting a job. Maybe their parents, sure, I mean they were discriminated against. But these kids have *every* opportunity that I do to do well.

In one generation, as Sam sees it, the color line has been erased. Like Sam's view that there are opportunities for all, there is, according to Tara, a reason to celebrate the current state of race relations.

> I mean, like you are not the only people that have been persecuted—I mean, yeah, you have been, but so has every group. I mean, if there's any time to be black in America, it's now.

Seeing society as race-neutral serves to decouple past historical practices and social conditions from present-day racial inequality. A number of respondents viewed society this way and pointed out that job discrimination had ended. Michelle was quite direct in her perception that the labor market is now free of discrimination, stating that "don't think people hire and fire because someone is black and white now." Ken also believed that discrimination in hiring did not occur since racial minorities now have legal recourse if discrimination occurs.

> I think that pretty much we got past that point as far as jobs. I think people realize that you really can't discriminate that way because you will end up losing . . . because you will have a lawsuit against you.

Critical race theorist David Theo Goldberg sees this narrative as part of the "continued insistence on implementing an ideal of color-blindness [that] either denies historical reality and its abiding contemporary legacies, or serves to cut off any claims to contemporary entitlements."[11] It also means that whites can picture themselves as victims of reverse discrimination and racism, as Anne, a woman in a focus group explained:

> Why is it so important to forget about, you know, white people's rights? I mean, not that, not being racist or anything, but why is it such a big deal that they have to have it their way or no way when it should be

a compromise between the two, and the whites should be able to voice their opinions as much as the blacks do.

There is the belief that whites have been silenced by race politics and as Jodie explains, "The tables have turned where they're getting more rights than we have. Like it never balanced out."

The logic inherent in the color-blind approach is circular; since race no longer shapes life opportunities in a color-blind world, there is no need to take race into account when discussing differences in outcomes between racial groups. This approach erases America's racial hierarchy by implying that social, economic, and political power and mobility are equally shared among all racial groups. Ignoring the extent or ways in which race shapes life opportunities validates whites' social location in the existing racial hierarchy while legitimating the political and economic arrangements that perpetuate and reproduce racial inequality and privilege.

Color Is Now a Matter of Choice

Leslie Carr suggests "the roots of color-blind ideology are found in classic liberal doctrines of freedom—the freedom of the individual created by the free capitalist marketplace."[12] Within the context of a free-market model, color blindness has come to mean that ignoring or attending to one's racial identity is a matter of individual choice, much like the ways in which whites can choose whether or not to emphasize part of their ethnic background. Many whites, for example, claim to be Irish on St. Patty's Day. Some Italian Americans feel purchasing a meal at the Olive Garden Restaurant is an ethnic dining experience that reconnects them to their immigrant past or fictive ethnic family tree. Some whites don kilts at Highlander Fairs or dress as medieval artisans or knights at Renaissance Festivals. These individuals experience their ethnicity as an option. There is no social cost to "being ethnic" for a day, nor does this voluntary behavior circumscribe opportunities in life. The color-blind narrative holds that affirming racial identity is, like whites who have the luxury of an optional ethnicity, an individual, voluntary decision.[13] If pride in one's ethnicity and by extension one's color is a matter of choice, then race no longer matters as an independent force which organizes social life, allocates resources, or creates obstacles to upward mobility.[14] In post-race, color-blind America, one can now consume images and products for, from, and about any racial or ethnic group. Racial styles, like clothing fashion, food choices, or musical preferences are like interchangeable, mix-and-match commodities for sale at the mall.

The color-blind narrative allows racial identity to be acknowledged in individual and superficial ways but using race to assert group demands violates the cherished notion that as a nation we recognize the rights of individuals rather than group rights. Within the color-blind perspective, it is understood that one does not choose one's race, but one should be conscious, or at least cautious, not to make race more than background cultural information. In a post-race, color-blind world, race can be seen, but pointing out race-based inequities should not be heard. The idea of identity, race, and the fluidity of individual choices was part of Jeff's explanation of race relations:

> It just seems like a gap's been bridged, where people don't have like separate things. You know, like in past generations there were things that each group had to itself, but now it's like there are plenty of things you can find in, like, black people that white people do. You know, there's music; rap music is no longer, . . . it's not a black thing anymore. . . . When it first came out, it

was black music, but now it's just music. It's another choice, just like country music can be considered like white hick music or whatever. You know, it's just a choice.

Tom makes the point that race categories exist, but assimilation allows any individual to become an American, if they so choose:

Blacks don't seem, poor blacks seem like they're more immigrant than we are.

Interviewer: In what way?

Because they try to keep pushing the differences. You know, like I said, the Asians just meld in a little bit better than the blacks.... Why do they have to be caught up in being African American? They've been in America all their lives. They were born here. They're not African Americans. That's just separate.

There was the perception that Asians did not embrace identity politics or use their racial identity to promote group rights. As Mike, a young white man in a focus group told me:

It's just becoming like really, really popular for black students to be black and proud and racist. But with Asians, it's not that way. I mean there is a magazine *Ebony* for strictly black people— I've never really read it. I mean there is no magazine for just Asian people. There's nothing saying, like, "Asian power."

Comedian Chris Rock points to how erasing the color line and color blindness are linked when he asked rhetorically "What does it say about America when the greatest golfer in the world [Tiger Woods] is black and the greatest rapper [Eminem] is white." Rock's message is clear: No role or occupation (at least in sports and music) is now determined by skin color. By allowing anyone to claim ownership of racial styles, colorblind narratives negate the ways in which race continues to circumscribe opportunities in life. The color-blind approach requires that these preferences, while racially

bracketed, be available to all for purchase or consumption. At its core, the color-blind philosophy holds that racial minorities can succeed if they rid themselves of any notion that their race entitles them to special treatment. Racial identity can still be expressed or acknowledged, but one's race should mean nothing more than a tendency towards individualistic expressions, like music, foods, or clothes.

Within the color-blind perspective, it is not race per se which determines upward mobility, but how much an individual *chooses* to pay attention to race that determines one's fate. According to this perspective, race is only as important as you allow it to be, as Kevin, a 33-year-old white male custodial worker in Colorado told me:

I never really look at anyone as a color, you know. Your skin's a color, but that doesn't mean, ... I don't know, I never look at someone being black or Chinese. Yeah, you're Chinese because of the way your eyes are slanted, but you talk just like me. You're just like me. I don't look at you any different than you being me. You know, that's how I've always looked at it. You know.

Implicit in this expression of color-blindness is that color does not matter as long as blacks and Chinese assimilate to the point where they are "just like" Kevin. As a member of the dominant group, Kevin has the privilege of defining color blindness as the expectation that racial minorities will mirror his own cultural and social experiences while denying how racism shapes the experiences of racial minorities.[15]

When racial identity shifts from being an individual expression to one that is used to organize politically or make group-based grievances, whites view it as racist. Mary believes that race is used to force whites to think about color and inequality:

I think that they are making it worse for themselves. I think that anybody can see in this country—I think it's you [blacks]. It doesn't matter what color you are. I mean, sure there are black things but why put it on a T-shirt? Why not just have a plain black T-shirt? Why would you have to make such a big statement that pushes people away, that threatens people. I would never want to threaten anybody.

As Mary's comments make clear, embracing racial symbols that serve to socially isolate and challenge the racial status quo is a "threat." Implicit in this exchange is that it is not very pleasurable for Mary to interact with those who would use race to promote a political agenda.

The respondents below were bothered by what they saw as a double standard concerning beauty pageants; blacks could have their own pageant but whites could not. Their anger is, at least based in part, on an understanding that the norm of color blindness has been violated. Jodie lamented that:

> You know, it's amazing. Like, even, like even, like the Miss America pageants. There's a black Miss America pageant. But there's also black contestants in the Miss America pageant and then there's a separate pageant for blacks only. And if we had a separate pageant for whites only I just think that things would be . . . more hell would be raised.

Michelle was also bothered by her perception that the idea of race was taken too seriously by blacks:

> You know, it just seems, even for silly things, even the fact that you have to have black women in the Miss America pageant but then they have their own Miss Black America pageant. You know, like that type of thing, and it's like, come on. . . .

John, a 22-year-old male from New Jersey, also felt that whites were held to a different set of social expectations than blacks:

> I watch Miss America and we've had what, a black Miss America three out of the last

five years, yet they do have a black Miss America (contest). They don't have white contestants, they only have black contestants. Now, I'm not saying that a black person can't enter the white contest, but it's just kind of ironic that here a black woman enters a predominately white contest and, you know, usually a Miss America's supposed to be representative of the whole population, yet only 12% of the population is black. . . . It just kind of seems strange that if a white person tried to enter a black contest, forget it, you'd have mayhem.

Viewed within the color-blind perspective, the Miss Black America pageant is a form of institutional racism because it denies all racial groups full access to participation. The Miss Black America pageant is, as suggested above, racist for excluding whites because of the color of their skin. The long history of racial minorities being excluded from white organizations and institutions as the reason behind why black, Latino, and Asian organizations were formed in the first place is now only viewed as irrelevant.

Like the anger expressed over what was perceived as a racial double standard concerning the Miss America pageant, Malcolm X also came to represent challenges to the color-blind perspective, which were viewed as illegitimate because they advocate group solutions to race-based inequities. As one respondent told me about Malcolm X:

> He got into Buddha [sic] and changed his violence. When he was younger, I think that's when he was violent but in the years before he was killed I think he definitely went towards peace, like Martin Luther King. I don't know why they can't wear Martin Luther King hats [instead of Malcolm X hats].

Color blindness has emerged as America's newest racial mythology because it provides a level-playing-field narrative that allows whites to inhabit a psychological space that is free of racial tension. This new era of color blindness is a respite from the racial identity movements which often result in white guilt, defensiveness, or the avoidance of racially charged issues. Color blindness provides whites with the belief that they live in an era that is free of racism. Convinced that these racist attitudes and practices are over, whites today are able to define themselves as racially progressive and tolerant. Within this universe where racial differences are almost meaningless, whites are able to claim that their privileged social position relative to racial minorities reflects individual achievement rather than the fruits of white supremacy. The constant barrage of color-blind messages and messengers reinforce and confirm that the egalitarian and meritocratic norms that undergird American culture are intact. Embracing color blindness allows whites to be blind to or ignore the fact that racial and ethnic minorities lag behind whites on almost every measure of quality of life. Color-blind pleasure means whites are able to think about contemporary race relations as a clean slate where the crimes of slavery, Jim Crow, institutional racism, and white privilege have been ended and the racist sins of their grandparents have been erased.

Our Survey Says — "Color-Blind Nation"

National survey data suggest that a majority of whites view race relations through the lens of color blindness. A 1997 Gallup poll found that a majority of whites believe that blacks have "as good a chance as whites" in their community in procuring employment (79%).[16] A Kaiser Family Poll (1997) found that a majority of whites believe that blacks are doing at least as well or better than whites in income and educational attainment. The poll found that "almost two-thirds (64%) of

whites do NOT believe that whites have benefited from past and present discrimination against African Americans."[17] In their study on racial attitudes, Schuman and associates found that when white Americans are asked to account for black disadvantage, the most popular explanation is that of black people's lack of motivation or will power to get ahead.[18] These surveys suggest a majority of whites view the opportunity structure as being open to all, regardless of color. Not only do whites see parity compared to blacks in access to housing, employment, education, and achieving a middle-class life style, but where differences do exist, whites attribute racial inequities to the individual shortcomings of blacks.

Reflecting on affirmative action, Monica articulates an all-is-now-equal argument as to why color should no longer matter in hiring decisions or school admissions:

> I think all the backgrounds have come a long way to where they don't need it any more. Basically everyone has equal opportunity to get a certain job, to get into a certain school, and now it should be based on your performance and not for what you are.

Drawing on an ideology of egalitarianism and meritocracy, Monica believes, as most white Americans do, that color is no longer a factor in obtaining employment or a quality education. Given the premise that racial equality has now been achieved, Monica is able to argue that achievement and not skin color should shape the allocation of resources. In other words, since the playing field is now level, any group claims to address real or imagined inequities are illegitimate. Joan voiced the anger that whites should in some way be held accountable for past or present racial inequities.

> That's what bothers me. They say "we" have been oppressed. They have not. The students here at the university right now have not been oppressed. They did not

experience the Watts riot, they didn't experience physically being hosed down by police. Granted, the white population was responsible for that, but we are not. We are not responsible. Therefore, we should not be put out because of that. We didn't do it. We're not doing it now, therefore they have no right to say, well, we've been oppressed.

Neither Joan, nor the white race, should be "put out" for past racist practices. The color-blind perspective is a historical rendering of the actions of the near and distant past as events which are disconnected from contemporary racial inequality.

James expresses a number of the trends found in the surveys cited earlier. After stating that "hey, everybody's got the same opportunity" when asked about what his views were on the idea of white privilege, James countered that:

> They say that I have white privileges. Uh, and if they say it's like because where I live, I live in a big house or something like that, they're wrong, because that's not a privilege. That's something my parents worked for. And if they don't live in a big fancy houses that's something that their parents didn't work for. And if they want to change that . . . I've got black people living across from me. Uh, they're no different than me. They're different from the black people down here because they worked for what they wanted. These people [blacks in a poor segregated part of the city], they don't have to live here. There's no one holding them back. They can get into school as well as everybody else can. I was lucky my parents could pay for school and I didn't need financial aid. . . . You know, the opportunity is there. You've just got to take hold of it.

James suggests that when class background is taken into account whites and blacks are the same. The blacks who are unable to leave poor, segregated neighborhoods

reflect individual shortcomings on the part of blacks, not structural obstacles. Rob implies that it is hard work and individual merit, not one's skin color that matters. Examining his own mobility, Rob remarks, "I don't know if their situation is any different than mine. I mean, I can only gauge on the fact that I've been busting my ass for the last ten years to get to where I want to be."

How Color Blind a Nation?

The beliefs voiced by whites in national survey data and my own interviews raise an empirical question; to what extent are we now a color-blind nation? If educational opportunity, occupational advancement, health, upward mobility, and equal treatment in the public sphere can be used as indicators of how color-blind we are as a nation, then we have failed. U.S. census figures present a picture of America that is far from color-blind. In 1999, over 73% of white households owned their own homes compared to 46% for blacks, 45% for Hispanics, 53% for Asians, and 56% for American Indians.[19] In 1993, whites had about ten times more in assets than blacks or Latinos.[20] Median family income in 1998 was $42,439 for whites, $25,351 for blacks, $27,330 for Latinos, and $46,637 for Asians. In 1997, almost 25% of whites over the age of 25 had four years of college or more compared to less than 14% for blacks and Latinos. In 1997, 8.6% of whites compared to 26.5% blacks, 27% of Latinos, and 14% of Asians lived at or below the poverty line.[21] A national study found that even after controlling for individual credit history, blacks in 33 states were charged more for car loans than whites.[22] Health statistics tell a similar tale. Whites have lower rates of diabetes, tuberculosis, pregnancy-related mortality, and sudden infant death syndrome (SIDS), and are more likely to have prenatal care in the first trimester than blacks, Latinos, or Asians. In

1997, 15% of whites did not have public or private health care coverage compared to 21.5% for blacks, 34% for Latinos, and 20.7% for Asians.[23]

In 1998, blacks and Latinos were also underrepresented as lawyers, physicians, professors, dentists, engineers, and registered nurses. AGlass Ceiling study commissioned by the federal government found that when one reaches the level of vice president and above at *Fortune* 1000 industrial companies and *Fortune* 500 service industries, 96.6% of the executives are white males. Nationally, white men comprise 90% of the newspaper editors and 77% of television news directors.[24] In 1999, the Department of Justice found that blacks and Latinos were twice as likely as whites to be subject to force when they encounter a police officer, were more likely to be subjected to car searches during a traffic stop, and were more likely to be ticketed than whites. Although blacks and whites are just as likely to use drugs, almost two-thirds of those convicted on drug charges are black.[25] Congress does not represent the racial and ethnic diversity of this country. In 2000, blacks were 13% of the population, Asians and Pacific Islanders 4%, and Latinos 12%. Yet the House of Representatives was only 9% black, 4% Latino, and 0.9% Asian. The U.S. Senate is 97% white and only 2% Asian and 1% American Indian, and therefore has no black or Latino members.[26] In early 2003, there were no black or Latino governors. According to another report, if you were black and living in Florida, you were four times as likely as whites to have your ballot invalidated in the 2000 presidential election.[27] We are not now, nor have we ever been, a color-blind nation.

The Cost of Racialized Pleasures

Being able to ignore or being oblivious to the ways in which almost all whites are privileged in a society cleaved on race has a number of implications. Whites derive pleasure in being told that the current system for allocating resources is fair and equitable. Creating and internalizing a color-blind view of race relations reflects how the dominant group is able to use the mass media, immigration stories of upward mobility, rags-to-riches narratives, and achievement ideology to make white privilege invisible. Frankenberg argues that whiteness can be "displaced," as is the case with whiteness hiding behind the veil of color blindness. It can also be made "normative" rather than specifically "racial," as is the case when being white is defined by white respondents as being no different than being black or Asian.[28] Lawrence Bobo and associates have advanced a theory of laissez-faire racism that draws on the color-blind perspective. As whites embrace the equality of opportunity narrative they suggest that

> laissez-faire racism encompasses an ideology that blames blacks themselves for their poorer relative economic standing, seeing it as a function of perceived cultural inferiority. The analysis of the bases of laissez-faire racism underscores two central components: contemporary stereotypes of blacks held by whites, and the denial of societal (structural) responsibility for the conditions in black communities.[29]

As many of my respondents make clear, if the opportunity structure is open ("It doesn't matter what color you are"), there must be something inherently wrong with racial minorities or their culture that explains group-level differences.

Leslie Carr argues "that color blindness is not the opposite of racism; it is another form of racism. . . ."[30] I would add that the form color blindness takes as the nation's hegemonic political discourse is a variant of laissez-faire racism. Historian David Roediger contends that in order for the Irish to have been absorbed into the white race in the mid-nineteenth century "the imperative to define themselves as whites came from the particular public and psychological wages whiteness offered" these new immigrants.[31] There is still a "wage" to whiteness, that element of ascribed status whites automatically receive because of their membership in the dominant group. But within the framework of color blindness the imperative has switched from whites overtly defining themselves or their interests as white, to one where they claim that color is irrelevant; being white is the same as being black, yellow, brown, or red. Some time ago, Ralph Ellison asked this important question about race relations that continues to go unanswered:

> What, by the way, is one to make of a white youngster who, with a transistor radio glued to his ear, screaming a Stevie Wonder tune, shouts racial epithets at black youngsters trying to swim at a public beach. . . . ?[32]

My interviews with whites around the country suggest that in this post-race era of color-blind ideology Ellison's keen observations about race relations need modification. The question now is what are we to make of a young white man from the suburbs who listens to hip-hop, wears baggy hip-hop pants, a baseball cap turned sideways, unlaced sneakers, and an oversized shirt emblazoned with a famous NBA player who, far from shouting racial epithets, lists a number of racial minorities as his heroes? It is now possible to define oneself as not being racist because of the clothes you wear, the celebrities you like, or the music you listen to while believing that blacks or Latinos are disproportionately poor or over-represented in low-pay, dead-end jobs because they are part of a debased, culturally deficient group. Having a narrative that smooths over the cognitive dissonance and oft time schizophrenic dance that whites

must do when they navigate race relations is likely an invaluable source of pleasure.

NOTES

1. FUBU (For Us By Us) is a black-owned manufacturer of urban, hip-hop style clothing.
2. For an excellent overview of how the media construct a view of race relations that is overly optimistic, see Benjamin DeMott, *The Trouble with Friendship: Why Americans Can't Think Straight About Race* (New York: The Atlantic Monthly Press, 1995).
3. The Gallup Organization, "Black/White Relations in the U.S." (June 10, 1997):1–5; David Shipler, *A Country of Strangers: Blacks and Whites in America* (New York: Vintage Books, 1998).
4. For an insightful discussion of how neoconservative writers like Dinesh D'Souza distort history and contemporary race relations, see David Theo Goldberg, "The New Segregation," *Race and Society* 1, no. 1 (1998).
5. Dinesh D'Souza, *The End of Racism: Principles for a Multiracial Society* (New York: Free Press, 1995); Ellis Cose, *Color-Blind: Seeing Beyond Race in a Race-Obsessed World* (New York: Harper Collins, 1997).
6. David Moore, "Americans Most Important Sources of Information: Local News," *The Gallup Poll Monthly*, 2–5 September 1995; David Moore and Lydia Saad, "No Immediate Signs That Simpson Trial Intensified Racial Animosity," *The Gallup Poll Monthly*, 2–5 October 1995; Kaiser Foundation, *The Four Americas: Government and Social Policy Through the Eyes of America's Multi-Racial and Multi-Ethnic Society* (Menlo Park, CA: Kaiser Family Foundation, 1995).
7. A. C. Nielsen, *Information Please Almanac* (Boston: Houghton Mifflin, 1997).
8. John Lewis and Sut Jhally, "Affirming Inaction: Television and the New Politics of Race," in *Marxism in the Postmodern Age: Confronting the New World Order*, edited by A. Callari, S. Cullenberg, and C. Biewener (New York: Guilford Press).
9. For an outstanding discussion of how color blindness is used politically by neoconservatives, see Amy Ansell, *New Right, New Racism: Race and Reaction in the United States* (New York: New York University Press, 1997);

Howard Winant, *Racial Conditions: Politics, Theory, Comparisons* (Minneapolis: University of Minneapolis Press, 1994); Stephen Steinberg, *Turning Back: The Retreat from Racial Justice in American Thought and Policy* (New York: Beacon Press, 1995); Eduardo Bonilla-Silva, *White Supremacy and Racism in the Post-Civil Rights Era* (Boulder: Lynne Rienner Publishers); and Michael Omi, "Racism," in *The Making and Unmaking of Whiteness,* edited by Birget Brander Rasmussen, Eric Klineberg, Irene J. Nexica, and Matt Wray (Durham: Duke University Press, 2001).

10. Ruth Frankenberg, "The Mirage of an Unmarked Whiteness," in *The Making and Unmaking of Whiteness,* edited by Birget Brander Rasmussen, Eric Klineberg, Irene J. Nexica, and Matt Wray (Durham: Duke University Press, 2001).

11. David Theo Goldberg, *Racial Subjects: Writing on Race in America* (Thousand Oaks: Routledge, 1997), 55; see also Charles Jaret, *Contemporary Racial and Ethnic Relations* (New York: Harper Collins, 1995), 265–270.

12. Leslie G. Carr, *Color-Blind Racism* (Thousand Oaks: Sage Publications), 108; see also David Carroll Cochran, *The Color of Freedom: Race and Contemporary American Liberalism* (New York: State University of New York Press).

13. Mary Waters, *Ethnic Options: Choosing Identities in America* (Berkeley: University of California Press); Charles A. Gallagher, "Playing the Ethnic Card: Using Ethnic Identity to Negate Contemporary Racism," in *Deconstructing Whiteness, Deconstructing White Supremacy,* edited by Ashley Doane and Eduardo Bonilla-Silva (Lynne Rienner Publishers, forthcoming 2002).

14. Ashley W. Doane Jr., "Dominant Group Identity in the United States: The Role of 'Hidden' Ethnicity in Intergroup Relations," *The Sociological Quarterly* 38, no. 3: 378.

15. Joe Feagin and Melvin Sikes, *Living With Racism: The Black Middle Class Experience* (Boston: Beacon Press, 1994).

16. The Gallup Organization, "Black/White Relations in the U.S.," 10 June 1997, 1–5.

17. Kaiser Foundation, *The Four Americas: Government and Social Policy Through the Eyes of America's Multi-Racial and Multi-Ethnic Society* (Menlo Park, CA: Kaiser Family Foundation, 1995).

18. Howard Schuman et al (1997), 193.

19. U.S. Bureau of the Census, *Housing Vacancies and Home Ownership Annual Statistics* (Washington D.C.: U.S. Government Printing Office, 1999).

20. U.S. Bureau of the Census, *Asset Ownership of Households* (Washington D.C.: U.S. Government Printing Office, 1993); see also *Black Wealth/White Wealth: A New Perspective on Racial Inequality* (New York: Routledge, 1995).

21. John J. Macionis, *Sociology,* 7th ed. (Saddle River, NJ: Prentice Hall, 1999).

22. Diana B. Henriques, *New York Times* 4 July, 2001, p. A1.

23. U.S. Department of Health and Human Services, *National Center for Chronic Disease Prevention and Health Promotion,* 1998; Centers for Disease Control and Prevention, National Center for Health Statistics, *Monthly Vital Statistics Report* 46.

24. Feagin, 2000.

25. Karen Gullo, *The Atlanta Journal and Constitution,* 12 March 2001, p. A7.

26. Jim Abrams, *The Atlanta Journal and Constitution,* 2 December 2000, p. A9.

27. Laura Parker and Peter Eisler, *USA Today,* 6–8 April 2001, p. A1.

28. Frankenberg (2001), p. 76.

29. Lawrence Bobo and James R. Kluegel, "Status, Ideology, and Dimensions of Whites' Racial Beliefs and Attitudes: Progress and Stagnation," in *Racial Attitudes in the 1990s: Continuity and Change,* edited by Steven A. Tuch and Jack K. Martin (Westport, CN: Praeger 1997), p. 95.

30. Carr, p. x.

31. David Roediger, *The Wages of Whiteness: Race and the Making of the American Working Class* (New York: Verso Press 1991), p. 137.

32. Cited in David Roediger, "The White Question," *Race Traitor* (Winter 1993): 104.

14

THE IDEOLOGY OF COLORBLINDNESS

Lani Guinier • *Gerald Torres*

QUESTIONS TO CONSIDER

Dr. Martin Luther King Jr.'s plea that one day his children would be judged "not by the color of their skin, but by the content of their character" is perhaps the single most quoted statement about the goals of the modern civil rights movement. There is however a huge gap between the expressed societal goals of what we "ought to be" and what we are. Guinier and Torres suggest that the very idea of colorblindness has become a way to turn a blind eye toward glaring racial inequality. What purpose is served by turning MLK's statement on colorblindness on its head? How and in what ways has the idea of colorblindness been appropriated by individuals or groups who believe race no longer matters in shaping individual or group socioeconomic outcomes?

The discourse of colorblindness focuses on managing the appearance of formal equality without worrying overmuch about the consequences of real-world inequality. Proponents of a colorblind ethos define freedom and equality exclusively in terms of the autonomous—some would say atomized—individual. This individual has no historical antecedents, no important social relationships, and no political commitments. By structuring the primary concerns around the idea of freedom for an everyman or everywoman, proponents of colorblind analysis locate that atomized individual in an abstract universe of rights and preferences rather than within an obdurate social structure that may limit or even predetermine a person's choices. In relationship to the state and to the market, the paramount virtue of the colorblind universe resides in treating each abstract individual the same as every other. By subjecting rules to this metric of simple sameness, people are legitimized through the appearance of abstract fairness.

Three rules seem to govern this colorblind universe. First, race is all about skin color. It is not a marker for social status, history, or power but is simply a false construction of phenotype that relies improperly on ascriptive physical identifiers of "blood" or ancestry. This is what some commentators call "formal race." Others refer to it as "biological race." Formal or biological race treats all race as pigmentation and grants all racial classifications symmetrical status. When race is only pigmentation, all racial classifications are equally bad, despite hierarchies of privilege or disadvantage that accompany the racial assignation.

Thus, the second rule of colorblindness is that recognizing race is the equivalent of holding onto unscientific notions of racial biology. If race is essentially "made-up," with no scientific basis, then critics of race argue that treating people differently based on these made-up categories is unacceptable. Even if members of different "races" are treated "the same," each person so identified is denied his or her essential individual humanity. Moreover, when one notices race, one is implicitly manifesting racial enmity or racial preference. Since racial classification enabled a Jim Crow legal system to perpetuate false assumptions about biological inferiority, noticing race is in essence a throwback to racism.

The third rule is that racism is a personal problem. Unlike capitalism or socialism which are economic system, or democracy which is a political arrangement, racism, racial hierarchy, or any institutionalized racial discrimination is not an economic or historic system, political arrangement, or social structure. Under the third rule of colorblindness, racism lacks any necessary nexus to power or privilege, and any observed connection is incidental, merely a result of the actions of people with a bad heart. Racism is a psychological disease of individuals, not a social plague. Racism is not produced by environmental toxins, nor is it reinforced by cultural forms or institutional practice. It is simply an irrational defect of the individual mind. It afflicts the aberrant soul who is vulnerable to prejudice or even self-hatred. The challenge for the judiciary, therefore, is to discern and eliminate to the greatest extent possible any public identification of race, since the identification is per se stigmatizing.

For those who believe we are already close to a colorblind society, formal fairness outweighs other concerns. They prefer rules like colorblindness even when such rules hide or reinforce relationships of privilege and subordination. The dangers of continuing to notice race are so profound that they justify doing nothing about the historic and present effects of the nexus between race and political and economic power. Not only is it wrong for the government to notice race, it is wrong for the political system to permit racially affected groups to mobilize in either their own self-interest or the larger public good.

• • •

In response to the claims of those who take a colorblind approach, we argue, as a practical matter, that it is impossible to be colorblind in a world as color-conscious as ours. Moreover, efforts to be colorblind are undesirable because they inhibit racialized minorities from struggling against their marginalized status. The rule of colorblindness disguises (sometimes deliberately) or normalizes (sometimes unwittingly) relationships of privilege and subordination. It gives those who have enjoyed little power in our society no mechanisms for understanding and challenging the systemic nature of their oppression. It affirms the existing imbalance in power relations; all that must change is for the privileged within the society to learn to tolerate on an individual basis those who were previously raced black or brown. Racial difference is relegated to celebratory holidays that capture the nostalgia of a time when we once thought we were different, but whose celebration reaffirms how essentially "the same" we truly are. This approach does not involve any fundamental rethinking of how race has socially and politically constructed privilege. The way race has been used both to distribute resources and to camouflage the unfairness in that distribution remains invisible. And the political space, where groups come together to give voice to their collective experience and mobilize to engage in fundamental social change, vanishes.

• • •

Racial Inequality Is Not a Problem of Individuals

Most people who oppose racism today believe that it is a psychological condition which distorts a person's thinking about people of a different "racial" phenotype. They believe in the changing-people's-thinking approach to racism. This approach, we argue, poses several dangers.

First, it reaffirms an essentialist view of race as merely a biological holdover from a less enlightened time that lacks any present political or social meaning. It suggests that racism is simply an inappropriate way that some individuals categorize groups of people who are in fact phenotypically different but whose physical differences amount to nothing important. This approach does not leave any space for other kinds of differences that people of color do in fact experience. These experiences are written off as some aberrational individual commitment to racialism that is obsessive and negative.

Second, the changing-people's-thinking approach not only locates the problem in the individual but it locates the remedy there as well. All that is necessary to overcome racism is for an individual to become better informed about different racial groups.

Third, in the changing-people's-thinking approach, either not speaking of race at all or speaking of it as a uniformly bad thing trumps all other options. This so-called neutral stance becomes almost inevitable after one has defined racism solely as an individual problem and an aberrant one at that. Racism is chased into the closet, and we are surprised when someone openly expresses intolerant views. Conservatives and progressives alike get caught in this trap and end up as speaking police, monitoring what people may say but feeling no compulsion to do anything about the racial hierarchy that shelters the root sources of bigotry. What surprises us about open bigotry is that it is public, not that it exists.

If we do not shift the locus of conversation to make visible the effects of such deeply held but unspoken attitudes, they will tend to normalize inequality. We will all then be tempted to explain the terrible condition of people of color as resulting from the behavior of the victims themselves. Having cleansed the social discourse of any mention of race and having policed expressions of bigotry, we will come to view any remaining racial dimension to observed injustices and inequities as a function of the way "those people" of color conceive of and structure their social life.

Colorblindness Masks Entrenched Racial Inequality

The colorblindness doctrine assumes that race is an individual attribute that should be of no consequence. For that reason, those advocating colorblindness as both means and end fail to recognize patterns of racial inequality and perceive no need to look more closely at data associated with these collective accidents of birth. They fail to see that an economy which is largely unaccountable to democratic institutions and principles of justice merely compounds inequality through the generations.

Stripped of concrete features like race, a black family earning $50,000 a year, for example, seems financially identical to a white family with the same income. Yet, this assumption of sameness does not take into account the effects of structural inequality compounded over time. Data on the generational effects of inequality show that blacks earning $50,000 or more have a median net worth that is barely one-half the median net worth of their white counterparts.

Most Americans have difficulty accumulating wealth. Income, understood principally as wages and salaries, does not easily convert into wealth because immediate necessities deplete available resources. Although income is distributed in a highly unequal manner in the United States (the top 20 percent of earners receives 43 percent of all income, while the poorest 20 percent of the population receives 4 percent of the total income), the distribution of wealth is even more unequal, and that inequality grows with each succeeding generation. In 1900, 39 percent of the wealthiest men in America emerged from wealthy families; by 1950, 68 percent of the wealthiest were born into wealth. By 1970, this figure climbed to 82 percent. That same year, only 4 percent of the richest men came from modest origins.

Income has been used as a surrogate for wealth at least in part due to the existence of little reliable data on wealth accumulation. But income alone offers an incomplete, skewed assessment of the inequality in life chances among different individuals and groups. The reality for most families is that while income may supply basic necessities, wealth is a critical resource for improving life chances, securing prestige, passing status along to the next generation, and influencing the political process. Wealth also provides financial stability during times in which needs overwhelm income.

Even at a time when the economy is good and when the unemployment rate for people of color is at an all-time low, blacks will not be able to sustain their economic gains until they can convert income into asset accumulation. Yet as the sociologist Dalton Conley points out: "At the lower end of the income spectrum (less than $15,000 per year), the median African American family has no assets, while the equivalent white family holds $10,000 worth of equity.

At upper income levels (greater than $75,000 per year), while families have a median net worth of $308,000, almost three times the figure for upper-income African American families ($114,600)." The median net worth of whites is twelve times that of blacks. Similarly, the average white household controls $6,999 in net financial assets while the average black household retains no net financial assets whatsoever.

Owning a home is the primary method of equity accumulation for most families in the United States. Not surprisingly, disparities in home-ownership rates contribute to the black-white wealth disparity. As of 1997, only 44 percent of blacks owned their homes, in contrast with 71 percent of whites. Not only are blacks less likely to own homes, but when they do own homes, their asset is less likely to accumulate value than that of white home-owners. The value of housing in black neighborhoods increases at a lower rate compared with similar units in predominantly white neighborhoods. Black households are less likely than white households to have their wealth invested in financial assets, rental property, and businesses or farms that are likely to produce income. Black assets more often are tied up in a home and consumables, such as a car or household goods. As a result, black families are less able to expand their income than white families, and thus the disparity in wealth perpetuates itself.

What these comparisons of income and wealth illustrate is not just the effects of historical discrimination in particular cases but the effects of an entire complex of social relations, reflected in poorer housing markets, less adequate schools, reduced access to banks and other sources of capital, hostile relations with police authority, and increased crime. The cumulative impact of these disparities requires an explanation that does not merely excuse the current distribution of assets.

Efforts to pass these effects off to class are unavailing. When trying to explain the wealth gap between blacks and whites, Melvin Oliver and Thomas Shapiro used a large number of controls in their work—income, age, sex, marriage, children, number of working people within the household, education, occupation, work history, and region. With these controls, Oliver and Shapiro confirmed that nonracial factors standing alone cannot explain the black-white wealth gap.

The status of both the black poor and the black middle class is much more precarious and unstable than that of their white peers. Between 1980 and 1996 the absolute incomes of the poorest blacks declined dramatically, as compared with a small decline in the income of the poorest white families. Even as poverty in the black community declined overall, those who remained poor became poorer still. The percentage of black men between ages 25 and 34 who earn less than the poverty line for a family of four jumped from about 20 percent in 1969 to just over 50 percent in 1991.

Even among blacks and whites who both start at low socioeconomic positions as measured by parental occupation, whites who make it into the middle class accumulate more wealth than blacks who have traveled the same path. Blacks' middle-class status entirely depends on income, whereas the status of the white middle class rests on the stability and security of assets. The writer DeNeen L. Brown illustrates this marginality and fragility when she explains what it means to be first-generation black middle-class: "To me that term doesn't mean anything other than someone who is one step out of poverty and two paychecks from being broke. I have income but not true wealth."

The average net worth of middle-class whites is nearly four times that of comparably situated blacks, and their average net financial assets are nearly 55 times greater than that of their black counterparts. This is true even within the context of real economic success. As Oliver and Shapiro note: "No matter how high up the mobility ladder blacks climb, their asset accumulation remains capped at inconsequential levels, especially when compared to that of equally mobile whites." As a result, each generation passes on a form of "asset poverty" regardless of the level of mobility or occupational attainment achieved. Social mobility does not fully counteract the effects of the intergenerational transmission of wealth.

Access to higher education has always been an indicator of both social mobility and the capacity of families to transfer wealth across generations. What we find when we compare the opportunities of white and black people is a continuing gap in access to higher education between these two groups. Because of the dramatic changes occurring in our economy, what this differential means is that the distribution of access to our knowledge-based economy will be color-coded.

Most people believe (and the data confirm) that education positively affects wealth accumulation: high educational achievement typically leads to better-paying jobs, which in turn result in greater wealth accumulation. What is less clear is the affect that wealth has upon education. While ample research has explored the effect of family and neighborhood income upon student performance and attainment, few studies have focused on wealth. The studies that do exist provide some insight into this relationship. Conley found that financial contributions of parents to their children's educational expenses have strong effects upon children's educational expectations. Yet African-American young adults receive less financial help from their parents and return more money to their parents' households than their white counterparts during the period immediately following high school. These data suggest that African-American young adults are substituting work for schooling.

Conley found that the most significant wealth-based predictor of educational performance is parents' liquid assets. (The most significant *overall* predictor, according to Conley, is parental educational level—another instance of the compounding of wealth over generations.) From this he infers that family-based educational financing is "probably more important than the differences in school districts associated with housing values." Conley states that wealth-based resource disparities at the district level (created by reliance on local property taxes, which fund the schools) account for approximately 10 percent of the gap in black and white standardized test scores. Furthermore, a decline in our social commitment to providing access to higher education for people of color is widening the gap. The declining support for public education compounds the problems in higher education. Black and other nonwhite communities feel the impact of this decreased support first and most powerfully, but it will affect all poor communities, regardless of color, in the long run. Everyone who depends on public education for upward mobility will suffer. Recent dramatic changes in the economy promise to magnify this disadvantage.

When Conley incorporated wealth factors into traditional educational analyses, a number of important elements in the cultural-deficit model for explaining educational disparities disappear. These include the pathologies supposedly created by female heads of households, receipt of welfare payments, parental age, parental occupational prestige, and parental income level. As the economist Marcellus Andrews puts it: "Working-class black people are muddling through an economy that no longer offers the prospect of middle-class life to hard working but modestly educated adults." There is a simple way to look at the confluence of these facts. Black people as a group not only have lower incomes than whites but also reduced access to the major avenue of wealth creation and transfer in the middle and working classes, namely high-quality higher education. Race in this society tracks wealth, wealth tracks education, and education tracks access to power.

Race provides an analytic tool for understanding significant dynamics of American economic life, such as the largely unremarked upon absence of any automatic escalator from one class to the next, despite the Horatio Alger myth. The linkages between race and black poverty tell us more about race than they do about individual black people. Moreover, the linkage between race and poverty tells us as much about white people as it does about black people. It tells us that the most potent determinant of economic success lies in the accumulated assets that are passed on from one generation to the next. Racial disparities cannot be explained by reference to any simple binary in which blacks are poor and whites are not. Instead, the mechanisms making it so hard for black people to accumulate assets in a way that changes their life chances are the same mechanisms that keep poor whites poor. These mechanisms are compounded by race, but they are not totally explained by race. Race is instructive in identifying the workings of class, but it cannot be swallowed up into class.

Hugh Price, President of the National Urban League, challenged us in his 1999 State of Black America address to look at race as "endogenous," that is, "something that is defined within a political-economic system and not at all natural or immutable." Race cannot be defined outside the economic or political system; "it is defined by the economic system, to grant or deny access to wealth accumulation." For the individual who is raced black, Price is pointing out links in a chain that may provide an important context for what otherwise might be interpreted as individual deficits, behavioral flaws, or cultural pathology.

• • •

SEEING THE BIG PICTURE

Briefly glance through the Appendix. Based on your observations of statistics on race in this section, can you make an argument that the United States is now colorblind? How might you reconcile the ideal of colorblindness with the trends in the data?

15

THE POSSIBILITY OF A NEW RACIAL HIERARCHY IN THE TWENTY-FIRST-CENTURY UNITED STATES

Herbert J. Gans

QUESTIONS TO CONSIDER

In a timely and provocative article, Herbert Gans suggests that racial categories, as currently understood, are undergoing fundamental changes. He argues that the current racial hierarchy will collapse into two categories: black and nonblack. How will this happen and which racial and ethnic groups will be placed in each of these two categories and why?

Over the last decade, a number of social scientists writing on race and ethnicity have suggested that the country may be moving toward a new racial structure (Alba 1990; Sanjek 1994; Gitlin 1995). If current trends persist, today's multiracial hierarchy could be replaced by what I think of as a dual or bimodal one consisting of "nonblack" and "black" population categories, with a third, "residual," category for the groups that do not, or do not yet, fit into the basic dualism.[1]

More important, this hierarchy may be based not just on color or other visible bodily features, but also on a distinction between undeserving and deserving, or stigmatized and respectable, races.[2] The hierarchy is new only insofar as the old white-nonwhite dichotomy may be replaced by a nonblack-black one, but it is hardly new for blacks, who are likely to remain at the bottom once again. I fear this hierarchy could develop even if more blacks achieve educational mobility, obtain professional and managerial jobs, and gain access to middle-class incomes, wealth, and other "perks." Still, the hierarchy could also end, particularly if the black distribution of income and wealth resembles that of the then-dominant races, and if interracial marriage eliminates many of the visible bodily features by which Americans now define race.

Since no one can even guess much less model the many causal factors that will influence the future, the observations that follow are not intended to be read as a prediction but as an exercise in speculative analysis. The weakness of such an analysis is its empirical reliance on the extrapolation of too many current trends and the assumed persistence of too many current phenomena. The analysis becomes a justifiable exercise, however, because it aims only to speculate about what future "scenarios" are possible, and what variables might shape these.

Obviously, the observations about such a hierarchy are not meant to suggest that it is desirable. Indeed, I wrote the paper with the hope that if such a future threatens to become real, it can be prevented.

The remainder of this paper elaborates the basic scenario, adds a set of qualifications, and considers the variables and alternative scenarios now most likely to be significant for the future. The paper concludes with observations about the contemporary construction of race in the United States raised by my analysis about a possible future.

The Dual Racial Hierarchy

Before what is now described, somewhat incorrectly, as the post-1965 immigration, the United States was structured as a predominantly Caucasian, or white, society, with a limited number of numerically and otherwise inferior races, who were typically called Negroes, Orientals, and American Indians—or blacks, yellows, and reds to go with the pinkish-skinned people called whites. There was also a smattering of groups involving a huge number of people who were still described by their national or geographic origins rather than language, including Filipinos, Mexicans and Puerto Ricans, Cubans, etc.[3]

After 1965, when many other Central and Latin American countries began to send migrants, the Spanish-speaking groups were all recategorized by language and called Hispanics. Newcomers from Southeast Asia were classified by continental origin and called Asians, which meant that the later Indian, Pakistani, and Sri Lankan newcomers had to be distinguished regionally, and called South Asians.

At the end of the twentieth century, the country continues to be dominated by whites. Nevertheless, both the immigrants who started to arrive after the end of World War II and the political, cultural, and racial changes that took place in the wake of their arrival have further invalidated many old racial divisions and labels. They have also set into motion what may turn out to be significant transformations in at least part of the basic racial hierarchy.

These transformations are still in an early phase but one of the first has been the elevation of a significant, and mostly affluent, part of the Asian and Asian-American population into a "model minority" that also bids to eradicate many of the boundaries between it and whites. Upward socioeconomic mobility and increasing intermarriage with whites may even end up in eliminating the boundary that now constructs them as a separate race. Thus, one possible future trend may lead to all but poor Asians and Asian-Americans being perceived and even treated so much like whites that currently visible bodily differences will no longer be judged negatively or even noticed, except when and where Asians or Asian-Americans threaten white interests (e.g., Newman 1993). The same treatment as quasi whites may spread to other successfully mobile and intermarrying immigrants and their descendants, for example Filipinos and white Hispanics.[4]

What these minorities have in common now with Asians, and might have in common even more in the future, is that they are all nonblack, although not as many are currently as affluent as Asians. Nonetheless, by the middle of the twenty-first century, as whites could perhaps become, or will worry about becoming, a numerical minority in the country, they might cast about for political and cultural allies.[5] Their search for allies, which may not even be conscious or deliberate, could hasten the emergence of a new, nonblack racial category, whatever it is named, in which skin color, or in the case of "Hispanics," racially constructed ethnic differences, will be ignored, even if whites would probably remain the dominant subcategory.

The lower part of the emerging dual hierarchy will likely consist of people classified as blacks, including African-Americans, as well as Caribbean and other blacks, dark skinned or black Hispanics, Native Americans, and anyone else who is dark skinned enough and/or possessed of visible bodily features and behavior patterns, actual or imagined, that remind nonblacks of blacks. Many of these people will also be poor, and if whites and other nonblacks continue to blame America's troubles on a low-status

scapegoat, the new black category will be characterized as an undeserving race.

In effect, class will presumably play nearly as much of a role in the boundary changes as race, but with some important exceptions. For example, if a significant number of very poor whites remain as the twenty-first-century equivalent of today's "white trash," they will probably be viewed as less undeserving than equally poor blacks simply because they are whites.[6]

Furthermore, the limits of class are indicated, at least for today, by the continued stigmatization of affluent and otherwise high-status blacks, who suffer some of the same indignities as poor blacks (Feagin and Sykes 1994).[7] So, of course, do moderate and middle-income members of the working class, who constitute the majority of blacks in America even if whites do not know it. The high visibility of "black" or Negroid physical features renders class position invisible to whites, so that even affluent blacks are suspected of criminal or pathological behavior that is actually found only among a minority of very poor blacks.

Despite continuing white hatreds and fears of blacks that continue almost 150 years after the Civil War, racial classification systems involving others have been more flexible. When the first Irish immigrants came to New York, they were so poor that they were perceived by Anglo-Saxon whites as the black Irish and often treated like blacks. Even so, it did not take the Irish long to separate themselves from blacks, and more important, to be so separated by the city's Anglo-Saxons. A generation later, the Irish were whites (Roediger 1991; Ignatiev 1995).

Perhaps their new whiteness was reinforced by the arrival of the next set of newcomers: people from Eastern and Southern Europe who were often described as members of "swarthy races." Even though the word *race* was used the way we today use *ethnicity*, the newcomers were clearly not white in the Anglo-Saxon sense, and Southern Italians were sometimes called "guineas" because of their dark skin. Nonetheless, over time, they too became white, thanks in part to their acculturation, their integration into the mainstream economy, and after World War II, their entry into the middle class. Perhaps the disappearance of their swarthiness was also reinforced by the arrival in the cities of a new wave of Southern blacks during and after World War II.

A less typical racial transformation occurred about that time in Mississippi, where whites began to treat the Chinese merchants who provided stores for poor blacks as near whites. As Loewen (1988) tells the story, increased affluence and acculturation were again relevant factors. Although whites neither socialized nor intermarried with the Chinese, they accorded them greater social deference and political respect than when they had first arrived. They turned the Chinese into what I previously called a residual category, and in the process created an early version of the nonblack-black duality that may appear in the United States in the next century.

As the Mississippi example suggests, changes in racial classification schemes need not require racial or class equality, for as long as scarce resources or positions remain, justifications for discrimination also remain and physical features that are invisible in some social settings can still become visible in others. Glass ceilings supply the best example, because they seem to change more slowly than some other hierarchical boundaries. Even ceilings for Jews, non-Irish Catholics, and others long classified as whites are still lower than those for WASPs in the upper reaches of the class and prestige structures.

I should note that the racial hierarchy I have sketched here, together with the qualifications that follow, are described both from the perspective of the (overtly) detached social scientist, and also from the perspective of the populations that end up as dominant in the structure. A longer paper would analyze how very differently the people who are fitted into the lower or residual parts of the hierarchy see it.[8]

Qualifications to the Dual Hierarchy

Even if the country would someday replace its current set of racial classifications, the result would not be a simple dual structure, and this model needs to be qualified in at least three ways.

Residuals

The first qualification is the near certainty of a residual or middle category that includes groups placed in a waiting position by the dominant population until it becomes clear whether they will be allowed to become nonblack, face the seemingly permanent inferiority that goes with being black, or become long-term residuals.

If such a structure were to develop in the near future, those likely to be placed in a residual category would include the less affluent members of today's Asian, Hispanic and Filipino, Central and South American Indian, and mixed Indian-Latino populations. The future of the dark-skinned members of the South Asian newcomers is harder to predict. Indeed, their treatment will become an important test of how whites deal with the race-class nexus when the people involved are very dark skinned but are not Negroid—and when their class position is so high that in 1990 it outranked that of all other immigrants (Rumbaut 1997, table 1.4).[9]

Who is classified as residual will, like all other categorizations, be shaped by both class and race. To borrow Milton Gordon's (1964) useful but too rarely used notion of "ethclass," what may be developing are "race-classes," with lower-class members of otherwise racially acceptable groups and higher-class members of racially inferior ones being placed in the residual category.

It is also possible for two or more residual categories to emerge, one for nonwhite and Hispanic populations of lower- and working-class position, and another for nonwhites and Hispanics of higher-class position, with the latter more likely to be eligible eventually to join whites in the nonblack portion of a dual hierarchy. Yet other variations are conceivable, however, for white America has not yet given any clues about how it will treat middle-class Latinos of various skin colors and other bodily features. Perhaps today's ad hoc solution, to treat nonblack Hispanics as a quasi-racial ethnic group that is neither white nor black, may survive for another generation or more, particularly if enough Hispanics remain poor or are falsely accused of rejecting linguistic Americanization.

Being placed in a residual classification means more than location in a middle analytic category; it is also a socially enforced, even if covert, category, and it will be accompanied by all the social, political, and emotional uncertainties that go with being placed in a holding pattern and all the pains these create (Marris 1996). True, residuals may not know they are waiting, but then the second-generation white ethnic "marginal men" identified by Stonequist (1937) did not know they were waiting for eventual acculturation and assimilation.

Multiracials

A second qualification to the dual model is created by the emergence of biracials or multiracials that result from the rising intermarriage rates among Asian, Hispanic,

and black and white immigrants as well as black and white native-born Americans.[10] Interra-cial marriages increased from 1 percent of all marriages in 1960 to 3 percent in 1990 (Harrison and Bennett 1995, 165).[11] They are expected to increase much faster in the future, particularly Asian-white ones, since even now, about a third of all Asian marriages, and more than half of all Japanese ones, are intermarriages.[12] If Hispanic-white marriages were also counted, they would exceed all the rest in current number and expected growth, but these are usually treated as ethnic rather than racial intermarriages.

Another set of recruits for a residual position includes the light-skinned blacks, once called mulattos, who today dominate the African-American upper class, some of whom may be sufficiently elite and light skinned to be viewed as nonblack. Even now, the most prominent among the light skinned black-white biracials, including business and civic leaders, celebrities and entertainers, are already treated as honorary whites, although many refuse this option and take special pride in their blackness and become "race leaders."[13]

Meanwhile, "multiracial" is in the process of slowly becoming a public racial category, and someday it could become an official one codified by the U.S. Census.[14] At this writing, however, many people of mixed race are not ready to define themselves publicly as such, and those who can choose which racial origin to use are sometimes flexible on instrumental grounds, or may choose different racial origins on different occasions.[15] How people of various racial mixtures construct themselves in the longer run is impossible to tell, since issues of their identification and treatment by others, their own identity, and the social, occupational, financial, and political benefits and costs involved cannot be predicted either.

As far as the country's long-term future racial structure is concerned, however, what matters most is how whites will eventually view and treat multiracial people. This will be affected by the variations in class and visible physical features among multiracial people— for example, how closely they resemble whites or other deserving races. Another question is the future of the traditional identification of race with "blood," which counts all nonwhites in halves, quarters, or even eighths, depending on how many and which ancestors intermarried with whom.[16] If the late twentieth-century belief in the power of genes continues, blood might simply be replaced by genes someday.

Mixed race is a particularly complex category, for several reasons. In any racial intermarriage with more than one offspring, each sibling is likely to look somewhat different racially from the others, ranging from darker to lighter or more and less nonwhite. Thus, one black-white sibling could be viewed as black and another as nonblack— even before they decide how they view themselves. What happens in subsequent generations is virtually unimaginable, since even if mixed-race individuals marry others of the same mixture, their children will not resemble their grandparents and some may barely resemble their parents. Eventually, a rising number will be treated as, and will think of themselves as, white or nonblack, but this is possible only when people of multiracial origin can no longer bear children who resemble a black ancestor.

Empirical evidence about the effects of racial intermarriage from countries where it has taken place for a long time is unfortunately not very relevant. The closest case, the Caribbean islands, are for the most part, tiny. They are also former plantation societies, with a small number of white and light-skinned elites, and a large number of nonwhites— and a differential conception of white and nonwhite from island to island.[17] Caribbean nonwhites appear to intermarry fairly freely but skin color does count and the darkest-skinned peoples are invariably lowest in socioeconomic class and status (Mintz 1989; Rodriguez 1989).

The only large country, Brazil, also began as a plantation society, and it differs from the United States particularly in that the Brazilian state eschewed racial legislation. As a result, Brazil never passed Jim Crow laws, but as of this writing (January 1998) it has not passed civil rights legislation either. Racial stratification, as well as discrimination and segregation, has persisted nonetheless, but it has been maintained through the class system. Drastic class inequalities, including a high rate of illiteracy among the poor, have enabled whites to virtually monopolize the higher class and status positions.

The absence of state involvement has given Brazil an undeserved reputation as a society that encourages intermarriage but ignores racial differences, a reputation the state has publicized as "racial democracy." The reality is not very different from that of the United States, however, for while there has been more intermarriage, it appears to have taken place mainly among blacks and black-white biracials, who together make up about half the country's population. Moreover, biracials gain little socioeconomic advantage from their lighter skins, even as the darkest-skinned blacks are kept at the bottom, forced into slums and prisons as in the United States.[18]

In effect, the Brazilian experience would suggest an empirical precedent for my hypothesis that blacks will remain a separate, and discriminated-against, population in the United States of the future. Indeed, in just about every society in which blacks first arrived as slaves, they are still at the bottom, and the political, socioeconomic, and cultural mechanisms to keep them there remain in place. Although blacks obtain higher incomes and prestige than Asians or white Hispanics in a number of American communities, the descendants of nonblack immigrants are, with some notable exceptions, still able to overtake most blacks in the long run.

Since parts of the United States were also a plantation society in which the slaves were black, the leftovers of the racial stratification pattern will likely continue here as well. Thus, children of black-white intermarriages who turn out to be dark skinned are classified as blacks, even if the United States is on the whole kinder to light-skinned biracials than Brazil.

The future of Asian-white biracials remains more unpredictable, in part because no empirical data exist that can be used to shore up guesses about them. The same observation applies to the endless number of other multiracial combinations that will be created when the children of multiracial parents intermarry with yet other multiracials. There will be few limits to new variations in bodily features, though which will be visible or noticed, and which of the latter will be stigmatized or celebrated as exotic cannot be guessed now.[19] Most likely, however, the larger the number of multiracials and of multiracial variations, the more difficult it will be for nonblacks to define and enforce racial boundaries, or to figure out which of the many darker-skinned varieties of multiracials had black ancestors. In that case, an eventual end to racial discrimination is possible.

If future racial self-identification patterns will also resemble today's ethnic ones, the racial equivalent of today's voluntary white ethnicity and its associated lack of ethnic loyalty may mean that many future triracial, quadriracial, and other multiracial people may eventually know little, and care even less, about the various racial mixtures they have inherited. It is even conceivable that this change will extend to black multiracials, and should race become voluntary for them as well, the possibility of an end to racial discrimination will

be increased. Unfortunately, at the moment such extrapolations are far closer to utopian thinking than to sociological speculation.

Regional Variations

A third qualification to the dual model is that the portrait I have drawn is national, but given the regional variations in old racial groups and new immigrant populations, it fits no single U.S. region. Moreover, some parts of the country are now still so devoid of new immigrants, with the exception of the handful who come to establish "ethnic" restaurants, that the present racial hierarchies, categories, and attitudes, many of them based on stereotypes imported from elsewhere, could survive unchanged for quite a while in such areas. Furthermore, some areas that have experienced heavy immigration from Asia and Latin America are currently seeing an outmigration of whites, especially lower-income ones (Frey 1996). Thus, even current patterns in the racial makeup of U.S. regions could change fairly quickly.

In addition, regional differences remain in the demography of the lowest strata. The racial hierarchy of the Deep South will probably continue to bear many direct marks of slavery, although the de facto black experience elsewhere in the country has so far not been totally different. Moreover, in some regions, Latin American and other poor nonblack immigrants have already been able to jump over the poor black population economically and socially, partly because whites, including institutions such as banks, are less hostile—or less necessary—to them than they are to blacks.

In the Southwest, Mexicans and other Hispanics remain at the socioeconomic bottom, although in California, they may be joined by the Hmong, Laotians, and other very poor Asians. And Native Americans still occupy the lowest socioeconomic stratum in the handful of mostly rural parts of the country where they now live, although tribes with gambling casinos may be able to effect some changes in that pattern.

Even though some of the new immigrants can by now be found just about everywhere in America, the Los Angeles and New York City areas not only remain the major immigrant arrival centers but also contain the most diverse populations. As a result, a number of the issues discussed in this paper will be played out there, even as they are barely noticeable in the many smaller American cities that may have attracted only a handful of the newcomers. Since these two cities are also the country's prime creators of popular culture, however, their distinctive racial and ethnic characteristics will probably be diffused in subtle ways through the country as a whole.

Alternative Scenarios

Speculating about the future also requires some explicit consideration of the variables that could affect the guesses I have made here, which in turn could lead to alternative scenarios. Generally speaking these variables are macrosociological—major changes in the economy, demographic patterns including internal migration and immigration, as well as political realignments and racial divisions of labor, among others. These in turn can result in changes in racial and ethnic relations as well as in classification systems.

As noted earlier, dominant groups can alter racial categories and constructions. Model minorities are "chosen" by the dominant population precisely because they appear to share, and thereby to uphold, that population's behavior or values. If new behavior or values need to be upheld, new model minorities may be recruited. Scapegoats are populations that can be blamed for social problems, although the dominant populations choose, or even create, the social problems for which scapegoats will be blamed. Scapegoats, or targets for blame, generally come in two varieties: *higher* scapegoats, usually recruited from higher status minority groups that can be blamed for obtaining too much economic or cultural power; and *lower* ones, typically the undeserving poor, who can be accused of deviant behavior or values said to hold back economic growth, require public expenditures that could bankrupt governmental budgets, threaten familial and sexual norms, or impair the moral fabric of the rest of society. Blaming both types of scapegoats is a politically easy way of responding to a crisis, particularly one for which immediate and feasible solutions are lacking.

During the long Cold War, the Soviets and other foreign scapegoats could be blamed for American problems, but now, domestic scapegoats have again become the primary target. While illegal and even legal American immigrants are once again joining poor blacks as the country's principal lower scapegoats, only a few states have sufficient immigrants to serve as targets for blame, which may help to explain why conservative politicians, particularly Republicans, have more often demonized poor blacks.

The most likely candidates for change in current racial categories, other than of model minorities, are the people whites now call Hispanics, as well as descendants of some now officially nonwhite populations in the new immigration. They will have to be allowed into the higher-status occupations in larger number if and when the supply of whites runs out, and in that case, today's forms of racial and ethnic discrimination against them, particularly those shaped by class considerations, would have to give way. In fact, by the middle of the twenty-first century, demographers and journalists may be amazed that fifty years earlier, whites expected to be swamped in 2050 by an aggregate of diverse peoples then all called Hispanics.

Two macrosocial factors are probably most important in thinking about alternative scenarios. One is the set of geopolitical and economic demographics that can be produced by cross-national population movements, including the one that has fueled the immigration from Central and Latin America, as well as Russia, Asia, and now Africa, during the last half century. These movements were controlled at least in part by U.S. government legislation, but world catastrophes could take place that could force even the United States to open its borders to much larger numbers of people who might alter the racial distribution significantly.

National demographics can also be changed by domestic political considerations, however, which could lead to a new search for white—and non-Hispanic—immigrants. The United States found its late-nineteenth-century industrial workforce in white Europe rather than among the newly freed slaves in the South. Likewise, Australia has recently looked for European immigrants to discourage the arrival of further Asians.

The second major factor is the state of the domestic economy. If late-twentieth century trends in the world economy and on Wall Street continue in their present forms, the further disappearance of American firms, jobs, and high wages, as well as related changes in the country's economy, would persist too.

Suppose, for example, that unemployment, or the decline of real income, or both, worsened in the first quarter of the twenty-first century, and Americans in large numbers conclude that the country's economy can never again supply full-time jobs paying a living wage for everyone. While the descendants of the poorer immigrants would be the first to experience what I once called "second

generation decline" (Gans 1992), other immigrants can also be dispatched into persistent poverty when not enough jobs are available, with the appropriate racial stereotypes invented or reinvented to justify their downward mobility. Even some middle-class descendants of Asian, Russian, and other newcomers could be transformed into lower scapegoats. Then, the dual racial hierarchy I have described would look very different or might not come to pass at all.

Should economic crises result in political crises as well, or raise religious and culture "wars" to more feverish pitches, the current movement toward a dual racial structure could also end quickly. Then, a modern version of the nineteenth-century American monoracial pattern might reappear, with the children of white newcomers joining older white ethnics and WASPs as the only acceptable race. Some members of the newly scapegoated races would probably react in turn, inaugurating political protest, intensifying identity politics and slowing down on intermarriage and other forms of acculturation and assimilation. Some descendants of today's newcomers might return to the old country.

What if a very different economic scenario were assumed, involving a return of old-style economic growth accompanied by a stronger U.S. position in the global economy, a shortage of domestic workers, and an upward trend in real income? In that case, the trend toward a dual structure might be hastened, and the erosion of perceived racial differences speeded up as well.

At that point, the now still visible bodily differences of Asian-Americans and their descendants might no longer be noticed, and these groups would repeat the post-World War II pattern by which Southern and Eastern European "races" were redefined as "ethnic groups." The reclassification of Hispanics, including the treatment of third-generation

Central and Latin Americans, would probably move in the same direction.

The fate of blacks is more difficult to imagine. If the economy created a seller's market for people with job skills at all levels from blue collar to professional and managerial, all poverty would decline sharply, including that of blacks. Moreover, blacks would be able to enter the upper middle and middle classes in such numbers as to disturb white America's long association of poverty with blackness. Indeed, in an economy with enough decent jobs for all, private and public affirmative action policies to assure the spread of blacks at all levels of the occupational and socioeconomic structure would be likely as well.

Under such conditions, those aspects of white racism due to fear of and anger at black poverty would begin to decline, and if the federal government was committed to fight racial discrimination and segregation, so would the construction of blacks as an undeserving race. Black-white intermarriage rates might also rise more quickly.

If the prosperity were long term, and it as well as other events in the society and the world reduced the country's resort to domestic scapegoats, a dual racial hierarchy might be replaced by the beginnings of a multiracial structure in which the boundaries of all races would become fuzzier and weaker. Since now-stigmatized visible bodily differences would then lose their negative connotations, they might not only be ignored but even come to be celebrated as positive contributions to American diversity, just as current ethnic differences among Europeans provide the country with nonthreatening cultural diversities.

Prosperity alone does not necessarily solve a society's other problems, however, and political, cultural, and religious conflicts could remain, encouraging dominant groups to choose and stigmatize an undeserving race, even if it is not a poor one. Anti-Semitic activities, for example, have occurred in prosperous times and societies, and in nations with minuscule Jewish populations.

Likewise, more economic prosperity and other positive economic tendencies alone do not necessarily produce more acculturation and assimilation of immigrants. Even the acculturation of large numbers of immigrants and their descendants does not automatically preclude identity politics, for today's college and university campuses are rife with rapidly acculturating newcomers who nevertheless feel strongly enough about their racial identity to become active in identity politics.

It is even possible that in a multiracial America, some latter-day descendants of WASPs and white ethnics will resort to identity politics as an attempt to retain or restore their political and cultural dominance.[20] And if a global economy also produced pressures toward global cultural and political homogeneities, nation-states or their successors might develop now unimagined forms of national identity politics or cultural revivals to maintain some kind of national distinctiveness. Immigrants and their descendants might be victimized by such developments more than blacks, however.

Three Tendencies in the Contemporary Construction of Race

Biological Constructions

The first tendency is the continuing construction of race from biological as well as social building blocks. Most scientific experts agree that there are no biologically definable races, and that race is therefore not a useful biological concept. The lay public, however, which is not ready to accept expert opinion, sees differences in visible bodily features, mostly facial, between people and treats them as racial differences caused by differences in "blood." People also racialize differences in personality traits such as "soul"—and national character in the case of immigrants.

The visible bodily differences are not imaginary, for people do differ by skin color, and the shapes or other characteristics of various body parts, including heads, eyelids, noses, hair, and others. To cite just a few examples, even in third-generation white ethnic America, one can find Irish and Welsh (or "Celtic") faces, southern Italian and Sicilian ones, and Slavic as well as Scandinavian ones.

What people notice are not scientifically defined races or subraces, but the descendants of once-isolated peoples who had been inbreeding for centuries.[21] Since most have now stopped doing so as a result of rural to urban and other migrations, their distinctiveness is disappearing with each new generation, but it has by no means disappeared.

Some of the variations in personality and social characteristics that laypeople correlate with race or "blood" can undoubtedly be traced in part to the societies and economies, as well as the racial hierarchies, in which these once-isolated peoples lived. The occupational and other social roles that immigrants play in their new societies also play a part, one reason why immigrant shopkeepers in "middlemen" roles are often seen as "clannish" by the populations they serve, for example.

Some visible bodily features that distinguish people are noticed and judged; some are noticed but not judged one way or another; and yet others are not even noticed, seeming to be virtually invisible. Although how features are judged can be traced in part to the popular Darwinisms of the last two centuries, in general, the bodily features of the most prestigious peoples are usually adopted as ideals of physical perfection, while features found among the lower social classes are judged pejoratively.[22]

Variations in skin color, as well as in head shapes, noses, eyes, lips, and hair, have been noticed in many societies, but differences in some bodily parts have been ignored, for example, the size of fingers and the shapes of ears and earlobes.[23] Yet other bodily features are not noticed because they are hidden by clothes; while a few are not noticed because people wear clothes to hide them. These often spur fantasies, for example about black penis size and other imagined racial differences in reproductive and other organs.[24]

A major ingredient of the social construction of race is the determination of which visible bodily features are noticed and used to delineate race and which remain unnoticed. In the process shaping that construction, various social constructors, including laypersons, experts, and, when relevant, commercial and political decision makers, take part. Unless explicit ideological, commercial, or political reasons are involved, the constructors may not be aware of the process in which they are involved, or the causes that shape the final determination. Usually, whites are the major constructors, but increasingly, representatives of the racial minorities to be constructed participate when they can politicize the process, or can frighten manufacturers or advertisers of national consumer goods.[25]

Strictly speaking, a biological construction should make racial characteristics and classifications relatively fixed, but lay biological construction is almost as flexible as social construction. The reason for the lack of fixity is not hard to find, for the choice of which visible bodily features are to be noticed has almost nothing to do with race and everything to do with stratification.

As the Brazilian and United States experiences indicate, the race of the lowest class became the lowest race because slaves were almost by definition the lowest class and race.

That captured blacks were the only population economically and otherwise powerless to prevent their becoming enslaved in recent centuries led whites to use their distinguishable skin color and facial features to translate their class inferiority into a racial one (Fields 1990). Similarly, the stigmatization of "yellow" skin resulted from the serflike status of Chinese "coolies" on railroad construction gangs; the stigmatization of "swarthiness" followed from the low status of the Southern and Eastern European newcomers; and a century later, white Hispanic immigrants are sometimes called a race because of their low class position.[26] That the ancestors of now-respected Americans were once damned for their swarthy skins has been quietly forgotten, both among their descendants and among the peoples who "invented" the original stigma.

Ethnicity as Racial

The second, and related, tendency is the continuing lay practice of identifying ethnic and national differences as racial, particularly in private self-naming. Census analysts have discovered that in the 1990 census, respondents to open-ended questions claimed membership in nearly three hundred races or ethnic groups, including seventy Hispanic categories (Morganthau 1995, 64). In many instances, they equated their race with their nationality—or with their tribes in the case of Native Americans.[27] As Eleanor Gerber and Manuel de la Puente pointed out in reporting on a study of test questions for the 2000 census: "Most respondents recognized the term 'ethnic group' but . . . would indicate it was 'the same thing' as race . . . [and] often coined the term 'ethnic race' during our discussions" (Gerber and de la Puente 1996, 21).

The two Bureau of Census researchers suggest lack of education as the causal factor in this conflation, indicating that only the college educated could distinguish ethnic group from race. However, as long as Americans notice visible bodily differences among people of the same official race, they will hold on to *private* constructions of race that differ from the official definitions.[28] Even among the third- and fourth-generation white multiethnics whose "ethnic options" Mary Waters (1990) studied, some chose their ethnicities on the basis of racial conceptions of national origin.[29] In effect, ethnicity continues to be a matter of "blood."[30]

Racial Tolerance

The third and perhaps most important tendency is the apparently increasing white tolerance for racial differences, except with respect to blacks. At the same time, whites seem to use race less often as an indicator of class, except when they are considering poor blacks. This trend may become more widespread as racial intermarriage among people of similar class increases further. Today, class homogamy is apparently outranking racial homogamy among college-educated young people (Kalmijn 1991).

If this pattern spreads to other Americans of the same age and if it becomes permanent, and if whites were willing and able to see that their hatreds and fears of blacks and other very poor nonwhites are so often reactions to their extreme and persistent poverty rather than their race, class could become more important and more overt as a boundary and a principle of stratification in the future. If Americans could also realize that class is more than a matter of "lifestyle" differences among near equals, class stratification might someday become a matter of general public discussion. In that case, the myth of a classless America might eventually be laid to rest.[31]

Even a more modest increase in awareness of class would be desirable, because class is after all an achieved status, while race is not, even in its reasonably flexible lay construction. However, the shift from race to class would also require Americans to develop a more fundamental understanding of the United States and to invent a new conception of the American dream and its underlying myth to replace that of the classless society. So far, there is no indication of this happening.

In fact, it would probably not happen until events in the political economy make it possible to achieve a drastic reduction of joblessness and poverty, so that the correlation of poverty with blackness is significantly lowered. If and when blacks become roughly equal economically to nonblacks, blacks can no longer be treated as an undeserving race.

If poverty and inequality are not lessened, however, and if more poor blacks are condemned to work for nothing but their welfare benefits, they could be treated as an ever more undeserving race, and other populations who cannot enter, or stay in, the middle class, including poor Hispanics and Asians, might join them. In that case, the racial hierarchy of the next century's United States would look very different from the one I have sketched here.

Conclusion

A society's reconstruction of racial categories appears to require at least the following conditions: (1) an influx of immigrants who do not fit the existing racial categories and their associated class backgrounds; (2) a healthy economy with sufficient opportunity for upward mobility even for poorer immigrants; (3) a lack of demand for new lower (and higher) racial scapegoats; and (4) an at least temporary demand for model minorities.

If these conditions are met, existing racial definitions and categories will be altered, sometimes even quickly if there is a proliferation of interracial marriages. However, in a society with a history of slavery, one possible effect is a dual racial hierarchy, in which one part consists mostly of ex-slaves. However, since even the effects of slavery should eventually be eliminated, at least in theory, the United States could become a predominantly interracial or multiracial society someday.

Even then, the more prestigious racial mixtures are apt to remain somewhat whiter for a while than the rest, and the less prestigious ones darker. But if the country's racial mixing ever became so thorough that skin color and other currently used bodily features were sufficiently unrecognizable or no longer of sufficient interest to be noticed, race would no longer be associated with social ranking. If Americans then still needed to rank each other, new criteria would have to be found.

NOTES

I am grateful for comments on earlier drafts of this paper from Margaret Chin, Jennifer Lee, an anonymous reviewer—and from my fellow authors in this volume.

1. These categories are constructions, but they also contain populations experiencing all the pleasures and pains of being located in a hierarchy. And although I am often discussing constructions, I will forgo the practice of putting all racial, national, and related names and labels between quotes, except for unusual racial stereotypes.

2. The two races may not be called that openly, but ambiguous pejoratives have long been part of the American vocabulary, for example *underclass* now, and *pauper* a century earlier (Gans 1995). Since races are social constructions, their names will depend in large part on who does the naming—and whose names become dominant in the public vocabulary.

3. Puerto Ricans are still often described as immigrants, even though they have been American citizens for a long time and their move from the island to the mainland is a

form of interstate mobility. Racial, class, and linguistic considerations have undoubtedly influenced this labeling.

The same dominant-race thinking led Irving Kristol and other neoconservatives to argue in the 1960s that blacks were similar enough to the white European immigrants to be able to adopt and act on immigrant values. They also assumed that blacks would then assimilate like immigrants, ignoring such facts as that blacks had originally come as slaves, not immigrants; had been here several centuries; and had not yet been allowed by whites to assimilate. Thirty years later, many whites ignore the same facts to propose the newest immigrants as role models for blacks.

4. Much less is said about black Hispanics, including Puerto Ricans, who suffer virtually all of the discriminatory and other injustices imposed on African-Americans.

5. Some highly placed whites are already worrying, for example in a *Time* cover story by William Henry III (1990), but then similar whites worried a century earlier what the then arriving Catholic and Jewish newcomers would do to *their* country. The current worries are as meaningless as the old ones, since they are based on extrapolations of current patterns of immigration, not to mention current constructions of (nonwhite) race and (Hispanic) ethnicity.

6. Hacker (1996) notes, for example, that the term "white trash" is no longer in common use. Indeed, for reasons worth studying, the more popular term of the moment is "trailer trash," which nonetheless seems to be applied solely to poor whites.

7. In this respect, the United States differs from many other countries in the Western hemisphere, where blacks who have managed to become affluent are treated, within limits, as whites.

8. Not only might they perceive it more angrily than I am here doing, but they might be angrier about it than about the present hierarchy, simply because it is new but no great improvement. One result could be their constructions of new racial identities for themselves that depart drastically from the ones future nonblacks consider reasonable.

9. Being far fewer than Asians in number, South Asians are nationally not very visible now.

Moreover, for religious and other reasons, South Asian immigrants have so far often been able to discourage their children from intermarrying.

10. My observations on multiracial constructions and people have benefited from many conversations with Valli Rajah.

11. Between 1970 and 1994, the number of people in interracial marriages grew from 676,000 to more than three million (Fletcher 1997). In 1990, biracial children made up 4 percent of all children, increasing from half a million in 1970 to about two million that year. The largest number were Asian-white children, followed by Native American-white and African American-white ones (Harrison and Bennett 1995).

12. Some observers currently estimate that 70 percent of all Japanese and Japanese-Americans are intermarried, mostly with whites. Since they came to the United States as families long before 1965, this estimate may supply a clue about what will happen to second-, third-, and later-generation descendants of other Asian-American populations.

13. Presumably class position will affect how other descendants of old Southern mulatto and creole populations (Dominguez 1986) will be classified.

14. In the political debates over the racial categories to be used in the Year 2000 Census, vocal multiracials preferred to be counted as and with various people of color. African-Americans and other officially recognized racial groups also indicated their opposition to a multiracial category, being reluctant to reduce the power of their numbers or the federal benefits that now go to racial minorities (e.g., Holmes 1996).

15. Kohne (1996) reports that light-skinned biracial Columbia University students who identify as whites also apply for scholarships as blacks. But then, four decades earlier, I met Italian-Americans in Boston's West End who took Irish names in order to obtain jobs in Irish-dominated city hall.

16. The practice of quantifying racial bloods has a long history in Europe and the United States, thanks to both eugenics and slavery. Perhaps it will disappear when enough people have to start counting three or more

races. However, people also still use blood fractions when they marry across religions, so that the notion of racial, ethnic, or religious "blood" is by no means obsolete.

17. They are also different, for "one and the same person may be considered white in the Dominican Republic or Puerto Rico . . . 'colored' in Jamaica, Martinique, or Curacao . . . [and] a 'Negro' in Georgia" (Hoetink 1967, xii).

18. This account is based mainly on the data summarized in Fiola 1990 and Skidmore 1992, the classic analysis of the Brazilian racial system in Skidmore 1993, Adamo's 1983 case study of race and class in Rio de Janeiro, and the sociopolitical analyses by Marx (1995, 1996). I am indebted to Anthony Marx for guiding me into the literature on Brazil, although there is still precious little social research, especially with current data, in English.

19. No one has so far paid much attention to who is constructed as exotic and why, except the multiracial people, mostly women, to whom it is applied. Some of them benefit because they are sought by industries that hire workers with exotic facial features; but women without these occupational interests resent such labeling because it turns them into sexual objects.

    Industries that employ workers with exotic features, facial and otherwise, such as the fashion and entertainment industries, play an interesting, and probably unduly influential, role in the country's public racial construction.

20. Even now, at the close of the twentieth century, whites who argue that America is a "Christian" nation are pursuing a politics of identity as much as of religious dominance.

21. I am indebted to my Columbia University colleague, biologist Robert Pollack, for my understanding of this phenomenon.

22. Originally, people drew on nineteenth-century and earlier comparisons of apes and humans, with those determined to be closer to apes in facial appearance being thought inferior. Brain size was also used, at least until scientific research debunked its relevance, and the researchers also discovered that it did not correlate with status. The final blow was the discovery that the much maligned Neanderthalers had larger brains than *Homo sapiens*.

23. Ears have served mainly as anchors for adornment, although protruding ones have sometimes been brought surgically closer to the head.

24. Now that some young women show their navels or wear bathing suits with uncovered buttocks, these could become eligible for racial typing.

25. Constructionists in the social sciences and the humanities have so far mainly emphasized that races, like other human notions, are socially constructed, but social scientists have paid little attention to the actual construction process and its participants. What we know about that process comes mostly from scholars who analyze racial images over time, in literature or the popular culture, and have collected process information as part of their work.

26. Forced Chinese labor was also recruited for the cotton plantations, but the Chinese workers turned out to be inefficient cotton pickers and thus managed to avoid becoming slaves.

27. I am indebted to Roderick Harrison and especially Manuel de la Puente of the U.S. Bureau of the Census for materials that clarified this set of responses.

28. Social scientists on the staff of the Census Bureau and the Bureau of Labor Statistics spend part of their time analyzing the large number of private races that people supply in answer to open-ended questions to produce the small number of public ones reported by the federal government.

29. For some similar practices by Jews in post-Holocaust Germany, see Rapaport 1997, 166–67.

30. For example, one of Waters's respondents explained that she traced her bad moods to "the Irish in me," while "all of the good things" were Italian (Waters 1990, 25). Embryo clinics are asked by some of their customers to supply sperm and egg donors of similar ethnic origin, in one case to obtain an "Irish background, or at least light hair and light eyes" (Kolata 1997, 34). As a result, ethnicity may be so racialized that it is not very voluntary, although voluntary ethnicity may also be used to achieve voluntarily chosen racial features.

31. Needless to say, traumatic and long-lasting economic decline is a more likely cause for a public recognition of class in America.

REFERENCES

Adamo, Samuel C. 1983. "The Broken Promise: Race, Health and Justice in Rio de Janeiro, 1890–1940." Ph.D. diss., University of New Mexico.

Alba, Richard D. 1990. *Ethnic Identity.* New Haven: Yale University Press.

Dominguez, Virginia R. 1986. *White by Definition.* New Brunswick: Rutgers University Press.

Feagin, Joe R., and Michael P. Sykes. 1994. *Living with Racism.* Boston: Beacon.

Fields, Barbara J. 1990. "Slavery, Race and Ideology in the United States of America." *New Left Review* 15:95–108.

Fiola, Jan. 1990. "Race Relations in Brazil: A Reassessment of the 'Racial Democracy' Thesis." Occasional Papers Series no. 34. University of Massachusetts Latin American Studies Program, Amherst.

Fletcher, Michael A. 1997. "More Than a Black-White Issue." *Washington Post National Weekly Edition,* May 26, 34.

Frey, William H. 1996. "Immigration, Domestic Migration and Demographic Balkanization in America." *Population and Development Review* 22:741–63.

Gans, Herbert J. 1992. "Second Generation Decline: Scenarios for the Economic and Ethnic Futures of the post-1965 American Immigrants." *Ethnic and Racial Studies* 15:173–92.

———. 1995. *The War against the Poor.* New York: Basic.

Gerber, Eleanor, and Manuel dela Puente. 1996. "The Development of and Cognitive Testing of Race and Ethnic Origin Questions for the Year 2000 Census." In Bureau of the Census, *1996 Annual Research Conference.* Washington: Government Printing Office.

Gitlin, Todd. 1995. *The Twilight of Common Dreams.* New York: Metropolitan.

Gordon, Milton M. 1964. *Assimilation in American Life.* New York: Oxford University Press.

Hacker, Andrew. 1996. Foreword to *The Coming Race War?* by Richard Delgado. New York: New York University Press.

Harrison, Roderick J., and Claudette Bennett. 1995. "Racial and Ethnic Diversity." In *State of the Union: America in the 1990s,* vol. 2, *Social Trends,* edited by Reynolds Farley. New York: Russell Sage Foundation.

Henry, William, III. 1990. "Beyond the Melting Pot." *Time,* April 9, 29–32.

Hoetink, Harry. 1967. *The Two Variants in Caribbean Race Relations.* London: Oxford University Press.

Holmes, Steven. 1996. "Census Tests New Category to Identify Racial Groups." *New York Times,* December 4, A25.

Ignatiev, Noel. 1995. *How the Irish Became White.* New York: Routledge.

Kalmijn, Matthijs. 1991. "Status Homogamy in the United States." *American Journal of Sociology* 93:496–523.

Kohne, Natasha G. 1996. "The Experience of Mixed-Race Women: Challenging Racial Boundaries." Unpublished senior thesis, department of sociology, Columbia University, New York.

Kolata, Gina. 1997. "Clinics Selling Embryos Made for 'Adoption.'" *New York Times,* November 23, 1, 34.

Loewen, James W. 1988. *The Mississippi Chinese.* 2d ed. Prospect Heights, Ill.: Waveland

Marris, Peter. 1996. *The Politics of Uncertainty.* New York: Routledge.

Marx, Anthony W. 1995. "Contested Citizenship: The Dynamics of Racial Identity and Social Movements." *International Review of History* 40, supplement 3: 159–83.

———. 1996. "Race-Making and the Nation-State." *World Politics,* January, 180–208.

Mintz, Sidney W. 1989. *Caribbean Transformations.* New York: Columbia University Press.

Morganthau, Tom. 1995. "What Color Is Black?" *Newsweek,* February 12, 63–67.

Newman, Katherine. 1993. *Declining Fortunes.* New York: Basic.

Rapaport, Lynn. 1997. *Jews in Germany after the Holocaust.* Cambridge: Cambridge University Press.

Rodriguez, Clara E. 1989. *Puerto Ricans: Born in the U.S.A.* Boston: Unwin Hyman.

Roediger, David R. 1991. *Wages of Whiteness.* London: Verso.

Rumbaut, Ruben G. 1997. "Ties That Bind: Immigration and Immigrant Families in the United States." In *Immigration and the Family,* edited by Alan Booth, Ann C. Crouter, and Nancy Landale. Mahwah, N.J.: Erlbaum.

Sanjek, Roger. 1994. "Intermarriage and the Future of the Races in the United States." In *Race,* edited by Steven Gregory and Roger Sanjek. New Brunswick: Rutgers University Press.

Skidmore, Thomas L. 1992. "Fact and Myth: Discovering a Racial Problem in Brazil." Working paper 173. Helen Kellogg Institute for International Studies, University of Notre Dame.

———. 1993. *Black into White*. Durham: Duke University Press.

Stonequist, Everett V. 1937. *The Marginal Man.* New York: Scribner's.

Waters, Mary. 1990. *Ethnic Options: Choosing Identities in America.* Berkeley: University of California Press.

PART II
Prejudice, Discrimination, and Racism

Imagine you are a fifty-seven-year-old white vice president with Friendly Bank. You earn a considerable amount of money, have large mortgage and car payments, and support four kids, two of whom are in college. You are the primary breadwinner in your family. At lunch, your boss asks you about the new manager you will be hiring. He hints to you in a subtle way, a way you could never prove in court, that he has had bad experiences working with Asian Americans and would be extremely upset if one was hired. You are not racist toward Asians. In fact, one of your best friends is an Asian American. You do, however, need this job, your family needs to eat, two of your children are in college, and you are at an age at which moving from one job to another would be very difficult and extremely costly. Of the three hundred people who apply for this position, several Asian American candidates appear to be highly qualified, and one unquestionably would make an excellent bank manager. Would you turn a blind eye to the resumes of the Asian Americans or would you hire the most qualified person, even if that meant hiring an Asian American and being marginalized or conveniently downsized by your boss?

How do feelings of antipathy toward or dislike of a group of people because of their skin color, ethnicity, or religion culminate in actions against members of that group? As the preceding example indicates, individuals may act in discriminatory ways and not be prejudiced or racist. Conversely, someone may be prejudiced and racist toward a group and not discriminate. The Asian or black shoe salesperson who does not like whites may still sell a white customer a pair of shoes in order to earn a commission.

Prejudice and discrimination are linked in complicated ways. Since World War II, whites' views on integration, interracial marriage, voting for nonwhite politicians, and sharing social space with blacks and Asians suggest that whites are gradually embracing the idea of a colorblind society. However, things, particularly attitudes through surveys, are not always as they seem. Such survey findings are encouraging only if you believe that respondents' answers are an accurate reflection of what they really think or feel. Perhaps these trends reflect pressure to conform to what respondents believe is a socially desirable attitude. Typically, individuals want to present themselves to others in a positive way. This pressure to conform may lead respondents to conveniently forget or tightly monitor racist or prejudiced beliefs. Are answers to questions about racial attitudes merely a reflection of what takes place in the abstract, unnatural interview setting, or are these responses a valid and reliable window into Americans' racial attitudes? Frankly, social scientists are not always sure. To further complicate matters, it's not clear what connection, if any, exists between attitudes and action or between prejudice and discrimination. Demonstrating a strong, consistent causal link between attitudes and actions has proved elusive in the social sciences. The proposition that actions flow from attitudes may seem straightforward, but as we will see in the readings, it is not. It seems logical that individuals would behave in a manner consistent with their attitudes, opinions, or beliefs about a particular topic.

If, for example, you define yourself as not being racist, you would not engage in racial discrimination. But as the example about the vice president of Friendly Bank suggests, various social and economic pressures mediate what we would like to do, what we should do, and what we actually do.

Prejudice and discrimination take many forms. The first five readings in Part II examine those forms and the way certain social and structural conditions can create an environment in which prejudice and discrimination are likely to emerge. In an insightful and classic piece of sociology, Herbert Blumer explains race prejudice (racism) as a reflection of how individuals place themselves in a racial hierarchy relative to other racial groups they encounter. That is, individuals attempt to maintain privilege and status by reserving the "prerogatives" of their racial group, even if they are not consciously aware of it. Robert Merton provides examples of the social context in which a nonprejudiced individual like our vice president at Friendly Bank might act in a discriminatory fashion. Like Blumer, Merton outlines how prejudice and discrimination are often rooted in efforts to maintain privileges or advantages that accrue to individuals because of their skin color. Susan Akram and Kevin Johnson discuss how Arab Americans and Muslims in the United States have been subject to discriminatory treatment, harassment, and increased surveillance by the government since the 9/11 terrorist attacks. The assumption among some, these authors point out, is that every Arab American

is viewed as a potential terrorist until proven otherwise. George Lipsitz chronicles how racism by the federal government in housing, bank lending, and huge subsidies to spur suburbanization (and white flight from the cities) after World War II should be understood as institutional practices that resulted in substantial long-term, intergenerational "investments" in the white population. Joe Feagin explores how racism directed at middle- and upper-middle-class blacks plays out in ways that nonblacks do not, cannot, or will not see.

The five articles in "How Space Gets Raced" reveals a nation highly segregated by race and ethnicity. Douglas Massey argues that residential segregation results in a loss of occupational and educational mobility for racial minorities and cuts off communities from "mainstream" America. Elijah Anderson explains how many poor, young African Americans use fear and intimidation as a way to gain respect among their peers. Robert Bullard details how poor and nonwhite neighborhoods are disproportionately exposed to toxic waste, perhaps the most obvious way in which social space gets raced to the detriment of a racial minority. Jonathan Kozol examines how structural inequality disproportionately affects racial minorities in schools in the United States. Shannon Zenk and associates expose the extent to which space gets raced in their study of which neighborhoods have access to large supermarkets and those who must rely on the corner store or bodega for their groceries.

UNDERSTANDING RACISM

16

RACE PREJUDICE AS A SENSE OF GROUP POSITION

Herbert Blumer

QUESTIONS TO CONSIDER

Herbert Blumer writes, "to characterize another racial group is, by opposition, to define one's own group." How does a "sense of group position" shape how we see other racial and ethnic groups? Have you ever defined your racial group membership in such a way as to heighten your group's status at the expense of another? What was the context?

In this paper I am proposing an approach to the study of race prejudice different from that which dominates contemporary scholarly thought on this topic. My thesis is that race prejudice exists basically in a sense of group position rather than in a set of feelings which members of one racial group have toward the members of another racial group. This different way of viewing race prejudice shifts study and analysis from a preoccupation with feelings as lodged in individuals to a concern with the relationship of racial groups. It also shifts scholarly treatment away from individual lines of experience and focuses interest on the col-

Herbert Blumer, "Race Prejudice as a Sense of Group Position" from *The Pacific Sociological Review*, Vol. 1, No. 1, Spring 1958, pp. 3–7. Reprinted by permission of Dean S. Dorn for the Pacific Sociological Association.

lective process by which a racial group comes to define and redefine another racial group. Such shifts, I believe, will yield a more realistic and penetrating understanding of race prejudice.

There can be little question that the rather vast literature on race prejudice is dominated by the idea that such prejudice exists fundamentally as a feeling or set of feelings lodged in the individual. It is usually depicted as consisting of feelings such as antipathy, hostility, hatred, intolerance, and aggressiveness. Accordingly, the task of scientific inquiry becomes two-fold. On one hand, there is a need to identify the feelings which make up race prejudice—to see how they fit together and how they are supported by other psychological elements, such as mythical beliefs. On the other hand, there is need of showing how the feeling complex has come into being. Thus, some scholars trace the complex feelings back chiefly to innate dispositions; some trace it to personality composition, such as authoritarian personality; and others regard the feelings of prejudice as being formed through social experience. However different may be the contentions regarding the make-up of racial prejudice and the way in which it may come into existence, these contentions are alike in locating prejudice in the realm of individual feeling. This is clearly true of the work of psychologists, psychiatrists, and social psychologists, and tends to be predominantly the case in the work of sociologists.

Unfortunately, this customary way of viewing race prejudice overlooks and obscures the fact that race prejudice is fundamentally a matter of relationship between racial groups. A little reflective thought should make this very clear. Race prejudice presupposes, necessarily, that racially prejudiced individuals think of themselves as belonging to a given racial group. It means, also, that they assign to other racial groups those against whom they are prejudiced. Thus, logically and actually, a scheme of racial identification is necessary as a framework for racial prejudice. Moreover, such identification involves the formation of an image or a conception of one's own racial group and of another racial group, inevitably in terms of the relationship of such groups. To fail to see that racial prejudice is a matter (a) of the racial identification made of oneself and of others, and (b) of the way in which the identified groups are conceived in relation to each other, is to miss what is logically and actually basic. One should keep clearly in mind that people necessarily come to identify themselves as belonging to a racial group; such identification is not spontaneous or inevitable but a result of experience. Further, one must realize that the kind of picture which a racial group forms of itself and the kind of picture which it may form of others are similarly products of experience. Hence, such

pictures are variable, just as the lines of experience which produce them are variable.

The body of feelings which scholars, today, are so inclined to regard as constituting the substance of race prejudice is actually a resultant of the way in which given racial groups conceive of themselves and of others. A basic understanding of race prejudice must be sought in the process by which racial groups form images of themselves and of others. This process, as I hope to show, is fundamentally *a collective process*. It operates chiefly through the public media in which individuals who are accepted as the spokesmen of a racial group characterize publicly another racial group. To characterize another racial group is, by opposition, to define one's own group. This is equivalent to placing the two groups in relation to each other, or defining their positions *vis-à-vis* each other. It is the *sense of social position* emerging from this collective process of characterization which provides the basis of race prejudice. The following discussion will consider important facets of this matter.

I would like to begin by discussing several of the important feelings that enter into race prejudice. This discussion will reveal how fundamentally racial feelings point to and depend on a positional arrangement of the racial groups. In this discussion I will confine myself to such feelings in the case of a dominant racial group.

There are four basic types of feeling that seem to be always present in race prejudice in the dominant group. They are (1) a feeling of superiority, (2) a feeling that the subordinate race is intrinsically different and alien, (3) a feeling of proprietary claim to certain areas of privilege and advantage, and (4) a fear and suspicion that the subordinate race harbors designs on the prerogatives of the dominant race. A few words about each of these four feelings will suffice.

In race prejudice there is a self-assured feeling on the part of the dominant racial group of being naturally superior or better. This is commonly shown in a disparagement of the qualities of the subordinate racial group. Condemnatory or debasing traits, such as laziness, dishonesty, greediness, unreliability, stupidity, deceit and immorality, are usually imputed to it. The second feeling, that the subordinate race is an alien and fundamentally different stock, is likewise always present. "They are not of our kind" is a common way in which this is likely to be expressed. It is this feeling that reflects, justifies, and promotes the social exclusion of the subordinate racial group. The combination of these two feelings of superiority and of distinctiveness can easily give rise to feelings of aversion and even antipathy. But in themselves they do not form prejudice. We have to introduce the third and fourth types of feeling.

The third feeling, the sense of proprietary claim, is of crucial importance. It is the feeling on the part of the dominant group of being entitled to either exclusive or prior rights in many important areas of life. The range of such exclusive or prior claims may be wide, covering the ownership of property such as choice lands and sites; the right to certain jobs, occupations or professions; the claim to certain kinds of industry or lines of business; the claim to certain positions of control and decision-making as in government and law; the right to exclusive membership in given institutions such as schools, churches and recreational institutions; the claim to certain positions of social prestige and to the display of the symbols and accoutrements of these positions; and the claim to certain areas of intimacy and privacy. The feeling of such proprietary claims is exceedingly strong in race prejudice. Again, however, this feeling even in combination with the feeling of superiority and the feeling of distinctiveness does not explain race prejudice. These three feelings are present frequently in societies showing

no prejudice, as in certain forms of feudalism, in caste relations, in societies of chiefs and commoners, and under many settled relations of conquerors and conquered. Where claims are solidified into a structure which is accepted or respected by all, there seems to be no group prejudice.

The remaining feeling essential to race prejudice is a fear or apprehension that the subordinate racial group is threatening, or will threaten, the position of the dominant group. Thus, acts or suspected acts that are interpreted as an attack on the natural superiority of the dominant group, or an intrusion into their sphere of group exclusiveness, or an encroachment on their area of proprietary claim are crucial in arousing and fashioning race prejudice. These acts mean "getting out of place."

It should be clear that these four basic feelings of race prejudice definitely refer to a positional arrangement of the racial groups. The feeling of superiority places the subordinate people *below;* the feeling of alienation places them *beyond;* the feeling of proprietary claim excludes them from the prerogatives of position; and the fear of encroachment is an emotional recoil from the endangering of group position. As these features suggest, the positional relation of the two racial groups is crucial in race prejudice. The dominant group is not concerned with the subordinate group as such but it is deeply concerned with its position *vis-à-vis* the subordinate group. This is epitomized in the key and universal expression that a given race is all right in "its place." The sense of group position is the very heart of the relation of the dominant to the subordinate group. It supplies the dominant group with its framework of perception, its standard of judgment, its patterns of sensitivity, and its emotional proclivities.

It is important to recognize that this sense of group position transcends the feelings of the individual members of the dominant group, giving such members a common orientation that is not otherwise to be found in separate feelings and views. There is likely to be considerable difference between the ways in which the individual members of the dominant group think and feel about the subordinate group. Some may feel bitter and hostile, with strong antipathies, with an exalted sense of superiority and with a lot of spite; others may have charitable and protective feelings, marked by a sense of piety and tinctured by benevolence; others may be condescending and reflect mild contempt; and others may be disposed to politeness and considerateness with no feelings of truculence. These are only a few of many different patterns of feeling to be found among members of the dominant racial group. What gives a common dimension to them is a sense of the social position of their group. Whether the members be humane, or callous, cultured or unlettered, liberal or reactionary, powerful or impotent, arrogant or humble, rich or poor, honorable or dishonorable—all are led, by virtue of sharing the sense of group position, to similar individual positions.

The sense of group position is a general kind of orientation. It is a general feeling without being reducible to specific feelings like hatred, hostility or antipathy. It is also a general understanding without being composed of any set of specific beliefs. On the social psychological side it cannot be equated to a sense of social status as ordinarily conceived, for it refers not merely to vertical positioning but to many other lines of position independent of the vertical dimension. Sociologically it is not a mere reflection of the objective relations between racial groups. Rather, it stands for "what ought to be" rather than for "what is." It is a sense of where the two racial groups *belong.*

In its own way, the sense of group position is a norm and imperative—indeed a very powerful one. It guides, incites, cows, and coerces. It should be borne in mind that this sense of group position stands for and involves a fundamental kind of group affiliation for the members of the dominant racial group. To the extent they recognize or feel themselves as belonging to that group they will automatically come under the influence of the sense of position held by that group. Thus, even though given individual members may have personal views and feelings different from the sense of group position, they will have to conjure with the sense of group position held by their racial group. If the sense of position is strong, to act contrary to it is to risk a feeling of self-alienation and to face the possibility of ostracism. I am trying to suggest, accordingly, that the locus of race prejudice is not in the area of individual feeling but in the definition of the respective positions of the racial groups.

The source of race prejudice lies in a felt challenge to this sense of group position. The challenge, one must recognize, may come in many different ways. It may be in the form of an affront to feelings of group superiority; it may be in the form of attempts at familiarity or transgressing the boundary line of group exclusiveness; it may be in the form of encroachment at countless points of proprietary claim; it may be a challenge to power and privilege; it may take the form of economic competition. Race prejudice is a defensive reaction to such challenging of the sense of group position. It consists of the disturbed feelings, usually of marked hostility, that are thereby aroused. As such, race prejudice is a protective device. It functions, however shortsightedly, to preserve the integrity and the position of the dominant group.

It is crucially important to recognize that the sense of group position is not a mere summation of the feelings of position such as might be developed independently by separate individuals as they come to compare themselves with given individuals of the subordinate race. The sense of group position refers to the position of group to group, not to that of individual to individual. Thus, *vis-à-vis* the subordinate racial group the unlettered individual with low status in the dominant racial group has a sense of group position common to that of the elite of his group. By virtue of sharing this sense of position such an individual, despite his low status, feels that members of the subordinate group, however distinguished and accomplished, are somehow inferior, alien, and properly restricted in the area of claims. He forms his conception as a representative of the dominant group; he treats individual members of the subordinate group as representative of that group.

An analysis of how the sense of group position is formed should start with a clear recognition that it is an historical product. It is set originally by conditions of initial contact. Prestige, power, possession of skill, numbers, original self-conceptions, aims, designs and opportunities are a few of the factors that may fashion the original sense of group position. Subsequent experience in the relation of the two racial groups, especially in the area of claims, opportunities and advantages, may mould the sense of group position in many diverse ways. Further, the sense of group position may be intensified or weakened, brought to sharp focus or dulled. It may be deeply entrenched and tenaciously resist change for long periods of time. Or it may never take root. It may undergo quick growth and vigorous expansion, or it may dwindle away through slow-moving erosion. It may be firm or soft, acute or dull, continuous or intermittent. In short, viewed comparatively, the sense of group position is very variable.

However variable its particular career, the sense of group position is clearly formed by a running process in which the dominant racial group is led to define and redefine the subordinate racial group and the relations between them. There are two important aspects of this process of definition that I wish to single out for consideration.

First, the process of definition occurs obviously through complex interaction and communication between the members of the dominant group. Leaders, prestige bearers, officials, group agents, dominant individuals and ordinary laymen present to one another characterizations of the subordinate group and express their feelings and ideas on the relations. Through talk, tales, stories, gossip, anecdotes, messages, pronouncements, news accounts, orations, sermons, preachments and the like definitions are presented and feelings are expressed. In this usually vast and complex interaction separate views run against one another, influence one another, modify each other, incite one another and fuse together in new forms. Correspondingly, feelings which are expressed meet, stimulate each other, feed on each other, intensify each other and emerge in new patterns. Currents of view and currents of feeling come into being; sweeping along to positions of dominance and serving as polar points for the organization of thought and sentiment. If the interaction becomes increasingly circular and reinforcing, devoid of serious inner opposition, such currents grow, fuse and become strengthened. It is through such a process that a collective image of the subordinate group is formed and a sense of group position is set. The evidence of such a process is glaring when one reviews the history of any racial arrangement marked by prejudice.

Such a complex process of mutual interaction with its different lines and degrees of formation gives the lie to the many schemes which would lodge the cause of race prejudice in the make-up of the individual— whether in the form of innate disposition, constitutional make-up, personality structure, or direct personal experience with members of the other race. The collective image and feelings in race prejudice are forged out of a complicated social process in which the individual is himself shaped and organized. The scheme, so popular today, which would trace race prejudice to a so-called authoritarian personality shows a grievous misunderstanding of the simple essentials of the collective process that leads to a sense of group position.

The second important aspect of the process of group definition is that it is necessarily concerned with *an abstract image* of the subordinate racial group. The subordinate racial group is defined as if it were an entity or whole. This entity or whole—like the Negro race, or the Japanese, or the Jews—is necessarily an abstraction, never coming within the perception of any of the senses. While actual encounters are with individuals, the picture formed of the racial group is necessarily of a vast entity which spreads out far beyond such individuals and transcends experience with such individuals. The implications of the fact that the collective image is of an abstract group are of crucial significance. I would like to note four of these implications.

First, the building of the image of the abstract group takes place in the area of the remote and not of the near. It is not the experience with concrete individuals in daily association that gives rise to the definitions of the extended, abstract group. Such immediate experience is usually regulated and orderly. Even where such immediate experience is disrupted the new definitions which are formed are limited to the individuals involved. The collective image of the abstract group grows up not by generalizing from experiences gained in close, first-hand contacts but through the transcending characterizations that are made of the group as an entity. Thus, one must seek the central stream of definition in those areas where the dominant group as such is characterizing the subordinate group as such. This occurs in the "public arena" wherein the spokesmen appear

as representatives and agents of the dominant group. The extended public arena is constituted by such things as legislative assemblies, public meetings, conventions, the press, and the printed word. What goes on in this public arena attracts the attention of large numbers of the dominant group and is felt as the voice and action of the group as such.

Second, the definitions that are forged in the public arena center, obviously, about matters that are felt to be of major importance. Thus, we are led to recognize the crucial role of the "big event" in developing a conception of the subordinate racial group. The happening that seems momentous, that touches deep sentiments, that seems to raise fundamental questions about relations, and that awakens strong feelings of identification with one's racial group is the kind of event that is central in the formation of the racial image. Here, again, we note the relative unimportance of the huge bulk of experiences coming from daily contact with individuals of the subordinate group. It is the events seemingly loaded with great collective significance that are the focal points of the public discussion. The definition of these events is chiefly responsible for the development of a racial image and of the sense of group position. When this public discussion takes the form of a denunciation of the subordinate racial group, signifying that it is unfit and a threat, the discussion becomes particularly potent in shaping the sense of social position.

Third, the major influence in public discussion is exercised by individuals and groups who have the public ear and who are felt to have standing, prestige, authority and power. Intellectual and social elites, public figures of prominence, and leaders of powerful organizations are likely to be the key figures in the formation of the sense of group position and in the characterization of the subordinate group. It is well to note this in view of the not infrequent tendency of students to regard race prejudice as growing out of the multiplicity of experiences and attitudes of the bulk of the people.

Fourth, we also need to perceive the appreciable opportunity that is given to strong interest groups in directing the lines of discussion and setting the interpretations that arise in such discussion. Their self-interests may dictate the kind of position they wish the dominant racial group to enjoy. It may be a position which enables them to retain certain advantages, or even more to gain still greater advantages. Hence, they may be vigorous in seeking to manufacture events to attract public attention and to set lines of issue in such a way as to predetermine interpretations favorable to their interests. The role of strongly organized groups seeking to further special interest is usually central in the formation of collective images of abstract groups. Historical records of major instances of race relations, as in our South, or in South Africa, or in Europe in the case of the Jew, or on the West Coast in the case of the Japanese, show the formidable part played by interest groups in defining the subordinate racial group.

I conclude this highly condensed paper with two further observations that may throw additional light on the relation of the sense of group position to race prejudice. Race prejudice becomes entrenched and tenacious to the extent the prevailing social order is rooted in the sense of social position. This has been true of the historic South in our country. In such a social order race prejudice tends to become chronic and impermeable to change. In other places the social order may be affected only to a limited extent by the sense of group position held by the dominant racial group. This I think has been true usually in the case of anti-Semitism in Europe and this country. Under these conditions the sense of group position tends to be weaker and more vulnerable. In turn, race prejudice has a much more variable and intermittent career, usually becoming pronounced only as a consequence of grave disorganizing events that allow for the formation of a scapegoat.

This leads me to my final observation which in a measure is an indirect summary. The sense of group position dissolves and race prejudice declines when the process of running definition does not keep abreast of major shifts in the social order. When events touching on relations are not treated as "big events" and hence do not set crucial issues in the arena of public discussion; or when the elite leaders or spokesmen do not define such big events vehemently or adversely; or where they define them in the direction of racial harmony; or when there is a paucity of strong interest groups seeking to build up a strong adverse image for special advantage—under such conditions the sense of group position recedes and race prejudice declines.

The clear implication of my discussion is that the proper and fruitful area in which race prejudice should be studied is the collective process through which a sense of group position is formed. To seek, instead, to understand it or to handle it in the arena of individual feeling and of individual experience seems to me to be clearly misdirected.

SEEING THE BIG PICTURE

Blumer explains that four "feelings" make up race prejudice. Are you able to come up with an example of each of these four feelings for a specific racial or ethnic group? Are you convinced by his argument that racism is "a fundamental matter of relationship between racial groups" rather than individual-level feelings of animosity?

17

DISCRIMINATION AND
THE AMERICAN CREED

Robert K. Merton

QUESTIONS TO CONSIDER

Have you ever been in a situation in which social, economic, or peer pressure forced you to treat someone from a different racial group in an inappropriate way? Robert Merton suggests that individuals who are not prejudiced often act in bigoted and discriminatory ways. How and why does this happen? Is it possible to live our lives in the category Merton calls the "unprejudiced non-discriminator"?

The primary function of the sociologist is to search out the determinants and consequences of diverse forms of social behavior. To the extent that he succeeds in fulfilling this role, he clarifies the alternatives of organized social action in a given situation and of the probable outcome of each. To this extent, there is no sharp distinction between pure research and applied research. Rather, the difference is one between research with direct implications for particular problems of social action and research which is remote from these problems. Not infrequently, basic research which has succeeded only in clearing up previously confused concepts may have an immediate bearing upon the problems of men in society to a degree not approximated by applied research oriented exclusively to these problems. At least, this is the assumption underlying the present paper:

clarification of apparently unclear and confused concepts in the sphere of race and ethnic relations is a step necessarily prior to the devising of effective programs for reducing intergroup conflict and for promoting equitable access to economic and social opportunities. . . .

The American Creed: As Cultural Ideal, Personal Belief and Practice

The American creed as set forth in the Declaration of Independence, the preamble of the Constitution and the Bill of Rights has often been misstated. This part of the cultural heritage does *not* include the patently false assertion that all men are created equal in capacity or endowment. It does *not* imply that an Einstein and a moron are equal in intellectual capacity or that Joe Louis and a small, frail Columbia professor (or a Mississippian Congressman) are equally endowed with brawny arms harboring muscles as strong as iron bands. It does *not* proclaim universal equality of innate intellectual or physical endowment.

Instead, the creed asserts the indefeasible principle of the human right to full equity—the right of equitable access to justice, freedom and opportunity, irrespective of race or religion or ethnic origin. It proclaims further the universalist doctrine of the dignity of the individual, irrespective of the groups of which he is a part. It is a creed announcing full moral equities for all, not an absurd myth affirming the equality of intellectual and physical capacity of all men everywhere. And it goes on to say that though men differ in innate endowment, they do so as individuals, not by virtue of their group memberships.

Viewed sociologically, the creed is a set of values and precepts embedded in American culture, to which Americans are expected to conform. It is a complex of affirmations, rooted in the historical past and ceremonially celebrated in the present, partly enacted in the laws of the land and partly not. Like all creeds, it is a profession of faith, a part of cultural tradition sanctified by the larger traditions of which it is a part.

It would be a mistaken sociological assertion, however, to suggest that the creed is a fixed and static cultural constant, unmodified in the course of time, just as it would be an error to imply that as an integral part of culture, it evenly blankets all subcultures of the national society. It is indeed dynamic, subject to change and in turn promoting change in other spheres of culture and society. It is, moreover, unevenly distributed throughout the society, being institutionalized as an integral part of local culture in some regions of the society and rejected in others.

. . . Learned men and men in high public positions have repeatedly observed and deplored the disparity between ethos and behavior in the sphere of race and ethnic relations. In his magisterial volumes on the American Negro, for example, Gunnar Myrdal called this gulf between creed and conduct "an American dilemma," and centered his attention

on the prospect of narrowing or closing the gap. The President's Committee on Civil Rights, in their report to the nation, and . . . President [Truman] himself, in a message to Congress, have called public attention to this "serious gap between our ideals and some of our practices."

But as valid as these observations may be, they tend so to simplify the relations between creed and conduct as to be seriously misleading both for social policy and for social science. All these high authorities notwithstanding, the problems of racial and ethnic inequities are not expressible as a discrepancy between high cultural principles and low social conduct. It is a relation not between two variables, official creed and private practice, but between three: first, the cultural creed honored in cultural tradition and partly enacted into law; second, the beliefs and attitudes of individuals regarding the principles of the creed; and third, the actual practices of individuals with reference to it.

Once we substitute these three variables of cultural ideal, belief and actual practice for the customary distinction between the two variables of cultural ideals and actual practices, the entire formulation of the problem becomes changed. We escape from the virtuous but ineffectual impasse of deploring the alleged hypocrisy of many Americans into the more difficult but potentially effectual realm of analyzing the problem in hand.

To describe the problem and to proceed to its analysis, it is necessary to consider the official creed, individuals' beliefs and attitudes concerning the creed, and their actual behavior. Once stated, the distinctions are readily applicable. Individuals may *recognize* the creed as part of a cultural tradition, *without having any private conviction of its moral validity or its binding quality.* Thus, so far as the beliefs of individuals are concerned, we can identify two types: those who genuinely believe in the creed and those who do not (although some of these may, on public or ceremonial occasions, profess adherence to its principles). Similarly, with respect to actual practices: conduct may or may not conform to the creed. But, and this is the salient consideration: *conduct may or may not conform with individuals' own beliefs concerning the moral claims of all men to equal opportunity.*

Stated in formal sociological terms, this asserts that attitudes and overt behavior vary independently. *Prejudicial attitudes need not coincide with discriminatory behavior.* The implications of this statement can be drawn out in terms of a logical syntax whereby the variables are diversely combined, as can be seen in the following typology.

By exploring the interrelations between prejudice and discrimination, we can identify four major types in terms of their attitudes toward the creed and their behavior with respect to it. Each type is found in every region and social class, though in varying numbers. By examining each type, we shall be better prepared to understand their interdependence and the appropriate types of action for curbing ethnic discrimination. The folklabels for each type are intended to aid in their prompt recognition.

Type I: The Unprejudiced Non-Discriminator or All-Weather Liberal

These are the racial and ethnic liberals who adhere to the creed in both belief and practice. They are neither prejudiced nor given to discrimination. Their orientation toward the creed is fixed and stable. Whatever the environing situation, they are likely to abide by their beliefs: hence, the *all-weather* liberal.

This is, of course, the strategic group which *can* act as the spearhead for the progressive extension of the creed into effective practice. They represent the solid foundation both for the measure of ethnic equities which now exist and for the future enlargement of these equities. Integrated with the creed in both belief and practice, they would seem most motivated to influence others toward the same democratic outlook. They represent a reservoir of culturally legitimatized goodwill which can be channeled into an active program for extending belief in the creed and conformity with it in practice.

Most important, as we shall see presently, the all-weather liberals comprise the group which can so reward others for conforming with the creed, as to transform deviants into conformists. They alone can provide the positive social environment for the other types who will no longer find it expedient or rewarding to retain their prejudices or discriminatory practices.

But though the ethnic liberal is a *potential* force for the successive extension of the American creed, he does not fully realize this potentiality in actual fact, for a variety of reasons. Among the limitations on effective action are several fallacies to which the ethnic liberal seems peculiarly subject. First among these is the *fallacy of group soliloquies.* Ethnic liberals are busily engaged in talking to themselves. Repeatedly, the same groups of like-minded liberals seek each other out, hold periodic meetings in which they engage in mutual exhortation and thus lend social and psychological support to one another. But however much these unwittingly self-selected audiences may reinforce the creed among themselves, they do not thus appreciably diffuse the creed in belief or practice to groups which depart from it in one respect or the other.

More, these group soliloquies in which there is typically wholehearted agreement among fellow-liberals tend to promote another fallacy limiting effective action. This is the *fallacy of unanimity.* Continued association with like-minded individuals tends to produce the illusion that a large measure of consensus has been achieved in the community at large. The unanimity regarding essential cultural axioms which obtains in these small groups provokes an overestimation of the strength of the movement and of its effective inroads upon the larger population which does not necessarily share these creedal axioms. Many also mistake participation in the groups of like-minded individuals for effective action. Discussion accordingly takes the place of action. The reinforcement of the creed for oneself is mistaken for the extension of the creed among those outside the limited circle of ethnic liberals.

Arising from adherence to the creed is a third limitation upon effective action, the *fallacy of privatized solutions* to the problem. The ethnic liberal, precisely because he is at one with the American creed, may rest content with his own individual behavior and thus see no need to do anything about the problem at large. Since his own spiritual house is in order, he is not motivated by guilt or shame to work on a collective problem. The very freedom of the liberal from guilt thus prompts him to secede from any *collective* effort to set the national house in order. He essays a *private* solution to a *social* problem. He assumes that numerous individual adjustments will serve in place of a collective adjustment. His outlook, compounded of good moral philosophy but poor sociology, holds that each individual must put his own house in order and fails to recognize that privatized solutions cannot be effected for problems which are essentially social in nature. For clearly, if each person *were* motivated to abide by the American creed, the problem would not be likely to exist in the first place. It is only when a social environment is established by conformists to the creed that deviants can in due course be brought to modify their behavior in the direction of conformity. But this "environment" can be constituted only through collective effort and not through private adherence to a public creed. Thus we have the paradox that the clear conscience of many ethnic liberals may promote the very social situation which permits deviations from

the creed to continue unchecked. Privatized liberalism invites social inaction. Accordingly, there appears the phenomenon of the inactive or passive liberal, himself at spiritual ease, neither prejudiced nor discriminatory, but in a measure tending to contribute to the persistence of prejudice and discrimination through his very inaction.

The fallacies of group soliloquy, unanimity and privatized solutions thus operate to make the potential strength of the ethnic liberals unrealized in practice.

It is only by first recognizing these limitations that the liberal can hope to overcome them. With some hesitancy, one may suggest initial policies for curbing the scope of the three fallacies. The fallacy of group soliloquies can be removed only by having ethnic liberals enter into organized groups not comprised merely by fellow-liberals. This exacts a heavy price on the liberal. It means that he faces initial opposition and resistance rather than prompt consensus. It entails giving up the gratifications of consistent group support.

The fallacy of unanimity can in turn be reduced by coming to see that American society often provides large rewards for those who express their ethnic prejudice in discrimination. Only if the balance of rewards, material and psychological, is modified will behavior be modified. Sheer exhortation and propaganda are not enough. Exhortation verges on a belief in magic if it is not supported by appropriate changes in the social environment to make conformity with the exhortation rewarding.

Finally, the fallacy of privatized solutions requires the militant liberal to motivate the passive liberal to collective effort, possibly by inducing in him a sense of guilt for his unwitting contribution to the problems of ethnic inequities through his own systematic inaction.

One may suggest a unifying theme for the ethnic liberal: goodwill is not enough to modify social reality. It is only when this goodwill is harnessed to social-psychological realism that it can be used to reach cultural objectives.

Type II: The Unprejudiced Discriminator or Fair-Weather Liberal

The fair-weather liberal is the man of expediency who, despite his own freedom from prejudice, supports discriminatory practices when it is the easier or more profitable course. His expediency may take the form of holding his silence and thus implicitly acquiescing in expresions of ethnic prejudice by others or in the practice of discrimination by others. This is the expediency of the timid: the liberal who hesitates to speak up against discrimination for fear he might lose status or be otherwise penalized by his prejudiced associates. Or his expediency may take the form of grasping at advantages in social and economic competition deriving solely from the ethnic status of competitors. This is the expediency of the self-assertive: the employer, himself not an anti-Semite or Negrophobe, who refuses to hire Jewish or Negro workers because "it might hurt business"; the trade union leader who expediently advocates racial discrimination in order not to lose the support of powerful Negrophobes in his union.

In varying degrees, the fair-weather liberal suffers from guilt and shame for departing from his own effective beliefs in the American creed. Each deviation through which he derives a limited reward from passively acquiescing in or actively supporting discrimination contributes cumulatively to this fund of guilt. He is, therefore, peculiarly vulnerable to the efforts of the all-weather liberal who would help him bring his conduct into accord with his beliefs, thus removing this source of guilt. He is the most amenable to cure, because basically he wants to be cured. His is a split conscience which motivates him to cooperate actively with those who will help remove the source of internal conflict.

He thus represents the strategic group promising the largest returns for the least effort. Persistent re-affirmation of the creed will only intensify his conflict; but a long regimen in a favorable social climate can be expected to transform the fair-weather liberal into an all-weather liberal.

Type III: The Prejudiced Non-Discriminator or Fair-Weather Illiberal

The fair-weather illiberal is the reluctant conformist to the creed, the man of prejudice who does not believe in the creed but conforms to it in practice through fear of sanctions which might otherwise be visited upon him. You know him well: the prejudiced employer who discriminates against racial or ethnic groups until a Fair Employment Practice Commission, able and willing to enforce the law, puts the fear of punishment into him; the trade union leader, himself deeply prejudiced, who does away with Jim Crow in his union because the rank-and-file demands that it be done away with; the businessman who forgoes his own prejudices when he finds a profitable market among the very people he hates, fears or despises; the timid bigot who will not express his prejudices when he is in the presence of powerful men who vigorously and effectively affirm their belief in the American creed.

It should be clear that the fair-weather illiberal is the precise counterpart of the fair-weather liberal. Both are men of expediency, to be sure, but expediency dictates different courses of behavior in the two cases. The timid bigot conforms to the creed only when there is danger or loss in deviations, just as the timid liberal deviates from the creed when there is danger or loss in conforming. *Superficial similarity in behavior of the two in the same situation should not be permitted to cloak a basic difference in the meaning of this outwardly similar behavior,* a difference which is as important for social policy as it is for social science. Whereas the timid bigot is under strain when he conforms to the creed, the timid liberal is under strain when he deviates. For ethnic prejudice has deep roots in the character structure of the fair-weather bigot, and this will find overt expression unless there are powerful countervailing forces, institutional, legal and interpersonal. He does not accept the moral legitimacy of the creed; he conforms because he must, and will cease to conform when the pressure is removed. The fair-weather liberal, on the other hand, is effectively committed to the creed and does not require strong institutional pressure to conform; continuing interpersonal relations with all-weather liberals may be sufficient.

This is the one critical point at which the traditional formulation of the problem of ethnic discrimination as a departure from the creed can lead to serious errors of theory and practice. Overt behavioral deviation (or conformity) may signify importantly different situations, depending upon the underlying motivations. Knowing simply that ethnic discrimination is rife in a community does not, therefore, point to appropriate lines of social policy. It is necessary to know also the distribution of ethnic prejudices and basic motivations for these prejudices as well. Communities with the same amount of overt discrimination may represent vastly different types of problems, dependent on whether the population is comprised by a large nucleus of fair-weather liberals ready to abandon their discriminatory practices under slight interpersonal pressure or a large nucleus of fair-weather illiberals who will abandon discrimination only if major changes in the local institutional setting can be effected. Any statement of the problem as a gulf between creedal ideals and prevailing practice is thus seen to be overly-simplified in the precise sense of masking this decisive difference between the type of discrimination exhibited by the fair-weather liberal and by the fair-weather illiberal.

That the gulf-between-ideal-and-practice does not adequately describe the nature of the ethnic problem will become more apparent as we turn to the fourth type in our inventory of prejudice and discrimination.

Type IV: The Prejudiced Discriminator or the All-Weather Illiberal

This type, too, is not unknown to you. He is the confirmed illiberal, the bigot pure and unashamed, the man of prejudice consistent in his departure from the American creed. In some measure, he is found everywhere in the land, though in varying numbers. He derives large social and psychological gains from his conviction that "any white man (including the village idiot) is 'better' than any nigger (including George Washington Carver)." He considers differential treatment of Negro and white not as "discrimination," in the sense of unfair treatment, but as "discriminating," in the sense of showing acute discernment. For him, it is as clear that one "ought" to accord a Negro and a white different treatment in a wide diversity of situations, as it is clear to the population at large that one "ought" to accord a child and an adult different treatment in many situations.

This illustrates anew my reason for questioning the applicability of the unusual formula of the American dilemma as a gap between lofty creed and low conduct. For the confirmed illiberal, ethnic discrimination does *not* represent a discrepancy between *his* ideals and *his* behavior. His ideals proclaim the right, even the duty, of discrimination. Accordingly, his behavior does not entail a sense of social deviation, with the resultant strains which this would involve. The ethnic illiberal is as much a conformist as the ethnic liberal. He is merely conforming to a different cultural and institutional pattern which is centered, not about the creed, but about a doctrine of essential inequality of status ascribed to those of diverse ethnic and racial origins. To overlook this is to overlook the well-known *fact* that our national culture is divided into a number of local subcultures which are not consistent among themselves in all respects. And again, to fail to take this fact of different subcultures into account is to open the door for all manner of errors of social policy in attempting to control the problems of racial and ethnic discrimination.

This view of the all-weather illiberal has one immediate implication with wide bearing upon social policies and sociological theory oriented toward the problem of discrimination. The extreme importance of the social surroundings of the confirmed illiberal at once becomes apparent. For as these surroundings vary, so, in some measure, does the problem of the consistent illiberal. The illiberal, living in those cultural regions where the American creed is widely repudiated and is no effective part of the subculture, has his private ethnic attitudes and practices supported by the local mores, the local institutions and the local power-structure. The illiberal in cultural areas dominated by a large measure of adherence to the American creed is in a social environment where he is isolated and receives small social support for his beliefs and practices. In both instances, the *individual* is an illiberal, to be sure, but he represents two significantly different *sociological types*. In the first instance, he is a *social conformist,* with strong moral and institutional reinforcement, whereas in the second, he is a *social deviant,* lacking strong social corroboration. In the one case, his discrimination involves him in further integration with his network of social relations; in the other, it threatens to cut him off from sustaining interpersonal ties. In the first cultural context, personal change in his ethnic behavior involves alienating himself from people significant to him; in the second context, this change of personal outlook may mean fuller incorporation in groups meaningful to him. In the first situation, modification of his

ethnic views requires him to take the path of greatest resistance whereas in the second, it may mean the path of least resistance. From all this, we may surmise that any social policy aimed at changing the behavior and perhaps the attitudes of the all-weather illiberal will have to take into account the cultural and social structure of the area in which he lives. . . .

Implications of the Typology for Social Policy

. . . In approaching problems of policy, two things are plain. First, these should be considered from the standpoint of the militant ethnic liberal, for he alone is sufficiently motivated to engage in positive action for the reduction of ethnic discrimination. And second, the fair-weather liberal, the fair-weather illiberal and the all-weather illiberal represent types differing sufficiently to require diverse kinds of treatment.

Treatment of the Fair-Weather Liberal

The fair-weather liberal, it will be remembered, discriminates only when it appears expedient to do so, and experiences some measure of guilt for deviating from his own belief in the American creed. He suffers from this conflict between conscience and conduct. Accordingly, he is a relatively easy target for the all-weather liberal. He represents the strategic group promising the largest immediate returns for the least effort. Recognition of this type defines the first task for the militant liberal who would enter into a collective effort to make the creed a viable and effective set of social norms rather than a ceremonial myth. . . .

Since the fair-weather liberal discriminates only when it seems rewarding to do so, the crucial need is so to change social situations that there are few occasions in which discrimination proves rewarding and many in which it does not. This would suggest that ethnic liberals self-consciously and deliberately seek to draw into the social groups where they constitute a comfortable majority a number of the "expedient discriminators." This would serve to counteract the dangers of self-selection through which liberals come to associate primarily with like-minded individuals. It would, further, provide an interpersonal and social environment for the fair-weather liberal in which he would find substantial social and psychological gains from abiding by his own beliefs, gains which would more than offset the rewards attendant upon occasional discrimination. It appears that men do not long persist in behavior which lacks social corroboration.

We have much to learn about the role of numbers and proportions in determining the behavior of members of a group. But it seems that individuals generally act differently when they are numbered among a minority rather than the majority. This is not to say that minorities abdicate their practices in the face of a contrary-acting majority, but only that the same people are subjected to different strains and pressures according to whether they are included in the majority or the minority. And the fair-weather liberal who finds himself associated with militant ethnic liberals may be expected to forgo his occasional deviations into discrimination; he may move from category II into category I. . . .

Treatment of the Fair-Weather Illiberal

Because his *beliefs* correspond to those of the full-fledged liberal, the fair-weather liberal can rather readily be drawn into an interpersonal environment constituted by those of a comparable turn of mind. This would be more difficult for the fair-weather illiberal, whose beliefs are so fully at odds with those of ethnic liberals that he may, at first, only

be alienated by association with them. If the initial tactic for the fair-weather liberal, therefore, is a change in interpersonal environment, the seemingly most appropriate tactic for the fair-weather illiberal is a change in the institutional and legal environment. It is, indeed, probably this type which liberals implicitly have in mind when they expect significant changes in behavior to result from the introduction of controls on ethnic discrimination into the legal machinery of our society.

For this type—and it is a major limitation for planning policies of control that we do not know his numbers or his distribution in the country—it would seem that the most effective tactic is the institution of legal controls administered with strict efficiency. This would presumably reduce the amount of *discrimination* practiced by the fair-weather illiberal, though it might *initially* enhance rather than reduce his *prejudices*. . . .

A second prevalent tactic for modifying the prejudice of the fair-weather illiberal is that of seeking to draw him into interethnic groups explicitly formed for the promotion of tolerance. This, too, seems largely ineffectual, since the deeply prejudiced individual will not enter into such groups of his own volition. As a consequence of this process of self-selection, these tolerance groups soon come to be comprised by the very ethnic liberals who initiated the enterprise.

This barrier of self-selection can be partially hurdled only if the ethnic illiberals are brought into continued association with militant liberals in groups devoted to significant common values, quite remote from objectives of ethnic equity as such. Thus, as our Columbia-Lavanburg researches have found, many fair-weather illiberals *will* live in interracial housing projects in order to enjoy the rewards of superior housing at a given rental. And some of the illiberals thus brought into personal contact with various ethnic groups under the auspices of prestigeful militant liberals come to modify their prejudices. It is, apparently, only through interethnic collaboration, initially enforced by pressures of the situation, for immediate and significant objectives (other than tolerance) that the self-insulation of the fair-weather illiberal from rewarding interethnic contacts can be removed.

But however difficult it may presently be to affect the *prejudicial sentiments* of the fair-weather illiberal, his *discriminatory practices* can be lessened by the uniform, prompt and prestigeful use of legal and institutional sanctions. The critical problem is to ascertain the proportions of fair-weather and all-weather illiberals in a given local population in order to have some clue to the probable effectiveness or ineffectiveness of anti-discrimination legislation.

Treatment of the All-Weather Illiberal

It is, of course, the hitherto confirmed illiberal, persistently translating his prejudices into active discrimination, who represents the most difficult problem. But though he requires longer and more careful treatment, it is possible that he is not beyond change. In every instance, his social surroundings must be assiduously taken into account. It makes a peculiarly large difference whether he is in a cultural region of bigotry or in a predominantly "liberal" area, given over to verbal adherence to the American creed, at the very least. As this cultural climate varies, so must the prescription for his cure and the prognosis for a relatively quick or long delayed recovery.

In an unfavorable cultural climate—and this does not necessarily exclude the benign regions of the Far South—the immediate resort will probably have to be that of working through legal and administrative federal controls over extreme discrimination, with full recognition that, in all probability, these regulations will be systematically evaded for some time to come. In such cultural regions,

we may expect nullification of the law as the common practice, perhaps as common as was the case in the nation at large with respect to the Eighteenth Amendment, often with the connivance of local officers of the law. The large gap between the new law and local mores will not *at once* produce significant change of prevailing practices; token punishments of violations will probably be more common than effective control. At best, one may assume that significant change will be fitful, and excruciatingly slow. But secular changes in the economy may in due course lend support to the new legal framework of control over discrimination. As the economic shoe pinches because the illiberals do not fully mobilize the resources of industrial manpower nor extend their local markets through equitable wage-payments, they may slowly abandon some discriminatory practices as they come to find that these do not always pay—even the discriminator. So far as discrimination is concerned, organized counteraction is possible and some small results may be expected. But it would seem that wishes father thoughts, when one expects basic changes in the immediate future in these regions of institutionalized discrimination.

The situation is somewhat different with regard to the scattered, rather than aggregated, ethnic illiberals found here and there throughout the country. Here the mores and a social organization oriented toward the American creed still have some measure of prestige and the resources of a majority of liberals can be mobilized to isolate the illiberal. In these surroundings, it is possible to move the all-weather illiberal toward Type III—he can be brought to conform with institutional regulations, even though he does not surrender his prejudices. And once he has entered upon this role of the dissident but conforming individual, the remedial program designed for the fair-weather illiberal would be in order.

18
<hr>

RACE AND CIVIL RIGHTS PRE-SEPTEMBER 11, 2001: THE TARGETING OF ARABS AND MUSLIMS

Susan M. Akram • *Kevin R. Johnson*

QUESTIONS TO CONSIDER

Most Americans believe that what makes the United States a great country is our ability to learn from our mistakes. We identify a social injustice, correct it, and vow that such behavior will never happen again. We interned—a nice word for jailed—Japanese Americans throughout World War II, only to release them after the war and pay reparations to survivors decades later. When racial profiling (Driving While Black) emerged as a civil rights issue, the federal government set up a task force to end this practice. As a nation we tell ourselves that such discriminatory, immoral, and un-American actions against one of our own will never happen again. Akram and Johnson argue that like the objects of Japanese American internment in the 1940s and black profiling in the 1990s, Arab Americans and Muslims are America's "new" targets. How is the idea of racialization linked to nationality, stereotypes, and post–9/11 national security and the treatment of Arab and Muslim Americans?

The federal government's response to the tragedy of September 11, 2001, demonstrates the close relationship between immigration law and civil rights in the United States. Noncitizens historically have been vulnerable to civil rights deprivations, in no small part because the law permits, and arguably encourages, extreme governmental conduct with minimal protections for the rights of noncitizens. Unfortunately, the current backlash against Arabs and Muslims fits comfortably into a long history of US government efforts to stifle political dissent.[1] This backlash is especially troubling because of the possibility—exemplified by the internment of persons of Japanese ancestry during World War II—that racial, religious, and other differences have fueled the animosity toward Arabs and Muslims.

It is in the context of a particular historical and legal environment that the post–September 11 targeting of Arabs and Muslims must be understood, as this context both explains Arab and Muslim fears in time of crisis and permits such targeting to be acceptable in the public eye. Such government,

Originally published as part of a longer article, "Race, Civil Rights, and Immigration Law after September 11, 2001: The Targeting of Arabs and Muslims," in the *NYU Annual Survey of American Law* 58, no. 3 (2002): 295–356 [58 N.Y.U. Ann. Surv. Am. L. 295 (2002)].

public, and private acts as the unjustified FBI investigations of Arab- or Muslim-owned businesses, or the closing of Muslim and Arab bank accounts, or the shutting down of Muslim charities, or FBI visits to mosques and Muslim/Arab academics, or "special registration" and other targeted monitoring of persons only of Arab origin or Muslim faith have become quite an accepted part of the "war on terrorism." Yet, should either the government or others target white Irish Catholics or Jews or another racial/ethnic minority in such a sustained manner, they would doubtless face significant and vociferous challenge for racial or religious profiling.

Commentators have observed how popular perceptions of racial and other minorities influence their treatment under the law.[2] As with other minority groups, this seems true for Arabs and Muslims. As Professor Natsu Saito summarizes,

> Arab Americans and Muslims have been "raced" as "terrorists": foreign, disloyal, and imminently threatening. Although Arabs trace their roots to the Middle East and claim many different religious backgrounds, and Muslims come from all over the world . . . , these distinctions are blurred and negative images about either Arabs or Muslims are often attributed to both. As Ibrahim Hooper of the Council on American-Islamic Relations notes, "The common stereotypes are that we're all Arabs, we're all violent and we're all conducting a holy war."[3]

The demonization of Arabs and Muslims in the United States, accompanied by harsh legal measures directed at them, began well before the tragedy of September 11, 2001.[4] It can be traced to popular stereotypes,[5] years of mythmaking by film and media,[6] racism during times of national crisis,[7] and a campaign to build political support for US foreign policy in the Middle East.[8] Since at least the 1970s, US laws and policies have been founded on the assumption that Arab and Muslim noncitizens are potential terrorists and have targeted this group for special treatment under the law.[9] The post–September 11 targeting of Muslims and Arabs is simply the latest chapter in this history.[10]

The Stereotyping of Arabs as Terrorists and Religious Fanatics

Similar to the animus toward other racial minorities, anti-Arab, anti-Muslim animus can be viewed as part of a dynamic process of "racialization."[11] Racialization, as used here, views "race" as "an unstable and 'decentered' complex of social meanings constantly being transformed by political struggle."[12] This understanding of race breaks with the traditional view that race is fixed by biology; it instead considers "racial formation" to explain how race operates in the United States.[13]

Defining race as a process in which racial difference is socially, not biologically, constructed assists in examining the treatment of Arabs and Muslims in the United States; their experiences show the severe damage that racialization can do and offer hope that the process can be reversed.[14] Recognizing that race is the product of social construction, the US Supreme Court held that different groups may be racialized and that Arabs can be discriminated against as members of a different "race" in violation of the civil rights laws.[15]

Through the process of racialization, Arabs and Muslims have been considered racially different from whites and other racial minorities. Professor Nabeel Abraham, a leading commentator on racism against Arabs and Muslims in the United States, identifies three distinct ways in which Arabs and Muslims have been racialized: (1) through political violence by extremist groups based on the

Arab-Israeli conflict in the Middle East, (2) by xenophobic violence targeting Arabs and Muslims at the local level, and (3) through the hostility arising from international crises affecting the United States and its citizens.[16] The law and its enforcement also have contributed to hostility toward Arabs and Muslims in the United States.[17]

The Silencing of Arabs Through Politically Motivated Violence and Intimidation

Conflict in the Middle East provokes violence against Arabs and Muslims in the United States, as well as the lesser-known intimidation tactics followed by some mainstream activist organizations. A Rand Corporation study conducted for the US Department of Energy concludes that the Jewish Defense League (JDL) was, for more than a decade, one of the most active terrorist groups, as classified by the FBI, in the United States.[18] The study reviews the violence known to have been committed by the JDL, as well as incidents in which the JDL's involvement was suspected, all of which was described as part of a strategy "to eliminate perceived enemies of the Jewish people and Israel."[19] The violence included bombings of Arab foreign offices and planting bombs in American-Arab Anti-Discrimination Committee offices across the country.[20] According to the FBI, Jewish extremist organizations were responsible for twenty terrorist incidents in the 1980s.[21]

Despite the many incidents of anti-Arab violence at the hands of Jewish extremist groups, influential hate-crime studies fail to include these groups as perpetrators of these crimes.[22] According to Professor Abraham, "Jewish extremist groups constitute an undeniable source of anti-Arab hate violence not discussed in conventional accounts of racist violence in the United States."[23]

Even less publicized than the anti-Arab violence of extremist groups is the campaign by mainstream organizations, such as the Anti-Defamation League of B'nai B'rith (ADL), to intimidate and silence Arabs and Muslims. Established in the early 1900s as an organization with the mission of fighting anti-Semitism, the ADL gained a reputation as a leading antidiscrimination organization in the United States. Unfortunately, after the creation of Israel in 1948, the ADL added a new mission: to discredit or silence critics of Israel or defenders of Palestinian human rights.[24] The ADL has aggressively engaged in efforts to intimidate Arabs, Muslims, and others with similar views on the Middle East conflict, discouraging them from participating in political debate. In 1983, for example, the ADL released a handbook entitled *Pro-Arab Propaganda in America: Vehicles and Voices*.[25] It lists as "anti-Israel propagandists" some of the most prominent scholars on Middle East issues, including Columbia University's Edward Said and Harvard University's Walid Khalidi, as well as humanitarian organizations dealing with the Middle East or Palestine. Alfred Lilienthal, an influential commentator on Middle East issues, himself on the ADL's blacklist, claims, "Many ADL charges against critics of Israel are totally inaccurate, questionable, or based upon half-truths," and the ADL often characterizes groups or individuals who criticize Israel or Zionism as "extremists" intent on eradicating Israel or inciting anti-Semitism in America.[26] The ADL handbook was widely distributed throughout the United States to, according to critics, challenge, harass, and silence groups and individuals on the list.

The ADL is not the only mainstream organization to distribute lists of Arab American individuals and groups and those working with them. The American Israel Public Affairs Committee (AIPAC) issued two similar lists.[27] Through a campaign, primarily on college campuses, organized against groups and individuals on these lists, AIPAC and the ADL have harassed and intimidated academics and activists for years.[28]

Aside from its campaign to discredit and silence academics on university campuses, the ADL has also sought to silence pro-Muslim and pro-Arab speakers from engaging in public debate concerning the Middle East. Most recently, the Florida ADL unsuccessfully lobbied the Florida Commission on Human Relations to exclude a Muslim representative from a panel at a civil rights conference.[29] Similarly, the American Jewish Committee sought to exclude Ghazi Khankan, executive director of the New York chapter of the Council on American-Islamic Relations (CAIR), from participating in a public forum on multicultural understanding because he was "anti-Israel."[30] The ADL demanded that CAIR's Northern California director be prevented from testifying about hate crimes before the California Select Committee on Hate Crimes.[31]

The full extent of the ADL's activities against Arabs did not come to light until January 1993, when the results of an FBI investigation of a veteran San Francisco Police Department officer and an ADL-paid undercover agent became public. Law enforcement authorities uncovered computerized files on thousands of Arab Americans and information on Arab organizations, as well as many other mainstream organizations.[32] These files reflected surveillance of organizations and leaders, including the NAACP, Greenpeace, the ACLU, the Asian Law Caucus, the National Lawyers Guild, the Rainbow Coalition, Jews for Jesus, and three current or past members of the US Congress.[33] The information included confidential law enforcement files and information from the Department of Motor Vehicles.[34] The FBI confirmed that the ADL provided information from the surveillance activities to the South African government.[35] The ADL's attorney admitted that

the ADL had passed surveillance information to Israel.[36] At least one US citizen of Arab descent who had been the subject of surveillance was arrested in Israel when he visited the Israeli-occupied Palestinian territories.[37] When the spying became public, an array of civil rights lawsuits was filed.[38] As part of the settlement of a class action, the ADL was permanently enjoined from illegal spying on Arab American and other civil rights groups.[39]

Despite the settlement and the permanent injunction, the damage to the civil liberties of Arabs in the United States from the ADL's surveillance activities has been done. The discovery of espionage has contributed to the climate of fear for Arab and Muslim Americans. US intelligence agencies may have obtained information from the ADL that could potentially place politically active Arab groups and individuals under heightened government scrutiny.[40] Consequently, Arab Americans may perceive that the US government is in collusion with Israeli and anti-Arab organizations. Such perceptions have been reinforced by the revelation that information provided by the ADL triggered the FBI investigation and arrest of the "LA Eight," a group of noncitizens, for alleged technical violations of the Immigration and Nationality Act (INA).[41] Furthermore, "no . . . major American Jewish organization has condemned the ADL for its political excesses or its documented association with Israeli intelligence organizations."[42] Our research has not discovered any publication in which the ADL admitted culpability or disavowed these activities.

In sum, the ADL has engaged in surveillance of Arab and Muslim groups in an apparent effort to intimidate and silence those voices it deems "anti-Semitic."[43] As Professor Abraham summarizes: "The overall effect of the ADL's practices is to reinforce the image of Arabs as terrorists and security threats, thereby creating a climate of fear, suspicion, and hostility towards Arab-Americans and others who espouse critical views of Israel, possibly leading to death threats and bodily harm."[44]

The Impact of Anti-Arab Images in Popular Culture

Racism against Arabs is not all the work of political activists. Importantly, media and film, feeding on existing stereotypes in US society about Arabs and Muslims, have found a ready audience for dangerous and one-dimensional images. Such depictions contribute to the racialization of Arabs and Muslims. In addition, in a study on anti-Arab racism, Professor Abraham documents a range of racial epithets, intolerant speech, and violence directed at Arabs by private citizens and public officials.[45]

Jack Shaheen's review of US films offers convincing evidence of the vilification of Arabs and Muslims by the movie industry. Shaheen catalogs hundreds of Hollywood movies in which Arabs or Muslims are portrayed as terrorists or otherwise placed in a negative, often nonhuman, light. Muslims are shown as hostile invaders or "lecherous, oily sheikhs intent on using nuclear weapons."[46] A far-too-common scene shows a mosque with Arabs at prayer, then cuts away to show civilians being gunned down.

These movies show Westerners hurling such epithets at Arabs as "assholes," "bastards," "camel-dicks," "pigs," "devil-worshipers," "jackals," "rats," "rag-heads," "towel-heads," "scum-buckets," "sons-of-dogs," "buzzards of the jungle," "sons-of-whores," "sons-of-unnamed goats," and "sons-of-she-camels."[47] Arab women are often portrayed as weak and mute, covered in black, or as scantily clad belly dancers.

The US Department of Defense has cooperated with Hollywood in making more than a dozen films showing US soldiers killing Arabs and Muslims. Audiences apparently embrace the demonization in these movies. As Shaheen notes,

> To my knowledge, no Hollywood WWI, WWII, or Korean War movie has ever shown America's fighting forces slaughtering children. Yet, near the conclusion of [the movie] Rules of Engagement, US marines open fire on the Yemenis, shooting 83 men, women, and children. During the scene, viewers rose to their feet, clapped and cheered. Boasts director Friedkin, "I've seen audiences stand up and applaud the film throughout the United States."[48]

One-sided film portrayals omit images of Arabs and Muslims as ordinary people with families and friends or as outstanding members of communities, scholars, writers, or scientists. Few US movies have depicted Arabs or Muslims in a favorable light and even fewer have included them in leading roles. Commentators rarely criticize the unbalanced depiction of Arabs and Muslims.[49] The stereotyping and demonization of Arabs and Muslims by American films may well have gone largely unnoticed because these characterizations are entirely consistent with widespread attitudes in US society.

Reinforcing the anti-Arab, anti-Muslim stereotypes in film, public officials have openly used intolerant speech toward Arabs and Muslims—speech that would be clearly unacceptable if directed at other minority groups.[50] For example, a mayoral candidate in Dearborn, Michigan, a suburb of Detroit, distributed a campaign brochure in which he claimed the city's Arab Americans "threaten our neighborhoods, the value of our property and a darned good way of life."[51] In 1981, the governor of Michigan proclaimed that Michigan's economic woes were due to the "damn Arabs."[52] Such statements by public officials fuel the perception that prejudice and animosity directed at Arabs and Muslims are socially acceptable.

Moreover, prominent politicians have returned financial contributions from Arab American and American Muslim groups, fearing the political risks of the acceptance of such monies. For example, in the 1984 presidential campaign, Walter Mondale returned five thousand dollars in contributions made by US citizens of Arab ancestry.[53] Philadelphia mayoral candidate Wilson Goode returned more than two thousand dollars in campaign contributions from Arab Americans.[54] In his first congressional race, Joe Kennedy returned one hundred dollars to James Abourezk, a former US senator who is Arab American.[55] New York senator Hillary Clinton returned fifty thousand dollars to Muslim organizations.[56] Although several of these politicians stated that they returned the funds because of the contributors' anti-Semitic remarks, the perception remains that Arabs and Muslims cannot participate in the body politic. For similar reasons, New York City mayor Rudolph Giuliani returned ten million dollars donated by a Saudi Arabian prince for the victims of the World Trade Center destruction due to a public outcry caused by the contributor's criticism of US foreign policy in the Middle East.[57]

Racism in Times of National Crisis

Hostility toward minorities often accompanies times of crisis in the United States. For Arabs and Muslims, this may be even more problematic. Perpetrators of hate crimes against Arabs and Muslims frequently fail to differentiate among persons based on religion or ethnic origin, from Pakistanis, Indians, Iranians, and Japanese to Muslims, Sikhs, and Christian Arabs.[58] The widespread perception in the United States is that Arabs and Muslims are identical and eager to wage a holy war against the United States. In fact, according to a 1993 report, only 12 percent of the Muslims in the United States are Arab,[59] and Arab Muslims at that time were

even a minority in the Arab American community.[60] Although there are Muslim extremists, the majority of Muslims are "decent, law-abiding, productive citizens."[61]

Because of the lack of differentiation between different types of Arabs and Muslims, terrorist acts by small groups of Arabs and Muslims often have been followed by generalized hostility toward entire communities of Arabs and Muslims in the United States. For example, after Lebanese Shiite gunmen in 1985 hijacked TWA Flight 847 to Beirut, beat an American on the plane to death, and held the remaining passengers hostage for more than two weeks,[62] violent attacks against persons of Arab and Muslim origin occurred across the United States. Islamic centers and Arab American organizations were vandalized and threatened. A Houston mosque was firebombed. A bomb exploded in the American-Arab Anti-Discrimination Committee office in Boston, severely injuring two police officers.[63] Later that same year, after terrorists hijacked the *Achille Lauro* cruise liner and murdered a passenger, a wave of anti-Arab violence swept the country, including the bombing of an American-Arab Anti-Discrimination Committee office that killed its regional executive director.[64]

In 1986, in apparent response to the Reagan administration's "war on terrorism" directed at Libya, another episode of anti-Arab harassment and violence broke out. The same night as a US bombing raid on Libya, the American-Arab Anti-Discrimination Committee national office in Washington received threats. Shortly thereafter, the Detroit American-Arab Anti-Discrimination Committee office, the Dearborn Arab Community Center, and the Detroit Arab American newspaper received bomb threats.[65] Threats, beatings, and other violent attacks on Arabs were reported across the United States. At this time, someone broke into a Palestinian family's home, set off a smoke bomb inside the house, and painted slogans such as "Go Back to Libya" on the walls.[66]

The first Gulf War intensified anti-Arab hostility in the United States. The American-Arab Anti-Discrimination Committee reported four anti-Arab hate crimes for 1990 before the invasion of Kuwait in August of that year. Between the invasion and February 1991, the committee reported 175 incidents.[67] When US intervention commenced in January 1991, Arab and Muslim businesses and community organizations were bombed, vandalized, and subjected to harrassment.[68]

The US Government and the Role of Law

Institutional racism through the law and its enforcement has contributed to the racialization and targeting of Arabs and Muslims. The federal government's actions taken in the name of fighting terrorism have been followed by indiscriminate threats and violence against Arabs and Muslims in the United States. This frightening pattern has repeated itself in the wake of September 11.[69]

The Nixon administration's "Operation Boulder" was an early effort of the US government to target Arabs in the United States for special investigation and discourage their political activism on Middle Eastern issues.[70] Ostensibly designed to confront the threat posed by terrorists who took hostages and murdered athletes at the 1972 Munich Olympics, the president's directives authorized the FBI to investigate people of "Arabic origin" to determine their potential relationship with "terrorist" activities related to the Arab-Israeli conflict.[71] The FBI admittedly wiretapped prominent Detroit lawyer Abdeen Jabara, then president of the Association of Arab-American University Graduates.[72]

Later in the 1970s, President Carter took numerous steps against Iranians and Iran in response to the crisis in which US citizens were held hostage in Tehran. In the 1980s, the Reagan administration's foreign policy also involved combating "terrorism." President Reagan in 1986 announced that the US government had evidence that Libyan leader Muammar Qaddafi was responsible for terrorist attacks, such as those at the Rome and Vienna airports, and was planning further attacks in the United States.[73] The US Navy later that year shot down two Libyan planes off the coast of Libya. President Reagan announced that "we have the evidence" that Qaddafi was sending hit teams to assassinate the US president.[74] Despite official responses from the Austrian, Italian, and Israeli governments that there was no evidence of Libyan involvement in the Rome and Vienna attacks or that any Libyan "hit squads" had been sent to the United States,[75] the United States bombed Libya. Violence against US residents of Arab or Middle Eastern origin and vandalism of their community centers, mosques, businesses, and homes followed the public announcements.

In the 1990s, after the US invasion of Kuwait, the US government's "war on terrorism" shifted focus to Iraq and its leader, Saddam Hussein. The Bush administration accused Iraqi forces of atrocities against Kuwaitis. The administration then launched a surveillance program directed at Arab Americans. The FBI interrogated Arab and Muslim leaders, activists, and antiwar demonstrators across the country.[76] The Department of Justice instituted fingerprinting of all residents and immigrants of Arab origin in the United States; the Federal Aviation Administration commenced a system of airline profiling of persons from the Arab world.[77] Private harassment and violence against Arab and Muslim communities followed.

Foreign policy has played a large role in immigration measures directed at Arabs and Muslims in the United States. The Immigration and Naturalization Service (INS)[78]

---

sought to deport noncitizens of Palestinian ancestry[79] at the same time that the federal government attempted to shut down Palestine Liberation Organization (PLO) offices in the United States and at the United Nations.[80] In the 1980s, President Reagan issued a secret National Security Decision Directive that authorized the creation of a network of agencies designed to prevent "terrorists" from entering or remaining in the United States. Under one proposal, intelligence agencies would provide the INS with "names, nationalities and other identifying data and evidence relating to *alien undesirables and suspected terrorists* believed to be in . . . the U.S."[81] The Alien Border Control Committee also considered an INS-created strategy outlined in a document entitled "Alien Terrorists and Undesirables: A Contingency Plan." The strategy called for mass arrests and detentions of noncitizens from Arab nations and Iran, and suggested using ideological exclusion grounds in the immigration laws to remove noncitizens from Arab countries and Iran already in the United States.[82]

Efforts to Stifle Political Dissent: The Case of the LA Eight

Critics long have pointed out that the United States has discriminated against Arabs and Muslims in applying the terrorist exclusion provisions of the INA, the comprehensive US immigration law.[83] Arabs, particularly Palestinians, are the primary groups subject to many of the terrorism provisions. During the first Gulf War crisis, for example, government officials fingerprinted and photographed all entrants to the US who held Iraqi or Kuwaiti passports without regard to evidence of past terrorist activities or sympathies.[84] Related to the terrorist provisions in the immigration laws are those permitting exclusion of noncitizens based on political beliefs or associations, passed during the anticommunist fervor of the McCarthy era.[85] The courts generally upheld application of the ideological exclusions, which provoked sharp academic criticism. In 1977, Congress enacted the McGovern Amendment, which permitted the attorney general to waive the exclusion of any noncitizen affiliated with an organization proscribed by the United States.[86] In 1979, Congress created a single exception to the McGovern Amendment that denied the exclusion waiver for only one group: PLO officials or representatives.[87] In any event, through a variety of means, consular officers could continue to exclude a person based on ideology.

The federal government's efforts to remove the LA Eight illustrate the extremes to which it will resort in order to deport political dissidents from the country.[88] The case began before dawn on January 26, 1987, when officers of the FBI, INS, and Los Angeles Police Department descended on the home of Khader Hamide, a US lawful permanent resident, and his Kenyan-born wife, Julie Mungai. They were handcuffed, told they were being arrested for "terrorism," and taken into custody while police blocked the street and an FBI helicopter hovered overhead.[89] Six other individuals were arrested that morning.

The INS sought to remove the LA Eight from the United States based on political ideology. Both the director of the FBI and the regional counsel of the INS testified before Congress that the sole basis of the government's efforts to deport the LA Eight was their political affiliations. In the words of FBI director William Webster, "All of them were arrested because they are alleged to be members of a world-wide Communist organization which under the [INA] makes them eligible for deportation . . . *If these individuals had been United States citizens, there would not have been a basis for their arrest.*"[90] The evidence underlying the government's charges amounted to a claim that the LA Eight read or distributed literature linked to the Popular Front for the Liberation of Palestine (PFLP), which the district court found was engaged in a wide range of lawful activities from providing education, health care, social services, and day care to cultural and political activities.[91] The district court ruled that the ideological exclusion grounds violated the First Amendment.[92]

In 1990, while the LA Eight case was pending, Congress repealed the ideological exclusion grounds from the immigration laws. The INS then instituted new proceedings against the LA Eight based on charges of terrorism, as well as other grounds. The INA permits removal of noncitizens who have "engaged in terrorist activity," which is defined as having committed "in an individual capacity or as a member of an organization, an act of terrorist activity or an act which the actor knows, or reasonably should know, *affords material support to any individual, organization, or government in conducting a terrorist activity at any time.*"[93] This broad language authorizes the INS to deport or exclude an individual who has donated money to an organization for its legal, social, or charitable activities, if any part of that organization also has engaged in terrorism, as broadly defined.[94]

The thrust of the INS case was based on the LA Eight's affiliation with the PFLP. Because this provision previously had never been used by the INS to seek to deport a noncitizen from the United States, the LA Eight claimed that the federal government selectively enforced the immigration laws against them for exercising their First Amendment rights. In the end, the Supreme Court ruled that the 1996 amendments to the immigration laws barred judicial review of their claim.[95]

Following the court's decision, the case was remanded to the immigration court. In 2001, the court dismissed the primary removal charges on the grounds that they were not meant to apply retroactively. Nonetheless, the federal government continues its efforts to deport the LA Eight, even relying on secret evidence in seeking removal of two of the eight.[96]

The Secret Evidence Cases

The INS also has selectively targeted Arabs and Muslims through the use of secret evidence—evidence that it refuses to disclose to the noncitizen or his or her counsel—to charge, detain, and deny bond or release in removal proceedings. By 1999, twenty-five secret evidence cases were pending.[97]

In *Rafeedie v. INS*,[98] Fouad Rafeedie, a twenty-year lawful permanent resident of Palestinian origin, was arrested open returning to the United States after a two-week trip to a conference in Syria sponsored by the Palestine Youth Organization. He was placed in summary exclusion proceedings based on ideological grounds. The INS claimed that disclosing its evidence against Rafeedie would be "prejudicial to the public interest, safety, or security of the United States."[99] The court of appeals rejected the INS position and required application of the ordinary due process analysis in deciding whether the federal government's national security interests outweighed Rafeedie's First Amendment rights. The court observed that the only way Rafeedie could have prevailed over the secret evidence proceeding would have been to "rebut the undisclosed evidence against him . . . It is difficult to imagine how even someone innocent of all wrong-doing could meet such a burden."[100]

Since repeal of the ideological exclusion provisions of the INA in 1990, the INS has relied on secret evidence to detain and deport Arabs and Muslims. Moreover, in response to the 1995 Oklahoma City bombing, Congress enacted antiterrorism legislation that has facilitated the targeting of Arab and Muslim noncitizens: the Antiterrorism and Effective Death Penalty Act (AEDPA)[101] and the Illegal Immigration Reform and Individual Responsibility Act (IIRIRA).[102] Both brought about radical changes to the immigration laws and effectively allowed for the possibility of ideological exclusion and removal through secret evidence proceedings.

Bolstered by the 1996 reforms curtailing the rights of noncitizens, the INS brought approximately two dozen deportation actions based on secret evidence, claiming that disclosing the evidence would compromise the security of the United States.[103] Although the INS denies that it selectively uses secret evidence against Arabs and Muslims, our research has not uncovered a single secret evidence case not involving an Arab or Muslim noncitizen.[104]

AEDPA established a special procedure for detaining and deporting "alien terrorists" that permits the use of secret evidence with certain procedural and constitutional safeguards designed to protect constitutional rights. The federal government, however, has not yet used the new procedure; instead, it has relied on preexisting regulations that it claims authorize the use of secret evidence in the immigration courts. By so doing, the government has avoided complying with AEDPA's safeguards, including requiring the production of an unclassified summary of the secret evidence to the noncitizen and having a federal court assess the constitutionality of the use of secret evidence. This strategy has allowed the US government to avoid charging the noncitizen under a substantive "terrorism" provision of the INA, which would require the government to prove such a charge.[105]

The cases of the "Iraqi Seven" arose out of the US government's resettlement of Iraqi Kurds after the Gulf War.[106] The Iraqi men, who had all worked for a CIA-funded Iraqi opposition group, were evacuated from Iraq by the United States. The INS commenced exclusion proceedings against them based on alleged visa violations. Fearing persecution if returned to Iraq, the seven sought asylum in the United States. Relying primarily on secret evidence, the immigration judge found them to be national security risks.

As a result of the litigation, the INS released five hundred pages of evidence used against the Iraqi Seven. James Woolsey, the former head of the CIA who directed the US government's efforts to organize the overthrow of Saddam Hussein, was one of the lawyers representing the Iraqis. Besides concluding that hundreds of pages had been erroneously classified, Woolsey found that the evidence was based on serious errors in Arabic-English translations; ethnic and religious stereotyping by the FBI; and reliance on unreliable information, including rumors and innuendo. He claimed that the US government made material misrepresentations to the immigration judge.[107] Despite the weakness of the government's case, the case was only concluded when five of the Iraqis entered into a settlement agreement, withdrawing their asylum claims in exchange for release from detention.

Mazen al-Najjar and Anwar Haddam experienced the longest detentions connected with secret evidence proceedings: Al-Najjar was detained for more than four years[108] and Haddam was jailed for four years,[109] both on allegations of association with terrorism. Al-Najjar, a stateless Palestinian, was editor of the journal of the World and Islam Studies Enterprise (WISE), a think tank based at the University of South Florida devoted to promoting discussion of Middle East issues. The INS arrested al-Najjar and placed him in removal proceedings as part of an FBI investigation against a former WISE administrator who became head of the Islamic Jihad. The arrest and detention was based on secret evidence.[110] Al-Najjar was held in custody for three years and seven months before his release in December 2000. He was then rearrested in November 2001, and remained in custody until his deportation in August 2002.[111] No terrorism charges were ever brought, but he was detained and his removal was sought on the basis of visa violations and on evidence the INS refused to disclose.[112]

Anwar Haddam was an elected member of the Algerian Parliament. A professor of physics at the University of Algiers, he ran for election as a member of the Islamic Salvation Front (FIS), a moderate Islamic party that swept the 1991 elections with 80 percent of the vote. The Algerian military staged a coup d'état, arrested the president of the FIS, and rounded up thousands of its members. Top FIS officials were killed or imprisoned, while thousands of FIS supporters were imprisoned, tortured, and executed. A civil war followed with tens of thousands of deaths. One of the few elected FIS officials who managed to escape Algeria, Haddam entered the United States on a valid nonimmigrant visa in 1992, and later filed an asylum claim. The INS took Haddam into custody and detained him based on secret evidence.[113]

In both the al-Najjar and Haddam cases, as the secret evidence was either unclassified or disclosed, it was demonstrated that the government's "terrorist" claims were based on unreliable evidence and apparently unfounded. Yet, the inability to challenge the secret evidence cost al-Najjar and Haddam years of their lives in custody.

Nasser Ahmed, a father of US-citizen children, was held in custody and denied bond for three-and-a-half years based on secret evidence.[114] Charged in April 1995 with overstaying his visa, he had been released on fifteen thousand dollars bond while he pursued a claim for political asylum. In 1996, while his own deportation proceedings were ongoing, Ahmed became the court-appointed translator for the attorneys representing Sheik Omar Abdel Rahman, later convicted

in the 1993 World Trade Center bombing attempt. As Ahmed was going to immigration court for his asylum hearing, the INS arrested him and opposed his release on bond. On remand, the immigration court dismissed the evidence of the government's remaining contentions on the grounds that it was based on an informant who had personal reasons for seeking Ahmed's deportation.

As the secret evidence cases have slowly moved toward conclusion, the government's claims in all of the cases have evaporated. No case has included sufficient evidence of terrorism-related charges necessary to justify the years of detention. Besides the individual loss of liberty, the cases have chilled Arab and Muslim political speech.

Conclusion

Stereotypes about Arabs and Muslims have influenced immigration law and its enforcement, as well as the civil rights of Arab and Muslim noncitizens in the United States. This discussion is by no means comprehensive. Other examples of the US government's response to perceived fears of Arab and Muslim terrorism are plentiful. For example, in the 1990s, the much-publicized case of asylum-seeker Sheik Omar Abdel Rahman[115] by itself resulted in changes to the immigration laws that narrowed the rights of all asylum applicants.[116] An episode of the popular television show *60 Minutes*,[117] focusing on his alleged abuse of the asylum system, triggered a chain reaction that culminated in 1996 asylum reforms. These reforms included a summary exclusion procedure by which a noncitizen could be excluded from the country without a hearing on an asylum or other claim to relief.[118]

As shown above, demonization of Arabs and Muslims has had an impact on the evolution of the law and encouraged harsh governmental efforts to remove Arabs and Muslims from the United States. The same stereotypes have affected the civil rights of all persons of Arab and Muslim ancestry in the United States since September 11, 2001. Importantly, the aftermath of the security measures taken since then threatens to have enduring impacts on the civil rights of all immigrants, and on US citizens as well.

NOTES

1. See Kevin R. Johnson, "The Antiterrorism Act, the Immigration Reform Act, and Ideological Regulation in the Immigration Laws: Important Lessons for Citizens and Noncitizens," *St Mary's Law Journal* 28 (1997): 841–69. See generally James Morton Smith, *Freedom's Fetters: The Alien and Sedition Laws and American Civil Liberties* (Ithaca, NY: Cornell University Press, 1956); see also James X. Dempsey and David Cole, *Terrorism and the Constitution: Sacrificing Civil Liberties in the Name of National Security* (Los Angeles: First Amendment Foundation, 1999).

2. Richard Delgado and Jean Stefancic, "Images of the Outsider in American Law and Culture: Can Free Expression Remedy Systemic Social Ills?" *Cornell Law Review* 77, no. 6 (1992): 1258; Cynthia Kwei Yung Lee, "Race and Self-Defense: Toward a Normative Conception of Reasonableness," *Minnesota Law Review* 81 (1996): 402–52; Margaret M. Russell, "Race and the Dominant Gaze: Narratives of Law and Inequality in Popular Film," *Legal Studies Forum* 15 (1991): 243; see also Jody Armour, "Stereotypes and Prejudice: Helping Legal Decisionmakers Break the Prejudice Habit," *California Law Review* 83, no. 3 (May 1995): 733.

3. Natsu Taylor Saito, "Symbolism Under Siege: Japanese American Redress and the 'Racing' of Arab Americans as 'Terrorists,'" *Asian Law Journal* 8, no. 1 (May 2001): 11–26.

4. See Susan M. Akram, "Scheherezade Meets Kafka: Two Dozen Sordid Tales of Ideological Exclusion," *Georgetown Immigration Law Journal* 14 (1999): 54.

5. Edward W. Said, "A Devil Theory of Islam," *The Nation*, August 12, 1996, 28; see also Ahmed Yousef and Caroline F. Keeble, *The Agent: The Truth Behind the Anti-Muslim Campaign in America* (UASR Publishing Group, 1999).

6. See Nabeel Abraham, "Anti-Arab Racism and Violence in the United States," in *The Development of Arab-American Identity*, ed. Ernest McCarus (Ann Arbor, MI: University of Michigan Press, 1994); Jack G. Shaheen, *Reel Bad Arabs: How Hollywood Vilifies a People* (New York: Olive Branch Press, 2001); see also the archived reports of the American-Arab Anti-Discrimination Committee on anti-Arab hate crimes, http://www.adc.org.

7. See Nabeel Abraham, "The Gulf Crisis and Anti-Arab Racism in America," in *Collateral Damage: The New World Order at Home and Abroad*, ed. Cynthia Peters (Boston: South End Press, 1991), 255–78; see also Michael J. Whidden, "Unequal Justice: Arabs in America and United States Antiterrorism Legislation," *Fordham Law Review* 69, no. 6 (May 2001): 2825, and Suad Joseph, "Against the Grain of the Nation—The Arab," in *Arabs in America: Building a New Future*, ed. Michael W. Suleiman (Philadelphia: Temple University Press, 1999).

8. Alfred M. Lilienthal, "The Changing Role of B'nai B'rith's Anti-Defamation League," *Washington Report on Middle East Affairs*, June 1993, 18; Anti-Defamation League of B'nai B'rith, *Pro-Arab Propaganda in America: Vehicles and Voices: A Handbook* (New York: Anti-Defamation League of B'nai B'rith, 1983). The Middle East Studies Association (MESA) has passed two resolutions criticizing the ADL for defaming students, teachers, and researchers as "pro-Arab propagandists." See Betsy Barlow, "Middle East Studies Association Condemns ADL Philadelphia Office," *Washington Report*, January–February 1997, 72; Phebe Marr, "MESA Condemns Blacklisting," *Washington Report*, December 17, 1984, 8.

9. See Ian F. Haney López, "Institutional Racism: Judicial Conduct and a New Theory of Racial Discrimination," *Yale Law Journal* 109, no. 8 (June 2000); see also Akram, "Scheherezade Meets Kafka," which traces the contemporary targeting of Arabs and Muslims in immigration enforcement (see n. 4).

10. For analysis of the balancing of necessary security measures and democratic values in response to terrorism, see Symposium, "Law and the War on Terrorism," *Harvard Journal of Law and Public Policy* 25 (Spring 2002); "Responding to Terrorism: Crime,

Punishment, and War," *Harvard Law Review* 115 (2002): 1217–38; Peter Margulies, "Uncertain Arrivals: Immigration, Terror, and Democracy after September 11," *Utah Law Review* (2002): 481.

11. Ian F. Haney López, "The Social Construction of Race: Some Observations on Illusion, Fabrication, and Choice," *Harvard Civil Rights-Civil Liberties Law Review* 29, no. 1 (Winter 1994).

12. Michael Omi and Howard Winant, *Racial Formation in the United States: From the 1960s to the 1980s* (New York: Routledge and Kegan Paul, 1986).

13. Ibid., 68–69.

14. See Saito, "Symbolism Under Siege" (see n. 3).

15. *St Francis Coll. v. Al-Khazraji*, 481 US 604, 610n4 (1987).

16. See Abraham, "Anti-Arab Racism and Violence" (see n. 6).

17. López, "Institutional Racism" (see n. 9); M. Cherif Bassiouni, introduction to *The Civil Rights of Arab-Americans*, ed. M. Cherif Bassiouni (Washington, DC: Association of Arab-American University Graduates, 1974). For analysis of the negative impacts of Operation Boulder (code name for Nixon's 1972 policy) on the civil rights of Arab Americans, see Abdeen M. Jabara, "Operation Arab: The Nixon Administration's Measures in the United States After Munich," in Bassiouni, *Civil Rights of Arab-Americans*, 1–14.

18. Bruce Hoffman, *Terrorism in the United States and the Potential Threat to Nuclear Facilities* (Santa Monica, CA: Rand Corporation, 1986), 11, 15.

19. Ibid., 16.

20. Ibid., 12–15.

21. "Domestic Terrorism in the 1980s," *FBI Law Enforcement Bulletin*, October 1987, 13.

22. Chris Lutz, ed., *They Don't All Wear Sheets: A Chronology of Racist and Far Right Violence, 1980–1986* (Atlanta, GA: Center for Democratic Renewal, 1987); Anti-Defamation League of B'nai B'rith, *Extremism on the Right: A Handbook* (New York: Anti-Defamation League of B'nai B'rith, 1988).

23. Abraham, "Anti-Arab Racism and Violence," 157 (see n. 6).

24. Lilienthal, 18 (see n. 8).

25. Anti-Defamation League, *Pro-Arab Propaganda* (see n. 8).

26. Lilienthal, 18 (see n. 8).

27. Amy Kaufman Goott and Steven J. Rosen, *The Campaign to Discredit Israel* (Washington, DC: American Israel Public Affairs Committee, 1983); Jonathan S. Kessler and Jeff Schwaber, *The AIPAC College Guide: Exposing the Anti-Israel Campaign on Campus* (Washington, DC: American Israel Public Affairs Committee, 1984).

28. Paul Findley, *They Dare to Speak Out: People and Institutions Confront Israel's Lobby* (Westport, CT: Lawrence Hill, 1985); Naseer Aruri, "The Middle East on the U.S. Campus," *The Link* 18, no. 2 (May–June 1985); Edward Tivnan, *The Lobby: Jewish Political Power and American Foreign Policy* (New York: Simon and Schuster, 1987); Rachelle Marshall, "PACmen," *The Nation*, June 6, 1987; Rachelle Marshall, "The Decline of B'nai B'rith: From Protector to Persecutor," *Washington Report on Middle East Affairs*, April 1989, 19.

29. Delinda C. Hanley, "ADL and AJC Demand Muslim Panelists Be Excluded," *Washington Report on Middle East Affairs*, January–February 2002, 83.

30. Ibid.

31. Ibid.

32. Rick Paddock, "A Spy for the Anti-Defamation League: Did a Liberal Civil Rights Group Get Caught with Its Binoculars Up?" *Cal. J.*, June 1, 1993, 2.

33. Abdeen Jabara, "The Anti-Defamation League: Civil Rights and Wrongs," *Covert Action*, no. 45 (Summer 1993): 28–29; see also San Francisco District Attorney's Office, "Organizational Victims of ADL Espionage" (1993), reprinted in *ADC Times*, May–June 1993, 21 (on file with Susan M. Akram).

34. Jabara, "The Anti-Defamation League," 30–31 (see n. 33).

35. Ibid., 31.

36. Ibid.; Jim McGee, "Jewish Group's Tactics Investigated," *Washington Post*, October 19, 1993.

37. Dennis Opatrny and Scott Winokur, "Israeli Man Held by Israel Linked to Spy Case," *San Francisco Examiner*, February 12, 1993; Jabara, "The Anti-Defamation League," 29 (see n. 33).

38. Bob Egelko, "Jewish Defense Group Settles S. F. Spying Suit," *San Francisco Chronicle*, February 23, 2002; Dennis King and Chip Berlet, "ADLgate," *Tikkun* 8 (July–August 1993): 31; Dennis Opatrny and Scott Winokur,

"Police Said to Help Spy on Political Groups," *San Francisco Examiner*, March 9, 1993.

39. Final Settlement, *American-Arab Anti-Discrimination Committee v. Anti-Defamation League*, Civil Action No. 93-6358 RAP (C.D. Cal. 1999).

40. See McGee, n. 36.

41. Jabara, "The Anti-Defamation League," 37 (see n. 33).

42. Michael Gillespie, "Los Angeles Court Hands Down Final Judgment in Anti-Defamation League Illegal Surveillance Case," *Washington Report on Middle East Affairs*, December 1999, 43.

43. An ADL advertisement in the *New York Times*, May 11, 1997, entitled "We Hate Keeping Files on Hate," claims: "For 83 years, ADL has considered it our duty to collect and process information on racists, anti-Semites and extremists by monitoring and analyzing publications of all kinds and to share our findings to help focus American public opinion on the dangers of bigotry and hatred" (copy on file with Susan M. Akram).

44. Abraham, "Anti-Arab Racism and Violence," 187 (see n. 6).

45. Ibid.

46. Shaheen, *Reel Bad Arabs*, 9 (see n. 6).

47. Ibid., 11.

48. Ibid., 15.

49. Ibid., 31–33.

50. Abraham, "Anti-Arab Racism and Violence," 188–92 (see n. 6).

51. Michael Guido, "Let's Talk About City Parks and the Arab Problem," cited in Abraham, "Anti-Arab Racism and Violence," 191 (see n. 6).

52. Governor Milliken quoted in Abraham, "Anti-Arab Racism and Violence," 196 (see n. 6).

53. *New York Times*, "Mondale Camp Returns Funds to U.S. Arabs," August 25, 1984.

54. Stephen Franklin, "Arab-Americans Fall Victim to Mideast: Kuwaiti Ship Flagging Sparks Fears," *Chicago Tribune*, July 12, 1987.

55. Editorial, "The Untouchables," *The Nation*, March 21, 1987.

56. Dean E. Murphy, "Mrs. Clinton Says She Will Return Money Raised by a Muslim Group," *New York Times*, October 26, 2000.

57. Neil MacFarquhar, "Saudi Sheik Regrets Giuliani Turning Down His Donation," *New York Times*, October 13, 2001.

58. Laurie Goodstein and Tamar Lewin, "Victims of Mistaken Identity, Sikhs Pay a Price for Turbans," *New York Times*, September 19, 2001; Tamar Lewin and Gustav Niebuhr, "Attacks and Harassment Continue on Middle Eastern People and Mosques," *New York Times*, September 18, 2001.

59. Lynne Duke, "Islam Is Growing in U.S. Despite an Uneasy Image," *Washington Post*, October 24, 1993.

60. Michael W. Suleiman, "The Arab Immigrant Experience," introduction to *Arabs in America*, 18 (see n. 7).

61. Editorial, "Don't Judge Islam by Verdicts," *Orlando Sentinel*, March 8, 1994.

62. Bernard Weinraub, "39 American Hostages Free After 17 Days," *New York Times*, July 1, 1985.

63. House Committee on the Judiciary, Subcommittee on Criminal Justice, *Ethnically motivated violence against Arab-Americans: Hearing before the Subcommittee on Criminal Justice of the Committee on the Judiciary*, 99th Cong., 1986, 57, 64.

64. *New York Times*, "Bomb Kills Leader of U.S. Arab Group," October 12, 1985.

65. Abraham, "Anti-Arab Racism and Violence," 171 (see n. 6).

66. Ibid., 172.

67. American-Arab Anti-Discrimination Committee, *1991 Report on Anti-Arab Hate Crimes: Political and Hate Violence Against Arab Americans* (Washington, DC: American-Arab Anti-Discrimination Committee Research Institute, 1992), 6.

68. Abraham, "Anti-Arab Racism and Violence," 204 (see n. 6).

69. Jim McGee, "Ex-FBI Officials Criticize Tactics on Terrorism," *Washington Post*, November 28, 2001.

70. Bassiouni, *Civil Rights of Arab-Americans* (see n. 17).

71. Elaine Hagopian, "Minority Rights in a Nation-State: The Nixon Administration's Campaign against Arab-Americans," *Journal of Palestine Studies 5*, nos. 1 and 2 (Autumn–Winter, 1975–76): 97–114.

72. Ibid., 102.

73. Noam Chomsky, *Pirates & Emperors: International Terrorism in the Real World* (Montreal: Black Rose Books, 1987), 117–30.

74. Ibid., 123.

75. Ibid., 118.

76. Emily Sachar, "FBI Grills NY Arab-Americans," *Newsday*, January 29, 1991.

77. Lisa Belkin, "For Many Arab-Americans, FBI Scrutiny Renews Fears," *New York Times*, January 12, 1991.

78. On March 1, 2003, the INS was reorganized into the US Immigration and Customs Enforcement (ICE) and the US Citizenship and and Immigration Services (CIS) agencies. For ease of reference this article will continue to refer to "INS" or "immigration services," because all events referred to occurred prior to the agency reorganization.

79. David Cole, "Guilt by Association: It's Alive and Well at INS," *The Nation*, February 15, 1993, 198–99.

80. *United States v. Palestine Liberation Organization*, 695 F. Supp. 1456 (S.D.N.Y. 1988), rejecting the US government's efforts to close the PLO office used in connection with its role as Permanent Observer to the United Nations; see also *Palestine Information Office v. Shultz*, 853 F.2nd 932 (D.C. Cir. 1988), and *Mendelsohn v. Meese*, 695 F. Supp. 1474 (S.D. N.Y. 1988), challenging the constitutionality of law requiring closure of the Palestine Information Office in Washington, DC.

81. House Committee on the Judiciary, Subcommittee on Administrative Law and Governmental Relations, *Legislation to Implement the Recommendations of the Commission on Wartime Relocation and Internment of Civilians: Hearing on HR 442 Before the Subcommittee on Administrative Law and Governmental Relations*, 100th Cong., 1987, 67 (submission of Investigations Division of the Immigration and Naturalization Service, emphasis added).

82. Memorandum from Investigations Division, Immigration and Naturalization Service, Alien Border Control (ABC) Group IV–Contingency Plans 16 (November 18, 1986), with attachments including INS, "Alien Terrorists and Undesirables: A Contingency Plan" (1986) (on file with Susan Akram).

83. John A. Scanlan, "American-Arab—Getting the Balance Wrong—Again!" *Administrative Law Review* 52, no. 1 (Winter 2000): 363–68.

84. Sharon LaFraniere and George Lardner, "U.S. Set to Photograph, Fingerprint all New Iraqi and Kuwaiti Visitors," *Washington Post*, January 11, 1991.

85. Immigration and Nationality Act (INA) Sec. 212(a) (27)–(29), 8 U.S.C. Sec. 1182(a) (27)–(29) (1952) (repealed 1990).

86. 22 U.S.C. Sec. 2691 (1988) (denying waiver to noncitizens connected with the Palestine Liberation Organization as well as representatives of organizations advocating totalitarian government).

87. The "PLO exception" is codified as INA Sec. 212(a), 8 U.S.C. Sec. 1182(a).

88. For the Supreme Court decision in the lengthy litigation, see *Reno v. American-Arab Anti-Discrimination Committee*, 525 US 471 (1999), citing other published federal court decisions in the case. For an example of the commentators on the implications of the case, see Hiroshi Motomura, "Judicial Review in Immigration Cases after AADC: Lessons from Civil Procedure," *Georgetown Immigration Law Journal* 14 (2000).

89. Dempsey and Cole, *Terrorism and the Constitution*, 33–34, discussing LA Eight case (see n. 1).

90. Senate Select Committee on Intelligence, *Nomination of William H. Webster: Hearings before the Select Committee on Intelligence of the United States Senate*, 100th Cong., 1st sess., 1987, 95 (emphasis added).

91. *American-Arab Anti-Discrimination Committee v. Reno*, 119 F. 3rd 1367, 1370 (9th Cir. 1997).

92. *American-Arab Anti-Discrimination Committee v. Meese*, 714 F. Supp. 1060 (C.D. Cal. 1989).

93. INA Sec. 212(a) (3) (B) (iii), 8 U.S.C. Sec. 1182(a) (3) (B) (iii) (emphasis added). After September 11, Congress further expanded the definition of "terrorist activity."

94. Gerald L. Neuman, "Terrorism, Selective Deportation and the First Amendment after *Reno v. AADC*," *Georgetown Immigration Law Journal* 14 (2000): 322–27.

95. *Reno v. American-Arab Anti-Discrimination Committee*, 525 US 471–72 (1999). In reaching that conclusion, the Court relied on INA Sec. 242(g), 8 U.S.C. Sec. 1252(g): "Except as provided in this section and notwithstanding any other provision of law, no court shall have jurisdiction to hear any cause or claim by or on behalf of any alien arising from the decision or action by the Attorney General to commence proceedings, adjudicate cases, or execute removal orders against any alien under this Act."

96. Stephen H. Legomsky, *Immigration and Refugee Law and Policy*, 3rd ed. (New York: Foundation Press, 2002), 86.

97. See Akram, "Scheherezade Meets Kafka," 52n4 (see n. 4).

98. *Rafeedie v. INS*, 688 F. Supp. 729 (D.D.C. 1988), *aff'd in part, rev'd in part, remanded*, 880 F.2nd 506 (D.C. Cir. 1989).

99. *Rafeedie v. INS*, 688 F. Supp., 734–35.

100. *Rafeedie v. INS*, 880 F.2nd, 516.

101. Antiterrorism and Effective Death Penalty Act of 1996, Public Law 104–132, *U.S. Statutes at Large* 110 (1996): 1213; see Whidden, "Unequal Justice," 2841–83, for summary of the genesis of AEDPA and analysis of its impact on Arabs and Muslims (see n. 7).

102. Illegal Immigration Reform and Immigrant Responsibility Act of 1996, Public Law 104-208, *U.S. Statutes at Large* 110 (1996): 3009.

103. Akram, "Scheherezade Meets Kafka," 52, 52n4, listing post-1996 secret evidence cases (see n. 4).

104. See *National Security Considerations Involved in Asylum Applications: Hearings Before the Senate Judiciary Committee on Technology, Terrorism, and Government Information*, 105th Cong., 1998, FDCH Political Transcripts, 5–14 (testimony of INS General Counsel Paul Virtue).

105. AEDPA at Sec. 303 (f) (2) (B) and at Sec. 504 (e) (3) (C).

106. For a general summary of the Iraqi Seven cases by the lead counsel, see Niels W. Frenzen, "National Security and Procedural Fairness: Secret Evidence and the Immigration Laws," *Interpreter Releases* 76 (1999): 1681n31.

107. *National Security Considerations Involved in Asylum Applications: Hearings Before the Senate Judiciary Committee on Technology, Terrorism, and Government Information*, 105th

108. ACLU of Florida, "Palestinian Professor Challenges His Detention by INS as Illegal," May 14, 2002, http://www.aclufl.org/alnajjarhabeasrelease051402.html.

109. *In re Anwar Haddam*, 2000 BIA LEXIS 20, 1 (BIA December 1, 2000).

110. *Al-Najjar v. Reno*, 97 F. Supp. 2nd 1329, 1333–34 (S.D. Fla. 2000).

111. *Al-Najjar v. Ashcroft*, 257 F.3rd 1330, 1336–68 (2001) (stating that the attorney general had the authority to detain al-Najjar indefinitely).

112. *Al-Najjar v. Ashcroft*, 257 F.3rd 1262, 1274 (11th Cir. 2001).

113. For discussion of the facts and legal decisions in the Haddam case, see *In re Haddam*, No. A22-751-813 (BIA September 10, 1998), *aff'd; In re Anwar Haddam*, 2000 BIA LEXIS 20, 1 (BIA December 1, 2000); Akram, "Scheherezade Meets Kafka," 79–81, analyzing the INS proceedings against Haddam (see n. 4).

114. *Matter of Nasser Ahmed*, No. A90-674-238 (Immigration Court, June 24, 1999) (decision following remand); see also Dempsey and Cole, *Terrorism and the Constitution*, 128–31, discussing case (see n. 1).

115. *United States v. Rahman*, 189 F.3rd 88, 103 (2nd Cir. 1999).

116. Philip G. Schrag, *A Well-Founded Fear: The Congressional Battle to Save Political Asylum in America* (New York: Routledge, 2000), 42–44, 134, 137, 148, 162, 164, 217.

117. "How Did He Get Here?" *60 Minutes*, CBS, March 14, 1993.

118. Thomas Alexander Aleinikoff, David A. Martin, and Hiroshi Motomura, *Immigration and Citizenship: Process and Policy*, 4th ed. (St. Paul, MN: West Group, 1998), 863–71, 1028–29 (discussing summary exclusion provisions of 1996 immigration reforms).

SEEING THE BIG PICTURE

The statistics on hate crimes in the Appendix (Section IV) show patterns that are analogous to the attacks on Arab Americans and Muslims in the United States as described by Akram and Johnson. How is the disproportionate number of hate crimes committed against racial minorities similar to what has happened to Arab Americans and Muslims since the 9/11 terrorist attacks?

19

THE POSSESSIVE INVESTMENT IN WHITENESS: RACIALIZED SOCIAL DEMOCRACY

George Lipsitz

QUESTIONS TO CONSIDER

What does George Lipsitz mean by a "possessive investment in whiteness"? How is it possible that being a member of a particular racial group could confer social and economic privileges (or disadvantages) that are both institutional and intergenerational? How many specific programs does Lipsitz identify as being party to institutional racism?

Shortly after World War II, a French reporter asked expatriate Richard Wright his opinion about the "Negro problem" in the United States. The author replied "There isn't any Negro problem; there is only a white problem."[1] By inverting the reporter's question, Wright called attention to its hidden assumptions—that racial polarization comes from the existence of blacks rather than from the behavior of whites, that black people are a "problem" for whites rather than fellow citizens entitled to justice, and that unless otherwise specified "American" means whites.[2] But Wright's formulation also placed political mobilization by African Americans in context, attributing it "to the systemic practices of aversion, exploitation, denigration, and discrimination practiced by people who think of themselves as white."

Whiteness is everywhere in American culture, but it is very hard to see. As Richard Dyer argues, "white power secures its dominance by seeming not to be anything in particular."[3] As the unmarked category against which difference is constructed, whiteness never has to speak its name, never has to acknowledge its role as an organizing principle in social and cultural relations.[4]

To identify, analyze, and oppose the destructive consequences of whiteness, we need what Walter Benjamin called "presence of mind." Benjamin wrote that people visit fortune-tellers not so much out of a desire to know the future but rather out of a fear of not noticing some important aspect of the present. "Presence of mind," he argued, "is an abstract of the future, and precise awareness of the present moment more decisive than foreknowledge of the most distant events."[5] In our society at this time, precise awareness of the present moment requires an understanding of the existence and the destructive consequences of "white" identity.

In recent years, an important body of American studies scholarship has started to

George Lipsitz, "The Possessive Investment in Whiteness: Racialized Social Democracy and the 'White' Problem in American Studies." *American Quarterly* 47:3 (1995), 369–387. Copyright © The American Studies Association. Reprinted with permission of The John Hopkins University Press.

explore the role played by cultural practices in creating "whiteness" in the United States. More than the product of private prejudices, whiteness emerged as a relevant category in American life largely because of realities created by slavery and segregation, by immigration restriction and Indian policy, by conquest and colonialism. A fictive identity of "whiteness" appeared in law as an abstraction, and it became actualized in everyday life in many ways. American economic and political life gave different racial groups unequal access to citizenship and property, while cultural practices including Wild West shows, minstrel shows, racist images in advertising, and Hollywood films institutionalized racism by uniting ethnically diverse European-American audiences into an imagined community—one called into being through inscribed appeals to the solidarity of white supremacy.[6] Although cross-ethnic identification and pan-ethnic antiracism in culture, politics, and economics have often interrupted and resisted racialized white supremacist notions of American identity, from colonial days to the present, successful political coalitions serving dominant interests have often relied on exclusionary concepts of whiteness to fuse unity among otherwise antagonistic individuals and groups.[7]

In these accounts by American studies scholars, cultural practices have often played crucial roles in prefiguring, presenting, and preserving political coalitions based on identification with the fiction of "whiteness." Andrew Jackson's coalition of the "common man," Woodrow Wilson's "New Freedom," and Franklin D. Roosevelt's New Deal all echoed in politics the alliances announced on stage and screen by the nineteenth-century minstrel show, by D. W. Griffith's cinema, and by Al Jolson's ethnic and racial imagery.[8] This impressive body of scholarship helps us understand how people who left Europe as Calabrians or Bohemians became something

called "whites" when they got to America and how that designation made all the difference in the world.

Yet, while cultural expressions have played an important role in the construction of white supremacist political alliances, the reverse is also true (i.e., political activity has also played a constitutive role in racializing U. S. culture). Race is a cultural construct, but one with sinister structural causes and consequences. Conscious and deliberate actions have institutionalized group identity in the United States, not just through the dissemination of cultural stories but also through systematic efforts from colonial times to the present to create a possessive investment in whiteness for European Americans. Studies of culture too far removed from studies of social structure leave us with inadequate explanations for understanding racism and inadequate remedies for combatting it.

From the start, European settlers in North America established structures encouraging possessive investment in whiteness. The colonial and early-national legal systems authorized attacks on Native Americans and encouraged the appropriation of their lands. They legitimated racialized chattel slavery, restricted naturalized citizenship to "white" immigrants, and provided pretexts for exploiting labor, seizing property, and denying the franchise to Asian Americans, Mexican Americans, Native Americans, and African Americans. Slavery and "Jim Crow" segregation institutionalized possessive identification with whiteness visibly and openly, but an elaborate interaction of largely *covert* public and private decisions during and after the days of slavery and segregation also produced a powerful legacy with enduring effects on the racialization of experience, opportunities, and rewards in the United States. Possessive investment in whiteness pervades public policy in the United States past and present—not just long ago during slavery and segregation but in the recent past and present as well—through the covert but no less systematic racism inscribed within U.S. social democracy.

Even though there has always been racism in American history, it has not always been the same racism. Political and cultural struggles over power shape the contours and dimensions of racism in any era. Mass mobilizations against racism during the Civil War and civil rights eras meaningfully curtailed the reach and scope of white supremacy, but in each case reactionary forces then engineered a renewal of racism, albeit in new forms, during successive decades. Racism changes over time, taking on different forms and serving different social purposes in different eras.

Contemporary racism is not just a residual consequence of slavery and *de jure* segregation but rather something that has been created anew in our own time by many factors including the putatively race-neutral liberal social democratic reforms of the past five decades. Despite hard-fought battles for change that secured important concessions during the 1960s in the form of civil rights legislation, the racialized nature of social democratic policies in the United States since the Great Depression has, in my judgment, actually increased the possessive investment in whiteness among European Americans over the past half-century.

The possessive investment in whiteness is not a simple matter of black and white; all racialized minority groups have suffered from it, albeit to different degrees and in different ways. Most of my argument here addresses relations between European Americans and African Americans because they contain many of the most vivid oppositions and contrasts, but the possessive investment in whiteness always emerges from a fused sensibility drawing on many sources at once—on antiblack racism to be sure, but also on the legacies of racialization left by federal, state, and local policies toward Native Americans, Asian Americans, Mexican Americans, and other groups designated by whites as "racially other."

During the New Deal, both the Wagner Act and the Social Security Act excluded farm workers and domestics from coverage, effectively denying those disproportionately minority sectors of the work force protections and benefits routinely channeled to whites. The Federal Housing Act of 1934 brought home ownership within reach of millions of citizens by placing the credit of the federal government behind private lending to home buyers, but overtly racist categories in the Federal Housing Administration's (FHA's) "confidential" city surveys and appraisers' manuals channeled almost all of the loan money toward whites and away from communities of color.[9] In the post–World War II era, trade unions negotiated contract provisions giving private medical insurance, pensions, and job security largely to the mostly white workers in unionized mass-production industries rather than fighting for full employment, universal medical care, and old age pensions for all or for an end to discriminatory hiring and promotion practices by employers.[10]

Each of these policies widened the gap between the resources available to whites and those available to aggrieved racial communities, but the most damaging long-term effects may well have come from the impact of the racial discrimination codified by the policies of the FHA. By channeling loans away from older inner-city neighborhoods and toward white home buyers moving into segregated suburbs, the FHA and private lenders after World War II aided and abetted the growth and development of increased segregation in U.S. residential neighborhoods. For example, FHA appraisers denied federally supported loans to prospective home buyers in the racially mixed Boyle Heights neighborhood of Los Angeles because it was a "'melting pot' area literally honeycombed with diverse and subversive racial elements."[11] Similarly, mostly white St. Louis County secured five times as many FHA mortgages as the more racially mixed city of St. Louis between 1943 and 1960. Home buyers in the county received six times as much loan money and enjoyed per capita mortgage spending 6.3 times greater than those in the city.[12]

In concert with FHA support for segregation in the suburbs, federal and state tax monies routinely provided water supplies and sewage facilities for racially exclusive suburban communities in the 1940s and 1950s. By the 1960s, these areas often incorporated themselves as independent municipalities in order to gain greater access to federal funds allocated for "urban aid."[13] At the same time that FHA loans and federal highway building projects subsidized the growth of segregated suburbs, urban renewal programs in cities throughout the country devastated minority neighborhoods.

During the 1950s and 1960s, federally assisted urban renewal projects destroyed 20 percent of the central city housing units occupied by blacks, as opposed to only 10 percent of those inhabited by whites.[14] Even after most major urban renewal programs had been completed in the 1970s, black central city residents continued to lose housing units at a rate equal to 80 percent of what had been lost in the 1960s. Yet white displacement declined back to the relatively low levels of the 1950s.[15] In addition, the refusal first to pass, then to enforce, fair housing laws, has enabled realtors, buyers, and sellers to profit from racist collusion against minorities without fear of legal retribution.

During the decades following World War II, urban renewal helped construct a new "white" identity in the suburbs by helping destroy ethnically specific European-American urban inner-city neighborhoods. Wrecking balls and bulldozers eliminated some of these sites, while others became transformed by an influx of minority residents desperately competing for a declining number of affordable housing units. As increasing numbers of racial minorities moved into cities, increasing numbers of European-American ethnics moved out. Consequently, ethnic differences among whites became a less important dividing line in American culture, while race became more important. The suburbs helped turn European Americans into "whites" who could live near each other and intermarry with relatively little difficulty. But this "white" unity rested on residential segregation and on shared access to housing and life chances largely unavailable to communities of color.[16]

During the 1950s and 1960s, local "pro-growth" coalitions led by liberal mayors often justified urban renewal as a program designed to build more housing for poor people, but it actually destroyed more housing than it created. Ninety percent of the low-income units removed for urban renewal were never replaced. Commercial, industrial, and municipal projects occupied more than 80 percent of the land cleared for these projects, with less than 20 percent allocated for replacement housing. In addition, the loss of taxable properties and tax abatements granted to new enterprises in urban renewal zones often meant serious tax increases for poor, working-class, and middle-class home owners and renters.[17] Although the percentage of black suburban dwellers also increased during this period, no significant desegregation of the suburbs took place. From 1960 to 1977, four million whites moved out of central cities, while the number of whites living in suburbs increased by twenty-two million.[18] During the same years, the inner-city black population grew by six million, but the number of blacks living in suburbs increased by only 500,000 people.[19] By 1993, 86 percent of suburban whites still lived in places with a black population below 1 percent. At the same time, cities with large numbers of minority residents found themselves cut off from loans by the FHA; in 1966, because of their growing black and Puerto Rican populations, Camden and Paterson, New Jersey, received no FHA-sponsored mortgages between them.[20]

Federally funded highways designed to connect suburban commuters with downtown places of employment destroyed already scarce housing in minority communities and often disrupted neighborhood life as well. Construction of the Harbor Freeway in Los Angeles, the Gulf Freeway in Houston, and the Mark Twain Freeway in St. Louis displaced thousands of residents and bisected previously connected neighborhoods, shopping districts, and political precincts. The process of urban renewal and highway construction set in motion a vicious cycle: population loss led to decreased political power, which made minority neighborhoods more likely to be victimized by further urban renewal and freeway construction, not to mention more susceptible to the placement of prisons, waste dumps, and other projects that further depopulated these areas.

In Houston, Texas—where blacks make up slightly more than one-quarter of the local population—more than 75 percent of municipal garbage incinerators and 100 percent of the city-owned garbage dumps are located in black neighborhoods.[21] A 1992 study by staff writers for the *National Law Journal* examined the Environmental Protection Agency's response to 1,177 toxic waste cases and found that polluters of sites near the greatest white population received penalties 500 percent higher than penalties imposed on polluters in minority areas—an average of $335,566 for white areas contrasted with $55,318 for minority areas. Income did not

account for these differences—penalties for low-income areas on average actually exceeded those for areas with the highest median incomes by about 3 percent. The penalties for violating all federal environmental laws about air, water, and waste pollution in minority communities were 46 percent lower than in white communities. In addition, Superfund remedies left minority communities with longer waiting times for being placed on the national priority list, cleanups that begin from 12 to 42 percent later than at white sites, and a 7 percent greater likelihood of "containment" (walling off a hazardous site) than cleanup, while white sites experienced treatment and cleanup 22 percent more often than containment.[22]

Urban renewal failed as a program for providing new housing for the poor, but it played an important role in transforming the U. S. urban economy away from factory production and toward producer services. Urban renewal projects subsidized the development of downtown office centers on land previously used for residences, and they frequently created buffer zones of empty blocks dividing poor neighborhoods from new shopping centers designed for affluent commuters. In order to help cities compete for corporate investment by making them appealing to high-level executives, federal urban aid favored construction of luxury housing units and cultural centers, such as symphony halls and art museums, over affordable housing for workers. Tax abatements granted to these producer-services centers further aggravated the fiscal crisis that cities faced, leading to tax increases on existing industries, businesses, and residences.

Workers from aggrieved racial minorities bore the brunt of this transformation. Because the 1964 Civil Rights Act came so late, minority workers who received jobs because of it found themselves more vulnerable to seniority-based layoffs when businesses automated or transferred operations overseas. Although the act initially made real progress in reducing employment discrimination, lessened the gaps between rich and poor and black and white, and helped bring minority poverty to its lowest level in history in 1973, that year's recession initiated a reversal of minority progress and a reassertion of white privilege.[23] In 1977, the U. S. Civil Rights Commission reported on the disproportionate impact of layoffs on minority workers. In cases where minority workers made up only 10 to 12 percent of the work force in their area, they accounted for from 60 to 70 percent of those laid off in 1974. The principle of seniority, a social democratic triumph, in this case worked to guarantee that minority workers would suffer most from technological changes because the legacy of past discrimination by their employers left them with less seniority than white workers.[24]

When housing prices doubled during the 1970s, white homeowners who had been able to take advantage of discriminatory FHA financing policies received increased equity in their homes, while those excluded from the housing market by earlier policies found themselves facing higher costs of entry into the market in addition to the traditional obstacles presented by the discriminatory practices of sellers, realtors, and lenders. The contrast between European Americans and African Americans is instructive in this regard. Because whites have access to broader housing choices than blacks, whites pay 15 percent less than blacks for similar housing in the same neighborhood. White neighborhoods typically experience housing costs 25 percent less expensive than would be the case if the residents were black.[25]

A recent Federal Reserve Bank of Boston study showed that minority applicants had a 60 percent greater chance of being denied home loans than white applicants with the same credit-worthiness. Boston bankers made 2.9 times as many mortgage loans per one thousand housing units in neighborhoods inhabited by low-income whites than they did to neighborhoods populated by low-income blacks.[26] In addition, loan officers were far more likely to overlook flaws in the credit records of white applicants or to arrange creative financing for them than they were with black applicants.[27]

A Los Angeles study found that loan officers more frequently used dividend income and underlying assets criteria for judging black applicants than they did for whites.[28] In Houston, the NCNB Bank of Texas disqualified 13 percent of middle-income white loan applicants but disqualified 36 percent of middle-income black applicants.[29] Atlanta's home loan institutions gave five times as many home loans to whites as to blacks in the late 1980s. An analysis of sixteen Atlanta neighborhoods found that home buyers in white neighborhoods received conventional financing four times as often as those in black sections of the city.[30] Nationwide, financial institutions get more money in deposits from black neighborhoods than they invest in them in the form of home mortgage loans, making home lending a vehicle for the transfer of capital away from black savers and toward white investors.[31] In many locations, high-income blacks were denied loans more often than low-income whites.[32]

Federal home loan policies have placed the power of the federal government behind private discrimination. Urban renewal and highway construction programs have enhanced the possessive investment in whiteness directly through government initiatives. In addition, decisions about the location of federal jobs have also systematically supported the subsidy for whiteness. Federal civilian employment dropped by 41,419 in central cities between 1966 and 1973, but total federal employment in metropolitan areas grew by 26,558.[33] While one might naturally expect the location of government buildings that serve the public to follow population trends, the federal government's policies in locating offices and records centers in suburbs helped aggravate the flight of jobs to suburban locations less accessible to inner-city residents. Since racial discrimination in the private sector forces minority workers to seek government positions disproportionate to their numbers, these moves exact particular hardships on them. In addition, minorities who follow their jobs to the suburbs generally encounter increased commuter costs because housing discrimination makes it harder and more expensive for them to relocate than for whites.

The racialized aspects of fifty years of these social democratic policies became greatly exacerbated by the anti–social democratic policies of neoconservatives in the Reagan and Bush administrations during the 1980s and 1990s. They clearly contributed to the reinforcement of possessive investments in whiteness through their regressive policies in respect to federal aid to education and their refusal to challenge segregated education, housing, and hiring, as well as their cynical cultivation of an antiblack, countersubversive consensus through attacks on affirmative action and voting rights legislation. In the U.S. economy, where 86 percent of available jobs do not appear in classified advertisements and where personal connections provide the most important factor in securing employment, attacks on affirmative action guarantee that whites will be rewarded for their historical advantages in the labor market rather than for their individual abilities or efforts.[34]

Yet even seemingly race-neutral policies supported by both neoconservatives and social democrats in the 1980s and 1990s have also increased the absolute value of being white. In the 1980s, changes in federal tax laws decreased the value of wage income and increased the value of investment income—a move harmful to minorities who suffer from an even greater gap between their total wealth and that of whites than in the disparity between their income and white income. Failure to raise the minimum wage between 1981 and 1989 and the more than one-third decline in value of Aid for Families with Dependent Children payments hurt all poor people, but they exacted special costs on nonwhites facing even more constricted markets for employment, housing, and education than poor whites.[35]

Similarly, the "tax reforms" of the 1980s made the effective rate of taxation higher on investment in actual goods and services than it was on profits from speculative enterprises. This encouraged the flight of capital away from industrial production with its many employment opportunities and toward investments that can be turned over quickly to allow the greatest possible tax write-offs. Consequently, government policies actually discouraged investments that might produce high-paying jobs and encouraged investors to strip companies of their assets in order to make rapid short-term profits. These policies hurt almost all workers, but they exacted particularly high costs from minority workers who, because of employment discrimination in the retail and small business sectors, were overrepresented in blue-collar industrial jobs.

On the other hand, while neoconservative tax policies created incentives for employers to move their enterprises elsewhere, they created disincentives for home owners to move. Measures such as California's Proposition 13 granting tax relief to property owners badly misallocate housing resources because they make it financially unwise for the elderly to move out of large houses, further reducing the supply of housing available to young families. While one can well understand the necessity for protecting senior citizens on fixed incomes from tax increases that would make them lose their homes, the rewards and punishments provided by Proposition 13 are so extreme that they prevent the kinds of generational succession that have routinely opened up housing to young families in the past. This reduction works particular hardships on those who also face discrimination by sellers, realtors, and lending institutions.

Subsidies to the private sector by government agencies also tend to reward the results of past discrimination. Throughout the country, tax increment redevelopment programs give tax-free, low-interest loans to developers whose projects use public services, often without having to pay taxes to local school boards or county governments. Industrial development bonds resulted in a $7.4 billion tax loss in 1983, a loss that ordinary tax payers had to make up through increased payroll taxes. Compared to white Americans, people of color, who are more likely to be poor or working class, suffer disproportionately from these changes as tax payers, as workers, and as tenants. A study by the Citizens for Tax Justice found that wealthy Californians spend less than eleven cents in taxes for every dollar earned, while poor residents of the state paid fourteen cents out of every dollar in taxes. As groups overrepresented among the poor, minorities have been forced to shoulder this burden in order to subsidize the tax breaks given to the wealthy.[36] While holding property tax assessments for businesses and some home owners to about half of their market value, California's Proposition 13 deprived cities and counties of $13 billion a year in taxes. Businesses alone avoided $3.3 billion to $8.6 billion in taxes per year under this statute.[37]

Because they are ignorant of even the recent history of the possessive investment in whiteness—generated by slavery and segregation but augmented by social democratic reform—Americans produce largely cultural explanations for structural social problems. The increased possessive investment in whiteness generated by dis-investment in America's cities, factories, and schools since the 1970s disguises the general problems posed to our society by de-industrialization, economic restructuring, and neoconservative attacks on the welfare state as *racial* problems. It fuels a discourse that demonizes people of color for being victimized by these changes, while hiding the privileges of whiteness by attributing them to family values, fatherhood, and foresight—rather than to favoritism.

The demonization of black families in public discourse since the 1970s is particularly instructive in this regard. During the 1970s, the share of low-income households headed by blacks increased by one-third, while black family income fell from 60 percent of white family income in 1971 to 58 percent in 1980. Even when adjusting for unemployment and for African-American disadvantages in life-cycle employment (more injuries, more frequently interrupted work histories, confinement to jobs most susceptible to layoffs), the wages of full-time year-round black workers fell from 77 percent of white workers' income to 73 percent by 1986. In 1986, white workers with high school diplomas earned three thousand dollars per year more than African Americans with the same education.[38] Even when they had the same family structure as white workers, blacks found themselves more likely to be poor.

Among black workers between the ages of twenty and twenty-four, 46 percent held blue-collar jobs in 1976, but that percentage fell to only 20 percent by 1984. Earnings by young black families had reached 60 percent of the amount secured by white families in 1973, but by 1986 they fell back to 46 percent. Younger African-American families experienced a 50 percent drop in real earnings between 1973 and 1986, with the decline in black male wages particularly steep.[39]

Many recent popular and scholarly studies have explained clearly the causes for black economic decline over the past two decades.[40] Deindustrialization has decimated the industrial infrastructure that formerly provided high-wage jobs and chances for upward mobility to black workers. Neoconservative attacks on government spending for public housing, health, education, and transportation have deprived African Americans of needed services and opportunities for jobs in the public sector. A massive retreat from responsibility to enforce antidiscrimination laws at the highest levels of government has sanctioned pervasive overt and covert racial discrimination by bankers, realtors, and employers.

Yet public opinion polls conducted among white Americans display little recognition of these devastating changes. Seventy percent of whites in one poll said that African Americans "have the same opportunities to live a middle-class life as whites."[41] Nearly three-fourths of white respondents to a 1989 poll believed that opportunities for blacks had improved during the Reagan presidency.[42]

Optimism about the opportunities available to African Americans does not necessarily demonstrate ignorance of the dire conditions facing black communities, but, if not, it then indicates that many whites believe that blacks suffer deservedly, that they do not take advantage of the opportunities offered them. In the opinion polls, favorable assessments of black chances for success often accompanied extremely negative judgments about the abilities, work habits, and character of black people. A National Opinion Research Report in 1990 disclosed that more than 50 percent of American whites viewed blacks as innately lazy and less intelligent and less patriotic than whites.[43] Furthermore, more than 60 percent of whites questioned in

that survey said that they believed that blacks suffer from poor housing and employment opportunities because of their own lack of willpower. Some 56.3 percent of whites said that blacks preferred welfare to employment, while 44.6 percent contended that blacks tended toward laziness.[44] Even more important, research by Mary and Thomas Byrne Edsall indicates that many whites structure nearly all of their decisions about housing, education, and politics in response to their aversions to black people.[45]

The present political culture in this country gives broad sanction for viewing white supremacy and antiblack racism as forces from the past, as demons finally put to rest by the passage of the 1964 Civil Rights Act and the 1965 Voting Rights Act.[46] Jurists, journalists, and politicians have generally been more vocal in their opposition to "quotas" and to "reverse discrimination" mandating race-specific remedies for discrimination than to the thousands of well-documented incidents every year of routine, systematic, and unyielding discrimination against blacks.

It is my contention that the stark contrast between black experiences and white opinions during the past two decades cannot be attributed solely to ignorance or intolerance on the part of individuals but stems instead from the overdetermined inadequacy of the language of liberal individualism to describe collective experience.[47] As long as we define social life as the sum total of conscious and deliberate individual activities, then only *individual* manifestations of personal prejudice and hostility will be seen as racist. Systemic, collective, and coordinated behavior disappears from sight. Collective exercises of group power relentlessly channeling rewards, resources, and opportunities from one group to another will not appear to be "racist" from this perspective because they rarely announce their intention to discriminate against individuals. But they work to construct racial indentities by giving people of different races vastly different life chances.

The gap between white perceptions and minority experiences can have explosive consequences. Little more than a year after the 1992 Los Angeles rebellion, a sixteen-year-old high school junior shared her opinions with a reporter from the *Los Angeles Times.* "I don't think white people owe anything to black people," she explained. "We didn't sell them into slavery, it was our ancestors. What they did was wrong, but we've done our best to make up for it."[48] A seventeen-year-old senior echoed those comments, telling the reporter:

> I feel we spend more time in my history class talking about what whites owe blacks than just about anything else when the issue of slavery comes up. I often received dirty looks. This seems strange given that I wasn't even alive then. And the few members of my family from that time didn't have the luxury of owning much, let alone slaves. So why, I ask you, am I constantly made to feel guilty?[49]

More ominously, after pleading guilty to bombing two homes and one car, to vandalizing a synagogue, and attempting to start a race war by murdering Rodney King and bombing Los Angeles's First African Methodist Episcopal Church, twenty-year-old Christopher David Fisher explained that "sometimes whites were picked on because of the color of their skin. . . . Maybe we're blamed for slavery."[50] Fisher's actions were certainly extreme, but his justification of them drew knowingly and precisely on a broadly shared narrative about the victimization of innocent whites by irrational and ungrateful minorities.

The comments and questions raised about the legacy of slavery by these young whites illumine broader currents in our culture that have enormous implications for understanding the enduring significance of race in our country. These young people

associate black grievances solely with slavery, and they express irritation at what they perceive as efforts to make them feel guilty or unduly privileged in the present because of things that happened in the distant past. Because their own ancestors may not have been slave owners or because "we've done our best to make up for it," they feel that it is unreasonable for anyone to view them as people who owe "anything" to blacks. On the contrary, Fisher felt that his discomfort with being "picked on" and "blamed" for slavery gave him good reason to bomb homes, deface synagogues, and plot to kill black people.

Unfortunately for our society, these young whites accurately reflect the logic of the language of liberal individualism and its ideological predispositions in discussions of race. They seem to have no knowledge of the disciplined, systemic, and collective *group* activity that has structured white identities in American history. They are not alone in their ignorance; in a 1979 law journal article, future Supreme Court Justice Antonin Scalia argued that affirmative action "is based upon concepts of racial indebtedness and racial entitlement rather than individual worth and individual need" and is thus "racist."[51]

Yet liberal individualism is not completely color blind on this issue. As Cheryl I. Harris demonstrates, the legacy of liberal individualism has not prevented the Supreme Court from recognizing and protecting the group interests of *whites* in the Bakke, Croson, and Wygant cases.[52] In each case, the Court nullified affirmative action programs because they judged efforts to help blacks as harmful to whites: to white expectations of entitlement, expectations based on the possessive investment in whiteness they held as members of a group. In the Bakke case, for instance, neither Bakke nor the court contested the legitimacy of medical school admissions standards that reserved five seats in each class for children of wealthy donors to the university or that penalized Bakke for being older than most of the other applicants. The group rights of not-wealthy people or of people older than their classmates did not compel the Court or Bakke to make any claim of harm. But they did challenge and reject a policy designed to offset the effects of past and present discrimination when they could construe the medical school admission policies as detrimental to the interests of whites as a group—and as a consequence they applied the "strict scrutiny" standard to protect whites while denying that protection to people of color. In this case, as in so many others, the language of liberal individualism serves as a cover for coordinated collective group interests.

Group interests are not monolithic, and aggregate figures can obscure serious differences within racial groups. All whites do not benefit from the possessive investment in whiteness in precisely the same way; the experiences of members of minority groups are not interchangeable. But the possessive investment in whiteness always affects individual and group life chances and opportunities. Even in cases where minority groups secure political and economic power through collective mobilization, the terms and conditions of their collectivity and the logic of group solidarity are always influenced and intensified by the absolute value of whiteness in American politics, economics, and culture.[53]

In the 1960s, members of the Black Panther Party used to say that "if you're not part of the solution, you're part of the problem." But those of us who are "white" can only become part of the solution if we recognize the degree to which we are already part of the problem—not because of our race, but because of our possessive investment in it. Neither conservative "free market" policies nor liberal social democratic reforms can solve the "white problem" in America because both of them reinforce the possessive investment

in whiteness. But an explicitly antiracist pan-ethnic movement that acknowledges the existence and power of whiteness might make some important changes. Pan-ethnic, antiracist coalitions have a long history in the United States—in the political activism of John Brown, Sojourner Truth, and the Magon brothers, among others—but we also have a rich cultural tradition of pan-ethnic antiracism connected to civil rights activism of the kind detailed so brilliantly in rhythm and blues musician Johnny Otis's recent book, *Upside Your Head! Rhythm and Blues on Central Avenue.*[54] These efforts by whites to fight racism, not out of sympathy for someone else but out of a sense of self-respect and simple justice, have never completely disappeared; they remain available as models for the present.[55]

Walter Benjamin's praise for "presence of mind" came from his understanding of how difficult it may be to see the present. But more important, he called for presence of mind as the means for implementing what he called "the only true telepathic miracle"—turning the forbidding future into the fulfilled present.[56] Failure to acknowledge our society's possessive investment in whiteness prevents us from facing the present openly and honestly. It hides from us the devastating costs of disinvestment in America's infrastructure over the past two decades and keeps us from facing our responsibilities to reinvest in human capital by channeling resources toward education, health, and housing—and away from subsidies for speculation and luxury. After two decades of disinvestment, the only further disinvestment we need is to disinvest in the ruinous pathology of whiteness that has always undermined our own best instincts and interests. In a society suffering so badly from an absence of mutuality, an absence of responsibility, and an absence of simple justice, presence of mind might be just what we need.

NOTES

1. Raphael Tardon, "Richard Wright Tells Us: The White Problem in the United States," *Action*, 24 Oct. 1946. Reprinted in Kenneth Kinnamon and Michel Fabre, *Conversations with Richard Wright* (Jackson, Miss., 1993), 99. Malcolm X and others used this same formulation in the 1960s, but I believe that it originated with Wright, or at least that is the earliest citation I have found so far.

2. This is also Toni Morrison's point in *Playing in the Dark: Whiteness in the Literary Imagination* (Cambridge, Mass., 1992).

3. Richard Dyer, "White," *Screen* 29 (fall 1988): 44.

4. I thank Michael Schudson for pointing out to me that since the passage of civil rights legislation in the 1960s whiteness dares not speak its name, cannot speak in its own behalf, but rather advances through a color-blind language radically at odds with the distinctly racialized distribution of resources and life chances in American society.

5. Walter Benjamin, "Madame Ariane: Second Courtyard on the Left," from *One-Way Street* (London, 1969), 98–99.

6. Richard Slotkin, *Gunfighter Nation: The Myth of the Frontier in Twentieth Century America* (New York, 1992); Eric Lott, *Love and Theft* (New York, 1993); David Roediger, *Wages of Whiteness* (New York, 1992); Michael Rogin, "Blackface White Noise: The Jewish Jazz Singer Finds His Voice," *Critical Inquiry* 18 (spring 1992).

7. Robin Kelley, *Hammer and Hoe* (Chapel Hill, N.C., 1990); Lizabeth Cohen, *Making A New Deal* (Cambridge, 1991); George Sanchez, *Becoming Mexican American* (New York, 1993); Edmund Morgan, *American Slavery, American Freedom* (New York, 1975); John Hope Franklin, *The Color Line: Legacy for the Twentyfirst Century* (Columbia, Mo., 1993).

8. Alexander Saxton, *The Rise and Fall of the White Republic* (New York, 1992); Roediger, *Wages;* Michael Rogin, *Ronald Reagan, the Movie: and Other Episodes in Political Demonology* (Berkeley, 1987); Michael Rogin, "Blackface"; Michael Rogin, "'Democracy and Burnt Cork': The End of Blackface, the Beginning of Civil Rights," presented at the University of California Humanities Research Institute Film Genres Study Group, November 1992.

9. See Kenneth Jackson, *Crabgrass Frontier: The Suburbanization of the United States* (New York, 1985); and Douglas S. Massey and Nancy A. Denton, *American Apartheid: Segregation and the Making of the Underclass* (Cambridge, Mass., 1993).

10. I thank Phil Ethington for pointing out to me that these aspects of New Deal policies emerged out of political negotiations between the segregationist Dixiecrats and liberals from the North and West. My perspective is that white supremacy was not a gnawing aberration within the New Deal coalition but rather an essential point of unity between southern whites and northern white ethnics.

11. Records of the Federal Home Loan Bank Board of the Home Owners Loan Corporation. City Survey File, Los Angeles, 1939, Neighborhood D-53, National Archives, Washington, D.C., box 74, records group 195.

12. Massey and Denton, *American Apartheid,* 54.

13. John R. Logan and Harvey Molotch, *Urban Fortunes: The Political Economy of Place* (Berkeley, 1987), 182.

14. Ibid., 114.

15. Ibid., 130.

16. See Gary Gerstle, "Working-Class Racism: Broaden the Focus," *International Labor and Working Class History* 44 (fall 1993): 36.

17. Logan and Molotch, *Urban Fortunes,* 168–69.

18. Troy Duster, "Crime, Youth Unemployment, and the Black Urban Underclass," *Crime and Delinquency* 33 (Apr. 1987): 308.

19. Ibid., 309.

20. Massey and Denton, *American Apartheid,* 55.

21. Logan and Molotch, *Urban Forunes,* 113.

22. Robert D. Bullard, "Environmental Justice for All," in *Unequal Protection: Environmental Justice and Communities of Color,* ed. Robert Bullard (San Francisco, 1994), 9–10.

23. Massey and Denton, *American Apartheid,* 61.

24. Gertrude Ezorsky, *Racism and Justice: The Case for Affirmative Action* (Ithaca, N.Y., 1991), 25.

25. Logan and Molotch, *Urban Fortunes,* 116.

26. Jim Campen, "Lending Insights: Hard Proof That Banks Discriminate," *Dollars and Sense* 191 (Jan.–Feb. 1991): 17.

27. Mitchell Zuckoff, "Study Shows Racial Bias in Lending," *The Boston Globe,* 9 October 1992, 1, 77, 78.

28. Paul Ong and J. Eugene Grigsby III, "Race and Life-Cycle Effects on Home Ownership in Los Angeles, 1970 to 1980," *Urban Affairs Quarterly* 23 (June 1988): 605.

29. Massey and Denton, *American Apartheid,* 108.

30. Gary Orfield and Carol Ashkinaze, *The Closing Door: Conservative Policy and Black Opportunity* (Chicago, 1991), 58, 78.

31. Logan and Molotch, *Urban Fortunes.*

32. Campen, "Lending Insights," 18.

33. Gregory Squires, "'Runaway Plants,' Capital Mobility, and Black Economic Rights," in *Community and Capital in Conflict: Plant Closings and Job Loss,* ed. John C. Raines, Lenora E. Berson, and David McI. Gracie (Philadelphia, 1982), 70.

34. Gertrude Ezorsky, *Racism and Justice: The Case for Affirmative Action* (Ithaca, N.Y., 1991), 15.

35. Orfield and Ashkinaze, *The Closing Door,* 225–26.

36. McClatchy News Service, "State Taxes Gouge the Poor, Study Says," *Long Beach Press-Telegram,* 23 April 1991, A1.

37. "Proposition 13," *UC Focus* (June–July 1993): 2.

38. William Chafe, *The Unfinished Journey* (New York, 1986), 442; Noel J. Kent, "A Stacked Deck: Racial Minorities and the New American Political Economy," *Explorations in Ethnic Studies* 14 (Jan. 1991): 11.

39. Kent, "Stacked Deck," 13.

40. Melvin Oliver and James Johnson, "Economic Restructuring and Black Male Joblessness in United States Metropolitan Areas," *Urban Geography* 12 (Nov.–Dec. 1991); Gerald David Jaynes and Robin M. Williams, Jr., eds., *A Common Destiny: Blacks and American Society* (Washington, D.C., 1989); Reynolds Farley and Walter R. Allen, *The Color Line and the Quality of Life in America* (New York, 1987); Melvin Oliver and Tom Shapiro, "Wealth of a Nation: A Reassessment of Asset Inequality in America Shows at Least $\frac{1}{3}$ of Households Are Asset Poor," *Journal of Economics and Sociology* 49 (Apr. 1990); Jonathan Kozol, *Savage Inequalities: Children in America's Schools* (New York, 1991); Cornell West, *Race Matters* (Boston, 1993).

41. Orfield and Ashkinaze, *Closing Door,* 46.

42. Ibid., 206.

43. Bart Landry, "The Enduring Dilemma of Race in America," in Alan H. Wolfe, *America at Century's End* (Berkeley, 1991), 206; Franklin, *Color Line,* 36–37.

44. Kathleen Hall Jamieson, *Dirty Politics: Deception, Distraction, and Democracy* (New York, 1992), 100.

45. Mary Edsall and Thomas Byrne Edsall, *Chain Reaction* (New York, 1991).

46. Nathan Glazer makes this argument in *Affirmative Discrimination* (New York, 1975).

47. I borrow the term "overdetermination" here from Louis Althusser, who uses it to show how dominant ideologies become credible to people in part because various institutions and agencies independently replicate them and reinforce their social power.

48. Rogena Schuyler, "Youth: We Didn't Sell Them into Slavery," *Los Angeles Times,* 21 June 1993, B4.

49. Ibid.

50. Jim Newton, "Skinhead Leader Pleads Guilty to Violence, Plot," *Los Angeles Times,* 20 Oct. 1993 A1, A15.

51. Antonin Scalia, quoted in Cheryl I. Harris, "Whiteness as Property," *Harvard Law Review,* 106 (June 1993): 1767.

52. Ibid.

53. The rise of a black middle class and the setbacks suffered by white workers during deindustrialization may seem to subvert the analysis presented here. Yet the black middle class remains fragile, far less able than other middle-class groups to translate advances in income into advances in wealth and power. Similarly, the success of neo-conservatism since the 1970s has rested on securing support from white workers for economic policies that do them objective harm by mobilizing counter-subversive electoral coalitions against busing and affirmative action, while carrying out attacks on public institutions and resources by representing "public" space and black space. See Oliver and Shapiro, "Wealth of a Nation." See also Logan and Harvey, *Urban Fortunes.*

54. Johnny Otis, *Upside Your Head! Rhythm and Blues on Central Avenue* (Hanover, N.H., 1993).

55. Mobilizations against plant shutdowns, for environmental protection, against cutbacks in education spending, and for reproductive

rights all contain the potential for pan-ethnic antiracist organizing, but, too often, neglect of race as a central modality for how issues of employment, pollution, education, or reproductive rights are experienced isolates these

social movements from their broadest possible base.

56. Walter Benjamin, "Madame Ariane: Second Courtyard on the Left," from *One-Way Street* (London, 1969), 98, 99.

SEEING THE BIG PICTURE

How do rates of homeownership (Section II in the Appendix) and occupations by race (Section VIII) point to historic investments that have privileged one group over another?

20

THE CONTINUING SIGNIFICANCE OF RACE: ANTIBLACK DISCRIMINATION IN PUBLIC PLACES

Joe R. Feagin

QUESTIONS TO CONSIDER

Joe Feagin suggests that being middle or upper-middle class does not necessarily insulate blacks from being the target of discriminatory behavior in public settings. How does racism manifest itself for this part of the African American population? What social resources or responses do some members of the black middle class use to minimize discrimination in public places?

Title II of the 1964 Civil Rights Act stipulates that "all persons shall be entitled to the full and equal enjoyment of the goods, services, facilities, privileges, advantages, and accommodations of

Joe R. Feagin, "The Continuing Significance of Race" from *American Sociological Review*, 1991, February, Vol. 56, pp. 101–116. Copyright © 1991 American Sociological Association. Reprinted by permission.

any place of public accommodation . . . without discrimination or segregation on the ground of race, color, religion, or national origin." The public places emphasized in the act are restaurants, hotels, and motels, although racial discrimination occurs in many other public places. Those black Americans who would make the greatest use of these public accommodations and certain other public places would be middle-class, i.e., those with the requisite resources. . . .

Discrimination can be defined in social-contextual terms as "actions or practices carried out by members of dominant racial or ethnic groups that have a differential and negative impact on members of subordinate racial and ethnic groups" (Feagin and Eckberg 1980, pp. 1–2). This differential treatment ranges from the blatant to the subtle (Feagin and Feagin 1986). Here I focus primarily on blatant discrimination by white Americans targeting middle-class blacks. Historically, discrimination against blacks has been one of the most serious forms of racial/ethnic discrimination in the United States and one of the most difficult to overcome, in part because of the institutionalized character of color coding. I focus on three important aspects of discrimination: (1) the variation in sites of discrimination; (2) the range of discriminatory actions; and (3) the range of responses by blacks to discrimination.

Sites of Discrimination

There is a spatial dimension to discrimination. The probability of experiencing racial hostility varies from the most private to the most public sites. If a black person is in a relatively protected site, such as with friends at home, the probability of experiencing hostility and discrimination is low. The probability increases as one moves from friendship settings to such outside sites as the workplace, where a black person typically has contacts with both acquaintances and strangers, providing an interactive context with greater potential for discrimination.

In most workplaces, middle-class status and its organizational resources provide some protection against certain categories of discrimination. This protection probably weakens as a black person moves from those work and school settings where he or she is well-known into public accommodations such as large stores and city restaurants where contacts are mainly with white strangers. On public streets blacks have the greatest public exposure to strangers and the least protection against overt discriminatory behavior, including violence. A key feature of these more public settings is that they often involve contacts with white strangers who react primarily on the basis of one ascribed characteristic. The study of the micro-life of interaction between strangers in public was pioneered by Goffman and his students, but few of their analyses have treated hostile discriminatory interaction in public places. A rare exception is the research by Gardner (1980; see also Gardner 1988), who documented the character and danger of passing remarks by men directed against women in unprotected public places. Gardner writes of women (and blacks) as "open persons," i.e., particularly vulnerable targets for harassment that violates the rules of public courtesy.

The Range of Discriminatory Actions

In his classic study, *The Nature of Prejudice*, Allport (1958, pp. 14–5) noted that prejudice can be expressed in a series of progressively more serious actions, ranging from antilocution to avoidance, exclusion, physical attack, and extermination. Allport's work suggests a continuum of actions from avoidance, to exclusion or rejection, to attack. In his travels in the South in the 1950s a white journalist who changed his skin color to black encountered discrimination in each of these categories (Griffin 1961). In my data, discrimination against middle-class blacks still ranges across this continuum: (1) avoidance actions, such as a white couple crossing the street when a black male approaches; (2) rejection actions, such as poor service in public accommodations; (3) verbal attacks, such as shouting racial epithets in the street; (4) physical threats and harassment by white police officers; and (5) physical threats and attacks by other whites, such as attacks by white supremacists in the street. Changing relations between blacks and whites in recent decades have expanded the repertoire of discrimination to include more subtle forms and to encompass discrimination in arenas from which blacks were formerly excluded such as formerly all-white public accommodations.

Black Responses to Discrimination

Prior to societal desegregation in the 1960s much traditional discrimination, especially in the South, took the form of an asymmetrical "deference ritual" in which blacks were typically expected to respond to discriminating whites with great deference. . . . Such rituals can be seen in the obsequious words and gestures—the etiquette of race relations—that many blacks, including middle-class blacks, were forced to utilize to survive the rigors of segregation (Doyle 1937). However, not all responses in this period were deferential. From the late 1800s to the 1950s, numerous lynchings and other violence targeted blacks whose behavior was defined as too aggressive (Raper 1933). Blauner's (1989) respondents reported acquaintances reacting aggressively to discrimination prior to the 1960s.

Deference rituals can still be found today between some lower-income blacks and their white employers. In her northeastern study Rollins (1985, p. 157) found black maids regularly deferring to white employers. Today, most discriminatory interaction no longer involves much asymmetrical deference, at least for middle-class blacks. Even where whites expect substantial deference, most middle-class blacks do not oblige. For middle-class blacks contemporary discrimination has evolved beyond the asymmetrical deference rituals and "No Negroes served" type of exclusion to patterns of black-contested discrimination. . . .

Some white observers have suggested that many middle-class blacks are paranoid about white discrimination and rush too quickly to charges of racism (Wieseltier 1989, June 5; for

male views of female "paranoia" see Gardner 1988). But the daily reality may be just the opposite, as middle-class black Americans often evaluate a situation carefully before judging it discriminatory and taking additional action. This careful evaluation, based on past experiences (real or vicarious), not only prevents jumping to conclusions, but also reflects the hope that white behavior is not based on race, because an act not based on race is easier to endure. After evaluation one strategy is to leave the site of discrimination rather than to create a disturbance. Another is to ignore the discrimination and continue with the interaction, a "blocking" strategy similar to that Gardner (1980, p. 345) reported for women dealing with street remarks. In many situations resigned acceptance is the only realistic response. More confrontational responses to white actions include verbal reprimands and sarcasm, physical counterattacks, and filing lawsuits. Several strategies may be tried in any given discriminatory situation. In crafting these strategies middle-class blacks, in comparison with less privileged blacks, may draw on middle-class resources to fight discrimination.

The Research Study

To examine discrimination, I draw primarily on 37 in-depth interviews from a larger study of 135 middle-class black Americans in Boston, Buffalo, Baltimore, Washington, D.C., Detroit, Houston, Dallas, Austin, San Antonio, Marshall, Las Vegas, and Los Angeles. . . .

Although all types of mistreatment are reported, there is a strong relationship between type of discrimination and site, with rejection/poor-service discrimination being most common in public accommodations and verbal or physical threat discrimination by white citizens or police officers most likely in the street. [Table 1] . . .

The most common black responses to racial hostility in the street are withdrawal

TABLE 1   Percentage Distribution of Discriminatory Actions by Type and Site: Middle-Class Blacks in Selected Cities, 1988–1990

| | Site of Discriminatory Action | |
Type of Discriminatory Action	*Public Accommodations*	*Street*
Avoidance	3	7
Rejection/poor service	79	4
Verbal epithets	12	25
Police threats/harassment	3	46
Other threats/harassment	3	18
Total	100	100
Number of actions	34	28

TABLE 2   Percentage Distribution of Primary Responses to Discriminatory Incidents by Type and Site: Middle-Class Blacks in Selected Cities, 1988–1990

| | Site of Discriminatory Incident | |
Response to Discriminatory Incident	*Public Accommodations*	*Street*
Withdrawal/exit	4	22
Resigned acceptance	23	7
Verbal response	69	59
Physical counterattack	4	7
Response unclear	—	4
Total	100	99
Number of responses	26	27

or a verbal reply [Table 2]. In many avoidance situations (e. g., a white couple crossing a street to avoid walking past a black college student) or attack situations (e.g., whites throwing beer cans from a passing car), a verbal response is difficult because of the danger or the fleeting character of the hostility. A black victim often withdraws, endures this treatment with resigned acceptance, or replies with a quick verbal retort. In the case of police harassment, the response is limited by the danger, and resigned acceptance or mild verbal protests are likely responses. Rejection (poor service) in public accommodations provides an opportunity to fight back verbally—the most common responses to public accommodations discrimination are verbal counterattacks or resigned acceptance. Some black victims correct whites quietly, while others respond aggressively

and lecture the assailant about the discrimination or threaten court action. A few retaliate physically. Examining materials in these 37 interviews . . . we will see that the depth and complexity of contemporary black middle-class responses to white discrimination accents the changing character of white-black interaction and the necessity of continual negotiation of the terms of that interaction.

Responses to Discrimination: Public Accommodations

Two Fundamental Strategies: Verbal Confrontation and Withdrawal

In the following account, a black news director at a major television station shows the interwoven character of discriminatory action and black response. The discrimination took the form of poor restaurant service, and the responses included both suggested withdrawal and verbal counterattack.

> He [her boyfriend] was waiting to be seated. . . . He said, "You go to the bathroom and I'll get the table. . . ." He was standing there when I came back; he continued to stand there. The restaurant was almost empty. There were waiters, waitresses, and no one seated. And when I got back to him, he was ready to leave, and said, "Let's go." I said, "What happened to our table?" He wasn't seated. So I said, "No, we're not leaving, please." And he said, "No, I'm leaving." So we went outside and we talked about it. And what I said to him was, you have to be aware of the possibilities that this is not the first time that this has happened at this restaurant or at other restaurants, but this is the first time it has happened to a black news director here or someone who could make an issue of it, or someone who is prepared to make an issue of it.
>
> So we went back inside after I talked him into it and, to make a long story short, I had the manager come. I made most of the people who were there (while conducting myself professionally the whole time) aware that I was incensed at being treated this way. . . . I said, "Why do you think we weren't seated?" And the manager said, "Well, I don't really know." And I said, "Guess." He said, "Well I don't know, because you're black?" I said, "Bingo. Now isn't it funny that you didn't guess that I didn't have any money" (and I opened up my purse) and I said, "because I certainly have money. And isn't it odd that you didn't guess that it's because I couldn't pay for it because I've got two American Express cards and a Master Card right here. I think it's just funny that you would have assumed that it's because I'm black." . . . And then I took out my card and gave it to him and said, "If this happens again, or if I hear of this happening again, I will bring the full wrath of an entire news department down on this restaurant." And

he just kind of looked at me. "Not [just] because I am personally offended. I am. But because you have no right to do what you did, and as a people we have lived a long time with having our rights abridged. . . ." There were probably three or four sets of diners in the restaurant and maybe five waiters/ waitresses. They watched him standing there waiting to be seated. His reaction to it was that he wanted to leave. I understood why he would have reacted that way, because he felt that he was in no condition to be civil. He was ready to take the place apart and . . . sometimes it's appropriate to behave that way. We hadn't gone the first step before going on to the next step. He didn't feel that he could comfortably and calmly take the first step, and I did. So I just asked him to please get back in the restaurant with me, and then you don't have to say a word, and let me handle it from there. It took some convincing, but I had to appeal to his sense of, this is not just you, this is not just for you. We are finally in a position as black people where there are some of us who can genuinely get their attention. And if they don't want to do this because it's right for them to do it, then they'd better do it because they're afraid to do otherwise. If it's fear, then fine, instill the fear.

This example provides insight into the character of modern discrimination. The discrimination was not the "No Negroes" exclusion of the recent past, but rejection in the form of poor service by restaurant personnel. The black response indicates the change in black-white interaction since the 1950s and 1960s, for discrimination is handled with vigorous confrontation rather than deference. The aggressive black response and the white backtracking underscore Brittan and Maynard's (1984, p. 7) point that black-white interaction today is being renegotiated. It is possible that the white personnel defined the couple as "poor blacks" because of their jeans, although the jeans were fashionable and white patrons wear jeans. In comments not quoted here the news director rejects such an explanation. She forcefully articulates a theory of rights—a response that signals the critical impact of civil rights laws on the thinking of middle-class blacks. The news director articulates the American dream: she has worked hard, earned the money and credit cards, developed the appropriate middle-class behavior, and thus has under the law a *right* to be served. There is defensiveness in her actions too, for she feels a need to legitimate her status by showing her purse and credit cards. One important factor that enabled her to take such assertive action was her power to bring a TV news team to the restaurant. This power marks a change from a few decades ago when very few black Americans had the social or economic resources to fight back successfully. . . .

The confrontation response is generally so costly in terms of time and energy that acquiescence or withdrawal are common options. An example of the exit response was provided by a utility company executive in an East Coast city:

> I can remember one time my husband had picked up our son . . . from camp; and he'd stopped at a little store in the neighborhood near the camp. It was hot, and he was going to buy him a snowball. And the proprietor of the store—this was a very old, white neighborhood, and it was just a little sundry store. But the proprietor said he had the little window where people could come up and order things. Well, my husband and son had gone into the store. And he told them, "Well, I can't give it to you here, but if you go outside to the window, I'll give it to you." And there were other [white] people in the store who'd been served [inside]. So, they just left and didn't buy anything.

. . . This site differed from the previous example in that the service was probably not of long-term importance to the black family passing through the area. In the previous site the possibility of returning to the restaurant

for business or pleasure may have contributed to the choice of a confrontational response. The importance of the service is a likely variable affecting black responses to discrimination in public accommodations. . . .

The complex process of evaluation and response is described by a college dean, who commented generally on hotel and restaurant discrimination encountered as he travels across the United States:

> When you're in a restaurant and . . . you notice that blacks get seated near the kitchen. You notice that if it's a hotel, your room is near the elevator, or your room is always way down in a corner somewhere. You find that you are getting the undesirable rooms. And you come there early in the day and you don't see very many cars on the lot and they'll tell you that this is all we've got. Or you get the room that's got a bad television set. You know that you're being discriminated against. And of course you have to act accordingly. You have to tell them, "Okay, the room is fine, [but] this television set has got to go. Bring me another television set." So in my personal experience, I simply cannot sit and let them get away with it [discrimination] and not let them know that I know that that's what they are doing. . . .
>
> When I face discrimination, first I take a long look at myself and try to determine whether or not I am seeing what I think I'm seeing in 1989, and if it's something that I have an option [about]. In other words, if I'm at a store making a purchase, I'll simply walk away from it. If it's at a restaurant where I'm not getting good service, I first of all let the people know that I'm not getting good service, then I [may] walk away from it. But the thing that I have to do is to let people know that I know that I'm being singled out for a separate treatment. And then I might react in any number of ways—depending on where I am and how badly I want whatever it is that I'm there for.

This commentary adds another dimension to our understanding of public discrimination, its cumulative aspect. Blacks confront not just isolated incidents—such as a bad room in a luxury hotel once every few years—but a lifelong series of such incidents. Here again the omnipresence of careful assessments is underscored. The dean's interview highlights a major difficulty in being black—one must be constantly prepared to assess accurately and then decide on the appropriate response. This long-look approach may indicate that some middle-class blacks are so sensitive to white charges of hypersensitivity and paranoia that they err in the opposite direction and fail to see discrimination when it occurs. In addition, as one black graduate student at a leading white university in the Southeast put it: "I think that sometimes timely and appropriate responses to racially motivated acts and comments are lost due to the processing of the input." The "long look" can result in missed opportunities to respond to discrimination.

Using Middle-Class Resources for Protection

One advantage that middle-class blacks have over poorer blacks is the use of the resources of middle-class occupations. A professor at a major white university commented on the varying protection her middle-class status gives her at certain sites:

> If I'm in those areas that are fairly protected, within gatherings of my own group, other African Americans, or if I'm in the university where my status as a professor mediates against the way I might be perceived, mediates against the hostile perception, then it's fairly comfortable. . . . When I divide my life into encounters with the outside world, and of course that's ninety percent of my life, it's fairly consistently unpleasant at those sites where there's nothing that mediates between my race and what I have to do. For example, if I'm in a grocery store, if I'm in my car, which is a 1970 Chevrolet, a real old ugly

car, all those things—being in a grocery store in casual clothes, or being in the car—sort of advertises something that doesn't have anything to do with my status as far as people I run into are concerned.
>
> Because I'm a large black woman, and I don't wear whatever class status I have, or whatever professional status [I have] in my appearance when I'm in the grocery store, I'm part of the mass of large black women shopping. For most whites, and even for some blacks, that translates into negative status. That means that they are free to treat me the way they treat most poor black people, because they can't tell by looking at me that I differ from that.

This professor notes the variation in discrimination in the sites through which she travels, from the most private to the most public. At home with friends she faces no problems, and at the university her professional status gives her some protection from discrimination. The increase in unpleasant encounters as she moves into public accommodations sites such as grocery stores is attributed to the absence of mediating factors such as clear symbols of middle-class status—displaying the middle-class symbols may provide some protection against discrimination in public places. . . .

Responses to Discrimination: The Street

Reacting to White Strangers

As we move away from public accommodations settings to the usually less protected street sites, racial hostility can become more fleeting and severer, and thus black responses are often restricted. The most serious form of street discrimination is violence. Often the reasonable black response to street discrimination is withdrawal, resigned acceptance, or a quick verbal retort. The difficulty of responding to violence is seen in this report by a man working for a media surveying firm in a southern industrial city:

> I was parked in front of this guy's house.... This guy puts his hands on the window and says, "Get out of the car, nigger."...So, I got out, and I thought, "Oh, this is what's going to happen here." And I'm talking fast. And they're, "What are you doing here?" And I'm, "This is who I am. I work with these people. This is the man we want to put in the survey." And I pointed to the house. And the guy said, "Well you have an out-of-state license tag, right?" "Yea." And he said, "If something happened to you, your people at home wouldn't know for a long time, would they?"...I said, "Look, I deal with a company that deals with television. [If] something happens to me, it's going to be a national thing."...So, they grab me by the lapel of my coat, and put me in front of my car. They put the blade on my zipper. And now I'm thinking about this guy that's in the truck [behind me], because now I'm thinking that I'm going to have to run somewhere. Where am I going to run? Go to the police? [laughs] So, after a while they bash up my headlight. And I drove [away].

Stigmatized and physically attacked solely because of his color, this man faced verbal hostility and threats of death with courage. Cautiously drawing on his middle-class resources, he told the attackers his death would bring television crews to the town. This resource utilization is similar to that of the news director in the restaurant incident. Beyond this verbal threat his response had to be one of caution. For most whites threatened on the street, the police are a sought-after source of protection; this is often not the case....

Responses to Discrimination by White Police Officers

Most middle-class blacks do not have such governmental authority as their personal protection. In fact, white police officers are a major problem. Encounters with the police can be life-threatening and thus limit the range of responses. A television commentator recounted two cases of police harassment when he was working for a survey firm in the mid-1980s. In one of the incidents, which took place in a southern metropolis, he was stopped by several white officers:

> "What are you doing here?" I tell them what I'm doing here.... And so me spread on top of my car. [What had you done?] Because I was in the neighborhood, I left this note on these peoples' house: "Here's who I am. You weren't here, and I will come back in thirty minutes." [Why were they searching you?] They don't know. To me, they're searching, I remember at that particular moment when this all was going down, there was a lot of reports about police crime on civilians.... It took four cops to shake me down, two police cars, so they had me up there spread out. I had a friend of mine with me who was making the call with me, because we were going to have dinner together, and he was black, and they had me up, and they had him outside.... They said, "Well, let's check you out."... And I'm talking to myself, and I'm not thinking about being at attention, with my arms spread on my Ford [a company car], and I'm sitting there talking to myself, "Man, this is crazy, this is crazy."
>
> [How are you feeling inside?] Scared. I mean real scared. [What did you think was going to happen to you?] I was going to go to jail.... Just because they picked me. Why would they stop me? It's like, if they can stop me, why wouldn't I go to jail, and I could sit there for ten days before the judge sees me. I'm thinking all this crazy stuff.... Again, I'm talking to myself. And the guy takes his stick. And he doesn't whack me hard, but he does it with enough authority to let me know they mean business. "I told you stand still; now put your arms back out." And I've got this suit on, and the car's wet. And my friend's hysterical. He's outside the car. And they're checking him out. And he's like, "Man, just be cool, man." And he had tears in his eyes. And I'm like, oh,

man, this is a nightmare. This is not supposed to happen to me. This is not my style!
And so finally, this other cop comes up and
says, "What have we got here Charlie?" "Oh,
we've got a guy here. He's running through
the neighborhood, and he doesn't want to do
what we tell him. We might have to run him
in." [You're "running through" the neighborhood?] Yeah, exactly, in a suit in the rain?!
After they got through doing their thing and
harassing me, I just said, "Man, this has been
a hell of a week."

And I had tears in my eyes, but it
wasn't tears of upset. It was tears of anger;
it was tears of wanting to lash back. . . .
What I thought to myself was, man, blacks
have it real hard down here. I don't care if
they're a broadcaster; I don't care if they're
a businessman or a banker. . . . They don't
have it any easier than the persons on skid
row who get harassed by the police on a
Friday or Saturday night.

It seems likely that most black men—including middle-class black men—see white police
officers as a major source of danger and death.
(See "Mood of Ghetto America" 1980, June 2,
pp. 32–34; Roddy 1990, August 26.) Scattered
evidence suggests that by the time they are in
their twenties, most black males, regardless
of socioeconomic status, have been stopped
by the police because "blackness" is considered a sign of possible criminality by police
officers (Moss 1990; Roddy 1990, August 26).
This treatment probably marks a dramatic
contrast with the experiences of young white
middle-class males. In the incident above the
respondent and a friend experienced severe
police maltreatment—detention for a lengthy
period, threat of arrest, and the reality of physical violence. The coping response of the respondent was resigned acceptance somewhat
similar to the deference rituals highlighted by
Goffman. The middle-class suits and obvious
corporate credentials (for example, survey
questionnaires and company car) did not
protect the two black men. The final comment
suggests a disappointment that middle-class

status brought no reprieve from police stigmatization and harassment. . . .

Conclusion

I have examined the sites of discrimination,
the types of discriminatory acts, and the
responses of the victims and have found the
color stigma still to be very important in
the public lives of affluent black Americans.
The sites of racial discrimination range from
relatively protected home sites, to less protected workplace and educational sites, to
the even less protected public places. The
1964 Civil Rights Act guarantees that black
Americans are "entitled to the full and equal
enjoyment of the goods, services, facilities,
privileges, advantages, and accommodations"
in public accommodations. Yet the interviews
indicate that deprivation of full enjoyment
of public facilities is not a relic of the past:
deprivation and discrimination in public accommodations persist. Middle-class black
Americans remain vulnerable targets in
public places. Prejudice-generated aggression
in public places is, of course, not limited to
black men and women—gay men and white
women are also targets of street harassment
(Benokraitis and Feagin 1986). Nonetheless,
black women and men face an unusually
broad range of discrimination on the street
and in public accommodations.

The interviews highlight two significant
aspects of the additive discrimination faced
by black Americans in public places and
elsewhere: (1) the cumulative character of an
individual's experiences with discrimination;
and (2) the *group's* accumulated historical
experiences as perceived by the individual.
A retired psychology professor who has
worked in the Midwest and Southwest commented on the pyramiding of incidents:

I don't think white people, generally,
understand the full meaning of racist discriminatory behaviors directed toward

Americans of African descent. They seem to see each act of discrimination or any act of violence as an "isolated" event. As a result, most white Americans cannot understand the strong reaction manifested by blacks when such events occur. They feel that blacks tend to "over-react." They forget that in most cases, we live lives of quiet desperation generated by a litany of *daily* large and small events that whether or not by design, remind us of our "place" in American society.

Particular instances of discrimination may seem minor to outside white observers when considered in isolation. But when blatant acts of avoidance, verbal harassment, and physical attack combine with subtle and covert slights, and these accumulate over months, years, and lifetimes, the impact on a black person is far more than the sum of the individual instances.

The historical context of contemporary discrimination was described by the retired psychologist, who argued that average white Americans

> . . . ignore the personal context of stimulus. That is, they deny the historical impact that a negative act may have on an individual. "Nigger" to a white may simply be an epithet that should be ignored. To most blacks, the term brings into sharp and current focus all kinds of acts of racism—murder, rape, torture, denial of constitutional rights, insults, limited opportunity structure, economic problems, unequal justice under the law and a myriad of . . . other racist and discriminatory acts that occur daily in the lives of *most* Americans of African descent—including professional blacks.

Particular acts, even antilocution that might seem minor to white observers, are freighted not only with one's past experience of discrimination but also with centuries of racial discrimination directed at the entire group, vicarious oppression that still includes racially translated violence and denial of access to the American dream. Anti-black discrimination is a matter of racial-power inequality

institutionalized in a variety of economic and social institutions over a long period of time. The microlevel events of public accommodations and public streets are not just rare and isolated encounters by individuals; they are recurring events reflecting an invasion of the microworld by the macroworld of historical racial subordination.

REFERENCES

Allport, Gordon. 1958. *The Nature of Prejudice.* Abridged. New York: Doubleday Anchor Books.

Benokraitis, Nijole, and Joe R. Feagin. 1986. *Modern Sexism: Blatant, Subtle and Covert Discrimination.* Englewood Cliffs, NJ: Prentice-Hall.

Blauner, Bob. 1989. *Black Lives, White Lives.* Berkeley: University of California Press.

Brittan, Arthur, and Mary Maynard. 1984. *Sexism, Racism and Oppression.* Oxford: Basil Blackwell.

Doyle, Bertram W. 1937. *The Etiquette of Race Relations in the South.* Port Washington, NY: Kennikat Press.

Feagin, Joe R., and Douglas Eckberg. 1980. "Prejudice and Discrimination." *Annual Review of Sociology* 6:1–20.

Feagin, Joe R., and Clairece Booher Feagin. 1986. *Discrimination American Style,* rev. ed. Melbourne, FL: Krieger.

Gardner, Carol Brooks. 1980. "Passing By: Street Remarks, Address Rights, and the Urban Female." *Sociological Inquiry* 50:328–56.

———. "Access Information: Public Lies and Private Peril." *Social Problems* 35:384–97.

Goffman, Erving. 1956. "The Nature of Deference and Demeanor." *American Anthropologist* 58: 473–502.

Griffin, John Howard. 1961. *Black Like Me.* Boston: Houghton Mifflin. "The Mood of Ghetto America." 1980. *Newsweek,* 2 June, pp. 32–4.

Moss, E. Yvonne. 1990. "African Americans and the Administration of Justice." Pp. 79–86 in *Assessment of the Status of African-Americans,* edited by Wornie L. Reed. Boston: University of Massachusetts, William Monroe Trotter Institute.

Raper, Arthur F. 1933. *The Tragedy of Lynching.* Chapel Hill: University of North Carolina Press.

Roddy, Dennis B. 1990. "Perceptions Still Segregate Police, Black Community." *The Pittsburgh Press,* 26 August, p. B1.

Rollins, Judith. 1985. *Between Women.* Philadelphia: Temple University Press.

Wieseltier, Leon. 1989. "Scar Tissue." *New Republic,* 5 June, pp. 19–20.

HOW SPACE GETS RACED

21

RESIDENTIAL SEGREGATION AND NEIGHBORHOOD CONDITIONS IN U.S. METROPOLITAN AREAS

Douglas S. Massey

QUESTIONS TO CONSIDER

Douglas Massey points out that almost all racial and ethnic groups are highly segregated in the United States. Racially integrated neighborhoods are an anomaly. Why is residential segregation the norm rather than the exception? Why are blacks subject to the most severe discrimination in the housing market?

Social scientists have long studied patterns of racial and ethnic segregation because of the close connection between a group's spatial position in society and its socioeconomic well-being. Opportunities and resources are unevenly distributed in space; some neighborhoods have safer streets, higher home values, better services, more effective schools, and more supportive peer environments than others. As people and families improve their socioeconomic circumstances, they generally move to gain access to these benefits. In doing so, they seek to convert past

Douglas S. Massey, "Residential Segregation and Neighborhood Conditions in U.S. Metropolitan Areas" from *America Becoming: Racial Trends and Their Consequences*, Vol. 1, pp. 391–434, National Academies Press. Copyright © 2001. Reprinted with permission from *America Becoming*.

socioeconomic achievements into improved residential circumstances, yielding tangible immediate benefits and enhancing future prospects for social mobility by providing greater access to residentially determined resources.

Throughout U.S. history, racial and ethnic groups arriving in the United States for the first time have settled in enclaves located close to an urban core, in areas of mixed land use, old housing, poor services, and low or decreasing socioeconomic status. As group members build up time in the city, however, and as their socioeconomic status rises, they have tended to move out of these enclaves into areas that offer more amenities and improved conditions—areas in which majority members are more prevalent—leading to their progressive spatial assimilation into society.

The twin processes of immigrant settlement, on the one hand, and spatial assimilation, on the other, combine to yield a diversity of segregation patterns across groups and times, depending on the particular histories of inmigration and socioeconomic mobility involved (Massey, 1985). Groups experiencing recent rapid inmigration and slow socioeconomic mobility tend to display relatively high levels of segregation, whereas those with rapid rates of economic mobility and slow rates of inmigration tend to be more integrated.

When avenues of spatial assimilation are systematically blocked by prejudice and discrimination, however, residential segregation increases and persists over time. New minorities arrive in the city and settle within enclaves, but their subsequent spatial mobility is stymied, and ethnic concentrations increase until the enclaves are filled, whereupon group members are forced into adjacent areas, thus expanding the boundaries of the enclave (Duncan and Duncan, 1957). In the United States, most immigrant groups experienced relatively few residential barriers, so levels of ethnic segregation historically were not very high. Using a standard segregation index (the index of dissimilarity), which varies from 0 to 100, European ethnic groups rarely had indexes of more than 60 (Massey, 1985; Massey and Denton, 1992).

Blacks, in contrast, traditionally experienced severe prejudice and discrimination in urban housing markets. As they moved into urban areas from 1900 to 1960, therefore, their segregation indices rose to unprecedented heights, compared with earlier times and groups. By mid-century, segregation indices exceeded 60 virtually everywhere; and in the largest Black communities they often reached 80 or more (Massey and Denton, 1989b, 1993).

Such high indices of residential segregation imply a restriction of opportunity for Blacks compared with other groups. Discriminatory barriers in urban housing markets mean individual Black citizens are less able to capitalize on their hard-won attainments

and achieve desirable residential locations. Compared with Whites of similar social status, Blacks tend to live in systematically disadvantaged neighborhoods, even within suburbs (Schneider and Logan, 1982; Massey et al., 1987; Massey and Fong, 1990; Massey and Denton, 1992).

In a very real way, barriers to spatial mobility are barriers to social mobility; and a racially segregated society cannot logically claim to be "color blind." The way a group is spatially incorporated into society is as important to its socioeconomic well-being as the manner in which it is incorporated into the labor force. It is important, therefore, that levels and trends in residential segregation be documented so that this variable can be incorporated fully into research and theorizing about the causes of urban poverty. To accomplish this, presented here is an overview and interpretation of historical trends in the residential segregation of Blacks, Hispanics, and Asians.

Long-Term Trends in Black Segregation

Massey and Hajnal (1995) examined historical trends in Black segregation at the state, county, municipal, and neighborhood levels. Their interpretation focused on two specific time periods—pre-World War II; 1900 to 1940; and postwar, from 1950 to 1990. Table 1 presents their data[1] on the geographic structure of Black segregation and racial isolation during the earlier period. Because of data limitations,

---

[1]Residential segregation was measured using the index of dissimilarity, and racial isolation was measured using the P* index (Massey and Denton, 1988). The index of dissimilarity is the relative number of Blacks who would have to change geographic units so that an even Black-White spatial distribution could be achieved. The P* index is the percentage of Blacks residing in the geographic unit of the average Black person.

TABLE 1   Indices of Black-White Segregation Computed at Three Geographic Levels, 1900 to 1940

	Years				
	1900	*1910*	*1920*	*1930*	*1940*
Between states					
Dissimilarity	64	65	61	54	52
Isolation	36	34	30	25	24
Between counties					
Dissimilarity	69	70	66	60	59
Isolation	45	43	38	33	32
Between wards					
Dissimilarity					
Boston	—	64	65	78	79
Buffalo	—	63	72	81	82
Chicago	—	67	76	85	83
Cincinnati	—	47	57	73	77
Cleveland	—	61	70	85	86
Philadelphia	—	46	48	63	68
Pittsburgh	—	44	43	61	65
St. Louis	—	54	62	82	84
Average	—	56	62	76	78
Isolation					
Boston	06	11	15	19	—
Buffalo	04	06	10	24	—
Chicago	10	15	38	70	—
Cincinnati	10	13	27	45	—
Cleveland	08	08	24	51	—
Philadelphia	16	16	21	27	—
Pittsburgh	12	12	17	27	—
St. Louis	13	17	30	47	—
Average	10	13	23	39	—

Source: Massey and Hajnal (1995).

segregation or isolation at the municipal level during this early period could not be measured.

As Table 1 shows, Blacks and Whites were distinctly segregated from one another across state boundaries early in the twentieth century. In 1900, for example, 64 percent of all Blacks would have had to move to a different state to achieve an even distribution across state lines, and most Blacks lived in a state that was 36 percent Black. These figures simply state the obvious, that in 1900, some 90 percent of Blacks lived in a handful of southern states, which contained only 25 percent of all Whites (U.S. Bureau of the Census, 1979).

The isolation index shows that in the South, most Blacks lived in rural counties that were approximately 45 percent Black, yielding a high degree of segregation and racial isolation at the county level as well. The dissimilarity index for 1900 reveals that nearly 70 percent of all Blacks would have had to shift their county of residence to achieve an even racial distribution across county lines.

At the beginning of this century, for Blacks, the typical residential setting was southern and rural; for Whites it was northern and urban. Under conditions of high state- and county-level segregation, race relations remained largely a regional problem centered in the South. Successive waves of Black migration out of the rural South into the urban North transformed the geographic structure of Black segregation during the twentieth century, however, ending the regional isolation and rural confinement of Blacks. From 1900 to 1940, the index of Black-White dissimilarity fell from 64 to 52 at the state level and from 69 to 59 at the county level. Black isolation likewise dropped from 36 to 24 within states, and from 45 to 32 within counties.

The movement of Blacks out of rural areas, however, was accompanied by their progressive segregation within cities. Although we lack indices of Black-White dissimilarity for 1900, research has demonstrated that blacks were not particularly segregated in northern cities during the nineteenth century. Ward-level dissimilarity for Blacks in 11 northern cities circa 1860 had average indices of approximately 46 (Massey and Denton, 1993).

By 1910, however, the eight cities listed in Table 1 had an average index of 56, and the level of Black-White dissimilarity increased sharply during each decade after 1910, suggesting the progressive formation of black ghettos in cities throughout the nation. As Lieberson (1980) has shown, the growth of Black populations in urban areas triggered the imposition of higher levels of racial levels of racial segregation within cities. Before the U.S. Supreme Court declared them unconstitutional in 1916, many U.S. cities actually passed apartheid laws establishing separate Black and White districts. Thereafter, however, segregation was achieved by less formal means (see Massey and Denton, 1993:26–42). Whatever the mechanism, the end result was a rapid increase in Black residential segregation, with the neighborhood segregation index rising from 56 to 78 between 1910 and 1940, a remarkable increase of 39 percent in just three decades.

The combination of growing urban Black populations and higher levels of segregation could only produce one possible outcome—higher levels of Black isolation. In 1900, the relatively small number of urban Blacks and the rather low level of Black-White segregation resulted in a low degree of racial isolation within neighborhoods. Among the eight cities shown in Table 1, the average isolation index was just 10; the typical urban Black resident lived in a ward that was 90 percent non-Black. Moreover, the index of isolation did not vary substantially from city to city. Urban Blacks early in the century were quite likely to know and interact socially with Whites (Massey and Denton, 1993:19–26). Indeed, on average they were more likely to share a neighborhood with a White person than with a Black person.

By 1930, however, the geographic structure of segregation had changed dramatically, shifting from state and county levels to the neighborhood level. The average isolation index was now 39 in neighborhoods, indicating that most Black residents in the cities under study lived in a ward that was almost 40 percent Black. In some cities, the degree of racial isolation reached truly extreme levels. The transformation was most dramatic in Chicago, where the isolation index went from 10 in 1900 to 70 in 1930, by which time, moreover, the dissimilarity index had reached 85. Similar conditions of intense Black segregation occurred in Cleveland, which by 1930 displayed a dissimilarity index of 85 and an isolation index of 51.

•   •   •

Despite the relative stability of segregation achieved by 1970 at the state, county, and neighborhood levels, a remarkable change was occurring at the city level. From 1950 onward, Blacks and Whites were becoming more and more segregated across *municipal* boundaries. After 1950, Blacks and Whites not only tended to live in different neighborhoods; increasingly they lived in different municipalities as well. After 1950, in other words, Blacks and Whites came to reside in wholly different towns and cities. From 1950 to 1980, the index of Black-White dissimilarity increased from 35 to 49 at the municipal level, a change of 40 percent in just 30 years, a shift that was remarkably similar to the rapid change observed in neighborhood-level segregation during the early period of ghetto formation. Black isolation went from an index of 19 to 35 at the municipal level, an increase of 84 percent. By the end of the 1970s, the average Black urban dweller lived in a municipality that was 35 percent Black; and one-half of all urban Blacks would have had to exchange places with Whites to achieve an even municipal distribution.

The emergence of significant municipal-level segregation in the United States reflects demographic trends that occurred in all parts of the urban hierarchy—in nonmetropolitan areas as well as central cities and suburbs. In 1950, there were no predominantly Black central cities in the United States. Among cities with more than 100,000 inhabitants, none had a Black percentage in excess of 50 percent. By 1990, however, 14 cities were at least 50 percent Black, including Atlanta, Baltimore, Detroit, Gary, Newark, New Orleans, and Washington; together they were home to 11 percent of all Blacks in the United States. In addition, another 11 cities were approaching Black majorities by 1990, with percentages ranging from 40 percent to 50 percent, including Cleveland, St. Louis, and Oakland. Among cities with populations of 25,000 or more, only two municipalities in the entire United States were more than 50 percent Black in 1950, both in the South; but by 1990 the number had increased to 40. Some of these cities—such Prichard, Alabama, Kinston, North Carolina; and Vicksburg, Mississippi— were located in nonmetropolitan areas of the South. Others—such as Maywood, Illinois; Highland Park, Michigan; and Inglewood, California—were suburbs of large central cities in the North and West.

Recent Trends in Black Segregation

Table 2 shows indicators of Black residential segregation for the 30 U.S. metropolitan areas with the largest Black populations. As in Table 1, these data are used to evaluate racial segregation from two vantage points. The first three columns show trends in the indices of spatial separation between Blacks and Whites using the index of dissimilarity, and the next three columns show trends in indices of Black residential isolation. The indices for 1970 and 1980, from Massey and Denton (1987), are metropolitan areas based on 1970 boundaries. Indices for 1990, from Harrison and Weinberg (1992), are based on 1990 geographic definitions. White and Black Hispanics were excluded, by both sets of researchers, from their subject sets of Whites and Blacks, and both sets of researchers computed indices using tracts as units of analysis.

Among the northern metropolitan areas shown, there is little evidence of any trend toward Black residential integration. Black segregation indices averaged about 85 in 1970, 80 in 1980, and 78 in 1990, a decline of only 8 percent in 20 years. Dissimilarity indices more than 60 are generally considered high, whereas those between 30 and 60 are considered moderate (Kantrowitz, 1973). At the rate of change observed between 1970 and 1990, the average level of Black-White segregation in northern areas would not reach the lower limits of the high range until the year 2043. At the slower rate of change prevailing from 1970 to 1980, it would take until 2067. As of 1990, no large northern Black community approached even a moderate level of residential segregation.

TABLE 2   Trends in Black Segregation and Isolation in the 30 Metropolitan Areas with the Largest Black Populations, 1970 to 1990

Metropolitan	Dissimilarity Indices			Isolation Indices		
	1970[a]	1980[a]	1990[b]	1970[a]	1980[a]	1990[b]
Northern						
Boston, MA	81.2	77.6	68.2	56.7	55.1	51.2
Buffalo, NY	87.0	79.4	81.8	71.2	63.5	68.1
Chicago, IL	91.9	87.8	85.8	85.8	82.8	83.9
Cincinnati, OH	76.8	72.3	75.8	59.1	54.3	61.0
Cleveland, OH	90.8	87.5	85.1	81.9	90.4	80.8
Columbus, OH	81.8	71.4	67.3	63.5	57.5	52.5
Detroit, MI	88.4	86.7	87.6	75.9	77.3	82.3
Gary-Hammond-E. Chicago, IL	91.4	90.6	89.9	80.4	77.3	84.2
Indianapolis, IN	81.7	76.2	74.3	64.5	62.3	61.0
Kansas City, MO	87.4	78.9	72.6	74.2	69.0	61.6
Los Angeles-Long Beach, CA	91.0	81.1	73.1	70.3	60.4	69.3
Milwaukee, WI	90.5	83.9	82.8	73.9	69.5	72.4
New York, NY	81.0	82.0	82.2	58.8	62.7	81.9
Newark, NJ	81.4	81.6	82.5	67.0	69.2	78.6
Philadelphia, PA	79.5	78.8	77.2	68.2	69.6	72.2
Pittsburgh, PA	75.0	72.7	71.0	53.5	54.1	53.1
St. Louis, MO	84.7	81.3	77.0	76.5	72.9	69.5
San Francisco-Oakland, CA	80.1	71.7	66.8	56.0	51.1	56.1
Average	84.5	80.1	77.8	68.7	66.1	68.9
Southern						
Atlanta, GA	82.1	78.5	67.8	78.0	74.8	66.5
Baltimore, MD	81.9	74.7	71.4	77.2	72.3	70.6
Birmingham, AL	37.8	40.8	71.7	45.1	50.2	69.6
Dallas-Ft. Worth, TX	86.9	77.1	63.1	76.0	64.0	58.0
Greensboro-Winston Salem, NC	65.4	56.0	60.9	56.1	50.1	55.5
Houston, TX	78.1	69.5	66.8	66.4	59.3	63.6
Memphis, TN	75.9	71.6	69.3	78.0	75.9	75.0
Miami, FL	85.1	77.8	71.8	75.2	64.2	47.1
New Orleans, LA	73.1	68.3	68.8	71.3	68.8	71.9
Norfolk-Virginia Beach, VA	75.7	63.1	50.3	73.5	62.8	55.9
Tampa-St. Petersburg, FL	79.9	72.6	69.7	58.0	51.5	51.0
Washington, DC	81.1	70.1	66.1	77.2	68.0	66.7
Average	75.3	68.3	66.5	69.3	63.5	64.9

[a]Indices are from Massey and Denton (1987).
[b]Indices are from Harrison and Weinberg (1992).

Indeed, in most metropolitan areas, racial segregation remained very high throughout the 20-year period. Dissimilarity indices were essentially constant in seven metropolitan areas—Cincinnati, Detroit, Gary, New York, Newark, and Philadelphia; in seven others— Buffalo, Chicago, Cleveland, Indianapolis, Milwaukee, Pittsburgh, and St. Louis—small declines still left Blacks extremely segregated. All the latter metropolitan areas had dissimilarity indices exceeding 70 in 1990, and in four cases, the index was more than 80. No other ethnic or racial group in the history of the United States has ever, even briefly, experienced such high levels of residential segregation (Massey and Denton, 1993).

A few metropolitan areas experienced significant declines in the level of Black-White segregation between 1970 and 1990, although the pace of change slowed considerably duringthe 1980s, compared with the 1970s. In Columbus, Ohio, for example, Black-White dissimilarity fell by more than 10 index points from 1970 to 1880 (from 82 to 71), but then dropped by only 4 points through 1990. Likewise, San Francisco dropped from 80 to 72 during the 1970s, but went to just 68 by 1990.

The only areas that experienced a sustained decline in Black-White segregation across both decades were Los Angeles and Boston; but in each case, the overall index of segregation remained well within the high range. The drop in Los Angeles probably reflects the displacement of Blacks by the arrival of large numbers of Asian and, particularly, Hispanic immigrants (Massey and Denton, 1987). By 1990, for example, Watts, the core of the 1960s Black ghetto, had become predominantly Hispanic (Turner and Allen, 1991). The arrival of more than a million new immigrants in Los Angeles County between 1970 and 1980 put substantial pressure on the housing stock, and increased intergroup competition for residential units, especially at the low end of the market, leading to considerable neighborhood flux and residential mixing (Frey and Farley, 1996).

When large Black communities are subject to high levels of segregation, intense racial isolation is inevitable. In 1990, six metropolitan areas—Chicago, Cleveland, Detroit, Gary, New York, and Newark—had isolation indices of 80 or more, meaning that most Black people lived in neighborhoods that were more than 80 percent Black. Detailed analyses of neighborhoods show, however, that this overall average is misleading, because it represents a balance between a small minority of Blacks who reside in highly integrated neighborhoods and a large majority of Blacks who live in all-Black neighborhoods (Denton and Massey, 1991). Moreover, in four of the six metropolitan areas, the level of Black isolation actually increased between 1970 and 1990.

In other northern areas, the prevailing pattern of change in racial isolation was one of stability, with shifts of less than 5 percent from 1970 to 1990. The average isolation index of 68.9 in 1990 was virtually identical to the index of 68.7 observed two decades earlier; in other words, 20 years after the Fair Housing Act, Blacks were still unlikely to come into residential contact with members of other groups. The large ghettos of the North have remained substantially intact and were largely unaffected by Civil Right legislation of the 1960s.

Trends in Black segregation and isolation are somewhat different in the South, where segregation levels traditionally have been lower because of the distinctive history and character of southern cities. With social segregation enforced by Jim Crow legislation, Blacks and Whites before 1960 often lived in close physical proximity, with Black-inhabited alleys being interspersed between larger, White-occupied avenues (Demerath and Gilmore, 1954). During the postwar housing boom, moreover, rural Black settlements were often overtaken by expanding White suburbs, thereby creating the appearance of racial integration. For these and other reasons, Black-White segregation scores in the South traditionally have averaged about 10 points lower than in the North (Massey and Denton, 1993).

This regional differential is roughly maintained, as shown in Table 1, but southern areas display considerably greater diversity, despite the regional averages, than in the North. In some metropolitan areas, such as Baltimore, Houston, and Tampa, significant declines in segregation occurred during the

1970s, but declines slowed during the 1980s. In others, such as Dallas, Miami, and Norfolk, steady declines occurred throughout both decades. In Memphis and New Orleans, relatively small changes occurred, no matter which decade one considers. Two southern areas displayed increasing levels of Black-White segregation—Birmingham, where the increase was very sharp after 1970, and Greensboro, where an initial decline during the 1970s was reversed during the 1980s.

In general, then, Black-White segregation scores in the South appear to be converging on indices from 60 to 70, yielding an average of 67 and maintaining the traditional differential compared with the North. Metropolitan areas with segregation indices higher than the 60 to 70 range in 1970 experienced decreasing segregation, whereas those with indices less than 60 to 70 displayed increasing segregation; and those with indices within that range did not change much.

Only Norfolk differed from this pattern, with a significant and sustained decline in segregation during both decades, producing by 1990 a level of Black-White dissimilarity well within the moderate range. Many Norfolk residents are in the military, which has been more successfully integrated than other institutions in American life (Moskos and Butler, 1996: see also Volume II, Chapter 8). Frey and Farley (1994) demonstrated that areas dominated, economically, by military bases have significantly lower levels of Black-White segregation than others, controlling for a variety of other factors.

Although indices of Black-White dissimilarity may be lower in the South, the relative number of Blacks in urban areas is greater; so the average level of racial isolation within neighborhoods is not much different than in the North. From 1970 to 1990, there was relatively little change in the overall degree of Black isolation, with the average index decreasing from 69 in 1970 to 65 in 1990.

In four southern areas—Baltimore, Memphis, Miami, and New Orleans—the Black isolation index was more than 70 in both decades; and in Birmingham, the index of Black isolation rose from 45 to 70 between 1970 and 1990. Only in Norfolk, which was rapidly desegregating, and in Tampa, which had relatively few Blacks, did isolation scores fall below 60. In most cities in the South, as in the North, Blacks were relatively unlikely to share neighborhoods with members of other racial or ethnic groups.

Thus, despite evidence of change in the South, Blacks living within the nation's largest urban Black communities are still highly segregated and spatially isolated from the rest of American society. Of the 30 northern and southern areas examined here, 19 still had Black-White dissimilarity indices in excess of 70 in 1990, and 12 had isolation indices in excess of 70. Either in absolute terms or in comparison to other groups, Blacks remain a very residentially segregated and spatially isolated people.

Recent Trends in Hispanic Segregation

Based on the historical experience of Blacks, recent demographic trends of Hispanics would be expected to have produced increasing levels of segregation during the 1970s and 1980s. In this period, there has been a remarkable resurgence of Hispanic immigration, yielding rapidly growing Hispanic populations in many metropolitan areas. In the Los Angeles metropolitan area, for example, the Hispanic population increased by 1.3 million between 1970 and 1990; Hispanics went from being 28 percent of the population to 38 percent. Because migrant networks channel new arrivals to neighborhoods where immigrants have already settled, such rapid in-migration could be expected to increase the concentration of Hispanics within enclaves and raise overall levels of isolation and segregation (Massey, 1985).

Although spatial assimilation may occur as income rises and the generations succeed one another, these socioeconomic mechanisms occur at a much slower pace than immigration and settlement. During periods of rapid immigration, therefore, segregation levels tend to rise; and the greater and more rapid the immigration, the more pronounced the increase in segregation.

Table 3 presents indicators of Hispanic-White dissimilarity and Hispanic residential isolation for the 30 metropolitan areas containing the largest Hispanic communities in the United States. In a significant subset of these metropolitan areas, Hispanics constitute an absolute majority of the total population, a condition that does not hold for any of the Black communities listed in Table 2. Because large minority populations increase the demographic potential for isolation, and because theorists hypothesize that high minority percentages foment greater discrimination on the part of majority members (Allport, 1958; Blalock, 1967), indices are tabulated separately for areas where Hispanics comprise a majority or near-majority (48 to 49 percent) of the population.

Despite the fact that demographic conditions in these metropolitan areas operate to maximize the potential for segregation, the degree of Hispanic-White residential dissimilarity proved to be quite moderate, and actually decreases over the two decades, going from an average of 55 in 1970 to 47 in 1990. Indices of Hispanic-White segregation were essentially constant in El Paso and Miami, and changed little in San Antonio and Corpus Christi. In Brownsville and McAllen, there were pronounced declines in segregation; but in no case was there an increase in Hispanic segregation from Whites within Hispanic-majority areas.

Indices of isolation, in contrast, were high and rose somewhat from 1970 to 1990. The increases did not stem from an increasing tendency for Whites and Hispanics to live apart, however, but from the large size and rapid growth of the Hispanic population. Isolation indices of 85 and 87 in Brownsville and McAllen mainly reflect the fact that Hispanics represent 82 and 85 percent of the metropolitan populations, respectively. Even if Hispanics were evenly distributed, high levels of Hispanic-White contact are impossible to achieve in areas that are so predominantly Hispanic.

Among Blacks, however, isolation indices in the 80s, as in Chicago and Detroit, generally reflect the intense segregation of Blacks, rather than high Black population percentages; in both these metropolitan areas, Blacks constitute about 22 percent of the population. The contrast in the indices between Hispanics and Blacks is put into perspective by comparing indices for Hispanics in San Antonio with indices for Blacks in northern areas (see Table 1). Although Hispanic constitute 48 percent of San Antonio's population, its Hispanic-White dissimilarity index of 54 is less than that for Black-White indices in any northern area; and San Antonio's Hispanic isolation index of 69 is less than it is for 7 of the 18 black isolation indices.

A better indication of what happens to Hispanics in U.S. cities can be seen by examining segregation measures computed for metropolitan areas where Hispanics do not constitute such a large percentage of the population. On average, indices of Hispanic-White dissimilarity changed little in these areas, moving upward slightly from 45 in 1970 to 50 in 1990. In about one-third of these metropolitan areas—Chicago, Denver, Houston, New York, Phoenix, Riverside, Sacramento, and Tucson—Hispanic segregation remained nearly constant from 1970 to 1990; and in three cases—Albuquerque, Jersey City, and

TABLE 3   Trends in Hispanic Segregation and Isolation in the 30 Metropolitan Areas with the Largest Hispanic Populations, 1970 to 1990

Metropolitan Area	Dissimilarity Indices			Isolation Indices		
	1970[a]	1980[a]	1990[b]	1970[a]	1980[b]	1990[b]
Hispanic majority						
Brownsville-Harlingen, TX	54.0[c]	42.0[d]	39.8	NA	NA	85.2
Corpus Christi, TX	55.9	51.6	47.5	63.5	63.6	67.8
El Paso, TX	49.6	51.2	49.7	71.5	74.1	80.0
McAllen-Pharr, TX	62.0[c]	48.0[d]	37.9	NA	NA	87.4
Miami, FL	50.4	51.9	50.3	46.5	58.3	73.4
San Antonio, TX	59.1	57.2	53.7	67.5	67.5	69.1
Other metropolitan						
Albuquerque, NM	45.7	42.5	41.9	54.4	50.6	53.4
Anaheim-Santa Ana, CA	32.0	41.6	49.9	19.4	31.0	50.1
Bakersfield, CA	5.8	54.5	55.4	34.9	42.1	55.7
Chicago, IL	58.4	63.5	63.2	25.1	38.0	51.3
Dallas-Ft. Worth, TX	42.5	47.8	49.5	18.6	24.0	41.1
Denver-Boulder, CO	47.4	47.4	46.5	27.4	27.5	33.8
Fresno, CA	40.8	45.4	47.8	37.6	44.6	58.7
Houston, TX	45.3	46.4	49.3	26.9	32.8	49.3
Jersey City, NJ	54.8	48.8	42.9	34.5	46.5	56.0
Los Angeles, CA	46.8	57.0	61.0	37.8	50.1	71.5
Nassau-Suffolk, NY	29.1	36.2	42.3	6.0	9.6	22.1
New York, NY	64.9	65.6	65.8	36.1	40.0	66.6
Newark, NJ	60.4	65.6	66.7	16.7	26.3	48.5
Oxnard-Simi Valley, CA	NA	NA	52.3	NA	NA	51.2
Philadelphia, PA	54.0	62.9	62.6	10.6	21.6	42.9
Phoenix, AZ	48.4	49.4	48.1	32.1	32.1	39.8
Riverside-San Bernardino, CA	37.3	36.4	35.8	30.2	31.6	42.7
Sacramento, CA	34.7	36.4	37.0	16.3	16.5	23.9
San Diego, CA	33.1	42.1	45.3	19.8	26.9	43.6
San Francisco-Oakland, CA	34.7	40.2	43.9	19.2	19.3	41.1
San Jose, CA	40.2	44.5	47.8	29.6	31.7	47.1
Tampa, FL	56.0	48.4	45.3	25.0	18.2	21.5
Tucson, AZ	52.6	51.9	49.7	46.7	43.1	48.8
Washington, DC	31.8	30.5	40.9	4.3	5.4	22.5
Average	45.3	48.0	49.6	26.5	30.8	45.1

Note: The Massey-Denton computations did not include several metropolitan areas that housed large Hispanic populations in 1990; therefore, additional indices have been taken from Lopez (1981) and Hwang and Murdock (1982). These figures, however, were computed for central cities rather than metropolitan areas and are therefore somewhat higher thus underestimating increases and overestimating declines in the level of Hispanic-White segregation.

[a]Indices are from Massey and Denton (1987).
[b]Indices from Harrison and Weinberg (1992).
[c]Indices are from Lopez (1981).
[d]Indices are from Hwang and Murdock (1982).

Tampa—indices of Hispanic-White dissimilarity decreased somewhat over the decades. In the remainder of the areas, indices of Hispanic segregation increased. In most cases, the increases were modest; but in several instances, segregation increased substantially over the two decades. In Los Angeles, for example, indices of Hispanic-White segregation increased from 47 to 61; in Anaheim the increase was from 32 to 50. Large increases were also recorded in Nassau-Suffolk, San Diego, San Francisco, and Washington, D.C. In all these metropolitan areas there were rapid rates of Hispanic population growth and immigration from 1970 to 1990.

Despite these increases, indices of Hispanic-White segregation still remained moderate in 1990. Only 5 of the 24 metropolitan areas displayed indices in excess of 60. In 3 of these—New York, Newark, and Philadelphia—Puerto Ricans predominated; and since 1970, this group has stood apart from other Hispanic populations in displaying uniquely high levels of segregation (Jackson, 1981; Massey, 1981), a pattern largely attributable to the fact that many Puerto Ricans are of African ancestry (Massey and Bitterman, 1985; Massey and Denton, 1989a). The two remaining areas are Los Angeles, which experienced more Hispanic immigration than any other metropolitan area in the country, and Chicago, which contained a large population of Puerto Ricans in addition to a rapidly growing Mexican immigrant community.

Reflecting the increase in the proportion of Hispanics in most metropolitan areas, Hispanic isolation indices rose markedly throughout the nation. In those few areas where rates of Hispanic population increase were relatively slow—Albuquerque, Denver, Phoenix, and Tucson—the level of Hispanic isolation hardly changed; but as the rate of Hispanic immigration increased, so did the extent of spatial isolation. Given its popularity as a destination for Hispanic immigration,

Hispanic isolation rose most strongly in Southern California cities, going from 19 to 50 in Anaheim, 38 to 72 in Los Angeles, and 20 to 40 in San Diego.

By the 1990, isolation indices equaled or exceeded 50 in about half of the metropolitan areas under consideration, but in only two cases—New York and Los Angeles, the two metropolitan areas with the largest Hispanic communities—did the index exceed 60. By way of contrast, only eight of the 30 Black communities examined earlier had Black isolation indices less than 60. Although contemporary demographic conditions suggest trends toward high segregation and rising isolation among Hispanics, they still do not display the high index ratings characteristic for Blacks in large urban areas.

Recent Trends in Asian Segregation

Although Asian immigration into U.S. urban areas accelerated rapidly after 1970, Asian populations are still quite small compared with either Black or Hispanic populations. Moreover, Asians are more highly concentrated regionally and found in a relatively small number of metropolitan areas. Table 4, therefore, presents indices of Asian segregation and isolation only for the 20 largest Asian communities, rather than the 30 largest.

Again demographic conditions for Asians favor substantial increases in segregation and isolation. In most metropolitan areas, immigration led to the rapid expansion of a rather small 1970 population base. In some areas, the number of post-1970 migrants actually exceeds the size of the original Asian community severalfold. Only 25,000 Asians lived in the Anaheim-Santa Ana metropolitan area in 1970, for example, but by 1990, their number had multiplied ten times, to 249,000. Over the same period, the Asian community of Los Angeles quadrupled, going from

TABLE 4   Trends in Asian Segregation and Isolation in the 20 Metropolitan Areas with the Largest Asian Populations, 1970 to 1990

Metropolitan Area	Dissimilarity Indices			Isolation Indices		
	1970[a]	1980[a]	1990[b]	1970[a]	1980[a]	1990[b]
Anaheim, CA	27.4	24.9	33.3	2.6	7.7	22.4
Boston, MA	49.9	47.4	44.8	8.0	10.5	12.9
Chicago, IL	55.8	43.9	43.2	7.6	8.7	15.9
Dallas, TX	43.9	29.1	40.5	1.7	2.6	9.6
Fresno, CA	35.1	22.9	43.4	5.7	5.3	33.1
Houston, TX	42.7	34.6	45.7	1.5	4.5	15.7
Los Angeles, CA	53.1	43.1	46.3	12.3	15.2	40.5
Minneapolis, MN	45.2	36.9	41.2	3.0	6.2	15.1
Nassau-Suffolk, NY	42.2	34.5	32.4	1.0	2.2	5.9
New York, NY	56.1	48.1	48.4	11.6	14.3	32.8
Newark, NJ	50.2	34.4	29.6	1.5	2.9	7.5
Paterson Clifton-Passaic, NJ	46.6	40.4	34.4	1.3	3.1	12.1
Philadelphia, PA	49.1	43.7	43.2	2.4	4.0	11.0
Riverside-San Bernardino, CA	31.9	21.5	32.8	2.5	4.1	10.2
Sacramento, CA	47.6	35.5	47.7	11.8	11.6	23.6
San Diego, CA	41.3	40.5	48.1	5.9	11.1	29.1
San Francisco-Oakland, CA	48.6	44.4	50.1	21.0	23.2	46.0
San Jose, CA	25.4	29.5	38.5	5.3	11.6	36.6
Seattle, WA	46.6	33.3	36.5	11.7	12.4	20.0
Washington, DC	36.5	26.8	32.3	2.2	5.7	12.6
Average	43.8	35.8	40.6	6.0	8.3	20.6

[a]Indices are from Massey and Denton (1987).
[b]Indices are from Harrison and Weinberg (1992).

243,000 to 943,000; and Chicago's Asian population grew from 62,000 to 230,000. In such cases where a sudden massive in-migration overwhelms a small, established community, indices of segregation often decrease initially as new arrivals distribute themselves widely, and then increase as these pioneers attract subsequent settlers to the same residential areas.

Such a patter of decreasing and then increasing Asian segregation is the most common pattern of change among the metropolitan areas shown in Table 4. The Asian-White dissimilarity index averaged 44 in 1970, decreased to 36 in 1980, and then increased to 41 in 1990. This basic trend occurred in 12 of the 20 metropolitan areas. In three more areas, an initial decline was followed by no change from 1980 to 1990.

Only one area—San Jose—experienced a sustained increase in Asian segregation; but it began from a very low level of segregation in 1970. Four areas displayed uninterrupted declines in segregation across both decades—Boston, Nassau-Suffolk, Newark, and Paterson.

Despite rapid immigration and population growth, Asian segregation indices remained quite moderate in 1990. Increases observed between 1980 and 1990 simply restored the indices to their 1970 levels, yielding little net change over the two decades. Thus, Asian-White dissimilarity indices ranged from the low 30s in Anaheim, Nassau-Suffolk, Newark, Riverside, and Washington to 50 in San Francisco-Oakland. In no metropolitan area did the index of Asian segregation approach the high levels characteristic of Blacks in the nation's largest metropolitan areas.

Rapid Asian immigration into moderately segregated communities did produce rather sharp increases in the extent of Asian isolation, however, consistent with a process of enclave consolidation. The most pronounced increases occurred in areas where southeast-Asian refugees settled in large numbers—Anaheim, where the isolation index rose from 3 in 1970 to 22 in 1990; Fresno, where the increase was from 6 to 33; and San Diego, where the increase was from 6 to 29. Despite these increases, however, Asians still are not very isolated anywhere, including San Francisco-Oakland, where they constitute a higher percentage of the population (21 percent) than in any other metropolitan area. The isolation index of 46 means that Asians in the Bay Area are more likely to share a neighborhood with non-Asians than with each other; and in Los Angeles, which received the highest number of Asian immigrants between 1970 and 1990, the isolation index rose to just under 41. Thus, the largest and most segregated Asian communities in the United States are much less isolated than the most integrated Black communities.

Black Hypersegregation

Despite their apparent clarity, the above data actually understate the extent of Black isolation in U.S. society, because the data only incorporate two dimensions of segregation: evenness, as measured by the dissimilarity index, and isolation, as measured by the P* index. Massey and Denton (1988, 1989b), however, conceptualize segregation as a multidimensional construct. They contend there are five dimensions of spatial variation; in addition to evenness and isolation, residential segregation should be conceptualized in terms of clustering, concentration, and centralization. This five-dimensional conceptualization of segregation recently has been updated and revalidated with 1990 data (Massey et al., 1996).

Clustering is the extent to which minority areas adjoin one another spatially. It is maximized when Black neighborhoods form one large, contiguous ghetto; and it is minimized when they are scattered, as in a checkerboard pattern. *Centralization* is the degree to which Blacks are distributed in and around the center of an urban area, usually defined as the central-business district. *Concentration* is the relative amount of physical space occupied by Blacks; as segregation increases, Blacks are increasingly confined to smaller, geographically compacted areas.

A high level of segregation on any single dimension is problematic because it isolates a minority group from amenities, opportunities, and resources that affect socioeconomic well-being. As high levels of segregation accumulate across dimensions, however, the deleterious effects of segregation multiply. Indices of evenness and isolation (i.e., dissimilarity and P*), by themselves, cannot capture this multidimensional layering of segregation; therefore, there is a misrepresentation of the nature of Black segregation and an understatement of its severity. Blacks are not only more segregated than other groups on any single dimension of segregation; they are more segregated across all dimensions simultaneously.

Massey and Denton (1993) identified a set of 16 metropolitan areas that were highly segregated—i.e., had an index higher than 60—on at least four of the five dimensions of segregation, a pattern they called "hypersegregation." These metropolitan areas included Atlanta, Baltimore, Buffalo, Chicago, Cleveland, Dallas, Detroit, Gary, Indianapolis, Kansas City, Los Angeles, Milwaukee, New York, Newark, and St. Louis. Within this set of areas, the Black-White dissimilarity index averaged 82, the average isolation index was 71, the mean clustering index was 58, the mean centralization index was 88, and the average concentration index was 83. By way of contrast, neither Hispanics nor Asians were hyper-segregated within *any* metropolitan area.

These 16 metropolitan areas are among the most important in the country, incorporating 6 of the 10 largest urban areas in the United States. Blacks in these areas live within large, contiguous settlements of densely inhabited neighborhoods packed tightly around the urban core. Inhabitants typically would be unlikely to come into contact with non-Blacks in the neighborhood where they live. If they were to travel to an adjacent neighborhood, they would still be unlikely to see a White face. If they went to the next neighborhood beyond that, no Whites would be there either. People growing up in such an environment would have little direct experience with the culture, norms, and behaviors of the rest of American society, and have few social contacts with members of other racial groups.

Denton (1994) reexamined the issue of hypersegregation using data from the 1990 Census. According to her analysis, not only has Black hypersegregation continued, in many ways it has grown worse. Of the 16 metropolitan areas defined as hypersegregated in 1980, 14 remained so in 1990. In Atlanta the index of spatial concentration decreased to 59, just missing the criteria for hypersegregation, and in Dallas the isolation index decreased to 58. But both these figures are *just* below the threshold index of 60. All other metropolitan areas that were hypersegrated in 1980 showed an increase on at least one dimension by 1990. In 10 areas, isolation increased; concentration grew more acute in 9 areas; and clustering increased in 8. In Newark and Buffalo, segregation increased in all five dimensions simultaneously; and in Detroit, segregation increased on all dimensions but one.

In short, areas that were hypersegregated in 1980 generally remained so in 1990, and there was little evidence of movement away from this extreme pattern. On the contrary,

hypersegregation appears to have spread to several new urban areas during the 1980s. Of the 44 nonhypersegregated metropolitan areas studied by Massey and Denton in 1980, Denton (1994) found that 6 had come to satisfy the criteria by 1990—Birmingham, Cincinnati, Miami, New Orleans, Oakland, and Washington, D.C.—bringing the total number of hypersegregated metropolitan areas to 20. Taken together, these 20 contain roughly 11 million Blacks and constitute 36 percent of the entire U.S. Black population. As already pointed out, the percentage of Hispanics and Asians who are hypersegregated is zero.

Explaining the Persistence of Racial Segregation

A variety of explanations have been posited to account for the unusual depth and persistence of Black segregation in American cities. One hypothesis is that racial segregation reflects class differences between Blacks and Whites—i.e., because Blacks, on average, have lower incomes and fewer socioeconomic resources than Whites, they cannot afford to move into White neighborhoods in significant numbers. According to this hypothesis, Back-White segregation, to some extent, reflects segregation on the basis of income, with poor households, which happen to be predominantly Black, living in different neighborhoods than affluent households, which happen to be disproportionately White.

This explanation has not been sustained empirically, however. When indices of racial segregation are computed within categories of income, occupation, or education, researchers have found that levels of Black-White segregation do not vary by social class (Farley, 1977; Simkus, 1978; Massey, 1979, 1981; Massey and Fischer, 1999). According to Denton and Massey (1988), Black families annually earning at least $50,000 were just as segregated as those earning less than $2,500. Indeed, Black families annually earning more than $50,000 were more segregated than Hispanic or Asian families earning less than $2,500. In other words, the most affluent Blacks appear to be more segregated than the poorest Hispanics or Asians; and in contrast to the case of Blacks, Hispanic and Asian segregation levels fall steadily as income rises, reaching low or moderate levels at incomes of $50,000 or more (Denton and Massey, 1988).

Another explanation for racial segregation is that Blacks prefer to live in predominantly Black neighborhoods, and that segregated housing simply reflects these preferences. This line of reasoning does not square well with survey evidence on Black attitudes, however. Most Blacks continue to express strong support for the ideal of integration. When asked on opinion polls whether they favor "desegregation, strict segregation, or something in-between," Blacks answer "desegregation" in large numbers (Schuman et al., 1985). Blacks are virtually unanimous in agreeing that "Black people have a right to live wherever they can afford to," and 71 percent would vote for a community-wide law to enforce this right (Bobo et al., 1986).

Black respondents are not only committed to integration as an ideal, survey results suggest they also strongly prefer it in practice. When asked about specific neighborhood racial compositions, Blacks consistently select racially mixed areas as most desirable (Farley et al., 1978, 1979, 1994; Clark, 1991). Although the most popular choice is a neighborhood that is half-Black and half-White, as late as 1992, nearly 90 percent of Blacks in Detroit would be willing to live in virtually any racially mixed area (Farley et al., 1994).

Although Blacks express a reluctance about moving into all-White neighborhoods, this apprehension does not indicate a rejection of White neighbors per se, but stems from well-founded fears of hostility and rejection.

Among Black respondents to a 1976 Detroit survey who expressed a reluctance to moving into all-White areas, 34 percent thought that White neighbors would be unfriendly and make them feel unwelcome, 37 percent felt they could be made to feel uncomfortable, and 17 percent expressed a fear of outright violence (Farley et al., 1979). Moreover, 80 percent of all Black respondents rejected the view that moving into a White neighborhood constituted a desertion of the Black community. More recently, Jackson (1994) linked the reluctance of Blacks to "pioneer" White areas not only to fears of rejection by White neighbors, but also to an *expectation* of discrimination by real estate agents and lenders.

Thus evidence suggests that racial segregation in urban America is not a voluntary reflection of Black preferences. If it were up to them, Blacks would live in racially mixed neighborhoods. But it is not up to them only, of course; their preferences interact with those of Whites and, thus, produce the residential configurations actually observed. Even though Blacks may prefer neighborhoods with an even racial balance, integration will not occur if most Whites find this level of racial mixing unacceptable.

On the surface, Whites seem to share Blacks' ideological commitment to open housing. The percentage of Whites on national surveys who agree that "Black people have a right to live wherever they can afford to" approached 90 percent in the late 1970s; and the percentage who disagreed with the view that "White people have a right to keep Blacks out of their[Whites'] neighborhoods," reached 67 percent in 1980. At present, few Whites openly call for the strict segregation of American society (Schuman et al., 1985, 1998; Sniderman and Piazza, 1993; Hochschild, 1995).

However, Whites remain quite uncomfortable with the implications of open housing in practice; only 40 percent, in 1980, said they would be willing to vote for a community-wide law stating that "a homeowner cannot refuse to sell to someone because of their race or skin color" (Schuman and Bobo, 1988). In other words, 60 percent of Whites would vote *against* an open housing law, which, in fact, has been federal law for 25 years.

White support for open housing generally declines as the hypothetical number of Blacks in their neighborhood increases. Whereas 86 percent of Whites in 1978 said they would not move if "a Black person came to live next door," only 46 percent stated they would not move if "Black people came to live in large numbers," and only 28 percent of Whites would be willing to live in a neighborhood that was half Black and half-White (Schuman et al., 1985). Likewise, the severity of White prejudice toward Blacks increases as the percentage of Blacks in the area increases, a relationship that is *not* observed for Hispanics or Asians (Taylor, 1998).

When questions are posed about specific neighborhood compositions, moreover, it becomes clear that White tolerance for racial mixing is quite limited. According to Farley et al. (1994), 16 percent of Whites responding to a 1992 Detroit survey said they would feel uncomfortable in a neighborhood where only 7 percent of the residents were Black; 13 percent would be unwilling to enter such an area. When the Black percentage reaches 20 percent, one-third of all Whites say they would be unwilling to enter, 30 percent would feel uncomfortable, and 15 percent would seek to leave. A neighborhood about 30 percent Black exceeds the limits of racial tolerance for most Whites; 59 percent would be unwilling to move in, 44 percent would feel uncomfortable, and 29 percent would try to leave. Beyond a 50:50 balance, a neighborhood becomes unacceptable to all except a small minority of Whites; 73 percent said they would not wish to move into such a neighborhood, 53 percent would try to leave, and 65 percent would feel uncomfortable. As was

stated, most Blacks feel a 50:50 racial mixture is desirable. This fundamental disparity between the two races has been confirmed by surveys conducted in Milwaukee, Omaha, Cincinnati, Kansas City, and Los Angeles (Clark, 1991).

The discrepancy between Whites' acceptance of open housing in principal and their reluctance to live among Blacks in practice yields a rather specific hypothesis about the nature of trends in Black-White segregation over the past 20 years. Hypothetically, declines in Black-White segregation should be confined primarily to metropolitan areas with relatively small Black populations, because in these places, desegregation can occur without Whites having to share their neighborhoods with too many Black people (Massey and Gross, 1991). If Black people make up 3 percent of the metropolitan population, for example, then complete desegregation yields an average of 3 percent Black within every neighborhood, which is well within most Whites' tolerance limits. If, however, Black people make up 20 percent of the metropolitan population, desegregation would produce neighborhoods that are 20 percent Black, on average, which exceeds the tolerance limits of many Whites, creates instability, and fuels a process of neighborhood turnover. In keeping with this hypothesis, Krivo and Kaufman (1999) show that desegregation between 1980 and 1990 was quite likely where the Black population was small but very unlikely where it was large. As a result, observed declines in segregation during the 1980s were confined largely to metropolitan areas that contained very few Blacks.

Over the last three decades, U.S. metropolitan areas have been transformed by immigration and many have moved well beyond the simple Black-White dichotomy of earlier years, necessitating new approaches to the measurement of racial attitudes. A recent survey in Los Angeles sought to replicate the Detroit survey within an ethnically diverse metropolis. Analysis of these data by Zubrinsky and Bobo (1996) showed that all non-Black groups—Whites, Asians, and Hispanics—attribute a variety of negative traits to Blacks and consider Blacks to be the least desirable neighbors (see, also, Bobo and Zubrinsky, 1996). Blacks experience by far the greatest likelihood of hostility from other groups, and are universally acknowledged to face the most severe housing discrimination. The end result is a clear hierarchy of neighborhood racial preferences in Los Angeles, with Whites at the top, followed by Asians and Hispanics, and Blacks at the bottom. Segregation does not result from Black ethnocentrism so much as from avoidance behavior by other groups, all of whom seek to circumvent potential coresidence with Blacks.

These contrasting racial attitudes create large intergroup disparities in the demand for housing in racially mixed neighborhoods. Given the violence, intimidation, and harrassment that historically have followed their entry into White areas, Blacks express reluctance at being first across the color line. After one or two Black families have moved into a neighborhood, however, Black demand grows rapidly, given the high value placed on integrated housing. This demand escalates as the Black percentage rises toward 50 percent, the most preferred neighborhood configuration; beyond this point, Black demand stabilizes and then falls off as the Black percentage rises toward 100 percent.

The pattern of white, Asian, and Hispanic demand for housing in racially mixed areas follows precisely the opposite trajectory. Demand is strong for homes in all-White areas, but once one or two Black families enter a neighborhood, demand begins to falter as some non-Black families leave and others refuse to move in. The acceleration in residential turnover coincides with the expansion of Black demand, making it likely that outgoing White, Hispanic, or Asian households

are replaced by Black families. As the Black percentage rises, overall demand drops ever more steeply, and Black demand rises at an increasing rate. By the time Black demand peaks at the 50 percent mark, practically no other groups are willing to enter and most are trying to leave. Thus, racial segregation appears to be created by a process of racial turnover fueled by the persistence of significant anti-Black prejudice on the part of virtually every other group.

This model of racial change was proposed two decades ago by Schelling (1971), who argued that integration is an unstable outcome because Whites prefer lower minority proportions than Blacks—even though Whites might accept some Black neighbors. Yet by itself, Schelling's explanation is incomplete. Whites can only avoid coresidence with Blacks if mechanisms exist to keep Blacks out of neighborhoods to which they might otherwise be attracted. Whites can only flee a neighborhood where Blacks have entered if there are other all- White neighborhoods to go to, and this escape will only be successful if Blacks are unlikely or unable to follow.

Racial discrimination was institutionalized in the real estate industry during the 1920s and well established in private practice by the 1940s (Massey and Denton, 1993). Evidence shows that discriminatory behavior was widespread among realtors at least until 1968, when the Fair Housing Act was passed (Helper, 1969; Saltman, 1979). After that, outright refusals to rent or sell to Blacks became rare, given that overt discrimination could lead to prosecution under the law.

Black home seekers now face a more subtle process of exclusion. Rather than encountering "White only" signs, they encounter a covert series of barriers. Blacks who inquire about an advertised unit may be told that it has just been sold or rented; they may be shown only the advertised unit and told that no others are available; they may only be shown houses in Black or racially mixed areas and led away from White neighborhoods; they may be quoted a higher rent or selling price than Whites; they may be told that the selling agents are too busy and to come back later; their phone number may be taken but a return call never made; they may be shown units but offered no assistance in arranging financing; or they simply may be treated brusquely and discourteously in hopes that they will leave.

Although individual acts of discrimination are small and subtle, they have a powerful cumulative effect in lowering the probability of Black entry into White neighborhoods. Because the discrimination is latent, however, it is not easily observable, and the only way to confirm whether or not it has occurred is to compare the treatment of both Black and White clients that have similar social and economic characteristics. If White clients receive systematically more favorable treatment, then one can safely conclude that discrimination has taken place (Fix et al., 1993).

Differences in the treatment of White and Black home seekers are measured by means of a housing audit. Teams of White and Black auditors are paired and sent to randomly selected realtors to pose as clients seeking a home or apartment. The auditors are trained to present comparable housing needs and family characteristics, and to express similar tastes; they are assigned equivalent social and economic traits by the investigator. After each encounter, the auditors fill out a detailed report of their experiences and the results are tabulated and compared to determine the nature and level of discrimination (Yinger, 1986, 1989).

Local fair-housing organizations began to conduct such studies at the end of the 1960s. These efforts revealed that discrimination was continuing despite the Fair Housing Act. A 1969 audit of realtors in St. Louis, for example, documented a pattern and practice of

discrimination sufficient to force four realty firms to sign a consent decree with the U.S. Department of Justice wherein they agreed to desist from certain biased practices (Saltman, 1979). Likewise, a 1971 audit study carried out in Palo Alto, California, found that Blacks were treated in a discriminatory fashion by 50 percent of the area's apartment complexes; and a 1972 audit of apartments in suburban Baltimore uncovered discrimination in more than 45 percent of the cases (Saltman, 1979).

Racial discrimination clearly persisted through the 1980s. In one 1983 Chicago study, suburban realtors showed homes to 67 percent of White auditors but only 47 percent of Black auditors (Hintzen, 1983). Another Chicago study done in 1985 revealed that Whites were offered financial information at nearly twice the rate it was offered to Blacks (Schroeder, 1985). One developer working in Chicago's south suburbs refused to deal with Blacks at all; Blacks were always told that no properties were available, even though 80 percent of Whites were shown real estate (Bertram, 1988). In the same study, realtors told 92 percent of Whites that apartments were available but gave this information to only 46 percent of Blacks.

Audit studies of other metropolitan areas reveal similar levels of racial discrimination. According to Yinger's (1986) review of studies conducted in metropolitan Boston and Denver during the early 1980s, Black home seekers had between a 38 and a 59 percent chance of receiving unfavorable treatment, compared to Whites, on any given real estate transaction. Through various lies and deceptions, Blacks were informed of only 65 of every 100 units presented to Whites, and they inspected fewer than 54 of every 100 shown to Whites.

• • •

Realtors were approached by auditors who inquired about the availability of the advertised unit; they also asked about other units that might be on the market. Based on the results, HDS provided evidence that discrimination against Blacks had declined little since 1977. Indeed, it appears the 1977 HUD study may have understated both the incidence and severity of housing discrimination in American cities (Yinger, 1995). According to HDS data, housing was made more available to Whites in 45 percent of the transactions in the rental market and in 34 percent of those in the sales market. Whites received more favorable credit assistance in 46 percent of sales encounters, and were offered more favorable terms in 17 percent of rental transactions. When housing availability and financial assistance were considered together, the likelihood of experiencing racial discrimination was 53 percent in both the rental and sales markets.

• • •

Compared with Blacks, relatively few studies of prejudice and discrimination against Hispanics have been conducted, and there are no national studies that examine attitudes and behaviors concerning Asians. Hakken (1979) found that discrimination against Hispanics in the rental housing market of Dallas was as likely as that against Blacks, and similar results were reported by Feins and colleagues for Boston (Feins et al., 1981). James and Tynan (1986) replicated these results in a study of Denver's sales market, but they found a substantially lower probability of discrimination against Hispanics in the rental market; and despite the relatively high likelihood of discrimination in home sales, in reality, severity of discrimination against Hispanics was not great; the average number of housing units offered to Hispanics was not significantly different than the number offered to non-Hispanic whites (James and Tynan, 1986).

As with Blacks, however, discrimination against Hispanics appears to have a racial basis. Hakken (1979) found that dark-skinned Chicanos were more likely to experience discriminatory treatment than Blacks, whereas light-skinned Hispanics were less likely to experience such treatment. Consistent with this finding, Massey and Denton (1992) found that Mexicans who identified themselves as mestizos (people of mixed European and Indian origin) were less likely to achieve suburban residence than those who identified themselves as White.

The extent of the racial effect is greater among Caribbean Hispanics, particularly Puerto Ricans, among whom the racial continuum runs from European to African. Denton and Massey (1989) showed that for Puerto Ricans who identified themselves as Black, housing was as segregated as for U.S. Blacks, whereas those who identified themselves as White experienced low-to-moderate levels of separation. Discrimination was mixed for Caribbean Hispanics who said they were of mixed Black-White origins, but were much closer to the high level of Black segregation. The degree of segregation experienced by racially mixed Caribbean Hispanics was generally greater than that experienced by racially mixed Mexicans, suggesting greater White antipathy toward Africans than Amerindians.

The most complete and systematic data on the treatment of Hispanics in urban real estate markets comes from HUD's 1988 HDS (Yinger, 1995). Results from this study indicate that the overall incidence of housing discrimination was greater for Hispanics than Blacks in the sale market (42 versus 34 percent), but less for Hispanics than Blacks in the rental market (32 versus 45 percent), replicating the earlier results of James and Tynan (1986) in Denver. Also in keeping with the findings of James and Tynan was the fact that the severity of discrimination in the sales market was considerably lower for Hispanics than for Blacks; whereas the marginal probability that an additional housing unit was denied to Blacks was 88 percent, it was only 66 percent for Hispanics. As in earlier research, in the 1988 HDS, race figured prominently in the treatment of Hispanics—dark-skinned Hispanics were much more likely to experience discrimination in the sales market than light-skinned Hispanics (Yinger, 1995). Paradoxically, therefore, recent research on discrimination involving Hispanics reaffirms the conclusion that race remains the dominant organizing principle in U.S. urban housing markets.

Segregation and the Concentration of Poverty

The past two decades have been hard on the socioeconomic well-being of many Americans. The structural transformation of the U.S. economy from goods production to service provision generated a strong demand for workers with high and low levels of schooling, but offered few opportunities for those with modest education and training. In the post-industrial economy that emerged after 1973, labor unions withered, the middle class bifurcated, income inequality grew, and poverty spread; and this new stratification between people was accompanied by a growing spatial separation between them. The stagnation of income proved to be remarkably widespread, and inequality rose not only for minorities—Blacks, Hispanics, and Asians—but also for non-Hispanic Whites (Danziger and Gottschalk, 1995; Levy, 1995; Morris et al., 1994). As a result of their continued racial segregation, however, the spatial concentration of poverty was especially severe for Blacks (Massey and Eggers, 1990; Massey et al., 1991; Krivo et al., 1998). High levels of income inequality paired with high levels of racial or ethnic segregation result in geographically concentrated poverty, because the poverty is localized in a small

number of densely settled, racially homogenous, tightly clustered areas, often in an older, urban core abandoned by industry. Had segregation not been in place, the heightened poverty would be distributed widely throughout the metropolitan area (Massey, 1990; Massey and Denton, 1993). By 1990, 83 percent of poor inner-city Blacks lived in neighborhoods that were at least 20 percent poor (Kasarda, 1993).

In a recent paper, Massey and Fischer (2000) broadened this theoretical perspective by arguing that racial segregation interacts with any structural shift that affects the distribution of income, or the spatial configuration of the classes, to concentrate poverty spatially. Specifically, they hypothesize that as racial segregation increases, decreasing incomes, increasing inequality, increasing class segregation, and increasing immigration are more strongly translated into geographic isolation of the poor. Thus, these structural trends produce high and increasing concentrations of poverty for highly segregated groups, but low and falling concentrations of poverty among nonsegregated groups.

Because more than 70 percent of urban Blacks are highly segregated, but 90 percent of all other groups are not, the population of poor experiencing high concentrations of poverty is overwhelmingly Black (Massey and Fischer, 2000). Given the interaction between racial segregation and the changing socioeconomic structure of American society, the issue of race cannot be set aside to focus on the politics of race versus class. Although the implementation of policies that raise average incomes, lower income inequality, and reduce class segregation would lower the spatial isolation of the urban poor, policies to promote the desegregation of urban society would probably have an even greater effect, given segregation's critical role in determining how these factors generate concentrated poverty.

The Consequences of Concentrated Poverty

The argument that the prevalence of concentrated poverty among Blacks decisively undermines the life chances of the Black poor was first made forcefully by Wilson (1987). He argued that class isolation, through a variety of mechanisms, reduced employment, lowered incomes, depressed marriage, and increased unwed childbearing *over and above any effects of individual or family deprivation.* At the time Wilson made this argument, relatively little evidence existed to support it (Jencks and Mayer, 1990), but over the past decade a growing number of studies have accumulated to sustain the basic thrust of Wilson's hypothesis.

In 1988, the Rockefeller and Russell Sage Foundations funded the Social Science Research Council (SSRC) to establish a program of research into the causes and consequences of persistent urban poverty. One SSRC subcommittee—the Working Group on Communities and Neighborhoods, Family Processes, and Individual Development—met regularly over the next eight years to conceptualize and then implement a program of research to determine how concentrated poverty affected social and cognitive development. The ultimate product was a recently published series of studies (Brooks-Gunn et al., 1997) examining the effect of neighborhood conditions on cognitive and social development at three points in the life cycle—early childhood (ages 3–7), late childhood/early adolescence (ages 11–15), and late adolescence (ages 16–19).

The empirical analyses clearly show that socioeconomic inequality is perpetuated by mechanisms operating at the neighborhood level, although the specific pathways are perhaps more complex than Wilson or others imagined. Not only do neighborhood effects vary in their nature and intensity at different stages of the life cycle, they are often conditioned by gender, mediated by family processes, and possibly interactive in how they combine with individual factors to determine social outcomes. Despite these complexities, however, research permits three broad generalizations.

- First, neighborhoods seem to influence individual development most powerfully in early childhood and late adolescence.
- Second, the spatial concentration of affluence appears to be more important in determining cognitive development and academic achievement than the concentration of poverty.
- Third, the concentration of male joblessness affects social behavior more than cognitive development, particularly among Blacks.

These effects persist even after controlling for unobserved heterogeneity. Thus, Wilson's (1987) theory is basically correct—there is something to the hypothesis of neighborhood effects.

One of the most important disadvantages transmitted through prolonged exposure to the ghetto is educational failure. Datcher (1982) estimates that moving a poor Black male from his typical neighborhood (66 percent Black with an average annual income of $8,500) to a typical White neighborhood (86 percent White with a mean income of $11,500) would raise his educational attainment by nearly a year. Corcoran and colleagues (1989) found similar results. Crane (1991) likewise shows that the dropout probability for Black teenage males increases dramatically as the percentage of low-status workers in the neighborhood increases. Residence in a poor neighborhood also decreases the odds of success in the labor market. Datcher (1982) found that growing up in a poor Black area lowered male earnings by at least 27 percent, although Corcoran and colleagues (1989) put the percentage at about 18 percent.

Exposure to conditions typical of the ghetto also dramatically increases the odds of pregnancy and childbirth among teenage girls. According to estimates by Crane (1991), the probability of a teenage birth increases dramatically as the percentage of low-status workers in the neighborhood increases. Similarly, Hogan and Kitagawa (1985) found that living in a very poor neighborhood raised the monthly pregnancy rate among Black adolescents by 20 percent and lowered the age at which they became sexually active. Furstenburg et al. (1987) have shown that attending school in integrated, rather than segregated, classrooms substantially lowers the odds that 15- to 16-year-old Black girls will experience sexual intercourse. Brooks-Gunn et al. (1993) found that the probability of giving birth before age 29 rose markedly as the percentage of high-income families fell.

In a dynamic longitudinal analysis that followed young Black men and women from ages 15 to 30, Massey and Shibuya (1995) found that young men who live in neighborhoods of concentrated male joblessness are more likely to be jobless themselves, controlling for individual and family characteristics, and that Black women in such neighborhoods were significantly less likely to get married.

Massey and Shibuya (1995) also linked concentrated disadvantage to higher probabilities of criminality, a link well-documented by Krivo and Peterson (1996) using aggregate data. The concentration of criminal activity that accompanies the concentration of deprivation accelerates the process of neighborhood transition and, for Blacks, resegregation (Morenoff and Sampson, 1997); it also helps drive up rates of Black-on-Black mortality, which have reached heights unparalled for any other group (Almgren et al., 1998; Guest et al., 1998). The spatial concentration of crime presents special problems for the Black middle class, who must adopt extreme strategies to insulate their children from the temptations and risks of the street (Anderson, 1990; Patillo, 1998).

The quantitative evidence thus suggests that any process that concentrates poverty within racially isolated neighborhoods will simultaneously increase the odds of socioeconomic failure within the segregated group. People who grow up and live in environments of concentrated poverty and social isolation are more likely to become teenage parents, drop out of school, achieve low educations, earn lower adult incomes, and become involved with crime—either as perpetrator or victim.

One study has directly linked the socioeconomic disadvantages suffered by individual minority members to the degree of segregation they experience in society. Using individual, community, and metropolitan data from the 50 largest U.S. metropolitan areas in 1980, Massey et al. (1991) showed that group segregation and poverty rates interacted to concentrate poverty geographically within neighborhoods, and that exposure to neighborhood poverty subsequently increased the probability of male joblessness and single motherhood among group members. In this fashion, they linked the structural condition of segregation to individual behaviors widely associated with the underclass through the intervening factor of neighborhood poverty, holding individual and family characteristics constant. As the structural factor controlling poverty concentration, segregation is directly responsible for the perpetuation of socioeconomic disadvantage among Blacks.

The Road Ahead

This review yields several well-supported conclusions about residential segregation in the United States at the end of the twentieth century.

- First, the extreme segregation of Blacks continues unabated in the nation's largest metropolitan areas, and is far more severe than anything experienced by Hispanics or Asians.

• Second, this unique segregation can in no way be attributed to class.

• Third, although Whites now accept open housing in principle, they have yet to come to terms with its implications in practice. Whites still harbor strong anti-Black sentiments and are unwilling to live with more than a small percentage of Blacks in the neighborhood. As a result, declines in Black-White segregation have been confined almost entirely to metropolitan areas where few Blacks live.

• Fourth, color prejudice apparently extends to dark-skinned Hispanics, and discrimination against both Blacks and Afro-Hispanics is remarkably widespread in U.S. housing markets. Through a variety of deceptions and exclusionary actions, Black access to housing in White neighborhoods is systematically reduced.

• Fifth, White biases and discrimination apparently do not extend to Asians or light-skinned Hispanics, at least to the same degree. In no metropolitan area are Asians or Hispanics hypersegregated; and despite the recent arrival of large numbers of immigrants and rapid rates of population growth, they display levels of segregation and isolation that are far below those of Blacks.

• Sixth, as a result of segregation, poor Blacks are forced to live in conditions of intensely concentrated poverty. Recent shifts in U.S. socio-economic structure and patterns of class segregation have interacted with Black segregation to produce unusual concentrations of poverty among Blacks. Poor Blacks are far more likely to grow up and live in neighborhoods surrounded by other poor people than poor Whites, Hispanics, or Asians.

• Finally, as a result of their prolonged exposure to high rates of neighborhood poverty, Blacks experience much higher risks of educational failure, joblessness, unwed childbearing, crime, and premature death compared with other groups.

Given the central role that residence plays in determining one's life chances, these results suggest the need to incorporate the effects of racial segregation more fully into theories about the perpetuation of poverty and the origins of the urban underclass. These results also suggest the need to incorporate desegregation efforts more directly into public policies developed to ameliorate urban poverty. All too often, U.S. policy debates have devolved into arguments about the relative importance of race versus class. The issue, however, is not whether race *or* class perpetuates the urban underclass, but how race *and* class *interact* to undermine the social and economic well-being of Black Americans.

• • •

REFERENCES

Allport, G. 1958. *The Nature of Prejudice.* Garden City, N.Y.: Doubleday Anchor.

Almgren, G., A. Guest, G. Imerwahr, and M. Spittel. 1998. Joblessness, family disruption, and violent death in Chicago: 1970–1990. *Social Forces* 76: 1465–1494.

Anderson, E. 1990. *Streetwise: Race, Class, and Change in an Urban Community.* Chicago: University of Chicago Press.

Bertram, S. 1988. *An Audit of the Real Estate Sales and Rental Markets of Selected Southern Suburbs.* Homewood, Ill.: South Suburban Housing Center.

Blalock, H.M., Jr. 1967. *Toward a Theory of Minority-Group Relations.* New York: Wiley.

Bobo, L., H. Schuman, and C. Steeh. 1986. Changing racial attitudes toward residential integration. Pp. 152–169 in *Housing Desegregation and Federal Policy,* ed. Chapel Hill; University of North Carolina Press.

Bobo, L., and C. Zubrinsky. 1996. Attitudes on residential integration: Perceived status differences, mere in-group preference, or racial prejudice? *Social Forces* 74:883–909.

Brooks-Gunn, J., G. Duncan, and J. Aber, eds. 1997. *Neighborhood Poverty: Context and Consequences for Children.* New York: Russell Sage.

Brooks-Gunn, J., G. Duncan, P. Klebanov, and N. Sealand. 1993. Do neighborhoods influence child and adolescent development? *American Journal of Sociology* 99:353–395.

Clark, W. 1991. Residential preferences and neighborhood racial segregation:A test of the Schelling segregation model. *Demography* 28:1–19.

Corcoran, M., R. Gordon, D. Laren, and G. Solon. 1989. Effects of family and community background on men's economic status. Working Paper 2896, National Bureau of Economic Research, Cambridge, Mass.

Crane, J. 1991. The epidemic theory of ghettos and neighborhood effects on dropping out and teenage childbearing. *American Journal of Sociology* 96:1226–1259.

Danziger, S., and P. Gottschalk. 1995. *America Unequal.* Cambridge: Harvard University Press and the Russell Sage Foundation.

Datcher, L. 1982. Effects of community and family background on achievement. *The Review of Economics and Statistics* 64:32–41.

Demerath, N., and H. Gilmore. 1954. The ecology of southern cities. Pp. 120–125 in *The Urban South*, R. Vance and N. Demerath, eds. Chapel Hill; University of North Carolina Press.

Denton, N. 1994. Are African Americans still hypersegregated? Pp. 49–81 in *Residential Apartheid: The American Legacy*, R. Bullard, J. Grigsby III, and C. Lee, eds. Los Angeles: CAAS Publications, University of California.

Denton, N., and D. Massey. 1988. Residential segregation of Blacks, Hispanics, and Asians by socioeconomic status and generation. *Social Science Quarterly* 69:797–817. 1989. Racial identity among Caribbean Hispanics: The effect of double minority status on residential segregation. *American Sociological Review* 54:790–808. 1991. Patterns of neighborhood transition in a multiethnic world. *Demography* 28:41–64.

Duncan, O., and B. Duncan. 1957. *The Negro Population of Chicago: A Study of Residential Succession.* Chicago: University of Chicago Press.

Farley, R. 1977. Residential segregation in urbanized areas of the United States in 1970: An analysis of social class and racial differences. *Demography* 14:497–518.

Farley, R., S. Bianchi, and D. Colasanto. 1979. Barriers to the racial integration of neighborhoods: The Detroit case. *Annals of the American Academy of Political and Social Science* 441:97–113.

Farley, R., H. Schuman, S. Bianchi, D. Colasanto, and S. Hatchett. 1978. "Chocolate city, vanilla suburbs": Will the trend toward racially separate communities continue? *Social Science Research* 7:319–344.

Farley, R., C. Steeh, M. Krysan, T. Jackson, and K. Reeves. 1994. Stereotypes and segregation: Neighborhoods in the Detroit area. *American Journal of Sociology* 100:750–780.

Feins, J., R. Bratt, and R. Hollister. 1981. *Final Report of a Study of Racial Discrimination in the Boston Housing Market.* Cambridge: Abt Associates.

Fix, M., G. Galster, and R. Struyk. 1993. An overview of auditing for discrimination. Pp. 1–68 in *Clear and Convincing Evidence: Measurement of Discrimination in America*, M. Fix and R. Struyk, eds. Washington, D.C.: The Urban Institute Press.

Frey, W., and R. Farley. 1994. Changes in the segregation of Whites from Blacks during the 1980s; Small steps toward a more integrated society. *American Sociological Review* 59:23–45. 1996. Latino, Asian, and Black segregation in U.S. metropolitan areas: Are multiethnic metros different? *Demography* 33:35–50.

Furstenberg, F. Jr., S. Morgan, K. Moore, and J. Peterson. 1987. Race differences in the timing of adolescent intercourse. *American Sociological Review* 52:511–518.

Galster, G. 1986. More than skin deep: The effect of housing discrimination on the extent and pattern of racial residential segregation in the United States. Pp. 119–138 in *Housing Discrimination and Federal Policy*, J. Goering, ed. Chapel Hill: University of North Carolina Press. 1987. The ecology of racial discrimination in housing: An exploratory model. *Urban Affairs Quarterly* 23:84–107. 1990a. Racial discrimination in housing markets during the 1980s: A review of the audit evidence. *Journal of Planning Education and Research* 9:165–175. 1990b. Racial steering by real estate agents: Mechanisms and motives. *The review of Black Political Economy* 19:39–63. 1990c. White flight from racially integrated neighborhoods in the 1970s: The Cleveland experience. *Urban Studies* 27:385–399. 1990d. Neighborhood racial change, segregationist sentiments, and affirmative marketing policies. *Journal of Urban Economics* 27:244–361.

Galster, G., F. Freiberg, and D. Houk. 1987. Racial differentials in real estate advertising practices: An exploratory case study. *Journal of Urban Affairs* 9:199–215.

Galster, G., and W. Keeney. 1988. Race, residence, discrimination, and economic opportunity: Modeling the nexus of urban racial phenomena. *Urban Affairs Quarterly* 24:87–117.

Guest, A., G. Almgren, and J. Hussey. 1998. The ecology of race and socioeconomic distress: Infant and working age mortality in Chicago. *Demography* 35:23–34.

Hakken, J. 1979. *Discrimination Against Chicanos in the Dallas Rental Housing Market: An Experimental Extension of the Housing Market Practices Survey.* Washington, D.C.: Office of Policy Development and Research, U.S. Department of Housing and Urban Development.

Harrison, R., and D. Weinberg. 1992. Racial and ethnic residential segregation in 1990. Paper presented at the annual meeting of the Population Association of America, Denver, April 13.

Helper, R. 1969. *Racial Policies and Practices of Real Estate Brokers.* Minneapolis: University of Minnesota Press.

Hintzen, H. 1983. *Report of an Audit of Real Estate Sales Practices of 15 Northwest Chicago Real Estate Sales Offices.* Chicago: Leadership Council for Metropolitan Open Communities.

Hochschild, J. 1995. *Facing up to the American Dream: Race, Class, and the Soul of the Nation.* Princeton: Princeton University Press.

Hogan, D., and E. Kitagawa. 1985. The impact of social status, family structure, and neighborhood on the fertility of Black adolescents. *American Journal of Sociology* 90:825–855.

Hwang, S., and S. Murdock. 1982. Residential segregation in Texas in 1980. *Social Science Quarterly* 63(1982):737–748.

Jackson, P. 1981. Paradoxes of Puerto Rican segregation in New York. Pp. 109–126 in *Ethnic Segregation in Cities,* C. Peach, V. Robinson, and S. Smith, eds. London: Croom Helm.

Jackson, T. 1994. The other side of the residential segregation equation: Why Detroit area Blacks are reluctant to pioneer integration. Paper presented at the Russell Sage Foundation Multi-City conference.

James, F., and E. Tynan. 1986. Segregation and discrimination against Hispanic Americans. Pp. 83–98 in *Housing Discrimination and Federal Policy,* J. Goering, ed. Chapel Hill: University of North Carolina Press.

Jencks, C., and S. Mayer. 1990. The social consequences of growing up in a poor neighborhood. Pp. 111–186 in *Inner City Poverty in the United States,* L. Lynn, Jr., and M. McGeary, eds. Washington, D.C.: National Academy of Sciences.

Kantrowitz, N. 1973. *Ethnic and Racial Segregation in the New York Metropolis.* New York: Praeger.

Kasarda, J. 1993. Inner city concentrated poverty and neighborhood distress; 1970–1990. *Housing Policy Debate* 4(3):253–302.

Krivo, L., and R. Kaufman. 1999. How low can it go? Declining Black-White segregation in a multi-ethnic context. *Demography* 36:93–110.

Krivo, L., and R. Peterson. 1996. Extremely disadvantaged neighborhoods and urban crime. *Social Forces* 75:619–648.

Krivo, L., R. Peterson, H. Rizzo, and J. Reynolds. 1998. Race segregation, and the concentration of disadvantage: 1980–1990. *Social Problems* 45:61–80.

Levy, F. 1995. Incomes and income inequality. Pp. 1–58 in *State of the Union: America in the 1990s,* Farley, ed. New York: Russell Sage.

Lieberson, S. 1980. *A Piece of the Pie: Blacks and White Immigrants Since 1880.* Berkeley: University of California Press.

Lopez, M. 1981. Patterns of interethnic residential segregation in the urban Southwest, 1960 and 1970. *Social Science Quarterly* 62:50–63.

Massey, D. 1979. Effects of socioeconomic factors on the residential segregation of Blacks and Spanish Americans in United States urbanized areas. *American Sociological Review* 44:1015–1022. 1981. Hispanic residential segregation: A comparison of Mexicans, Cubans, and Puerto Ricans. *Sociology and Social Research* 65:311–322. 1985. Ethnic residential segregation: A theoretical synthesis and empirical review. *Sociology and Social Research* 69:315–350. 1990. American apartheid: Segregation and the making of the underclass. *American Journal of Sociology* 96:329–358.

Massey, D., and B. Bitterman. 1985. Explaining the paradox of Puerto Rican segregation. *Social Forces* 64:306–331.

Massey, D., G. Condran, and N. Denton. 1987. The effect of residential segregation on Black social and economic well-being. *Social Forces* 66:29–57.

Massey, D., and N. Denton. 1987. Trends in the residential segregation of Blacks, Hispanics, and Asians. *American Sociological Review* 52:802–825. 1988. The dimensions of residential segregation.

Social Forces 67:281–315. 1989a. Residential segregation of Mexicans, Puerto Ricans, and Cubans in U.S. metropolitan areas. *Sociology and Social Research* 73:73–83. 1989b. Hypersegregation in U.S. metropolitan areas: Black and Hispanic segregation along five dimensions. *Demography* 26:373–393. 1992. Racial identity and the spatial assimilation of Mexicans in the the United States. *Social Science Research* 21:235–260. 1993. *American Apartheid: Segregation and the Making of the Underclass*. Cambridge: Harvard University Press.

Massey, D., and M. Eggers. 1990. The ecology of inequality: Minorities and the concentration of poverty, 1970–1980. *American Journal of Sociology* 95:1153–1189.

Massey, D., and M. Fischer. 1999. Does rising income bring integration? New results for Blacks, Hispanics, and Asians in 1990. *Social Science Research* 28:316–326. 2000. How segregation concentrates poverty. *Ethnic and Racial Studies* 23:670–691.

Massey, D., and E. Fong. 1990. Segregation and neighborhood quality: Blacks, Hispanics, and Asians in the San Francisco metropolitan area. *Social Forces* 69:15–32.

Massey, D., and A. Gross. 1991. Explaining trends in residential segregation 1970–1980. *Urban Affairs Quarterly* 27:13–35.

Massey, D., A. Gross, and M. Eggers. 1991. Segregation, the concentration of poverty, and the life chances of individuals. *Social Science Research* 20:397–420.

Massey, D., and Z. Hajnal. 1995. The changing geographic structure of Black-White segregation in the United States. *Social Science Quarterly* 76:527–542.

Massey, D., K. Shibuya. 1995. Unraveling the tangle of pathology: The effect of spatially concentrated joblessness on the well-being of African Americans. *Social Science Research* 24:252–366.

Massey, D., M. White, and V. Phua. 1996. The dimensions of segregation revisited. *Sociological Methods and Research*. 25:172–206.

Morenoff, J., and R. Sampson. 1997. Violent crime and the spatial dynamics of neighborhood transition: Chicago, 1970–1990. *Social Forces* 76:31–64.

Morris, M., A. Bernhardt, and M. Hancock. 1994. Economic inequality: New methods for new trends. *American Sociological Review* 59:205–219.

Moskos, C., and J. Butler. 1996. *All That We Can Be: Black Leadership and Racial Integration the Army Way*. New York: Basic Books.

Patillo, M. 1998. Sweet mothers and gangbangers: Managing crime in a Black middle-class neighborhood. *Social Forces* 76:747–774.

Pearce, D. 1979. Gatekeepers and homeseekers: Institutional patterns in racial steering. *Social Problems* 26:325–342.

Rosenbaum, J. 1991. Black pioneers: Do their moves to suburbs increase economic opportunity for mothers and children? *Housing Policy Debate* 2:1179–1214.

Rosenbaum, J., M. Kulieke, and L. Rubinowitz. 1988. White suburban schools' responses to low-income Black children: Sources of success and problems. *The Urban Review* 20:28–41.

Rosenbaum, J., and S. Popkin. 1991. Employment and earnings of low-income Blacks who move to middle class suburbs. Pp. 342–56 in *The Urban Underclass*, C. Jencks and P. Peterson, eds. Washington, D.C.: The Brookings Institution.

Saltman, J. 1979. Housing discrimination: Policy research, methods, and results. *Annals of the American Academy of Political and Social Science.* 441:186–196.

Schelling, T. 1971. Dynamic models of segregation. *Journal of Mathematical Sociology* 1:143–186.

Schneider, M., and J. Logan. 1982. Suburban racial segregation and Black access to local public resources. *Social Science Quarterly* 63:762–770.

Schroeder, A. 1985. *Report on an Audit of Real Estate Sales Practices of Eight Northwest Suburban Offices.* Chicago: Leadership Council for Metropolitan Open Communities.

Schuman, H., and L. Bobo. 1988. Survey-based experiments on White racial attitudes toward residential integration. *American Journal of Sociology* 2:273–299.

Schuman, H., C. Steeh, and L. Bobo. 1985. *Racial Attitudes in America: Trends and Interpretations.* Cambridge: Harvard University Press.

Schuman, H., C. Steeh, L. Bobo, and M. Krysan. 1998. *Racial Attitudes in America: Trends and Interpretations.* Cambridge: Harvard University Press.

Simkus, A. 1978. Residential segregation by occupation and race in ten urbanized areas, 1950–1970. *American Sociological Review* 43:81–93.

Sniderman, P., and T. Piazza. 1993. *The Scar of Race.* Cambridge: Harvard University Press.

Taylor, M. 1998. The effect of racial composition on racial attitudes of Whites. *American Sociological Review* 63:512–535.

Turner, E. and J. Allen. 1991. *An Atlas of Population Patterns in Metropolitan, Los Angeles and Orange Counties.* Occasional Publication in Geography No. 8. Northridge, Calif.: Center for Geographical Studies, California State University at Northridge.

Turner, M., J. Edwards, and M. Mikelsons. 1991. *Housing Discrimination Study: Analyzing Racial and Ethnic Steering.* Washington, D.C.: U.S. Department of Housing and Urban Development, Office of Policy Development and Research.

U.S. Bureau of the Census. 1979. The Social and Economic Status of the Black Population in the United States: An Historical View, 1790–1978. Current Population Reports, Special Studies Series P–23, No. 80. Washington, D.C.: U.S. Government Printing Office.

White, M. 1987. *American Neighborhoods and Residential Differentiation.* New York: Russell Sage Foundation.

Wienk, R., C. Reid, J. Simonson, and F. Eggers. 1979. *Measuring Racial Discrimination in American Housing Markets: The Housing Market Practices Survey.* Washington, D.C.: U.S. Department of Housing and Urban Development.

Wilson, W. 1987. *Truly Disadvantaged: The Inner City, the Underclass, and Public Policy.* Chicago: University of Chicago Press.

Yinger, J. 1986. Measuring racial discrimination with fair housing audits: Caught in the act. *American Economic Review* 76:991–993. 1985. The racial dimension of urban housing markets in the 1980s. Pp. 43–67 in *Divided Neighborhoods: Changing Patterns of Racial Segregation,* G.A. Tobin, ed. Newbury Park, Calif.: Sage Publications. 1989. Measuring discrimination in housing availability. Final Research Report No. 2 to the U.S. Department of Housing and Urban Development. Washington, D.C.: The Urban Institute. 1995. *Closed Doors, Opportunities Lost: The Continuing Costs of Housing Discrimination.* New York: Russell Sage.

Zubrinsky, C., and L. Bobo. 1996. Prismatic metropolis: Race and residential segregation in the City of Angels. *Social Science Research* 25: 335–374.

SEEING THE BIG PICTURE

The index of dissimilarity is a measure of how residentially segregated one population is from another. A score of zero would mean groups are randomly distributed throughout a particular area while a score of one hundred would mean groups share no social space with one another. What does the index of dissimilarity numbers in Section II of the Appendix tell us about residential segregation in the United States?

22
_____

THE CODE OF THE STREETS

Elijah Anderson

QUESTIONS TO CONSIDER

In "The Code of the Streets" Elijah Anderson chronicles how an individual's environment can create a set of expectations that are at odds with the "dominant" culture. How is "oppositional culture" often detrimental to children and young adults in these communities? How is oppositional culture linked to Anderson's discussion of "street" and "decent" families?

Of all the problems besetting the poor inner-city black community, none is more pressing than that of interpersonal violence and aggression. It wreaks havoc daily with the lives of community residents and increasingly spills over into downtown and residential middle-class areas. Muggings, burglaries, carjackings, and drug-related shootings, all of which may leave their victims or innocent bystanders dead, are now common enough to concern all urban and many suburban residents. The inclination to violence springs from the circumstances of life among the ghetto poor—the lack of jobs that pay a living wage, the stigma of race, the fallout from rampant drug use and drug trafficking, and the resulting alienation and lack of hope for the future.

Simply living in such an environment places young people at special risk of falling victim to aggressive behavior. Although there are often forces in the community which can counteract the negative influences, by far

Elijah Anderson, "The Code of the Streets" from *The Code of the Streets.* Originally in *The Atlantic Monthly*, 273, No. 5, May 1994. Copyright © 1994 by Elijah Anderson. Reprinted with the permission of Elijah Anderson.

the most powerful being a strong, loving, "decent" (as inner-city residents put it) family committed to middle-class values, the despair is pervasive enough to have spawned an oppositional culture, that of "the streets," whose norms are often consciously opposed to those of mainstream society. These two orientations—decent and street—socially organize the community, and their coexistence has important consequences for residents, particularly children growing up in the inner city. Above all, this environment means that even youngsters whose home lives reflect mainstream values—and the majority of homes in the community do—must be able to handle themselves in a street-oriented environment.

This is because the street culture has evolved what may be called a code of the streets, which amounts to a set of informal rules governing interpersonal public behavior, including violence. The rules prescribe both a proper comportment and a proper way to respond if challenged. They regulate the use of violence and so allow those who are inclined to aggression to precipitate violent encounters in an approved way. The rules have been established and are enforced mainly by the street-oriented, but on the streets the distinction between street and decent is often irrelevant; everybody knows that if the rules are violated, there are penalties. Knowledge of the code is thus largely defensive; it is literally necessary for operating in public. Therefore, even though families with a decency orientation are usually opposed to the values of the code, they often reluctantly encourage their children's familiarity with it to enable them to negotiate the inner-city environment.

At the heart of the code is the issue of respect—loosely defined as being treated "right," or granted the deference one deserves. However, in the troublesome public environment of the inner city, as people increasingly feel buffeted by forces beyond their control, what one deserves in the way of respect becomes more and more problematic and uncertain. This in turn further opens the issue of respect to sometimes intense interpersonal negotiation. In the street culture, especially among young people, respect is viewed as almost an external entity that is hard-won but easily lost, and so must constantly be guarded. The rules of the code in fact provide a framework for negotiating respect. The person whose very appearance—including his clothing, demeanor, and way of moving—deters transgressions feels that he possesses, and may be considered by others to possess, a measure of respect. With the right amount of respect, for instance, he can avoid "being bothered" in public. If he is bothered, not only may he be in physical danger but he has been disgraced or "dissed" (disrespected). Many of the forms that dissing can take might seem petty to middle-class people (maintaining eye contact for too long, for example), but to those invested in the street code, these actions become serious indications of the other person's intentions. Consequently, such people become very sensitive to advances and slights, which could well serve as warnings of imminent physical confrontation.

This hard reality can be traced to the profound sense of alienation from mainstream society and its institutions felt by many poor inner-city black people, particularly the young. The code of the streets is actually a cultural adaptation to a profound lack of faith in the police and the judicial system. The police are most often seen as representing the dominant white society and not caring to protect inner-city residents. When called, they may not respond, which is one reason many residents feel they must be prepared to take extraordinary measures to defend themselves and their loved ones against those who are inclined to aggression. Lack of police accountability has in fact been incorporated into the status system: the person who is believed capable of "taking care of himself" is accorded a certain deference, which translates into a sense of physical and psychological control. Thus the street code emerges where the influence of the police ends and personal responsibility for one's safety is felt to begin. Exacerbated by the proliferation of drugs and easy access to guns, this volatile situation results in the ability of the street-oriented minority (or those who effectively "go for bad") to dominate the public spaces.

Decent and Street Families

Although almost everyone in poor inner-city neighborhoods is struggling financially and therefore feels a certain distance from the rest of America, the decent and the street family in a real sense represent two poles of value orientation, two contrasting conceptual categories. The labels "decent" and "street," which the residents themselves use, amount to evaluative judgments that confer status on local residents. The labeling is often the result of a social contest among individuals and families of the neighborhood. Individuals of the two orientations often coexist in the same extended family. Decent residents judge themselves to be so while judging others to be of the street, and street individuals often present themselves as decent, drawing distinctions between themselves and other people. In addition, there is quite a bit of circumstantial behavior—that is, one person may at different times exhibit both decent and street orientations, depending on the circumstances. Although these designations result from so much social jockeying, there do exist concrete features that define each conceptual category.

Generally, so-called decent families tend to accept mainstream values more fully and attempt to instill them in their children. Whether married couples with children or single-parent (usually female) households, they are generally "working poor" and so tend to be better off financially than their street-oriented neighbors. They value hard work and self-reliance and are willing to sacrifice for their children. Because they have a certain amount of faith in mainstream society, they harbor hopes for a better future for their children, if not for themselves. Many of them go to church and take a strong interest in their children's schooling. Rather than dwelling on the real hardships and inequities facing them, many such decent people, particularly the increasing number of grandmothers raising grandchildren, see their difficult situation as a test from God and derive great support from their faith and from the church community.

Extremely aware of the problematic and often dangerous environment in which they reside, decent parents tend to be strict in their child-rearing practices, encouraging children to respect authority and walk a straight moral line. They have an almost obsessive concern about trouble of any kind and remind their children to be on the lookout for people and situations that might lead to it. At the same time, they are themselves polite and considerate of others, and teach their children to be the same way. At home, at work, and in church, they strive hard to maintain a positive mental attitude and a spirit of cooperation.

So-called street parents, in contrast, often show a lack of consideration for other people and have a rather superficial sense of family and community. Though they may love their children, many of them are unable to cope with the physical and emotional demands of parenthood, and find it difficult to reconcile their needs with those of their children. These families, who are more fully invested in the code of the streets than the decent people are, may aggressively socialize their children into it in a normative way. They believe in the code and judge themselves and others according to its values.

In fact the overwhelming majority of families in the inner-city community try to approximate the decent-family model, but there are many others who clearly represent the worst fears of the decent family. Not only are their financial resources extremely limited, but what little they have may easily be misused. The lives of the street-oriented are often marked by disorganization. In the most desperate circumstances people frequently have a limited understanding of priorities and consequences, and so frustrations mount over bills, food, and, at times, drink, cigarettes, and drugs. Some tend toward self-destructive behavior; many street-oriented women are crack-addicted ("on the pipe"), alcoholic, or involved in complicated relationships with men who abuse them. In addition, the seeming intractability of their situation, caused in large part by the lack of well-paying jobs and the persistence of racial discrimination, has engendered deep-seated bitterness and anger in many of the most desperate and poorest blacks, especially young people. The need both to exercise a measure of control and to lash out at somebody is often reflected in the adults' relations with their children. At the least, the frustrations of persistent poverty shorten the fuse in such people—contributing to a lack of patience with anyone, child or adult, who irritates them.

In these circumstances a woman—or a man, although men are less consistently present in children's lives—can be quite aggressive with children, yelling at and striking them for the least little infraction of the rules she has set down. Often little if any serious explanation follows the verbal and physical punishment. This response teaches children a particular lesson. They learn that to solve any kind of interpersonal problem one must quickly resort to hitting or other violent behavior. Actual peace and quiet, and also the appearance of calm, respectful children conveyed to her neighbors and friends, are often what the young mother most desires, but at times she will be very aggressive in trying to get them. Thus she may be quick to beat her children, especially if they defy her law, not because she hates them but because this is the way she knows to control them. In fact, many street-oriented women love their children dearly. Many mothers in the community subscribe to the notion that there is a "devil in the boy" that must be beaten out of him or that socially "fast girls need to be whupped." Thus much of what borders on child abuse in the view of social authorities is acceptable parental punishment in the view of these mothers.

Many street-oriented women are sporadic mothers whose children learn to fend for themselves when necessary, foraging for food and money any way they can get it. The children are sometimes employed by drug dealers or become addicted themselves. These children of the street, growing up with little supervision, are said to "come up hard." They often learn to fight at an early age, sometimes using short-tempered adults around them as role models. The street-oriented home may be fraught with anger, verbal disputes, physical aggression, and even mayhem. The children observe these

goings-on, learning the lesson that might makes right. They quickly learn to hit those who cross them, and the dog-eat-dog mentality prevails. In order to survive, to protect oneself, it is necessary to marshal inner resources and be ready to deal with adversity in a hands-on way. In these circumstances physical prowess takes on great significance.

In some of the most desperate cases, a street-oriented mother may simply leave her young children alone and unattended while she goes out. The most irresponsible women can be found at local bars and crack houses, getting high and socializing with other adults. Sometimes a troubled woman will leave very young children alone for days at a time. Reports of crack addicts abandoning their children have become common in drug-infested inner-city communities. Neighbors or relatives discover the abandoned children, often hungry and distraught over the absence of their mother. After repeated absences, a friend or relative, particularly a grandmother, will often step in to care for the young children, sometimes petitioning the authorities to send her, as guardian of the children, the mother's welfare check, if the mother gets one. By this time, however, the children may well have learned the first lesson of the streets: survival itself, let alone respect, cannot be taken for granted; you have to fight for your place in the world.

Campaigning for Respect

These realities of inner-city life are largely absorbed on the streets. At an early age, often even before they start school, children from street-oriented homes gravitate to the streets, where they "hang"—socialize with their peers. Children from these generally permissive homes have a great deal of latitude and are allowed to "rip and run" up and down the street. They often come home from school, put their books down, and go right back out the door. On school nights eight- and nine-year-olds remain out until nine or ten o'clock (and teenagers typically come in whenever they want to). On the streets they play in groups that often become the source of their primary social bonds. Children from decent homes tend to be more carefully supervised and are thus likely to have curfews and to be taught how to stay out of trouble.

When decent and street kids come together, a kind of social shuffle occurs in which children have a chance to go either way. Tension builds as a child comes to realize that he must choose an orientation. The kind of home he comes from influences but does not determine the way he will ultimately turn out—although it is unlikely that a child from a thoroughly street-oriented family will easily absorb decent values on the streets. Youths who emerge from street-oriented families but develop a decency orientation almost always learn those values in another setting—in school, in a youth group, in church. Often it is the result of their involvement with a caring "old head" (adult role model).

In the street, through their play, children pour their individual life experiences into a common knowledge pool, affirming, confirming, and elaborating on what they have observed in the home and matching their skills against those of others. And they learn to fight. Even small children test one another, pushing and shoving, and are ready to hit other children over circumstances not to their liking. In turn, they are readily hit by other children, and the child who is toughest prevails. Thus the violent resolution of disputes, the hitting and cursing, gains social reinforcement. The child in effect is initiated into a system that is really a way of campaigning for respect.

In addition, younger children witness the disputes of older children, which are often resolved through cursing and abusive talk, if not aggression or outright violence. They see that one child succumbs to the greater physical and mental abilities of the other. They are also alert and attentive witnesses to the verbal and physical fights of adults, after which they compare notes and share their interpretations of the event. In almost every case the victor is the person who physically won the altercation, and this person often enjoys the esteem and respect of onlookers. These experiences reinforce the lessons the children have learned at home: might makes right, and toughness is a virtue, while humility is not. In effect they learn the social meaning of fighting. When it is left virtually unchallenged, this understanding becomes an ever more important part of the child's working conception of the world. Over time the code of the streets becomes refined.

Those street-oriented adults with whom children come in contact—including mothers, fathers, brothers, sisters, boyfriends, cousins, neighbors, and friends—help them along in forming this understanding by verbalizing the messages they are getting through experience: "Watch your back." "Protect yourself." "Don't punk out." "If somebody messes with you, you got to pay them back." "If someone disses you, you got to straighten them out." Many parents actually impose sanctions if a child is not sufficiently aggressive. For example, if a child loses a fight and comes home upset, the parent might respond, "Don't you come in here crying that somebody beat you up; you better get back out there and whup his ass. I didn't raise no punks! Get back out there and whup his ass. If you don't whup his ass, I'll whup your ass when you come home." Thus the child obtains reinforcement for being tough and showing nerve.

While fighting, some children cry as though they are doing something they are ambivalent about. The fight may be against their wishes, yet they may feel constrained to fight or face the consequences—not just from peers but also from caretakers or parents, who may administer another beating if they back down. Some adults recall receiving such lessons from their own parents and justify repeating them to their children as a way to toughen them up. Looking capable of taking care of oneself as a form of self-defense is a dominant theme among both street-oriented and decent adults who worry about the safety of their children. There is thus at times a convergence in their child-rearing practices, although the rationales behind them may differ.

Self-Image Based on "Juice"

By the time they are teenagers, most youths have either internalized the code of the streets or at least learned the need to comport themselves in accordance with its rules, which chiefly have to do with interpersonal communication. The code revolves around the presentation of self. Its basic requirement is the display of a certain predisposition to violence. Accordingly, one's bearing must send the unmistakable if sometimes subtle message to "the next person" in public that one is capable of violence and mayhem when the situation requires it, that one can take care of oneself. The nature of this communication is largely determined by the demands of the circumstances but can include facial expressions, gait, and verbal expressions—all of which are geared mainly to deterring aggression. Physical appearance, including clothes, jewelry, and grooming, also plays an important part in how a person is viewed; to be respected, it is important to have the right look.

Even so, there are no guarantees against challenges, because there are always people around looking for a fight to increase their share of respect—or "juice," as it is sometimes called on the street. Moreover, if a person is assaulted, it is important, not only in the eyes of his opponent but also in the eyes of his "running buddies," for him to avenge himself. Otherwise he risks being "tried" (challenged) or "moved on" by any number of others. To maintain his honor he must show he is not someone to be "messed with" or "dissed." In general, the person must "keep himself straight" by managing his position of respect among others; this involves in part his self-image, which is shaped by what he thinks others are thinking of him in relation to his peers.

Objects play an important and complicated role in establishing self-image. Jackets, sneakers, gold jewelry, reflect not just a person's taste, which tends to be tightly regulated among adolescents of all social classes, but also a willingness to possess things that may require defending. A boy wearing a fashionable, expensive jacket, for example, is vulnerable to attack by another who covets the jacket and either cannot afford to buy one or wants the added satisfaction of depriving someone else of his. However, if the boy forgoes the desirable jacket and wears one that isn't "hip," he runs the risk of being teased and possibly even assaulted as an unworthy person. To be allowed to hang with certain prestigious crowds, a boy must wear a different set of expensive clothes—sneakers and athletic suit—every day. Not to be able to do so might make him appear socially deficient. The youth comes to covet such items—especially when he sees easy prey wearing them.

In acquiring valued things, therefore, a person shores up his identity—but since it is an identity based on having things, it is highly precarious. This very precariousness gives a heightened sense of urgency to staying even with peers, with whom the person is actually competing. Young men and women who are able to command respect through their presentation of self—by allowing their possessions and their body language to speak for them—may not have to campaign for regard but may, rather, gain it by the force of their manner. Those who are unable to command respect in this way must actively campaign for it—and are thus particularly alive to slights.

One way of campaigning for status is by taking the possessions of others. In this context, seemingly ordinary objects can become trophies imbued with symbolic value that far exceeds their monetary worth. Possession of the trophy can symbolize the ability to violate somebody—to "get in his face," to take something of value from him, to "dis" him, and thus to enhance one's own worth by stealing someone else's. The trophy does not have to be something material. It can be another person's sense of honor, snatched away with a derogatory remark. It can be the outcome of a fight. It can be the imposition of a certain standard, such as a girl's getting herself recognized as the most beautiful. Material things, however, fit easily into the pattern. Sneakers, a pistol, even somebody else's girlfriend, can become a trophy. When a person can take something from another and then flaunt it, he gains a certain regard by being the owner, or the controller, of that thing. But this display of ownership can then provoke other people to challenge him. This game of who controls what is thus constantly being played out on inner-city streets, and the trophy—extrinsic or intrinsic, tangible or intangible—identifies the current winner.

An important aspect of this often violent give-and-take is its zero-sum quality. That is, the extent to which one person can raise himself up depends on his ability to put another person down. This underscores the alienation that permeates the inner-city ghetto community. There is a generalized sense that very little respect is to be had, and therefore everyone competes to get what affirmation he can of the little that is available. The craving for respect that results gives people thin skins. Shows of deference by others can be highly soothing, contributing to a sense of security, comfort, self-confidence, and self-respect. Transgressions by others which go unanswered diminish these feelings and are believed to encourage further transgressions. Hence one must be ever vigilant against the transgressions of others or even *appearing* as if transgressions will be tolerated. Among young people, whose sense of self-esteem is particularly vulnerable, there is an especially heightened concern with being disrespected. Many inner-city young men in particular crave respect to such a degree that they will risk their lives to attain and maintain it.

The issue of respect is thus closely tied to whether a person has an inclination to be violent, even as a victim. In the wider society people may not feel required to retaliate physically after an attack, even though they are aware that they have been degraded or taken advantage of. They may feel a great need to defend themselves *during* an attack, or to behave in such a way as to deter aggression (middle-class people certainly can and do become victims of street-oriented youths), but they are much more likely than street-oriented people to feel that they can walk away from a possible altercation with their self-esteem intact. Some people may even have the strength of character to flee, without any thought that their self-respect or esteem will be diminished.

In impoverished inner-city black communities, however, particularly among young males and perhaps increasingly among females, such flight would be extremely difficult. To run away would likely leave one's self-esteem in tatters. Hence people often feel constrained not only to stand up and at least attempt to resist during an assault but also to "pay back"—to seek revenge—after a successful assault on their person. This may include going to get a weapon or even getting relatives involved. Their very identity and self-respect, their honor, is often intricately tied up with the way they perform on the streets during and after such encounters. This outlook reflects the circumscribed opportunities of the inner-city poor. Generally people outside the ghetto have other ways of gaining status and regard, and thus do not feel so dependent on such physical displays.

By Trial of Manhood

On the street, among males these concerns about things and identity have come to be expressed in the concept of "manhood." Manhood in the inner city means taking the prerogatives of men with respect to strangers, other men, and women—being distinguished as a man. It implies physicality and a certain ruthlessness. Regard and respect are associated with this concept in large part because of its practical application: if others have little or no regard for a person's manhood, his very life and those of his loved ones could be in jeopardy. But there is a chicken-and-egg aspect to this situation: one's physical safety is more likely to be jeopardized in public *because* manhood is associated with respect. In other words, an existential link has been created between the idea of manhood and one's self-esteem, so that it has become hard to say which is primary. For many inner-city youths, manhood and respect are flip sides of the same coin; physical and psychological well-being are inseparable, and both require a sense of control, of being in charge.

The operating assumption is that a man, especially a real man, knows what other men know—the code of the streets. And if one is not a real man, one is somehow diminished as a person, and there are certain valued things one simply does not deserve. There is thus believed to be a certain justice to the code, since it is considered that everyone has the opportunity to know it. Implicit in this is that everybody is held responsible for being

familiar with the code. If the victim of a mugging, for example, does not know the code and so responds "wrong," the perpetrator may feel justified even in killing him and may feel no remorse. He may think, "Too bad, but it's his fault. He should have known better."

So when a person ventures outside, he must adopt the code—a kind of shield, really—to prevent others from "messing with" him. In these circumstances it is easy for people to think they are being tried or tested by others even when this is not the case. For it is sensed that something extremely valuable is at stake in every interaction, and people are encouraged to rise to the occasion, particularly with strangers. For people who are unfamiliar with the code—generally people who live outside the inner city—the concern with respect in the most ordinary interactions can be frightening and incomprehensible. But for those who are invested in the code, the clear object of their demeanor is to discourage strangers from even thinking about testing their manhood. And the sense of power that attends the ability to deter others can be alluring even to those who know the code without being heavily invested in it—the decent inner-city youths. Thus a boy who has been leading a basically decent life can, in trying circumstances, suddenly resort to deadly force.

Central to the issue of manhood is the widespread belief that one of the most effective ways of gaining respect is to manifest "nerve." Nerve is shown when one takes another person's possessions (the more valuable the better), "messes with" someone's woman, throws the first punch, "gets in someone's face," or pulls a trigger. Its proper display helps on the spot to check others who would violate one's person and also helps to build a reputation that works to prevent future challenges. But since such a show of nerve is a forceful expression of disrespect toward the person on the receiving end, the victim may be greatly offended and seek to retaliate with equal or greater force. A display of nerve, therefore, can easily provoke a life-threatening response, and the background knowledge of that possibility has often been incorporated into the concept of nerve.

True nerve exposes a lack of fear of dying. Many feel that it is acceptable to risk dying over the principle of respect. In fact, among the hard-core street-oriented, the clear risk of violent death may be preferable to being "dissed" by another. The youths who have internalized this attitude and convincingly display it in their public bearing are among the most threatening people of all, for it is commonly assumed that they fear no man. As the people of the community say, "They are the baddest dudes on the street." They often lead an existential life that may acquire meaning only when they are faced with the possibility of imminent death. Not to be afraid to die is by implication to have few compunctions about taking another's life. Not to be afraid to die is the quid pro quo of being able to take somebody else's life—for the right reasons, if the situation demands it. When others believe this is one's position, it gives one a real sense of power on the streets. Such credibility is what many inner-city youths strive to achieve, whether they are decent or street-oriented, both because of its practical defensive value and because of the positive way it makes them feel about themselves. The difference between the decent and the street-oriented youth is often that the decent youth makes a conscious decision to appear tough and manly; in another setting—with teachers, say, or at his part-time job—he can be polite and deferential. The street-oriented youth, on the other hand, has made the concept of manhood a part of his very identity; he has difficulty manipulating it—it often controls him.

Girls and Boys

Increasingly, teenage girls are mimicking the boys and trying to have their own version of "manhood." Their goal is the same—to get respect, to be recognized as capable of setting or maintaining a certain standard. They try to achieve this end in the ways that have been established by the boys, including posturing, abusive language, and the use of violence to resolve disputes, but the issues for the girls are different. Although conflicts over turf and status exist among the girls, the majority of disputes seem rooted in assessments of beauty (which girl in a group is "the cutest"), competition over boyfriends, and attempts to regulate other people's knowledge of and opinions about a girl's behavior or that of someone close to her, especially her mother.

A major cause of conflicts among girls is "he say, she say." This practice begins in the early school years and continues through high school. It occurs when "people," particularly girls, talk about others, thus putting their "business in the streets." Usually one girl will say something negative about another in the group, most often behind the person's back. The remark will then get back to the person talked about. She may retaliate or her friends may feel required to "take up for" her. In essence this is a form of group gossiping in which individuals are negatively assessed and evaluated. As with much gossip, the things said may or may not be true, but the point is that such imputations can cast aspersions on a person's good name. The accused is required to defend herself against the slander, which can result in arguments and fights, often over little of real substance. Here again is the problem of low self-esteem, which encourages youngsters to be highly sensitive to slights and to be vulnerable to feeling easily "dissed." To avenge the dissing, a fight is usually necessary.

Because boys are believed to control violence, girls tend to defer to them in situations of conflict. Often if a girl is attacked or feels slighted, she will get a brother, uncle, or cousin to do her fighting for her. Increasingly, however, girls are doing their own fighting and are even asking their male relatives to teach them how to fight. Some girls form groups that attack other girls or take things from them. A hard-core segment of inner-city girls inclined toward violence seems to be developing. As one thirteen-year-old girl in a detention center for youths who have committed violent acts told me, "To get people to leave you alone, you gotta fight. Talking don't always get you out of stuff." One major difference between girls and boys: girls rarely use guns. Their fights are therefore not life-or-death struggles. Girls are not often willing to put their lives on the line for "manhood." The ultimate form of respect on the male-dominated inner-city street is thus reserved for men.

"Going for Bad"

In the most fearsome youths such a cavalier attitude toward death grows out of a very limited view of life. Many are uncertain about how long they are going to live and believe they could die violently at any time. They accept this fate; they live on the edge. Their manner conveys the message that nothing intimidates them; whatever turn the encounter takes, they maintain their attack—rather like a pit bull, whose spirit many such boys admire. The demonstration of such tenacity "shows heart" and earns their respect.

This fearlessness has implications for law enforcement. Many street-oriented boys are much more concerned about the threat of "justice" at the hands of a peer than at the hands of the police. Moreover, many feel not only that they have little to lose by going to prison but that they have something to gain. The toughening-up one experiences in prison can actually enhance one's reputation on the streets. Hence the system loses influence over the hard core who are without jobs, with little perceptible stake in the system. If mainstream society has done nothing *for* them, they counter by making sure it can do nothing *to* them.

At the same time, however, a competing view maintains that true nerve consists in backing down, walking away from a fight, and going on with one's business. One fights only in self-defense. This view emerges from the decent philosophy that life is precious, and it is an important part of the socialization process common in decent homes. It discourages violence as the primary means of resolving disputes and encourages youngsters to accept nonviolence and talk as confrontational strategies. But "if the deal goes down," self-defense is greatly encouraged. When there is enough positive support for this orientation, either in the home or among one's peers, then nonviolence has a chance to prevail. But it prevails at the cost of relinquishing a claim to being bad and tough, and therefore sets a young person up as at the very least alienated from street-oriented peers and quite possibly a target of derision or even violence.

Although the nonviolent orientation rarely overcomes the impulse to strike back in an encounter, it does introduce a certain confusion and so can prompt a measure of soul-searching, or even profound ambivalence. Did the person back down with his respect intact or did he back down only to be judged a "punk"—a person lacking manhood? Should he or she have acted? Should he or she have hit the other person in the mouth? These questions beset many young men and women during public confrontations. What is the "right" thing to do? In the quest for honor, respect, and local status—which few young people are uninterested in—common sense most often prevails, which leads many to opt for the tough approach, enacting their own particular versions of the display of nerve. The presentation of oneself as rough and tough is very often quite acceptable until one is tested. And then that presentation may help the person pass the test, because it will cause fewer questions to be asked about what he did and why. It is hard for a person to explain why he lost the fight or why he backed down. Hence many will strive to appear to "go for bad," while hoping they will never be tested. But when they are tested, the outcome of the situation may quickly be out of their hands, as they become wrapped up in the circumstances of the moment.

An Oppositional Culture

The attitudes of the wider society are deeply implicated in the code of the streets. Most people in inner-city communities are not totally invested in the code, but the significant minority of hard-core street youths who are have to maintain the code in order to establish reputations, because they have—or feel they have—few other ways to assert themselves. For these young people the standards of the street code are the only game in town. The extent to which some children—particularly those who through upbringing have become most alienated and those lacking in strong and conventional social support—experience, feel, and internalize racist rejection and contempt from mainstream society may strongly encourage them to express contempt for the more conventional society in turn. In dealing with this contempt

and rejection, some youngsters will consciously invest themselves and their considerable mental resources in what amounts to an oppositional culture to preserve themselves and their self-respect. Once they do, any respect they might be able to garner in the wider system pales in comparison with the respect available in the local system; thus they often lose interest in even attempting to negotiate the mainstream system.

At the same time, many less alienated young blacks have assumed a street-oriented demeanor as a way of expressing their blackness while really embracing a much more moderate way of life; they, too, want a non-violent setting in which to live and raise a family. These decent people are trying hard to be part of the mainstream culture, but the racism, real and perceived, that they encounter helps to legitimate the oppositional culture. And so on occasion they adopt street behavior. In fact, depending on the demands of the situation, many people in the community slip back and forth between decent and street behavior.

A vicious cycle has thus been formed. The hopelessness and alienation many young inner-city black men and women feel, largely as a result of endemic joblessness and persistent racism, fuels the violence they engage in. This violence serves to confirm the negative feelings many whites and some middle-class blacks harbor toward the ghetto poor, further legitimating the oppositional culture and the code of the streets in the eyes of many poor young blacks. Unless this cycle is broken, attitudes on both sides will become increasingly entrenched, and the violence, which claims victims black and white, poor and affluent, will only escalate.

23

ENVIRONMENTAL JUSTICE IN THE 21ST CENTURY: RACE STILL MATTERS

Robert D. Bullard

QUESTIONS TO CONSIDER

Where is the trash dump, the water treatment plant, or the power plant in your community? In this reading Robert Bullard argues that in all likelihood these environmental dangers are in low-income, black and brown neighborhoods. Why do some communities get "dumped on" while others remain free of any toxic waste sites?

Hardly a day passes without the media discovering some community or neighborhood fighting a landfill, incinerator, chemical plant, or some other polluting industry. This was not always the case. Just three decades ago, the concept of environmental justice had not registered on the radar screens of environmental, civil rights, or social justice groups.[1] Nevertheless, it should not be forgotten that Dr. Martin Luther King, Jr., went to Memphis in 1968 on an environmental and economic justice mission for the striking black garbage workers. The strikers were demanding equal pay and better work conditions. Of course, Dr. King was assassinated before he could complete his mission.

Another landmark garbage dispute took place a decade later in Houston, when African-American homeowners in 1979 began a bitter fight to keep a sanitary landfill out of their suburban middle-income neighborhood.[2] Residents formed the Northeast Community

Action Group or NECAG. NECAG and their attorney, Linda McKeever Bullard, filed a class-action lawsuit to block the facility from being built. The 1979 lawsuit, *Bean v. Southwestern Waste Management, Inc.*, was the first of its kind to challenge the siting of a waste facility under civil rights law.

The landmark Houston case occurred three years before the environmental justice movement was catapulted into the national limelight in the rural and mostly African-American Warren County, North Carolina. The environmental justice movement has come a long way since its humble beginning in Warren County, North Carolina, where a PCB landfill ignited protests and over 500 arrests. The Warren County protests provided the impetus for a U.S. General Accounting Office study, *Siting of Hazardous Waste Landfills and Their Correlation with Racial and Economic Status of Surrounding Communities.*[3] That study revealed that three out of four of the off-site, commercial hazardous waste landfills in Region 4 (which comprises eight states in the South) happen to be located in predominantly African-American communities, although African-Americans made up only 20% of the region's population.

Robert D. Bullard, "Environmental Justice in the 21st Century: Race Still Matters" from *Phylon*, 2001, Vol. 49, No. 3–4, pp. 151–171. Copyright © 2001 *Phylon*. Reprinted by permission.

More important, the protesters put "environmental racism" on the map. Fifteen years later, the state of North Carolina is required to spend over $25 million to clean up and detoxify the Warren County PCB landfill.

The Warren County protests also led the Commission for Racial Justice to produce *Toxic Waste and Race*,[4] the first national study to correlate waste facility sites and demographic characteristics. Race was found to be the most potent variable in predicting where these facilities were located—more powerful than poverty, land values, and home ownership. In 1990, *Dumping in Dixie: Race, Class, and Environmental Quality* chronicled the convergence of two social movements—social justice and environmental movements—into the environmental justice movement. This book highlighted African-Americans, environmental activism in the South, the same region that gave birth to the modern civil rights movement. What started out as local and often isolated community-based struggles against toxics and facility siting blossomed into a multiissue, multiethnic, and multiregional movement.

The 1991 First National People of Color Environmental Leadership Summit was probably the most important single event in the movement's history. The Summit broadened the environmental justice movement beyond its early antitoxics focus to include issues of public health, worker safety, land use, transportation, housing, resource allocation, and community empowerment.[5]

The meeting also demonstrated that it is possible to build a multiracial grassroots movement around environmental and economic justice.[6]

Held in Washington, DC, the four-day Summit was attended by over 650 grassroots and national leaders from around the world. Delegates came from all fifty states including Alaska and Hawaii, Puerto Rico, Chile, Mexico, and as far away as the Marshall Islands. People attended the summit to share their action strategies, redefine the environmental

movement, and develop common plans for addressing environmental problems affecting people of color in the United States and around the world.

On September 27, 1991, Summit delegates adopted 17 "Principles of Environmental Justice." These principles were developed as a guide for organizing, networking, and relating to government and nongovernmental organizations (NGOs). By June 1992, Spanish and Portuguese translations of the Principles were being used and circulated by NGOs and environmental justice groups at the Earth Summit in Rio de Janeiro.

In response to growing public concern and mounting scientific evidence, President Clinton on February 11, 1994 (the second day of the national health symposium), issued Executive Order 12898, "Federal Actions to Address Environmental Justice in Minority Populations and Low-Income Populations." This Order attempts to address environmental injustice within existing federal laws and regulations.

Executive Order 12898 reinforces the 35-year-old Civil Rights Act of 1964, Title VI, which prohibits discriminatory practices in programs receiving federal funds. The Order also focuses the spotlight back on the National Environmental Policy Act (NEPA), a twenty-five-year-old law that set policy goals for the protection, maintenance, and enhancement of the environment. NEPA's goal is to ensure for all Americans a safe, healthful, productive, and aesthetically and culturally pleasing environment. NEPA requires federal agencies to prepare a detailed statement on the environmental effects of proposed federal actions that significantly affect the quality of human health.

The Executive Order calls for improved methodologies for assessing and mitigating impacts, health effects from multiple and cumulative exposure, collection of data on low-income and minority populations who may be disproportionately at risk, and impacts on subsistence fishers and wildlife consumers. It also encourages participation of the impacted populations in the various phases of assessing impacts—including scoping, data gathering, alternatives, analysis, mitigation, and monitoring.

The Executive Order focuses on "subsistence" fishers and wildlife consumers. Everybody does not buy fish at the supermarket. There are many people who are subsistence fishers, who fish for protein, who basically subsidize their budgets, and their diets by fishing from rivers, streams, and lakes that happen to be polluted. These subpopulations may be underprotected when basic assumptions are made using the dominant risk paradigm.

Many grassroots activists are convinced that waiting for the government to act has endangered the health and welfare of their communities. Unlike the federal EPA, communities of color did not first discover environmental inequities in 1990. The federal EPA only took action on environmental justice concerns in 1990 after extensive prodding from grassroots environmental justice activists, educators, and academics.[7]

People of color have known about and have been living with inequitable environmental quality for decades—most without the protection of the federal, state, and local governmental agencies. Environmental justice advocates continue to challenge the current environmental protection apparatus and offer their own framework for addressing environmental inequities, disparate impact, and unequal protection.

An Environmental Justice Framework

The question of environmental justice is not anchored in a debate about whether or not decision makers should tinker with risk management. The framework seeks to prevent environmental threats before they occur.[8] The environmental justice framework incorporates other social movements that seek to eliminate harmful practices (discrimination harms the victim) in housing, land use, industrial planning, health care, and sanitation services. The impact of redlining, economic disinvestments, infrastructure decline, deteriorating housing, lead poisoning, industrial pollution, poverty, and unemployment are not unrelated problems if one lives in an urban ghetto or barrio, rural hamlet, or reservation.

The environmental justice framework attempts to uncover the underlying assumptions that may contribute to and produce unequal protection. This framework brings to the surface the ethical and political questions of "who gets what, why, and how much." Some general characteristics of the framework include:

1. *The environmental justice framework incorporates the principle of the "right" of all individuals to be protected from environmental degradation.* The precedents for this framework are the Civil Rights Act of 1964, Fair Housing Act of 1968 and as amended in 1988, and Voting Rights Act of 1965.

2. *The environmental justice framework adopts a public health model of prevention (elimination of the threat before harm occurs) as the preferred strategy.* Impacted communities should not have to wait until causation or conclusive "proof" is established before preventive action is taken. For example, the framework offers a solution to the lead problem by shifting the primary focus from *treatment* (after children have been poisoned) to *prevention* (elimination of the threat via abating lead in houses).

Overwhelming scientific evidence exists on the ill effects of lead on the human body. However, very little action has been taken to rid the nation of childhood lead poisoning in urban areas. Former Health and Human

Secretary Louis Sullivan tagged this among the "number one environmental health threats to children."[9]

The Natural Resources Defense Council, NAACP Legal Defense and Educational Fund, ACLU, and Legal Aid Society of Alameda County joined forces in 1991 and won an out-of-court settlement worth $15–20 million for a blood-lead testing program in California. The *Matthews v. Coye* lawsuit involved the State of California not living up to the federally mandated testing of some 557,000 poor children for lead who receive Medicaid. This historic agreement triggered similar actions in other states that failed to live up to federally mandated screening.[10]

Lead screening is an important element in this problem. However, screening is not the solution. Prevention is the solution. Surely, if termite inspections can be mandated to protect individual home investment, a lead-free home can be mandated to protect public health. Ultimately, the lead abatement debate, public health (who is affected) vs. property rights (who pays for cleanup), is a value conflict that will not be resolved by the scientific community.

3. *The environmental justice framework shifts the burden of proof to polluter/dischargers who do harm, discriminate, or who do not give equal protection to racial and ethnic minorities, and other "protected" classes.* Under the current system, individuals who challenge polluters must "prove" that they have been harmed, discriminated against, or disproportionately impacted. Few impacted communities have the resources to hire lawyers, expert witnesses, and doctors needed to sustain such a challenge.

The environmental justice framework would require the parties that are applying for operating permits (landfills, incinerators, smelters, refineries, chemical plants, etc.) to "prove" that their operations are not harmful to human health, will not disproportionately impact racial and ethnic minorities and other protected groups, and are nondiscriminatory.

4. *The environmental justice framework would allow disparate impact and statistical weight, as opposed to "intent," to infer discrimination.* Proving intentional or purposeful discrimination in a court of law is next to impossible, as demonstrated in *Bean v. Southwestern Waste*. It took nearly a decade after *Bean v. Southwestern Waste* for environmental discrimination to resurface in the courts.

5. *The environmental justice framework redresses disproportionate impact through "targeted" action and resources.* This strategy would target resources where environmental and health problems are greatest (as determined by some ranking scheme but not limited to risk assessment). Reliance solely on "objective" science disguises the exploitative way the polluting industries have operated in some communities and condones a passive acceptance of the status quo.

Human *values* are involved in determining *which* geographic areas are worth public investments. In the 1992 EPA report, *Securing Our Legacy,* the agency describes geographic initiatives as "protecting what we love."[11]

The strategy emphasizes "pollution prevention, multimedia enforcement, research into causes and cures of environmental stress, stopping habitat loss, education, and constituency building."[12] Geographic initiatives are underway in the Chesapeake Bay, Great Lakes, Gulf of Mexico programs, and the U.S.-Mexican Border program. Environmental justice targeting would channel resources to "hot spots," communities that are overburdened with more than their "fair" share of environmental and health problems.

The dominant environmental protection paradigm reinforces instead of challenges the stratification of people (race, ethnicity, status, power, etc.), place (central cities, suburbs, rural areas, unincorporated areas, Native American reservations, etc.), and work (i.e., office workers are afforded greater protection than farm workers). The dominant paradigm exists to manage, regulate, and distribute risks. As a result, the current system has (1) institutionalized unequal enforcement, (2) traded human health for profit, (3) placed the burden of proof on the "victims" and not the polluting industry, (4) legitimated human exposure to harmful chemicals, pesticides, and hazardous substances, (5) promoted "risky" technologies such as incinerators, (6) exploited the vulnerability of economically and politically disenfranchised communities, (7) subsidized ecological destruction, (8) created an industry around risk assessment, (9) delayed cleanup actions, and (10) failed to develop pollution prevention as the overarching and dominant strategy.[13]

The mission of the federal EPA was never designed to address environmental policies and practices that result in unfair, unjust, and inequitable outcome. EPA and other government officials are not likely to ask the questions that go to the heart of environmental injustice: What groups are most affected? Why are they affected? Who did it? What can be done to remedy the problem? How can the problem be prevented? Vulnerable communities, populations, and individuals often fall between the regulatory cracks.

Impetus for a Paradigm Shift

The environmental justice movement has changed the way scientists, researchers, policy makers, and educators go about their daily work. This bottom-up movement has redefined environment to include where people live, work, play, go to school, as well as how these things interact with the physical and natural world. The impetus for changing the dominant environmental protection paradigm did not come from within regulatory agencies, the polluting industry, academia, or the "industry" that has been built around risk management. The environmental justice movement is led by a loose alliance of grassroots and national environmental and civil rights leaders who question the foundation of the current environmental protection paradigm.

Despite significant improvements in environmental protection over the past several decades, millions of Americans continue to live, work, play, and go to school in unsafe and unhealthy physical environments.[14] During its 30-year history, the U.S. EPA has not always recognized that many of our government and industry practices (whether intended or unintended) have adverse impact on poor people and people of color. Growing grass roots community resistance emerged in response to practices, policies, and conditions that residents judged to be unjust, unfair, and illegal. Discrimination is a fact of life in America. Racial discrimination is also illegal.

The EPA is mandated to enforce the nation's environmental laws and regulations equally across the board. It is also required to protect all Americans—not just individuals or groups who can afford lawyers, lobbyists, and experts. Environmental protection is a right, not a privilege reserved for a few who can vote with their feet and escape or fend off environmental stressors that address environmental inequities.

Equity may mean different things to different people. Equity is distilled into three broad categories: procedural, geographic, and social equity.

Procedural equity refers to the "fairness" question: the extent that governing rules, regulations, evaluation criteria, and enforcement are applied uniformly across the board and in a nondiscriminatory way. Unequal protection might result from nonscientific and undemocratic decisions, exclusionary practices, public hearing held in remote locations and at inconvenient times, and use of English-only material as the language to communicate and conduct hearings for non-English speaking publics.

Geographic equity refers to location and spatial configuration of communities and their proximity to environmental hazards, noxious facilities, and locally unwanted land uses (LULUs) such as landfills, incinerators, sewer treatment plants, lead smelters, refineries, and other noxious facilities. For example, unequal protection may result from land-use decisions that determine the location of residential amenities and disamenities. Unincorporated, poor, and communities of color often suffer a "triple" vulnerability of noxious facility siting.

Social Equity assesses the role of sociological factors (race, ethnicity, class, culture, life styles, political power, etc.) on environmental decision making. Poor people and people of color often work in the most dangerous jobs, live in the most polluted neighborhoods, and their children are exposed to all kinds of environmental toxins on the playgrounds and in their homes.

The nation's environmental laws, regulations, and policies are not applied uniformly—resulting in some individuals, neighborhoods, and communities being exposed to the elevated health risks. A 1992 study by staff writers from the *National Law Journal* uncovered glaring inequities in the way the federal EPA enforces its laws. The authors write:

> There is a racial divide in the way the U.S. Government cleans up toxic waste sites and punishes polluters. White communities see faster action, better results and stiffer penalties than communities where blacks, Hispanics and other minorities live. This unequal protection often occurs whether the community is wealthy or poor.[15] These findings suggest that unequal protection is placing communities of color at special risk.
>
> The *National Law Journal* study supplements the findings of earlier studies and reinforces what many grassroots leaders have been saying all along: not only are

people of color differentially impacted by industrial pollution they can expect different treatment from the government. Environmental decision-making operates at the juncture of science, economics, politics, special interests, and ethics. This current environmental model places communities of color at special risk.

The Impact of Racial Apartheid

Apartheid-type housing, development, and environmental policies limit mobility, reduce neighborhood options, diminish job opportunities, and decrease choices for millions of Americans.[16] The infrastructure conditions in urban areas are a result of a host of factors including the distribution of wealth, patterns of racial and economic discrimination, redlining, housing and real estate practices, location decisions of industry, and differential enforcement of land use and environmental choices, and diminished job communities for African Americans.

Race still plays a significant part in distributing public "benefits" and public "burdens" associated with economic growth. The roots of discrimination are deep and have been difficult to eliminate. Housing discrimination contributes to the physical decay of inner-city neighborhoods and denies a substantial segment of the African-American community a basic form of wealth accumulation and investment through home ownership.[17] The number of African-American homeowners would probably be higher in the absence of discrimination by lending institutions.[18] Only about 59 percent of the nation's middle-class African Americans own their homes, compared with 74 percent of whites.

Eight out of every ten African Americans live in neighborhoods where they are in majority. Residential segregation decreases for most racial and ethnic groups with additional education, income, and occupational status. However, this scenario does not hold true for African Americans. African Americans, no matter what their educational or occupational achievement or income level, are exposed to higher crime rates, less effective educational systems, high mortality risks, more dilapidated surroundings, and greater environmental threats because of their race. For example, in the heavily populated South Coast air basin of the Los Angeles area, it is estimated that over 71 percent of African Americans and 50 percent of whites live in highly polluted areas.[19]

It has been difficult for millions of Americans in segregated neighborhoods to say "not in my backyard" (NIMBY) if they do not have a backyard.[20] Nationally, only about 44 percent of African Americans own their homes compared to over two-thirds of the nation as a whole. Homeowners are the strongest advocates of the NIMBY positions taken against locally unwanted uses or LULUs such as the construction of garbage dumps, landfills, incinerators, sewer treatment plants, recycling centers, prisons, drug treatment units, and public housing projects. Generally, white communities have greater access than people-of-color communities when it comes to influencing land use and environmental decision making.

The ability of an individual to escape a health-threatening physical environment is usually related to affluence. However, racial barriers complicate this process for many Americans.[21] The imbalance between residential amenities and land uses assigned to central cities and suburbs cannot be explained by class factors alone. People of color and whites do not have the same opportunities to "vote with their feet" and escape undesirable physical environments.

Institutional racism continues to influence housing and mobility options available to African Americans of all income levels— and is a major factor that influences quality of neighborhoods they have available to them. The "web of discrimination" in the housing market is a result of action and inaction of local and federal government officials, financial institutions, insurance companies, real estate marketing firms, and zoning boards. More stringent enforcement mechanisms and penalties are needed to combat all forms of discrimination.

Uneven development between central cities and suburbs combined with the systematic avoidance of inner-city areas by many businesses have heightened social and economic inequalities. For the past two decades, manufacturing plants have been fleeing central cities and taking their jobs with them. Many have moved offshore to Third-World countries where labor is cheap and environmental regulations are lax or nonexistent.

Industry flight from central cities had left behind a deteriorating urban infrastructure, poverty, and pollution. What kind of replacement industry can these communities attract? Economically depressed communities do not have a lot of choices available to them. Some workers have become so desperate that they see even a low-paying hazardous job as better than no job at all. These workers are forced to choose between unemployment and a job that may result in risks to their health, their family's health, and the health of their community. This practice amounts to "economic blackmail." Economic conditions in many people-of-color communities make them especially vulnerable to this practice.

Some polluting industries have been eager to exploit this vulnerability. Some have even used the assistance of elected officials in obtaining special tax breaks and government operating permits. Clearly, economic development and environmental policies flow from forces of production and are often dominated and subsidized by state actors. Numerous examples abound where state actors have targeted cities and regions for infrastructure improvements and amenities such as water irrigation systems, ship channels, road and bridge projects, and mass transit systems. On the other hand, state actors have done a miserable job in protecting central city residents from the ravages of industrial pollution and nonresidential activities valued as having a negative impact on quality of life.[22]

Racial and ethnic inequality is perpetuated and reinforced by local governments in conjunction with urban-based corporations. Race continues to be a potent variable in explaining urban land use, streets and highway configuration, commercial and industrial development, and industrial facility siting. Moreover, the question of "who gets what, where, and why" often pits one community against another.[23]

Zoning and Land Use

Some residential areas and their inhabitants are at a greater risk than the larger society from unregulated growth, ineffective regulation of industrial toxins, and public policy decisions authorizing industrial facilities that favor those with political and economic clout.[24] African Americans and other communities of color are often victims of land-use decision making that mirrors the power arrangements of the dominant society. Historically, exclusionary zoning (and rezoning) has been a subtle form of using government authority and power to foster and perpetuate discriminatory practices.

Zoning is probably the most widely applied mechanism to regulate urban land use in the United States. Zoning laws broadly define land for residential, commercial, or industrial uses, and may impose narrower land-use restrictions (e.g., minimum and maximum lot size, number of dwellings per acre, square feet and height of buildings, etc.). Zoning ordinances, deed restrictions, and other land-use mechanisms have been widely used as a "NIMBY" tool, operating through exclusionary practices. Thus, exclusionary zoning has been used to zone against something rather than for something. With or without zoning, deed restrictions or other devices, various groups are unequally able to protect their environmental interests. More often than not, people-of-color communities get shortchanged in the neighborhood protection game.

In Houston, Texas, a city that does not have zoning, NIMBY was replaced with the policy of PIBBY (place in black's back yard).[25] The city government and private industry targeted landfills, incinerators, and garbage dumps for Houston's black neighborhoods for more than five decades. These practices lowered residents' property values, accelerated physical deterioration, and increased disinvestment in the communities. Moreover, the discriminatory siting of landfills and incinerators stigmatized the neighborhoods as "dumping grounds" for a host of other unwanted facilities, including salvage yards, recycling operations, and automobile "chop shops."[26]

The Commission for Racial Justice's landmark *Toxic Wastes and Race* study found race to be the single most important factor (i.e., more important than income, home ownership rate, and property values) in the location of abandoned toxic waste sites.[27] The study also found that (1) three out of five African Americans live in communities with abandoned toxic waste sites; (2) sixty percent (15 million) African Americans live in communities with one or more abandoned toxic waste sites; (3) three of the five largest commercial hazardous waste landfills are located in predominately African American or Latino communities and accounts for 40 percent of the nation's total estimated landfill capacity; and (4) African Americans are heavily overrepresented in the population of cities with the largest number of abandoned toxic waste sites, which include Memphis, St. Louis, Houston, Cleveland, Chicago, and Atlanta.

Waste facility siting imbalances that were uncovered by the U.S. General Accounting Office (GAO) in 1983 have not disappeared.[28] The GAO discovered three out of four of the offsite commercial hazardous waste landfills in Region IV (Alabama, Florida, Georgia, Kentucky, Mississippi, North Carolina, South Carolina, and Tennessee) were located in predominately African American communities. African Americans still made up about one-fifth of the population in EPA Region IV. In 2000, 100 percent of the off-site commercial hazardous wastes landfills in the region is dumped in two mostly African-American communities.

Environmental Racism

Many of the differences in environmental quality between black and white communities result from institutional racism influences local land use, enforcement of environmental regulations, industrial facility siting, and where people of color live, work and play. The roots of institutional racism are deep and have been difficult to eliminate. Discrimination is a manifestation of institutional racism and causes life to be very different for whites and blacks. Historically, racism has been and continues to be a major part of the American sociological system, and as a result, people of color find themselves at a disadvantage in contemporary society.

Environmental racism is real. It is just as real as the racism found in the housing industry, educational institutions, employment arena, and judicial system. What is environmental racism and how does one recognize it?

Environmental racism refers to any policy, practice, or directive that differentially affects or disadvantages (whether intended or unintended) individuals, groups, or communities based on race or color. Environmental racism combines with public policies and industry practices to provide benefits for whites while shifting costs to people of color.[29] Environmental racism is reinforced by government, legal, economic, political, and military institutions.

Environmental decision making and policies often mirror the power arrangements of the dominant society and its institutions. Environmental racism disadvantages people of color while providing advantages or privileges for whites. A form of illegal "exaction" forces people of color to pay costs of environmental benefits for the public at large. The question of who *pays* and who *benefits* from the current environmental and industrial policies is central to this analysis of environmental racism and other systems of domination and exploitation.

Racism influences the likelihood of exposure to environmental and health risks as well as accessibility to health care.[30] Many of the nation's environmental policies distribute the costs in a regressive pattern while providing disproportionate benefits for whites and individuals who fall at the upper end of the education and income scale. Numerous studies, dating back to the seventies, reveal that people of color have borne greater health and environmental risk burdens than the society at large.[31]

Elevated public health risks are found in some populations even when social class is held constant. For example, race has been found to be independent of class in the distribution of air pollution,[32] contaminated fish consumption,[33] location of municipal landfills and incinerators,[34] toxic waste dumps,[35] cleanup of superfund sites,[36] and lead poisoning in children.[37]

Lead poisoning is a classic example of an environmental health problem that disproportionately impacts children of color at every class level. Lead affects between 3 to 4 million children in the United States—most of whom are African-American and Latinos who live in urban areas. Among children 5 years old and younger, the percentage of African-American children who have excessive levels of lead in their blood far exceeds the percentage of whites at all income levels.

In 1988, the federal Agency for Toxic Substances Disease Registry (ATSDR) found that for families earning less than $6,000, 68 percent of African-American children had lead poisoning, compared with 36 percent for white children. In families with income exceeding $15,000, more than 38 percent of African-American children suffer from lead poisoning compared with 12 percent of whites. The average blood-lead level has dropped for all children with the phasing out of leaded gasoline. Today, the average blood-lead level for all children in the U.S. is under 6 ug/dl.[38] However, these efforts have not had the same positive benefits on all populations. There is still work to be done to address the remaining problem. The lead problem is not randomly distributed across the nation. The most vulnerable populations are low income African-American and Hispanic-American children who live in older urban housing.[39]

Figures reported in the July 1994 *Journal of American Medical Association* on the Third National Health and Nutrition Examination Survey (NHANES III) revealed that 1.7 million children (8.9 percent of children aged 1 to 5) are lead poisoned, defined as blood-lead levels equal to or above 10 ug/dl.[40] Lead-based paint (chips and dust) is the most common source of lead exposure for children. Children may also be exposed through soil and dust contamination built up from vehicle exhaust, lead concentration in soils in urban areas, lead dust brought into the home on parents work clothes, lead used in ceramics and pottery, folk medicines, and lead in plumbing.

The Right to Breathe Clean Air

Urban air pollution problems have been with us for some time now. Before the federal government stepped in, issues related to air pollution were handled primarily by states and local government. Because states and local governments did such a poor job, the federal government set out to establish national clean air standards. Congress enacted the Clean Air Act (CAA) in 1970 and mandated the U.S. Environmental Protection Agency (EPA) to carry out this law. Subsequent amendments (1977 and 1990) were made to the CAA that form the current federal program. The CAA was a response to states' unwillingness to protect air quality. Many states used their lax enforcement of environmental laws as lures for business and economic development.[41]

Central cities and suburbs do not operate on a level playing field. They often compete for scarce resources. One need not be a rocket scientist to predict the outcome between affluent suburbs and their less affluent central city competitors.[42] Freeways are the lifeline for suburban commuters, while millions of central-city residents are dependent on public transportation as their primary mode of travel. But recent cuts in mass transit subsidies and fare hikes have reduced access to essential social services and economic activities. Nevertheless, road construction programs are booming—even in areas choked with automobiles and air pollution.[43]

The air quality impacts of transportation are especially significant to people of color who are more likely than whites to live in urban areas with reduced air quality. National Argonne Laboratory researchers discovered that 437 of the 3,109 counties and independent cities failed to meet at least one of the EPA ambient air quality standards.[44] Specifically, 57 percent of whites, 65 percent of African Americans, and 80 percent of Hispanics live in 437 counties with substandard air quality. Nationwide, 33 percent of whites, 50 percent of African Americans, and 60 percent of Hispanics live in the 136 counties in which two or more air pollutants exceed standards. Similar patterns were found for the 29 counties designated as nonattainment areas for three or more pollutants. Again, 12 percent of whites, 20 percent of African Americans, and 31 percent of Hispanics resided in the worse nonattainment areas.

Asthma is an emerging epidemic in the United States. The annual age-adjusted death rate from asthma increased by 40% between 1982 through 1991, from 1.34 to 1.88 per 100,000 population,[45] with the highest rates being consistently reported among blacks aged 15–24 years of age during the period 1980–1993.[46] Poverty and minority status are important risk factors for asthma mortality.

Children are at special risk from ozone.[47] Children also represent a considerable share of the asthma burden. It is the most common chronic disease of childhood. Asthma affects almost 5 million children under 18 years. Although the overall annual age-adjusted hospital discharge rate for asthma among children under 15 years old decreased slightly from 184 to 179 per 100,000 between 1982 and 1992, the decrease was slower compared to other childhood diseases[48] resulting in a 70% increase in the proportion of hospital admissions related to asthma during the 1980s.[49] Inner-city children have the highest rates for asthma prevalence, hospitalization, and mortality.[50] In the United States, asthma is the fourth leading cause of disability among children aged less than 18 years.[51]

The public health community has insufficient information to explain the magnitude of some of the air pollution-related health problems. However, they do know that persons suffering from asthma are particularly sensitive to the effects of carbon monoxide, sulfur dioxide's particulate matter, ozone, and nitrogen oxides. Ground-level ozone may

exacerbate health problems such as asthma, nasal congestions, throat irritation, respiratory tract inflammation, reduced resistance to infection, changes in cell function, loss of lung elasticity, chest pains, lung scarring, formation of lesions within the lungs, and premature aging of lung tissues.[52]

Nationally, African Americans and Latino Americans have significantly higher prevalence of asthma than the general population. A 1996 report from the federal Centers for Disease Control shows hospitalization and deaths rates from asthma increasing for persons twenty-five years or less.[53] The greatest increases occurred among African Americans. African Americans are two to six times more likely than whites to die from asthma.[54] Similarly, the hospitalization rate for African Americans is 3 to 4 times the rate for whites.

A 1994 CDC-sponsored study showed that pediatric emergency department visits at Atlanta Grady Memorial Hospital increased by one-third following peak ozone levels. The study also found that asthma rate among African-American children is 26 percent higher than the asthma rate among whites.[55] Since children with asthma in Atlanta may not have visited the emergency department for their care, the true prevalence of asthma in the community is likely to be higher.

Exploitation of Land, Environment, and People

Environmental decision-making and local land-use planning operate at the juncture of science, economics, politics, and special interests that place communities of color at special risk.[56] This is especially true in America's Deep South. The Deep South has always been thought of as a backward land based on its social, economic, political, and environmental policies. By default, the region became a "sacrifice zone," a sump for the rest of the nation's toxic waste.[57] A colonial mentality exists in the South where local government and big business take advantage of people who are politically and economically powerless. Many of these attitudes emerged from the region's marriage to slavery and the plantation system—a brutal system that exploited humans and the land.[58] The Deep South is stuck with this unique legacy—the legacy of slavery, Jim Crow, and white resistance to equal justice for all. This legacy has also affected race relations and the region's ecology. Southerners, black and white, have less education, lower incomes, higher infant mortality, and lower life expectancy than Americans elsewhere. It should be no surprise that the environmental quality that Southerners enjoy is markedly different from that of other regions of the country.

The South is characterized by "look-the-other-way environmental policies and give-away tax breaks."[59] It is our nation's Third World where "political bosses encourage outsiders to buy the region's human and natural resources at bargain prices."[60] Lax enforcement of environmental regulations have left the region's air, water, and land the most industry-befouled in the United States.

Toxic waste discharge and industrial pollution are correlated with poorer economic conditions. Louisiana typifies this pattern. Nearly three-fourths of Louisiana's population—more than 3 million people—get their drinking water from underground aquifers. Dozens of the aquifers are threatened by contamination from polluting industries.[61] The Lower Mississippi River Industrial Corridor has over 125 companies that manufacture a range of products including fertilizers, gasoline, paints, and plastics. This corridor has been dubbed "Cancer Alley" by environmentalists and local residents.[62] Ascension Parish typifies what many people refer to as a toxic "sacrifice zone." In two parish towns of Geismer and St. Gabriel, 18 petrochemical plants are crammed into a nine-and-a-half-square mile area. Petrochemical plants discharge millions of pounds of pollutants annually into the water and air.

Louisiana citizens subsidize this corporate welfare with their health and the environment. Tax breaks given to polluting industries have created a few jobs at high cost. Nowhere is the polluter-welfare scenario more prevalent than in Louisiana. The state is a leader in doling out corporate welfare to polluters. A 1998 *Time Magazine* article reported that in the 1990s, Louisiana wiped off the books $3.1 billion in property taxes to polluting companies.[63] The state's top five worse polluters received $111 million dollars over the past decade.

Global Dumping Grounds

There is a direct correlation between exploitation of land and exploitation of people. It should not be a surprise to anyone to discover that Native Americans have to contend with some of the worst pollution in the United States.[64] Native American nations have become prime targets for waste trading.[65] More than three dozen Indian reservations have been targeted for landfills, incinerators, and other waste facilities.[66] The vast majority of these waste proposals were defeated by grassroots groups on the reservations. However, "radioactive colonialism" is alive and well.[67] The legacy of institutional racism has left many sovereign Indian nations without an economic infrastructure to address poverty, unemployment, inadequate education and health care, and a host of other social problems. In 1999, Eastern Navajo reservation residents filed suit against the Nuclear Regulatory Commission to block uranium mining in Church Rock and Crown Point communities.

Hazardous waste generation and international movement of hazardous waste pose some important health, environmental, legal, and ethical dilemmas. It is unlikely that many of the global hazardous waste proposals can be effectuated without first addressing the social, economic, and political context in which hazardous wastes are produced (industrial processes), controlled (regulations, notification and consent documentation), and managed (minimization, treatment, storage, recycled, transboundary shipment, pollution prevention, etc.). The "unwritten" policy of targeting Third-World nations for waste trade received international media attention in 1991. Lawrence Summers, at the time he was chief economists of the World Bank, shocked the world and touched off an international scandal when his confidential memorandum on waste trade was leaked. Summers writes: "'Dirty' Industries: Just between you and me, shouldn't the World Bank be encouraging MORE migration of the dirty industries to the LDCs?"[68]

Consumption and production patterns, especially in nations with wasteful "throwaway" life styles as the United States, and the interests of transnational corporations create and maintain unequal and unjust waste burdens within and between affluent and poor communities, states, and regions of the world. Shipping hazardous wastes from rich communities to poor communities is not a solution to the growing global waste problem. Not only is it immoral, but it should be illegal. Moreover, making hazardous waste transactions legal does not address the ethical issues imbedded in such transactions.[69] The practice is a manifestation of power arrangements and a larger stratification system where some people and some places are assigned greater value than others.

In the real world, all people, communities, and nations are not created equal. Some populations and interests are more equal than others. Unequal interests and power

arrangements have allowed poisons of the rich to be offered as short term remedies for poverty of the poor. This scenario plays out domestically (as in the United States where low-income and people-of-color communities are disproportionately impacted by waste facilities and "dirty" industries) and internationally (where hazardous wastes move from OECD states flow to non-OECD states).

The conditions surrounding the more than 1,900 maquiladoras, assembly plants operated by American, Japanese, and other foreign countries, located along the 2,000-mile U.S.-Mexico border may further exacerbate the waste trade.[70] The industrial plants use cheap Mexican labor to assemble imported components and raw material and then ship finished products back to the United States. Nearly a half million Mexican workers are employed in the maquiladoras.

A 1983 agreement between the United States and Mexico required American companies in Mexico to return waste products to the United States. Plants were required to notify the federal EPA when returning wastes. Results from a 1986 survey of 20 of the plants informed the U.S. EPA that they were returning waste to the United States, even though 86 percent of the plants used toxic chemicals in their manufacturing process. Much of the waste ends up being illegally dumped in sewers, ditches, and the desert. All along the Lower Rio Grande River Valley maquiladoras dump their toxic wastes into the river, from which 95 percent of the region's residents get their drinking water.[71]

The disregard for the environment and public safety has placed border residents' health at risk. In the border cities of Brownsville, Texas, and Matamoras, Mexico, the rate of anecephaly—babies born without brains—is four times the national average. Affected families have filed lawsuits against 88 of the area's 100 maquiladoras for exposing the community to xylene, a cleaning solvent that can cause brain hemorrhages, and lung and kidney damage.

Contaminated well and drinking water looms as major health threats. Air pollution has contributed to a raging asthma and respiratory epidemic. The Mexican environmental regulatory agency is understaffed and "ill-equipped to adequately enforce its environmental laws."[72] Only time will tell if the North American Free Trade Agreement (NAFTA) will "fix" or exacerbate the public health, economic, and environmental problems along the U.S.-Mexico border.

Setting the Record Straight

The environmental protection apparatus is broken and needs to be fixed. The environmental justice movement has set out clear goals of eliminating unequal enforcement of environmental, civil rights, and public health laws. Environmental justice leaders have made a difference in the lives of people and the physical environment. They have assisted public decision makers in identifying "at risk" populations, toxic "hot spots," research gaps, and action models to correct existing imbalances and prevent future threats. However, impacted communities are not waiting for the government or industry to get their acts together. Grassroots groups have taken the offensive to ensure that government and industry do the right thing.

Communities have begun to organize their own networks and force their inclusion into the mainstream of public decision making. They have also developed communication channels among environmental justice leaders, grassroots groups, professional associations (i.e., legal, public health, education, etc.), scientific groups, public policy makers to assist them in identifying "at-risk" populations, toxic "hot spots," research gaps, and work to correct imbalances.

In response to growing public concern and mounting scientific evidence, President Clinton signed Executive Order 12898. The Executive Order is not a new law. It only reinforces what has been the law of the land for over three decades. Environmental justice advocates are calling for vigorous enforcement of civil rights laws and environmental laws.

The number of environmental justice complaints is expected to escalate against industry, government, and institutions that receive funds. Citizens have a right to challenge discrimination—including environmental discrimination. It is a smokescreen for anyone to link Title VI or other civil rights enforcement to economic disinvestment in low-income and people-of-color communities. There is absolutely no empirical evidence to support the contention that environmental justice hurts Brownfields redevelopment efforts.

The ERA has awarded over 200 Brownfield grants. In 1998, the agency had received some five dozen Title VI complaints. It is worth noting that not a single Title VI complaint involves a Brownfields site. On the other hand, two decades of solid empirical evidence documents the impact of racial redlining by banks, savings and loans, insurance companies, grocery chains, and even pizza delivery companies thwarts economic vitality in black communities—not enforcement of civil rights laws. Racial redlining was such a real problem that Congress passed the Community Reinvestment Act in 1977.

States have had three decades to implement Title VI of the Civil Rights Act of 1964. Most states have chosen to ignore the law. States need to do a better job assuring non-discrimination in the application and the implementation of permitting decisions, enforcement, and investment decisions. Environmental justice also means sharing in the benefits. Governments must live up to their mandate of protecting all people and the environment. Anything less is unacceptable. The solution to environmental injustice lies in the realm of equal protection of all individuals, groups, and communities. No community, rich or poor, urban or suburban, black or white, should be allowed to become a "sacrifice zone" or the dumping ground.

Hazardous wastes and "dirty" industries have followed the "path of least resistance." Poor people and poor communities are given a false choice of "no jobs and no development" versus "risky low-paying jobs and pollution." Industries and governments (including the military) have often exploited the economic vulnerability of poor communities, poor states, poor regions, and poor nations for their "risky" operations. The environmental racism, and the international toxics trade at home and abroad.

NOTES

1. Robert D. Bullard, 1994, *Dumping in Dixie: Race, Class and Environmental Quality.* Boulder, CO: Westview Press.

2. Robert D. Bullard, "Solid Waste Sites and the Black Houston Community," *Sociological Inquiry* 53 (Spring 1983): 273–288.

3. U.S. General Accounting Office (1983), *Siting of Hazardous Waste Landfills and Their Correlation with Racial and Economic Status of Surrounding Communities,* Washington, DC: Government Printing Office.

4. Commission for Racial Justice (1987), *Toxic Wastes and Race in the United States,* New York: United Church of Christ.

5. Charles Lee, 1992, *Proceedings: The First National People of Color Environmental Leadership Summit.* New York: United Church of Christ Commission for Racial Justice.

6. Dana Alston, "Transforming a Movement: People of Color Unite at Summit against Environmental Racism," *Sojourner* 21 (1992), pp. 30–31.

7. William K. Reilly, "Environmental Equity: EPA's Position," *EPA Journal* 18 (March/April 1992): 18–19.

8. R. D. Bullard and B. H. Wright, "The Politics of Pollution: Implications for the Black Community," *Phylon* 47 (March 1986): 71–78.

9. Robert D. Bullard, "Race and Environmental Justice in the United States," *Yale Journal of International Law* 18 (Winter 1993): 319–335; Robert D. Bullard, "The Threat of Environmental Racism," *Natural Resources & Environment* 7 (Winter 1993): 23–26, 55–56.

10. Louis Sullivan, "Remarks at the First Annual Conference on Childhood Lead Poisoning," in Alliance to End Childhood Lead Poisoning: Final Report. Washington DC: Alliance to End Childhood Lead Poisoning, October, 1991, p. A-2.

11. Bill Lann Lee, "Environmental Litigation on Behalf of Poor, Minority Children, *Matthews v. Coye:* A Case Study." Paper presented at the Annual Meeting of the American Association for the Advancement of Science, Chicago (February 9, 1992).

12. Ibid., p. 32.

13. Ibid.

14. Robert D. Bullard, "The Environmental Justice Framework: A Strategy for Addressing Unequal Protection." Paper presented at Resources for the Future Conference on Risk Management, Annapolis, MD (November 1992).

15. Paul Mohai and Bunyan Bryant, "Race, Poverty, and the Environment," *EPA Journal* 18 (March/April 1993): 1–8; R. D. Bullard, "In Our Backyards," *EPA Journal* 18 (March/April 1992): 11–12; D. R. Wernette and L. A. Nieves, "Breathing Polluted Air," *EPA Jounal* 18 (March/April 1992): 16–17; Patrick C. West, "Health Concerns for Fish-Eating Tribes?" *EPA Journal* 18 (March/April 1992): 15–16.

16. Marianne Lavelle and Marcia Coyle, "Unequal Protection," *National Law Journal* (September 21, 1992): S1–S2.

17. Robert D. Bullard, ed., *Confronting Environmental Racism: Voices from the Grassroots.* Boston: South End Press. 1993, chapter 1; Robert D. Bullard, "Waste and Racism: A Stacked Deck?" *Forum for Applied Research and Public Policy* 8 (Spring 1993): 29–35; Robert D. Bullard (ed.), *In Search of the New South—The Black Urban Experience in the 1970s and 1980s* (Tuscaloosa, AL: University of Alabama Press, 1991).

18. Florence Wagman Roisman, "The Lessons of American Apartheid: The Necessity and Means

of Promoting Residential Racial Integration," *Iowa Law Review* 81 (December 1995): 479–525.

19. Joe R. Feagin, "A House Is Not A Home: White Racism and U.S. Housing Practices," in R. D. Bullard, J. E. Grigsby, and Charles Lee, eds., *Residential Apartheid: The American Legacy*. Los Angeles: UCLA Center for Afro-American Studies Publication, 1994, pp. 17–48.

20. Eric Mann, *L.A.'s Lethal Air: New Strategies for Policy, Organizing, and Action*. Los Angeles: Labor/Community Strategy Center, 1991, p. 31.

21. Jim Motavalli, "Toxic Targets: Polluters that Dump on Communities of Color are Finally Being Brought to Justice," *E Magazine*, 4 (July/August 1997): 29–41.

22. Joe Bandy, "Reterritorializing Borders: Transnational Environmental Justice on the U.S./Mexico Border," *Race, Gender, and Class* 5 (1997): 80–103.

23. Bunyan Bryant and Paul Mohai, *Race and the Incidence of Environmental Hazards* (Boulder, CO: Westview Press, 1992); Bunyan Bryant, ed., *Environmental Justice*, pp. 8–34.

24. R. Pinderhughes, "Who Decides What Constitutes a Pollution Problem?" *Race, Gender, and Class* 5 (1997): 130–152.

25. Diane Takvorian, "Toxics and Neighborhoods Don't Mix," *Land Use Forum: A Journal of Law, Policy and Practice* 2 (Winter 1993): 28–31; R. D. Bullard, "Examining the Evidence of Environmental Racism," *Land Use Forum: A Journal of Law, Policy, and Practice* 2 (Winter 1993): 6–11.

26. For an in-depth examination of the Houston case study, see R. D. Bullard, 1987, *Invisible Houston: The Black Experience in Boom and Bust*. College Station, TX: Texas A&M University Press, pp. 60–75.

27. Ruth Rosen, "Who Gets Polluted: The Movement for Environmental Justice," *Dissent* (Spring 1994): 223–230; R. D. Bullard, "Environmental Justice: It's More than Waste Facility Siting," *Social Science Quarterly* 77 (September 1996): 493–499.

28. Commission for Racial Justice, *Toxic Wastes and Race in the United States*, pp. xiii–xiv.

29. U.S. General Accounting Office, *Siting of Hazardous Waste Landfills and Their Correlation with Racial and Economic Status of Surrounding Communities*. Washington, DC: U.S. General Accounting Office, 1983, p. 1.

30. Robert D. Bullard, ed., *Confusing Environmental Racism: Voices from the Grassroots* Boston: South End, 1993; Robert D. Bullard, "The Threat of Environmental Racism," *Natural Resources & Environment* 7 (Winter 1993): 23–26; Bunyan Bryant and Paul Mohai, eds., *Race and the Incidence of Environmental Hazards*. Boulder, CO: Westview Press, 1992; Regina Austin and Michael Schill, "Black, Brown, Poor and Poisoned: Minority Grassroots Environmentalism and the Quest for Eco-Justice." *The Kansas Journal of Law and Public Policy* 1 (1991): 69–82; Kelly C. Colquette and Elizabeth A. Henry Robertson, "Environmental Racism: The Causes, Consequences, and Commendations." *Tulane Environmental Law Journal* 5 (1991): 153–207; Rachel D. Godsil, "Remedying Environmental Racism." *Michigan Law Review* 90 (1991): 394–427.

31. Bullard and Feagin, "Racism and the City," pp. 55–76; Robert D. Bullard, "Dismantling Environmental Racism in the USA," *Local Environment* 4 (1999): 5–19.

32. W. J. Kruvant, "People, Energy, and Pollution." Pp. 125–167 in D. K. Newman and Dawn Day, eds., *The American Energy Consumer*. Cambridge, Mass.: Ballinger, 1975; Robert D. Bullard, "Solid Waste Sites and the Black Houston Community." *Sociological Inquiry* 53 (Spring 1983): 273–288; United Church of Christ Commission for Racial Justice, *Toxic Wastes and Race in the United States*. New York: Commission for Racial Justice, 1987; Dick Russell, "Environmental Racism," *The Amicus Journal* 11 (Spring 1989): 22–32; Eric Mann, *L.A.'s Lethal Air: New Strategies for Policy, Organizing, and Action*. Los Angeles: Labor/Community Strategy Center, 1991; D. R. Wernette and L.A. Nieves, "Breathing Polluted Air: Minorities are Disproportionately Exposed." *EPA Journal* 18 (March/April 1992): 16–17; Bryant and Mohai, Race and the Incidence of Environmental Hazards; Benjamin Goldman and Laura J. Fitton, *Toxic Wastes and Race Revisited*. Washington, DC: Center for Policy Alternatives; NAACP, and United Church of Christ, 1994.

33. Myrick A. Freedman, "The Distribution of Environmental Quality." In Allen V. Kneese and Blair T. Bower (eds.), *Environmental Quality Analysis*. Baltimore: Johns Hopkins

University Press for Resources for the Future, 1971; Michael Gelobter, "The Distribution of Air Pollution by Income and Race." Paper presented at the Second Symposium on Social Science in Resource Management, Urbana, Illinois (June 1988); Gianessi et al., "The Distributional Effects of Uniform Air Pollution Policy in the U.S." *Quarterly Journal of Economics* (May 1979): 281–301.

34. Patrick C. West, J. Mark Fly, and Robert Marans, "Minority Anglers and Toxic Fish Consumption: Evidence from a State-Wide Survey in Michigan." In Bryant and Mohai, *Race and the Incidence of Environmental Hazards,* pp. 100–113.

35. Robert D. Bullard, "Solid Waste Sites and the Black Houston Community." *Sociological Inquiry* 53 (Spring 1983): 273–288; Robert D. Bullard, *Invisible Houston: The Black Experience in Boom and Bust.* College Station, TX: Texas A&M University Press, 1987, chapter 6; Robert D. Bullard, "Environmental Racism and Land Use." *Land Use Forum: A Journal of Law, Policy & Practice* 2 (Spring 1993): 6–11.

36. United Church of Christ Commission for Racial Justice, *Toxic Wastes and Race;* Paul Mohai and Bunyan Bryant, "Environmental Racism: Reviewing the Evidence." In Bryant and Mohai, *Race and the Incidence of Environmental Hazards;* Paul Stretesky and Michael J. Hogan, "Environmental Justice: An Analysis of Superfund Sites in Florida," *Social Problems* 45 (May 1998): 268–287.

37. Marianne Lavelle and Marcia Coyle, "Unequal Protection: The Racial Divide in Environmental Law." *National Law Journal,* September 21, 1992.

38. Agency for Toxic Substances Disease Registry, *The Nature and Extent of Lead Poisoning in Children in the United States: A Report to Congress.* Atlanta: U.S. Department of Health and Human Resources, 1988, pp. 1–12.

39. J. Schwartz and R. Levine, "Lead: An Example of the Job Ahead," *EPA Journal* 18 (March/April 1992): 32–44.

40. Centers for Disease Control and Prevention, "Update: Blood Lead Levels—United States, 1991–1994," *Mortality and Morbidity Weekly Report* 46, no. 7 (February 21, 1997): 141–146.

41. James L. Pinkle, D. J. Brody, E. W. Gunter, R. A. Kramer, D. C. Paschal, K. M. Glegal, and T. D. Matte, "The Decline in Blood Lead Levels in the United States: The National Health and Nutrition Examination Survey (NHANES)," *Journal of the American Medical Association* 272 (1994): 284–291.

42. Arnold W. Reitze, Jr., "A Century of Air Pollution Control Law: What Worked; What Failed; What Might Work," *Environmental Law* 21 (1991): 1549.

43. For an in-depth discussion of transportation investments and social equity issues, see R. D. Bullard and G. S. Johnson, eds., *Just Transportation: Dismantling Race and Class Barriers to Mobility.* Gabriola Island, BC: New Society Publishers, 1997.

44. Sid Davis, "Race and the Politics of Transportation in Atlanta," in R. D. Bullard and G. S. Johnson, *Just Transportation,* pp. 84–96; Environmental Justice Resource Center, *Sprawl Atlanta: Social Equity Dimensions of Uneven Growth and Development.* A Report prepared for the Turner Foundation, Atlanta: Clark Atlanta University (January 1999).

45. D. R. Wernette and L. A. Nieves, "Breathing Polluted Air: Minorities Are Disproportionately Exposed," *EPA Journal* 18 (March 1992): 16–17.

46. CDC, "Asthma—United States, 1982–1992." *MMWR* 43 (1995): 952–955.

47. CDC, "Asthma morality and hospitalization among children and young adults—United States, 1980–1993." *MMWR* 45 (1996): 350–353.

48. Anna E. Pribitkin, "The Need for Revision of Ozone Standards: Why Has the EPA Failed to Respond?" *Temple Environmental Law & Technology Journal* 13 (1994): 104.

49. CDC/NCHS, *Health United States* 1994. DHHS Pub. No. (PHS) 95-1232; Tables 83, 84, 86 & 87.

50. CDC, "Asthma—United States, 1982–1992." *MMWR* 43 (1995): 952–955.

51. CDC, "Disabilities among children aged less than or equal to 17 years—United States, 1991–1992." *MMWR* 44 (1995): 609–613.

52. U.S. EPA, "Review of National Ambient Air Quality Standards for Ozone, Assessment of Scientific and Technical Information," OAQPS Staff Paper. Research Triangle Park, NC: EPA, 1996; Haluk Ozkaynk, John D. Spengler, Marie O'Neil, Jianping Xue, Hui Zhou, Kathy Gilbert, and Sonja Ramstrom, "Ambient Ozone Exposure and Emergency Hospital Admissions and Emergency Room Visits for Respiratory Problems in Thirteen

U.S. Cities," in American Lung Association, *Breathless: Air Pollution and Hospital Admissions/Emergency Room Visits in 13 Cities.* Washington, DC: American Lung Association, 1996; American Lung Association, *Out of Breath: Populations-at-Risk to Alternative Ozone Levels.* Washington, DC: American Lung Association, 1995.

53. Centers for Disease Control and Prevention, National Center for Environmental Health, Division of Environmental Hazards and Health Effects, Air Pollution and Respiratory Branch, "Asthma Mortality and Hospitalization Among Children and Young Adults— United States, 1980–1993," *Morbidity and Mortality Weekly Report,* 45 (1996)

54. Centers for Disease Control, "Asthma: United States, 1980–1990,"*MMWR* 39 (1992): 733–735.

55. Mary C White, Ruth Etzel, Wallace D. Wilcox, and Christine Lloyd, "Exacerbations of Childhood Asthma and Ozone Pollution in Atlanta," *Environmental Research* 65 (1994), p. 56.

56. R. D. Bullard, "The Legacy of Apartheid and Environmental Racism," *St. John's Journal of Legal Commentary* 9 (Spring, 1994): 445–474.

57. Donald Schueler, "Southern Exposure," *Sierra* 77 (November/December 1992): 45.

58. Robert D. Bullard, "Ecological Inequities and the New South: Black Communities Under Siege." *Journal of Ethnic Studies* 17 (Winter 1990): 101–115; Donald L. Bartlett and James B. Steele, "Paying a Price for Polluters," *Time* (November 23, 1998), pp. 72–80.

59. Schueler, "Southern Exposure," p. 46.

60. Ibid., pp. 46–47.

61. James O'Byrne and Mark Schleifstein, "Drinking Water in Danger," *The Times Picayune,* February 19, 1991, p. A5.

62. Conger Beasley, "Of Poverty and Pollution: Keeping Watch in Cancer Alley," pp. 39–45.

63. Bartlett and Steele, "Paying a Price for Polluters," p. 77.

64. Conger Beasley, "Of Pollutions and Poverty: Deadly Threat on Native Lands," *Buzzworm,* 2 (5) (1990): 39–45; Robert Tomsho, "Dumping Grounds: Indian Tribes Contend with Some of the Worst of America's Pollution," *The Wall Street Journal* (November 29, 1990); Jane Kay, "Indian Lands Targeted for Waste Disposal Sites," *San Francisco Examiner* (April 10, 1991); Valerie Taliman, "Stuck Holding the Nation's Nuclear Waste," *Race, Poverty & Environment Newsletter* (Fall 1992): 6–9.

65. Bradley Angel, *The Toxic Threat to Indian Lands: A Greenpeace Report.* San Francisco: Greenpeace, 1992; Al Geddicks, *The New Resource Wars: Native and Environmental Struggles Against Multinational Corporations.* Boston: South End Press, 1993.

66. Jane Kay, "Indian Lands Targeted for Waste Disposal Sites," *San Francisco Examiner* (April 10, 1991).

67. Ward Churchill and Winona la Duke, "Native America: The Political Economy of Radioactive Colonialism," *Insurgent Sociologist* 13 (1) (1983): 61–63.

68. Greenpeace, "The Logic Behind Hazardous Waste Export," *Greenpeace Waste Trade Update* (First Quarter 1992): 1–2.

69. Dana Alston and Nicole Brown, "Global Threats to People of Color," pp. 179–194 in R. D. Bullard, ed., *Confronting Environmental Racism: Voices from the Grassroots.* Boston: Southend Press, 1993.

70. Roberto Sanchez, "Health and Environmental Risks of the Maquiladora in Mexicali," *Natural Resources Journal* 30 (1) (1990): 163–186.

71. Beatriz Johnston Hernandez, "Dirty Growth," *The New Environmentalist* (August 1993).

72. T. Barry and B. Simms, *The Challenge of Cross Border Environmentalism: The U.S. Mexico Case,* Albuquerque, NM: The Inter-Hemispheric Education Resource Center, 1994.

24

SAVAGE INEQUALITIES

Jonathan Kozol

QUESTIONS TO CONSIDER

It is a core belief in the United States that every child has the right to a high-quality education. We also subscribe to the belief that education is the path to upward, intergenerational mobility. In this reading Jonathan Kozol compares schools in poor, overwhelmingly nonwhite communities and middle-class, primarily white communities and finds that they are grossly and "savagely" unequal. Schools in poor neighborhoods lack basic supplies and are dirty and overcrowded; schools located in affluent suburbs have the newest textbooks, up-to-date libraries, advanced placement classes, and small student-to-teacher ratios. How do race, class, schooling, and the potential for upward socioeconomic mobility intersect in Kozol's study?

I n a country where there is no distinction of class," Lord Acton wrote of the United States 130 years ago, "a child is not born to the station of its parents, but with an indefinite claim to all the prizes that can be won by thought and labor. It is in conformity with the theory of equality . . . to give as near as possible to every youth an equal stake in life."[1] Americans, he said, "are unwilling that any should be deprived in childhood of the means of competition."

It is hard to read these words today without a sense of irony and sadness. Denial of "the means of competition" is perhaps the single most consistent outcome of the education offered to poor children in the schools of our large cities; and nowhere is this pattern

of denial more explicit or more absolute than in the public schools of New York City.

Average expenditures per pupil in the city of New York in 1987 were some $5,500. In the highest spending suburbs of New York (Great Neck or Manhasset, for example, on Long Island) funding levels rose above $11,000, with the highest districts in the state at $15,000.[2] "Why . . .", asks the city's Board of Education, "should our students receive less" than do "similar students" who live elsewhere? "The inequity is clear."[3]

But the inequality to which these words refer goes even further than the school board may be eager to reveal. "It is perhaps the supreme irony," says the nonprofit Community Service Society of New York, that "the same Board of Education which perceives so clearly the inequities" of funding between separate towns and cities "is perpetuating similar inequities" right in New York. And, in comment on the Board of Education's final statement—"the inequity is clear"—the

From *Savage Inequalities* by Jonathan Kozol. Copyright © 1991 by Jonathan Kozol. Used by permission of Crown Publishers, a division of Random House, Inc.

CSS observes, "New York City's poorest . . . districts could adopt that eloquent statement with few changes."

New York City's public schools are subdivided into 32 school districts. District 10 encompasses a large part of the Bronx but is, effectively, two separate districts. One of these districts, Riverdale, is in the northwest section of the Bronx. Home to many of the city's most sophisticated and well-educated families, its elementary schools have relatively few low-income students. The other section, to the south and east, is poor and heavily nonwhite.

The contrast between public schools in each of these two neighborhoods is obvious to any visitor. At Public School 24 in Riverdale, the principal speaks enthusiastically of his teaching staff. At Public School 79, serving poorer children to the south, the principal says that he is forced to take the "tenth-best" teachers. "I thank God they're still breathing," he remarks of those from whom he must select his teachers.

Some years ago, District 10 received an allocation for computers. The local board decided to give each elementary school an equal number of computers, even though the schools in Riverdale had smaller classes and far fewer students. When it was pointed out that schools in Riverdale, as a result, had twice the number of computers in proportion to their student populations as the schools in the poor neighborhoods, the chairman of the local board replied, "What is fair is what is determined . . . to be fair."

The superintendent of District 10, Fred Goldberg, tells *The New York Times* that "every effort" is made "to distribute resources equitably." He speculates that some gap might exist because some of the poorer schools need to use funds earmarked for computers to buy basic supplies like pens and paper. Asked about the differences in teachers noted by the principals, he says there are no differences, then adds that next

year he'll begin a program to improve the quality of teachers in the poorer schools. Questioned about differences in physical appearances between the richer and the poorer schools, he says, "I think it's demographics."[4]

Sometimes a school principal, whatever his background or his politics, looks into the faces of the children in his school and offers a disarming statement that cuts through official ambiguity. "These are the kids most in need," says Edward Flanery, the principal of one of the low-income schools, "and they get the worst teachers." For children of diverse needs in his overcrowded rooms, he says, "you need an outstanding teacher. And what do you get? You get the worst."

In order to find Public School 261 in District 10, a visitor is told to look for a mortician's office. The funeral home, which faces Jerome Avenue in the North Bronx, is easy to identify by its green awning. The school is next door, in a former roller-skating rink. No sign identifies the building as a school. A metal awning frame without an awning supports a flagpole, but there is no flag.

In the street in front of the school there is an elevated public transit line. Heavy traffic fills the street. The existence of the school is virtually concealed within this crowded city block.

In a vestibule between the outer and inner glass doors of the school there is a sign with these words: "All children are capable of learning."

Beyond the inner doors a guard is seated. The lobby is long and narrow. The ceiling is low. There are no windows. All the teachers that I see at first are middle-aged white women. The principal, who is also a white woman, tells me that the school's "capacity" is 900 but that there are 1,300 children here. The size of classes for fifth and sixth grade children in New York, she says, is "capped" at 32, but she says that class size in the school goes "up to 34." (I later see classes, however, as large as 37.) Classes for younger children, she goes on, are "capped at 25," but a school can go above this limit if it puts an extra adult in the room. Lack of space, she says, prevents the school from operating a pre-kindergarten program.

I ask the principal where her children go to school. They are enrolled in private school, she says.

"Lunchtime is a challenge for us," she explains. "Limited space obliges us to do it in three shifts, 450 children at a time."

Textbooks are scarce and children have to share their social studies books. The principal says there is one full-time pupil counselor and another who is here two days a week: a ratio of 930 children to one counselor. The carpets are patched and sometimes taped together to conceal an open space. "I could use some new rugs," she observes.

To make up for the building's lack of windows and the crowded feeling that results, the staff puts plants and fish tanks in the corridors. Some of the plants are flourishing. Two boys, released from class, are in a corridor beside a tank, their noses pressed against the glass. A school of pinkish fish inside the tank are darting back and forth. Farther down the corridor a small Hispanic girl is watering the plants.

Two first grade classes share a single room without a window, divided only by a blackboard. Four kindergartens and a sixth grade class of Spanish-speaking children have been packed into a single room in which, again, there is no window. A second grade bilingual class of 37 children has its own room but again there is no window.

By eleven o'clock, the lunchroom is already packed with appetite and life. The kids line up to get their meals, then eat them in ten minutes. After that, with no place they can go to play, they sit and wait until it's time to line up and go back to class.

On the second floor I visit four classes taking place within another undivided space. The room has a low ceiling. File cabinets and movable blackboards give a small degree of isolation to each class. Again, there are no windows.

The library is a tiny, windowless and claustrophobic room. I count approximately 700 books. Seeing no reference books, I ask a teacher if encyclopedias and other reference books are kept in classrooms.

"We don't have encyclopedias in classrooms," she replies. "That is for the suburbs."

The school, I am told, has 26 computers for its 1,300 children. There is one small gym and children get one period, and sometimes two, each week. Recess, however, is not possible because there is no playground. "Head Start," the principal says, "scarcely exists in District 10. We have no space."

The school, I am told, is 90 percent black and Hispanic; the other 10 percent are Asian, white or Middle Eastern.

In a sixth grade social studies class the walls are bare of words or decorations. There seems to be no ventilation system, or, if one exists, it isn't working.

The class discusses the Nile River and the Fertile Crescent.

The teacher, in a droning voice: "How is it useful that these civilizations developed close to rivers?"

A child, in a good loud voice: "What kind of question is that?"

In my notes I find these words: "An uncomfortable feeling—being in a building with no windows. There are metal ducts across the room. Do they give air? I feel asphyxiated. . . ."

On the top floor of the school, a sixth grade of 30 children shares a room with 29 bilingual second graders. Because of the high class size there is an assistant with each teacher. This means that 59 children and four grown-ups—63 in all—must share a room that, in a suburban school, would hold no more than 20 children and one teacher. There are, at least, some outside windows in this room—it is the only room with windows in the school—and the room has a high ceiling. It is a relief to see some daylight.

I return to see the kindergarten classes on the ground floor and feel stifled once again by lack of air and the low ceiling. Nearly 120 children and adults are doing what they can to make the best of things: 80 children in four kindergarten classes, 30 children in the sixth grade class, and about eight grown-ups who are aides and teachers. The kindergarten children sitting on the worn rug, which is patched with tape, look up at me and turn their heads to follow me as I walk past them.

As I leave the school, a sixth grade teacher stops to talk. I ask her, "Is there air conditioning in warmer weather?"

Teachers, while inside the building, are reluctant to give answers to this kind of question. Outside, on the sidewalk, she is less constrained: "I had an awful room last year. In the winter it was 56 degrees. In the summer it was up to 90. It was sweltering."

I ask her, "Do the children ever comment on the building?"

"They don't say," she answers, "but they know."

I ask her if they see it as a racial message.

"All these children see TV," she says. "They know what suburban schools are like. Then they look around them at their school. This was a roller-rink, you know. . . . They don't comment on it but you see it in their eyes. They understand."

On the following morning I visit P.S. 79, another elementary school in the same district. "We work under difficult circumstances," says the principal, James Carter, who is black. "The school was built to hold one thousand students. We have 1,550. We are badly over-crowded. We need smaller classes but, to do this, we would need more space. I can't add

five teachers. I would have no place to put them."

Some experts, I observe, believe that class size isn't a real issue. He dismisses this abruptly. "It doesn't take a genius to discover that you learn more in a smaller class. I have to bus some 60 kindergarten children elsewhere, since I have no space for them. When they return next year, where do I put them?

"I can't set up a computer lab. I have no room. I had to put a class into the library. I have no librarian. There are two gymnasiums upstairs but they cannot be used for sports. We hold more classes there. It's unfair to measure us against the suburbs. They have 17 to 20 children in a class. Average class size in this school is 30.

"The school is 29 percent black, 70 percent Hispanic. Few of these kids get Head Start. There is no space in the district. Of 200 kindergarten children, 50 maybe get some kind of preschool."

I ask him how much difference preschool makes.

"Those who get it do appreciably better. I can't overestimate its impact but, as I have said, we have no space."

The school tracks children by ability, he says. "There are five to seven levels in each grade. The highest level is equivalent to 'gifted' but it's not a full-scale gifted program. We don't have the funds. We have no science room. The science teachers carry their equipment with them."

We sit and talk within the nurse's room. The window is broken. There are two holes in the ceiling. About a quarter of the ceiling has been patched and covered with a plastic garbage bag.

"Ideal class size for these kids would be 15 to 20. Will these children ever get what white kids in the suburbs take for granted? I don't think so. If you ask me why, I'd have to speak of race and social class. I don't think the powers that be in New York City understand, or want to understand, that if they do not give these children a sufficient education to lead healthy and productive lives, we will be their victims later on. We'll pay the price someday—in violence, in economic costs. I despair of making this appeal in any terms but these. You cannot issue an appeal to conscience in New York today. The fair-play argument won't be accepted. So you speak of violence and hope that it will scare the city into action."

While we talk, three children who look six or seven years old come to the door and ask to see the nurse, who isn't in the school today. One of the children, a Puerto Rican girl, looks haggard. "I have a pain in my tooth," she says. The principal says, "The nurse is out. Why don't you call your mother?" The child says, "My mother doesn't have a phone." The principal sighs. "Then go back to your class." When she leaves, the principal is angry. "It's amazing to me that these children ever make it with the obstacles they face. Many *do* care and they *do* try, but there's a feeling of despair. The parents of these children want the same things for their children that the parents in the suburbs want. Drugs are not the cause of this. They are the symptom. Nonetheless, they're used by people in the suburbs and rich people in Manhattan as another reason to keep children of poor people at a distance."

I ask him, "Will white children and black children ever go to school together in New York?"

"I don't see it," he replies. "I just don't think it's going to happen. It's a dream. I simply do not see white folks in Riverdale agreeing to cross-bus with kids like these. A few, maybe. Very few. I don't think I'll live to see it happen."

I ask him whether race is the decisive factor. Many experts, I observe, believe that wealth is more important in determining these inequalities.

"This," he says—and sweeps his hand around him at the room, the garbage bag, the ceiling—"would not happen to white children."

In a kindergarten class the children sit cross-legged on a carpet in a space between two walls of books. Their 26 faces are turned up to watch their teacher, an elderly black woman. A little boy who sits beside me is involved in trying to tie bows in his shoelaces. The children sing a song: "Lift Every Voice." On the wall are these handwritten words: "Beautiful, also, are the souls of my people."

In a very small room on the fourth floor, 52 people in two classes do their best to teach and learn. Both are first grade classes. One, I am informed, is "low ability." The other is bilingual.

"The room is barely large enough for one class," says the principal.

The room is 25 by 50 feet. There are 26 first graders and two adults on the left, 22 others and two adults on the right. On the wall there is the picture of a small white child, circled by a Valentine, and a Gainsborough painting of a child in a formal dress.

"We are handicapped by scarcity," one of the teachers says. "One fifth of these children may be at grade level by the year's end."

A boy who may be seven years old climbs on my lap without an invitation and removes my glasses. He studies my face and runs his fingers through my hair. "You have nice hair," he says. I ask him where he lives and he replies, "Times Square Hotel," which is a homeless shelter in Manhattan.

I ask him how he gets here.

"With my father. On the train," he says.

"How long does it take?"

"It takes an hour and a half."

I ask him when he leaves his home.

"My mother wakes me up at five o'clock."

"When do you leave?"

"Six-thirty."

I ask him how he gets back to Times Square.

"My father comes to get me after school."

From my notes: "He rides the train three hours every day in order to attend this segregated school. It would be a shorter ride to Riverdale. There are rapid shuttle-vans that make that trip in only 20 minutes. Why not let him go to school right in Manhattan, for that matter?"

At three o'clock the nurse arrives to do her recordkeeping. She tells me she is here three days a week. "The public hospital we use for an emergency is called North Central. It's not a hospital that I will use if I am given any choice. Clinics in the private hospitals are far more likely to be staffed by an experienced physician."

She hesitates a bit as I take out my pen, but then goes on: "I'll give you an example. A little girl I saw last week in school was trembling and shaking and could not control the motions of her arms. I was concerned and called her home. Her mother came right up to school and took her to North Central. The intern concluded that the child was upset by 'family matters'—nothing more—that there was nothing wrong with her. The mother was offended by the diagnosis. She did not appreciate his words or his assumptions. The truth is, there was nothing wrong at home. She brought the child back to school. I thought that she was ill. I told her mother, 'Go to Montefiore.' It's a private hospital, and well respected. She took my advice, thank God. It turned out that the child had a neurological disorder. She is now in treatment.

"This is the kind of thing our children face. Am I saying that the city underserves this population? You can draw your own conclusions."

Out on the street, it takes a full half hour to flag down a cab. Taxi drivers in New York are sometimes disconcertingly direct in what they say. When they are contemptuous of poor black people, their contempt is unadorned. When they're sympathetic and compassionate, their observations often go right to the heart of things. "Oh . . . they neglect these children," says the driver. "They leave them in the streets and slums to live and die." We stop at a light. Outside the window of the taxi, aimless men are standing in a semicircle while another man is working on his car. Old four-story buildings with their windows boarded, cracked or missing are on every side.

I ask the driver where he's from. He says Afghanistan. Turning in his seat, he gestures at the street and shrugs. "If you don't, as an American, begin to give these kids the kind of education that you give the kids of Donald Trump, you're asking for disaster."

Two months later, on a day in May, I visit an elementary school in Riverdale. The dog woods and magnolias on the lawn in front of P.S. 24 are in full blossom on the day I visit. There is a well-tended park across the street, another larger park three blocks away. To the left of the school is a playground for small children, with an innovative jungle gym, a slide and several climbing toys. Behind the school there are two playing fields for older kids. The grass around the school is neatly trimmed.

The neighborhood around the school, by no means the richest part of Riverdale, is nonetheless expensive and quite beautiful. Residences in the area—some of which are large, free-standing houses, others condominiums in solid red-brick buildings—sell for prices in the region of $400,000; but some of the larger Tudor houses on the winding and tree-shaded streets close to the school can cost up to $1 million. The excellence of P.S. 24, according to the principal, adds to the value of these homes. Advertisements in *The New York Times* will frequently inform prospective buyers that a house is "in the neighborhood of P.S. 24."

The school serves 825 children in the kindergarten through sixth grade. This is approximately half the student population crowded into P.S. 79, where 1,550 children fill a space intended for 1,000, and a great deal smaller than the 1,300 children packed into the former skating rink; but the principal of P.S. 24, a capable and energetic man named David Rothstein, still regards it as excessive for an elementary school.

The school is integrated in the strict sense that the middle- and upper-middle-class white children here do occupy a building that contains some Asian and Hispanic and black children; but there is little integration in the classrooms since the vast majority of the Hispanic and black children are assigned to "special" classes on the basis of evaluations that have classified them "EMR"—"educable mentally retarded"—or else, in the worst of cases, "TMR"—"trainable mentally retarded."

I ask the principal if any of his students qualify for free-lunch programs. "About 130 do," he says. "Perhaps another 35 receive their lunches at reduced price. Most of these kids are in the special classes. They do not come from this neighborhood."

The very few nonwhite children that one sees in mainstream classes tend to be Japanese or else of other Asian origins. Riverdale, I learn, has been the residence of choice for many years to members of the diplomatic corps.

The school therefore contains effectively two separate schools: one of about 130 children, most of whom are poor, Hispanic, black, assigned to one of the 12 special classes; the other of some 700 mainstream students, almost all of whom are white or Asian.

There is a third track also—this one for the students who are labeled "talented" or "gifted." This is termed a "pull-out" program since the children who are so identified remain in mainstream classrooms but are taken out for certain periods each week to be provided with intensive and, in my opinion, excellent instruction in some areas of reasoning and logic often known as "higher-order skills" in the contemporary jargon of the public schools. Children identified as "gifted" are admitted to this program in first grade and, in most cases, will remain there for six years. Even here, however, there are two tracks of the gifted. The regular gifted classes are provided with only one semester of this specialized instruction yearly. Those very few children, on the other hand, who are identified as showing the most promise are assigned, beginning in the third grade, to a program that receives a full-year regimen.

In one such class, containing ten intensely verbal and impressive fourth grade children, nine are white and one is Asian. The "special" class I enter first, by way of contrast, has twelve children of whom only one is white and none is Asian. These racial breakdowns prove to be predictive of the school-wide pattern.

In a classroom for the gifted on the first floor of the school, I ask a child what the class is doing. "Logic and syllogisms," she replies. The room is fitted with a planetarium. The principal says that all the elementary schools in District 10 were given the same planetarium ten years ago but that certain schools, because of overcrowding, have been forced to give them up. At P.S. 261, according to my notes, there was a domelike space that had been built to hold a planetarium, but the planetarium had been removed to free up space for the small library collection. P.S. 24, in contrast, has a spacious library that holds almost 8,000 books. The windows are decorated with attractive, brightly colored curtains and look out on flowering trees. The principal says that it's inadequate, but it appears spectacular to me after the cubicle that holds a meager 700 books within the former skating rink.

The district can't afford librarians, the principal says, but P.S. 24, unlike the poorer schools of District 10, can draw on educated parent volunteers who staff the room in shifts three days a week. A parent organization also raises independent funds to buy materials, including books, and will soon be running a fund-raiser to enhance the library's collection.

In a large and sunny first grade classroom that I enter next, I see 23 children, all of whom are white or Asian. In another first grade, there are 22 white children and two others who are Japanese. There is a computer in each class. Every classroom also has a modern fitted sink.

In a second grade class of 22 children, there are two black children and three Asian children. Again, there is a sink and a computer. A sixth grade social studies class has only one black child. The children have an in-class research area that holds some up-to-date resources. A set of encyclopedias (World Book, 1985) is in a rack beside a window. The children are doing a Spanish language lesson when I enter. Foreign languages begin in sixth grade at the school, but Spanish is offered also to the kindergarten children. As in every room at P.S. 24, the window shades are clean and new, the floor is neatly tiled in gray and green, and there is not a single light bulb missing.

Walking next into a special class, I see twelve children. One is white. Eleven are black. There are no Asian children. The room is half the size of mainstream classrooms. "Because of overcrowding," says the principal, "we have had to split these rooms in half." There is no computer and no sink.

I enter another special class. Of seven children, five are black, one is Hispanic, one is white. A little black boy with a large head sits in the far corner and is gazing at the ceiling.

"Placement of these kids," the principal explains, "can usually be traced to neurological damage."

In my notes: "How could so many of these children be brain-damaged?"

Next door to the special class is a woodworking shop. "This shop is only for the special classes," says the principal. The children learn to punch in time cards at the door, he says, in order to prepare them for employment.

The fourth grade gifted class, in which I spend the last part of the day, is humming with excitement. "I start with these children in the first grade," says the teacher. "We pull them out of mainstream classes on the basis of their test results and other factors such as the opinion of their teachers. Out of this group, beginning in third grade, I pull out the ones who show the most potential and they enter classes such as this one."

The curriculum they follow, she explains, "emphasizes critical thinking, reasoning and logic." The planetarium, for instance, is employed not simply for the study of the universe as it exists. "Children also are designing their own galaxies," the teacher says.

A little girl sitting around a table with her classmates speaks with perfect poise: "My name is Susan. We are in the fourth grade gifted program."

I ask them what they're doing and a child says, "My name is Laurie and we're doing problem-solving."

A rather tall, good-natured boy who is half-standing at the table tells me that his name is David. "One thing that we do," he says, "is logical thinking. Some problems, we find, have more than one good answer. We need to learn not simply to be logical in our own thinking but to show respect for someone else's logic even when an answer may be technically incorrect."

When I ask him to explain this, he goes on, "A person who gives an answer that is not 'correct' may nonetheless have done some interesting thinking that we should examine. 'Wrong' answers may be more useful to examine than correct ones."

I ask the children if reasoning and logic are innate or if they're things that you can learn.

"You know some things to start with when you enter school," Susan says. "But we also learn some things that other children don't."

I ask her to explain this.

"We know certain things that other kids don't know because we're *taught* them."

She has braces on her teeth. Her long brown hair falls almost to her waist. Her loose white T-shirt has the word TRI-LOGIC on the front. She tells me that Tri-Logic is her father's firm.

Laurie elaborates on the same point: "Some things you know. Some kinds of logic are inside of you to start with. There are other things that someone needs to teach you."

David expands on what the other two have said: "Everyone can think and speak in logical ways unless they have a mental problem. What this program does is bring us to a higher form of logic."

The class is writing a new "Bill of Rights." The children already know the U.S. Bill of Rights and they explain its first four items to me with precision. What they are examining today, they tell me, is the very *concept* of a "right." Then they will create their own compendium of rights according to their own analysis and definition. Along one wall of the classroom, opposite the planetarium, are seven Apple II computers on which children have developed rather subtle color animations that express the themes—of greed and domination, for example—that they also have described in writing.

"This is an upwardly mobile group," the teacher later says. "They have exposure to whatever New York City has available. Their parents may take them to the theater, to museums. . . ."

In my notes: "Six girls, four boys. Nine white, one Chinese. I am glad they have this class. But what about the others? Aren't there ten black children in the school who could enjoy this also?"

The teacher gives me a newspaper written, edited and computer-printed by her sixth grade gifted class. The children, she tells me, are provided with a link to kids in Europe for transmission of news stories.

A science story by one student asks if scientists have ever falsified their research. "Gregor Mendel," the sixth grader writes, "the Austrian monk who founded the science of genetics, published papers on his work with peas that some experts say were statistically too good to be true. Isaac Newton, who formulated the law of gravitation, relied on unseemly mathematical sleight of hand in his calculations. . . . Galileo Galilei, founder of modern scientific method, wrote about experiments that were so difficult to duplicate that colleagues doubted he had done them."

Another item in the paper, also by a sixth grade student, is less esoteric: "The Don Cossacks dance company, from Russia, is visiting the United States. The last time it toured America was 1976. . . . The Don Cossacks will be in New York City for two weeks at the Neil Simon Theater. Don't miss it!"

The tone is breezy—and so confident! That phrase—"Don't miss it!"—speaks a volume about life in Riverdale.

"What makes a good school?" asks the principal when we are talking later on. "The building and teachers are part of it, of course. But it isn't just the building and the teachers. Our kids come from good families and the neighborhood is good. In a three-block area we have a public library, a park, a junior high. . . . Our typical sixth grader reads at eighth grade level." In a quieter voice he says, "I see how hard my colleagues work in schools like P.S. 79. You have children in those neighborhoods who live in virtual hell. They enter school five years behind. What do they get?" Then, as he spreads his hands out on his desk, he says: "I have to ask myself why there should be an elementary school in District 10 with fifteen hundred children. Why should there be an elementary school within a skating rink? Why should the Board of Ed allow this? This is not the way that things should be."

Stark as the inequities in District 10 appear, educators say that they are "mild" in comparison to other situations in the city. Some of the most stunning inequality, according to a report by the Community Service Society, derives from allocations granted by state legislators to school districts where they have political allies. The poorest districts in the city get approximately 90 cents per pupil from these legislative grants, while the richest districts have been given $14 for each pupil.

Newspapers in New York City have reported other instances of the misallocation of resources. "The Board of Education," wrote the *New York Post* during July of 1987, "was hit with bombshell charges yesterday that money earmarked for fighting drug abuse and illiteracy in ghetto schools was funneled instead to schools in wealthy areas."

In receipt of extra legislative funds, according to the *Post*, affluent districts were funded "at a rate 14 times greater than low-income districts." The paper said the city's poorest areas were underfunded "with stunning consistency."

The report by the Community Service Society cites an official of the New York City Board of Education who remarks that there is "no point" in putting further money "into some poor districts" because, in his belief, "new teachers would not stay there." But the report observes that, in an instance where beginning teacher salaries were raised by nearly half, "that problem largely disappeared"—another interesting reminder of the difference money makes when we are willing to invest it. Nonetheless, says the report, "the perception that the poorest districts are beyond help still remains. . . ." Perhaps the worst result of such beliefs, says the report, is the message that resources would be "wasted on poor children." This message "trickles down to districts, schools, and classrooms." Children hear and understand this theme—they are poor investments—and behave accordingly. If society's resources would be wasted on their destinies, perhaps their own determination would be wasted too. "Expectations are a powerful force . . . ," the CSS observes.

Despite the evidence, the CSS report leans over backwards not to fuel the flames of racial indignation. "In the present climate," the report says, "suggestions of racism must be made with caution. However, it is inescapable that these inequities are being perpetrated on [school] districts which are virtually all black and Hispanic. . . ." While the report says, very carefully, that there is no "evidence" of "deliberate individual discrimination," it nonetheless concludes that "those who allocate resources make decisions over and over again which penalize the poorest districts." Analysis of city policy, the study says, "speaks to systemic bias which constitutes a conspiracy of effect. . . . Whether consciously or not, the system writes off its poorest students."[5]

NOTES

1. Lord Acton cited: George Alan Hickrod, "Reply to the 'Forbes' Article," *Journal of School Finance* 12 (1987).
2. Per-pupil spending, New York City and suburbs: Office for Policy Analysis and Program Accountability, New York State Board of Education, "Statistical Profiles of School

Districts" (Albany: 1 January 1989). Numbers cited are for 1986–1987 school year.

3. Question asked by New York City Board of Education and response of Community Service Society: Community Service Society of New York, "Promoting Poverty: The Shift of Resources Away from Low-Income New York City School Districts" (New York: 1987).

4. Contrasts between Schools in District 10, statements of principals and superintendent: *The New York Times,* January 2, 1987. District 10 Superintendent Fred Goldberg resigned under pressure in 1991. A highly respected veteran of the New York City public schools, he struck me, in the course of an April 1990 interview, as an enlightened educator caught up in a compromising situation that was not of his own making. Educators in New York believe that he was made to pay an unfair price for the profound racism rooted in the city's public schools.

5. Inequities in New York City Schools: *The New York Times,* 2 July 1987; *New York Post,* 2 July 1987; *The* (New York) *City Sun,* 15–21 July 1987; "Promoting Poverty" (Community Service Society of New York), cited above.

25

WHY ARE THERE NO SUPERMARKETS IN MY NEIGHBORHOOD?: THE LONG SEARCH FOR FRESH FRUIT, PRODUCE, AND HEALTHY FOOD

Shannon N. Zenk (et al.)

QUESTIONS TO CONSIDER

In a typical middle- to upper-middle-class white suburban neighborhood it is not uncommon to find two, three, or even four supermarkets within a mile or two of one another. Because of their close proximity these stores engage in cutthroat competition. The result is a cheap abundance of fresh fruits, vegetables, and a staggering array of healthy foods. Now think about a poor neighborhood in an inner city. Corner stores, not supermarkets, are the source for grocery shopping. How, according to Professor Zenk and associates, is race and class implicated in having access to large supermarkets? What are the health consequences of having to purchase groceries from corner stores or bodegas rather than a huge supermarket?

From "Neighborhood Composition, Neighborhood Poverty, and the Spatial Accessibility of Supermarkets in Metropolitan Detroit" by Shannon Zenk (et al.) *American Journal of Public Health,* April 2005, Vol. 95. No. 4, pp. 660–667. Copyright © American Public Health Association. Reprinted with permission of The American Public Health Association.

Four of the 10 leading causes of death in the United States are chronic diseases for which diet is a major risk factor.[1] Racial disparities in the burden of these chronic, diet-related diseases are well documented, with African Americans often having the highest morbidity and mortality.[2-5] Because health risks and resources are spatially and socially structured and African Americans disproportionately live in economically disadvantaged neighborhoods, increased attention has been focused on how residential environments shape health and contribute to racial disparities in health.[6-9] An extensive body of literature now associates residence in economically disadvantaged neighborhoods, after control for individual socioeconomic status, with a variety of adverse diet-related health outcomes.[10-12]

Despite numerous research efforts that have examined neighborhood variations in health, relatively little is known about the mechanisms by which neighborhood environments affect health.[13-15] One hypothesis is that economically and socially disadvantaged neighborhoods have inadequate access to healthy foods, thus negatively affecting dietary quality and health. Although the presence of supermarkets may not always be beneficial for neighborhood residents (e.g., if supermarkets displace smaller stores with owners who had positively contributed to and invested in the neighborhood), such large stores can be neighborhood health resources providing generally better availability and selection, higher quality, and lower cost of foods compared with smaller food stores.[16] These food resource factors influence dietary patterns.[17-24] Previous studies have found that fewer supermarkets are located in African American neighborhoods compared with White neighborhoods[25,26] and are located in economically disadvantaged neighborhoods compared with affluent neighborhoods.[16,26-29] Other studies have found no differences in the accessibility of supermarkets according to racial or socioeconomic characteristics of neighborhoods.[30-32] This discrepancy could reflect either differences in the definition of supermarkets or true variability in results across time and place that may be caused by differences in the degree of racial or economic segregation. Lower purchasing power is an often-cited but disputed explanation for the relative scarcity of supermarkets in economically disadvantaged neighborhoods.[33-35]

Analysis of the role of race without regard to poverty and of poverty without regard to race offers an incomplete picture of the potential importance of these factors in shaping the spatial accessibility of supermarkets. Understanding these relationships is critical for informing intervention and policy efforts. Such an understanding is particularly important, given the roles of racial residential segregation and economic restructuring in concentrating poverty in African American neighborhoods of older industrial cities of the Northeast and Upper Midwest.[36-40] Therefore, we sought to determine whether supermarkets are located at farther distances from the center of African American neighborhoods compared with White neighborhoods regardless of neighborhood economic conditions or if racial disparities in supermarket accessibility occur only in higher poverty contexts.

Methods

Setting and Sample

The setting for this study was the Detroit metropolitan area in Michigan. Metropolitan Detroit is characterized by extreme economic inequalities across neighborhoods.[36] Economic inequalities can be traced to the period just after World War II, when highway construction and cheap land outside the city led many industries to relocate to the suburbs.[39,41-43] Between 1950 and 1990, the city of Detroit lost approximately 350,000 jobs,[41,43,44] largely owing to the relocation of industries to the suburbs, deindustrialization, and other facets of economic restructuring. At the same time, discriminatory federal housing policies and lending practices, racial steering (the act of real estate agents systematically showing African Americans to different neighborhoods than Whites), restrictive covenants, and violence created and reinforced racial residential segregation in metropolitan Detroit. In effect, African Americans were confined to the least desirable, older residential neighborhoods of the city, whereas Whites were able to move to more desirable, newer suburban locations.[35,37,41,44-47] The city of Detroit shifted from 16.2% African American in 1950 to 81.2% African American in 2000,[43,48] a sharp contrast with the 84.8% of metropolitan Detroit residents outside the city limits who identified as non-Hispanic White in 2000.[48] Metropolitan Detroit remains one of the most racially segregated areas in the United States—ranked second overall in residential segregation of African Americans in 2000.[49] The sample for this study was 869 neighborhoods (we used census tracts as proxies) in the tricounty Detroit metropolitan area. These neighborhoods are located in the city of Detroit and in the tricounty Detroit metropolitan area (Wayne, Oakland, Macomb counties) within a 10-mile buffer of Detroit.

Measures

We used 2000 decennial census data to characterize the neighborhoods. Population density was computed as the total population per square mile (median = 5367.44). Racial composition was defined as the percentage of non-Hispanic African American residents (median = 6.06%). Neighborhood poverty was defined as the percentage of residents below the poverty line (median = 8.21%). . . . Given that 92% of residents in tricounty metropolitan Detroit were either non-Hispanic White (67.3%) or non-Hispanic African American (24.9%), neighborhoods with low proportions of African Americans generally correspond with predominately White neighborhoods.

Supermarkets were defined as supercenters (e.g., Meijer, Super Kmart) and full-line grocery stores (e.g., Farmer Jack, Kroger) associated with a national or regional grocery chain, i.e., a chain with 11 or more retail stores.[50] To identify supermarkets, we obtained a 2001 list of grocery stores from the Michigan Department of Agriculture. We used 2001–2002 paper telephone directories, as well as online telephone directories and company Web sites, in the fall of 2002 to verify the addresses of these supermarkets and to identify additional supermarkets. We confirmed the address of any supermarket not on the Michigan Department of Agriculture list by telephoning the store. One hundred and sixty supermarkets were identified in Detroit and in the metropolitan area within a 15-mile buffer of Detroit. . . . The additional 5-mile buffer of supermarkets around the sampled neighborhoods helped to ensure that we could calculate supermarket accessibility for neighborhoods at the periphery.

• • •

The nearest supermarket was significantly further away in neighborhoods with a high proportion of African Americans and in the most impoverished neighborhoods compared with neighborhoods with a low proportion of African Americans and the least impoverished neighborhoods, respectively. (These results were adjusted for population density.)

• • •

Among the most impoverished neighborhoods, distance to the nearest supermarket varied considerably by percentage

African American, with the nearest supermarket averaging 1.10 to 1.15 miles farther in neighborhoods with medium . . . and high . . . proportions of African Americans, respectively, than in neighborhoods with low proportions of African Americans. . . .

Discussion

Disparities in Supermarket Accessibility

The relationship between neighborhood racial composition and supermarket accessibility varied according to neighborhood poverty level in metropolitan Detroit. The distance to the nearest supermarket was similar among the least impoverished neighborhoods across the 3 tertiles of percentage African American. However, disparities in supermarket accessibility on the basis of race were evident among the most impoverished neighborhoods: the most impoverished neighborhoods in which African Americans resided, on average, were 1.1 miles farther from the nearest supermarket than were the most impoverished White neighborhoods. Most African Americans in tricounty metropolitan Detroit reside in neighborhoods that are in the upper tertile for percentage poor and that have either a high proportion of African Americans (60%) or a medium proportion of African Americans (20%), as defined in this study.

Inadequate accessibility to supermarkets may contribute to less-nutritious diets and hence to greater risk for chronic, diet-related diseases. In a recent qualitative study, Detroit residents reported that lack of access to supermarkets was a barrier to healthy eating[50] At least 3 previous quantitative studies, all of which examined chain supermarkets, have suggested that closer proximity to supermarkets is associated with better-quality diets.[51–53] The observation that the nearest supermarket averaged 1.1 miles further in the most impoverished neighborhoods in which African Americans resided . . . compared with the most impoverished White neighborhoods . . . is particularly salient, given that 23% and 28% . . . of households in the most impoverished neighborhoods in which African Americans resided did not own a car in 2000.

We began the study with 3 measures of supermarket accessibility: distance to the nearest supermarket, number of supermarkets within a 3-mile radius (considered reachable by car), and potential supermarket accessibility . . . [54] Because the patterns of these relationships were similar, we present only distance to the nearest supermarket. For all 3 measures, supermarket accessibility was comparable among the least impoverished neighborhoods regardless of neighborhood racial composition, whereas disparities were evident among the most impoverished neighborhoods. The most impoverished neighborhoods in which African Americans resided . . . averaged 2.3 and 2.7 (respectively) fewer supermarkets within a 3-mile radius and had lower potential supermarket accessibility relative to the most impoverished White neighborhoods . . .

Race appears to be an important factor with respect to supermarket accessibility in the context of more impoverished neighborhoods; 76% of neighborhoods with a high proportion of African Americans were among the most impoverished. The disproportionate representation of African Americans in more impoverished neighborhoods in Detroit can be traced historically. Until the 1940s—a decade in which Detroit's African American population doubled from 149,119 to 300,506 because of the influx of African Americans from the South for manufacturing jobs—African Americans generally resided in central Detroit and east central Detroit.[35,36] Facing overcrowded and substandard housing, African Americans began moving to other parts of the city.[39,55,57] Nevertheless, institutional racism—specifically racial residential segregation—confined African Americans to Detroit neighborhoods that began losing employment opportunities, particularly in the manufacturing industry, in the 1950s.[39,41,44] Between 1948 and 1967, Detroit lost nearly 130,000 manufacturing jobs.[39]

Often confronting strong resistance from Whites, African Americans first moved to nearby neighborhoods in central Detroit.[46,58] Hence, many neighborhoods located in central Detroit[57] transitioned from White to African American in the 1950s and 1960s when African Americans moved in and Whites moved out to newly constructed housing in northeast and northwest Detroit and the suburbs. Businesses closed soon thereafter, particularly after the 1967 racial discord, further compounding the adverse economic impact of the loss of manufacturing jobs.[39,44,59] Hence, the number of abandoned homes and businesses, including grocery stores, grew, and poverty increased substantially.

This pattern of White flight and economic divestment was repeated during several decades across Detroit neighborhoods. Residential patterns of African Americans generally expanded outward in a stepwise progression from central and east central Detroit toward the northern city boundaries and eventually to Southfield, a suburb adjacent to northwest Detroit.[39,44,58] Neighborhoods located in the northernmost portion of Detroit near Eight Mile Road, the infamous African American–White racial dividing line of metropolitan Detroit, and particularly in northwest and northeast Detroit were among the most recent neighborhoods to transition from White to African American. Some neighborhoods, such as those in the far northwest Detroit community of Redford, shifted to African American as late as the 1990s.[44,58,60,61] Similarly, in the suburb of Southfield, the African American population has grown

tremendously, from 102 people (0.1% of the population) in 1970 to 42,259 people (54%) in 2000.[58] The number of African Americans in Southfield increased by 48% between 1990 and 2000 alone, despite an increase of only 3% in the city's total population.

This social history of metropolitan Detroit neighborhoods is relevant to our study because, among the least impoverished neighborhoods, all but 1 of the predominately African American neighborhoods with supermarket accessibility equivalent to that of their predominately White counterparts were located in northwest and north central Detroit and in Southfield. An optimistic interpretation of our findings is that supermarkets have newly opened or have remained open in or nearby these middle-income, yet racially transitioning, neighborhoods. This interpretation provides hope that supermarkets will invest or stay invested in African American neighborhoods as long as the residents have sufficient purchasing power to make these outlets profitable. An alternative interpretation of the findings is that among the least impoverished neighborhoods, African American neighborhoods have supermarket accessibility equivalent to that of predominantly White neighborhoods only because the supermarkets located in and nearby are remnants of historically White neighborhoods. Longitudinal data are needed to empirically test these different theories. If these areas remain African American, if they maintain a middle-income population, and if supermarkets remain open in or near these neighborhoods, then economic development may be a key intervention strategy to improve supermarket accessibility in African American neighborhoods. If, conversely, supermarkets close or do not open new sites in these economically stable African American neighborhoods, then factors associated with race are a more likely cause of disparities in supermarket accessibility. Indeed, our finding of disparate supermarket accessibility among the most impoverished neighborhoods by neighborhood racial composition warrants further investigation to identify contributing factors.

• • •

Practice and Policy Implications

The results of the study have several practice and policy implications. Pursuit of these strategies would benefit from a partnership approach between public health professionals and community members to ensure the local relevance of intervention strategies and to enhance community capacity for future intervention efforts.[62] In the first of these implications, the results suggest the critical importance of working to redress fundamental inequalities between African Americans and Whites in order to reduce chronic, diet-related diseases among African Americans.[63] For example, the economic development of African American neighborhoods could be enhanced by policies of creating jobs that pay a fair wage, to improve educational quality and opportunities for adults to increase job skills, to subsidize child care, and to attract new businesses. Second, working to attract supermarkets to economically disadvantaged African American neighborhoods in Detroit is a specific economic development strategy that may directly improve food access. Supermarket development can enhance local economic vitality by (1) providing jobs for residents, (2) increasing the local tax base, (3) making foods available at lower prices, thereby increasing the spending power of residents, and (4) attracting other forms of retail.[34,35,64] Supporting African American ownership of and employment at these supermarkets may be critical to their acceptance and success.[65]

Third, a metropolitanwide planning approach to the food system needs to be pursued.[66] Ideally, the food system would be evaluated holistically to ensure that all communities are served equitably. Fourth, in the short term, inadequate transportation is a significant barrier for residents of economically disadvantaged African American neighborhoods' gaining access to supermarkets.[50] Affordable public transportation needs to be improved by integrating transportation routes with supermarket locations.[67,68]

Fifth, on the basis of our findings of disparate access to supermarkets among the most impoverished neighborhoods by percentage African American residents, efforts to expand the Community Reinvestment Act, a law designed to combat discrimination in commercial real estate lending, may be warranted. Finally, given that racial ideologies are likely to shape the political will to pursue these intervention strategies, public health researchers and practitioners need to work to challenge racial stereotypes in public discourse.[42,43,69]

Helping to contextualize the plight of African Americans historically and spatially and to identify its ramifications for health were the primary intents of this study. We found that the historically influenced concentration of African Americans in higher-poverty neighborhoods in Detroit adversely affects spatial access to supermarkets, a resource of potential great importance in promoting the health of African Americans.

About the Authors

Shannon N. Zenk is with the Program in Cancer Control and Population Sciences, University of Illinois at Chicago Cancer Center, Chicago. Amy J. Schulz and Barbara A. Israel are with the Department of Health Behavior and Health Education, University of Michigan, Ann Arbor. Sherman A. James is with the Terry Sanford Institute of Public Policy, Duke University, Durham, NC. Shuming Bao is with the China

Data Center, University of Michigan. Mark I. Wilson is with the Department of Epidemiology, University of Michigan.

Requests for reprints should be sent to Shannon N. Zenk, PhD, University of Illinois at Chicago, Institute for Health Research and Policy, 1747 W Roosevelt Rd, M/C 275, Chicago, IL 60608 (e-mail: szenk@uic.edu).

This article was accepted June 14, 2004.

Contributors

S. N. Zenk developed the study, collected the data, and led the data analysis and writing. A. J. Schulz, B. A. Israel, S. A. James, and M. L. Wilson contributed to the conceptualization of the study and interpretation of the results. S. Bao participated in the data analysis and interpretation of results. All authors reviewed and helped to revise drafts of the article.

Acknowledgments

Preparation of this article was supported by the National Cancer Institute Cancer Education and Career Development Program (5 R25 CA57699-12).

We thank Sonya Jones for sharing insights on accessibility measurement and spatial regression. We also thank Kami Pothukuchi for providing raw data on names and locations of supermarkets in metropolitan Detroit. Richard T. Campbell's helpful comments are appreciated.

Human Participant Protection

No human participant protocol approval was needed for this study.

NOTES

1. National Center for Health Statistics, Centers for Disease Control and Prevention. Deaths—leading causes. Available at: http://www.cdc.gov/nchs/fastats/lcod.htm. Accessed February 13, 2004.

2. Fried VM, Prager K, MacKay AP, Xia H. Chartbook on trends in the health of Americans. In: *Health, United States, 2003*. Hyattsville, Md: National Center for Health Statistics, 2003.

3. Jemal A, Thomas A, Murray T, Thun M. Cancer statistics, 2002. *CA Cancer J Clin*. 2002; 52:23–47.

4. Ries Lag, Eisner MP, Kosary CL, et al., eds. SEER cancer statistics review, 1973–1999. Bethesda, Md: National Cancer Institute; 2002. Available at: http://seer.cancer.gov/csr/1973–1999. Accessed February 13, 2004.

5. *Healthy People 2010: Understanding and Improving Health*. Washington, DC: US Dept of Health and Human Services, 2001. Also available at: http://web.health.gov/healthypeople/document. Accessed January 1, 2005.

6. Fitzpatrick K, LaGory M. *Unhealthy Places: The Ecology of Risk in the Urban Landscape*. New York, NY: Routledge; 2000.

7. Lillie-Blanton M, LaVeist T. Race/ethnicity, the social environment, and health. *Soc Sci Med*. 1996;43: 83–91.

8. Macintyre S, Maciver S, Sooman A. Area, class, and health: should we be focusing on places or people? *J Soc Policy*. 1993;22:213–234.

9. Yen J, Syme SL. The social environment and health: a discussion of the epidemiologic literature. *Annu Rev Public Health*. 1999;20: 287–308.

10. Ellen I, Mijanovich GT, Dillman K. Neighborhood effects on health: exploring the links and assessing the evidence. *J Urban Aff*. 2001; 23:391–408.

11. Pickett KE, Pearl M. Multilevel analyses of neighborhood socioeconomic context and health outcomes: a critical review. *J Epidemiol Community Health*. 2000; 55:111–122.

12. Robert SA. Socioeconomic position and health: the independent contribution of community socioeconomic context. *Annu Rev Sociol* 1999; 25:489–516.

13. Diez Roux AV. Investigating neighborhood and area effects on health. *Am J Public Health*. 2001;91:1783–1789.

14. Hillemeier MM, Lynch J, Harper S, Casper M. Measuring contextual characteristics for community health. *Health Serv Res*. 2004; 38:1645–1717.

15. Macintyre S, Ellaway A, Cummins S. Place effects on health: how can we conceptualize, operationalize, and measure them? *Soc Sci Med.* 2002;55:125–139.

16. Mantovani RE, Daft L, Macaluso TF, Welsh J, Hoffman K. *Authorized Food Retailers' Characteristics and Access Study* Alexandria, Va: US Dept of Agriculture; 1997.

17. Cheadle A, Psaty BM, Curry S, et al. Community-level comparisons between the grocery stone environment and individual dietary practices. *Prev Med* 1991; 20:250–261.

18. Cohen NL, Stoddard AM, Sarouhkhanians S, Sorensen G. Barriers toward fruit and vegetable consumption in a multiethnic worksite population. *J Nutr Educ.* 1998;30:381–386.

19. Drewnowski A, Specter SE. Poverty and obesity: the role of energy density and energy costs. *Am J Clin Nutr* 2004; 79:6–16.

20. French SA, Story M, Jeffery RW. Environmental influences on eating and physical activity. *Annu Rev Public Health.* 2001; 22: 309–335.

21. Furst T, Connors M, Bisogni CA, Sobal J, Falk LW. Food choice: a conceptual model of the process. *Appetite.* 1996;26:247–266.

22. Glanz K, Basil M, Mailbach E, Goldberg J, Snyder D. Why Americans eat what they do: taste, nutrition, cost, convenience, and weight control concerns as influences on food consumption. *J. Am Diet Assoc.* 1998;98:1118–1126.

23. Huang K. Role of national income and prices. In: Frazao E, ed. *America's Eating Habits: Changes and Consequences.* US Dept of Agriculture, 1999;161–171. Agriculture Information Bulletin No. 750.

24. Reicks M, Randall J, Haynes B. Factors affecting vegetable consumption in low-income households. *J Am Diet Assoc.* 1994;94: 1309–1311.

25. Race and place matter for major Chicago area grocers. Chicago, Ill: Metro Chicago Information Center: Available at http://www.mcic.org. Accessed January 3, 2005.

26. Morland K, Wing S, Diez Roux A, Poole C. Neighborhood characteristics associated with the location of food stores and food service places. *Am J Prev Med.* 2002;22:23–29.

27. Alwitt LF, Donley TD. Retail stores in poor urban neighborhoods. *J Consum Aff.* 1997;31: 139–164.

28. Chung C, Myers SL. Do the poor pay more for food? An analysis of grocery store availability and food price disparities. *J Consum Aff.* 1999; 33:276–296.

29. Cotterill RW, Franklin AW. *The Urban Grocery Store Gap.* Storrs, Conn: Food Marketing Policy Center, University of Connecticut; 1995.

30. Cummins S, Macintyre S. A systematic study of an urban foodscape: the price and availability of food in Greater Glasgow. *Urban Stud.* 2002;39:2115–2130.

31. Cummins S, Macintyre S. "Food deserts"— Evidence and assumption in health policy making. *BMJ.* 2002; 325:436–438.

32. Jones SJ. *The Measurement of Food Security at the Community Level: Geographic Information Systems and Participating Ethnographic Methods* [dissertation]. Chapel Hill, NC. University of North Carolina at Chapel Hill, 2002.

33. Donohue RM. *Abandonment and Revitalization of Central City Retailing: The Case of Grocery Stores* [dissertation]. Ann Arbor, Mich: University of Michigan, 1997.

34. The business case for pursuing retail opportunities in the inner city. Boston, Mass: The Boston Consulting Group and The Initiative for a Competitive Inner City; 1988. Available at: http://www.icic.org. Accessed January 3, 2005.

35. The changing models of inner city grocery retailing. Boston, Mass: The Initiative for a Competitive Inner City; 2002. Available at: http://www.icic.org. Accessed January 3, 2005.

36. Jargowsky PA. *Poverty and Place: Ghettos, Barrios, and the American City.* New York, NY: Russell Sage Foundation, 1997.

37. Massey DS, Denton NA. *American Apartheid: Segregation and the Making of the Underclass.* Cambridge, Mass: Harvard University Press; 1993.

38. Massey, DS, Fischer MJ. How segregation concentrates poverty. *Ethn Racial Stud.* 2000; 23:670–691.

39. Sugrue TJ. *The Origins of the Urban Crisis: Race and Inequality in Postwar Detroit.* Princeton, NJ. Princeton University Press; 1996.

40. Wilson WJ. *The Truly Disadvantaged: The inner City, the Underclass, and Public Policy.* Chicago, Ill: University of Chicago Press; 1987.

41. Farley R, Danziger S, Holzer HJ. *Detroit Divided.* New York, NY: Russell Sage Foundation; 2000.

42. Geronimus AT. To mitigate, resist, or undo: addressing structural influences on the health

of urban populations. *Am J Public Health.* 2000; 90:867–872.

43. Schulz A, Williams DR, Israel B, Lempert LB. Racial and spatial relations as fundamental determinants of health in Detroit. *Milbank Q.* 2002;80:677–707.

44. Darden JT, Hill RC, Thomas J, Thomas R. *Detroit: Race and Uneven Development.* Philadelphia, Pa: Temple University Press; 1987.

45. Collins CA, Williams DR. Segregation and mortality: the deadly effects of racism. *Social Forum.* 1999;14:495–523.

46. Thomas JM. *Redevelopment and Race: Planning a Finer City in Postwar Detroit.* Baltimore, Md: The Johns Hopkins University Press; 1997.

47. Williams DR, Collins CA. Racial residential segregation: a fundamental cause of racial disparities in health. *Public Health Rep.* 2001; 116:404–416.

48. *Michigan Metropolitan Information Center 2000 Census Demographic Characteristics.* Detroit, Mich: The Center for Urban Studies, Wayne State University. Available at: http://www.cus .wayne.edu/census/censuspubs.aspx. Accessed January 3, 2005.

49. Iceland J, Weinberg DH, Steinmetz E. *Racial and Ethnic Residential Segregation in the United States: 1980–2000.* Washington, DC: US Government Printing Office; 2002, US Census Bureau. Series CENSR-3.

50. Kieffer E, Willis S, Odoms-Young A, et al. Reducing disparities in diabetes among African American and Latino residents of Detroit: the essential role of community planning focus groups. *Ethn Dis.* 2004;14:S1-27–S1-37.

51. Laraia BA, Siega-Riz AM, Kaufman JS, Jones SJ. Proximity to supermarkets is positively associated with diet quality index for pregnancy. *Prev Med.* 2004;39:869–875.

52. Morland K, Wing S, Diex Roux A. The contextual effect of the local food environment on residents' diets: the atherosclerosis risk in communities study. *Am J Public Health.* 2002; 92:1761–1767.

53. Wrigley N, Warm D, Margetts B, Whelan A. Assessing the impact of improved retail access on diet in a "food desert": a preliminary report. *Urban Stud.* 2002; 39:2061–2082.

54. Zenk SN. *Neighborhood Racial Composition, Neighborhood Poverty, and Food Access in Metropolitan Detroit: Geographic Information Systems and Spatial Analysis* [dissertation]. Ann Arbor, Mich: University of Michigan; 2004.

55. Hartigan J. *Racial Situations: Class Predicaments of Whiteness in Detroit.* Princeton, NJ: Princeton University Press, 1999.

56. Zunz O. *The Changing Face of Inequality: Urbanization, Industrial Development, and Immigrants in Detroit, 1880–1920.* Chicago, Ill: University of Chicago Press; 1982.

57. McWhirter C. Life of one street mirrors city's fall: racial fears trigger white flight in '50s. *The Detroit News.* June 17, 2001. Available at: http://www.detnews.com/specialreports/ 2001/elmhurst. Accessed January 5, 2005.

58. Metzger K, Booza J. *African Americans in the United States, Michigan, and Metropolitan Detroit.* Detroit, Mich: Center for Urban Studies, Wayne State University; 2002. Center for Urban Studies Working Paper Series, No. 8.

59. McWhirter C. 1967 riot sent street into wrenching spiral: once stable block withers as property owners desert. *The Detroit News.* June 18, 2001. Available at: http://www.detnews .com/specialreports/2001/elmhurst. Accessed January 5, 2005.

60. *1990 Census Subcommunity Profiles for the City of Detroit.* Detroit, Mich: Southeast Michigan Census Council: 1993.

61. *2000 Census Subcommunity Profiles for the City of Detroit.* Detroit, Mich: United Way Community Services; 2001.

62. Israel BA, Schulz AJ, Parker EA, Becker AB. Review of community-based research: assessing partnership approaches to improve public health. *Annu Rev Public Health.* 1998; 19:173–201.

63. James SA. Primordial prevention of cardiovascular disease among African Americans: a social epidemiological perspective. *Prev Med.* 1999;29:S84–S89.

64. Pothukuchi K. Attracting supermarkets to inner city neighborhoods: economic development out of the box. *Econ Dev Q.* In press.

65. *The African American Grocery Shopper 2000.* Washington DC: Food Marketing Institute; 2000.

66. Pothukuchi K, Kaufman JL. Placing the food system on the urban agenda: the role of municipal institutions in food system planning. *Agric Human Values.* 1999;16:213–224.

67. Ashman L, Vega J, Dohan M, Fisher A, Hipper R, Romain B. *Seeds of Change: Strategies for Food*

Security for the Inner City. Los Angeles, Calif: University of California Los Angeles; 1993.

68. Gottlieb R, Fisher A, Dohan M, O'Connor L, Parks V. *Homeward Bound: Food-Related Transportation Strategies for Low Income and Transit Dependent Communities.* Los Angeles, Calif: University of California Transportation Center: 1996. Available at: http://www.foodsecurity.org/homewardbound.pdf. Accessed February 13, 2004.

69. Cohen HW, Northridge ME. Getting political: racism and urban health. *Am J Public Health* 2000;90:841–842.

SEEING THE BIG PICTURE

Compare health outcomes by race in Section III (diabetes, obesity, hypertension) with rates of poverty by race in Section VI of our Appendix. What role do poverty and residential segregation by racial groups play in having access to "healthy foods" found in a supermarket compared to the processed, salty, and fatty foods that dominate corner stores or bodegas?

PART III

Racialized Opportunity in Social Institutions

Answer the questions that follow.

1. As of 2000, what percentage of the United States do you think was
   a. Black _____%
   b. White _____%
   c. Asian _____%
   d. American Indian _____%
   e. Latino _____%

2. Who are your three best friends? (1)_____ (2)_____ (3)_____

3. Does the unemployment rate in the United States vary by color or ethnicity?_____

Each of your answers, whether you realize it or not, reflects how you have been shaped by social institutions. Compare your answers on item 1 to the correct percentages as enumerated by the U.S. Bureau of the Census (2003): 12.1 percent black, 75 percent white, 3.6 percent Asian/Pacific Islander, 0.9 percent American Indian, and 12.5 percent Latino. (These numbers add up to more than 100 percent because Latinos can be any race.)

Did your estimates of the size of these groups differ from the actual numbers? If you said that the black population was around 30 percent or that the Asian population was 10 percent, your answer was similar to the average American response. Why do you suppose most people in the United States almost triple-count the black and Asian population? From a sociological perspective, what does the over-counting of the nonwhite population mean?

Item 2 asked you to list your three best friends. How many of the people you listed are from a different race? How many are the same sex as you? If you don't have any best friends who are from a racial background different from your own, why not? Is it that you do not like people from other races? Does this mean you are a racist? Do you only have friends of the same sex? Why?

With regard to item 3, the unemployment rate in the United States does vary by color or ethnicity, with blacks and Latinos twice as likely as whites to be unemployed. Explain the link between the unemployment rate and how close people live to areas of high job growth. How are both of these factors linked to race and ethnicity?

The answers to these questions reflect the ways institutions shape how we view the world. Your beliefs, opinions, and attitudes, and the "commonsense" knowledge that guides your moment-to-moment understanding of the world—all may seem to be highly individualistic. Upon closer sociological inspection, however, we see that institutions and other social arrangements influence, mediate, and structure how we think about and come to understand the world in which we live. Think for a moment about your answers to the preceding questions. People of all colors typically overestimate the nonwhite population and underestimate the white population. Perhaps you overestimated the nonwhite population because you live in an all-black or all-Latino neighborhood. When you look out the window or walk down the street, you see that everyone in your neighborhood is like you. You then use that local information to make a judgment about the, rest of the United States. But what if you are white and you overestimated the nonwhite population? How do you explain doubling or tripling the black or Asian population? Do you get your information about other racial groups secondhand, from watching television? Might there be a difference between the media's portrayal of race and ethnic relations and what is actually taking place in society? Do you watch professional sports, music videos, or the local television news? Might your estimates reflect something about your television viewing habits? If you do live in a racially segregated neighborhood, might that explain why your best friends are all the same color as you? Do you think you might have close friends from different racial backgrounds if your high school or neighborhood was racially integrated? Why are jobs often not as plentiful or as well paying in black or Latino neighborhoods as they are in white areas or the suburbs?

In Part III, we focus on how race and ethnic identity intersect with the criminal justice system, the labor market, where individuals live and why they live there, and how the media shape our views on race and ethnic relations. The four readings in "Race and Criminal Justice: Oxymoron or an American Tragedy?" examine the influence of race and class in the American justice system. In reading 26, law professor David Cole examines racial disparities in capital punishment sentencing. His research found that courts are more likely to sentence to death a black person who kills a white person than a white person who kills a black individual. Who is likely to live and die, controlling for the type of crime committed, varies by race. In reading 27, scholar-activist Angela Davis links the "war on drugs" and the skyrocketing number of incarcerated young black and brown men to the growth of the extremely profitable "prison industrial complex." Jeffrey Reiman

examines a very obvious but unstated fact: people in prison tend to be quite poor. Put another way, rich people can pay for outstanding legal counsel. It is not, as Reiman argues, that poor people are more prone to criminal behavior. He asserts that the criminal justice system is rife with racial and economic bias. Devah Pager's findings about the employment prospects of men with and without criminal records raise troubling questions about the role of race and racism in employment opportunities.

The section "How Race Shapes the Workplace" examines the sociological reasons that economic and occupational outcomes vary by race and ethnicity. The short research summary by Amy Braverman details how a name can signal racial identity and the way employers use this information. Roger Waldinger provides historical and contemporary examples of how employment opportunities have changed over time by examining the different occupational niches that ethnic and racial groups occupied in New York City and the conditions that allowed upward mobility for some and economic stagnation for others. In reading 32 Katherine Newman and Catherine Ellis document the work strategies used by fast-food workers in Harlem. The "McJob" experiences of two hundred black and brown respondents in their study challenge a number of "commonsense" assumptions about work at a fast-food restaurant and workers' attitudes about upward mobility. Xiaolan Bao, writing about Chinese laborers in New York City sweatshops, and William Kandel and Emilio Parrado, describing Latinos in poultry plants in the southeast, together chronicle the experiences of these two newly arrived immigrant groups as part of an unregulated and exploited workforce—experiences that are becoming all too common.

The next section, "Race, Representations, and the Media," explores the influence of the media on our views of race and ethnicity. In the subsection "Drug Dealers, Maids, and Mammies: The Role of Stereotypes in the Media," Roger Klein and Stacy Naccarato discuss racial bias in local news coverage. Justin Lewis and Sut Jhally use a research project examining exposure to *The Cosby Show* to demonstrate the effect of the television shows people watch on their racial attitudes and perceptions of mobility. The readings by S. Robert Lichter and Daniel R. Amundson focus on the depiction of blacks in the nightly news and Latinos in television programming, noting how frequently these portrayals are reduced to a series of degrading stereotypes. Each of these readings asks us to consider how representations of race and ethnicity on the nightly news or on situation comedies shape our worldview. The subsection "Crazy Horse Malt Liquor and Athletes: The Tenacity of Stereotypes" takes two examples of stereotypes that refuse to go away: the images of the savage Indian and the violent black athlete. Debra Merskin deconstructs the meaning of American Indians in popular culture and the consequences of such stereotypical and racist imagery. Finally, Richard Lapchick reports on one unintended consequence of America's romance with professional sports: the cementing of racial stereotypes. Athletes, particularly college athletes, are often subjected to a double standard because their lives are so closely scrutinized by the media.

RACE AND CRIMINAL JUSTICE: OXYMORON OR AN AMERICAN TRAGEDY?

26

NO EQUAL JUSTICE: THE COLOR OF PUNISHMENT

David Cole

QUESTIONS TO CONSIDER

In McClesky v. Kemp, *the Supreme Court ruled that even though sentencing disparities were found to be significantly correlated with the race of the defendant, those findings did not necessarily mean there was racist intent in the sentencing. David Cole's research, however, challenges the deeply held belief that the rule of law should be and is applied to all citizens without regard to race, creed, status, or lineage. How do you explain differences in sentencing by race? What would happen if there were a "war on drugs" and the suburbs, rather than the city, were the target? What would white America's response be if millions of young, white middle-class suburbanites were arrested, sentenced, and put in jail for an extended period of time for recreational marijuana or ecstasy use?*

Tonya Drake, a twenty-five-year-old mother of four on welfare, needed the money. So when a man she hardly knew gave her a $100 bill and told her she could keep the change if she mailed a package for him, she agreed, even though she suspected it might contain drugs. The change amounted to $47.40. The package contained crack cocaine. And for that, Tonya Drake, whose only prior offenses were traffic violations, received a ten-year

David Cole, *No Equal Justice: Race and Class in the American Criminal Justice System.* Copyright © 1998 by David Cole. Reprinted by permission of The New Press, (800) 233–4830.

mandatory minimum prison sentence. When federal judge Richard A. Gadbois, Jr., sentenced her, he said, "This woman doesn't belong in prison for 10 years for what I understand she did. That's just crazy, but there's nothing I can do about it." Had the cocaine in the package been in powder rather than crack form, she would have faced a prison sentence of less than three years, with no mandatory minimum.[1]

Tonya Drake is joined by thousands of prisoners serving lengthy mandatory prison terms for federal crack cocaine violations.[2] What unites them is skin color. About 90 percent of federal crack cocaine defendants are black. Indeed, a 1992 U.S. Sentencing

Commission study found that in seventeen states, not a single white had been prosecuted on federal crack cocaine charges.[3]

Crack cocaine is nothing more than powder cocaine cooked up with baking soda. Wholesalers deal in powder; retailers deal in crack. But under the federal sentencing guidelines, a small-time crack "retailer" caught selling 5 grams of crack receives the same prison sentence as a large-scale powder cocaine dealer convicted of distributing 500 grams of powder cocaine. The U.S. Sentencing Commission has estimated that 65 percent of crack users are white.[4] In 1992, however, 92.6 percent of those convicted for crimes involving crack cocaine were black, while only 4.7 percent were white; at the same time, 45.2 percent of defendants convicted for powder cocaine crimes were white, and only 20.7 percent were black.[5] In Minnesota, where state sentencing guidelines drew a similar distinction between crack and powder cocaine, African Americans made up 96.6 percent of those charged with possession of crack cocaine in 1988, while almost 80 percent of those charged with possession of powder cocaine were white.[6] Sentencing guidelines were ostensibly adopted to eliminate disparity in sentencing, yet the crack/powder distinction has ensured that significant racial inequities remain.

Black defendants have challenged the crack/powder disparity on constitutional grounds, but every federal challenge has failed.[7] The courts, echoing the Supreme Court in *McCleskey*, have held that "mere" statistical disparities do not prove that Congress or the Sentencing Commission adopted the disparities for the purpose of harming African Americans. And it is not wholly irrational to treat crack as more harmful than powder cocaine, because crack is more often associated with violence, is more potent as typically ingested, and is more accessible to low-income people. Accordingly, even

though black cocaine offenders in the federal system serve sentences on average five years longer than white cocaine offenders, the courts see no constitutional problem.

In 1995, however, the U.S. Sentencing Commission, which administers the federal sentencing guidelines, concluded that the disparities could not be justified by qualitative differences between the two drugs, particularly as powder cocaine distributors provide the raw material for crack. It proposed to reduce the differential, noting the racial disparities and their corrosive effect on criminal justice generally.[8] Congress and President Clinton responded like politicians; they reframed the issue as whether we should be "tough on crime," and opposed any change. For the first time since the sentencing guidelines were created in 1984, Congress passed a law overriding a Sentencing Commission recommendation to alter the guidelines.[9]

In 1995, the Georgia Supreme Court very briefly took a different approach. Georgia has a "two strikes and you're out" sentencing scheme that imposes life imprisonment for a second drug offense. As of 1995, Georgia's district attorneys, who have unfettered discretion to decide whether to seek this penalty, had invoked it against only 1 percent of white defendants facing a second drug conviction, but against more than 16 percent of eligible black defendants. The result: 98.4 percent of those serving life sentences under the provision were black. On March 17, 1995, the Georgia Supreme Court ruled, by a 4-3 vote, that these figures presented a thres hold case of discrimination, and required prosecutors to explain the disparity.[10]

Instead of offering an explanation, however, Georgia Attorney General Michael Bowers took the unusual step of filing a petition for rehearing signed by every one of the state's forty-six district attorneys, all of whom were white. The petition warned that the Court's approach was a "substantial step toward invalidating" the death penalty, and would "paralyze the criminal justice system," presumably because racial disparities in other areas might also have to be explained. Thirteen days later, the Georgia Supreme Court took the highly unusual step of reversing itself, and held that the figures established no discrimination and required no justification. The court's new decision relied almost exclusively on the U.S. Supreme Court's decision in *McCleskey*.[11]

The crack/powder differential and the Georgia experience with "two strikes and you're out" life sentences are but two examples of the widespread racial disparities caused by the war on drugs. Between 1986 and 1991, arrests of members of racial and ethnic minorities for all crimes increased by twice as much as nonminority arrests.[12] Yet when that figure is broken down by type of crime, drug offenses were the *only* area in which minority arrests actually increased more than nonminority arrests. The five-year increase in arrests of minorities for drug offenses was *almost ten times* the increase in arrests of white drug offenders.[13]

In 1992, the United States Public Health Service estimated, based on self-report surveys, that 76 percent of illicit drug users were white, 14 percent black, and 8 percent Hispanic—figures which roughly match each group's share of the general population[14] Yet African Americans make up 35 percent of all drug arrests, 55 percent of all drug convictions, and 74 percent of all sentences for drug offenses.[15] In Baltimore, blacks are five times more likely than whites to be arrested for drug offenses.[16] In Columbus, Ohio, black males are less than 11 percent of the population, but account for 90 percent of drug arrests; they are arrested at a rate eighteen times greater than white males.[17] In Jacksonville, Florida, black males are 12 percent of the population, but 87 percent of drug arrests.[18] And in Minneapolis, black males

are arrested for drugs at a rate twenty times that for white males.[19]

Similar racial disparities are found in incarceration rates for drug offenses. From 1986 to 1991, the number of white drug offenders incarcerated in state prisons increased by 110 percent, but the number of black drug offenders increased by 465 percent.[20] In New York, which has some of the most draconian drug laws in the country—selling two ounces of cocaine receives the same sentence as murder—90 percent of those incarcerated for drugs each year are black or Hispanic.[21] The "war on drugs" is also responsible for much of the growth in incarceration since 1980. Federal prisoners incarcerated for drug offenses increased nearly tenfold from 1980 to 1993, and that increase accounted for nearly three-quarters of the total increase in federal prisoners.[22] The number of state prisoners incarcerated for drug offenses during the same period increased at a similar rate.[23]

The same pattern emerges in the treatment of juveniles. Between 1986 and 1991, arrests of minority juveniles (under age eighteen) for drug offenses increased by 78 percent, while arrests of nonminority juveniles for drugs actually *decreased* by 34 percent.[24] As with adults, black youth are also treated progressively more severely than whites at each successive stage of the juvenile justice process. In 1991, white youth were involved in 50 percent of all drug-related cases, while black youth accounted for 48 percent.[25] Yet blacks were detained for drug violations at nearly twice the rate of whites.[26] Four times as many black juvenile drug cases were transferred to criminal courts for adult prosecution as white cases.[27] And black youth involved in drug-related cases were placed outside the home almost twice as often as white youth. These disparities are only getting worse: from 1987 to 1991, such placement for black juveniles in drug cases increased 28.5 percent, while placement for whites *decreased*

30 percent.[28] The situation in Baltimore is illustrative. In 1980, eighteen white juveniles and eighty-six black juveniles were arrested for selling drugs—already a fairly stark five-to-one disparity. In 1990, the number of white juveniles arrested on drug charges fell to thirteen, while the number of black juveniles arrested grew to 1,304—a disparity of more than one hundred to one.[29]

Thus, the victims of the war on drugs have been disproportionately black. Some argue that this is neither surprising nor problematic, but simply reflects the unfortunate fact that the drug problem itself disproportionately burdens the black community.[30] If more blacks are using and selling drugs, equal enforcement of the drug laws will lead to disproportionate arrests and incarceration of African Americans. Even if that were the case, the fact that the disparities increase at each successive stage of both the criminal and juvenile justice processes suggests that greater drug use by blacks is not the whole story. In addition, as noted earlier, official estimates of drug use by race do not reflect the disparities evident in the criminal justice system, and in fact suggest very little racial disparity in drug use.

The effects of the drug war are difficult to measure. Critics contend that drugs are just as prevalent and cheap today as they were before the crackdown began in the mid-1980s. Proponents point to signs that crack use has declined, and that teen use of drugs generally has also fallen. But it is extremely difficult to say whether these trends are a result of the war on drugs. Scholars find that drug use goes in cycles, but they have never been able to find a correlation between fluctuations in drug use and criminal-law enforcement. One thing is certain, however: the stigmatization and incarceration of such a high proportion of young African-American males for drug crimes will have significant adverse long-term effects on the black community. A criminal record makes it much more difficult to find a legitimate job. We are disabling tens of thousands of young black men at the outset of their careers. The short-term "benefits" of removing offenders from the community may well come back to haunt us in the long term.

Three Strikes

Not so long ago, "three strikes and you're out" was just a baseball slogan. Today, it passes for a correctional philosophy. And here again, African Americans are disproportionately the losers. Between 1993 and 1995, twenty-four states and the federal government adopted some form of "three strikes and you're out" legislation, under which repeat offenders face life sentences for a third felony conviction.[31] (Georgia and South Carolina went even further, adopting "two strikes and you're out" laws.) California's three-strikes law, one of the first, was sparked by a repeat offender's abduction and murder of twelve-year-old Polly Klaas in Petaluma in 1993.[32] Under California's version, a second felony conviction doubles the sentence otherwise authorized, and a third felony conviction receives a mandatory twenty-five-year-to-life term, no matter how insubstantial the third conviction, so long as the prior convictions were for "violent" or "serious" crimes. The "three strikes" idea has been wildly popular; 72 percent of California's voters approved it in a popular referendum, and President Clinton himself jumped on the three-strikes bandwagon during the 1994 mid-term election campaign.[33] But the implementation of the laws has led to many problems.

First, the laws lead to draconian results. Jerry Dewayne Williams, for example, received a twenty-five-year sentence for stealing a slice of pizza from four young men at a

Los Angeles beach.[34] Another defendant's third strike consisted of stealing five bottles of liquor from a supermarket.[35] In its first two years, California's law led to life sentences for twice as many marijuana users as murderers, rapists, and kidnappers combined.[36] A California Department of Corrections study reported that 85 percent of those sentenced under the law were convicted most recently of a nonviolent crime.[37] Some have argued that focusing on the third strike is an unfair basis for criticism, because most offenders sentenced under the law have long criminal histories.[38] But the law is triggered even where a defendant's prior offenses are in the distant past, the third conviction is for a minor offense, and there is little likelihood that public safety required anything like a life sentence. Robert Wayne Washington, for example, received twenty-five years to life for a minor cocaine possession charge; his prior offenses were two eight-year-old burglaries and an intervening conviction for possession of contraband.[39]

Second, if the purpose of the law is to incapacitate those who would otherwise repeatedly prey on society, it is overinclusive. Most violent criminals have a relatively limited "criminal career," tailing off after ten years or so.[40] An individual's third strike often will not occur until his criminal career is on the wane. Thus, the three-strikes laws will impose life sentences on many offenders who pose little future danger to the community.

Third, such laws increase the costs of administering the criminal justice system. They make police work more dangerous, because a repeat offender facing a life sentence, in the words of Los Angeles Police Department spokesman Anthony Alba, is like "a cornered animal. If he knows he is going to get life in jail, he is definitely going to up the ante in eluding his captors."[41] Once apprehended, many defendants facing a third strike are unwilling to plead guilty, leading to a marked increase in criminal trials. Michael Judge, the chief public defender for Los Angeles County, said, "The law has created the single greatest increase in workload in the thirty years since I've been associated with the criminal justice system."[42] Two years into the California law's existence, an auditor estimated that it had cost Los Angeles County alone an extra $169 million.[43] The increase in criminal trials causes backlogs in the civil justice system, as the courts must increas-ingly devote themselves to criminal trials; as of 1996, 47 of California's 125 civil courts had to be diverted to hearing criminal cases.[44]

Three-strikes and other mandatory minimum laws have contributed to startling growth in our prison population. From 1980 to 1994, the national prison and jail population increased 195.6 percent.[45] By comparison, the general population increased from 1980 to 1990 by only 9.8 percent.[46] If the prison population continues to grow at the rate of increase from 1995–96, it would top 3.2 million in 2009. California alone has built sev enteen new jails in the last fifteen years. Its prison spending has increased over that period from 2 percent to almost 10 percent of its state budget, and it now spends more on corrections than on higher education.[47]

Despite these problems, the three-strikes approach remains extraordinarily popular. Why? One possibility is that, as with many other "get tough" policies, its direct burdens fall disproportionately on minorities. The Georgia case discussed above involving racially disparate application of a two-strikes law is not unique. In California, for example, blacks make up only 7 percent of the general population, yet as of 1996 they accounted for 43 percent of the third-strike defendants sent to state prison. Whites, by contrast, make up 53 percent of the general population in California, but only 24.6 percent of third-strike prisoners. This means that blacks are being imprisoned under California's three-strikes law at a rate 13.3 times that of the rate for whites. And because three-strikes convicts serve such long sentences, their proportion of the prison population will steadily increase; third-strikers comprised 8 percent of the total prison population in 1996, but the California Department of Corrections estimates that by 2024 they will amount to 49 percent.[48] Without a change in direction, the already stark racial disparities in our nation's prisons will only get worse. Yet it is precisely for that reason that there is unlikely to be a change in direction. As long as the effects of this get-tough measure are felt principally in minority communities, there is not likely to be sufficient political pressure for change.

When Is Disparity Discrimination?

As the figures above illustrate, it is beyond dispute that criminal sentencing is marked by stark racial *disparities.* But does this amount to *discrimination*? Everyone agrees that black defendants should not receive harsher penalties simply because they are black, and that criminals who attack white victims should not be punished more severely because the victims were white. But the disparities identified above may be attributable to factors other than race discrimination. Perhaps blacks commit more serious crimes per capita than whites. Social scientists and criminologists have long sought to determine through statistical analysis whether criminal sentencing is impermissibly affected by race, and have reached contradictory conclusions.

In the death penalty setting, as we have seen, most studies conclude that there is discrimination based on the race of the victim, even after controlling for other possible factors. In non-death penalty cases, however, the results are more mixed. In a 1993 study of the racial impact of the federal sentencing guidelines, for example, the U.S. Justice Department's Bureau of Justice Statistics found that although blacks on average received sentences that were almost two years longer than whites, the bulk of this disparity was due to the crack/cocaine sentencing disparity.[49] The study concluded that other racial differences in sentencing for drug trafficking, fraud, and embezzlement could be explained by nonracial factors such as prior prison records, guilty pleas, and severity of offense.[50] But the study also found that even after controlling for such factors, black offenders were 50 to 60 percent more likely to be sentenced for larceny than white offenders, and twice as likely as whites to be sentenced for weapons offenses.[51] Several other studies have concluded that racial disparities in sentencing are largely attributable to race-neutral factors, such as offense severity or prior criminal record.[52] Most criminologists agree that a substantial part—but not all—of sentencing disparity is attributable to blacks committing more serious crimes than whites.[53] However, all of these findings—both those that find discrimination and those that do not—are plagued by several inescapable problems.

First, in order to determine whether a racial *disparity* is the result of racial *discrimination,* one must compare similar cases. Where defendants similar in all respects but race are treated differently, one may reasonably conclude that discrimination has occurred. The rub lies in defining "similar." As Barbara Meierhoefer has argued,

> There is no disagreement that similar offenders should be sentenced similarly. The problem . . . is that there is no consensus as to what defines "similar offenders." Even outwardly empirical assessments of whether unwarranted disparity has been

reduced will be strongly influenced by which offense and offender characteristics are selected to define "similarly situated" offenders.[54]

Thus, for example, critics of the Baldus study used in *McCleskey* have argued that it did not sufficiently identify "similar" cases, and that therefore its conclusion that the remaining disparities were racial in nature was flawed.[55]

Second, even if we could identify and agree on all relevant race-neutral factors that might conceivably explain a disparity, no study can possibly measure all such factors.[56] Some of the most important factors, such as strength of evidence, credibility of witnesses, or the effectiveness of a lawyer's representation, are simply not susceptible to quantification. Quantifiable factors may be missing from available data. No study can absolutely eliminate the possibility that some unaccounted-for race-neutral variable that correlates with race has caused the apparent racial disparity.

Third, statistical studies may also err in the opposite direction, by concealing racial discrimination. A study of sentencing decisions that found that all racial disparities could be explained by offense severity and prior criminal records, for example, might conceal racial discrimination in police or prosecutorial practices. If police officers observe, stop, and arrest blacks at a higher rate than whites because of their race, blacks are more likely to develop criminal records, all other things being equal. Similarly, if prosecutors offer more generous plea bargains to white than black defendants because of their race, black defendants' sentencing reports will reflect higher "offense severity" and more serious criminal records. By focusing only on one stage of the criminal justice system, a statistician may miss discrimination occurring at another stage. At the same time, statistical studies may miss

discrimination if, in the aggregate, two forms of discrimination cancel each other out. For example, some biased sentencers might assign a longer sentence for a black-on-black crime because the *defendant* is black; others might impose a shorter sentence because the *victim* is black. If these biases cancel each other out in the aggregate, statistics may conceal actual discrimination.

For these reasons, statistical studies can rarely prove intentional discrimination. But even if none of the sentencing disparities outlined above is attributable to discrimination as the Supreme Court has defined it, they nonetheless raise serious questions about the racial fairness of our criminal justice policy. To see that this is so, one need only imagine the public response if the current racial disparities in criminal justice were reversed. Imagine what kind of pressure legislatures would feel, for example, if one in three young *white* men were in prison or on probation or parole. Imagine what the politics of the death penalty would look like if prosecutors sought the death penalty 70 percent of the time when whites killed blacks, but only 19 percent of the time when blacks killed whites. Or imagine what our juvenile justice policies would be like if white youth charged with drug offenses were four times as likely as black youth to be tried as adults, and twice as likely to be placed outside the home. One thing is certain: the nation would not accept such a situation as "inevitable."

Indeed, turning the tables on some of these statistics is almost beyond comprehension. If the per capita incarceration rate for whites were equal to that for blacks, more than 3.5 million white people would be incarcerated today, instead of 570,000, and we would need more than three times the prison capacity (and prosecution and court capacity) that we currently have. And because white people comprise about 80 percent of the general population, it would be literally impossible for whites to be overrepresented in the prison population to the same degree that black people currently are—four times their representation in the general population.

To see what happens when the criminal law begins to affect large numbers of white middle- and upper-class people, one need only look at the history of marijuana laws. The country's first marijuana users were largely nonwhite, mostly Mexicans.[57] By 1937, every state had criminalized marijuana. In the 1950s, federal penalties for the sale of marijuana ranged from two to five years imprisonment; a second offense brought a sentence of five to ten years; and a third brought ten to twenty years. State penalties followed suit. In 1956, Congress imposed mandatory minimum sentences for marijuana possession and sale.

In the 1960s, however, marijuana spread to the white middle and upper classes. By 1970, some college campuses reported that at least 70 percent of their student population had tried marijuana. As one author wrote in 1970, "Vast numbers of people have recently adopted the drug as their principal euphoriant; however, by all estimates, the new users are the sons and daughters of the middle class, not the ethnic minorities and ghetto residents formerly associated with marijuana."[58] The harsh penalties imposed when their effect was primarily felt by minorities were no longer acceptable, and marijuana laws were liberalized. As Dr. Stanley Yolles explained in 1970,

> Nobody cared when it was a ghetto problem. Marijuana—well, it was used by jazz musicians or the lower class, so you didn't care if they got 20 years. But when a nice, middle-class girl or boy in college gets busted for the same thing, then the whole community sits up and takes notice. And that's the name of the game today. The problem has begun to come

home to roost—in all strata of society, in suburbia, in middle-class homes, in the colleges. Suddenly, the punitive, the vindictive approach was touching all classes of society. And now the most exciting thing that's really happening is the change in attitude by the people. Now we have a willingness to examine the problem, as to whether it's an experimentation, or an illness rather than an "evil."[59]

Police and prosecutors began to leave users alone, and instead targeted dealers and sellers. The courts limited enforcement, using their discretion to invalidate convictions on a variety of grounds. And the legislatures amended the laws, eliminating strict penalties for possession. As one commentator described the development, "In response to the extraordinary explosion in marijuana consumption and the penetration of its use into the mainstream of American life, every state amended its penalties in some fashion between 1969 and 1972, the overall result being a massive downward shift in penalties for consumption-related offenses. Simple possession of less than one ounce was classified as a misdemeanor in all but eight states by the end of 1972."[60] In 1973, Oregon went further and actually decriminalized possession of small amounts of marijuana, and by 1981 ten other states had followed suit.[61]

When the effects of a criminal law reach the sons and daughters of the white majority, our response is not to get tough, but rather to get lenient. Americans have been able to sustain an unremittingly harsh tough-on-crime attitude precisely because the burden of punishment falls disproportionately on minority populations. The white majority could not possibly maintain its current attitude toward crime and punishment were the burden of punishment felt by the same white majority that prescribes it.

NOTES

1. Jim Newton, "Judges Voice Anger over Mandatory U.S. Sentences," *L.A. Times,* 21 August 1993, A1.

2. As of 1995, there were 14,000 people in prison for federal crack convictions, 80 percent of whom were black. Ronald Smothers, "Wave of Prison Uprisings Provokes Debate on Crack," *N.Y. Times,* 24 October 1995, A18.

3. H. R. Rep. No. 104-272 at 20 (1995), reprinted in 1995 U.S.C.C.A.N. 335,353 (citing U.S. Sentencing Commission study).

4. *United States v. Armstrong,* 517 U.S. 456 (1996) (Stevens, J., dissenting) (citing United States Sentencing Commission, Special Report to Congress: *Cocaine and Federal Sentencing Policy,* 39, 161 (1995).

5. *United States v. Clary,* 846 F. Supp. 768, 787 (E. D. Mo. 1994); see also *United States v. Walls,* 841 F. Supp. 24, 28 (D.D.C. 1994).

6. *State v. Russell,* 477 N.W.2d 886, 887 n.1 (Minn. 1991). In the Eastern District of Missouri, 98.2 percent of defendants convicted of crack cocaine charges from 1988 to 1992 were black. *United States v. Clary,* 846 F. Supp. at 786.

7. See, e.g., *United States v. Richardson,* 130 F.3d 765 (7th Cir. 1997); *United States v. Andrade,* 94 F.3d 9 (1st Cir. 1996); *United States v. Teague,* 93 F.3d 81 (2d Cir. 1996), *cert. denied,* 117 S. Ct. 708 (1997); *United States v. Lloyd,* 10 F.3d 1197 (6th Cir. 1993), *cert. denied,* 513 U.S. 883 (1994); *United States v. Jackson,* 67 F.3d 1359 (8th Cir. 1995), *cert. denied,* 517 U.S. 1192 (1996).

8. United States Sentencing Comm., Special Report to the Congress, *supra* note 4.

9. In 1997, the Sentencing Commission recommended reducing rather than eliminating the disparity, and the Clinton Administration supported the proposal. As of this writing, Congress has not acted on the recommendation.

10. *Stephens v. State,* 1995 WL 116292 (Ga. S. Ct. Mar. 17, 1995).

11. *Stephens v. State,* 456 S.E.2d 560 (Ga. 1995).

12. American Bar Association, *The State of Criminal Justice,* 9 (February 1993) (23 percent minority increase, 10 percent nonminority).

13. Id.

14. Jerome G. Miller, *Search and Destroy: African American Males in the Criminal Justice System,* 81 (New York: Cambridge Univ. Press, 1996).

15. Marc Mauer & Tracy Juling, The Sentencing Project, *Young Black Americans and the Criminal Justice System: Five Years Later,* 12 (1995).

16. David J. Rothman, "The Crime of Punishment," *New York Rev. of Books,* 17 February 1994, 34, 37.

17. Jerome G. Miller, *Search and Destroy, supra* note 14.

18. Id.

19. Id.

20. Marc Mauer, *Intended and Unintended Consequences: State Racial Disparities in Imprisonment,* 10 (Sentencing Project, Jan. 1997).

21. Human Rights Watch, *Cruel and Unusual: Disproportionate Sentences for New York Drug Offenders,* 2 (March 1997).

22. Dep't of Justice, Bureau of Justice Statistics Bulletin, *Prisoners in 1994,* 10, Table 13 (1995).

23. Id. at 11, Table 14 (state prisoners incarcerated on drug offenses increased from 19,000 in 1980 to 186,000 in 1993).

24. American Bar Association, *State of Criminal Justice, supra* note 12.

25. Office of Juvenile Justice and Delinquency Programs, *Juvenile Court Statistics 1991,* 25, Table 35, 71, Table 114 (May 1994). In this source, Hispanic youth were included in the "white" racial category.

26. 13,800 black juveniles were detained for drug violations, as compared to 7,400 white juveniles. Id. at 74, Table 118, 28, Table 39.

27. Id. at 29, Table 40.

28. Id. at 25, Table 37.

29. National Center on Institutions and Alternatives, *Hobbling a Generation: Young African American Males in the Criminal Justice System of America's Cities: Baltimore, Maryland* (September 1992).

30. See, e.g., Randall Kennedy, "The State, Criminal Law, and Racial Discrimination: A Comment," 107 Harv. L. Rev. 1255 (1994). For a detailed response, see David Cole, "The Paradox of Race and Crime: A Comment on Randall Kennedy's 'Politics of Distinction,'" 83 Geo. L.J. 2547 (1995); see also Randall Kennedy, "A Response to Professor Cole's 'Paradox of Race and Crime,'" 83 *Geo. L.J.* 2573 (1995).

31. National Institute of Justice, Department of Justice, *Three Strikes and You're Out: A Review of State Legislation*, 1 (September 1997); Tom Rhodes, "Third Strike and Pizza Thief Is Out for 25 Years," *The Times*, 4 April 1996 (available on NEXIS).

32. Maura Dolan & Tony Perry, "Justices Deal Blow to '3 Strikes,'" *L.A. Times*, 31 June 1996, A1.

33. Id.; see also The President's Radio Address, Weekly Comp. Pres. Doc. 1493 (July 16, 1994) (supporting "three strikes and you're out" provision in federal crime bill).

34. Rhodes, *supra* note 31.

35. Daniel B. Wood, "Softer Three-Strikes Law Brings Wave of Appeals," *Christian Science Monitor*, 24 June 1996, 3.

36. Christopher Davis, Richard Estes, and Vincent Schiraldi, *"Three Strikes:" The New Apartheid* (Report of the Center on Juvenile and Criminal Justice, San Francisco, March 1996).

37. Fox Butterfield, "Tough Law on Sentences is Criticized," *N.Y. Times*, 8 March 1996, A14.

38. See, e.g., Andy Furillo, "Most Offenders Have Long Criminal Histories," *Sacramento Bee*, 31 March 1996, A1.

39. Id.

40. William Spelman, *Criminal Incapacitation*, 15 (New York: Plenum Press, 1994) ("the typical criminal career lasts only 5 to 10 years"); 1 *Criminal Careers and Career Criminals*, 94 (Alfred Blumstein et al., eds.) (Washington, D.C.: National Academy Press, 1986) (same).

41. Daniel B. Wood, "LA Police Lash Out Against Three Strikes," *Christian Science Monitor*, 29 March 1996, 3.

42. Fox Butterfield, *supra* note 37.

43. Id.

44. Ian Katz, "Bull Market in Prisons and Knee-Jerk Politics," *The Guardian*, 25 May 1996 (available on NEXIS).

45. Bureau of Justice Statistics, *Sourcebook of Criminal Justice Statistics—1995*, Table 6.11 (1996).

46. Ann Golenpaul, ed., *Information Please Almanac*, 829 (Boston: Houghton Mifflin, 1997).

47. Ian Katz, *supra* note 44.

48. Christopher Davis, et al., *supra* note 36.

49. Douglas C. McDonald & Kenneth F. Carlson, *Sentencing in the Federal Courts: Does Race Matter? The Transition to Sentencing Guidelines, 1986–90: Summary*, 1–2 (Washington, D.C.: Bureau of Justice Statistics, 1993).

50. Id. at 13–17.

51. Id. at 16–17.

52. See, e.g. Stephen Klein, Joan Petersilia, and Susan Turner, "Race and Imprisonment Decisions in California," 247 *Science* 812–16 (Feb. 16, 1990) (studying California sentences and concluding that race did not improve the accuracy of predicting what type of punishment offenders would receive); Alfred Blumstein, "On the Racial Disproportionality of United States Prison Populations," 73 J. of Crim. L. & Crim. 1259 (1983) (finding little evidence of racial bias in incarceration for serious crimes); but see Jerome Miller, *Search and Destroy*, *supra* note 14 (reviewing studies finding evidence of racial discrimination); Crutchfield, et. al, "Analytical and Aggregation Biases in Analysis of Imprisonment: Reconciling Discrepancies in Studies of Racial Disparity," 31 J. of Res. In Crime & Delinquency 178 (1994) (critiquing prior studies for aggregating information in a way that might conceal discrimination; finding evidence of discrimination).

53. Michael H. Tonry, *Malign Neglect: Race, Crime, and Punishment in America*, 29 (New York: Oxford Univ. Press, 1995).

54. Barbara S. Meierhoefer, "Individualized and Systemic Justice in the Federal Sentencing Process," 29 Am. Crim. L. Rev. 889, 891 (1992).

55. William Wilbanks, *The Myth of a Racist Criminal Justice System* (Monterey, CA: Brooks/Cole, 1986).

56. Stephen P. Klein, *Racial Disparities in Sentencing Decisions*, 5 (Santa Monica, CA: Rand, 1991).

57. Unless otherwise indicated, the information in the next two paragraphs is drawn from Bonnie Whitebread, "Marijuana Prohibition," 56 U.Va. L. Rev. 983 (1970).

58. Whitebread, 56 Va. L. Rev. at 1096.

59. Gertrude Samuels, "Pot, Hard Drugs, and the Law," *N.Y. Times Magazine*, 15 February 1970, 14.

60. Richard J. Bonnie, "The Meaning of 'Decriminalization': A Review of the Law," Contemporary Drug Problems 277, 278 (Fall 1981).

61. Id. at 279; see also Bureau of Justice Statistics, U.S. Dept of Justice, *Drugs, Crime and the*

Justice System, 84–85 (1992) (reporting that when large numbers of white middle-class youth were arrested for marijuana possession in the late 1960s and early 1970s, public complaints led Congress and eleven states to decriminalize or reduce substantially the penalties for that crime).

SEEING THE BIG PICTURE

Look at Juvenile Drug Offenses in the section on Crime in Section IV of the Appendix. How might Cole explain the huge difference in arrest statistics between blacks and other racial groups?

27

RACE AND CRIMINALIZATION: BLACK AMERICANS AND THE PUNISHMENT INDUSTRY

Angela Y. Davis

QUESTIONS TO CONSIDER

Angela Davis links the growth of the prison industrial complex to the "war on drugs" and to institutional racism. How do race and racism figure into in her analysis of who gets targeted for America's "war on drugs"? How might racial stereotypes and the huge profits generated by the "prison industrial complex" shape the ways legislation is written by corporate lobbyists and lawmakers?

I n this post–civil rights era, as racial barriers in high economic and political realms are apparently shattered with predictable regularity, race itself becomes an increasingly proscribed subject. In the

dominant political discourse it is no longer acknowledged as a pervasive structural phenomenon, requiring the continuation of such strategies as affirmative action, but rather is represented primarily as a complex of prejudicial attitudes, which carry equal weight across all racial boundaries. Black leadership is thus often discredited and the identification of race as a public, political issue itself called into question through the invocation of, and application of the epithet "black racist" to, such figures as Louis Farrakhan and Khalid Abdul Muhammad. Public debates about the role of the state that once focused very sharply and openly on issues of "race" and racism are now expected to unfold in the absence of any direct acknowledgment of the persistence and indeed further entrenchment—of racially structured power relationships. Because race is ostracized from some of the most impassioned political debates of this period, their racialized character becomes increasingly difficult to identify, especially by those who are unable—or do not want—to decipher the encoded language. This means that hidden racist arguments can be mobilized readily across racial boundaries and political alignments. Political positions once easily defined as conservative, liberal, and sometimes even radical therefore have a tendency to lose their distinctiveness in the face of the seductions of this camouflaged racism.

President Clinton chose the date of the Million Man March, convened by Minister Louis Farrakhan of the Nation of Islam, to issue a call for a "national conversation on race," borrowing ironically the exact words of Lani Guinier (whose nomination for assistant attorney general in charge of civil rights he had previously withdrawn because her writings focused too sharply on issues of race).[1] Guinier's ideas had been so easily dismissed because of the prevailing ideological equation of the "end of racism" with the removal of all allusions to race. If conservative positions argue that race consciousness itself impedes the process of solving the problem of race—i. e., achieving race blindness—then Clinton's speech indicated an attempt to reconcile the two, positing race consciousness as a means of moving toward race blindness. "There are too many today, white and black, on the left and the right, on the street corners and radio waves, who seek to sow division for their

own purposes. To them I say: 'No more. We must be one.'"

While Clinton did acknowledge "the awful history and the stubborn persistence of racism," his remarks foregrounded those reasons for the "racial divide" that "are rooted in the fact that we still haven't learned to talk frankly, to listen carefully and to work together across racial lines." Race, he insisted, is not about government, but about the hearts of people. Of course, it would be absurd to deny the degree to which racism infects in deep and multiple ways the national psyche. However, the relegation of race to matters of the heart tends to render it increasingly difficult to identify the deep structural entrenchment of contemporary racism.

When the structural character of racism is ignored in discussions about crime and the rising population of incarcerated people, the racial imbalance in jails and prisons is treated as a contingency, at best as a product of the "culture of poverty," and at worst as proof of an assumed black monopoly on criminality. The high proportion of black people in the criminal justice system is thus normalized and neither the state nor the general public is required to talk about and act on the meaning of that racial imbalance. Thus Republican and Democratic elected officials alike have successfully called for laws mandating life sentences for three-time "criminals," without having to answer for the racial implications of these laws. By relying on the alleged "race-blindness" of such laws, black people are surreptitiously constructed as racial subjects, thus manipulated, exploited, and abused, while the structural persistence of racism—albeit in changed forms—in social and economic institutions, and in the national culture as a whole, is adamantly denied.

Crime is thus one of the masquerades behind which "race," with all its menacing ideological complexity, mobilizes old public fears *and* creates new ones. The current anti-crime debate takes place within a reified mathematical realm—a strategy reminiscent of Malthus's notion of the geometrical increase in population and the arithmetical increase in food sources, thus the inevitability of poverty and the means of suppressing it: war, disease, famine, and natural disasters. As a matter of fact, the persisting neo-Malthusian approach to population control, which, instead of seeking to solve those pressing social problems that result in real pain and suffering in people's lives, calls for the elimination of those suffering lives—finds strong resonances in the public discussion about expurgating the "nation" of crime. These discussions include arguments deployed by those who are leading the call for more prisons and employ statistics in the same fetishistic and misleading way as Malthus did more than two centuries ago. Take for example James Wooten's comments in the *Heritage Founda-tion State Backgrounder:*

> If the 55% of the 800,000 current state and federal prisoners who are violent offenders were subject to serving 85% of their sentence, and assuming that those violent offenders would have committed 10 violent crimes a year while on the street, then the number of crimes prevented each year by truth in sentencing would be 4,000,000. That would be over $^2/_3$ of the 6,000,000 violent crimes reported.[2]

In *Reader's Digest,* Senior Editor Eugene H. Methvin writes:

> If we again double the present federal and state prison population—to somewhere between 1 million and 1.5 million and leave our city and county jail population at the present 400,000, we will break the back of America's 30 year crime wave.[3]

The real human beings—a vastly disproportionate number of whom are black and Latino/a men and women—designated by these numbers in a seemingly race-neutral way are deemed fetishistically exchangeable with the crimes they have or will allegedly commit. The real impact of imprisonment on their lives never need be examined. The inevitable part played by the punishment industry in the reproduction of crime never need be discussed. The dangerous and indeed fascistic trend toward progressively greater numbers of hidden, incarcerated human populations is itself rendered invisible. All that matters is the elimination of crime—and you get rid of crime by getting rid of people who, according to the prevailing racial common sense, are the most likely people to whom criminal acts will be attributed. Never mind that if this strategy is seriously and consistently pursued, the majority of young black women spend a good portion of their lives behind walls and bars in order to serve as a reminder that the state is aggressively confronting its enemy.[4]

While I do not want to locate a response to these arguments on the same level of mathematical abstraction and fetishism I have been problematizing, it is helpful, I think, to consider how many people are presently incarcerated or whose lives are subject to the direct surveillance of the criminal justice system. There are already approximately 1 million people in state and federal prisons in the United States, not counting the 500,000 in city and county jails or the 600,000 on parole or the 3 million people on probation or the 60,000 young people in juvenile facilities. Which is to say that there are presently over 5.1 million people either incarcerated, on parole, or on probation. Many of those presently on probation or parole would be behind bars under the conditions of the recently passed crime bill. According to the Sentencing Project, even before the passage of the crime bill, black people were 7.8 times more likely to be imprisoned than whites.[5] The Sentencing Project's most recent report[6] indicates that 32.2 percent of young black men and 12.3 percent of young Latino men between the ages of twenty and twenty-nine are either in prison, in jail, or on probation or parole. This is in comparison with 6.7 percent of young white men. A total of 827,440 young African-American males are under the supervision of the criminal justice system, at a cost of $6 billion per year. A major strength of the 1995 report, as compared to its predecessor, is its acknowledgment that the racialized impact of the criminal justice system is also gendered and that the relatively smaller number of African-American women drawn into the system should not relieve us of the responsibility of understanding the encounter of gender and race in arrest and incarceration practices. Moreover, the increases in women's contact with the criminal justice system have been even more dramatic than those of men.

> The 78% increase in criminal justice control rates for black women was more than double the increase for black men and for white women, and more than nine times the increase for white men. . . . Although research on women of color in the criminal justice system is limited, existing data and research suggest that it is the combination of race and sex effects that is at the root of the trends which appear in our data. For example, while the number of blacks and Hispanics in prison is growing at an alarming rate, the rate of increase for women is even greater. Between 1980 and 1992 the female prison population increased 276% compared to 163% for men. Unlike men of color, women of color thus belong to two groups that are experiencing particular dramatic growth in their contact with the criminal justice system.[7]

It has been estimated that by the year 2000 the number of people imprisoned will surpass 4 million, a grossly disproportionate number of whom will be black people, and

that the cost will be over $40 billion a year,[8] a figure that is reminiscent of the way the military budget devoured—and continues to devour—the country's resources. This out-of-control punishment industry is an extremely effective criminalization industry, for the racial imbalance in incarcerated populations is not recognized as evidence of structural racism, but rather is invoked as a consequence of the assumed criminality of black people. In other words, the criminalization process works so well precisely because of the hidden logic of racism. Racist logic is deeply entrenched in the nation's material and psychic structures. It is something with which we are all very familiar. The logic, in fact, can persist, even when direct allusions to "race" are removed.

Even those communities that are most deeply injured by this racist logic have learned how to rely upon it, particularly when open allusions to race are not necessary. Thus, in the absence of broad, radical grassroots movements in poor black communities so devastated by new forms of youth-perpetuated violence, the ideological options are extremely sparse. Often there are no other ways to express collective rage and despair but to demand that police sweep the community clean of crack and Uzis, and of the people who use and sell drugs and wield weapons. Ironically, Carol Moseley-Braun, the first black woman senator in our nation's history, was an enthusiastic sponsor of the Senate Anticrime Bill, whose passage in November 1993 paved the way for the August 25, 1994, passage of the bill by the House. Or perhaps there is little irony here. It may be precisely because there is a Carol Moseley-Braun in the Senate and a Clarence Thomas in the Supreme Court—and concomitant class differentiations and other factors responsible for far more heterogeneity in black communities than at any other time in this country's history—that implicit consent to antiblack racist logic (not to speak of racism toward other groups) becomes far more widespread among black people. Wahneema Lubiano's explorations of the complexities of state domination as it operates within and through the subjectivities of those who are the targets of this domination facilitates an understanding of this dilemma.[9]

Borrowing the title of Cornel West's recent work, race *matters*. Moreover, it matters in ways that are far more threatening and simultaneously less discernible than those to which we have grown accustomed. Race matters inform, more than ever, the ideological and material structures of U.S. society. And, as the current discourses on crime, welfare, and immigration reveal, race, gender, and class matter enormously in the continuing elaboration of public policy and its impact on the real lives of human beings.

And how does race matter? Fear has always been an integral component of racism. The ideological reproduction of a fear of black people, whether economically or sexually grounded, is rapidly gravitating toward and being grounded in a fear of crime. A question to be raised in this context is whether and how the increasing fear of crime—this ideologically produced fear of crime—serves to render racism simultaneously more invisible and more virulent. Perhaps one way to approach an answer to this question is to consider how this fear of crime effectively summons black people to imagine black people as the enemy. How many black people present at this conference have successfully extricated ourselves from the ideological power of the figure of the young black male as criminal—or at least seriously confronted it? The lack of a significant black presence in the rather feeble opposition to the "three strikes, you're out" bills, which have been proposed and/or passed in forty states already, evidences the disarming effect of this ideology.

California is one of the states that has passed the "three strikes, you're out" bill. Immediately after the passage of that bill, Governor Pete Wilson began to argue for a "two strikes, you're out" bill. Three, he said, is too many. Soon we will hear calls for "one strike, you're out." Following this mathematical regression, we can imagine that at some point the hardcore anticrime advocates will be arguing that to stop the crime wave, we can't wait until even one crime is committed. Their slogan will be: "Get them before the first strike!" And because certain populations have already been criminalized, there will be those who say, "We know who the real criminals are— let's get them before they have a chance to act out their criminality."

The fear of crime has attained a status that bears a sinister similarity to the fear of communism as it came to restructure social perceptions during the fifties and sixties. The figure of the "criminal"—the racialized figure of the criminal—has come to represent the most menacing enemy of "American society." Virtually anything is acceptable—torture, brutality, vast expenditures of public funds—as long as it is done in the name of public safety. Racism has always found an easy route from its embeddedness in social structures to the psyches of collectives and individuals precisely because it mobilizes deep fears. While explicit, old-style racism may be increasingly socially unacceptable—precisely as a result of antiracist movements over the last forty years— this does not mean that U.S. society has been purged of racism. In fact, racism is more deeply embedded in socioeconomic structures, and the vast populations of incarcerated people of color is dramatic evidence of the way racism systematically structures economic relations. At the same time, this structural racism is rarely recognized as "racism." What we have come to recognize as open, explicit racism has in many ways begun to be replaced by a secluded, camouflaged kind of racism, whose influence on people's daily lives is as pervasive and systematic as the explicit forms of racism associated with the era of the struggle for civil rights.

The ideological space for the proliferations of this racialized fear of crime has been opened by the transformations in international politics created by the fall of the European socialist countries. Communism is no longer the quintessential enemy against which the nation imagines its identity. This space is now inhabited by ideological constructions of crime, drugs, immigration, and welfare. Of course, the enemy within is far more dangerous than the enemy without, and a black enemy within is the most dangerous of all.

Because of the tendency to view it as an abstract site into which all manner of undesirables are deposited, the prison is the perfect site for the simultaneous production and concealment of racism. The abstract character of the public perception of prisons militates against an engagement with the real issues afflicting the communities from which prisoners are drawn in such disproportionate numbers. This is the ideological work that the prison performs—it relieves us of the responsibility of seriously engaging with the problems of late capitalism, of transnational capitalism. The naturalization of black people as criminals thus also erects ideological barriers to an understanding of the connections between late-twentieth century structural racism and the globalization of capital.

The vast expansion of the power of capitalist corporations over the lives of people of color and poor people in general has been accompanied by a waning anticapitalist consciousness. As capital moves with ease across national borders, legitimized by recent trade agreements such as NAFTA and GATT,

corporations are allowed to close shop in the United States and transfer manufacturing operations to nations providing cheap labor pools. In fleeing organized labor in the U.S. to avoid paying higher wages and benefits, they leave entire communities in shambles, consigning huge numbers of people to joblessness, leaving them prey to the drug trade, destroying the economic base of these communities, thus affecting the education system, social welfare—and turning the people who live in those communities into perfect candidates for prison. At the same time, they create an economic demand for prisons, which stimulates the economy, providing jobs in the correctional industry for people who often come from the very populations that are criminalized by this process. It is a horrifying and self-reproducing cycle.

Ironically, prisons themselves are becoming a source of cheap labor that attracts corporate capitalism—as yet on a relatively small scale—in a way that parallels the attraction unorganized labor in Third World countries exerts. A statement by Michael Lamar Powell, a prisoner in Capshaw, Alabama, dramatically reveals this new development:

> I cannot go on strike, nor can I unionize. I am not covered by workers' compensation or the Fair Standards Act. I agree to work late-night and weekend shifts. I do just what I am told, no matter what it is. I am hired and fired at will, and I am not even paid minimum wage: I earn one dollar a month. I cannot even voice grievances or complaints, except at the risk of incurring arbitrary discipline or some covert retaliation.
>
> You need not worry about NAFTA and your jobs going to Mexico and other Third World countries. I will have at least five percent of your jobs by the end of this decade.
>
> I am called prison labor. I am The New American Worker.[10]

This "new American worker" will be drawn from the ranks of a racialized population whose historical superexploitation—from the era of slavery to the present—has been legitimized by racism. At the same time, the expansion of convict labor is accompanied in some states by the old paraphernalia of ankle chains that symbolically links convict labor with slave labor. At least three states—Alabama, Florida, and Arizona—have reinstituted the chain gang. Moreover, as Michael Powell so inclusively reveals, there is a new dimension to the racism inherent in this process, which structurally links the superexploitation of prison labor to the globalization of capital.

In California, whose prison system is the largest in the country and one of the largest in the world, the passage of an inmate initiative in 1990 has presented businesses seeking cheap labor with opportunities uncannily similar to those in Third World countries. As of June 1994, a range of companies were employing prison labor in nine California prisons. Under the auspices of the Joint Venture Program, work now being performed on prison grounds includes computerized telephone messaging, dental apparatus assembly, computer data entry, plastic parts fabrication, electronic component manufacturing at the Central California Women's facility at Chowchilla, security glass manufacturing, swine production, oak furniture manufacturing, and the production of stainless steel tanks and equipment. In a California Corrections Department brochure designed to promote the program, it is described as "an innovative public-private partnership that makes good business sense."[11] According to the owner of Tower Communications, whom the brochure quotes,

> The operation is cost effective, dependable and trouble free. . . . Tower Communications has successfully operated a message center utilizing inmates on the grounds of

California state prison. If you're a business leader planning expansion, considering relocation because of a deficient labor pool, starting a new enterprise, look into the benefits of using inmate labor.

The employer benefits listed by the brochure include

> federal and state tax incentives; no benefit package (retirement pay, vacation pay, sick leave, medical benefits); long term lease agreements at far below market value costs; discount rates on Workers Compensation; build a consistent, qualified work force; on call labor pool (no car breakdowns, no babysitting problems); option of hiring job-ready ex-offenders and minimizing costs; becoming a partner in public safety.

There is a major, yet invisible, racial supposition in such claims about the profitability of a convict labor force. The acceptability of the superexploitation of convict labor is largely based on the historical conjuncture of racism and incarceration practices. The already disproportionately black convict labor force will become increasingly black if the racially imbalanced incarceration practices continue.

The complicated yet unacknowledged structural presence of racism in the U.S. punishment industry also includes the fact that the punishment industry which sequesters ever-larger sectors of the black population attracts vast amounts of capital. Ideologically, as I have argued, the racialized fear of crime has begun to succeed the fear of communism. This corresponds to a structural tendency for capital that previously flowed toward the military industry to now move toward the punishment industry. The ease with which suggestions are made for prison construction costing in the multi-billions of dollars is reminiscent of the military buildup: economic mobilization to defeat communism has turned into economic mobilization to defeat crime. The ideological construction of crime is thus complemented and bolstered by the material construction of jails and prisons. The more jails and prisons are constructed, the greater the fear of crime, and the greater the fear of crime, the stronger the cry for more jails and prisons, ad infinitum.

The law enforcement industry bears remarkable parallels to the military industry (just as there are anti-Communist resonances in the anti-crime campaign). This connection between the military industry and the punishment industry is revealed in a *Wall Street Journal* article entitled "Making Crime Pay: The Cold War of the, '90s":

> Parts of the defense establishment are cashing in, too, scenting a logical new line of business to help them offset military cutbacks. Westinghouse Electric Corp., Minnesota Mining and Manufacturing Co., GDE Systems (a division of the old General Dynamics) and Alliant Techsystems Inc., for instance, are pushing crime-fighting equipment and have created special divisions to retool their defense technology for America's streets.

According to the article, a conference sponsored by the National Institute of Justice, the research arm of the Justice Department, was organized around the theme "Law Enforcement Technology in the 21st Century." The secretary of defense was a major presenter at this conference, which explored topics like "the role of the defense industry, particularly for dual use and conversion":

> Hot topics: defense-industry technology that could lower the level of violence involved in crime fighting. Sandia National Laboratories, for instance, is experimenting with a dense foam that can be sprayed at suspects, temporarily blinding and deafening them under breathable bubbles. Stinger Corporation is working on "smart

guns," which will fire only for the owner, and retractable spiked barrier strips to unfurl in front of fleeing vehicles. Westinghouse is promoting the "smart car," in which mini-computers could be linked up with big mainframes at the police department, allowing for speedy booking of prisoners, as well as quick exchanges of information.[12]

Again, race provides a silent justification for the technological expansion of law enforcement, which, in turn, intensifies racist arrest and incarceration practices. This skyrocketing punishment industry, whose growth is silently but powerfully sustained by the persistence of racism, creates an economic demand for more jails and prisons and thus for similarly spiraling criminalization practices, which, in turn fuels the fear of crime.

Most debates addressing the crisis resulting from overcrowding in prisons and jails focus on male institutions. Meanwhile, women's institutions and jail space for women are proportionately proliferating at an even more astounding rate than men's. If race is largely an absent factor in the discussions about crime and punishment, gender seems not even to merit a place carved out by its absence. Historically, the imprisonment of women has served to criminalize women in a way that is more complicated than is the case with men. This female criminalization process has had more to do with the marking of certain groups of women as undomesticated and hypersexual, as women who refuse to embrace the nuclear family as paradigm. The current liberal-conservative discourse around welfare criminalizes black single mothers, who are represented as deficient, manless, drug-using breeders of children, and as reproducers of an attendant culture of poverty. The woman who does drugs is criminalized both because she is a drug user and because as a consequence, she cannot be a good mother. In some states, pregnant women are being imprisoned for using crack because of possible damage to the fetus.

According to the U.S. Department of Justice, women are far more likely than men to be imprisoned for a drug conviction.[13] However, if women wish to receive treatment for their drug problems, often their only option, if they cannot pay for a drug program, is to be arrested and sentenced to a drug program via the criminal justice system. Yet when U.S. Surgeon General Jocelyn Elders alluded to the importance of opening discussion on the decriminalization of drugs, the Clinton administration immediately disassociated itself from her remarks. Decriminalization of drugs would greatly reduce the numbers of incarcerated women, for the 278 percent increase in the numbers of black women in state and federal prisons (as compared to the 186 percent increase in the numbers of black men) can be largely attributed to the phenomenal rise in drug-related and specifically crack-related imprisonment. According to the Sentencing Project's 1995 report, the increase amounted to 828 percent.[14]

Official refusals to even consider decriminalization of drugs as a possible strategy that might begin to reverse present incarceration practices further bolsters the ideological staying power of the prison. In his well-known study of the history of the prison and its related technologies of discipline, Michel Foucault pointed out that an evolving contradiction is at the very heart of the historical project of imprisonment.

> For a century and a half, the prison has always been offered as its own remedy: . . . the realization of the corrective project as the only method of overcoming the impossibility of implementing it.[15]

As I have attempted to argue, within the U.S. historical context, racism plays a pivotal role in sustaining this contradiction. In fact, Foucault's theory regarding the prison's tendency to serve as its own enduring justification becomes even more compelling if the role of race is also acknowledged. Moreover, moving beyond the parameters of what I consider the double impasse implied by his theory—the discursive impasse his theory discovers and that of the theory itself—I want to conclude by suggesting the possibility of radical race-conscious strategies designed to disrupt the stranglehold of criminalization and incarceration practices.

In the course of a recent collaborative research project with U.C. Santa Barbara sociologist Kum-Kum Bhavnani, in which we interviewed thirty-five women at the San Francisco County Jail, the complex ways in which race and gender help to produce a punishment industry that reproduces the very problems it purports to solve become dramatically apparent. Our interviews focused on the women's ideas about imprisonment and how they themselves imagine alternatives to incarceration. Their various critiques of the prison system and of the existing "alternatives," all of which are tied to reimprisonment as a last resort, led us to reflect more deeply about the importance of retrieving, retheorizing, and reactivating the radical abolitionist strategy first proposed in connection with the prison-reform movements of the sixties and seventies.

We are presently attempting to theorize women's imprisonment in ways that allow us to formulate a radical abolitionist strategy departing from, but not restricted in its conclusions to, women's jails and prisons. Our goal is to formulate alternatives to incarceration that substantively reflect the voices and agency of a variety of imprisoned women. We wish to open up channels for their involvement in the current debates around alternatives to incarceration, while not denying our own role as mediators and interpreters and our own political positioning in these debates. We also want to distinguish our explorations of alternatives from the spate of "alternative punishments" or what are now called "intermediate sanctions" presently being proposed and/or implemented by and through state and local correctional systems.

This is a long-range project that has three dimensions: academic research, public policy, and community organizing. In other words, for this project to be successful, it must build bridges between academic work, legislative and other policy interventions, and grassroots campaigns calling, for example, for the decriminalization of drugs and prostitution—and for the reversal of the present proliferation of jails and prisons.

Raising the possibility of abolishing jails and prisons as the institutionalized and normalized means of addressing social problems in an era of migrating corporations, unemployment and homelessness, and collapsing public services, from health care to education, can hopefully help to interrupt the current law-and-order discourse that has such a grip on the collective imagination, facilitated as it is by deep and hidden influences of racism. This late-twentieth-century "abolitionism," with its nineteenth-century resonances, may also lead to a historical recontextualization of the practice of imprisonment. With the passage of the Thirteenth Amendment, slavery was abolished for all except convicts—and in a sense the exclusion from citizenship accomplished by the slave system has persisted within the U.S. prison system. Only three states allow prisoners to vote, and approximately 4 million people are denied the right to vote because of their present or past incarceration. A radical strategy to abolish jails and prisons as the normal way of dealing with the social problems of late capitalism is not a strategy for abstract abolition. It is designed to force a rethinking of the increasingly repressive role of the state during this era of late capitalism and to carve out a space for resistance.

NOTES

1. See, for instance, the *Austin-American Statesman,* October 17, 1995.

3. Charles S. Clark, "Prison Overcrowding," *Congressional Quarterly Researcher* 4, no. 5 (Feb. 4, 1994): 97–119.

3. Ibid.

4. Marc Mauer, "Young Black Men and the Criminal Justice System: A Growing National Problem," Washington, D.C.: The Sentencing Project, February 1990.

5. Alexander Cockburn, *Philadelphia Inquirer,* August 29, 1994.

6. Marc Mauer and Tracy Huling, "Young Black Americans and the Criminal Justice System: Five Years Later," Washington, D. C.: The Sentencing Project, October 1995.

7. Ibid., 18.

8. *See* Cockburn.

9. *See* Lubiano's essay in this volume, as well as "Black Ladies, Welfare Queens, and State Minstrels: Ideological War by Narrative Means," in *Race-ing Justice, En-gendering Power: Essays on Anita Hill, Clarence Thomas, and the Construction of Social Reality,* ed. Toni Morrison (New York: Pantheon, 1992), 323–63.

10. Unpublished essay, "Modern Slavery American Style," 1995.

11. I wish to acknowledge Julie Brown, who acquired this brochure from the California Department of Correction in the course of researching the role of convict labor.

12. *Wall Street Journal,* May 12, 1994.

13. Lawrence Rence, A. Greenfield, Stephanie Minor-Harper, *Women in Prison* (Washington, D.C.: U.S. Dept. of Justice, Office of Justice Programs, Bureau of Statistics, 1991).

14. Mauer and Huling, "Young Black Americans," 19.

15. Michel Foucault, *Discipline and Punish: The Birth of the Prison,* trans. Alan Sheridan (New York: Vintage, 1979), 395.

28

...AND THE POOR GET PRISON

Jeffrey Reiman

QUESTIONS TO CONSIDER

Contrary to the high-profile cases that have recently rocked Wall Street (Enron, Global Crossing, Tyco), few Chief Executive Officers (CEO) or white-collar administrators serve lengthy (for that matter, any!) jail time for their white-collar crimes. A corporate CEO who has raided his company's pension fund and destroyed the future of thousands of workers typically receives a fine and/ or community service for his crime whereas low-level, nonviolent drug dealers are often sentenced to long and hard time in a federal penitentiary. Wealthy lawbreakers, agues Jeffrey Reiman, rarely see the inside of a prison. Why? How is this pattern linked to race?

Weeding Out the Wealthy

The offender at the end of the road in prison is likely to be a member of the lowest social and economic groups in the country.[1]

This statement in the *Report of the President's Commission on Law Enforcement and Administration of Justice* is as true today as it was over three decades ago when it was written. Our prisons are indeed, as Ronald Goldfarb has called them, the "national poorhouse."[2] To most citizens this comes as no surprise— recall the Typical Criminal and the Typical Crime. Dangerous crimes, they think, are committed mainly by poor people. Seeing that prison populations are made up primarily of the poor only makes them surer of

this. They think, in other words, that the criminal justice system gives a true reflection of the dangers that threaten them.

In my view, it also comes as no surprise that our prisons and jails predominantly confine the poor. This is not because these are the individuals who most threaten us. It is because the criminal justice system effectively weeds out the well-to-do, so that at *the end of the road in prison,* the vast majority of those we find there come from the lower classes. This weeding-out process starts before the agents of law enforcement go into action. [I argue] that our very definition of crime *excludes* a wide variety of actions at least as dangerous as those included and often worse. Is it any accident that the kinds of dangerous actions excluded are the kinds most likely to be performed by the affluent in America? Even before we mobilize our troops in the war on crime, we have already guaranteed that large numbers of upper-class individuals will never come within their sights.

This process does not stop at the definition of crime. It continues throughout each level of the criminal justice system. At each step, from arresting to sentencing, the likelihood of being ignored or released or treated lightly by the system is greater the better off one is economically. As the late U.S. Senator Philip Hart wrote:

> Justice has two transmission belts, one for the rich and one for the poor. The low-income transmission belt is easier to ride without falling off and it gets to prison in shorter order.
>
> The transmission belt for the affluent is a little slower and it passes innumerable stations where exits are temptingly convenient.[3]

This means that the criminal justice system functions from start to finish in a way that makes certain that "the offender at the end of the road in prison is likely to be a member of the lowest social and economic groups in the country."

For the same criminal behavior, the poor are more likely to be arrested; if arrested, they are more likely to be charged; if charged, more likely to be convicted; if convicted, more likely to be sentenced to prison; and if sentenced, more likely to be given longer prison terms than members of the middle and upper classes.[4] In other words, the image of the criminal population one sees in our nation's jails and prisons is distorted by the shape of the criminal justice system itself. It is the face of evil reflected in a carnival mirror, but it is no laughing matter.

The face in the criminal justice carnival mirror is also, as we have already noted, very frequently a black face. Although blacks do not make up the majority of the inmates in our jails and prisons, they make up a proportion that far outstrips their proportion in the population.[5] Here, too, the image we

see is distorted by the processes of the criminal justice system itself. Edwin Sutherland and Donald Cressey write in their widely used textbook *Criminology* that

> . . . numerous studies have shown that African-Americans are more likely to be arrested, indicted, convicted, and committed to an institution than are whites who commit the same offenses, and many other studies have shown that blacks have a poorer chance than whites to receive probation, a suspended sentence, parole, commutation of a death sentence, or pardon.[6]

William Wilbanks has attacked this conclusion in *The Myth of a Racist Criminal Justice System.*[7] He uses as "perhaps the most important criticism" of the charge that there is discrimination against blacks in arrests the work of Michael Hindelang, which compares the rate at which respondents to the National Crime Survey report being victimized by assailants perceived to be black with the rate at which blacks are arrested for the relevant crimes according to the *UCR,* and finds "that the racial gap in *offending* for robbery, assault, and rape (whether or not an arrest occurred) was almost equal to that found for *arrest* statistics." Wilbanks concludes, "these results indicate that police select black and white arrestees in approximately the same proportion as they are found in the pool of offenders," and thus "argue against police bias in the arrest process."[8] Recent statistics, however, suggest quite the opposite. Consider the following.

In 1998, respondents to the *National Criminal Victimization Survey* reported that approximately 22 percent of their assailants in violent victimizations (rape, robbery, simple and aggravated assault) were perceived to be black. That same year, the *UCR* indicates that 42 percent of the individuals arrested for these crimes were black. If we drop simple assault on the assumption that it is less often reported to the police than the other violent crimes, the figures change only slightly: 25 percent of violent victimizers are perceived to be black, whereas 44 percent of those arrested for rape, robbery, and aggravated assault are black. These figures indicate that police are arresting blacks almost two times more frequently than the occurrence of their perceived offenses.[9] Because arrest determines the pool from which charged, convicted, and imprisoned individuals are selected, this suggests that deep bias persists throughout the criminal justice system.

I am aware that there are various problems with comparing *UCR* and *NCVS* statistics and various possible explanations for the divergence of black-white arrest rates from the rate at which blacks and whites are perceived offenders. Thus I do not claim that the results just presented prove definitively the presence of racism. Nonetheless, because they come from the statistics that Wilbanks uses as "the most important criticism" of the discrimination thesis, I think they suffice to cast significant doubt on Wilbanks's claim. Thus, I shall treat his thesis as currently unsubstantiated and continue to follow the majority of researchers in holding that the criminal justice system is widely marked by racial discrimination as well as by economic bias.[10] Moreover, I shall shortly present the results of numerous studies that demonstrate this point.

Curiously enough, statistics on differential treatment of races are available in greater abundance than our statistics on differential treatment of economic classes. For instance, although the FBI tabulates arrest rates by race (as well as by sex, age, and geographic area), it omits class or income. Similarly, both the President's Crime Commission report and Sutherland and Cressey's *Criminology* have index entries for race or racial discrimination but none for class or income of offenders. It would seem that both independent and government data gatherers are more willing to own up to America's racism than to its class bias. Nevertheless, it does not pay to look at these as two independent forms of bias. It is my view that, at least as far as criminal justice is concerned, racism is simply one powerful form of economic bias. I use evidence on differential treatment of blacks as evidence of differential treatment of members of the lower classes. There are five reasons for this.

1. First and foremost, black Americans are disproportionately poor. In 1996, while slightly more than one of every ten white Americans received income below the poverty line, nearly three of every ten black Americans did.[11] The picture is even worse when we shift from income to wealth (property such as a home, land, stocks). Blacks in America own one-fifth of the wealth that whites do.[12] Moreover, "the homeownership rate among non-Hispanic whites is more than 50 percent higher than that of blacks." Among homeowners, in 1993, the median equity "was about $50,000 for whites (in 1993 dollars) [and] $29,000 for blacks." Only about 5 percent of black households owned stocks. Compared to 25 percent of white households.[13] Unemployment figures give a similarly dismal picture: In 1997, 2.8 percent of white workers were unemployed and 6.5 percent of blacks were. Among those in the crime-prone ages of 16 to 24, 12.7 percent of white youngsters (with no college) and 31.6 percent of black youngsters (with no college)—nearly one of every three—were jobless.[14]

2. The factors most likely to keep one out of trouble with the law and out of prison, such as a suburban living room instead of a tenement alley to gamble in or legal counsel able to devote time to one's case instead of an overburdened public defender, are the kinds of things that money can buy regardless of one's race, creed, or national origin. For example, as

we shall see, arrests of blacks for illicit drug possession or dealing have sky-rocketed in recent years, rising way out of proportion to drug arrests for whites—though research shows no greater drug use among blacks than among whites. However, drug arrests are most easily made in "disorganized inner-city" areas, where drug sales are more likely to take place out of doors, and dealers are more willing to sell to strangers. Blacks are (proportionately) more likely than whites to live in such inner-city areas and thus more likely than whites to be arrested on drug charges.[15] And one very important reason that blacks are more likely than whites to live in disorganized inner-city areas is that a greater percentage of blacks than whites are poor and unemployed. What might at first look like a straightforward racial disparity turns out to reflect economic status.

3. Blacks who travel the full route of the criminal justice system and end up in jail or prison are close in economic condition to whites who do. In 1978, 53 percent of black jail inmates had pre-arrest incomes below $3,000, compared with 44 percent of whites.[16] In 1983, the median pre-arrest income of black jail inmates was $4,067 and that of white jail inmates was $6,312. About half of blacks in jail were unemployed before arrest, and 44 percent of whites were.[17] In 1991, 30 percent of whites in the prison population and 38 percent of blacks reported no full- or part-time employment during the month before their arrest.[18]

4. Some studies suggest that race works to heighten the effects of economic condition on criminal justice outcomes, so that "being unemployed *and* black substantially increase[s] the chances of incarceration over those associated with being either unemployed or black."[19] This

means that racism will produce a kind of selective economic bias, making a certain segment of the unemployed even more likely to end up behind bars.

5. Finally, it is my belief that the economic powers that be in America have sufficient power to end or drastically reduce racist bias in the criminal justice system. To the extent that they allow it to exist, it is not unreasonable to assume that it furthers their economic interests.

For all these reasons, racism will be treated here as either a form of economic bias or a tool that achieves the same end.

In the remainder of this chapter, I show how the criminal justice system functions to *weed out the wealthy* (meaning both middle- and upper-class offenders) at each stage of the process and thus produces a distorted image of the crime problem. Before entering into this discussion, however, three points are worth noting.

First, it is not my view that the poor are all innocent victims persecuted by the evil rich. The poor do commit crimes, and my own assumption is that the vast majority of the poor who are confined in our prisons are guilty of the crimes for which they were sentenced. In addition, there is good evidence that the poor do commit a greater portion of the crimes against person and property listed in the FBI Index than the middle and upper classes do, relative to their numbers in the national population. What I have already tried to prove is that the crimes in the FBI Index are not the only acts that threaten us nor are they the acts that threaten us the most. What I will try to prove in what follows is that the poor are arrested and punished by the criminal justice system much more frequently than their contribution to the crime problem would warrant—thus the criminals who populate our prisons as well as the public's imagination are disproportionately poor.

Second, the following discussion has been divided into three sections that correspond to the major criminal-justice decision points. As always, such classifications are a bit neater than reality, and so they should not be taken as rigid compartments. Many of the distorting processes operate at all criminal-justice decision points. So, for example, while I will primarily discuss the lighthanded treatment of white-collar criminals in the section on charging and sentencing, it is also true that white-collar criminals are less likely to be arrested or convicted than are blue-collar criminals. The section in which a given issue is treated is a reflection of the point in the criminal justice process at which the disparities are the most striking. Suffice it to say, however, that the disparities between the treatment of the poor and the nonpoor are to be found at all points of the process.

Third, it must be borne in mind that the movement from arrest to sentencing is a funneling process, so that discrimination that occurs at any early stage shapes the population that reaches later stages. Thus, for example, some recent studies find little economic bias in sentence length for people convicted of similar crimes.[20] When reading such studies, however, one should remember that the population that reaches the point of sentencing has already been subject to whatever discrimination exists at earlier stages. If, for example, among people with similar offenses and records, poor people are more likely to be charged and more likely to be convicted, then even if the sentencing of convicted criminals is evenhanded, it will reproduce the discrimination that occurred before.

Arrest and Charging

The problem with most official records of who commits crime is that they are really statistics on who gets arrested and convicted. If, as I will show, the police are more likely to arrest some people than others, these official statistics may tell us more about the police than about criminals. In any event, they give us little reliable data about those who commit crimes and do not get caught. Some social scientists, suspicious of the bias built into official records, have tried to devise other methods of determining who has committed a crime. Most often, these methods involve an interview or questionnaire in which the respondent is assured of anonymity and asked to reveal whether he or she has committed any offenses for which he or she could be arrested and convicted. Techniques to check reliability of these self-reports also have been devised; however, if their reliability is still in doubt, common sense dictates that they would understate rather than overstate the number of individuals who have committed crimes and never come to official notice. In light of this, the conclusions of these studies are rather astounding. It seems that crime is the national pastime. The President's Crime Commission conducted a sur-vey of 10,000 households and discovered that "91 percent of all Americans have violated laws that could have subjected them to a term of imprisonment at one time in their lives."[21]

A number of other studies support the conclusion that serious criminal behavior is widespread among middle- and upper-class individuals, although these individuals are rarely, if ever arrested. Some of the studies show that there are no significant differences between economic classes in the incidence of criminal behavior.[22] The authors of a recent review of literature on class and delinquency conclude that "Research published since 1978, using both official and self-reported data suggests . . . that there is no pervasive relationship between SES [socioeconomic status] and delinquency."[23] This conclusion is echoed by Jensen and Thompson, who argue that

The safest conclusion concerning class structure and delinquency is the same one that has been proposed for several decades: class, no matter how defined, contributes little to explaining variation in self-reports of common delinquency.[24]

Others conclude that while lower-class individuals do commit more than their share of crimes, arrest records overstate their share and understate that of the middle and upper classes.[25] Still other studies suggest that some forms of serious crime—forms usually associated with lower-class youth—show up *more frequently* among higher-class persons than among lower.[26] For instance, Empey and Erikson interviewed 180 white males aged 15 to 17 who were drawn from different economic strata. They found that "virtually all respondents reported having committed not one but a variety of different offenses." Although youngsters from the middle classes constituted 55 percent of the group interviewed, they admitted to 67 percent of the instances of breaking and entering, 70 percent of the instances of property destruction, and an astounding 87 percent of all the armed robberies admitted to by the entire sample.[27] Williams and Gold studied a national sample of 847 males and females between the ages of 13 and 16.[28] Of these, 88 percent admitted to at least one delinquent offense.

Even those who conclude "that more lower status youngsters commit delinquent acts more frequently than do higher status youngsters"[29] also recognize that lower-class youth are significantly overrepresented in official records. Gold writes that "about five times more lowest than highest status boys appear in the official records; if records were complete and unselective, we estimate that the ratio would be closer to 1.5:1."[30] The simple fact is that for the same offense, *a poor person is more likely to be arrested and, if arrested, charged, than a middle- or upper-class person.*[31]

This means, first of all, that poor people are more likely to come to the attention of the police. Furthermore, even when apprehended, the police are more likely to formally charge a poor person and release a higher-class person *for the same offense*. Gold writes that

... boys who live in poorer parts of town and are apprehended by police for delinquency are four to five times more likely to appear in some official record than boys from wealthier sections who commit the same kinds of offenses. These same data show that, at each stage in the legal process from charging a boy with an offense to some sort of disposition in court, boys from different socioeconomic backgrounds are treated differently, so that those eventually incarcerated in public institutions, that site of most of the research on delinquency, are selectively poorer boys.[32]

From a study of self-reported delinquent behavior, Gold finds that when individuals were apprehended, "if the offender came from a higher status family, police were more likely to handle the matter themselves without referring it to the court."[33]

Many writers have commented on the extent and seriousness of "white-collar crime," so I will keep my remarks to a minimum. Nevertheless, for those of us trying to understand how the image of crime is created, four points should be noted.

1. White-collar crime is costly; it takes far more dollars from our pockets than all the FBI Index crimes combined.
2. White-collar crime is widespread, probably much more so than the crimes of the poor.
3. White-collar criminals are rarely arrested or charged; the system has developed kindlier ways of dealing with the more delicate sensibilities of its higher-class clientele.

4. When white-collar criminals are prosecuted and convicted, their sentences are either suspended or very light when judged by the cost their crimes have imposed on society.

The first three points will be discussed here, and the fourth will be presented in the section on sentencing below.

Everyone agrees that the cost of white-collar crime is enormous. In 1985, *U.S. News & World Report Report* reported that "Experts estimate that white-collar criminals rake in a minimum of $200 billion annually."[34] Marshall Clinard also cites the $200 billion estimate in his recent book, *Corporate Corruption: The Abuse of Corporate Power.*[35] Nonetheless, $200 billion probably understates the actual cost. Some experts place the cost of white-collar crime for firms doing business in the government sector alone at $500 billion a year.[36] Tax evasion alone has been estimated to cost from 5 to 7 percent of the gross national product. For 1997, that would be between $403 and $564 billion.[37]

Let me close with one final example that typifies this particular distortion of justice policy. Embezzlement is the crime of misappropriating money or property entrusted to one's care, custody, or control. Because the poor are rarely entrusted with tempting sums of money or valuable property, this is predominantly a crime of the middle and upper classes. The U.S. Chamber of Commerce estimate of the annual economic cost of embezzlement, adjusted for inflation and population growth, is $12.42 billion—more than four-fifths the total value of all property and money stolen in all FBI Index property crimes in 1997. (Don't be fooled into thinking that this cost is imposed only on the rich or on big companies with lots of resources. They pass on their losses—and their increased insurance costs—to consumers in the form of higher prices. Embezzlers take money out of the very same pockets that muggers do: yours!) Nevertheless, the FBI reports that in 1997, when there were 1,805,600 arrests for property crimes, there were 17,100 arrests for embezzlement nationwide.[38] Although their cost to society is comparable, the number of arrests for property crimes was *more than 100 times greater* than the number of arrests for embezzlement. Roughly, this means there was one property crime arrest for every $8,000 stolen, and even the language becomes more delicate as we deal with a "better" class of crook.

The clientele of the criminal justice system forms an exclusive club. Entry is largely a privilege of the poor. The crimes they commit are the crimes that qualify one for admission—and they are admitted in greater proportion than their share of those crimes. Curiously enough, the crimes the affluent commit are not the kind that easily qualify one for membership in the club.

And as we have seen, the reluctance to use the full force of the criminal justice system in pursuit of white-collar criminals is matched by a striking reluctance to use the full force of current public and private research organizations to provide up-to-date es-timates of its cost. This coincidence is worth pondering by anyone interested in how criminal justice policy gets made and how research and statistics function in the process.

Conviction

Between arrest and imprisonment lies the crucial process that determines guilt or innocence. Studies of individuals accused of similar offenses and with similar prior records show that the poor defendant is more likely to be adjudicated guilty than is the wealthier defendant.[39] In the adjudication process the only thing that *should* count is whether the accused is guilty and whether the prosecution can prove it beyond a reasonable doubt. Unfortunately, at least two other factors that are irrelevant to the question of guilt or innocence significantly affect the outcome: One is the ability of the accused to be free on bail prior to trial, and the second is access to legal counsel able to devote adequate time and energy to the case. Because both bail and high-quality legal counsel cost money, it should come as no surprise that here as elsewhere the poor do poorly.

The advantages of access to adequate legal counsel during the adjudicative process are obvious but still worthy of mention. In 1963, the U.S. Supreme Court handed down the landmark *Gideon v. Wainwright* decision, holding that the states must provide legal counsel to the indigent in all felony cases. As a result, no person accused of a serious crime need face his or her accuser without a lawyer. However, the Supreme Court has not held that the Constitution entitles individuals to lawyers able to devote equal time and resources to their cases. Even though *Gideon* represents significant progress in making good on the constitutional promise of equal treatment before the law, we still are left with two transmission belts of justice: one for the poor and one for the affluent. There is an emerging body of case law on the right to effective assistance of counsel[40]; however, this is yet to have any serious impact on the assembly-line legal aid handed out to the poor.

Needless to say, the distinct legal advantages that money can buy become even more salient when we enter the realm of corporate and other white-collar crime. Indeed, it is often precisely the time and cost involved in bringing to court a large corporation with its army of legal eagles that is offered as an excuse for the less formal and more genteel treatment accorded to corporate crooks. This excuse is, of course, not equitably distributed to all economic classes, any more than quality legal service is. This means that, regardless of actual innocence or guilt, one's chances of beating the rap increase as one's income increases. Regardless of what fraction of crimes are committed by the poor, the criminal justice system is distorted so that an even greater fraction of those convicted will be poor. And with conviction comes sentencing.

Sentencing

The simple fact is that the criminal justice system reserves its harshest penalties for its lower-class clients and puts on kid gloves when confronted with a better class of crook. We will come back to the soft treatment of S&L crooks shortly. For the moment, note that the tendency to treat higher-class criminals more leniently than lower-class criminals has been with us for a long time. In 1972, *The New York Times* did a study on sentencing in state and federal courts. The *Times* stated that "crimes that tend to be committed by the poor get tougher sentences than those committed by the well-to-do," that federal "defendants who could not afford private counsel were sentenced nearly twice as severely as defendants with private counsel," and that a "study by the Vera Institute of Justice of the courts in the Bronx indicates a similar pattern in the state courts."[41]

More recently, D'Alessio and Stoltzenberg studied a random sample of 2,760 offenders committed to the custody of Florida Department of Corrections during fiscal year 1985. Although they found no greater sentence severity for poor offenders found guilty of property crimes, they found that poor offenders did receive longer sentences for violent crimes, such as manslaughter, and for moral offenses, such as narcotics possession. Nor, by the way, did sentencing guidelines reduce this disparity.[42] A study of individuals convicted of drunk driving found that increased education (taken as an indicator of higher occupational status) "increase[d] the rate of movement from case filing to probation and decrease[d] the rate of movement to prison." And though, when probation was given, more-educated offenders got longer probation, they also got shorter prison sentences, if sentenced to prison at all.[43]

Chiricos and Bales found that, for individuals guilty of similar offenses and with similar prior records, unemployed defendants were more likely to be incarcerated while awaiting trial, and for longer periods, than employed defendants. They were more than twice as likely as their employed counterparts to be incarcerated upon a finding of guilt. And defendants with public defenders experienced longer periods of jail time than those who could afford private attorneys.[44] McCarthy noted a similar link between unemployment and greater likelihood of incarceration.[45] In his study of 28,315 felony defendants in Tennessee, Virginia, and Kentucky, Champion also found that offenders who could afford private counsel had a greater likelihood of probation, and received shorter sentences when incarceration was imposed.[46] A study of the effects of implementing Minnesota's determinate sentencing program shows that socio-economic bias is "more subtle, but no less real" than before the new program.[47]

Tillman and Pontell examined the sentences received by individuals convicted of Medicaid provider fraud in California. Because such offenders normally have no prior arrests and are charged with grand theft, their sentences were compared with the sentences of other offenders convicted of grand theft and who also had no prior

records. While 37.7 percent of the Medicaid defrauders were sentenced to jail or prison time, 79.2 percent of the others convicted of grand theft were sentenced to jail or prison. This was so even though the median dollar loss due to the Medicaid frauds was $13,000, more than ten times the median loss due to the other grand thefts ($1,149). Tillman and Pontell point out that most of the Medicaid defrauders were health professionals, while most of the others convicted of grand theft had low-level jobs or were unemployed. They conclude that "differences in the sentences imposed on the two samples are indeed the result of the different social statuses of their members."[48]

As usual, data on racial discrimination in sentencing tell the same story of the treatment of those who cannot afford the going price of justice. A study of offender processing in New York State counties found that, for offenders with the same arrest charge and the same prior criminal records, minorities were incarcerated more often than comparably situated whites.[49] A study of sentencing in Miami concludes that when case-related attributes do not clearly point to a given sentence, sentencing disparities are more likely to be based on race.[50] A study of 9,690 males who entered Florida prisons in 1992 and 1993, and who were legally eligible for stricter sentencing under the habitual offender statute, shows that, for similar prior records and seriousness of crime, race had a "significant and substantial" effect: Black defendants were particularly disadvantaged "for drug offenses and for property crimes."[51]

Most striking perhaps is that, in 1993, 51 percent of inmates in state and federal prisons were black and 44 percent of inmates of jails were black, whereas blacks make up only 36.5 percent of those arrested for serious (FBI Index) crimes.[52] Furthermore, when we look only at federal prisons, where there is reason to believe that racial and economic discrimination is less prevalent than in state institutions, we find that in 1986, nonwhite inmates were sentenced, on average, to 33 more months for burglary than white inmates and 22 more months for income tax evasion. In 1989, the average federal sentence for blacks found guilty of violent offenses was 10 months longer than that for whites.[53]

Here must be mentioned the notorious "100-to-1" disparity between sentences for possession of cocaine in powder form (popular in the affluent suburbs) and in crack form (popular in poor inner-city neighborhoods). Federal laws require a mandatory five-year sentence for crimes involving 500 grams of powder cocaine or 5 grams of crack cocaine. This yields a sentence for the first-time offenders (with no aggravating factors, such as possession of a weapon) that is longer than the sentence for kidnapping, and only slightly shorter than the sentence for attempted murder![54] About 90 percent of those convicted of federal crack offenses are black; about 4 percent are white. "As a result, the average prison sentence served by Black federal prisoners is 40 percent longer than the average sentence for Whites."[55] In 1995, the United States Sentencing commission recommended ending the 100-to-1 disparity between powder and crack penalties, and, in an unusual display of bipartisanship, both the Republican Congress and the Democratic President rejected their recommendation.[56]

Sentencing disparities between the races are, of course, not new. An extensive study by the *Boston Globe* of 4,500 cases of armed robbery, aggravated assault, and rape found that "blacks convicted in the superior courts of Massachusetts receive harsher penalties than whites for the same crimes."[57] The authors of a study of almost 1,200 males sentenced to prison for armed robbery in a southwestern state found that "in 1977 whites incarcerated for armed robbery had a greater than average chance of receiving the least severe sentence, while nonwhites had a greater than average chance of receiving a moderately severe sentence."[58] A study of 229 adjudicated cases in a Florida judicial district yielded the finding that "whites have an 18 percent greater chance in the predicated probability of receiving probation than blacks when all other things are equal."[59] A recent study of criminal justice systems in California, Michigan, and Texas by Petersilia confirms the continuation of this trend. "Controlling for the factors most likely to influence sentencing and parole decisions," she writes, "the analysis still found that blacks and Hispanics are less likely to be given probation, more likely to receive *prison* sentences, more likely to receive longer sentences, and more likely to serve a greater portion of their original time."[60] Myers found that "harsher treatment of persons with fewer resources (e.g., female, unemployed, unmarried, black) is . . . pronounced in highly unequal counties."[61]

The federal government has introduced sentencing guidelines and mandatory minimum sentences that might be expected to eliminate discrimination, and many states have followed suit. The effect of this however, has been not to eliminate discretion but to transfer it from those who sentence to those who decide what to charge—that is, from judges to prosecutors. Prosecutors can charge in a way that makes it likely that the offender will get less than the mandatory minimum sentence. Says U.S. District Judge J. Lawrence Irving of San Diego, "the system is run by the U.S. attorneys. When they decide how to indict, they fix the sentence."[62] And discrimination persists. To examine the effects of mandatory minimum sentences, Barbara Meierhoefer studied 267,178 offenders sentenced in federal courts from January 1984 to June 1990. She found that whites were consistently more-likely than blacks to be sentenced to less than the minimum sentence. The disparity varied from year to year, reaching a high point in 1988, when blacks were 30 percent more likely than whites to receive at least the minimum. Hispanics fared even worse than blacks. Concludes Meierhoefer,

> . . . despite the laws' emphasis on offense behavior, sentences still vary by offender characteristics. . . . Further, both black and Hispanic offenders now receive notably more severe sentences than their white counterparts.
>
> The latter trend suggests that there may be questions to be considered concerning the impact of shifting discretion affecting sentencing from the court to the prosecutor's office.[63]

A growing number of judges are speaking out against the system of sentencing guidelines and mandatory minimum sentences. According to U.S. District Judge Terry Hatter of Los Angeles, "the toughest sentences are now strictly 'applied to basically one group of people: poor minority people.'" Appellate Judge Gerald W. Heaney of Duluth, Minnesota, conducted his own study "and found that young black men got longer sentences than their white counterparts for similar crimes. Using 1989 data, he compared sentences under the new system with those under the old. The average sentence for black males was 40 months longer, he found, while the average sentence for white males was 19 months longer."[64]

There is considerable evidence that *double discrimination*—by race of the victim and of the offender—affects death penalty sentencing. In Florida, for example, blacks "who kill whites are nearly forty times more likely to be sentenced to death than those who kill blacks." Moreover, among "killers of whites, blacks are five times more likely

than whites to be sentenced to death." This pattern of double discrimination was also evidenced, though less pronouncedly, in Texas, Ohio and Georgia, the other states surveyed. Together, these four states "accounted for approximately 70 percent of the nation's death sentences" between 1972 and 1977.[65]

More recent studies have shown the same pattern. It was on the basis of such research that what may have been the last constitutional challenge to the death penalty was raised and rejected. In the 1987 case of *McCleskey v. Kemp*, evidence of discriminationon the basis of the victim's race was provided by a study by Professor David Baldus, of the University of Iowa, who examined 2,484 Georgia homicide cases that occurred between 1973 (when the current capital murder law was enacted) and 1979 (a year after McCleskey received his death sentence).[66] After controlling for all legitimate nonracial factors—such as severity of crime and the presence of aggravating factors—Baldus found that "murderers of white victims are still being sentenced to death 4.3 times more often than murderers of black victims."[67] The justices of the Supreme Court acknowledged the systemic disparities, but a majority held that the disparities would not invalidate death penalty convictions unless discrimination could be shown in the individual case at hand.

A 1990 report of the General Accounting Office to the Senate and House Committees on the Judiciary reviewed 28 studies on racial disparities in death penalty sentencing and concluded that the race of the victim strongly influenced the likelihood of a death penalty: "[T]hose who murdered whites were found to be more likely to be sentenced to death than those who murdered blacks."[68] Note that all these discriminatory sentences were rendered under statutes that had passed constitutional muster and were therefore presumed free of the biases that led the Supreme Court to invalidate all American death penalty statutes in *Furman v. Georgia* in 1972.

Another study has shown that among blacks and whites on death row, whites are more likely to have their sentences commuted. Also, blacks or whites who have private counsel are more likely to have their execution commuted than condemned persons defended by court-appointed attorneys.[69]

As I have already pointed out, justice is increasingly tempered with mercy as we deal with a better class of crime. The Sherman Antitrust Act is a criminal law. It was passed in recognition of the fact that one virtue of a free enterprise economy is that competition tends to drive consumer prices down, so agreements by competing firms to refrain from price competition is the equivalent of stealing money from the consumer's pocket. Nevertheless, although such conspiracies cost consumers far more than lower-class theft, price fixing was a misdemeanor until 1974.[70] In practice, few conspirators end up in prison, and when they do, the sentence is a mere token, well below the maximum provided in the law.

In the historical *Electrical Equipment* cases in the early 1960s, executives of several major firms met secretly to fix prices on electrical equipment to a degree that is estimated to have cost the buying public well over $1 billion. The executives involved knew they were violating the law. They used plain envelopes for their communications, called their meetings "choir practice," and referred to the list of executives in attendance as the "Christmas card list." This case is rare and famous because it was one in which the criminal sanction was actually imposed. Seven executives received and served jail sentences. In light of the amount of money they had stolen from the American public, however, their sentences were more an

indictment of the government than of themselves. ~~thirty days in jail!~~

Speaking about the record of federal antitrust prosecution, Clinard and Yeager write that

> . . . even in the most widespread and flagrant price conspiracy cases, few corporate executives are ever imprisoned; of the total 231 cases with individual defendants from 1955 to 1975, prison sentences were given in only 19 cases. Of a total of 1,027 individual defendants, only 49 were sentenced to prison.[71]

There is some (slight) indication of a toughening in the sentences since antitrust violations were made a felony in 1974 and penalties were increased. "In felony cases prosecuted under the new penalties through March 1978, 15 of 21 sentenced individuals (71 percent) were given terms averaging 192 days each."[72] Nevertheless, when the cost to society is reckoned, even such penalties as these are hardly severe.

After the "anything goes" attitude of the Reagan era, which brought us such highly publicized white collar skullduggery as the multibillion dollar savings and loan scandal, the 1990s have seen a kind a backlash, with the government under pressure to up the penalties for corporate offenders. Here too, however, progress follows a slow and zigzagging course. Consider, for example, the following series of titles of articles from *The Washington Post:* March 2, 1990. "Criminal Indictments: Training Bigger Guns on Corporations"; April 1, 1990, "Going Soft on Corporate Crime"; April 28, 1990, "Justice Dept. Shifts on Corporate Sentencing" ("Attorney General Dick Thornburgh last month withdrew the Justice Department's longstanding support for tough mandatory sentences for corporate criminals following an intense lobbying campaign by defense contractors, oil companies and other *Fortune*

500 firms."); April 27, 1991, "Corporate Lawbreakers May Face Tougher Penalties."[73] Lest this last one be taken as truly reversing the trend to leniency, note that it reports new sentencing guidelines approved by the U.S. Sentencing Commission, and it points out: "The only penalties set forth by the guidelines are fines and probation because the defendants in such cases are not individuals." Compare this with a statement from Ira Reiner, Los Angeles district attorney, quoted in the first of the articles just listed: "A fine, no matter how substantial, is simply a cost of doing business for a corporation. But a jail term for executives is different. What we are trying to do is to change the corporate culture." Good luck, Ira.

Studies have shown that even though corporate and white-collar lawbreakers are being more frequently brought to justice and more frequently being sanctioned, they still receive more lenient sentences than do those who are sentenced for common property crimes.[74] A study by Hagan and Palloni, which focuses particularly on the differences between pre- and post-Watergate treatments of white-collar offenders, concludes that likelihood of prosecution after Watergate was increased, but that the effect of this was canceled out by the leniency of the sentences meted out:

. . . the new incarcerated white-collar offenders received relatively light sentences that counterbalanced the increased use of imprisonment. Relative to less-educated common criminals, white-collar offenders were more likely to be imprisoned after Watergate than before, but for shorter periods.[75]

Even after the heightened public awareness of white-collar crime that came in the wake of Watergate and the S&L scandals, it remains the case that crimes of the poor lead to stiffer sentences than the crimes of the well-to-do (see Table 1). Keep in mind while looking at these figures that *each* of the "crimes of the affluent" costs the public more than *all* of the "crimes of the poor" put together.

I do not deny that there has been some toughening of the treatment of white-collar offenders in recent years. Nonetheless, this toughening has been relatively mild, especially when compared with the treatment dealt out to lower-class offenders. Before turning to the "great" scandals of Watergate and the savings and loan industry, here are two "small" cases that illustrate the new developments.

In September 1991, a fire destroyed a chicken-processing plant in Hamlet, North Carolina. When the 100 employees in the

TABLE 1   Sentences Served for Different Classes of Crime, 1996—97

	Percent Sentenced to Prison	Average Time Served (in months)
Crimes of the poor		
Robbery	99	60
Burglary	89	28
Auto Theft	63	24
Crime of the affluent		
Fraud	63	16
Tax Law Violation	42	15
Embezzlement	58	9

Source: Sourcebook—1998 (compiled from Tables 5.28 and 6.54, and rounded off).

plant tried to escape, they found that the company executives had ordered the doors locked "to keep out insects and to keep employees from going outside for coffee breaks, or stealing chickens." Twenty-five workers died in the fire; some were found burned to death at the doors they couldn't open. Another 50 people were injured. The owner of the company and two plant managers were charged with involuntary manslaughter. The outcome: The owner pleaded guilty and was sentenced to 19 years and 6 months in prison. You may or may not think this is severe as a punishment for someone responsible for 25 very painful deaths, but note three revealing facts. First, as part of the plea agreement, the involuntary manslaughter cases against the two plant managers were dismissed, though they surely knew the doors were locked and what the risks were. Second, the owner is eligible for parole after $2^{1}/_{2}$ years. And third, the sentence is "believed to be the harshest judgment ever handed out for a workplace safety violation."[76]

We have seen in this chapter and the one before that the criminal justice system is triply biased against the poor. First, there is the economic class bias *among harmful acts* as to which get labeled crimes and which are treated as regulatory matters, as we saw in the previous chapter. Second, there is economic class bias *among crimes* that we have already seen in this chapter. The crimes that poor people are likely to commit carry harsher sentences than the "crimes in the suites" committed by well-to-do people. Third, *among defendants convicted of the same crimes,* the poor receive less probation and more years of confinement than well-off defendants, assuring us once again that the vast majority of those put behind bars are from the lowest social and economic classes in the nation. On either side of the law, the rich get richer . . .

. . . and the Poor Get Prison

At 9:05 A.M. on the morning of Thursday, September 9, 1971, a group of inmates forced their way through a gate at the center of the prison, fatally injured a guard named William Quinn, and took 50 hostages. The Attica uprising had begun. It lasted four days, until 9:43 A.M. on the morning of Monday, September 13, when corrections officers and state troopers stormed the prison and killed 29 inmates and 10 hostages.[77] During those four days the nation saw the faces of its captives on television—the hard black faces of young men who had grown up on the streets of Harlem and other urban ghettos. Theirs were the faces of crime in America. The television viewers who saw them were not surprised. Here were faces of dangerous men who should be locked up. Nor were people outraged when the state launched its murderous attack on the prison, killing many more inmates and guards than did the prisoners themselves. Maybe they were shocked—but not outraged. Neither were they outraged when two grand juries refused to indict any of the attackers, nor when the mastermind of the attack, New York Governor Nelson Rockefeller, was named vice president of the United States three years after the uprising and massacre.[78]

They were not outraged because the faces they saw on the TV screens fit and confirmed their beliefs about who is a deadly threat to American society—and a deadly threat must be met with deadly force. How did those men get to Attica? How did Americans get their beliefs about who is a dangerous person? These questions are interwoven. People get their notions about who is a criminal at least in part from the occasional television or newspaper picture of who is inside our prisons. The individuals they see there have been put in prison because people believe certain kinds of individuals are dangerous and should be locked up.

I have agued in this chapter that this is not a simple process of selecting the dangerous and the criminal from among the peace-loving and the law-abiding. It is also a process of *weeding out the wealthy* at every stage, so that the final picture—a picture like that that appeared on the TV screen on September 9, 1971—is not a true reflection of the real dangers in our society but a distorted image, the kind reflected in a carnival mirror.

It is not my view that the inmates in Attica were innocent of the crimes that sent them there. I assume they and just about all the individuals in prisons in America are probably guilty of the crime for which they were sentenced and maybe more. My point is that people who are equally or more dangerous, equally or more criminal, are not there; that the criminal justice system works systematically not to punish and confine the dangerous and the criminal, *but to punish and confine the poor who are dangerous and criminal.*

It is successful at all levels. In 1973, there were 204,211 individuals in state and federal prisons, or 96 prisoners for every 100,000 individuals (of all ages) in the general population. By 1979, state and federal inmates numbered 301,470, or 133 per 100,000 Americans. By 1998, there were a total of 1,825,400 persons in state and federal prisons and in the local jails, a staggering 672 for every 100,000 in the population. One in 149 U.S. residents (of all ages and both sexes) was behind bars in 1998. However, of the 1,825,400 inmates in federal and state prisons and in jails, some 1,715,000 are men, virtually all above the age of 18. Because the adult male population in the United States is about 94 million, *this means that roughly one out of every 55 American adult men is behind bars.*[79] This enormous number of prisoners is, of course, predominantly from the bottom of society.

Of the estimated 1.2 million people in state prisons in 1998, one-third were not employed at all (full or part time) prior to their arrests. Just over half were employed at all, thus nearly half were without full-time employment prior to arrest. These statistics are comparable to those in 1986, when 31 percent of state inmates had no pre-arrest employment at all, and 43 percent had no full-time pre-arrest employment.[80] Among jail inmates in 1996, 36 percent were not employed prior to arrest—20 percent were looking for work and 16 percent were not. Approximately half of jail inmates reported pre-arrest incomes below $7,200 a year.[81]

To get an idea of what part of society is in prison, we should compare these figures with comparable figures for the general population. Because more than 90 percent of inmates are male, we can look at employment and income figures for males in the general population in the mid-1990s.

In 1994, 5.4 percent of males, 16 years old and above, in the labor force were unemployed and looking for work. Since it is normally thought that the number of unemployed people who are not looking for work is something less than equal to the number looking, doubling this rate will give us a conservative estimate of the percentage of males above age 16 who are unemployed, looking and not looking. Then, whereas one-third of state prison inmates and 36 percent of jail inmates were unemployed (looking and not looking for work) in the year prior to their arrest, the rate for unincarcerated males above the age of 16, was approximately 11 percent. Prisoners were unemployed at a rate more than three times that of their counterparts in the general population.[82] In 1994, the median income for males, 15 years old and above, with any income at all, was $22,995.[83] This means that half of these males in the general population with any income at all were earning this amount or less. Compare this to jail inmates, about half of whom earned $7,200 a year or less in the year before they were arrested.

Our prisoners are not a cross section of America. They are considerably poorer and considerably less likely to be employed than the rest of Americans. Moreover, they are also less educated, which is to say less in possession of the means to improve their sorry situations. Of all U.S. prison inmates, 41 percent did not graduate from high school, compared to 20 percent of the U.S. adult population.[84]

The criminal justice system is sometimes thought of as a kind of sieve in which the innocent are progressively sifted out from the guilty, who end up behind bars. I have tried to show that the sieve works another way as well. It sifts the affluent out from the poor, so it is not merely the guilty who end up behind bars, but the *guilty poor*.

. . . The criminal justice system does not simply weed the peace-loving from the dangerous, the law-abiding from the criminal. At every stage, starting with the very definitions of crime and progressing through the stages of investigation, arrest, charging, conviction, and sentencing, the system *weeds out the wealthy*. It refuses to define as "crimes" or as serious crimes the dangerous and predatory acts of the well-to-do—acts that, as we have seen, result in the loss of thousands of lives and billions of dollars. Instead, the system focuses its attention on those crimes likely to be committed by members of the lower classes. Thus, it is no surprise to find that so many of the people behind bars are from the lower classes. The people we see in our jails and prisons are no doubt dangerous to society, but they are not *the danger* to society, not the gravest danger to society. Individuals who pose equal or greater threats to our well-being walk the streets with impunity.

. . . In the present chapter I have argued that the criminal justice system works to make crime appear to be the monopoly of the poor by . . . more actively pursuing and prosecuting the poor rather than the well off for the acts that are labeled crime. *The . . . effect . . . is to maintain a real threat of crime that the vast majority of Americans believes is a threat from the poor.* The criminal justice system is a carnival mirror that throws back a distorted image of the dangers that lurk in our midst—and conveys the impression that those dangers are the work of the poor.

NOTES

1. *Challenge*, p. 44.
2. Ronald Goldfarb, "Prisons: The National Poorhouse," *New Republic*, November 1, 1969, pp. 15–17.
3. Philip Hart, "Swindling and Knavery, Inc.," *Playboy*, August 1972, p. 158.
4. Compare the statement, written more than half a century ago, by Professor Edwin H. Sutherland, one of the major luminaries of twentieth-century criminology:

   First, the administrative processes are more favorable to persons in economic comfort than to those in poverty, so that if two persons on different economic levels are equally guilty of the same offense, the one on the lower level is more likely to be arrested, convicted, and committed to an institution. Second, the laws are written, administered, and implemented primarily with reference to the types of crimes committed by people of lower economic levels [E. H. Sutherland, Principles of Criminology (Philadelphia: Lippincott, 1939), p. 179].

5. For example, in 1991, when blacks made up 12 percent of the national population, they accounted for 46 percent of the U.S. state prison population. BJS, *Survey of State Prison Inmates*, 1991, p. 3.
6. Edwin H. Sutherland and Donald R. Cressey, *Criminology*, 9th ed. (Philadelphia: Lippincott, 1974), p. 133. The following studies are cited in support of this point (p. 133, note 4): Edwin M. Lemert and Judy Roseberg, "The Administration of Justice to Minority Groups in Los Angeles County," University of California Publications in Culture and Society 2, no. 1 (1948), pp. 1–28; Thorsten Sellin, "Race

Prejudice in the Administration of Justice," *American Journal of Sociology* 41 (September 1935), pp. 212–217; Sidney Alexrad, "Negro and White Male Institutionalized Delinquents," *American Journal of Sociology* 57 (May 1952). Pp. 569–74; Marvin E. Wolfgang, Arlene Kelly and Hans C. Nolde, "Comparisons of the Executed and the Commuted among Admissions to Death Row," *Journal of Criminal Law, Criminology, and Police Science* 53 (September 1962), pp. 301–11; Nathan Goldman, *The Differential Selection of Juvenile Offenders for Court Appearance* (New York: National Council on Crime and Delinquency, 1963); Irving Piliavin and Scott Briar, "Police Encounters with Juveniles," *American Journal of Sociology* 70 (September 1964), pp. 206–14; Robert M. Terry, "The Screening of Juvenile Offenders," *Journal of Criminal Law, Criminology, and Police Science* 58 (June 1967), pp. 173–81. See also Ramsey Clark, *Crime in America* (New York: Simon & Schuster, 1970), p. 51: "Negoes are arrested more frequently and on less evidence than whites and are more often victims of mass or sweep arrests"; and Donald Taft, *Criminology,* 3rd ed. (New York: Macmillan, 1956), p. 134:

> Negroes are more likely to be suspected of crime than are whites. They are also more likely to be arrested. If the perpetrator of a crime is known to be a Negro the police may arrest all Negroes who were near the scene–a procedure they would rarely dare to follow with whites. After arrest Negroes are less likely to secure bail, and so are more liable to be counted in jail statistics. They are more liable than whites to be indicted and less likely to have their case nol prossed or otherwise dismissed. If tried, Negroes are more likely to be convicted. If convicted they are less likely to be given probation. For this reason they are more likely to be included in the count of prisoners. Negroes are also more likely than whites to be kept in prison for the full terms of their commitments and correspondingly less likely to be paroled.

7. William Wilbanks, *The Myth of a Racist Criminal Justice System* (Monterey, Calif.: Brooks/Cole, 1987).
8. Ibid., pp. 64–65.
9. *Sourcebook–1998,* p. 186, Table 3.26; p. 342, Table 4.10, *UCR–1998;* pp. 228.
10. For an overview of this double distortion, see Thomas J. Dolan, "The Case for Double Jeopardy: Black and Poor," *International Journal of Criminology and Penology* 1 (1973), pp. 129–50.
11. *StatAbst–1998,* p. 480, Table 762. See also Karen Pennar, "The Rich Are Richer—And America May Be the Poorer," *Business Week,* November 18, 1991, pp. 85–88.
12. Francine Blau and John Graham, "Black-White Differences in Wealth and Asset Composition," *Quarterly Journal of Economics* (May 1990), p. 323; David Swinton, "The Economic Status of African Americans during the Reagan-Bush Era: Withered Opportunities, Limited Outcomes, and Uncertain Outlook," in *The State of Black America* (New York: National Urban League, 1993), p. 138.
13. *Economic Report of the President,* February 1998, pp. 130–31.
14. *StatAbst–1998,* p. 407, Table 651.
15. Michael Tonry, "Racial Politics, Racial Disparities, and the War on Crime," *Crime & Delinquency* 40, no. 4 (October 1994), pp. 483, 485–86.
16. *Sourcebook–1981,* p. 463.
17. *StatAbst–1988,* p. 175, Table 304.
18. BJS, *Profile of Inmates in the United States and England and Wales, 1991* (October 1994, NCJ-145863), p. 13.
19. Theodore Chiricos and William Bales, "Unemployment and Punishment: An Empirical Assessment," *Criminology* 29, no. 4 (1991), p. 718.
20. "An offender's socioeconomic status . . . did not impact sentence length for any of the property offenses." Stewart J. D'Alession and Lisa Stolzenberg, "Socioeconomic Status and the Sentencing of the Traditional Offender," *Journal of Criminal Justice* 21 (1993), p. 73. The same study did find that lower-socioeconomic status offenders received harsher sentences for violent and moral-order crimes. Another study that finds no greater likelihood of incarceration based on socioeconomic status is Michael Benson and Esteban Walker, "Sentencing the White-Collar Offender," *American Sociological Review* 53 (April 1988),

pp. 294–302. And yet another found higher-status offenders to be more likely to be incarcerated: David Weisburd, Elin Waring, Stanton Wheeler, "Class, Status, and the Punishment of White Collar Criminals," *Law and Social Inquiry* 15 (1990), pp. 223–41. These last two studies are limited to offenders convicted of white-collar crimes, and so they deal with a sample that has already been subject to whatever discrimination exists in the arrest, charging, and conviction of white-collar offenders.

21. Isidore Silver, "Introduction to the Avon edition of *The Challenge of Crime in a Free Society*" (New York: Avon, 1968), p. 31.

22. This is the conclusion of Austin L. Porterfield, *Youth in Trouble* (Fort Worth, Tex.: Leo Potishman Foundation, 1946); Fred J. Murphy, M. Shirley, and H. L. Witmer, "The Incidence of Hidden Delinquency," *American Journal of Orthopsychiatry* 16 (October 1946), pp. 686–96; James F. Short, Jr., "A Report on the Incidence of Criminal Behavior, Arrests, and Convictions in Selected Groups," *Proceedings of the Pacific Sociology Society, 1954*, pp. 110–18, published as vol. 22, no. 2 of *Research Studies of the State College of Washington* (Pullman: State College of Washington, 1954); F. Ivan Nye, James F. Short, Jr., and Virgil J. Olson, "Socioeconomic Status and Delinquent Behavior," *American Journal of Sociology* 63 (January 1958), pp. 381–89; Maynard L. Erikson and Lamar T. Empey, "Class Position, Peers and Delinquency," *Sociology and Social Research* 49 (April 1965), pp. 268–82; William J. Chambliss and Richard H. Nagasawa, "On the Validity of Official Statistics; A Comparative Study of White, Black, and Japanese High-School Boys," *Journal of Research in Crime and Delinquency* 6 (January 1969), pp. 71–77; Eugene Dolescal, "Hidden Crime," *Crime and Delinquency Literature* 2, no. 5 (October 1970), pp. 546–72; Nanci Koser Wilson, *Risk Ratios in Juvenile Delinquency* (Ann Arbor, Mich.: University Microfilms, 1972); and Maynard L. Erikson, "Group Violations, Socioeconomic Status, and Official Delinquency," *Social Forces* 52, no. 1 (September 1973), pp. 41–52.

23. Charles R. Tittle and Robert F. Meier, "Specifying the SES/Delinquency Relationship," *Criminology* 28, no. 2 (1990), p. 292.

24. Gary F. Jensen and Kevin Thompson," What's Class Got to Do With It? A Further Examination of Power-Control Theory," *American Journal of Sociology* 95, no. 1 (January 1990), p. 1021.

25. This is the conclusion of Martin Gold, "Undetected Delinquent Behavior," *Journal of Research in Crime and Delinquency* 3, no. 1 (1966), pp. 27–46; and of Sutherland and Cressey, *Criminology*, pp. 137, 220.

26. Cf. Larry Karacki and Jackson Toby, "The Uncommitted Adolescent: Candidate for Gang Socialization," *Sociological Inquiry* 32 (1962), pp. 203–15; William R. Arnold, "Continuities in Research—Scaling Delinquent Behavior," *Social Problems* 13, no. 1 (1965), pp. 59–66; Harwin L. Voss, "Socio-economic Status and Reported Delinquent Behavior," *Social Problems,* 13, no. 3 (1966), pp. 314–24; LaMar Empey and Maynard L. Erikson, "Hidden Delinquency and Social Status," *Social Forces* 44, no. 4 (1966), pp. 546–54; Fred J. Shanley, "Middle-Class Delinquency As a Social Problem," *Sociology and Social Research* 51 (1967), pp. 185–98; Jay R. Williams and Martin Gold, "From Delinquent Behavior to Official Delinquency," *Social Problems* 20, no. 2 (1972), pp. 209–29.

27. Empey and Erikson, "Hidden Delinquency and Social Status," pp. 549, 551. Nye, Short, and Olson also found destruction of property to be committed most frequently by upperclass boys and girls, "Socioeconomic Status and Delinquent Behavior," p. 385.

28. Williams and Gold, "From Delinquent Behavior to Official Delinquency."

29. Gold, "Undetected Delinquent Behavior," p. 37.

30. Ibid., p. 44.

31. Comparing socioeconomic status categories, "scant evidence is found that would support the contention that group delinquency is more characteristic of the lower-status levels than other socioeconomic status levels. In fact, only arrests seem to be more characteristic of the low-status category than the other categories." Erikson, "Group Violations, Socioeconomic Status and Official Delinquency," p. 15.

32. Gold, "Undetected Delinquent Behavior," p. 28 (emphasis added).

33. Ibid., p. 38.

34. "Stealing $200 Billion the Respectable Way," *U.S. News & World Report,* May 20, 1985, p. 83.

35. Marshall B. Clinard, *Corporate Corruption: The Abuse of Corporate Power* (New York: Praeger, 1990), p. 15.

36. August Bequai, "High-Tech Security and the Failings of President Clinton's Commission on Critical Infrastructure Protection," *Computer and Security* 17 (1998), pp. 19–21.

37. Michael Levi, *Regulating Fraud: White-Collar Crime and the Criminal Process* (London: Tavistock, 1987), p. 33; *StatAbst–1998,* p. 456, Table 721.

38. *UCR–1998,* p. 210, Table 29.

39. See, for example, Theodore G. Chiricos, Philip D. Jackson, and Gordon P. Waldo, "Inequality in the Imposition of a Criminal Label," *Social Problems* 19, no. 4 (Spring 1972), pp. 553–72.

40. A good summary of these developments can be found in Joel Jay Finer, "Ineffective Assistance of Counsel," *Cornell Law Review* 58, no. 6 (July 1973), pp. 1077–1120.

41. Lesely Oelsner, "Wide Disparities Mark Sentences Here," *The New York Times,* September 27, 1972, p. 1.

42. Stewart J. D'Alession and Lisa Stolzenberg, "Socioeconomic Status and the Sentencing of the Traditional Offender," *Journal of Criminal Justice* 21 (1993), pp. 71–74.

43. Barbara C. Nienstedt, Marjorie Zatz, and Thomas Epperlein, "Court Processing and Sentencing of Drinking Drivers," *Journal of Quantitative Criminology* 4, no. 1 (1988), pp. 39–59.

44. Theodore Chiricos and William Bales, "Unemployment and Punishment: An Empirical Assessment," *Criminology* 29, no. 4 (1991), pp. 701–24.

45. Belinda R. McCarthy, "A Micro-Level Analysis of Social Control: Intrastate Use of Jail and Prison Confinement," *Justice Quarterly* 7, no. 2 (June 1990), pp. 334–35.

46. Dean J. Champion, "Private Counsels and Public Defenders: A Look at Weak Cases, Prior Records, and Leniency in Plea Bargaining," p. 143.

47. T. Miethe and C. Moore, "Socioeconomic Disparities under Determinate Sentencing Systems: A Comparison of Preguideline and Postguideline Practices in Minnesota," *Criminology* 23, no. 2 (1985), p. 358.

48. Robert Tillman and Henry Pontell, "Is Justice 'Collar-Blind'?: Punishing Medical Provider Fraud," *Criminology* 30, no. 4 (1992), pp. 547–73, quote from p. 560.

49. James F. Nelson, "Hidden Disparities in Case Processing: New York State, 1985–1986," *Journal of Criminal Justice* 20 (1992), pp. 181–200.

50. J. D. Unnever and L.A. Hembroff, "The Prediction of Racial/Ethnic Sentencing Disparities," *Journal of Research in Crime and Delinquency* 25 (1988), p. 53.

51. C. Crawford, T. Chiricos, and G. Kleck, "Race, Racial Threat, and Sentencing of Habitual Offenders," *Criminology* 36, no. 3 (1998), pp. 481–511.

52. BJS, *Prisoners in 1994,* August 1995 (NCJ-151654), p. 9; BJS, *Prison and Jail Inmates, 1995,* p. 10; *Sourcebook–1994,* Table 4.11, p. 388.

53. *Sourcebook–1987,* pp. 376, 491, 518; *Sourcebook–1992,* p. 492, Table 5.21.

54. *Criminal Justice Newsletter,* March 1, 1995, p. 3; *Criminal Justice Newsletter,* April 17, 1995, p. 5.

55. McDonald, Douglas, and Ken Carlson, *Sentencing in the Federal Courts: Does Race Matter?* (Washington, D.C.: BJS, 1993), cited in Michael Tonry, "Racial Politics, Racial Disparities, and the War on Crime," *Crime & Delinquency* 40, no. 4 (October 1994), p. 487.

56. Ronald Smothers, "Wave of Prison Uprisings Provokes Debate on Crack," *The New York Times,* October 24, 1995, p. A12.

57. "Blacks Receive Stiffer Sentences," *Boston Globe,* April 4, 1979, pp. 1, 50f.

58. Randall Thomson and Matthew Zingraff, "Detecting Sentencing Disparity: Some Problems and Evidence," *American Journal of Sociology* 86, no. 4 (1981), pp. 869–80, especially p. 875.

59. J. Unnever, C. Frazier, and J. Henretta, "Race Differences in Criminal Sentencing," *Sociological Quarterly* 21 (Spring 1980), pp. 197–205, especially p. 204.

60. J. Petersillia, "Racial Disparities in the Criminal Justice System: A Summary," *Crime & Delinquency* 31, no. 1 (1985), p. 28. See also G. Bridges and R. Crutchfield, "Law, Social Standing and Racial Disparities in

Imprisonment," *Social Forces* 66, no. 3 (1988), pp. 699–724.

61. M. Myers, "Economic Inequality and Discrimination in Sentencing," *Social Forces* 65, no. 3 (1987), p. 761.

62. Mary Pat Flaherty and Joan Biskupic, "Rules Often Impose Toughest Penalties on Poor, Minorities," *The Washington Post,* October 9, 1996, p. A26.

63. Barbara S. Meierhoefer, *The General Effect of Mandatory Minimum Prison Terms: A Longitudinal Study of Federal Sentences Imposed* (Washington, D.C.: Federal Judicial Center, 1992), especially pp. 1, 20, 25. Between October 1989 and 1990, 46 percent of whites received federal sentences below the mandatory minimum, but 32 percent of blacks did. *Sourcebook—1991,* p. 542, Table 5.43.

64. Mary Pat Flaherty and Joan Biskupic, "Rules Often Impose Toughest Penalties on Poor, Minorities."

65. William J. Bowers and Glenn L. Pierce, "Racial Discrimination and Criminal Homicide under Post-Furman Capital Statutes," in H. A. Bedau, ed., *The Death Penalty in America* (New York: Oxford University Press, 1982), pp. 206–24.

66. *McCleskey v. Kemp,* 107 S. Ct. 1756 (1987). The research central to this case was that of David Baldus, reported in D. Baldus, C. Pulaski, and G. Woodworth, "Comparative Review of Death Sentences: An Empirical Study of the Georgia Experience," *Journal of Criminal Law and Criminology* 74 (1983), pp. 661–725. Other studies that support the notion of discrimination in capital sentencing based on race of victim are R. Paternoster, "Race of Victim and Location of Crime: The Decision to Seek the Death Penalty in South Carolina," *Journal of Criminal Law and Criminology* 74, no. 3 (1983), pp. 754–88; R. Paternoster, "Prosecutorial Discretion in Requesting the Death Penalty: A Case of Victim Based Racial Discrimination," *Law and Society Review* 18 (1984), pp. 437–78; S. Gross and R. Mauro, "Patterns of Death: An Analysis of Racial Disparities in Capital Sentencing and Homicide Victimization," *Stanford Law Review* 37 (1984), pp. 27–120; Radelet and Pierce, "Race and Prosecutorial Discretion in Homicide Cases," *Law and Society Review* 19 (1985), pp. 587, 615–19.

67. Anthony G. Amsterdam, "Race and the Death Penalty," in S. Gold, ed., *Moral Controversies* (Belmont, Calif.: Wadsworth, 1993), pp. 268–69.

68. U.S. General Accounting Office, Report to the Senate and House Committees on the Judiciary, *Death Penalty Sentencing: Research Indicates Pattern of Racial Disparities* (February 1990), especially p. 5.

69. Marvin E. Wolfgang, Arlene Kelly, and Hans C. Nolde, "Comparison of the Executed and the Commuted among Admissions to Death Row," in *Crime and Justice in Society,* ed. Quinney. Pp. 508, 513.

70. "Antitrust: Kauper's Last Stand," *Newsweek,* June 21, 1976, p. 70. On December 21, 1974, the Antitrust Procedures and Penalty Act was passed, striking out the language of the Sherman Antitrust Act, which made price fixing a misdemeanor punishable by a maximum sentence of one year in prison. According to the new law, price fixing is a felony punishable by up to three years in prison. Because prison sentences were a rarity under the old law and usually involved only 30 days in jail when actually imposed, there is little reason to believe the new law will strike fear in the hearts of corporate crooks.

71. Marshall Clinard and Peter Yeager, *Corporate Crime* (New York: Free Press, 1980), pp. 291–92.

72. Ibid., p. 153.

73. *The Washington Post,* March 2, 1990, pp. A1, A20; April 1, 1990, p. C3; April 28, 1990, pp. A1, A14; April 27, 1991, p. A6.

74. K. Johnson, "Federal Court Processing of Corporate, White Collar, and Common Crime Economic Offenders over the Past Three Decades," *Mid-American Review of Sociology* 11, no. 1 (1986), pp. 25–44.

75. J. Hagan and P. Palloni, "'Club Fed' and the Sentencing of White-Collar Offenders Before and After Watergate," *Criminology* 24, no. 4 (1986), pp. 616–17. See also J. Hagan and P. Parker, "White-Collar Crime and Punishment: The Class Structure and Legal Sanctioning of Securities Violations," *American Sociological Review* 50 (1985), pp. 302–16.

76. John P. Wright, Francis T. Cullen, and Michael B. Blankenship, "The Social Construction of Corporate Violence: Media Coverage of the

Imperial Food Products Fire," *Crime & Delinquency* 41, no. 1 (January 1995), pp. 23–24; Laurie Grossman, "Owner Sentenced to Nearly 20 Years over Plant Fire," *The Wall Street Journal,* September 15, 1992, p. A10.

77. Tom Wicker, *A Time to Die* (New York: Quadrangle, 1975), pp. 311, 314.

78. Ibid., p. 310.

79. *Sourcebook—1987,* p. 486, BJS, *Correctional Populations in the United States, 1985,* p. 10, Table 2.6; *StatAbst—1988,* p. 13, Table 13; BJS, *Prisoners in 1998* (NCJ175687); BJS, Prison and Jail Inmates at Midyear 1998 (NCJ173414); U.S. Bureau of the Census, Current Population Reports, Series PPL-57, U.S. Population Estimates by Age, Sex, Race, and Hispanic Origin: 1990–1996.

80. BJS, *Survey of State Prison Inmates,* 1991, p. 3.

81. BJS, *Criminal Offender Statistics,* at http:// www.ojp.usdoj.gov/bjs/crimoff.htm (last revised December 5, 1999); and BJS, *Profile of Jail Inmates 1996* (April 1998, NCJ164620).

82. *Economic Report of the President,* February 1998, p. 331, Table B-43.

83. *Economic Report of the President,* February 1998, p. 320, Table B-33.

84. BJS, *Criminal Offender Statistics,* "Comparing Federal and State Prison Inmates."

REFERENCES

Anderson, David. *Crime and the Politics of Hysteria: How the Willie Horton Story Changed American Justice.* New York: Times Books, 1995.

Clinard, Marshall. *Corporate Corruption: The Abuse of Power.* New York: Praeger, 1990.

Day, Kathleen. *S & L Hell: The People and the Politics Behind the $1 Trillion Savings and Loan Scandal.* New York: Norton, 1993.

Lusane, Clarence. *Pipe Dream Blues: Racism and the War on Drugs.* Boston: South End Press, 1991.

Lynch, Michael, and E. Britt Patterson. *Race and Criminal Justice.* New York: Harrow & Heston, 1991.

Miller, Jerome. *Search and Destroy: African-American Males in the Criminal Justice System.* New York: Cambridge University Press, 1996.

Pearce, Frank, and Lauren Snider. *Corporate Crime.* Toronto: University of Toronto Press, 1995.

Pizzo, Stephen et al. *Inside Job: The Looting of America's Savings and Loans.* New York: McGraw-Hill, 1989.

Simon, David, and Stanley Eitzen. *Elite Deviance,* 6th ed. Boston: Allyn & Bacon, 1999.

Timmer, Doug, and Stanley Eitzen. *Crimes in the Streets and Crimes in the Suites.* Boston: Allyn & Bacon, 1989.

29

THE MARK OF A CRIMINAL RECORD

Devah Pager

QUESTIONS TO CONSIDER

The rate of recidivism (convicts who return to jail) is extremely high in the United States. Poverty, a lack of formal education, and the disappearance of employment opportunities in the inner city of jobs that pay a living wage create conditions that researchers believe are linked to criminal activity. How difficult is it for someone with a criminal record, a "mark" as this author describes it, to secure employment? Furthermore, how might race play out among those with and without a criminal "mark"? Devah Pager's research findings are shocking.

"The Mark of a Criminal Record," by Devah Pager, *Focus* 23, no. 2, Summer 2004. Focus, newsletter for the Institute of Research on Poverty, © 2004 by the Regents of the University of Wisconsin.

Among those recently released from prison, nearly two-thirds will be charged with new crimes and 40 percent will return to prison within three years. Those who are not reincarcerated have poorer employment and incomes than those without criminal records. But there is strong disagreement over the reasons that ex-offenders do so poorly after release. Does incarceration itself actually lead to lower employment and income? Or do the poor outcomes of ex-offenders merely arise from the environmental and personal histories that sent them to prison in the first place—the broken families, the poor neighborhoods, the lack of education and absence of legitimate opportunities, the individual tendencies toward violence or addiction?[1]

Survey research has consistently shown their incarceration is linked to lower employment and income. Many hypotheses have been proposed for this relationship: the labeling effects of criminal stigma, the disruption of social and family networks, the loss of human capital, institutional trauma, and legal barriers to employment. It is, however, difficult, using survey data, to determine which of these mechanisms is at work and whether, for any given mechanism, the results are due to the effect of imprisonment or to preexisting characteristics of people who are convicted. A further issue, given racial disparities in imprisonment rates, is whether the effect of a criminal record is more severe for African American that it is for white ex-offenders.

In the research reported here I sought to answer three primary questions about the mechanisms driving the relationship between imprisonment and employment.[2] First, to what extent do employers use information about criminal histories to make hiring decisions? Second, does race, by itself, remain a major barrier to employment? Its continued significance has been questioned in recent policy debates.[3] Third, does the effect of a criminal record differ for black and white applicants? Given that many Americans hold strong and persistent views associating race and crime, does a criminal record trigger a more negative response for African American than for white applicants?

The Employment Audit

Just as a college degree may serve as a positive credential for those seeking employment, a prison term attaches a "negative credential" to individuals, certifying them in ways that may qualify them for discrimination or social exclusion. Using an experimental audit design, I have been able to isolate that institutional effect, holding constant many background and personal characteristics that otherwise make it very difficult to disentangle cause and effect.[4]

In an employment audit, matched pairs of individuals ("testers") apply for real job openings to see whether employers respond differently to applicants on the basis of selected characteristics. The methodology combines experimental methods with real-life contexts. It is particularly valuable for those with an interest in discrimination, and has primarily been used to study characteristics such as race, gender, and age that are protected under the Civil Rights Act.

Several states, including Wisconsin, have expanded fair employment legislation to protect individuals with criminal records from discrimination by employers, because of their concern about the consequences of the rapid expansion and the skewed racial and ethnic composition of the ex-offender population over the last three decades. Under this legislation, employers are warned that past crimes may be taken into account only if they closely relate to the specific duties required by the job—as, for example, if a convicted embezzler applies for a book-keeping position, or a sex offender for

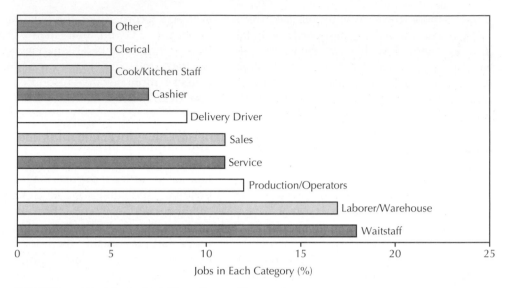

FIGURE 1 The jobs in the Milwaukee audit sample.

a job at a day care center. Because of the Wisconsin legislation barring discrimination on the basis of a criminal record, we might expect circumstances to be, if anything, more favorable to the employment of ex-offenders than in states without legal protections.

This audit was conducted between June and December, 2001, in Milwaukee, Wisconsin, which in population, size, racial composition, and employment rate is typical of many major American cities. At the time, the local economy was moderately strong and unemployment rates ranged between 4 and 5.2 percent.[5]

I used two audit teams of 23-year-old male college students, one consisting of two African Americans and the other of two whites. All were bright and articulate, with appealing styles of self-presentation. Characteristics that were not already identical, such as education and work experience, were made to appear identical for the purposes of the audit. Within each team, one auditor was randomly assigned a "criminal record" for the first week; then week by week auditors took turns playing the ex-offender role. The "criminal record" consisted of a nonviolent, felony drug

conviction (possession of cocaine with intent to distribute). If the employment application did not request information about previous convictions, ways were found to include that information—for example, by reporting work experience in the correctional facility and citing a parole officer as a reference.

The audit teams applied to separate sets of jobs drawn from the Sunday classified section of the city's major daily newspaper, the *Milwaukee Journal Sentinel*, and from Jobnet, a state-sponsored Web site for employment listings. Since nearly 90 percent of state prisoners have no more than a high school diploma, the job openings chosen were for entry-level positions requiring no previous experience and no education beyond high school (see Figure 1). All openings were within 25 miles of downtown Milwaukee; a majority were in the suburbs or surrounding counties.[6] The survey audited 350 employers, 150 by the white audit team and 200 by the black team.

The audit study focused only on the first stage in the employment process—the stage most likely to be affected by the barrier of a criminal record. Auditors visited the employers, filled out applications, and went as far as they could during that first interview. They did not return for a second visit. Thus our critical variable of interest was the proportion of cases in which employers called the applicant after the first visit. Reference checks were included as an outcome, in the belief that it would be important to have a former employer or parole officer vouch for applicants with criminal records. As it turned out, employers paid virtually no attention to references; only 4 out of 350 actually checked.

Even though employers are not allowed to use criminal background information to make hiring decisions, about three-quarters of employers in this sample explicitly asked if the applicant had ever been convicted of a crime and, if so, for details. A much smaller proportion, just over a quarter, indicated that they would perform a background check (employers are not required to say if they intend to, and this doubtless represents a lower-bound estimate). The use of background checks by employers has been increasingly steadily, however, because of greater ease of access to criminal history information and growing concerns over security.

To what extent are applicants with criminal backgrounds dropped at the beginning of the process? For answers, we turn to the results of the audit.

The Effects of a Criminal Record and Race on Employment

Given that all testers presented nearly identical credentials, the different responses they encountered can be attributed fully to the effects of race and criminal background.

The results in Figure 2 suggest that a criminal record has severe effects. Among whites, applicants with criminal records were only half as likely to be called back as equally qualified applicants with no criminal record.

The second question involved the significance of race, by itself, in shaping black men's employment prospects, and here too the audit offered an unequivocal answer (Figure 2). The effect of race was very large, equal to or greater than the effect of a criminal record. Only 14 percent of black men without criminal records were called back, a proportion equal to or less than even than the number of whites *with* a criminal background. The magnitude of the race effect

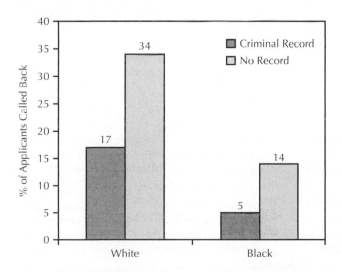

FIGURE 1 The effect of a criminal record in the Milwaukee audit sample.

found here corresponds very closely to effects found in previous audit studies directly measuring racial discrimination.[7] Since 1994, when the last major audit was reported, very little has changed in the reaction of employers to minority applicants, at least in Milwaukee.

In addition to the strong independent effects of race and criminal record, evidence suggests that the combination of the two may intensify the negative effects: black ex-offenders are one-third as likely to be called as black applicants without a criminal record. It seems that employers, already reluctant to hire blacks, are even more wary of those with proven criminal involvement. None of our white testers was asked about a criminal record before submitting his application, yet on three occasions black testers were questioned. Our testers were bright, articulate young men, yet the cursory review that entry-level applicants receive leaves little room for these qualities to be noticed.

In some cases, testers reported that employers' levels of responsiveness changed dramatically once they had glanced down at the criminal record questions. Employers seemed to use the information as a screening mechanism, without probing further into the context or complexities of the applicant's situation. But in a few circumstances employers expressed a preference for workers who had recently been released from prison because (in one case) "they tend to be more motivated and are more likely to be hard workers" and (in the case of a janitorial job) the job "involved a great deal of dirty work." Despite these cases, the vast majority of employers were reluctant to take a chance on applicants with a criminal record.

The evidence from this audit suggests that the criminal justice system is not a peripheral institution in the lives of young disadvantaged men. It has become a dominant presence, playing a key role in sorting and stratifying labor market opportunities for such men. And employment is only one of the domains affected by incarceration. Further research is needed to understand its effects on housing, family formation, and political participation, among others, before we can more fully understand its collateral consequences for social and economic inequality

NOTES

1. For discussions of the effect of incarceration, see, e.g., J. Grogger, "The Effect of Arrests on the Employment and Earnings of Young Men," *Quarterly Journal of Economics* 110 (1995): 51–72; B. Western, "The Impact of Incarceration on Wage Mobility and Inequality," *American Sociological Review* 67, no. 4 (2002): 526–46.

2. This research is reported in D. Pager, "The Mark of a Criminal Record," *American Journal of Sociology* 108, no. 5 (2003): 937–75. IRP thanks the University of Chicago Press for permission to summarize the article.

3. See, for example, D. Neal and W. Johnson, "The Role of Premarket Factors in Black-White Wage Differences," *Journal of Political Economy* 104, no. 5 (1996): 869–95; S. Steele, *The Content of Our Character: A New Vision of Race in America* (New York: Harper Perennial, 1991).

4. The method of audit studies was pioneered in the 1970s with a series of housing audits conducted by the Department of Housing and Urban Development, and was modified and applied to employment by researchers at the Urban Institute in the early 1990s. M. Turner, M. Fix, and R. Struyk, *Opportunities Denied, Opportunities Diminished: Racial Discrimination in Hir-ing* (Washington, DC: Urban Institute Press, 1991).

5. Bureau of Labor Statistics, Local Area Unemployment Statistics. Last accessed March 2003. http://www.bls.gov/lau/home.htm.

6. Over 90 percent of recent, entry-level job openings in Milwaukee were located in the outlying counties and suburbs, and only 4 percent in the central city. J. Pawasarat and L. Quinn, "Survey of Job Openings in the Milwaukee Metropolitan Area: Week of May 15, 2000," *Employment and Training Institute Report*, University of Wisconsin–Milwaukee, 2000.

7. M. Bendick, Jr., C. Jackson, and V. Reinoso, "Measuring Employment Discrimination through Controlled Experiments," *Review of Black Political Economy* 23 (1994): 25–48.

SEEING THE BIG PICTURE

In the Appendix look at the unemployment statistics in Section VII, the bachelor's degrees conferred by race in Section I, and the crime statistics in Section IV. How do you think these trends are linked?

HOW RACE SHAPES THE WORKPLACE

30

KRISTEN v. AISHA; BRAD v. RASHEED: WHAT'S IN A NAME AND HOW IT AFFECTS GETTING A JOB

Amy Braverman

QUESTIONS TO CONSIDER

We tend to think of racial discrimination as the denial of rights or opportunities to someone because of his or her race. Is it possible that race discrimination could also include denying someone employment opportunities because that person has a black-sounding name?

Could the name at the top of a résumé prompt racial discrimination? According to Marianne Bertrand, associate professor in the Graduate School of Business, and MIT economist Sendhil Mullainathan, it can. Answering more than 1,300 help-wanted ads in Boston and Chicago, the researchers sent four résumés—two higher quality, two lower quality, one of each with a black-sounding name—to companies seeking sales, administrative-support, clerical, and customer-service employees. Overall, "white" applicants were called back 50 percent more often than "black" applicants. Brad and Kristen were the top performing white-sounding names, while Jermaine and Ebony got the most callbacks among black-sounding names. Neil, Emily, Rasheed, and Aisha received the fewest callbacks.

From "Why Brad and Kristen Beat Out Jermaine and Ebony." *University of Chicago Magazine* 95(3). February 2003. Reprinted with permission.

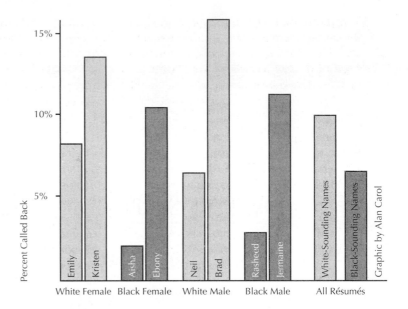

FIGURE 1 Why Brad and Kristen beat out Jermaine and Ebony.

31

WHEN THE MELTING POT BOILS OVER: THE IRISH, JEWS, BLACKS, AND KOREANS OF NEW YORK

Roger Waldinger

QUESTIONS TO CONSIDER

Roger Waldinger makes a number of astute observations about how racial and ethnic groups get sorted into certain occupations. How and in what ways does the historical timing of a group's entry (for example, Irish, Jews, Italians, and Afro-Caribbeans) into the United States affect its economic and social mobility? How does one group come to monopolize one trade or occupation? How are race, ethnicity, upward mobility, and control of local politics linked to upward mobility?

Roger Waldinger, "When the Melting Pot Boils Over: The Irish, Jews, Blacks, and Koreans of New York" from *The Bubbling Cauldron*, pp. 265–281, Michael Peter Smith, Joseph R. Feagin (eds.). Copyright © 1995 by the Regents of the University of Minnesota. Reprinted by permission.

ssimilation is the grand theme of American immigration research. The classic sociological position provided an optimistic counter to the dim assessments of the new immigrants prevalent at the early part of the century. Notwithstanding the marked differences that impressed contemporaries, Robert Park, Ernest Burgess, W. I. Thomas, and others contended that the new immigrant groups would lose their cultural distinctiveness and move up the occupational hierarchy. Milton Gordon's now classic volume distilled the essence of the sociological view: immigrant-ethnic groups start at the bottom and gradually move up; their mobility takes place through individual advancement, not group collective action; in the process of moving up, ethnic groups lose their distinctive social structure; and as ethnics become like members of the core group, they become part of the core group, joining it in neighborhoods, in friendship, and eventually in marriage.

But the image of immigrants moving onward and upward is hard to reconcile with the darker, conflictual side of American ethnic life. Conflict, often of the fiercest kind, runs like a red thread through the history of American ethnic groups. Certainly New Yorkers evince an extraordinary propensity to come to blows over racial and ethnic differences. The latest conflicts pitting blacks against Hasidim and Koreans in Brooklyn or Chinese against Puerto Ricans in Manhattan are but the latest episodes in a longer saga, extending from the anti-Catholic crusades of the 1850s to the school conflicts of the 1890s, to the controversies engendered by the Coughlinites and the German Bund of the 1930s, to the school integration struggles of the 1960s, right up to this day.

The contradiction between ethnic assimilation and ethnic conflict is more apparent than real. Where the classic sociological model goes wrong is not in its depiction of an upward trajectory, but rather in its individualistic assumptions about the process of ethnic change. The story of ethnic progress in America can be better thought of as a collective search for mobility, in which the succession of one migrant wave after another ensures a continuous competitive conflict over resources. Groups move up from the bottom by specializing in and dominating a particular branch of economic life; that specialization goes unchallenged as long as the newest arrivals are con-tent to work in the bottom-level jobs for which they were initially recruited. This [reading] develops the story in the form of brief episodes from the New York experience of four ethnic groups—Irish, Jews, African Americans, and Koreans. Each group is associated with the four successive waves of migration that have swept over New York in the past two hundred years.

The Irish

Nearly one and a half million Irish flocked to the United States between 1846 and 1855 in flight from famine; they converged on the eastern port cities of Boston, Philadelphia, and New York, where, lacking resources, about a quarter stayed. Low levels of education, lack of exposure to industrial or craft work, and lack of capital led the Irish into the lower ranges of manual work, with women taking domestic work and men engaging in insecure, low-paid itinerant employment, especially in construction. Irish progress from the bottom proceeded at a slow pace.

By 1900, however, the Irish had already established themselves in public employment. At the time, the public sector provided relatively few jobs, but this was soon to change. Irish employment in New York City government almost quadrupled between 1900 and 1930, increasing from just under 20,000 to 77,000, while the total number of city workers climbed from 54,000 to 148,000 less than a factor of three.[1]

Irish penetration into the public sector reflected the growing political power of the Democratic machine, which remained Irish dominated. But the machine's hold on local government was met by opposition from WASP reformers. Seeking to break the machine's power by severing the link between political activity and government employment, the reformers installed a civil service system—to little avail. The Irish encountered few effective competitors for city jobs. There was never any serious threat that WASPs would dislodge the Irish. Moreover, the increasingly numerous Poles, Jews, Italians, and others who were just off the boat had little chance of doing well in essay-type exams against the Irish, who were, after all, native English speakers.

The liabilities of the new immigrants lasted hardly a generation; with the Jews' rapid educational and occupational advancement, another competitor entered the scene. But as long as the Irish, through Tammany Hall's grip over city government, could control municipal hiring, interethnic competition posed little threat. Competition was structured in such a way as to minimize the value of Jews' educational advantages. The patronage system functioned unencumbered throughout Tammany's dominance between 1917 and 1933.

The depression severely challenged Irish control over public jobs; LaGuardia's election in 1933 delivered the coup de grace. Keeping control of City Hall required LaGuardia to undermine the material base of Tammany's power and consolidate his support among groups not firmly under Tammany's tow—the most important of which were the Jews, who had split between LaGuardia and his Tammany opponent in 1933. Both goals could be accomplished in the same way, namely pursuing the administrative changes long championed by the reformers.[2]

The depression and LaGuardia's reforms made city jobs more attractive to highly educated workers, which, under the circumstances, mainly meant Jews. One door at which Jewish competitors knocked was teaching, previously an Irish reserve (as the 1900 statistics show). If Jewish entrance into teaching produced antagonism, far more explosive was the situation in the police force. Twenty-nine thousand men sat for the exam held in April 1939, from whom three hundred were selected to enter the department in 1940. Of these, over one-third were Jews. Not surprisingly, this class of 1940 constituted the first significant proportion of Jews to enter the police.[3]

Jewish-Irish competition produced some other episodes, but conflict between them abated, thanks to the prosperity of the postwar era and the new opportunities it provided. Outmigration to the suburbs and the Sun Belt and mobility into the middle class depleted the ranks of the city's Irish population. By the late 1950s, as Nathan Glazer and Daniel Moynihan noted, so profound was the sense of displacement that the remaining Irish New Yorkers reminded themselves, "There are still some of us left."[4]

Those who are left have kept up the long-established Irish occupational ways. Although the commissioners of the police and fire departments are black and Puerto Rican, respectively, the top brass retains a strongly Irish cast, as does the rank and file. Indeed, the fire department presents a glimpse of New York gone by, with a workforce that is 93 percent white and 80 percent Catholic. Some unions still have a distinctly Irish makeup.[5]

In the 1980s, some of the old niches at last gained new blood, as an influx of new, illegal Irish immigrants fled unemployment in the Republic of Ireland for better times in New York. Whereas black Americans still found the doors of construction unions closed, the new arrivals, dubbed "JFK carpenters," were warmly welcomed by their aging compatriots. Women also retraced the steps of the past, as could be seen from the classified pages of the *Irish Echo*, with its columns of ads for nannies, babysitters, and housekeepers.

The Jews

Although the Jewish presence in New York extends far back, almost to the city's founding, Jews did not become an important, visible element in the city's economic life until the 1880s. Rising anti-Semitism, combined with the pressures of modernization, led to a huge outflow of Jews from Eastern Europe. By 1920, New York, with two million Jews, had become the world's largest Jewish city.

The new arrivals came just when the demand for factory-made clothing began to surge. Many had been tailors in the old country, and although most had worked with needle and thread, they quickly adapted themselves to machine production. As the various components of the clothing industry grew in synergistic fashion, the opportunities for mobility through the ethnic economy multiplied. Through rags, some immigrants found riches; the sweatshop workers who moved to contracting and then to manufacturing, or possibly careers in retailing, filled the newly formed ranks of New York's *alrightniks*.[6]

The Jewish concentration in commerce and clothing manufacture defined their initial place in the ethnic division of labor. Jewish specializations seldom overlapped with the Irish: domestic service and general labor were rarities among the Russians but were common Irish pursuits; by the same token, tailoring and retailing, whether by merchant or peddler, were far more likely to engage Russians than Irish.

As Jews sought to move beyond the ethnic economy, interethnic competition and antagonism grew more intense. The relatively rapid educational progress of younger immigrants and of the second generation prepared them to work outside the ethnic economy, but gentile employers were rarely eager to hire Jews. One study, completed just before the Great Depression, found that the doors of New York's large, corporate organizations—"railroads, banks, insurance companies, lawyers' offices, brokerage houses, the New York Stock Exchange, hotels . . . and the home offices of large corporations of the first rank"—were infrequently opened to Jews.[7] The surge into the schools, and through the schools into the professions, met with resistance from the older, largely Protestant population that dominated these institutions.

In the 1930s, depression and discrimination outside the ethnic economy led many second-generation Jews to seek an alternative in public employment. Although the quest for government jobs, and in particular teaching positions, had started earlier, the straitened circumstances of the 1930s accelerated this search. The quality and quantity of Jews vying for government employment increased, heightening the competitive pressure on the Irish and yielding the antagonism we've already observed.

Jewish-Irish conflict reached its height in the late 1930s; it gradually subsided, replaced by a more explosive, deeply antagonistic relationship with blacks. Although black occupations were more similar to those of the Irish than they were to the Jews', the economic pursuits of Jews put them at odds with blacks on various counts. The Jews dominated small retail activity throughout the city and were particularly prominent in Harlem. The Jewish storeowners in Harlem sold to blacks but preferred not to employ them until protests in the mid-1930s finally forced them to relent. Antagonism toward Jewish shopkeepers in Harlem rose during the 1930s, fueled by the depression and by Jews' broader role as middlemen in the Harlem economy. Frustration boiled over in the riot of 1943, when black Harlemites burned down the stores of Jews in a fury that presaged events to come.[8] Hostility simmered thereafter, reaching the boiling point during the 1960s.

The transformation of the ethnic economy also engendered black-Jewish conflict, Rapid Jewish social mobility meant a dwindling Jewish working class; the diminishing supply of Jewish workers had a particularly notable effect on the garment industry, where Jewish factory owners were forced to hire outsiders in growing numbers—first Italians, then blacks. In World War II, desperate for workers, Jewish employers hired blacks in great numbers. By 1950, there were 25,000 African American garment workers, 20,000 more than were working in clothing factories ten years before.[9]

But relations between blacks and Jews proved uneasy. Blacks moved into less-skilled, poorer-paying positions, from which mobility into better-remunerated positions proved difficult. Although the garment unions made explicit efforts to organize black workers and integrate them into union structures, few blacks moved up to elected offices, and none high up in the union hierarchy. To protect jobs from southern competitors, the unions adopted a policy of wage restraint, which inevitably meant a softened stance on union employers at home—much to the dismay of black New York garment workers.[10]

The garment business was the Jewish enclave of the past; Jewish mobility into the middle class had made teaching the Jewish niche of the mid-1960s. As the schools came to serve a growing black population, their role was increasingly contested by black students, parents, and protest organizations.

The complaints were various, and not all directly linked to the Jews' prominent role in the school system; but the situation in which so many Jews were teachers and so many schools in black neighborhoods were staffed by Jews inevitably led to conflict. In 1968, a black-dominated school board in Brooklyn dismissed a group of white, largely Jewish teachers and replaced them with a mainly black staff; these actions set off a three-month-long strike by the Jewish-led teachers' union. Although the union eventually won, its victory was pyrrhic, at least concerning black-Jewish relations. Memory of the strike and the resentments it fueled have not significantly changed, even a generation later.[11]

What has altered, however, is the economic position of the Jews. The ethnic economy of the immigrant days remains, but in vestigial form. Although Jews are still active in the garment industry, they mainly concentrate in the designing and merchandising ends. "Goldberg" no longer runs clothing factories; his place has been taken by "Kim" and "Wong," who only employ compatriots, not blacks. The same transformations have changed the face of petty retailing and small landlording—the older flash points of black-Jewish conflict. The Jewish presence in the public sector is also fading fast: working as a city engineer or accountant used to be a Jewish occupation; now these careers engage far many more Patels than Cohens.[12] Only in teaching and in higher education do the Jewish concentrations of the past remain in full force.[13]

A distinctive Jewish role in New York's economy still lives on. It is to be found in the professions, in the persistently high rate of Jewish self-employment, in the prominence of Jews in law, real estate, finance, and the media. But the current Jewish pursuits differ crucially from the older ethnic economy in that they are detached from the dynamics of interethnic composition that characterized earlier periods. In a sense, the material basis that underlay anti-Semitic currents in New York for most of the twentieth century is gone. But its legacy and the many other resources around which groups can compete—status, politics, and territory—ensure continued conflict between Jews and their ethnic neighbors.

The Blacks

In 1890, the black share of the New York population was 1.6 percent—just about what it had been on the eve of the Civil War. But in the 1890s the South started losing blacks due to outmigration, and that loss quickly translated into New York's gain. By 1920, New York housed 150,000 black residents—who, although only 3 percent of the city's population, made New York the country's largest black urban concentration. In the next twenty years, as European immigration faltered and then stopped, and bad conditions in the rural South provided additional reasons to leave, the number of black New Yorkers tripled. Postwar prosperity and a new wave of mechanization down South launched a final, massive flow northward: by 1960, the African American population of New York numbered 1,088,000, of whom approximately 320,000 had moved to the city from other areas (mainly the South) in the previous ten years.[14]

It was not until 1940 that black New Yorkers moved out of the peripheries of the New York economy. At the turn of the century, blacks mainly found work in domestic labor, with 90 percent of black women and 55 percent of black men working in some type of domestic service occupation. Blacks' confinement to domestic service reflected, in part, the unfavorable terms of competition with immigrants, who had evicted them

from trades where they had previously been accepted. The continued expansion of New York's economy slowly opened doors in a few manufacturing industries; the shut-off of immigration during World War I and its permanent demise after 1924 further accelerated dispersion into other fields.[15]

But the depression largely put an end to these gains. By 1940, 40 percent of blacks still worked in personal service—a far greater proportion than among the workforce overall.[16] With the advent of World War II doors to other jobs were finally unlocked; manufacturing, in particular, saw very large black employment gains. Yet unlike the case in Chicago or Detroit, the black sojourn in New York's manufacturing sector proved short-lived. Lacking auto factories or steel mills, New York's goods-producing sector was a concentration of low-wage jobs; white workers remained ensconced in the better-paying, more skilled positions. Opportunities for blacks were more easily found in the burgeoning service sector—for example, health care—and in government; hence, blacks quickly dispersed into other fields.

Government, where 35 percent of native-born black New Yorkers worked in 1990,[17] has become the black niche par excellence. The history of black employment in the public sector provides yet another example of the continuing, interethnic competitive conflicts over jobs and economic resources in which New York's ethnic groups have been engaged.

In the early years of the twentieth century, local government, like most other New York employers, closed its doors to blacks: in 1911, the city only employed 511 blacks, almost all of whom were laborers. In the early 1920s, Tammany installed the leader of its black client organization, the United Colored Democracy, as a member of the three-person Civil Service Commission, but black access to public jobs changed marginally. By the late 1920s, the city counted

2,275 black workers on its payroll of whom 900 were in laboring jobs and an additional 700 were in other noncompetitive or per diem positions.[18] The reform regime did more for blacks, pushing black employment above parity by 1940.[19] But these effects occurred as a result of the government's burgeoning payrolls, and they were mainly felt in the black concentrations of hospitals, sanitation, and public works, where more than 80 percent of the city's black job holders workers in 1935.[20] Moreover, blacks remained vulnerable to discriminatory practices, as in the city-owned subway system, where blacks only worked as porters, with the exception of a few stations in Harlem. Most important, the employment system that emerged during the depression put blacks at a structural disadvantage in competition with whites. Lacking the educational skills and credentials needed to qualify for most city jobs, blacks and Puerto Ricans found themselves channeled into noncompetitive positions, of which the single largest concentration was found in the municipal hospital system. From here there were few routes of movement upward, as these bottom-level positions were disconnected from the competitive system, which promoted from within.

Race didn't reach the top of government's agenda until 1965, when John Lindsay arrived in office, the first reformer elected mayor since LaGuardia.[21] Elected with the votes of liberals and minorities, Lindsay lacked his predecessors' commitments to the interests of the largely white, civil service workforce and pledged to increase black and Puerto Rican employment in city agencies. But the new mayor quickly discovered that the civil service structure was not easily amenable to change. Lindsay gradually made progress in reducing the inflated eligibility requirements inherited from the depression, but resistance proved severe when his reforms threatened established white ethnic workers in the better-paid ranks.

Lindsay's main focus, in contrast to earlier reform administrations, was to evade the civil service system and its unionized defenders. The Lindsay administration created new, less-skilled positions for which minority residents could be more easily hired. But this approach never involved large numbers and, more important, left existing eligibility requirements unchallenged, shunting minority recruits into dead-end jobs, where they were marooned.

Lindsay backed off from his confrontations with the civil service system and its defenders in the aftermath of the disastrous 1968 teachers' strike. Where the mayor could both accommodate the unions and pursue his earlier goals of increasing minority employment, he did—mainly by tripling the number of exempt workers and shifting them from agency to agency to avoid the requirement of taking an examination. But in other instances, pressure from civil service interests proved overwhelming. With Abraham Beame's accession to City Hall in 1973, followed in 1977 by Edward Koch, mayoral support for black employment gains vanished for the next sixteen years.

The 1970s and 1980s nevertheless saw dramatic gains in black government employment. Like earlier white ethnic groups that had developed a concentration in public jobs, blacks benefited from simultaneous shifts in the structure of employment and in the relative availability of competing groups.

Changes in the structure of employment came from a variety of sources. The Equal Employment Opportunity (EEO) Act of 1972 prohibited discrimination in local government. By requiring local governments to maintain records on all employees by race and gender and to submit them to the Equal Employment Opportunity Commission, with the clear expectation that governments would show improvement over time, the act also led to institutional changes. As

EEO functions were established in each city agency, recruitment and personnel practices changed in ways that benefited previously excluded groups, as recruitment became focused on minority and immigrant communities.

Moreover, the 1972 act provided minority employees with levers to act on more recalcitrant agencies, which they used with greatest effectiveness in the uniformed services. For example, in 1973 the Vulcan Society (the organization of black firefighters) successfully challenged the results of a 1971 exam, leading to an imposition of a 1:3 quota for the duration of that list (1973–79). In 1979, the Guardians and the Hispanic Society challenged the 1979 police officer's exam; court findings of disparate impact led to the imposition of a 33.3 percent minority quota for the duration of the list.

While the advent of affirmative action helped increase access for blacks and other minorities, other changes on the supply side hastened the growth of black employment. Although the city's attraction to its traditional white ethnic labor force had begun to diminish by the 1960s, the fiscal crisis of the mid-1970s decisively exacerbated and extended the city's recruitment difficulties among its traditional workforce. By the time large-scale hiring resumed in the early 1980s, public employment had become a less attractive option than before. Moreover, municipal salaries and benefits took a severe beating during the fiscal crisis; although compensation edged back upward during the 1980s, real gains never recaptured the losses endured during the 1970s. The strength enjoyed by New York's private sector during the 1980s pulled native white workers up the hiring queue and out of the effective labor supply for many city agencies.[22]

In a situation where "the City was hiring a great deal and not turning away anyone who was qualified," as one deputy commissioner told me in an interview, the disparity in the availability of minority and white workers led to rapid recruitment of minority workers. Minorities had constituted only 40 percent of the new workers hired in 1977, making up the majority in only two low-paid occupational categories. By 1987, minorities made up 56 percent of all hires, dominating the ranks of new recruits in five out of eight occupational categories.[23]

Thus, the Koch years of 1977 to 1989 saw the ethnic composition of the municipal workforce completely transformed, notwithstanding the mayor's opposition to affirmative action and the disfavor with which minority leaders greeted his hiring policies. By 1990, whites constituted 48 percent of the 375,000 people working for the city and just slightly more— 50 percent—of the 150,000 people working in the agencies that the mayor directly controlled.[24] The declining white presence in municipal employment chiefly benefited blacks. Blacks constituted 25 percent of the city's population and a still smaller proportion of residents who were older than eighteen and thus potentially employable, but made up 36 percent of the city's total workforce and 38 percent of those who worked in the mayoral agencies. Although blacks were still underrepresented in some of the city's most desirable jobs, the earlier pattern of concentration at the bottom was overcome. The municipal hospital system, which employed two-thirds of the city's black employees in the early 1960s, in 1990 employed less than one-fifth, reflecting the dispersion of blacks throughout the municipal sector. And higher-level jobs showed clusters of considerable black overrepresentation as well, with blacks accounting for 40 percent of the administrators and 36 percent of the professionals employed in the direct mayoral agencies.

By 1990, when David Dinkins became New York's first black mayor, the phase of black-for-white succession in municipal employment was nearly complete. Blacks held just over 35 percent of all city jobs; although unevenly represented among the city's many agencies, they were often a dominant presence, accounting for more than 40 percent of employment in six of the ten largest agencies, and more than 50 percent of employment in three of the largest ten.

The comparison with Latinos underlines blacks' advantage in the new ethnic division that has emerged in city government. Whereas the city's Latinos and black populations are equal in number, Latinos hold one-third as many municipal jobs as do blacks. The discrepancies are even greater as one moves up the occupational hierarchy into the ranks of managers and professionals. And blacks have been far more successful than Latinos in gaining new permanent civil service jobs, rather than the provisional appointments on which Latinos have mainly relied. The disparity has not gone unnoticed, as the Commission on Hispanic Concerns pointed out in a 1986 report.[25] Of course, other answers might be invoked to explain Latinos' municipal jobs deficit relative to blacks'. But whatever the precise explanation, Mayor Dinkins's continuing conflicts with the Hispanic community suggest that earlier patterns of interethnic competition over municipal jobs remain alive and well.

The Koreans

In the mid-1960s, just when New York could no longer retain its native population, it reverted back to its role as an immigrant mecca. Immigrants began flocking to New York immediately after the liberalization of U.S. immigration laws in 1965. Their arrival has been the principal driving force of demographic and ethnic change in New York ever since—and will continue to be for the foreseeable future.

In 1965, what no one expected was the burgeoning of Asian immigration. The reforms tilted the new system toward immigrants with kinship ties to permanent residents or citizens. Since there had been so little Asian immigration in the previous fifty years, how could Asian newcomers find settlers with whom to seek reunification? The answer is that kinship connections were helpful, but not essential. The 1965 reforms also created opportunities for immigrants whose skills—as engineers, doctors, nurses, pharmacists—were in short supply. Along with students already living in the United States and enjoying easy access to American employers, these professionals made up the first wave of new Asian immigrants, creating the basis for the kinship migration of less well educated relatives.

Thus, well-educated, high skilled immigrants have dominated the Korean influx to the United States and to New York in particular. Although Koreans constitute a small portion of New York's new immigrants—rarely more than 3 percent of the eighty thousand to ninety thousand legal immigrants who come to New York each year—they play an important and very visible role. As middle-aged newcomers with poor English-language skills and often lacking professional licenses, relatively few Koreans have managed to steer a route back into the fields for which they trained. Instead they have turned to small business, setting up new businesses at a rate that few other groups can rival.

Koreans started in fruit and vegetable stores, taking over shops in all areas of the city, regardless of neighborhood composition or customer clientele. From there, Koreans moved on to other retail specialties—dry cleaning, fish stores, novelty shops, and nail salons. By 1980, a third of New York Korean males were already self-employed. The *1991 Korean Business Directory* provides a ready indicator of commercial growth over the

1980s, listing over 120 commercial special-ties in which Korean firms are to be found.[26]

The roots of the Korean ethnic economy are found in several sources. The competi-tive field was open. By the middle to late 1960s, the sons and daughters of Jewish and Italian storekeepers had better things to do than mind a store, and their parents, old, tired, and scared of crime, were ready to sell out to the newcomers from Korea. By the 1980s, the supply of new, native-born white entrepreneurs had virtually dried up. One survey of neighborhood businesses in Queens and Brooklyn found that almost half of the white-owned shops were run by immigrants and that most white busi-nesses were long-established entities, in contrast to the newly founded Korean shops with which they competed.[27]

Another spur to growth came from within the ethnic community. Koreans, like every other immigrant group, have special tastes and needs that are best served by an insider: the growth of the Korean population has created business for Korean accountants, doctors, brokers, hair stylists, and restaurant owners. Although the Korean community is too small to support a huge commercial infrastructure oriented to ethnic needs, the community has utilized its ethnic connec-tions to Korea to develop commercial activ-ities oriented toward non-Korean markets. Active trade relations between South Korea and the United States have provided a springboard for many Korean-owned import-export businesses, of which 119 are listed in the *1991 Korean Business Directory.*

Finally, the social structure of the Korean community itself generates advantages for business success that few other immigrant groups share. Many Koreans emigrate with capital, and those who are cash poor can raise money through rotating credit associa-tions known as *gae.* Because Koreans migrate in complete family units, family members

provide a supply of cheap and trusted labor. The prevalence of self-employment means that many Koreans have close ties to other business owners, who in turn are a source of information and support, and the high organizational density of the Korean community—which is characterized by an in-credible proliferation of alumni clubs, chur-ches, businessman's associations—provides additional conduits for the flow of busi-ness information and the making of needed contacts. These community resources distin-guish the Koreans from their competi-tors, who are less likely to be embedded in ethnic or family ties that can be drawn upon for help with business information, capital assis-tance, or staffing problems.

The Koreans have discovered that conflict *need not* be interethnic; there are other sources of threat, and in the 1980s they mobilized Korean merchants on a considerable scale. Like other small business owners, Koreans were unhappy with local government, usually with something that government was doing or was threatening to do. Fruit and vegetable store owners felt that sanitation officials were too conscientious about sidewalk cleanliness, especially since the result of the officials' de-mands was often a fine that the Korean store owner had to pay. Pressuring the city to relax inspections became a high priority for Korean organizations. In the late 1980s, as the city's fiscal crisis led it to search for new sources of revenue, fiscal planners thought of placing a special tax on dry cleaners. So Korean dry cleaners entered an unusual coalition with the white owners of commercial laundries, and the union that represented the laundryworkers, to roll back the planned tax. Like other small business owners, Korean merchants could also become dissatisfied with government's *failure* to act. The prosperity of the 1980s gave com-mercial landlords license to raise rents to the maximum, much to the distress of small busi-ness owners throughout the city. Koreans joined with their non-Korean counterparts to push for commercial rent control—to no avail.

Although Italians and Jews have largely deserted petty retail trade, they have remained in wholesaling, where the businesses are larger and profits more sizable. Thus Jewish and Italian fruit and vegetable or fish wholesalers have acquired a substantial Korean trade. The encounter has not always been a happy one, as Illsoo Kim recounted in his pathbreaking book: "Especially in their first years of emergence into the fruit and vegetable business, Koreans reported many incidents at the Hunts Point [wholesale] Market. The incidents ranged from unfair pricing and sale of poor-quality produce by the Italian and Jewish wholesalers, to physical threats and beatings administered by competing white retailers."[28] Such conflicts sparked the first mass demonstration by Koreans ever in New York. Although Kim reports that Koreans were subsequently accepted by the wholesaling community, there have been continued incidents and protests, including a recent boycott by Koreans of one of the city's largest fish wholesalers.[29]

In New York, as in almost every other major American city, black neighborhoods have provided new immigrants from Asia and the Middle East with an important economic outlet. To some extent, Koreans and other immigrants have simply replaced older white groups that had long sold to blacks and were now eager to bail out of an increasingly difficult and tense situation. By opening stores in black neighborhoods Koreans were also filling the gap left by the departure of large, nonethnic chain stores, which were steadily eliminating the low-margin, high-cost operations involved in serving a ghetto clientele. Selling to black customers proved fraught with conflict. Small protests erupted in the late 1970s. In 1981 a boycott erupted along 125th Street, Harlem's main commercial thoroughfare, with black leaders calling

Korean shop owners "vampires" who came to Harlem to "suck black consumers dry."[30]

Repeated security problems as well as more organized clashes led Korean store owners to establish neighborhood prosperity associations, in addition to those organizations that grouped merchants in a particular retail branch. Thus, alongside groups like the Korean Produce Association or the Korean Apparel Contractors Associations, one finds neighborhood groups like the Korean Merchant Association of the Bronx or the Uptown Korean Merchants Association, which seek "to improve Korean merchants' relations with local residents or communities" while lobbying local police for more effective support.[31]

In 1990 antagonism between black shoppers and Korean merchants erupted in picket lines set up in front of two Korean stores in the Flatbush section of Brooklyn. The clash started with a dispute between a Korean store owner and a black Haitian customer who charged assault; that claim then provoked black activist groups—of fairly dubious repute[32]—to establish a boycott that targeted not only the offending owner, but a neighboring Korean merchant against whom no injury was ever charged.

The boycott lasted for months, choking off business at both stores. Although customers disappeared, the two stores were kept alive by contributions from the organized Korean community, which perceived a broader danger to its economic viability should the boycott succeed. As time went on, government officials were inevitably involved. The boycott became a crisis for Mayor Dinkins, who was widely criticized for not actively seeking an end to the dispute.

The boycott ground to a halt, and a court threw out the legal suit brought by the aggrieved Haitian shopper. Other, fortunately short-lived boycotts were started in New York even while the Flatbush dispute lingered on. A clash in a nearby Brooklyn area between blacks and a small group of

Vietnamese refugees—possibly mistaken for Koreans—showed how quickly tensions generated in one arena could move to another.

Conclusion

The story of New York's Irish, Jews, blacks, and Koreans is richer and more complicated than the occupational histories I've recounted in the preceding pages. But if the [reading's] deliberately one sided focus provides only a partial account, it reminds us of ethnicity's continuing importance, and not simply because of feelings for one's own kind or animosities toward outsiders. Rather, ethnicity's centrality stems from its role as the mechanism whereby groups of categorically different workers have been sorted into an identifiably distinct set of jobs. In this sense, the ethnic division of labor has been the central division of labor in modern New York. Now, as in the past, distinctive roles in the ethnic division of labor impart a sense of "we ness" and group interest—ensuring the persistence of ethnic fragmentation and conflict.

NOTES

1. Stephen Erie, *Rainbow's End* (Berkeley: University of California Press, 1988), 88–89.

2. Thomas Kessner, *Fiorella H. LaGuardia* (New York: McGraw-Hill, 1989); Charles Garrett, *The LaGuardia Years* (New Brunswick, NJ: Rutgers University Press, 1961).

3. A survey of the surviving members of the class indicates that 38 percent were Catholic and 36 percent Jewish, with Russia and Ireland the leading countries of origin of the respondents grandparents (Richard Herrnstein et al., "New York City Police Department Class of 1940: A Preliminary Report" [unpublished manuscript, Department of Psychology, Harvard University, n. d.])

4. Nathan Glazer and Daniel P. Moynihan, *Beyond the Melting Pot* (Cambridge, MA: MIT Press, 1969).

5. Data on the ethnic composition of the fire department are from *Equal Employment Opportunity Statistics: Agency Full Report* (New York: New York City Department of Personnel, 1990); data on the religious composition are from Center for Social Policy and Practice in the Workplace, *Gender Integration in the Fire Department of the City of New York* (New York: Columbia University School of Social Work, 1988), p. 41.

6. Roger Waldinger, *Through the Eye of the Needle* (New York: New York University Press, 1986).

7. Heywood Broun and George Britt, *Christians Only* (New York: Vantage Press, 1931), 244.

8. Dominic Capeci, *The Harlem Riot of 1943* (Philadelphia: Temple University Press, 1977), 177.

9. Waldinger, *Through the Eye of the Needle*, 109–10. Employment data calculated from the census apply to employed persons twenty-five to sixty-four years old only. "Blacks" refers to native-born African Americans only. Data calculated from the Public Use Microdata Samples (U.S. Bureau of the Census, *Census of Population, 1940*, Public Use Microdata Samples [Computer file] [Washington, DC: U.S. Dept. of Commerce, Bureau of the Census, producer, 1983; Ann Arbor, MI: Inter-university Consortium for Political and Social Research, distributor, 1984]; U.S. Bureau of the Census, Census of Population, 1950, Public Use Microdata Samples [computer file] [Washington, DC: U.S. Dept. of Commerce, Bureau of the Census, and Madison: University of Wisconsin, Center for Demography and Ecology, producers, 1984; Ann Arbor, MI: Inter-university Consortium for Political and Social Research, distributor, 1984]).

10. Hasia Diner, *In the Almost Promised Land* (Westport, CT: Greenwood Press, 1977), presents a favorable account of the response among the Jewish trade union elite to the black influx into the garment industry; see chap. 6. Herbert Hill has offered a far more critical account in numerous writings, most important, "The Racial Practices of Organized Labor: The Contemporary Record," in *Organized Labor and the Negro*, edited by Julius Jacobson (New York: Doubleday, 1968), 286–337. For a judicious balancing of the issues, see Nancy Green, "Juifs et noirs aux etats-unis: La rupture d'une 'alliance naturelle,'" *Annales, E.S.C.,* 2 (March–April 1987): 445–64.

11. Diane Ravitch, *The Great School Wars* (New York: Basic Books, 1974).

12. Roger Waldinger, "The Making of an Immigrant Niche," *International Migration Review* 28(1)(1994).

13. "The Debate Goes On," *Alumnus: The City College of New York* 87(1) (Winter 1992):8–11.

14. Emmanuel Tobier, "Population," in *Setting Municipal Priorities*, edited by Charles Brecher and Raymond Horton (New York: New York University Press, 1981), 24.

15. Data are from U.S. Bureau of the Census, *Occupations at the 1900 Census* (Washington, DC: GPO, 1904). See also Herman Bloch, *The Circle of Discrimination* (New York: New York University Press, 1969).

16. Data are from the U.S. Bureau of the Census, *Census of Population, 1940.*

17. Calculated from the U.S. Bureau of the Census, *Census of Population and Housing, 1990*, Public Use Microdata Sample (a Sample): 5-Percent Sample (computer file) (Washington, DC: U.S. Dept. of Commerce, producer, 1993; Ann Arbor, MI: Inter-university Consortium for Political and Social Research, distributor, 1993).

18. Colored Citizens' Non-Partisan Committee for the Re-election of Mayor Walker, *New York City and the Colored Citizen* (n.d. [1930?]), LaGuardia Papers, Box 3530, New York Municipal Archives.

19. Calculated from U.S. Bureau of the Census, *Census of Population, 1940*, Public Use Microdata Samples. Also see Edwin Levinson, *Black Politics in New York City* (New York: Twayne, 1974).

20. Ira Katznelson, *Black Men, White Cities* (New York: Oxford University Press, 1973), 82.

21. For a more detailed discussion of the Lindsay period, see Roger Waldinger, "The Ethnic Politics of Municipal Jobs," working paper no. 248, UCLA Institute of Industrial Relations, Los Angeles, 1993.

22. Raymond Horton, "Human Resources," in *Setting Municipal Priorities*, edited by Charles Brecher and Raymond Horton (New York: New York University Press, 1986). See also Roger Waldinger, "Changing Ladders and Musical Chairs," *Politics and Society* 15 (4) (1986–87): 369–402, and "Making of an Immigrant Niche."

23. City of New York, Citywide Equal Employment Opportunity Committee, *Equal Employment Opportunity in New York City Government, 1977–1987* (New York: Citywide Equal Employment Opportunity Committee, 1988), 6.

24. Data are from unpublished EEOC reports from the New York City Department of Personnel, New York Board of Education, New York City Transit Authority, and New York City Health and Hospitals Corporation.

25. City of New York, Mayor's Commission on Hispanic Concerns, *Report* (New York: Mayor's Commission on Hispanic Concerns, 1986), 109.

26. *1991 Korean Business Directory* (Long Island City, NY: Korean News, 1991).

27. Roger Waldinger, "Structural Opportunity or Ethnic Advantage: Immigrant Business Development in New York," *International Migration Review* 23(1)(1989):61.

28. Illsoo Kim, *The New Urban Immigrants* (Princeton, NJ: Princeton University Press, 1981), 51.

29. Pyong Gap Min, "Cultural and Economic Boundaries of Korean Ethnicity: A Comparative Analysis," *Ethnic and Racial Studies* 14(2) (1991):235.

30. Lucie Cheng and Yen Espiritu, "Korean Businesses in Black and Hispanic Neighborhoods," *Sociological Perspectives* 32(4) (1989):521.

31. Illsoo Kim, "The Koreans: Small Business in an Urban Frontier," in *New Immigrants in New York*, edited by Nancy Foner (New York: Columbia University Press, 1987), 238.

32. Tamar Jacoby, "Sonny Carson and the Politics of Protest," *NY: The City Journal* 1(4)(1991): 29–40.

SEEING THE BIG PICTURE

Look at Section VIII on Occupations in the Appendix. Which racial and ethnic groups monopolize which occupations? How might these trends reflect Waldinger's thesis concerning control of occupations and upward mobility?

32

"THERE'S NO SHAME IN MY GAME": STATUS AND STIGMA AMONG HARLEM'S WORKING POOR

Katherine S. Newman • Catherine Ellis

QUESTIONS TO CONSIDER

Katherine Newman and Catherine Ellis ask us to imagine what life is like working a "McJob." How do individuals maintain self-respect working at a job that provides little in the way of social status? Is it possible for these workers to find employment that pays a living wage (about $16 an hour in New York City)? What does "No Same in My Game" mean, and what does this phrase suggest about our attitude toward work?

In the early 1990s, the McDonald's Corporation launched a television ad campaign featuring a young black man named Calvin, who was portrayed sitting atop a Brooklyn stoop in his golden-arches uniform while his friends passed by to hard-time him about holding down a "McJob." After brushing off their teasing with good humor, Calvin is approached furtively by one young black man who asks, sotto voce, whether Calvin might help him get a job. He allows that he too could use some earnings and that, despite the ragging he has just given Calvin, he thinks the uniform is really pretty cool—or at least that having a job is pretty cool.

Every fast-food worker we interviewed for this study knew the Calvin series by heart: Calvin on the job; Calvin in the street; Calvin helping an elderly woman cross the street on his way to work; Calvin getting promoted to management. They knew what McDonald's was trying to communicate to young people by producing the series in the first place. Fast-food jobs are burdened by a lasting stigma, but one that can be overcome in time. Eventually, so the commercial suggests, the public "dissing" will give way to private admiration as the value of sticking with a job eclipses the stain of a burger flipper's lowly reputation.

One of the moral maxims of American culture is that work defines the person. We carry around in our heads a rough tally that tells us what kinds of jobs are worthy of respect or of disdain, a pyramid organized by the income attached to a particular job, the educational credentials it demands, and the social characteristics of an occupation's

in cumbents. We use this system of stratification (ruthlessly at times) to boost the status
of some and humiliate others.[1]

Given our tradition of equating moral
value with employment, it stands to reason
that the most profound dividing line in our
culture is that which separates the working
person from the unemployed.[2] Only after
this line has been crossed do we begin to
make the finer gradations that distinguish
a white-collar worker from his blue-collar
counterpart, a CEO from a secretary. A whole
host of moral virtues—discipline, personal
responsibility, pragmatism—are ascribed to
those who have found and kept a job, almost any job, while those who have not are
dismissed in public discourse as slothful
and irresponsible.[3]

We inhabit an unforgiving culture that
fails to acknowledge the many reasons some
people cross that employment barrier and
others are left behind. We may remember, for
a time, that unemployment rates are high;
that particular industries have downsized
millions of workers right out of their jobs;
or that racial barriers or negative attitudes
toward teenagers make it harder for some
people to get jobs than others. Yet in the end
American culture wipes out these background truths in favor of a simpler dichotomy: the worthy and the unworthy, the
working folk and the lazy deadbeats.

For those on the positive side of the
divide, those who work for a living, the rewards are far greater than a paycheck. The
employed enter a social world in which their
identities as mainstream Americans are
shaped, structured, and reinforced. The workplace is the main institutional setting—and
virtually the only one after one's school career
is over—in which individuals become part
of the collective American enterprise that
lies at the heart of our culture: the market.
We are so divided in other domains—race,
geography, family organization, gender roles,

and the like—that common ground along
almost any other lines is difficult to achieve.
For our diverse and divided society, participation in the world of work is the most
powerful source of social integration.

It is in the workplace that we are most
likely to mix with those who come from different backgrounds, are under the greatest
pressure to subordinate individual idiosyn-
crasy to the requirements of an organization,
and are called upon to contribute to goals
that eclipse the personal. All workers have
these experiences in common, even as segregation constrains the real mix of workers,
conformity is imposed on some occupations
more than others, and the goals to which we
must subscribe are often elusive, unreach-
able, or at odds with personal desire.

The creation of a workplace identity is
rarely the task of the self-directed individualist, moving along some preordained path.
It is a miracle worked by organizations,
firms, supervisors, fellow workers, and by
the whole long search that leads from the
desire to find a job to the endpoint of landing one. This transformation is particularly
fraught for ghetto youth and adults, for they
face a difficult job market, high hurdles in
convincing employers to take a chance on
them, and relatively poor rewards—from a
financial point of view—for their successes.
But the crafting of an identity is an important
developmental process for them, just as it is
for their more privileged counterparts.

Powerful forces work to exclude African-
Americans, Latinos, and other minorities
from full participation in American society.
From the schools that provide a substandard education for millions of inner-city kids,
to an employment system rife with discrimination, to a housing market that segregates
minority families, there is almost no meaning to the notion that Americans all begin
from the same starting line.[4] Precisely because this is the case, blasting one's way

through the job barrier and starting down that road of acquiring a common identity as mainstream worker is of the greatest importance for black and brown youth in segregated communities. It may be one of the few accessible pipelines into the core of American society and the one with the greatest payoff, symbolic and material.

This paper draws upon a two-year study of fast-food workers and job seekers in central and northern Harlem. Two hundred African-American and Latino workers participated in this study by participating in face-to-face interviews. Sixty of them completed extensive life histories, and a smaller group contributed yearlong personal diaries and permitted the members of our research group to spend extensive periods of time with them, their family members, and their friends. We draw upon all of these data here to explore the nature of values among the working poor in the inner city.

The Social Costs of Accepting Low-Wage Work

While the gainfully employed may be honored over those who stand outside the labor force, all jobs are not created equal. Fast-food jobs, in particular, are notoriously stigmatized and denigrated. "McJob" has become a common epithet meant to designate work without redeeming value. The reasons for this heavy valence are numerous and worthy of deconstruction, for the minority workers who figure in this study have a mountain of stigma to overcome if they are to maintain their self-respect. Indeed, this is one of the main goals of the organizational culture they join when they finally land a job in the restaurant chain we will call "Burger Barn."

Fast-food jobs epitomize the assembly line structure of deskilled service jobs: they are highly routinized, and appear to the untutored observer to be entirely lacking in discretion—almost military in their scripted nature. The symbolic capital of these routinized jobs can be measured in negative numbers. They represent the opposite of the autonomous entrepreneur who is lionized in popular culture (from *Business Week* to hip-hop).

Burger Barn workers are told that they must, at all cost to their own dignity, defer to the public. Customers can be unreasonably demanding, rude, and demeaning, and workers must count backwards from one hundred in an effort to stifle their outrage. Servicing the customer with a smile is music to management's ears because making money depends on keeping the clientele happy, but it can be an exercise in humiliation for inner-city teenagers. It is hard for them to refrain from reading this public nastiness as another instance of society's low estimation of their worth. But if they want to hold on to these minimum-wage jobs, they soon realize that they have to tolerate comments that would almost certainly provoke a fistfight outside the workplace.

It is well known among ghetto consumers that fast-food crew members have to put up with whatever verbiage comes across the counter. That knowledge occasionally prompts nasty exchanges designed explicitly to anger workers, to push them to retaliate verbally. Testing those limits is an outlet for customers down on their luck, and a favorite pastime of teenagers in particular. This may be the one opportunity they have to put someone else down in public, knowing there is little the worker can do in return.

It is bad enough to be on the receiving end of this kind of abuse from adults, especially white adults, for that has its own reading along race lines. It is, in some respects, even worse to have to contend with it from minority peers, for there is much more

366 Katherine S. Newman • Catherine Ellis

personal honor at stake, more pride to be lost, and an audience whose opinion matters more. This no doubt is why harassment is a continuous problem for fast-food workers. It hurts. Their peers, with plenty of anger bottled up for all kinds of reasons extraneous to the restaurant experience, find counterparts working the cash register convenient targets for venting.

Roberta Sampson[5] is a five-year veteran of Burger Barn who has worked her way up to management. A formidable African-American woman, Roberta has always prided herself on her ability to make it on her own. Most of Roberta's customers have been perfectly pleasant people; many have been long-time repeat visitors to her restaurant. But she has also encountered many who radiate disrespect.

> Well, I had alcoholics, derelicts. People that are aggravated with life. I've had people that don't even have jobs curse me out. I've dealt with all kinds.
> Sometimes it would get to me. If a person yelled out [in front of] a lobby full of people, "Bitch, that's why you work at Burger Barn," I would say [to myself], "I'm probably making more than you and your mother." It hurts when people don't even know what you're making and they say those things. Especially in Harlem, they do that to you. They call you all types of names and everything.

Natasha Robins is younger than Roberta and less practiced at these confrontations. But she has had to contend with them nevertheless, especially from age-mates who are (or at least claim to be) higher up the status hierarchy than she is. Hard as she tries, Natasha cannot always control her temper and respond the way the firm wants her to:

> It's hard dealing with the public. There are good things, like old people. They sweet. But the younger people around my age are always snotty. Think they better than you because

they not working at Burger Barn. They probably work at something better than you.

How do you deal with rude or unfriendly customers? They told us that we just suppose to walk to the back and ignore it, but when they in your face like that, you get so upset that you have to say something. . . . I got threatened with a gun one time. 'Cause this customer had threw a piece of straw paper in the back and told me to pick it up like I'm a dog. I said, "No." And he cursed at me. I cursed at him back and he was like, "Yeah, next time you won't have nothing to say when I come back with my gun and shoot your ass." Oh, *excuse* me.

Ianna Bates, who had just turned sixteen the summer she found her first job at Burger Barn, has had many of the same kinds of problems Natasha Robins complains of. The customers who hard-time her are just looking for a place to vent their anger about things that have nothing to do with buying lunch. Ianna recognizes that this kind of thing could happen in any restaurant, but believes it is a special problem in Harlem, for ghetto residents have more to be angry about and fewer accessible targets for one-upmanship. Cashiers in fast-food shops catch the results:

> What I hate about Burger Barn is the customers, well, some of them that I can't stand. . . . I don't want to stereotype Harlem . . . , but since I only worked in Harlem that's all I can speak for. Some people have a chip on their shoulders. . . . Most of the people that come into the restaurant are black. Most of them have a lot of kids. It's in the ghetto. Maybe, you know, they are depressed about their lifestyles or whatever else that is going on in their lives and they just. . . . I don't know. They just are like *urff!*
> And no matter what you do you cannot please them. I'm not supposed to say anything to the customer, but that's not like me. I have a mouth and I don't take no short from nobody. I don't care who it is, don't take anybody's crap.

Despite this bravado, Ianna well knows that to use her mouth is to risk her job. She has had to work hard to find ways to cope with this frustration that do not get her into trouble with management:

> I don't say stuff to people most of the time. Mostly I just look at them like they stupid. Because my mother always told me that as long as you don't say nothin' to nobody, you can't never get in trouble. If you look at them stupid, what are they going to do? If you roll your eyes at somebody like that, I mean, that's really nothing [compared to] . . . cursing at them. Most of the time I try to walk away.

As Ianna observes, there is enough free-floating fury in Harlem to keep a steady supply of customer antagonism coming the way of service workers every day of their work lives. The problem is constant enough to warrant official company policies on how Burger Barn's crew members should respond to insults, what managers should do to help, and the evasive tactics that work best to quell an incendiary situation without losing business.[6] Management tries to minimize the likelihood of such incidents by placing girls on the registers rather than boys, in the apparent belief that young men will attract more abuse and find it harder to quash their reactions than their female counterparts.

Burger Barn does what it can to contend with these problems on the shop floor. But the neighborhood is beyond its reach and there too fast-food workers are often met with ridicule from the people they grew up with. They have to learn to defend themselves against the criticism that they have lowered themselves in taking these jobs coming from people they have known all their lives. Stephanie Harmon, who has worked at Burger Barn for over a year, explains that here too she leans on the divide between the worker and the do-nothing:

> People I hang out with, they know me since I was little. We all grew up together. When they see me comin', they laugh and say, "Here come Calvin, here come Calvin sister." I just laugh and keep on going. I say, "You're crazy. But that's OK cause I got a job and you all standing out here on the corner." Or I say, "This is my job, it's legal." Something like that. That Calvin commercial show you that even though his friends tease him and he just brushed them off, then he got a higher position. Then you see how they change toward him.

As Stephanie indicates, the snide remarks of peers and neighbors when a worker first dons a Burger Barn uniform are often replaced with requests for help in getting hired and a show of respect when that worker sticks with the job, shows up with money in her pockets and, best of all, moves into management. Still, the scorn is a burden to endure.

Tiffany Wilson, also a teen worker in a central Harlem Burger Barn, thinks she knows why kids in her community who don't work give her such a hard time. They don't want her to succeed because if no one is making it, then no one needs to feel bad about failing. But if someone claws their way up and looks like they have a chance to escape the syndrome of failure, it must mean everyone could, in theory, do so as well. The teasing, a thinly veiled attempt to enforce conformity, is designed to push would-be success stories back into the fold:

> What you will find in any situation, more so in the black community, is that if you are in the community and you try to excel, you will get ridicule from your own peers. It's like the "crab down" syndrome. . . . If you put a bunch of crabs in a big bucket and one crab tries to get out, what do you think the other crabs would do now? According to my thinking, they should pull him up or push him or help him get out. But the crabs pull him back in the barrel. That's just an

analogy for what happens in the community a lot.

Keeping everyone down prevents any particular person from feeling that creeping sense of despair that comes from believing things could be otherwise but aren't.

Swallowing ridicule would be a hardship for almost anyone in this culture, but it is particularly hard on minority youth in the inner city. They have already logged several years' worth of interracial and cross-class friction by the time they climb behind a Burger Barn cash register. More likely than not, they have also learned from peers that no self-respecting person allows themselves to be "dissed" without striking back. Yet this is precisely what they must do if they are going to survive on the shop floor.

This is one of the main reasons why these jobs carry such a powerful stigma in American popular culture: they fly in the face of a national attraction to autonomy, independence, and the individualist's right to respond in kind when their dignity is threatened. In ghetto communities, this stigma is even more powerful because—ironically—it is in these enclaves that this mainstream value of independence is elaborated and embellished. Film characters from the Superfly variety to the political version (e.g., Malcolm X)—rap stars, and local idols base their claims to notoriety on stan-ding above the crowd, going their own way, being beyond the ties that bind ordinary mortals. There are white parallels, to be sure, but this is a powerful genre of icons in the black community, not because it is a disconnected subculture, but because it is an intensified version of a perfectly recognizable American middle- and working-class fixation.

It is therefore noteworthy that thousands upon thousands of minority teens, young adults, and even middle-aged adults line up for jobs that will subject them, at least potentially, to a kind of character assassination. They do so not because they start the job-hunting process with a different set of values, one that can withstand society's contempt for fast-food workers. They take these jobs because in so many inner-city communities, there is nothing better in the offing. In general, they have already tried to get better jobs and have failed, landing instead at the door of Burger Barn as a last resort.

The stigma of these jobs has other sources beyond the constraints of enforced deference. Low pay and poor prospects for mobility matter as well. Fast-food jobs are invariably minimum-wage positions.[7] Salaries rise very little over time, even for first-line management. In ghetto areas, where jobs are scarce and the supply of would-be workers chasing them is relatively large, downward pressure keeps these jobs right down at the bottom of the wage scale.[8]

The public perception (fueled by knowledge of wage conditions) is that there is very little potential for improvement in status or responsibility either. Even though there are Horatio Algers in this industry, there are no myths to prop up a more glorified image. As a result, the epithet "McJob" develops out of the perception that a fast-food worker is not likely to end up in a prestigious position as a general manager or restaurant owner; she is going to spend her whole life flipping burgers.

As it happens, this is only half true. The fast-food industry is actually very good about internal promotion. Shop floor management is nearly always recruited from the ranks of entry-level workers. Carefully planned training programs make it possible for people to move up, to acquire transferable skills, and to at least take a shot at entrepreneurial ownership. Industry leaders, like McDonald's, are proud of the fact that half of their present board of directors started out on the shop floor as crew members. One couldn't say as much for most other Fortune 500 firms.

Nevertheless, the vast majority of workers never even get close to management. The typical entry-level worker cycles through the job in short order, producing an industry average job tenure of less than six months. Since this is just an average, it suggests that a large number of employees are there and gone in a matter of weeks. It is this pattern, a planned operation built around low skills and high turnover, that has given fast-food jobs such a bad name. Although it is quite possible to rise above the fray and make a very respectable living in fast-food management, most crew members remain at the entry level and leave too soon to see much upward movement. Observing this pattern on such a large scale— in practically every town and city in the country—Americans naturally conclude that there is no real future in a job of this kind and anyone with more on the ball wouldn't be caught dead working behind the counter.

The stigma also stems from the low socioeconomic status of the people who hold these jobs. This includes teenagers, immigrants who often speak halting English, those with little education, and (increasingly in affluent communities afflicted with labor shortages) the elderly. To the extent that the prestige of a job refracts the social characteristics of its average incumbents, fast-food jobs are hobbled by the perception that people with better choices would never purposively opt for a McJob. We argue that entry-level jobs of this kind don't merit this scorn: a lot more skill, discretion, and responsibility are locked up in a fast-food job than meets the public eye. But this truth hardly matters where public perception is concerned. There is no faster way to indicate that a person is barely deserving of notice than to point out that they hold a "chump change" job in Kentucky Fried Chicken or Burger King.

We "know" this is the case just by looking at the age, skin color, or educational credentials of the people already on the job: the tautology has a staying power that even the most expensive public relations campaign cannot shake.

It is hard to know the extent to which this stigma discourages young people in places like central Harlem from knocking on the doors of fast-food restaurants in search of employment. It is clear that the other choices aren't much better and that necessity drives thousands, if not millions, of teens and older job seekers to repudiate the stigma associated with fast-food work or learn to live with it.[9] But no one comes into the central Harlem job market without having to contend with the social risks to their identity that come with approaching stigmatized ground.

Tiffany Wilson started working in the underground economy bagging groceries when she was little more than ten years old because her mother was having trouble supporting the family, "checks weren't coming in," and there was "really a need for food" in the family. She graduated to summer youth by the time she was fourteen and landed a job answering phones in a center that dealt with domestic violence cases, referring terrified women to shelters. By the time she was sixteen, Tiffany needed a real job that would last beyond the summertime, so she set about looking—everywhere. As a black teenager, she quickly discovered there wasn't a great deal open to her. Tiffany ended up at Burger Barn in the Bronx, a restaurant two blocks from her house and close enough to her high school to make after-school hours feasible.

> The first Burger Barn I worked at was because nobody else would take me. It was a last resort. I didn't want to go to Burger Barn. You flip burgers. People would laugh at you. In high school, I didn't wanna be in that kind of environment. But lo and

behold, after everything else failed, Martin Paints, other jobs, Burger Barn was welcoming me with open arms. So I started working there.

Tiffany moved to Harlem when she finished high school and found she couldn't commute back to the Bronx. Reluctant to return to the fast-food business, Tiffany tried her luck at moving up, into a service job with more of a white-collar flavor. She looked everywhere for a position in stores where the jobs are free of hamburger grease and hot oil for French fries, stores where clerks don't wear aprons or hair nets. Nothing panned out, despite her best efforts:

> I'm looking at Lerners and Plymouth [clothing stores] and going to all these stores and lo and behold Burger Barn is there with open arms because I had two years of experience by then.

The new Burger Barn franchise was right in the middle of Harlem, not far from the room she rents over a storefront church. It had the additional appeal of being a black-owned business, something that mattered to Tiffany in terms of the "more cultural reasons why [she] decided to work there." But she confesses to a degree of disappointment that she was not able to break free of entry-level fast-food jobs. With a high-school diploma in hand, Tiffany was hoping for something better.

William Johnson followed a similar pathway to Burger Barn, graduating from summer youth jobs in the middle of high school and looking for something that would help pay for his books and carfare. The Department of Labor gave him a referral to Burger Barn, but he was reluctant at first to pursue it:

> To go there and work for Burger Barn, that was one of those real cloak-and-dagger kind of things. You'll be coming out [and your friends say], "Yo, where you going?" You be,

"I'm going, don't worry about where I'm going." And you see your friends coming [to the restaurant] and see you working there and now you be [thinking], "No, the whole [housing] project gonna know I work in Burger Barn." It's not something I personally proclaim or pride and stuff. . . . If you are a crew member, you really aren't shit there. . . . You got nothing there, no benefits, nothing. It was like that [when I was younger] and it's like that now.

William tried every subterfuge he could think of to conceal his job from the kids he knew. He kept his uniform in a bag and put it on in the back of the restaurant so that it would never be visible on the street. He made up fake jobs to explain to his friends where his spending money was coming from. He took circuitous routes to the Barn and hid back by the gigantic freezer when he spotted a friend coming into the store. The last thing William wanted was to be publicly identified as a shift worker at Burger Barn.

In this, William was much like the other teen and young adult workers we encountered. They are very sensitive to stigma, to challenges to their status, and by taking low-wage jobs of this kind they have positioned themselves to receive exactly the kind of insults they most fear. But the fact is that they do take these risks and, in time, latch onto other "narratives" that undergird their legitimacy.

Breaking the Stigma

One of the chief challenges of an organization like Burger Barn is how to take people who have come to them on the defensive and turn them into workers who at least appear on the surface, if not deep in their souls, to enjoy their work. Customers have choices; they can vote with their feet. If ordering french fries at Burger Barn

requires them to run a gauntlet of annoy-
ance, rudeness, or diffidence from the person who takes their order, they can easily
cross the street to a competitor the next
time. It is clearly in the company's interest
to find ways to turn the situation around.
Ideally, from the industry's viewpoint, it
would be best if the whole reputation of
these jobs could be reversed. This is what
McDonald's had in mind when it launched
the Calvin series. But for all the reasons outlined earlier in this chapter, that is not likely
to happen, for the conditions that give rise
to the stigma in the first place—low wages,
high turnover, enforced deference—are not
likely to change. Beyond publicizing the
opportunities that are within reach, much
of which falls on deaf ears, there is little the
industry can do to rehabilitate its workers
in the eyes of the public and thereby dampen
the tension across the counter.

Yet behind the scenes, managers and
workers, and peers working together in restaurant crews, do build a moral defense of
their work. They call upon timeless American
values, values familiar to many, including
conservatives, to undergird their respect-
ability. Pointing to the essential virtues of the
gainfully employed, Burger Barn workers
align themselves with the great mass of men
and women who work for a living. "We are
like them," they declare, and in so doing
separate themselves from the people in their
midst who are not employed.

They have plenty of experience with
individuals who don't work, often including
members of their own families: beggars who
come around the restaurants looking for
handouts every day; fast-talkers who come
into Burger Barn hoping for free food; and
age-mates who prefer to deal drugs. In general, these low-wage workers are far less
forgiving, and far less tolerant, of these
people than are the liberals who champion
the cause of the working poor. Since they

hold hard, exhausting, poorly paid jobs, they
see little reason why anyone ought to get a
free ride. What the indigent should do, on
this account, is to follow their example: get
a job, any job.

Ianna Bates is an articulate case in point.
She has had to confront the social degradation
that comes from holding a "low job" and has
developed a tough hide in response. Her
dignity is underwritten by the critique she has
absorbed about the "welfare dependent":

> I'm not ashamed because I have a job.
> Most people don't and I'm proud of myself
> that I decided to get up and do something
> at an early age. So as I look at it, I'm not on
> welfare. I'm doing something.
> I'm not knocking welfare, but I know
> people that are on it that can get up and
> work. There's nothing wrong with them.
> And they just choose not to. . . . They don't
> really need to be on [welfare]. They just want
> it because they can get away with it. I don't
> think it's right because that's my tax dollars
> going for somebody who is lazy, who don't
> wanna get up. I can see if a woman had three
> children, her husband left her and she don't
> have no job cause she was a housewife. OK.
> But after a while, you know, welfare will
> send you to school. Be a nurse assistant, a
> home attendant, something!
> Even if you were on welfare, it should be
> like, you see all these dirty streets we have?
> Why can't they go out and sweep the streets,
> clean up the parks. I mean, there is so much
> stuff that needs to be done in this city. They
> can do that and give them their money. Not
> just sit home and not do anything.

Patricia Hull, a mother of five children in her
late thirties, couldn't agree more. Patty has
worked at Burger Barn for five years now,
having pulled herself off of welfare by the
sheer determination to be a decent role model
for her children. One might imagine that she
would be more tolerant of AFDC recipients,
since she has been there. She moved up to the
Big Apple from Tennessee after her husband

walked out on her, hoping to find more job opportunities than the few that were available in the rural south. It took a long time for her to get on her feet and even Patty would agree that without "aid" she would not have made it this far. Still, having finally taken the hard road to a real job, she sees no reason why anyone else should have an easier ride:

> There's so much in this city; it's always hiring. It may not be what you want. It may not be the pay you want. But you will always get a job. If I can work at Burger Barn all week and come home tired and then have to deal with the kids and all of that, and be happy with $125 a week, so can you. Why would I give quarters [to bums on the street]? My quarter is tax-free money for you! No way.

Or, in a variation on the same theme, Larry Peterson reminds us that any job is better than no job. The kids who would dare to hard-time Larry get nothing but a cold shoulder in return because Larry knows in his soul that he has something they don't have: work for which he gets paid.

> I don't care what other people think. You know, I just do not care. I have a job, you know. It's my job. You ain't puttin' *no* food on my table; you ain't puttin' *no* clothes on my back. I will walk tall with my Burger Barn uniform on. Be proud of it, you know.

These views could have come straight from the most conservative Republicans in the country, bent on justifying draconian cuts in the welfare budget. For they trade on a view held by many of the ghetto-based working poor: that work equals dignity and no one deserves a free ride. The difference between them is simply that the working poor know whereof they speak: they have toiled behind the hot grease pits of french-fry vats, they have stood on their feet for eight or nine hours at a stretch, all for the magnificent sum of $4.25 an hour. Virtually all they have to show for their trouble is the self-respect that comes from being on the right side of that gaping cavern that separates the deserving (read working) and the undeserving (read nonworking) poor (Katz 1989).

Other retorts to status insults emerge as well. Flaunting financial independence often provides a way of lashing back at acquaintances who dis young workers for taking Burger Barn jobs. Brian Gray, born in Jamaica but raised in one of Harlem's tougher neighborhoods, knows that his peers don't really think much of his job. "They just make fun," he says. "Ah, you flipping burgers. You gettin' paid $4.25. They'd go snickering down the street." But it wasn't long after Brian started working that he picked up some serious money, serious at least for a teenager in his neighborhood.

> What I did was made Sam [the general manager] save my money for me. Then I got the best of clothes and the best sneakers with my own money. Then I added two chains. Then [my friends] were like, "Where you selling drugs at?" And I'm like, "the same place you said making fun of me, flipping burgers. That's where I'm getting my money from. Now, where are you getting yours from?" They couldn't answer.

Contrary to public perception, most teenagers in Harlem are afraid of the drug trade and won't go near it. They know too many people who are six feet under, in jail, or permanently disabled by the ravages of drugs. If you aren't willing to join the underground economy, where are you going to get the money to dress yourself, go out on the town, and do the other things teens throughout the middle class do on Mom and Dad's sufferance? Most of Harlem's youth cannot rely on their parents' financial support to meet these needs. Indeed, this is one of the primary pressures that pushes young people out into the labor market in the first place, and at an early age. Most workers we interviewed had their first job by the age of fourteen.

What Brian does, then, is to best his mates at their own game by showing them that he has the wherewithal to be a consumer, based on his own earnings. He derives no small amount of pleasure from turning these tables, upending the status system by outdoing his friends on style grounds they value as much as he does.

It might be comforting to suggest that these hard-working low-wage workers were, from the very beginning, different from their nonworking counterparts, equipped somehow to withstand the gauntlet of criticism that comes their way when they start out on the bottom of the labor market. It would be comforting because we would then be able to sort the deserving, admirable poor (who recognize the fundamental value of work and are willing to ignore stigma) from the undeserving (who collapse in the face of peer pressure and therefore prefer to go on the dole). This is too simplistic. Burger Barn workers of all ages and colors fully admit that their employment is the butt of jokes and that it has subjected them to ridicule. Some, like Larry Peterson, argue that they don't care what other people think, but even these brave souls admit that it took a long time for them to build up this confidence.

Where, then, does the confidence come from? How do ghetto residents develop the rejoinders that make it possible to recapture their dignity in the face of peer disapproval? To some degree, they can call on widely accepted American values that honor working people, values that float in the culture at large.[10] But this is not enough to construct a positive identity when the reminders of low status—coming from customers, friends, and the media—are abundant. Something stronger is required: a workplace culture that actively works to overcome the nega-

tives by reinforcing the value of the work ethic. Managers and veteran employees on the shop floor play a critical role in the reinforcement process by counseling new workers distressed by bad-mouthing.

Kimberly Sampson, a twenty-year-old African-American woman, began working at Burger Barn when she was sixteen and discovered firsthand how her "friends" would turn on her for taking a low-wage job. Fortunately, she found a good friend at work who steadied her with a piece of advice:

> Say it's a job. You are making money. Right? Don't care what nobody say. You know? If they don't like it, too bad. They sitting on the corner doing what they are doing. You got to work making money. You know? Don't bother with what anybody has to say about it.

Kim's advisor, a workplace veteran who had long since come to terms with the insults of his peers, called upon a general status hierarchy that places the working above the nonworking as a bulwark against the slights. His point was later echoed by Kim's manager in the course of a similar episode, as she explained:

> Kids come in here . . . they don't have enough money. I'll be like, "You don't have enough money; you can't get [the food you ordered]." One night this little boy came in there and cursed me out. He [said], "That's why you are working at Burger Barn. You can't get a better job. . . ."
> I was upset and everything. I started crying. [My manager] was like, "Kim, don't bother with him. I'm saying, *you got a job*. You know. It is a *job*."

Absorbing this defensive culture is particularly important for immigrant workers in Harlem who often find fast-food jobs the first venue where they have sustained interaction with African-Americans who resent the fact that they have jobs at all, much less jobs in their community. Marisa Gonzalez, a native of Ecuador, had a very difficult time when she first began working as a hostess at Burger Barn. A pretty, petite nineteen-year-old, she was selected for the job because she has the kind of sparkle and vivaciousness that any restaurant would want customers to see. But some of her more antagonistic black customers saw her as an archetype: the immigrant who barely speaks a word of English who snaps up a job some native-born English speaker ought to have. Without the support of her bilingual, Latino manager, she would not have been able to pull herself together and get on with the work:

> I wasn't sent to the grill or the fries [where you don't need to communicate with customers]. I was sent to the cash register, even though the managers knew I couldn't speak English. That was only one week after my arrival in the United States! So I wasn't feeling very well at all. Three weeks later I met a manager who was Puerto Rican. He was my salvation. He told me, "Marisa, it's not that bad." He'd speak to me in English, even though he knows Spanish. He'd tell me, "Don't cry. Dry off those tears. You'll be all right, you'll make it." So he encouraged me like no other person in that Burger Barn, especially when the customers would curse at me for not knowing English. He gave me courage and after that it went much better.

Among the things this manager taught Marisa was that she should never listen to people who give her a hard time about holding a job at Burger Barn. Having been a white-collar clerical worker in her native country, it did bother Marisa that she had slipped down the status hierarchy—and it still does. She was grateful, nevertheless, to have a way to earn money and her family was desperate for her contribution. When customers would insult her, insinuating

that someone who speaks limited English was of lowly status, she turned to management for help. And she found it in the form of fellow Latino bosses who told her to hold her head up because she was, after all, working, while her critics on the whole were not.

Once these general moral values are in place, many Burger Barn workers take the process one step further: they argue their jobs have hidden virtues that make them more valuable than most people credit. Tiffany Wilson, the young black woman who reluctantly settled for a Burger Barn job when none of the clothing stores she wanted to work for would take her, decided in the end that there was more substance to her job than she credited initially:

> When I got in there, I realized it's not what people think. It's a lot more to it than flipping burgers. It's a real system of business. That's when I really got to see a big corporation at play. I mean, one part of it, the foundation of it: cashiers, the store, how it's run. Production of food, crew workers, service. Things of that nature. That's when I really got into it and understood a lot more.

Americans tend to think of values as embedded in individuals, transmitted through families, and occasionally reinforced by media images or role models. We tend not to focus on the powerful contribution that institutions and organizations make to the creation and sustenance of beliefs. Yet it is clear that the workplace itself is a major force in the creation of a rebuttal culture among these workers. Without this line of defense it would be very hard for Burger Barn employees to retain their dignity. With the support of fellow workers, however, they are able to hold their heads up, not by defining themselves as separate from society, but by calling upon the values they hold in common with the rest of the working world.

This is but one of the reasons why exclusion from the society of the employed is such a devastating source of social isolation. We could hand people money, as various guaranteed income plans of the past thirty years have suggested. But we can't hand out honor. For a majority of Americans, honor comes from participation in this central setting in our culture and from the positive identity it confers.

Franklin Roosevelt understood this during the Great Depression and responded with the creation of thousands of publicly funded jobs designed to put people to work building the national parks, the railway stations, the great highways that criss-cross the country, and the murals that decorate public walls from San Francisco to New York. Social scientists studying the unemployed in the 1930s showed convincingly that people who held WPA jobs were far happier and healthier than those who were on the dole, even when their incomes did not differ significantly. WPA workers had their dignity in the midst of poverty; those on the dole were vilified and could not justify their existence or find an effective cultural rationale for the support they received.

This historical example has its powerful parallels in the present. Joining the workforce is a fundamental, transforming experience that moves people across barriers of subculture, race, gender, and class. It never completely eradicates these differences and in some divisive settings it may even reinforce consciousness of them—through glass ceilings, discriminatory promotion policies, and the like. But even in places where pernicious distinctions are maintained, there is another, overarching identity competing with forms that stress difference: a common bond within the organization and across the nation of fellow workers. This is what makes getting a job so much more than a means to a financial end. It becomes a

crucial developmental hurdle, especially for people who have experienced exclusion before, including minorities, women, the elderly, and teenagers. Any experience that can speak back to the stigma that condemns burger flippers as the dregs, resurrecting them as exemplars of the American work ethic, has extraordinary power.

Those who choose to earn a living in the legitimate job market receive few material rewards for their effort, but they can claim moral legitimacy from the traditional American work ethic. They can't flash large rolls of cash before the eyes of their neighbors, but they can pride themselves on "doing the right thing," avoiding the dangers of the drug trade and the sloth of welfare recipients. While they understand that some people have a legitimate need to receive government assistance, they don't see the payoff of dealing drugs, and this in not an opinion they keep to them-selves. Workers with friends or family in the drug trade often implore them to get out, warning them of the dangers, and reasoning that they each make about the same amount of money in a week, while the one involved with drugs has to work longer hours.

Nadine Stevens has worked at Burger Barn since graduating from high school five years ago. By all accounts she lives in one of the most dangerous neighborhoods in Harlem. Her apartment building is the home of an active drug trade and, indeed, the mailboxes were recently removed from the building by police because they were being used for drug transactions. She knows most of the drug dealers who sit on her stoop every day and night, having grown up with them. She and her mother and sister, whose ground-floor apartment faces the street, have seen many young women they know wasted by drugs, and young men killed in their hallway.

Nadine tries to convince the dealers she knows to get out of the trade, and to shoot for getting into management at Burger Barn. She and her sister, Rachael, with whom she works at Burger Barn, recently accosted a young teen they knew on the street whom they suspected of drug running. They told her that if she was desperate for money they'd get her a job at Burger Barn. Sensing the girl's reluctance, Nadine cried, "There's no shame in my game! Come work with me."

The dealers they know argue that the Burger Barn employee is working in a poorly paid, demeaning job and that, furthermore, they couldn't get hired there if they tried. Although their work is dangerous, illegal, and despised by neighbors, they brandish the accoutrements of success glorified in the United States: expensive cars, stylish clothes, and lots of cash. Their honor is measured in dollars, a common American standard that competes for the attention of people otherwise destined to earn little more than the minimum wage.

Anthony Vallo has had to choose on which side of the law to work and, once he secured his Burger Barn job, had to decide what to do about his friends and acquaintances who chose the wrong side. Two of his best friends are in jail. Another friend is dealing drugs and probably isn't far from a jail term himself. What Anthony does is try to maintain a cordial relationship with these guys, but to put as much distance between himself and them as he can without giving offense:

> This friend of mine is selling and stuff like that, but he's my friend. We used to go to school back then. He was like, "Damn, you still doin' that Burger Barn shit? I can get you a real job!" I think he respects me; at least he don't criticize me behind my back. But I try to avoid him, you know.

Drug dealers are not the only problem cases with which Harlem workers must contend. At least until welfare reform began to force women on AFDC back into the labor force, many young mothers working low wage jobs were faced with the fork in the road that led either to a job at a place like Burger Barn or public assistance. Since most know a fair number of women who have elected, or had no choice but to opt for, the latter, it takes no small amount of fortitude to go for a minimum-wage job.[11] Indeed, given that AFDC offered greater financial benefits—when health coverage, food stamps, and subsidized housing are part of the package—than these jobs provide, it takes a strong attachment to the work ethic and a willingness to sacrifice elements of one's financial well-being in favor of the dignity that goes with holding a real job.

The Importance of Going to Work

Although having a well-paid, respected career is prized above all else in the United States, our culture confers honor on those who hold down jobs of any kind over those who are outside of the labor force. Independence and self-sufficiency—these are virtues that have no equal in this society. But there are other reasons why we value workers besides the fact that their earnings keep them above water and therefore less in need of help from government, communities, or charities. We also value workers because they share certain common views, experiences, and expectations. The work ethic is more than an attitude toward earning money—it is a disciplined existence, a social life woven around the workplace.

For all the talk of "family values," we know that in the contemporary period, family often takes a backseat to the requirements of a job, even when the job involves flipping burgers. What we are supposed to orient toward primarily is the workplace and its demands. This point could not be made more forcefully than it is in the context of the welfare reform bills of 1996. Public policy in the late 1990s makes clear that poor women are now supposed to be employed even if they have young children.[12] With a majority of women with children, even those under a year of age, in the labor force, we are not prepared to cut much slack to those who have been on welfare. They can and should work like the rest of us, or so the policy mantra goes. This represents no small change in the space of a few decades in our views of what honorable women and mothers should do. But it also reflects the growing dominance of work in our understanding of adult priorities.

We could think of this increasingly work-centered view of life as a reflection of America's waning economic position, a pragmatic response to wage stagnation, downsizing, and international competition: we must work harder. And this it may be. But it is also part of a secular transformation that has been ongoing for decades as we've moved away from home-centered work lives in the agricultural world to employment-centered lives outside the domestic sphere altogether. The more work departs from home, the more it becomes a social system of its own, a primary form of integration that rivals the family as a source of identity, belonging, and friendship. Women like Antonia Piento are not content only to take care of children at home. They want a life that is adult centered, where they have peers they can talk to. Where they might once have found that company in the neighborhood, now they are more likely to find it on the shop floor. Those primary social ties are grounded in workplace relations, hence to be a worker is also to be integrated into a meaningful community of fellow workers, the community that increasingly becomes the source of personal friends, intimate relations and the world view that comes with them.

Work is therefore much more than a means to a financial end. This is particularly the case when the work holds little intrinsic satisfaction. No one who gets paid for boiling french fries in hot oil thinks they are playing a world-shattering role. They know their jobs are poorly valued; they can see that in their paychecks, in the demeanor of the people whom they serve across the counter, even among some managers. But what they have that their nonworking counterparts lack is both the dignity of being employed and the opportunity to participate in a social life that increasingly defines their adult lives. This community gives their lives structure and purpose, humor and pleasure, support and understanding in hard times, and a backstop that extends beyond the instrumental purposes of a fast-food restaurant. It is the crucible of their values, values that we have argued here are decidedly mainstream.

The working poor sit at the bottom of the occupational structure and feel the weight of disapproval coming down upon their shoulders from better paid, more respectable employees. Yet they stand at the top of another pyramid and can look down the slope toward people they know well who have taken another pathway in the world.

NOTES

The research for this chapter was made possible by generous grants from the Russell Sage, Ford, Rockefeller, Spencer, and William T. Grant Foundations. A revised version of this chapter appears in Newman 1999.

1. See Michèle Lamont's chapter in this volume for an analysis of the way working-class men bolster their self-worth by evaluating individuals according to moral criteria such as honesty and self-reliance rather than by socioeconomic characteristics like income and education. They may sit below the elite in this country based on standards of wealth, power, and education, but they see themselves as

sitting atop another hierarchy, a moral one, which they consider most important.

2. There are further shades of gray below the line of the employed that distinguish those who are searching for work and those who have accepted their fate as nonworkers, with the latter suffering the greatest stigma of all.

3. For more on the moral structure associated with work and achievement of the American dream, see Hochschild 1995.

4. See Wilson 1996, Massey and Denton 1993, Hacker 1992, and Urban Institute 1991.

5. All names and identifying information have been changed to protect confidentiality.

6. Hochschild 1983 documents similar attempts in the airline industry. One airline holds a mandatory seminar for flight attendants to teach them "anger-desensitization" when dealing with rude and demeaning customers.

7. In areas experiencing exceptionally tight labor markets—including much of the Midwest in the late 1990s—wages for these jobs are climbing above the minimum-wage line.

8. This is one of the many reasons why increasing the minimum wage is so important. Ghettos have such impoverished job bases to begin with that they are almost always characterized by slack labor markets. Only when the labor supply outside ghetto walls has tightened down to almost impossible levels do we begin to see this tide lift inner-city boats. Eventually employers do turn to the workers who are low on their preference queues (as we learned in the 1980s during the Massachusetts miracle), but these conditions are, sadly, rare and generally short-lived.

9. Indeed, over a five-month period in 1993 there were fourteen job applicants for every job opening at two different Burger Barns in Harlem (Newman and Lennon 1995).

10. The fact that Harlem residents rejected for these jobs hold these values is some evidence for the preexisting nature of this mind-set—although these rejects had already piled up work experience that may have contributed to the sharpening of this alternative critique.

11. It should be noted that women on welfare and women in low-wage jobs are not necessarily two distinct groups. Many women find it necessary to go back and forth between holding a low-wage job and relying solely on welfare, and many supplement one form of income with the other (not to mention other income from friends, family, and unreported work), since neither source alone provides enough money to support a family (see Edin 1994).

12. As Jane Mansbridge mentions in her chapter discussing race, activism, and the evolution of feminist ideas in this volume, this expectation is nothing new for many black women. Julia Wrigley indicates the same thing in her discussion of the historic relationship between black domestic workers and white employers in this volume.

REFERENCES

Anderson, Elijah. 1990. *Streetwise*. Chicago: University of Chicago Press.
Edin, Kathryn. 1994. "The Myths of Dependency and Self-Sufficiency: Women, Welfare, and Low-Wage Work." Unpublished paper. Department of Sociology and Center for Urban Policy Research, Rutgers University.
Hacker, Andrew. 1992. *Two Nations*. New York: Ballantine.
Hochschild, Arlie. 1983. *The Managed Heart*. Berkeley: University of California Press.
Hochschild, Jennifer L. 1995. *Facing Up to the American Dream*. Princeton: Princeton University Press.
Katz, Michael. 1989. *The Undeserving Poor*. New York: Pantheon.
Massey, Douglas S., and Nancy A. Denton. 1993. *American Apartheid*. Cambridge: Harvard University Press.
Newman, Katherine S. 1999. *No Shame in My Game: The Working Poor in the Inner City*. New York: Knopf/Russell Sage Foundation.
Newman, Katherine S., and Chauncy Lennon. 1995. "The Job Ghetto." *American Prospect*, summer, 66–67.
Urban Institute. 1991. *Opportunities Denied, Opportunities Diminished*. Report 91–9. Washington: Urban Institute Press.
Waller, Maureen. 1996. "Redefining Fatherhood: Paternal Involvement, Masculinity, and Responsibility in the 'Other America.'" Ph.D. diss., Princeton University.
Wilson, William Julius. 1996. *When Work Disappears*. New York: Knopf.

33
———————

SWEATSHOPS IN SUNSET PARK: A VARIATION OF THE LATE TWENTIETH-CENTURY CHINESE GARMENT SHOPS IN NEW YORK CITY

Xiaolan Bao

QUESTIONS TO CONSIDER

Imagine working twelve hours a day, seven days a week, under physical conditions that are brutal: exposure to lint, physical confinement, sleep deprivation, and chemicals that constantly burn your throat. Your take-home pay at the end of an eighty-four-hour week is about $55. This is not a Jacob Riis description of New York City in 1890 but New York City one hundred years later in the 1990s. Bao's ethnography documents the modern sweatshop and the new immigrants who supply the labor and large profits to the entrepreneurs who are quick to take advantage of young women new to the United States.

On March 12, 1995, the *New York Times* carried a report on the Chinese garment shops in the Sunset Park area of Brooklyn, a neighborhood that houses the new Chinese garment production center in New York City. Unlike most of the Chinatown garment shops in Manhattan, many of the Chinese shops in Sunset Park are not unionized. The weak influence of organized labor and law enforcement agencies in the area had virtually turned the industry there into a safety valve for some Chinese employers to extract quick profits while not complying with any labor laws. Incidents of exploitation increased with the expansion of the Chinese garment shops in the area.

From *Sweatshop USA: The American Sweatshop in Historical and Global Perspective*, edited by Daniel E. Bender and Richard A. Greenwald. Routledge, 2003.

The report in the *New York Times*, written by reporter Jane H. Lii, largely confirmed the above observation. The vivid description of life in the shops, based on the reporter's first-hand experience, gripped the hearts of its readers. According to Lii, the shop she worked in for an entire week was "typical of the small, new shops outside Manhattan":

> The steel doors opened into a dim, dusty warehouse. Red and blue rags covered the four windows, shutting out all natural light. Bundles of cut cloth sat piled in haphazard mounds, some stacked taller than a worker. Under fluorescent lights swinging from chains, rows of mid-aged Chinese women hunched over sewing machines, squinting and silent.

Were the working conditions there as horrific as those that splashed across the headlines in city newspapers? Lii's reply indicated that there was "something more complex at work." What, then, was the complexity? Lii reported that the owner of the shop was "actually benevolent, albeit in a harsh way." "She does not pay minimum wage, but she serves her workers tea. She makes them work until midnight, but she drives them home afterward. She uses child laborers, but she fusses over them, combing their ponytails, admiring their painted fingernails, even hugging them." According to Lii, the boss had opened the business only to save her family's honor, for her brother had, among many things, absconded with close to $80,000 owed to his workers in back wages. The shop also was reopened, according to its present owner, in order to provide jobs for those who came from the same region in China and whom she called "our people."

As Lii reported, the situation of the workers in the shop was also complicated. They "sewed virtually nonstop" because they wanted to make money and had no other alternatives without speaking English. They brought their children into the shop to care for them while working. Several children, however, toiled by their mothers' sides to supplement their incomes. It was said that their mothers wanted to instill in them a work ethic by allowing them to do so.

Lii reported that both the employer and her workers considered American labor laws ideal and laudable, but impractical. The workers considered their employer a good boss "precisely because she was willing to violate labor laws and allow their children to work by their sides." The situation was, therefore, "a miserable complicity born of necessity in an insular, immigrant world" or, simply, "a grim conspiracy of the poor," as the reporter concluded. No wonder that the result of working at Sunset Park was pitiful:

> Seven days later, after 84 hours of work,
> I got my reward, in the form of a promise
> that in three weeks I would be paid $54.24
> or 65 cents an hour (minimum wage is

$4.25). I also walked away from the lint-filled factory with aching shoulders, a stiff back, a dry cough and a burning sore throat.

How representative is Lii's seven-day experience in the shops, and how valid is her analysis? In what ways are the conditions in the Sunset Park Chinese shops similar to the union shops in Manhattan's Chinatown, the hub of the Chinese industry in New York City? In what ways are they different? To what extent are the conditions in Sunset Park similar to those of the city's garment shops at the turn of the twentieth century? What are the factors that have led to these similarities and differences? In the era of globalization, what can the conditions in Sunset Park Chinese garment shops tell us about the impact of globalization in the U.S.? This study attempts to answer these questions.

This article is primarily based on the author's historical research of the Chinese garment industry in New York City over the last ten years, her visits to a number of shops in Sunset Park in the late 1990s, and her interviews with several dozen workers in the area.[1] It gives a brief account of the working conditions in the shops and discusses several highly controversial issues in the Sunset Park Chinese community that relate to the garment industry. By presenting a more differentiated picture of the industry, it argues that while labor organizing and law enforcement remain important ways to address labor abuse in the industry, it is imperative for law enforcement agencies, organized labor, and all concerned individuals to understand the complexity embedded in the highly competitive structure of the garment industry, the multidimensional impact of labor legislation and law enforcement, and the need to develop new forms of labor organizing that are informed and responsive to the challenges of the time. Without such an understanding, any effort to curb the sweating phenomenon is likely to be sporadic and without lasting effect on the industry.

Working Environments

The shop where Jane Lii worked and reported is, in large part, typical of the Chinese garment shops in the Sunset Park area. Many of them are housed in former warehouses or converted garages. Because these shops are often hidden behind a steel door and have no sign on the front, one can hardly tell from the outside the nature of the activities inside the shops or, simply, whether there is any activity at all.

Sunset Park offers the Chinese garment industry many advantages. First, the former warehouses and the converted garages there are spacious. Even though they do not provide comfortable working conditions, they offer much more production space than industrial lofts in Manhattan's Chinatown.[2] The 1983 Chinatown Garment Industry Study reports that in 1981, Chinese shops with about 30 sewing machines occupied an average of 6,070 square feet in Soho. These shops were and are still the largest garment shops in the Chinatown area.[3] However, shops in Sunset Park with a similar number of sewing machines can cover as much as 10,000 square feet.[4] The spacious environment of the shops not only allows an effective flow of production, but also provides shop owners with enough space to expand their businesses.

In addition, rents and maintenance fees for buildings in Sunset Park are relatively inexpensive. In the spring of 1998, for example, the owner of a shop, located between Fort Hamilton Parkway and 43rd Street and covering more than 10,000 square feet, told me that she paid only $2,500 a month for a space that accommodates forty workers. For the same money, she could afford only a 4,000-square-foot shop in Manhattan's

Chinatown. Maintenance fees are also low. For an additional yearly payment of $100 to $200, the gas and other equipment and utility lines would be checked by the building owner.[5]

There are, however, many characteristics that Sunset Park shops share with their counterparts in Manhattan's Chinatown. Besides bundles of cut cloth piled up in haphazard mounds in almost any open floor space, there are severe problems with ventilation. Shops that were converted from former warehouses and garages have very few or virtually no windows at all. Conditions are even worse when the employers cover the few windows with rags or newspapers or simply lock the main entrance to conceal operations. In these shops the air is stifling and filled with lint and dust, while workers sew under fluorescent lights in the daytime.[6]

However, unlike Chinatown shops that generally suffer from space limitations, the physical size and working conditions of Sunset Park shops are not all the same. There are shops that have more than thirty workers and cover a space of over 10,000 square feet. There are also shops packed with a dozen sewing machines and piles of cut garments but covering less than 4,000 square feet. These small and big shops are located side by side. However, regardless of the differences, they have something in common. Like their counterparts in Manhattan's Chinatown, there is virtually no space reserved for workers' activities other than sewing. Even in the relatively spacious shops, workers eat their lunch at their sewing machines or at the desks where they work.

Division of Labor

Although the shops in Sunset Park, like those in Manhattan's Chinatown, work on various lines of garments from manufacturers or other contractors, workers mostly produce sportswear and other low-priced women's apparel. The division of labor in the shops varies according to the size of the shop and the line of the garments they produce, but there are in general five kinds of workers on the floor: the sorter, the foreperson, machine operators, pressers, and floor workers.

Garment production starts with the sorter, who separates the cut-up fabrics according to the style of the garments and decides where the work should begin. The cut fabrics are then sent to the machine operators for either sewing or hemming. Machine operators include those workers who sew minor parts of the garments, such as zippers, collars, cuffs and pockets. The garment then passes to the hands of the foreperson, who checks the quality of the sewed or hemmed garments. A quality garment will be sent to buttoners and trimmers who attach buttons, sew buttonholes, and trim extra threads. In its final stage, the garment will be sent to floor workers who hang tags, eliminate irregularities, and put the garments in a transparent plastic bag for shipping.

Like its counterparts elsewhere in the city, the Chinese garment industry in Sunset Park is characterized by its gender hierarchy. The rationale used to justify it is always inconsistent and contradictory. For example, the sorter and pressers, the two highest paid jobs on the shop floor, are almost invariably men. Trimmers, the lowest paid workers, are virtually all women. This arrangement is said to have its basis in women's lack of physical strength to move the bundles of cut-up materials around, and women's intellectual inability to sort the cut-up pieces and to lay out a workable schedule for production. Women are also believed to be too weak to operate the heavy pressing machines and endure the heat generated by them. As a result, they are denied the opportunity to work as a sorter or a presser. What is forgotten in this

ungrounded rationale for the gender division of labor on the floor is the duration of strength, which the Chinese call *yin li*, and the extraordinary wisdom to figure out the way to sew the garments with their ever-changing styles. Both of these are necessary qualities of machine operators, who are overwhelmingly women.

It is said that women constitute the majority of machine operators in the shops because the flexible work hours, made possible by the piece-rate system and the larger number of operators in the shops, allow them to fulfill their family responsibilities while working in the shops. This justification ignores the highly competitive environment among the large number of machine operators that is generated by the piece-rate system. Since garment production is seasonal and work tends to be limited in most of the shops, in order to make ends meet, women workers are most likely to utilize every minute available to compete with one another in seizing work and to produce as many garments as they can. This work atmosphere is likely to deprive them of the flexibility that the piece-rate system is supposed to offer.

In addition, as known in the shops, workers' earnings depend not only on the piece rates and the speed at which they work, but also on the kind of work they do. The more mechanical and simple the work is, the faster they can produce, and the more money they can earn. There is no denying that pressers work under extremely stressful conditions, because there are usually only two or three of them in a shop of thirty or more machines and they have to press all the finished garments within a given time. However, their work is simpler than that of machine operators, so they can easily speed up their work after they become used to the structure of the garments and thus increase their incomes. Because there are only a few pressers in a shop, they are protected from the frenetic competition that is a routine part of the lives of machine operators.[7]

Unlike the pressers, machine operators' incomes fluctuate a great deal. Since styles are transient due to the unpredictable nature of fashion, it tends to take much longer for machine operators to get familiar with their work before they can speed up their production. The unpredictable nature of their work also creates more opportunities for their employers to keep wages low by constantly changing their piece rates, which are allegedly based on styles.

Family wages are always invoked to justify not only the higher pay of some traditionally men's work, but also the special payment arrangements in such sections as buttoning and bagging (putting the finished garments into bags). Since piece rates in these two sections are much lower than other sections, employers would subcontract the entire workload to one or two married male workers and allow them to complete the work with the assistance of their families. It used to be said that this arrangement was made to help the men fulfil their traditional gender roles as "rice winners" and to respect Chinese traditional culture. However, this rationale was cast aside in the early 1990s when the male workers left for higher paying jobs and women replaced them in these sections.

As Nancy Green and Susan Glenn have cogently argued, the gender division of labor in the garment industry has never been static.[8] Take the operation of sewing machines for example. Although most sewing machine operators are women, an increasing number of undocumented male workers have taken over these positions in Sunset Park over the last few years. Gender remains at work, however. The recently arrived men could easily take over the traditionally female jobs from women, but the gender identity of their jobs continued to subject them to a position inferior to those in the traditionally men's sections. They are generally believed to be less skilled, physically weak, and hence less manly than the rest of the male workers in the shops.

Fluidity between class and gender lines, generated by the structural flexibility of the garment industry, does not preclude opportunities for upward mobility for female as well as male workers, albeit in different ways and to different degrees. Although most Chinese employers are men and had been workers themselves, an increasing number of women workers have become owners of the garment shops in recent years. This was the case in the shop where reporter Lii worked. Many women employers learned English by attending the free language classes offered by their union or other public institutions. Speaking from fair to good English, they operate their businesses successfully, without the assistance of men. Their past experience as workers and their gender identity may enable them to better understand their women employees. However, this does not guarantee that they will be benevolent bosses, as implied in Lii's report. Recent cases of labor law violations in the Chinese garment shops owned by women have demonstrated that, situated in a highly competitive and marginal position in the city's industry, women employers can be as unscrupulous as their male counterparts.[9]

Wages and Hours

Workers' wages in the Sunset Park garment shops fluctuate greatly, contingent upon the type of work they produce, the level of skill, and the quality and adequacy of work their employer provides. A new hand may earn practically nothing for the first day, while a skilled long-stitch machine operator can earn as much as $600 a week in the high season. In general, as in the case of most Chinatown shops in Manhattan, the sorter, the fore-person, the cleaner(s), and the floor workers are paid by the hour. My interviews show that in 1998 a full-time foreperson or a sorter earned an average of more than six dollars per hour, and the finished garment checkers and cleaners, about three dollars. The rest of the workers in the shops are paid at piece rates. Their incomes vary greatly, ranging from weekly averages of $600 to $700 for a presser; $400 to $500 for a hemmer; $300 to $400 for a single machine operator and buttoner; $250 to $300 for a general machine operator, and $150–$200 for a trimmer. Compared with the union's minimum wages, the above wages of the Sunset Park Chinese garment workers may appear desirable. However, most of these weekly wages are in fact the result of workers' working ten to twelve hours a day. Their work hours are even longer during the busy seasons, with competition mounting in recent years.

Forms of payment are also factors that affect workers' incomes. Like their counter-parts in Manhattan's Chinatown, most em-ployers in Sunset Park issue payments in a combination of checks and cash. The portion of the payment received by check is deter-mined by the worker's status or need. For union members, whose number is small in the area, employers tailor the amount of their checks strictly according to the union minimum income requirement for benefit eligibility. However, for nonunion workers, who form the overwhelming majority of the workforce in Sunset Park, the amounts of their checks are either kept below the pov-erty threshold so that they can maintain eli-gibility for welfare benefits, or kept in line with the US Immigration and Naturalization Service's basic requirement for financial eligi-bility for sponsoring the immigration of their family members or relatives into the United States. Working underground, undocument-ed workers are paid invariably by cash.

Chinese employers argue that workers themselves request various forms of payment. However, my interviews reveal that all work-ers, regardless of their status, are forced to accept a reduction in their wages, because checks are issued with a deduction of a five to seven percent "handling fee." The same is true for cash payments. Furthermore, piece rates are often not announced before the comple-tion of work and in some shops employers reserve their rights to reduce workers' wages if they consider the wages to be too high.

Researcher Mark Levitan reports that in 1990, 72 percent of the reported incomes of less-skilled blue-collar workers, apparel workers included, were below the poverty threshold for a family of four ($12,674).[10] Underreporting might be a factor in leading to the low-income status of some workers' families. However, what Levitan reported did not appear to be far from reality in the case of Chinese garment workers in New York. My interviews suggest that in the late 1990s the actual average annual income of most Sunset Park Chinese garment workers was only about $20,000.[11] To sustain their families, many have to work long hours, in violation of U.S. labor laws.

In the shops where the employers still bother to concern themselves with the inves-tigations of law enforcement agencies, work-ers were required to punch their work cards to show that they were working eight hours a day, even before they start their day's work. My interviews, however, reveal that 90 percent of the workers employed in Sunset Park are working ten to twelve hours a day. During the busy seasons or when orders have to be rushed out, it is not unusual for workers to work unusually long hours, or as Lii indicated, even labor around the clock.

Long hours of work, coupled with the hazardous environment of the shops severely damages workers' health. What happened to Bao Zhi Ni is, indeed, not an isolated case. Her written testimony at a public hearing held by the New York State Assemb-ly Subcommittee on Sweatshops on October 2, 1997, is illustrative of workers' situations:

> My name is Bao Zhi Ni. I am a garment worker. I have worked in the garment factories for close to ten years. For many long hours, I work without proper safety equipment, and under filthy conditions. I work at least ten to twelve hours everyday, but because the bosses depress the wages so low we can only make $20, $30 a day, even though we're working over ten hours . . .
>
> For many long hours I sit at the sewing machine repeating the same motions. I also have to handle heavy bundles of garments every day. Each day at work is an exhausting day. My eyes are tired, and my vision is blurry. My fingers, wrists, shoulders, neck, back, spine, all these parts of my body are inflicted with pain. I started feeling the pain in my lower back five years ago, but I continued to work in the sweatshops. I have no medical benefits.
>
> My shoulders and back hurt constantly. Because I have been forced to work for such long hours, the cartilage between the bones in my back has rubbed away, and I have a pinched nerve. With the pain and the numbness in my left leg, I know that I have muscular and nervous problems. My fingers and wrists hurt. Now, even after just one or two hours of work, my back aches so much that I can barely stand straight. . . . In order to make a living I have no choice but to force myself to work through this pain. Sometimes I can't do it, but I have no choice but to take one or two days off.
>
> Sometimes I have to take one or two weeks off. When I take this time off to heal just a little, my boss gets angry. The boss will call my house to scold me and say that I'm lazy, tell me that I must go back to work as soon as possible.[12]

My interviews reveal that almost all the garment workers who worked in the industry for more than five years have various health problems. Deng Ying Yi, a longtime labor activist at the Workers Center in Brooklyn run by the Union of Needletraders, Industrial and Textile Employees (UNITE!), is virtually disabled after working in the garment industry for more than ten years, with her nervous system partially damaged. Her case is not unique among workers in Sunset Park. However, most of these nonunionized workers are not covered by any form of health insurance.

To survive in their new homeland, nonunionized workers have to develop their own system to cope with the situation. Many rely heavily on their family ties and community networks. The experience of a Mr. Zhang, who had been a middle-rank official in Guangzhou but who became a finished garment checker in a Sunset Park Chinese garment shop, is indicative of this phenomenon:

> I was already fifty-two when I immigrated to this country. I worked in a garment shop as *cha yi* (Cantonese: a finished garment checker) and my wife *jin sin* (Cantonese: a trimmer). Together, we earned an average of less than $400 a week and we still had to raise a daughter, our youngest daughter who was in her teens and was eligible to come with us when we immigrated to this country. She had to eat, to dress and to go to school. In addition, we had to save money in order to sponsor our two older children to come to the United States. How did we manage to do all this? Well, we relied on our family. . . .
>
> I came with my other five siblings under the sponsorship of a brother. Each of us came with his or her own family. Altogether, it was more than twenty of us who came to New York City on the same day on the same plane. We rented three two-bedroom apartments in this part of Brooklyn because the brother who came earlier told us that rents are much less expensive in this area. Each apartment was shared by two families. My family and my brother's family shared a two-bedroom apartment and we paid a total of $700 for rent and utilities but we ate separately. My family spent a little more

than $100 each month on groceries. How did we manage to do this? We bought the cheapest possible food at the market, say, the thirty-nine-cent-a-pound chicken on sale at Key Foods and the four-head-for-one-dollar broccoli at the street stands in this neighborhood. In addition, my wife and I also picked up empty soda cans and other stuff on our way home from work. If we were lucky, the monthly income from that part of our labor could cover our groceries for an entire week.

For eight years after we came to this city, we never ate out and never stopped working, eleven to twelve hours a day and seven days a week. Whenever we did not have work to do in our shop my wife and I went to work in another shop.[13]

While family ties are important resources for immigrant workers who came with their families, community networks are the most important assets for undocumented immigrant workers, most of whom did not come with their families. For example, undocumented workers from Wenzhou have contributed money to establish their own "mutual funds." These funds can be used by any member in time of need. This practice has proved to be the most effective way for these workers to survive in time of adversity, since they are denied any social services and benefits in the United States.

As elsewhere in the world, the gendered definitions of roles in the Sunset Park Chinese garment shops, their hierarchical order, and the rationale applied to justify them are shaped by the flexible but highly competitive structure of the garment industry, and have been inherently unstable. This fluidity generates dynamics in the industry, but has also taken a toll on those who labor in the industry. It is by exhausting human resources among the workers and in their community that the nonregulated segment of the garment industry has managed to thrive. Sunset Part is a case in point.

"Co-Ethnic Conspiracy?"

One major aspect of the Chinese garment industry in New York that has generated great interest among some scholars is its co-ethnic nature. Although in recent years more and more garment shops in New York have employers and workers who do not share the same ethnic identity, this is not the case with many of the Chinese garment shops in Manhattan's Chinatown and Brooklyn's Sunset Park. Most Chinese employers continue to hire only workers from major Chinese settlements.

As many studies have pointed out, this co-ethnic nature of the industry has benefited both workers and management.[14] Like their Eastern European counterparts at the turn of the twentieth century, Chinese workers do not have to learn to speak or understand English to work in a garment shop. They can also learn the trade on site and from scratch. In truth, without the industry, many working-class Chinese immigrant families may not have been able to survive.

The co-ethnic nature of the industry is also said to have simplified and humanized management of the shops. Many studies have discussed the particular recruitment pattern of the Chinese shops. Although in recent years a growing number of new immigrant workers have begun to seek employment through advertisements in community newspapers or the help-wanted signs posted in the front of the shops, most employers continue to rely on the recommendations of their workforce for new recruits, and most new immigrant workers obtain their first jobs through their families, friends, and relatives. Some employers also hire job applicants on the spot, without giving them much of a background check. New recruits, especially those who are employed with the recommendations from workers already in the shop, are allowed to use the facilities in the shop to receive on-site training.

Workers can maintain their cultural practices at their workplaces. They celebrate major Chinese festivals in the shops. They also share Chinese food and cooking with one another, listen to the blasting of the closed-circuit Chinese radio broadcasts, and share news about their homeland while working. As Lii noted, although employers in most Chinese shops do not offer their employees overtime payments when they expect workers to work long hours or on weekends, they offer them free rice and water, or even tea in some shops, to eat and drink with their lunch. They also provide lunch or afternoon tea to compensate workers' working on weekends. It is also widely known that most employers in Sunset Park will drive their employees home if their work ends after 11:00 P.M.

Workers who are unfamiliar with the labor laws and their rights in the United States feel obligated to work hard for their employers if their employers are willing to accommodate their needs. The undocumented workers feel particularly grateful to their employers if their employers have offered them any form of protection during immigration or other law enforcement raids. Employers in Sunset Park are known to cover workers up with piles of cut-garments scattered on the floor, or allow them to use the ladder in the shop to climb to the skylight. These gestures foster gratitude on the workers' part, which they feel obligated to reciprocate.

Many workers find it easy to identify with their employers if they are immigrants and have been workers themselves. Workers who desire upward social mobility look up to their employers as role models, a mirror of their future in the land of opportunity. Workers' empathy with their employers' situation, generated by a mixture of gratitude, fear, and admiration, has often led to their acquiescence to their employers' unscrupulous practices on the shop floor. In some cases this relationship of empathy has become so entrenched that law enforcement agents from outside the Chinese community and Chinese union organizers find it difficult to break. No wonder observers of the industry, like reporter Lii, do not hesitate to call the Sunset Park shop "a miserable complicity born of necessity in an insular, immigrant world." However, this conspiracy theory is too simplistic to explain the complex interdependent relationship between the workers and their employers in the ethnic enclave economy of the United States. It also fails to highlight the imbalance of power embedded in this relationship. Failing to locate the ultimate beneficiaries of this relationship, this theory cannot explain fully the causes of sweated labor in the shops.

Clearly, employers' various forms of accommodation benefit themselves rather than the workers. Let's take the special form of recruitment, for example. Since workers' incomes are based on the work they have accomplished, it will only hurt the new recruits if they are slow to learn their routine of work. However, on-site training allows employers to strengthen their personal ties with the newly hired as well as those who are already in the shop. Paying wages in a mixture of cash and checks or simply by cash also enables the employers to avoid paying taxes, the amounts of which are likely to be much larger than their workers'. A closer investigation of the situation in the industry also reveals that accommodations offered by employers are not unconditional. They are given only to workers who follow the rules they set. Those who refuse to do so are fired, blacklisted, physically assaulted, or subjected to other forms of retaliation.

Most Chinese employers do not force their workers to work long hours. However, production is organized in such a way that workers who do not stay as long as the rest will find themselves in an extremely disadvantageous position. Since there is no limit on work hours in most of the shops and workers who are willing to maximize their work hours can work as long as they wish, those who refuse to do so will end up having only "pork neckbones" (a slang in the Chinatown garment industry, referring to garments difficult to sew), or simply no garments to work on the next morning when they return.

Similar situations occur if a worker is ill and takes sick leave, or refuses to work on Sunday. Employers will hire a replacement worker almost immediately after a laborer fails to show up. Employers will also distribute "chickens in soy sauce" (another slang in the Chinatown garment industry, referring to work easy to sew) or paychecks on Sunday. Under these situations, workers who take a sick day are likely to lose their jobs, and those who do not work on Sunday will miss not only an important opportunity to increase their incomes, but also to get paid in a timely manner. Since workers' wages tend to be withheld by their employers for months in Sunset Park, failing to be present on payday will mean another indefinitely long delay in getting paid. It's no wonder that workers in Sunset Park tend to lament, "We have the option to die but we don't have the option to take a sick day or a rest."

Some employers have also blatantly taken advantage of their workers' acquiescence to maximize their profit. Instances of *zhen jia lao ban* (real and fake bosses) and *yi guo liang zhi* (one country, two systems), stories told by labor activist Deng Ying Yi, are indications of how far employers would go.[15] As Deng recalled, one day workers of a shop came to the UNITE! Workers' Center to seek assistance in collecting their wages. It turned out that their employer had closed the shop after owing them several hundred thousands of dollars in back wages and had vanished without a trace. However, when the State Department of Labor finally undertook this case, the department found it difficult to file charges against the real owner of the shop.

The owner, an undocumented immigrant himself, had registered the shop with the name and social security number of an elderly worker and had been signing all the legal doccuments under this worker's name without informing him. Filing charges against owner of the shop would mean charges against this worker, who was not the real owner of the shop.[16]

The story of "one country, two systems" is about a peculiar phenomenon in some unionized shops in Sunset Park. According to Deng, although union contracts stipulate that all workers in a union shop are union members and entitled to union benefits, employers of some unionized shops refuse to register their new recruits as union members and keep their wages in the books. Consequently, there are both union and nonunion members in the same shop who are working under very different systems of employment.

My interviews further reveal other forms of discrimination on the floor. For example, some employers offer different piece rates to workers of different immigration status and from different regions in China. Cantonese immigrant workers, who form the majority of the workforce, tend to receive higher piece rates and work relatively regular hours, while non-Cantonese or undocumented workers are denied all these "privileges." Discriminatory treatments have taken a different form in a small number of shops that hire several skilled workers from other ethnic groups. The non-Chinese workers are offered wages and other working conditions that comply with labor laws, while their Chinese fellow workers, who work side by side with them, have to struggle against the grim reality of low pay and long hours of work.[17]

Chinese employers have been so reckless in exploiting workers in their own community that it reinforces the stereotypical image of Chinese workers as the docile "willing slaves" in the Sunset Park area. This image of the workers subjects them to exploitation not only by Chinese employers, but also by shop owners of other ethnic groups. In 1997, the *Sing Tao Daily* reported that seven Chinese workers from a Jewish-owned garment shop came to seek help from the UNITE! Workers' Center. They complained that they had been discriminated against by their Jewish employer who had closed the shop and refused to pay them according to labor laws, as he did to his Hispanic workers.[18]

The most common problem workers face, however, is the failure to receive compensation for their work in a timely manner. Employers benefit tremendously from withholding their workers' wages. Community labor activists estimate that a shop of average size in Sunset Park has thirty-five workers and the lowest wage of garment workers in the area is about $150 per week. If the owner of a shop withholds his/her employees' wages for eight weeks, which is not uncommon in the area, the employer will have more than $40,000 in hand by the end of the eighth week, even if workers in the shop earned the lowest wage in the area. With this $40,000, an employer can open another shop without having to pay interest as they would if borrowing money from a bank.

Regrettably, as union organizers and law enforcement agencies have pointed out, workers tend not to take any legal action against their employers until their employers close down the shops. The reasons are varied. One major reason is the workers' lack of knowledge about their rights and the political operation in their new homeland. With few employment alternatives, many immigrant workers fear that any form of cooperation with law enforcement agencies or organized labor will cost them their jobs. This was particularly the situation before the signing of the Hot Goods Bill by the New York State governor in 1996.[19] Prior to the adoption of this bill, law enforcement

agencies had difficulty in helping workers retrieve their back wages if a shop was closed and the employer was hard to locate. As a result, the longer wages were withheld, the more reluctant workers were to report their cases. They feared that their reporting would lead their employers to close the shop for good.

Workers' reluctance to report labor violations on the floor is also compounded by a lack of understanding about the U.S. income tax system. Many are afraid that the amount of money they receive will be reduced by paying taxes if they seek assistance from law enforcement agencies and have to report their back wages to the Internal Revenue Service. Understandably, undocumented workers have additional concerns. Working underground, they fear that a visit from the Department of Labor to their work place will bring in a raid by the Immigration and Naturalization Service.

While workers are often reluctant to take action against their employers, employers are not hesitant to take advantage of workers' fear. According to longtime observers of the community, many employers in the garment industry engage in speculative financial activities with the money they have withheld from their workers, such as gambling or buying high-return but high-risk stocks. Since most of these activities will not lead to their expected outcomes, the employers close down their shops to avoid payments they owe their employees.

There are also employers who simply try to extract larger profits by closing down operations, absconding with the money they have withheld from their employees, and reopening their business under a different name. This was the case where reporter Lii worked. Hence, labor violations are widespread and the turnover rate of many Sunset Park Chinese garment shops is at a record high.[20] This highly unstable situation makes it even more difficult to enforce labor laws in the area, especially in recent years when most of these agencies are understaffed.

Tensions and exploitation in many Chinese garment shops in Sunset Park lay bare the limits of ethnic solidarity in the garment industry. Relegated to the same ethnic economic sector, Chinese employers have to rely on workers in their own community to run their businesses and accommodate workers' needs. However, situated in a marginal position of a highly competitive industry, many employers also do not hesitate to exploit their community ties to maintain their competitive edge in the industry. As in the case with their predecessors in the city's industry, the garment industry offers new Chinese immigrant workers many advantages in working among their own, but it also makes them more vulnerable to exploitation by management on all levels. The degree of labor violation in many Chinese garment shops demonstrates not only the limits of ethnic solidarity but also the devastating impact of the frenetic search for cheap labor on the Chinese community. This impact, as well as the limited nature of ethnic solidarity, will be further explored in the following section.

"The Cantonese vs. the Fujianese"?

One major issue that surfaced constantly during my interviews with workers is their concern about the increasing number of undocumented workers in the industry, most of whom are believed to be from Fuzhou, a major city in the province of Fujian in southeastern China. These newcomers, who speak their own dialect, are often blamed for worsening labor conditions on the shop floor and deteriorating living standards in Sunset Park. They also are charged with undermining workers' solidarity in the industry. Many Cantonese

workers believe that there is no way for them to get along well with the Fujianese.

In the course of interviewing workers in Sunset Park, however, I came to know many Cantonese and Fujianese workers who are good friends. I also came to see that although a large number of undocumented workers came from Fuzhou, Fuzhou is not the only place that has sent undocumented Chinese immigrants to the United States. Undocumented Chinese workers also come from Wenzhou, Guangdong, and almost all the coastal areas of China. There are also some from Malaysia and other Southeast Asian countries. Nevertheless, there is a pronounced tendency in New York's Chinese community to identify all undocumented workers as Fujianese. Stories about how fanatically hardworking they are became a recurring theme in the narratives of almost all the non-Fujianese workers. Fujianese workers were said to be so money-crazy that they would bring their rice cookers to the shops, cook and eat there while working, and even spend the night in the shops if they found any work there.

These undocumented workers are also blamed for having eroded the image of the Chinese in the Sunset Park area. It is said that since they spend so many hours at work, they could even do without a place to stay. It is a general belief in the Sunset Park Chinese community that several dozen immigrants from Fuzhou would share a single one-bedroom apartment, either only spending the night there or using it just for bathing and other purposes while spending their nights in the garment shops. I heard little sympathy for their plight in my interviews with non-Fujianese workers.

Anecdotal as these stories are, recycled repeatedly, they have fostered a profound prejudice against workers from Fuzhou. This prejudice is so prevalent that it often blinds non-Fujianese workers to class conflicts on the shop floor. For example, I came across a group of Cantonese workers who had just been fired by their employer for refusing to work as many hours as he wanted. Rather than blaming their unscrupulous employer, they blamed their unemployment on the workers from Fuzhou whom their employer had hired for lower rates and longer hours of work.

Although all prejudices are unjustified, factors that have contributed to the prejudice against Fujianese workers are worth exploring. My conversation with a Mrs. Deng, a Taishanese worker and a staunch opponent of "those hateful Fujianese," is revealing:[21]

A: As you know, the Chinese garment shops in Sunset Park have a bad name as sweatshops these days. Our lives are miserable. It was all because of those hateful Fujianese. They have taken our jobs. The bosses love them because they don't have family responsibilities and can work twenty-four hours a day in the shop. They are very greedy. What is in their eyes is only money, money, money. Recently we Cantonese have been losing ground in my shop. The Fujianese are taking over. They are everywhere in my shop.

Q: Could you tell me how many workers from Fuzhou are exactly in your shop?

A: Well, I never counted them, but, never mind, let me try. There are a total of about forty machine operators in my shop, one, two, three, yes, three are Cantonese, three are Mandarin speaking from Shanghai and Wuhan, and . . . [It turned out that only eight out of a total of thirty-five workers in her shop were from Fuzhou and only five out of the nine undocumented workers in her shop came from Fuzhou.]

Q: So the majority in your shop is not Fujianese and the undocumented workers in your shop are not all from Fuzhou.

A: Yes, you are right. My impression was wrong. But still I am nervous about them. Let me tell you something, actually, there are also undocumented workers from Taishan. A village in Taishan is now almost empty, you know, because they had a smuggler in that village, and he had connections with those snakeheads in New York City. The conditions of the undocumented workers from that village are deplorable. I always think that my situation is already miserable enough. [She was collecting welfare benefits at the time of this interview. Her husband just had a surgery and could not work and she had four schoolchildren to raise.] But theirs are even worse. However, I have been told that compared with those from Fuzhou, they seem to be doing fine because many of them have family members or relatives in New York. Those from Fuzhou don't seem to have this advantage and they owe the snakeheads much more money than those from Taishan. Anyway, I should admit that I don't know very much about them because I don't talk to them and they don't talk to me either.

Q: What then made you so angry with them?

A: They work too hard! Whenever there is some work in the shop, especially the easy jobs, they are there. Very often we don't have any work left when we return in the morning. They have finished all the work at night! But we can't do this. We have to go home at night to take care of our families and to have a little rest. We are human beings, you know. But work is money. They have taken away all our money. They are so hateful!

Q: Did your boss ever close the door of the shop at a time like that?

A: No, how could you expect them to do
so? Of course not; for the bosses, the
sooner they can get the work done the
better. So they love those illegal immigrants from Fuzhou. In the past, many
garment shop owners had signs on the
gates of their shops, saying "Cantonese
only," because they were afraid that
they would be harassed by the Fujianese
gangsters, who are well known for their
fearlessness, if they had Fujianese
workers in their shops. But now they
don't care. They need workers who can
work twenty-four hours a day. So the
sign on their gates has also changed. It
reads "Fujianese only."

The situation has made me really
mad. To be honest, who doesn't need
money? I too wish that I could work
around the clock, if I did not have a
family to take care of. I need money too. I
don't mind working hard. I was a peasant in China. Rain or shine, I worked
outdoors, under conditions much worst
than sewing in a garment shop. I wish I
could make more money for my family.

But, wait a minute, I sense something
wrong with myself in answering your
questions. Haven't I somewhat mis-
judged those undocumented workers
from Fuzhou? Yes, I think I have.

Obviously, tension among the workers,
ignited by the highly competitive nature of
garment organization and accelerated by the
manipulation of management, has led to their
misjudgment of reality in the shop.

Ungrounded as the stories about undocumented workers from Fuzhou are, generated by a mixture of myth and reality, they
take a toll on all workers from the same place.
This can be seen in the response of a Ms. Wong:

I think we immigrants from Fuzhou have
been treated very unfairly by our own Chinese community. I am not an illegal immigrant. I came with all the papers as a legal

immigrant. In addition, unlike the majority
of illegal immigrants from the Fuzhou area,
I came from the city and with my family.
But still, I am looked at as an illegal immigrant because I came from Fuzhou.

I don't speak Cantonese, so I could not
find a job in a restaurant or other place.
That's how I ended up working in a garment shop.

My husband and I had a hard time looking for a place for our family to stay when
we first came. Landlords from other parts
of China refused to rent to us, because we
are from Fuzhou. People in the community
said we lived like pigs, with several dozen
people usually packed in one apartment but
registered under only one or two names.
So the landlords were scared. Landlords
from Fuzhou did not treat us well either.
They charged us much higher rents
because they knew that we had no choice.

My husband and I finally got to rent this
place because we decided to speak Mandarin and pretended to be from other parts
of China when we first met our landlady,
who is Cantonese. Yes, now, she knows
that we are from Fuzhou but she doesn't
care anymore because we have become
very good friends, and she says we are the
best tenants she has ever had.[22]

Many immigrant workers from Fuzhou
whom I interviewed shared her experience.
Although almost all immigrant workers from
Fuzhou have been affected by the prejudice
against them, the undocumented ones among
them are the most victimized. A Mr. Dong's
response was typical:

I don't understand why we should be
treated like this! We are human beings too!
Yes, we work very hard, because we need
money to pay back our debts! Yes, many of
us share an apartment, because we want to
save money. Do we enjoy our lives in this
country? Of course not. We are separated
from our families and working underground. We are bullied by our bosses, even
including those from Fuzhou. They make
us work long hours but pay us much less

than other workers in the shops. I don't think anyone would like to live a life like ours! But, still, we are not going to give up because we are working for a better life for our families.

My family lives in a village along the Ming River, and I was a fisherman in the village before I came to the United States. I left my home village because the water there was so seriously polluted that there were no edible fish left. I could not make a living for my family by fishing.

Some people ask, "Why don't you go home if life is so hard for you?" But can we? My family has borrowed a lot of money to send me here. My wife and my kids have pinned their hopes on me, yearning for me to bring them to *meiguo* [the beautiful land, which refers to the United States].

In addition, what will folks in my village say if I return home penniless? I remember when I was in the village, I envied those who returned home from the United States. They looked so successful, squandering money like dirt. I wished I could be like them one day. Of course, after I came to the United States, I got to know that many of them too had been working in a sweatshop, as I do now. If they can make it, I can make it, too. So, I work hard. It is none of anyone's business if I don't eat, don't sleep, and work nonstop.[23]

The strong desire to improve the well-being of their families, reinforced by a degree of vanity for a glamorous return, led the undocumented workers to leave their native land and fall prey to the sweating system in the United States. Although the living conditions of their native land have "pushed" them out of China, it was the underground economy in the United States that has "pulled" them in and lured them to violate U.S. immigration laws.

The experience of the Fujianese garment workers in Sunset Park reminds one of what has happened to each group of newcomers in New York's garment industry. While the constant search for cheap labor brings in different groups of ethnic workers at different points in history, newcomers are always blamed for the cutthroat competition in the industry. This "finger pointing" takes place even within the same ethnic group. As national characteristics were used in the past as a convenient way of explaining the deterioration of working conditions, today regional and dialectal differences, immigration status, and even the location of one's family have become indexes in the Chinese garment industry for differentiating the old from the new, the "human" from the "inhuman," and thereby the excusers from the excused.[24] Labor solidarity in the community is thus undermined by conflicts of interest among workers, as well as elements in the cultural repertoire of the community.

Will Too Much Law Enforcement Kill the Chinese Garment Industry in New York City?

In the late 1990s, a number of Chinese employers in Sunset Park began to react strongly when the New York State Apparel Industry Task Force carried out its mission to enforce labor laws in the city's garment industry. In October 1996, after the task force completed its investigation and charged many Chinese garment shops with labor violations, Chinese employers in Sunset Park launched a massive demonstration to protest the state operation. They called it "adding salt to the wound." Claiming that the law enforcement agency had unjustly labeled all Chinese shops as "sweatshops," Chinese employers held the state investigation accountable for causing the further decline of Chinese garment industry in the city by providing manufacturers with the justification for withdrawing their work from the Chinese community.

According to the Chinese employers, manufacturers should be blamed for the deteriorating working conditions in the Chinese shops. Since they suppressed piece rates to such an intolerable degree and demanded such quick production and delivery of finished garments, Chinese employers were forced to reduce the piece rates they offered to their workers and expect them to work longer hours in order to remain competitive. In addition, since manufacturers frequently delayed payments for finished work, Chinese employers had to withhold wages to their own workers. Labor law enforcement will kill the Chinese garment industry, they asserted, because only by reducing wages and extending work hours could the industry survive in the highly competitive environment of garment production in New York.[25]

The Chinese employers' accusation against manufacturers is not entirely groundless, given manufacturers' frantic efforts to reduce the costs of labor in recent years. However, as many concerned individuals in the community have rightly pointed out, even though the Chinese garment industry has been hit hard by the outflow of garment production from the city, the sweatshop conditions in the industry are what allow the manufacturers to put a human face on their move from the city.[26]

What has happened since the State Department of Labor established its Apparel Industry Task Force in 1987? Did the efforts of the Task Force lead to the decline of the Chinese garment industry in New York City? Did the industry really decline?

Statistics show that despite the shrinking of the city's share in the U.S. garment industry, the absolute numbers of Chinese shops and their workforce in the past decade or more did not suggest any sign of decline; indeed, they grew. In the early 1980s, there were approximately 500 Chinese shops in the city, largely concentrated in Manhattan's

Chinatown and employing an estimated 25,000 Chinese workers. In 1998, there was an estimate of more than 800 Chinese shops, scattered in various parts of the city and employing more than 30,000 Chinese workers.[27]

One specific segment of the Chinese garment industry has declined significantly in recent years, however. It is the number of the unionized shops in Manhattan's Chinatown. Between 1992 and 1997 the number of garment shops in Manhattan's Chinatown dropped from 608 to 555 and employment declined from 21,015 to 14,887, a loss of more than 6,000 jobs.[28] The decline in the Manhattan's Chinatown garment industry coincided with the rapid growth of the Chinese garment shops in other parts of the city, in particular, Sunset Park in Brooklyn. Although Manhattan's Chinatown remains the center of the Chinese garment industry in New York, with about 500 Chinese shops still clustered in this area, its importance has been significantly reduced by the rapid growth of the Chinese garment industry in other boroughs.

The decline of Manhattan's Chinatown shops has also led to the weakening of union influence on the entire Chinese garment industry in New York City. In the early 1980s, when shops in Chinatown represented an overwhelming majority of the Chinese garment shops in New York City, more than 90 percent of them were unionized. By the end of the 1990s, it is estimated that the UNITE! Local 23-25 represented only half of the Chinese garment shops in the city.[29] The union's influence has declined even in Manhattan's Chinatown, with the percentage of Chinese union shops dropping from more than 90 percent in the early 1980s to fewer than 80 percent by 1997.[30] As a result, membership of the UNITE! Local 23-25—the largest local of the union, with an 85 percent Chinese membership—dropped from 28,083 in 1992 to 22,995 in 1996, a loss of more than 5,000 members.[31]

Despite problems embedded in the unionization of the Chinatown garment industry in earlier years, there are still many significant differences in working conditions between union and nonunion shops. The shrinking percentage of union shops in the Chinese garment industry indicates that more and more Chinese garment workers have been deprived of the benefits and protection to which union members are entitled. It should, therefore, come as no surprise that labor violations are rampant in many nonunion Chinese shops, which have, in turn, undercut working conditions in the union shops.

There is little doubt that manufacturers and retailers should be held accountable for the deteriorating working conditions in the city's garment industry. However, many individuals in the community are also correct in pointing out that it is the sweating system in some Chinese garment shops that has provided them with the most convenient excuse to pull production out of New York City. This is particularly true when politicians of all stripes have recognized a political advantage in promoting the elimination of sweatshops in the U.S., and manufacturers and retailers have also been pressured by consumer groups as well as labor to distance themselves from contract shops labeled as sweatshops.

The Chinese employers' argument that "too much law enforcement will kill the Chinese garment industry in New York City" reminds one of the situations at the turn of the twentieth century. As Nancy Green has noted, during that time when progressive reformers, labor leaders, and state legislators endeavored to improve labor conditions by passing new legislation and enforcing laws, manufacturers also argued that too many constraints would make the landscape of the garment industry disappear altogether from the city.[32] However, the garment industry remains in New York City, and so will the Chinese garment industry, at least for the decade to come.

Some Reflections

Driven by the search for cheap nonunion labor, runaway shops and sweated labor are not unique to the Chinese garment industry, nor are they new in the history of the city's industry. As early as the 1920s the dispersion of garment shops from Manhattan into various parts of the city already became a peculiar aspect in the landscape of New York's garment industry.[33] The Chinese garment industry, as a major part of the city's industry, is no exception in these regards.

The experience of Chinese workers is in many ways similar to that of their predecessors in the city's garment industry, but there are also differences. Particularly in the 1980s and 1990s, these differences were caused by the challenge of the times rather than simply by the cultural characteristics of the Chinese workers. Garment workers in the first half of the twentieth century were able to enjoy improved working conditions, thanks to the strong influence of labor unions and the continuous growth of the city's garment industry. However, Chinese workers in the late twentieth century were increasingly subjected to abusive labor conditions as the city's industry declined rapidly. Their union, plagued by its entrenched bureaucratic culture, could hardly respond to their needs.

As in the case of the city's garment industry in the early twentieth century, law enforcement and labor organizing remain the two most powerful ways to address the problems in the Chinese garment industry. Both law enforcement agents and labor organizers face the challenge of how to understand the complex reality of the garment industry beyond the highly politicized representations of it in political arenas. However, they also have to address different issues in their own realms.

As Mark Levitan has aptly put it, one of the major factors that has undermined significantly the efforts to eliminate sweated labor in the city is that "there are not enough cops on the beat." Despite the growth of sweated labor in the city's garment industry and the politicians' highly emotional pledges to eliminate it, both New York State and federal investigation teams are severely understaffed. According to Levitan, in 1998, there were only twenty-three investigators in the federal office of the Wage and Hour Division that had responsibility for the entire New York City metropolitan area, and only twenty-three out of thirty-four positions in New York City's Apparel Industry Task Force were filled.[34] As a result, in addition to improving their understanding of the dynamics generated by the highly competitive structure of the garment industry, the history and culture of each ethnic group, and the multifaceted impact of their operations, law enforcement agents still have to battle the shortage of hands in carrying out their tasks, a difficult situation that is indeed not of their own making.

Organized labor faces another type of challenge. Never before has UNITE!, the major labor union of the U.S. garment industry, been under so much pressure to reform itself. The parochialism and the culture of business unionism that UNITE! shares with other traditional trade unions have proved to be impotent in this new age of the global economy. Today, with the impressive growth of the community-based labor organizations in New York's Chinatown and other ethnic communities, the question UNITE! faces is no longer whether it is willing to change but whether the change is adequate to maintain its legitimacy as a labor union in the industry.[35] In this era when capital has already globalized its search for inexpensive labor, how can we develop effective organizing strategies that are not only responsive to the needs of U.S. workers but also allow them to join forces with workers in other parts of the world? This is a question very much on the agendas of trade unions as well as concerned individuals in the Chinese community and the city.

NOTES

1. Unless otherwise noted, the following discussion is primarily based on these sources and the information provided by Liang Huan Ru, the former veteran union organizer in Brooklyn.

2. I use "Manhattan's Chinatown" because new Chinatowns have recently emerged in other boroughs of New York City, such as Queens and Brooklyn.

3. Abeles, Schwartz, Haechel & Silverblatt, Inc., *The Chinatown Garment Industry Study* (hereafter *Study*) (New York: International Ladies' Garment Workers' Union Local 23–25 and the New York Skirt and Sportswear Association, 1983), 55. For the sizes of the shops in Manhattan's Chinatown, see *Study*, 49–59.

4. See for example, the weekly special issue of the *Sing Tao Daily* (hereafter *STD*), March 8, 1998, 7.

5. My visit to the shop and interview with the shop owner.

6. One woman worker told me in an interview that it was so hot inside her shop in summer that sometimes she simply could not help crying while trying to rush out her work.

7. Experienced pressers began to lose this advantage in more and more Chinese garment shops in recent years, largely due to the increased competition from undocumented male workers. Unable to compete with the low wages accepted by the latter, they too had to face economic insecurity in the industry. I am indebted to a reminder from Liang Huan Ru, an organizer of UNITE! Local 23–25, and May Ying Chen, vice president of UNITE!, for this piece of information. What, however, must be kept in mind is that while competition has mounted among pressers in recent years, women machine operators also faced competition from undocumented workers.

8. See Susan Glenn, *Daughters of the Shtetl: Life and Labor in the Immigrant Generation* (Ithaca, New York: Cornell University Press, 1990), 90–131, and Nancy Green, *Ready-to-Wear and Ready-to-Work: A Century of Industry and Immigrants in Paris and New York* (Durham: Duke University Press, 1997), 161–87.

9. The most recent case was the one at 446 Broadway in November 1997, in which a young woman employer closed her shop after withholding a large sum of money in back wages from her employees. The case was covered by most major newspapers inside and outside the Chinese community. See, for example, *New York Times*, December 14, 1997.

10. See "Opportunity at Work: The New York City Garment Industry" (New York: Community Service Society of New York, 1998), 39.

11. This observation has been supported by recent coverage in Chinese community newspapers. For example, as covered in *World Journal* (hereafter *WJ*) in 1996, the monthly income of an elderly couple who worked in a Chinese garment shop was $1,800 and $2,200, respectively. Given the depressed piece rates in the last two years and the seasonal nature of the industry, this observation, based on interviews with workers in Sunset Park, does not seem to be far away from reality.

12. Directly quoted from "Behind Closed Doors: A Look into the Underground Sweatshop Industry," a report by the New York State Assembly Sub-Committee on Sweatshops (New York, November 1997), 59–61.

13. Interview by the author on April 13, 1998.

14. See, for example, Bernard Wong, "The Role of Ethnicity in Enclave Enterprises: A Study of the Chinese Garment Factories in New York City." *Human Organization* 46 (2), 1987: 120–9.

15. "One country, two systems" is the Chinese state policy in Hong Kong after the former British colony was returned to China in 1997.

16. Cases like this are not unheard of in the Chinese garment industry in Manhattan's Chinatown as well as other boroughs of the city. See, for example. The Chinese Staff and Workers Association, *Zhi Gong Zhi Sheng* (January 1994).

17. I was told that this small number of workers from other ethnic groups were likely to have worked for the former owner of the shop and the Chinese employer employed them as part of the deal when he/she purchased the business. I was also told that some Chinese employers deliberately kept these workers to protect their businesses from harassment by Chinese gangsters, who tended not to attack shops with non-Chinese workers for fear that their illicit activities would be known beyond the Chinese community.

18. *STD*, December 19, 1997.

19. The "Hot Goods Bill" was signed into law on July 2, 1996. This bill has established "additional methods of obtaining restitution for unpaid apparel industry workers from contractors, manufacturers, and retailers." For a further discussion of this bill, see "Behinds Closed Doors," 4.

20. The *Study* has reported that at the end of 1981, 28 percent of all Chinese shops in Chinatown had been in business for less than one year and close to half of them had been in operation for less than two years (p. 68). However, in the late 1990s, as many workers have pointed out, the Chinese garment shops in Sunset Park are often opened and closed down within months.

21. Taishan is a county in Guangdong Province. Immigrants from this county are also generally called "Cantonese."

22. Interview by the author on July 2, 1998.

23. Interview by the author on June 21, 1998.

24. Immigration status and whether one is living with their family have become important indexes because much of the Chinese community has chosen to believe that legal immigration and family life are the norms throughout the history of the community, however invalid this belief is.

25. For a summary of their arguments, see *STD*, April 22, 1998.

26. For different voices in the community, see, for example, the weekly special issues of *STD*, May 17, 1998 and June 28, 1998.

27. The estimate of 800 Chinese shops is based on an adding of the approximate 500 shops in Manhattan and the more than 300 shops in Brooklyn and other boroughs. More than 30,000 workers were estimated by the community press in the end of 1997. See *STD*, December 22, 1997.

28. These statistics are provided by the Research Department of the New York State Department of Labor.

29. In 1997, when the union signed a new contract with Chinese employers, the three Chinese contractors' associations represented only 406 shops in the city. This was later reported in most Chinese community newspapers. See, for example, *STD*, February 23, 1998.

30. This percentage of Chinatown union shops in 1997 is based on a comparison of the number of garment shops in the Chinatown area provided by the state labor department, which is not classified according to ethnicity, and the estimate of Chinatown union organizers and the Chinese newspapers. See, for example, *STD*, December 22, 1997 and April 29, 1998 and *WJ*, February 28, 1998.

31. These statistics are provided by the UNITE! Research Department. The estimated percentage of the local's Chinese membership in this study is consistent with the numbers provided by the local.

32. Green, *Ready-To-Wear*, 50.

33. See Nancy Green, "Sweatshop Migrations: The Garment Industry between Home and Shop," in *The Landscape of Modernity: Essays on New York City, 1900–1940*, eds. David Ward and Olivier Zunz (New York: Russell Sage Foundation, 1992), 213–32.

34. Mark Levitan, *Opportunity at Work: The New York City Garment Industry* (New York: Community Service Society of New York, 1998), 59.

35. One of the most active community-based labor organizations in New York's Chinatown in the last two decades is the Chinese Staff and Workers' Association.

34

HISPANICS IN THE AMERICAN SOUTH AND THE TRANSFORMATION OF THE POULTRY INDUSTRY

William Kandel • Emilio A. Parrado

QUESTIONS TO CONSIDER

In 2000, half our nation's foreign born were from Latin America. This segment represents only about 10% of the total U.S. population—less than the 15% of the population made up of foreign born individuals in 1890, but there is an important difference. Early migrations to the United States consisted of mostly white people from Europe. The most recent waves of immigrants are Latino and Asian. Another major difference from past migration patterns is that Latinos from Mexico and Central America are no longer concentrated only in the states that border Mexico. William Kandel and Emilio Parrado examine the ways Latino migration to the southeastern part of the United States has invigorated regions that had been in economic decline, noting that the economic resurgence has resulted largely from the creation of jobs that are dangerous, dirty, unregulated, and exploitive. Do these jobs present new immigrants with a path toward upward mobility or a life of poverty wages?

Findings from the 2000 Census indicate two important trends affecting the Hispanic population. The first is the extraordinarily high rate of Hispanic population increase outside of urban areas over the past decade, with growth rates exceeding both metropolitan and nonmetropolitan growth rates for all other racial and ethnic groups (Cromartie 1999; Pérez 2001). In addition, for the first time in U.S. history, half of all nonmetropolitan Hispanics currently live outside the five southwestern states of Arizona, California, Colorado, New Mexico, and Texas (Cromartie and Kandel 2002). The diversity of new rural areas raises questions about forces outside of the Southwest that are attracting migrants, the Hispanic population's assimilation patterns into communities unaccustomed to dealing with immigration, and the connection between structural economic change and Hispanic population growth.

The main objective of this chapter is to link changes in the poultry industry with the growth of the Hispanic population in nonmetropolitan counties in nine southeastern states: Alabama, Arkansas, Georgia, Louisiana, Mississippi, North Carolina, South Carolina, Tennessee, and Virginia. We document the restructuring of the poultry industry and spatially correlate poultry production and areas of Hispanic settlement. Next, given the impact of these population changes on local communities, we examine two case studies to elaborate more directly on the implications of Hispanic growth for the culture, organization, and everyday life of two nonmetropolitan counties in Virginia and North Carolina. Finally, we derive implications for further research to address relations between Hispanics and other minority groups.

New Destinations in Nonmetropolitan America

The degree to which Hispanic residential settlement has expanded outside of traditional migrant-receiving states can be illustrated with 1990 and 2000 Census data. Table 1 presents state-level nonmetropolitan population in absolute and percentage terms for the top seventeen states, sorted by Hispanic population growth rate. Eight of the nine southeastern poultry-producing states appear among the ten states with the fastest-growing nonmetropolitan Hispanic populations; the remaining seven include midwestern states with large beef and pork meatpacking industries.

While Hispanics continue to be overwhelmingly located in metropolitan areas, during the 1990s their nonmetropolitan growth of 70.4 percent exceeded their metropolitan growth rate of 60.4 percent (Cromartie and Kandel 2002). By the decade's end, according to Census 2000 data, Hispanics represented approximately 5.5 percent of the nonmetropolitan population, but had accounted for over 25.0 percent of its growth during the decade. Moreover, Hispanic population growth during the 1990s surpassed total population growth in nonmetropolitan areas in every state except Hawaii.

Widespread media attention on Hispanics in new destinations, however, owes more to their geographic concentration. In 2000, over a third of the 3.2 million rural Hispanics lived in just 109 of all 2,288 nonmetropolitan counties (Cromartie and Kandel 2002).

Since the 1990s, a number of ethnographic studies have documented the immigrants' reception in relatively small communities with few foreign-born residents (Griffith 1995; Guthey 2001; Hernández-León and Zúñiga 2000). The growing nonmetropolitan pres-ence of Hispanics can be attributed to several concurrent trends. First, increased enforce-ment policies by the Immigration and Naturalization Service to reduce undocumented immigration, ironically, have pushed undoc-umented migrants away from the traditional migrant-receiving states of California, Arizona, and Texas and

TABLE 1 Nonmetropolitan State Populations Ranked by Hispanic Population Growth

Rank	State	Nonmetro Hispanic Population			Nonmetro Population			Hispanic Share (%)	
		1990	2000	% Change	1990	2000	% Change	1990	2000
1	North Carolina	16,714	98,846	491	2,252,775	2,612,257	16	1	4
2	Delaware	1,221	6,915	466	113,229	156,638	38	1	4
3	Alabama	5,198	26,155	403	1,330,857	1,453,233	9	0	2
4	South Carolina	5,830	27,853	378	1,064,088	1,205,050	13	1	2
5	Georgia	26,270	124,296	373	2,126,654	2,519,789	18	1	5
6	Tennessee	7,119	32,737	360	1,579,336	1,842,679	17	0	2
7	Arkansas	9,559	36,504	282	1,310,724	1,434,529	9	1	3
8	Virginia	8,136	28,258	247	1,407,096	1,550,447	10	1	2
9	Mississippi	7,774	24,321	213	1,797,542	1,932,670	8	0	1
10	Minnesota	11,283	34,860	209	1,364,205	1,456,119	7	1	2
11	Iowa	11,807	35,611	202	1,576,857	1,600,191	1	1	2
12	Indiana	12,260	36,921	201	1,581,713	1,690,582	7	1	2
13	Kentucky	8,479	24,465	189	1,905,535	2,068,667	9	0	1
14	Nebraska	16,641	44,564	168	791,050	811,425	3	2	5
15	Wisconsin	11,098	28,893	160	1,560,597	1,723,367	10	1	2
16	Missouri	10,822	27,807	157	1,626,202	1,800,410	11	1	2
17	Pennsylvania	11,004	27,403	149	1,798,645	1,889,525	5	1	1

Sources: U.S. Bureau of the Census 1990, 2000.

Note: Shaded columns are the eight southeastern states highlighted in the study.

into southeastern and midwestern states that previously had few Hispanic migrants (Durand, Massey, and Charvet 2000).

Second, several informants and anecdotal accounts describe labor market saturation in the traditional migrant gateway cities of Los Angeles, Houston, and Chicago and suggest that growing numbers of "pioneer migrants" are seeking employment in new parts of the country. Hispanic settlement in nonmetropolitan areas also was facilitated by an economic recession in the early 1990s in the urban Southwest and other U.S. metropolitan centers. In addition to looking for employment opportunities in nonmetropolitan areas, many Hispanic immigrants may seek to escape problems associated with urban settings, such as poor schools, youth gangs, violence, and expensive and crowded housing.

Third, immigrants are also moving to nontraditional areas because of employers' recruiting efforts to sustain the number of workers needed in industries with less-than-desirable jobs (Johnson-Webb 2002). Consequently, the proportion of Hispanics in industries with low wages and harsh working conditions—meat processing, carpet manufacturing, oil refining, and forestry, to name a few—has increased dramatically since the 1990s (Broadway 1994; Engstrom 2001; Gouveia and Stull 1995; Hernández-León and Zúñiga 2000; Díaz McConnell forthcoming; McDaniel 2002). Because the U.S. Department of Labor does not classify these positions as temporary or highly skilled, firms cannot use special immigration provisions, such as the H2A or H2B visas, to obtain foreign workers. Information on recruitment practices consists of mostly qualitative journalistic accounts that, nevertheless, describe a host of practices that firms use to recruit workers (Carlin 1999; Katz 1996a, 1996b; Smothers 1996; Taylor and Stein 1999).

An influx of immigrants and newcomers into rural communities often generates conflicting feelings among local residents. Hispanic population growth in many nonmetropolitan places coincides with revived economic activity and reversals of stagnant or declining demographic patterns of previous decades (Broadway 1994; Brown 1993). Nevertheless, immigrant population growth may challenge the ability of rural communities to meet increased demands for social services, particularly schooling for immigrant children, and often increases poverty rates and income inequality (Reed 2001). While immigrants undoubtedly hold the least-desirable and most poorly paid jobs, their presence may exert downward wage pressure on native-born residents working in other low-skilled industries (Massey, Durand, and Malone 2002). Ethnic diversity is viewed by many Americans as a public good that introduces different cultures, languages, and cuisines to native-born residents and reinforces America's cherished self-image as a nation built on the energy and hopes of immigrants (Lapinski et al. 1997). Yet, popular reports suggest a significant level of social conflict in and municipal response from communities that have experienced influxes of immigrants in a relatively short time (Grey 1995; Guthey 2001; Studstill and Nieto-Studstill 2001). We return to these oppositional perspectives that use qualitative descriptions of poultry-producing communities below.

Trends in Poultry Consumption

To see how Hispanic migration to new regions in the southeastern U.S. is related to industrial restructuring, we first consider changes in one of the region's dominant low-skill industries, poultry processing. The poultry industry has been a mainstay in the Southeast for many decades, but since the 1970s, a number of trends have aggregated to influence the demand for labor

FIGURE 1   Per capita consumption of chicken, turkey, and beef, 1960–1999. *Source:* U.S. Department of Agriculture 1960–2000.

and, consequently, the settlement patterns of Hispanics. These include (1) increased consumption; (2) increased demand for value-added production; (3) industry consolidation and vertical integration, leading to larger firms; (4) increasing location of production facilities in the Southeast; and (5) the relative attractiveness of meat-processing jobs.

The impetus for changes in the poultry industry began with three consumption trends that strongly influenced the demand for labor. The first was domestic consumption, which grew as the result of two somewhat contradictory trends. In 1977, when beef consumption far exceeded poultry consumption, widely publicized findings from the Framingham Study explicitly outlined health risks associated with red meat in the diet (Dawber 1980). The report's implications were not lost on the American public, which began to eat less beef and more poultry. Per capita poultry consumption doubled between 1977 and 1999, while beef consumption dropped 30 percent over the same period (Fig. 1).

Yet, while the Framingham Study represents a milestone event, increasing consumption of fast food in the United States coincided with the growing demand for convenience food. Growth in fast-food franchises such as Kentucky Fried Chicken and marketing through nontraditional outlets

such as McDonald's created an enormous demand for a wide variety of chicken products. Within a little over a decade, per capita consumption of poultry surpassed that of beef for the first time since World War II (U.S. Department of Agriculture [USDA] 1960–2000).

The second consumption trend, growth in poultry exports, paralleled domestic demand. Following domestic consumer demand for further-processed products, poultry firms began supplementing their slaughtering plants with production facilities that cut up chickens and packaged the parts for different segments of the market. Breasts and other white meat met domestic consumption preferences, and dark meat was reserved for the export market. By the mid-1970s, chicken exports had increased significantly, and between 1987 and 2002, they skyrocketed, from 500 million to 6.5 billion pounds (USDA 1960–2000).

The demand for more convenient prepared food generated a precipitous increase in the sale of cut-up poultry and an equally precipitous decline in the sale of whole birds. In 1963, the poultry product mix sold in American supermarkets consisted of 85 percent whole birds and 15 percent cut-up poultry products; by 1997, that proportion was exactly the reverse (Ollinger, MacDonald, and Madison 2000). Consequently, many poultry producers appended "cut-up" operations to their meat-processing plants. The structural shift of value-added production from the retail sector (supermarkets) to the production sector (meat-slaughtering and -processing plants) has had profound consequences for labor demand, and, consequently, for labor supply.

Poultry Industry Concentration and Consolidation

Significant increases in both industry concentration and average poultry plant size have accompanied the trend toward increased consumption. Industrial concentration can often be measured using the "four firm concentration ratio," the proportion of total production controlled by the four largest firms (Ollinger, MacDonald, and Madison 2000). For the slaughter of chickens, this ratio more than doubled, from 14 percent to 41 percent, between 1963 and 1992; for turkey slaughter, the ratio increased from 23 percent to 45 percent over the same period. Concentration of poultry-processing firms fluctuated, but it also shows an upward trend during the same period. Data after 1992 are not available, but industry reports suggest that this trend continued throughout the 1990s.

Beginning in the late 1940s, firms began to realize greater scale economies by integrating all facets of operation. Under this mode of production, firms contract out to formerly independent chicken farms and provide the chicks, feed, medicines, veterinary services, and other inputs; contracted growers later return grown birds of consistent size and quality to the plant for slaughter (Bugos 1992). Slaughter operations also became more complex as firms responded to increasingly varied consumer and industry demands by adopting cut-up operations and packaging their products in ready-to-sell containers.

By controlling all phase of poultry production, such vertically integrated firms could increase their overall profitability while lowering prices; in real terms, the price of poultry dropped by just over 50 percent between 1960 and 1999 (USDA 1960–2000).

Industry consolidation and production have led to larger plants. To measure the extent of industry consolidation, we use proportion of production from firms with four hundred or more employees, a widely used measure developed by the U.S. Bureau of the Census. Beginning in 1967, the proportion of chicken produced by such large plants tripled; by 1992, they accounted for three-quarters of all poultry slaughter and processing (Ollinger, MacDonald, and Madison 2000).

Increased consumer demand, growing exports, and industry consolidation trends have combined to expand the demand for labor in the poultry industry. Figure 2 presents employment figures in both the poultry industry and the red meat industry for comparison. The above-noted trends in industry consolidation and plant size also occurred to roughly the same extent in the redmeat-processing industry (MacDonald et al. 2000). Yet, as Figure 2 demonstrates, employment in the red meat industry has not grown at all since 1970. In contrast, employment in the poultry industry has grown by 150 percent during the same period, and today it actually exceeds that of the beef industry (U.S. Department of Labor [DOL] 1972–2001).

Geographic Context of Poultry Production

Structural changes in the poultry industry occur in a geographic context. As in most industrial sectors, there is a distinct logic behind the poultry business's economic geography. Poultry can be raised in most areas, and

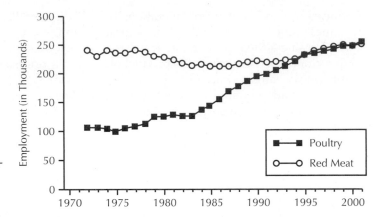

FIGURE 2 Employment in poultry and red meat products industry, 1972–2001. *Source:* U.S. Department of Labor, 1972–2001.

before large firms took over, it was a very competitive industry, because almost anyone could grow chickens almost anywhere. Some locations, however, have certain advantages, and in a competitive market, one seeks advantage by minimizing the most expensive inputs. For poultry, the key inputs are feed and climate. The Southeast, it turns out, has both an ideal climate for raising chickens and access to low-cost grain. Data from the Census of Agricul-ture show that the Southeast was producing over half of the nation's chicken slaughter products as early as 1963; in recent years, the proportion has increased to roughly two-thirds (USDA 1960– 2000).

The expansion and consolidation of the poultry industry in the Southeast has occurred within the context of a simultaneous economic transformation that, in just a few decades, changed the American South from a relatively depressed region to an economi-cally booming destination (Cobb 1982; Griffith 1995). This economic growth began in the 1960s with the active recruitment of manufacturing industries and promotion of the South as a competitive location for firms seeking a low-wage, nonunionized work-force. With the rediscovery of the Sunbelt as a vacation and retirement destination, the tourism and retirement-community indus-tries expanded significantly.

Tourists and retirees embody two popu-lations which economic development offi-cials everywhere hope to attract, because they use relatively few social services and inject much of their disposable income into the local economy. However, they may un-balance local labor markets, because while they create a large demand for service, con-struction, and other types of workers, they contribute little, if anything, to the local labor supply.

Hispanics in The Poultry Industry

Attracting workers to the poultry industry is a growing challenge. Nationwide, wages paid in the industry are significantly higher than the minimum wage. However, at $7.39 an hour as of 1997, they had not changed in real terms in more than thirty years and remained among the lowest for manufacturing and food industry employment (Hetrick 1994; U.S. Department of Commerce [DOC] 1967–1997). The wage data we used do not specify region, but wages in southern states were probably below the average. Unionization rates, never high in the South in general, have remained well below 5 percent in meat-processing industries since the early 1980s, according to the Current Population Survey.

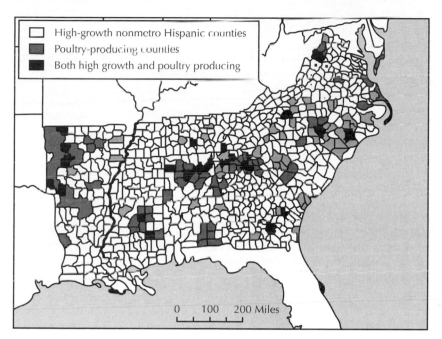

FIGURE 3   Poultry-producing and high-growth Hispanic counties, nine south-eastern states, 1990–2000. *Sources:* U.S. Department of Agriculture, 1987, 1992, 1997; U.S. Bureau of the Census 1990, 2000.

Poultry processing, like other meat processing, is a relatively hazardous and unattractive occupation, with harsh working conditions that have been continually exposed as bad in media and scholarly accounts (Bjerklie 1995; Sun and Escobar 1999). Moreover, economic growth that began in the early 1980s and continued for almost two decades created employment options that diminished relative incentives for working in the poultry industry.

Under these circumstances, it is not surprising that the poultry industry in the southeastern states has experienced difficulty finding a sufficient supply of local workers willing to accept their wages and working conditions. Consequently, the industry's expansion and concentration within a geographic region whose economic development was already creating an immense demand for low-skilled workers forced the sector to look elsewhere.

As with other low-skill, low-wage industries, the poultry business began actively recruiting immigrants, most coming from Mexico and Central America. Numerous reports have documented the extreme lengths firms have gone to recruit workers for their plants (Barboza 2001). For a region that had low absolute numbers of Hispanics, the size of the poultry-processing workforce has grown significantly.

The results of these recruiting efforts can be seen in Figure 3, which maps the confluence of the location of significant poultry production with Hispanic settlement within the nine southeastern states. Areas denoted by light shading represent counties in these states which, according to the U.S. Census of Agriculture, ranked, in 1987, 1992, and 1997, within the top 100 chicken-producing counties in the nation. Areas with crosshatching represent rapid-growth nonmetropolitan

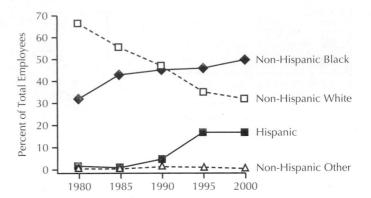

FIGURE 4 Racial and ethnic composition of meat-processing industry employees, nine southeastern states, 1980–2000. *Source:* U.S. Department of Commerce, 1963–1997.

Hispanic counties, defined as those in which the Hispanic population grew in absolute and percentage terms by one thousand persons and 150 percent, respectively, between 1990 and 2000. Combining the two patterns yields counties that overlap, shown in solid black. Note that while the rapid Hispanic growth counties are nonmetropolitan, the poultry-growing counties include nonmetropolitan as well as metropolitan counties. Since the Census of Agriculture data refer to where poultry is raised, as opposed to where it is slaughtered and processed, we would expect most of the poultry counties to be in rural, nonmetropolitan areas. Moreover, because of the economics of poultry transportation, we can reasonably assume that most are close to poultry-processing facilities. Thus, contiguous counties in Figure 3 account for a significant number of all counties highlighted.

The proximity of the Hispanic population to poultry-producing regions is unmistakable, and when combined with the qualitative evidence on recruiting practices, it provides a clear picture of the close connection between the poultry industry and Hispanic population growth. Duplin County in North Carolina, for example, has seen its Hispanic population increase by almost seven thousand since the 1990s, owing in no small part to the demand for labor in its Carolina Turkey, Nash Johnson, and Butterball

Turkey plants. The Hispanic population in Hall County, Georgia, has grown by twenty-three thousand, not only because of its proximity to Atlanta, but also because of the poultry plants in the town of Gainsville. Marshall County in Alabama employs over three thousand poultry workers, owing to a Tyson Poultry plant in Guntersville, and its Hispanic population has grown by forty-three hundred in the same period.

We have argued that the transformations in this industry correlate with Hispanic population growth in the area. As such, we would expect important changes in the racial and ethnic composition of the labor force working in the poultry industry. However, it is unclear whether Hispanics are replacing or complementing blacks and whites. Figure 4 presents changes in the racial and ethnic composition of the labor force in the meat-processing industry between 1980 and 2000, using Current Population Survey (CPS) data (DOC 1963–1997). Meat processing is a broad category that includes the processing of red meat, pork, turkey, and chicken. However, outside of some pork processing in Mississippi, North Carolina, and Virginia, almost all meat processing in the nine southeastern states consists of poultry processing.

Changes in the racial and ethnic composition of the industry are telling of the potential differential effect of migration on racial groups. Whites have dropped from just under 70 percent to just over 30 percent of the workforce. The proportion of blacks has increased from 30 percent to 50 percent, and the proportion of Hispanics has increased from one percent to 17 percent. Figure 2 shows that the actual number of workers in the poultry industry nationwide had more than doubled between 1980 and 2001, so the lower percentage of whites does not necessarily indicate that there are fewer whites involved in poultry processing, but it does indicate that there are many more blacks and Hispanics.

Because the CPS tends to undercount Hispanics, these percentages are conservative. To provide some sense of the potential understatement, consider the case of hired farmworkers, another employment group with a high proportion of Hispanics. The National Agricultural Workers Survey, considered the most representative survey of farmworkers, places the Hispanic composition of the agricultural farmworker population at more than double the proportion estimated by the CPS.

The National Agricultural Workers Survey evaluates the degree to which immigrant labor complements or substitutes for domestic workers. Hispanics may be replacing non-Hispanic whites, which, assuming the latter are moving into higher-paying jobs, leaves everyone better off. Non-Hispanic blacks may also be leaving the poultry industry in absolute numbers, but their increasing proportion suggests that immigrants may be competing for the same low-skill jobs.

We now turn to case studies of two poultry-producing counties in the Southeast to illustrate how some of the issues noted above—the rapid incorporation of Hispanics into the American South and the consequent impact on receiving communities—manifest in real places. We consider one county in Virginia and one in North Carolina that typ-ify the economic and demographic patterns that we suggest are occurring throughout the southeastern United States.

Accomack County, Virginia, and Duplin County, North Carolina

Accomack County, along the eastern shoreline of Virginia, is the northern part of a slender peninsula at the base of the well-known Delmarva (Delaware-Maryland-Virginia) poultry-producing region. Duplin County, along the southeastern coastal plain of North Carolina, is among the leading turkey-producing counties in the country.

These two nonmetropolitan counties reflect similar population and economic conditions. By 2000, Accomack and Duplin Counties had populations of thirty-eight thousand and forty-nine thousand, respectively, and their 1997 median household incomes of roughly $25,000 and $27,000 were well below the $40,000 and $35,000 averages for Virginia and North Carolina, respectively. Temperate climates in both areas are well suited for raising poultry and growing corn, soybeans, and other feed grains used by the industry. In addition, both counties have long been known for their production of cash crops, including vegetables, fruit, nursery and greenhouse crops, and tobacco. As one drives south from the Maryland border along Virginia's Highway 13 or along I-40 across North Carolina, farmland, food stands, and the occasional tourist billboard interrupt the rural landscape. Few locations have sizable populations or notable geographies beyond one or two traffic lights; according to one Accomack County resident, "There isn't any town here, there are towns."

Poultry Plants

Virginia ranks eighth or ninth in broiler output, and Accomack County produces about

10 percent of that. Two processing plants, the Tyson plant in Temperanceville and the Perdue plant in the town of Accomac, have been in business for over thirty years and together employed roughly twenty-six hundred persons in 2002. Both Tyson and Perdue are among the top four poultry-producing firms in the nation, and their plants are among the largest in the Delmarva region (Delmarva Poultry Industry [DPI] 2002). Temperanceville is not incorporated; since Accomac is the county seat, it is there that most of the poultry regulation and social-service provision occurs.

North Carolina's annual output of forty-one million turkeys ranks second in the nation, and Duplin County produces one-quarter of that. The poultry industry in the county began in the early 1950s and soon became Duplin County's largest industry. In 1986, Carolina Turkeys built the nation's largest turkey-processing plant in the town of Mount Olive. In 2002, the plant employed close to three thousand workers and had become the world's largest turkey-processing facility, with integrated operations that combined diagnostic labs, research farms, breeder farms, hatcheries, growing farms, and feed mills. Additional poultry plants include Nash Johnson & Sons, Butterball Turkey, and House of Raeford, which together employ an additional twenty-two hundred workers.

Hispanics

Hispanic population growth in Accomack and Duplin Counties during the 1990s illustrates the dramatic inflow of Latinos into southern communities. In 1990, the census counted 450 and 1,015 Hispanics in Accomack and Duplin Counties, respectively. By 2000, the numbers were 1,680 and 7,426, representing increases of 272 and 633 percent, respectively.

These changes altered the racial and ethnic makeup of both counties as they rapidly moved from a biracial white-black population to a multiethnic population with significant Hispanic representation. As of 2000, the population of Accomack had become 62.0 percent white, 31.0 percent black, and 5.5 percent Hispanic, while that of Duplin County had became 55.0 percent white, 29.0 percent black, and 15.0 percent Hispanic. Disaggregating by national origin shows that most Latinos are Mexicans and represent around 65 percent of the Latino population in both counties. Next in line are Guatemalans, 20 percent of Accomack County's Hispanic population, and Hondurans, 15 percent of the same in Duplin County. Differences in the country of origin of the Latino population reflect the highly structured process guiding migration decisions and the role work, friends, and family networks in determining the destinations of individual migrants (Massey and Espinosa 1997). For example, informants in Accomack County indicate that a sizable portion of the Guatemalan population actually originates from a single *departamento* (province) of the country.

Moreover, while the census captures permanently settled Hispanics, it often undercounts the large number of seasonal agricultural migrant workers who pass through both counties. These annual migratory streams usually begin in Florida or Texas and continue through Georgia and the Carolinas before stopping in the Delmarva Peninsula. Seasonal workers typically work for farm-labor contractors and accompany them from one location to another. While traveling through these counties, in either direction, some migrants find work in the poultry plants and decide to stay. Since poultry work is year-round, those who switch from agricultural work to poultry processing have a greater likelihood of settling permanently.

An example from Duplin County illustrates the close connection between seasonal and permanent migration. One of our interviewees, currently a high-ranking administrator coordinating housing services for one poultry plant, initiated his migration experience when a relative, a former seasonal farmworker, decided to settle in North Carolina. In the late 1970s, growing employment opportunities in the poultry industry provided seasonal workers a channel for upward mobility. After settling in Duplin County, the relative sent word to the interviewee's family about promising employment opportunities in the United States, triggering our interviewee's first U.S. trip in 1980. Most of his brothers and sisters, using his settlement, family networks, and waves of legalizations in the 1980s, followed by the end of the decade. In 2000, his mother immigrated with his youngest sister. Thus, after twenty-two years of experience in the United States, this Mexican family from the State of Veracruz was reconstituted in North Carolina. Only his father remains in Mexico, despite our interviewee's assurances that life in the United States is not so bad and that the whole family awaits his arrival.

Employment Context

The majority of Hispanic immigrants in Accomack County work in agriculture, not poultry processing, even though the relative size of both industries in the county is roughly the same. In Duplin County, the mix is about equal. Agricultural work typically pays the current minimum wage of $5.15 per hour, although piece-rate pay scales during the harvest season may roughly double this. Poultry plant employment, on the other hand, is year-round work with a starting wage of about $8.00 per hour and includes health and retirement benefits. Any employment progression from agriculture to poultry processing tends to convert residency tenure from temporary to permanent. Some selectivity of legal status occurs;

agricultural farmworkers are more likely to be unauthorized than are poultry workers, whose legal documents are more carefully reviewed.

While the processing of poultry is considered year-round work, a significant portion of the workforce cycles through for short periods (Griffith 1995; Horowitz and Miller 1999). Workers may leave because they don't like the work, are using poultry work as stopgap employment between farm-labor jobs, visit family in their home countries, or because they have violated attendance rules. Some also leave to maintain seasonal migration patterns with their undocumented family members. Firms, anticipating that a significant number of hires will leave within months of starting, adjust their wage and benefits structures to reward workers who stay for over six months. According to unofficial estimates and anecdotal reports, turnover rates in poultry plants average from 70 percent annually, with considerable variation by plant. In North Carolina, the high turnover rates permit poultry workers to qualify for programs providing assistance to seasonal workers.

The dynamics of migration and working conditions contribute to the high turnover rate. In addition, crackdowns on undocumented migrants after September 11, 2001, have also affected the stability of poultry employment. There are increasing reports of employees and employers receiving letters from the Social Security Administration notifying them of violations. Employees are notified first, usually because they have used a false or incorrect Social Security number. If the employee does not correct the situation, a letter is sent to the employer, who must notify the employee and terminate employment.

The racial composition of agricultural and poultry workers in Accomack County resembles that found in the nine southeastern states surveyed. Although exact figures do not exist, industry officials estimate the makeup of the poultry-processing workforce nationwide at approximately 50 percent black, 40 percent white, and 10 percent Hispanic. In Duplin County, the Hispanic component in poultry is far greater, approaching 65 percent in one plant.

Within plants, fairly rigid racial and ethnic divisions characterize productive activities, with most whites and some blacks occupying managerial positions and Hispanics confined to manual work in production, packing, mailing, and housekeeping. These divisions have several sources. As one of our informants observed, inability to speak English and low levels of education are central factorsin maintaining Hispanics in manual positions. At the same time, what he considered cultural differences also facilitate segrega-tion of activities along racial and ethnic lines.

Labor Market and Demographic Impacts

A central question driving most arguments in favor of or against immigration is the extent to which Hispanic inflows displace or complement local workers. Particularly important is the interaction between Hispanic employment and labor-market outcomes of other minority groups, especially African Americans. While this question well exceeds the scope of this chapter, we contend that labor-market compositional shifts are intertwined with industrial transformations. When such shifts are applied to the poultry industry, we can expect growth in product demand, industrial concentration, and production variability to facilitate demand for Hispanic workers. In this process, Hispanic population inflows do not necessarily imply worker displacement, because all three macrotrends create additional employment.

Some of these expectations are confirmed by our two case studies. Despite very rapid population growth, the unemployment rate declined in Accomack and Duplin Counties, from 9.6 percent to 4.2 percent, and from 8.6 percent to 5.0 percent, respectively, between 1992 and 2000 (DOC 2002). In fact, in 2001, the unemployment rates in both counties were much lower than the nationwide nonmetropolitan average. In addition, when asked why poultry companies were increasingly hiring Hispanic workers, our informants consistently replied that new jobs were opening up and that nobody else wanted them. This is especially true in Duplin County, with its large, new Carolina Turkeys processing plant. In such a context, the expectation of worker displacement may not be reasonable.

Moreover, informants acknowledged the creation of many skilled positions in, for example, administrative, government, or educational employment for which Hispanics do not qualify. Overall, evidence suggests that while industrial transformations in the poultry industry expanded the demand for low-skilled workers and thus attracted Hispanics, the concomitant and multiplicative effect of economic growth and population increase also facilitated upward occupational mobility and better employment for more educated local residents.

In addition to their racial and ethnic impact on the labor market, Hispanic inflows change the demography of Accomack and Duplin Counties in other ways. Two changes are particularly relevant: gender composition and age distribution.

Gender ratios in these counties vary significantly by racial and ethnic group. According to the 2000 Census, the number of men per 100 women in Accomack County is 94 for whites, 85 for blacks, and 166 for Hispanics. In Duplin County, the gender ratio is 95 for whites, 84 for blacks, and 156 for

Hispanics. For the United States as a whole, the gender ratio for Hispanics is 105 men per 100 women. Clearly, the two counties are anomalies within the United States, reflecting the predominantly male component of recent immigration there.

In addition, differences in gender ratios highlight a diverging pattern between Hispanics and blacks. The relative undersupply of women in the Hispanic case contradicts their relative oversupply among African Americans. Studies have found that gender ratios have significant importance in marriage patterns, particularly among blacks, making it more difficult for individuals to find partners in contexts of unbalanced gender markets (Lichter, LeClere, and McLaughlin 1991; Lichter et al. 1992). It is unclear how these patterns will affect the marriage behavior of single Hispanic men and women (Oropesa and Lichter 1994; Parrado and Zenteno In press). If Hispanic men try to find partners in the United States, the relative undersupply of Hispanic women may promote interracial marriage. Alternatively, to the extent that marriage is still constrained across racial and ethnic lines, single men may be forced to return to their local communities to find a partner (Parrado 2002). In this scenario, gender imbalances can also affect patterns of return migration. Given their cultural background, forming a union is still a central personal objective among Hispanics, particularly Mexicans. Conversations with immigrants in these communities suggest that gender imbalances and the difficulties in finding a partner, above and beyond economic success, critically affect settlement decisions.

In addition, gender imbalances have an effect on broader sexual behaviors. Immigrant communities are particularly vulnerable to the proliferation of prostitution and other forms of sexually risky behaviors. Use of prostitutes is particularly prevalent among single and married migrants who leave their families behind, which increases the risk of spreading sexually transmitted diseases, including AIDS. In fact, researchers have hypo thesized that migration to the United States is a central contributor to the diffusion of the AIDS epidemic in Mexico, even in rural areas (McQuiston and Parrado 2002; Mishra, Conner, and Magaña 1996). Within the guidelines of the Healthy People objectives established by the U.S. Department of Health and Human Services, Latino organizations in Duplin County have begun to address sexually risky behavior by developing training programs and educational campaigns promoting condom use and AIDS prevention.

The other demographic trait with striking community impacts, age distribution, varies similarly across racial and ethnic groups. Figure 5 plots the percentage of the population in different age groups by race and ethnicity in Duplin County; patterns for Accomack County are very similar. Hispanics represent a much younger population than either blacks or whites. If we look at migration dynamics, the percentage Hispanic peaks very early, zero to nine years old and again at twenty to twenty-four; it declines at older ages. The two peaks reflect the fact that labor migration is initiated in the early twenties, while children migrate early on or are born following their parents' settlement. The age distribution of blacks and whites is more even, with relatively higher proportions above age forty.

The age distribution of the Hispanic population has affected local communities in these counties in two ways. First, the rapid arrival of school-aged children has increased demand for educational facilities and contributed to school overcrowding. In addition, given the lack of knowledge of English among students and their parents, their arrival has suddenly increased the need for English as a second language (ESL) classes

FIGURE 5 Age distribution, by race and ethnicity, Duplin County, North Carolina, 2000. *Source:* U.S. Bureau of the Census 2000.

as well as interpreters to facilitate parent-teacher communication. The challenges that immigrants pose for public education systems are particularly relevant; some schools in Duplin County have become 50 percent Hispanic within the space of just a few years. Educators in both counties often find that the new arrivals have little educational background or familiarity with the U.S. educational system. Financing is particularly problematic. In Duplin County, for instance, Carolina Turkeys has recognized the tremendous burden that ESL classes pose on school budgets and now provides financial assistance for their provision.

Second, younger populations increase the prevalence of certain risk behaviors, including crime, alcoholism, and motor vehicle accidents. The higher representation of Hispanics in younger groups makes them particularly vulnerable to such problems, and special programs to address these issues might be required. In addition, age can also affect racial and ethnic relations. Research on neighborhood transitions in cities like Chicago shows that resistance to ethnic change stems not only from the different ethnicity of the arriving population but also from its youth (Flippen 2001). Elderly residents, in particular, may feel threatened by the arrival of younger groups, who they

sense can disrupt their way of life or increase their vulnerability to crime. Such feelings can fuel anti-immigrant sentiments among native residents.

Community Impacts and Reaction

Signs of a Hispanic influx into Accomack County in the 1990s generally appeared muted, with only an occasional store sign in Spanish to suggest the presence of Hispanics. From the perspective of social-service delivery, however, indications of a Hispanic presence have cropped up in many small ways. The county court now has a certified court interpreter; previously, anyone with some bilingual ability would be asked to volunteer a translation for defendants. The two health clinics in the area now have Spanish-speaking personnel. The local hospital now uses a commercial phone service to automatically translate conversations. Some county schools have begun canvassing other districts for Spanish-speaking teachers. Employees at the Virginia Employment Commission frequently help Hispanic workers find new or better-paying jobs and often provide emergency food aid, a benefit frequently requested by those just arriving. However, other services, such as securing a driver's license or alcohol counseling, still require people to find their own translator or interpreter. At the community level, Hispanics now enjoy soccer matches all day each Sunday, a local weekly radio program in Spanish, a small Spanish-language newspaper, and church services in Spanish.

In Duplin County, where community impacts are more noticeable, several institutions have emerged that specifically attend to the needs of the Hispanic population and facilitate assimilation and incorporation into U.S. society. Latinos Unidos, for example, provides information about health and legal issues, offers ESL classes, and trains community members to serve local communities. County government has also adapted to the growing Latino community. A leadership program offered through a local college to promote entrepreneurship is now being reformatted into Spanish, an effort that has had a measurable impact on the emergence of Hispanic businesses. Small grocery, video, and music stores cater directly to the Hispanic community and can easily be identified when visiting the counties. In addition, Carolina Turkeys donated two lots to local Hispanic residents on which to construct churches.

Not surprisingly, Hispanic growth is changing the cultural landscape of these communities, from the types of food and consumer goods being sold in stores to the festivities that are celebrated. These changes sometimes occur in conjunction with shifts within the companies that hire Hispanics. For instance, in September 2000, workers from Carolina Turkeys in Duplin County organized an international festival to recognize the growing diversity of the county's Hispanic population. During the successful Semana de la Hispanicidad (Hispanic Heritage Week) in 2001, flags from every Latin American country were posted throughout the company's hallways. Following their lead, black employees decided to celebrate

African-American Week in January 2002. In 2002, Carolina Turkeys invited the Mexican consul to give a speech in Duplin County, a widely publicized event that drew over three hundred people, garnered media attention for the Latino population, and created closer links with other groups. Many hope these kinds of initiatives will increase awareness and understanding of the growing diversity of Duplin County's population.

None of the informants we interviewed in Accomack and Duplin Counties suggested that the growth of the Hispanic population had caused concern among community residents, and they offered several reasons for the amenable reception. As part of the Delmarva region, Accomack County has been accustomed for decades to hosting migrants who work in the area's vegetable and grain farms. Moreover, the growth of the Hispanic population here was never as dramatic as it has been in some southeastern towns, such as Siler City, North Carolina, or Dalton, Georgia, where large numbers of Hispanics have recently settled in areas with relatively smaller base populations. In addition, there is increasing recognition of the contribution of the Hispanic population to the local economies. As one informant acknowledged, "We understand that without them, our vegetables wouldn't be picked because we don't have domestic workers that can do the job—or that would want to do the job."

When pressed, however, some of our informants mentioned hearing gripes about job competition between the Hispanic migrant workers and local blacks. Another issue that disturbs local residents in both counties is the trafficking in false driver's licenses, particularly because some of the recipients have little or no driving experience. Hispanic residents, on the other hand, are worried about crime and being targeted for robbery, in particular, because they often carry their money with them or keep their savings in their houses instead of in banks.

Racial and ethnic inequalities in access to housing also create tension. In Accomack County, 82 percent of white households live in owner-occupied housing units, compared with 63 percent of black households, and only 36 percent of Hispanic households. Figures for Duplin County are almost identical. In addition, Hispanics tend to live in overcrowded conditions in both counties, with an average household size of 4.5 persons compared with 2.5 for blacks and whites. Management at Carolina Turkeys in Duplin County and the Tyson and Perdue plants in Accomack County recognize the companies' role in providing adequate rental housing for Hispanic workers and have built homes or purchased house trailers close to their plants.

Conclusions and Policy Implications

In this chapter, we have presented evidence to illustrate how industrial restructuring correlates with changes in labor force composition and, by implication, with patterns of international migration and settlement. If similar trends in industrial development occur in other industries, we can expect them to generate further migration and population change. The visibility of prominent manufacturing firms will require greater attention by policy makers to labor-recruitment practices and the growing number of proposals for changing current immigration policies.

To show how industrial restructuring of the poultry industry plays out at the local level, we presented two case studies of poultry-producing counties in the Southeast, both with similar structural characteristics, but at different phases in their incorporation of Hispanic workers. To the extent that recent local history has been relatively incident free, these vignettes offer some degree of guarded optimism for the incorporation of Hispanic immigrants into the rural South as they create what Haverluk (1998) calls "new communities."

Nevertheless, a central concern of researchers is the degree to which outcomes of industrial development, such as international migration, differentially affect native residents. A sizable literature suggests that the presence of immigrant labor can be significant for wages, benefits, and working conditions (U.S. Department of Labor 1989). Moreover, as the relatively rapid settlement of immigrants in rural communities continues, it may also exacerbate existing patterns of spatial separation and inequality. This may require greater local expenditures on social services and programs that facilitate social integration between new and established residents. Given the geographic proximity of Mexico to the United States, increasing economic integration resulting from the North American Free Trade Agreement, age-specific migration, immigration laws favoring family reunification, and relatively high fertility, Hispanic demographic growth in rural areas will invariably increase. Consequently, many of the issues discussed above will likely continue for the foreseeable future.

SEEING THE BIG PICTURE

In the Appendix, examine the high school dropout rates for Latinos in the Education section (Section I), then look at the occupations where Latinos are clustered, shown in the Occupations section (Section VIII). What does a "good" job require in a postindustrial service economy and what might this mean for Latino immigrants?

RACE, REPRESENTATIONS, AND THE MEDIA— DRUG DEALERS, MAIDS, AND MAMMIES: THE ROLE OF STEREOTYPES IN THE MEDIA

35

BROADCAST NEWS PORTRAYAL OF MINORITIES: ACCURACY IN REPORTING

Roger D. Klein • Stacy Naccarato

QUESTIONS TO CONSIDER

Think for a moment about your favorite local television news station. How does this news program portray racial minorities in your community? Which groups are likely to be portrayed as victims or criminals? Who is portrayed as being demanding, aggressive, or dangerous? What color are the heroes, authority figures, or experts? Which groups are portrayed negatively and which are portrayed favorably? How and why does this happen? Roger Klein and Stacy Naccarato explain that biased and sensational news coverage is not what viewers want but reflect the subtle bias in and out of the newsroom.

A study reported late last year by the Project for Excellence in Journalism (Rosenstiel, Gottlieb, & Brady, 2000) suggests that local television news is in trouble. Viewers are abandoning local news in droves, leaving what was once considered "the most popular and trusted source of information in the country" (p. 84). Why are viewers leaving? The report concludes that it is a lack of quality. Carl Gottlieb (personal communication, June 2001), a former televi-

sion news director and a coauthor of the study, noted that viewers want information, they want value, and they resent the tricks that local news plays to try and hook viewers. The authors believe that local television news is at a crossroad, and they are not particularly optimistic.

But the heart of their report focuses on what successful local news stations do to increase ratings. Surprisingly, the answer is improved quality. One small part of what many successful stations do to improve quality is to reduce crime coverage. They also provide greater context for the crime stories they do cover. They explain crime stories and rather than scaring the audience, they provide

Klein/Naccarato, *American Behavioral Scientist,* Vol. 46, Issue 12, pp. 1612–1616, Copyright © 2003 by Sage Publications. Reprinted with permission of Sage Publications.

balance and relevance. Those findings, we believe, are reasons for optimism. They also connect to the major theme of this article.

How are minorities portrayed on local television news? Studies surveying local news in Chicago (Linton & LeBailly, 1998), Los Angeles (Dixon & Linz, 2000), and Philadelphia (Romer, Jamieson, & deCoteau, 1998) have come to similar conclusions. Blacks and Latinos are more likely than Whites to be portrayed as perpetrators. In addition, in two of these studies (Dixon & Linz, 2000; Romer et al., 1998), it has been shown that Whites are overrepresented as homicide victims, compared to crime statistics, whereas Blacks and Latinos are underrepresented as victims. Even local television news stations have acknowledged a problem in the portrayal of minorities. In 1999, San Francisco's KRON-TV produced a two-part series on racism in the news, examining local coverage of minorities and examining race-related issues in their own newsroom (http://www.sfgate.com/cgi-bin/ramhurl .cgi?file=1991/10/21-race_kronv.rm).

In Pittsburgh, we examined 3 weeks of local television newscasts last year and found almost 80% of the references to Blacks, the area's largest minority, to be negative. By contrast, less than two thirds of references to Whites were rated as negative. Put differently, only 22% of stories about Blacks were positive. An almost four-to-one negative-to-positive ratio is troubling.

An equally troubling problem is a lack of context in the crime stories reported on local television news. For example, a rash of murders in Pittsburgh in the spring of 2001 resulted in the total number of homicides through mid-August, exceeding the total in all of 2000. Naturally, there was consider-able media attention given to the increase. Local television news presented the bare facts and there was little context. On the other hand, the major local Pittsburgh

newspaper, *The Pittsburgh Post-Gazette,* provided context. The focus on context is an importan one. Throughout the past two years, about 80% of both the murder victims and the suspects in Pittsburgh have been Black. The broader newspaper coverage, along with editorial coverage (e.g., Craig, 2001), helped readers to understand that the majority of these Black-on-Black homicides appear to have been committed by a small number of people in the African American community. The newspaper also outlined some of the possible causes. Dorfman and Schiraldi (in press) note that White Americans exaggerate the threat of victimization by minorities. They note that Whites believe that they are more likely to be victimized by a member of a minority group, whereas statistics show that they are actually 3 times more likely to be victimized by another White person. The Pittsburgh newspaper does not encourage the readership to view Blacks as dangerous. But television news, with its lack of context, may well contribute to viewers' fears.

Some researchers (e.g., Dixon & Linz, 2000) believe that ethnic misrepresentation on local television news may result in a belief by viewers that the real world is similar to the television world. In data we have collected with different age groups ranging from middle-school students to senior citizens, between 70% and 97% of respondents agree with the statement "Local TV news shows me the way the world really is" (Klein & Cox, 1992, p. 4). One way to interpret these data is by concluding that for many of these Pittsburgh respondents, the television news world has become the real world. Have their attitudes toward African Americans been shaped by the negative-to-positive story ratio described above? Perhaps.

It isn't only adult minorities who are portrayed as criminals on local news.

Minority youth are shown as criminals far more often than young Whites (Dorfman & Schiraldi, in press). Actually, it has been shown that the media portray youth of all races as violent, and one study in California (Dorfman, 1993, cited in Dorfman & Schiraldi, in press) demonstrated that less than 2% of stories about youth show their accomplishments. Dorfman (personal communication, June 2001) has suggested that people who have little personal contact with youth tend to view them as violent if they get most of their information about them from print and electronic media.

Are audiences aware of minority misrepresentation? Yes. One study (Linton, 1995) showed that African Americans' main complaint about news coverage was that it contained too much negativity about Blacks and excessive emphasis on crime. A national poll by CNN/*USA Today*/Gallup (Sharp & Puente, 1994) concluded that almost 40% of Hispanics were upset with news coverage of issues important to them and two thirds of African Americans reported being upset at least once per week by news coverage of Black issues. A national poll of 1,200 children in 1998 conducted by Children Now found that in all of the racial groups surveyed (African American, Asian, Latino, and White), children reported that news media tend to portray African American and Latino people more negatively than White and Asian people, particularly when the news is about young people. A survey of 100 graduate students at the University of Pittsburgh (Klein & Smith, 2000) adds to these findings. Half of the respondents were Black and half were White. Almost 80% of White students and 96% of Blacks agreed that local television news misrepresents minorities, but only 16% of Whites and 30% of Blacks believed that news misrepresents White people. Many of the students also believe that the media intentionally misrepresent minorities. Eighty-

six percent of Blacks and 40% of Whites believe misrepresentation is intentional. Although the Black/White opinion difference for this question is statistically significant, the fact that 40% of Whites agreed that news intentionally misrepresents Blacks is itself impressive. Contrast that with only 6% of Whites and 20% of Blacks agreeing that local television news intentionally misrepresents Whites.

Why does local news overrepresent minorities as criminals? First, we should ask why local news overrepresents crime stories in general. The two most common explanations are ratings and convenience: Crime sells and crime stories are easy to do; at least they are easy to do the way most stations do them.

The most common explanations offered for minority misrepresentation are racism and economic gain. Some researchers (e.g., Romer et al., 1998) believe that stations participate in a policy of ethnic blame. They note that Whites own most of the mass media organizations, they influence news content, they want to portray their group favorably, and they blame people of color for their problems. Heider (2000) suggests that some stations and advertisers believe that this ethnic blame approach appeals to a largely White television news audience. The Project for Excellence in Journalism (Rosenstiel et al., 2000) report noted that one third of the local stations surveyed claimed that news content was influenced by advertiser wishes. Finally, Heider has argued that news directors, who are mostly White, suffer from what he calls "incognizant racism"—they are not intentionally racist but rather are simply unaware of their own attitudes.

Given all of these problems, what can be done to try and change local television news? Continuing with Heider's (2000) belief that some news people may be unaware of their behavior, we find the work behind the scenes at KRON-TV to be an excellent example of how news personnel can be made aware. The station formed a committee to examine race relations within the news division and worked with San Francisco State University to assess the accuracy and fairness of coverage of the different racial groups living within the viewing area. Such commitment takes time, cooperation, trust, and management support, and obviously KRON provided that sort of environment. More local news stations should try and follow in their footsteps, but we believe that is much easier to say than do.

Of course, in local television news, ratings and profits are the name of the game. Here, we believe the results of the Project for Excellence in Journalism study are again germane. As mentioned before, they concluded that quality journalism sells. They ranked stations from "A" to "F" based on quality and concluded that "64% of 'A' quality stations were building ratings, a higher percentage than any other grade and nearly double most grades" (Rosenstiel et al., 2000, p. 84). There were some key elements that went into an "A" rating, including greater coverage of the community and longer stories. But master stations (those with consistently high quality rankings and rising ratings over 3 years), as noted before, also aired fewer crime stories. Fewer crime stories may translate into greater profits.

Many local television news stations, however, are set in their ways. For years, news consulting organizations have been promoting emotionalism and sensationalism, and many of the stations have listened. In fact, Carl Gottlieb (personal communication, June 2001) noted that if he were still a news director and was reading his own report recommending quality journalism and less crime coverage, he'd say, "What, are you kidding?" In other words, change will not be easy. But Gottlieb added that out of desperation, out of fear of losing even more viewers, local stations are just beginning to listen.

Notice that it is not suggested that local television news stations eliminate crime stories. But fewer crime stories will almost certainly mean fewer opportunities to misrepresent minorities. Of course, an overall reduction in negative stories does not necessarily mean that the relative imbalance between Black and White crime stories will be reduced.

Again, the Project for Excellence in Journalism found that quality sells and that providing context is also important. By offering context rather than just a very brief 20 seconds of post-homicide or post-robbery video, stations can help to better educate viewers. By focusing more on information and less on sensationalism, there also might be less focus on skin color. Dorfman (1997) has written a handbook on crime coverage for journalists. In the handbook, she encourages reporters covering a homicide to ask a question they often ask when covering a car crash: "Was alcohol involved?" Dorfman says most reporters are not trained to ask the alcohol question at a homicide, but as a public health researcher, Dorfman knows that alcohol is as likely to be involved in a homicide as in a car crash. By improving the nature of crime coverage, reporters can better inform the public about issues that really matter and possibly reduce some of the biases mentioned earlier.

A nationwide study of local news directors (Driscol & Splichal, 1998) supports the belief that news directors are concerned. More than 70% of the 147 news directors responding agreed that their newscasts are scaring members of the community, and 52% agreed that audiences are fed up with this approach. Because local stations are losing viewers and because news directors are sensitive to some of these issues, the time may be ripe for change. But because news is first and foremost a business, it will be more effective to approach stations from a financial angle. Along these lines, recent data from a study by Bushman and Bonnaci (2001) suggest that television viewers are less likely to recall commercial messages when programming has violent content. Although Bushman did not specifically study televisionnews, it is possible that the same principle applies. Advertisers might be interested in these findings.

We also should consider the work of Urban Affairs Professor Danilo Yanich. Yanich (personal communication, June 2001) goes into the community and trains news viewers in critical viewing skills. He suggests that as they watch a news story they use a mental stop—called a critical pause—and that they question a story's purpose and its value. Yanich suggests viewers call local stations when they are concerned or upset by a story. Yanich, who is at the University of Delaware, also has fostered good relationships with local news directors and has been successful in discussing with them the problems created by biased and inadequate crime coverage.

There are also efforts by major news organizations. For example, the Radio and TV News Directors Association (RTNDA) has taken a proactive stand. They have supported efforts to hire people of color in news management roles, promoted the need for diversity in the newsroom, and conducted annual surveys assessing the number of minorities working in news broadcasting. For the current year, the number of minorities in television news hit a record high of 24.6%. Eight percent of news directors were minorities. However, in radio news, minority participation was 10.8%, barely above the decade low set in 2000 (http://www.rtndf.org/news/2001/minsurvey.shtml).

In concluding, we would like to propose that more psychologists become involved in researching television news. Quite a few psychologists study television in general but not the news. We are unclear as to why that is the case. Notice that many of the experts cited herein come from the fields of communications, public health, and urban affairs. We believe that psychologists can make valuable contributions to the research literature and can help to implement change.

REFERENCES

Bushman, B., & Bonnaci, A. (2001). *Sex and violence impair memory for commercials.* Unpublished manuscript, Iowa State University.

Children Now. (1998, May 6). *A different world: Children's perceptions of race and class in media.* Oakland, CA: Author.

Craig, J. G. (2001, August 12). Murder most murky. *Pittsburgh Post-Gazette,* p. E-3.

Dixon, T. L., & Linz, D. (2000). Race and the misrepresentation of victimization on local television news. *Communication Research, 27,* 547–573.

Dorfman, L. (1997). *Reporting on violence: A handbook for journalists.* Berkeley, CA: Berkeley Media Studies Group.

Dorfman, L., & Schiraldi, V. (in press). Off balance: Youth, race and crime in the news. *Crime and Delinquency.*

Driscol, P., & Splichal, S.L. (1998). *Legal concerns in TV newsrooms: A national survey of local television news directors.* Paper presented at the annual convention of the Association for Educators in Journalism and Mass Communication, Baltimore.

Heider, D. (2000). *White news: Why local news programs don't cover people of color.* Mahwah, NJ: Lawrence Erlbaum Associates.

Klein, R. D., & Cox, R. C. (1992). *Audience reactions to local TV news: An extension.* Paper presented at the annual meeting of the American Psychological Association, Washington, DC.

Klein, R. D., & Smith, B. (2000). *Reactions of Black and White students to local TV news.* Unpublished manuscript, University of Pittsburgh.

Linton, C. (1995). *Multicultural news in Chicago: Does it make the grade? Ethnic leaders rate the* Chicago Tribune *and* Sun-Times. Evanston, IL: Gannett Urban Journalism Center, Northwestern University.

Linton, C. C., & LeBailly, R. K. (1998). *African-American and Latino views of local Chicago TV news*

(Working Paper WP-98-15). Chicago: Institute of Policy Research, Northwestern University.

Romer, D., Jamieson, K. H., & deCoteau, N. J. (1998). The treatment of persons of color in local television news. *Communication Research, 25,* 286–305.

Rosenstiel, T., Gottlieb, C., & Brady, L. E. (2000). Time of peril for TV news. *Columbia Journalism Review, 39,* 84–92.

Sharp, D., & Puente, M. (1994, July 26). Minorities consider the media unfair. *USA Today,* p. 1A.

SEEING THE BIG PICTURE

Section VIII on Occupations in the Appendix shows the racial composition of editors and reporters in the United States. Which groups are over- and underrepresented in these fields? How does a lack of racial minorities in the news production room shape the way racial minorities are presented in the mass media?

36

TELEVISION AND THE POLITICS OF REPRESENTATION

Justin Lewis • Sut Jhally

QUESTIONS TO CONSIDER

Justin Lewis and Sut Jhally use The Cosby Show *as a way to deconstruct the meaning of race, racial representations, and the role of social class in television. The authors argue that* The Cosby Show, *far from just being a well-written and successful situation comedy, sent a number of messages that were both positive and negative. What were they?*

O ne of the abiding concerns in contemporary North American culture has been the many attempts to deal with race and racial inequality. Because racism is often understood as a perception dependent on negative or stereotypical images, debates about race often have centered on the issue of representation, with analytical glances increasingly cast toward television, as the main image-maker in our culture.

To make sense of the many competing claims about the way black people are represented on television, we carried out an extensive study based on a content analysis of prime time television together with a series of 52 focus group interviews (made up of 26 white, 23 black, and 3 Latino groups) from a range of class backgrounds. The interviews were designed to probe attitudes about race and the media representation thereof. To facilitate these discussions, each interview began with the viewing of an episode of *The Cosby Show*.

The Cosby Show was chosen because it has, in many ways, changed the way television thinks about the portrayal of African Americans. During the time it took for *The Cosby Show* to go from being innovative to institutional, African Americans became a fairly common sight on network television in the United States. And not just any African Americans: Our content analysis confirmed that we now see a plethora of middle- and upper-middle-class black characters populating our screens. Major black characters—from *ER* to *Sportsnight*—are now much more likely to be well-heeled professionals than blue-collar workers. In this sense, Bill Cosby can be credited with spurring a move toward racial equality on television. Fictional characters on U.S. television always have tended to be middle or upper-middle class—and since the late 1980s, black people have become an equal and everyday part of this upwardly mobile world.

The Cosby Show was, in this sense, more than just another sitcom. It represents a turning point in television culture, to a new era in which black actors have possibilities beyond the indignities of playing a crude and limited array of black stereotypes, an era in which white audiences can accept TV programs with more than just an occasional "token" black character. There is, it seems, much to thank Bill Cosby for. He has, quite literally, changed the face of network television.

At first reading, our study suggested that the upward mobility of black representation precipitated by *The Cosby Show* was an unambiguously positive phenomenon. It appeared, from our focus groups, to promote an attitude of racial tolerance among white viewers, for whom black television characters have become ordinary and routine, and to generate a feeling of pride and relief among black viewers. But *The Cosby Show* and the new generation of black professionals on U.S. television are caught up in a set of cultural assumptions about race and class that complicates the political ramifications of such a trend.

It is true that, in recent decades, the size of the black middle class in the U.S. has grown. This much said, the social success of black TV characters in the wake of *The Cosby Show* does not reflect any overall trend toward black prosperity in the world beyond television. On the contrary, the period in which *The Cosby Show* dominated television ratings— 1984 to 1990—witnessed a comparative decline in the fortunes of most African Americans in the United States. The racial inequalities that scarred the United States before the civil rights movement could only be rectified by instituting major structural changes in the nation's social, political, and economic life—an idea informing Great Society interventions in the 1960s and 1970s. Since the election of Ronald Reagan in 1980, both Republican and Democratic administrations generally have withdrawn from any notion of large-scale public intervention in an iniquitous system, committing themselves instead to promoting a global free enterprise economy. This laissez-faire approach has resulted in the stagnation or gradual erosion of advances made by black people during the 1960s. For all the gains made in the fictional world of TV, by almost all demographic measures (such as education, health, levels of incarceration, income, and wealth), the United States remains a racially divided society.

As William Julius Wilson (1987) has documented, maintaining these divisions are a set of socioeconomic conditions that keep most people in their place. The "American Dream" of significant upward mobility is an aspiration that few can or will ever realize. It is an idea sustained by fictions and by anecdotes that focus on the exceptions rather than the rule of class division. If we are to begin any kind of serious analysis of racial inequalityin the United States, we must acknowledge the existence of the systematic disadvantages that exclude most people on low incomes in poor neighborhoods—a condition in which black people in the United States have disproportionately been placed—from serious economic advancement.

Left unchecked, it is the laws of free market capitalism—rather than more overt, individual forms of racial discrimination—that reproduce a racially skewed class structure. Most major institutions in the United States have officially declared themselves nonracist and invited black citizens to compete alongside everyone else. This is important but insufficient. If three white people begin a game of Monopoly, a black player who is invited to join the game halfway through enters at a serious disadvantage. Unless blessed by a disproportionate degree of good luck, the black player will be unable to overcome these economic disadvantages and compete on equal terms. This is, in effect if not in intention, how the United States has treated most of its black citizens: It offers the promise of equal opportunity without providing the means—good housing, good education, good local job opportunities—to fulfill it.

There is a wealth of evidence about the operation of these structural inequalities (see, e.g., Wilson 1987; Hacker 1992). What is remarkable about our culture is that it refuses to acknowledge the existence of class structures, let alone understand how they influence racial inequalities. And yet, at certain moments, we do accept these things as obvious. We expect rich white children to do better than poor black children. We expect it, because we know that they will go to better schools, be brought up in more comfortable surroundings, and be offered more opportunities to succeed. And our expectations would, most often, be proved quite right. The child who succeeds in spite of these odds is a glamorous figure in our culture precisely because he or she has defied these expectations. Unfortunately, our culture teaches us to ignore these social structures and offers us instead a naive obsession with individual endeavor. Instead of a *collective* war on poverty, we have welfare reforms that increase poverty and homelessness in the name of *individual* responsibility.

We would argue that U.S. television—and popular culture generally—is directly culpable for providing an endless slew of apocryphal stories that sustain a cultural refusal to deal with class inequalities and the racial character of those inequalities.

The Upscale World of Television Fiction

Televison in the United States is notable for creating a world that shifts the class boundaries upward. If the path to heaven is more arduous for the rich than the poor, the opposite can be said of entry to the ersatz world of television. Data from the University of Pennsylvania's Cultural Indicators project suggest that, in recent decades, television gives the overwhelming majority of its main parts to characters from middle- and professional class backgrounds, whereas significant working class roles are few and far between (Jhally and Lewis 1992). This is in notable contrast to the norms of other English-speaking television programs from countries like Britain and Australia, where working-class characters are much more commonplace. In the United States, the TV world is skewed to such an extent that the definition of what looks normal on television no longer includes the working class. The bias is neither obvious nor clearly stated. On the contrary, television's professionals are generally universalized so that the class barriers that divide working class viewers from upper-middle TV characters melt away. As some of our working class viewers said of Cliff Huxtable, he may be a doctor, but he's not as aloof as some of the real doctors they encounter in the non-TV world. This is seen in the words of two respondents:

> I guess he doesn't really seem professional, you know, not the way a doctor would be. The ones I meet are very uppity and they really look down on the lower class.

> They don't play the status they are in the show. You expect them to be living a much higher class, flashing the money, but they're very down to earth.

Television's characters are thus well-off but accessible. These are pictures of the American Dream, and they are paraded in front of us in sitcoms and drama series night after night. On television, most people, or most people with an ounce of merit, are making it.

But surely, it is only television, isn't it? Most people realize that the real world is different, don't they? Well, yes and no. Our study suggested that the line between the TV world and the world beyond the screen has become, for most people, exceedingly hazy. Many of the respondents in our study would shift from immersion in television's world to critical distance in the same interview, praising *The Cosby Show* at one moment for its realism and criticizing it at another for its lack of realism. Thus, for example, one respondent began with an endorsement of the show's realism: "I think that Cosby is much more true to life; you can put yourself right into the picture. Just about everything they do has happened to you, or you've seen it happen."

Later in the interview, the same respondent criticized the show:

> It's totally a fantasy to me, a fairy tale. . . . I think if you bring the real humdrum of what really life is all about, it would be a total bore. I would much prefer to see a little bit of fairy tale and make-believe.

It seems we watch at one moment with credulity and at another with disbelief. We mix skepticism with an extraordinary faith in television's capacity to tell us the truth. We know that the succession of doctors, lawyers, and other professionals that dominate television's stories is not real, yet we continually think about them as if they were. We have thereby learned to live in the dreams of network executives.

Exceptions to this—perhaps the most notable in recent television history being *Roseanne*—become conspicuous because (at least until the last show in the series when the family wins the lottery) they defy this norm. Simply by being sympathetic and assertively working class, the characters in *Roseanne* stood out from the sea of upscale images that surrounded them. In the United States, there are nearly twice as many janitors as all the lawyers and doctors put together, and yet, on television, the legal or medical professions are run of the mill, whereas to portray a major character as a janitor seems "ostentatiously" class-conscious. The negative response to *thirtysomething* in the 1980s was, in this context, extremely revealing. Here was a show that dealt, fairly intimately, with the lives of a group of middle- and upper-middle-class people. In demographic terms, these characters were the standard fare offered by network television, where most characters of any importance are middle or upper-middle class. Why, then, was this show in particular invariably described, often pejoratively, as a yuppie drama?

The answer tells us a great deal about the way class is represented on television.

The show *thirtysomething* was unusual not because it was about young professionals but because it was self-consciously about young professionals. It was difficult to watch an episode without being aware that this was a group of people who were, in class terms, fairly privileged. Here was a show that was conspicuously and unapologetically class-conscious. When most TV characters display a liberal concern for the poor or the homeless, we are invited to applaud their altruism. When characters on *thirtysomething* did so, we were more likely to cringe with embarrassment at the class contradictions thrown up by such philanthropic gestures. Thus, *thirtysomething*'s principal sin was not that it showed us yuppies, but that it made them appear part of an exclusive world that many people will never inhabit. With its coy realism, *thirtysomething* was killjoy television, puncturing the myth of the American Dream.

Although we see echoes of this class consciousness on shows like *Frasier,* they are represented in ways that tend to elide rather than confirm class distinctions. It is not just that Frasier and Niles Crane's high cultural, upper-middle-class affectations are often parodied, but the constant presence of their working-class father reminds us that class background is unimportant.

The prosperous, comfortable world in which most television characters live is generally welcoming, and it is into this world that upscale black characters—from the Huxtables onward—fit like the proverbial glove. It is, we would argue, hard to underestimate the significance of this in the politics of representation. Thus, we can say that to be "normal" on television—the prerequisite for a "positive image"—black characters are necessarily presented as middle or upper-middle class. Indeed, *The Cosby Show* itself used two of television's favorite professions—what, after all, could be more routine than a household

headed by a lawyer and a doctor? But unlike *thirtysomething,* it also had to look normal, to portray these wealthy professionals as a regular, "everyday" family. The respondents in our study suggested that the show was particularly skillful and adroit in absorbing this contradiction; indeed, its popularity depends on this combination of accessibility and affluence. Professionals and blue-collar workers can both watch the show and see themselves reflected in it. Social barriers, like class or race are absent from this world. They have to be. To acknowledge the presence of such things would make too many viewers uncomfortable. Television has thereby imposed a set of cultural rules on us that give us certain expectations about the way the TV world should be.

The bombardment from this image world makes it difficult for people schooled in the evasive language of North American television to comprehend the world around them seriously. If a serious analysis of class structures is generally absent from our popular vocabulary, then that absence is confirmed by a television environment that makes upward mobility desirable but class barriers irrelevant. As a consequence, when our respondents tried to make sense of class issues thrown up by a discussion of *The Cosby Show,* many were forced to displace the idea of class onto a set of racial categories. This was often the case for our black respondents, who often became enmeshed in the debate about whether the show was "too white" (an idea that, incidentally, the great majority repudiated). Yet, we would argue, the very terms of such a debate involve a misleading syllogism, one that declares that because black people are disproportionately less likely to be upper-middle class, if they become so they have not entered a class category (upper-middle class) but a racial one (white). One of our black middle-class respondents revealed the confusion involved in this way of thinking when he said, "What's wrong with showing a black family who has those kind of values? I almost said *white* values but *that's not the word I want*" (italics added). The context of a portrayal like *The Cosby Show* is not so much "white culture" (whatever that may be), but "upper-middle-class culture." It is partly by echoing the stilted discourse of U.S. television that many of our respondents found it difficult to make such a distinction.

In creating *The Cosby Show* Bill Cosby can hardly be blamed for playing by the rules of network television. Indeed, what our study makes clear is that it was only by conforming to these cultural limitations that he was able to make a black family so widely acceptable to white TV viewers. This discomfort or distance that most of the white viewers in our study expressed about black television characters was articulated not only in racial terms, but also—albeit indirectly—in class terms. What many white viewers found off-putting about other black sitcoms was not blackness per se but working-class blackness:

> I mean it's not a jive show, like *Good Times*. I think those other shows are more jive, more soul shows, say as far as the way the characters are with making you aware that they are more separate. Where Cosby is more of American down the line thing, which makes everybody feel accepted.

> I remember that it (*The Jeffersons*) was a little bit more slapstick, a little bit more stereotypical. They were concerned with racial issues. And it was much more interested in class, and the difference between class, middle-class versus working class.

> They talk with the slick black accent, and they work on the mannerisms, and I think they make a conscious effort to act that way like they are catering to the black race in that show. Whereas Cosby, you know, definitely doesn't do that. He's upper

middle class and he's not black stereotypical. There's a difference in the tone of those shows, completely.

The Price of Admission and Its Political Consequences

Although there may be dimensions to this race/class inflection that go beyond television, the difficulty some white viewers have in inviting black working-class characters into their living rooms is partly a function of television's class premise, in which normalcy is middle and upper-middle class and where working-class characters are, to some extent, outsiders. In terms of the politics of representation, our study raises a difficult question: If black characters must be upscale to be accepted into this image world, is such an acceptance worth the price of admission? To answer this question, we must consider the broader consequences of this representational move.

Among white people, the repeated appearance of black characters in TV's upwardly mobile world gives credence to the idea that racial divisions, whether perpetuated by class barriers or by racism, do not exist. Most white people are extremely receptive to such a message. It allows them to feel good about themselves and about the society of which they are a part. The many black professionals who easily inhabit the TV world suggest to people that, as one of our respondents put it, "There really is room in the United States for minorities to get ahead, without affirmative action."

If affirmative action has become a hot issue in contemporary politics, it is because the tide has turned against it, with states and universities (including our own) buckling under to pressure to abandon the policy. As Gray (1996) suggested in his analysis of the Reagan years, conservatives are able to use their opposition to such policies as a way of mobilizing white votes. Indeed, our study reveals that the opposition to affirmative action among white people is overwhelming. What was particularly notable was that although most white people are prepared to acknowledge that such a policy was once necessary, the prevailing feeling was that this was no longer so.

> I think I've become less enamored of it. I think that when the whole idea was first discussed, it was a very good idea. . . . In recent years, I don't think it's necessarily getting anybody anywhere.

> I think in a lot of respects it's carried too far and that it results in reverse discrimination because you have quotas to meet for different job positions and that kind of stuff, it's like, a white person no longer has equal opportunity towards a job because you have to fill a quota.

> Well, I think it has gone too far, where the white people don't have the opportunities. I think it has come to a point where people should be hired now, not because of their color or their race, but because of what they're able to do. I mean there are people who are much better qualified but can't get hired because they are white, and I don't think that's right. Maybe in the beginning, they needed this . . . but it has gone too far.

There are, of course, circumstances in which a qualified black person will receive a warm reception from employees concerned to promote an "equal opportunities" image. Any cursory glance at social statistics, however, demonstrates that this is because employers are sheepish or embarrassed by current levels of inequality in the workplace. Almost any social index suggests that we live in a society in which black and white people are not equal, whether in terms of education, health, housing, employment, or wealth. So why is affirmative action suddenly no longer necessary? Partly, we would

suggest, because our popular culture tells us so.

During our content analysis of the three main networks, we came across only one program that offered a glimpse of these racial divisions. What was significant about this program, however, was that it did not take place in the present, but in the past, during the early days of the civil rights movement. TV was only able to show us racial divisions in the United States by traveling back in time to the "bad old days." Most of the black characters in television's here-and-now seemed blissfully free of such things. Attempts by Hollywood to deal with racial inequality adopt the same strategy. Racism, whether in *Driving Miss Daisy, The Long Walk Home,* or *Amistad,* is confined to the safe distance of history. There are some notable exceptions— such as Spike Lee's work— but the general impression is clear: The social causes of racial inequality are behind us.

Television, despite—and in some ways because of—the liberal intentions of many who write its stories, has pushed our culture backward. White people are not prepared to deal with the problem of racial inequality because they are no longer sure if or why there is a problem. James Patterson and Peter Kim (1992) conducted a survey of contemporary American belief systems:

> In the 1990s, white Americans hold blacks, and blacks alone, to blame for their current position in American society. "We tried to help," whites say over and over, "but blacks wouldn't help themselves." This is the basis for what we've called the new racism. Everything flows from it. It is a change from the hardcore racism that existed in our country's earlier years. It is also a dramatic contrast to the attitude of the 1960s, when many whites, from the President on down, publicly stated that black people were owed compensation for centuries of oppression. (P. 183)

The use of upscale black television characters, our study made increasingly clear, is an intrinsic part of this process. Television becomes Dr. Feelgood, indulging its white audience so that their response to racial inequality becomes a guilt-free, self-righteous inactivity.

This has saddled us, as Patterson and Kim (1992) suggest, with a new, repressed form of racism. For although television now portrays a world of equal opportunity, most white people know enough about the world to see that black people achieve less, on the whole, than do white people—a discourse emphasized by television news (Entman 1990). They know that black people are disproportionately likely to live in poor neighborhoods, drop out of school, or be involved in crime. Indeed, overall, television's representation of black people is bifurcated—a Jekyll-and-Hyde portrayal in which the bulk of ordinary working-class black Americans have few images of themselves outside of those connected with crime, violence, and drugs.

Media Images: Accentuating the Positive and the Negative

The most striking aspect of the interviews with black Americans in our study was the ubiquity of comments about the role that media images play in how white America looks at them—of how stereotypical images of blacks as criminals affected their own everyday interaction with white society and institutions, as one person put it:

> Nobody can believe that you can actually have the intelligence, the fortitude, the dedication and the determination to go out and earn a decent living to afford you some nice things. The mentality today is that if you're black and you get something, you either got it through drugs or through prostitution.

The role that the media played in the cultivation of this perception was clearly understood. As another of our respondents stated, "We seem to be the only people in the world that TV tries to pick out the negative to portray as characteristic of us. What television is doing to us, I think, is working a hell of a job on us."

For minority groups, then, living in the kind of residential and social apartheid that characterizes much of contemporary America, media images are vital, as they are the primary way that the broader society views them. Black America, after all, is well aware of what white perception of black males in particular can lead to. In the Rodney King case, an all-white suburban jury acquitted four LAPD officers for a brutal beating on the basis that the person receiving the beating was, in the words of one of the jurors, "controlling the action." When your image of black people is as subhuman criminals, muggers, drug addicts, gang members, and welfare cheats, then even when a black man is lying hogtied on the ground, he is still dangerous, and any action to subdue him becomes justified.

It is not surprising, in this framework, that Bill Cosby's self-conscious attempt to promote a series of very different black images was so well received by the black respondents in our study. But if it is a kind of representational rescue mission, it is one with an almost fairy-tale script. Thus, we can move away from news images of black criminals to fictional images of black lawyers and judges in a matter of network minutes.

In this way, the media images turn real and complex human beings into crude one-dimensional caricatures, which then come to define minority populations for the majority. Perhaps the apotheosis of this bifurcated imagery was the figure of O.J. Simpson. If many white Americans were bemused by the degree to which black Americans felt they had a stake in the innocence of a rich TV celebrity, it was because they did not understand the representational issues at stake. The rush to a judgment of innocence was a mechanism of self-defense against a popular culture that offers a limited and bifurcated view of black life, one that can be symbolized by two characters in the recent history of black representation: Bill Cosby and Willie Horton.

The Cosby Show epitomized and inspired a move in network television toward the routine presentation of black professionals in drama and situation comedy. The flip side to this is the world of the news or so-called reality programming (like *Cops*), in which it is blacks as violent criminals, drug dealers, crackheads, and welfare mothers that dominate the screen. Perhaps the embodiment of this side of the story is Willie Horton, the image used by the Bush presidential campaign in 1988 to scare white America away from voting for Mike Dukakis. (In a now infamous TV campaign ad that is credited with turning the election around, Horton was represented as a crazed murderer, whom the Dukakis prison furlough program, in a moment of foolish liberal dogoodery, allowed out of prison.)

These are the two predominant images of black Americans with which the majority of white people are familiar. The O.J. case was pivotal, as Simpson came to be located precisely at the conjuncture between the two. He *was* Bill Cosby (affluent, friendly, smiling, cultured). If he was guilty of brutal double murder, he would *become* Willie Horton. The representational identity of black America as a whole, given the incredible visibility of the case, was the prize at stake.

Writer Anthony Walton (1989) commented on what is at stake in these battles over representation:

I am recognizing my veil of double consciousness, my American self and my black self. I must battle, like all humans, to see myself. I must also battle, because I am black, to see myself as others see me; increasingly my life, literally, depends upon it. I might meet Bernard Goetz in the subway. . . . The armed security guard might mistake me for a burglar in the lobby of my building. And they won't see a mild-mannered English major trying to get home. They will see Willie Horton. (p. 77)

In this context, it is little wonder that black Americans took the Simpson case so personally. His innocence would, in some ways, maintain the representational progress forged by Bill Cosby, whereas his guilt would tilt it back to Willie Horton. He *had* to be innocent because African Americans, like all people, want the world to recognize their humanity and their dignity. In a context in which their identity is at stake, the "evidence" had little relevance. Any story—however implausible—of conspiracy and racism would eradicate the forensics, the DNA tests, and so forth. That is precisely what Johnny Cochran offered the jury and black America, and it was accepted with thanks.

But for white viewers, how can sense be made of this bifurcated world? How can black failure in reality programming be reconciled with television's fictions, so replete with images of black success? How to explain racial inequalities in the context of the racial equality of television's upscale world? Without some acknowledgment that the roots of racial inequality are embedded in our society's class structure, there is only one way to reconcile this paradoxical state of affairs. If black people are disproportionately unsuccessful, then they must be disproportionately less deserving. Although few of our respondents were prepared to be this explicit (although a number came very close), their failure to acknowledge class or racial barriers means that this is the only explanation available. The consequence, in the apparently enlightened welcome white viewers extend to television's black professionals, is a new, sophisticated form of racism. Their success casts a shadow across the majority of black people who, by these standards, have failed. Television, which tells us very little about the structures behind success or failure (Iyengar 1991), leaves white viewers to assume that the black people who do not match up to their television counterparts have only themselves to blame.

In a rather different way, the effect of *The Cosby Show* on its black audience is also one of flattering to deceive. The dominant reaction of our black viewers to the show was "for this relief, much thanks." After suffering years of negative media stereotyping, most black viewers were delighted by a show that portrayed African Americans as intelligent, sensitive, and successful:

> I admire him. I like his show because it depicts black people in a positive way. It's good to see that black people can be professionals.
> Thank you Dr. Cosby for giving us back ourselves.

The problem with this response is that it embraces the assumption that, on television, a positive image is a prosperous image. This dubious equation means that African Americans are trapped in a position in which any reflection of more typical black experience—which is certainly not upper-middle class—is "stereotypical." As one of our respondents said, even though he was painfully aware that *The Cosby Show* presented a misleading picture of what life was like for most black Americans, "There's part of me that says, in a way, I don't want white America to see us, you know,

struggling or whatever." On TV, there is no dignity in struggling unless you win.

This analysis of stereotyping dominates contemporary thought. It is the consequence of a television world that has told us that to be working class is to be marginal. Thus, it is that viewers in our study were able to see the Huxtable family on *The Cosby Show* as both "regular" and "everyday" *and* as successful, well-heeled professionals.

For black viewers, this deceit amounts to a form of cultural blackmail. It leaves two choices, either to be complicit partners in an image system that masks the deep racial divisions in the United States or forced to buy into the fiction that, as one respondent put it, "there are black millionaires all over the place," thereby justifying *The Cosby Show* as a legitimate portrayal of average African American life.

The Structural Confines of Network Television

If our story tells us anything, it is that we need to be more attentive to the attitudes cultivated by "normal" everyday television. In the case of representations of race, these attitudes can affect the way we think about "issues" like race and class and, in so doing, even influence the results of elections.

As we have suggested, it does not have to be this way. There is no reason why TV characters cannot be working class and dignified, admirable—or even just plain normal. Bill Cosby's more recent sitcom—*Cosby*—is one attempt to do this, although his enormous popularity as a performer gives him a license that other shows, such as the short-lived *Frank's Place*, do not have. Other television cultures have managed to avoid distorting and suppressing the class structure of their societies; why can't we manage it in the United States?

The American Dream is much more than a gentle fantasy; it is the dominant discourse in the United States for understanding (or misunderstanding) class. It is a cultural doctrine that encompasses vast tracts of American life. No politician would dare question our belief in it, any more than they would publicly question the existence of God. Even though politicians of many different persuasions pay lip service to the dream (it is, in conventional wisdom, "what's great about America"), it is not a politically neutral idea. It favors those on the political right to say that anyone, regardless of circumstance, can make it if they try. In such an egalitarian world, the free market delivers a kind of equity, making public intervention and regulation an unnecessary encumbrance. For government to act to eradicate the enormous social problems in the United States is to defy the logic of the dream. Intervention implies, afterall, that the system is not naturally fair, and opportunity is not universal.

The American Dream is, in this context, insidious rather than innocent. It is part of a belief system that allows people in the United States to disregard the inequalities that generate its appalling record on poverty, crime, health, homelessness, and education. It is not surprising that the more fortunate cling to the self-justifying individualism the dream promotes. One of the saddest things about the United States is that sometimes, the less fortunate do too.

The ideological dominance of the American Dream is sustained by its massive presence in popular culture. The television and film industries churn out fable after fable, thereby reducing us to a state of spellbound passivity in which decades of stagnating incomes for many Americans have been accepted with little protest. The success we are encouraged to strive for is always linked to the acquisition of goods,

a notion fueled by the ubiquitous language of advertising, in which consumers do not usually see themselves in commercials; rather, they see a vision of a glamorous and affluent world to which they aspire. Underlying the preponderance of middle- and upper-middle class characters on display is the relentless message that this is what the world of happiness and contentment looks like. In this context, ordinary settings seem humdrum or even depressing. Not only do we expect television to be more dramatic than everyday life, but, in the United States, we also expect it to be more affluent. We do not want a good story; we want a "classy" setting.

> I liked the background. I like to look at the background on a TV program, I enjoy that. The setting, the clothes, that type of thing. I don't enjoy dismal backgrounds.
>
> This is nice, it looks good and it's kind of, you accept it; they have a beautiful home and everything is okay.

This is the language of advertising. It is also, now, the discourse of the American Dream. This language is now so much a part of our culture that these attitudes seem perfectly natural. It is only when we look at other television cultures that we can see that they are not.

Few other industrial nations leave their cultural industries to be as dependent on advertising revenue as they are in the United States. In the United States, very little happens in our popular culture without a commercial sponsor. This takes place in a lightly regulated free market economy in which cultural industries are not accountable to a notion of public service but to the bottom line of profitability.

Apart from tiny grants to public broadcasting, the survival of radio and television stations depends almost entirely on their ability to sell consumers (viewers or listeners) to advertisers. Moreover, broadcasters in the United States are required to do little in the way of public service. There are no regulations that encourage quality, diversity, innovation, or educational value in programming. This means that the influence of advertising is twofold. Not only does it create a cultural climate that influences the form and style of programs that fill the spaces between commercials; it also commits television to the production of formulaic programming. Once cultural patterns are established, it is difficult to deviate from them without losing the ratings that bring in the station's revenue.

This is not merely a tyranny of the majority and the logic of the lowest common denominator. A ratings system driven by advertising does not so much favor popularity as the quest for the largest pockets of disposable income. The 1999 season of *Dr. Quinn, Medicine Woman* was cancelled by CBS even though it was regularly the most popular show during its Saturday night time slot. The problem was simply that its viewers were generally not wealthy enough to be of interest to advertisers. The ad-driven chase for well-heeled demographics thereby gives network television an in-built class bias, creating a climate in which portrayals of working-class black characters may make good television but are an unlikely way to attract television's most sought-after demographic group.

Which brings us back to the many representational offshoots of *The Cosby Show*. To be successful and to stay on the air, *The Cosby Show* had to meet certain viewers' expectations. This, as we have seen meant seducing viewers with the vision of comfortable affluence the Huxtables epitomized. Once television has succumbed to the discourse of the American Dream, where a positive image is a prosperous one, it cannot afford the drop in ratings that will accompany a

redefinition of viewers', expectations. TV programs that do so are necessarily short-lived. Programs like *Frank's Place, Cop Rock,* or *Twin Peaks* all deviated from a norm, and, although still watched by millions of viewers, they did not attain the mass audience required to keep them on the air. This puts us on a treadmill of cultural stagnation. It is a system in which the bland repetition of fantasies tailored to the interests of wealthier viewers makes sound business sense.

In such a system, *The Cosby Show*'s survival depended on meeting the demands of a formula that pleases as many people as possible and especially its more upscale audience. Our study suggests that it did so with consummate success, pleasing black and white people, blue-collar workers and professionals, all in slightly different ways. The more blue-collar *Cosby* has been less universally embraced, and in this context we should applaud Bill Cosby's attempt to use his popularity to offer audiences a less upscale image.

When our book *Enlightened Racism: The Cosby Show, Audiences, and the Myth of the American Dream* was first published in 1992, we were widely credited with holding *The Cosby Show* responsible for promoting the routine fiction of effortless black success. But this was not the thrust of our argument. *The Cosby Show* and many black professionals portrayed in its wake are genuine attempts to make television's upscale world more racially diverse. The problem is not with individual instances of black success but with a television environment whose structural conditions make a wider array of images less profitable.

REFERENCES

Entman, R. 1990. "Modern Racism and the Images of Blacks in Local Television News." *Critical Studies in Mass Communication* 7 (4, December): 332–345.

Gray, H. 1996. *Watching Race: Television and the Struggle for Blackness.* Minneapolis: University of Minnesota Press.

Hacker, A. 1992. *Two Nations: Black and White, Separate, Hostile, Unequal.* New York: Scribner.

Iyengar, S. 1991. *Is Anyone Responsible?* Chicago: University of Chicago Press.

Jhally, S. and J. Lewis. 1992. *Enlightened Racism: The Cosby Show, Audiences, and the*
Myth of the American Dream. Boulder, CO: Westview.

Patterson, J. and P. Kim. 1992. *The Day America Told the Truth.* New York: Dutton.

Walton, A. 1989. "Willie Horton and Me." *The New York Times Magazine,* August 20, section 6, p. 77.

Wilson, W. J. 1987. *The Truly Disadvantaged.* Chicago: University of Chicago Press.

37

DISTORTED REALITY: HISPANIC CHARACTERS IN TV ENTERTAINMENT

S. Robert Lichter • Daniel R. Amundson

QUESTIONS TO CONSIDER

Latinos now represent a larger proportion of the total population than do black individuals, but they are mostly invisible on prime time television. Robert Lichter and Daniel Amundson provide a historical overview of the ways Latinos have been characterized by the media. Have stereotypical depictions of Latinos changed in recent years? Are you able to name five main characters appearing on prime time television (8 P.M. to 11 P.M. slot) who are Latino? Are these representations favorable? What are the occupations of these Latino characters?

The Past as Prologue

It takes diff'rent strokes to move the world.
—"Diff'rent Strokes" Theme Song

When Kingfish uttered his last "Holy Mackerel, Andy!" in 1953, it marked the end of television's most controversial depiction of blacks. Ironically, the departure of "Amos 'n' Andy" also signaled the end of a brief

period of ethnic diversity that would not reappear in prime time for two decades. Several of the earliest family sitcoms were transplanted radio shows set in America's black or white ethnic subcultures. "The Goldbergs" followed the lives of a Jewish immigrant family in New York for twenty years on radio before switching to the new medium in 1949. It featured Gertrude Berg as Molly Goldberg, everyone's favorite Jewish mother. An even more successful series that premiered the same year was "Mama," which chronicled a Norwegian immigrant family in turn-of-the-century San Francisco. Theme music by Grieg added to

S. Robert Lichter and Daniel R. Amundson, "Distorted Reality" from *Latin Looks: Images of Latinas and Latinos in the U.S. Media* by Clara Rodriguez. Copyright © 1997 by Westview Press, a division of Perseus Books, LLC. Reprinted by permission.

the "ethnic" atmosphere, as did accents that made Aunt "Yenny" into a popular character. These white ethnic shows were soon joined by the all-black "Amos 'n' Andy" as well as "Beulah," which starred the black maid of a white middle-class family.

All these shows relied on stereotypical dialogue and behavior for much of their humor. But social standards were changing, and the new medium created its own demands and perceptions. For example, not only Amos and Andy but even Beulah had been portrayed on radio by white males. When the popular radio show "Life with Luigi" made the switch to TV in 1952, Italian American groups protested its stereotyped portrayal of Italian immigrants. Black groups were equally outraged over "Amos 'n' Andy," which had been an institution on radio since 1929. As the program evolved, it centered on the schemes of George "King-fish" Stevens, who combined the soul of Sgt. Bilko with the fate of Ralph Kramden. A small-time con man with big plans that never panned out, he became an immensely popular, lovable loser. His schemes usually pulled in the ingenuous cabbie Andy and the slow-moving janitor Lightnin'.

From Kingfish's fractured syntax ("I'se regusted") to Lightnin's shuffle and falsetto "yazzuh," the series drew on overtly racial stereotypes. The NAACP blasted the portrayal of blacks as "inferior, lazy, dumb, and dishonest," and urged a boycott of Blatz beer, the sponsor. The pressure from civil rights groups probably helped bring the series to a premature end, since it attracted sizeable audiences throughout its two year run.

• • •

While controversy surrounded "Amos and Andy," little debate attended television's earliest and most high profile Latino portrayal. From 1950 through 1956, Ziv productions sold 156 episodes of "The

Cisco Kid" in syndication to individual stations across the country. Resplendent in his heavily embroidered black costume, Cisco rode across the southwest righting wrongs and rescuing damsels in distress. He was accompanied by his portly sidekick, Pancho, who served as a comic foil. Pancho was loyal and brave, but his English was every bit as fractured as the Kingfish's. Further, although Cisco and Pancho were positive and even heroic characters, they were often outnumbered by evil and frequently criminal Latino adversaries. In its simplistic presentation that combined positive and negative ethnic stereotypes, "Cisco" set the tone for the "Zorro" series that would follow it on ABC from 1957 through 1959. Thus, these early high-profile representations of Latinos proved a mixed bag, as television's conventions of the day were applied to both network and syndicated fare.

The All-White World

"Cisco" and "Zorro," which were aimed at children, outlasted the first generation of ethnic sitcoms for general audiences. By the 1954 season "Mama" was the only survivor of this once-thriving genre. Thus, by the time our study period began, TV's first era of ethnic humor had already come and gone. The urban ethnic sitcoms were replaced by homogeneous suburban settings. There was nothing Irish about the life of Chester Riley, nothing Scandinavian about Jim and Margaret Anderson. The new family shows were all-American, which meant vaguely northern European and carefully noncontroversial. The few remaining ethnics were mostly relegated to minor roles or single episodes.

Just how homogeneous was this electronic neighborhood? From 1955 through

1964, our coders could identify only one character in ten as anything other than northern European on the basis of name, language, or appearance. Such a small slice of the pie got cut up very quickly, and many groups got only crumbs. Just one character in fifty was Hispanic, fewer than one in a hundred was Asian, and only one in two hundred was black.

● ● ●

Hispanics had virtually no starring roles. For most Hispanic characters, life consisted of lounging in the dusty square of a sleepy Latin town, waiting for the stars to come on stage. Occasionally Hispanics would show up as outlaws in the Old West, but even then mostly as members of someone else's gang. Their comic roles were epitomized by Pepino Garcia, a farmhand for "The Real McCoys," who functioned mainly as a target of Grandpa Amos McCoy's tirades. Pepino and "The Real McCoys" were replaced in 1963 by Jose Jimenez in the "Bill Dana Show."

Like their black colleagues, a few stars stood out in a sea of marginal and insignificant roles. A notable exception was Cuban band leader Ricky Ricardo in "I Love Lucy," played by Desi Arnaz. As the co-star of one of the most popular shows on TV (and coowner of Desilu Productions, along with wife Lucille Ball), Arnaz was a prominent figure in Hollywood. When exasperated by Lucy's schemes and misadventures, Ricky added a comic touch with displays of "Latin" temper and lapses into Spanish. "I Love Lucy" made its mark on television comedy and TV production in general, but it did little for Hispanic characters. The same could be said of another early show with a Hispanic setting, which nonetheless cast Anglos in the major roles. Guy Williams played Don Diego, alias Zorro, the masked champion of the poor and oppressed in old Los Angeles. Their oppressors were evil, greedy Spanish governors and landowners. In one episode Annette Funicello, fresh from the Mickey Mouse Club, showed up as the singing senorita Anita Cabrillo. Despite its "Hispanic" characters, the show was not a generous portrayal of either the people or the culture.

The departure of "Amos and Andy" and "Beulah" all but eliminated black stars. Jack Benny's valet Rochester was one of the few major roles still held by a black in the late 1950s. Black characters didn't even show up in the backgrounds of early shows. Urban settings might feature a black delivery man, porter, or waiter, but black professionals and businessmen were virtually nonexistent. Some westerns like "Rawhide" and "Have Gun, Will Travel" presented a few black cowboys riding the range with their white counterparts. Aside from such occasional and insignificant roles, black characters were simply not a part of the early prime time world.

The Return of Race

In the mid-1960s, the portrayal of ethnic and racial minorities underwent major changes. The proportion of non–northern European roles doubled over the next decade. Before 1965, all racial and ethnic groups to the south or east of England, France, and Germany had scrambled for the one role in ten available to them. Now nonwhite characters alone could count on better than one role in ten. From the first to the second decade in our study [1955–1975], the proportion of English characters was cut in half, while Hispanics became half again as numerous and the proportion of Asians doubled. Blacks were the biggest winners, gaining a dramatic fourteen-fold increase in what had been virtually an all-white landscape.

The invisibility of Hispanics during this period remained more than metaphorical. They were simply not part of television's new ethnic "relevance." Latinos had few continuing prime time roles of any sort during the late 1960s, and certainly no major star parts like Bill Cosby's Alexander Scott. In fact, most Latinos who were cast during this period showed up in episodes of international espionage series that used Central and South American locales. "I Spy" had many episodes set in Mexico, bringing the agents into contact with some positive and many more negative Hispanic characters. In other espionage shows, such as "Mission Impossible," the action often centered on a fictitious Central American country, which was inevitably run by a jack-booted junta that could only be stopped by the enlightened Anglo-led team from north of the border.

One of the few exceptions to this pattern was the western "High Chaparral." Rancher John Cannon had settled in the Arizona territory to found a cattle empire. When his first wife was killed by Apaches, John married Victoria Montoya, the daughter of a wealthy Mexican rancher. The marriage was as much a business move as a romance, since it united the two families. Once tied by marriage, Don Montoya helped John build his herds and produce good breeding stock. Together the two families fought off Apaches and other marauders. Culture clashes between the two families occurred, but usually as a minor part of the plot. Unlike most Mexicans shown in previous westerns, the Montoyas were rich, powerful, sophisticated, and benevolent. In most episodes, Victoria attempted to civilize her more rustic husband and establish a proper home on the range. To be sure, this series still presented semiliterate Hispanic

ranchhands, but these portrayals were overshadowed by the Montoyas.

The other exception was the short-lived social relevancy series "Man and the City." This series presented more contemporary problems of Latinos in an unnamed southwestern city. The show was notable for frequently asserting the dignity and rights of Latinos. For example, in a 1971 segment, a cop is killed in the city's barrio. The police department pulls out all the stops to catch the killers, imposing a curfew and holding suspects incommunicado without legal counsel. All the suspects are Hispanics from the barrio who have little connection to the case. The mayor is forced to intervene and remind the police chief that the city has laws. He demands that all suspects, including minority groups, be given their full rights. The police are reluctant, believing this will impede their investigation. The mayor insists and the police obey his order. They eventually capture a key suspect who helps them catch the killers. There is no indication that racial tensions in the city have ended, merely that one violent episode is over. The groups involved have not learned to like each other; nor are they presented as peacefully coexisting. The point here is that all people have rights and deserve to be treated with dignity and equality. This seems to be the only series that attempted to derive socially relevant plotlines from the barrio.

Not only did the proportion of black characters jump to 7 percent between 1965 and 1975, but the range and quality of roles expanded even more dramatically. In adventure series like "I Spy" and "Mission: Impossible," blacks moved into their first starring roles in over a decade. Not only were these roles more prominent, they offered a new style of character. Alexander Scott of "I Spy" and Barney Collier of "Mission: Impossible" were competent, educated professionals. These men were highly successful agents whose racial backgrounds were clearly secondary to their bravery and skill. They opened the way for blacks to appear in roles that did not require the actor to be black. There was no more use of poor English, servile shuffling, or popeyed double takes for comic effect. Instead, Collier was presented as an electronics expert and Scott as a multilingual Rhodes Scholar.

The new visibility of blacks quickly moved beyond the secret agent genre. In 1968 the first of television's relevance series managed to convert a negative stereotype into a positive one by casting a young black rebel as a member of "The Mod Squad." Linc Hayes' militant credentials included an afro haircut, aviator sunglasses, and an arrest during the Watts riots. Not to worry, though. This brooding black rebel was working with the good guys on the L.A.P.D.'s undercover "youth squad," where the dirty dozen met the counterculture every Tuesday at 7:30.

While ABC was coopting the Black Panthers into the establishment, NBC looked to the black middle class for "Julia," the first black-oriented sitcom in fifteen years. As a dedicated nurse and loving mother in an integrated world, the Julia Baker character looked ahead to "The Cosby Show" rather than backward to "Amos 'n' Andy." She certainly had more in common with Claire Huxtable than with Kingfish's nagging wife, Sapphire. Unfortunately, she also lacked the vitality and wit of either Sapphire or future mother figures who would be more firmly rooted in black culture, like "Good Times" Florida Evans.

"Julia" suffered from the dullness of being a prestige series, just as "The Mod Squad" labored under the hype that attended the relevance series. What they had in common with better-written shows like "I Spy" and "Mission Impossible" was a tendency to replace the old negative black stereotypes with new positive ones. The authors of *Watching TV* wrote with a touch of hyperbole, "They were no longer bumbling, easygoing, po' folk like Beulah, but rather articulate neo-philosophers just descended from Olympus, though still spouting streetwise jargon."[1] Having discovered that blacks didn't have to be cast as valets and janitors, white writers turned them into James Bonds and Mary Tyler Moores. Thus, as blacks suddenly began to appear on the tube after a decade's absence, they remained invisible in Ralph Ellison's sense. The frantic search for positive characters smothered individuality with good intentions.

Let a Hundred Flowers Bloom

In the early 1970s TV began to broadcast a different message about minorities. The unlikely agent of change was an equal opportunity bigot named Archie Bunker, who excoriated "spics," "jungle bunnies," "chinks," "yids," and every other minority that ever commanded an epithet. When "All in the Family" became the top-rated show within five months of its 1971 premiere, it attracted a barrage of criticism for making the tube safe for ethnic slurs. The producer of public television's "Black Journal" found it "shocking and racist."[2] Laura Hobson, who wrote "Gentlemen's Agreement," an attack on anti-Semitism, decried its attempt to sanitize bigotry, "to clean it up, deodorize it, make millions of people more comfy about indulging in it."[3] Of course, the point of the show was to poke fun at Archie and all he stood for, as the script and laugh track tried to make clear.

Norman Lear's strategy was to educate audiences by entertaining them instead of preaching at them. So he created a kind of politicized Ralph Kramden, whom audiences could like in spite of his reactionary views, not because of them. He intended that the contrast between Archie's basic decency and his unattractive rantings would prod viewers to reexamine the retrograde ideas they permitted themselves. As Lear put it, the show "holds up a mirror to our prejudices. . . . We laugh now, swallowing just the littlest bit of truth about ourselves, and it sits there for the unconscious to toss about later."[4] As a tool for improving race relations, this approach may have been too subtle for its own good. Several studies suggest that liberals watched the show to confirm their disdain for Archie's views, while conservatives identified with him despite his creator's best intentions.[5] But another legacy of the program was to pioneer a more topical and (by television's standards) realistic portrayal of ethnic relations.

An immediate consequence of "All in the Family" was to introduce the first sitcoms populated by black families since "Amos 'n' Andy." A year after demonstrating the audience appeal of a white working class milieu not portrayed successfully since "The Honeymooners," Lear and his partner Bud Yorkin transferred the setting to a black ghetto in "Sanford and Son." Unlike the integrated middle class world of TV blacks in the late 1960s, "Sanford and Son" revolved around the foibles of a junk dealer in a poor black section of Los Angeles. "Sanford" proved so popular that it soon trailed only "All in the Family" in the Nielsen ratings.

Meanwhile, in an irony Archie would not have appreciated, "All in the Family" spawned not one but two additional black family sitcoms. "The Jeffersons" featured Archie's one-time neighbor George Jefferson as an upwardly mobile businessman whose snobbishness and inverted racism

made him almost a black Archie Bunker. "Good Times" was actually a second generation spinoff. When Archie's liberal nemesis Maude got her own show in 1972, the scriptwriters gave her a quick-witted and tart-tongued black maid named Florida Evans. Two years later the popular Florida got her own show as the matriarch of a family living in a Chicago housing project. This series developed the "Sanford" technique of finding sometimes bitter humor among lower status characters trying to cope with life in the ghetto while looking for a way out of it. Scripts featured ward heelers, loan sharks, abused children, and other facets of life on the edge, in sharp contrast to the comfortable middle class world of "Julia" or the glamorous and exotic locales of "I Spy."

By this time, other producers, stimulated by Norman Lear's enormous success, were providing sitcoms that drew their characters from minority settings. "What's Happening!!" followed the adventures of three big city high school kids. "Diff'rent Strokes" created an unlikely "accidental family" in which a wealthy white man raised two black kids from Harlem in his Park Avenue apartment, without any serious clash of cultures. This trend almost never extended from the ghetto to the barrio. The one great exception was "Chico and the Man," a generation-gap sitcom that paired an ebullient young Mexican American with an aging Bunkerish Anglo garage owner. This odd couple clicked with audiences, but the show's success was cut short by the suicide of comedian Freddy Prinze (Chico) in 1977.

Like the black sitcoms, "Chico" used minority culture as a spark to enliven a middle class white world that seemed bland or enervated by comparison. Minority characters of the early 1970s prided themselves not on their similarity to mainstream culture, but on their differences from it. Assimilated characters like Alexander Scott, Barney Collier, and Julia Baker gave way to the racial pride of George Jefferson, Fred of "Sanford and Son," and Rooster on "Starsky and Hutch." Where would Fred Sanford or George Jefferson be without their jive talk and street slang? Language was just one way of stressing the differences between racial and ethnic groups.

Minority characters also picked up flaws as they took on more complete roles. Fred Sanford was domineering and could appear foolish. George Jefferson could be as stubborn and narrow-minded as his one-time next-door neighbor. By badgering the interracial couple living upstairs and labelling their daughter a "zebra," he left no doubt about his views. But the thrust of the ethnic sitcom was not to ridicule minority cultures. Instead, racial and ethnic backgrounds were used as an educational tool. The religious, cultural, and other traditions that differentiate minorities from the mainstream were now treated as beneficial rather than problematic. Removed from the confines of the melting pot, these groups offered new approaches to old problems. Television charged them with the task of teaching new ways to the often obstinate world around them. Blacks and Hispanics participated in this era of racial and cultural re-education. It was Chico Rodriguez who taught Ed Brown to relax and be more tolerant on "Chico and the Man." Benson, the sharp-tongued butler, tried to maintain order amidst the chaos of "Soap," while steering his employers onto the right track. In one episode he even saved young Billy from the clutches of a religious cult.

The most spectacularly successful effort to combine education with entertainment was a hybrid of the miniseries and "big event" genres. Indeed, "Roots" became the biggest event in television history. This adaptation of Alex Haley's best-selling novel traced the history of four generations of a black family in America, beginning with Kunta Kinte, an African tribesman sold into slavery. It ran for eight consecutive nights in January 1977. When it was over, 130 million Americans had tuned in, including 80 million who viewed the final episode. Seven of the eight episodes ranked among the all-time top ten at that point in television's history. "Roots" created a kind of national town meeting comparable to the televised moon landing or the aftermath of President Kennedy's assassination. It was blamed for several racial disturbances but credited for stimulating a productive national debate on the history of American race relations.

While blacks could look to the high-profile presentation of African American history presented by "Roots," there was no similar presentation of Hispanic history. If Anglos relied exclusively on Hollywood for information on Latino contributions to American history, their knowledge would extend little further than John Wayne's defense of "The Alamo" against the Mexican "invaders." Illustrations of Latino culture were equally rare. In fact, the only high-profile Hispanic character during this period was Chico Rodriguez. Despite its popularity, "Chico and the Man" was not known as a series that explored Latino culture or Hispanic contributions to American history and culture.

Despite occasional failures, ethnic comedies became the hottest new programming trend of the 1970s. "All in the Family" was the top-rated show for an unprecedented five straight seasons, surpassing previous megahits "I Love Lucy" and "Gunsmoke." Other top twenty regulars included "Sanford and Son," "The Jeffersons," black comic Flip Wilson's variety show, and "Chico and the Man." The ethnic wave crested during the 1974–75 season, when a remarkable six of the seven top-rated shows were ethnic sitcoms—"All in the Family," "Sanford," "Chico," "Jeffersons," "Rhoda," and "Good Times."

If the new decade offered an unaccustomed array of new roles for minorities, it contained some traps as well. Ethnic characters gained more prominent and desirable roles, but also more unflattering ones. Bumblers, buffoons, and bimbos took their place alongside heroes and sages. For example, Vinnie Barbarino and Juan Epstein were two of the uneducated underachievers on "Welcome Back Kotter." Barbarino's Italian heritage added ethnic color to his machismo image, while Epstein's ethnic background was contrived for comic effect. He was presented as Buchanan High School's only Puerto Rican Jew. "Good Times" created some negative black characters, such as insensitive building supervisors and abusive politicians. In "What's Happening," the Thomas family made do without their con man father after he walked out on them. His occasional visits home were usually in search of money for some new scheme. A steady stream of minority characters began to show up as criminals in cop shows like "Kojak," "Baretta," and "Barney Miller."

"Barney Miller" also deserves note as one of the most multicultural shows of the time. In the 1975–76 season the squad room contained Polish detective Wojohowicz, Asian American Nick Yemana, African American Harris, and Puerto Rican Chano Amenguale. While Chano was far from perfect he appeared to be a capable officer and no more eccentric than his colleagues on the squad. In the next season Chano was replaced by Detective Baptista, who was a fiery Latina, but not as significant in the squad as Chano. These characters at least served to offset the Hispanic criminals they often arrested.

The late 1970s retained a mix of ethnic heroes and fools in some of the most popular shows of the day. But ethnic characters were beginning to lose their novelty. For instance, "CHiPs" ran from 1977 through 1983 and one of the starring characters was Officer Frank Poncherello. Even though Poncherello was played by the well-known Eric Estrada, Poncherello's Hispanic heritage was all but invisible. It no longer mattered in this series that one of the leads was a Latino. During the 1979 season, three dramatic series were launched with black leads, but none came close to the ratings necessary for renewal. "Paris" starred James Earl Jones as a supercop who ran the station house during the day and taught criminology at night. "The Lazarus Syndrome" featured Louis Gossett as the chief of cardiology in a large hospital. "Harris and Company" focused on the problems of a single parent raising a family. The twist was that this black family was held together not by a matriarch but a middle-aged widower. Thus, Hollywood was at least trying to create some positive role models for black males. But no such efforts extended to Latinos. There were no network series built around a Latino family, Hispanic high school kids, or any of the other patterns found in sitcoms featuring blacks. It would be several years before the short-lived ABC series "Condo" would prominently cast Latinos as middle class characters.

Overall, the 1980s offered little that was new to racial or ethnic minority portrayals in the wake of TV's ethnic revival. These groups continued to be presented more or less as they were in the late 1970s. Despite the continuing presence of racial and ethnic diversity, however, racial themes were no longer in vogue. Integration was assumed as a backdrop, as the prime time world became less polarized. The age of pluralism had arrived, but the thrill was gone.

The riots were over, the battles won, and characters got back to their other plot functions. Among these were crime and other wrongdoing. Comedies like "Taxi," "White Shadow," and "WKRP in Cincinnati" continued to present integrated casts, but ethnic characters in dramatic series were often on the dark side of the law.

Ironically, television's multicultural world of the 1980s provided an updated version of the stereotypical Hispanic banditos who populated the westerns thirty years earlier. In the fall of 1980, ABC's controversial sitcom "Soap" introduced a remake of Frito Bandito. Carlos "El Puerco" Valdez was a South American revolutionary playing a love interest of Jessica Tate. They had met when his band kidnapped her for ransom. This plan failed, but after things took a passionate turn, she became a benefactor of his revolution. "El Puerco" led a bumbling, low-budget revolution and he was not above taking time out to romance his new gringo benefactor. "El Puerco" was both Latin lover and bandito with a measure of Jerry Lewis buffoonishness thrown in. Thus, it was down this line that the Frito Bandito's sombrero had been passed—to a fatigue-wearing ne'er-do-well.

There were also more sinister turns in Latino portrayals. Crime shows like "Miami Vice," "Hill Street Blues," and "Hunter" presented Hispanic drug lords as a major nemesis. Trafficking in human misery made these characters rich enough to own cities and sometimes even small countries. They were among the nastiest criminals on TV in the 1980s. There were also petty Hispanic criminals in the slums of "Hill Street Blues" and "Cagney & Lacey." These small-time hoods, drug addicts, and pimps were less flamboyant than their big-league counterparts, but no less unsavory. Altogether, TV's latest crop of Hispanics included a cruel and vicious group of criminals.

"Miami Vice" was not only a source of criminal Hispanics—after all the squad was led by the enigmatic Lieutenant Martin Castillo and on the distaff side of the unit was detective Gina Navarro. However inconsistently, the show did attempt to show successful law-abiding Latinos mixed in with the criminal crop. For all of its flaws "Miami Vice" at least attempted to reflect the presence of Latinos in Miami. Contrast this attempt with more contemporary shows like "Baywatch," "Acapulco H.E.A.T.," and others that rarely if ever reference the Hispanic populations in their host cities.

There were occasional attempts to base shows on Hispanic casts, but all proved unsuccessful. In 1983 the Lear-wannabee sitcom "Condo" briefly pitted a bigoted WASP against his Latino next-door neighbors. The following season, the equally short-lived "A.K.A. Pablo" dealt somewhat more seriously with ethnic questions. Focusing on struggling young comic Pablo Rivera and his extended family, the series wrestled with questions about ethnic humor and the preservation of Hispanic culture. Pablo made many jokes about his family and his Mexican American heritage in his nightclub act. This frequently offended his traditionalist parents, who expected him to treat his heritage more respectfully. Despite its brief run, this series was one of the few to deal explicitly with aspects of Latino culture.

A more mixed portrayal appeared in the 1987 series "I Married Dora." In this fractured fairy tale, Dora Calderon was the housekeeper for widower Peter Farrell and his family. When faced with deportation, Dora and Peter joined in a marriage of convenience. Like many television housekeepers before her, Dora was the voice of wisdom and compassion in the household, but her own illegal status gave her role an ambiguous twist. In 1988, a series called

"Trial and Error" was based on Latino characters from the barrio in East Los Angeles. The show revolved around a free-wheeling entrepreneur who ran a souvenir T-shirt company and his upwardly mobile roommate, who was a newly minted lawyer. This series had a lighter touch with less attention to Hispanic culture, but it met with the same quick demise as its predecessors.

Both "A.K.A. Pablo" and "Trial and Error" sprang from the efforts of comedian Paul Rodriguez. It is not uncommon for bankable stars to get their own television series. This is particularly true for stand-up comics, who have taken their nightclub acts into successful series like "Roseanne," "Home Improvement," "Grace Under Fire," and "Seinfeld." This approach has proven to be a very important avenue onto the screen for blacks. Several exclusively black shows currently on the air are the result of the work of a bankable star. Among those who have followed in the footsteps of Bill Cosby are Keenan Ivory Wayans of "In Living Color," Martin Lawrence of "Martin," Mark Curry of "Hangin' with Mr. Cooper," and Charles Dutton of "Roc." Unfortunately, this approach has so far been a dead end for Latinos.

Blacks fared better in the 1980s, largely escaping the criminal portrayals of other minorities. When black characters did turn to crime, they were usually small-time criminals driven by desperation. There were even times when their criminal acts were presented as social commentary. For instance, in an episode of "Hill Street Blues," a black militant occupies a housing project and takes hostages. He threatens to kill them unless the city agrees to keep the project open and fix it up. The man is frustrated and angry that weeks of negotiating led to nothing. The city simply set a new closing date and moved on. Rage and desperation drive him to act and a tense standoff ensues.

In the end, he is mistakenly shot by a police sniper. Everyone is shocked by his desperate act and his tragic death.

Meanwhile, TV turned out numerous positive black role models as diverse as "The Cosby Show's" Heathcliff Huxtable, Mary Jenkins of "227," Rico Tubbs on "Miami Vice," and Bobby Hill of "Hill Street Blues." These shows suggest the diversity of major roles that were at last becoming available to blacks. "227" and "Amen" continued the sharp-tongued tradition of 1970s sitcoms, without the abrasive or objectionable images that had brought criticism. Tubbs and Hill both carried on the tradition of "salt and pepper" law enforcement teams. Hill also represented the educative function of minorities by helping to wean his partner Renko, a southerner, away from residual racist tendencies.

Of course, "Cosby" was the biggest hit of all. This series further developed the lowkey humanistic colorblind approach that Bill Cosby has popularized over two decades as "I Spy's" Alexander Scott, high school teacher Chet Kincaid on "The Bill Cosby Show," and finally in a black version of "Father Knows Best." The enormous success of this venture led some critics to snipe at Cosby for playing black characters in whiteface to maximize audience appeal. Black psychiatrist Alvin Pouissant, retained by the show to review scripts for racial authenticity, notes that the criticisms come from white reporters more often than black viewers: "Sometimes it seems they want the show to be 'culturally black' . . . and sometimes it seems they would be happier to see them cussing out white people, a sort of protest sitcom. Some seem to feel that because the family is middle class with no obvious racial problems, that constitutes a denial or dismissal of the black person."[6]

Compared to the plight of TV's Hispanics, debates over whether the Huxtables are divorced from the black experience may seem a luxury, a sign that a one-time outgroup has reached a mature phase in its relationship with the Hollywood community. In 1979 organized opposition even persuaded Norman Lear to withdraw a new comedy series at the last minute. "Mister Dugan," a sitcom about a black congressman, was scheduled to premier on CBS a week after Lear arranged a special screening for the Congressional Black Caucus. The screening was a disaster, with Congressman Mickey Leland calling the lead character "a reversion to the Steppin' Fetchit syndrome."

Lear promptly pulled the show from the schedule. He remarked at the time, "We have a high social conscience, and we want to get the story right. We do not favor the short-term gain over the long-term public interest. Dropping the show was an exercise in that commitment."[7] This was an extraordinary episode in a business often excoriated for caring only about the bottom line. When the medium's most successful producer is willing to withdraw a series on the eve of its broadcast, writing off a $700,000 investment, it shows the power of social commitment in television. The only question is the strength and direction of that commitment.

Moreover, such criticism is belied by the top ten ratings obtained by such diverse families as the Sanfords, Jeffersons, and Evans, not to mention Kunta Kinte and his kin. The success of upper and lower class, matriarchal and patriarchal black family series suggests that television has gone beyond using black characters as a sign of racial diversity. It has begun to show diversity within the black community as well, at last recognizing both the cultural distinctiveness and the universal humanity of this group of Americans. Unfortunately, Hispanics have never played a significant role in television's debate over race relations. When television has explored discrimination, prejudice, or the appropriateness of inter-racial relationships, it has almost always staged them as a black versus white issue. Whatever racial tensions exist between Latinos and other groups in American society, they have very rarely made it to the small screen.

A Tale of Two Minorities

Black representation continued to increase during the 1990s, as the number of shows with all-black or mostly black casts jumped. Driven largely by the Fox network's quest for new audiences and trademark shows, these new series drew heavily on the struttin' and jivin' characters of the 1970s. Both the 1992 and 1993 seasons featured ten such series, including hits like "Hangin' with Mr. Cooper," "Family Matters," "Martin," and "Fresh Prince of Bel Air." Intense debate has ensued over the quality of these roles and portrayals, which critics disparage as latterday minstrel show stereotypes. However, such complaints have not diminished the popularity of these shows, particularly among black audiences.

Despite continuing controversy, television's portrayal of blacks is in many ways more diverse and substantive than ever before. For instance, on Monday nights viewers could contrast the wealthy Banks family on "Fresh Prince of Bel Air" with the working class Cumberbatches in "704 Hauser Street." On Tuesday, they could see the struggles of a single mother in "South Central," followed by the stable two-parent extended family in "Roc." Then there were the Winslows, a comfortably middle class black family that was a cornerstone of Friday night viewing for years. In addition there were numerous black characters in integrated series such as "L.A. Law," "Law & Order," "Evening Shade," "Love & War," "NYPD Blue," "In the Heat of the Night," and "sea Quest DSV." African Americans were seen as lawyers, judges, police captains, and a host of other roles in these shows.

While shows that were exclusively or mainly about blacks comprised about one eighth of the prime time schedule in 1992–93, only one series in the previous three seasons was based on a Latino family or character. Moreover, that series—the short-lived "Frannie's Turn"—mainly used Hispanic traditions as a comic foil for feminist putdowns. This series revolved around the marriage of a Cuban emigré named Joseph Escobar and his wife, Frannie, an Anglo of unclear ethnic origins. Whatever ethnic and cultural differences may have existed between them were rarely played upon, since most of the plots dealt with Frannie's quest for equality. However, when aspects of her itage did come up, they frequently reflected poorly on Latinos. For instance, the first episode dealt with Frannie's discovery that Joseph has been sending money to a Cuban liberation movement while telling her to cut the household budget. At one point in the ensuing argument, she suggests sarcastically, "Who knows, maybe they'll send you the Bay of Pigs decoder ring." In the few episodes that aired, the couple's children seemed oblivious to their heritage, and no effort was made to teach them about their father's culture. Overall, this series made no greater use of ethnicity than "I Love Lucy" did almost forty years earlier.

Otherwise, Latino characters remained largely supporting players or background figures in the prime time schedule. The highest profile in 1992–93 was enjoyed by Daniel Morales, who replaced Victor Sifuentes on "L.A. Law." Most other recent Latino roles involved lower status jobs or far less airtime in low-rated series. Examples include Chuy Castillo, the cook at the "Golden Palace"; Jennifer Clemente, a very junior attorney in the U.S. Justice Department on "The Round Table"; and detective Rafael Martinez on the "Hat Squad." There was also Mahalia Sanchez, a bus station cashier in the "John Larroquette Show," rookie detective James Martinez in "NYPD Blue," and Paco Ortiz in "Nurses," none of them starring roles.

The cultural diversity within the Latino community was almost completely absent from prime time. Most Hispanic characters on television came from a "generic" background without reference to national origin or past. Television has rarely pointed out the cultural, historical, or economic differences among different groups within the Latino community. The few shows to make such distinctions, from "Miami Vice" to "Frannie's Turn," usually did so to place a particular nationality in a negative light. In "Miami Vice," differing national origins were connected with different types of illegal activities, while in "Frannie's Turn" a Cuban heritage was not a badge of honor. Sadly, the highest-profile Latino characters of the season were Eric and Lyle Menendez, whose murder trial was featured in two made-for-television movies.

An Update

As we have seen, before 1965, prime time was a nearly all-white world populated mainly by generic northern Europeans, save for the occasional black servant or Mexican bandito. Soon thereafter, the spectrum widened to embrace an array of ethnic and cultural traditions. But various minority groups shared unequally in television's new search for ethnic roots.

Some of these disparities are summarized in Table 1. As the table makes clear,

TABLE 1   Traits of TV Characters, 1955–1986

	White	Black	Latino
All characters	89%	6%	2%
*Social background**			
Attended college	72	44	**
Lacked high school diploma	25	49	**
Low economic status	22	47	40
Professional or executive	22	17	10
Unskilled laborer	13	16	22
Plot functions			
Starring role	17	15	8
Character succeeded	65	72	54
Character failed	23	16	34
Positive portrayal	40	44	32
Negative portrayal	31	24	41
Committed crime	11	7	22

*Characters were coded only if their backgrounds were clearly indicated by the script.
**Two few characters were coded for meaningful comparisons.
Source: Based on a content analysis of 7,639 prime time characters that appeared in 620 entertainment programs between 1955 and 1986.

between 1955 and 1986, proportionately fewer Hispanic characters were professionals or executives and more were unskilled laborers. Fewer Hispanics had starring roles, were positively portrayed, or succeeded in attaining their goals. Indeed, according to our 1994 study,[8] the more villainous the character, the sharper the group differences that emerged. Hispanic characters were twice as likely as whites and three times as likely as blacks to commit a crime. Once TV's roster of Hispanic stereotypes solely included the grinning bandito criss-crossed with ammunition belts. More recently, as scriptwriter Ben Stein has observed, "Any time a Cuban or Colombian crosses the tube, he leaves a good thick trail of cocaine behind."[9]

In addition, because of their negative and criminal roles, Latinos stood apart from other characters in the methods they adopted to attain their goals. They were more likely than either whites or blacks to use violence and deceit. If Latinos were distinctive in the means they used to pursue

their goals, they also differed in their motivations. Hispanic characters were much more likely to be driven by greed than other characters. More broadly, black characters managed to attain whatever they strove for more often than either whites or Hispanics. In fact, the failure rate among Hispanics was more than double that of blacks. Perusing these figures, it is difficult to resist the conclusion that Hollywood has cracked open the door to black concerns while letting Hispanics serve as window dressing.

Examining character portrayals in 1992, we found that compared to both Anglos and African Americans, television's Hispanics were low in number, low in social status, and lowdown in personal character, frequently portraying violent criminals. The worst offenders were "reality" shows, whose version of reality often consisted of white cops chasing black and Hispanic robbers. Utilizing the same scientific content analysis approach, we examined the more recent 1994–95 season. We focused on a composite month of prime time entertainment programs broadcast on the four major broadcast networks and in first-run syndication. We found some welcome progress in television's portrayal of Hispanics, combined with some lingering sins of both omission and commission. (These results reflect our analysis of 5,767 characters who appeared on 528 different episodes of 139 prime time series.)

The proportion of Hispanic characters was up but still far below the proportion of Hispanic Americans in the real world. Latinos were "ghettoized" in a handful of series, few of which are still on the air, and few portrayed prosperous, well-educated, authoritative characters. The most striking and hopeful result, however, was a dramatic decline in the portrayal of Hispanics as criminals. Among the major findings:

- *Visibility.* TV's Hispanic presence doubled from 1992 levels. And these characters were more likely to play major roles when they appeared. But the rise was from only 1 to 2 percent of all characters, far below the 10 percent of Americans with Hispanic ancestry in real life. And a majority appeared in only two series, one of which has been canceled.
- *Criminality.* Hispanic characters were less likely to play villains than they were in the 1992 network prime time schedules. The drop in criminal portrayals was down 63 percent (from 16 percent of all Hispanic characters in 1992 and 6 percent in 1994). But even this level of criminality was higher than the 4 percent we found among whites and 2 percent among blacks
- *New "Realities."* The most striking changes appeared in the cops-and-robbers "reality" shows, such as "COPS" and "America's Most Wanted." In 1992, a staggering 45 percent of all Hispanics and 50 percent of African Americans who appeared in these shows committed crimes. In 1994–95, the "crime rate" for both minorities plummeted to less than half the previous levels—down from 45 to 16 percent of Latinos and from 50 to 20 percent of blacks portrayed.

NOTES

1. Harry Castleman and Walter Podrazik, *Watching TV: Four Decades of American Television* (New York: McGraw-Hill, 1982), 208.
2. Ibid., 226.
3. Laura Z. Hobson, quoted in Christopher Lasch, "Archie Bunker and the Liberal Mind," *Channels*, October/November 1981, 34.
4. Quoted in Castleman and Podrazik, *Watching TV*, 227.
5. See Richard Adler, ed., *All in the Family: A Critical Appraisal* (New York: Praeger, 1979).
6. Quoted in William Raspberry, "Cosby Show: Black or White?" *Washington Post*, 5 November 1984.
7. Quoted in *Time*, 19 March 1979, 85.
8. S. Robert Lichter and Daniel R. Amundson, *Distorted Reality: Hispanic Characters in TV Entertainment* (Washington, DC: Center for Media and Public Affairs, 1994).
9. Quoted in *Time*, 19 March 1979, 85.

CRAZY HORSE MALT LIQUOR AND ATHLETES: THE TENACITY OF STEREOTYPES

38

WINNEBAGOS, CHEROKEES, APACHES, AND DAKOTAS: THE PERSISTENCE OF STEREOTYPING OF AMERICAN INDIANS IN AMERICAN ADVERTISING BRANDS

Debra Merskin

QUESTIONS TO CONSIDER

Driving your Winnebago recreational vehicle (fully loaded 2001 Chieftan model) with Jeep Cherokee in tow, you pull into the Navajo National Park in New Mexico for your much-needed vacation. You sit down, light up a Natural American Spirit Cigarette, open a forty-ounce bottle of Crazy Horse Malt Liquor, and get ready to watch the World Series match between the Atlanta Braves (with their "Tomahawk Chop") and the Cleveland Indians. Each of there products draws on extremely stereotypical imagery of American Indians. Why, according to Debra Merskin, do these stereotypes continue, and what effect do these images have on the way individuals view American Indians?

From early childhood on, we have all learned about "Indianness" from textbooks, movies, television programs, cartoons, songs, commercials, fanciful paintings, and product logos.[1] Since the turn of the century, American Indian images, music, and names have been incorporated into many American advertising campaigns and product images. Whereas patent medicines of the past featured "coppery, feather-topped visage of the Indian" (Larson, 1937, p. 338), butter boxes of the present show the doe-eyed, buckskin-clad Indian "princess." These stereotypes are pervasive, but not necessarily consistent—varying over time and place from the "artificially idealistic" (noble savage) to present-day images of "mystical environmentalists or uneducated, alcoholic bingo-players confined to reservations"

(Mihesuah, 1996, p. 9). Yet today a trip down the grocery store aisle still reveals ice cream bars, beef jerky, corn meal, baking powder, malt liquor, butter, honey, sour cream, and chewing tobacco packages emblazoned with images of American Indians. Companies that use these images of Indians do so to build an association with an idealized and romanticized notion of the past through the process of branding (Aaker & Biel, 1993). Because these representations are so commonplace (Land O' Lakes maiden, Jeep Cherokee, Washington Redskins logo), we often fail to notice them, yet they reinforce long-held stereotypical beliefs about Native Americans.

Trade characters such as Aunt Jemima (pancake mix), Uncle Rastus (Cream of Wheat), and Uncle Ben (rice) are visual reminders of the subservient occupational positions to which Blacks often have been relegated (Kern-Foxworth, 1994). Similarly, Crazy Horse Malt Liquor, Red Chief Sugar, and Sue Bee Honey similarly remind us of an oppressive past. How pictorial metaphors on product labels create and perpetuate stereotypes of American Indians is the focus of this study. McCracken's (1993) Meaning Transfer Model and Barthes's (1972) semiotic analysis of brand images serve as the framework for the analysis of four national brands. The following sections discuss how stereotypes are constructed and how they are articulated in, and perpetuated through, advertising.

Background

To understand how labels on products and brand names reinforce long-held stereotypical beliefs, we must consider beliefs already in place that facilitated this process. Goings (1994), in his study of African American stereotypes, points out that, "Racism was not a byproduct of the Civil War; it

had clearly been around since the founding of the nation" (p. 7) Similarly, anti-Indian sentiments did not begin with the subjugation and dislocation efforts of the 1800s. Racial and ethnic images, part of American advertising for more than a century, were created in "less enlightened times" but have become a part of American popular culture and thought (Graham, 1993, p. 35) and persist today. The system of representation thereby becomes a "stable cultural convention that is taught and learned by members of a society" (Kates & Shaw-Garlock, 1999, p. 34).

Part of the explanation for the persistent use of these images can be found in the power and persuasiveness of popular culture representations. Goings's (1994) analysis of Black collectibles and memorabilia from the 1880s to the 1950s is a useful analogy for understanding the construction of Native American stereotypes in popular culture. He suggests that "collectible" items such as salt and pepper shakers, trade cards, and sheet music with images of happy Sambos, plump mammies, or wide-eyed pickaninnies served as nonverbal articulations of racism made manifest in everyday goods. By exaggerating the physical features of African American men and women, and making them laughable and useable in everyday items, these household objects reinforced beliefs about the place of Blacks in American society. Aunt Jemima, the roly-poly mammy; and Uncle Rastus, the happy slave chef (ironically both remain with us today) helped make Whites feel more comfortable with, and less guilty about, maintenance of distinctions on the basis of race well after Reconstruction. These items were meant for daily use, hence constantly and subtly reinforcing stereotypical beliefs.

Similarly, Berkhofer (1979) suggests that "the essence of the white image of the Indian has been the definition of American

Indians in fact and in fancy as a separate and single other. Whether evaluated as noble or ignoble, whether seen as exotic or downgraded, the Indian as image was always alien to white." (p. xv) White images of Native Americans were similarly constructed through children's games, toys, tales, art, and theater of the 1800s. Whereas "Little Black Sambo" tales reinforced the construction of racist beliefs about Blacks, songs such as "Ten Little Indians" or "cowboy and Indian" games similarly framed Indian otherness in the White mind. Goings (1994) makes an important point about the source of the construction of objects that represent this way of thinking:

> It is important to note that Black memorabilia are figures from white American history. White Americans developed the stereotypes; white Americans produced the collectibles; and white American manufacturers and advertisers disseminated both the images and the objects to a white audience. (p. xix)

The maintenance of these kinds of beliefs satisfies the human need for psychological equilibrium and order, finding support and reinforcement in ideology. Defined as "typical properties of the 'social mind' of a group" (van Dijk, 1996, p. 56), ideologies provide a frame of reference for understanding the world. *Racist* ideologies serve several social functions operating to reproduce racism by legitimating social inequalities, thereby justifying racially or ethnically constructed differences. Racist ideology is used to (1) organize specific social attitudes into an evaluative framework for perceiving otherness, (2) provide the basis for "coordinated action and solidarity among whites," and (3) define racial and ethnic identity of the dominant group (van Dijk, 25–27). These beliefs and practices are thereby articulated

in the production and distribution of racist discourse.

Theoretical Foundation

To every ad they see or hear, people bring a shared set of beliefs that serve as frames of reference for understanding the world around them. Beyond its obvious selling function, advertising images are about making meaning. Ads must "take into account not only the inherent qualities and attributes of the products they are trying to sell, but also the way in which they can make those properties mean something to us" (Williamson, 1978, p. 12).

Barthes (1972) describes these articulations as myth, that is, "a type of speech" or mode of signification that is conveyed by discourse that consists of many possible modes of representation including, but not limited to, writing, photography, publicity, and advertising. Myth is best described by the process of semiology (Barthes, 1972). Semiology "postulates a relation between two terms, a signifier and a signified" (Barthes, 1972, p. 112). The correlation of the terms *signifier, signified,* and *sign* is where associative meaning is made. What we see in an advertisement or product label, at first glance, are basic elements composed of linguistic signs (words) and iconic signs (visuals). Barthes (1972) uses a rose, for example, as a symbol of passion. Roses are not passion per se, but rather the roses (signifier) + concept of passion (signified) = roses (sign). He states that "the signifier is empty, the sign is full, it is a meaning" (Barthes, 1972, p. 113). Another example that involves race is the use of Aunt Jemima for maple syrup. We see the representation of a bandana-clad Black woman who suggests the mammy of the Deep South (signified). When placed on the bottle of syrup (sign), meaning is transferred to the otherwise ambiguous product—care giving, home cooking, and food sharing. The sign is formed at the intersection between a brand name and a meaning system that is articulated in a particular image. Quite simply, a sign, whether "object, word, or picture," has a "particular meaning to a person or group of people. It is neither the thing nor the meaning alone, but the two together" (Williamson, 1978, p. 17).

McCracken (1993, p. 125), who defines a brand as a "bundle or container of meaning," expanded on the Barthesian analysis and developed a framework for understanding the cultural relationship that brands have within society. His anthropological model . . . illustrates the meanings of brands. McCracken shows how brands assume meaning through advertising, combined with consumption behavior, and the nature of common knowledge that consumers bring to this system. The present study expands on this process by adding a reinforcement loop from consumer back to the culture where stereotypes are experienced and re-circulated through the system.

A brand can have gendered meaning (maleness/femaleness), social standing (status), nationality (country meaning), and ethnicity/race (multicultural meaning). A brand can also stand for notions of tradition, trustworthiness, purity, family, nature, and so on. McCracken (1993) uses the Marlboro man as an example of these components with which a simple red and white box came to signify freedom, satisfaction, competence, maleness, and a quintessentially American, Western character. The product becomes part of the constellation of meanings that surrounds it and thereby "soaks up" meanings. When the rugged Marlboro man is situated on his horse, on the open plain, almost always alone, the meanings of the constellation become clear—freedom, love of the

outdoors, release from the confines of industrialized society—he is a "real man," self-sufficient and individualistic. These meanings become part of a theme made up of prototypical content while simultaneously being "idealizations and not reality itself" (Schmitt & Simonson, 1997, p. 124).

Advertisements are created in such a way as to boost the commodity value of brand names by connecting them to images that resonate with the social and cultural values of a society. These images are loaded with established ideological assumptions that, when attached to a commodity, create the commodity sign. Tools of branding are thereby used to create a particular image in the mind of the consumer. According to van Dijk (1996), this pattern often serves to present an US versus THEM dichotomy, with US being White, "positive, tolerant, modern," and THEM being minorities who are "problematic, deviant and threatening" (pp. 26–27). Hence, attitudes, beliefs, and behavior that are racist serve to support a dominant ideology that focuses on difference and separatism.

These ideas and values are articulated through the construction, maintenance, and perpetuation of stereotypes. Stereotypes are overgeneralized beliefs that

> get hold of the few simple, vivid,
> memorable, easily grasped, and widely
> recognized characteristics about a person,
> reduce everything about the person to
> those traits, exaggerate and simplify
> them, and fix them without change or
> development to eternity. (Hall, 1997,
> p. 258)

An example is the way the "Indian problem" of the 1800s has been shown in "cowboy and Indian" films. In his analysis of the representation of Indians in film, Strickland (1998, p. 10) asks, "What would we think the American Indian was like if we had only the celluloid Indian from which to reconstruct history?" (Strickland, 1998, p. 10). The cinematic representation includes the Indian as a

> bloodthirsty and lawless savage; the Indian as enemy of progress; the Indian as tragic, but inevitable, victim; the Indian as a lazy, fat, shiftless drunk; the Indian as oil-rich illiterate; the Indian as educated half-breed unable to live in either a white or Indian world; the Indian as nympho-maniac; the Indian as noble hero; the Indian as stoic and unemotional; the Indian as the first conservationist. (Strickland, 1998, p. 10)

Champagne's (1994) analysis of Indians in films and theater suggests that the longevity of James Fenimore Cooper's *Last of the Mohicans*, evidenced by its many film treatments, demonstrates that "Hollywood prefers to isolate its Indians safely within the romantic past, rather than take a close look at Native American issues in the contemporary world" (p. 719).

Natty Bumppo, in James Fenimore Cooper's *Deerslayer*, is a literary example of the male who goes from a state of "uncultured animality" to a state of "civilization and culture" (Green, 1993, p. 327). Larson (1937) describes how this stereotype was translated into a tool for marketing patent medicines:

> No sooner had James Fenimore Cooper romanticized the Indian in the American imagination in his novels than patent-medicine manufacturers, quick to sense and take advantage of this new enthusiasm, used the red man as symbol and token for a great variety of ware. How the heart of the purchaser—filled, like as not, with the heroic exploits of Cooper's Indians—must have warmed as he gazed at the effigy, symbolic of "Nature's Own Remedy." (p. 338)

The female savage becomes an Indian princess who "renounces her own family, marries someone from the dominate culture and assimilates into it" (Green, 1993, p. 327), for example, Pocahontas. From this perspective, Indians are thought of as childlike and innocent, requiring the paternalistic care of Whites; that is, they are tamable. In her study of Indian imagery in *Dr. Quinn, Medicine Woman*, Bird (1996, p. 258) suggests that what viewers see is a White fantasy filled with White concerns around "guilt and retrospective outrage." Green's (1993) analysis of the use of male Indian images in ads posits that Natives continue to be portrayed according to stereotypical images: (1) noble savage (the stoic, innocent, child of nature), (2) civilizable savage (redeemable, teachable), and (3) bloodthirsty savage (fierce, predatory, cultureless, animalistic). Taken together, these studies suggest that historically constructed images and beliefs about American Indians are at the essence of stereotypical thinking that are easily translated into product images.

Method

To study the articulation of racist ideology in brand images, four currently available national products (Land O' Lakes butter, Sue Bee Honey, Big Chief [Monitor] Sugar, and Crazy Horse Malt Liquor) were analyzed according to Barthes's (1972) semiotic analysis. First, the material object was identified (signifier); second, the associative elements were identified (signified); and, third, these were brought together in what we as consumers recognize as the sign. Company websites, press releases, and product packages were used for visual and textual information. Several attempts to communicate directly with the companies yielded no response. Through this method of analysis we can see how these meanings are transferred to the different products on the basis of both race and gender.

Results

The following section presents a descriptive analysis of Land O' Lakes, Sue Bee Honey, Big Chief (Monitor) Sugar, and Crazy Horse Malt Liquor brand images.

Land O' Lakes

Although not the first national manufacturer to draw on the mystique of Indianness (that honor goes to Red Man Tobacco in 1904), Land O' Lakes is certainly one of the more prominent. In 1921, the Minnesota Cooperative Creameries Association opened for business in Arden Hills, Minnesota. This company served as the central shipping agent for a small group of small, farmer-owned dairy cooperatives (Morgan, 1986, p. 63). In 1924, the group wanted a different name and solicited ideas from farmers. Mrs. E. B. Foss and Mr. George L. Swift came up with the winning name—Land O' Lakes, "a tribute to Minnesota's thousands of sparkling lakes" (p. 63). The corporate website opens with a photograph of a quiet lake amid pine trees and blue sky. The copy under the photograph reads:

> Welcome to Land O' Lakes. A land unlike anywhere else on earth. A special place filled with clear, spring-fed lakes. Rivers and streams that dance to their own rhythms through rich, fertile fields. It's the land we call home. And from it has flowed the bounty and goodness we bring to you, our neighbors and friends.
> (Land O' Lakes, 2000)

In addition, "The now famous Indian maiden was also created during the search for a brand name and trademark. Because the regions of Minnesota and Wisconsin were the legendary lands of Hiawatha and Minnehaha, the idea of an Indian Maiden took form" (Land O' Lakes, 2000). A painting was sent to the company of an Indian maiden facing the viewer, holding a butter carton with a background filled with lakes, pines, flowers, and grazing cows.

At the Land O' Lakes corporate website, the director of communications includes a statement about the maiden image, where he agrees that the logo, the "Indian Maiden," has powerful connotations (Land O' Lakes). Hardly changed since its introduction in the 1920s, he says that Land O' Lakes has built on the "symbolism of the purity of the products" (Burnham, 1992). The company "thought the Indian maiden would be a good image. She represents Hiawatha and the Land of Gitchygoomee and the names of Midwest towns and streets that have their roots in the American Indian population" (Burnham, 1992).

The signifier is thereby the product, be it butter, sour cream, or other Land O' Lakes products. The Indian woman on the package is associated with youth, innocence, nature, and purity. The result is the generic "Indian maiden." Subsequently, the qualities stereotypically associated with this beaded, buckskinned, doe-eyed young woman are transferred to the company's products. Green's "noble savage" image is extended to include the female stereotype.

Sue Bee Honey

The Sioux Honey Association, based in Sioux City, Iowa, is a cooperative of honey producers, yielding 40 million pounds of honey annually (Sioux Honey Association, 2000). Corporate communications describe a change of the product name in 1964 from Sioux Bee to Sue Bee, "to reflect the correct pronunciation of the name" (Sioux Honey Association, 2000). The brand name and image are reinforced on trucks (both real and toys), on the bottles and jars in which the honey is sold, and through collectibles such as coffee mugs and recipe books.

Sue Bee Honey also draws upon the child-of-nature imagery in an attempt to imbue qualities of purity into their products. If we were to view Sue Bee in her full form (as she is shown on many specialty items such as mugs, glasses, and jars) we would see that she is an Indian maiden on top, with braided hair and headband, and a bee below the waist. Changing the spelling of her name from "Sioux Bee" to "Sue Bee" could be interpreted in a variety of ways—possibly simply as a matter of pronunciation, as the company asserts, or as an effort to draw attention away from the savage imagery stereotypically attributed to members of this tribe and more toward the little girlishness of the image. In this case, the product is honey, traditionally associated with trees and forests and natural places. This association works well with the girl–child Indian stereotype. By placing the girl bee on the package of honey, consumers can associate the innocence, purity, and naturalness attributed to Native American females with the quality of the product.

In the tradition of Pocahontas, both the Land O' Lakes and the Sue Bee maidens symbolize innocence, purity, and virginity—children of nature. The maiden image signifies a female "Indianness." She is childlike, as she happily offers up perhaps honey or butter (or herself) that "is as pure and healthy as she is" (Dotz & Morton, 1996, p. 11). The maiden's image is used to represent attempts to get back to nature, and the association is that this can be accomplished through the healthy, wholesome products of Land O' Lakes. Both images are encoded with socially constructed meanings about female Indian sexuality, purity, and nature.

Monitor Sugar Company

Founded in 1901, the Monitor Sugar Company processes approximately 4% of U.S. beet production into sugar (granulated, powdered, brown, and icing; Monitor Sugar Company, 2000). For 60 years, the company has been producing sugar from beets, relying on the image of an American Indians in full headdress to sell the sugar goods. The products are available on grocery store shelves and in bulk for institution, delivered by trucks with the Big Chief logo emblazoned on the sides.

So, who is this Chief said to represent? Is he a bona fide tribal leader or a composite Indian designed to communicate naturalistic characteristics associated with Indians with the sugar? Green's (1993) savage typology suggests that this individual is a combination of the noble savage (natural) and the bloodthirsty savage (ferocious). He is proud, noble, and natural and yet he is wearing a ceremonial headdress that communicates strength and stoicism.

Crazy Horse Malt Liquor

A 40-ounce beverage that is sold in approximately 40 states (Metz & Thee, 1994), Crazy Horse Malt Liquor is brewed by the Heilman Brewing Company of Brooklyn, New York. Crazy Horse Malt Liquor employs the image of Tasunke Witko (Crazy Horse) on the label of its malt liquor. On the front of the bottle is an American Indian male wearing a headdress that appears to be an eagle feather bonnet, and there is a symbol representing a medicine wheel—both sacred images in Lakota and other Native cultures (1994).

Image analysis shows that the sign is that of an actual Indian chief. Signified, however, are beliefs about Indians as warriors, westward expansion, how mighty the consumer might be by drinking this brand,

and wildness of the American Western frontier.

This brand, perhaps more than any other, has come under public scrutiny because it is the image of a particular person. A revered forefather of the Oglala Sioux tribe of South Dakota, Crazy Horse died in 1877 (Blalock, 1992). The labels feature the prominent image of Chief Crazy Horse, who has long been the subject of stories, literature, and movies. Larger than life, he has played a role in American mythology.

Signifying Green's (1993) bloodthirsty savage image, Crazy Horse Malt Liquor makers use of American myths through image and association. Ironically, Crazy Horse objected to alcohol and warned his nation about the destructive effects of liquor (Specktor, 1995). As a sign, Crazy Horse represents a real symbol of early American life and westward expansionism. He was, according to the vice president of the Oglala Sioux Tribe, a "warrior, a spiritual leader, a traditional leader, a hero who has always been and is still revered by our people" (Hill, 1992; Metz & Thee, 1994, p. 50). This particular image brings together some interesting aspects of branding. Not only is the noble and bloodthirsty savage stereotype brought together in a proud, but ultimately defeated, Indian chief, but also this is an image of a real human being. The association of alcohol with that image, as well as targeting the Indian population, draws on assumptions of alcohol abuse.[2]

Discussion and Conclusions

Although there are dozens of possible examples of Native images on product labels, ranging from cigarette packages to sports utility vehicles, the examples discussed above illustrate the principles behind semiotics. The four presented here are significant examples of national brands employing stereotypical representations. When people are made aware of these products, they see how these images are consistently found in many products that employ Indian stereotypes either in product names or in their logos.

Many of these signs and symbols have been with us so long we no longer question them. Product images on packages, in advertisements, on television, and in films are nearly the only images non-Indians ever see of Native Americans. The covers of romance novels routinely feature Indian men sweeping beautiful non-Indian women off their feet as their bodices are torn away. These stereotypical representations of American Indians denies that they are human beings, and presents them as existing only in the past and as single, monolithic Indians (Merskin, 1998).

American Indians are certainly not the only racial or ethnic group to be discriminated against, overtly or covertly. Aunt Jemima and Rastus certainly have their origins in dehumanizing, one-dimensional images based on a tragic past. Yet, like Betty Crocker, these images have been updated. Aunt Jemima has lost weight and the bandana, and the Frito Bandito has disappeared (Burnham, 1992). But the Indian image persists in corporate marketing and product labeling.

These are highly visible and perhaps more openly discussed than images that appear on the products we see in grocery store aisles. An Absolut Vodka ad shows an Eskimo pulling a sled of vodka and a GreyOwl Wild Rice package features an Indian with braids, wearing a single feather, surrounded by a circle that represents (according to GreyOwl's distribution manager) the "oneness of nature" (Burnham, 1992). A partial list of others includes Apache helicopter, Jeep Cherokee, Apache rib doormats, Red Man Tobacco, Kleek-O the Eskimo (Cliquot Club ginger ale),

Dodge Dakota, Pontiac, the Cleveland Indians, Mutual of Omaha, Calumet Baking Powder, Mohawk Carpet Mills, American Spirit cigarettes, Eskimo pies, Tomahawk mulcher, Winnebago Motor Homes, Indian Motorcycles, Tomahawk missiles, many high school sports teams, and the music behind the Hamm's beer commercials that begins "From the land of sky blue waters." And the list goes on.

Change is coming, but it is slow. For one thing, American Indians do not represent a significant target audience to advertisers. Representing less than 1% of the population, and the most economically destitute of all ethnic minority populations, American Indians are not particularly useful to marketers. Nearly 30% live below the official poverty line, in contrast with 13% of the general U.S. population (Cortese, 1999, p. 117). Without the population numbers or legal resources, it is nearly impossible for the voices of Natives to be heard, unlike other groups who have made some representational inroads. According to Westerman (1989), when minority groups speak, businesses are beginning to listen: "That's why Li'l Black Sambo and the Frito Bandito are dead. They were killed by the very ethnic groups they portrayed" (p. 28).

Not only does stereotyping communicate inaccurate beliefs about Natives to Whites, but also to Indians. Children, all children, are perhaps the most important recipients of this information for it is during childhood that difference is first learned. If, during the transition of adolescence, Native children internalize these representations that suggest that Indians are lazy, alcoholic by nature, and violent, this misinformation can have a life-long impact on perceptions of self and others. As Lippmann (1922/1961) wrote,

> The subtlest and most pervasive of all influences are those which create and maintain the repertory of stereotypes. We are told about the world before we see it. We imagine most things before we experience them. (p. 89)

By playing a game of substitution, by inserting other ethnic groups or races into the same situation, it becomes clear that there is a problem. Stereotypical images do not reside only in the past, because the social control mechanisms that helped to create them remain with us today.

Future research should continue to examine how the advertising and marketing practice of branding contributes to the persistent use of racist images on product labels. This study adds to the sparse literature on media representations of Native Americans in general and adds to Green's (1993) typology by including female counterparts to the male savage stereotypes. Future research could explore more images of Native Americans in ads and on products. Qualitative research with members of different tribes would add depth to this area of study.

NOTES

1. Many people have preferences about terms used to describe America's indigenous peoples. "American Indian" is commonly used, as is "Native American, Native, and Indian." These terms are used interchangeably in recognition of individual preferences, without disregarding the weight each word carries.

2. Lawsuits are currently underway to limit Heilman Breweries use of the name Crazy Horse Liquor (Specktor, 1995). Several states have outlawed the sale of the beverage (Specktor, 1995). Also under review are important legal issues such as a tribe's sovereign power to exercise civil jurisdiction and the Witko family's right to protect the image of their ancestor.

REFERENCES

Aaker, D., & A. L. Biel. (1993). *Advertising's role in building strong brands*. Matwah, NJ: Lawrence Erlbaum.

Barthes, R. (1972). *Mythologies*. New York: The Noonday Press.

Berkhofer, R., Jr. (1979). *The white man's Indian: Images of the American Indian from Columbus to the present*. New York: Vintage Books.

Bird, S. E. (1996). Not my fantasy: The persistence of Indian imagery in *Dr. Quinn, Medicine Woman*. In S. E. Bird (Ed.), *Dressing in feathers: The construction of the Indian in American popular culture* (pp. 245–262). Boulder, CO: Westview Press.

Blalock, C. (1992). Crazy Horse controversy riles Congress: Controversies over Crazy Horse Malt Liquor and Black Death vodka. *Beverage Industry, 83*(9), 1–3.

Burnham, P. (1992, 27 May). Indians can't shake label as guides to good buys. *The Washington Times*, p. E1.

Champagne, D. (1994). *Native America: Portrait of the peoples*. Detroit: Visible Ink.

Cortese, A. J. (1999). *Provocateur: Images of women and minorities in advertising*. New York: Rowman & Littlefield Publishers, Inc.

Dotz, W., & Morton, J. (1996). *What a character! 20th century American advertising icons*. San Francisco: Chronicle Books.

Goings, K. W. (1994). *Mammy and Uncle Mose: Black collectibles and American stereotyping*. Bloomington, IN: Indiana University Press.

Graham, R. (1993, 6 January). Symbol or stereotype: One consumer's tradition is another's racial slur. *The Boston Globe*, p. 35.

Green, M. K. (1993). Images of American Indians in advertising: Some moral issues. *Journal of Business Ethics, 12*, 323–330.

Hall, S. (1997). *Representation: Cultural representations and signifying practices*. London: Sage.

Hill, R. (1992). The non-vanishing American Indian: Are the modern images any closer to the truth? *Quail* (May), 35–37.

Kates, S. M., & Shaw-Garlock, G. (1999). The ever-entangling web: A study of ideologies and discourses in advertising to women. *Journal of Advertising 28*(2), 33–49.

Kern-Foxworth, M. (1994). *Aunt Jemima, Uncle Ben, and Rastus: Blacks in advertising yes-terday, today, and tomorrow*. Westport, CT: Praeger.

Land O' Lakes. (2000). [On-line]. Available: http://www.landolakes.com

Larson, C. (1937). Patent-medicine advertising and the early American press. *Journalism Quarterly, 14*(4), 333–339.

Lippmann, W. (1922/1961). *Public opinion*. New York: McMillan & Company.

McCracken, G. (1993). The value of the brand: An anthropological perspective. In D. Aaker & A. L. Biel (Eds.), *Brand Equity is advertising: Advertising's role in building strong brands*. Matwah, NJ: Lawrence Erlbaum.

Merskin, D. (1998). Sending up signals: A survey of American Indian media use and representation in the mass media. *The Howard Journal of Communications, 9*, 333–345.

Metz, S., & Thee, M. (1994). Brewers intoxicated with racist imagery. *Business and Society Review, 89*, 50–51.

Mihesuah, D. A. (1996). *American Indians: Stereotypes and realities*. Atlanta, GA: Clarity Press.

Monitor Sugar Company. (2000) [On-line]. Available: http://members.aol.com/asga/mon.htm.

Morgan, H. (1986). *Symbols of America*. New York: Penguin Books.

Schmitt, B., & Simonson, A. (1997). *Marketing aesthetics: The strategic management of brands, identity, and image*. New York: The Free Press.

Sioux Honey Association. (2000). [On-line]. Available: http://www.suebeehoney.com.

Specktor, M. (1995, January 6). Crazy Horse exploited to peddle liquor. *National Catholic Reporter, 31*(10), 3.

Strickland, R. (1998). The celluloid Indian. *Oregon Quarterly* (Summer), 9–10.

van Dijk, T. A. (1996). *Discourse, racism, and ideology*. La Laguna: RCEI Ediciones.

Westerman, M. (1989, March). Death of the Frito bandito: Marketing to ethnic groups. *American Demographics, 11*, 28–32.

Williamson, J. (1978), Decoding advertisements: Ideology and meaning in advertising. New York: Marion Boyars.

SEEING THE BIG PICTURE

Look though the Appendix and notice the relative quality-of-life measures of American Indians. What is the link between this group's socioeconomic standing and the way they are portrayed in the media?

39

SPORT IN AMERICA: THE NEW
RACIAL STEREOTYPES

Richard E. Lapchick

QUESTIONS TO CONSIDER

Richard Lapchick asks why athletes are subject to such an intense level of scrutiny by the press. What argument does he make that links race, stereotypes, and celebrity culture to the attitudes most Americans have about student and professional athletes?

Athletes and Crime

The beginning of the twenty-first century brought the hope that many social injustices would be rectified. However, surveys taken throughout the 1990s indicated that many inaccurate perceptions persisted such as the majority of whites surveyed continuing to believe that most African-Americans are less intelligent, more prone to drug use, more violent, and more inclined towards violence against women than whites are.

Sport culture, as it is currently interpreted, now provides whites with the chance to talk about athletes in a way that reinforces these stereotypes of African-Americans. Because African-Americans dominate the most popular sports, whites tend to "think black" when they think about the major sports.

Richard E. Lapchick, "Sport in America: The New Racial Stereotypes" from *Smashing Barriers: Race and Sport in the New Millennium*, pp. 265–280. Copyright © 2001 by Madison Books. Reprinted by permission of Rowman & Littlefield Publishers, Inc.

Each time any athlete gets into trouble, I receive many calls from writers and television producers seeking comments. After a fight involving a basketball or football player, the interrogation invariably includes, "What makes football or basketball players more inclined to get into fights?" I have never been asked this question of a hockey or baseball player, despite the fact that there are as many game fights in those sports.

After a reported incident of domestic violence involving a basketball or football player, the inevitable question is, "What makes football or basketball players more inclined to abuse women?" Equal numbers of hockey and baseball players are accused of domestic violence, yet I have never been asked this question about them.

Each year during the professional drafts in each sport I am asked, "What do you think about colleges and even high school football and basketball players jumping to the pros and missing their chance for an education?" I have never been asked that question about baseball or hockey, tennis or golf players who put higher education on hold to pursue athletic careers.

Shawn Fanning left Northeastern University early to turn pro and earn millions; he was called a genius for founding Napster. The Dean of Northeastern University's School of Engineering told me that one of his biggest problems comes from companies attempting to lure away his top students each year. They leave for the money.

I believe that at least part of the systematic coupling of athletes and crime revolves around racial stereotyping. The media has persistently and consistently suggested that basketball and football players, who happen to be overwhelmingly African-American, are more violent than athletes in other sports and people in society in general. The result is that nearly everyone, including the police, women, fans, the media, sports administrators, and athletes themselves, believes that certain athletes, especially basketball or football players, are more inclined to be violent in general and violent against women in particular.

Rosalyn Dunlap, an African-American who was a five-time All American sprinter who now works on social issues involving athletes, including gender violence prevention, said, "perpetrators are not limited to any category or occupation. The difference is that athletes who rape or batter will end up on television or in the newspapers. Such images of athletes in trouble create a false and dangerous mindset with heavy racial overtones. Most other perpetrators will be known only to the victims, their families, the police, and the courts."

Once, while speaking to a group of distinguished international fellows at an elite academic institution, I asked members of the audience to write down five words that they would use to describe American athletes. In addition to listing positive adjectives, not one missed including one of the following words: dumb, violent, rapist or drug-user. I regularly meet with NBA and NFL players,

as well as with college student-athletes on dozens of campuses. There are a lot of angry athletes who are convinced the public is stereotyping them because of the criminal acts of a few.

Many American men have grown to dislike athletes. A typical man might crave the money and the fame that a pro athlete enjoys, but he recognizes that such athletic success is unattainable for him. After reading all the negative press about athletes, he doesn't want to read that Mike Tyson felt he was treated unfairly by the justice system, knowing full well that Tyson made a reported hundred million dollars in his post-release rehabilitation program. He has little sympathy for the large number of pro athletes signing contracts worth more than ten million dollars a year. He is a micro-thought away from making egregious stereotypes about the "other groups" perceived as stealing his part of the American pie.

Big-time athletes fit the "other groups" category. Whether it is an African-American athlete or coach, or a white coach of African-American athletes, when something goes wrong with a player, a national reaction is likely to be immediate. Tom "Satch" Sanders, who helped the Boston Celtics win eight world championships, is now vice president for player programs for the NBA. His office encourages and guides players to finish their education, prepare for careers after basketball, and adjust to all the attention that NBA stars attract. Sanders presents a view complementary to Dunlap's. He proposes that the public has made a link between the stereotypes for athletes and African-Americans: "Everyone feels that athletes have to take the good with the bad, the glory with the negative publicity. However, no one appreciates the broad-brush application that is applied in so many instances. Of the few thousand that play sports on the highest level, if four or five individuals in each sport—particularly if they are black—have problems with the law, people won't have long to wait before some media people are talking about all those athletes."

APBnews.com released two revealing studies in 2000. The first was a study of NFL players on two teams that made it to the 2000 Super Bowl. The second was a study of the sixteen NBA teams in the 2000 playoffs. In the NFL study, 11 percent of the players had a criminal history. That stood in dramatic contrast to the 35 to 46 percent lifetime arrest rate (taken from extensive studies in California and New York) for adult males under thirty, the same age group as most NFL players. Most NFL players are between 18 and 30 years old although most of those are between the ages of 21 and 30. In the study of NBA players, the arrest rate of those on the sixteen playoff teams was 18 percent, again a fraction of the national figures for their comparable age group of males.

Jeff Benedict's book *Pros and Cons* created a sensation in 1998 by saying that 21 percent of NFL players had arrest records. In an article he coauthored in 1999 for the statistics journal *Chance,* he said that the lifetime arrest rates for the NFL players he documented in *Pros and Cons* was less than half the arrest rate in the general population.

Fans build stereotypes of athletes from media coverage of the athletes and the games. Fans, who are mostly white, observe sport through a media filter that is created by an overwhelming number of white men. There are 1,600 daily newspapers in America employing only nineteen African-American sports columnists. There are only two African-American sports editors who work on newspapers in a city that has professional sports franchises. The fact that the number of sports columnists, as reported in the 2000 conference of the National Asso-

ciation of Black Journalists, has almost doubled from 11 since 1998 is a positive sign. However, there are no African-American sports writers on 90 percent of the 1,600 daily newspapers.

I am not suggesting, nor would I ever suggest, that most or even many of the white news writers are racist. However, they were raised in a culture in which many white people have strong beliefs about what it means to be African-American. The obvious result is that their reporting provides reinforcement of white stereotypes of African-American athletes. According to the National Opinion Research Center Survey, sponsored by the National Science Foundation for the University of Chicago, whites surveyed share the following attitudes:

- Fifty-six percent of whites think African-Americans are more violent.
- Sixty-two percent of whites think African-Americans do not work as hard as whites.
- Seventy-seven percent of whites think most African-Americans live off welfare.
- Fifty-three percent think African-Americans are less intelligent.

Some white writers may have picked up these stereotypes in their own upbringing. When they write about an individual African-American athlete or several African-American athletes who have a problem, it becomes easy to unconsciously leap to the conclusion that fits the stereotype. Sanders said, "Blacks in general have been stereotyped for having drugs in the community as well as for being more prone to violence, However, now more than ever before, young black athletes are more individualistic and they resist the 'broad brush.' They insist on being judged as individuals for everything." But even that resistance can't be misinterpreted by the public and by the writers as off-the-court trash talking.

The athletes of the twenty-first century come from a generation of despairing youth cut adrift from the American dream. When the Center for the Study of Sport in Society started in 1984, one of its primary missions was to help young people balance academics and athletics. Since 1990, its mission has been extended to help young people lead healthy and safe lives.

Today our colleges are recruiting athletes:

- who have witnessed violent death. If an American child under the age of sixteen is killed every two hours with a handgun, then there is a good chance that young athletes will have a fallen family member or friend.
- who are mothers and fathers when they arrive at our schools. There are boys who helped 900,000 teenage girls get pregnant each year. Some student-athletes will leave after four years of college with one or more children who are four or five years old.
- who have seen friends or family members devastated by drugs.
- who have seen battering in their homes. An estimated 3 percent of American men are batterers and an estimated 3 million women are battered each year.
- who were victims of racism in school. Seventy-five percent of all students surveyed by Lou Harris reported seeing or hearing about racially or religiously motivated confrontations with overtones of violence very or somewhat often.
- who grew up as latchkey kids. Either a single parent or two working parents head 57 percent of American families, black and white alike.

Not enough campuses or athletic departments have the right people to help guide these young men and women into their adult lives. College campuses desperately need professionals that can deal with these nightmarish factors.

Academic Issues in College Sport

The amount of media coverage devoted to student-athlete literacy problems seem unique to athletes. The media rarely reports that 30 percent of *all* entering freshmen must take remedial English or mathematics. The same holds true for the media's portrayal of student-athlete graduation rates. Although college athletic departments should strive to increase the number of student-athletes who graduate, graduation rates for the student body as a whole have changed. Only 14 percent of entering freshmen graduated in four years. If an athlete does not graduate in four years, some call him dumb; others say the school failed him. Few note that he may be typical of college students.

Don McPherson nearly led Syracuse University to a national championship when he was their quarterback in the 1980s. After seven years in the NFL and CFL, McPherson worked until 1999 directing the Mentors in Violence Prevention (MVP) Program, the nation's largest program using athletes as leaders to address the issue of men's violence against women.

McPherson reflected on the image that associates athletes with a lack of intelligence: "When whites meet an uneducated black athlete who blew opportunities in college or high school, they think he is dumb. They don't question what kind of school he may have had to attend if he was poor, or how time pressures from sport may have affected him. If they don't make it as a pro athlete, they're through without a miracle. I met lots of 'Trust Fund Babies' at Syracuse. They blew opportunities. No one called them dumb, just rich. We knew they would not need a miracle to get a second chance. I played at Syracuse at a time when being a black quarterback had become more acceptable. But the stereotypes still remained. As a player, people still remember me as a great runner and scrambler. I had not dented their image of the physical vs. intelligent black athlete."

McPherson led the nation in passing efficiency over Troy Aikman and won many awards, including the Maxwell Award, but he was most proud of being the quarterback with the highest passing efficiency rating in the nation. "I should have shattered the image of the athletic and mobile black quarterback and replaced it with the intelligent black quarterback. Unfortunately, stereotypes of football players, mostly black, still prevail. They make me as angry as all the stereotypes of black people in general when I was growing up."

McPherson wore a suit to class and carried the *New York Times* under his arm. But McPherson said that those whites that recognize his style were "surprised and said I was 'a good black man,' as if I were different from other black men. Most students assumed I was poor and that football was going to make me rich. Like many other blacks on campus, I was middle class. My father was a detective and my mother was a nurse."

Irrespective of color or gender, student-athletes graduate at higher rate than non student-athletes, yet it is difficult to get accurate reporting of this in the press. According to the NCAA's 1999 report:

- Fifty-eight percent of white male Division I student-athletes graduated vs. 57 percent of white male nonathletes. Forty-two percent of African American male Division I student-athletes graduated vs. 33 percent of African American male nonathletes.
- Seventy-one percent of white female Division I student-athletes graduated

compared to 61 percent of white female nonathletes. Fifty-seven percent of African American female Division I student-athletes graduated vs. only 43 percent of African American female nonathletes.

Some disparities do appear when we compare white student-athletes to African American student-athletes:

- Fifty-three percent of white male Division I basketball student-athletes graduated versus 37 percent of African American male Division I basketball student athletes.
- Seventy percent of white female Division I basketball student-athletes graduated compared to only 56 percent of African American female Division I basketball student-athletes.

College sport does not own problems of illiteracy and low graduation rates. They belong to higher education in general and its inheritance of the near bankruptcy of secondary education in some communities.

The publication of graduation rates, long feared by athletic administrators, reveals scandalous rates, but it also shows poor graduation rates specifically for students of color. The predominantly white campuses of most colleges and universities are not welcoming environments for people of color. African American student-athletes arrive on most campuses and see that only 10 percent of the student body, 3 percent of the faculty, and less than 5 percent of top athletics administrators and coaches look like them. Unless there is a Martin Luther King Center or Boulevard, all of the buildings and streets are named after white people.

In many ways, the publication of graduation rates for student-athletes helped push the issue of diversity to the forefront of campus-wide discussions of issues of race, ethnicity, and gender. Educators finally recognized how they were failing students of color by not creating a conducive, welcoming educational environment.

Drugs and Alcohol Use Among Athletes

A common stereotype depicts athletes as abusing drugs and alcohol. Some athletes do use drugs. CNN Headline news broadcasts stories about famous athletes caught with drugs. Repeated exposure to such reports inflates the size of the problem, but the facts do not reveal widespread abuse among athletes at the professional, college or even high school level.

According to an extensive 1995 *Los Angeles Times* survey of athletes and the crimes they committed, a total of twenty-two professional and college athletes and three coaches were accused of drug use or a drug-related crime that year. On average, the media reported a story about a new sports figure with a drug problem every two weeks. Center estimates now put the number of sports figures accused of drug-related crimes at fifty per year or one media story per week on average.

Stories about athletes accused of drug use or drug-related crime are and should be disturbing. But those stories are rarely, if ever, put in the context of the 1.9 million Americans who use cocaine each month or the 12.1 million who use heroin throughout their lives. A total of 13 million individuals (6 percent of the American population) use some illicit drug each month, and 17 percent of men in the eighteen-to-twenty-five age group are drug users. Whether it is twenty-two or fifty, athletes who use drugs make up a small fraction of a single percent of the more than 400,000 athletes who play college and professional sports in America.

The NBA's drug policy, which leaves open the possibility of a lifetime ban for any athlete who is caught using drugs, is generally recognized as a model for the sports world. The policy may have stopped a substance abuse problem that predated its inception. According to an APBnews.com report, *Crime in the NBA*, released in June 2000, forty-one players were charged, booked, or arrested in eighty-two instances of crimes more serious than traffic tickets over the course of their time on the rosters of the sixteen NBA playoff teams. The story noted that "it is perhaps a credit to the NBA's antidrug policy that none of the eighty-two incidents noted in the APBnews.com study were related to hard drugs." (Marijuana was cited in six cases.) The forty-one players put the NBA's arrest rate at 18 percent. APB News.com reported that, "By way of comparison, the lifetime arrest rate of the general population as measured in four different studies ranges from 31 to 50 percent."

On the subject of alcohol abuse, the same 1995 *Los Angeles Times* survey of athletes and the crimes they committed, reported that twenty-eight college and professional athletes and four coaches were charged with alcohol-related infractions. None of these thirty-two cases were put in the context of the 13 million Americans who engage in binge drinking at least five times per month. Yet we read about a new athlete with an alcohol problem every eleven days. Such images can fuel an exaggerated sense of crisis in athletics when they are not viewed in full social context.

McPherson remembered being "shocked" when he arrived on Syracuse's campus at how much drinking went on each night among the student body. He felt compelled to call football players he knew on other campuses. "It was the same everywhere. Now when I go to speak on college campuses I always ask. It is worse today. Athletes are part of that culture, but insist that practice and academics crowd their schedules too much to be in bars as often as other students." Student personnel administrators on college campuses acknowledge that abusive drinking is the number one issue on college campuses today.

Athletes and Violence

Media coverage of professional, college, and even high school athletes consistently implies that the violence of sport makes its participants more violent in society.

Are sports any more violent today than they were twenty years ago when no one would have made such an assertion? I don't think so. But the streets and schools across America surely are more violent than they were twenty years ago—there are 2,000 assaults in schools across the nation every hour of every day. The number of American children killed by guns in the 1900s has exceeded the total number of soldiers who died in the Vietnam War. Gun violence obeys no boundaries of race, class, or geography. School shootings occurred in Pearl (Mississippi), Paduka (Kentucky), Jonesboro (Arkansas), and Littleton (Colorado). Violence seems part of the school day.

If one were to put together a lowlights tape of the fights in sports that the public best remembers, I guarantee that most people would list Kermit Washington hitting Rudy Tomjanovich, Latrell Sprewell choking P. J. Carlesimo, and Roberto Alomar spitting at umpire John Hirschbeck. Fear of men of color attacking whites in our society is part of the culture. There is no doubt that the treatment afforded to Washington, Sprewell and Alomar was measurably different than that given Denver Bronco Bill Romanowski, who is white, after he spit in the face of a black player in 1999.

Most of the stories written about specific athletes who are violent or gender violent are about African American athletes. Stories about them that appear without appropriate filters of what is going on in society reinforce racial stereotyping.

Athletes and Gender Violence

In the wake of the O. J. Simpson case, any incident involving an athlete assaulting a woman has received extraordinary publicity. The individual cases add up to another stereotype of the new millennium: athletes, especially basketball and football players, are more inclined to be violent towards women than nonathletes are.

Joyce Williams-Mitchell has worked extensively in this field, most recently as the executive director of the Massachusetts Coalition of Battered Women's Service Groups. As an African American woman, she abhors the image of athletes being more prone to violence against women. "It is a myth. The facts do not bear this out. All the studies of patterns of batterers defined by occupation point to men who control women through their profession. We hear about police, clergy, dentists, and judges. I only hear about athletes as batterers when I read the paper. They are in the public's eye. Men from every profession have the potential to be batterers."

There have been, of course, too many cases of athletes committing assaults on girls and women. As I wrote this section, I received a voice mail message from a reporter: "Have you heard that Corey Dillion is the latest case of an athlete hitting a woman? I guess that depends on when you pick up the message. There may have already been another case!" His message implied that attacks on women by athletes took place hourly.

However, there has never been a thorough, scientific study conclusively showing that athletes are more inclined to violence. Jeffrey Benedict, Todd Crossett, and Mark McDonald wrote the only study that comes close. It was based on sixty-five cases of assault against women that took place on ten Division I campuses over a three year period. Thirteen of the cases involved athletes; seven of the athletes were basketball or football players.

Despite the authors' acknowledgment of both the small number of cases revealed and the fact that the survey did not control for alcohol and tobacco use or the man's attitude toward women (then three main predictors of a male's inclination to gender violence), the press regularly quoted their study without qualification. Media reports never stated that the study came up with only thirteen abusive athletes over three years. They simply said that the study concluded that student-athletes, in particular basketball or football players, committed nearly 20 percent of all campus assaults. Rosalyn Dunlap pointed out that, "This is a racially loaded conclusion. When I was a student-athlete at the University of Missouri, I never thought of keeping myself safe from a 260-pound football player any more than any other man on the street. In fact, male athletes on campus protected me."

The following is a list of data usually missing in the debate about athletes and violence against women.

- In 1994, 1,400 men killed their significant others. In that year, O. J. Simpson was the only athlete accused of murder.
- In 1998, an estimated 3 million women were battered and close to one million were raped. According to various reports in the press in the five years between 1995 and 2000, between seventy and one hundred athletes and coaches were ac-cused of assault against a woman each year.
- The 1999 *Chronicle of Higher Education*'s annual campus crime survey showed that there were a total of 1,053 forcible sex offenses reported in 1997. Fewer than thirty-five student-athletes were arrested in conjunction with these crimes.

Gender violence is a serious problem among American men. The cost of crime to America is pegged at $500 billion per year, according to a National Institute for Justice research report for the Justice Department released in March 1996. Gender assault and child abuse accounted for $165 billion—more than one third of that total.

Rosalyn Dunlap, who worked with The National Consortium for Academics and Sport to create more awareness about the issue, said, "There are no men who should be exempted from being educated about the issue of gender violence although many believe they are. It is a problem for naval commanders, daycare providers, fraternities, guys in a bar, in corporations, in halls of higher education and, yes, on athletic teams. But no more so on athletic teams."

There have been numerous cases in which women brought suits against corporations from harassment and/or assault. The *Boston Globe* gave extensive coverage in the late 1990s to the case against Astra USA, Inc., a chemical company, where women lodged sixteen formal complaints for incidents ranging from sexual harassment to rape. Twenty-nine women brought suit against Mitsubishi for the same reasons. None of the press about Astra suggested that working in a chemical company produced a climate of sexual aggression. At Mitsubishi, no one suggested any relationship between the manufacturing process and gender assault. So why do stories about athletes imply such a linkage to athletics? Does it fit white America's racial imagery?

McPherson believes it does: "Football and basketball mean black. When the public talks about gender violence and athletes, it talks black. No one discusses the problems of golfer John Dailey or Braves manager Bobby Cox. Warren Moon was another story altogether. Problems about athletes hit the papers and people think they detect a pattern because of the seeming frequency. But no one else's problems get in the papers. How do we make legitimate comparisons? With Astra and Mitsubishi, we look at the corporate climate and don't generalize about individuals. But with athletes, especially black athletes, we look at players and look for patterns to add up."

Some observers say athletes are trained to be violent and that we can expect that training to carry over into their homes. If this is true, then what about the training in lethal force we give the police, the Army, the Air Force, the Navy, and the Marines? Will these men also come home and kill? McPherson adds, "There is no logic to connect these cases, but we do fit our stereotypes of African-Americans with such images when we carry through the implication for athletes."

With all the recent publicity about the horrors of gender violence, it would be easy to forget that it was America's big, dirty secret until the O. J. Simpson case made it a notorious subject. Before that trial, few Americans were willing to talk about gender violence. The same unwillingness to confront racism diminishes society's ability to eradicate it. But the situation will never change if it remains unconfronted.

Athletes should take a leadership role on this issue, just as they have on drug abuse and educational opportunity. The MVP Program, organized in 1992 by Northeastern University's Center for the Study of Sport in

Society and now headed by Jeff O'Brien, a former football player, has worked on more than sixty-five campuses training male and female athletes to be spokespeople on the issue of gender violence. Each of those schools has become proactive on an issue that has hurt so many women and their families.

Don McPherson insists that "we have to do more to help our youth survive by including our athletes rather than excluding them in helping our youth. The stereotyping of our athletes does not help. We need to be ready with facts to dispute the easy labels."

McPherson and Tom Sanders both argue vigorously that America's athletes not only don't fit the emerging stereotypes about athletes and crime, but the vast majority of professional athletes are extremely positive role models. Sanders said, "when I look at the many NBA players who have their own foundations and who are very involved with giving back to the communities where they play and where they came from, I know they are hurt by the stereotypes." McPherson asserts that "most of the players in the NFL are deeply religious, family-centered men who are constantly giving back to their communities with time and money."

Rosalyn Dunlap wonders when the public and the media will stop being cynical about athletes. "I hear so many people say that if athletes do something in the community that they do it for publicity. Why can't we accept that athletes want to help? Sport and those who play it can help educate us and sensitize us. While we can't ignore the bad news, we should also focus on the overwhelming good news of what athletes do to make this a better world."

I do not believe the stereotypes. However, I do believe the high profile of all professional sports makes it incumbent on those involved to call on sports institutions to demand a higher standard for athletes.

Athletes, once challenged, have played a leading role in the battle to educate our children; in the life and death fight against alcohol and drug abuse; and in the attempt to resolve conflicts with reason and not with fists or weapons. Now it is time to challenge them to fight the long overdue battle against gender violence.

The challenge to athletes involved a starting point of confronting the behavior of an individual athlete. Some universities had to make star athletes academically ineligible or expel them from school to convince others that they were serious about education and would not tolerate either poor academic records or athletes violating social norms.

After the tragic death of Len Bias, the nation was forced to recognize that cocaine was not "recreational," but lethal. Schools began random drug testing; the NBA promised to uphold a lifetime ban for players who ignored league drug policies. This ban was necessary to show players as well as their young fans that there could be no tolerance for the use of life-threatening drugs.

The ban will always seem unfair to the player caught with drugs. I am sure Michael Ray Richardson, who was the first NBA player banned for life, still looks in the mirror and asks, "Why me? There were other guys." But the discipline had to start somewhere. What was unfortunate for Richardson was fortunate for the NBA and for society. Action, no matter how symbolic, was critical.

Likewise, when street violence began to invade our rinks, courts, and fields, sport had to take a stand with automatic and serious sanctions that cost players money and cost teams their playing services. No commissioner or director of a players association wanted their entire league and all of its athletes branded as thugs because of those who acted out during the game.

The New England Patriots bit the bullet for all professional sports and decided not to sign draftee Christian Peter, the University of Nebraska's highly acclaimed football player, who carried numerous criminal charges on his record. It was a milestone decision. Patriot owner Robert Kraft felt compelled to take a strong stand immediately after they drafted Peter, despite the fact that he would lose dollars in the draft and could have faced lawsuits from Peter's representatives. The importance of his decision was not only that players would see clear consequences for their actions, but also that children who idolize those players would also see such consequences as relevant to their own choices in life.

Sports figures are in a unique position to effect change. Keith Lee, a six-year NFL veteran who is now the chief operating officer of the National Consortium for Academics and Sport, works to improve race relations among young people. He states, "We need positive role models who can help young people to believe in what they cannot yet see. We need them now more than ever."

PART IV
How America's Complexion Changes

A nationally distributed, full-page magazine advertisement placed by IBM depicts nine of the company's employees at a business meeting. The employees, presumably managers, are focusing on a white-haired man who is pointing to a chart. The activity portrayed is rather mundane—meetings of this type take place thousands of times every business day. What makes this ad exceptional is what it is selling. In large letters across the top of the page, the text of the ad announces "Diversity Works." The employees shown in the hand-drawn advertisement consist, in order, of an older white woman, a black woman, an Asian woman, a white man, an older black man with white hair, two men of ambiguous racial identity, and a white woman in a wheelchair. The racial and ethnic makeup of the cartoon characters in this ad is intended to convey to readers that IBM, as the supporting text tells us, "values individual differences." What is particularly interesting is the lack of white men in this rendering of the inner workings of a large corporation.

IBM may indeed value diversity, but the reality is that the upper ranks of corporate management are still the domain of white men. The bipartisan Glass Ceiling Commission found that white men "hold about 95 of every 100 senior management positions, defined as vice president or above." How corporate America presents its workforce to the public and how diverse the organization actually is, especially as one moves up the occupational ranks, is a contradiction. Perhaps there is a reason this advertisement was a drawing and not an actual photograph of a diverse work environment. What occupations or organizations can you name in which high-status positions reflect the racial, ethnic, and gender composition of the United States? Think about the racial and ethnic composition of members of Congress, or the CEOs of the Fortune 500 companies, or the fifty state governors, or tenured college professors. What is the race and gender of your university or college president? What about the racial or ethnic background of sports or entertainment celebrities? What patterns emerge, and what do they mean?

We are an incredibly diverse nation. We are reminded of this by the advertisements promoting diversity from corporations like IBM, McDonald's, Texaco, Denny's, and DuPont. We are reminded of this when we are repeatedly told that by the year 2050, about half of U.S. residents will be white and the other half will be black, Asian, and Latino. We are reminded of this when we debate the relative merits of affirmative action, bilingual education, or immigration quotas.

In the public imagination, the idea of ethnic and racial diversity seems to be simultaneously celebrated, feared, and reviled. The United States is promoted as the land of opportunity, but some groups have had more opportunity than others. Why? The United States is defined as a country of immigrants, yet many citizens are fearful that the "new wave" of immigrants will radically change "American" culture. Why? The United States is proclaimed a colorblind nation, yet inequities based on race and ethnicity are still the norm for a sizable part of the population. If we are a colorblind nation why is it very likely that you will marry someone from your same racial background?

The readings in Part IV examine these contradictions. The four readings in the first section of Part IV, "Race, Ethnicity, and Immigration," focus on the changing complexion of the United States. Stephen Steinberg calls into question the assertion that the United States is a melting pot by pointing out that some groups have never been "melted" into the stew because they were not allowed in the pot. Min Zhou maps changes in the immigration flows to the United States over the last thirty years and discusses the sociological implications of these changes, noting that immigrants now come mostly from Asia and Central and South America. Michael Suleiman examines a community that until very recently received very little attention from the mainstream media. He describes the ebb and flow of Arab immigrants to the United States and their socioeconomic success relative to other immigrant groups. Mary Waters looks at mobility and racial identity construction in exploring the influence of race, ethnicity, and opportunity on the experiences of Afro-Caribbeans in New York City.

The section "Race and Romance: Blurring Boundaries" explores historical and contemporary trends in interracial marriage. Law Professor Randall Kennedy uses popular representations of interracial couples in the media to examine just how much progress we have made in the area of interracial romance. Heather Dalmage explains how and why "racial borders" are patrolled to promote racial endogamy. Frank Wu discusses the cultural contradictions of interracial marriages among Asians and Asian Americans and presents a critique of the "mixed race movement." Based on her extensive research of mix-raced couples around the country, Maria Root outlines what she calls "ten truths" about interracial marriage.

Finally, in "Living with Less Racism: Strategies for Individual Action," Charles A. Gallagher suggests ten things we can do to ameliorate racism as we go about our lives.

RACE, ETHNICITY, AND IMMIGRATION

40

THE MELTING POT AND THE COLOR LINE

Stephen Steinberg

QUESTIONS TO CONSIDER

According to the theory of the melting pot, diverse ethnic and racial groups will be thrown together and meld into a new American amalgam that represents the finest cultural aspects of each community. Food is perhaps the easiest way to understand the melting pot perspective. Salsa, not ketchup, is now the number one condiment. There are almost 64,000 pizzerias, almost 7,000 Taco Bells, and 30,000 Asian restaurants in the United States according to experts in the food industry. But as sociologist Stephen Steinberg argues, not everyone has been allowed into the pot. He suggests "America's melting pot has been inclusive of everybody but blacks." Is his statement about black exclusion from the melting pot justified when we consider African American contributions to popular culture?

E very nation, upon examination, turns out to have been a more or less successful melting pot." So wrote Robert Park, the founder of the famed Chicago School of Sociology, in 1930. It is a testament to Park's prescience that he was able to imagine the melting pot at a time when the United States was ethnically more diverse, and more fragmented, than ever before. During the previous half-century, the nation had absorbed some 24 million immigrants, mostly from Eastern and Southern Europe. These "new immigrants"—Italians, Poles,

Russian Jews, Ukrainians, Hungarians and others, far removed geographically and culturally from the people who settled the United States during its first century—were widely believed to be "unassimilable." In Chicago, for example, 70 percent of the population consisted of immigrants and the children of immigrants, and the city was divided into a patchwork of ethnic neighborhoods. In 1921 and 1924, Congress responded with legislation that cut the volume of immigration and instituted national quotas biased against further immigration from Southern and Eastern Europe.

Against this background, Park's dictum provided reassurance that the intermingling of peoples was a universal process and that

America's ethnic discord would resolve itself over time. This optimism was shared by Chicago sociologists W. Lloyd Warner and Leo Srole, who conducted field studies of immigrant communities in the 1940s. Warner and Srole argued that appearances were deceptive, that the ethnic enclave, though it seemed to nurture isolation and separatism, actually functioned as a decompression chamber, helping immigrants adjust to their new surroundings and preparing the next generation to venture into the mainstream. Whatever its original raison d'etre, the ethnic community actually functioned as an instrument of assimilation.

But if early sociologists were confident about assimilation, a later generation rejected the idea of the melting pot. Ironically, many of these scholars were themselves children of immigrants who have risen to the top of the academic ladder. Their revisionist view of the melting pot can be seen as part of a broader trend among second-generation immigrants: assimilation breeds nostalgia. First-generation immigrants, who are most authentically steeped in ethnic culture, tend to throw it away, often with both hands, as they pursue the opportunities that led them to come to America in the first place. Decades later, their largely assimilated children engage in desperate, but usually futile, efforts to recover the very culture that their parents relinquished. As the children of immigrants entered the ranks of social science, they brought this same nostalgia to their analysis of ethnic trends.

The turning point came with the publication of *Beyond the Melting Pot* in 1970. Scholars Nathan Glazer and Daniel Patrick Moynihan, who had each ascended from immigrant poverty to the ivory tower, concluded from their study of New York City that "the most important thing about the melting pot was that it did not happen." The syntax of this much-quoted passage

warrants a moment's reflection. To say that the melting pot "did not happen" is not the same as saying that it was not happening. After all, Park and other theorists of assimilation never claimed that the melting pot was a fait accompli; nor did they project a deadline for the completion of this evolutionary process. Nevertheless, the book's title and argument found a receptive audience. Aside from selling over half a million copies, *Beyond the Melting Pot* marked the beginning of a paradigm shift in the study of ethnicity.

Other books soon appeared that trumpeted the survival of ethnicity over the sinister forces of assimilation. Their titles celebrated *The Decline of the WASP* (1971) and *The Rise of the Unmeltable Ethnics* (1971). A year later, an article in the *New York Times Magazine* proclaimed, "America Is NOT a Melting Pot." Indeed, these writers contended that the United States was undergoing an "ethnic revival" that would resuscitate immigrant cultures. Again, there is a striking historical irony. When ethnic groups were intact and cultural differences pronounced, leading sociologists held that assimilation was inevitable. Several decades later, when these groups had undergone profound transformation, forsaking major elements of their ancestral cultures and assuming comfortable identities as Americans, the prevailing view was that the melting pot had "never happened."

But such attempts to turn black the clock of assimilation would prove difficult. With the exception of Native Americans, ethnic groups in America are transplanted peoples, far removed in time and space from their original homelands. The necessity of adapting to life in America made assimilation, in Park's words, "progressive and irreversible." By the late 1970s, a number of scholars, myself among them, had begun to argue that the so-called ethnic revival was in fact a symptom of decline, a dying gasp of ethnic consciousness. In fact, all the long-term trends suggested that the melting pot was working as predicted: during the twentieth century, immigrants largely lost their original language and culture, ethnic enclaves dispersed as economic and occupational mobility increased, and the rate of ethnic and religious intermarriage accelerated.

It may be that some observers deny the evident fact of assimilation simply because of the ambiguous terminology that we use to describe it. "Melting pot" conjures up an image of a bubbling cauldron into which immigrants descend—whether they jump or are pushed is another matter—and are quickly dissolved into oblivion. Though rhetorically effective, this imagery obscures the evolutionary nature of assimilation. Correctly understood, it is a process that occurs incrementally across generations. To argue that ethnicity is still an active force in American life—as Glazer and Moynihan did in 1970 and other scholars have repeated ever since—is to beg the crucial question. Just because assimilation isn't complete doesn't mean that it isn't taking place.

How we view assimilation also depends on our conception of culture. Revisionists argue that the melting pot theory is based on a static view, in which the original culture of an immigrant's homeland is simply replaced by American culture. Such critics concede that Italian-Americans, for example, bear little resemblance to Italians in Italy, but they argue that Italian-Americans are nevertheless a distinct community, forged on American soil, complete with its own identity and subculture.

Yet melting pot theorists also realize that immigrant cultures evolve and take new forms as newcomers adapt to life in America. The crucial issue is not whether change occurs, but rather the direction and the end result of that change. The key question is this: will the ethnicity of formerly hyphenated Americans endure, or is it merely a transitional stage in a long-term assimilation? My position has long been that, even if we assume a greater tolerance for diversity than actually exists in American society, the conditions were never promising for a genuine and lasting pluralism.

• • •

Today there is an emerging consensus that the descendants of the great waves of European immigration have reached an advanced stage of assimilation. The most striking evidence is provided by the soaring rates of intermarriage across ethnic lines. According to a 1990 study by sociologist Richard Alba, the percentage of white ethnics aged twenty-five to thirty-four who married outside their own groups was as follows: Germans, 52 percent; Irish, 65 percent; English, 62 percent; Italians, 73 percent; French, 78 percent; Scots, 82 percent; Poles, 84 percent. Even in the case of Jews, for whom intermarriage was historically low, the figure is now thought to approach 50 percent. The conclusion seems inescapable that the melting pot, in the most literal sense, is a reality for groups of European ancestry.

Indeed, sociologists now lump these groups together under the rubric of "Euro-American," thus resolving with a single word the assimilation question that was debated for half a century. It is now conceded that the various nationalities of European descent have become simply "white." As a result, ethnic pluralists and opponents of the melting pot have retreated to a new position: the melting pot does exist, but it is "for whites only." On this view, the common "whiteness" of the Irish, Italians, Poles, Jews and other groups destined them to "melt," even though they were once regarded as distinct races whose cultural and genetic differences rendered them unassimilable. A new genre of "whiteness studies" has documented the process through which these erstwhile pariahs were incorporated into the white majority. The core argument is encapsulated in the titles of several recent books, including *How the Irish Became White, How Jews Became White Folks* and *Whiteness of a Different Color.*

But this argument goes on to hold that the current wave of immigrants, composed mainly of "people of color" from Asia, Latin America and the Caribbean, will not be able to follow in the footsteps of the white ethnics. The fault line dividing ethnic groups in America is no longer nationality or religion, but race. Indeed, a number of scholars have declared that "assimilation theory is dead," since its Eurocentric bias renders it useless for understanding the condition and destiny of people of color.

Aside from racism, the new ethnic pluralists cite several positive factors that, they argue, will spare the new immigrants from the dreaded melting pot. Today's immigrants enter a society that is far more tolerant of ethnic diversity. The ideology of multiculturalism extols ethnic difference and provides institutional mechanisms, such as bilingual education, for the preservation of immigrants' language and culture. As a result, the Asians, Latinos and Caribbeans who make up the new immigration have formed cohesive ethnic communities with flourishing economies and foreign-language media, including cable television, that provide institutional anchorage for language and culture. Furthermore, compared to earlier immigrants, the new immigrants have easy access to their homelands, thanks to telecommunications and cheap airfare. And finally, many new immigrants arrive with education and skills, and often capital as well, and therefore are not forced to compromise their ethnic identities for the sake of economic survival. Indeed, in today's global economy, it is not a handicap but an asset to be multilingual and multicultural.

These are all valid points. The question is whether they add up to the conclusion that assimilation is dead, and that the new immigrants will not "melt" as did their predecessors from Europe. It must be conceded that this is a possible scenario, given what we know about racism as a divisive force in America history. One cannot immediately discount the argument that the melting pot is "for whites only," and that today's immigrants will be prevented from assimilating.

In fact, however, this proposition receives little empirical support from the large body of research on today's immigrants. Indeed, the most compelling evidence leads to the conclusion that, notwithstanding their racial difference, the new immigrants are not only assimilating but are doing so at an even faster rate than did earlier immigrants from Europe.

In retrospect, an early indicator of the eventual assimilation of European immigrants was the rapidity with which they lost their native languages. A pattern emerges with stubborn consistency. Immigrants, of course, retained their native tongues; their children typically were bilingual; and by the third generation, the vast majority were monolingual in English. The virtual eradication of languages in only two generations shows just how fragile culture is, at least once it loses its "survival value" and is severed from the institutions that nourish it. Needless to say, immigrants and their bilingual children were not indifferent to the snuffing out of their native language. But the lesson of history is that sentiment—even passionate loyalty—is not enough to withstand the powerful forces of assimilation.

This process is being reenacted—if anything, at an accelerated pace—among the new immigrants. In a study of Los Angeles based on 1990 census data, David Lopez found that, among Asians, the shift to English monolingualism was nearly universal by the third generation. Consider what this means for family relations. Unless the immigrant grandparents acquire a basic fluency in English, which often is not the case, then grand children cannot converse with their grandparents except through the mediation of their bilingual parents.

The picture is somewhat more complex among Latinos, though the overall pattern is still one of rapid language loss. If retention of Spanish were to occur anywhere in the United States, it would be in Los Angeles. Not only do most L.A. Latinos live in predominantly Latino neighborhoods, but the city also has a thriving ethnic press and electronic media. Furthermore, Los Angeles has had an official policy of promoting multiculturalism, including bilingual education and bilingual ballots. Yet Lopez found that 57 percent of third-generation Latinos spoke only English at home. Closer examination of the data revealed that Spanish was retained mainly in households where a foreign-born person—presumably that all-important immigrant grandparent—was present. In the case of Mexican-American youth living in households with no immigrants, only 20 percent spoke Spanish at home.

A study of Cubans in South Florida also found that most young people preferred to speak English at home, even when they were bilingual. Nor was this true only of the middle classes. Among second-generation youth who classified themselves as working class or poor, three-quarters preferred to speak English. Clearly, even though today's society is nominally more conducive to language retention, the new immigrants are moving very rapidly to English monolingualism.

If loss of a native language marks the beginning of the assimilation process, marriage across ethnic lines represents the last (or next to last) stage. Here again, the data do not support either the assumptions or the hopes of the new ethnic pluralists. A study based on the 1990 census found that 40 percent of Asians born in the United States married non-Asians—and these are mostly the children, not even the grandchildren, of immigrants. The figures ranged from 22 percent among Vietnamese to 31 percent among Japanese, 38 percent among Asian Indians, 46 percent among Chinese, 65 percent among Filipinos and 72 percent among Koreans. These figures are so high that they call into question the very category of race in describing Asian-Americans. Indeed, the level of marriage between Asians of different nationalities is strikingly low, suggesting that they do not see themselves as members of a pan-ethnic Asian "race." Rather, most Asians who intermarry do so with whites, giving rise to speculation that Asians are in the process of "becoming white."

Rates of intermarriage for Latinos are lower than for Asians, but they are high nevertheless. Almost one-third of U.S.-born Hispanics between the ages of twenty-five and thirty-four are married to non-Hispanic whites. Indeed, marriage across racial lines has become so commonplace that some commentators have raised the possibility of a "mestizo America"—a racial mixture that blurs the boundaries among ethnic groups. On this view, it is not a question of minorities being absorbed into the white majority, but rather of a fusing of these diverse peoples into a new amalgam. This is the literal meaning of a "melting pot," and a fulfillment of Robert Park's prescient observation that every nation is a "more or less successful melting pot." Like it or not, and the dissent of the ethnic pluralists is clear, assimilation does appear to be progressive and irreversible, the inexorable byproduct of forces put into motion by the very act of immigrating.

• • •

Admittedly, this sweeping conclusion, while it captures the main thrust of American ethnic history, does not tell the whole story:

in particular, it does not account for the African-American experience. Here we speak of a group that came to America in slave ships, not immigrant steamers. While successive waves of immigrants flowed into the country, first to settle the land and later to provide labor for burgeoning industries, blacks were trapped in the South in a system of feudal agriculture. Even in the North, a rigid color line excluded them from the manufacturing sector. In short, the Industrial Revolution was "for whites only," depriving blacks of the jobs and opportunities that delivered Europe's huddled masses from poverty.

This was the historic wrong that was supposed to be remedied by landmark civil rights legislation in the 1960s. But by the time most blacks arrived in Northern cities, the manufacturing sector was undergoing a permanent decline, reflecting the impact of labor-saving technology and the export of jobs to low-wage countries. Not only did blacks encounter far less favorable opportunities than did immigrants, not only did they suffer from the economic consequences of past discrimination, and not only did they encounter pervasive racism in the world of work, but they also experienced intense labor competition from yet another huge wave of immigrants, which began in the 1960s and continues to this day.

Though these new immigrants are conspicuous for their "racial" difference, they are not subjected to the all-encompassing system of racial discrimination that was the legacy of slavery. Furthermore, many of these immigrants arrived with education and skills—and sometimes capital as well—that accelerated their mobility and social integration. As noted earlier, Asians and Latinos already display a far greater degree of "residential assimilation" than blacks. And at a time when marriage across racial lines is soaring for Asians and Latinos, it has inched up only slightly for blacks, again indicating

that a fundamentally different dynamic is at work. The conclusion is unavoidable: America's melting pot has been inclusive of everybody but blacks.

This is not to deny the obvious fact that there has been enormous progress over the past half-century. Jim Crow is a thing of the past, thanks largely to the black protest movement. The emergence of a large black middle class is another encouraging development, though in my view this does not reflect the deracialization of labor markets so much as the favorable impact of affirmative action policy over several decades. Finally, there has been an unmistakable shift in America's fundamental attitudes toward race. The prominence of blacks among the nation's elites, as well as its pantheon of folk heroes, is stark proof that skin color is no longer a badge of inferiority.

Nevertheless, ours is still a society riven by race. Claims of "progress" invariably depend on comparing the situation today to a retrograde past. The problem here, as James Baldwin observed, is that the crimes of the past are used to gloss over the crimes of the present. When comparisons are made between blacks and whites today, a far less sanguine picture emerges. For example, blacks today earn only three-fifths as much as whites. Furthermore, although the income gap between blacks and whites closed somewhat in the 1960s, there has been little or no progress since the mid-1970s. So long as nearly a quarter of blacks, and half of black youth, live below the poverty line, these class factors will continue to engender and reinforce racial division.

Even more germane to the question of whether America is a melting pot, black and white Americans are as residentially segregated as ever. Nor is this true only of inner-city blacks. Middle-class blacks also encounter pervasive discrimination in housing, and their arrival into white suburbs usually triggers white flight, resulting in re-segregation. It is a mark of the melting pot's failure that African-Americans, whose roots go back to the founding of the nation, are more segregated than even recent immigrants from Asia and Latin America.

In short, despite "progress," ghettoization is still a fact of life. And here we confront a great historical paradox—for these ghettos, the enforced "home" of the nation's racial pariahs, also nourished a vibrant African-American subculture. As sociologist Bob Blauner has observed, while immigrant ghettos "functioned as way stations on the road to acculturation and assimilation," the black ghetto has been permanent, "a continuing crucible for ethnic development and building." And unlike immigrants, who clung to vestiges of cultures ripped from their moorings in distant places, black culture evolved out of the lived experience of black people in America. Instead of isolated fragments selected precisely because they did not interfere with mainstream American culture, black culture is an integral part of the everyday lives of black people. As a result, black culture displays a vitality and dynamism that is generally lacking among the ossifying cultures of the nation's immigrant groups.

Ironically, generations of sociologists have taken precisely the opposite position, on the one hand celebrating the cultures of the nation's immigrant groups and, on the other, holding that blacks were merely "white Americans in black skin," lacking a culture of their own. In the same book where they declared that the melting pot "never happened," Glazer and Moynihan wrote that "it is not possible for Negroes to view themselves as other ethnic groups viewed themselves because—and this is the key to much in the Negro world—the Negro is only an American and nothing else. He has no values and culture to guard and protect." Under a barrage of criticism, Glazer subsequently explained that he meant blacks had no *foreign* culture to guard or protect. However, this only compounds the error, since these foreign cultures—and precisely because they were foreign—were destined to a gradual but inexorable decline. On the other hand, as an indigenous product of the American experience, black culture continues not only to thrive in segregated black communities but also to exert a powerful influence on mainstream American culture.

• • •

Throughout this essay, I have emphasized that the melting pot is still at work and that, like past immigrants, today's immigrants from outside the Western Hemisphere will also be fully assimilated at some indeterminate point in the future. The problem, of course, is that we live in the present. It may be our national destiny to become a melting pot, but today the United States is a remarkably polyglot society in which ethnicity flourishes. Despite an overriding trend toward assimilation, ethnic loyalties and attachments remain strong even among segments of older immigrant groups. New immigrants, freshly arrived on American soil, are only at the early stages of the assimilation process. To turn a blind eye to these realities by focusing on long-term trends runs the risk of blotting out the lives and sensibilities of entire communities.

Nor does this warning apply only to ideologues on the political right who, in the name of the melting pot, have waged a relentless crusade against bilingualism, multicultural education and affirmative action. In recent years, a left discourse has emerged that looks "beyond race" and "beyond ethnicity," imagining a post-ethnic future where people are not defined by genes or ancestry. This vision promotes intermarriage across racial and ethnic lines as a way of eliminating, once and for all, the dissonances and conflicts attending racial and ethnic diversity.

For example, historian Gary Nash, a pioneer of multicultural education, has published an essay titled "The Hidden History of Mestizo America," in which he argues that we "need new ways of transcending America's Achilles' heel of race, now that a certain amount of progress has been achieved in living up to our own credo." Like Nash, sociologist Orlando Patterson advocates miscegenation as the ultimate solution to America's intractable race problem. Never mind that African-Americans—not to speak of other ethnic groups—may not wish to miscegenate themselves out of existence. Never mind that it would take generations, if not centuries, to produce the hybrid nation that they envision. Instead of confronting the urgent problems of race in America and addressing the challenges of a multicultural society, these visionaries are throwing in the towel. They use a utopian vision of the melting pot as a façade for moral capitulation.

Let me be clear. There is compelling evidence that the United States will one day become a melting pot, and that this day is approaching faster than ethnic pluralists are willing to acknowledge. From a moral standpoint, however, it is imperative that this melting pot evolve through the operation of historical forces rather than through public policy interventions. It is wrong—to continue the metaphor—to turn up the temperature under the melting pot, or to nudge, cajole or push people into the bubbling cauldron. Any use of state power to undermine ethnicity or to force assimilation is incompatible with democratic principles and violates the rights of ethnic minorities to hold onto their languages and cultures.

The irony of the matter is that, like earlier waves of immigrants, today's newcomers will find their way to the melting pot in due course. So, presumably, will African-Americans, but not until the structures of American apartheid are thoroughly dismantled and the persistent inequalities are resolved. These groups will pursue the personal and social integration that is the promise of the melting pot. But they must do so of their own accord, and not on somebody else's timetable. Here we can take another lesson from history: the carrot, not the stick, has always been the more effective instrument of assimilation.

SEEING THE BIG PICTURE

In Section X of the Appendix, do rates of intermarriage support the assertion that the United States is a melting pot? What does the popularity of hip-hop and rap say about the theory of the melting pot?

41
_____

THE CHANGING FACE OF AMERICA: IMMIGRATION, RACE/ETHNICITY, AND SOCIAL MOBILITY

Min Zhou

QUESTIONS TO CONSIDER

A century ago, immigrants to the United States were overwhelmingly white and from Europe. Since the 1980s, most immigrants have been arriving from Asia and the Americas (excluding Canada). How have these new waves of immigrants shaped U.S. culture? How have these newcomers transformed urban areas? Which models discussed earlier (assimilation, ethnic pluralism, and melting pot) might best describe the current and future experiences of recent arrivals to the United States? Why do some groups in the United States feel threatened about current trends in immigration?

Contemporary immigration refers to the period of large-scale, non-European immigration to the United States that has begun to accelerate since the late 1960s after a long hiatus of restricted immigration (Massey 1995). Between 1971 and 1995, the United States admitted approximately 17.1 million immigrants, including 1.6 million formerly unauthorized aliens and 1.1 million "special agricultural workers" (SAWs) who were granted permanent resident status under the provisions of the Immigration Reform and Control Act of 1986 (IRCA). The scale of contemporary immigration almost

matched that during the first quarter of the century (17.2 million admissions between 1901 and 1925), when immigration to the United States was at its peak. Although similar in numbers, the annual admission trends in these two peak periods looked quite different. During the first twenty-five years of the century, annual admission numbers fluctuated drastically with several noticeable ebbs and flows. In contrast, during the twenty-five years near the end of the millennium, the inflows were fairly steady, which had been kept under the half-million mark until 1978 and then gradually increased from 1978 to 1988. The year 1989 witnessed a sudden surge beyond the one-million mark that lasted for the next three consecutive years. This surge was almost entirely represented by the legalization of the formerly undocumented population permitted by IRCA. Clearly, had it not been for IRCA, immigration trends would have been stable, though heading in a gradual, upward direction.[1]

Just as the turn-of-the-century immigration dramatically transformed America, contemporary immigration has repeated history, changing the face of America in ways that are unique and challenging the traditional views of immigrant incorporation. In this chapter, I specifically examine the following issues: 1) the historical trends of immigration to the United States, 2) the settlement patterns of contemporary immigrants in America's largest metropolitan regions, 3) the nature of racial and ethnic relations in areas of high immigration, and 4) the key determinants of social mobility for new immigrants and their offspring. The chapter aims at understanding how contemporary immigration differs from turn-of-the-century immigration and how such differences may affect our approach to the issues and concerns over the changing face of America in the new millennium.

Distinctive Features of Contemporary Immigration

Trends

Several distinctive features of contemporary immigration are noteworthy in historical perspective. First, despite a similarity in the absolute numbers, the rate of contemporary immigration relative to the total U.S. population is much lower than that of the earlier period since the U.S. population has more than tripled during the course of the twentieth century (3.9 vs. 11.7 per thousand) (Smith and Edmonston 1997). The comparatively low rate of contemporary immigration implies a more modest overall impact on the U.S. population today than in the past. However, such an impact is disproportionately localized in areas of high immigration, not only in historic gateway cities but

also in smaller urban or suburban areas in which few immigrants had settled in the past. Second, the rate of contemporary emigration is considerably lower today than in the past. It was estimated that, for every one hundred immigrants during the first two decades of high immigration, thirty-six had returned to their homelands. In contrast, between 1971 and 1990, less than a quarter had returned (U.S. Immigration and Naturalization Service 1997; Warren and Kraly 1985). This trend suggests a more steady growth today than in the past, indicating that contemporary immigrants are more likely than their earlier counterparts to stay in the United States permanently. Third, unlike immigration then, contemporary immigration is accompanied by a much larger number of undocumented immigrants because of historical patterns of reliance on Mexican labor migration, especially in agriculture, as well as the operation of migration networks that has facilitated undocumented immigration through back-door channels (Massey 1995; Massey et al. 1987). Fourth, compared to immigration then, today's inflows are made up of a much more visible proportion of refugees and asylees.[2] During past thirty-five years (1961–1995), annual admission of refugees averaged 68,150, compared to the average annual admission of 47,000 over the fifteen-year span immediately after World War II. The admission of refugees today implies a much enlarged base for later immigration through family reunification.

Last but not least, the all-time high presence of nonimmigrants arriving in the United States temporarily each year also bears a broad implication for potential immigration, both legal and illegal. Statistics from the Immigration and Naturalization Service (INS) showed that 22.6 million nonimmigrant visas were issued in 1995: 17.6 million (78 percent) were tourists who came for short visits for business or pleasure; the rest were on long-term nonimmigrant visas, including 395,000 foreign students (along with their spouses and children), 243,000 temporary workers or trainees (along with their immediate relatives), and a smaller number of traders and investors. These latter groups of nonimmigrants contain a significant pool of potential immigrants. The majority of those who initially entered as students can freely seek employment in the United States after the completion of their studies, which in turn increases the probability of later adjusting to permanent resident status. Among those who entered as tourists, the great majority will depart on time. However, a relatively small proportion, but a quantitatively large number, of those who might qualify for family-sponsored immigration may overstay their visas and wait in the United States to have their status adjusted. In 1995, almost half the legal immigrants admitted had their nonimmigrant visas adjusted in the United States. About 40 percent of the total undocumented immigrant population was "nonimmigrant overstays" (U.S. Immigration and Naturalization Service 1997).

In sum, a lower rate of emigration, greater numbers of undocumented immigrants and refugees or asylees, and the larger pool of potential immigrants among nonimmigrants imply the complexity of contemporary immigration. Another significant implication for immigrant America is that it is a more challenging task than ever before to accurately measure the scale and impact of immigration and to manage or control the inflows.

Diversity

Compared with the turn-of-the-century immigrants, contemporary immigrants are markedly different in national origins, types of admission, spatial distribution, and socioeconomic characteristics. The newcomers are predominantly from non-European countries.

Since the 1980s, more than 85 percent of the immigrants admitted to the United States come from Asia and the Americas (excluding Canada) and only 10 percent from Europe compared to more than 90 percent at the earlier peak. In particular, the share of immigrants from the Americas as a proportion of total legal immigrant admissions has risen substantially from 25 percent in the 1950s, moving to 39 percent in the 1960s, and jumping up to 50 percent since the 1980s. Similarly, the share of immigrants from Asia as a proportion of the total admissions grew from a tiny 5 percent in the 1950s, to 11 percent in the 1960s and 33 percent in the 1970s, and stayed at 35 percent since 1980, except for 1991, when the Asian share dropped to 18 percent because of the sudden increase in the legalizees under IRCA, most of whom were of Latin origins (U.S. Immigration and Naturalization Service during 1997). The top five sending countries during the period between 1981 and 1995 were Mexico, the Philippines, China/Taiwan, the Dominican Republic, and India, compared to Italy, Austria–Hungary, the Soviet Union, Canada, and the United Kingdom during the first two decades of the century. Mexico alone accounted for more than one-fifth of the total legal admissions since the 1980s. In fact, Mexico was on the INS list of the top five countries of last residence between 1921 and 1960 and was number one after 1960 (U.S. Immigration and Naturalization Service 1997).

The composition of contemporary immigration has a lasting effect on the growth and composition of the general U.S. population. During the past thirty years, immigration accounted for more than a third of the total population growth. Asian- and Latin-origin populations grew particularly fast in both absolute and relative sizes. Some groups—Salvadorans, Guatemalans, Dominicans, Haitians, Jamaicans, Asian Indians, Koreans, Vietnamese, Cambodians, and Laotians—

grew at spectacular rates, mainly as a result of immigration. It is estimated that, at the current levels of net immigration, intermarriage, and ethnic affiliation, the size of the Asian population will grow from nine million in 1995 to thirty-four million in 2050 (growing from 3 to 8 percent of the total U.S. population) and that the Hispanic population will grow from twenty-seven million in 1995 (about 9 percent of the population) to ninety-five million (or 25 percent of the population) in 2050 (Smith and Edmonston 1997).

Spatially, the turn-of-the-century immigrants were highly concentrated along the northeastern seaboard and the Midwest. For them, the top five most-preferred state destinations were New York, Pennsylvania, Illinois, Massachusetts, and New Jersey, and the top most-preferred immigrant urban destinations were New York, Chicago, Philadelphia, St. Louis, and Boston (Waldinger and Bozorgmehr 1996). In contrast, today's newcomers are highly concentrated, not simply in states or urban areas traditionally attracting most immigrants, but also in states or urban areas that had few immigrants in the past. Since 1971, the top five states of immigrant-intended residence have been California, New York, Florida, Texas, and New Jersey, accounting for almost two out of every three newly admitted immigrants. California was the leading state of immigrant destination since 1976. In 1995, the five leading urban areas of high immigrant concentration were New York, Los Angeles –Long Beach, Chicago, Miami–Hialeah, and Orange County (U.S. Immigration and Naturalization Service 1997).

The new immigrants also differ from the turn-of-the-century inflows in their diverse socioeconomic backgrounds. The image of the poor, uneducated, and unskilled "huddled masses," used to depict the turn-of-the-century European immigrants, no longer applies to today's newcomers. The 1990 U.S. census attests to the vast differences in levels of education, occupation, and income by national origins. For example, more than 60 percent of foreign-born persons (aged twenty-five years or older) from India reported having attained college degrees, three times the proportion of average Americans, but less than 5 percent of those from El Salvador and Mexico so reported. Among employed workers (aged sixteen years or older), more than 45 percent of the foreign-born persons from India held managerial or professional occupations, more than twice the proportion of average American workers, but less than 7 percent of those from El Salvador, Guatemala, and Mexico so reported. Moreover, immigrants from India reported a median household income of $48,000, compared to $30,000 for average American households; those from the Dominican Republic and the Soviet Union reported a median household income below $20,000. Poverty rates varied, ranging from a low of 5 percent for Indians and Filipinos to a high of 33 percent for Dominicans and an extreme high of more than 40 percent for Cambodians and 60 percent for Hmongs, compared to about 10 percent for average American families.

The New Second Generation

Spatial concentration, diverse origins, and socioeconomic status of new immigrants hinge not only on the fate of immigrants but also on their children. Because of the recency of contemporary immigration, a new generation of immigrant children and children of immigrant parentage is just coming of age. This new second generation is not only disproportionately young but also ethnically diverse. The Current Population Survey (CPS) for the period 1994–1998 shows that almost 40 percent of the second generation are under eighteen years of age, in contrast to 28 percent of the U.S. population. In the second generation, more than a third are of

Latin American ancestry and 7 percent of Asian ancestry, compared with 12 and 4 percent, respectively, in the total U.S. population reported in the 2000 census. If it were distributed randomly across America's urban landscape, the new second generation would not be of great interest since it is relatively small in absolute numbers. However, historical and contemporary patterns of immigrant settlement suggest that immigrants and their children are highly concentrated in just a handful of metropolitan regions. For example, California alone accounted for some 45 percent of the nation's immigrant student population, more than one out of ten school-aged children in the state were foreign born, and more than a third of the state's school-aged children spoke a language other than English at home (Cornelius 1995). In Los Angeles County, two-thirds of the public schools have a numerical majority of nonwhite students, and 39 percent are represented by more than three-quarters of U.S.- or foreign-born minority students. In major immigrant-receiving cities, such as Los Angeles, San Francisco, New York, and Miami, more than a third of the students in the entire school system speak a language other than English at home.

These changes, impacted by a massive immigration during the past three decades, along with the changes in local cultures, economies, and neighborhoods, have created diverse receiving contexts quite different from the ones in which European immigrants entered a century ago. The challenge for the adaptation of immigrant offspring into postindustrial America is profound. Differing from their immigrant parents, immigrant children lack meaningful connections to their "old" world. Thus, they are unlikely to consider a foreign country as a place to return to or as a point of reference. Instead, they are prone to evaluate themselves or to be evaluated by others by the standards of their new

country (Gans 1992; Portes 1995; Portes and Zhou 1993). Nonetheless, the encounter in any metropolitan context is likely to invoke one of two, if not more, scenarios: The child either succeeds in school and moves ahead or falls behind (or remains the same as) the modest, often low status of the parents' generation. The latter scenario is labeled by the sociologist Herbert Gans (1992) as "second-generation decline." Thus, a more pressing issue is whether the new second generation will be able to incorporate into middle-class America, following the path taken by the "old" second generation arriving at the turn of the century, and to advance beyond their parents' generation.

Transforming Urban America: Old and New Immigrant Metropolises

Like earlier waves of European immigrants, contemporary immigrants are overwhelmingly urban bound, but they differ from their earlier counterparts in geographic distribution. While about 94 percent of immigrants from Asia and close to 90 percent of Latin American immigrants live in urban areas (compared to just over 70 percent of the native-born U.S. population), they are concentrated not only in metropolitan areas in the West and Northeast but also in the Southeast and the Southwest. New immigrants, like their fellow Americans, are spatially distributed not only by social class and race but also by social networks and family or kinship ties. The settlement patterns of contemporary immigrants are characteristic of dispersion and concentration. New immigrants are more spread out than ever before, yet they continue to be highly concentrated within the metropolitan region of settlement. Next, I focus on describing the particular patterns of spatial concentrations in selected metropolitan areas—New

York, Los Angeles, Miami, San Francisco, and Chicago[3]—and examine how different national origin groups converge on particular urban centers and how these urban centers are in turn impacted by the arrival of newcomers.

The Old and New "Ellis Islands"

Ellis Island, where the Statue of Liberty stands, has been the historic gateway to immigrant America. Seeking a better life or an alternative means of livelihood in a new land, millions of European immigrants entered the United States through this gateway in the late nineteenth and early twentieth centuries. Many made New York City their new home, even though thousands returned to their homelands after a lengthy period of sojourning (Moch 1992; Morawska 1990). Since the 1970s, immigration has transformed the "old" Ellis Island and given rise to new ones. While New York remains the most popular immigrant-receiving center, Los Angeles has surpassed it as the largest immigrant metropolis in absolute and relative terms. In absolute numbers, Los Angeles metropolitan region had 600,000 more foreign-born persons than New York as of 1990. Relatively, a third of Los Angeles' residents are immigrants, compared to 27 percent in New York, whose immigrant share was as high as 40 percent at the turn of the century (Waldinger and Bozorgmehr 1996). Miami and San Francisco, though much smaller in size, have become more densely populated by new immigrants than any other U.S. metropolitan area, with a share of 34 and 27 percent, respectively. In contrast, Chicago, the second-largest immigrant metropolis in 1910, dropped a few places down the list in 1990 when measured by the immigrant share of the total population (13 percent).

Compared to the old urban centers, new immigrant-receiving centers take a much larger share of the country's foreign-born population. In 1910, the foreign-born shared 15 percent of the U.S. total population. About a quarter of them lived in the top five largest metropolises—New York, Chicago, Philadelphia, St. Louis, and Boston (Waldinger and Bozorgmehr 1996). The foreign stock's (immigrants and their children's) share of the total population in 1990 was much smaller, less than 9 percent. However, a much higher proportion (37 percent) of the immigrants were concentrated in the top five largest metropolitan areas—Los Angeles, New York, San Francisco, Miami, and Chicago. In addition, the majority of urban immigrants lived in the central city.

Preferred Destinations

Different immigrant urban centers today attract immigrants from different countries. Table 1 displays the top ten national origin groups in each of the selected metropolitan areas. As shown, immigrants of different national origins are not evenly distributed across the urban landscape. New York, an urban center that received primarily European immigrants across the Atlantic Ocean at the turn of the century, has become the center for Caribbean immigrants. The three main Caribbean groups comprise almost a fifth of the area immigrant population. What is more striking is that none of these groups outnumbered others by an overwhelming margin and that none, except for the Chinese, appeared on the national top ten list, an indicator of extremely high concentration in just one area. In fact, 66 percent of Dominican immigrants, 36 percent of Haitian immigrants, and 39 percent of Jamaican immigrants in the United States lived in New York alone.

The picture in Los Angeles is drastically different. Mexican immigrants are the largest national origin group, comprising 40 percent of the area's foreign stock, 5.5 times larger than the second-largest group on the metropolis'

TABLE 1 Top-Ten Foreign-Born, National Origin Groups by Selected PMSAs, 1990 (in 1,000s)

Number	United States	N	New York	N	Los Angeles	N	Miami	N	San Francisco	N	Chicago	N
1	Mexico	4,298	Dominican Republic	232	Mexico	1,167	Cuba	429	China[1]	95	Mexico	238
2	Philippines	913	China[1]	166	El Salvador	213	Nicaragua	67	Philippines	60	Poland	76
3	China[1]	774	Jamaica	129	Philippines	161	Haiti	45	Mexico	48	Philippines	43
4	Canada	745	Italy	122	China[1]	136	Colombia	43	El Salvador	26	India	34
5	Cuba	737	Soviet Union	84	Korea	114	Jamaica	31	Vietnam	17	Italy	28
6	Germany	712	Haiti	80	Guatemala	108	Dominican Republic	16	Nicaragua	14	Germany	28
7	United Kingdom	640	Guyana	77	Vietnam	76	Honduras	16	United Kingdom	11	Korea	25
8	Italy	580	Colombia	71	Iran	67	Peru	15	Germany	11	China[1]	24
9	Korea	568	Poland	66	Soviet Union	51	Mexico	10	Soviet Union	9	Greece	18
10	Vietnam	543	Ecuador	64	Japan	40	Spain	10	Canada	9	Yugoslavia	18
Top Ten		10,510		1,092		2,102		682		300		532
Total		19,767		2,236		2,895		875		441		797

[1]Includes Hong Kong and Taiwan.
Source: U.S. Census Bureau (1993).

top ten list and on the national top ten list. Also noticeable are immigrants from El Salvador and Guatemala, making up 11 percent of the area's immigrant population. Although these two Central American groups are not on the national top list, they are disproportionately concentrated in Los Angeles, which is home to 48 percent of Guatemalan immigrants and 46 percent of Salvadoran immigrants in the United States. Compared to immigrant New York, Los Angeles appears to be less diverse ethnically, though it may have as many national origins groups as one can count. It is also less diverse in class status because of the strong correlation between national origins and the skill levels of the newcomers.

The dominance of Cubans in Miami is a different story. Though Miami is a much smaller metropolitan area, not only does it have the highest proportion of immigrants, but it is also a metropolis with the largest presence of Cuban Americans. More than half of Miami's foreign stock is of Cuban origin, and the group is 6.5 times larger than the second-largest group on the metropolitan top ten list. Unlike Mexicans in Los Angeles, Cubans in Miami are not simply the largest group in size, but also socioeconomically diverse with a significantly large middle class and strong influence in the area's political and economic matters.

Like Miami, San Francisco is also a much smaller metropolis. Though no single national origin group is dominant, the Asian presence is impressive, making up more than 40 percent of the foreign stock. In contrast, Chicago is a much larger metropolis, but its foreign-born stock is only 13 percent. Interestingly, Mexican immigrants form the largest national origin group, three times larger than the second group on the metropolitan top ten list. However, their visibility is blurred by the area's relatively large native-born population.

Demographic Transformation in Immigrant-Receiving Urban Centers

The diversity of contemporary immigrants and their geographic concentration, combined with recent trends of deindustrialization and suburbanization, have reshaped the demographic profiles of both old and new immigrant-receiving centers. Figure 1 illustrates the racial composition of the three largest metropolitan areas between 1980 and 2000. During the last two decades of the twentieth century, demographic transformation is drastic: The proportions of the "colored" components other than "black" in the general population increased corresponding to the decreasing dominance of the "white" component. In both New York and Los Angeles, non-Hispanic white populations had become a numerical minority by the year 2000. Even in Chicago, the diminishing dominance of the white population is significant. What have altered the racial composition in these metropolises are the obvious influxes of Asians and Latinos. Past research on internal migration patterns in the United States has also shown consistent findings that, in high-immigration metropolitan areas, there is a significantly large out-migration and that out-migrants are predominantly non-Hispanic whites (Frey 1995). At the metropolitan level, therefore, the demographic impact of immigrant influx is singularly on whites. But whether whites are pushed out by new immigrants or by other economic forces is debatable and may be a topic for yet another chapter.

Just thirty years ago, America's urban landscape, including the areas with high immigrant density, was predominantly white. The racial hierarchy was dictated by a black–white dichotomy with an unquestionable, all-encompassing white dominance. Although there were various immigrant groups co-existing within the urban social structure,

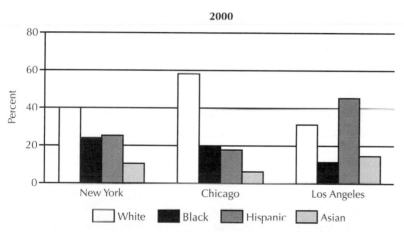

FIGURE 1 Population Growth by Race/Ethnicity, Selected Metropolitan Areas, 1980–2000 (PMSAS) *Source:* U.S. Census of Population (2000).

these immigrants were expected to eventually become assimilated into the dominant white Anglo-Saxon Protestant (WASP) culture. Immigrant enclaves or ghettos did exist, mostly in the central city, but they did not constitute a permanent problem because they were considered transitional stops or springboards and would eventually die down with time. Indeed, with the span of only two or three generations and a long hiatus of low immigration, the white ethnics, such as the

Irish, Jews, and Italians, who were once designated as inferior "races," have now become indistinguishably "white" (Alba and Nee 1997). Meanwhile, the majority of second-and third-generation Asian and Latin Americans also quietly dispersed into the white middle class without much public notice because they represented only a tiny fraction of the population.

In the first generation, the racial composition in major immigrant-receiving centers reflects the patterns of contemporary immigrant settlement I have just discussed: American cities have now become less "white" (but no less "black") and more "colored" than ever before. Los Angeles and Miami have turned into "Latin-dominant" cities. The middle chart displays racial/ethnic composition of the children of immigrants. Only Los Angeles contains a "Latin-dominant" second generation, with the same shift in Miami slowed down by its large concentration of white second-generation retirees, making Miami's second-generation population an ethnically diverse group. New York and Chicago contain a second-generation population that can only be described as "white dominant," a reflection of the impact of these regions' earlier immigration histories. San Francisco, the singularly "Asian-dominant" region, stands out as different, boasting the greatest variety in the ethnic composition of its second generation as well as the most pronounced Asian tilt.

It should be noted that changes in racial composition that were impacted by immigration have occurred also in areas historically receiving relatively few immigrants. The U.S. census data shows that, between 1990 and 2000, Hispanic and Asian populations grew at 631 and 172 percent, respectively, in Raleigh–Durham–Chapel Hill; 388 and 197 percent in Atlanta; and 189 and 111 percent in Minneapolis–St. Paul. These recent demographic trends suggest that new immigrants are more dispersed across America than earlier waves.

The Changing Dynamics of Race and Ethnicity

What is more striking about these demographic changes is that the arrival of new immigrants and the concurrent trend of rapid out-migration of non-Hispanic whites in immigrant metropolitan areas significantly alter the dynamics of race and ethnicity. They make ethnicity more salient and pose new challenges to all Americans—native-born whites, blacks, Asian and Latin Americans alike, as well as the newcomers themselves.

Non-Hispanic Whites

The non-Hispanic white population comprises primarily of the grandchildren or great-grandchildren of European immigrants. Decreasing numbers notwithstanding, non-Hispanic whites still hold dominant political and economic power in immigrant-receiving centers, and the shift of the black–white paradigm does not change this dominance. How, then, have non-Hispanic whites been affected by immigration? Perhaps the most significant impact has involved the notion of American identity, as many fear that newcomers would overtake America and that Americans would be un-Americanized by them. The hotly contested issues of multiculturalism, bilingualism, and immigration reform in the political arena reflect some of these deeply rooted fears. In areas of immigrant concentration, many whites are confronted with a new dilemma of becoming a minority with a majority mentality in a multiethnic society (Horton 1995). In affluent suburban communities with a large and sudden influx of middle-class newcomers, such fears are more pronounced. For example, in Monterey Park, California, whites used to be able to drop their hyphens as unqualified Americans. But in the wave of a large influx of affluent Asian immigrants, they find themselves on the defensive without an ethnic culture of resistance and empowerment to express their fears (Horton 1995). However, nativist fears manifest themselves differently in different metropolitan settings. For example, in Mexican Los Angeles, the Spanish language is stigmatized and is being banned from instruction in schools, whereas in Cuban

Miami, the same language is considered an important marketable skill, and bilingualism is celebrated as the American way.

Non-Hispanic Blacks

The foreign-born component of non-Hispanic blacks is relatively small, though migration from the Afro-Caribbean region has been on the rise, and Afro-Caribbean immigrants tend to concentrate in New York and Miami. As essentially a native-born population and the most American of the Americans, non-Hispanic blacks have been socially affected by the influx of other "colored" immigrants in different ways. In the wake of immigration's surge, non-Hispanic blacks have experienced increasing differentiation in socioeconomic characteristics at the individual level and bifurcation between the middle class and the poor (Grant et al. 1996; Oliver and Shapiro 1995). These patterns of differentiation and bifurcation are caused primarily by the drastic economic restructuring of America's urban labor markets that is simultaneous with rapid growth in immigration. Uneducated and poor blacks have been trapped in the inner city, where ladders of social mobility have disappeared and where the entry to low-skilled jobs is barred by employer discrimination and immigrant employment networks (Waldinger 1996; Wilson 1996). Middle-class blacks have experienced unprecedented social mobility, yet many have continued to face racial discrimination, especially in the housing market that constrains their residential mobility (Clark 1996; Massey and Denton 1987).

The arrival of large numbers of nonwhite immigrants has significantly changed the racial composition of the urban population, rendering the black–white paradigm outdated. However, such a change has not moved blacks up the racial hierarchy. Instead, blacks' racial caste status has been pushed down further by the internalization of other colored immigrants into, unfortunately, the "moral problem in the hearts and minds of Americans" (Myrdal 1962). For example, the widely publicized black–Korean conflicts in America's inner cities and the 1992 Los Angeles civil unrest were not caused by economic competition but rather by the realignment of race relations, manifested in the tension over "turf," which has continued to constrain blacks in virtually every aspect of their lives (Min 1996; Morrison and Lowry 1994). In their struggle for racial equality, many native-born blacks are confronted with a daunting dilemma: how to deal with being a minority competing with other new minorities whose members have come from different backgrounds and headed for many directions.

Native Americans of Asian and Latin Origin

The children and grandchildren of Asian and Latin immigrants have also felt the powerful social impact of contemporary immigration. Almost overnight, native-born Americans of Asian and Latin origin, especially those already "assimilated" or "melted" into white middle-class suburban communities, are confronted with the renewed image of "foreigners." Their American identity is constantly questioned because they look like the newcomers who do not fit the old characterization of an American as "either an European or the descendant of an European" (De Crevecoeur 1904) or as an "immaculate, well-dressed, accent-free Anglo" (Zangwill 1914). These phenotypical definitions of "American," widely and often unconsciously held, make it harder for some native-born people to feel fully American if they happen to be Native Americans or Mexican Americans, whose ancestors settled on this land long before the *Mayflower* reached shore.

Stereotyping images of an "American" create special problems for native-born Americans of non-European ancestry whose national origin groups contain a disproportionately large number of recent arrivals. Incidents of harassing a native-born Mexican American suspected of being an undocumented immigrant or comments about a third-generation Japanese American's "good English" are frequently heard. The children, U.S.-born and similar to other American children, have found to suffer from persistent disadvantages merely because they look "foreign" (U.S. Commission on Civil Rights 1988, 1992).

While they are infuriated by the unfair treatment as foreigners, native-born Hispanic and Asian Americans are also caught in a dilemma of inclusion versus exclusion in their struggle for racial equality. Similar to other Americans in speech, thought, and behavior, native-born Hispanic and Asian Americans and their foreign-born counterparts often hold contradictory values and standards over labor rights, individualism, civil liberty, and ultimately the ideology of assimilation. These differences, intertwined with the acculturation gap between immigrant and native-born generations, have impeded ethnic coalition and ideological consensus. For example, the picketing of restaurants in New York's Chinatown in 1994 and Los Angeles' Koreatown in 1998 was a conscious effort mostly by second-generation Asian Americans fighting for immigrant rights. But it was perceived by the ethnic community as a group of "whitened" kids trying to "destroy their parents' businesses" and the ethnic community. Ironically, the parent generation consciously struggles to push children to become "white" by moving their families into white neighborhoods, sending their children to white schools, and discouraging their children to play basketball and mimic hip-hop culture. For Afro-Caribbean immigrants, the parents even push their children to adopt certain strategies, such as

invoking their accents or other references to French or British colonial culture to differentiate themselves from native-born blacks and to avoid the stigma of "blackness" (Portes and Stepick 1993; Waters 1994, 1996). But becoming "white" is politically incorrect and thus unacceptable for the native-born generation.

The Newcomers

The social impact of contemporary immigration is perhaps most intense on the newcomers themselves. Earlier labor migrants of Asian or Latin American origin were mostly sojourners with an intention of eventually returning to their homelands. In contrast, most new immigrants are permanent settlers, even though there is a significantly visible presence of transnationals who have maintained their homes or led their regular lives simultaneously in their countries of origin and destination. Most permanent settlers have made concerted efforts to assimilate first economically and then culturally. No matter how much they want to be like other Americans, however, the newcomers often find themselves facing an ambivalent public that questions their willingness to assimilate and doubts their assimilability. They also face the unrealistically high expectation that they should assimilate quickly. It took earlier European immigrants two or three generations to assimilate into the middle class, and such a pace was facilitated by economic expansion, industrialization, and a long hiatus of restricted immigration (Alba 1985; Alba and Nee 1997; Perlmann and Waldinger 1997). Today, the second generation of contemporary immigrants is just coming of age, and predictions about their future outcome of assimilation are only estimates.

Today's immigrants also encounter various structural constraints that limit their chances of integration. On the one hand, the continuous high volume of immigration has affected new arrivals in ways similar to their native-born coethnics. However assimilated they may have become, they are still likely to be viewed as foreigners "fresh off the boat." On the other hand, many newcomers, especially the low-skilled poor, lack contact with and exposure to the segment of American society into which they aspire to assimilate. In this case, they may either allow themselves and their children to assimilate into the inner city or build ethnic communities to help shield coethnic members from being trapped in the inner city (Portes and Zhou 1993). Either way, the process is viewed as a rejection to assimilation.

In real life, immigrants must first deal with the issue of economic survival. New immigrants arrived in cities where economic restructuring and globalization have created bifurcated labor markets with numerous labor-intensive and low-paying jobs on the one end and a growing sector of knowledge-intensive and well-paying jobs on the other. This bifurcated labor market renders many immigrants underemployed with substandard wages or occupational overqualification (Zhou 1997a). The 1990 census data reveal that immigrant men of all groups displayed fairly low rates of labor force nonparticipation (below 8 percent), except for Southeast Asians (16 percent) (Rumbaut 1995; Zhou and Bankston 1998).[4] In particular, Mexican men, who were most handicapped of all immigrant groups by the lack of skills and English proficiency, showed the lowest labor force nonparticipation rate, probably because of the fact that most of Mexican immigrant workers arrived through extensive employment and migrant networks (Massey 1996). Among those who were in the labor force, all male immigrants, except for the Europeans, were more likely than native white workers to be underemployed, with over half the immigrants—more than 60 percent of the Asians among them—experiencing underemployment measured by partial employment, low-wage employment, and overqualified

employment. Mexicans were almost twice as likely as other groups to be underemployed by low wages. By contrast, Africans, Asians, and Europeans were more likely to be underemployed by being educationally overqualified for the jobs they held. It is clear that disadvantages in labor market status do not necessarily affect immigrant groups in the same manner. For those who are not able to obtain adequate employment, Mexican immigrants are more likely to be absorbed in partial or low-wage employment, while African and Asian immigrants are more likely to be occupationally overqualified in occupations.

The underemployment patterns among employed men were similar to those among employed women. Overall, however, gender expectations about employment are different. For example, male workers who are discouraged to seek work may be viewed as being forced to detach themselves from the labor market. But the same view may not be applicable to unemployed women because they may voluntarily withdraw from the labor force because of marriage or childbearing. By the same token, partial employment among men may be viewed as an imposed disadvantage, but partial employment among women may be voluntary or a strategy for supplementing husbands' underpaid family wages. Whether all forms of underemployment accrue to economic disadvantages remains a matter of debate. I would argue that unemployment is an absolute disadvantage. Partial employment or low-wage employment does not help much because their jobs are usually inadequate for sustaining a decent living, much less for moving up the socioeconomic ladder. This disadvantage affects Mexican immigrants disproportionately. Although Mexican immigrants have relatively easy access to the U.S. labor market, their employment stability is heavily affected by the uncertain demands of the highly competitive, volatile industries in which they work. These conditions in turn constrain Mexican immigrants' ability to achieve economic success commensurate with their high rate of labor force participation.

While many immigrant workers start out as low-wage workers and gradually move up in the labor market, others may be "stuck" in dead-end jobs. Of course, whether one can successfully move out of their underemployment depends not simply on individual human capital or incentive because the effects of human capital may be intervened by factors beyond the control of individual group members. Immigration selectivity is one such factor. Immigrants who have arrived with strong human capital may be able to overcome labor market disadvantages by overqualification. Those who have arrived with little human capital are likely to be employed in low-wage and "bad" jobs. They usually have few economic resources and cannot afford the time for the kind of reeducation and retraining that can possibly move them up in the labor market. However, it would be premature to conclude that those who initially hold entry-level, low-wage jobs are necessarily "trapped" at the bottom of the labor market. In fact, as immigrants gain labor market experience, many are able to advance within and across industries to better-paying positions and even to self-employment (Portes and Zhou 1992, 1996; Zhou 1992). Thus, the long-term outcomes of underemployment as an alternative means to upward social mobility or as a dead-end street trapping immigrants in their starting point or pushing them further down toward the bottom are speculative but not mutually exclusive scenarios.

The Impact of Race/Ethnicity on Immigrant Incorporation

Classical sociological theories about immigrant adaptation predict a linear trajectory in which immigrants, starting their American life at disadvantaged positions, eventually converge toward the mean and become indistinguishable Americans (Alba 1985; Gordon 1964; Park 1928; Warner and Srole 1945). This conclusion is based on two assumptions. One is that there is a natural process by which diverse and initially disadvantaged ethnic groups come to share a common culture and to gradually gain equal access to the opportunity structure of the host society. The other is that this process consists of gradually deserting old cultural and behavioral patterns in favor of new ones and that, once set in motion, this process moves inevitably and irreversibly toward assimilation (Warner and Srole 1945).

Immigrants' intergenerational mobility has been empirically measured by the extent to which immigrant groups achieve parity with the society's dominant group in education, occupation, income and wealth, and political power, which is, in Gordon's (1964) term, "secondary structural assimilation." Looking back in history from the present standpoint, the experiences of the children and grandchildren of earlier European immigrants appear to confirm the assimilationist prediction about structural assimilation. Between the 1920s and the 1950s, when America experienced a long hiatus of restricted immigration, the host country seemed to have absorbed the great waves of immigrants who had experienced significant upward mobility across immigrant generations, as determined by the length of stay since immigration, the mastery of the English language, the acquisition of human capital, and increasing exposure to American culture (Alba 1985; Chiswick 1977; Greeley 1976; Sandberg 1974; Wytrwal 1961).

However, it remains an open question whether new immigrants and their offspring will follow the path of their European predecessors. In terms of the direction of intergeneration mobility, the distinctions between yesterday's European immigrants and today's newcomers may not be as sharp as they appear to be. However, with regard to the rate of structural assimilation—the degree to which immigrant groups achieve parity with the dominant group—the classical assimilationist paradigm shows its constraints. The historiography of the turn-of-the-century European immigrants reveals divergent rather than convergent outcomes among different national origin groups (Perlmann 1988). Past studies on intergenerational mobility have found persistent interethnic differences in the rate of progress even after controlling for measurable human capital characteristics and contextual factors. In a study of the Irish, Italian, Jewish, and African Americans in Providence, Rhode Island, Perlmann (1988) found that, with family background factors held constant, ethnic differences in levels of schooling and economic attainment persisted in the second and later generations. He also found that schooling did not equally commensurate with occupational advancement for African Americans as for other European Americans across generations. Recent studies have also indicated that the distance between immigrant offspring and the native-born population in key socioeconomic measures varies among different national origin groups and that for some it continues to remain substantial (Model 1991; Tang 1993; Tienda and Lii 1987; Zhou and Kamo 1994). Even the direction of intergenerational mobility does not appear to be linear, and research has found both general and group-specific trends of second- or third-generation decline (Gans 1992; Landale and Oropesa 1995). These findings about past and present immigrant experiences have suggested that the direction and the rate of social mobility are two distinct dimensions of the adaptational outcomes and that what determines the direction may not necessarily be what determines the rate. Next, I highlight the ways in which race and

ethnicity impact the prospects of immigrant incorporation.

Ethnicity and Class

Ethnicity, which is intrinsically linked to national origin, has been found to be one of the most salient factors influencing social mobility of new immigrants. Classical assimilationist theories often treat ethnicity as a measure of old-country ways and consider it an impediment to structural assimilation, but acknowledge that ethnicity does more in predicting the rate than in predicting the direction of mobility (Park 1928; Warner and Srole 1945). Yet empirical research indicates significant differences in the magnitude of progress across different ethnic or national origin groups. Steinberg (1996) revealed a surprisingly prominent and strong role that ethnicity played in structuring the lives of adolescents, both in and outside of school. He found that students of Asian origin outperformed non-Hispanic white students, who in turn out-performed black and Hispanic students by significantly large margins. He also found that the ethnic differences remained marked and consistent across nine different high schools under study after controlling for social class, family structure, and place of birth of parents. He also found similar ethnic effects on other important predictors of school success, such as the belief in the payoff of schooling, attribution styles, and peer groups. A study reported in *Ethnic Los Angeles,* conducted by a research team at the University of California, Los Angeles, and headed by Roger Waldinger and Mehdi Bozorgmehr, showed significant intergroup differences in the rate of intergenerational progress while revealing trends of upward mobility for all immigrant groups. This study found that native-born Mexicans and Central Americans experienced greater earnings and educational disparities with non-Hispanic whites relative to their Asian and Middle Eastern counterparts (Bozorgmehr et al. 1996; Cheng and Yang 1996; Lopez et al. 1996; Ortiz 1996). Portes and Rumbaut (1996) attributed these differences to the interplay of premigration conditions, individual characteristics, host reception, and group adaptational patterns. They argue that the diverse socioeconomic characteristics on arrival among new immigrants give rise to varied modes of incorporation that in turn affect the rate as well as the direction of progress among second and later generations.

Ethnicity and the Ethnic Hierarchy

While ethnicity is intrinsically intertwined with national origin, it is deeply rooted in America's ethnic stratification system, exerting positive as well as negative effects on adaptational outcomes. What makes ethnicity favor some groups while penalizing others? One way to interpret the varied effects of ethnicity is to examine its interaction with class. Socioeconomic status has an independent effect on mobility outcomes because it influences where people live, where they go to school, with whom they are in close contact, and what kind of family and community resources are available. Wealthier and skilled immigrants are able to integrate into better sectors of the host economy with relative ease and settle directly in suburban middle-class communities, albeit with temporary downward mobility. Poorer and unskilled immigrants have few options but take up low-wage jobs and settle in declining urban areas, starting their American life either in poverty or on welfare. Becker (1963) found that early and insignificant differentials in class status can result in substantial differences in educational and occupational mobility in later years. The strong correlation between national origins and skill levels of contemporary immigrants also has a significant bearing on

the varied effects of ethnicity. For example, the children of Mexican immigrants lag far behind their peers of Asian origins in academic performance and educational attainment, partly because of socioeconomic differences (Perlmann and Waldinger 1997) and partly because of differential resources generated in the family and the ethnic community (Caplan et al. 1989; Gibson 1989; Rumbaut and Ima 1988).

However, controlling for the interactive effect between class and national origin does not seem to reduce the significance of ethnicity. Recent studies on the new second generation are a case in point. Using language proficiency as a proxy for the nativity or immigration status in a large-scale study in the San Diego School District during the 1986–1987 and 1989–1990 school years, Rumbaut found that first-generation Chinese, Korean, Japanese, Vietnamese, and Filipino students had the highest grade-point averages of all students in the district. More remarkable, even the Hmong, who came from preliterate peasant background, and the more recently arrived Cambodians outperformed all native-born English-only American students (Rumbaut 1995). Given the drastic differences in socioeconomic backgrounds of these Asian national origin groups, this finding complicates the effect of class. Portes and his associates reported findings from the Children of Immigrants Longitudinal Survey (CILS) showing that parents' socioeconomic status, length of U.S. residence, and homework hours significantly affected academic performance but that controlling for these factors did not eliminate the effect of ethnicity. More systematic analyses of the educational progress of children of immigrants using the CILS data generally confirmed these findings (Rumbaut and Portes 2001).

The fact that ethnicity continues to shape the American experience of immigrant groups implies that ethnicity also interacts with broader structural factors that produce and reinforce specific advantages or disadvantages in ethnic group membership and that the outcomes of adaptation may be segmented with potential and real risks of downward mobility (Portes and Zhou 1993). Portes and MacLeod (1996), using the National Educational Longitudinal Survey, reported that the negative effect of disadvantaged group memberships among immigrant children was reinforced rather than reduced in suburban schools but that the positive effect of advantaged group memberships remained significant even in inner-city schools. Using the same data set but employing a two-stage least-squares method, Hao and Bonstead-Bruns (1998) found that immigrant status increases educational expectations for Chinese, Koreans, and Filipino families more than for Mexican families. They also found that Chinese background consistently exerted positive effects on educational achievement, while Mexican background showed significantly negative effects, and that the ethnic effects persisted after controlling for important individual and contextual factors.

Why is it that ethnicity exerts opposite effects on the same outcome measures for different national origin groups? Existing literature has suggested that the advantages and disadvantages of ethnic group membership lie not merely in the class status and the corresponding modes of incorporation from which the first generation start life in America, but also in different levels of the social structures in which individuals and groups participate. At the macro level, the system of ethnic stratification functions to provide different ethnic groups with unequal access to economic resources and political power. At the micro level, the networks of social ties, which are often ethnically based, prescribe different strategies to cope with structural disadvantages and mobilize different types of social capital to provide support for group

members. Either the members of disadvantaged ethnic groups accept an inferior status and a sense of basic inferiority as part of their collective self-definition or they create a positive view of their heritage on the basis of cultural and ethnic distinction, thereby establishing a sense of collective dignity (Ogbu 1974). If a socially defined ethnic group wishes to assimilate but finds that normal paths of integration are blocked on the basis of ethnicity, the group may be forced to take alternative survival strategies that enable its members to cope psychologically with structural barriers but that do not necessarily encourage structural assimilation. The group may also react to structural disadvantages by constructing resistance to assimilation (Fordham 1996; Kohl 1994). In this case, symbolic expressions of ethnicity and ethnic empowerment hinder rather than facilitate social mobility among group members.

As immigrants and their children are absorbed into different segments of American society, becoming American may not always be an advantage. When immigrants enter middle-class communities directly or after a short transition, they may find it advantageous to acculturate and assimilate. If the social environment surrounding immigrant children is rich in resources and if its goals are consistent with those of the immigrant family, then ethnic resources may be relatively less important, but those ethnic resources may still count. For example, many middle-class immigrant parents move into affluent white neighborhoods and send their children to schools attended mainly by white students from similar or more affluent socioeconomic backgrounds. But they still insist on enrolling their children in ethnic institutions during after-school hours and weekends or involving them in religious or cultural activities. The children then benefit both from privileged socioeconomic contacts with members of the dominant group in mainstream American society and from the group-specific expectations of and opportunities for intellectual development.

Thus, when immigrant children enter the bottom of the ethnic hierarchy, where the forces of assimilation come mainly from the underprivileged, acculturation and assimilation are likely to result in distinct disadvantages, viewed as maladjustment by both mainstream society and the ethnic community. Immigrant children from less fortunate socioeconomic backgrounds have a much harder time than middle-class children succeeding in school. A significant number of the children of poor, especially dark-skinned, immigrants can be trapped in permanent poverty in the era of stagnant economic growth, for in the process of Americanization, these immigrant children "will either not be asked, or will be reluctant, to work at immigrant wages and hours as their parents did but will lack job opportunities, skills and connections to do better" (Gans 1992: 173–174). The prospects facing children of the less fortunate may be high rates of unemployment, crime, alcoholism, drug use, and other pathologies associated with poverty and the frustration of rising expectation.

This new reality defines the world that confronts the children of new immigrants. Children growing up in households headed by poor, low-skilled immigrants face uncertain prospects for moving ahead through school success. The parents, of course, have few of the economic resources that can help children do well in school. The environment does not help when neighborhoods are poor and beset by violence and drugs and local schools do not function well. To add to this difficulty, immigrant children receive conflicting signals, hearing at home that they should achieve at school while learning a different lesson on the street—that of rebellion against authority and rejection of goals

of achievement. At the same time, both real life and television expose children to the wage and consumption standards of U.S. society, and children come to expect more than their parents ever had. As a result, children of the foreign born are unwilling to work the low-paying, low-status jobs of their parents, but they do not have the education, skills, or opportunities to do better (Gans 1992). This mismatch between rising aspirations and shrinking opportunities will either lead to second-generation decline or provoke "second-generation revolt" (Perlmann and Waldinger 1997). However, young immigrants or children of immigrants may benefit from cultivating social ties within ethnic communities to develop forms of behavior likely to break the cycle of disadvantage and to lead to upward mobility. The extent to which young people are integrated into this community also becomes a major determinant of school adaptation, especially when the social environment otherwise places children at risk (Zhou and Bankston 1998).

Conclusion

The significant differences between contemporary and turn-of-the-century European immigration necessitate a reconceptualization of the phenomenon and the development of alternative theories. Because of the diverse socioeconomic backgrounds of new immigrants, the pathways toward integration into American society may be as rugged as they are segmented. Many new immigrants continue to follow the traditional rugged route, starting from the bottom rungs of the socioeconomic ladder and gradually working their way up. A visible proportion of them, however, manage to bypass the bottom starting line, incorporating directly into mainstream professional occupations and dispersing into suburban middle-class communities. Still, a significant number may be permanently "trapped" at the bottom, either unable to find work or working at "dead-end" jobs with little hope for social mobility.

Increasing diversity also poses challenges for Americans as they experience the drastic changes in the dynamics of race and ethnicity in an era of rapid social and economic transformations. Again, the old framework of assimilation has become outmoded. In multiethnic metropolises today, all native-born racial/ethnic groups are facing the challenge of adjustment to the new reality. Growing tensions are arising from an urgent need to negotiate the culture of diversity and to redefine oneself in the new racial/ethnic stratification system.

Finally, the future of new immigrants and their children is intrinsically linked to the diversity of immigration and to the current social stratification system into which today's immigrant children are assimilating. The American public still seems to allude to the idea that all immigrant children should move up and melt into the middle class. Because there are poor whites who have never assimilated into the white middle class, it is natural that some immigrant children may not make it, either, as immigrants are incorporating into a highly stratified society that accords individuals with varied life chances. Gans (1992) questions the American faith that mystifies an eventual immigrant success, particularly in regards to the new second generation. While children of the middle class have a better chance for success, the poor, especially the darker skinned, may not fare equally well. Consequently, assimilation as a widespread outcome for contemporary immigrant groups is possible for some but questionable for others. Indeed, for most Europeans, assimilation did not take place until the third or even the fourth generation. Thus, while the new second-generation immigrants may not assimilate, their children or grandchildren may. But with scenarios of second-generation decline still a matter of speculation, it seems clear that assimilation no longer means that everyone will eventually succeed.

NOTES

The original version of this chapter was presented at the Research Conference on Racial Trends in the United States, National Research Council, Washington, DC, October 15–16, 1998. Some of the main ideas were drawn from my previously published work (Zhou 1997b, 2001). I thank Roger Waldinger and Mary Waters for their helpful comments and Vincent Fu and Diana Lee for their research assistance.

1. In theory, all the IRCA legalizees should have been residing in the country for a considerable period of time prior to 1989, though a substantial portion of those legalized under the SAW program turned out to be relatively recent arrivals.
2. Refugees and asylees can be anyone with a well-founded fear of prosecution on the basis of race, religion, membership in a social group, political opinion, or national origin. Refugees are those seeking protection outside the United States, while asylees are those seeking protection once already in the United States.
3. These are Census Bureau–designated principal metropolitan statistical areas rather than cities proper.
4. African immigrants also include a significant component of refugees from Ethiopia who had a higher labor force participation rate than Southeast Asian refugees. African refugees, as well as European refugees, tend to have higher educational attainment, more fluent English proficiency, and better access to community-based employment networks than Southeast Asian refugees.

REFERENCES

Alba, Richard D. 1985. *Italian Americans: Into the Twilight of Ethnicity*. Englewood Cliffs, NJ: Prentice Hall.
Alba, Richard D., and Victor Nee. 1997. "Rethinking Assimilation Theory for a New Era of Immigration." *International Migration Review* 31 (4): 826–874.

Becker, Howard S. 1963. *Outsiders: Studies in the Sociology of Deviance.* New York: The Free Press.

Bozorgmehr, Mehdi, Claudia Der-Martirosian, and Georges Sabagh. 1996. "Middle Easterners: A New Kind of Immigrant." In *Ethnic Los Angeles,* edited by Roger Waldinger and Mehdi Bozorgmehr. New York: Russell Sage Foundation.

Caplan, Nathan, Marcella H. Choy, and John K. Whitmore. 1989. *The Boat People and Achievement in America: A Study of Family Life, Hard Work, and Cultural Values.* Ann Arbor: University of Michigan Press.

Cheng, Lucie, and Philip Q. Yang. 1996. "Asian: The 'Model Minority' Deconstructed." In *Ethnic Los Angeles,* edited by Roger Waldinger and Mehdi Bozorgmehr. New York: Russell Sage Foundation.

Chiswick, Barry R. 1977. "Sons of Immigrants: Are They at an Earnings Disadvantage?" *American Economic Review* 67 (February): 376–380.

Clark, William A. V. 1996. "Residential Patterns: Avoidance, Assimilation, and Succession." In *Ethnic Los Angeles,* edited by Roger Waldinger and Mehdi Bozorgmehr. New York: Russell Sage Foundation.

Cornelius, Wayne A. 1995. "Educating California's Immigrant Children: Introduction and Overview." In *California's Immigrant Children: Theory, Research, and Implications for Educational Policy,* edited by Rubén Rumbaut and Wayne A. Cornelius. La Jolla, CA: Center for U.S.-Mexican Studies, University of California, San Diego.

De Crevecoeur, J. Hector St. John. 1904 [1782]. *Letters from an American Farmer.* New York: Fox, Duffield.

Fordham, Signithia. 1996. *Blacked Out: Dilemmas of Race, Identity, and Success at Capital High.* Chicago: University of Chicago Press.

Frey, William H. 1995. "Immigration and Internal Migration 'Flight' from U.S. Metropolitan Areas: Toward a New Demographic Balkanization." *Urban Studies* 32 (4–5): 733–757.

Gans, Herbert J. 1992. "Second-Generation Decline: Scenarios for the Economic and Ethnic Futures of the Post-1965 American Immigrants." *Ethnic and Racial Studies* 15 (2): 173–192.

Gibson, Margaret A. 1989. *Accommodation without Assimilation: Sikh Immigrants in an American High School.* Ithaca, NY: Cornell University Press.

Gordon, Milton M. 1964. *Assimilation in American Life: The Role of Race, Religion, and National Origins.* New York: Oxford University Press.

Grant, David M., Melvin L. Oliver, and Angela D. James. 1996. "African Americans: Social and Economic Bifurcation." In *Ethnic Los Angeles,* edited by Roger Waldinger and Mehdi Bozorgmehr. New York: Russell Sage Foundation.

Greeley, Andrew M. 1976. "The Ethnic Miracle." *The Public Interest* 45: 20–36.

Hao, Lingxin, and Melissa Bonstead-Bruns. 1998. "Parent-Child Differences in Educational Expectations and the Academic Achievement of Immigrant and Native Students." *Sociology of Education* 71: 175–198.

Horton, John. 1995. *The Politics of Diversity: Immigration, Resistance, and Change in Monterey Park, California.* Philadelphia: Temple University Press.

Kohl, Herbert. 1994. *"I Won't Learn from You" and Other Thoughts on Creative Maladjustment.* New York: The New Press.

Landale, Nancy S., and R. S. Oropesa. 1995. "Immigrant Children and the Children of Immigrants: Inter- and Intra-Group Differences in the United States." Research Paper. Population Research Group, Michigan State University.

Lopez, David E., Eric Popkin, and Edward Tells. 1996. "Central Americans: At the Bottom, Struggling to Get Ahead." In *Ethnic Los Angeles,* edited by Roger Waldinger and Mehdi Bozorgmehr. New York: Russell Sage Foundation.

Massey, Douglas S. 1995. "The New Immigration and Ethnicity in the United States." *Population and Development Review* 21 (3): 631–652.

———. 1996. "The Age of Extremes: Concentrated Affluence and Poverty in the Twenty-First Century." *Demography* 33 (4): 395–412.

Massey, Douglas S., Rafael Alarcon, Jorge Durand, and Humberto Gonzalez. 1987. *Return to Aztlan: The Social Process of International Migration from Western Mexico.* Berkeley and Los Angeles: University of California Press.

Massey, Douglas S., and Nancy A. Denton. 1987. "Trends in Residential Segregation of Black, Hispanics, and Asians: 1970–1980." *American Sociological Review* 52: 802–825.

Min, Pyong Gap. 1996. *Caught in the Middle: Korean Communities in New York and Los Angeles.* Berkeley and Los Angeles: University of California Press.

Moch, Leslie Page. 1992. *Moving Europeans.* Bloomington: Indiana University Press.

Model, Suzanne. 1991. "Caribbean Immigrants: A Black Success Story?" *International Migration Review* 25: 248–276.

Morawska, Ewa T. 1990. "The Sociology and Historiography of Immigration." In *Immigration*

Reconsidered: History, Sociology, and Politics, edited by Virginia Yans-McLaughlin. New York: Oxford University Press.

Morrison, Peter A., and Ira S. Lowry. 1994. "A Riot of Color: The Demographic Setting." In *The Los Angeles Riot,* edited by Mark Baldassare. Boulder, CO: Westview Press.

Myrdal, Gunnar. 1962 [1944]. *An American Dilemma: The Negro Problem and Modern Democracy.* New York: Harper & Row.

Ogbu, John U. 1974. *The Next Generation: An Ethnography of Education in an Urban Neighborhood.* New York: Academic Press.

Oliver, Melvin L., and Thomas M. Shapiro. 1995. *Black Wealth/White Wealth: A New Perspective on Racial Inequality.* New York: Routledge.

Ortiz, Vilma. 1996. "The Mexican-Origin Population: Permanent Working Class or Emerging Middle Class?" In *Ethnic Los Angeles,* edited by Roger Waldinger and Mehdi Bozorgmehr. New York: Russell Sage Foundation.

Park, Robert E. 1928. "Human Migration and the Marginal Man." *American Journal of Sociology* 33: 881–893.

Perlmann, Joel. 1988. *Ethnic Differences: Schooling and Social Structure among the Irish, Jews, and Blacks in an American City, 1988–1935.* New York: Cambridge University Press.

Perlmann, Joel, and Roger Waldinger. 1997. "Second Generation Decline? Immigrant Children Past and Present—A Reconsideration." *International Migration Review* 31 (4): 893–922.

Portes, Alejandro. 1995. "Economic Sociology and the Sociology of Immigration: A Conceptual Overview." In *The Economic Sociology of Immigration: Essays on Networks, Ethnicity, and Entrepreneurship,* edited by Alejandro Portes. New York: Russell Sage Foundation.

Portes, Alejandro, and Dag MacLeod. 1996. "The Educational Progress of Children of Immigrants: The Roles of Class, Ethnicity, and School Context." *Sociology of Education* 69 (4): 255–275.

Portes, Alejandro, and Rubén G. Rumbaut. 1996. *Immigrant America: A Portrait.* 2nd ed. Berkeley and Los Angeles: University of California Press.

Portes, Alejandro, and Alex Stepick. 1993. *City on the Edge: The Transformation of Miami.* Berkeley and Los Angeles: University of California Press.

Portes, Alejandro, and Min Zhou. 1992. "Gaining the Upper Hand: Economic Mobility among Immigrant and Domestic Minorities." *Ethnic and Racial Studies* 15: 491–522.

——. 1993. "The New Second Generation: Segmented Assimilation and Its Variants among Post-1965 Immigrant Youth." *Annals of the American Academy of Political and Social Science* 530 (November). 74–98.

——. 1996. "Self-Employment and the Earnings of Immigrants." *American Sociological Review* 61: 219–230.

Rumbaut, Rubén G. 1995. "Vietnamese, Laotian, and Cambodian Americans." In *Asian Americans: Contemporary Trends and Issues,* edited by Pyong Gap Min. Thousand Oaks, CA: Sage Publications.

Rumbaut, Rubén G., and Kenji Ima. 1988. *The Adaptation of Southeast Asian Refugee Youth: A Comparative Study.* Washington, DC: U.S. Office of Refugee Resettlement.

Rumbaut, Rubén G., and Alejandro Portes, eds. 2001. *Ethnicities: Coming of Age in Immigrant America.* Berkeley and Los Angeles and New York: University of California Press and Russell Sage Foundation.

Sandberg, N. C. 1974. *Ethnic Identity and Assimilation: The Polish-American Community.* New York: Praeger.

Smith, James P., and Barry Edmonston, eds. 1997. *The New Americans: Economic, Demographic and Fiscal Effects of Immigration.* Washington, DC: National Academy Press.

Steinberg, Laurence. 1996. *Beyond the Classroom.* New York: Simon & Schuster.

Tang, Joyce. 1993. "The Career Attainment of Caucasian and Asian Engineers." *Sociological Quarterly* 34: 467–496.

Tienda, Marta, and D. T. Lii. 1987. "Minority Concentration and Earnings Inequality: Blacks, Hispanics and Asians Compared." *American Journal of Sociology* 2: 141–165.

U.S. Census Bureau. 1993. *1990 Census of the Population: The Foreign Born Population in the United States.* Washington, DC: U.S. Government Printing Office.

U.S. Commission on Civil Rights. 1988. *The Economic Status of Americans of Asian Descent: An Exploratory Investigation.* Washington, DC: Clearinghouse Publications.

——. 1992. *Civil Rights Issues Facing Asian Americans in the 1990s: A Report.* Washington, DC: U.S. Government Printing Office.

U.S. Immigration and Naturalization Service. 1997. *Statistical Yearbook of the Immigration and Naturalization Service, 1995.* Washington, DC: U.S. Government Printing Office.

Waldinger, Roger. 1996. *Still the Promised City? African-Americans and New Immigrants in*

Postindustrial New York. Cambridge, MA: Harvard University Press.

Waldinger, Roger, and Mehdi Bozorgmehr. 1996. "The Making of a Multicultural Metropolis." In *Ethnic Los Angeles.* New York: Russell Sage Foundation.

Warner, W. Lloyd, and Leo Srole. 1945. *The Social Systems of American Ethnic Groups.* New Haven, CT: Yale University Press.

Warren, Robert, and Ellen Percy Kraly. 1985. "The Elusive Exodus: Emigration from the United States." Population Trends and Public Policy Occasional Paper No. 8 (March). Washington, DC: Population Reference Bureau.

Waters, Mary C. 1994. "Ethnic and Racial Identities of Second-Generation Black Immigrants in New York City." *International Migration Review* 28 (4): 795–820.

———. 1996. "Immigrant Families at Risk: Factors That Undermine Chances of Success." In *Immigration and the Family: Research and Policy on U.S. Immigrants,* edited by Alan Booth, Ann C. Crouter, and Nancy Landale. Hillsdale, NJ: Lawrence Erlbaum Associates.

Wilson, William J. 1996. *When Work Disappears: The World of the New Urban Poor.* New York: Knopf.

Wytrwal, J. A. 1961. *America's Polish Heritage: A Social History of Poles in America.* Detroit: Endurance Press.

Zangwill, Israel. 1914. *The Melting Pot: Drama in Four Acts.* New York: Macmillan.

Zhou, Min. 1992. *Chinatown: The Socioeconomic Potential of an Urban Enclave.* Philadelphia: Temple University Press.

———. 1997a. "Employment Patterns of Immigrants in the U.S. Economy." Paper presented at the Conference on International Migration at Century's End: Trends and Issues, International Union for Scientific Study of the Population, Barcelona, Spain, May 7–10.

———. 1997b. "Growing up American: The Challenge Confronting Immigrant Children and Children of Immigrants." *Annual Review of Sociology* 23: 63–95.

———. 2001. "Contemporary Immigration and the Dynamics of Race and Ethnicity." In *America Becoming: Racial Trends and Their Consequences,* edited by Neil Smelser, William Julius Wilson, and Faith Mitchell. Washington, DC: National Academy Press.

Zhou, Min, and Carl L. Bankston III. 1998. *Growing up American: The Adaptation of Vietnamese Adolescents in the United States.* New York: Russell Sage Foundation.

Zhou, Min, and Yoshinori Kamo. 1994. "An Analysis of Earnings Patterns for Chinese, Japanese and Non-Hispanic Whites in the United States." *Sociological Quarterly* 35 (4): 581–602.

42

THE ARAB IMMIGRANT EXPERIENCE

Michael W. Suleiman

QUESTIONS TO CONSIDER

Since 9/11 the media seem to have discovered the Arab American population in the United States, but this group has had significant presence in this country for almost 150 years. In this article Suleiman maps Arab migration to the United States and the "Americanization" process this group, like almost all immigrant groups to this country, has experienced. He suggests that an ambiguous racial status and racism were used to deny citizenship to Arab immigrants. How and why did this happen?

Introduction

In 1977, William E. Leuchtenburg, the prominent American historian, remarked, "From the perspective of the American historian, the most striking aspect of the relationship between Arab and American cultures is that, to Americans, the Arabs are a people who have lived outside of history."[1] Professor Leuchtenburg could have just as accurately made the same observation about Arabs in America.

Ignorance about Arab Americans among North Americans at large means that, before looking at more detailed accounts of the Arab-American experience, we may benefit from a quick overview of Arab immigration to North America and what the Arab-American communities here have been like.

There have been two major waves of Arab immigration to North America. The first lasted from the 1870s to World War II and the second from World War II to the present. Members of the two waves of immigrants had somewhat different characteristics and faced different challenges in the social and political arena. Any examination of the immigrant communities must take into account these differences. As we shall see, the two communities began to come together in the 1960s, especially after the 1967 Arab-Israeli war,[2] and this rapprochement must also be taken into account.

The term "Arab Americans" refers to the immigrants to North America from the Arabic-speaking countries of the Middle East and their descendants. The Arabic-speaking countries today include Algeria, Bahrain, Egypt, Iraq, Jordan, Kuwait, Lebanon,

From "The Arab Immigrant Experience," by Michael Suleiman as it appears in *Arabs in America: Building a New Future,* edited by Michael Suleiman. Reprinted by permission of Temple University Press. Copyright © 1999 by Temple University. All rights reserved.

Libya, Mauritania, Morocco, Oman, pre-1948 Palestine and the Palestinians, Qatar, Saudi Arabia, Sudan, Syria, Tunisia, United Arab Emirates, and Yemen. Somalia and Djibouti are also members of The League of Arab States and have some Arabic-speaking populations. Most Arab immigrants of the first wave came from the Greater Syria region, especially present-day Lebanon, and were overwhelmingly Christian; later immigrants came from all parts of the Arab world, but especially from Palestine, Lebanon, Syria, Egypt, Iraq, and Yemen, and had large numbers of Muslims among them. Although most Muslim Arab immigrants have been Sunni (reflecting the population in the region), there is a substantial Shi'a minority. Druze started immigrating in small numbers late in the nineteenth century.

Immigrants from the Arabic-speaking countries have been referred to and have referred to themselves by different names at different times, including Arabs or Arabians, but until World War II the designation Syrian or Syrian-Lebanese was used most often. The changeability of the name may indicate the absence of a definite and enduring identity, an issue that is discussed later. For the purposes of this chapter, the various names are used interchangeably, but the community primarily is referred to as Arab or Arab American.[3]

It is impossible to determine the exact number of Arab immigrants to North America, because U.S. and Canadian immigration officials have at different times used different classification schemes. Until 1899 in the United States, for instance, immigration statistics lumped the Arabs with Greeks, Armenians, and Turks. For this and other reasons, only estimates can be provided.

According to U.S. immigration figures, which generally are considered to be low, about 130,000 Arabs had immigrated to the United States by the late 1930s.[4] Estimates of the size of the Arab-American community by scholars and community leaders vary widely. A conservative estimate is that there were approximately 350,000 persons of Arab background in the United States on the eve of World War II.[5] In the 1990s, the size of the Arab community in the United States has been estimated at less than one million to the most frequently cited figure of two and one-half to three million.[6]

Numerous reasons have been given for the first wave of Arab immigration to America, which began in large numbers in the 1880s, but the reasons usually fall into two categories: push and pull factors, with the push factors accorded greater weight.

Most scholars argue that the most important reasons for emigration were economic necessity and personal advancement.[7] According to this view, although the economy in geographic or Greater Syria (a term encompassing the present-day countries and peoples of Syria, Lebanon, the Palestinians, Israel, Jordan, and possibly Iraq) registered some clear gains in the late nineteenth and early twentieth centuries, this progress was uneven in its impact and did not manifest itself in a sustained manner until "after emigration to the New World began to gather momentum."[8] The economy of Mount Lebanon suffered two major crippling blows in the mid-1800s. The first was the opening of the Suez Canal, which sidetracked world traffic from Syria to Egypt and made the trip to the Far East so easy and fast that Japanese silk became a major competitor for the Lebanese silk industry. The second blow came in the 1890s, when Lebanese vineyards were invaded by phylloxera and practically ruined.[9]

Also contributing to the economic stress in the Syrian hinterland was a rapid increase in population without a commensurate increase in agricultural or industrial productivity. Many families found that the subsistence economy could support only one child, who eventually inherited the farm or household. Other male children had to fend for themselves, and emigration to a New World of great wealth became an irresistible option.[10]

Many Lebanese Christians, who constituted most of the early Arab arrivals in North America, emphasize religious persecution and the lack of political and civil freedom as the main causes of their emigration from lands ruled by an oppressive Ottoman regime.[11] Under Ottoman rule, Christians in the Syrian province were not accorded equal status with their Muslim neighbors. They were subjected to many restrictions on their behavior and often suffered persecution. These oppressive conditions worsened and discriminatory actions occurred more often as the Ottoman rulers became weaker and their empire earned the title of the "Sick Man of Europe." As the power of the sultan declined, the local rulers began to assert greater author-ity and power, which they at times used to suppress and oppress further their subjects, particularly Christians. In part, this persecution took place in response to the increased power and prestige of "Christian" Europe and the encroachment of its rulers on Ottoman sovereignty. This effect, combined with the Christian population's desire for greater equality, threatened the Muslim public's sense of security. Like the "poor white trash" of the American South at the time of the Civil War and the Civil Rights Movement, the Muslim population in the Syrian province was poor and oppressed— but it still enjoyed a social status that was superior to that of the non-Muslims, particularly the Christians. The threat of losing that "high" status made many Muslims susceptible to suggestions from local Ottoman rulers that their Christian neighbors were the cause of rather than companions in their troubles. The worsened social and economic conditions in Syria in the mid-1800s and the beginning of the disintegration of feudalism, especially among the Druze, produced social turmoil that erupted in sectarian riots in which thousands of Christians perished.[12] Many Christian Lebanese, especially Maronites, cite the 1860 disturbances and massacres as the main factor contributing to the exodus from their homeland.

In addition to the economic, political, and social causes of the early Arab immigration to North America, some incidental factors should be cited. Among these are improved transportation and communication facilities worldwide, development of steam navigation that made the sea voyage safer and shorter, and aggressiveness of agents of the steamship companies in recruiting new immigrant passengers. Although American missionaries often actively discouraged Syrians or Arabs from migrating to the United States, their very presence as model Americans, their educational activities, and their reports about American life ignited a desire, especially among the graduates of American schools and colleges in Syria, to emigrate to America.

After the feasibility and profitability of immigration to the United States and to "America" in general were well established, chain migration became the norm, with immigrants making it possible for the ambitious and the disgruntled in the old homeland to seek newer horizons. Those wanting to escape military service in the Ottoman army and those craving freedom from oppression and the liberty to speak and publish without censorship or reprisal left their homeland quickly and stealthily and sought what they thought would be a temporary refuge in America.

The Early Arab Community in America

Before World War II, most Arabs in America were Christians who came from the Mount Lebanon region of geographic Syria. Especially until the turn of the century, these travelers were mainly poor, uneducated, and illiterate in any language. They were not trained for a particular profession. As unskilled workers, after they learned the rudiments of the English language, they could work in factories and mines. However, such jobs were taxing and monotonous and, most importantly, did not offer opportunities for the fast accumulation of wealth, which was the primary objective of these early Arab arrivals. Farming presented them with the added hardships of isolation, loneliness, and severe weather conditions. Peddling therefore was an attractive alternative. It did not require much training, capital, or knowledge of English. With a few words of English learned on the run, a suitcase (*Kashshi*) full of notions (e.g., needles, thread, lace) provided by a better-established fellow Lebanese or other Arab supplier, probably a relative who helped bring them to the New World, many new arrivals often were on the road hawking their wares only a day or so after they landed in America. Success in peddling required thrift, hard work, very long hours, the stamina to endure harsh travel conditions (mostly walking the countryside on unpaved roads), and not infrequently, the taunting and insults from children or disgruntled customers. These conditions were made tolerable for most early Arab arrivals by their vision of a brighter economic future and the concomitant prestige they and their families would eventually acquire in the old country. When they could afford to do so, they switched to the "luxury" of a horse and buggy and later to a dry-goods store.[13]

Before World War I, Arabs in North America thought of themselves as sojourners, as people who were in, but not part of, American society. Their politics reflected and emulated the politics of their original homeland in substance and style, because they were only *temporarily* away from home.

In New York, *Kawkab America* (*Kawkab Amirka*), the first Arabic-language newspaper established in North America, declared in its very first issue its unequivocal support for the Ottoman sultan, whose exemplary virtues it detailed at length.[14] All other newspapers had to define in one way or another their attitude toward and their relationship with the Ottoman authorities. Although *Kawkab America* was pro-Ottoman, at least initially, *Al-Ayam* (*al-Ayyam*) was the most vehement opponent of the Ottoman authorities, a role it later shared with *Al-Musheer* (*al-Mushir*).[15] It excoriated the cruelty and corruption of Ottoman rulers, especially in the Mount Lebanon region. It also called for rebellion against the Turkish tyrants and urged its readers to exercise their freedom in America to call for freedom back home. Other newspapers, including *Al-Hoda* (*al-Huda*) and *Meraat-ul-Gharb* (*Mir'at al-gharb*), fell between these two extremes of total support or clear rejection of Ottoman authority.

The orientation of early Arab Americans toward their homeland meant that their political activities were also focused on issues that were important in their country or village of origin. There was communal solidarity, but the community was a collective of several communities. The sectarian and regional disputes that separated the Arabs back home were also salient in this "temporary" residence. The newspapers they established were in the main socializing agencies conveying the messages of their sectarian leadership. Because the Orthodox already had their *Kawkab America, Al-Hoda* was set up to represent and speak for the Maronites. Later, *Al-Bayan* (*al-Bayan*) proclaimed itself the newspaper of the Druze.[16] Within each community there were rivalries and competing newspapers, each claiming to be the best defender or representative of its sect.

World War I was a watershed event for Arabs in North America, cutting them off from their people back home. This separation from the homeland became almost complete with the introduction of very restrictive quota systems in the United States and Canada after World War I, which practically cut off emigration from Arab regions. These developments intensified the community's sense of isolation and separation, simultaneously enhancing its sense of solidarity. One consequence was a strengthening of the assimilationist trend—a trend already reinforced by the American-born children of these Arab immigrants.

The substance and style of the Arab community's politics changed after the war, with a clear realization that they had become part of American society. Intersectarian conflicts became less intense and fewer in number. Calls for unity were heeded more often. For instance, Syrian-Lebanese clubs formed regional federations that joined together to form a national federation.[17] A process of socialization into American politics resulted in greater participation in voting and party membership and in public and political service at local or state levels. "Syrian" Republican and Democratic Clubs were formed in the United States, and the arena for political competition changed as the Arab community became part of the American body politic. There also emerged a clear change in matters of style—generally for the better. By the 1930s and 1940s, conflicts became fewer and somewhat less personal, and the language of discourse became much less offensive.

Whereas first-generation Arabs in America managed as best they could in an alien environment, their children were thoroughly immersed in American society and culture—and their first or only language was English. Consequently, English-language newspapers and journals were established to cater to young Americans of Arab heritage.[18] Eastern churches began to translate some of the liturgy and conduct part of the services in English to prevent the loss of members,[19] although many members left the church nonetheless. Some intellectuals, including some of the most celebrated Arab-American writers and poets, took advantage of the blessings of freedom and democracy in North America to attack the tyranny and corruption of the clergy, especially in the old homeland but also in America. Some also expressed atheistic or agnostic views, and others left their old churches and joined new ones.[20]

As Arabs assimilated in American society, they also worked harder for a better image of themselves and their people in the old homeland. More effort was spent on campaigns to inform Americans about the rich Arab heritage. In the political arena, especially in the United States, there were many, serious efforts to get the government to support foreign policy positions favored by the Arab community, especially in regard to Palestine. During World War I and its aftermath, the main political preoccupation of the Arabic-speaking groups in North America was to achieve the liberation of their homelands from Ottoman rule and to provide economic assistance to their starving relatives, especially in the Mount Lebanon region. To accomplish these objectives, their leaders set up relief committees, raised funds, and sent money and supplies whenever it was possible to do so. They also urged Arab young men in the United States to join the American armed forces to help their new country and to liberate their old homeland.[21] Leaders organized campaigns to have their people buy American Liberty bonds to help with the war effort.[22]

After the war, the Arabs in America were divided over the destiny of the regions liberated from Ottoman rule. In general, there was a strong sentiment among the Maronites to support French control over Syria and Lebanon under the League of Nations' Mandate.[23] Others argued for complete independence, viewing France as a new occupying power.[24] On the question of Palestine, there was general agreement in support of the Palestinian-Arab population and for eventual, if not immediate, independence. There was widespread opposition to Zionism as a movement bent on establishing a Jewish state there.[25] Arabs in America showed their support for the Palestinians through lectures, publications, fund raising, and political lobbying, especially with U.S. government officials.[26]

Until World War I, Arabs in North America may be considered sojourners exhibiting many traits of a middleman minority a community whose members primarily engage in one particular specialized activity such as migrant farm work or peddling. Substantial numbers of Arabs in America engaged in commerce, most often beginning as peddlers commissioned by their own countrymen. Their objective was to make the greatest amount of money in the shortest possible time to help their families in the old country and eventually to retire in comfort in their village or neighborhood. In the meantime, they spent as little as possible of their income in America, often living in crowded tenements and, while on the road, in barns or shacks to avoid expensive hotel costs. They did not live rounded lives, allowing themselves no luxuries and finding contentment and solace in family life. Because they could pull up stakes anytime, they sought liquidity in their economic enterprises. Long-term investments were avoided. For that reason, in addition to other advantages, they preferred peddling, dry goods stores, restaurants, the professions, and a cottage industry in lace and needlework. In all of these activities, their primary contacts were with other Arab Americans, especially relatives or people from the same town, religious sect, or geographic region.[27] They developed few lasting relationships with "Americans." *Al-Nizala*, the term the Arab-American community used to refer to itself, is a name that clearly describes its status and purpose. It means a temporary settlement, and it was used in contrast to "the Americans" to indicate the alien or stranger status of Arabs in America. At first, Arabs in America formed their own residential colonies, especially in New York and Boston. Even when they did not, they encouraged within-group marriage, frequently praising its virtues and especially pointing out the disadvantages of marrying "American" girls. In other words, they resisted assimilation, even after their intellectuals began to urge acculturation to life in America.[28]

Arabs in America, sharing an attitude common to other middleman or sojourner communities, were charged with being "clannish, alien, and unassimilable."[29] Such attitudes were fairly common among influential American journalists and public officials, who also viewed Arabs as inferior to whites. In the economic field, Arabs were sometimes seen as parasites, because they allegedly did not engage in any productive industry, merely being engaged in trade. They were sometimes attacked as a drain on the American economy, because they sent part of their income back home.[30]

The Process of Americanization

Arab immigrants soon found out that the land of opportunity was also strewn with hardship and an "unwelcome" mat. In response to insults and charges of inferiority, they did occasionally defend themselves.[31] However, to add injury to insult, the U.S. and Canadian authorities began to claim that Arabs had no right to naturalization and citizenship because they allegedly were Asian and did not belong to the white race.[32] This problem of racial identification and citizenship

traumatized the Arabic-speaking community. In their attempt to resolve this crisis, the "Syrians" searched for their roots and found them in their *Arab* background, which ensured them Caucasian racial status and therefore eligibility for U.S. citizenship—or so they argued.[33] Beginning in 1909, Arabic-speaking individuals from geographic Syria began to be challenged in their citizenship petitions. It was not until 1914, however, that George Dow was denied a petition to become a U.S. citizen because, as a "Syrian of Asiatic birth," he was not a free white person within the meaning of the 1790 U.S. statute.[34] In 1915, the Dow decision was reversed based on the argument that the pertinent binding legislation was not that of 1790 but the laws of 1873 and 1875, and in accordance with these, Syrians "were so closely related to Europeans that they could be considered 'white persons.'"[35] Despite this precise and authoritative language, "Syrians" in the United States continued to be challenged and to feel insecure about their naturalization status until the period of 1923 to 1924.[36]

Even during World War II, the status of Arabs remained unclear. In 1942, a Muslim Arab from Yemen was denied U.S. citizenship because "Arabs as a class are not white and therefore not eligible for citizenship," especially because of their dark skin and the fact that they are "part of the Mohammedan world," separated from Christian Europe by a wide gulf.[37] On the other hand, in 1944, an "Arabian" Muslim was granted citizenship status under the 1940 Nationality Act, because "as every schoolboy knows, the Arabs have at various times inhabited parts of Europe, lived along the Mediterranean, been contiguous to European nations and been assimilated culturally and otherwise by them."[38]

Apart from the legal battles to ensure they were allowed to reside in their new homelands, especially in the United States, Arabic-speaking persons had to figure out what identity best fit their indeterminate status. They knew who they were and had a very strong sense of personal identity centered first and foremost in the family. There were, however, other lesser but still important identities related to clan, village, or sect. Because these identities were strong, a "national" identity could remain amorphous or at least indeterminate, shifting from one orientation to another with relative ease and without much psychological dislocation. In practical terms, the Arabic-speaking people in North America functioned as a collective of communities whose bonds of solidarity beyond the family were mainly related to sect or country, such as Maronite, Orthodox, Muslim, Druze, and Palestinian affiliations. Before World War II, the primary or most acceptable designation for the group was "Syrian." However, when Lebanon emerged as a country in the 1920s, some Maronites, especially N. Mokarzel, the editor and publisher of *Al-Hoda,* spearheaded a campaign to get the community to change its name to Lebanese, because Lebanon was where most of its members originally came from.[39] The campaign was not a big success, although, many of the clubs did change their name to Syrian-Lebanese.[40]

Another and more important identity crisis occurred when these peripatetic sojourners realized that they had to decide whether to become "settlers" or return to the old homeland. It had become increasingly difficult for them to function as temporary aliens. After World War I, it became clear to large numbers of Arabs in North America that it was not possible to go "home" again and that the United States and Canada were their homes.[41] This change from sojourner to permanent settler necessitated and was accompanied by other changes in the way Arabs in America thought and in the way they behaved. The substantial investments they had made in homes, property, and real estate in the old country lost their original purpose, and much more attention was paid to material improvements and investments in their new countries. In the United States, one manifestation was the migration by substantial numbers of the New York Arab community from the rundown and extremely crowded tenements of Manhattan to the nicer environment of South Ferry in Brooklyn and beyond.[42]

Arabs in America saw that they had to become full-fledged Americans. Assimilation became strongly and widely advocated, and citizenship training and naturalization were greatly encouraged. Although outmarriage was still not favored, some now claimed that success in such situations was possible if the American partner (usually female) was a "good" person who behaved in a conservative or traditional manner.[43] Along the same lines, Arab women were told to retain the modesty code of the old homeland.[44]

Although Arab women in America constituted a major asset to their kinfolk, they also presented the community with many difficulties, primarily related to issues of honor and modesty. This problem was most acute among the Druze, some of whom asked to restrict or totally ban the immigration of Druze women to America. Among Christians, women peddlers were a big concern. The complaints and areas targeted for reform included the act of peddling itself, the personal appearance and dress of the woman peddler, the distance she covered and whether she had to stay away from home overnight, and her demeanor or behavior. These problems were viewed as especially serious because large numbers had decided to stay in America and wanted to become "acceptable" to the host society. The preference was for Arab women to help their kinfolk by crocheting or sewing at home or by minding their family's store. Work in factories was also acceptable, although not favored, especially among the rising middle-class Arab Americans.[45]

The decision to settle in America meant setting a higher priority on children's education for boys and girls. This was viewed as more important than any contribution the children might make to the family's economic welfare. The result was a marked improvement in women's education and an increase in the number of male and female graduates from universities and professional institutions.

Another consequence of the decision to stay in America was that parents and children had to learn to be good Americans, and they flocked to citizenship classes. Parents attended English-language classes and studied the American governmental system in preparation for their new role as American citizens. Americanization was seen as a process of shedding old loyalties, the traditional culture, and the Arabic language. The children therefore grew up barely aware of their Arabic heritage.

Although the assimilationist approach began to gain favor and was encouraged by the leadership, it was not presented in ideological terms. Often, it took the form of a suggestion that Arabs should no longer feel like strangers in their new country and that they should make a positive contribution to American society.[46] Nevertheless, in the heyday of the melting pot approach to assimilation, the Arabs in America strove to remove any differences, except perhaps food and music, that separated them from the general American population. They also neglected or chose not to teach their children Arabic or to instill into them much pride of heritage.[47] The result was that, by World War II, Arabs in North America were, for all practical purposes, an indistinguishable group from the host society. It took a second wave of immigration and other developments to rekindle interest in their Arab heritage and to revive them as an ethnic community.

Post–World War II Immigration

The second wave of Arab immigration brought to North America a much more diverse population, one that differed greatly from the early pioneering group. Whereas the first-wave immigrants came almost exclusively from the area of Greater Syria and were overwhelmingly Lebanese, the new immigrants came from all parts of the Arab world, including North Africa. Unlike early arrivals, who were predominantly Christian, the new immigrants were Christians and Muslims.

The two groups' reasons for immigration were also somewhat different. In addition to economic need and the attraction of a major industrial society, new immigrants often were driven out of their homes as a result of regional conflicts (e.g., Palestine-Israel, Arab-Israeli, Iraq-Iran, Iraq-Kuwait) or civil wars (e.g., Lebanon, Yemen) or as a consequence of major social and political changes in the homeland that made life difficult, especially for the wealthy or the middle class in Egypt, Iraq, Syria, and other countries. The search for a democratic haven, where it is possible to live in freedom without political or economic harassment and suppression by the government was a strong motivation, even more so than during the earlier period, that affected much larger numbers of individuals. To these political and economic motivations can be added a psychological one. The great improvements in transportation and communication facilitated the process of immigration, and by making the world seem smaller, they made it much easier for people to accept the notion of migration to other parts of the world, especially to the United States and Canada.

Whereas the early Arab immigrants were mainly uneducated and relatively poor, the new arrivals included large numbers of relatively well-off, highly educated professionals:

lawyers, professors, teachers, engineers, and doctors. Many of the new immigrants began as students at American universities who decided to stay, often as a result of lack of employment opportunities back home or because of the unstable political conditions in the homeland—conditions that often threatened imprisonment or death for returnees.[48] Besides these comparatively affluent immigrants, especially in the 1990s, relatively large numbers of semieducated Arabs, primarily engaged in commerce, came to North America as political refugees or as temporary residents to escape the wars and violence of the Middle East region.

An important difference between members of the two immigration waves is the way each group thought of itself in terms of American society and politics. First-wave immigrants were viewed and thought of themselves as mere sojourners staying in the United States on a temporary basis with the primary or sole purpose of making a fortune they could enjoy back home. This orientation remained dominant at least until World War I and probably well into the 1920s. Such a stance meant that they avoided participation in American society beyond taking care of basic needs such as commerce. They were "Syrians" or "Arabians" and sought to establish their own churches, clubs, or newspapers. They sought (and preached to their people) not to "meddle" in the affairs of the host society. They were anxious not to offend their hosts, not to break the law, and not to behave in a manner offensive to Americans, but they also tried not to imitate American social customs (i.e., Americanize), not to mix socially with Americans, and not to intermarry. Although most did not participate in politics much beyond voting, they nevertheless expressed pride in the occasional Arab who was able to make it as a city alderman, political party functionary, or a candidate for local political office.

The change from these conditions came slowly and as a result of changes in the world around them, especially World War I, the Ottomans' oppressive treatment of their subjects in the Syria-Lebanon region, and the success of Zionism in securing Western, especially British and American, support for its objective of establishing a Jewish homeland in Palestine.

Immigrants who arrived after World War II came with a well-defined view of democracy and the role of citizens in it—ideas they had learned in their homeland but that had originally been imported from Europe and America. Their higher level of education and social status gave them greater confidence about participating in American politics almost as soon as they arrived in their new country. Even when they thought about returning to their Arab homeland, they were anxious to live full and productive lives in the United States or Canada for themselves and their children. The Arab-American community today constitutes a combination of the diversities of the early and more recent immigrants. In addition to the sectarian and mainly social clubs that the early immigrants formed, new political organizations were gradually established. In the United States, Syrian Democratic and Syrian Republican clubs were formed in the 1920s and 1930s. These were, as the Arab Democratic and Arab Republican clubs are today, adjuncts to the main two major parties designed to encourage political participation and to integrate Arabs into the American body politic. What was new and significant was the establishment of bona fide Arab-American pressure groups and voluntary associations whose main function has been to protect themselves against harassment from private groups or public agencies and to influence policy in the United States and Canada concerning different parts of the Arab World or Middle East.

As World War I had marked a watershed for the early Arab immigrants, the 1967 Arab-Israeli war did for the entire community. The older and newer Arab-American communities were shocked and traumatized by the 1967 war. In particular, they were dismayed and extremely disappointed to see how greatly one-sided and pro-Israeli the American communications media were in reporting on the Middle East.[49] The war itself also produced soul-searching on the part of many Arab Americans, old and new, and often reinforced or strengthened their Arab identity. This group included many members already active in various Palestinian, Syrian, and Lebanese clubs, which were mainly social in nature.

By 1967, members of the third generation of the early Arab immigrants had started to awaken to their own identity and to see that identity as Arab, not "Syrian." Elements of this third generation combined with politically sophisticated immigrants to work for their ethnic community and the causes of their people in the old homelands. The result was establishment of the Association of Arab-American University Graduates (AAUG) in late 1967, which was the first post–World War II national, credible, nonsectarian organization seeking to represent diverse elements of the Arab-American community and to advance an Arab rather than regional or country orientation.

To the AAUG, however, American hostility to "Arabs" and the concept of Arabism was so extreme and so widespread among policy makers and the general public that influencing the political process or public policy, especially in the United States, seemed futile. The Republican and Democratic parties were almost completely and solidly one sided in their support of Israel and in their hostility to Arab causes, even though the United States had huge economic and military assets in the region and was on the friendliest terms with most leaders and countries of the Arab world. The AAUG sought support from or identified with other individuals and groups. Among these were a few politicians such as Senator William Fulbright and others who were courageous enough to voice criticism of U.S. policy in the Middle East, other minority or disenfranchised groups in American society, and some intellectuals who began to criticize the administration and its policies.

The AAUG's first priority was the need to provide accurate information about the Arab world and Arabs in North America and to distribute this literature to the public at large, wherever access was possible. It sought to educate the Arab countries and people about the true nature of the problems facing the region and to educate Arab intellectuals and political leaders about U.S. and Canadian policies and the American political process. While the AAUG sought mainly to inform and educate, it also performed other tasks, because no other organizations existed to perform them. Among the tasks to which the AAUG devoted some time and effort were political lobbying, attacks against defamation of and discrimination against Arabs and Arab Americans, and activism among Arab Americans to get them to participate in politics.

These ancillary tasks were later championed and performed by newer organizations. The National Association of Arab Americans (NAAA) was formed in 1972 in the United States to act as a political lobby to defend and advance Arab-American interests and causes. In 1980, in response to the continuing slanders and attacks against Arabs and Arab Americans, the American-Arab Anti-Discrimination Committee (ADC) was established and quickly drew widespread support from the varied elements of the Arab community. In 1985, the Arab American Institute (AAI) was formed, primarily to encourage Arab Americans to become active in the American political arena.[50]

Building a New Future

To get a feel for how the Arab community has fared in America, it is useful to review some of the challenges and concerns that Arabs have faced in their new homeland and how they have coped with building a new future. Among the most important issues with which Arabs in America have had to wrestle is the definition of who they are, their sense of identity as a people, especially as they encountered and continue to encounter bias and discrimination in their new homeland.

Although Arabs in the United States and Canada constitute an ethnic group, they were not an ethnic minority in their old homeland. Their new identity has been shaped by many factors but especially by continuing interactions between conditions in the old and new homelands and by the interplay between their perceptions of themselves and how others see them. The early immigrants spoke Arabic and came from a predominantly Arabic culture and heritage, but they did not think of themselves as "Arabs." The main bond of solidarity among them at that time was based on familial, sectarian, and village- or region-oriented factors. The plethora of names by which they were known in the New World reflects their lack of "national" identity and ignorance or confusion on the part of the host society. Another factor in this process was the American, especially U.S., obsession with the idea of race and the various attempts early in this century to classify every immigrant group, no matter how small, by its racial composition.[51] The early Arabic-speaking groups were called Asians, "other Asians," Turks from Asia, Caucasian, white, black, or "colored."

Although immigration officials and the general press looked down on Arabic-speaking peoples, they nevertheless viewed them as part of the "white race," at least for the first thirty years or so of their presence in North America.

These authorities then decided those immigrants were not white. With their very identity questioned and maligned, the reaction of the early Arab Americans was to try to refute what they saw as demeaning and untrue charges. They argued that they were very much part of the white race.[52] Stung by accusations of inferiority in terms of scientific and technological accomplishments, Syrian-Arab Americans developed a two-cultures thesis long before C. P. Snow discussed it.[53] Their argument, which became popular in the community, especially among Arab literati, was that, although America was the most advanced country in the world in science, technology, and industrialization, the East was spiritually superior.[54] Coming from the Holy Land, they offered themselves as guides and instructors to Americans in their search for and desire to experience the life and times of Jesus—where he was born, preached, was crucified, and rose from the dead.[55] Arab Americans spoke and wrote about the "spiritual" East in terms that suggested perpetuity: it was always so and would always be so. By accident or not, these writers in essence condemned the East to an absence of material progress and desire to produce such for all time.

The emphasis on Eastern spirituality, although useful in making Arabs feel good about themselves compared with "materialist" Americans, still left Arabs in America with little cultural heritage to offer their American-born children. The result often was to ignore their Arab heritage and, especially beginning in the 1920s, to emphasize almost full assimilation in American society. As the children grew up immersed in American society and culture while simultaneously exposed to a smattering of Arabic words at home and some Arabic food and music, they often found themselves experiencing an identity crisis of some kind, mainly resulting in rootlessness, ambiguity, and a fractionalized personality.[56] These were the reactions of some of the Arab-American literati of the post–World War II period. The very culture of their own country denied them the privilege of being openly proud of their heritage. They sometimes dealt with this awkward situation by complaining about American prejudice and discrimination against Arabs and by simultaneously denigrating their own people and heritage—if only to ingratiate themselves with their readers, their fellow Americans.[57]

The 1967 war changed the situation radically. Israel, in the short period of seven days, defeated the Arab armies. The Arab people generally felt let down and humiliated. Arabs in America, both newcomers and third-generation descendants of the early pioneers, deeply resented the extreme partisanship America and Americans (especially the U.S. government and people) showed toward Israel and the occasional hostility toward Arabs. The consequence was for Arab Americans to shake off their malaise and to organize. Their first goal was to fight against the negative stereotyping of Arabs. Their second was to help modify American policy toward the Middle East and make it more balanced. In the process, sectors of the well-established older community de-assimilated. They began openly to call themselves Arab and to join political groupings set up to defend Arab and Arab-American causes.[58] Arab Americans also began to organize conferences and publish journals and books in defense of their cause. They wrote fiction, poetry, and memoirs declaring pride in and solidarity with Arabs and the Arab community in America.

Open Arab-American pride in their heritage and activism on behalf of their cause does not, however, mean that prejudice against them ceased. On the contrary, many in the community feel that prejudice and discrimination have increased. Different reasons have been advanced to explain the prejudice

and discrimination that Arabs encounter in North America, and different individuals and groups have emphasized what they believe to be the main cause or the one most pertinent to their situation.

The most popular explanation for the negative stereotypes Americans hold about Arabs is that they are ignorant of the truth because they have not read or have read inaccurate and false reports about Arabs and have not come into contact with Arabs. According to this view, the stereotypes are mainly the result of propaganda by and on behalf of Zionist and pro-Israeli supporters. The primary objective of this propaganda has been to deprive Arabs, especially Palestinians, from presenting their case to the American public and the American political leadership.[59]

In this view, the attempt to deny Arabs and Arab Americans a public voice also extends to the political arena. In this way, it becomes a "politics of exclusion" in an attempt to prevent debate on any issues that reflect poorly on Zionists or Israel. It also smears and defames Arab candidates for political office to defeat them and exclude them from effective participation in political decision making. This "political racism" is presumed to be ideological in nature and not necessarily directed against Arabs or Arab Americans as a people or as an ethnic community.[60]

Another view sees hostility and violence against Arabs and Arab Americans as anti-Arab racism. This hostility is seen as part of the native racist attitudes and is believed to be present in all sectors of American society, not just among fringe groups. Somewhat related to this view is "jingoistic racism," which is directed at whatever foreign enemy is perceived to be out there.[61] Because of the many recent conflicts in the Middle East in which the United States directly or indirectly became involved and where incidents of hijacking and hostage taking occurred, many Americans reacted negatively against a vaguely perceived enemy next door, often not distinguishing between Arabs and Muslims or between Arabs and any foreigner who "looks" Arab.[62]

Still another view of negative Arab stereotypes, at least in the United States, argues that these ideas are "rooted in a core of hostile archetypes that our culture applies to those with whom it clashes."[63] According to this argument, most of the elements that constitute the Arab image in America are not unique to Arabs but also have been applied to other ethnic groups, especially blacks and Jews in the form of racism and anti-Semitism. These negative stereotypes have been transferred to a new group, the Arabs or Arab Americans.

Part of the negative stereotyping and hostility many Americans harbor toward Arabs is based on the latter's alleged mistreatment of their women. It is rather ironic, therefore, that Arab-American women find themselves the subject of prejudice, discrimination, and hostility at the hands of American men and women. This is often the result of hostility based on race, color, or religion.[64]

Arab-American women have had more problems than their male counterparts in defining an acceptable or comfortable identity. The problem is multifaceted and affects different sectors differently. Women who have come from the most traditional countries of the Arab world have experienced a greater restriction of their freedom in the United States. This is primarily the result of an inability on the part of traditional husbands, fathers, and brothers to deal with the nearly complete freedom accorded to women in American society. Just as important is the inability of the women to participate fully in the United States because they do not know the language, lack the necessary education, and are unfamiliar with American customs. They are not psychologically ready to countenance, let alone internalize, certain mores pertaining to the public display of affection and male-female interaction. Because many cannot drive and probably do not have a car, they find themselves much more isolated than they were back home, where they often had a vibrant and full life, albeit within the confines of the family and female friends.[65]

Among middle-class, first-generation Arab-American women, there is perhaps not much adjustment necessary. They usually follow the somewhat liberal mores they brought with them from the old homeland. On the other hand, Arab girls reaching their adolescence in the United States are likely to experience more problems as a result of the potential clash between traditional child-rearing practices and the freer atmosphere found in North America.[66]

Among better-educated, young Arab-American women, the issue of identity is both more subtle and more openly discussed. Like their male Arab-American counterparts, these women suffer from and are offended by the hostility against Arabs and Arab Americans. They also find American views of how women are allegedly treated in the Arab world to be inaccurate and grotesque. Nevertheless, they would like to expand the rights of Arab women and to improve the quality of their lives. They resent and reject any attempt on the part of Arab-American men to define what their role should be in maintaining Arab culture and mores in North America. In particular, they want to reject the notion that family honor resides in women and that the way a woman behaves, especially concerning her modesty and sexuality, can bring honor or dishonor to the family. They do not wish to be the conveyors or transmitters of tradition and culture—at least not as these are defined by men or as they prevail in the old homeland.[67]

Women and men in the Arab-American community of the 1990s find that the "white" racial classification that the early Syrian-Arab community worked so hard to attain is flawed. In practical daily interactions, Arabs in America are often treated as "honorary whites" or "white but not quite."[68] In reaction to this situation, at least four different orientations have been advocated. For the majority, especially among the older and well-established Christian community, there is some disgruntlement but general passivity about the discrimination and the prejudice that accompany their "white but not quite" status, and they work to remove these negative attitudes. Others, especially the Arab American Institute, have argued for a special designation of Arabs in the United States as a minority (e.g., the Hispanics) or as a specific census category encompassing all peoples of the Middle East.[69] Still others, especially some young, educated Arab-American women, have expressed a preference for the designation "people of color."[70] This would place them as part of a larger category that includes most of the federally recognized minorities in the United States. There are also those who resent being boxed into one category. Their sense of identity is multifaceted; they are men or women; Arab, American, Muslim or Christian; white or dark skinned; and so on. They think of themselves in different ways at different times or in different contexts, and they argue for getting rid of such categories or for the use of more descriptive categories that recognize different aspects of their background, culture, or physical appearance.[71]

The search for an adequate or comfortable identity for Arabs in America has been guided and perhaps complicated by the need to feel pride in their heritage and simultaneously avoid prejudice and discrimination in their new homeland. For most, the search is neither successful nor final. They continue to experience marginality in American society and politics, and they try to overcome this in various ways. Some resort to ethnic denial; they de-emphasize their Arab or Islamic background by claiming a connection with what they believe is a more acceptable appearance in America. Instead of proclaiming their Arabism, for instance, they claim that they are Lebanese or Egyptian. Some may even deny their heritage altogether, claiming to be Greek or Italian. Some new arrivals instead choose ethnic isolation. They are unwilling to change themselves and do not believe they can change the host society.

Among those who want full integration or assimilation into American society, especially middle-class Arab Americans, many emphasize the strong cultural link between Arabs and Americans. They refuse to give up and continue to work hard to show where the dominant American view is wrong. For most, accommodation is the easiest and most comfortable stance. These men and women consciously or subconsciously act in ways that reduce their difference from the American dominant group. They attempt "to pass."[72] Others, especially those who seek material success, especially those who are in public professions (e.g., television, radio, movies), often give in and convert to the prevailing view. Not infrequently, the very individuals who are looked down on by the Arab-American community are selected to speak for and represent the Arabs in America.[73]

The Arab-American Community in the 1990s

After more than a century of immigration, it is clear that the basic reasons Arabs came are no different from those that drove or attracted other groups to come here. They came because of the promise of a quick fortune and a sense of adventure; the threat of war or economic disaster; education, training, technology; and the thrill of living in a free democratic system. Whatever their reasons, true integration and full assimilation have eluded them. In part, this is the result of the many developments leading to the debunking of the notion of a melting pot and the greater tolerance of a multicultural society. The more important reason, however, has been the hostility the host society has shown toward Arab immigrants.[74]

Nevertheless, Arabs in America have done very well. Since the 1960s, there has always been at least one representative of Arab background in the U.S. Congress (e.g., James Abourezk, Mary Rose Oakar, Mark Joe [Nick] Rahall II). Others have served as state governors (e.g., Victor Atiyeh, OR) or on the White House staff (e.g., John H. Sununu). Similarly, individuals of Arab descent have been elected to the Canadian parliament (e.g., Mac Harb, Mark Assad) and to provincial legislatures. Many of these individuals have faced difficulties in attaining their positions because they were of Arab background. Some have found it useful to de-emphasize or deny that background to get or maintain their positions. Most also have not been strong or vocal supporters of Arab or Arab nationalist causes. Nonetheless, ethnic pride is more openly displayed by an increasing number of political candidates at local, state, and national levels.[75]

Arab Americans have done well and fared better economically than the general population average in many areas. The 1980 and 1990 U.S. census data show that Arab Americans reach a higher educational level than the American population as a whole. According to the 1990 census, 15.2 percent of Arab Americans have "graduate degrees or higher"—more than twice the national average of 7.2 percent. Household income among Arab Americans also tends to be higher than the average. Arab Americans have also done well in professional, management, and sales professions.[76]

Although many Arabs in America have reached the highest level of their profession in

almost all professions,[77] the American media primarily highlight the negative achievements of Arabs and Muslims. Quite often, the media announce the Arab or Islamic origin or affiliation of anyone accused of a terrorist act—even before they know whether the perpetrator is Arab or Muslim. In the case of positive role models such as Michael DeBakey or Ralph Nader, the media often never mention their Arab background. One reason is that "some [too many] have found it necessary to hide their origins because of racism."[78] Lists of prominent Arab Americans occasionally are published in the press to inform the public about the community's accomplishments, but the fact that such lists are compiled indicates that Arab Americans feel the sting of negative stereotyping and try to correct the bad publicity. Despite the fact that Arabs have lived in America for more than a century and despite their major successes, they are still struggling to be accepted in American society. Full integration and assimilation will not be achieved until that happens.[79]

NOTES

1. See William E. Leuchtenburg, "The American Perception of the Arab World." In George N. Atiyeh, ed., *Arab and American Cultures* (Washington, DC: American Enterprise Institute for Public Policy Research, 1977), p. 15.

2. Although it is possible to speak of several waves of Arab immigration to North America (e.g., 1880s to World War I, World War I to World War II, 1945 to 1967, 1968 to the present), there have been two main waves: from the 1880s to World War II and from World War II to the present. The major differences in the character and composition of the immigrant populations can be detected primarily between these two groups.

3. Unless otherwise indicated, references to the Arab community include the Arabs in Canada and those in the United States. Because of the much smaller numbers of Arabs in Canada, leadership on major issues

usually has come from the Arab community in the United States.

4. See appendixes 1 and 2 in Gregory Orfalea, *Before the Flames: Quest for the History of Arab Americans* (Austin, TX: University of Texas Press, 1988), pp. 314–15. There were about 11,000 Arabs in Canada in 1931. For more on the subject of Arab immigration to Canada, see Baha Abu-Laban, *An Olive Branch on the Family Tree: The Arabs in Canada* (Toronto: McClelland and Stewart, 1980).

5. This is the official U.S. government figure cited in Philip Hitti's "The Emigrants," published in the 1963 edition of the *Encyclopedia of Islam* and reproduced in *Al-Hoda, 1898–1968* (New York: Al-Hoda Press, 1968), p. 133. A much larger estimate of 800,000 (Lebanese) was given by Ashad G. Hawie, *The Rainbow Ends* (New York: Theo. Gaus' Sons, 1942), pp. 149, 151.

6. This figure does not include the Arab community in Canada, which has fewer than 400,000 persons today. For estimates of Arab immigration to Canada, see Baha Abu-Laban, *An Olive Branch on the Family Tree: The Arabs in Canada* (Toronto: McClelland and Stewart, 1980) and Ibrahim Hayani's chapter in this book. Philip M. Kayal gave the low estimate in 1974 for Arabs in the United States but provided a revised estimate much closer to the generally accepted figure in 1987. See his "Estimating Arab-American Population," *Migration Today* 2, no. 5 (1974): 3, 9, and "Report: Counting the 'Arabs' Among Us," *Arab Studies Quarterly* 9, no. 1 (1987): 98–104.

7. See Philip K. Hitti, *The Syrians in America* (New York: George H. Doran, 1924), p. 48; Alixa Naff, *Becoming American: The Early Arab Immigrant Experience* (Carbondale, IL: Southern Illinois University Press, 1985), p. 83; Samir Khalaf, "The Background and Causes of Lebanese/Syrian Immigration to the United States before World War I." In Eric J. Hooglund, ed., *Crossing the Waters: Arabic-Speaking Immigrants to the United States before 1940* (Washington, DC: Smithsonian Institution Press, 1987), pp. 17–35; and Charles Issawi, "The Historical Background of Lebanese Emigration: 1800–1914." In Albert Hourani and Nadim Shehadi, eds., *The Lebanese in the World: A Century of Emigration* (London: I.B. Tauris, 1992), pp. 13–31. See also

Baha Abu-Laban, "The Lebanese in Montreal." In Albert Hourani and Nadim Shehadi, eds., *The Lebanese in the World: A Century of Emigration* (London: I.B. Tauris, 1992), pp. 227–42.

8. Charles Issawi, "The Historical Background of Lebanese Emigration: 1800–1914." In Albert Hourani and Nadim Shehadi, eds., *The Lebanese in the World: A Century of Emigration* (London: I.B. Tauris, 1992), p. 22.

9. Philip K. Hitti, *The Syrians in America* (New York: George H. Doran, 1924), pp. 49–50. See also Akram Fouad Khater, "'House' to 'Goddess of the House': Gender, Class, and Silk in 19th-Century Mount Lebanon," *International Journal of Middle East Studies* 28, no. 3 (1996): 325–48.

10. For an informed and intelligent discussion on this and related issues, see Louise Seymour Houghton's series of articles entitled "Syrians in the United States," *The Survey* 26 (1 July, 5 August, 2 September, 7 October, 1911), pp. 480–95, 647–65, 786–803, 957–68.

11. For an early account of Arab immigration to the United States and to North America in general, which cites religious persecution as the reason for migration, see Basil M. Kherbawi, "History of the Syrian Emigration," which is part seven of Kherbawi's *tarikh al-Wilayat al-Muttahida* (*History of the United States*) (New York: al Dalil Press, 1913), pp. 726–96, published in Arabic.

12. See Leila Tarazi Fawaz, *An Occasion for War: Civil Conflict in Lebanon and Damascus in 1860* (Berkeley, CA: University of California Press, 1995). See also, Mikha'il Mishaqa, *Murder, Mayhem, Pillage and Pluder: The History of Lebanon in the 18th and 19th Centuries.* Translated by Wheeler M. Thackston, Jr. (Albany, NY: State University of New York Press, 1988).

13. See Louise Seymour Houghton's series of articles entitled "Syrians in the United States," *The Survey,* 26 (1911), pp. 480–95; and Alixa Naff, *Becoming American: The Early Arab Immigrant Experience* (Carbondale, IL: Southern Illinois University Press, 1985), pp. 128–200. For Canadian statistics, see Baha Abu-Laban, *An Olive Branch on the Family Tree: The Arabs in Canada* (Toronto: McClelland and Stewart, 1980).

14. *Kawkab America* (15 April 1892): 1, English section. The English titles of Arabic newspapers cited here are provided as originally used. The titles in parentheses are the transliterations used by the Library of Congress.

15. Even though *Kawkab America* was published for about seventeen years, only copies of the first four years are available, the others have been lost.

16. See Motaz Abdullah Alhourani, "The Arab-American Press and the Arab World: News Coverage in Al-Bayan and Al-Dalil" (master's thesis, Kansas State University, Manhattan, KS, 1993).

17. For a history of the organizational and political activities of Arabic-speaking groups in the United States during this period, see James Ansara, "The Immigration and Settlement of the Syrians" (master's thesis, Harvard University, Cambridge, MA, 1931).

18. Among these, the most important journal was *The Syrian World,* published and edited by Salloum Mokarzel. A useful publication is the *Annotated Index to the Syrian World, 1926–1932* by John G. Moses and Eugene Paul Nassar (Saint Paul, MN: Immigration History Research Center, University of Minnesota, 1994).

19. See Philip M. and Joseph M. Kayal, *The Syrian-Lebanese in America: A Study in Religion and Assimilation* (Boston, MA: Twayne Publishers, 1975).

20. A good account of the most prominent of these writers is provided by Nadira Jamil Sarraj, *Shu'ara' al-Rabitah al-Qalamiyah* (Poets of the Pen League) (Cairo, Egypt: Dar al-Ma'arif, 1964), published in Arabic.

21. See, for instance, Ameen Rihani, "To Syrians in the [American] Armed Forces," *As-Sayeh* (*al-Sa'ih*) (16 September 1918): 2, published in Arabic.

22. Advertisements and editorials in support of American Liberty bonds were found in most Arabic publications of that period, including *Al-Hoda* and *Meraat-ul-Gharb.*

23. See, in particular, *Syria Before the Peace Conference* (New York: Syrian-Lebanese League of North America, 1919).

24. This was the view often voiced after French entrenchment in Syria and Lebanon in the late 1920s and the 1930s.

25. For a summary of these views, see "Editors and Arabian Newspapers Give Opinions on Zionism," *The Jewish Criterion* (5 July 1918): 16–17.

26. Among the more active participants in public lectures and writings on this issue were Ameen Rihani and F. I. Shatara. The Arab National League was established in 1936, and members spoke out on Palestine and other issues. For coverage of these and other activities related to the Palestine issue, see *Palestine & Transjordan* for that period. See also "A Communique from the Arab National League," *As-Sayeh* (6 August 1936): 9.

27. On the occupations of emigrant Arabs, especially in North America and specifically about those engaged in commerce, see Salloum Mokarzel, *Tarikh al-tijara al-Suriyya fi al-mahajir al-Amrikiyya* (The History of Trade of Syrian Immigrants in the Americas) (New York: Syrian-American Press, 1920), published in Arabic. On peddling activity, see Alixa Naff, *Becoming American: The Early Arab Immigrant Experience* (Carbondale, IL: Southern Illinois University Press, 1985), pp. 128–200.

28. The Arabic press of the period was replete with such advice.

29. Edna Bonacich, "A Theory of Middleman Minorities," *American Sociological Review* 38 (1973): 591.

30. Prejudice against Arabs in America was widespread, and there was also some discrimination, especially in the southern United States. See, for instance, Nancy Faires Conklin and Nora Faires, " 'Colored' and Catholic: The Lebanese in Birmingham, Alabama." In Eric J. Hooglund, ed., *Crossing the Waters: Arabic-Speaking Immigrants to the United States before 1940* (Washington, DC: Smithsonian Institution Press, 1987), pp. 69–84.

31. See, for instance, H. A. El-Kourie, "Dr. El-Kourie Defends Syrian Immigrants," *Birmingham Ledger* (20 September 1907) and "El-Kourie Takes Burnett to Task," *Age-Herald* (Birmingham, AL) (20 October 1907): 6.

32. In 1908, Canada issued the Order-in-Council, P.C. 926, which severely restricted Asiatic immigration. Negative attitudes about "Syrians," mistaking them for "Turks," also were a factor in reducing the level of Arab immigration to Canada. See Baha Abu-Laban, "The Lebanese in Montreal." In Albert Hourani and Nadim Shehadi, eds., *The Lebanese in the World: A Century of Emigration* (London: I.B. Tauris, 1992), p. 229.

33. See Kalil A. Bishara, *The Origins of the Modern Syrian* (New York: Al-Hoda Publishing House, 1914), published in English and Arabic.

34. See *Ex Parte Dow*, 211 F. 486 (E.D. South Carolina 1914) and *In Re Dow*, 213 F. 355 (E.D. South Carolina 1914).

35. *Dow v. United States et al*, 26 F. 145 (4th Cir. 1915).

36. See Joseph W. Ferris, "Syrian Naturalization Question in the United States: Certain Legal Aspects of Our Naturalization Laws," Part II, *The Syrian World* 2, no. 9 (1928): 18–24.

37. *In Re Ahmed Hassan*, 48 F. Supp. 843 (E.D. Michigan 1942).

38. *Ex Parte Mohriez*, 54 F. Supp. 941 (D. Massachusetts 1944).

39. See the Arabic edition of *Al-Hoda, 1898–1968* (New York: Al-Hoda Press, 1968).

40. *The Syrian Voice* changed its name to *The Syrian and Lebanonite Voice* in the late 1930s.

41. See M[ichael A.] Shadid, "Syria for the Syrians," *Syrian World* 1, no. 8 (1927): 21–24, and see "'Syria for the Syrians' Again: An Explanation and a Retraction," *Syrian World* 3, no. 4 (1928): 24–28.

42. For an excellent early study of New York Arabs, see Lucius Hopkins Miller, "A Study of the Syrian Communities of Greater New York," *Federation* 3 (1903): 11–58.

43. This was the message often presented in *Al-Akhlaq* (*al-Akhlaq*) (Character) in the 1920s.

44. See the various articles in the Arabic press by Afifa Karam and Victoria Tannous.

45. This issue occupied the Arab community for a long time and was almost a weekly subject in the main newspapers until peddling activity dwindled in the late 1920s. See, for instance, Afifa Karam's (untitled) article about women peddlers and the *Kashshi* in *Al-Hoda* (14 July, 1903): 2.

46. See, for instance, Habib I. Katibah, "What Is Americanism?" *The Syrian World* 1, no. 3 (1926): 16–20; W. A. Mansur, "The Future of Syrian Americans," *The Syrian World* 2, no. 3 (1927): 11–17, and see "Modern Syrians' Contributions to Civilization," *The Syrian World* 4, no. 5 (1930): 7–14.

47. The question about whether to teach Arabic to their children was a controversial issue in the 1920s and hotly debated in two main journals, *The Syrian World* and *Al-Akhlaq.*

48. See Michael W. Suleiman, "A Community Profile of Arab-Americans: Major Challenges and Concerns," *Arab Perspectives* (September 1983): pp. 6–13.

49. See Ibrahim Abu-Lughod, ed., *The Arab-Israeli Confrontation of June, 1967: An Arab Perspective* (Evanston, IL: Northwestern University Press, 1970).

50. Michael W. Suleiman, "Arab-Americans and the Political Process." In Ernest McCarus, ed., *The Development of Arab-American Identity* (Ann Arbor, MI: University of Michigan Press, 1994), pp. 37–60.

51. See "Dictionary of Races or Peoples." In *United States Reports of the Immigration Commission* (Washington, DC: Government Printing Office, 1911).

52. The details of these appeals are discussed in Michael W. Suleiman, "Early Arab-Americans: The Search for Identity." In Eric J. Hooglund, ed., *Crossing the Waters: Arabic-Speaking Immigrants to the United States before 1940* (Washington, DC: Smithsonian Institution Press, 1987), pp. 37–54.

53. C. P. Snow, *The Two Cultures and the Scientific Revolution* (Cambridge, England: Cambridge University Press, 1961).

54. This became a popular theme among many Arab-American writers. See, for instance, Abraham Mitry Rihbany, *A Far Journey* (Boston, MA: Houghton-Mifflin, 1914).

55. Abraham Mitrie Rihbany, *The Syrian Christ* (Boston, MA: Houghton-Mifflin, 1916).

56. See Evelyn Shakir, "Pretending to Be Arab: Role-Playing in Vance Bourjaily's 'The Fractional Man,'" *MELUS* 9, no. 1 (1982): 7–21. See also Vance Bourjaily, *Confessions of a Spent Youth* (New York: Bantam Books, 1961).

57. See, for instance, William Peter Blatty, *Which Way to Mecca, Jack?* (New York: Bernard Geis Associates, 1960).

58. See Ali Shteiwi Zaghel, "Changing Patterns of Identification among Arab Americans: The Palestine Ramallites and the Christian Syrian-Lebanese" (Ph.D. diss., Northwestern University, 1977).

59. Much has been written in this vein. For a lengthy bibliography, see Michael W. Suleiman, *The Arabs in the Mind of America* (Brattleboro, VT: Amana Books, 1988). For a Canadian-Arab activist's view, see Sheikh Muhammad Said Massoud, *I Fought as I Believed* (Montreal: Sheikh Muhammad Said Massoud, 1976).

60. Helen Hatab Samhan, "Politics and Exclusion: The Arab American Experience,"

Journal of Palestine Studies 16, no. 2 (1987): 11–28.

61. Nabeel Abraham, "Anti-Arab Racism and Violence in the United States." In Ernest McCarus, ed., *The Development of Arab-American Identity* (Ann Arbor, MI: University of Michigan Press, 1994), pp. 155–214.

62. For documentation, see, for instance, *1990 ADC Annual Report on Political and Hate Violence* (Washington, DC: American-Arab Anti-Discrimination Committee, 1991). For Canadian statistics, see Zuhair Kashmeri, *The Gulf Within: Canadian Arabs, Racism and the Gulf War* (Toronto: James Lorimer & Co., 1991).

63. Ronald Stockton, "Ethnic Archetypes and the Arab Image." In Ernest McCarus, ed., *The Development of Arab-American Identity* (Ann Arbor, MI: University of Michigan Press, 1994), p. 120.

64. See the various essays and poems in Joanna Kadi, ed., *Food for Our Grandmothers: Writings by Arab-American and Arab-Canadian Feminists* (Boston, MA: South End Press, 1994).

65. See Louise Cainkar, "Palestinian Women in the United States: Coping with Tradition, Change, and Alienation" (Ph.D. diss., Northwestern University, 1988).

66. See Charlene Joyce Eisenlohr, "The Dilemma of Adolescent Arab Girls in an American High School" (Ph.D. diss., University of Michigan, 1988).

67. For an excellent study on Arab-American women, see Evelyn Shakir, *Bint Arab: Arab and Arab American Women in the United States* (Westport, CT: Praeger, 1997).

68. Joseph Massad, "Palestinians and the Limits of Racialized Discourse," *Social Text* 11, no. 1 (1993): 108.

69. The attempt has failed, at least so far. See the 16 September 1997 letter to Katherine K. Wellman of the Office of Management and Budget sent on Arab American Institute (AAI) stationery and signed by Helen Hatab Samhan (AAI), Samia El Badry (Census 2000 Advisory Committee), and Hala Maksoud, American-Arab Anti-Discrimination Committee.

70. Lisa Suhair Majaj, "Two Worlds: Arab-American Writing," *Forkroads* 1, no. 3 (1996): 64–80. See also different entries in Joanna Kadi, ed., *Food for Our Grandmothers: Writings by Arab-American and Arab-Canadian Feminists* (Boston, MA: South End Press, 1994).

71. See, for instance, Pauline Kaldas, "Exotic." In Joanna Kadi, ed., *Food for Our Grandmothers: Writings by Arab-American and Arab-Canadian Feminists* (Boston, MA: South End Press, 1994), pp. 168–69.

72. See Nabeel Abraham, "Arab-American Marginality: Mythos and Praxis." In Baha Abu-Laban and Michael W. Suleiman, eds., *Arab Americans: Continuity and Change* (Belmont, MA: AAUG Press, 1989), pp. 17–43.

73. See Michael W. Suleiman, "American Views of Arabs and the Impact of These Views on Arab Americans," *Al-Mustaqbal Al-Arabi* 16 (1993): 93–107, published in Arabic.

74. Milton Gordon states that the absence of a hostile attitude on the part of the host society is a key factor in the integration and assimilation of immigrants. See his *Assimilation in American Life: The Role of Race, Religion, and National Origins* (New York: Oxford University Press, 1964).

75. These attitudes were evident in a 1998 survey of Arabs active in U.S. politics, an analysis of which I plan to publish.

76. For analyses of some of the 1980 and 1990 U.S. census data, see John Zogby, *Arab America Today: A Demographic Profile of Arab Americans* (Washington, DC: Arab American Institute, 1990), and Samia El-Badry, "The Arab-American Market," *American Demographics* (January 1994): 22–27, 30. See also "CPH-L-149 Selected Characteristics for Persons of Arab Ancestry: 1990," U.S. Bureau of the Census, 1990 Census of Population and Housing, C-P-3-2, Ancestry of the Population in the United States: 1990.

77. Examples include Michael DeBakey in medicine (heart surgery); Elias Corey in chemistry (1990 Nobel Prize winner); Casey Kasem, Danny Thomas, and Paula Abdul in entertainment; Helen Thomas in journalism; Doug Flutie in sports (1984 Heisman Trophy winner); and Ralph Nader in consumer advocacy.

78. Casey Kasem, "We're Proud of Our Heritage," *Parade* (*Kansas City Star*) (16 January 1994): 1.

79. See Lisa Suhair Majaj, "Boundaries: Arab/American." In Joanna Kadi, ed., *Food for Our Grandmothers: Writings by Arab-American and Arab-Canadian Feminists* (Boston, MA: South End Press, 1994), pp. 65–84.

43

ETHNIC AND RACIAL IDENTITIES OF SECOND-GENERATION BLACK IMMIGRANTS IN NEW YORK CITY

Mary C. Waters

QUESTIONS TO CONSIDER

Based on her research of West Indians and Haitian Americans in New York City, Mary Waters found that first-generation black immigrants "tended to distance themselves from American blacks." Why? What does this "distancing" strategy say about the way American blacks are perceived by new immigrant groups? How is racism within *a racial group possible?*

The growth of nonwhite voluntary immigrants to the United States since 1965 challenges the dichotomy that once explained different patterns of American inclusion and assimilation—the ethnic pattern of assimilation of European immigrants and the racial pattern of exclusion of America's nonwhite peoples. The new wave of immigrants includes people who are still defined racially in the United States but who migrate voluntarily and often under an immigrant preference system that selects for people with jobs and education that puts them well above their coethnics in the economy. Do the processes of immigration and assimilation for nonwhite immigrants resemble the processes for earlier white immigrants? Or do these immigrants and their children

face very different choices and constraints because they are defined racially by other Americans?

This [reading] examines a small piece of this puzzle—the question of the development of an ethnic identity among the second generation of black immigrants from the Caribbean. While there has been a substantial amount of interest in the identities and affiliations of these immigrants, very little research has been conducted on the identities of their children. The children of black immigrants in the United States face a choice about whether to identify as black American or whether to maintain an ethnic identity reflecting their parents' national origins. First-generation black immigrants to the United States have tended to distance themselves from American blacks, stressing their national origins and ethnic identities as Jamaican or Haitian or Trinidadian, but they also face overwhelming pressures in the United States to identify only as blacks (Foner 1987; Kasinitz 1992; Stafford 1987; Sutton and

Makiesky 1975; Woldemikael 1989). In fact, they have been described as "invisible immigrants," because rather than being contrasted with other immigrants (for example, contrasting how Jamaicans are doing relative to Chinese), they are compared with black Americans. The children of black immigrants, because they lack their parents' distinctive accents, can choose to be even more invisible as ethnics than their parents. Second-generation West Indians in the United States most often will be seen by others as merely "American"—and must actively work to assert their ethnic identities.

The types of racial and ethnic identities adopted by a sample of second-generation West Indians[1] and Haitian Americans in New York City are explored here, along with subjective understandings these youngsters have of being American, being black American, and being their ethnic identity. After a short discussion of current theoretical approaches to understanding assimilation among the second generation, three types of identities adopted by the second generation are described and the different experiences of race relations associated with these identities are traced. Finally this [reading] suggests some implications for future patterns of identity development. . . .

Interviews with first-generation immigrants and their American coworkers reveal a great deal of tension between foreign-born and American-born blacks in both the working-class and the middle-class work sites. Long-standing tensions between newly arrived West Indians and American blacks have left a legacy of mutual stereotyping. (See Kasinitz 1992.) The immigrants see themselves as hardworking, ambitious, militant about their racial identities but not oversensitive or obsessed with race, and committed to education and family. They see black Americans as lazy, disorganized, obsessed with racial slights and barriers, with a dis-

organized and laissez-faire attitude toward family life and child raising. American blacks describe the immigrants as arrogant, selfish, exploited in the workplace, oblivious to racial tensions and politics in the United States, and unfriendly and unwilling to have relations with black Americans. The first generation believes that their status as foreign-born blacks is higher than American blacks, and they tend to accentuate their identities as immigrants. Their accent is usually a clear and unambiguous signal to other Americans that they are foreign born.

The dilemma facing the second generation is that they grow up exposed to the negative opinions voiced by their parents about American blacks and to the belief that whites respond more favorably to foreign-born blacks. But they also realize that because they lack their parents' accents and other identifying characteristics, other people, including their peers, are likely to identify them as American blacks. How does the second generation handle this dilemma? Do they follow their parents' lead and identify with their ethnic identities such as Jamaican or Haitian or West Indian? Or do they try to become "American" and reject their parents' ethnic immigrant identities? . . .

Theoretical Approaches to Assimilation

Theories derived from the experiences of European immigrants and their children in the early twentieth century predicted that the more time spent in the United States, the more likely second-generation youths were to adopt an "American identity" and to reduce ties to the ethnic identities and culture of their parents. This "straight-line" assimilation model assumes that with each succeeding generation, the groups become more similar to mainstream Americans and more economically successful. For instance, Warner and Srole's (1945) study of ethnic groups in Yankee City (Newburyport, Massachusetts) in the early 1930s describes the generational march from initial residential and occupational segregation and poverty to residential, occupational, and identificational integration and Americanization.

However, the situation faced by immigrant blacks in the 1990s differs in many of the background assumptions of the straight-line model. The immigrants do not enter a society that assumes an undifferentiated monolithic American culture but rather a consciously pluralistic society in which a variety of subcultures and racial and ethnic identities coexist. In fact, if these immigrants assimilate, they become not just Americans but black Americans. The immigrants generally believe that it is higher social status to be an immigrant black than to be an American black. Second, the economic opportunity structure is very different now from what it was at the beginning of the twentieth century. The unskilled jobs in manufacturing that enhanced job mobility for immigrants' children at the turn of the century have been lost as economic restructuring in the United States has shifted to a service economy (Gans 1992). The immigrants also are quite varied in the skills they bring with them. Some arrive with advanced educations and professional qualifications to take relatively well-paying jobs, which put them ahead of native American blacks (for example, Jamaican nurses). Others are less skilled and face difficulties finding work in the United States. Finally, the degree of residential segregation faced by blacks in the United States, whether foreign born or American born, has always been, and continues to be, of a much higher order than the segregation faced by foreign-born white immigrants (Lieberson 1980; Massey 1990). Thus, even with occupational mobility, it is not clear that blacks would be able to

move into higher-status neighborhoods in the orderly progression that Warner and Srole (1945) describe in their Yankee City study of European ethnic succession. A further complication for the black second generation is that part of being a black American involves dealing with American racism. Because immigrants and black Americans report a large difference in the perception and expectation of racism in American society, part of becoming American for the second generation involves developing a knowledge and perception of racism and its subtle nuances. . . .

Patterns in the Second Generation

The interviews suggest that while the individuals in this study vary a great deal in their identities, perceptions, and opinions, they can be sorted into three general types: identifying as Americans, identifying as ethnic Americans with some distancing from black Americans, or identifying as an immigrant in a way that does not reckon with American racial and ethnic categories.

A black American identity characterized the responses of approximately 42 percent of the eighty-three second-generation respondents interviewed. These youngsters identified with other black Americans. They did not see their "ethnic" identities as important to their self-image. When their parents or friends criticized American blacks or described what they perceived as fundamental differences between Caribbean-origin people and American blacks, these youngsters disagreed. They tended to downplay a national-origin identity and described themselves as American.

Another 30 percent of the respondents adopted a very strong ethnic identity that involved a considerable amount of distancing from American blacks. It was important for these respondents to stress their ethnic identities and for other people to recognize that they were not American blacks. These respondents tended to agree with parental judgments that there were strong differences between Americans and West Indians. This often involved a stance that West Indians were superior to American blacks in their behaviors and attitudes.

A final 28 percent of respondents had an immigrant attitude toward their identities, as opposed to American-identified youth or ethnic-identified youth. Most, but not all, of these respondents were more recent immigrants themselves. A crucial factor for these youngsters is that their accents and styles of clothing and behavior clearly signaled to others that they were foreign born. In a sense, their identity as an immigrant people precluded having to make a "choice" about what kind of American they were. These respondents had a strong identity, such as Jamaican or Trinidadian, but did not evidence much distancing from American blacks. Rather their identities were strongly linked to their experiences on the islands, and they did not worry much about how they were seen by other Americans, white or black.

A number of factors influence the type of identity the youngsters develop. They include the class background of the parents, the social networks in which the parents are involved, the type of school the child attends, and the family structure. All of these factors affect the ability of parents and other family members to shield children from neighborhood peer groups that espouse antischool values.

The type of identity and outlook on American race and ethnic relations that the youngsters developed was strongly related to their social class and its trajectory. The ethnic-identified youngsters were most likely to come from a middle-class background. Of the eighty-three second-generation teens

and young adults interviewed, 57 percent of the middle-class teens identified ethnically, whereas only 17 percent of the working-class and poor teens identified ethnically.[2] The poorest students were the most likely to be immigrant or American identified. Only one out of the twelve teens whose parents were on public assistance identified ethnically. The American identified, perhaps not surprisingly, were also more likely to be born in the United States—67 percent of the American identified were born in the United States, as opposed to only 13 percent of the immigrant identified and 42 percent of the ethnically identified.

Parents with more education and income were able to provide better schools for their offspring. Among the respondents, some of the middle class had moved from the inner-city neighborhoods they had originally settled in to middle-class neighborhoods in the borough of Queens or to suburban areas where the schools were of higher academic quality and more likely to be racially integrated. Other middle-class parents sent their children to Catholic parochial schools or to citywide magnet schools such as Brooklyn Tech or Stuyvesant. Thus, the children were far more likely to attend schools with other immigrant children and with other middle-class whites and blacks, although some of the Catholic high schools were all black in enrollment.

The children of middle-class parents who did attend the local high schools were likely to be recent immigrants who had an immigrant identity. Because of their superior education in the West Indies, these students were the best in the local high schools, attended honors classes, and were bound for college. The children of middle-class parents who identified as American and were pessimistic about their own future opportunities and adopted antischool ideologies were likely to have arrived early in their lives and to have attended New York City public schools in inner-city areas from an early age.

The social networks of parents also influenced the type of identity the children developed. Regardless of social class, parents who were involved in ethnic voluntary organizations or heavily involved in their churches seemed to instill a strong sense of ethnic identity in their children. Parents whose social networks transcended neighborhood boundaries seemed to have more ability to provide guidance and social contacts for their children.

The two neighborhood schools where we interviewed the teenagers were among the five most dangerous schools in New York City—they were inadequate facilities with crumbling physical buildings, high dropout rates, and serious problems with violence. Both schools were all minority, with over 90 percent of the student body composed of black students, both American and foreign born. The students who attended these schools and were not in the separate honors tract (which was overwhelmingly filled with newly arrived immigrants) faced very limited future options, even if they managed to graduate.

Finally, the family structure and the experience of migration itself have a profound effect on the degree of control parents have over teenage children. Many families are composed of single working mothers and children. These mothers have not been able to supervise their children as much as they would like, and many do not have any extended family or close friends available to help with discipline and control. Even families with two spouses present often have been apart for long periods because one spouse preceded the family in migration. Often children have been left in the islands or sent ahead with relatives to New York, with the parents often struggling to reassert authority after the family reunites. The generational

conflict that ensues tends to create greater pressure for students to want to be "American" to differentiate themselves from parents.

Ethnic Response

All of the teenage respondents reported comments by their parents about American blacks that were very similar to those recorded in our interviews with the first generation. The differences were in how the teens interpreted what their parents were saying. In general, the ethnic-identified teens agreed with their parents and reported seeing a strong difference between themselves and black Americans, stressing that being black is not synonymous with being black American. They accept their parents' and the wider society's negative portrayals of poor blacks and wanted to avoid any chance that they will be identified with them. They described the culture and values of lower-class black Americans as lacking discipline, a work ethic, good child-rearing practices, and respect for education. They contrast these failures with the values of their parents' ethnic groups, which include an emphasis on education, strict discipline for children, a strong work ethic, and social mobility. They try to impress that they are Jamaican or Haitian and most definitely not black American. This allows them less dissonance with their parents' negative views of American blacks. They do not reject their parents' culture and identities but rather reject the American social system that would identify them as black American and strongly reject the African American peer group culture to which they would be assigned by whites and others if they did not consciously transmit their ethnic identities.

Although society may define the second generation on the basis of skin color, the second-generation ethnic teens believed that being black American involves more than merely having black skin. One young woman criticized American blacks in this way:

> Some of them [black Americans] think that their heritage includes not being able to speak correctly or walk correctly, or act loud and obnoxious to make a point. I don't think they have to do that. Just when I see black Americans, it depends on how I see you on the street. Walking down the street with that walk that moves a little bit too much. I would say, I'd think you dropped out of high school.

These teens also differentiated themselves from black Americans in terms of their sensitivity to racism, real or imagined. Some of the ethnic-identified second generation echo the feelings we heard from the first generation that American blacks are too quick to use race as an explanation or excuse for not doing well:

> There was a time back in the, '40s and, '50s and, '60s or whenever when people was actually trying to keep down black people and stuff like that. But, you know, some black people now, it's like they not actually trying to make it better, you know? Some are just like, people are like, oh, this place is trying to keep me down, and they sulk and they cry about it, and they're not really doing that much to help themselves.
> . . . It's just like hyping the problem if they keep [saying] everything is racial, everything is racial.

The second-generation teens who are doing well try to understand how it is that they are so successful when black Americans are not—and often they chalk it up to family values. They say that their immigrant families have close-knit family values that stress education. Aware of, and sometimes sharing, the negative images of black Americans that the whites they encounter believe, the second generation also perceives that whites treat them better when they realize they are not

"just" black Americans. When asked if they benefited ever from their ethnicity, they responded "yes": "It seems white Americans don't tend to put you in the same category as black Americans." Another respondent said:

> The West Indians tend to go that extra step because they, whites, don't usually consider them really black Americans, which would be working class. They don't consider them, I guess, as black. They see them as a person.

The dilemma for the second generation is that while they have a strong sense of their own identities as very different from black Americans, this was not clear to other people. Often both whites and blacks saw them as just black Americans and did not notice that they were ethnically different. When people did comment on their ethnic difference it was often because of the way they talked and the way they walked. These two characteristics were cited as reasons that whites and other blacks gave for thinking those of the second generation were not "really black." Whites tend to let these children know that they think of them as exceptions to the rule, with the rule being that most blacks are not good people. However, these young people also know that unless they tell people of their ethnicity, most whites have no idea they are not black Americans.

Many of these teens coped with this dilemma by devising ways to telegraph their identities as second-generation West Indians or Haitians. One girl carried a Guyanese map as part of her key chain so that when people looked at her keys they would ask her about it and she could tell them that her parents were from Guyana. One young woman described having her mother teach her an accent so that she could use it when she applied for a job or a place to live. Others just try to work it into conversation when they meet someone. This means that their self-identification is almost always at odds with the identifications others make of them in impersonal encounters in American society and that, as a result, they must consciously try to accentuate their ethnic identity:

Q: When a form or survey asks for your race what do you put down?

A: Oh boy, that is a tough one. It's funny because, you know, when we fill applications I never know what to check off, you know. I'm serious. 'Cause they have Afro-American, but they never have like Caribbean. They do have white, Chinese. To tell the truth, I would like to be called Caribbean, West Indian. Black West Indian.

The teens who were around many black Americans felt pressure from their peers to be part of the group and identify as black American. These teens would consciously talk about passing for American at some points and passing for Haitian or Jamaican at others by changing the way they talked or acted:

> When I'm at school and I sit with my black friends and, sometimes I'm ashamed to say this, but my accent changes. I learn all the words. I switch. Well, when I'm with my friends, my black friends, I say I'm black, black American. When I'm with my Haitian-American friends, I say I'm Haitian. Well, my being black, I guess that puts me when I'm with black Americans, it makes people think that I'm lower class. . . . Then, if I'm talking like this [regular voice] with my friends at school, they call me white.

American-Identified Second Generation

The American-identified second-generation teenagers differed in how little they stressed their immigrant or ethnic identities to the interviewers. They follow a path that is more similar to the model posed in the straight-line theory. They stress that they are American because they were born here, and they are disdainful of their parents' lack of understanding of the American social system. Instead of rejecting black American culture, it becomes their peer culture, and they embrace many aspects of it. This brings them in conflict with their parents' generation, most especially with their parents' understandings of American blacks. They most definitely assimilate to black America; they speak black English with their peers, they listen to rap music, and they accept the peer culture of their black American friends. They are aware of the fact that they are considered black American by others and that they can be accused of "acting white" if they don't speak black English and behave in particular ways. Most included their ethnic identities as background, but none of them adopted the stance that they were not, in a major sense, black American. When asked about ethnic background and how other people think of it, one respondent replied:

Q: What is your ethnic background?

A: I put down American because I was born up here. I feel that is what I should put down. . . .

Q: What do other people think you are?

A: Black American because if I don't say. . . . Like if they hear my parents talk or something they always think they are from Jamaica. . . . But they just think I am black American because I was born up here.

Many of these teens discuss how they do not control how others see them:

> Some people just think I am American because I have no accent. So I talk like American people. I don't talk Brooklynese. They think I am from

down south or something. . . . A lot of people say you don't look Haitian. I think I look Haitian enough. I don't know, maybe they are expecting us to look fresh off the boat. I was born here and I grew up here, so I guess I look American and I have an American accent.

Q: If people think you are black American do you ever do anything about it?

A: No, I don't. If they ask me if I am American, I say yes. If they ask me where my parents are from, I tell them Haiti.

In fact, they imply that being a black American is more stylish and "with it" than being from the islands:

I consider myself a black American. When I think of a black American I don't think of them as coming from the West Indies.

Q: Any characteristics that come to mind?

A: I would not think of someone in a suit. I would think of a regular teenager. I would think of a regular person. I think of someone that is in style.

Q: What about someone from the islands?

A: Jamaicans. They dress with neon colors. Most of the girls wear gold and stuff like that.

Some of the young people told us that they saw little if any difference between the ethnic blacks and the American blacks. Many stressed the Caribbeanization of black New York and described how all the Americans were interested in being Caribbean now:

It use to be Jamaicans and American blacks did not get along because everyone was afraid of Jamaicans. But now I guess we are closer now. You tell an American that you are Jamaican and it is no big deal. Americans are acting more

like Jamaicans. Jamaicans are acting like Americans.

Q: What do you mean by acting like each other?

A: Sure there are a lot of Americans out there speaking patois. And then all the Jamaicans are coming over here and they are like "Yo, what's up" and they are like that. Pretty soon you can't really tell who is Jamaican and who is American.

However, the parents of the American-identified teens have expressed to their children the same negative impressions of American blacks that the ethnic-identified teens reported. These teenagers report many negative appraisals of American blacks by their parents:

They always say Haiti is better in this way or in that way. They say the kids here have no respect. The kids here are brought up without any supervision. My father is always talking about they [American blacks] be hanging out on the corner. And he says you won't find Haitians doing that. My mom always says you will marry a Haitian. Why are you talking to those American boys?

This young Haitian American teen tries to disagree with her mother and to temper her mother's interpretations of American blacks:

Q: Are there any characteristics or traits that come to mind about Haitian Americans?

A: Not really. I don't really—cause most people are Haitian American if they are born here. . . . Like me, I don't know if I act like a Haitian or do I have Haitian characteristics, but I'm mostly—like everything I do or like is American. My parents, they do not like American blacks, but they feel that they are lazy. They don't want to work and stuff like that from what they see. And I feel that, um, I feel that way too, but sometimes it won't be that person's fault, so I try to stick up for them. And my mother is like, yeah, you're just too American.

In marked contrast to the ethnic-identified teens, though, the American-identified teens disagreed with their parents' statements about American blacks, reluctantly agreed with some of it but provided qualifications, or perhaps, most disturbingly, accepted the appraisals as true of American blacks in general and themselves as American blacks. This young Trinidadian American swallows her parents' stereotypes and applies them directly to herself:

Q: How close do you feel in your ideas about things to West Indians?
A: Not very close. My feelings are more like blacks than theirs. I am lazy. I am really lazy and my parents are always making comments and things about how I am lazy. They are always like, in Trinidad you could not be this lazy. In Trinidad you would have to keep on working.

The fact that the teens are identifying as American and that their parents have such negative opinions of Americans causes some conflict. The teens either adopt a negative opinion of themselves or disagree with their parents' assessments of American blacks. But it is not just their parents who criticize black Americans. These youngsters are very aware of the generalized negative view of blacks in the wider culture. In answer to the question, "Do whites have an image of blacks?" all of them responded that whites have a negative view of blacks, seeing them as criminal, lazy, violent, and uncaring about family. Many of the teenagers prefaced their remarks by saying that they did not know any whites but that they knew this is what whites thought

through the mass media and through the behaviors of whites they encountered in buses, trains, and stores. This mostly involved incidents such as whites protecting their handbags when the teenagers arrived or store clerks following them and expecting them to shoplift. This knowledge that the society in which they live devalues them because of their skin color and their identity affected these teens deeply.

Immigrant-Identified Teens

The more recently arrived young people who still identify as immigrant differed from both the ethnic- and the American-identified youth. They did not feel as much pressure to "choose" between identifying with or distancing from black Americans as did either the American or the ethnic teens. Strong in their national-origin identities, they were neutral toward American distinctions between ethnics and black Americans. They tended to stress their nationality or their birthplace as defining their identity. They also pointed to their experiences growing up and attending school in a different country. This young man had dreadlocks and a strong Jamaican accent. He stresses his African roots and lets his Jamaican origin speak for itself:

Q: What is your ethnicity? For example, when forms or surveys ask what your ethnic group or ancestry is what do you put?
A: African.
Q: Do you ever put Jamaican or anything?
A: No, not really. Only where Jamaican comes up is if someone asks where you're from. I'll say I am from Jamaica.
Q: What do people usually think you are?
A: They say I am Jamaican.
Q: They know that immediately?
A: Yeah.

Q: How do they know?

A: I change my voice. I don't have to tell them. I think it's also because of my locks sometimes and the way I carry myself, the way I dress.

While an ethnic-identified Jamaican American is aware that she might be seen by others as American and thus actively chooses to present herself as Jamaican, an immigrant-identified Jamaican could not conceive of herself as having a choice, nor could she conceive of being perceived by others as American. While an ethnic-identified teen might describe herself as Jamaican American, for the immigrant teen Jamaican would be all the label needed. Most teens in this category were recent immigrants. The few U.S.-born teens classified as immigrant identified had strong family roots on the islands, were frequent visitors to the islands, and had plans to return to live there as adults. A crucial factor that allows these youngsters to maintain this identity is that their accents and styles of clothing and behavior clearly signaled to others that they were foreign born.

Q: How important is it to you that your friends think of you in terms of your ethnicity?

A: Oh, very important. You know, I try hard not to lose my roots, you know, when I come to the United States. A lot of people who come here try to lose their accent, you know. Even in the workplace, you know, because they fear what other people might think of them. Even in the workplace. Me, I never try to change, you know, the way I am. I always try to, you know, stay with them, the way of my culture.

Q: So it's something you want people to recognize?

A: Yeah, definitely, definitely, absolutely.

Q: Why?

A: Why? I'm proud of who I am, you know. I'm proud of where I'm from and I'm not going to change because somebody might not like the way I walk, talk or dress, you know.

The importance of birthplace was stressed repeatedly by the immigrant identified as they stressed their difference from American-born coethnics:

Q: What would you put on a form or survey that asked about your ethnicity?

A: I'll say I'm Jamaican. You gotta say where you come from.

Q: And do you think of yourself more as a Jamaican or more as an American?

A: I think of more of a Jamaican' cause it's, I wasn't born here. I was born in Jamaica and was there for fourteen years.

Q: And what about kids who are born in America, but their parents were born in Jamaica?

A: Well, you see that is the problem. You see, kids whose parents are Jamaican, they think that, well, they are Jamaican. They need to recheck that they're Americans 'cause they was born in the country and they wasn't born outside the country. So I think they should, you know, know more about American than Jamaican.

Some who adopt this strong identity with the immigrant country were born in the United States, but the combination of strong family roots on the island, frequent visits, and plans to go live there when they are older allows them to think of themselves as not really American at all. This is especially easy to do in the public high schools where there are large numbers of freshly arrived youngsters from the islands.

Q: What do you think your race is?

A: Well, I'm black. I consider myself black. I don't consider myself black American, Afro-American and stuff like that because it's hard to determine, you know, for a person as an individual to determine himself to be Afro-American. . . . I'll be more a Guyanese person because certain things and traditions that I am accustomed to back home, it's still within the roots of me. And those things have not changed for a long period of time, even though you have to adapt to the system over here in order to get ahead and cope with what is going on around you.

While the ethnics tended to describe people as treating them better when they described their ethnic origins, and the Americans tended to stress the antiblack experiences they have had and the lack of difference between the foreign born and the American, the immigrant teens spoke about anti-immigrant feelings and discrimination and responded with pride in their national origins.

Contrasting Identities

In some sense one can see each of these identities as an embrace of one identity and an opposition to another. The American-identified youth are assimilating, in fact, to the American black subculture in the neighborhood. They are adapting to American black cultural forms, and they do so in distinction to their parents' ethnic identities and the wider mainstream white identities. These students adopt some of the "oppositional" poses that American black teenagers show toward academic achievement: the idea of America, the idea of opportunity, and the wider society (Fordham 1988; Ogbu 1990; Portes and Zhou 1993). They also are opposed to their parents' outlooks and ideas, stressing that what worked as a life strategy and a child-raising technique in the islands does not work in the United States. These teens tend to adopt a peer culture of racial

solidarity and opposition to school authorities. What is clear from the interviews is that this stance is in part a socialized response to a peer culture, but the vast majority of it comes about as a reaction to their life experiences. Most specifically, the teens respond to their experiences with racial discrimination and their perceptions of blocked social mobility. The lives of these youngsters basically lead them to reject their parents' immigrant dream of individual social mobility and to accept their peers' analysis of the United States as a place with blocked social mobility where they will not move far.

The American-identified teens do not seem aware of the scholarly literature and the perceptions among ethnic- and immigrant-identified youngsters that the foreign born are of higher social status than the American born. In the peer culture of the neighborhood and the school, these teenagers describe a situation in which being American offers higher social status than being ethnic. For instance, several youngsters described "passing" as black American in order not to be ridiculed or picked on in school:

> I used to be scared to tell people that I was Haitian. Like when I was in eighth grade there were lots of Haitians in the ESL classes, and people used to beat them up. They used to pick on them. I said to myself I am going to quiet down, say I am American.

When asked about the images others held of being from the islands, most of the teens described neutral attributes, such as styles of dress. However, many who identified as Americans also described negative associations with the immigrants' identities. The Jamaicans said most people thought of drug dealers when they thought of Jamaicans. A few of the teens also intimated that people from the islands were backward in not knowing how to live in a big city, both in appreciating the wonders of the city and being street smart to avoid crime and hassles with other people. In terms of the former attribute, the teens described people from the islands who were not accustomed to shopping in big malls or having access to a wide variety of consumer goods.

Not one of the American-identified teens voiced the opinion of the overwhelming majority of the ethnic teens that whites were more likely to like the foreign born. In part, this reflected the differences the groups had in their contact with whites. Most of the inner-city ethnic-identified teens had almost no contact with whites, except for teachers. They also are in schools where the vast majority of the students are foreign born or second generation. The larger number of middle-class teens who were ethnic-identified were more likely to have white classmates in citywide magnet high schools, in parochial schools, or in suburban schools or workplaces.

The inner-city American-identified teens also voiced more positive appraisals of black Americans than did the immigrant- or the ethnic-identified teens. Their descriptions reflect the reality of living in neighborhoods where there is crime and violence. A majority of the American-identified teens said that a good trait of black Americans is that they work hard and they struggle. These are the very same children whose parents describe black Americans primarily as lazy and unwilling to take advantage of the opportunities available to them. The children seem to be perceiving a reality that the parents cannot or will not.

Many of these teens live in neighborhoods that are all black and also attend schools that are all black. So, aside from teachers, these young people have almost no contact with white Americans. This does not stop them from absorbing the fact that whites have negative stereotypic views of blacks. But unlike the middle-class blacks who come in contact with whites who tell them that they are "good blacks," these

youths live in the urban areas associated with crime, they dress like the typical black urban youth, and they talk with Brooklyn accents and black American slang. When they do encounter whites in public places, the whites do not ask about their parents' backgrounds.

Q: Have you ever experienced any discrimination or hostility in New York?

A: From being Trinidadian no. But because of being black, you know, everybody stereotypes. And they say "blacks, they tend to steal, and stuff like that." So, like, if I am walking down the street and a white lady go by and they smile and I smile. They put their bag on the other side.

The parents of these teens grew up in situations where blacks were the majority. The parents do not want their children to be "racial" in the United States. They define "being racial" as being overly concerned with race and with using race as an excuse or explanation for lack of success at school or on the job. The first generation tends to believe that, while racism exists in the United States, it can be overcome or circumvented through hard work, perseverance, and the right values and attitudes. The second generation experiences racism and discrimination constantly and develops perceptions of the overwhelming influence of race on their lives. These teens experience being hassled by police and store owners, not being given jobs, even being attacked on the streets if they venture into white neighborhoods. The boys adopt black American culture in their schools, wearing flattops, baggy pants, and certain types of jewelry. This contributes to the projection of the "cool pose," which in turn causes whites to be afraid of them. This makes them angry and resentful. The media also tells these youngsters that blacks are disvalued by American society. While parents tell their children to strive for upward mobility and to work harder in the face of discrimination, the American-identified teens think the rewards for doing so will be very slim.

This causes a wide gulf between the parents and their children. These parents are absolutely terrified of their children becoming Americans. For the children, to be American is to have freedom from the strict parental controls of the immigrant parents. This is an old story in the immigrant saga, one visible in novels and movies about conflicts between Jewish and Italian immigrants and their children. But the added dimension here is that these parents are afraid of the downward social mobility that becoming an American black represents to them. And this idea is reinforced constantly to these parents by whites who tell them that they are better than American blacks.

One question about how things had changed since the civil rights movement shows the different perceptions of the teens about race in American society. The ethnically identified gave answers I suspect most white Americans would give. They said that things are much better for blacks now. They state that blacks now can ride at the front of the bus and go to school with whites. The irony, of course, is that I was sitting in an all black school when they told this story. The vast majority of the American-identified teens state that things are not better since the civil rights movement; the change is that discrimination now is "on the down low," covered up, more crafty. Some pointed out that we were in an all-black school. The result of these different world views is that the parents' view of an opportunity structure that is open to hard work is systematically undermined by their children's peer culture and, more important, by the actual experience of these teens.

On the other hand, the ethnic-identified teens, whose parents are more likely to be middle class and doing well or who attend parochial or magnet schools, see clearer opportunities and rewards ahead, despite the existence of racism and discrimination. Their parents' message that hard work and perseverance can circumvent racial barriers does not fall on unreceptive ears. The ethnic-identified youngsters embrace an identity derived directly from their parents' immigrant identity. Such an identity is in opposition to their peers' identities and in solidarity with their parents' identities. These youngsters stress that they are Jamaican Americans and that, while they may be proud of their racial identity as black, they see strong differences between themselves and black Americans. They specifically see their ethnic identities as keys to upward social mobility, stressing, for instance, that their parents' values of hard work and strict discipline help them to succeed in the United States when black Americans fail. This ethnic identity is very much an American-based identity—it is in the context of American social life that these youngsters base their assumptions of what it means to be Jamaican or Trinidadian. In fact, the pan-ethnic identities of Caribbean or West Indian often are the most salient label for these youngsters, as they see little differences among the groups and it is more important to differentiate themselves as second-generation Americans. The distancing that these teens show from black Americans often leads them to accept many negative stereotypes of black Americans. These youngsters tend to have ethnic friends from a West Indian background, white American friends, and very few, if any, black American friends.

The immigrant-identified teens are different from either of the other two, because of how they think about who they are not as well as how they think about who they are. These teens have a strong identity as Jamaican or Trinidadian, but this identity tends to be related to their interactions with other Jamaicans or Trinidadians rather than their interactions with black or white Americans.

These youngsters identify with their home-lands or their parents' homelands, but not in opposition to black Americans or in opposition to white Americans. They tend to be immersed in the immigrant community, to have friends who are all the same ethnicity or from other islands. They tend to be more recent arrivals. Unlike the ethnically identified, however, they do not distance themselves from American blacks, and they have neutral or positive attitudes and relations with them. At the same time, they see themselves as different from, but not opposed to, black Americans.

These identities are fluid and change over time and in different social contexts. We found cases of people who describe identifying very strongly as black American when they were younger and who became more immigrant identified when they reached high school and found a large immigrant community. Most new arrivals to the United States start out as immigrant identified, and the longer they stay in the United States, the more they begin to think of themselves in terms of American categories. The kind of social milieu the child faces, especially the school environment, has a strong influence on the outcome. A school with many black Americans creates pressure to identify racially; likewise a neighborhood and school with many immigrants makes it possible to avoid thinking much about American categories. In the face of much pressure not to follow the rules and not to succeed academically, youngsters who are doing well in school and do value education increasingly come to stress their ethnic backgrounds as an explanation for their ambition and success.

The American racial classification system that pushes toward an either/or—"black or white"—designation of people makes the immigrant option harder to hold onto. When others constantly identify the individual as black and refuse to make distinctions based on black ethnicity, pressure builds for the individual to adapt his or her identity to that outside identification—either to say "Yes, I am black," and to accept categorization with black Americans or to resent the characterization and strongly make an ethnic identification as Trinidadian American. The American myopia about ethnic differences within the black community makes the middle-ground immigrant identity unstable. Because every young person is aware of the negative images held by whites and the wider society of black Americans, the acceptance of an American black identity also means the acceptance of the oppositional character of that identity. Oppositional identities, as Ogbu (1990) clearly argues, are self- and group-affirming identities for stigmatized groups— defining as good and worthy those traits and characteristics that are the opposite of those valued by the majority group. This tends to draw the aspirations of the teens downward.

Implications of the Patterns

Some of the distancing shown by the ethnic-identified teens vis-à-vis underclass black identity is the same as that exhibited by middle-class black Americans. Elijah Anderson (1990) has noted that middle-class blacks in a gentrifying neighborhood in Philadelphia use various verbal and nonverbal strategies to convey to others that they are not from the ghetto and that they disapprove of the ghetto-specific behaviors of the blacks who live there. Being an ethnic black in interactions with whites seems to be a shorthand way of conveying distance from the ghetto blacks. Thus, the second generation reserves their ethnic status for use as an identity device to stress their distance from poor blacks and to stress their cultural values, which are consistent with American middle-class values. This same use of an ethnic identity is present among first-generation immigrants of all social classes, even those in racially segregated poor neighborhoods in New York.

The second generation in the segregated neighborhoods, with little chance for social mobility, seems to be unaware that status as a black ethnic conveys higher social status among whites, in part because they have not had much contact with whites. The mass media conveys to them the negative image of American blacks held by whites but does not convey to them the image among intellectuals, middle-class whites, and conservative scholars, such as Thomas Sowell, that they have cultural capital by virtue of their immigrant status. They do get the message that blacks are stereotyped by whites in negative ways, that the all-black neighborhoods they live in are violent and dangerous, and that the neighborhoods of whites are relatively safe. They also encounter a peer culture that values black American cultural forms. The immigrant culture of struggle, hard work, and educational success that their parents try to enforce is experienced in negative ways by these youngsters. They see their parents denying them privileges that their American peers enjoy and, unlike the middle-class youth, they do not automatically associate hard work, lack of dating and partying, and stress on scholastic achievement with social mobility. In the peer culture of the school, immigrant- and ethnic-identified teens tend to be the best students. In the neighborhood inner-city schools, newly arrived immigrants who have attended better schools in the islands tend to outperform the students who have spent their lives in substandard New York City public schools. This tends to reinforce the association between ethnicity and school success—and the more American-identified teens adopt an adversarial stance toward school.

Warner and Srole (1945), in their study of Yankee City in the 1930s, report that it is the socially mobile white ethnics whose ties to the ethnic group and the ethnic identity decline. In their work, those individuals stuck in the lower classes turned to their ethnic identities and groups as a sort of consolation prize:

> Our class system functions for a large proportion of ethnics to destroy the ethnic subsystems and to increase assimilation. The mobile ethnic is much more likely to be assimilated than the nonmobile one. The latter retains many of the social characteristics of his homeland. . . . Some of the unsuccessfully mobile turn hostile to the host culture, develop increasing feelings of loyalty to their ethnic traditions, become active in maintaining their ethnic subsystems, and prevent others from becoming assimilated. But, generally speaking, our class order disunites ethnic groups and accelerates their assimilation. (p. 284)

It could be that the process will be exactly the opposite for black immigrants and black ethnics. In this case, the more socially mobile cling to ethnic identity as a hedge against their racial identity. The less mobile blacks see little advantage to stressing an ethnic identity in the social worlds in which they travel, which are shared mostly with black Americans. Stressing an ethnic identity in that context risks being described as "acting white," being seen as rejecting the race and accepting the white stereotypes, which they know through their everyday lives are not true.

The changes in race relations in the United States since the 1960s are very complicated and most surely involve a mixing of class and race. Some white Americans are trying to see the difference between ghetto inner-city blacks, whom they fear and do not like, and middle-class blacks, whom they do not fear and with whom they would like to have contact, if only to prove to themselves that they are not racist or, in a more formal sense, to meet their affirmative goals.

Middle-class blacks realize this and try to convey their class status in subtle and not so subtle ways (Feagin 1991). The immigrants also utilize the fact that New Yorkers tend to use foreign-born status as a proxy for the class information they are seeking. The white New Yorkers we interviewed do notice differences among blacks, and they use ethnic differences as clues for class differences. If the association found here between social class and ethnic identity is widespread, this perception could become a self-fulfilling prophesy. It could be that the children of poor parents will not keep an ethnic identity and the children whose parents achieve social mobility will keep the ethnic identity. This will reinforce the image in the minds of whites that the "island people" are "good blacks," thus giving the edge in employment decisions and the like to ethnic blacks over American blacks.

On the other hand, it remains to be seen how long the ethnic-identified second generation will continue to identify with their ethnic backgrounds. This also is related to the fact that whites tend to make racial judgments about identity when it comes to blacks. The second generation does not have an accent or other clues that immediately telegraph their ethnic status to others. They are aware that, unless they are active in conveying their identities, they are seen as black Americans, and that often in encounters with whites, the status of their black race is all that matters. It could be that by the time they have children, they will have decided that the quest not to be seen as a black American will be a futile one.

NOTES

1. The families of the teens were from twelve different countries including Jamaica (31 percent); Trinidad (21 percent); Guyana (16 percent); Barbados (10 percent); Haiti (10 percent), Grenada (5 percent); and a few each from the smaller islands of Montserrat, Saint Thomas, Anguilla, Saint Lucia, Dominica, and Nevis.

2. Middle class was defined as having at least one parent with a college degree or a professional or business position. Working class was defined as a parent with a low-skill job; poor were students whose parents were not currently employed.

REFERENCES

Anderson, E. 1990. *Streetwise: Race, Class, and Change in an Urban Community.* Chicago: University of Chicago Press.

Feagin, J. R. 1991. "The Continuing Significance of Race—Antiblack Discrimination in Public Places." *American Sociological Review* 56(1): 101–116.

Foner, N. 1987. "The Jamaicans: Race and Ethnicity Among Migrants in New York City." In *New Immigrants in New York,* edited by N. Foner. New York: Columbia University Press.

Fordham, S. 1988. "Racelessness as a Factor in Black Students' School Success: Pragmatic Strategy or Pyrrhic Victory?" *Harvard Education Review* 58(1) (February).

Gans, H. J. 1992. "Second-Generation Decline: Scenarios for the Economic and Ethnic Futures of Post-1965 American Immigrants." *Ethnic and Racial Studies* 15 (April):173–192.

Kasinitz, P. 1992. *Caribbean New York: Black Immigrants and the Politics of Race.* Ithaca, NY: Cornell University Press.

Lieberson, A. 1980. *A Piece of the Pie: Blacks and White Immigrants Since 1980.* Berkeley: University of California Press.

Massey, D. 1990. "American Apartheid: Segregation and the Making of the Underclass." *American Journal of Sociology* 96(2) (September): 329–357.

Ogbu, J. U. 1990. "Minority Status and Literacy in Comparative Perspective." *Daedulus* 119(2) (Spring):141–168.

Portes, A., and M. Zhou. 1993. "The New Second Generation: Segmented Assimilation and Its Variants." *Annals of the American Academy of Political and Social Sciences* 530 (November): 74–96.

Stafford, S. B. 1987. "Language and Identity: Haitians in New York City." In *Caribbean Life in New York City: Sociocultural Dimensions,* edited by C. R. Sutton and E.M. Chaney. New York: Center for Migration Studies.

Sutton, C. R., and S. P. Makiesky. 1975. "Migration and West Indian Racial and Ethnic Consciousness." In *Migration and Development: Implications for Ethnic Identity and Political Conflict,* edited by H. I. Safa and B. M. Du Toit. Paris: Mouton.

Warner, W. L., and L. Srole. 1945. *The Social Systems of American Ethnic Groups.* New Haven, CT: Yale University Press.

Woldemikael, T. M. 1989. *Becoming Black American: Haitian and American Institutions in Evanston, Illinois.* New York: AMS Press.

RACE AND ROMANCE: BLURRING BOUNDARIES

44

CAPTAIN KIRK KISSES LIEUTENANT UHURA: INTERRACIAL INTIMACIES—THE VIEW FROM HOLLYWOOD

Randall Kennedy

QUESTIONS TO CONSIDER

How many television shows and movies can you name in which the love interests are interracial couples? Now list the number of those interracial couples that were a black man and a white woman. Is it still true, as Law Professor Randall Kennedy suggests, that the only way Hollywood would pair a black man, even a superstar like Denzel Washington, with a white woman, would be for him to be "paralyzed from the waist down" as in the movie The Bone Collector *(1999)?*

• • •

In 1960 there were about 51,000 black-white married couples in the United States; in 1970, 65,000; in 1980, 121,000; in 1991, 213,000; and in 1998, 330,000. In other words, between 1960 and 2000, black-white mixed marriages increased more than sixfold.

But not only are mixed marriages becoming more numerous; they are also becoming more common among people who are younger and more fertile. Previously, participants in such marriages tended to be older than other brides and grooms. Frequently they were veterans of divorce, embarking on second or third marriages. In recent years, though, interracial couples have been marrying at younger ages than their pioneering predecessors, and have shown a greater inclination to raise children and pursue all of the other "normal" activities that married life offers.

Given the low historical baselines against which trends today are measured, it is easy to exaggerate the scope of black-white marital integration. It should therefore be stressed that mixed marriages remain remarkably rare, comprising a mere .6 percent of the total marriages in 1998, for instance, when 330,000 couples out of 55,305,000 overall had one black and one white partner. Moreover, blacks' racial isolation on the marriage market appears to eclipse that of other people of color. The percentages of Native Americans and Asian Americans marrying whites are much larger than the percentage of blacks doing the same.* Professor Nathan Glazer is correct, then, in stating that "blacks stand out uniquely among the array of ethnic and racial groups in the degree to which marriage remains within the group." Among the complex reasons for this social isolation are aggregate subjective evaluations of marriageability, beauty, personality, comfort, compatibility, and prestige that favor certain groups over others. At the dawn of the twenty-first century, a wide array of social pressures continue to make white-black marital crossings more difficult, more costly, and thus less frequent than other types of interethnic or interracial crossings.

Still, even taking into account the peculiar persistence of the black-white racial divide, the trajectory of this form of miscegenation is clear: through turbulent times and in the face of considerable opposition, the number of black-white marriages has been increasing consistently (albeit slowly) for at least forty years. Reinforcing this growth is the fact that interracial marriage has become compatible with lofty ambitions across a variety of fields—not only entertainment but government service, scholarship, the philanthropic sector, business, and the professions. The Thomas-Lamp marriage is indicative of this trend. So, too, are the unions of William Cohen (former senator from Maine and secretary of defense in the Clinton administration) and his black wife; Peter Norton (inventor of widely used computer software) and his black wife;[†] and Franklin Raines (former director of the Office of Management and Budget and chief executive officer of Fannie Mae) and his white wife. Furthermore, despite the substantial influence of the black-power backlash, some African Americans whose positions make them directly dependent upon black public opinion have managed to marry whites without losing their footing. A good example is Julian Bond, the chairman of the board of directors of the NAACP, whose wife is white.

There are other signs, too, that black-white interracial romance has become more broadly accepted and even, in certain contexts, quite fashionable. One such indicator is advertising. Advertisers seek to persuade people to buy goods and services by increasing awareness of them and associating them with imagined pleasures. In the past, advertisers targeting general audiences with the lure of romance have typically—indeed,

---

*"Over 93 percent of whites and of blacks marry within their own groups, in contrast to about 70 percent of Asians and of Hispanics and less than one-third of American Indians." Roderick J. Harrison and Claudette E. Bennett, "Racial and Ethnic Diversity," in Reynolds Farley, ed., *State of the Union: America in the 1990s—Vol. Two: Social Trends* (1995), 165.

When people of Latino and Asian ancestry marry exogamously, "their spouses are very likely to be white; interracial marriages in the United States [have seldom] involved the mixing of two minority groups" (Ibid.).

[†]Reflecting on his marriage, Peter Norton once mused, "Other than sex itself, why do you want to spend your life in the company of a woman as opposed to a best male friend? Part of the answer has to do with the wonderful, bizarre, inexplicable differences between male psychology and female psychology. Well, in the same vein, why would you want to spend your life with a person from the same ethnic background? You miss the frisson" (quoted in David Owen, "The Straddler," *The New Yorker*, January 30, 1995).

overwhelmingly—used couples of the same race. But these days, at least occasionally, interracial couples are being deployed as enticements to shop at Nordstrom's, Club Monaco, or Wal-Mart, or to purchase furniture from IKEA, jeans from Guess, sweaters from Tommy Hilfiger, cologne from Calvin Klein, shampoo from Procter & Gamble, or watches from Gucci.

Television programming also signals important changes in sexual attitudes. Prior to the 1960s, portrayals or even insinuations of black-white interracial romance were virtually nonexistent on TV. The November 22, 1968, episode of the popular science-fiction series *Star Trek* marked a breakthrough in showing a kiss shared by the legendary (white) Captain James T. Kirk and (black) Lieutenant Uhura. Remarkably, however, the characters were not portrayed as actively *wanting* to kiss each other; instead they were *forced* to do so by a villain who captured Kirk's vessel, the starship *Enterprise*, and usurped the will of its crew. Not until 1975 did network television portray a married black-white couple, Tom and Helen Willis, who occupied a prominent place on the popular sitcom *The Jeffersons*. The show, a spinoff of Norman Lear's *All in the Family*, was about an eponymous black family whose patriarch, the hardworking but obnoxious George Jefferson, was obsessed with upward mobility, or what the theme song referred to as "movin' on up." The Willises lived in the same expensive apartment building as the Jeffersons. Although George constantly taunted the couple, calling them zebras, the families ultimately merged when the Jeffersons' son married the Willises' daughter.[*] Since the

_____

*Roxie Roker, the black actress who played Helen Willis, was herself married to a white man. The popular musician Lenny Kravitz is their son. See Lynn Norment, "Am I Black, White, or in Between?," *Ebony*, August 1995; "Roxie Roker, 66, Who Broke Barrier in Her Marriage on TV's *Jeffersons*," *New York Times*, December 6, 1995.

1970s, depictions of interracial intimacies have remained rare on commercial television, though they do surface occasionally. In 1989 the short-lived *Robert Guillaume Show* presented viewers with a romance between a divorced black marriage counselor and his white secretary. The following year, the upstart Fox television network reluctantly aired *True Colors*, a situation comedy centered on the marriage of a black dentist (with two teenage sons) and a white schoolteacher (with a live-in mother and a teenage daughter). According to the show's creator, executives at the three older networks (ABC, CBS, and NBC) expressly stated that they were afraid the interracial marriage would alienate potential advertisers and dissuade at least some local affiliates from broadcasting the program. Notwithstanding cold feet at the top, writers have in the last decade or so succeeded in convincing television executives to air more entertainment fare featuring, or at least noting the existence of, interracial intimacy. Indeed, several of the most popular and influential shows of the 1990s portrayed transracial romances. Sometimes the racial aspect of the relationship was highlighted, as in *L.A. Law*'s dramatization of a black lawyer feeling that he must choose between his white lover and his job as an elected representative of a mainly black constituency. Sometimes it was ignored, as on *Ally McBeal*, where race matters seldom if ever arose in conversations between the white woman attorney and the black male physician with whom she was infatuated. On occasion, on-screen interracial relationships failed. The producers of *ER*, for example, terminated a romance between a black male doctor and a white colleague, not in deference to viewer opposition but because the black actor involved objected. He complained that whereas his character had always been obnoxious in his dealings with black women, he was now being shown as sympathetic in his treatment of the white woman. On other programs, interracial romance was permitted to blossom. In 1994, for example, on *In the Heat of the Night,* the white sheriff of a town in the Deep South married a black woman on-screen,[*] and in 1997, a network production of *Cinderella* paired a black actress in the title role with a Filipino Prince Charming, to great popular acclaim.[†]

In some venues, nonfictional portrayals of interracial intimacy have been sensationally negative, as on confessional talk shows that, for a while at least, uniformly depicted transracial relationships as troubled, weird, or pathological.[‡] In other contexts, however, television programs have acknowledged the gamut of personalities and emotions to be found among those who happen to be involved in interracial intimacies. In the fall of 1999, the Public Broadcasting System (PBS) aired *An American Love Story,* a ten-hour documentary film by Jennifer Fox that chronicled the lives of an interracial family: Bill Sims, a black man, Karen Wilson, a white woman, and their two daughters, Cecily and Chaney. Wilson and Sims first met in 1967, at a resort where he was playing piano in a rhythm-and-blues band and she was vacationing with her parents. He was the son of a cleaning woman and a steelworker who was also a Baptist minister; her father was a machinist, and her mother was a grocery clerk. When their courtship began, Bill was eighteen and Karen seventeen. Neither set of parents objected to the relationship, and both urged the couple to marry after Wilson got pregnant (though they in fact did not do so until the child was six years old).

Whites in Wilson's hometown of Prospect, Ohio, strongly condemned her romance with Sims. Her supposed friends ostracized the couple, and the local sheriff jailed Sims on several occasions for no other reason than to harass him. In 1972 they moved with their baby daughter to Columbus, but even in this larger, less isolated locale, they encountered overt hostility. They suspected bigots of killing their dog and setting their car afire in a successful campaign to frighten them away. They moved again, this time to Flushing, New York, where they hoped to find a more openminded community.

Over the years, the Wilson-Sims family subsisted largely on Karen's reliable earnings as a manager, supplemented by Bill's spotty wages as, among other things, a carpenter, mail carrier, and musician. At the price of some tedium, *An American Love Story* shows its subjects engaged in all the quotidian tasks of daily life—cooking, cleaning, resting, seeking comfort, venting frustration—that have little or nothing to do with racial differences. It also shows them facing various nonracial

---

[*]Denise Nicholas, who played the character whom the sheriff married, actively shaped the public image of her role, particularly with respect to the interracial relationship. Nicholas felt that the characters "should either break [the relationship] off or get married because oftentimes, historically, interracial relationships were back-alley affairs, hidden and lied about, particularly in the South. It became really important to me that the [characters] do something dignified; I didn't want my character to be cheap" ("Denise Nicholas and Carroll O'Connor Wed on TV Drama 'In the Heat of the Night,'" *Jet,* May 9, 1994). It should be recalled that the basis for the television series was the film of the same name (1967), which featured a thoroughly bigoted white sheriff (played by Rod Steiger, in an Academy Award-winning performance).

[†]ABC's hugely successful musical production starred Brandy as Cinderella and Paolo Montalban as the prince. Taking the role of Prince Charming's mother, the queen, was a black actress, Whoopi Goldberg, while the king was played by a white actor, Victor Garber. See Veronica Chambers, "The Myth of Cinderella," *Newsweek,* November 3, 1997; "Cinderella TV Music Special Produces Spectacular Rating for ABC," *Jet,* November 24, 1997.

[‡]Such depictions were no accident. When television producers sought guests for these programs, they advertised for people who had had *bad* experiences in or on account of interracial relationships. It was this bias that gave rise to episodes such as "Woman Disowned by Her Family for Dating a Black Man" on *Jenny Jones* and "Blacks and Blondes: White Girls Dating Black Guys for Sex, Style, and Status" on *Geraldo.*

crises, including Karen's hysterectomy and Bill's alcoholism. Almost inevitably, though, racial difficulties surface to menace the couple and their children. Among the most poignant segments of the series are wrenching scenes from Cecily's years as an undergraduate at Colgate College, where tyrannical black classmates tell her, essentially, that if she wants to be their friend, she must refuse to join a predominantly white sorority and, more generally, defer to their black-separatist sensibilities. She declines their terms, and they retaliate; she is hurt. Throughout, the television audience is privy to the conflict.[*]

The creators of *An American Love Story* wanted to document an interracial marriage that spanned the final decades of the twentieth century. Its subjects, for their part, wanted to change perceptions through education; this ambition constituted the principal explanation offered by the Sims-Wilson clan for permitting their family life to be examined in such a public manner. Education was also the primary aim cited by the program's director, Jennifer Fox, a white woman who credited her own love affair with a black man with opening her eyes to important areas of American life to which she had previously been blind.[†]

On the big screen, too, recent years have seen an increase in both the number and the quality of depictions of interracial intimacy. There was a time, not so long ago, when the scarcity of such portrayals made keeping track of them easy; now, because of their increasing numbers and variety, that task is much more difficult. True, the fear of an adverse audience response can still cause cautious film producers to suppress interracial romance, not only through their choice of projects but even in their handling of plot points. In John Grisham's novel *The Pelican Brief* (1992), for instance, the protagonists become lovers, but in the screen version (1993), there is no romance; the relationship remains resolutely platonic. The reason for this alteration is obvious: the male lead is played by a black actor (Denzel Washington), and the female lead by a white actress (Julia Roberts). There are, moreover, scores of other examples of black actors apparently being singled out for Hollywood's cold shower treatment lest they mirror real-life interracial erotic excitement. Prominent among these desexualized roles are Will Smith's character in *Men in Black* (1997) and Wesley Snipes's in *Murder at 1600* (1997). This approach led one wag to remark, in reference to *The Bone Collector* (1999), that the only way Denzel Washington would ever be shown "getting the girl" was if he played a man paralyzed from the waist down. That being said, a number of major motion pictures released in the past decade have followed actors and actresses of all complexions in their pursuit of sexual pleasures across color lines, and have done so with a boldness that probably would not have been tolerated in the environment that generated *Guess Who's Coming to Dinner?* Examples include the explicit erotic grapplings of Lawrence Fishburne and Ellen Barkin in *Bad Company* (1995), Wesley Snipes and Natassia Kinski in *One Night Stand* (1997), Reese Witherspoon and Bookeem Woodbine in *Freeway* (1996), Warren Beatty and Halle Berry in *Bulworth* (1998), Tom Cruise and Thandie Newton in *Mission Impossible 2* (2000), Julia Stiles and Sean Patrick Thomas in *Save the Last Dance* (2000), and Halle Berry

---

[*]Several months after *An American Love Story* aired, Cecily Wilson married a white union organizer whom she had met on a blind date. See "Weddings: Cecily Wilson, Gregory Speller," *New York Times,* May 7, 2000.

[†]Fox has stated that she was surprised by some of her relatives' negative reactions to her interracial relationship, and surprised, too, by the regularity of the racial mistreatment her black lover suffered. In retrospect, she observes, "it was almost like I was deluded or something; I thought I was living in a different world than I was living in" (quoted in Paula Span, "Modern Family Life in Black and White: PBS Documentary Chronicles an Interracial Marriage," *Washington Post,* September 9, 1999).

and Billy Bob Thornton in *Monster's Ball* (2001).[*] In increasing numbers of films, moreover, interracial intimacy has been emerging as simply one part of a larger story in which racial difference is of little or no significance. This is an important development because presuming the normalcy of interracial intimacy—treating it as "no big deal"—may be more subversive of traditional norms than stressing the racial heterodoxy of such relationships. Although examples of this presumption can be found in several films (e.g., *Pulp Fiction* [1994], *Cruel Intentions* [1999], and *Mystery Men* [1999]), the most significant was the blockbuster *The Bodyguard* (1992), which starred Kevin Costner and Whitney Houston.

• • •

Perhaps the most potent influence in creating new possibilities for interracial intimacy is that wielded by individuals engaged in (or born of) transracial dating, marriage, and parenting. This population, numbering in the hundreds of thousands, exhibits tremendous variety. One generalization that can properly be made about it, however, is that it is becoming increasingly vocal. There was a time, not so long ago, when the vast majority within this group sought invisibility; now, by contrast, many of its members seek recognition and are establishing or joining advocacy organizations devoted to publicizing their views and institutionalizing their presence. Announcing the formation of the Association of Multi-Ethnic Americans (AMEA) in November 1988, Carlos Fernandez declared:

> We who embody the melting pot . . . stand up, not merely as neutrals in interethnic conflicts, but as intolerant participants

against racism from whatever quarter it may come. . . . We are the faces of the future. Against the travails of regressive interethnic division and strife, we can be a solid core of unity bonding the peoples of all cultures together in the common course of human progress.

People involved in interracial intimacies used to voice quiet requests for simple protection against intimidation and violence. Now their demands are becoming more ambitious. One of these has to do with racial labeling. Many interracial couples object to standardized forms that compel them to designate their children either merely "black" or merely "white." Similarly, many who identify themselves as "mixed"—or "mulatto" or "half-and-half" or "multiracial"—bridle at classificatory regimes that impose singular racial identifications, as if everyone must be *only* white *or* black *or* Latino *or* Asian (etc., etc.). Prior to the census of 2000, the United States Census Bureau counted individuals according to that assumption. But after a good deal of prodding by AMEA and similar groups, the bureau decided to broaden the menu boxes available for indicating racial affiliation. Rather than being limited to only one box, respondents are now authorized to check whatever boxes they deem applicable, though the census bureau continues to decline to offer a separate "multiracial" box.[†]

---

[*]Two excellent coming-of-age films that evoke the hazards and rewards of teenage interracial dating in the 1950s are Robert De Niro's *A Bronx Tale* (1993) and Barry Levinson's *Liberty Heights* (2000).

[†]Although they failed to persuade the United States Census Bureau to offer the "multiracial" box for the 2000 census, multiracialist reformers have succeeded in convincing a number of state governments—including those of Georgia, Illinois, Florida, Indiana, Michigan, and Ohio—to require that such a box be provided on state forms that collect racial data. They have also managed to convince several important private institutions, among them Harvard University, to add a "multiracial" category alongside the other, more familiar and established, choices. See Tanya Kateri Hernandez, "'Multiracial' Discourse: Racial Classifications in an Era of Color-Blind Jurisprudence," *Maryland Law Review* 57 (1998): 97, 98 n. 4.

One complaint leveled against the traditional "check one box" regime is that it fosters confusion and inaccuracy—describing as "black," for example, people who are also partly white or partly Native American or partly Asian. Susan Graham, the (white) founder of Project RACE (Reclassify All Children Equally) notes that her "child has been white on the U.S. Census, black at school, and multiracial at home, all at the same time." Beyond the issue of statistical inaccuracy, the system has more personal ramifications, in that it compels mixed individuals to select for recognition only one aspect of their composite background, and thereby subordinate all the other aspects.

The census bureau's multiple-box-checking initiative addresses some but by no means all of the objections raised by critics.[†] Some contend that even the option of checking several boxes indicates, in effect, that multiracial individuals are only parts of other communities, rather than constituent members of a distinct multiracial community of their own. Some observers protest, moreover, the continuation of *any* racial scheme of classification, however it may be supplemented or repackaged. Whatever one may think of the ideas propounded by these various dissidents, it is clear that they are flexing their political muscles as never before and affecting hearts and minds in fundamental ways. They are not content to accept inherited conventions but insist instead on adding their own preferences to America's cultural mix. Professor Maria P. P. Root has demanded a Bill of Rights for racially mixed people, which would include the rights to identify one's race

differently in different situations, to change one's racial identity over a lifetime (and more than once), to have loyalties to and identifications with more than one racial group, and to be able freely to choose whom to befriend and love. The winner of the 1995 Miss USA beauty pageant objected to being pegged as "black." "If people are going to know me," Chelsi Smith explained, "it's important for them to know that I'm black and white and that it hasn't been a disadvantage." Tiger Woods likewise does not enjoy being referred to as the first "black" or "African American" golf superstar, believing that those labels obscure other aspects of his ancestry that are just as important to him. He has therefore coined the term "'Cablinasian'—[for] Caucasian, Black, Indian, Asian"—to describe himself.[‡] The coinage has proved controversial.[§] Many people, mainly blacks, have accused him of wanting to flee an African American identity that whites will impose upon him regardless of his preferences. ("When the black truck comes around," one observer quipped, "they're gonna haul his ass on it.")

[†]When the racial-classification issue was decided for the 2000 census, the person in charge of the supervisory agency was Franklin Raines, a black man married to a white woman. Franklin and Wendy Raines had two children who themselves faced this classification dilemma. See Julia Malone, "Facing the Racial Question: More Categories in the Census," *The Atlanta Journal and Constitution,* October 15, 1997.

[‡]Woods made his views known on Oprah Winfrey's television show soon after he won the prestigious Masters golf tournament. See Greg Couch, "Woods: I'm More Than Black," *Chicago Sun-Times,* April 22, 1997, p. 1.

[§]In a satirical essay entitled "The Mulatto Millennium," Danzy Senna facetiously defined "Cablinasian" thus:

> A rare exotic breed found mostly in California. This is the mother of all mixtures. . . . A show mulatto, with great performance skills, the Cablinasian will be whoever the crowd wants him to be, and can switch at the drop of a dime. Does not, however, answer to the name Black. . . . Note: If you spot a Cablinasian, please contact the Benetton Promotions Bureau. [In Claudine Chiawei O'Hearn, ed., *Half and Half: Writers on Growing Up Biracial and Bicultural* (1998), 26.]

For a powerful defense of Woods's position, see Gary Kamiya, "Cablinasian like Me," Salon.com, April 1997. For a critique, see Leonard Pitts, "Is There Room in This Sweet Land of Liberty for Such a Thing as 'Cablinasian'? Face It, Tiger: If They Say You're Black, Then You're Black," *Baltimore Sun,* April 29, 1997.

Such reactions notwithstanding, the real point here is that Root, Smith, Woods, and tens of thousands more like them have felt sufficiently self-assured to speak up, and have received substantial support in doing so. Their conduct mirrors and strengthens a new force in America: the will of people engaged in or born of multiracial relationships, who have begun to insist upon public recognition of the full complexity of their lives.

Across the country, scores of interracial support groups have sprung up, among them MOSAIC (Multiethnics of Southern Arizona in Celebration), A Place for Us (North Little Rock, Arkansas), I-Pride (Interracial Intercultural Pride, Berkeley, California), MASC (Multiracial Americans of Southern California, Los Angeles, California), F.C. (Families of Color) Communiqué (Fort Collins, Colorado), Interracial Family Alliance (Augusta, Georgia), Society for Interracial Families (Troy, Michigan), 4c (Cross Cultural Couples & Children, Plainsboro, New Jersey), the Interracial Club of Buffalo, the Interracial Family Circle of Washington, D.C., and HONEY (Honor Our New Ethnic Youth, Eugene, Oregon). On college campuses, students can join organizations such as FUSION (Wellesley), Kaleidoscope (University of Virginia), Students of Mixed Heritage and Culture (SMHAC, Amherst), Half 'n' Half (Bryn Mawr), and Mixed Plate (Grinnell). These groups offer forums in which people can meet others in their situation, disseminate relevant information, debate, and organize. Although most of these organizations lack deep roots, many display a vigor and resourcefulness that suggest they will survive into the foreseeable future. They stem from and represent a community in the making. It is a community united by a common demand that the larger society respect and be attentive to people who either by descent or by choice fall outside the conventional racial groupings—people who are partners in interracial couples, parents of children whose race is different from their own, and children whose race differs from their parents'. The members of this community want whites to cease viewing them as products or agents of an alarming mongrelization. They want blacks to stop regarding them as inauthentic and unstable in-betweeners. They want security amid the established communities from which they have migrated. They want to emerge from what the writer Lise Funderberg has aptly called the "racial netherworld." They want to enjoy interaction with others without regret or fear, defensiveness or embarrassment. They want respect.

SEEING THE BIG PICTURE

Look at Section X in the Appendix. All things being equal, one would think that if people choose to marry across the color line these unions would be randomly distributed—that is, we would observe similar marriage rates across racial categories. But we don't. What do these data suggest about intergroup relations?

45
——————

DISCOVERING RACIAL BORDERS

Heather M. Dalmage

QUESTIONS TO CONSIDER

Heather Dalmage explains how racial borders are "policed" to discourage individuals from falling in love across the color line. How and in what ways (if any) were racial borders enforced in your own life so that dating across the color line was not very likely to happen? How would your family react if your new romantic partner was from a racial category different from your own? Given that such unions are often stigmatized, what strategies do interracial couples employ, according to Dalmage, to dismiss such views and normalize their own relationship?

Border Patrolling

The belief that people ought to stick with their own is the driving force behind efforts to force individuals to follow prescribed racial rules. Border patrollers often think (without much critical analysis) that they can easily differentiate between insiders and outsiders. Once the patroller has determined a person's appropriate category, he or she will attempt to coerce that person into following the category's racial scripts. In *Race, Nation, Class: Ambiguous Identities,* Etienne Balibar and Immanuel Wallerstein observe that "people shoot each other every day over the question of labels. And yet, the very people who do so tend to deny that the issue is complex or puzzling or indeed anything but self-evident."[1] Border patrollers tend to take race

and racial categories for granted. Whether grounding themselves in essentialist thinking or hoping to strengthen socially constructed racial categories, they believe they have the right and the need to patrol. Some people, especially whites, do not recognize the centrality and problems of the color line, as evinced in color-blind claims that "there is only one race: the human race" or "race doesn't really matter any more." Such thinking dismisses the terror and power of race in society. These individuals may patrol without being aware of doing so. In contrast, blacks generally see patrolling the border as both problematic and necessary.

While border patrolling from either side may be scary, hurtful, or annoying, we must recognize that blacks and whites are situated differently. The color line was imposed by whites, who now have institutional means for maintaining their power; in contrast, blacks must consciously and actively struggle for liberation. Repeatedly, people in multiracial families have told me, "The one thing that David Duke and Louis Farrakhan agree on is that we should not exist." What is not analyzed are the different historical legacies that bring both men to the same conclusion. The only form of borderism in which blacks engage is border patrolling, although they can act on prejudicial feelings and discriminate. After centuries of systemic control, only whites can be racist. As Joe Feagin and Hernán Vera explain, "black racism would require not only a widely accepted racist ideology directed at whites, but also the power to systematically exclude whites from opportunities and rewards in major economic, cultural, and political institutions."[2] White and black border patrollers may both dislike interracial couples and multiracial families, but their dislike comes from different historical and social perspectives. Moreover, border patrolling tends to take place intraracially: whites patrol whites, and blacks patrol black and multiracial people.

White Border Patrolling

Despite the institutional mechanisms in place to safeguard whiteness, many whites feel both the right and the obligation to act out against interracial couples. If a white person wants to maintain a sense of racial superiority, then he or she must attempt to locate motives and explain the actions of the white partner in the interracial couple. A white person who crosses the color line threatens the assumption that racial superiority is essential to whites. The interracially involved white person is thus often recategorized as inherently flawed—as "polluted."[3] In this way, racist and essentialist thinking remains unchallenged.

Frequently white families disown a relative who marries a person of color, but several people have told me that their families accepted them again once their children were born. The need to disown demonstrates the desire to maintain the facade of a pure white family.[4] By the time children are born, however, extended family members have had time to shift their racial thinking. Some grant acceptance by making an exception to the "rule," others by claiming to be color blind. Neither form of racial thinking, however, challenges the color line or white supremacy. In fact, both can be painful for the multiracial family members, who may face unending racist compliments such as "I'll always think of you as white."

The myth of purity is maintained by controlling white women's wombs. Thus, white women are patrolled more harshly than white men are. The regulations women face have not always been overtly displayed but have developed within the culture's conception of the *family ethic,* an ideal extant since the arrival of the early settlers that has influenced perceptions of proper work and home roles for white, middle-class family members.[5] The proper family should have a male breadwinner and patriarch and a female who makes her husband and obedient children her life's central work. According to Mimi Abramowitz, the family ethic "has made [women] the guardians of family and community morality, expected them to remain pious and chaste and to tame male sexuality, and defined them as weak and in need of male protection and control."[6] Ultimately, the family ethic has kept white women under the control of white men. In *Whiteness Visible: The Meaning of Whiteness in American Literature and Culture,* Valerie Babb notes that images depicting white women as helpless and in need of white men's protection grew against a backdrop of a developing patriarchy. White women faced particularly harsh regulations because the "loss of sexual purity through intercourse with other races endangers visible race difference, a key driving force behind an ideology of whiteness that gives political, economic, and social advantage to those with 'appropriate' race lineage."[7] The myth of white racial purity required white women to give birth to the offspring of white men—and only white men. Unfortunately, many white women have played active roles in maintaining this myth of purity. For instance, in 1897 one wrote: "If it takes lynching to protect women's dearest possession from drunken, ravening beasts, then I say lynch a thousand a week if it becomes necessary."[8] Today many white women who give birth to children of color give them up for adoption, fearing that as mothers of children of color they will become pariahs in their families and society at large.[9] Such complicity has worked to strengthen the color line and white-supremacist abuses.

It has been argued that white women should be protected because they are the gatekeepers of racial purity.[10] Any white woman who would trade in her white privilege and connections to white male power must be dismissed as unnaturally bad and bizarre. Julie, a white mother recently divorced from her black husband, has contended with white border patrolling and its underlying images. One incident (although not the only one) occurred while she was on a date with a white physician:

> He asked to see a picture of my daughter. I handed it to him. He was very clever; he asked, "Is her dad from the U.S.?"
>
> I think he was praying her dad was Spanish, and he could deal with that, anything but black. I could tell it bothered him, so I said, "Listen, I can see by the look on your face that there is obviously a problem here, so why don't we just talk about it right now."
>
> He said, "You want to know the truth? Well, I have a real problem with the fact that you slept with a black man." Then he went on with the whole, "You're such a pretty and intelligent woman; why would you marry a black man?"

Her date was drawing on the interlocking imagery of race and sex and what it means to be a good white woman. In his attempt to explain away Julie's behavior, he searched for motives, implying that only unattractive, unintelligent white women sleep with and marry black men. Further, the fact that she slept with a black man removed her eligibility as a white woman. She is assumed to be fundamentally and essentially changed. Perhaps he feared that his white purity would be contaminated with blackness through this bad white woman. Perhaps he felt threatened because he could not immediately detect her racial flaw. He may have begun to discover the mutability of race, which could undermine his own sense of racial superiority. While all people of color face some form of racist imagery in a white racist society, Julie notes the centrality and power given to racist images directed specifically against black people and interracially involved whites and blacks: "I think he was praying her dad was Spanish, and he could deal with that, anything but black."

Black men are seen "as a constant threat" to patriarchal whiteness.[11] Abby Ferber writes: "A photograph of a white woman with an Asian American man, for example, does not have the same symbolic power. The image of interracial sexuality between a white woman and a black man is pregnant with meaning in the American imagery. Powerful enough to serve as a symbol of all interracial sexuality."[12] White women who enter into interracial relationships with black men are often treated as aberrant, misguided white trash who are in this relationship solely for sex or rebellion. Barbara gained forty pounds because she "got tired of being mistaken for a prostitute." She explains, "It's assumed that the only reason you're involved in the relationship is because you're sexually depraved . . . that you've got to be the dregs of society to get involved or you want to hurt somebody." Women may be explained away as money or status seekers.[13] Often when we are out, people will ask Philip what he does for work. After learning he's an attorney, they don't bother to ask me what I do. This could be a gender issue; in a patriarchal world men are seen as the subjects, women the objects. But I often wonder how much it has do with assumptions about uncovering the motive behind our relationship—that I have traded my white status for his occupational and class status.[14]

The strength of racist images is manifested in the comments directed at women who are assumed to be good, upstanding white women. June, a businesswoman who is raising two biracial sons in suburban New Jersey, commented, "I think America still hates [white] women who sleep with black men. And when they see you with these children, they want to believe you adopted them, which is usually the first question people will ask: 'Did you adopt them?' I always just say, 'No, I slept with a black man.'"

June's comments highlight a few issues. First, she does not specify who constitutes "America." Whites may hate these women because they threaten the color line that maintains white privilege and power. At the same time, blacks may hate them because they threaten the unity of African Americans. Second, several white women talked to me about the frequency of the adoption question—one more attempt to explain their behavior. If women who appear to be good turn out to be polluted, white border patrollers become nervous. Their inability to tell "us" from "them" calls into question their own racial identity. The more the border patroller clings to an identity of racial superiority, the more he or she looks for ways to explain away these aberrant white women. Third, like June, many interracially married white women resist allowing whites to recategorize them in an attempt to regain or

maintain a sense of superiority. "No, I used the good-old fashioned method" is a common retort to such questioners.

Not all white women resist border patrollers. Many succumb to the hostility and end their relationships with black men. Several white women told me they had temporarily ended their interracial relationship, each citing border patrolling as the reason. For instance, Barbara, the woman who gained forty pounds to avoid being seen as a prostitute, said:

> When I met my husband, he was the sweetest, kindest—he was a wonderful human being, everything I was looking for except for the color and at one point I was really apprehensive about it. The race thing really bothered me 'cause I didn't like being stared at and I didn't like people hating me. I didn't like how black women viewed me, and to white men I was a possession. It's like, "you crossed the line." You know the feeling, like you have to be the lowest of the low to be with an African American. "Who are you trying to hurt?" It was just really sick. So I went away for a while.

Although she did eventually marry this "wonderful human being," she needed time away to think about race on a more sophisticated level—time to question her internalization of racist images and the color line.

The stereotype of black male sexuality converges with the myth of the chaste and virtuous good white woman, making white female–black male relationships the ones most patrolled by whites.[15] White men contend with a different type of border patrolling in a society that privileges both whiteness and maleness. Historically, white men who interracially marry were reported to come from lower economic classes and were at times designated as crazy.[16] Today the more common image that white interracially married men face is of being in the relationship solely for sex. These men may be seen as committing an individual transgression but are not held responsible for protecting whiteness. In her study of white supremacist publications, Abby Ferber found that "while relationships between white women and black men are condemned, and described as repulsive, relationships between white men and black women were common and remain beyond condemnation."[17] The lack of imagery about white male–black female relations reflects a history of silence among whites concerning their complicity in the rape of black women. Moreover, in a society in which whiteness (and maleness) represents power, privilege, and unearned advantage, many white men view their privilege in the world as normal. They risk "outing" these taken-for-granted privileges when they talk about race.[18]

The white men with whom I spoke were split about the importance of—even the existence of—border patrolling. Unlike black men, black women, and white women, they did not consistently talk about the effects of racialized images. When I asked, "As an interracially married white man, how do you think others view you?" responses were split: half the men spoke of border patrollers; the other half denied the importance of race in their lives and society. The first few times I heard white men deny or disregard the importance of racism and border patrolling, I was surprised. It took me some time and several more interviews to make sense of this.

Joe, the first interracially married white man I interviewed, lived in a predominantly white, upper-class community about an hour from New York City. With his infant daughter on his lap and a tape recorder on the table, he began to unfold the details of his life. I asked how he thinks others view him. He responded, "I can't worry about what other people think. For a long time my wife worried, but once she got over that, we had a big wedding. . . . It took a lot to convince her

that's how we should think about it, and I think she's more comfortable with that." He said that they do not have problems as an interracial couple, that everything is smooth. We were chatting after the interview when his wife walked into the room. She began to cite several problems they had faced because of their interracial relationship. When she referred to each incident, he nodded in agreement.

Several months later I interviewed Raymond, a white interracially married man living on Chicago's north side. Drinking coffee in a local café, he discussed the meaning of race in his life. When I asked him about how others view him, he replied staunchly, "I don't know, and I don't care. I never thought about it. I don't think about it. What do they think when they see my wife and me together? Pardon my language, but I don't give a shit what they think; I just don't give a shit. I go for months, and that never occupies my mind."

These men may be proving masculinity through a show of strength, rugged individualism, and disinterest and thus verbally disregard border patrolling and racial images. Each, however, repeatedly claimed that race does not matter. Instead, they believed the focus "should be on ethnic backgrounds" or on the fact that "we are all Americans." Men who did not want to recognize racial images tended not to recognize the privilege associated with whiteness, drawing instead on notions of meritocracy. Whether or not they recognized differences, they did not recognize power. Nevertheless, they used their power as white males to create a racial discussion with which they felt comfortable. For instance, Joe's comfort came from not having to hear any racially derogatory comments: "If somebody would make a derogatory comment, I would just say, 'My wife is black.' Usually I wouldn't even have to say, 'I don't want to hear comments like that'—they would just stop." Whiteness is about privilege and power. It is a privilege to be able to set the parameters of racial discussions and expect that others will comply. Moreover, the power of these professional white men overrides the power that white border patrollers may have to influence them.

In addition to proving masculinity, these men may be attempting to downplay the prevalent stereotype that interracial couples are together for sexual reasons only. For instance, Raymond repeatedly stated that his relationship was not about "jungle fever," a phrase that filmmaker Spike Lee popularized to suggest that interracial couples are attracted only because of sexual curiosity. At the end of our interview I asked Raymond if there was anything else he wanted to say. He answered, "Let people know that this is not about jungle fever. Race does not matter. I love my wife." His repeated references to jungle fever reflected his awareness of border patrolling despite his claim of color-blindness. Rather than critically thinking about race and the origins of such stereotypes, he defensively dismisses the significance of race.

Some white men did recognize and address the importance of racial images, border patrollers, and the relationship between race and power. The common thread for these men was that they had friendships and networks with black males before meeting their spouse. Through these male friends they began to recognize the privileges that remain invisible to so many other white men. The importance of friendships with black males cannot be understated. White men sit in a position of power because of both their race and sex. When sex differences are removed as a factor in their relationships, they can understand more clearly the ways in which race mediates power relations. This is not as obvious to white men who are introduced to blackness (and thus whiteness) through intimate relations with a woman.

Clancy, a fifty-year-old white man who grew up outside Chicago, had black roommates and friends in college. By the time he met his wife he understood from his buddies the effects of racism in society. He spoke in detail about the border patrolling he faced from the white teachers at the Chicago elementary school where he taught after getting married: "My wife and I walked into a meeting with the white teachers and the people from the neighborhood, and it sent those people into conniptions. I won't forget that. It was my first year teaching there, and from then on it was like, 'God have mercy on my soul,' I was a dead person in that school and that stayed with me for seventeen years—the whole time I was there." In this case, Clancy's teaching position was continually threatened by white border patrollers.

Peter, a white minister living on Chicago's South Side, had graduated from a black seminary in the southern United States. As the only white in many situations, he was immersed in black culture. The privileges and power bestowed to whites in a system of whiteness and the richness of black culture became visible to him. Like Clancy, he recognized and addressed the border patrolling he encountered from whites. In the following case, Peter had just been named the pastor of a white church in a white working-class neighborhood in Cleveland: "I had gotten moved to a white church. That turned out to be two years from hell. The church did not want me to be appointed there. They actually had a special meeting after they got wind of who was coming; 95 percent of the church did not want me there because I was interracially married. The first church meeting I was at, the chair asked for further motions. One person said, 'I make a motion that the reverend resign from this church.'" Peter laughed about the absurdity of the situation and then continued:

"The first sermon, attendance was over one hundred; everyone came out to see the show. From then on, attendance never got above sixty, so basically about forty people boycotted the whole time I was there. I had people who still attended but resigned all their offices." In addition, church members began a letter-writing campaign to the bishop accusing Peter of various wrongdoings—for example, claiming he had taken all the Bibles out of the church. Peter and his family eventually moved to a black church in Chicago. The Ohio church members who had resigned their offices returned to them after he left.

Privileges granted to people with white skin have been institutionalized and made largely invisible to the beneficiaries. With overwhelming power in society, why do individual whites insist on border patrolling? As economic insecurity heightens and demographics show that whites are losing numerical majority status, the desire to scapegoat people of color, especially the poor, also heightens. As whites lose their economic footing, they claim white skin as a liability. Far from recognizing whiteness as privilege, they become conscious of whiteness only when defining themselves as innocent victims of "unjust" laws, including affirmative action.[19] In their insecurity they cling to images that promote feelings of superiority. This, of course, requires a racial hierarchy and a firm essentialist color line. Border patrolling helps to maintain the myth of purity and thus a color line created to ensure that whites maintain privileges and power.

Black Border Patrolling

Some blacks in interracial relationships discover, for the first time, a lack of acceptance from black communities. Others experienced border patrolling before their marriage, perhaps because of hobbies and interests, class, politics, educational goals, skin tone, vernacular, or friendship networks. Patrolling takes on new proportions, however, when they go the "other way" and marry a white person. While all relationships with individuals not seen as black are looked down on, relationships with whites represent the gravest transgression. Interracially married black women and men often believe they are viewed as having lost their identity and culture—that they risk being seen as "no longer really black." Before their interracial marriage, most called black communities their home, the place from which they gained a sense of humanity, where they gained cultural and personal affirmation. During their interracial relationship many discovered black border patrolling. Cathy Cohen suggests that "those failing to meet indigenous standards of blackness find their life chances threatened not only by dominant institutions or groups, but also by their lack of access to indigenous resources and support."[20] Interracially involved blacks needed to carefully weigh their decision to cross the color line.

George, a black man, lives with his wife, Dorothy, a white woman, and their two young children in Montclair, New Jersey, a racially mixed suburb of New York City. I drove along the town's big, clean, tree-lined streets one Sunday morning to meet with George in his home. During our interview he explained that he had dated a white girl in high school and was aware of how blacks and whites respond to such a relationship. Nonetheless, a recent event at his Manhattan workplace troubled him. Bill, a black male coworker, told him:

"I couldn't marry a white woman. How about you?"

I said, "I am married to a white woman."

"You joking me, George! Big strong handsome brother like you!"

I said, "Yo, man, I don't know what all that handsome stuff you comin' with."

He said, "All jokes aside, George, you telling me you went the other way?"

I said, "There's nothing wrong with that."

And he's like "Oh, George, I don't believe it."

He was just solemn after that and looked down, so I said, "Bill, does that mean we're not going to be friends anymore?"

He goes, "No, man, you still my man."

He gave me the ole handshake; I said, "Bill, no, man, you frontin' now."

He said, "I'm just surprised, you know. You never told me about your wife."

The implication here is that a "strong brother" would not sell out his community like this; only weak men would do that. Before this confrontation George had been an integral part of many conversations at work about race, racism, and black culture. After it he found "they'll be talking about something totally in the black culture. I come into the room and be listening; and when I would put my opinion in, the conversation would end—just like that. The room goes empty. . . . because I'm married to a white woman, blacks figure my culture is gone; it's shot." He is accused of having lost connectedness to African Americans, being weak, and marrying a white woman to escape his blackness.

Blacks in interracial relationships defend themselves against accusations of weakness, neurosis, and betrayal. In *Black Skin, White Masks,* Frantz Fanon writes about black men in interracial relationships: "I marry white culture, white beauty, white whiteness. When my restless hands caress those white breasts, they grasp white civilization and dignity and make them mine."[21] In his psychoanalytic interpretation of the effects of colonization and racism, Fanon suggests that many black men who intermarry suffer from neurosis created in a world in which black men are not valued and thus do not value themselves. They think that a relationship with a white woman will validate them—that is, whiten them. Of black women, Fanon writes, "It is because the Negress feels inferior that she aspires to win admittance into the white world."[22] Without acknowledging the pain caused by border patrolling and the desire many interracially married blacks have to maintain strong ties with other blacks, Fanon labels black men and black women in interracial relationships as pathological and neurotic.

More recently, Paul Rosenblatt and his colleagues conducted a study of forty-two multiracial couples in the Minneapolis–St. Paul area. They conclude that many African Americans feel that "it is inappropriate to choose as a partner somebody from the group that has been oppressing African Americans."[23] Many black border patrollers have an overriding concern about loyalty to the race. If an individual is not being loyal, then he or she is explained away as weak, acting in ways that are complicit with the oppression of other black Americans. In "Essentialism and the Complexities of Racial Identity," Michael Eric Dyson suggests, "Loyalty to race has been historically construed as primary and unquestioning allegiance to the racial quest for freedom and the refusal to betray that quest to personal benefit or the diverting pursuit of lesser goals. Those who detour from the prescribed path are labeled 'sell-outs,' 'weak,' 'traitors,' or 'Uncle Toms.'"[24] Thus, black men and women face differing social realities and forms of patrolling.

An overwhelming percentage of black-white couples involve a black male and a white female at a time when there are "more single women in the black community than single men."[25] Many black men are hindered by a racist educational system and job market that make them less desirable for marriage. Many others are scooped into the prison industrial complex. High-profile athletes and entertainers who marry white women confirm for many that black men who are educated and earn a good living sell out, attempting to buy white status through their interracial relationship.[26] Beyond issues of money and status, many black women see black male-white female interracial relationships "as a rejection of black women's beauty, [and] as a failure to acknowledge and reward the support that black women give black men."[27] In *Rooted against the Wind,* Gloria Wade-Gayles writes about the pain and feeling of rejection that black women experience when they see black men with white women:

> We see them, and we feel abandoned. We feel abandoned because we have been abandoned in so many ways, by so many people, and for so many centuries. We are the group of women furthest removed from the concept of beauty and femininity which invades almost every spot of the planet, and as a result, we are taught not to like ourselves, or, as my student said, not to believe that we can ever do enough or be enough to be loved or desired.[28]

Black women and men may both feel a sense of rejection when they see an interracial couple, but for each that sense of rejection comes from a different place. In a society in which women's worth is judged largely by beauty—more specifically, Eurocentric standards of beauty—black women are presumed to be the farthest removed from such a standard. Men's worth is judged largely by their educational and occupational status, two primary areas in which black men are undermined in a racist system. Black men with few educational and job opportunities lack status in the marriage market. Thus, when black men see a black woman with a white man, they may be reminded of the numerous ways in which the white-supremacist system has denied them opportunities. The privilege and power granted to whites, particularly to white males, is paraded in front of them; and

they see the black women in these relationships as complicit with the oppressor.

I met Parsia, a successful businesswoman and a black interracially married mother living in Connecticut, through a family friend. Having grown up in a close-knit African American community, she was uncertain if she wanted to marry interracially and risk losing the support of that community. Now happily married and the mother of a beautiful little girl, she is still very aware of border patrolling. For this reason she prefers not to bring her husband to some areas in Harlem and to black-centered events:

> African Americans do view blacks in interracial relationships as turncoats. There is a pervasive belief in the African American community that it is much more difficult to maintain your identity in an interracial relationship. I believe that once blacks see me as part of an interracial couple, it changes their perception of me right away. They disrespect me as another black person, and then they just disregard my belonging to the community, and suddenly I become the outsider—an outsider because I am with him.

Her fears are not unfounded. One day she and her husband were walking in Philadelphia when a young black man accosted them:

> If I had been alone and this young brother was hassling me in any way, I would have stopped, turned around, and said, "Look, why are you bothering me? What's the deal here?" But I didn't feel at all that I could have this conversation with this young man. He was so hostile, and the source of his hostility was totally his perception of black-white relationships, and there was nothing I could say to change that perception.

This young border patroller may be responding to a belief that Parsia is a race traitor. She is no longer an insider worthy of respect but an outsider who signifies neurosis in the form of self-hate and community betrayal—perhaps the highest form of betrayal. The prospect of rejection by other African Americans is enough for many blacks to deny, hide, or avoid interracial relationships. Border patrolling from other blacks, racism from whites, and the prospect of struggling alone in a racist society seem too high a price; so many who enter interracial relationships end them in short time.

Today there are no longer legal sanctions against interracial marriage, but de facto sanctions remain. At times, family and friends exert pressure to end the interracial relationship; at other times, pressure may come from the border patrolling of strangers. Even if the relationship is clandestine, thoughts of how friends, family members, co-workers, employers, and the general public might respond can deter people from moving forward in a relationship. In each of the following cases the couples did get back together eventually, but all the black women took some time away from the relationship to make this choice.

Lisa met her white husband when she was a college student at a historically black college in the South.

> [I was] the only female in the jazz orchestra, [so] there were all these [black] guys saying, "Why are you with this white guy?" And one band member would make racial comments about "Don't marry whitey, don't trust whitey, don't do this for whitey." This guy in the band tried to talk me out of marrying Peter. I had some apprehension, so I broke up with him and told him I did not want to develop a relationship.

Parsia explains why she temporarily ended her relationship before finally deciding to marry her white husband, Joe:

> When I met Joe, I was really resistant to dating across racial lines. No way would I do that. It took me a very long time to get over that and deal with those feelings,

biases, and expectations. I expected friends would feel very uncomfortable socializing with us. I still do believe that there is a certain language that blacks have when we are apart from other races, when we are alone socially. That's a very important part of my life, and I expected that I might lose that, and that was a very fearful thing for me. The more I felt him getting closer, the more I started seeing the possibility of longevity in the relationship, the more afraid I got. I was terrified that I would be in an interracial relationship for the rest of my life, so I pulled back in a big way and we broke up. There was definitely a shame and a guilt I had to get over because I felt that by dating interracially I was betraying black men.

Her fear reflects her reliance on other African Americans for mutual support in a white-supremacist system. Moreover, her observation that "there is a certain language that blacks have when we are apart from other races" indicates a shared cultural identity that creates and demands the enforcement of borders.

In some cases parents and family reinforce reservations about crossing over. Quisha, like Parsia, broke up with her white boyfriend, Raymond, because she needed time to think about what life would be like in an interracial relationship. "I was really excited about him and told my mom, and she just had a heart attack because he was white. I totally did not expect this from her. She would call everyday and was just hammering it into me to just forget this—and so I really badly and abruptly broke it off with Raymond. He was a real gentleman; he kept calling to find out what happened, and I totally blew him off." She explained her underlying fears as she discussed how she handles people staring at her: "I can feel my grandmother and my mother and my aunts disapproving in those stares, so that's intimidating." Lisa, Parsia, and Quisha all married the men they had left, but they needed time to think about risks, their own understandings of race and community, and what it means to be a black woman in the United States.

They are three of the many black women in interracial relationships who challenge the idea that white men are responsible for the low number of black female–white male interracial marriages. Theorists attempting to explain motives behind interracial marriages have often pointed to the low number of these marriages as evidence that white men are choosing not to marry black women.[29] These theorists suggest that white men are least likely to intermarry with black women because they would gain nothing in these marriages: no money, no status. My research, however, demonstrates the power of black women. The stories they share directly challenge longheld motive myths that imply that black women would marry white men if only white men would choose them. On the contrary, in each of the relationships just discussed, the black woman instigated a breakup. Perhaps their understanding of what it means to be strong, dedicated, and connected to black communities is responsible for the lower numbers of black female–white male marriages.

Border patrolling plays a central role in life decisions and the reproduction of the color line. As decisions are made to enter and remain in an interracial relationship, the color line is challenged and racial identities shift. Many blacks spoke of the growth they experienced because of their interracial relationship and border patrolling. Parsia explains, "I used to be real concerned about how I would be perceived and that as an interracially married female I would be taken less seriously in terms of my dedication to African American causes. I'm not nearly as concerned anymore. I would hold my record up to most of those in single-race relationships, and I would say, 'Okay, let's go toe to toe, and you tell me who's making the biggest

difference,' and so I don't worry about it anymore." Identities, once grounded in the presumed acceptance of other black Americans, have become more reflective. Acceptance can no longer be assumed. Definitions of what it means to be black are reworked. Likewise, because of border patrolling, many whites in interracial relationships began to acknowledge that race matters. Whiteness becomes visible in their claims to racial identity.

Conclusion

Unlike transracially adopted and multiracial people who are raised across the color line, people in interracial relationships discover borderism when they decide to cross the line. This unique form of discrimination, grounded in a racist and segregated society, is always at work even when multiracial family members are not present. Yet by examining the experiences of multiracial family members, we can see the myriad ways in which the color line is both reproduced and resisted. Because interracially married people are often raised in single-race worlds, they have internalized borderism. Thus, part of the decision to become involved interracially includes the need to overcome internalized borderist thoughts. Most of them begin questioning color-blind and essentialist perspectives and learn to understand race as more fluid and complex. Skin color and physical features become just one set of criteria used to think about community and belonging. Many of the people I interviewed referred to this growth process (although not all interracially married people accept the invitation to rethink race).

In a society that often rejects people who cross the color line, individuals involved in such relationships have much to consider before making a permanent commitment. Given the significance of race in our society, a basic choice that all couples contend with is whether or not to stay together in the face of borderism. A few individuals claimed that there was no decision; they fell in love, and that was it. For most others, however, a life across the color line and facing borderism did not look all that inviting and in fact was enough to cause some to terminate their relationships.[30] While the number of people involved in interracial relationships is not known, we do know that in 1995 the census bureau estimated that there were only 246,000 black-white interracial marriages in the United States.[31] This is quite a small percentage considering that in the same year there were more than 50 million total marriages.[32] Borderism and its various components are strong and painful enough to keep black-white interracial marriages the least common marriage pattern for both blacks and whites.

NOTES

1. Etienne Balibar and Immanuel Wallerstein, *Race, Nation, Class: Ambiguous Identities* (New York: Verso, 1991), 71.

2. Joe Feagin and Hernán Vera, *White Racism* (New York: Routledge, 1995), ix–x.

3. Ferber, *White Man Falling,* 100.

4. Naomi Zack, *Race and Mixed Race* (Philadelphia: Temple University Press, 1994).

5. Mimi Abramowitz, *Regulating the Lives of Women: Social Welfare Policy from Colonial Times to the Present* (Boston: South End Press, 1996).

6. Ibid., 3.

7. Valerie Babb, *Whiteness Visible: The Meaning of Whiteness in American Literature and Culture* (New York: New York University Press, 1998), 76.

8. Hale, *Making Whiteness,* 109.

9. See, for instance, Gail Folaron and McCartt Hess, "Placement Considerations for Children of Mixed African American and Caucasian Parentage," *Child Welfare League of America* 72, 3 (1993): 113–135.

10. See for instance, Ferber, *White Man Falling.*

11. Ibid.

12. Ibid., 104.

13. Robert Merton, "Intermarriage and the Social Structure: Fact and Theory," *Psychiatry* 4 (1941): 361–374; see also Matthijs Kalmijn, "Trends in Black/White Intermarriage," *Social Forces* 72, 1 (1996): 119–146.

14. Merton, "Intermarriage"; Kingsley Davis, "Intermarriage in Caste Societies," *American Anthropologist* (September 1941): 388–395.

15. Ferber, *White Man Falling.*

16. Zack, *Race and Mixed Race;* Joel Williamson, *New People: Miscegenation and Mulattoes in the United States* (New York: New York University Press, 1984); Spikard, *Mixed Blood.*

17. Ferber, *White Man Falling,* 103.

18. Kate Davy, "Outing Whiteness," *Theatre* 47, 2 (1995): 189–205.

19. Charles Gallagher, "White Reconstruction in the University," *Socialist Review* 24, 1 and 2 (1995): 165–188.

20. Cathy J. Cohen, "Contested Membership: Black Gay Identities and the Politics of AIDS," in *Queer Theory/Sociology,* ed. Steven Seidman (Cambridge, Mass.: Blackwell, 1996), 365.

21. Frantz Fanon, *Black Skins, White Masks* (New York: Grove), 83.

22. Ibid., 60.

23. Paul C. Rosenblatt, Terri A. Karis, and Richard D. Powell, *Multiracial Couples: Black and White Voices* (Thousand Oaks, Calif.: Sage, 1995), 155.

24. Dyson, "Essentialism," 222.

25. Rosenblatt et al., *Multiracial Couples,* 150.

26. Ibid., 151.

27. Ibid.

28. Gloria Wade-Gayles, *Rooted against the Wind* (Boston: Beacon, 1996), 110.

29. David Heer, "Negro-White Marriages in the United States," *Journal of Marriage and the Family* 28 (1966): 262–273; Kalmijn, "Trends"; Merton, "Intermarriage"; Davis, "Intermarriage in Caste Societies."

30. Although many people break up permanently, I interviewed individuals who eventually made the decision to commit to an interracial marriage.

31. Claudette Bennett, "Interracial Children: Implications for a Multiracial Category" (paper presented at the annual meeting of the American Sociological Association, Washington, D.C., 1995).

32. Rosenblatt et al., *Multiracial Couples,* 5.

46

THE CHANGING FACE OF AMERICA: INTERMARRIAGE AND THE MIXED RACE MOVEMENT

Frank Wu

QUESTIONS TO CONSIDER

Frank Wu examines the interracial "out" marriage rates for Asian and Asian Americans. Who are Asians Americans most likely to marry when they marry across the color line, and what do these trends suggest about racial group perceptions? What is the author referring to when he discusses the "passing of Asian Americans"?

I am a white American female. My husband is Chinese, born in Vietnam. He has a permanent resident visa. My question: What nationality does that make our children? Someone told me that they are white American, but to me that means that they are ignoring their Oriental heritage. My daughter says she is half-Chinese and half-American. Please straighten this out, as we never know how to fill out the forms when this question is asked.

—Letter to "Dear Abby" advice
column, *Chicago Tribune,*
June 24, 1991

The Chinese Girl in the Sixth Grade

When I was a boy, I once asked my mother if she would love me if I married an American girl. She answered that she would love me if

I married a foreigner. But she added that she would love me more if I married a Chinese girl.

I'm not sure how I would have avoided marrying somebody white, if I wanted to be married at all. In elementary school, there was only one grade in which an Asian American girl was in the same class as me. Everyone teased us that we were supposed to be married someday, but she avoided me. Without her, I was left with nobody. I had not learned it, but as much as boys and girls didn't play together as children, whites and non-whites didn't marry one another as adults.

When I was much older, I dated a woman who was white but spoke Chinese fluently. Her father was a Scottish immigrant; her mother was from the impeccable WASP milieu of mainline Philadelphia. She had studied Mandarin in college and Japanese in graduate school; lived in China, Taiwan, and Japan for extended periods of time; and earned advanced degrees with a concentration in Asian studies. Her accent was perfect; her vocabulary was extensive. She was literate. She could pass the "telephone test," meaning that a listener who could not see her would be fooled into believing that she was Chinese. She even had a job once as a radio broadcaster in Japan, using her similarly impressive Japanese. Her expertise with all matters Asian surpassed that of most Asian Americans, and she was better able than I to chat with my parents. She is an "egg": white outside, yellow inside.

I enjoyed more than she did surprising people at restaurants or overseas, who made assumptions about race and gender and expected me to communicate with them in Chinese only to find that she was in charge. There are enough whites who are fluent in Asian languages that in major cities abroad they are no longer even commended for having learned the native tongue, even though they are novel even now here at home.

Eventually, I married a Japanese American woman. On her paternal side, she is second generation (*nisei*); on her maternal side, she is third generation (*sansei*). As we started dating, I traveled with her to meet her mother in St. Louis. After we were introduced, my girlfriend's mother said to her, "He's good looking. . . . He looks Japanese."

By the time we were engaged, my parents had realized I would follow my own course in life. From their perspective, their prospective daughter-in-law might as well have been white. But they were relieved I would not end up an eccentric bachelor, never mind that the woman I had found was not Chinese.

Both my nieces by marriage have husbands who are white. Anybody familiar with Japanese Americans would find the family photographs shown off atop the mantelpiece to be quite ordinary. Japanese Americans can be distinguished from white Americans who lead otherwise similar lives, albeit only barely. My brother-in-law and sister-in-law have memories of the internment camp, but

their children are as integrated as can be. The whiteness of their daughters' spouses is insignificant, in a good sense. The *hakujin* husbands have included themselves in the Asian American community, such as it is.

I remember a white friend I had in elementary school. (I only had white friends in elementary school, because there were no other Asian Americans or any people of color for that matter in any of my classes, other than that one girl.) Like many of my white friends whom I made and lost, a few of whose parents did not want them playing with me, he asked me what my nationality was. I can still recall it, because, although I had developed my vocabulary from almost no English when I'd enrolled in kindergarten, I did not know the word "nationality." Once I figured it out, I gave myself too much credit for being clever in returning the favor with the question, "Well, what nationality are you?" I was puzzled by his answer, which used a metaphor that was restricted to white mixtures, "I'm Heinz 57. . . . Like the ketchup, 57 varieties."

In just my lifetime, intermarriage has become the taboo that binds. Mixed race individuals are accustomed to hearing "what are you?" rather than "Who are you?" and being fixed in an unwelcome gaze, but the mixed race movement is informing others that the "What are you?" inquiry is inappropriate even if it cannot ensure that it becomes irrelevant.

The future of race relations is mixed, literally as well as figuratively. Gradually, interracial relationships have become normal rather than forbidden, and the progeny of such relationships are accepted for their varied ancestries rather than rejected as abominations whose very existence violates natural laws. Although Asian Americans as a group may challenge the prevailing black-white racial paradigm, mixed race persons as individuals confound the concept of such straightforward racial opposites. For better or worse, they personify ambiguities because they demonstrate that race is not always hereditary.

Because the families of America are changing, the self-conception of America itself is changing. The 1960 Census, taken at a time when intermarriage was criminal conduct in more than a dozen states, showed only 149,000 interracial marriages within a total population of 179 million. The 1990 Census, taken when the number of multi-racial babies being born was growing at a higher rate than the number of mono-racial babies being born, showed more than 1.46 million interracial marriages within a total population of 281 million. Mixed marriages constituted about 3 percent of all marriages in 1980 nationwide and an estimated 5 percent in 1990. In California, which leads the mainland United States, about one out of six marriages now brings together couples of different racial or ethnic backgrounds. Among Asian Americans under the age of thirty-five who are married, half have found a spouse of a non-Asian background. Experts forecast that more than 20 percent of all marriages will be mixed by 2050. By 1990, more than 60 percent of Hawaiian babies were mixed race; by 2000, more than 20 percent of the Hawaiian population was mixed race. The 2000 Census counted about 6.8 million people of mixed race background, making up 2.4 percent of the population.

The transformation is recent. It was only in 1967 that the Supreme Court struck down legal bans on intermarriage in a case involving the aptly named Loving couple.[1] Since then, states have slowly repealed the bars that they had on the books. Alabama did not revise its statutes until 1999.[2] Local authorities reportedly were enforcing the rules in violation of the mandate from the highest court in the land. They did so by referring to the nullification doctrine of the antebellum era by which their predecessors had tried to ignore federal legislation against slavery by appealing to states' rights.

In the less than two generations since the *Loving* case, what social scientists have called "exogamy" or "outmarriage" has proliferated by an order of magnitude. Because of the personal nature of the relationships, the unions symbolize much more. Yet as with other demographic patterns, as a society we are only beginning to comprehend the complexities that they bequeath us. However sanguine we are about intermarriage and mixed race children, the success of all marriages and the future of any child depend on many factors. Intermarriage and the mixed race movement are positive, but they are no panacea. Both can reflect the effects of racial discrimination in the most intimate manner. Jeanne Wakatsuki Houston, author of a popular memoir about the internment, *Farewell to Manzanar,* writes that she saw her white husband as her "Anglo Samurai" who by "wielding his sword of integrity" would "slay the dragons that prevented my acceptance as an equal human being in his world."[3]

In this chapter, I begin by considering white opposition to interracial marriage and white attraction to people of color. I then turn to the ambivalence toward mixed marriages expressed by minority communities, both racial and religious. Finally, I consider the mixed race movement and its implications specifically for Asian Americans.

The Core of the Heart of the Race Problem

Both proponents and opponents of racial justice grasped that intermarriage was the culmination of racial equality. James Weldon Johnson, composer of the hymn "Lift Every Voice and Sing" (sometimes referred to as the black national anthem) and author of the novel *The Autobiography of an Ex-Colored*

Man,[4] once wrote, "in the core of the heart of the race problem the sex factor is rooted."[5] Gunnar Myrdal ranked "intermarriage" and in particular "sexual contacts with white women" as the area of greatest racial discrimination.[6]

When Abraham Lincoln signed the Emancipation Proclamation, his adversaries were fixated on the probability of legal equality leading to social equality.[7] When he ran for reelection in 1864, two pro-slavery writers sought to associate him with a fake Republican pamphlet purporting to endorse miscegenation, to inspire backlash. They coined the term "miscegenation" from Latin roots for mixture and race. Earlier, abolitionist Wendell Phillips actually had issued a similar call in earnest.[8] He preached "amalgamation" as the best means of uniting a divided nation.

A century later, as integration actually began in earnest, the paranoid fear that whites articulated again was the possibility that race mixing would proceed apace from the classroom to the bedroom. Foreseeing the impending upheaval of the old South, Theodore G. Bilbo, twice the governor of Mississippi and a three-term U.S. Senator, penned a book, *Take Your Choice: Separation or Mongrelization,*[9] in which he argued for "repatriation" of blacks to Africa specifically to avoid intermarriage. "The incontrovertible truths of this book and its sincere warnings," he wrote, "are respectfully inscribed to every white man and woman, regardless of nationality, who is a bona fide citizen of the United States of America."[10] He inveighed against what he believes to be false interpretations of democracy and Christianity, which would require recognizing African Americans as equal persons. He stated that intermarriage is "totally destructive to the white race" because "the Negro race is physically, mentally, and morally inferior."[11] Even if the mulatto might be the equal of the white man, "amalgamation must be condemned"

because "it cannot be said to be a matter of trial and error . . . corrupted blood cannot be redeemed."[12] He concluded his book with his own bill for "voluntary resettlement" of African Americans on the African continent.[13]

The official end of racial segregation in public education, decreed by the Supreme Court decision in *Brown v. Board of Education,* was thought to be the harbinger of a sexual calamity. Congressman Jon Bell Williams of Mississippi called the issuance of the *Brown* decision "black Monday," and Judge Thomas Brady of the same state borrowed the phrase for the title of his pamphlet, issued by the white supremacist Citizens' Councils of Mississippi, in which he asserted that the Supreme Court is tending toward Communism and proposes either that a new state be created and blacks transported there for their own benefit or that all public schools be closed and African Americans left to their own devices. Insisting that he would like harmony between races, Brady predicted that white Southern men would fight to the death to preserve racial purity, defined as whiteness and the honor of their women. "We say to the Supreme Court and to the entire world," he wrote, "'you shall not make us drink from this cup.'"[14] He warned, "those who do not believe this may try through force of arms to accomplish it. If this happens, then it will take an army of one hundred million men to compel it." He concluded, "You shall not mongrelize our children and grand-children!"[15]

The defining occasion of desegregation came in 1957, as federal troops had to be ordered out to enable blacks to attend Little Rock Central High School.[16] State officials were heading the campaign of massive resistance to school integration. A list of seven questions circulated by white leaders in Little Rock at the time began with, "Would the Negro boys be permitted to solicit the white girls for dances at school-soirees?" It ended with, "When the script calls for the enactment of tender love scenes, will these parts be assigned to negro boys and white girls without respect to race and color in drama classes?"

Such segregationist propaganda, like the hoax perpetrated against Lincoln, was based on the premise that whites who backed racial integration would blanch at sexual contact between their white daughters and black men. A popular line of reasoning was that segregationists were willing to abide integration, but integrationists would have to understand that their morality would necessitate Southern belles bedding black men indiscriminately. The presumption was that once such an abhorrent result became apparent, even selfproclaimed liberals would come to their senses. Novelist Norman Mailer explained that, "The white man fears the sexual potency of the Negro. . . . The white loathes the idea of the Negro attaining equality in the classroom because the white feels that the Negro already enjoys sensual superiority."[17]

In reply, African American men were reduced to pledging that, even as they sought to be admitted to all spheres of public life on equal terms, they would not aspire to the hands of white women, and to assuring whites that not all black men were superstuds. They did not wish to appear like Bigger Thomas, the African American male in Richard Wright's 1940 novel, *Native Son.* Thomas accidentally kills the wealthy young white woman for whom he works, and toward whom he is attracted, but Thomas also brutally kills his black girlfriend, the latter crime being both the more intentional and insignificant in the context of his wretched life.[18] They knew the strategic advantage of stopping short of intermarriage. Michael Lind, in *The Next American Nation: The New Nationalism and the Fourth American Revolution,*[19] argues that intermarriage is crucial to the

future of a diverse democracy. He observes that "even Martin Luther King Jr. dared dream, at least in public, only of black and white children playing together in the red hills of Birmingham, Alabama, instead of dreaming of weddings of mixed-race couples in the churches of Birmingham." In 1971, Robert E. Kuttner (a leading racialist not to be confused with the liberal economist of the same name) published in the now-defunct *American Mercury* magazine a think piece entitled, "Race Mixing: Suicide or Salvation?" Kuttner left no doubt that he considered it the former: "Legalized pornography teaches that the height of sexual pleasure can be attained only with Negro partners. . . . Who has not seen teenage girls with pale blond hair carrying Negro babies in Hippie settlements or in the drug communes around our elite universities?" He concluded, "Racial instincts in man deserve objective investigation by the methods of modern psychology" because white men prefer white women and "cannot be dismissed merely because womanless soldiers, explorers and colonizers mated with native women." In sum, "Race mixing between advanced and lower stocks is of no benefit to the higher type."[20]

Whites could be as upset by Asian Americans joining the family as they were by African Americans doing so. In the Western states, their dread of an Asian California was exceeded only by their horror at an Asian and Caucasian Pacific Coast. A white minister named Ralph Newman, living in Sacramento, said in 1931:

> Near my home is an eighty-acre tract of as fine land as there is in California. On that tract lives a Japanese. With that Japanese lives a white woman. In that woman's arms is a baby. What is that baby? It isn't white. It isn't Japanese. It is a germ of the mightiest problem that ever faced this state; a problem that will make the black problem of the South look white.[21]

Newman could have been confident that whites would back up his sentiments virtually unanimously. Whites from ardent segregationists to moderate integrationists opposed intermarriage. President Harry S Truman replied frankly to a reporter who asked whether intermarriage would become common, "I hope not; I don't believe in it."[22] Truman, who had taken incremental steps to dismantle segregation, was known to ask "Would you want your daughter to marry a Negro?"[23] In 1958, the Gallup organization reported that 96 percent of whites were against intermarriage.

With the civil rights movement, approval and disapproval of intermarriage have switched places in the polls, but the figures still show discrepancies by racial group. When the Gallup poll broke out separate figures for whites and blacks on this issue for the first time in 1972, the results were mirror images: 27 percent of whites approved of intermarriage and 73 percent disapproved of it; 76 per cent of blacks approved of intermarriage and 24 percent disapproved of it. Since then, the attitudes of whites and blacks have converged, as have the attitudes in the North and the South and of the college educated and the non-college educated. By 1997, the last year for which data are available, a majority of respondents approved of intermarriage: 67 percent of whites approved of intermarriage and 33 percent disapproved of it; 83 percent of blacks approved of intermarriage and 17 percent disapproved of it. According to a survey published in 2001 by *The Washington Post,* Harvard University, and the Kaiser Foundation, approval of intermarriage is rising, but "nearly half of all whites—more than any other group—still believe it is better for people to marry someone of their own race."[24]

Among Asian Americans, intermarriage is as pervasive as resistance to it. A 1998 study by the Organization of Chinese Americans found that 69 percent of Chinese American parents strongly agreed or agreed with the statement "I prefer that my children marry someone in the same ethnic group."[25] Among children, only 50 percent agreed with that sentiment.

As salutary as the overall statistics may appear, they are likely to be inflated.[26] Social science data are often distorted by preference falsification. Interviewees give answers they suppose will be acceptable to society or pleasing to the interviewer, tending not to disclose their true outlook. In any event, attitudes and behavior are not the same. Inter marriage rates are well below what they would be if people acted on their stated willingness to intermarry, and progress has come slower than appearances would suggest.

Yellow Fever and Trophy Boyfriends

Inequality runs as a theme through the literature of mixed race liaisons. Poet Langston Hughes wrote a poem, entitled "Cross," about mixed parentage, ending with the stanza:

> My old man died in a fine big house.
> My ma died in a shack.
> I wonder where I'm gonna die,
> Being neither white nor black?[27]

The most famous such relationship in American history involved a white man and a black woman; he was as powerful as she was not.[28] As was rumored in the press in his time and verified by genetic testing in ours, founding father Thomas Jefferson carried on a long-term affair with his slave Sally Hemings.[29] Until the genetic testing resolved the matter, as Mount Holyoke College historian Joseph Ellis has noted, the Jefferson-Hemings relationship was rejected as a scurrilous rumor by the mostly white academic community as much as it was repeated as common knowledge in the black oral tradition.[30] The relationship between the future president and the woman who was his late wife's half-sister probably began when she was an adolescent serving as a nanny in his household. They may have been passionate and devoted. It is inspirational to imagine that they worked out a semblance of parity through mutual commitment. The truth may be disheartening.

Whatever their private personas, their public roles were grossly unequal. When Jefferson demanded that Hemings return from France, where he was serving as ambassador, to Virginia and his Monticello estate, both of them knew that she was free overseas but would be held in bondage once back home. Jefferson owned her. The children born to them were his chattel property, too.

Intermarriage still occurs in distinct configurations, and not all individuals have the same ability to engage in it. Races come together asymmetrically. Intermarriage may reinforce rather than break down the color line that separates whites from blacks, because intermarriage has risen primarily due to alliances among whites, Asian Americans, and Latinos, not African Americans. White-black intermarriage lags behind as the least frequent. Whites are much more likely to marry Asian Americans than African Americans. The Asian American intermarriage rate is triple the African American rate.

Asian Americans generally marry up. Just as the idea of "marrying up" is an admission of socioeconomic hierarchy, so is "marrying up" interracially an acknowledgment of racial hierarchy. For most Asian Americans, a white spouse ranks higher than a black spouse. Whites and blacks may both be "foreign devils," but whites are the more sought-after foreign devils. Halford Fairchild, a noted psychologist who is of African American and Hawaiian Japanese descent, has said that "the black community,

in general, has been a lot more accepting of racial differences than other communities."[31] His Japanese American mother's family disowned her for marrying a black man, cautioning her that when they returned to his home in California, she would find "he has nothing."

In 1990, thirty times as many intermarried Asian Americans had white spouses as had black spouses, even though years ago intermarriage between Chinese Americans and African Americans in Harlem was not unheard of. The 1992 independent movie *Mississippi Masala* by director Mira Nair, about a South Asian woman from Uganda who falls in love with an African American man who owns a carpet-cleaning business (essayed by Denzel Washington, whom women of all races have pursued to the box office), is abnormal even within the atypicality of interracial romances. The 1997 Disney remake of Rodgers and Hammerstein's *Cinderella,* starring African American television actress Brandy in the title role and Asian American stage actor Paolo Montalban as Prince Charming, is anomalous in the opposite direction.

White Americans also rank above other Asian Americans. Although Asian Americans are marrying across Asian ethnicities more often than before—as my wife and I did—they are more likely to intermarry with white Americans than with Asian Americans of a different ethnicity. Few fail to grasp that it is the white look, not the Asian look, that is in demand. In John Updike's short story, "Metamorphosis," the white male protagonist is naïve in his infatuation with his Asian American female doctor. Fantasizing that he can capture her attention, he asks for reverse eyelid surgery to give himself almond eyes. In the O. Henry-style surprise ending, however, once he has undergone the painful operation, he spies on her desk her family photograph showing her husband "not old, exactly, probably younger than [him] by some years, but craggy, Caucasian, grinning, big-nosed, rather monstrously bumpy and creased." As he leaves the office, he ponders "how foolish he must look!" and he is grateful that he still has his right tear duct.[32]

The various pairings also exhibit the mutual influence of race and gender. Among African American-white married couples, an African American husband with a white wife remains more widespread than a white husband with an African American wife. According to the 1990 Census, 72 percent of African American-white couples consist of an African American male and a white female. It appears that the African American man who marries a white woman is exchanging his higher economic status for her higher social status. He is augmenting his material success with a woman who is regarded as belonging to a superior class; she is acquiring access to his affluence.

Terry McMillan's best-selling novel *Waiting to Exhale*[33] chronicled the love lives of a quartet of African American women. Among them was Bernadine Harris, whose trauma of being left by her African American husband was aggravated by the identity of the "other woman." Bernadine and her friends list the problems with black men: "with white women" comes second in the litany, after "scared to make a damned commitment," before "gay," and well ahead of ugly, stupid, and in prison.[34] After Bernadine had supported him as he struggled through his career, her husband left her for a younger white woman once his business became profitable. In the book, Bernadine reviews her mistake of trusting him: "Kathleen the bookkeeper, who was fresh out of some two-year college and California pretty" was "not at all a threat because, number one, she was white and you knew [he] would never look at a white girl and number two, he loved you and the kids."[35] In the movie, Angela Bassett

in the role of Bernadine was cheered by audiences as she acted on her anger: she visited her husband's office, slapped her rival, and confronted her husband, before returning home, clearing out the contents of his closet, dumping his fancy shirts and expensive suits into his luxury car, and setting it all ablaze.

The modern white-black intermarriage that prompted record outcry, from whites and blacks alike, was the 1949 marriage of Walter White and Poppy Cannon.[36] White, the long-time secretary of the NAACP, divorced his African American wife to take up with Cannon, a white businesswoman. Many whites found in the two of them proof of the conspiracy of black men to steal their women. Some black women deplored the dumping of a black woman for a white woman, treating the divorce and remarriage as an exercise in crass racial upward mobility. What White and Cannon should have made apparent was the fabrication of race. When they traveled, they were regarded as an interracial couple, but people made assumptions that reversed their racial roles.[37] White fit his name: He was light-skinned, blonde, and blue-eyed; both of his parents could have passed as white and his daughter was so light she had problems pursuing an acting career because she could not credibly play a black person but could not be cast as a white person.[38] Cannon was darker all-around, blacker in a physical sense.

Shortly thereafter, the widower Thurgood Marshall wed Cecile "Cissy" Suyatt. Known as Mr. Civil Rights for his courtroom victories against racial segregation, Marshall served for many years as the general counsel for the NAACP Legal Defense Fund prior to his historic appointment to the U.S. Supreme Court. Suyatt was a Filipina secretary at his office. She initially turned down his proposal for fear of the likely reactions. She reported whispers against her that she was a "foreigner," and she worried about what her family would say about an African American husband. Like White's marriage, Marshall's met the censure of some Southern whites. In response to the newspaper editorial that called him a racist for marrying a white woman, Marshall said, "I just think you ought to be accurate. . . . I've had two wives and both of 'em are colored."[39] In 1995, *Ebony* magazine listed the Marshall-Suyat wedding among its fifty "best" of the past half-century.[40]

In a reversal of the black-white interaction, 72 percent of Asian American-white couples consist of an Asian American wife and a white husband. Writing in *American Demographics* magazine, journalist Robert Suro reported that Asian women are intermarrying at twice the rate of Asian men.[41] In a 2000 California survey of Asian-white intermarriages, Filipina-white intermarriages were the most common. In the Golden State throughout the 1990s, there were 16,503 births of children to Filipina mothers and white fathers and only 5,556 births to white mothers and Filipino fathers. The former occurred almost three times as often as the latter.

The data produce a puzzle, however: Unless there are many more Asian American women than there are Asian American men, there must be enormous numbers of single Asian American men compared to single Asian American women. The solution to the conundrum of uneven rates of outmarriage is immigration. It appears to be foreign-born Asian women who are intermarrying as much as it is Asian American women.

Tiger, Keanu, and the Passing of Asian Americans

Support for the mixed race movement can be blended with caution about its implications. As compelling as the desire to define oneself may be, the mixed race movement poses the risk of increasing rather than decreasing the invidious forms of color consciousness. A range of color categories expands the reach of prejudice. By a Creole or mestizo sensibility, half-white may come to look better than all-black. Just as African Americans straighten their hair, Asian Americans perm theirs; just as African Americans have cosmetic surgery for a "classical" nose and Asian Americans do so for round eyes, the mixed race movement may promote, even if inadvertently, the practices of whitening.

University of North Carolina professor Jon Michael Spencer, who happens to be mixed race himself, argues against the ambitions of the mixed race movement in his 1997 book, *The New Colored People: The Mixed-Race Movement in America.*[42] Spencer believes that race can bring together oppressed peoples. He notes that historically and even at present, in areas with large numbers of individuals who are both black and white, such as nineteenth-century New Orleans, apartheid South Africa, or contemporary Hawaii and Brazil, the gradations among hues can be much finer in distinction than black and white but no less odious as discrimination against the darker skinned. None of the places whose populations have multiplied creatively have become racial nirvanas. The various methods of classifying people according to pedigree—for example, by the moons of fingernails—have in common the placement of whites at the top and the ordering of everyone else from swarthy to tawny in descending order. The expressions for every ancestral assortment are no better for being archaic. In addition to the official terms allocating with false precision the admixture of heredity, from "mulatto" to "quadroon" to "octoroon," were slang terms that could be decidedly uncomplimentary, such as "Sambo," which originally meant three-quarters black, and "high yellow" or "yella."

As much as some of us might proclaim enthusiastically, "There is only one race, the human race," few of us live up to the belief through our actions. Among African Americans, the colorism of "lighter is righter" has copied white prejudice.[43] Under slavery, white owners might choose lighter-skinned slaves for household duties instead of the toil of field work, and white men might take the lighter women as mistresses. Light-skinned mulattos, many of whom were freed through the wills of their white fathers, could have contempt for their darker brethren. Some of them even became slaveholders themselves, occupying a middle position between black and white. One of the most scathing attacks on black culture, *The American Negro,* was written a century ago by William Hannibal Thomas about his darker fellows. His vitriolic comments were scarcely distinguishable from those of white supremacists.[44] Even up to the civil rights era, an emphasis by some "blue veined" mixed race individuals on their white derivation can harken back to the "paper bag" test. A few "bougie"—"bougie" is a vernacular derivation of "bourgeois"— social clubs within African American communities, such as the Bon Ton Society of Washington, D.C., were said to employ a "paper bag" test for membership: Successful applicants had to be as light as the pallid brown of a paper bag.

The practice of passing, or "crossing over," bears out the pecking order. People of color who have the requisite skin tone and facial features are able to pretend that they are exclusively white so that they can enjoy the tangible advantages. They may even become white permanently, leaving behind their family, friends, and community, as they follow the excruciating path of forsaking their identity for their livelihood.

Passing usually occurs in only one direction. People who are white rarely try to disguise themselves as people of color and would have few reasons to do so. There are only a handful of people who became what was dubbed a "voluntary Negro": Morehouse College founder William Jefferson White, who had black ancestors and was raised within the black community; turn-of-the-century novelist Charles W. Chesnutt, who used the honorific "FMC," an antebellum term for "free man of color"; Adam Clayton Powell, who was virtually blonde and blue-eyed, but as a minister and Congressman was an advocate of black power; and jazz musician Mezz Mezzrow, nee Milton Mesirow, the Russian Jewish author of an autobiography, *Really the Blues.*[45]

The opposite is much more common. Whites even sued to avoid being classified as black. Until recently, it was considered libel of the worst form to call a white person black. It was an offense because it offended; black was decidedly inferior. In 1982, a well-to-do woman named Susie Guillory Phipps filed suit as an anonymous "Jane Doe" to challenge a Louisiana statute that made anyone with black ancestry automatically black.[46] She wanted to be white, not black or multiracial. Snubbing some of her relatives, she maintained she had had no idea she was even remotely black. Recalling her devastation at the revelation, she said she took sick for three days. "I was brought up white, I married white twice," she said. She lost. But publicity about her case prompted the state to amend its laws so that parents were allowed to list the race of newborns and an individual could adjust her birth certificate upon a showing that she was white by a preponderance of the evidence.

In the nineteenth and early twentieth centuries, the Asian population would have been driven out of existence by a combination of the rules on immigration and those on intermarriage. Immigration laws made it difficult for Asian women to come to the country. The ratio of Chinese men to Chinese women exceeded one hundred to one. Anti-miscegenation laws passed by states prevented Asian men from marrying white women. The Cable Act passed by Congress stripped non-Asian women of their citizenship if they married Asian men. Asian-black children were black. The government argued against granting of birthright citizenship to the few native-born children of Asian parents. If the mutually reinforcing public policies had been fully effective, Asian Americans could not have reproduced themselves.

Nowadays, Asian Americans are melting away voluntarily. Even as Asian Americans are continuing to appear through immigration, we are constantly disappearing through intermarriage. Japanese Americans, who have outmarried in the highest proportions, are joined by very few new arrivals from Japan. The Yasui family of Hood River, Oregon, is typical. The subject of Lauren Kessler's *Stubborn Twig: Three Generations in the Life of a Japanese-American Family*,[47] only one of eighteen third-generation cousins of the clan married another Japanese American (and then only in a second marriage). As go the Yasuis's children, so go Japanese Americans. They are likely to vanish as a distinctive ethnic group within another generation unless large numbers of mixed race individuals in the fourth and fifth generations choose an Asian American identity rather than a white identity. Some have said that Japanese American integration was hastened by the internment, but other Asian American ethnic groups also are intermarrying at high rates.

So for Asian Americans, passing presents a dilemma. Few are as unique as sculptor Isamu Noguchi, whose father was Yone Noguchi, a Japanese (not Japanese American) poet, and whose mother was Leonie Gilmour, a white American. Noguchi grew up in Japan and the United States; lived in Paris, where he was an apprentice to sculptor Constantin Brancusi; worked with choreographer Martha Graham while also designing the lamps for which he is best known; and became an internationally renowned artist representing the United States at the Venice Biennial and being recognized as a national treasure by Japan. Many Asian Americans are forced toward whiteness or blackness as two extremes along a spectrum with a preferred pole. Tiger Woods and Keanu Reeves show the effects of such dispersion.

Golf sensation Tiger Woods has become a reluctant poster child for the mixed race movement. (The unsuccessful legislation that would have required the Census to include a multiracial category was dubbed the "Tiger Woods bill.") As an athlete who has revitalized his sport as no other single competitor has ever done for any game, Woods can hardly be considered average in any terms. Just as it is inappropriate to make an individual the representative of everyone else of his specific racial background, it is unseemly to turn a single person into a symbol for everyone of mixed race background. He may be the product of the fusion of diverse cultures, but it would be absurd to give him the mixed man's burden of leading us to racial reconciliation.

Indeed, Woods reveals the contradictions of the mixed race movement. Even for international celebrities whose lives are known in every detail by total strangers, private and public racial identities do not align neatly.

In 1997, the twenty-one-year-old Woods became the youngest player ever to win the Masters Tournament as he began his ascent toward legendary status. Having left Stanford University as the top-rated amateur golfer, he defeated the professional field with a seemingly invincible superiority. Again and again, he defeated all comers while drawing a swelling crowd of spectators, many of whom would not have idolized Arnold Palmer or Jack Nicklaus as they putted on the links of exclusive country clubs. Shoal Creek in Birmingham, Alabama, was excluding blacks as late as 1990. Its rules prompted the PGA to adopt an antidiscrimination policy. In response, some clubs decided to give up their affiliation with the PGA.

Woods was different from his seniors. Poised and telegenic, he thrilled spectators by coming back to win even if he had had a poor start well over par. He graded himself after he played his rounds, to the irritation of his peers. His "C" game beat everybody else's "A" game. He was extraordinary even when he wasn't bothering to try too much. His most spectacular television advertisement used footage that was filmed accidentally. Before he was about to shoot the scripted material, he was goofing off by bouncing a ball on his club head two dozen times in a row without dropping it, before hitting it into the air and sending it flying several hundred yards.

Immediately, the story of his life introduced his fans to the mixed race movement. The son of Earl Woods, an African American Green Beret lieutenant colonel, and Kultida Punsawad, a well-to-do Thai secretary who was raised as a devout Buddhist near the bridge on the River Kwai (as in the movie of that title), Eldrick Woods was nicknamed Tiger in honor of Phong Nguyen, a Vietnamese officer who had saved his father's life more than once.

Woods was imitating his father's golf swing before he was a year old. By the time he was three, he had won against a club professional and appeared on television with Bob Hope. He shot his first hole in one when he was six. Because his mother wanted him to develop academically as well, she allowed him to play golf only if he had finished his homework.

From time to time, Woods has returned to his mother's homeland as a conquering hero. There he is said to be Asian "from the eyes up." He has even led a Thai national golf team in Asian regional contests. He also believes in most of the principles of Buddhism. But Woods is not simply African American some of the time and Asian American the rest of the time. His background is more complicated, and societal reactions to it more problematic, than that.

Appearing on Oprah Winfrey's television program just after his record victory at the Masters, Woods talked about his lineage at length. He told a nationwide viewership that he had invented a term for himself, "Cablinasian," to unify verbally his Caucasian, Black, Indian, and Asian heritage. To be precise, if it is possible to be precise in these matters, his father is half black, one-quarter Native American, and one-quarter Chinese; his mother is half Thai, one-quarter Dutch, and one-quarter Chinese. Woods said, "I just am who I am." Asked whether it bothered him to be labeled as an African American, he said, "It does." He checked off the official boxes on forms for both African American and Asian American, because, "Those are the two I was raised under, and the only two I know."

Winfrey christened him "America's son." But the episode proved controversial. As soon as Tiger became a precious commodity, Asian Americans and African Americans began an unbecoming dispute over who would claim him as one of their own. Asian Americans noted that technically, as half Thai and one-quarter Chinese, Woods was three-quarters Asian, and that was the largest portion of his makeup. African Americans were dismayed that someone who paid homage to black golfers of the past and alluded to continuing racial segregation seemed to be disowning his blackness when presented with the chance and selecting a paler self.

The tension between Asian Americans and African Americans was made superfluous, even if it was not quite resolved, thanks to the intervention of a white observer.

Notwithstanding the intense publicity over Woods's compound bloodlines, in most people's eyes, Woods turned out to be effectively black.

The pivotal incident came when Fuzzy Zoeller, a veteran of the PGA tour who happens to be white, made remarks about Woods to a television crew. Referring to the winner's prerogative of setting the dinner menu for the festivities at the Masters, Zoeller referred to Woods's race in a nonchalant remark. Calling Woods "that little boy," Zoeller said he should be told not to serve fried chicken or collard greens "or whatever it is they serve."[48] Even aside from the use of "that little boy," Zoeller was undoubtedly talking about race by referring to stereotypical Southern black cuisine.

Released by his major sponsor, K-Mart, as a spokesperson, Zoeller then delivered a tearful explanation about his penchant for being "a jokester"; he added, "I just didn't deliver the line well."[49] He even withdrew temporarily from the professional tour.

Woods accepted Zoeller's apology. But giving Zoeller the benefit of the doubt and treating him as a decent man acting in good faith only makes the mistake of his perception worse. It is as if he cannot help himself: When he looks at Woods he sees race; he sees blackness. He is cued to talk about soul food. He does not bring up curry chicken or lemongrass soup. That would have been equally (in)apt.

Woods may be one of the most well-known people on the face of the earth. He may even be renowned for his mixed race status and acquainted personally with the observer who is engrossed with race. Whatever Woods declared for himself and however Asian Americans and African Americans calculated their fractions, the real test of his race is how he is treated by strangers on the street who don't recognize his celebrity status. Woods himself has said, "I am 90 percent Oriental,

more Thai than anything." But he also has said that while he was in college, "What I realized is that even though I'm mathematically Asian—if anything—if you have one drop of black blood in the United States, you're black."[50]

The one drop rule to which Woods referred was a legal rule. On the theory that a single drop of black blood would contaminate white virtue, any person whose ancestry could be traced back to a black person was deemed to be black no matter how distant the relationship. The one drop rule, which has no basis in biology, has been abolished legally but not culturally. Somebody who is like Woods but who is not instantly identifiable from shoe advertisements is for practical purposes black. In a recent anthology of essays on being "half and half," one writer said of Woods, "'When the black truck comes around, they're going to haul his ass on it.'"[51]

Movie actor Keanu Reeves provides a contrasting example. He played the epitome of a clueless Californian in the teen favorite *Bill and Ted's Excellent Adventure.* He has been the Buddha and the son of the Devil in other films. He earned raves for his Hamlet on stage and he turned in an admirable Don Juan in Kenneth Branagh's cinematic version of Shakespeare's *Much Ado About Nothing* (with Denzel Washington as his better brother). He emerged as an action superstar with the thriller *Speed,* one of the highest-grossing movies of the 1990s.

Billed by *Vanity Fair* as "Hollywood's hottest heartthrob," Reeves was born in 1964 in Beirut. His father was a wealthy geologist of Hawaiian-Chinese extraction. His mother was a British showgirl who became a costume designer for rock musicians. Readers of sensational accounts of his life know that his father was estranged from the family and imprisoned for drug possession and that his mother raised him in Toronto with a series of stepfathers. His first name is based on a

Hawaiian term for the wind over the mountains. He was a high school hockey player of some talent. A serious motorcyclist, he rides a vintage Norton Commando even after two accidents. He has opted to tour with his band, Dogstar, in obscure venues instead of taking on lucrative but unsatisfying acting roles.

Reeves is a closeted Asian American. He has become a Caucasian Asian. To most moviegoers, he is an average white guy. He is an archetypal dude. He can easily be accepted as white. There is no reason for him to publicize that he is anything else. Only a fanatical devotee of tabloid news would even know his paternity. Neither his facial features nor his family name are obviously Asian. His father, however, can be readily identified as Asian from the few published photographs. He peers out from the shadows as an enigmatic figure.

There would be no reason other than excessive ethnic pride for Reeves to out himself as Asian. But the ease with which he has adopted whiteness is fascinating. To the extent that he has chosen to be white and has consciously selected his whiteness, he confirms that whiteness is beneficial. Other than Reeves, whose martial arts exploits were enhanced by "bullet time" special effects in the science fiction blockbuster *The Matrix,* Asian men are leading men and heroes only in the kung fu chop socky genre; unless Reeves is regarded as Asian American, the highest-grossing movie ever made without a white male lead is the Jackie Chan-Chris Tucker buddy flick *Rush Hour.* To the extent that Reeves has not selected whiteness but has stumbled into it, he indicates how whiteness is the default mode. Unless he deviates blatantly from the norm, he is assumed to be white.

Even though Reeves is essentially white, the uniformly negative commentary of film critics on his work unwittingly echoes the classic line about Asians. To many reviewers, ironically, he is inscrutable. Reeves himself once said about his skills as thespian, "I don't know anything, man."

It should give us pause that Woods is black and Reeves is white and neither is Asian. They are not even Eurasian or Amerasian. The terms have become antiquated exactly as they were on the cusp of becoming commonly applicable.

In the Mississippi Delta, where a few thousand Chinese laborers were brought during Reconstruction, many of their descendants intermarried long ago.[52] Families with Chinese roots came to have both white branches and black branches. With successive intermarriage, the Chinese roots have been forgotten, and the white branches and the black branches have grown apart. The same has happened to the little-known community of Punjabi Mexican Americans in California.[53]

Mixed race individuals do not leave race behind. A study conducted using 1980 Census data showed wide divergences in the racial identity of mixed race children. Among children with white mothers, only 35 percent of those with Chinese fathers were identified by their parents as white, but 74 percent of those with Asian Indian fathers were; conversely, among children with white fathers, about 62 percent of those with Chinese mothers were identified by their parents as white but 93 percent of those with Asian Indian mothers were.

Although the research on these topics is just beginning, the only summary that can be made thus far is that matters seem to be complicated and dynamic. The point should not be some sort of futile effort to make Woods and Reeves, along with the groups in Mississippi and California, into Asians through the dubious transmogrification of racial alchemy. In truth, they are no more Asian than they are black or white. They cannot be reduced to race with any coherence. Darby Li Po Price, a comedian with a doctorate in ethnic studies, tells the following opening joke: "I am of Chinese descent from my mother, and Scots-Irish, Welsh, and Cherokee descent from my father, so in the United States that means I'm Latino."[54] Yet as mixed race people take on their own identities, their cumulative choices create a new identity, such as Japanese, white, and Jewish combined.

As mixed race status becomes hip, however, individuals start to make superficial claims to be part this or part that, without any actual appreciation of the minority culture or acceptance of the consequences of affinity with it. The Native American population is growing much faster than its birthrate (and, needless to say, it has no immigration), thanks to people who are outsiders to Indian culture suddenly discovering their Indianness. When Disney released its animated movie *Pocahontas,* it inspired many such superficial Indians to fantasize about identity.[55]

Many Native Americans have contempt for ersatz Native Americans who are not enrolled in a tribe who casually say that they had a great-grandparent who was an Indian brave or an Indian maiden, some of whom seem to be doing nothing more than trolling for government benefits or speculating that they can cash in on the exaggerated riches of casino gambling. Most Native Americans grant that it is possible to be a bona fide Indian without being a pureblood, but they have had more than enough experience, largely catastrophic, with outsiders defining who is an Indian and what it means to be an Indian.[56]

The wannabees who announce that they are Native Americans but who have no actual experience as a Native American have not grappled with the alcoholism, poverty, and suicide of reservations.[57] They know nothing of the difficulty of enforcing treaty rights or the humiliation of seeing skeletons of their ancestors displayed in museums and caricatures of themselves as sports mascots. (They are not like the "black Seminoles," African Americans who more than a century ago took on the customs of neighboring Native Americans, part of the largely neglected integration of African Americans and Native Americans.)

Among Asian immigrants, the poignant case of children fathered by U.S. military personnel in Vietnam shows how the standing of mixed race individuals depends on the situation.[58] From their birth, they were snubbed as *bui doi,* the dust of life. Their mothers were considered prostitutes. With passage of the Homecoming Act by Congress in 1987, allowing them and their families to come here, they became *con van,* golden children. They could be the ticket to the United States for the relatives who rushed to claim them.

Our expectations of the mixed race movement should not be naïve. The mixed race movement can conceal a pessimistic message, namely that American society is most likely to flourish if it is monoracial rather than if it is multiracial. Few of its current adherents state their belief this way, but earlier enthusiasts of intermarriage candidly doubted that any culture could be sustained with numerous races. For them, intermarriage was the only hope and not the best hope. Cultural critic (then on the left, now on the right) Norman Podhoretz wrote that the "Negro problem" would not be solved unless we "let the brutal word come out—miscegenation."[59] Podhoretz would have been mortified if "a daughter of mine" were "'to marry one'," and he "would rail and rave and rant and tear my hair." However, he would hope to "have the courage to curse myself for raving and ranting, and to give her my blessing."[60] Political philosopher Hannah Arendt once made the same recommendation. Even though Arendt's argument was implicit rather than explicit, according to Harvard professor Werner Sollors, "she had a hard time getting her views published and generated a venomous debate." Even *Dissent* magazine, where the essay originally appeared, published a disclaimer and two separate rebuttals.[61] Intermarriage was the means of achieving a single racial identity. Native Americans, for example, could be rescued only if their cultures were destroyed and they were absorbed into white society. The Reverend Jedidiah Morse, an orthodox Calvinist, could try to save Indian souls by ensuring that they become "literally of one blood with us."[62]

The mixed race movement could bring about an unfortunate rediscovery: The most bitter enemies are your kin. Cousins can hate one another with an intensity not summoned against the unfamiliar. The great tragedies are family tragedies. Blood is the proper metaphor for race, even if it does not comport with biological fact.[63] Whites and blacks of the old South, masters and slaves, were often ill-fated relations. The world has witnessed, in the vengeful repetitiveness of divisive ethnic conflicts that emerge repeatedly, that people who know history can be damned to repeat it, as groups who seem to be the same to outsiders become all the more fierce for their similarity in their avowal that they are special and each is better than the other. It was their fellow Greeks, the Spartans, and not their foreign enemies, the Persians, who demolished the Athenian democracy; the hubris of the Athenians themselves hastened their downfall in the Peloponnesian War. Veteran political consultant Kevin Phillips argued in *The Cousin's Wars: Religion, Politics, and the Triumph of Anglo-America* that it was fratricide of the English Civil War, the American Revolution and the Civil War, that formed our national spirit.[64] The latest research has turned up intriguing hints that the Japanese and the Korean royal families

may once have been the same; their enmity becomes a feud like that of the British and the French.[65]

Our familiarity with other races also should not lead us to premature self-congratulation.[66] The clichéd rejoinder "many of my friends are black" is not persuasive, because that very friendship may mislead a person into treating those who are close to them as exceptions who prove the rules of race. Marrying someone of a different race provides no immunity from prejudice, as exposed by the ongoing case involving serial rapes of Asian American women in the Chicago area, the suspect in which was arrested in the Philippines when he visited his Filipina wife. Dating someone of a different race does not even grant a license to take liberties, as actor Ted Danson found out when he was dating comedian Whoopi Goldberg and he performed an embarrassing skit in blackface at the 1993 Friars Club roast in her honor. Having children who were of mixed racial background did not much move most of the white masters of slaves, other than to perform the gesture of manumitting them in a will.

At its best, the mixed race movement makes us think. Race may be fictional, but racism is real.[67] Although most of us may be reluctant to blame people who yearn for the benefits of passing, seeking privileges that many whites are not even aware of, we also may be hesitant to receive them as people of color, if they can conceal their identities when it is convenient.

The mixed race movement and passing give to some individuals who were assumed to be members of a stigmatized group the wherewithal to disassociate themselves from the group. It would be better if society recognized their right to belong to the groups of their choosing rather than coercing them into groups with whom they may have nothing in common. But it would be best if we stopped subjugating whole groups to the point where those who can would rather leave them. We will know we have achieved genuine racial equality when people who could claim to be white if they wanted to would rather stand up to say that they are proud to be black and they will lead lives within black communities. If everyone makes the same choice—white— then it is clear that there is no meaningful choice.

Perhaps the mixed race movement can be of lasting importance not by elevating some individuals out of the darker boxes but by persuading us that racial classifications in general are pernicious. If intermarriage and the mixed race movement are to live up to the optimistic claims that they are the future of race relations, they must hold out a greater promise than that some individuals can make a good match and a few individuals are able by themselves to ascend to whiteness. We will have accepted the mixed race movement as another form of our manifest diversity only when we know in our bones that "they" are "us."

NOTES

1. *Loving v. Virginia,* 388 U.S. 1 (1967).
2. David Greenberg, "White Weddings," *Slate,* June 14, 1999.
3. Jeanne Wakatsuki Houston, *Beyond Manzanar: Views of Asian American Womanhood* (Santa Barbara, Calif.: Capra Press, 1985), 20. This essay is reprinted in Russell Endo et al., *Asian Americans: Social Psychological Perspectives,* vol. 2 (Palo Alto, Calif.: Science and Behavior Books, 1980), 17–25.
4. James Weldon Johnson, *Along This Way* (New York: Viking, 1934).
5. Ibid., 170.
6. Gunnar Myrdal, *An American Dilemma: The Negro Problem and Modern Democracy* (New York: Harper & Row, 1944), 60–61.
7. Sidney Kaplan, "The Miscegenation Issues in the Election of 1864)" in Werner Sollors, ed., *Interracialism: Black-White Intermarriage in American History, Literature, and the Law* (Oxford: Oxford University Press, 2000), 219.
8. Michael Lind, *The Next American Nation: The New Nationalism and the Fourth American Revolution* (New York, Free Press, 1995), 291.
9. Theodore G. Bilbo, *Take Your Choice: Separation or Mongrelization* (Poplarville, Miss.: Dream House Publishing Co., 1947).
10. Ibid., frontispiece.
11. Ibid., 198.
12. Ibid., 201.
13. Ibid., appendix A.
14. Tom Brady, *Black Monday* (Winona, Miss.: Association of Citizens' Councils, 1954), 88.
15. Ibid., 89.
16. Charles Herbert Stember, *Sexual Racism: The Emotional Barrier to an Integrated Society* (New York: Elsevier, 1976), 24–25.
17. Norman Mailer, *Advertisements for Myself* (New York: G.P. Putnam's Sons, 1959), 332. Mailer also says in his famous "White Negro" essay that "the deeper issue is not desegregation but miscegenation." Ibid., 356.
18. Richard Wright, *Native Son* (New York: Literary Classics of America, 1991), 525–26, 667–68.
19. Lind, *Next American Nation,* 290.
20. Robert E. Kuttner, "Race Mixing: Suicide or Salvation," *American Mercury* (Winter 1971): 45–48.
21. Paul R. Spickard, *Mixed Blood: Intermarriage and Ethnic Identity in Twentieth-Century America* (Madison, Wis.: University of Wisconsin Press, 1989), 25.
22. William D. Zabel, "Interracial Marriage and the Law," in Sollors, *Interracialism,* 54.
23. Sollors, *Interracialism,* 13.
24. Darryl Fears and Claudia Deane, "Biracial Couples Report Tolerance; Survey Finds Most Are Accepted by Families," *Washington Post,* July 5, 2001, A1.
25. Flavia Tam et al., *Inter-Generational Paper on Asian American Attitudes Towards Family Values, Interracial Dating and Marriage* (Washington, D.C.: Organization of Chinese Americans, 1998). *See also* Betty Lee Sung, *Chinese American Intermarriage* (New York: Center for Migration Studies, 1990).
26. Timur Kuran, *Private Truths, Public Lies: The Social Consequences of Preference Falsification*

(Cambridge, Mass.: Harvard University Press, 1995).

27. Arnold Rampersad, ed., *The Collected Poems of Langston Hughes* (New York: Alfred A. Knopf, 1995), 305. The "tragic mulatto" was a recurring theme of Hughes's; he later turned "Cross" into a play.

28. Fawn M. Brodie, *Thomas Jefferson: An Intimate History* (New York: W.W. Norton, 1974); Annette Gordon-Reed, *Thomas Jefferson and Sally Hemings: An American Controversy* (Charlottesville: University Press of Virginia, 1997).

29. Leef Smith, "Tests Link Jefferson, Slave's Son; DNA Suggests a Monticello Liaison," *Washington Post,* November 1, 1998, A1. The scientific data were reported in Eugene A. Foster et al., "Jefferson Fathered Slave's Last Child," *Nature* 396 (November 5, 1998): 27–28 and Eric S. Lander and Joseph J. Ellis, "Founding Father," *Nature* 396 (November 5, 1998): 13–14.

30. Joseph J. Ellis, *American Sphinx: The Character of Thomas Jefferson* (New York: Knopf, 1997), 20. For an example of the pre-genetic testing debate, *see* Edwin McDowell, "Jefferson Liaison Is Disputed Again," *New York Times,* June 2, 1981, C7.

31. Itabari Njeri, "The Challenge of Diversity in an L.A. Cultural Crucible; In Crenshaw Neighborhood, Japanese-American, Blacks Have Forged a History of Complex Relationships," *Los Angeles Times,* May 2, 1990, E1.

32. John Updike, "Metamorphosis," *New Yorker,* August 9, 1999, 66–70. The title alludes to Franz Kafka's short story of the same name in which Gregor Samsa awakes to find himself transformed into a giant cockroach.

33. Terry McMillan, *Waiting to Exhale* (New York: Viking Productions, 1992).

34. Ibid., 329.

35. Ibid., 29–30.

36. Poppy Cannon, *A Gentle Knight: My Husband, Walter White* (New York: Rhinehart & Co., 1956), 12–13. The O.J. Simpson murder trial, in which he was acquitted of the murders of his ex-wife Nicole and her friend Ronald Goldman, also focused attention on the complexities of interracial marriages. *See* Jacqueline Adams, "The White Wife," *New York Times Magazine,* September 18, 1994, 36–38.

37. Cannon, *Gentle Knight,* 14.

38. Walter White, *A Man Called White: The Autobiography of Walter White* (New York: Viking Press, 1948), 338.

39. Juan Williams, *Thurgood Marshall: American Revolutionary* (New York: Times Books, 1998), 244.

40. Lynn Norment, "The Best Weddings of the Last 50 Years," *Ebony* (June 1995): 82.

41. Robert Suro, "Mixed Doubles," *American Demographics* (November 1999): 58.

42. Jon Michael Spencer, *The New Colored People: The Mixed-Race Movement in America* (New York: New York University Press, 1997).

43. Kathy Russell, Midge Wilson and Ronald Hall, *The Color Complex: The Politics of Skin Color Among African Americans* (New York: Doubleday, Anchor Books, 1992).

44. William Hannibal Thomas, *The American Negro: What He Was, What He Is, and What He May Become: A Critical and Practical Discussion* (New York: Macmillan, 1901). *See also* John David Smith, *Black Judas: William Hannibal Thomas and the American Negro* (Athens: University of Georgia Press, 2000).

45. Mezz Mezzrow, *Really the Blues: An Autobiography* (New York: Random House, 1946).

46. Associated Press, "Slave Descendant Fights Race Listing," *New York Times,* September 15, 1982, A1; Calvin Trillin, "American Chronicles: Black or White," *New Yorker,* April 14, 1986, 62–78.

47. Lauren Kessler, *Stubborn Twig: Three Generations in the Life of a Japanese-American Family* (New York: Random House, 1993).

48. Woods ultimately decided on cheeseburgers and French Fries, an historic first. Thomas Bonk, "It's Food That's Fit for This Golf King; The Masters: Wood's Choice for the Traditional Tournament Dinner Includes Cheeseburgers and Fries," *Los Angeles Times,* April 7, 1998, C1.

49. Hal Bock, "The Inside Track; Say What You Mean, Mean What You Say," *Los Angeles Times,* April 27, 1997, C2.

50. Gary Smith, "The Chosen; Tiger Woods Was Raised to Believe That His Destiny Is Not Only to Be the Greatest Golfer Ever, But Also to Change the World. Will the Pressures of Celebrity Grind Him Down First?" *Sports Illustrated,* December 23, 1996, 28.

51. Claudine Chiawei O'Hearn, *Half and Half: Writers on Growing Up Biracial and Bicultural* (New York: Pantheon Books, 1998), xxxiv.

52. Lucy M. Cohen, *Chinese in the Post Civil-War South: A People Without A History* (Baton Rouge. La.: University of Louisiana Press, 1984); James Loewen, *The Mississippi Chinese: Between Black and White* (Cambridge, Mass.: Harvard University Press, 1971).

53. Karen Isaksen Leonard, *Making Ethnic Choices: California's Punjabi Mexican Americans* (Philadelphia: Temple University Press, 1992).

54. Darby Li Po Price, "Mixed Laughter," in Paul Spickard and W. Jeffrey Burroughs, eds., *We Are a People: Narrative and Multiplicity in Constructing Ethnic Identity* (Philadelphia: Temple University Press, 2000), 179.

55. Leef Smith, "A Powhatan Princess in Their Past; Disney's 'Pocahontas' Inspires Virginians to Shake the Family Tree," *Washington Post,* July 3, 1995, B1. Regarding Indian identity, *see generally* Joane Nagel, *American Indian Ethnic Renewal: Red Power and the Resurgence of Identity and Culture* (New York: Oxford University Press, 1986).

56. For a discussion of these issues, *see* William S. Penn, *As We Are Now: Mixblood Essays on Race and Identity* (Berkeley: University of California Press, 1997).

57. For a contemporary account of Indian life, *see* Ian Frazier, *On the Rez* (New York: Farrar, Straus & Giroux, 2000).

58. Kieu-Linh Caroline Valverde, "From Dust to Gold: The Vietnamese Amerasian Experience," in Maria P.P. Root, ed., *Racially Mixed People in America* (Newbury Park, Calif.: Sage, 1992), 144–61.

59. Norman Podhoretz, "My Negro Problem— And Ours," *Commentary* (February 1963): 93–101. He wrote a postscript to this famous essay thirty years later. *See* Mark Gerson, ed., *The Essential Neoconservative Reader* (Reading, Mass.: Addison-Wesley, 1996), 18–22.

60. Ibid., 101

61. Hannah Arendt, "Reflections on Little Rock," in Sollors, *Interracialism,* 492–502. Sollors's account of the reaction to Arendt's article is in Werner Sollors, *Neither Black Nor White Yet Both: Thematic Explorations of Interracial Literature* (Cambridge: Harvard University Press, 1997), 316.

62. Robert William Fogel, *The Fourth Great Awakening and the Future of Egalitarianism* (Chicago: University of Chicago Press, 2000), 96.

63. Michael Ignatieff, *Blood and Belonging: Journeys into the New Nationalism* (New York: Farrar, Straus & Giroux, 1993).

64. Kevin Phillips, *The Cousins' Wars: Religion, Politics, and the Triumph of Anglo-America* (New York: Basic, 1999).

65. Alissa Quart, "The Lost Emperors: Japanese Scholars Struggle to Unearth the Past," *Lingua Franca* (December 2000/January 2001): 55–59.

66. Benjamin DeMott, *The Trouble with Friendship: Why Americans Can't Think Straight About Race* (New York: Atlantic Monthly Press, 1995).

67. Race has been dead for some time as a serious concept in the hard sciences. For a recent survey of the literature, I have relied on Joseph L. Graves Jr., *The Emperor's New Clothes: Biological Theories of Race at the Millennium* (New Brunswick, N.J.: Rutgers University Press, 2001).

47
_____

TEN TRUTHS OF INTERRACIAL MARRIAGE

Maria Root

QUESTIONS TO CONSIDER

In her extensive research on interracial dating and marriage patterns in the United States Maria Root was finally moved to ask "what distinguished families who could take in a racially different family member from those who could not." How does she answer this question? How did her list, "ten truths about interracial marriage," challenge your own beliefs about love across the color line?

I n 1944 the Swedish sociologist Gunnar Myrdal published his classic study of race relations, *An American Dilemma: The Negro Problem and Modern Democracy*. In identifying race as the American dilemma, Myrdal echoed W.E.B. Du Bois's observation half a century earlier that the color line would be the problem of the twentieth century. At the dawn of the twenty-first century, with Jim Crow laws and other legal barriers gone but not forgotten, we still struggle with the problem of race in America. And while race is no longer an issue only for black and white Americans, it remains defined by a long history that constructed black and white relations. This explains why even though only one-quarter of interracial marriages take place between black and white partners, intermarriage still predominantly conjures up images of black and white. Ironically, some of the younger participants in my

study, who had not learned all the old, harmful rules of race, did not see their relationship as interracial because it was not black and white.

One of the obstacles to progress may be that racism and sexism, and the power struggles within each sphere, have been regarded as separate. Psychologist Aida Hurtado observes that the difficulties of feminist theory in analyzing gender subordination are similar to the difficulties of race theorists analyzing race. Whereas both are analyzed as evidence of institutionalized imbalances in structural power, they are not constructed simultaneously.[1] Sociologist Abby Ferber[2] and philosopher Naomi Zack[3] also observe how imperative it is to understand the simultaneous influences and intersections of race and gender. My study demonstrates that when we see race and gender as master statuses connected by sex and fear of interracial sexuality, we gain a better understanding of the ways in which race and gender are constructed. This finding helps us understand why interracial marriage is not more common and why we seem to be moving toward increased possibilities of interracial intimacy, dissolving centuries of racial apartheid in intimate relationships and kinship networks.

Interracial relationships, and particularly interracial marriage, leave a permanent record of a transgression against what has been considered normal, "sticking with your own kind." They challenge the privilege and property of whiteness and any other rigid category of race—or gender. Some people fear that opening the way to interracial marriage might open the door to same-sex marriage and violate other cultural norms. Thus interracial marriage is a vehicle for examining race and gender relations as well as the structures that shape them. Anthropologist Roger Sanjek notes that "Race, sex and power remain the essential ingredients of the continuing 'American dilemma' of the United States . . . the power of race has long been expressed and mediated through sex. Rape, forced disruption of black conjugal ties and kinship networks, sexual mythology and fear, and legal bars to interracial marriage, and the overriding of kinship by race are historic features of the race-sex-power equation."[4]

Although the "colors of race" have expanded through imported labor and immigration, we see that race has achieved a more rapid transformation from a fictional category based on real or imagined physical features, essence of character, and capabilities to ethnicity for virtually all groups except blacks. And with this transformation from a racial caste category to an ethnic class category, objections based on "essences" recede. Thus, although there are objections to all forms of intermarriage, the strongest objections still pertain to black-white marriage.

Participants in my study repeatedly illustrated the point that race is a social and cultural invention, a make-believe tale that is hard to stop believing. Americans even today have countless devices that we use to convince ourselves that race is more than a fiction, that it is a real division between people that must be observed and respected. Afro-American Studies Professor Henry Louis Gates lists these devices that proclaim race to be real: birth certificates, biographical sketches, treatises, certificates, pamphlets, and so on.[5] The result is that race becomes very confusing, its boundaries simultaneously real and unreal. The meaning placed on interracial marriage, biracial children, or multiple and simultaneous racial alliances is part of the struggle to come to terms with the race fiction Europeans and Americans invented. President Clinton's Race Advisory Board chairman John Hope Franklin wrote, "stereotypes remain because Americans cling to the idea that it is best to try to ignore race. That, in turn, forces people to bury—and therefore harbor—beliefs they form from stereotypes heard at school, in the media and from family members."[6] In the public discussions hosted by this advisory board, comments on interracial marriage and the classification of multiracial children were conspicuous for their absence. The board contained no representatives of the various multiracial groups in this country. Even in a progressive attempt to discuss race, race was bounded and bordered, creating a fiction that race mixing is inconsequential to the American landscape of race, gender, and politics despite a history of legislative struggle for civil rights against a backdrop of fear.[7] Bigotry, fear, and denial are still formidable forces in this country's racial culture. Lynnette, a white woman, reflected on how racial boundaries were reinforced by her black husband, even in her own interracial family:

> I think it is the way we view ourselves as interracial. My husband, though, is not very accepting of white people. He doesn't view me as white, he never really kinda has. I don't know what kind of perception he has. So in some ways that has been a split in providing some more unity to the

family. He's very color conscious. He says a lot of things at home that could be divisive and the kids don't feel comfortable with . . . my daughter will go around and tease him with things like, "I'm going to marry somebody white, and know the color of this family."

This husband probably had no intention of creating an interracial family. But, ironically, by in effect using the one-drop rule invented to serve white male privilege, his family becomes a black family and he remains authentically black. He has also applied male privilege in denying his wife's racial identity, knowing that his racial identity will dominate hers, rather than the other way around. The experience of the younger generation, raised in the aftermath of civil rights reforms, confirms that race is socially constructed by the majority.

Families are the initial socializing agent, in questions of race as in everything else. As a psychologist, my prime interest in developing this study was to understand the process of political, social, and spiritual transformation that interracial marriages instigate in families. It seems that the theories of the past were limited by the attitudes of the era in which they evolved. Female gender roles in this American drama were either passive roles or victim roles, pawns rather than agents. Women have always been central to the creation and maintenance of families, and my research strongly suggests that current theories must make the role of women central in race relations, racial construction, and interracial marriage. A year after her daughter's wedding to a black man, Ann, a white woman from Seattle, had gained new respect for her daughter's ability to make independent decisions and saw her as an embodiment of the changing roles of women.

Probably extended family members would have more concern than her own parents, since we know her well. In a sense, we were

more surprised than upset about the dating going on. But she has also, for two summers, gone fishing on a commercial fishing boat, so what I am saying is she's probably broken ground in other areas by being the first. . . . My sisters and I would never have been on a commercial fishing boat with four or five men. But a new generation. I guess she is more of a risk taker than perhaps myself. . . . We had visiting students in our home where we raised our kids. So I think that added to her feeling she could come to us and share this. Our home was open. So I was surprised, but I wasn't offended. I didn't go home or cry or stew or anything. I think probably behind doors some of our extended family did. For example, we had a grandpa who was in his eighties, and so there may have been some rolling of the eyes, so to speak. But my husband and I were anxious to meet him . . . [and] he is wonderful. They were married about a year ago. He enhances our family, and if the others don't see it, that's their problem. But they came to the wedding, and grandpa came.

One of the main questions I sought to answer was what distinguished families who could take in a racially different family member from those who could not. As T. W. Adorno and his colleagues showed, the definition of who can belong to a family and who cannot is a way of asserting and maintaining authority and privilege. But in order to do this, tremendous self-deception must be practiced, for it involves the rewriting of the character and contributions of whole groups of people.[8] It became clear in thinking about families as variations of closed or open systems that the key element in distinguishing these families was the degree to which racial reproduction was considered a significant product of the family. This led me to realize that even in modern America, families are about business: mergers, franchises, and acquisitions. And when one becomes a liability to the business of family, the pain and rejection that follow can cause deep and lasting wounds. Regardless of what happens to a marriage, whether it is a lifelong success or a short-lived fiasco, one cannot go home the same person who was banished from the original corporation.

The dynamics that prevailed in closed, pseudo-closed, and even pseudo-open families had the elements of psychologist Gordon Allport's ten sociocultural laws of prejudice.[9] Allport noted that at the root of discrimination, ten conditions fed and sustained prejudice. The more conditions that were present in any particular place or time, the more likely we would be to see prejudiced personalities. Allport defined these conditions as follows:

> Where the social structure is marked by heterogeneity;
>
> Where vertical mobility is permitted;
>
> Where rapid social change is in progress;
>
> Where there are ignorance and barriers to communication;
>
> Where the size of a minority group is large or increasing;
>
> Where direct competition and realistic threats exist;
>
> Where exploitation sustains important interests in the community;
>
> Where customs regulating aggression are favorable to bigotry;
>
> Where traditional justifications for ethnocentrism are available; and
>
> Where neither assimilation nor cultural pluralism is favored.[10]

Allport's conclusions are important to this study. We live in a period of rapidly changing gender roles, technological development and expansion, and increased global and cultural exchange—in an increasingly competitive world. Many of Allport's conditions prevail now. Simultaneously, we have a young generation of people operating under some changing principles of competition, discrimination, and gender role expansion.

Discussions of interracial marriage through the past century have replicated the very dynamics that are central to it; that is, they usually take place intraracially rather than interracially. The black feminist scholar bell hooks notes that racial reality looks quite different when constructed from a white perspective than it does from a black perspective.[11] Historian Paul Spickard's research on intermarriage documented the significant protest in communities of color against aspects of integration and miscegenation.[12] In the course of his work as an attorney for the NAACP before his appointment to the U.S. Supreme Court, Thurgood Marshall noted that the difficulty with repealing Jim Crow laws and reversing *Plessy v. Ferguson* was the opposition from black communities.[13] The audible voice of protest, whether white or non-white, has been male. The voices of people of color and women have been muffled and marginalized, though they are so central to the phenomenon.[14]

Racial intermarriage looks quite different from a male perspective than from a female perspective. Women's primary responsibility for childbearing and child rearing makes them central to any discussion of interracial mixing. In these discussions, women and their bodies have historically been seen as the property of men. Rod, a black man in his thirties, provided a glimpse of this double standard in black families and communities when I asked him how his family was likely to react if his sisters married interracially. Rod was married to a white woman.

> Well, you know, honestly, they would probably not be accepted. We're all educated and cordial, but then again, when our family gets together, there's no telling

who's going to say what or who's going to
do what and if there's something like this
introduced that's upsetting, anything can
happen. You know, a person might, he
might be called a white boy or he might
be caught in a deep conversation that
you're not normally exposed to black
perception—real black perception. And
it's oftentimes difficult for someone of a
different race to socialize with the family
because those real realities come and so
that's uncomfortable. So for the men, most
of the men, we have had relationships,
have brought the women to a family
gathering, but not for my sisters. Too much
negative response from the family. I
believe that a lot of that has to do with how
the women's role is perceived by the men in
our family and that the rules [for] women
[with] regard to interracial relationships is
generally not something the men in our
family saw. The history of white men using
black women. We're suspicious.

My research has led me to conclude that
women will become central gatekeepers of
race and racial construction, reconstruction,
and deconstruction. Women, rather than
being pawns, are central figures in the growth
of interracial marriage. Increased female
financial independence, access and options
for birth control—even abortion—as well as
geographic mobility and relocation, provide
more control over a woman's choice of partners. Already intermarriage rates for Asian
American women, Hispanic women, and
American Indian women are substantial, and
often higher than for their male counterparts.
With the sex-ratio imbalances in the African
American communities across the country,
with more women of marriageable age than
available men; with the advanced education
of a growing number of African American
women; with the inscription of blackness
on mixed-race children regardless of the sex
of the parent who is black; and with the
assignment of child cultural socialization to

women, African American women will become significant to the discussion on interracial marriage as their rates of intermarriage
increase. This will be a direct contrast to their
forced interracial experiences in previous
eras.[15] I believe that the current reconstruction of black femininity will be related to
continued examinations of race and gender
and their intersection through sex and interracial relationships and marriage. White
women will continue to make choices across
color lines; when both gender and race are
taken into account, white women's power in
its totality is not that different from that of
men of color. Thus, the potential outcome
of such transformations may be that discussions of race will increasingly have a female
voice.

Sanjek suggests that the transformation
of race to ethnicity will likewise allow some
people of color to assume privileges that were
previously reserved for whiteness. Recall that
Roberta, the white grandmother introduced
earlier, has a biracial Asian-white grandson.
When I asked if she now saw her family as an
interracial or mixed family, she replied, "Oh,
yes. . . . We're all white." By defining race in
black and white terms—even though her
Japanese son-in-law is not considered white
by U.S. racial classifications, and her grandson is not considered "really" white by those
who patrol the borders of whiteness—Roberta
makes her daughter's marriage less objectionable. Her answer, ironically, can be seen
as a way of reconstructing race by broadening
the boundaries of whiteness. But can these
boundaries be broadened to include mixing
with the black population? Without this
expansion, we will not accomplish true racial
deconstruction but only the reconstruction of
whiteness. Attempts to retain a white ethnic
identity—for example, Polish American, Irish
American, Italian American—do not have to
feed white supremacist notions or reinforce
the fiction of race. Unfortunately, whiteness

as race in the U.S. seems to tolerate only symbolic ethnicity, particularly for newer immigrant groups.[16] Perhaps this is also part of the explanation for the distance between black and white—that many if not most blacks will not willingly give up their African American identity.

Though they make strange bedfellows, love and prejudice can coexist between partners, as I saw again and again in my research. Sometimes this was manifested in acts of collusion in which partners left their spouses standing alone to take their family's racial prejudice and abuse. I doubt that intermarriage is the solution to all of America's race problems in America. But it does provide one avenue for the challenging of stereotypes, particularly when it involves an extended kinship network of different-race and mixed-race kin. It is an opportunity to move into a different dialogue about race, a dialogue in which the voices of multiracial adult children and women and people of color can also be heard. Intermarriage will soon affect a substantial portion of Americans of all colors.

Individual and family identities may be transformed through these marriages. In her recent work, bell hooks has emphasized love as action and attitude that can inspire us to end oppressive practices. Whereas Martin Luther King, Jr. and others stressed the political uses and meanings of love, we hear love discussed less frequently in these terms as a powerful and transcendent force.[17] Joseph Campbell spoke to the transformation that marriage heralds when he wrote, "Marriage is not a simple love affair, it's an ordeal, and the ordeal is the sacrifice of ego to a relationship in which two have become one."[18] Campbell's statement is reflected in Martin Luther King, Jr.'s observation that "all men [and women] are caught in an inescapable network of mutuality, tied in a single garment of destiny. Whatever affects one directly affects all indirectly."[19] At its most

intense, love provides a reminder that two people have merged their lives and that they are having to negotiate some new boundaries and definitions of self. In the case of interracial love, some fictions around race must be challenged. People are resilient when they are deeply in love. They are open to new ideas and experiences because their love can override fear. Thus they promise hope of transformation in attitudes. The partnership between individualism, so highly prized by American culture, and romantic love makes interracial marriage an increasing possibility for most families now that legal barriers have been removed.

The psychologist Robert Sternberg found that three components form romantic love, the major motivating force in the marriage decisions of almost all of the participants in my study. The degree of their presence determines the quality or definition of love in a relationship.[20] First, he notes that there is an intimacy component from which connectedness arises. The intimacy involved in a lasting love relationship has several dimensions that are neither defined nor limited by race. Prager observes that intimacy can occur at different levels: (1) the frequency of personal sharing; (2) the depth and risk involved in the sharing; and (3) the amount of sharing that takes place and continues over time.[21] Conversations about racial experiences, culture, gender, and class were part of the experiences that provided a depth to the intimacy many participants had with their partners.

Second, there is a passion component that drives the initial physical attraction and sexual desire. In stereotypes of interracial relationships, the first component—intimacy—is often dismissed and only sexual desire and attraction are given credence as motivating forces. The third component is commitment, which requires a person to distinguish between liking and loving, infatuation and love, and lust and love.

When an interracial marriage or engage-ment is met with hostility, its opponents assume that the individuals involved lack the capacity to make the commitment that is Sternberg's third component of romantic love. Instead, interracial love is constructed as an immature form of attachment motivated by anger, rebellion, and pathology, rather than as an engulfing, embracing form of love that John Welwood describes as a soul con-nection. Two people come together to realize their deepest potential—to be the best people *they* can be.[22] When motivations and indi-viduals are stereotyped in a dismissive way, all individuals who love across color lines are seen as more similar than dissimilar. But research offers little data to support the notion that there is a consistent profile or type that is more inclined than others to intermarriage.[23]

In one of the few empirical studies designed to examine profiles of persons who intermarry, a longitudinal family study in Hawaii, Johnson and colleagues found few differences between groups. Among women who intermarried and women who did not, Asian American women who married inter-racially tended to be more independent than Asian American women who did not. Men who intermarried were less domineering than men who did not.[24] Even though this study was conducted almost twenty years ago, it captured an important aspect of flexibility in gender roles that I think contributes to the possibility of intermarriage. Many of the white men married to women of color in the study seemed willing to give up some aspects of white male privilege. Many were willing to be minorities in racial or ethnic communities. While I do not suggest that a white man in a black or Asian or Hispanic community suffers the same discrimination that a black or Asian or Hispanic or Indian man does in a white community, Johnson's findings suggest that these white men had less investment in maintaining a special sense of self through their whiteness.

With flexibility to redefine masculine and feminine roles in relationships, the heart of what might be exchanged between people may be more difficult to pinpoint. Such changes may also redefine standards of phys-ical attractiveness. For example, an attrac-tive man does not have to be tall; an attrac-tive woman does not have to be small or thin. If standards of attractiveness can extend beyond European standards of beauty, so, perhaps, can our motivation to know persons who would otherwise not be of interest. If our culture ever reaches the point where height is not associated with power, we might also see more frequent exceptions to one of the rules of heterosexual coupling, that is, that the male is supposed to be taller than the female. The ability to break this rule would reflect an expansion of the definitions of masculinity and femininity. Just as we have invented fic-tions about race and gender, we maintain many fictions about physical attractiveness as well. Race, ethnicity, and class influence what we consider acceptable and desirable gender roles. Living in a more pluralistic way could make physical attraction that much more mysterious, because we would become that much more aware of how socially and culturally conditioned attraction is.

It is no wonder that love is difficult to study. Although it can be a psychological state of mind, a judgment, an action, or an orientation, the meaning of love can be so individualistic as to make its study frustrat-ingly complicated. Seldom is the love that binds people together the subject of studies of interracial marriage. Yet I observed that despite cultural, class, gender, religious, and racial differences, people satisfied essential needs through their partners that seemed to transcend these categories.

Despite the human drama that accom-panies every search for love, companionship, and understanding, interracial marriage is most often depicted as foolhardy and irrational rather than heroic. At some level it seems easy for many people to dismiss interracial love as irrationality, infatuation, curiosity, or immaturity—a stage that will pass. Or else it is simply fetishized—she has a thing for black men, he has a thing for Asian women.

The irrationality of love has been associated with "addiction" or "fatal attraction"—and interracial love has certainly been depicted as irrational, addictive, even fetishistic. Fortunately, Peele and Brodsky untangle these issues in their book *Love and Addiction*.[25] They offer eight ways that infatuation and sustained love can be distinguished. In contrast to addiction, love is

1. an expansive experience rather than total focus on another person;
2. a helping relationship rather than idealization of another person;
3. an opportunity for enhanced growth rather than retreat to a private world;
4. the intensification of pleasure in life rather than intensification of pain;
5. a productive and beneficial experience rather than an incapacitating one;
6. a natural outcome of one's self and life rather than purely accidental and tentative;
7. an experience that continues and intensifies friendship and affection rather than an all-or-nothing experience; and
8. a responsibility that has an attendant heightened awareness rather than an uncontrollable urge or unconscious motivation.

The participants in my study all spoke of love as a motivating force for their choices. Although some divorced and some married persons reflected on their naïveté or youthful optimism at the time of their marriage, these marriages were about love. Participants referred to the psychological needs they thought their relationships provided. When both partners had the ability to work, emotional and relational needs took precedence over instrumental needs.

The hundreds of hours of interviews and background research I conducted can be distilled into what I call "Ten Truths About Interracial Marriage."

1. The civil rights movement and subsequent patterns of racial desegregation created opportunities for people to interact in meaningful ways, which has resulted in an increased rate of interracial marriage.
2. In the past twenty-five years, women's decreased financial dependence on their families has given them freedom to choose mates regardless of family approval.
3. Love, shared vision, and common values compel an interracial couple to marry, just as they do other couples.
4. The motives behind interracial marriage seldom include the desire to rebel or to make a political or social statement.
5. Families that reject an interracial marriage value the reproduction of their race over love, integrity, and commitment.
6. In order to live in an affirming emotional climate, an interracial couple may have to replace estranged blood kin with a fictive family of friends.
7. Conflicts within interracial marriages are more likely to arise from cultural, gender, class, social, and personal differences than from racial ones.
8. Irreconcilable differences within interracial marriages are similar to those within same-race marriages: loss of respect, unwillingness to compromise, hurtful actions, lack of responsibility, dishonesty, and conflicting values.

9. The rate of divorce for interracial marriages is only slightly higher than for same-race couples in the continental United States; the gap is quickly closing as divorce rates rise for all marriages.

10. Interracial couples can and do produce healthy, well-adjusted children.

In Puccini's last opera, *Turandot,* set in legendary Peking, the Chinese princess Turandot declares that she will accept the hand of the suitor who can answer three riddles. Those who try and fail will be executed, allowing Turandot to avenge an ancestor who was raped and murdered by a Tartar prince. Unbeknownst to her, one of the suitors, Prince Calaf, is the son of the exiled king of Tartary. Turandot lives in the past and Calaf in the future, as she reminds him that failure to solve the three riddles results in death and he reminds her of the possibility of life. "Turandot poses the first enigma: what rises at night, invoked by all the world, only to die at dawn reborn in the heart? Calaf rightly answers: hope. The second riddle is: what darts like a flame but is not a flame, that grows cold with death yet blazes with dreams of conquest? Turandot is furious when Calaf solves it with the answer: blood. Thirdly she demands what inflames you, white yet dark, that enslaves if it wants you free, but in taking you captive makes you king. Calaf, after hesitation, answers: Turandot."[26] Seeing her fear and fury at losing her superior position, he offers her his head nonetheless if she can discover his identity by dawn. No one in the kingdom sleeps that night as his identity is sought. Just before dawn, his father and his attendant, Liù, are brought before her. Liù, protective of the exiled king and pressed by Turandot to explain why she would endure torture or even death for him, answers "love." The concept is foreign to Turandot, but she is nevertheless moved momentarily. She soon recovers herself, however, and has Liù's tongue cut out.

Calaf appears and reveals his identity as the son of the exiled king. Turandot believes she has turned the tables and has restored her power over him. Fearless in the face of death, he kisses her as a challenge to experience his love. With his identity in her possession, Turandot surprises all. She opens her heart after years of lovelessness and reveals Calaf's name to the court as Love, thus sparing his life and starting hers anew, freed from her fear and hatred of Tartars.

Whereas the riddles are solved with the answers hope, blood, and love, these are indeed real-life enigmas when it comes to discussions of interracial marriage. Interracial marriage gives us hope that love can transcend some of the barriers that legislation has not. Its power to transform us, one at a time, cannot be underestimated, allowing us to release the hate, fear, and guilt of the past and move into the future with love as a political device. Despite some almost universal propensities for stratification, competition, and ethnocentrism, I believe that with stealth and persistence the people in my study demonstrated that love has the capacity to erode the fear and hate that have blemished many a participant's family landscape. Interracial marriage and its children provide an opportunity for a different discussion of race relations within the power matrices formed by race, gender, and ethnicity. Today's children are tomorrow's adults. I hope we teach them well.

NOTES

1. A. Hurtado, *The Color of Privilege: Three Blasphemies on Race and Feminism* (Ann Arbor: The University of Michigan Press, 1996), p. 33.

2. Ferber, *White Man Falling.*

3. N. Zack, *Race/Sex: Their Sameness, Difference, and Interplay* (New York: Routledge, 1997).

4. Sanjek, "Intermarriage," p. 103.

5. H. L. Gates, Jr., *Thirteen Ways of Looking at a Black Man* (New York: Vintage Books, 1997), pp. 207–8.

6. *Seattle Post-Intelligencer,* "Race Advisory Board."

7. H. Ball, *A Defiant Life: Thurgood Marshall and the Persistence of Racism in America* (New York, Crown Publishers, 1998); I. Bernstein, *Guns or Butter: The Presidency of Lyndon Johnson* (New York: Oxford University Press, 1996).

8. Adorno et al., *The Authoritarian Personality.*

9. G. W. Allport, *The Nature of Prejudice* (Reading, Mass.: Addison-Wesley, 1954; 1979).

10. Ibid., p. 221.

11. hooks, "Representing Whiteness."

12. Spickard, *Mixed Blood.*

13. Ball, *A Defiant Life.*

14. Frankenburg, *White Women, Race Matters.*

15. Spickard, *Mixed Blood;* Wyatt, *Stolen Women.*

16. Waters, *Ethnic Options.*

17. b. hooks, *All about Love: New Visions* (New York, William Morrow, 2000).

18. Quoted in Erlich and de Bruhl, eds., *Thesaurus of Quotations,* p. 411.

19. Ibid., p. 143.

20. R. J. Sternberg, "A Triangular Theory of Love," *Psychological Review* 93: 119–35.

21. K. Prager, *The Psychology of Intimacy* (New York: Guilford Press, 1995), pp. 259–66.

22. Welwood, *Love and Awakening.*

23. Tucker and Mitchell-Kernan, "New Trends in Black American Interracial Marriage."

24. Nagoshi et al., "Assortative Mating"; see also Ahern et al., "Personality Attributes."

25. S. Peele, "Fools for Love: The Romantic Ideal, Psychological Theory, and Addictive Love," in *The Psychology of Love,* ed. R. J. Sternberg and M. L. Barnes (New Haven: Yale University Press, 1988), pp. 179–82, a review of some of the earlier work of Peele and Brodsky.

26. Earl of Harewood and Antony Peattie, eds., *The New Kobbe's Opera Book* (New York, Putnam, 1997), p. 610.

LIVING WITH LESS RACISM: STRATEGIES FOR INDIVIDUAL ACTION

48

TEN SIMPLE THINGS YOU CAN DO TO IMPROVE RACE RELATIONS

Charles A. Gallagher

QUESTIONS TO CONSIDER

Photocopy and pass along my "Ten Things You Can Do to Improve Race Relations" to family, friends, teachers, spiritual leaders, brothers, and sisters. Please contact me with any additions you might have for my list. I can be reached at cgallagher@gsu.edu.

The study of race and ethnic relations in the United States can be a rather depressing and disempowering undertaking. Ongoing institutional racism in education, employment, housing, lending, and law enforcement; continued wealth and income disparities between racial groups; and the persistence of racial prejudice and discrimination in most spheres of social life may leave one with the impression that nothing can be done to improve race relations. The modern civil rights movement was three hundred years in the making, and while movement toward racial equality has been substantial, racism and racial inequality still infect our nation and poison civic life. Such prejudice and inequality persist in part because changing the institutional barriers that allocate occupational and educational opportunity is a slow and difficult task. Upward mobility for different racial and ethnic groups is typically measured in generations rather than decades or years. One is tempted to throw one's hands in the air and yell, "There is nothing I can do!!!" But there is. You have the power to influence your family, friends, and peers by discussing the topics raised in this class. At the individual, interpersonal, and community level you can engage in activities to promote equal opportunity while building bridges between people from different racial backgrounds. Understanding the root causes of ethnic and racial inequality in the United States and examining in this class the facts, theories, evidence, and examples that pertain to such inequality will allow you to explain to others why racism and racial and ethnic inequality remain so stubbornly part of our culture. You now have the sociological tools to calmly, intelli-

gently, and rationally engage in conversations with other adults about racism in America and what individuals, institutions, and the government *could* and *should* do to fashion a society where equal opportunity exists for all groups. Following are ten simple things you can do as you go about your day to raise your own and other people's consciousness about race relations and racial justice in America.

1. Talk to Your Family

Respectfully engage your friends and family in what you learned in this class. If you have family members that are racist or use stereotypes, ask them politely and nonjudgmentally why they harbor such animosity towards a whole group of people. Did they have a bad experience with someone from that group? Ask them if they have ever been the target of animosity or hatred because of their race, ethnic background, religion, or nationality. How did such an encounter make them feel? Were their parents or grandparents ever subject to such prejudice or discrimination? Why? Ask them if they think their prejudice or racism violates the American creed of equal treatment and opportunity for all regardless of group membership. If they believe in the American creed, how do they reconcile their racism or prejudice? Ask them if they believe in the golden rule that states "do unto others as you would have them do unto you."

2. Avoid Sterotypical Language

Be mindful that certain words or phrases typically mean the person is about to use stereotypes to describe a group. When you hear someone say "All black people do this . . . ," or "Latinos always like to . . . ," or "I never met a white person who could . . . ," a red flag should go up that stereotypes are in use. Politely ask if they are referring to an individual encounter with someone from another group or if they mean to speak for thirty-eight million blacks, forty million Latinos, ten million Asians, two hundred million whites or 2.5 million American Indians in this country. Ask the person if they really believe *all people* in that group actually share the same behaviors and attitudes. Is it possible that certain behaviors or beliefs only appear in one racial or ethnic group and not another?

3. Racism Isn't Funny

Don't tolerate racist jokes. If you hear a joke being told that disparages someone because of his or her group membership, stop the person from telling the joke. If they insist on finishing, ask them why they don't like black people or white people or Asians or Catholics or whomever they are ridiculing in their attempt at humor. You have many retorts to such simplistic and retrograde behavior. You might say "Hey, I don't think putting down other people is funny," or "I have gay friends, I don't want to hear you trashing them," or "My brother-in-law is black (or white or Asian or Catholic or Jewish, etc.) and I think he's great." Be willing to "take the stand" about what is appropriate public discourse. If you do not speak up and let the person know that such remarks are socially inappropriate, you are condoning their beliefs and behavior. Inaction is a form of action.

4. Be Introspective

Think back to reading 17, in which Robert Merton discussed the unprejudiced nondiscriminator. This person was not prejudiced, nor did she discriminate against anyone in any way. How can we live our lives

so social or peer pressure do not push us toward racist, prejudiced, or bigoted beliefs or actions? If you find yourself being a prejudiced nondiscriminator (fair-weather illiberal) or an unprejudiced discriminator (fair-weather liberal), ask yourself how you got there. Be introspective and honest about why you acted or behaved a certain way toward someone from a different ethnic or racial group. What scared you about the situation that made you deviate from your core beliefs or values? Did you overreact? Were you defensive? If you could relive that experience, what would you do differently? Is it possible you were socialized or taught to react the way you did? What role did peer pressure play in your actions? The most important thing you can do is to think critically about the root causes of your anxieties, attitudes, and actions. Be introspective and be willing to change how you think about groups different from your own.

5. Be a Good Citizen—Vote

Vote in every election. Take the time to find out candidates' positions on policies that have implications for race relations. Do not support a politician whose campaign rhetoric is racially divisive or attempts to win votes by manipulating racial (or class) fears. Knowing what the issues are (and are not) requires reading a newspaper everyday.

6. TV, Rap, Rock: Appeals to the Lowest Common Denominator

When you watch television, realize that you are under constant bombardment by the most simplistic and stereotypical images of ethnic and racial groups. Ask yourself which racial and ethnic groups are on prime time and how those groups are represented. Are whites, blacks, Asians, Latinos, or American Indians in a wide range of roles, or are some groups more likely to be maids, gangbangers, exotics, or lawyers? Why? What you watch on television is not just entertainment. The mass media provide the images, symbols, and narratives that shape the way we understand society. The media cement existing stereotypes and construct expectations about where groups should be placed in America's racial hierarchy. The television industry uses stereotypes to make racial inequality look like the "normal" order of society. How are you are being manipulated by the programs you watch?

7. Learn Your Family's History

Take time to talk to the elderly people in your life. Ask your parents, aunts and uncles, neighbors, and spiritual leaders in your community about how race relations have changed since they were children. Ask your parents, grandparents, and other relatives about the *Brown* decision, the Civil Rights movement, Martin Luther King, Jr.'s assassination, the American Indian Movement (AIM), La Raza, and the L.A. riots. How do they explain these events? What were they doing as these monumental events unfolded? Your elders are resources. Talk to them about the past and the present.

8. Teach through Example

Be a positive role model to all the younger people in your life. If you are of college age or older, you probably have a number of children and young adults who look up to you for moral guidance. If they hear you use foul language, then in all likelihood they will too. If you speak and act in a racist manner,

they will learn your racism. Explain to those who view you as a role model what it means to live in a multiracial, multi-ethnic society. Explain to them what the American creed and the "golden rule" mean.

9. Step Out of Your Comfort Zone

Involve yourself in activities that place you in an environment where you will be exposed to people from different racial and ethnic backgrounds. Think about attending museums, music events, ethnic festivals, restaurants, supermarkets, shops, or any other public place where you will share space with people different from yourself.

10. Know Thyself

Did you grow up in a community that was racially homogenous? Was your house of worship pretty much composed of people who looked like you? Are your best friends all of the same race? Was your elementary school segregated? How about your high school? What did it look like in terms of racial composition? Do you think being raised in a segregated environment shapes racial attitudes? How? How do you think being the only racial minority in most social settings might shape a person's views of race relations? Have your ideas about race changed since you were fifteen years old? How and why? Reflect on these questions and write your answers as an essay. Circulate what you write to your friends and family. Set up a meeting to have a discussion on what you wrote and what their views on race relations in the United States are.

"If You're Not Part of the Solution, You're Part of the Problem."

Appendix

Introduction

How are the race categories used in Census 2000 defined?

"White" refers to people having origins in any of the original peoples in Europe, the Middle East, or North Africa. It includes people who indicated their race or races as "White" or wrote in entries such as Irish, German, Italian, Lebanese, Near Easterner, Arab, or Polish.

"Black or African American" refers to people having origins in any of the black racial groups of Africa. It includes people who indicated their race or races as "Black, African Am., or Negro" or wrote in entries such as African American, Afro American, Nigerian, or Hatian.

"American Indian and Alaska Native" refers to people having origins in any of the original peoples of North and South America (including Central America), and who maintain tribal affiliation or community attachment. It includes people who indicated their race or races by marking this category or writing in their principal or enrolled tribe, such as Rosebud Sioux, Chippewa, or Navajo.

"Asian" refers to people having origins in any of the original peoples of the Far East, Southeast Asia, or the Indian subcontinent. It includes people who indicated their race or races as "Asian Indian," "Chinese," "Filipino," "Korean," "Japanese," "Vietnamese," or "Other Asian," or wrote in entries such as Burmese, Hmong, Pakistani, or Thai.

"Native Hawaiian and Other Pacific Islander" refers to people having origins in any of the original peoples of Hawaii, Guam, Samoa, or other Pacific Islands. It includes people who indicated their race or races as "Native Hawaiian," "Guamanian or Chamorro," "Samoan," or "Other Pacific Islander," or wrote in entries such as Tahitian, Mariana Islander, or Chuukese.

"Some other race" was included in Census 2000 for respondents who were unable to identify with the five Office of Management and Budget race categories. Respondents who provided write-in entries such as Moroccan, South African, Belizean, or a Hispanic origin (for example, Mexican, Puerto Rican, or Cuban) are included in the Some other race category. (U.S. Census 2000)

US Population is 75.1% white, 12.3 Black, 12.5% Latino, 3.6% Asian, American Indian 1%.

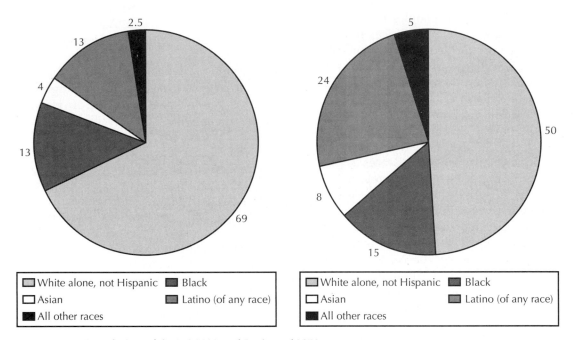

FIGURE 1   Population of the US 2000 and Projected 2050. *Source:* Data from U.S. Census Bureau, 2004, "U.S. Interim Projections by Age, Sex, Race, and Hispanic Origin," http://www.census.gov/ipc/www/usinterimproj/.

US Population is 75.1% white, 12.3 Black, 12.5% Latino, 3.6% Asian, American Indian 1%.

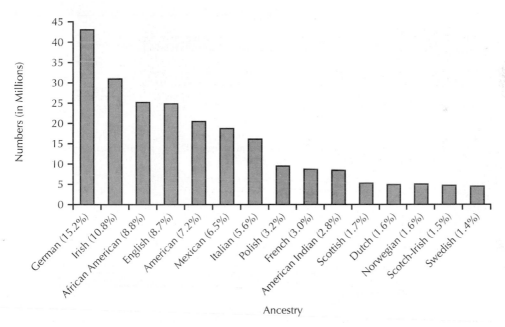

FIGURE 2   Fifteen Largest Ancestries. *Source:* Data from U.S. Census Bureau, Census 2000 special tabulation. *Note:* Percent of total population in parenthesis. Data based on sample.

US Population is 75.1% white, 12.3 Black, 12.5% Latino, 3.6% Asian, American Indian 1%.

Section I: Education

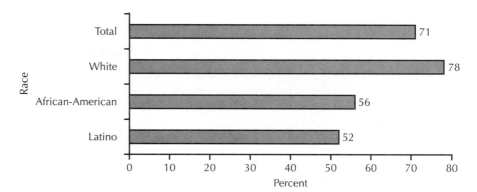

FIGURE 3   High School Graduation Rates for 2002. *Source:* Data from Manhattan Institute, Education Working Paper No. 8, February 2005.

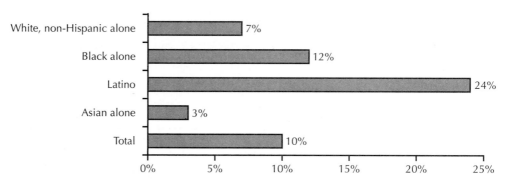

FIGURE 4   High School Dropout Rates for 2004. *Source:* Data from Child Trends' calculations of U.S. Census Bureau, *School Enrollment—Social and Economic Characteristics of Students: October 2004: Detailed Tables:* Table 1.

US Population is 75.1% white, 12.3 Black, 12.5% Latino, 3.6% Asian, American Indian 1%.

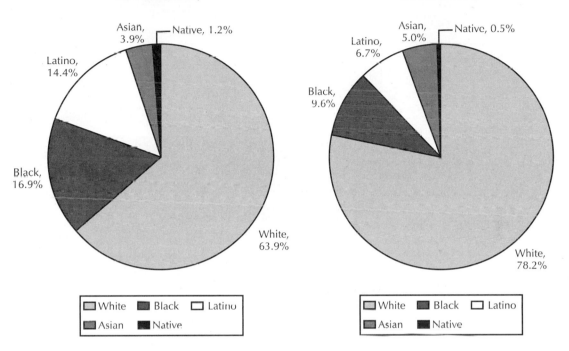

Public School Enrollments by Race and Ethnicity*

Asian, 3.9%
Native, 1.2%
Latino, 14.4%
Black, 16.9%
White, 63.9%

White Black Latino
Asian Native

Private School Enrollments by Race and Ethnicity**

Asian, 5.0%
Native, 0.5%
Latino, 6.7%
Black, 9.6%
White, 78.2%

White Black Latino
Asian Native

*90% of all school age children attend public school.

**10% of all school age children attend private school.

FIGURE 5 Racial Composition of Public and Private Schools. *Source:* Data from Common Core of Data, 1997–98 and Private School Survey, 1997–98

FIGURE 6 Degrees Conferred

Racial/Ethnic Group	BA	MA	Law	MD	PhD
White	70.0	60.3	83.0	68.6	81.0
Black	8.7	7.8	4.4	6.7	7.0
Latino	6.3	4.4	6.6	6.4	5.0
Asian	6.2	4.8	7.4	15.6	6.0
Native American	0.7	0.5	0.5	1.4	<1

Source: Data from U.S. Department of Education, National Center for Education Statistics, Integrated Postsecondary Education Data System (IPEDS), Fall 2003, National Postsecondary Student Aid Study (NPSAS: 2000), and NSF/NIH/USED/USDA/NASA, Survey of Earned Doctorates by US Citizens, 2003.

US Population is 75.1% white, 12.3 Black, 12.5% Latino, 3.6% Asian, American Indian 1%.

Section II: Housing

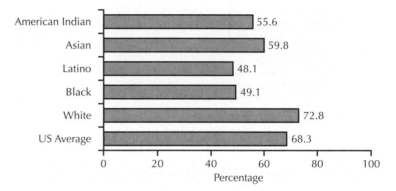

FIGURE 7   Homeownership Rates for 2003. *Source:* Data from U.S. Bureau of the Census: Home Ownership Rates by Race and Ethnicity of Householder, Annual Statistics 2003.

US Population is 75.1% white, 12.3 Black, 12.5% Latino, 3.6% Asian, American Indian 1%.

FIGURE 8   Index of Dissimilarity for the USA

	Black	Latino	Asian	Native American
Dissimilarity Index 2000 (weighted averages)	64	51	41	33

Source: Data from U.S. Bureau of the Census, 2000 Summary File 1.
Note: A zero on this index would mean that racial groups are evenly integrated throughout a city. A score of one hundred means complete racial segregation among groups.

FIGURE 9   Segregation from Whites in the Largest 10 Metropolitan Areas

Metropolitan Area	Population (Millions)	Black	Latino	Asian
Los Angeles–Long Beach	9.5	67.5	63.2	48.3
New York	9.3	81.8	66.7	50.5
Chicago	8.3	80.8	62.1	44.4
Philadelphia	5.1	72.3	60.2	43.8
Washington, DC	4.9	63.1	48.4	39.0
Detroit	4.4	84.7	45.7	45.9
Houston	4.2	67.5	55.7	49.4
Atlanta	4.1	65.6	52.5	45.2
Dallas	3.5	59.4	54.1	45.0
Boston	3.4	65.7	58.8	44.9

Source: Data from John R. Logan, Brian Stults, and Reynolds Farley. 2004. "Segregation of Minorities in the Metropolis: Two Decades of Change" Demography 41: 1–22. For more information, see http://browns4.dyndns.org/cen2000_s4. *Note:* A zero on this index would mean that racial groups are evenly integrated throughout a city. A score of one hundred means complete racial segregation among groups.

US Population is 75.1% white, 12.3 Black, 12.5% Latino, 3.6% Asian, American Indian 1%.

Section III: Health

FIGURE 10   **Health Disparities by Race**

	White	Black	Latino	Asian	AI/NA
Heart disease (%)	26.9	40.1	27.7	5.4	n/a
Premature deaths (%)	14.7	31.5	23.5	n/a	36.0
High blood pressure (%)	31.1	43.2	18.6	16.3	20.7
Overweight and obesity rate (%)	55.3	65.8	57.6	35.9	61.6
Birthrate (births/1000)	11.7	16.1	22.6	16.5	13.8
Infant mortality (death/1000)	5.7	13.5	5.4	4.7	9.7
Rate of teen births (births/1000)	28.5	68.3	83.4	18.3	53.8
Cases of HIV (rates 100K)	12.3	18.4	39.7	8.6	16.9
Distribution of new AIDS cases (%)	31.1	48.2	18.5	1.3	0.5
Tuberculosis (rates 100K)	1.5	12.6	10.4	27.8	6.8
Cigarette Smoking (%)	23.3	21.7	18.5	13.7	38.4

Source: Data from U.S Bureau of the Census, updated July 2005.

FIGURE 11   **Percentage of Americans Uninsured by Race**

	Uninsured Non-Elderly	Uninsured Children
White	13%	6%
Black	21%	9%
Latino	34%	20%
Other	19%	15%
USA	16%	10%

Source: Data from National Health Interview Survey, 2003.

US Population is 75.1% white, 12.3 Black, 12.5% Latino, 3.6% Asian, American Indian 1%.

Section IV: Crime

FIGURE 12   Percentage of Crime in the US by Race and Ethnicity

	White	Black	Asian	Native American
Murder & non-negligent manslaughter	42.5	55.4	1.4	0.7
Forcible rape	58.7	38.7	1.5	1.1
Robbery	42.8	55.4	1.2	0.6
Aggravated assault	61.7	36.0	1.3	1.0
Burglary	67.2	30.8	1.1	0.9
Larceny-theft	67.9	29.2	1.6	1.4
Motor vehicle theft	57.4	39.8	1.8	0.9
Arson	74.7	23.6	0.8	0.9
Violent crime	57.5	40.3	1.3	0.9
Property crime	66.9	30.4	1.5	1.2

Source: Data from U.S. Bureau of Justice Statistics, 2002.

US Population is 75.1% white, 12.3 Black, 12.5% Latino, 3.6% Asian, American Indian 1%.

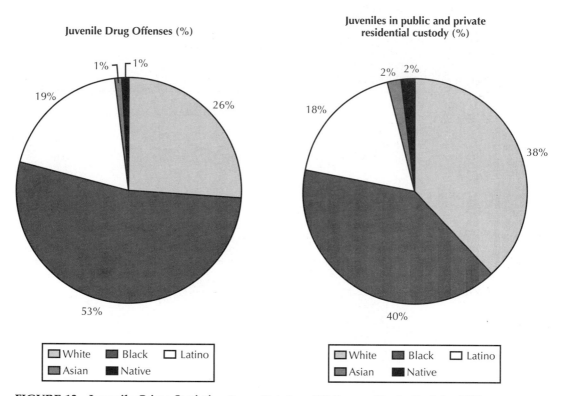

FIGURE 13   Juvenile Crime Statistics. *Source:* Data from U.S. Bureau of Justice Statistics, 2002.

US Population is 75.1% white, 12.3 Black, 12.5% Latino, 3.6% Asian, American Indian 1%.

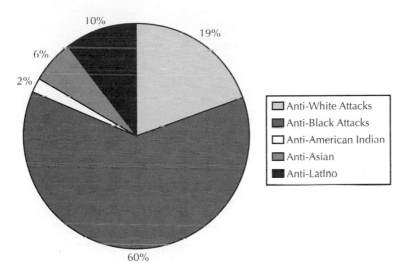

FIGURE 14   Hate Crimes by Race. *Source:* FBI's Uniform Crime Report, 2003.

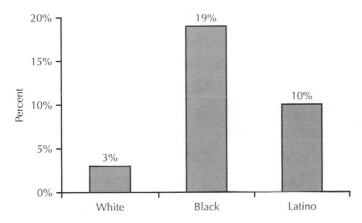

FIGURE 15   Lifetime Chances of Going to Prison. *Source:* Data from U.S. Bureau of Justice Statistics, 2001.

US Population is 75.1% white, 12.3 Black, 12.5% Latino, 3.6% Asian, American Indian 1%.

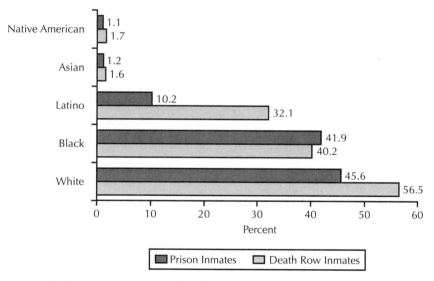

FIGURE 16   Prison and Death Row Inmates. *Source:* Data from U.S. Department of Justice and Death Row USA Spring 2004.

US Population is 75.1% white, 12.3 Black, 12.5% Latino, 3.6% Asian, American Indian 1%.

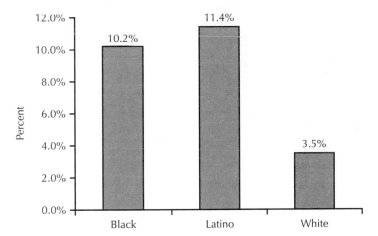

FIGURE 17   Likelihood of Being Searched During a Traffic Stop. *Source:* Data from U.S. Bureau of Justice Statistics, 2002.

US Population is 75.1% white, 12.3 Black, 12.5% Latino, 3.6% Asian, American Indian 1%.

Section V: Computers

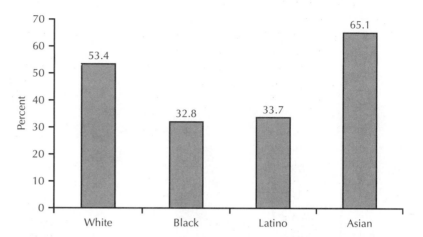

FIGURE 18   Families who own computers (*Income $15–30K, 2000).
Source: Data from U.S. Bureau of the Census.

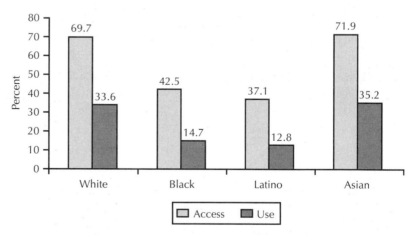

FIGURE 19   Computer Access & Use of Children 3–17 Years Old.
Source: Data from U.S. Bureau of the Census.

US Population is 75.1% white, 12.3 Black, 12.5% Latino, 3.6% Asian, American Indian 1%.

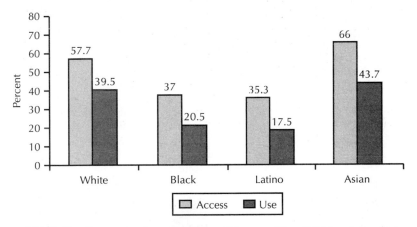

FIGURE 20 Computer Access & Use of Persons 18 and Older. *Source:* Data from U.S. Bureau of the Census.

US Population is 75.1% white, 12.3 Black, 12.5% Latino, 3.6% Asian, American Indian 1%.

Section VI: Income, Wealth and Poverty

FIGURE 21   Median Household Income, 2002

White	Black	Latino	Asian
$47,041	$29,939	$34,099	$54,488

Source: U.S. Census Bureau Population Survey, 2003.

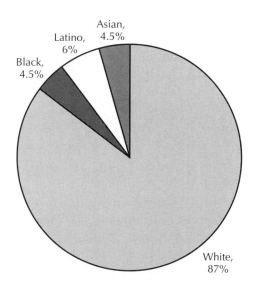

The Poor: Households with Incomes between $2500 and $4999

Asian, 14%
Latino, 9%
Black, 26%
White, 51%

The Rich: Households with Incomes Over $250,000

Asian, 4.5%
Latino, 6%
Black, 4.5%
White, 87%

FIGURE 22   Who Is Rich, Who is Poor

US Population is 75.1% white, 12.3 Black, 12.5% Latino, 3.6% Asian, American Indian 1%.

FIGURE 23   Poverty in the US

	White	Black	Latino	Asian
% of population living in poverty (2002)	17.6	29.9	13.4	24.5
Related kids under 18 in families living in poverty (2001)	8.9	30.0	27.4	11.1
Working Poor (%) (1998)	6.9	13.6	19.2	n/a
Poverty (%) (2003)	8.2	24.3	22.5	11.8

Source: Data from U.S. Bureau of the Census, 2001–2003.

US Population is 75.1% white, 12.3 Black, 12.5% Latino, 3.6% Asian, American Indian 1%.

Section VII: Employment

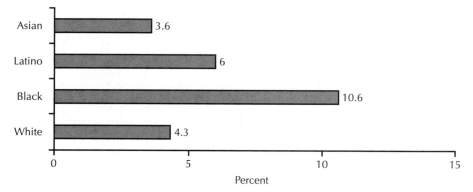

FIGURE 24   Unemployment Statistics. *Source:* U.S. Bureau of Labor Statistics, 2004–2005.

US Population is 75.1% white, 12.3 Black, 12.5% Latino, 3.6% Asian, American Indian 1%.

Section VIII: Occupations

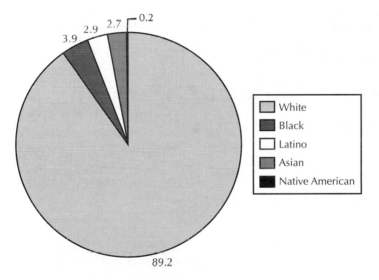

FIGURE 25   **Lawyers by Race and Ethnicity.** *Source:* Data from U.S. Census Bureau 1 Percent Public Use Microdata Sample Surveys, 201. *Note:* Numbers are the percent of the population.

US Population is 75.1% white, 12.3 Black, 12.5% Latino, 3.6% Asian, American Indian 1%.

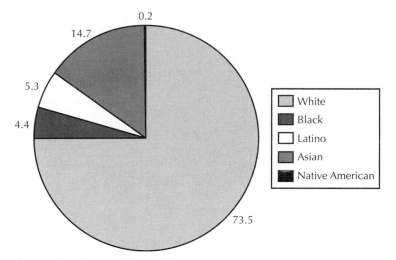

FIGURE 26   Physicians and Surgeons by Race and Ethnicity.
Source: Data from U.S. Census Bureau 1 Percent Public Use Microdata
Sample Surveys, 201. *Note:* Numbers are the percent of the population.

US Population is 75.1% white, 12.3 Black, 12.5% Latino, 3.6% Asian, American Indian 1%.

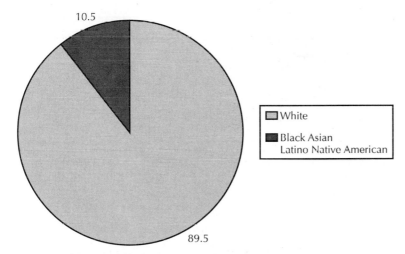

10.5

89.5

White

Black Asian
Latino Native American

FIGURE 27   Washington D.C. National Press Corps Reporters and Editor by Race and Ethnicity. *Source:* Data from Unity, 2004. *Note:* Numbers are the percent of the population.

US Population is 75.1% white, 12.3 Black, 12.5% Latino, 3.6% Asian, American Indian 1%.

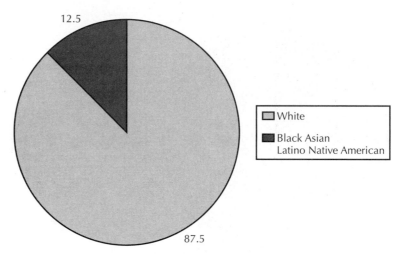

12.5

87.5

White

Black Asian
Latino Native American

FIGURE 28   Newsrooms Nationwide by Race and Ethnicity.
Source: Data from Unity, 2004. *Note:* Numbers are the percent of the
population.

US Population is 75.1% white, 12.3 Black, 12.5% Latino, 3.6% Asian, American Indian 1%.

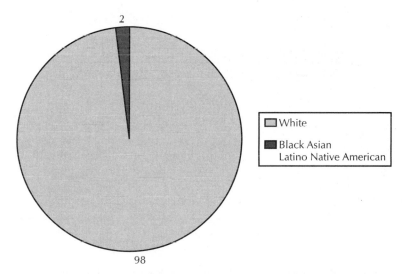

FIGURE 29 CEOs of Fortune 500 Companies by Race and Ethnicity.
Source: Data from Christian Science Monitor, October 31, 2005. *Note:* Numbers are the percent of the population.

US Population is 75.1% white, 12.3 Black, 12.5% Latino, 3.6% Asian, American Indian 1%.

FIGURE 30   Other Occupations by Race and Ethnicity

	White	Black	Latino	Asian	Native American
Registered Nurses	80.4	8.9	3.4	5.5	0.4
Engineers	80.9	4.2	3.9	9.2	0.3
Police Supervisors	81.4	9.5	6.1	0.5	0.9
Police/Detectives	76.6	11.4	8.5	1.4	0.7
College Instructors	79.7	5.6	4.5	8.1	0.4
Judges/Hearing Examiners/JPs/some Arbitrators	82.1	12.0	3.4	1.4	0.9
Clergy	81.8	8.4	3.9	4.1	0.7
Information Technology	73.8	7.6	5.1	11.4	0.3
School Teachers	81.8	9.0	5.7	1.8	0.5

Source: Data from U.S. Census Bureau 1 Percent Public Use Microdata Sample Surveys, 201.

US Population is 75.1% white, 12.3 Black, 12.5% Latino, 3.6% Asian, American Indian 1%.

Section IX: Government

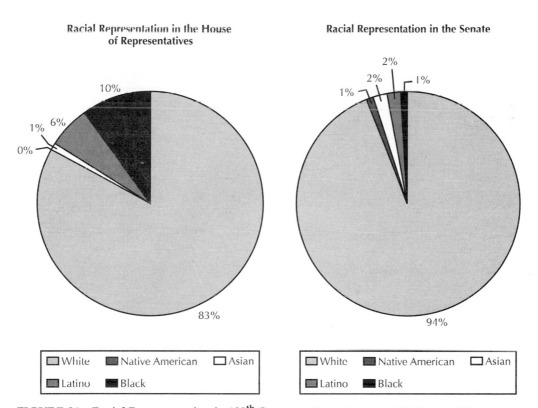

Racial Representation in the House of Representatives

10%

1% 6%

0%

83%

White   Native American   Asian
Latino   Black

Racial Representation in the Senate

2%
2%
1%   1%

94%

White   Native American   Asian
Latino   Black

FIGURE 31   Racial Representation in 109th Congress. *Source:* Data from U.S. House of Representatives, House Press Gallery; U.S. Senate, Daily Press Gallery, Minority Senators.

US Population is 75.1% white, 12.3 Black, 12.5% Latino, 3.6% Asian, American Indian 1%.

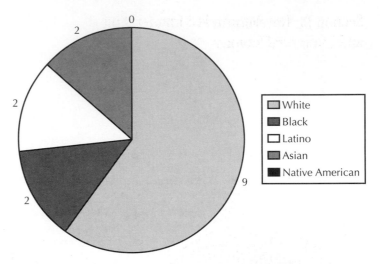

FIGURE 32   Racial Representation in the Presidential Cabinet 2005. *Source:* House Press Gallery: *The President's Cabinet;* The White House.

FIGURE 33   Race of Presidents in the United States

US Population is 75.1% white, 12.3 Black, 12.5% Latino, 3.6% Asian, American Indian 1%.

Section X: New Boundaries: Immigration and Interracial Couples

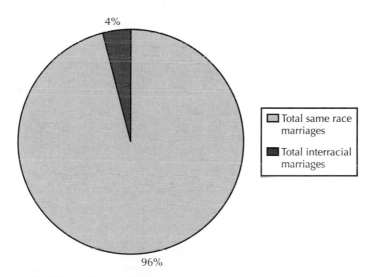

4%

96%

Total same race marriages

Total interracial marriages

FIGURE 34   Interracial Married Couples 2003. *Source:* Data from U.S. Census Bureau, *Statistical Abstract of the United States: 2004–2005.*

US Population is 75.1% white, 12.3 Black, 12.5% Latino, 3.6% Asian, American Indian 1%.

FIGURE 35   Ten Largest Cities and their Multiracial Populations 2000

Place	Total population		Two or more races population		
	Rank	Number	Rank	Number	Percent
New York, NY	1	8,008,278	1	393,959	4.9
Los Angeles, CA	2	3,694,820	2	191,288	5.2
Chicago, IL	3	2,896,016	3	84,437	2.9
Houston, TX	4	1,953,631	4	61,478	3.1
Philadelphia, PA	5	1,517,550	10	33,574	2.2
Phoenix, AZ	6	1,321,045	8	43,276	3.3
San Diego, CA	7	1,223,400	5	59,081	4.8
Dallas, TX	8	1,188,580	12	32,351	2.7
San Antonio, TX	9	1,144,646	9	41,871	3.7
Detroit, MI	10	951,270	18	22,041	2.3
Honolulu, HI	46	371,657	6	55,474	14.9
San Jose, CA	11	894,943	7	45,062	5.0

Source: Data from U.S. Census Bureau, Census 2000 Restricting Data (Public Law 94–171) Summary File, Table PL1.

US Population is 75.1% white, 12.3 Black, 12.5% Latino, 3.6% Asian, American Indian 1%.

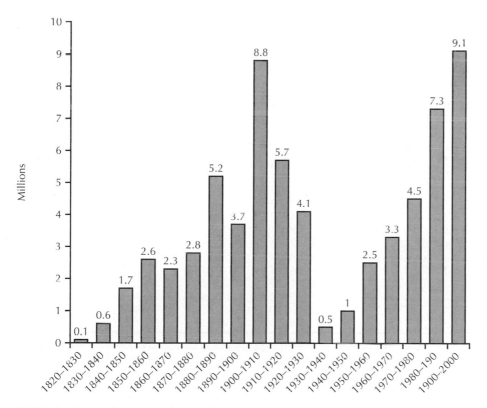

FIGURE 36 **Total Immigration to the United States from 1820 to 2000, by Decade.**
Source: Data from U.S. Immigration and Naturalization Service.

US Population is 75.1% white, 12.3 Black, 12.5% Latino, 3.6% Asian, American Indian 1%.

FIGURE 37

		Immigrants		Share of Population	
		2000	1990	2000	1990
1	Los Angeles-Long Beach	3,449,444	2,892,456	36.2%	32.7%
2	New York, NY	3,139,647	2,285,024	33.7%	26.8%
3	Chicago, IL	1,425,978	885,081	17.2%	11.9%
4	Miami, FL	1,147,765	874,569	50.9%	45.1%
5	Houston, TX	854,669	440,321	20.5%	13.3%
6	Orange County, CA	849,899	575,108	29.9%	23.9%
7	Washington, DC	832,016	489,641	16.9%	11.6%
8	Riverside-San Bernardino, CA	612,359	360,643	18.8%	13.9%
9	San Diego, CA	606,254	428,810	21.5%	17.2%
10	Dallas, TX	591,169	234,522	16.8%	8.8%
11	Oakland, CA	573,144	337,435	24.0%	16.2%
12	San Jose, CA	573,130	347,201	34.1%	23.2%
13	San Francisco, CA	554,819	441,290	32.0%	27.5%

Source: Data from John R. Logan. 2006. "Settlement Patterns of Immigrants in Metropolitan America" in Mary Waters and Reed Ueda (editors), The New Americans: A Handbook to Immigration Since 1965. Harvard University Press, forthcoming.

US Population is 75.1% white, 12.3 Black, 12.5% Latino, 3.6% Asian, American Indian 1%.